A DICTIONARY OF
INDIAN HISTORY

A

DICTIONARY

OF

INDIAN HISTORY

by

SACHCHIDANANDA
BHATTACHARYA

GEORGE BRAZILLER
NEW YORK

TO

ALL ORIENTALISTS, EASTERN AND WESTERN,

WHO BY THEIR LEARNED LABOUR

HAVE CONTRIBUTED TO THE ADVANCEMENT

OF OUR KNOWLEDGE OF THE HISTORY

OF THIS ANCIENT LAND OF OURS

FOREWORD

THE present work is the result of the life-long labour of a distinguished Professor of History in our country to assist students as well as general readers in acquiring an exact knowledge about the main personalities and places connected with the history of India during its dated period i.e. from about the middle of the first millennium B.C. down to modern times. Professor Sachchidananda Bhattacharya has to my mind very well succeeded in achieving his objective. Without being detailed and dry-as-dust he has noted down alphabetically the broad facts in the careers of the most important persons who have a place in Indian history, and also he has treated all important places as well as peoples and institutions which are almost equally important.

Such a book has been a desideratum, and to my knowledge I cannot think of any suitable book which will meet with the requirements of people interested in Indian history both from the point of view of serious study and the usually cultured man's curiosity. Prof. Bhattacharya has done well in placing his material in an alphabetical order and in a way his book may be compared with that very useful handbook on Hindu Mythology which was long ago published in Truebner's Oriental Series by Dowson. We can rely upon a responsible scholar like Prof. Bhattacharya who has spent his whole life in weaning our young men and women in India to take to the study of the history of their country seriously to be exact and accurate according to the best of his knowledge and understanding of the essentials. He has carefully avoided entering into controversy in some disputed matters, but he has given references to various views whenever it was necessary to do so.

I have found his book quite fascinating reading, and though not a professed student of history I have been interested in the subject also in connection with my own studies in linguistics, which as a human science is closely linked up with human history. I am sure, to dip into this book will be to obtain information, and quite a lot of it too, which we never knew before, and we shall also find matters which we did not understand in their proper bearings. The extent of his work, considering the total number of entries (this comes up to near about 3000), is, for a popular handbook of this type, quite inclusive and comprehensive, and I can only recommend Prof. Bhattacharya's work to our students and to the general public.

SUNITI KUMAR CHATTERJI
Emeritus Professor of Comparative Philology, University
Calcutta, *of Calcutta; Ex-Chairman, West Bengal Legislative*
7. 2. 1967 *Council and National Professor of India in Humanities*

PREFACE

INDIAN history has not reached the very high level of maturity of European studies but it has been on the whole factually built up. The idea of compiling a dictionary of Indian history therefore very naturally occurred to Mr. Sachchidananda Bhattacharya. He was told by many that the task was much too arduous for any single scholar and that it was a very bold attempt to tackle Indian history down the ages, unaided by others. Money was another hurdle. But Mr. Bhattacharya would not give up his cherished plan and began to work steadily. In the course of a conversation with me he referred to the financial difficulty of publishing this projected dictionary of Indian history. I could see from what he had done how useful this dictionary would be, if it could be completed. The University of Calcutta and the University Grants Commission were approached. They expressed readiness to sponsor the scheme and share the expense of publication. Mr. Bhattacharya's work gathered momentum. His dictionary comprises 2785 entries concerning persons, places, institutions, literary and historical works covering ancient, medieval and modern periods of Indian history. Mr. Bhattacharya's age has exceeded the limit of three score and ten. When we think of the strenuous labour which this venture involved we feel that a sense of achievement—something attempted, something done every day—sustained his strength. Traditional historical scholarship—wide reading, wide learning and a sound dose of common sense—was his equipment for his task. The factual content is adequate and helpful. There may be errors or omissions. The author does not certainly claim know-all-ness as a dictionary-maker of Indian history.

N. K. SINHA
*Asutosh Professor of Medieval
and Modern Indian history,
University of Calcutta*

5. 2. 1967

INTRODUCTION

A Dictionary of Indian History is intended to be a handy book of reference for students, teachers, journalists and general readers who may be interested in the study of Indian history. It deals with the dated period of Indian history, commencing from the ancient times, and covers all the periods of the history of India, ancient, medieval and modern.

The topics, 2785 in number, are arranged alphabetically and include names of persons, places, works and institutions significant in the evolution and development of the history of India. With rare exceptions references to living persons have been avoided. A chronologically arranged list of important dates forms the concluding section of the Dictionary. It does not claim to be exhaustive but will, on the whole, be found comprehensive.

In the spelling of proper names the system indicated in the publications of the Oxford University Press has generally been followed; but diacritical marks have been avoided.

Ploetz' *Manual of Universal History* by Tillinghast and *An Encyclopedia of World History* by W. L. Langer (Harvard University) suggested to me the idea of arranging the main historical figures and events in our country in the form of a dictionary. My method of approach and my arrangement are, however, entirely different. In place of the chronological method followed in those two works the topical method has been adopted here. Further, India has necessarily received very little space in the *Manual* as well as in the *Encyclopedia*, whereas this work is devoted entirely to Indian history which so far has lacked a dictionary of this kind. It thus aims at filling up a long-standing gap in the historiography of India.

The work was taken up as a labour of love in 1961, but a few months before my retirement from active teaching work in Universities it attracted the attention of Dr. N. K. Sinha, Asutosh Professor and Head of the Department of History, Calcutta University, who was pleased to get the University of Calcutta interested in its publication. It has since been sponsored by the University of Calcutta and the University Grants Commission of India. To both these bodies who, between them, have shared the entire cost of production, and to Dr. N. K. Sinha, who has been also pleased to add a preface, I offer my grateful thanks.

Dr. Suniti Kumar Chatterji, National Professor of India in Humanities, has laid me under a profound obligation by kindly contributing a Foreword.

My thanks are also due to Dr. Sukumar Bhattacharya, Professor of History, Visva-Bharati, for various helpful suggestions and to my pupil Maharajkumar Saurish Chandra Roy of Nadia (West Bengal), who very generously placed at my disposal the collections in the private library of the Nadia Raj. I must also thank the staff of the National Library, Calcutta, and of the Central Library of Calcutta University, for the readiness with which they supplied me with books and materials necessary for my purpose. To Sri P. K. Ghosh, of Eastend Printers, Calcutta, I record my special thanks for his many constructive suggestions.

In the preparation of this book, standard works on Indian History in its different aspects have been consulted. No special bibliography has, therefore, been added. On controversial topics, however, I have given references to the authorities relied upon. References to books with long titles have been given in abbreviated forms. A list of such abbreviations is appended.

The work has been rather strenuous for a man of my age, working without any assistance. Moreover, as it was to be completed within a specific period of time, some mistakes may have crept in. Any suggestion for improvement will be gratefully acknowledged and utilised if the book reaches a second edition.

Though the work has been generally written objectively, it may not have been possible to keep back the subjective element altogether. Opinions expressed on these rare occasions are entirely mine and I hope they will be found based on established facts.

I have put into this *Dictionary of Indian History* the fruits of my labour as a College and University teacher for half a century. I shall feel amply rewarded if this work is found useful by those who are interested in the history of India.

SACHCHIDANANDA BHATTACHARYA

62, Ballygunge Place,
Calcutta, India,
15 February, 1967

A DICTIONARY OF INDIAN HISTORY

Abastanoi—were a people who dwelt, on the eve of Alexander's invasion, in the north-western part of India, on the Chinab above its confluence with the Indus. Their name is the Greek form of the Sanskrit Ambastha who are mentioned in the *Aitareya Brahmana*, the *Mahabharata* and the *Barhaspatya Artha-sastra*. They were a tribe or clan who were at first mainly a fighting race, but some of them later on adopted other professions like those of priests, farmers and physicians. (*PHAI*, pp. 255-56)

Abdali, Ahmad Shah—an Afghan chief belonging to the Durrani clan who occupied the throne of Afghanistan in 1747 after the assassination of Nadir Shah (*q.v.*). He ruled from 1747 till his death in 1773. During this period he invaded India eight times, occupied the Panjab, and won a tremendous victory over the Marathas in the Third Battle of Panipat in 1761. The refusal of his Afghan soldiers to proceed against Mathura where four years ago they had suffered heavily from an outbreak of cholera and other disorders amongst them compelled him to withdraw to Afghanistan soon after this victory and frustrated his scheme of seizing the empire of Hindu-sthan. The menace of his invasion continued till 1767 and greatly influenced Anglo-Indian politics for several years. Ahmad Shah Abdali died in 1773. (Sarkar, J. N., *Fall of the Mughul Empire*, II, p. 376)

Abdul Gaffar Khan—known as the 'Frontier Gandhi'. He is a nationalist Muslim leader of the North-West Frontier Province. He at first started a militant organisation known as the 'Red Shirt' and later on joined the non-violent Civil Disobedience Movement (*q.v.*) started by Gandhi (*q.v.*). His party won the elections in 1937 and established a Congress Ministry in the North-West Frontier Province with his brother Dr. Khan Shaheb as the Chief Minister. After the partition following Indian independence he continued to live in the North-West Frontier state which became a part of Pakistan. He started a movement for Paktoonistan, incurred thereby the displeasure of the Pakistan Government and was put in prison. He is under detention at the time of writing.

Abdul Hamid Lahori—official historian of the time of Shah Jahan (*q.v.*). His work called *Padshahnamah* is an authoritative account of the reign of Shah Jahan.

Abdullah Barha Sayyid—the elder of the two Sayyid brothers (*q.v.*) who controlled the administration of the Mughul empire from 1713 when they put on the throne Furruksiyar till their fall in 1719. During this short period Abdullah with the help of his brother Husain did as he liked. In 1719 they deposed and killed Emperor Furruksiyar and in the course of the same year made and unmade four other successive Mughul emperors until at last they placed on the throne their fifth *protege* Muhammad Shah who was clever enough to remove Husain by assassination and to defeat and imprison Abdullah who was killed by poisoning in 1722.

Abdur Rahman, Amir—was placed on the throne of Afghanistan in 1880 with the support of the English after the Second Afghan War (*q.v.*). He was an astute politician who ruled from 1880 till his death in 1901, maintaining friendly relations both with England and Russia. He was also an able administrator who maintained the integrity of Afghanistan. It was during his time that the Durand line was drawn up in 1893 marking the Indo-Afghan boundary.

Abdur Rahim, Khan-i-Khanan—son of Bairam Khan. He was a minor at the time of his father's death in 1561, rose high in Akbar's service, became the Khan-i-Khanan or premier noble man in his court, and took part in many campaigns. He was a literary man, translated Babur's *Memoirs* into Persian and patronised literary men like Abdul Baqi who wrote the *Maasir-i-Rahimi*. He lived long, dying in the reign of Jahangir.

Abdur Razzak Lari—was a faithful noble and general of Abul Hasan, the last sultan of Golkunda. When in 1687 Aurangzeb made the final attack on Golkunda, he tried his best to bribe Abdur Razzak but he spurned all offers of temptation, bravely fought in the defence of Golkunda till he fell covered with seventy wounds. He was nursed back to recovery by order of Aurangzeb and at last accepted a high rank under the Mughul Emperor.

Abdur Razzak of Herat—came to India in 1448 as the ambassador of Sultan Shahrukh of Persia. He first came to Calicut and proceeded to Vijayanagar of which he has left an interesting account.

Abdus Samad—was Akbar's drawing master who was later on put in charge of the mint. He was a celebrated artist.

Abhiras, the—were a tribal people who are first mentioned in the *Mahabhasya* of Patanjali. They occupied the tract in the lower Indus Valley and western Rajputana and is mentioned in the *Periplus* and in the geography of Ptolemy. In the third quarter of the second century A.D. Abhira chieftains served as generals of the Saka rulers of western India. An Abhira chief named Iswardatta became the *Mahakshatrapa* (*q.v.*). Kings of Abhira tribe played an important part in bringing about the fall of the Satavahana dynasty in the middle of the third century A.D. The Abhiras are mentioned in the Allahabad inscription of Samudragupta as one of the many tribes who rendered homage to the great Gupta Emperor. (*PHAI*, p. 545)

Abhisaras, the—were a tribal people who dwelt in the Punch and some adjoining districts of Kashmir and some part of the Hazara district of the North-West Frontier Province on the eve of the invasion by Alexander the Great. (*PHAI*, p. 249)

Abhisares—was the king of the Abhisaras at the time of Alexander's invasion. He was a shrewd politician who informed Alexander the Great on his arrival at Taxila that he was ready to submit to the Greek invader, but he also carried on negotiations with Poros for joining his forces with those of Poros against Alexander. Eventually the alliance did not take place and Abhisares had to surrender to Alexander the Great. (*PHAI*, pp. 248-49, Chinnock, *Arrian*, p. 276)

Abhisheka—literally 'besprinkling'. It was an essential feature of the coronation of a king who was consecrated with seventeen kinds of liquids which were sprinkled on him by a Brahmana priest, a kinsman or brother of the king-elect, a friendly lord and a *vaisya*. (*PHAI*, pp. 167ff.)

Abu-l Fazl—son of Shaikh Mubarak, was a profoundly learned man with untiring industry and commanding intellect. He was a faithful officer of Akbar and was for many years his confidential secretary and adviser. He was not only a courtier and a man of affairs but was also a great scholar and learned author. His *Ain-i-Akbari* is a statistical account of Akbar's empire and his *Akbarnama* is an authoritative account of the history of India in Akbar's time. His brother Faizi was Akbar's court-poet. He was murdered in 1602 by a Bundela chief at the instigation of Prince Salim.

Abul-l Hasan—was the last Kutb Shahi sultan or king of Golkunda. He incurred the displeasure of the Mughul Emperor Aurangzeb for various reasons and in 1687 he was defeated by Aurangzeb who deposed him and kept him as a prisoner in the fort of Daulatabad till his death several years later.

Abyssinians, the—was the general name for negro slaves who were converted to Islam and were brought to India. They became a large body and were generally known as *habshies*. One such negro slave raised himself to the throne of Bengal and assumed the name of Sams-ud-din Muzzaffar Shah. He proved to be a tyrant and was deposed and killed in 1493. The Abyssinians also became very influential in the Bahmani kingdom as well as in the Sultanates which rose out of it. They joined with the Deccanee Muhammadans in those states and resisted the growth of the power and influence of the Muhammadans of foreign origin like the Arabs and the Persians. A band of the Abyssinians established themselves at Jinjee which they soon turned into a strong piratical centre. They opposed Shivaji until at last they were conquered by him in 1677. Many Abyssinian slaves were turned into eunuchs and employed at guarding the harems of the Muhammadan rulers in India. (*See poste* Malik Ambar, an Abyssinian slave of great ability who served at Ahmadnagar.)

Achyuta—was one of the many kings of Aryavarta who, according to the Allahabad inscription, was defeated and deposed by Samudragupta (A.D. 330-75). Achyuta was probably a king of Ahichchatra, modern Ramnagar, in the Bareilly district. (*PHAI*, p. 536)

Achyutaraya—king of Vijayanagar from 1529 to 1542. He was the brother and successor of Krishnadevaraya (1509-29). He was a man of weak and tyrannical character who lacked in personal courage and lost the fortresses of Mudgal and Raichur to Ismail Adil Shah, the sultan of Bijapur.

Adali—nephew of Sher Shah, who succeeded Sher Shah's son and immediate successor Islam Shah in 1554. His full title was Muhammad Adil Shah. He retired to eastern India after the Second Battle of Panipat (1557) and was subsequently killed in a conflict with the king of Bengal.

Adam, John—a senior member of the Governor-General's Council. He officiated as Governor-General for seven months (January-July, 1823). During his short administration John Silk Buckingham, editor of the *Calcutta Journal*, was expelled for undue criticism of public officials. This marked the advent of the Press into the public life of India.

Adham Khan—son of Maham Anaga, chief nurse ranking as a foster mother of Emperor Akbar. He joined with others in rousing the anger of Akbar against Bairam Khan who was dismissed by Akbar in 1560. For the next two years Adham Khan wielded great influence over Akbar and conquered Malwa for the Mughul Emperor. But in 1562 he stabbed to death within the palace Shams-ud-din Atga Khan whom Akbar had appointed as his prime minister. This act of violence very much enraged Akbar who had Adham Khan thrown over the battlements and thus executed.

Adhisima Krishna—pre-historic king of Hastinapura, mentioned in the *Vayu* and *Matsya Puranas*. He was the great-great-grandson of Parikshit, the famous Kuru king who came to the throne after the Bharata War. (*PHAI*, pp. 31ff.)

Adhirajendra—the last Chola king in the direct line of succession from Parantaka (*q.v.*). He ruled only for three years (1072-74) and was assassinated. He was a Saiva by faith and was so hostile to the famous Vaishnava saint Ramanuja that the latter had to stay away from his residence at Srirangam during the reign of Adhirajendra.

Adhyaksha—is an official designation used in Kautilya's *Arthasastra* to indicate heads of Departments, e.g. *Nagaradhyakshas* (magistrates in charge of cities) and *Baladhyakshas* (officers in charge of military affairs). (*PHAI*, pp. 284ff.)

Adi Granth—or the First Sacred Book is the scripture of the Sikhs. It was compiled in 1604 by the fifth Guru, Arjan Mal (1581-1606) by collecting select verses from the works of Guru Nanak and his three successors as well as of some Hindu and Jain saints.

Adil Shahi dynasty, the—was established in Bijapur in 1489 by Yusuf Adil Khan, originally a Georgian slave who by dint of his own ability rose high in the service of the Bahmani sultan, Mahmud (1482-1518) and was appointed by him governor of Bijapur, but later on set himself up as an independent ruler with Bijapur as his capital. His dynasty ruled over Bijapur from 1489 to 1685 when the last Adil Shahi sultan, Sikandar, was defeated and made a captive by Aurangzeb. The rulers of this dynasty were—Yusuf, Ismail, Mallu, Ibrahim I, Ali, Ibrahim II, Muhammad Ali II and Sikandar. It took part in the various wars of the Deccan, especially in the combined Muhammadan invasion on Vijayanagar culminating in the battle of Talikota (1585) in which Vijayanagar was defeated and was eventually destroyed. The Adil Shahi sultans of Bijapur were great builders and their works like the wall round the city, the principal mosque at Bijapur, the audience-hall or Gagan Muhall, the tomb of Ibrahim II (1580-1626) and the mausoleum of his successor Muhammad (1626-56) were all marked by grandeur of conception and boldness of execution. Some of the sultans, especially the sixth sultan, Ibrahim II,

were good and tolerant administrators. He was also a patron
of literature and the famous historian Muhammad Kasim,
surnamed Firishta, wrote his excellent history *Tarikh-i-Firishta*
under the patronage of this Adil Shahi Sultan.

Adisura—was, according to Bengal literary tradition, king of
Gaura or Lakshnavati who sought to revive in Bengal the
Brahmanical religion which had suffered from Buddhist pre-
dominance. He is believed to have imported into Bengal five
Brahmans from Kanauj, who taught orthodox Hinduism and
became the ancestors of *Radhiya* and *Varendra* Brahmans of
Bengal. He has been assigned to some date after A.D. 700.
But in the absence of contemporary records his existence as
an historical figure has been doubted.

Aditya—early Chola raja (A.D. 880-907) who defeated Aparajita
Pallava, put an end to the Pallava supremacy and thus facilitated
the foundation of the Chola supremacy by his son and successor.

Adityasena—son of Madhava Gupta, was the sovereign of Madhya-
desa in A.D. 672. He performed an *asvamedha* (horse-sacrifice)
(*q.v.*) ceremony and gave his daughter in marriage to Bhogavarman Maukhari. His daughter's daughter was married to
Sivadeva, king of Nepal, and their son Jayadeva married
Rajyamati, the daughter of Harshadeva, king of Kamarupa.

Adityavamsa—was, according to Kambuja tradition, a king
of Indraprastha whose son was Kaundinya who founded the
royal dynasty of Kambuja. There is no Indian record to confirm
this tradition.

Adivaraha—"primaeval boar", was a title assumed by King Mihira
Bhoja (A.D. 840-90) of the Gurjara-Pratihara dynasty of Kanauj.
This title has been found inscribed on his silver coins found in
abundance in northern India.

Afghanistan—is the country lying just on the north-western
frontier of West Pakistan, beyond Peshawar and extending
from the Durand line up to the Hindu Kush. It has been
closely connected with India in all ages. According to the
Mahabharata the Kuru king Dhritarastra married a princess
of Gandhara which has been identified with Qandahar. On
the eve of Alexander's invasion it was divided into the three
provinces of Paropanisadai, Aria and Arachosia corresponding
respectively to the modern Kabul, Herat and Qandahar regions.
Alexander overran and conquered the country which, on his
death, fell to the share of his general Seleucos Nikator who, in
his turn, was obliged to cede it to Chandragupta Maurya.
Afghanistan thus became an integral part of India and the

recent discovery of Asokan inscriptions near Jelalabad and Qandahar show how deeply it was influenced by Indian culture. Indeed it became a highway for Buddhist missionaries and a centre of Buddhism. It continued to be a part of the Kushana empire, but on the fall of the Kushanas it passed under the rule of the Persians in the third century of the Christian era. The Guptas could not recover it and in the eighth century Afghanistan, like the countries to the west and north of it, passed under Muslim rule. The new religion inspired the sturdy hill people with a missionary zeal and the wealth of India excited their greed. As a result, the successive Muslim dynasties of Ghazni and Ghur made repeated invasions into India until at last Shihabuddin Muhammad Ghuri conquered Delhi in 1193 and laid the foundation of the Muslim rule in India. The Delhi sultans, who are called Pathans, though mostly Turks, could not long keep under their control Afghanistan which became a foothold for the ferocious and stronger Mongols who used it as a base for invading India until at last in 1504 Babur made himself the master of the kingdom. It was from his capital at Kabul that Babur invaded India, won the First Battle of Panipat in 1526 and laid the foundation of the Mughul empire in India. In 1595 Akbar conquered Qandahar and thus brought Afghanistan within the Mughul empire. But Qandahar was lost by Jahangir in 1622, recovered by Shah Jahan in 1638 and lost again by him in 1648. All his subsequent efforts to recover Qandahar failed, but Kabul continued to be part of the Mughul empire until 1739 when Nadir Shah, who had become the king of Persia in 1736, conquered Kabul and invaded and plundered Delhi. Afghanistan was thus severed from the Indian monarchy. But separation did not mean immunity. Ahmad Shah Abdali or Durrani, an Afghan chief, made himself the ruler at Afghanistan after the death by assassination of Nadir Shah in 1747. Ahmad Shah proved as much a source of trouble to the Mughul emperors of Delhi, conquered and annexed the Panjab and administered the *coup de grace* to the Mughul empire by his victory at the third battle of Panipat in 1761. Though Ahmad Shah's ambition to become the emperor of Delhi was not fulfilled Afghanistan was never again to be a part of the Indian empire. It continued to be ruled by Afghan princes and to be a source of danger to India. Zaman Shah (1793-1800) occupied Lahore in 1798 and cherished the dream of invading the interior of India, but was himself deposed in 1800. Then followed a period of

disorder in Afghanistan which continued till the accession of
Dost Muhammad (1826-63) who restored order in Afghanistan.
But the foreign relations of Afghanistan came henceforth to be
largely influenced by the rivalry between Russia in Central
Asia and England in India, and each of the two powers wanted
to bring Afghanistan under its control. Afghanistan in its turn
wanted to avert the control of either by playing the one power
against the other. These contradictory forces led to the outbreak of two wars between Afghanistan and the British Government in India (*see* Anglo-Afghan Wars) in the nineteenth century
as the result of the last of which Afghanistan became more or
less subordinate in its foreign relations to India. Eventually
in 1893 the boundary was marked by what came to be known
as the Durand line. But in 1904 Amir Habibullah (1901-19)
was conceded the title of "His Majesty" and practically recognised as an independent ruler. During the First World
War Afghanistan maintained a policy of strict neutrality which
was very helpful to the British. Habibullah's successor, King
Amanullah fought the Third Anglo-Afghan War (April-May,
1919) in which Afghanistan was defeated. Afghanistan ceased
to have the right of importing arms and ammunition through
India and was not also to receive any subsidy from the British
Indian Government, but she was to have full control over
her own foreign policy and both powers were to respect each
other's independence. Amanullah then paid a visit to Europe
and on his return embarked on a policy of introducing certain
social, educational and legal reforms. This policy of reform
was strongly resented by the conservative section of the Afghans
and a civil war began in May 1929. Amanullah was compelled
to abdicate and the throne was for a time occupied by an
adventurer named Bachai-i-Saqqao. The British Government
maintained a policy of non-intervention. Eventually Bachai-i
Saqqao was defeated and killed by Muhmud Nadir Shah, a
scion of the old royal family, and an able officer of Amir
Amanullah. Nadir Shah became the ruler of Afghanistan by
general choice and administered Afghanistan with great tact
and ability till his death by assassination in 1933. His son
Muhammud Zahir peacefully succeeded him. Relations between
Afghanistan and India continued to be satisfactory under
Nadir Shah and his son and successor, King Zahir. Since
independence and partition Pakistan has been standing between
India and Afghanistan but friendly relations have existed between
the two countries.

Afghans, the—a generic term used to denote the many hill tribes who inhabit not only Afghanistan but also the north-west frontiers of India. They are very virile peoples who maintained peaceful as well as warlike contact with India since the beginning of history. The wealth of India had always tempted them and they came to India both as traders and raiders. Sultan Mahmud was the first Afghan ruler to invade India and Shihabuddin Muhammad Ghuri was the first Afghan ruler to establish Muslim rule in India. But the sultans of Delhi who ruled in India from 1200 to 1526 and who are generally called Afghans, or more popularly, Pathans, were mostly Turks. The sultans of the Lodi dynasty (1450-1526) alone were truly speaking Afghans. Babur, the first Mughul emperor, overthrew the Afghan power in the first battle of Panipat (1526). Afghan rule was re-established by Sher Shah (1539-42) and was finally overthrown as the result of Akbar's victory at the second battle of Panipat (1556).

Afridis, the—are a warlike tribe of frontier people inhabiting the Khyber region. They had always been a source of trouble to the government of India. They rose against Aurangzeb in 1667 and could be put down only after a prolonged conflict. Since 1893 after the boundary between Afghanistan and India was fixed by the Durand line they passed under British rule which could be enforced only at the cost of a series of tribal compaigns and by adopting a policy of paying subsidies to the tribal leaders.

Afzal Khan—a Muhammadan general whom the sultan of Bijapur sent in 1659 with an army of 10,000 men to suppress Shivaji who was then fast rising into power. At first Afzal carried everything before him and within a fortnight reached Wai, twenty miles north of Satara. But Shivaji remained safe within the fort of Pratapgarh. Failing to bring him out of his fort Afzal opened negotiations with Shivaji and a conference was arranged between the two. Shivaji sensed treachery on the part of the Muhammadan general and he went to the conference apparently unarmed but with concealed weapons and clad in armour, with a view to meeting craft with craft, if necessary. According to the Marathas, as the two embraced each other the strong and stalwart Muslim general tried to throttle Shivaji to death and Shivaji immediately killed Afzal by ripping up his belly with his *baghnakh* (tiger's claws) which he had been secretly carrying with him. The Marathas then defeated the Bijapur army in an open battle.

Agalassoi, the—a tribal people who lived in the lower Indus Valley next to the Siboi. Alexander the Great met them on his retreat down the Indus. The Agalassoi who could muster an army of 40,000 foot and 3,000 horse, offered stout resistance to Alexander, but were decisively defeated by him. According to the classical accounts the inhabitants of one of their towns to the number of 20,000 set fire to their dwellings and cast themselves with their wives and children into the flames in order to escape subordination to the Greeks.

Agathokles—an Indo-Greek prince who ruled in the Taxila region (*c*. 190-180 B.C.). Some of his coins have been found in that locality. They contain his name both in Greek and a kind of Prakrit.

Agesilos—a Greek who was the superintending engineer of the Kushan King Kanishka. His name has been found mentioned in the celebrated relic-casket found amongst the ruins of the relic tower that was built by Kanishka's orders at Peshawar. (*J.R.A.S.*, 1908, p. 1109)

Aga Khan, the—is the title of the religious head of the Borah Ismailian community of the Muhammadans in India. The present Aga Khan, Prince Aly, is the fourth successor to the title. It was first conferred on Hasan Aly Shah who claimed descent from the Prophet through his daughter. His son Aga Aly Shah bore the title for three years (1881-84) and was succeeded by his son Sultan Muhammad Aga Khan III on whom was conferred the title of "His Highness". (Dumasia, Naoroji—*The Aga Khan and His Ancestors*)

Agnikulas, the—were the four Rajput clans, viz. the Pawar (Pramara), Parihar (Pratihara), Chauhan (Chahumana) and Solanki or Chalukya. According to tradition as preserved in the *Chand Raisa* these four tribes were 'fire-born' and originated from a fire-pit at Mount Abu in southern Rajputana. The tradition suggests that the four clans were related and all arose in southern Rajputana. It also suggests that there was a rite of purgation by fire, somewhere in southern Rajputana, whereby some foreigners were purified and made fit to enter the Hindu caste system. (*J. R. Anthrop. Inst.*, 1911, p. 42)

Agnimitra—was the son and successor of Pushyamitra, the founder of the Sunga dynasty (*q.v.*). During his father's reign he was the viceroy in the Narmada region with his capital at Vidisa, the modern Bhilsa. He defeated his southern neighbour, the king of Vidarbha (Berar) and extended the Sunga dominions up to the Warda river. He succeeded his father in about 149 B.C.

and ruled, according to the Puranas, for eight years. His love affairs formed the theme of Kalidas's drama *Malvikagrimitra*. His name has also been found on several coins. (Pargiter, *Dynasties of the Kali Age*, pp. 30-70)

Agni Purana—is one of the eighteen *Puranas*. It contains the most systematic record of Indian historical tradition.

Agra-Mahisi—was the designation of the chief queen during the Scythian epoch, e.g. Naganika. (*PHAI*, p. 517)

Agrammes—variant Xandrames, is the name given by classical writers like Curtius to the king of Magadha who was the contemporary of Alexander the Great and whom the latter did not attack. He was the son of a usurper who was a barber by caste and was born after his father had become the king of the Prasii. The name is perhaps a Greek distortion of the Sanskrit term *Augrasainya*, i.e. the son of Ugrasena who was, according to the *Mahabodhivamsa*, the founder of the Nanda dynasty. (*PHAI*, p. 232; Mc Crindle, *The Invasion of India by Alexander*, p. 222)

Agronomoi, the—were magistrates who, according to Strabo, in the time of Chandragupta Maurya, "had the care of the rivers, measured the land and inspected the closed reservoirs from which water is distributed by canals, so that all may have an equal share of it. These persons have charge also of the hunters, and have the power of rewarding or punishing those who merit either. They collect the taxes, and superintend the occupations connected with land. They superintend the public roads and place a pillar at every ten stadia to indicate the by-ways and distances". They were magistrates in charge of rural administration and have been equated with the *Adhyakshas* mentioned in Kautilya's *Arthasastra* and the Rajukas referred to in Asokan edicts. (Strabo, Vol. III, p. 103 and *PHAI*, pp. 284 and 318)

Ahalya Bai, the Rani—was the widowed daughter-in-law of Malhar Rao Holkar (1728-64). Malhar Rao had been predeceased by his son, Khande Rao, in 1754. So on her father-in-law's death Ahalya Bai became the ruler of the vast Holkar state with its capital at Indore and administered the state with great success till her death in 1795. She was one of the most exemplary rulers that ever ruled and is still remembered by many benevolent works and temples that she built in different parts of India. The high road from Calcutta to Benares, the temple of Annapurna at Benares and that of Vishnu at Gaya were all built by her. She also played a leading part in the stirring events of the time. She had one son, Malle Rao, who died in 1766 and in 1767 Ahalya Bai appointed Tukoji Holkar as the commander of the Holkar's army. Eventually on the death of Ahalya Bai in 1795 Tukoji Holkar ascended the *gadi* of the Holkar raj. (*Prog. Ind. Hist. Records Commn.*, Dec., 1930)

Ahavamalla—was the title of the Chalukya king Somesvara I of Kalyani (A.D. 1053-68). He restored the power and prestige of the Chalukyas by defeating the contemporary Chola king Rajadhiraja in the battle of Koppam. He also stormed Dhara in Malwa and Kanchi in the south. Being seized by an incurable fever he put an end to his life by drowning himself in the Tunga-bhadra river, while reciting his faith in Siva.

Ahichhhatra—ancient city, modern Ramnagar, in the Bareilly district was, according to the *Mahabharata*, the capital of northern Panchala which fell to the share of Drona. It was a considerable town when Hiuen Tsang visited the country in the seventh century.

Ahmad Shah Bahmani—ninth sultan of the Bahmani kingdom, ascended the throne in 1422 after murdering his brother, the eighth sultan Firoz, and ruled till 1435. He waged a long war with Vijayanagar, ravaged the country and put to death thousands of men, women and children. He also destroyed the independence of the Hindu kingdom of Warangal in 1425 and fought wars with the sultans of Malwa and Gujarat and the Hindu rulers of Konkan. He transferred the capital from Kulbarga to Bidar.

Ahmad Shah, Emperor—fifteenth Mughul emperor (1748-54) of Delhi. As Prince he had repulsed the first invasion of Ahmad Shah Abdali just a month before the death of his father Emperor Muhammad Shah whom he succeeded. But Abdali renewed his invasion in 1750 and again in 1751 and compelled Emperor Ahmad Shah to cede the Punjab. Ahmad's reign was inglorious and in 1754 he was blinded and deposed by the *wazir* Gazi-uddin.

Ahmad Shah Durrani—*see ante* Ahmad Shah Abdali.

Ahmad Shah of Gujarat—was the third independent Muhammadan ruler or sultan of Gujarat (1411-41). The rule of his father and grandfather had been confined to the neighbourhood of Ahmadabad. It was Sultan Ahmad Shah who extended his rule over the whole of Gujarat and thus really laid the foundation of the independent kingdom of Gujarat. He fought with the sultans of Malwa and the princes of Rajputana and never suffered a defeat. He built the city of Ahmadabad near the old Hindu town of Aswal and made it a beautiful, splendid and charming city.

Ahmadabad—is the name of two cities, one in Gujarat and the second in the Deccan. Both were founded by rulers having the name of Ahmad. Ahmadabad in the Deccan was founded by the ninth Bahmani sultan Ahmad Shah (1422-35) (*q.v.*) who transferred his capital from Kulbarga to Bidar and named it Ahmadabad after himself. It declined after the fall of the Bahmani kingdom. Ahmadabad in Gujarat was founded by Sultan Ahmad Shah (1411-41) (*q.v.*) of Gujarat near the site of the old Hindu city of Aswal. It continued to be the capital of Gujarat from its foundation in the fifteenth century till the absorption of Gujarat in the Presidency of Bombay in the eighteenth century. It passed from the hands of the sultans into those of the Mughul emperor when Akbar conquered Gujarat in 1572, then into the hands of the Marathas in 1758 and lastly was incorporated within the British Indian Empire. It is particularly rich in noble buildings and was in its days of glory one of the foremost cities in the world. At one time it had a population of 900,000 and it is the home of many millionaire merchant princes. Its prosperity is said to hang on three threads—silk, gold and cotton. At present it is the capital of the newly constituted state of Gujarat and is the centre of of the cotton textile industry in India.

Ahmadnagar—was the capital of the Nizam Shahi dynasty which set up in the Deccan in 1490 a kingdom independent of the Bahmani sultanate. It was founded by the first sultan Ahmad Nizam Shah (*q.v.*). Akbar conquered it after overcoming the gallant resistance of Chand Bibi. It declined in importance after the conquest and annexation of the kingdom of Ahmadnagar by Emperor Shah Jahan in 1637. It is, however, still a large town and the head-quarters of the district bearing its name.

Ahmad Nizam Shah—original name Malik Ahmad, was a son of Nizamu-l-Mulk Bahri, leader of the Deccanee party in Bidar who had contrived in 1481 the death of Muhammad Gawan, the chief minister of the Bahmani sultan, Muhammad Shah Bahmani. On the death of his father Malik Ahmad he defeated the last Bahmani sultan Mahmud (1482-1518), established himself as an independent sovereign and founded his capital at Ahmadnagar so called after him. He also assumed the title of Ahmad Nizam Shah and his dynasty came therefore to be known as the Nizam Shahi dynasty of Ahmadnagar. In 1499 he conquered and annexed the strong fortress of Deogiri or Daulatabad and thus consolidated his dominions. He ruled till 1508.

Ahoms, the—were a people of Shan tribe of Upper Burma. Led by Sukapha they invaded and occupied the north-eastern part of Assam in about A.D. 1228, about the time when the Muhammadans invaded India from the north-west. The Ahoms gradually acquired sovereignty over Assam comprising the modern districts of Lakhimpur, Sibsagar, Darang, Nowgong and Kamrup. The district of Goalpara which is now included in Assam was never a part of the Ahom kingdom nor were the districts of Cachar and Sylhet. These three districts were joined with Assam only after British conquest in 1824. The Ahoms had the unique distinction of keeping off from the north-eastern part of India the Muslim invaders, Pathans as well as Mughuls, even though the latter conquered the rest of India. The Ahom rule in Assam lasted for over six centuries (1228-1825) during which thirty-nine kings sat on the throne. The kings bore the royal title of *Svargadeo* or lord of the Heaven. The more prominent of these kings were the seventeenth, named Pratap Singh (1603-41) (*q.v.*) and the twenty-ninth named Gadadhar Singh (1681-86) (*q.v.*). The earlier Ahom kings bore only Ahom names, but Pratap Singh was the first to assume a Sanskritised name and from his time onwards all the succeeding kings bore two names, one Ahom and the other Sanskritic. The Ahoms brought with them their own religion which they later on abandoned in favour of Hinduism. They also brought with them a language with a script of its own. But this language and script also gradually gave way to the Assamese language and script which is akin to Sanskrit and Bengali. The Ahoms established in Assam an efficient system of administration, based more or less on a form of feudalism with all its merits and demerits. The Ahom rulers maintained official records called *Buranjies* of their activities and thus promoted the production of much historical literature in Ahom as well as in Assamese. The Ahom capital was at Garhgaon near modern Jorhat in Sibsagar district. The last independent Ahom king of Assam was Jogeswar Singh, the thirty-ninth ruler of the dynasty founded by Sukapha in A.D. 1228. Jogeswar ruled just for one year (1819) and was overthrown by the Burmese. But the Burmese rule in Assam lasted only five years (1819-24) at the end of which the province passed under British rule by the treaty of Yandabo which closed the first Anglo-Burmese war and the Ahom rule in Assam practically ended. In 1832 the British established as a protected prince Purandar Singh who belonged to the old Ahom royal family as the ruler of upper Assam, but deposed

him in 1838 on account of his misgovernment. This marked
the final end of Ahom rule in Assam. The Ahoms are now a
part of the mixed population of Assam and form a very small
minority amongst them. (*See* Assam.)

Ahsanabad—*see* Kulbarga or Gulbarga.

Ahsan Shah, Jalaluddin—governor of Ma'bar, who rose in rebellion
against Sultan Muhammad Tughluq (*q.v.*) and proclaimed
himself independent in 1335. He founded the independent
Muslim kingdom of Madura which was, however, annexed
to the Hindu kingdom of Viyayanagar in 1377-78.

Ain-i-Akbari—is a unique work in Persian written by Emperor
Akbar's friend and minister Abu-l-Fazl. It is a survey of Akbar's
empire and of the imperial system and contains, unlike most
other historical records in Persian, a good deal of statistical
account and throws a flood of light on the economic condition
and administrative system of the Mughuls. It was translated
and annotated by Blochmann and Jarratt in 1873 and is a
most reliable source of information about India in Akbar's time.

Aix-la-chapelle, the treaty of—ended the war of Austrian succession in Europe in 1748 and the consequent First Anglo-French
War in India on the basis of mutual restitution of conquests.
Madras which had been conquered by the French during the
course of the war was therefore restored to the English.

Ajanta, caves and frescos at—represent the highest development
of the art of fresco-painting in India. Several caves in the
Ajanta valley in the Bombay Presidency were illuminated with
pictures drawn in colours representing various aspects of life
as well as flora and fauna. The paintings began to be drawn
up in the fifth century A.D. and were continued till the seventh
century. The lines of the drawings are very vigorous, the
knowledge of the pigments, and of the standard of mixture show
very great skill. The art is mainly decorative and is superior
to the contemporary art of Italy and southern Europe. The
human figures and the scenery depicted in the frescos at Ajanta
are typically southern; the architecture also is southern and
show little connexion with northern Indian architecture and
fresco painting. (Fergusson and Burgess, *The Cave Temples of
India*; Havell, *Indian Sculpture and Painting*; Smith, *History of Fine
Art in India and Ceylon*; *Ajanta Frescos*, O.U.P. On the question
of date—Smith, *Vakataka Dynasty of Berar* (*J.R.A.S.*, April 1914).

Ajatasatru—also called Kunika, was the son and successor of
Bimbisara, the king of Magadha and contemporary of Gautama
Buddha. According to tradition Ajatasatru killed his father and

ascended the throne. He proved to be a powerful king who extended the rule of Magadha by conquering Vaisali, by humbling Prasenajit, the king of Kosala and compelling him to cede to him the Kasi village and to give to him a Kosalan princess in marriage. He built a fortress at Pataligrama at the confluence of the Ganges and the Son and thus laid the foundation of the famous city of Pataliputra. Mahavira, the founder of Jainism and Gautama Buddha, the founder of Buddhism are said to have died early in his reign. Ajatasatru was a friend of the Jainas as well as of the Buddhists, though he was the patron of Devadatta, the schismatic cousin of Gautama Buddha. The first Buddhist Council is said to have been held in his reign, soon after the death of Gautama Buddha, at Rajagriha. The approximate date of his reign is from 516 B.C. to 489 B.C.

Ajayadeva—king of Gujarat (A.D. 1174-76), began his reign by a merciless persecution of the Jains and tortured their leader to death. (*Archaeol. S.W.* 1., Vol. IX, p. 16)

Ajayadeva—was the Chouhan king who founded Ajmer in about A.D. 1100. He and his queen Somaladevi issued coins some of which are extant. (*Ind. Ant.*, 1912, p. 209)

Ajit Singh—posthumous son of Raja Jaswant Singh of Marwar (Jodhpur), was born in Lahore in 1679. Ajit was brought to Delhi where Emperor Aurangzeb thought of converting him to Islam. He was, however, escorted out of Delhi to Marwar by the daring and courage of a Rathor chief named Durgadas. The case of Ajit Singh was taken up not only by the Rathor chiefs of Marwar but also by the the Rana of Mewar and led to a prolonged war between Emperor Aurangzeb and the Rajputs which dragged on till 1709 when peace was made between Ajit Singh and Aurangzeb's son and successor, Emperor Bahadur Shah I. By this peace Ajit Singh was recognised as the Rana of Marwar. In 1714 Ajit Singh gave one of his daughters in marriage to Emperor Farruksiyar and this alliance greatly increased his influence in the Mughul Court. His support was sought by the Sayyid brothers who at this time controlled the imperial administration and Ajit Singh became the governor of Ajmer and Gujarat. His dominions thus extended from Ajmer to the western coast and he had a fine opportunity for rallying the Hindu opposition to the Mughul and for overthrowing them. But he could not fully utilise the opportunities and eventually met with a tragic and mysterious death at the hands of his son, Bhakt Singh.

Ajivikas—were a religious sect founded by Gosala, a contemporary of Gautama Buddha and Mahavira. Their beliefs are expounded in two works *viz.* the *Samanna-phala-Sutta* and the *Bhagavati Sutra*. The Ajivikas did not believe in human efforts and they held that conditions of all human beings were caused by an inexorable fate. Theirs was a thorough-going determinism denying the free will of man and his moral responsibility for any so-called good or evil. They never became a large sect in India strong enough to influence her politics, though in Asoka's time they attracted the attention of the monarch who conferred upon them three cave-temples in the Barabar Hill near Gaya.

Ajmer—(also spelt Ajmir) a city founded in A.D. 1100 by the Chouhan king Ajaya Deva. It passed under Muslim rule after the defeat of Prithviraj in 1192 at the second battle of Tarain at the hands of Shihabuddin Muhammad of Ghur. It continued to be under Muslim rule and was constituted into a *suba* by Akbar.

Ajodhya—(see Ayodhya)

Akbar—the third Mughul Emperor (1556-1605), was the real founder of the Mughul empire and dynasty in India. At his accession on the death of his father, Humayun, in 1556, Akbar possessed no definite territory. Late in the same year his victory in the second battle of Panipat over Himu who represented the cause of the Afghan Sur dynasty, made him the master of the Panjab, Delhi, Agra and of the adjacent territories. Within the next five years he not only consolidated his hold over these territories but also established his sway over the valley of the Ganges and the Jumna as far east as Allahabad as well as over Gwalior in central India and Ajmer in Rajasthan. Within the next twenty years Akbar conquered the whole of northern India except Kashmir, Sind and Orissa. These three kingdoms also he annexed to his dominions by 1592. Already in 1581 he had reduced to submission his younger brother Hakim who ruled as an independent king in Kabul which became a part of Akbar's empire on Hakim's death in 1585. Ten years later he acquired Qandahar and annexed Baluchistan. Having thus completed the conquest of northern India, Akbar sought to conquer southern India. He stormed Ahmadnagar in 1600 and captured Asirgarh in Khandesh in 1601. That was his last conquest. At his death four years later Akbar's empire extended from Kabul in the west to Bengal in the east and from the foot of the Himalayas in the north to the river Narmada in the south. It was a vast empire which Akbar divided into the following fifteen *subas* or provinces: (1) Kabul; (2) Lahore (Panjab) including Kashmir; (3) Multan including Sind; (4) Delhi;

(5) Agra; (6) Awadh (Oudh); (7) Allahabad; (8) Ajmer; (9) Ahmadabad (Gujarat); (10) Malwa; (11) Bihar; (12) Bengal including Orissa; (13) Khandesh; (14) Berar and (15) Ahmadnagar. Akbar was great not only as a conqueror but also as an administrator and empire-builder. He gave to his empire an administrative system which was much superior to the one that had prevailed before. His was an autocracy organised on a bureaucratic basis. Its chief aim was the enhancement and maintenance of the personal authority and revenue of the monarch. The Emperor's will was carried out by a body of officials called *mansabdars*. They were divided into thirty-three classes, from *mansabdars* of 10 to those of 5,000. They were paid salaries in cash. Various rules were drawn up to prevent malpractices, especially the practice of fraudulent musters. Over each suba there was a Subadar, also called *Nawab Nazim*, who exercised a great deal of power and held his miniature court, as under the Turko-Afghans; but Akbar put an effective check on their powers by creating a new post of the *Diwan* who was placed in charge of the provincial finances. To improve his finances Akbar with the assistance of Raja Todar Mall organised the land-revenue system on the basis of survey according to a uniform standard of measurement, settlement directly with the *ryots* or cultivators, assessment at the rate of one-third of the produce which could be paid either in cash on in kind and was collected by officers appointed and paid by the State.

Akbar stands pre-eminent amongst the Indo-Muslim rulers as an empire-builder. Earlier Muslim rulers of India had not cared at all for their non-Muslim subjects, and the relation between them and their Hindu subjects who formed the majority of the population, was one of chronic warfare and hostility. Very early in his career Akbar realised that the Emperor of Hindustan must not be the king of the Muslims only. His rule, if it was to be firmly established, must be broad-based on the foundation of general loyalty, accorded willingly by the Hindus and the Musalmans alike. He, therefore, adopted a policy of conciliation and liberalism. He abolished the policy of condemning to slavery the members of the families of rulers defeated and dethroned by him. He treated their women folk with honour and offered the vanquished princes honourable careers in his own service. He abolished sectarian taxes like the pilgrims' tax and the *jaziya* which were imposed only on the Hindus, appointed them to high offices according to their talents, intermarried with the Hindu princes and accepted them as members of the royal family instead of imposing upon them the obligation to embrace Islam. This liberal and conciliatory attitude turned the Hindu Rajputs into his staunch supporters and it was Rajput valour that co-operated with the Muhammadan soldiers of Akbar to extend his dominion from Kabul to Bengal. Last, but not the least, Akbar dreamt of creating an Indian nation out of the fighting Hindus and Muhammadans in India. Feeling that it was religion which, more than anything else, tended to keep them apart he wanted to give them a new religion which would contain the best principles of all religions. It was with this grand object in view that in 1581 he promulgated a new religion called the *Din Ilahi* (*q.v.*). Its principles were taken partly from the Quran, partly from Hindu scriptures and partly from the Bible. Akbar believed in the principle of universal toleration, made no attempt to force his religion on others, and he left its acceptance to the inner feelings of man. As religion is more a matter of faith than of reason his new religion made few converts and the *Din Ilahi* failed in its object. But the effort to promulgate it "assured to him (Akbar) for all time a pre-eminent place among the benefactors of humanity—greatness and universal tolerance in matters of religion". (V. A. Smith, *Akbar the Great Moghul*; Von Noer, *Emperor Akbar*.)

Akbar II—was the eighteenth and penultimate Mughul Emperor of Delhi. He was the son of Emperor Shah Alam II (*q.v.*) and ruled from 1806-37. The British had already become the practical rulers of the greater part of India and Delhi had come under their control in 1803. Emperor Shah Alam II had lived virtually as a pensioner of the East India Company during the latter part of his reign (1769-1806), and his son and successor Emperor Akbar II was only a titular sovereign at the sufferance of the East India Company. He was asked "to give up all ceremonial implying supremacy over the Company's dominions" by the Governor-General Lord Hastings (1813-23) who stopped the presentation of *nazars* (*nuzzurs*) or formal presents which it had so long been the practice for the head of the East India Company in India to offer to the Delhi Emperor. His son and successor Emperor Bahadur Shah II (1837-58) was the last of the Mughul Emperors of India.

Akbar, Prince—was a son of Emperor Aurangzeb and his consort Dilras Bano Begum. The third and favourite son of Emperor

Aurangzeb, he was employed by the Emperor to lead the Mughul army in the war against the Rajputs in 1679. His army which was then in Chitor was surprised by the Rajputs and Aurangzeb transferred him to Marwar. Smarting under the disgrace of this removal Prince Akbar dreamt that with the assistance of Rajput arms he could replace his father just as the latter had displaced Shah Jahan. The Rajput chiefs also encouraged him in his hopes and it was believed that backed by Rajput arms he would make "a truly national King of India". He, therefore, wrote a very outspoken letter to his imperial father charging him with the folly of abandoning the wise policy of toleration followed by Akbar, drawing his attention to the prevailing misgovernment and asking him to retire from the world because he should not expect from his sons any better treatment than what he had meted out to his own father. With an army of 70,000 men including many Rajputs Akbar arrived near Ajmer on January 15, 1681, when Aurangzeb's army was away at Chitor and elsewhere. If Akbar had attacked his father at this moment the Emperor would have been caught at a disadvantage, but the Prince whiled away valuable time in indolence and pleasure. The time thus gained enabled Emperor Aurangzeb to sow distrust between his rebellious son Akbar and the Rajputs and the latter deserted him. Prince Akbar then fled from Rajputana to the Deccan where he took refuge with Shambhuji, son and successor of Shivaji. This threatened combination of Prince Akbar with the Marathas led Aurangzeb to proceed personally to the Deccan where Prince Akbar soon found it useless to continue to stay. He therefore quitted India and retired to Persia. In 1695 Prince Akbar made an attempt to invade India with Persian help. He advanced with twelve thousand Persian horsemen to the neighbourhood of Multan but was beaten back by a superior Mughul army led by his eldest brother Prince Muazzam. Defeated and baffled, Prince Akbar retired again to Persia where he died in exile in 1704.

Akbar Hydari, Sir—(1869-1941), started career as a subordinate officer in the Finance Department of the Government of India and rose to be the first Indian Controller of Treasuries. In 1937 he became the Chief Minister of the Nizam in whose dominions he introduced some reforms. Later on he became a Member of the Viceroy's Executive Council.

Akbar Khan—was a son of Amir Dost Muhammad of Afghanistan. He took a prominent part in organising Afghan resistance to the British army of occupation during the First Anglo-Afghan War (1841-43).

Akbar-namah, the—is a historical account of the reign of Emperor Akbar, written by his friend and courtier, Abul Fazl (*q.v.*). It is a very authoritative account of the reign of Akbar written by a contemporary historian who had personal knowledge of many of the incidents narrated by him and had full access to all state-papers of the time. It is very reliable about dates and topography, though partial in the estimate of Akbar.

Akesines, the—one of the Panjab rivers mentioned in the *Nadi-stuti* (*In Praise of the Rivers*) hymn of the Rigveda where it is called Asikni. Classical historians called it Akesines. Its modern name is Chinab. King Poros who opposed the passage of Alexander the Great ruled in the valley lying between this river on the east and the Hydaspes or the Jhelum on the west.

Akmal Khan—Afridi chieftain, raised the Afridis in revolt against the Mughul Emperor Aurangzeb in 1672 and crowned himself king. He defeated a Mughul army at Ali Masjid and succeeded for a time in establishing his rule over the whole of the Pathan land from Attock to Qandahar. In 1674 Aurangzeb personally went to Peshawar to supervise the operations against Akmal Khan and by a combination of diplomacy and arms reduced Akmal Khan and the Pathans to submission.

Alauddin I—was the first sultan of the Bahmani dynasty of the Deccan. His full official title was Sultan Alauddin Hasan Shah al-wali al Bahmani. Previously known as Hasan, entitled Zafar Khan, he was an Afghan or Turki officer of the Delhi sultan Muhammad bin Tughluq (1325-51), and was employed in the Deccan. The Muslim nobles in the Deccan, driven to rebellion by the eccentric policy of Sultan Muhammad bin Tughlaq, seized the fort of Daulatabad, accepted Hasan or Zafar Khan as the king who now assumed the title of Sultan Alauddin Bahman Shah and set up a new dynasty of kings with Kulbarga as his capital in 1347. The story related by Firishta about Hasan's origin to the effect that he was originally a menial in the service of Gangu, a Brahman astrologer of Delhi, who enjoyed the favour of Muhammad bin Tughluq, and later on, rose to prominence owing to the patronage of his Brahman master in whose honour he assumed title of Bahmani, is not correct as it finds no support either from coins or from inscriptions. The earlier Muhammadan chronicle *Burhan-i-Maasir* states that in consequence of his descent Hasan was known as Bahman after his coronation. In fact Hasan claimed descent from the famous Persian hero Bahman and the dynasty that he founded came to be known as the Bahmani dynasty. Hasan was a successful warrior and before his death in February, 1358, he left a kingdom extending from the river Wain Ganga on the north to the river Krishna on the south. He divided this kingdom into four provinces, namely, Kulbarga, Daulatabad, Berar and Bidar and gave it an efficient system of administration. According to the *Burhan-i-Maasir* he was a just king who did much towards propagating the Islamic faith.

Alauddin II—was the tenth sultan of the Bahmani dynasty of the Deccan. He ruled from 1435 to 1457, fought a war with Deva Raya II, the neighbouring Hindu king of Vijayanagar and forced him to make a peace favourable to the Sultan. Alauddin II was a zealous champion of Islam and was benevolent to his co-religionists. He founded many public schools, mosques and charitable institutions including a well-provided hospital at his capital at Bidar. It was, however, during his reign that the rivalry between the Deccanee Muhammadans backed by the Abyssinians who were mostly Sunnis and the foreign Muhammadans who were mostly Shias, became very acute and led to a brutal murder, with the approval of the Sultan, of a very large number of foreign Muhammadans, 'Sayyids and Mughuls', in the fort of Chakan, near Poona.

Alauddin Hussain Shah—was the sultan of Bengal from 1493 to 1518 and founder of the Hussain Shahi dynasty of Bengal. He was a Sayyid of Arab descent and proved to be a very successful and popular king of Bengal. He restored order in the internal administration, suppressed the power of the palace-guards, expelled the Abyssinian mercenaries, extended the limits of his kingdom to the borders of Orissa, recovered Bihar from the ruler of Jaunpur and captured Kamtapur in Cooch Behar. He built many mosques and alms-houses in his dominions and particularly at Gaur (*q.v.*). He was tolerant and appointed many Hindus like Purandar Khan, Rup and Sanatan to high offices. No insurrection or rebellion occurred during his reign of twenty-four years and he died at Gaur, beloved by his subjects and respected by his neighbours. He was succeeded by his son Nusrat Shah.

Alauddin Khalji—Sultan of Delhi (1296-1316), was the nephew and son-in-law of Jalaluddin Khalji, the founder of the Khalji dynasty of Delhi. Before his accession he was given the fief of Kara in the district of Allahabad. In this capacity and without the knowledge of the Sultan of Delhi Alauddin led the first

Muhammadan invasion into the Deccan in 1295 and invaded the kingdom of Devagiri then ruled by Ramachandradeva of the Yadava dynasty. Ramachandra sought in vain the help of the other Hindu rulers of the Deccan and was forced to submit by paying a large tribute in gold, silver, pearls and precious stones. The acquisition of this vast wealth roused the ambition of Alauddin Khalji who on his return brought about the murder of Sultan Jalaluddin Khalji and ascended the throne of Delhi in 1296. The sons of the late Sultan were killed and their adherents were bribed into silence and inaction. Alauddin had, however, immense odds to overcome. The Mongols invaded his dominions several times and on one occasion in 1299 they arrived in the vicinity of Delhi. They were however beaten back on all these occasions with severe casualties and ceased to give any further trouble to Alauddin after their defeat in 1308. A batch of the Mongols who had invaded India earlier in the reign of Jalaluddin, had been allowed to settle near Delhi after they had accepted Islam. They became known as the New Mussulmans and continued to be a discontented and restless lot. They hatched a conspiracy against the Sultan who came to know of it and wreaked a terrible vengeance on them ordering their wholesale massacre which was committed on one single day. Later on some of his near relations attempted to rise in revolt against him. But all of them were reduced to submission and sent to cruel deaths. It has been said that with the accession of Alauddin Khalji began the 'imperial period of the Sultanate'. A year after his accession his army led by his brother Ulugh Khan and his *wazir* Nusrat Khan overran and conquered the Hindu kingdom of Gujarat, drove the Hindu king Karnadeva to flee with his daughter Devala Devi to the court of Ramachandradeva, the Yadava king of Devagiri and brought back to Delhi an immense booty along with two important captives. One was queen Kamala Devi of Devagiri who later on became one of the favourite wives of Alauddin and the other was a young slave named Kafur who soon rose in the estimate of the Sultan and became the most influential noble in the state under the title of Malik Naib (or Lieutenant). Other conquests soon followed: Ranthambhor in 1301, Chitor in 1303, Malwa in 1305, and thereafter Ujjain, Dhar, Mandu and Chanderi in quick succession. The invasion of the Deccan was then resumed under the leadership of Kafur, now entitled Malik Naib (or Lieutenant) and Khwaja Haji. Devagiri was overrun and conquered a second time in 1307, and the Kakatiya kingdom of Warangal was reduced in 1310. This was soon followed by the reduction of the Hoysala kingdom of Dvarasamudra and the extension of the Muhammadan arms along both the coasts up to Cape Comorin. The victorious army returned to Delhi in 1311 carrying with it a vast booty of 612 elephants, 20,000 horses, 96,000 maunds of gold and many boxes of jewels and pearls. Never was the Delhi Sultan richer and more powerful: he now stood out as the paramount ruler of the whole of India from the Himalayas to Cape Comorin.

Alauddin was no mere soldier. He was probably illiterate, but he was a man of strong commonsense who knew what he wanted and also how to get it. According to the Muslim historian Barani, the Sultan had noticed the many rebellions that had disturbed the peace in the early part of his reign. He attributed these rebellious tendencies to four causes, namely, (i) disregard of the affairs of the state by the Sultan, (ii) the use of wine, (iii) intimacy and alliances amongst the nobles which enabled them to organise conspiracies, and (v) abundance of wealth which engendered pride and disloyalty. He took a series of strong and effective remedial measures. A strong system of espionage was introduced and marriages and other alliances amongst the nobles without the previous permission of the Sultan were strictly forbidden. Wine-drinking, wine-selling and wine-making were all strictly prohibited. Lastly, all kinds of private property were assailed. Pensions, endowments and free gifts were all appropriated to the state. People were heavily taxed and the taxes were so rigorously collected that the tax-collectors came to be despised and people refused to give their daughters in marriage to them. But Alauddin had attained his object. Conspiracies and rebellions ceased to disturb him any more. Alaudin frankly ruled by the sword and would not suffer either the Muhammadan ecclesiastics or the people to interfere with the business of administration which he carried on according to his will. He, therefore, maintained a large strong army which he appeared to have paid directly from the state. He fixed the salary of a foot-soldier at about Rs. 234/- per year and would pay him an additional yearly salary of about Rs. 78/- if he maintained two horses. In order to enable the soldiers to live on their scanty salaries he fixed the prices of all articles from the absolute necessaries of life like rice to articles of luxury like slaves and concubines. Elaborate measures were taken to enforce these rates and so long as he lived nobody dared to transgress them.

Alauddin was the patron of poets like Amir Khusrav and Hasan. He was also fond of architecture and built several forts and many mosques.

His old age was unhappy. He had had no success after 1312. His health broke and he fell a victim to dropsy. His intellect became blurred and his judgement became defective. He could not place much trust either on any of his wives or on his sons and Malik Kafur whom he had raised from the position of a captive to the rank of the Lieutenant of the Sultan, practically carried on the administration during the closing years of his reign which came to an end with his death on January 2, 1316.

Alauddin Masud—was the seventh sultan (1242-46) of the Slave dynasty (*q.v.*). He was the son of Sultan Rukn-ud-din, the second son and immediate successor of Sultan Iltutmish (1211-36). He was placed on the throne two years after the deposition of his aunt Sultana Raziya (*q.v.*) (1236-40). He proved to be an incompetent ruler and was deposed in 1246 by the nobles who then placed on the throne Nasir-ud-din (*q.v.*).

Alam Khan—was the third son of Sultan Buhlul Lodi (1451-89), and uncle of the last Delhi sultan Ibrahim Lodi (1517-26). He claimed that he had a better title to the throne of Delhi than his nephew and having failed by his own resources to depose Ibrahim Lodi he joined with Daulat Khan Lodi, governor of Lahore, in inviting Babur to invade India. Eventually Babur invaded India, defeated and killed Ibrahim Lodi in the first battle of Panipat (1526) and himself occupied the throne of Delhi. Alam Khan died of a broken heart.

Alam Shah I—*See* Bahadur Shah I.

Alam Shah II or **Shah Alam II**—was the seventeenth Mughul emperor (1759-1806). Prince Ali Gauhar was the name by which he was known before he succeeded his father Emperor Alamgir II in 1759. There after he assumed the title of Alam Shah II and is known in history as Shah Alam II. Emperor Shah Alam II reigned at a very critical period of Indian history. His father and predecessor Emperor Alamgir II had been deposed by his over-ambitious and unscrupulous *wazir* Ghazi-ud-din who was determined to be the master of the new emperor as well. Two years before his accession the East India Company had fought the battle of Plassey which had practically made the English East India Company rulers of Bengal, Bihar and Orissa. In the north-west Ahmad Shah Abdali had already begun his invasions of India, had sacked Delhi in 1756 and definitely occupied the Panjab in 1759 after driving away the

Marathas who had occupied the province in 1758. In the south the Marathas under the leadership of Peshwa Balaji Baji Rao (1740-61) were thinking of establishing their rule in place of that of the Mughuls. Thus at his accession Shah Alam II was confronted with an overweening and disloyal *wazir* in his own capital, with the rising power of the East India Company in Bengal, with the equally ambitious Ahmad Shah Abdali in the Panjab. In these circumstances Shah Alam II considered Abdali to be the greatest danger and he turned to the Marathas for protection against Abdali who, however, decisively defeated the Marathas at the third battle of Panipat in 1761. Abdali left Emperor Shah Alam II on the throne of Delhi and though his subsequent efforts to establish his sovereignty in Delhi failed, Emperor Shah Alam II was no gainer by Abdali's failure. In 1764 he made his second main effort to recover some of his power, entered into a alliance with Nawab Sujauddaula of Oudh and Mir Kasim, the fugitive Nawab of Bengal, for the purpose of driving away the English from Bengal. But the allied army was defeated by the English in the battle of Buxar (1764) and Emperor Shah Alam II made peace with the East India Company by the treaty of Allahabad by which he gained the districts of Kora and Allahabad from Oudh and granted to the East India Company the *Diwani* (or right of collection of revenue) over Bengal, Bihar and Orissa on condition of being paid an annual revenue of twenty-six lakhs of rupees. But the gain was temporary. The power of the Marathas which had been scotched but not destroyed as the result of the third battle of Panipat soon revived and Emperor Shah Alam II who was being kept out of his capital by the intrigues of the *wazir*, Najib-ud-daula (Ghazi-ud-din) and was anxious to return to Delhi, secured Maratha help by handing over to the Maratha chief Mahadaji Sindhia the districts of Kora and Allahabad. This enabled Shah Alam II to return to his capital in 1771, but he was no better than a puppet in the hands of the Marathas. The East India Company therefore violated the treaty of Allahabad, took away from him the districts of Kora and Allahabad and also stopped paying him the annual revenue of 26 lakhs of rupees which the Company had promised to pay him in lieu of the grant of the Diwani of Bengal in 1764. Emperor Shah Alam II was thus reduced to great straits and continued to be under Maratha control till the Second Anglo-Maratha War (1803-05) in the course of which Sindhia's army was defeated by the Company's army under General Lake in a battle fought near Delhi. Emperor Shah Alam II now passed with his capital under the protection of the East India Company. Old and blinded he was capable of no further action and was glad to accept from the East India Company a pension which he enjoyed till his death in 1806.

Alamgir—*see* under Aurangzeb.

Alamgir II—was the sixteenth Mughul emperor (1754-59). Son of the eighth Mughul emperor Jahandar Shah (1712-13) he was placed on the throne in 1754, many years after his father's death, by the *wazir* Ghazi-ud-din who blinded and deposed the fifteenth Mughul emperor Ahmad Shah and who wanted him to be no more than a puppet in his hands. The times were hard. Ahmad Shah Abdali invaded India for the fourth time in 1756, sacked Delhi, seized Sind and left his son Timur to govern the Panjab on his behalf. The Marathas soon followed suit and in 1758 they drove away Timur and occupied the Panjab. Emperor Alamgir II was a helpless spectator and as he began to make efforts to free himself from the control of the *wazir* Ghazi-ud-din the latter had him murdered in 1759. The battle of Plassey had already (1757) been fought and won by the East India Company and Emperor Alamgir II could do nothing to uphold the imperial authority over Bengal where the foundation of the British Empire in India was being laid.

Alberuni—(A.D. 973-1048) was a native of Khiva. He was brought to Ghazni in Sultan Mahmud's time (A.D. 997-1030) either as a prisoner or as a hostage. He came to India in Sultan Mahmud's train and lived in the Panjab for several years. His original name was Abu-Rihan Muhammad but he is generally known as Alberuni meaning 'the Master'. He was a profoundly learned scholar. While in India he learnt Sanskrit and made a thorough study of Hindu philosophy and other branches of Indian science. The results of his studies he embodied in his famous work entitled *Tahkik-i-Hind* ('An Enquiry into India') which is a truly scientific treatise. It records numerous accurate observations on the history, character, manners, customs and scientific knowledge of the Hindus and is a very important source-book of knowledge about Indian history and culture on the eve of the Muhammadan conquest. Some of his writings have been lost, but what remains like *'The Chronology of Ancient Nations'* (translated by Sachau) bears eloquent testimony to his erudition.

Al-Hajjaj—was the Muhammadan governor of Iraq during the Khalifate of Walid. Sind was then being ruled by King Dahir. Incensed by the operations of some pirates of Sind Al-Hajjaj sent several punitive expeditions to Sind. These were repulsed by Dahir. Al-Hajjaj then sent a larger expedition to Sind under his nephew and son-in-law Muhammad-ibn Kasim who eventually defeated and killed King Dahir in the battle of Raor (A.D. 712) and established Muslim rule in Sind.

Al-Jurz—early Arabic name for Gurjjara territory round Bhinmal or Broach.

Al-Masudi—early Arab traveller, visited in A.D. 915 the Pratihara kingdom which was then being ruled by King Mahipala I and wrote about his horses and camels.

Albuquerque, Affonso de—the second governor (1509-15) of the Portuguese possessions in India, aimed at founding a Portuguese empire in the East by occupying and directly ruling certain important places for trading purposes, by colonising selected districts, by encouraging mixed marriages between the Portuguese and the Indians, by building fortresses in places which could not be either colonised or conquered and, where even this last process was impracticable, by inducing Indian princes to recognise the supremacy of the king of Portugal and to pay him tribute. In pursuit of this policy he captured Goa in 1510 from the Sultan of Bijapur, Malacca in 1511, and Ormuz in 1515. Albuquerque was extremely unscrupulous in his methods and procured by poisoning the death of the Zamorin of Calicut who had befriended the Portuguese when they had first arrived in India. His policy of mixed marriages between the Portuguese who would stay in India and Indian women who would be converted to Christianity, failed in its objects and led to the production of a degenarate race of half-castes who could impart no real strength to the Portuguese empire in the East. His policy of systematic and cruel persecution of the Muhammadans estranged Indian sympathy from the Portuguese, and the Portuguese empire that Albuquerque dreamt of building up in the East, declined and fell soon after his death.

Alexander, A. V. (later Viscount)—was a member of the Cabinet Mission (*q.v.*) led by Lord Pethwick-Lawrence which visited India in April, 1946.

Alexander of Epirus—(272-255 B.C.) is believed to be referred to as Alikasuddara by Asoka in his Rock Edict XIII. The Alikasuddara (i.e. Alexander) mentioned in the edict might also have been Alexander of Corinth (252-244 B.C.). In either case the reference is of some help in fixing the date of Asoka.

Alexander the Great—King of Macedon (356-323 B.C.), in pursuit of his schemes of conquest, invaded unoffending India in

February or March 326 B.C. after crossing the Indus by a bridge
of boats at Ohind. The Panjab and Sind were at that time
divided into a large number of warring states, some of which
were monarchical, some tribal republics and others autonomous
states. Not only was there no unity amongst them, but there
existed mutual hostilities and rivalries which led some of them
to join the foreign invader in the expectation not only of getting
territorial rewards but also of wreaking vengeance on their
neighbours. Such a ruler was Ambhi, king of Taxila, who
went over to the side of Alexander who was thus enabled to
give his army not only the rest that it badly needed but
also the necessary training in the method of fighting with
elephants on which the strength of the Indian army largely
depended and of which the Greeks were mightily afraid. Having
been thus materially helped by the Taxilian king Ambhi, who
thus betrayed his duty as the gate-keeper of India, Alexander
crossed the Jhelum river and defeated on its banks in a hard-
fought battle King Poros whose dominions lay between the
Jhelum and the Chinab. Here Alexander's victory was due
to the greater mobility of his army which depended mainly on
the cavalry and mounted archers for its attack as against the
less mobile Indian army depending mainly on elephants,
infantrymen and archers on foot. Alexander then proceeded
eastword crossing successively the Chinab and the Ravi until
at last he reached the bank of the Bias (Hyphasis) beyond which
lay the dominions of the Prasii, that is to say, of the Nanda king
of Magadha. Though Alexander had by now subdued all the
Panjab states and peoples that lay between the Indus and the
Bias who could not unite against him, yet he had met
with much stubborn resistance from individual chiefs and
clans. Poros, though wounded in nine different places on his
body, did not flee from the battlefield and had to be, therefore,
treated with politic generosity. The Assakenians also had
fought with great valour and their stronghold Massaga was
stormed with great difficulty after Alexander had treacherously
massacred a mercenary army of 7,000 Indians whom he had
promised a safe conduct on condition of their leaving Massaga.
At Massaga, according to Diodorus, the women took up the
arms of the fallen and fought side by side with men. The sight
and experience of such valour on the part of the Indians combined with the reported enormous strength of the king or
the Prasii whose dominions lay beyond the Bias, struck terror,
as Plutarch observes, in the minds of Alexander's army and

they refused to proceed any further. Alexander, therefore, stopped on the bank of the Bias, retraced his steps to the Jhelum and marched down that river, accompanied by a large fleet, till he reached the mouths of the Indus reducing all this while the numerous states and peoples of the lower Panjab and Sind who were brave enough to offer him resistance, but not organised enough to unite against the common foreign enemy. Thus were subdued the Malavas, the Khudrakas and the Brahmanas of the kingdom of Mousikanos. The Malavas (the Malloi of the Greeks), who occupied the country about 90 miles north-east of Multan, succeeded in severely wounding Alexander himself and were punished for their daring by a general massacre which spared neither man, woman nor child. Having reached the mouths of the Indus Alexander divided his army into three parts—the fleet under Admiral Nearchos to sail along the coast into the Persian Gulf as far as the mouth of the Euphrates, one part of the army under Krateros to march along the coast and the other under the direct leadership of Alexander to march through Gedrosia (Mekran) back to Persia; and in September 325 B.C. Alexander the Great left India, nineteen months after he had first entered into India in March 326 B.C. The fleet and both parts of his army successfully completed their tasks and reached Susa in Persia in May 324 B.C. Alexander died a year later at Babylon in June 323 B.C.

The importance of Alexander's Indian invasion has sometimes been exaggerated. As a military feat it was some achievement no doubt to have overrun and conquered the Panjab and Sind in a campaign which lasted only nineteen months. But it must be remembered that it was possible largely because of the want of union amongst his Indian opponents. Then, again, his conquests did not last long. Even when he was marching back through Karmania (324 B.C.) his satrap Philippos whom he had left in charge of the upper Indus Province, was murdered. Shortly afterwards the Macedonian garrison was also overpowered and no effective control could be established by Alexander over his Indian conquests even before his death in 323 B.C. After his death these conquests soon slipped away from the hands of his successors. The colonies which he founded in India took no root. As V. A. Smith observes, "the campaign was in actual effect no more than a brilliantly successful raid which left upon India no marks save the horrid scars of bloody war. India remained unchanged and she was not hellenised." All her authors, Hindu, Buddhist or Jain, have ignored him, apparently because he was no better, in the estimate of Indiá, than a barbarian free-booter who killed a large number of unoffending men, women and children just to satisfy his vain craze for conquests and glory. His invasion, however, opened up new routes of communication between India and the Hellenic world and some of the Greek settlements that he established on the north-western frontier of India eventually became centres where the Indians and the Hellenic cultures met and influenced each other. (*E.H.I.*, pp. 52-120)

Alexandria—was the name of two Greek settlements established by Alexander the Great in the course of his invasion of India. One was in Afghanistan near Kabul and the second was in Sind near the confluence of the Chinub and the Indus. Both disappeared in later times.

Ali Adil Shah I—was the fifth sultan (1557-80) of the Adil Shahi dynasty of Bijapur. He professed the Shia form of Islam and was particularly intolerant of the Sunnis. In 1558 he made an alliance with the Hindu kingdom of Vijaynagar and invaded Ahmadnagar. The combined armies mercilessly ravaged Ahmadnagar. But the excesses perpetrated by the Hindus on the Muhammadans of Ahmadnagar soon estranged the relations between Sultan Adil Shah I and Rama Raja (*q.v.*) of Vijaya-nagar. Eventually an alliance was made amongst the four Muslim rulers of Bijapur, Ahmadnagar, Bidar and Golkunda and their combined forces defeated Vijayanagar at the battle of Talikota (1565). The victorious Adil Shah then took part in invading, plundering and destroying Vijayanagar for all time. Then in 1570 Sultan Ali Adil Shah I, in alliance with Ahmad-nagar for the purpose of driving out the Portuguese from their possessions in the western coast of India, besieged Goa with a large army, but the Portuguese foiled him. Ali Adil Shah's consort was the famous Chand Bibi of Ahmadnagar who showed great bravery in defending that city, where she had returned after the death of her husband, against Emperor Akbar.

Ali Adil Shah II—was the eighth sultan (1656-73) of the Adil Shahi dynasty of Bijapur. He was only eighteen years of age at the time of his accession. Taking advantage of his youth Emperor Shah Jahan ordered his son Aurangzeb, who was then his viceroy in the Deccan, to conquer Bijapur. So the Mughuls invaded Bijapur, defeated the young Sultan's armies in several engage-ments and forced him to purchase peace (1657) by surrendering a large portion of his territories including Bidar, Kalyani and Parenda. On the conclusion of peace with the Mughuls Sultan

Ali Adil Shah II decided to reduce to submission the Maratha leader Shivaji who had already captured some of his forts. In 1659 he sent against Shivaji a large army under Afzal Khan, who was, however, killed by Shivaji who also subsequently defeated the Bijapur army. Sultan Ali Adil Shah II never succeeded in limiting, far less reducing, the growing power of Shivaji and, pitch-forked between the Mughuls and the Marathas, he could only maintain a precarious throne till his death in 1673.

Ali Barid—was the third ruler of the Barid Shahi dynasty (*q.v.*) of Bidar, an off-shoot of the Bahmani kingdom. He was the grandson of Kasim Barid who founded the dynasty in 1492 and the son of the second Sultan Amir Barid. Ali Barid ascended the throne in A.D. 1539 and was the first of the Barid Shahi rulers to assume the title of Sultan.

Ali Gauhar, Prince—*see* under Alam Shah II.

Aligarh—a city in Uttar Pradesh, played a prominent part in modern Indian history. It had a strong fortress the capture of which in 1803 by the English from the Marathas in the course of the Second Anglo-Maratha War (*q.v.*) was an important incident as it facilitated the conquest of Delhi by the English. It was a prominent centre in the days of Sepoy Mutiny. It has a very large Muslim population and became a centre of Muslim culture in India from 1875 when by the efforts of Sir Syed Ahmad the Anglo-Oriental College was founded at Aligarh. This institution soon became the most important centre of Western education for the Indian Muslim community. In 1920 the Aligarh College was raised to the status of a University which has rendered immense services for the promotion of higher education and modern culture among the Indian Muslims. Aligarh was also the centre of what is known as the Aligarh Movement which aimed at reforming the Islamic faith by promoting western education amongst the Indian Muslims, by removing the acknowledged abuses that had crept into the Indian Muslim community and by standing away from the nationalistic movement that had been started by the Indian National Congress in 1885. This anti-nationalistic attitude of some of the patrons and products of Aligarh College led it to be considered as a seat of reaction in India. In 1906 some graduates of Aligarh organised the Muslim League to voice the aspirations of the Indian Muslim community. For some years the league worked along with the Indian National Congress in demanding a liberal constitution for India, but eventually it became more and more a communal body, took up the demand for Pakistan and ultimately became responsible for the division of India in 1947.

Ali Mardan Khalji—was appointed governor of Bengal by Sultan Qutb-ud-din (*q.v.*) in 1206. He revolted after the death of Qutb-ud-din in 1210, set himself up as the independent ruler of Bengal and assumed the title of Ala-ud-din. He was reduced to submission by Sultan Iltutmish (*q.v.*) in 1230.

Ali Mardan Khan—a Persian general and governor of Qandahar under Shah Abbas the Great. When Shah Jahan invaded Qandahar in 1638 its governor Ali Mardan Khan treacherously betrayed it to the Mughul Emperor who rewarded him with a high post in the Mughul army. Ali Mardan Khan then joined with Prince Murad in a campaign for the conquest of Balkh, but the enterprise failed. He continued to hold high offices under the Mughuls till his death and built or repaired the Ravi Canal in 1639.

Ali, Muhammad—prominent Muhammadan scholar and political leader. His translation of the Quran is a most authoritative version of it in translation. He along with his brother Shaukat Ali took a prominent part in the nationalistic political movement in India in the years following the First World War. He was a leader of the Khilafat movement which resulted from the humiliating terms imposed upon Turkey at the end of the World War I and joined with Mahatma Gandhi in starting and leading the Non-Co-operation Movement (1920-24). He became the President of the Indian National Congress in 1923, but he parted company with Mahatma Gandhi when he started the Civil Disobedience Movement in 1930. He, however, continued to be a nationalistic leader till his death.

Ali Naqi—was the *Diwan* of Gujarat while Emperor Shah Jahan's fourth son, Prince Murad, was the governor of the province. It was on a trumped up charge of having murdered Ali Naqi that Murad was executed in 1661.

Ali, Muhammad Ruhela—was the founder of the power of the Ruhelas in Rohilkhand lying at the base of the Himalayas to the north-west of Oudh. In 1774 at the end of the Rohilla War and death of their leader Hafiz Rahamat Khan the East India Company placed his son Faizullah Khan in possession of a small part of Rohilkhand, together with Rampur. Thus was founded the family of the Nawabs of Rampura.

Ali Shah—the seventh sultan (1416-20) of Kashmir. He was succeeded by his famous brother sultan Zain-ul-Abidin (1420-70) known as the Akbar of Kashmir.

Ali, Shaukat—*see* Shaukat Ali.

Alingar, the treaty of—was concluded on the 9th February, 1757, between Nawab Siraj-ud-daulah of Bengal and the East India Company represented by Clive and Watson after the recapture of Calcutta by the English. By this treaty peace was re-established between the Nawab and the East India Company on the basis of the following terms: restoration to the Company of all trading facilities as granted by the imperial *farman*, permission to repair the fort in Calcutta, right of minting coins in Calcutta, and payment by the Nawab of compensation to the English for the losses incurred by them at the capture of Calcutta by the Nawab, and maintenance of peace by both the parties in Bengal. A month after the conclusion of this treaty and in violation of it the English under Clive and Watson invaded and conquered the French possession of Chander-nagore a few miles up the Ganges above Calcutta. Further, in the following month of June the English again violated the treaty of Alinagar by entering into a conspiracy with Mir Jafar and other disaffected officers of the Nawab with the object of deposing Nawab Siraj-ud-daulah. This conspiracy culminated in the battle of Plassey (23rd June, 1757) and the defeat and eventual murder of Nawab Siraj-ud-daulah.

Alivardi Khan,—originally known as Mirza Muhammad Khan, was raised from obscurity by Shuja-u-din, Nawab of Bengal (1725-39), and came to be known as Alivardi or Allahvardi Khan. At the time of the death of Nawab Shuja-ud-din Alivardi Khan was the *naib nazim* (or chief of the Finance department) in Bihar which was then a part of the province of Bengal. Shuja-ud-din's son Sarfaraz Khan succeeded his father as the Nawab of Bengal. Shortly before, Nadir Shah (*q.v.*) had invaded and sacked Delhi and the whole of the Mughul central administration was thrown into confusion. Taking advantage of this disorganisation Alivardi Khan secured by corrupt means orders from the Delhi court appointing him as governor of Bengal in place of Sarfaraz Khan. Backed by his brother Haji Ahmad and the rich banker Jagat Set he rose in revolt against Nawab Sarfaraz Khan whom he defeated and killed in the battle of Giria, near Rajmahal, in 1740, and occupied the *masnad* of the Nawab of Bengal. By further lavish presents he secured imperial confirmation of his new authority as the Nawab of Bengal which province he ruled for the next sixteen years (1740-56) practically as an independent ruler and never sent any revenue to Delhi. Though he got the Nawabship by treachery he had some good qualities. In his early life he was a good administrator and valiant soldier. With the European trading companies which had already been established in Bengal, he maintained a strictly impartial attitude and did not allow them to violate the peace of the state by their mutual fightings. But he was greatly troubled by the Marathas who invaded Bengal practically every year. Having failed to repel the Marathas even though he treacherously assassinated the Maratha general, Bhaskar Pandit, Alivardi made peace with them in 1751 by ceding to them a part of the revenues of Orissa and by promising to pay an annual tribute of 12 lakhs of rupees as *Chauth*. He reigned in moderate peace for the next six years and died at the age of eighty in 1756. He was succeeded by his daughter's son, Siraj-ud-daula.

Aliwal, the battle of—was fought on January 28, 1848, in the course of the First Anglo-Sikh War (*q.v.*). The Sikhs were defeated; they lost their guns and were driven across the river Sutlej.

Aliya Begum—*see* under Mumtaz Mahal.

Allahabad—situated at the site of the confluence of the Ganges and the Jumna, is a city occupying a very important strategic position. The site was known in ancient times as Prayag which is considered as a very holy place by the Hindus. It was one of the capitals of the Gupta emperors in the fourth and fifth centuries of the Christian era. In the seventh century Emperor Harsavardhana held here his famous quinquennial assemblies, one of which was attended by the Chinese pilgrim Hiuen Tsang in A.D. 643. The oldest historical monument to be found at Allahabad is a pillar containing a version of the first six Pillar Edicts of Asoka (*c.* 273 B.C. - 232 B.C.) and an inscription composed by Harishena commemorating the conquests of the second Gupta Emperor Samudragupta (*c.* A.D. 330-80). Recognising the strategic importance of the site Akbar built here a fort in 1583 and the name Allahabad came to replace the much older name of Prayag. It was the headquarters of a *suba* or province bearing the same name from Akbar's time. It is now the capital of the state of Uttara Pradesha and is the seat of an important University.

Allahabad, the treaty of—was concluded in 1765 between Clive representing the East India Company and Emperor Shah Alam II. By this treaty the East India Company agreed to hand over to the Emperor the districts of Kora and Allahabad and also to pay him an annual tribute of twenty-six lakhs of rupees and the Emperor, in his turn, granted to the East India Company the *Diwani* of Bengal, Bihar and Orissa.

Allami Sadullah Khan—the Prime Minister of Emperor Shah Jahan (*q.v.*), was efficient as an administrator as well as a general and successfully led the Mughul army on various occasions. He died in harness in 1656.

Allard, General—French by nationality, had fought under Napoleon and was later on employed by Maharaja Ranjit Singh (A.D. 1798-1839) for the purpose of re-organising and training the Sikh army.

Almeida, Don Francisco de—the first Portuguese Viceroy (1505-09) of the Portuguese possessions in the East, believed that Portugal's success in the East depended on her naval supremacy and considered as visionary any idea of the establishment of a Portuguese empire in the East.

Alor—the capital of Sind during the rule of its last Hindu Raja Dahir, was conquered and occupied by the Arabs under Muhammad-ibn Kasim in A.D. 712. This marked the conquest of Sind by the Muhammadans.

Alp Khan—was appointed by Sultan Ala-ud-din Khalji governor of Gujarat after its conquest in 1297. In 1307 Alp Khan accompanied the Muslim forces led by Kafur and Khwaja Haji in their second campaign against Devagiri and succeeded in making a captive of Princess Devala Devi, who, on the conquest of Gujarat, had taken refuge along with her father, Karnadeva, in the court of Ramchandradeva, king of Devagiri. Alp Khan sent Princess Devala Devi to Ala-ud-din's court in Delhi where she was married to the Sultan's eldest son Khizr Khan.

Alp Khan—was the son and successor of Dilawar Khan Ghuri who set himself up as the independent sultan of Malwa in 1401. Alp Khan assumed the title of Hoshang Shah and ruled till his death in 1435. He was a man of restless spirit, took delight in adventurous enterprises and wars and fought against the sultans of Delhi, Jaunpur, Gujarat and even against the Bahmani sultan Ahmad Shah. But he failed in most of his campaigns.

Alphabets—the earliest Indian alphabets so far known are those found in the Piprawah vase and the inscriptions of Asoka (*c.* 273 B.C. - 232 B.C.). These are known as Brahmi script and the current Indian alphabets are all derived from them. How these earliest Indian alphabets came to be evolved is still a mystery. According to one view these are derived from various types of alphabets that were current in the countries of Western

Asia, while according to another view the origin of these earliest Indian Brahmi alphabets is to be traced to the numerous seals with pictorial writings found in the pre-historical monuments at Mohenjo-daro and Harappa in Sind. Asokan inscriptions found in the north-western frontier region of India are written in Kharosthi script and two of his inscriptions found recently in Afghanistan are bilingual—written both in Kharosthi and Aramaic Greek. Thus Brahmi, Kharosthi and Aramaic were the three kinds of alphabets in use in India as early as the third century of the pre-Christian era; and of these three again the Brahmi script was known all over India and was the parent of most of the kinds of later Indian alphabets. In the seventh century of the Christian era when Tibet was being ruled by King Srong-tsan-Gampo (A.D. 629-98) Buddhism was introduced into Tibet and along with Buddhism Indian alphabets also went to Tibet and formed the basis of Tibetan alphabets.

Alptigin—formerly a slave of the Samanid rulers of Central Asia, made himself the independent ruler of Ghazni in A.D. 962. He conquered a part of the kingdom of Kabul and thus established a Muhammadan kingdom just across the north-western boundary of India which was then being ruled by various Indian Hindu princes. Alptigin died in A.D. 963.

Alptigin—was a general of Sultan Balban (A.D. 1266-86) and was entitled Amir Khan. He was sent by Sultan Balban to suppress the rebellion of Tughril Khan in Bengal. Alptigin was defeated by Tughril who won over by lavish gifts many of the soldiers of Alptigin. This failure of the general so much enraged Sultan Balban that he had Alptigin hanged over the gate of Delhi. Alptigin was a capáble general and a rather popular nobleman and his execution roused strong feelings of resentment amongst the contemporary nobility.

Alvars, the—the earliest of the Vaishnava sects in the Tamil land in South India, flourished in the seventh and eighth centuries of the Christian era. Their leaders were known as *Acharyas* and included such men as Nathamuni, Yamunacharya and Ramanuja, the founder of *Visishtadvaitavada* or qualified monism as opposed to the absolute monism of Sankaracharya.

Amanullah—king of Afghanistan (1919-29) in succession to his father King Habibullah (1901-19), embarked soon after his accession on a war (the third Anglo-Afghan War) with British India, but was easily defeated by the much superior British Indian army which was equipped with modern military equipments like aeroplanes, wireless and high explosives. King

Amanullah asked for peace which was made in August 1919 and confirmed in 1921. By this treaty Amanullah ceased to receive any subsidy from the British but was given complete control over his foreign policy. Afghanistan received and sent ambassadors from and to England. Anglo-Afghan relations were much improved. King Amanullah subsequently made a European tour and on his return from the tour he began to introduce a series of internal reforms on the European model. These reforms infuriated the orthodox section of the Afghans; a civil war broke out and Amanullah was compelled to abdicate in 1929. He went to exile with his Queen Suriya in Europe where he lived till his death.

Amar Singh—Rana of Mewar (1597-1620). Son and successor of the famous Rana Pratap (*q.v.*) of Mewar, he tried to carry on the heroic war of independence against Emperor Akbar, but was defeated after a gallant resistance in 1599. Though he thus could not recover the lost territories of Mewar he maintained a desultory war with the Mughul empire till 1614, when tired of repeated failures and unable to resist the continued pressure of the Mughuls, he submitted to Emperor Jahangir who gave him very generous terms, did not require his personal attendance at the imperial court and did not insist on taking a princess of Mewar into the Mughul harem. Mewar continued to be on friendly terms with the Mughul empire till Aurangzib's policy alienated her.

Amar Singh Thapa—general of the king of Nepal during the Anglo-Nepal War of 1814-16, bravely defended the fort of Malaon against the British army led by General Ochterlony till the 15th May 1815 when he was compelled to surrender the fort. A few months later the war was concluded by the treaty of Sagauli, 1815.

Amaravati—a city in the Guntur district of Madras Presidency, became a centre of Hindu culture under the Satavahana kings who ruled in the Deccan for about four centuries after the death of Asoka. A new and purely indigenous school of art, architecture and sculpture developed in Amaravati. The sculptured figures found at Amaravati are remarkable for their slim and blithe features which are represented in most difficult poses and curves. Each individual figure has a distinct charm and the plants and flowers, especially the lotuses, are most admirably executed. Buddha is represented more often by a symbol than by a human image and this circumstance suggests that the Amaravati school of art and sculpture preceded the Mathura and Gandhara schools. At any rate, it is free from any trace of Greek influence.

Amardas—the third Guru (1552-74) of the Sikhs, was a man of high character and did much to promote the Sikh religion.

Amarkot—a town and state in Sind where Akbar was born on the 23rd November 1542 under the protection of its Hindu Raja, Rana Prasad by name. Its occupation in March 1843 by an Anglo-Indian army under Sir Charles Napier practically marked the completion of the British conquest of Sind.

Amatya—a generic term for a high official under the Guptas. It was also adopted by Shivaji, the Maratha king, in his administrative system. The *Amatya* in Shivaji's time meant the Finance Minister whose duty was to check and countersign all public accounts.

Ambaji—a Maratha leader who operated over Rajputana. In the course of eight years (1809-17) he extracted about two crores of rupees from Mewar alone.

Ambar, Malik—an Abyssinian slave who settled in Ahmadnagar, rose to be its chief administrator sometime after the death of Chand Sultana (*q.v.*). He organised the resources of Ahmadnagar in resisting the attempts of Emperor Jahangir to conquer Ahmadnagar. He was a born leader of men and one of the greatest statesmen that was produced in medieval India. He re-organised the revenue of the state, trained the Ahmadnagar army in the guerrilla method of fighting and thus enabled Ahmadnagar to stave off the Mughul conquest. But the imperial forces were much too strong and in 1616 Malik Ambar had to surrender the fort of Ahmadnagar to the Mughuls led by Prince Khurram. Malik Ambar lived in honour till his death in 1626 at an advanced age.

Ambedkar, Dr. Bhimrao Ramji—a prominent leader of the Indian scheduled castes, was educated in America and England, began his life as a clerk in a Govt. office, but was soon hounded out of it by the hostility of the caste Hindus. Sorely embittered he succeeded in building up a party of the untouchables, became a member of the Constituent Assembly and piloted through it the Indian Constitution Act which declared India to be a Republic. He also piloted the Hindu Code through the Indian Legislature.

Ambhi—was the king of Taxila in 327-26 B.C. when Alexander the Great invaded India. His territories lay between the Indus and the Jhelum and he was a great rival of king Poros whose dominions lay to the east of the Jhelum. Out of his grudge against

King Poros and also on account of his own cowardice he voluntarily submitted to Alexander and helped him in various ways in his war with Poros. He was rewarded by Alexander who first recognised him as the rightful king of Taxila and then appointed him as his governor over the valley of the Indus up to its confluence with the Chinab. His power was eventually overthrown probably by Chandragupta Maurya who liberated the Panjab from the Greek rule and was in possession of it when Alexander's general Seleucos who had succeeded to his eastern dominions, invaded India. Nothing is known about the end of Ambhi's career.

Amboyna, the massacre of—was perpetrated by the Dutch in 1623. Amboyna is in Java. When the Dutch found that the English East India Company were fast developing into a powerful rival body they suddenly fell upon the small English establishment at Amboyna and killed all the English settlers there after cruel persecution. This massacre scared away the English from Java and the Spice Islands and they henceforth concentrated their attention on India where they gradually overthrew the power of the Dutch.

Ambur, the battle of—was fought between Chanda Shahib (*q.v.*) backed by his French allies and Nawab Anwaruddin (*q.v.*) of the Carnatic in 1749. The Nawab was defeated and killed.

Amherst, Lord—was Governor-General in India (1823-28). During his administration the First Burmese War (1824-28) was fought as a result of which Assam, Arakan and Tenasserim were annexed to the British dominions. Lord Amherst failed to direct the operations properly and the Indo-British army suffered heavy losses. The war dragged on too long. While the war was proceeding two incidents occurred. First, the sepoys of the 47th Native Infantry rose in mutiny in protest against being compelled to sail across the sea and also against other material grievances, were fired upon by the British artillery and two British regiments and were ruthlessly suppressed. Secondly, Durjan Sal, a pretender to the *gadi* of Bharatpur (*q.v.*), rose in revolt in 1824 and proclaimed himself as the Raja. The fort was stormed and captured early in 1825. During Lord Amherst's administration the Government Sanskrit College in Calcutta was established in 1824. Lord Amherst resigned on account of domestic reasons.

Amin Chand—*see* under Omichand.

Amin Khan—the Mughul governor in Afghanistan in 1672 when the Afridis rose in revolt against Emperor Aurangzeb, was badly defeated by the rebels in a battle at Ali Masjid.

Amin Khan—was the *Wazir* at Delhi after the fall of the Sayyid Brothers early in the reign of Emperor Muhammad Shah (1719-48). He died in 1721.

Amir Ali, Syed (1849-1928)—was the first Indian to be appointed a judge of the Privy Council. Beginning his career as an advocate he was raised to the Bench in 1890 and continued to be a judge of the Calcutta High Court till 1904. In 1909 he was appointed to the Judicial Committee of the Privy Council in England where he died. His works included '*History of the Saracens* and several legal treatises.

Amir Khan—a general under Emperor Aurangzeb, was the governor of Kabul for twenty-one years (1677-98) and ably discharged his duties there.

Amir Khan—a leader of the Pathan mercenaries and bandits in central India in the early part of the nineteenth century on the eve of the Third Anglo-Maratha War, was at first a protégé and supporter of the Holkar and was a leader of the Pindaris. But he was won over to the side of the British Indian Government and was recognised as the Nawab of Tonk where his family continued to rule till integration and merger in 1948.

Amir Khusrav—surnamed 'Parrot of India', was a famous poet and author who wrote in Persian, Urdu and Hindi. He was a prolific writer who wrote poetry and prose and also composed music. He lived long and enjoyed the patronage of successive sultans of Delhi from Balban (*q.v.*) to Ghiyas-ud-din Tughluq (*q.v.*). He died in 1324-25. His extant works include many poems, historical *masnavis* and two historical works named the *Tughluqnamah* and the *Tarikh-i-Alai*. (*Cal. Rev.*, 1935)

Amirs of Sind—belonged to the Talpura tribe of Baluchistan who established themselves as rulers of Sind in the last quarter of the eighteenth century. They soon became divided into three important branches with their headquarters at Hyderabad, Khairpur and Mirpur and were theoretically under the rule of Afghanistan. As the nineteenth century advanced the Amirs of Sind practically ignored the supremacy of the Afghans but found themselves confronted with the ambitious designs over Sind of Ranjit Singh of the Panjab and of the Indo-British Government. The Amirs wanted to exclude them both from Sind, but British diplomacy gradually brought them under subordination. In 1831 the Indus was first surveyed by an

English squadron under Alexander Burnes and the British
Indian Government began to recognise the importance of
Sind and of the Indus as a highway not only of commerce
but also of imperial expansion. The Amirs of Sind were therefore persuaded to conclude in 1832 a treaty with the British
Indian Government by which they agreed to open up the
rivers and roads of Sind to the merchants and traders of Hindusthan, but no military stores or armed vessels of the English
were to enter into Sind. It was also specifically laid down that
neither the Amirs nor the English should covet each other's
territories. This treaty was renewed in 1834 and in 1838 the
British Indian Government thwarted an attempt of Ranjit
Singh to annex Sind and extorted as a price of their protection,
the right of placing a British Resident in Sind. On the outbreak
of the First Anglo-Afghan War (1838-42) the British Indian
Government sent an armed force through Sind in violation of
the treaty of 1832, exacted from the Amirs a heavy sum of
money in payment of arrears of their tribute payable to the
Amir of Afghanistan, imposed upon them in 1839 a fresh treaty,
in complete violation of the treaty of 1832, requiring the Amirs
to pay to the British Indian Government an annual tribute
of three lakhs of rupees and formally placing Sind under British
protection. In spite of their abhorrence for this treaty the
Amirs remained loyal to it during the critical years of the
first Anglo-Afghan War and the British Indian Government
freely and fully utilised Sind as a base of operations. After the
conclusion of the war the British Indian Government under
Lord Ellenborough unjustly charged the Amirs of Sind with
disaffection and hostility towards the English and appointed
Sir Charles Napier, a haughty general, as the British Resident
in Hyderabad. Sir Charles Napier imposed upon the Amirs a
new treaty (1842) which obliged them to cede certain parts of
Sind in lieu of the annual tribute of three lakhs of rupees, to
provide fuel for British vessels plying on the Indus and to
surrender their right of coining money. These terms which
practically implied the surrender of their independence by the
Amirs, were attempted to be enforced by Sir Charles with so
much harshness that in despair the warlike Baluchi subjects of
the Amirs attacked the British Residency at Hyderabad. This
supplied the Government of Ellenborough with a plausible
causus belle and a war was declared on the Amirs in February,
1843. It proved to be a short affair. The Amirs were defeated in
the battles of Miani and Dabo (February-March 1843) and

were exiled from Sind. By June 1843 the war came to a close and Sind was annexed to the British Indian empire.

Amir Timur—*see* under Timur.

Amir Umar—son of the sister of Sultan Alauddin Khalji, rose in revolt against the Sultan in Badaun and was easily suppressed and executed.

Amitrachates—*see* under *Amitraghāta*. The word may also be restored in Sanskrit as Amitrakhada, or 'devourer of enemies'. (*J.R.A.S.*, January 1928)

Amitraghata—literally meaning 'slayer of enemies' is a restoration in Sanskrit of the Greek name *Amitrachates* given by some classical historians to Bindusara, the son of Chandragupta Maurya.

Amoghavarsha—was the name borne by three kings of the Rashtrakuta dynasty of the Deccan. Amoghavarsha I had a long reign (A.D. 814-77). He was frequently engaged in wars with the eastern Chalukya kings of Vengi. He transferred his capital from Nasik to Manyakheta, now Malkhed. The Arab merchant Sulaiman, writing in A.D. 851, referred to him as Balhárá and reckoned him to be the fourth of the great kings of the world. In his old age Amoghavarsa I abdicated his throne in favour of his son Krishna II and devoted the rest of his life to ascetic practices. He was a patron of Jainism.

Amoghavarsha II—was the grandson of the grandson of Amoghavarsha I. He ruled only for a year (A.D. 917-18) and was deposed by his brother Govinda IV (A.D. 918-34).

Amoghavarsha III or **Vaddiga**—was the second son of the grandson of Amoghavarsha II. He succeeded Govinda IV in A.D. 934 and ruled for five years (A.D. 934-39). During his reign hostilities began between the Rashtrakutas of the Deccan and the Chola kings of the Far South.

Ampthill, Lord—was Governor of Madras and officiated for six months in 1904 as Viceroy of India during the absence on leave of Lord Curzon.

Amrakarddava—a general of the third Gupta Emperor, Chandra Gupta II (A.D. 381-413), "was covered with the glory of victory in many wars". He accompanied his royal master in the latter's campaign in eastern Malwa and helped him in overthrowing the power of the Sanakanika chief as well as of the Saka rulers in western Malwa and Kathiawar. He was a Buddhist, at any rate a pro-Buddhist, who made gifts for the promotion of Buddhism in his days.

Amrit Rao—was an adopted son of Raghunath Rao (Raghoba), the second son of Peshwa Baji Rao I, who ruled as Peshwa for only one year (1773). Amrit Rao was set up as the Peshwa after the flight of Peshwa Baji Rao II (1796-1818) to Bassein in October, 1802 following the battle of Poona, offered no resistance to the restoration of Peshwa Baji Rao II early in 1803 by the English and retired to Benares with a pension.

Amritsar—the holy city of the Sikhs in the Panjab. The site was bestowed on the fourth Guru Ramdas in 1577 by Emperor Akbar (1556-1605). It was later on developed into a beautiful city with its Golden Temple by the piety and generosity of generations of Sikhs.

Amritsar, the treaty of—was concluded on the 25th April, 1809, between Ranjit Singh and the East India Company during the administration of Lord Minto I (1807-13). By this treaty the cis-Sutlej states of the Panjab came definitely under British protection while Ranjit Singh was recognised as the king of the Panjab west of the Sutlej.

Amritsar, the treaty of—was concluded at Amritsar on the 16th March, 1846 at the end of the First Anglo-Sikh war (1845-46). By this treaty Kashmir which was a part of Ranjit Singh's kingdom was taken away from king Dalip Singh (*q.v.*) and was given by the English to Golab Singh, a Sardar of the Lahore Darbar, in return for ten lakhs of rupees, which he paid to the English.

Ananda or **Ananta Devi**—queen of Kumaragupta I (A.D. 415-55) (*q.v.*) and mother of Purugupta (*q.v.*).

Anandapal—son and successor of Raja Jaipal (or Jayapala) of the Hindu Shahiya dynasty of Udbhandapur (Waihand) or Ohind on the Indus. He ascended the throne in about A.D. 1002. Sultan Mahmud of Ghazni had inflicted a crushing defeat on his father, King Jaipal, in A.D. 1001. The primary duty of Anandapal after his accession was therefore to oppose and repel Sultan Mahmud. But in spite of his opposition Sultan Mahmud took Multan in A.D. 1006 and again invaded Anandapal's territories in A.D. 1008. Anandapal organised a league of the Indian princes including the rulers of Ujjain, Gwalior, Kanauj, Delhi and Ajmer and met the Sultan's army in the plain of Peshawar. The two hostile armies watched each other for forty days at the end of which the Sultan's camp was rushed and stormed by the allied Indian army. Victory seemed to be within the grasp of the Hindus when it was snatched by an unlucky accident. The elephant carrying either Anandapal or his son Brahmanpal turned and fled. On seeing this the allied Indian army broke in disorder and fled. Prince Brahmanpal was killed. The victorious Sultan advanced further into the country and attacked and plundered the fortress and temples of Kangra or Bhimnagar. Anandapal, however, would not submit and he continued to offer resistance to the Muhammadans from the fastnesses of the Salt Range till his death some years later.

Ananda Ranga Pillai—was the *dubash* of Dupleix, kept an account of what happened at Pondicherry and also recorded other historical events that had repercussions in the French Indian capital. Twelve volumes of his Tamil *Diary* have been translated into English. He sometimes recorded mere bazar rumours or gave to trivial things an exaggerated importance.

Ananda Vikrama Era—is a variety of Indian eras used in *Chand-Raisa* or *Prithviraj-Raisa* by the poet Chand Bardai who was the court-poet of Prithviraj, the king of Delhi, on the eve of its conquest by the Muhammadans (A.D. 1192). *Ananda* means 'devoid of nine' (Nandas), i.e. 100 minus 9 equivalent to 91 or 90 years after the Sananda Vikrama era of 58-57 B.C. It, therefore, dates from A.D. 33. (*J.R.A.S.*, 1906, p. 500)

Anangapala—a king belonging to the Tomara dynasty, flourished in the middle of the eleventh century of the Christian era, built the Red Fort in Delhi where the Qutb Mosque now stands and thus gave permanence to the city of Delhi. (*J.R.A.S.*, 1897, p. 13 & *E.H.I*, p. 401)

Anantavarman Choda Ganga—the most notable king belonging to the Eastern Ganga dynasty, ruled over Kalinga for seventy-one years (A.D. 1076-1147) and at one time ruled over a kingdom extending from the Ganges to the Godavari. He built the temple of Jagannath at Puri as well as the great temple of the Sun-God at Konarak in Puri District in Orissa. He was a great patron of Hindu religion and of Sanskrit and Telugu literatures.

Anarkali—a lady with whom Prince Salim, later Emperor Jahangir (1605-27), was in secret love. The Emperor built a beautiful marble tomb on her grave at Lahore in 1615 and inscribed on it a couplet expressing his passionate love for her.

Anderson—a Lieutenant in the Bombay European Regiment, was sent by the Lahore Darbar in March 1848 along with a civilian named Vans Agnew in the company of Sardar Khan Singh who was to replace Diwan Mulraj, governor of Multan. Soon after his arrival at Multan, Lieut. Anderson and his colleague, Vans Agnew, were murdered on the 20th April, 1848, at the instigation, it was believed, of the dismissed Diwan

Mulraj. This incident was followed by the outbreak of violent disturbances in Multan which eventually culminated in the Second Anglo-Sikh war (1848-49).

Andhra—is the land extending along the eastern coast of India from the mouth of the Godavari to that of the Krishna. The people speak mostly Telugu and have been inhabiting that region from ancient times. During the British rule the Andhra country was merged in the Tamil speaking Madras Presidency. In recent times after India won her independence the people claimed, on linguistic grounds, to be separated from Madras, and formed into a separate state. This demand was conceded after an outbreak of violence and the Andhra State was created with its capital at Hyderabad. The creation of the State of Andhra is the first example of the division of India on a linguistic basis and it has undoubtedly promoted the movement for such a division of India.

Andhra dynasty, the—*see* under Sátavahana dynasty.

Anga—ancient name of East Bihar, had its capital at Champa near the modern city of Bhagalpur on the Ganges. It was annexed in the 5th century B.C. to the kingdom of Magadha which then comprised the districts of Patna and Gaya in southern Bihar and has ever since remained a part of Magadha which later on came to be known as Bihar.

Angad—the second Guru of the Sikhs, was nominated to the dignity by Guru Nanak (*q.v.*) himself who esteemed him very high amongst his disciples and nominated him as his successor to the exclusion of his two sons. Guru Angad was a man of very high character and was the leader and preceptor of the Sikhs for fourteen years (1438-52).

Angkor Vat—is a magnificent monument of the contact of India with Cambodia which is called Kambuja in old local inscriptions. It is situated in the city of Angkor Thom which was in earlier times called Yasodharapura and was the capital of Cambodia during the reign of Jayavarman II (A.D. 1181-1205). It was one of the grandest cities in the world in that age and the temple known as Angkor Vat is the grandest of the monuments found at Angkor Thom. It was built by King Suryavarman II (A.D. 1049-66) of Kambuja. It was originally dedicated to God Vishnu. It stands on the top of a terraced structure. There are three terraces, each adorned with beautiful sculptures and each leading to the next higher one by means of a staircase. Each terrace is like a covered gallery. There are numerous spires and towers, the third and the last gallery having at the four angles eight towers, each 180 feet high. The central shrine is on the third terrace. It has a tower 213 feet high and it dominates the entire region. The whole structure is surrounded by a stone enclosure measuring two-thirds of a mile east to west and half a mile north to south. The enclosure is surrounded by a ditch 700 feet wide which is spanned over in one place by a stone causeway, 36 feet wide, which is continued as a broad paved road from the gate of the enclosure to the gate of the first terrace. The whole edifice has hardly an equal in the world and bears eloquent testimony to the development of art, architecture and sculpture in South East Asia as the result of her contact with India. (Majumdar, R. C., *Kambuja-Desa*, pp. 135-37)

Anglo-Afghan Wars—were three in number. The *First Anglo-Afghan war* (1838-42) was fought by the East India Company during the administration of Lord Auckland and it continued on to that of his successor Lord Ellenborough. In 1838 Shah Shuja, a former Amir of Afghanistan, was living as a British pensioner at Ludhiana in the Panjab and a Persian army, secretly backed by Russia, was besieging Herat on the Perso-Afghan frontier. Herat was considered as a very important strategical place which was the gateway to India and its capture by Persia, backed by Russia, was considered by the Government of England to be a menace to the British Indian Empire though the latter was then separated from Persia by the independent states of the Panjab under Maharaja Ranjit Singh and Afghanistan ruled by Amir Dost Mohammad and inhabited by the freedom-loving Afghans. Amir Dost Mohammad also felt alarmed at Russian aggression which was supposed to have inspired the Persian attack on Herat, and he felt that his safety lay in an alliance with the British Indian Government. But the Amir desired at the same time some guarantee of security against his eastern neighbour, Maharaja Ranjit Singh, who had recently captured Peshawar and suggested an Anglo-Afghan alliance on condition that the English would help him in recovering Peshawar from Ranjit Singh and the Amir, in his turn, would keep away all Russian influence from his court and country. The Government of Lord Auckland had a healthy fear of Maharaja Ranjit Singh and did not agree to put any pressure on him. Burnes, who had been sent by Auckland to Kabul to talk matters over with the Amir, failed to achieve anything and left Kabul in April, 1838. The Amir then showed some civilities to an informal Russian agent who had been in his court for some time past but who had been so long treated

indifferently. This was considered by the Government of Lord
Auckland as a definite act of hostility by the Amir, and, in
July, 1838 the Government of Lord Auckland made a Tripartite
Treaty with Maharaja Ranjit Singh of the Panjab and Shah Shuja,
the refugee Amir, who had been living in Ludhiana, with the
object of restoring Shah Shuja to the throne of Afghanistan.
It was expected that Shah Shuja, on his restoration to the
throne of Kabul, would be controlled in his foreign relations,
especially with Russia, by the British Indian Government
acting according to instructions sent from England. An Anglo-
Afghan war was bound to follow this definitely aggressive and
entirely unjustifiable Tripartite Alliance. Whatever justification, if at all any, the alliance had at the time of its conclusion
in July,1838, ceased to exist in the following month of September
when the Persians were obliged to raise the siege of Herat and
withdraw from Afghan territories. But Lord Auckland would
not be stopped and he began the first Anglo-Afghan War in
the following October. It was a most indefensible aggressive
war, involved flagrant violation of the treaty concluded in
1832 with the Amirs of Sind through whose territories the
British army marched into Afghanistan and was very badly
conducted. At the beginning the invading English army had
some successes. Qandahar was occupied in April 1839, Ghazni
was stormed in July and Kabul was captured in August. Dost
Mohammad evacuated his capital and eventually surrendered
to the Indo-British army which sent him as a prisoner to Calcutta
and Shah Shuja was restored to the throne of Afghanistan.
But troubles soon began. Having restored Shah Shuja the British
army should have withdrawn. But that was not done. Shah
Shuja was kept up only as the nominal ruler and the administration of the country was really conducted by Sir William
Macnaghten whom Lord Auckland appointed as the political
officer. As the Afghans who had never liked Shah Shuja, deeply
resented his restoration by British bayonets so the British army
of occupation had to be kept in Kabul. The war had raised
prices which hit hard every section of the people and the
lapses of the army of occupation aggravated popular discontent.
This was cleverly exploited by Akbar Khan, son of Dost
Mohammad, and in 1841 widespread disturbances broke out
against Shah Shuja and his patrons, the British army. Alexander
Burnes, the principal adviser of Macnaghten who had incurred
the special disfavour of the Afghans for his immoral acts, and
his brother were dragged out of their house and murdered by

an Afghan mob in November, 1841. Macnaghten and General Elphinstone, who was at the command of the army of occupation in Kabul, showed great indecision and weakness and in December entered into a treaty with Akbar Khan by which they agreed to the withdrawal of the British army from Afghanistan and to the restoration of Dost Mohammad. Macnaghten was soon afterwards found guilty of bad faith in respect of this treaty and was slain with three companions by the order of Akbar Khan. The dispirited British army of occupation numbering 16,500 persons left Kabul on the sixth January, 1841 on its way to Jalalabad which was being held by a British army under General Sale. The march proved a disaster. The retreating army was attacked from all sides by the Afghans who destroyed practically the whole of it except one person, named Dr. Brydon, who reached Jalalabad, severely wounded and utterly exhausted, on the 13th January. This appalling disaster severely shocked the complacency of Governor-General Lord Auckland as well as of the Government of England. The latter now recalled Lord Auckland and during the administration of his successor, Lord Ellenborough (1842-44), General Pollock relieved Jalalabad in April, 1842 and General Nott re-established British authority in the Qandahar region in May. The two armies then proceeded from their respective stations, reduced all opposition on their ways and reached Kabul which they occupied in September, 1842. The surviving British prisoners were rescued and in celebration of the British triumph, the great bazar of Kabul was blown up with gun powder. The British also ruthlessly sacked the city of Kabul, plundering and killing thousands of unoffending Afghans. These barbarous proceedings marked the end of a most unjustifiable and fruitless war. The British army of occupation soon withdrew and Dost Mohammad who was released from his detention in Calcutta, returned to Afghanistan where he resumed in 1842 his throne from which he had been so needlessly and unjustifiably displaced. He retained his throne till his death at eighty years of age in 1863. There is no doubt that the first Afghan War was an entirely unjustifiable proceeding on the part of the British Indian Government, that it was conducted in a very inefficient manner by the Government of Lord Auckland, and that it was an entirely futile adventure which cost the lives of 20,000 Indo-British soldiers and fifteen millions of rupees extracted from the poor tax-payers in India.

The Second Anglo-Afghan War (1878-80)—began during the viceroyalty of Lord Lytton I (1876-80) and was concluded

during the administration of his successor, Lord Ripon (1880-84).
Amir Dost Mohammad of Afghanistan died in 1863 and a war
of succession ensued amongst his sons. This war lasted for five
years (1863-68) during which the Government of India followed
what was called a policy of "masterly inactivity" and did
not take any part in the war amongst the rivals for the throne
of Kabul. When at last in 1868 Sher Ali, the third son of Dost
Mohammad, triumphed over all the other claimants and established himself on the throne of Kabul the Government of
India recognised him as the Amir of Afghanistan and agreed
to help him with arms and money. But in the meantime Russian
influence had greatly increased in Central Asia. Bukhara was
annexed in 1866, Tashkend in 1867 and Samarkhand in 1868.
This rapid expansion of Russian dominion in Central Asia was
a matter of common concern to Afghanistan and the British
Indian Government. Amir Sher Ali was anxious to stop
further Russian expansion in Central Asia and the British
Indian Government was anxious to keep Afghanistan free
from Russian control. In the circumstances a meeting was
arranged at Ambala in the Panjab in 1869 between Amir Sher
Ali and the then Viceroy Lord Mayo (1869-72). The Amir
would have conceded the British demand for control over his
foreign relations in return for an English guarantee that the
British Government would support him against Russia and
would acknowledge none but himself and his nominee as the
Amir of Afghanistan. Acting under instructions from England
Lord Mayo refused to give such a guarantee though he promised
to help Amir Sher Ali with money and arms. Naturally Amir
Sher Ali felt no attraction for a definite alliance with the Government of India on such terms. But in 1873 the Russians captured
K' iva and thus advanced further towards Afghanistan. Being
alarmed at this development Sher Ali made in 1873 to the
Viceroy, Lord Northbrook (1872-76), a definite proposal for
an Anglo-Afghan alliance which would assure Afghanistan
that if Russia or any of its protected states invaded Afghanistan
the British Government would not only help Afghanistan with
money and arms but also with troops. Acting on instructions
received from the ministry of Gladstone which was then in
power in England, Lord Northbrook could not agree to this
proposal. Nor would Lord Northbrook accept the Amir's
request to recognise as the Amir's heir-apparent his son, Abdullah
Jan. All these proceedings estranged Sher Ali from the English
and he desired to establish a good understanding with Russia

with whom he, therefore, opened correspondence and Russian agents came to frequent Kabul. In 1874 Disraeli succeeded Gladstone and in 1877 a Russo-Turkish war broke out which so strained the relations between England and Russia that a war between the two was apprehended at any moment. In these circumstances it was now decided to keep a firm hold on Afghan affairs so that Russia might not threaten India through Afghanistan. In pursuit of this policy Quetta, which controlled the route to Qandahar, was annexed in 1877 and Lord North-brook's successor, Lord Lytton I (1876-80), acting under instructions from the ministry of Disraeli, proposed to send to the court of Kabul a British mission for negotiating with the Amir an alliance on the terms that the Amir himself had offered in 1873 with the additional condition that a British Resident was to be stationed at Herat. But the Amir refused to accept the proposed British mission on the ground that the acceptance of a British mission would oblige him to receive a similar mission from Russia. Matters thus appeared to have reached a stalemate when a Russian mission under General Stolietoff entered Afghanistan in 1878, in spite of the Amir's prohibitory order, and negotiated with the Amir Sher Ali a treaty in Kabul on 22nd July, 1878 offering him a Russian guarantee against foreign invasion. The reception of the Russian mission in Kabul by the Amir infuriated Lord Lytton I who, with the approval of the Government of England, insisted on the acceptance of a British mission in Kabul by the Amir by a certain date, viz. the 20th November, 1878. The Amir appealed to Russia for help according to the very recently concluded alliance; but as in the meantime the Russo-Turkish war had been ended and peace and amity in Europe had been established between England and Russia by the Treaty of Berlin (1878), Russia could not enter into a war with England and advised Sher Ali to make terms with the British. It was now too late for Amir Sher Ali to do so, for a British Indian army had invaded Afghanistan on the 20th November, 1878 and the Second Anglo-Afghan War had begun.

As in the First Anglo-Afghan War (1838-42) the invading British Indian army had great initial successes. Deserted by Russia Sher Ali could offer but poor resistance to the organised invasion by the English. Three British armies converged on Kabul—one under General Browne through the Khyber Pass, a second under General (later on Lord) Roberts from the Kurram Valley and a third under General Biddulph from

Quetta. Further Qandahar was occupied by a fourth army under General Stewart. Within a month Sher Ali found his position so desperate that he fled from Afghanistan to Turkistan where he died shortly after. His power passed to his son Yakub Khan who opened negotiations with the British and concluded peace by the Treaty of Gandamak in May, 1879. The treaty conceded all the British demands and more—a permanent British envoy was to be established at Kabul, the foreign policy of Afghanistan was to be conducted on the advice of the Viceroy of India and the districts of Kurram, Pishi and Sibi were to be ceded to the British. Cavagnari, the first British envoy, accordingly, arrived at Kabul in July and the British appeared to have completely succeeded. But on the 3rd September a mutiny broke out in Kabul amongst the Afghan troops, Cavagnari was murdered and hostilities were renewed. The British, however, acted more promptly and effectively on this occasion. Roberts occupied Kabul in October, 1879 and Amir Yakub Khan now virtually became his prisoner. His brother, Ayub Khan now claimed to be the Amir and he even succeeded in defeating a British army in July, 1880 at the battle of Maiwand, near Qandahar. But Roberts soon marched with a large army from Kabul to Qandahar and with the substantial help given by Sher Ali's nephew Abdur Rahman Khan soon completely defeated Ayub Khan. In the meantime the administration in England had passed from the hands of Disraeli to those of Gladstone who recalled Lord Lytton and appointed Lord Ripon as the Viceroy (1880-84). The new Viceroy brought the Second Anglo-Afghan War to a close by concluding a treaty with Abdur Rahman whom he recognised as the Amir and who, in his turn, agreed, in return for an annual subsidy, to allow his foreign policy to be controlled by the Government of India. The three Afghan districts ceded by the treaty of Gandamak remained in British Indian possession.

The Second Anglo-Afghan War was the result of the interaction of two policies. One was that of what is known as the Forward Policy, which aimed at the expansion of the Indian boundary to the Hindu Kush which was held to be the natural boundary of India on the north-west and thus include within the British Indian Empire both Qandahar and Kabul which are considered as the twin gates to, and out of, India. The second was the desire of Russia and England, rivals in imperialism in the East, to establish their influence on Afghanistan. The English, especially the Conservative party amongst them, were actuated by a great dread of Russian expansion into India through Afghanistan. It never became a reality, but it was always dreaded and coloured and shaped British policy in Afghanistan throughout the nineteenth century.

The Third Anglo-Afghan War (April-May, 1919)—was short and sharp. Amir Abdur Rahman whom Lord Ripon acknowledged as the Amir of Afghanistan, ruled till his death in 1901. His successor Amir Habibullah (1901-19) who assumed the title of King of Afghanistan, remained on friendly terms with the British Indian Government. But his son and successor, King Amanullah (1919-29), partly under the pressure of internal troubles and partly under the influence of the anti-British party which had always existed in Afghanistan, declared a war against the British Indian Government soon after his accession. In this *Third Anglo-Afghan War* which lasted barely two months (April-May, 1919) the Afghans were defeated severely by the British Indian army armed with bombs, aeroplanes, wireless and other arms of modern warfare which the Afghans completely lacked. The Afghans were, therefore, compelled to sue for peace which was granted by the Treaty of Rawalpindi (August, 1919). According to this treaty Afghanistan was to import no arms or munitions of war through India and the King of Afghanistan was not to receive any subsidy from the Government of India. But Afghanistan would have complete freedom in her foreign relations and India and Afghanistan should respect each other's independence. Lastly Afghanistan would be represented in London by her own ambassador and an English ambassador would reside in Kabul. Anglo-Afghan relations since then have been generally cordial.

Anglo-French Wars—*see* under Carnatic Wars.

Anhilwara—was the chief city of Gujarat from the eighth century to the fifteenth century. It is now represented by the town of Patan. Its king Mularaja defeated and repulsed an invasion by Shihabuddin Muhammad Ghuri in 1178. This saved Gujarat from Muhammadan occupation for a century.

Ansari, Dr. (1880-1936)—a prominent Muhammadan nationalist leader. Born in Bihar, he graduated in medicine from Edinburgh and settled as a physician in Delhi. In 1912-13 he organised in India a medical mission which he sent to Turkey to help her in her wars. He took a leading part in organising the Muslim League over which he presided in its 1920 session. He was, however, no communalist and presided over the Madras session of the Indian National Congress in 1927. He co-operated with

Mahatma Gandhi in the Non-Cooperation Movement started by him and suffered imprisonment twice under the British rule in 1930 and 1932.

Antialkidas—was an Indo-Greek king who ruled at Taxila. An inscription found on a column at Besnagar (Vidisha) near modern Bhilsa in Central India shows that he sent a Greek ambassador named Heliodoros (*q.v.*) to the court of the king of Besnagar. The inscription has been assigned to between 140 B.C. and 130 B.C.

Antigonos Gonatas—referred to as Antikini in an Asokan inscription (R.E. XIII) as one of the Hellenistic kings with whom Emperor Asoka maintained friendly relations, was the king of Macedonia from 277 B.C. to 239 B.C.

Antikini—a Hellenistic king mentioned by Asoka in R.E. XIII, has been identified with Antigonos Gonatas, king of Macedonia (277 B.C. - 239 B.C.).

Antiochus I Soter—son of Seleucos Nikator, was the king of Syria when the second Maurya Emperor Bindusara was ruling in India. According to Strato, Antiochus I sent to Bindusara as ambassador a Greek named Deimachos. Antiochus was on friendly terms with Bindusara who wrote to Antiochus requesting him to buy and send to the Indian ruler sweet wine, dried figs and a sophist. Antiochus wrote in reply that figs and wine would be sent but not a sophist, as the laws forbade a sophist to be sold.

Antiochus II Theos—was the Greek king of Syria and western Asia (261 B.C. - 246 B.C.) who is referred to in Asoka's Rock Edict XIII as the Yona king Antiyoko who ruled beyond the boundary of the empire of Asoka and with whom he maintained friendly relations and in whose kingdom he made converts to *dhama* (*q.v.*) and established hospitals for men and beasts and planted medicinal herbs (R.E. II).

Antiochus III the Great—was the Greek king who ruled over Syria and western Asia towards the end of the third century B.C. It was during his time that Bactria became independent under Euthydemos. Shortly afterwards Antiochus III crossed the Hindu Kush and attacked an Indian prince named Subhagasena (Sophagasenas of the classical writers) who ruled over the Kabul valley. Antiochus III defeated Subhagasena, extorted from him a large cash indemnity and many elephants before he went back to his country. This invasion produced no permanent effect.

Anuruddha—was, according to the Ceylonese Chronicles, the successor to the throne of Magadha immediately after Udayi, the son and successor of king Ajatasatru (554 B.C. - 527 B.C.). The Puranas do not mention him and nothing is known about him even from the Ceylonese Chronicles except that he was a parricide.

Anwaruddin (1743-49)—began his career in the service of Asaf Jha, Nizam-ul-Mulk, and was appointed by the Nizam as the Nawab of the Carnatic in 1743 with Arcot as his capital to the exclusion of the son and other relatives of the previous Nawab, Dost Ali. The Carnatic was then in a disturbed state, as the Marathas made repeated raids into it and the relatives of the late Nawab Dost Ali created much trouble for the new Nawab. The confusion was further increased when, some time after the outbreak of the War of the Austrian Succession (1740-48) the French and the English merchants who had their respective settlements at Pondicherry and Madras, both in the Carnatic, began to fight amongst themselves in the Carnatic. Anwaruddin, as the Nawab of the Carnatic, was, theoretically at least, the protector of both the French and the English and was, therefore, expected to prevent them from fighting within his own dominions. Both the English and the French openly recognised his paramount position in times of need. Thus, when at the beginning of the war, the English were all powerful at sea and were plundering French ships, Dupleix, the French governor of Pondicherry, appealed to the Nawab to protect the French ships. But as the Nawab had no ships the English ignored with impunity his protest against their warlike activities against the French. But when in 1746 the French besieged Madras the English, who had so long ignored the authority of the Nawab, sought his protection against the French. Nawab Anwaruddin, true to his role as the protector, repeatedly asked Dupleix to raise the siege of Madras and to maintain peace. But as his protests and orders were unheeded by the French and as the war was now being fought on land for fighting which Anwaruddin had a large army, so Anwaruddin sent a large army to force the French to raise the siege of Madras. But the French had captured Madras before the arrival of the Nawab's army which, therefore, besieged the French in Madras. But the tiny French force that was within the fort made a sally and scattered the unwieldy army of the Nawab. The Nawab's army retired to St. Thome where again it was defeated by another small French army which came to re-inforce the French in Madras. These defeats not only reduced Nawab Anwaruddin to the position of a helpless spectator during the remaining period of the War of the Austrian Succession but had another more important consequence. They convinced Dupleix that a small trained French army could easily defeat a much larger Indian army. Dupleix further felt that he could easily exploit this superiority by interfering in the internal affairs of the Indian Princes. On the termination of the war with the English, Dupleix, therefore, entered into a secret agreement with Chand Shahib, the son-in-law of the previous Nawab of the Carnatic, to place him on the throne of the Carnatic. Anwaruddin was defeated and killed by the allied army at the battle of Ambur, to the south-west of Vellore, in August, 1749.

Aornos—was a fort situated, according to the classical historians, on the further bank of the Indus. Its site has not been satisfactorily identified. It was captured by Alexander the Great on his way to India and before he crossed the Indus at Ohind. Alexander entrusted the command of the fort to an Indian adventurer named Sisikottos (Sasigupta) who had already joined the Greek army.

Aparajita Pallava—was the last of the Pallava kings of Kanchi. He ruled in the second half of the ninth century. In A.D. 862-63 he defeated the Pandya king, Varaguna Varman at the battle of Sri Purambiya, but later on, towards the close of the ninth century, he himself was defeated and killed by the Chola king Aditya I (A.D. 880-907). With the death of Aparajita the long line of the Pallava kings came to an end.

Apollodotos—an Indo-Greek king, son of Eukratides (175 B.C.-156 B.C.), murdered his own father and gloried in his monstrous crime by driving his chariot-wheels through the blood of his father, to whose corpse he refused the poor honour of a burial. He issued many coins. According to some he was a contemporary and rival and not a son of Eukratides. (*P.H.A.I.*, p. 386)

Appa Shahib—was a son of Vyankoji, younger brother of Raghuji II, the Bhonsla Raja (1788-1816). On the death of Raghuji II in 1816 Appa Shahib first became the Regent as Parsoji, the son and successor of Raghuji Bhonsla II, was an imbecile. To strengthen his position Appa Shahib then entered into a treaty of subsidiary alliance with the English in May, 1816. Thus the Nagpur state which under Raghuji Bhonsla II had avoided the subsidiary system, lost its independence under the administration of Appa Shahib. But when Peshwa Baji Rao II rose against the English in 1817 Appa Shahib also followed suit. His army was defeated by the English in November, 1817 at the battle of Sitabaldi. Appa Shahib first fled to the Panjab and then to Jodhpur where he died in 1840.

Aquaviva, Father Ridolfo—was a Jesuit missionary working at Goa. In September, 1579 at the request of Emperor Akbar for two learned priests capable of explaining to him the Gospels Father Aquaviva was sent, along with Father Monserrate, by the Portuguese Government of Goa to Akbar's Court at Fatepur-Sikri. They arrived there in February, 1580 and were received with great honour by the Emperor. Aquaviva was a very learned scholar who earned the esteem of Emperor Akbar and lived long in his Court as an honoured member of it.

Arabs, the—had become a strong and united people soon after the rise of Islam. They were a sea-faring and trading people and had their eyes on the rich ports of western India and the out-lying parts of its north-west borderland. As early as A.D. 637, they made a raid on Thana near Bombay. This was repulsed, but other raids followed on Broach, Gulf of Debal in Sind and Kalat. Towards the close of the seventh century the Arabs conquered Makran in Baluchistan. This paved the way for the conquest of Sind by the Arabs. Arab merchant ships were plundered off the cost of Sind by pirates who found shelter at Debal in Sind. The aggrieved Arab merchants complained to Al-Hajjaj, the Governor of Arabia, who sent several expeditions to Sind which was then being ruled by King Dahir (*q.v.*). The early raids were all repulsed, but in A.D. 711 an Arab expedition into Sind was led by Muhammad-ibn Kasim, the son-in-law of Al-Hajjaj. Muhammad-ibn Kasim defeated and killed Dahir at the battle of Raor in A.D. 712 and captured his capital Alor. The Arabs then conquered Multan and Arab rule was established over Sind. The Arabs made many efforts to extend their dominions in India and often raided Cutch, Surashtra or Kathiawar and western Gujarat. But their progress beyond Sind was stopped by the Chalukyas in the south, the Pratiharas in the east and the Karkotas in the north. The Arab rule in India thus remained confined to Sind over which, however, the Arabs held sway till they were dispossessed by Shihabuddin Muhammad Ghuri in 1175 and Sind passed under the rule of the Delhi sultanate. The Arab conquest of Sind has been described as 'a triumph without results' in the sense that it did not lead to the eventual conquest of India by the Muhammadans.

Arachosia—name for the Qandahar region used by classical historians.

Arakan—a strip of land on the eastern coast of the Bay of Bengal, was an independent kingdom till 1784 when it was conquered by the Burmese. This territorial expansion of Burma so near Bengal was considered unsafe by the British Indian Government and was one of the circumstances that led to the First Burmese War (1824-26) at the end of which Arakan was ceded to the British Indian Government by the treaty of Yandabo (*q.v.*).

Aram Shah—sultan of Delhi (1206-11), was successor of Qutb-ud-din, the first sultan of Delhi. Sultan Aram did not inherit the abilities of his predecessor with whom his relationship is also uncertain. According to some historians he was Qutb-ud-din's son. Abu-l Fazl said that he was Qutb-ud-din's brother and, according to some, he was no relation of the first Sultan. He was selected for some unknown reasons only to be deposed soon in favour of Qutb-ud-din's son-in-law, Iltutmish.

Aravidu (or **Karnata**) **Dynasty, the**—was founded after the destruction of Vijayanagar (*q.v.*) following the battle of Talikota (1565), by Tirumala, brother of Ram Raja who had led the Vijayanagar army to its defeat and destruction at the battle of Tilikota. He established his capital at Penugonda and restored to some extent the power and prestige of the Hindu kingdom. The dynasty founded by him ruled in the Deccan till 1684 and produced several kings of whom the third king Venkata II was the most remarkable. He transferred his capital to Chandragiri and patronised Telugu poets and Vaishnava authors. A later ruler, also bearing the name of Venkata, granted in 1639-40 the site of Madras to Mr. Day of the East India Company. The grant was subsequently confirmed by King Ranga III who was practically the last of the rulers of the Aravidu dynasty.

Architecture—*see* Art and Architecture.

Arcot—a town in the Carnatic, was the capital of the Nawab Anwaruddin (*q.v.*) of the Carnatic (1743-49), and figured prominently in the Second Carnatic War (1751-54). It had a strong fort which after the death and defeat of Anwaruddin at the battle of Ambur in 1749 passed under the control of Chanda Shahib who, backed by the French, besieged Trichinopoly where his rival Muhammad Ali, son of Anwaruddin, had taken shelter. In order to relieve Trichinopoly Robert Clive at the head of an army of 200 Europeans and 300 sepoys took Arcot by surprise. Immediately Chanda Shahib besieged Arcot with a large army. Clive and his army stood the siege for 56 days (September 23 to November 14) and ultimately repulsed the besiegers. This siege of Arcot laid the foundation of Robert Clive's reputation as a general and secured the Carnatic for the English.

Argaon, the battle of—was fought on November 29, 1803 between the army of the Maratha leader, the Bhonsla Raja of Nagpur, and the English army under Arthur Wellesley in the Second Maratha War. The Bhonsla's army was decisively defeated and the English victory enabled them to capture the fort of Gawilgarh. The Bhonsla Raja made peace by the treaty of Deogarh in December 1803 and accepted the subsidiary alliance.

Aria—the name given by classical historians to Herat.

Ariana—Greek name for Afghanistan.

Arhat—is the general name for Buddhist and Jaina saints who have spiritually advanced very far. A Buddhist monk who has attained *nirvana* (*q.v.*) in this life is called an *Arhat.*

Arjumand Banu Begum—*see* Mumtaj Mahal.

Arjan—the fifth Guru (1581-1606) of the Sikhs, was the son and successor of Ramdas the fourth Guru. He compiled the *Adi Granth* by collecting select verses from the works of the four preceding Gurus as well as of many other Hindu and Muhammadan saints. He required the Sikhs to pay a "spiritual tribute", that is to say, a sort of a religious cess and thus laid the foundation of the wealth of the Sikh Guru. He helped Prince Khusru out of pity, when the latter was in revolt against his father, Emperor Jahangir. As a consequence Jahangir had him executed on a charge of treason.

Art and architecture of Ancient India—have a glorious tradition and magnificent achievements. Beginning from the pre-historic period to the modern times art and architecture in India have passed through many changes. The extant monuments of the Indus Valley civilisation (*c.* 3000 B.C. to 1500 B.C.) show that large palaces with modern amenities like market-places and communal baths with clearing pits and man-holes, all built of baked bricks, existed in Mohenjodaro as well as in Harappa and other cities of the Indus Valley. The art of executing seals with pictographs which probably stand for a system of writing as well as that of iconography was well known. But during the centuries that followed the destruction of the Indus Valley civilisation the art of building with stone appears to have been given up and in the beginning of the historical period (*c.* 320 B.C.) Indians built with timber. Thus the palace of Chandragupta Maurya (*c.* 322 B.C. to 298 B.C.) which Megasthenes warmly admired and considered as excelling the palaces of Susa

and Ecbatana, was built of timber which was also used in
building the pallisade which surrounded the city. Stone, however, came to be prolifically used during the reign of Chandragupta's grandson, Asoka (*c.* 270 B.C. to 232 B.C.) who inscribed
many inscriptions on excellently executed stone-pillars which
were so well polished that they were mistaken for iron-pillars
many centuries later. He also used stones in building numerous
stupas and his own palace at Pataliputra which looked so magnificent even after a lapse of six hundred years that Fa-Hien who
visited India in A.D. 405-11 and saw it, considered that it was
built by genii. The decorations used in Asokan pillars also
show a high degree of skill which suggests that the art of chisel-
ling and polishing stone must have been already an old art in
the time of Asoka, though some hold that these reveal Greek
influence on Indian art. Early Indian art in which stone was
used as the medium, was wedded to religion and no palace of
any early Indian king, whether of the north or of the south
India, has come down to modern times. But numerous temples,
Hindu, Buddhist and Jaina, were executed in the period between
A.D. 120 and 1193. Unfortunately most of these buildings and
temples with their exquisite artistic displays which were situated
in north India were destroyed by the Muhammadan invaders,
but the few that have survived the ravages of men and time,
e.g. the temples at Deoghar in Jhansi district and Bhitargaon
in Cawnpore district and at Khajuraho in Chhatarpur district,
all in U.P., show the excellence that was attained by the Hindu
artists in north India. It is, however, to south India that one has
to turn in order to appreciate the greatness of ancient Indian art
and architecture. Indeed south India has correctly been described
as the land of temples. Those of Conjeeveram, Tanjore, Tiruchi-
paly, Madura and Rameswaram are particularly magnificent
and are examples of pure Hindu art and architecture. Receding
terraces, spiral tops called *shikharas* and fine sculptures on the
wall depicting human as well as natural objects with a rare
fidelity are some of their characteristics. The paintings in the
cave temples at Ajanta, Ellora and Nasik form a class by themselves. The most unique edifice that has come down to modern
times from ancient India is the *Kailasha* rock-cut temple at
Ellora (A.D. 770) which is hewn out of the side of a whole block
of gneiss rock and is so well chiselled and polished that the
walls and the floors still, after all these centuries, throw clear
reflections. It is one of the most marvellous works of human
labour and skill in the world.

The principles and models of ancient Indian art, architecture and sculpture crossed the seas and influenced the art, architecture and sculpture in Indonesia, Indo-China, and Cambodia as is shown in the *Barabudhur* in Java and the *Angkor-Vat* in Cambodia, the two most magnificent edifices in south-eastern Asia. (Wheeler, M., *The Indus Civilisation;* Coomarswamy, A. K., *Hist. of Indian and Indonesian Art;* Fergusson, J., *Hist. of Indian and Eastern Architecture;* Smith, V. A., *Hist. of Fine Art in India and Ceylon*)

Arthasastra—*see* Kautilya.

Arya Samaj—a social reform body, was founded by Swami Dayananda Saraswaty (*q.v.*) in 1875. Under the influence of western education and science many amongst the educated Indians were tending to become Christian. The Arya Samaj, like the Brahma Samaj and the Prarthana Samaj, was started to stop this process and largely succeeded in its efforts. Its motto was 'Go back to the Vedas' and it wanted to reform society on the model of the Vedas and discard all later outgrowths. It upheld monotheism, condemned polytheism and the use of images. It was opposed to caste restrictions and child-marriages and it supported sea-voyage, female education and re-marriage of widows. It aimed at uplifting the down-trodden classes or castes amongst the Indians. It claimed that Hinduism was a proselytising religion and by what is known as the *suddhi* (purification) movement it converted many non-Hindus to Hinduism and thus gave a new dynamic force to Hinduism. It has done a great deal of social and educational work, especially in the Panjab. At first it confined its educational efforts to Sanskritic studies only, but later on one section of it led by Lala Hansraj supported the cultivation of western education as well and founded the Dayananda Anglo-Vedic College at Lahore. The orthodox section continued to believe in the necessity of reviving the Vedic ideal in modern life and founded the Gurukul at Hardwar in 1902. It has still a large following in Upper India.

Aryabhata—a premier Indian mathematician and astronomer, born in A.D. 476, wrote at the age of 23 his book called *Aryabhata-Tantra* in Sanskrit when he was residing at Kusumapura or Patna. He discovered the diurnal motion of the earth causing the division of time into night and day. Long before the time of Copernicus he discovered the truth that the earth moves round the sun. He also knew the real reason for the eclipses of the sun and the moon, that the moon and other planets have no light of their own and are illuminated with the reflected light of the sun and that the earth and other planets move round the sun along elliptical ways. (Dutt, B. B., *Hindu Contribution to Mathematics* and L. Rodet, *Lecons de Calcul Aryabhata*)

Aryadeva—a Buddhist author who flourished in the second century A.D., was one of the earliest exponents of the Mahayana form of Buddhism.

Aryavarta—literally means the territory inhabited by the Aryans. In the *Institute of Manu* (*c.* A.D. 200) the term is applied to the whole space of northern India between the Himalayas and the Vindhyas from sea to sea. When exactly this region came to be occupied by the Aryans has not been fixed with any precision. It must have been many centuries later than the Rig Vedic Age (*c.* 2000 B.C.) when the Aryans occupied Afghanistan and the Panjab only. The migration eastward and occupation of the whole of Aryavarta must have taken many centuries after the Aryans had made their first establishment in the Panjab.

Asad Khan—was the minister of Ibrahim Adil Shah I, Sultan of Bijapur (1535-57). He was a very capable administrator and diplomat. His greatest achievement was a diplomatic victory won in 1543. In that year the sultans of Ahmadnagar and Golkunda entered into an alliance with the Hindu kingdom of Vijayanagar with a view to attacking Bijapur. Asad Khan concluded peace separately with Ahmadnagar and Vijayanagar and thus broke up the coalition. Bijapur was saved for the time.

Asad Khan—was the Prime Minister for many years of Emperor Aurangzeb (1659-1707) during the latter part of his reign. His son Zulfikar Khan was one of the best generals of Aurangzeb.

Asaf Jah (Chin Qilich Khan)—was a prominent member of the Turani party of Mughul nobles who had their original homes in some part of Central Asia and who occupied important positions in the court of the later Mughul Emperors. His full name was Mir Qamar-ud-din Chin Qilich Khan. His father Gazi-ud-din Firuz Jang came to India during the reign of Aurangzeb and held high posts in the imperial service. Mir Qamar-ud-din first entered into the imperial service at the age of thirteen, quickly earned promotion, was given the title of Chin Qilich Khan and was at the time of Aurangzeb's death in command of the imperial army at Bijapur. He maintained perfect neutrality during the war of succession among the sons of Aurangzeb. Aurangzeb's son and successor Emperor Bahadur Shah (1707-12) made him the governor of Oudh and conferred on him his father's title of Gazi-ud-din Firuz Jang. Later on in 1713 he was appointed the governor of the Deccan with the

title of Nizam-ul-Mulk by Emperor Farruksiyar (1713-19).
As the viceroy in the Deccan he tried to check the growing
power of the Marathas, but he soon incurred the displeasure
of the Sayyid Brothers (*q.v.*), the King-Makers, and was transferred first to Muradabad and then to Malwa where he began
to gather strength and power. This aroused the hostility of the
Sayyid Brothers whom however Nizam-ul-Mulk succeeded in
getting defeated and killed. Nizam-ul-Mulk again became the
viceroy in the Deccan in 1720. In 1721 he was appointed *Wazir*
by Emperor Muhammad Shah (1719-48), but he left this office
in 1723 and returned to the viceroyalty in the Deccan in 1724.
Emperor Muhammad Shah made an attempt to remove him
by force, but having failed in his effort recognised him as the
Viceroy of the South and conferred upon him the title of Asaf
Jha. He now practically became the independent ruler of the
Deccan and founded the dynasty of the Nizams of Hyderabad.
He ruled over this territory very efficiently. He found a strong
rival in Peshwa Baji Rao I (1720-40) and supported his rival
the Commander-in-Chief, Trimbak Rao Dhabade, but was
forced, after Dhabade's defeat and death in 1731, to come to
terms with Baji Rao I on condition of leaving him a free hand
in the North. The Nizam violated this treaty in 1737 when at
the call of Emperor Muhammad Shah he proceeded to the
North to resist the expansion of the power of Peshwa Baji Rao I
in that region: but he was defeated by the Peshwa in a battle
fought near Bhopal and obliged to make peace on condition
of leaving Malwa and the territory between the Narmada and
the Chambal to the Peshwa. The Nizam-ul-Mulk was spared
by the element of distance from the disastrous effects of Nadir
Shah's invasion in 1739 and used it later on to further strengthen
his position in the Deccan. He died in 1748 at the age of ninety-
one.

Asaf Khan—Mughul general, was governor of Kara at the beginning
of the reign of Emperor Akbar (1556-1605). In 1564 he conquered, according to the orders of Akbar, the kingdom of
Gondwana, roughly corresponding to the northern districts of
the Madhya Pradesh, after defeating the Regent, Rani Durgavati
and her son the reigning minor king, Bir Narayan. For some
time Asaf Khan administered the newly conquered country
but later on he was transferred and in 1576 he was, along with
Raja Man Singh, the commander of the Mughul army which
fought with and defeated Rana Pratap at the battle of Haldighat
in April, 1576.

Asaf Khan—was the son of Mirza Ghiyas Beg, a Persian immigrant who came to India in the reign of Akbar, and brother of Mihr-un-nisa, better known as Nur Jahan, the queen of Emperor Jahangir (1605-27). Asaf Khan entered into the Mughul imperial service and became a prominent person in the imperial court. Asaf Khan's daughter was Mumtaz Mahal who was married to Emperor Jahangir's third son, Prince Khurram, better known as Shah Jahan. On the death of Jahangir in 1627 Asaf Khan frustrated the plan of Nur Jahan to place on the Mughul throne Jahangir's youngest son, Shahryar, who had married Nur Jahan's daughter and succeeded in securing the succession of Shah Jahan. The grateful son-in-law after his installation as the Emperor raised Asaf Khan to the high post of the *Wazir* of the Empire which position he held till his death.

Asaf-ud-daulah (1775-97)—son and successor of Nawab Suja-ud-daulah of Oudh, was an inefficient administrator who, first, made with the East India Company the treaty of Faizabad by which he agreed to pay to the Company an annual subsidy of 74 lakhs of rupees on condition that the Company should maintain two regiments of troops within Oudh in order to uphold his rule. The Nawab, however, mismanaged the finances and soon fell into arrears. In 1781 when the Company was engaged in wars with the Marathas Warren Hastings, the Company's Governor-General, demanded the payment of the arrears. The Nawab pleaded inability to clear up the dues unless he was placed in possession of a large part of the wealth that had passed from his father, the late Nawab Suja-ud-daulah, to his Begums. This provoked the notorious affair of the Begums of Oudh (*q.v.*) who were placed by the directions of Warren Hastings under restraint within their palace at Faizabad and whose eunuch-officers were subjected to bodily tortures until the Begums paid what was demanded of them. Nawab Asaf-ud-daulah thus played the infamous part of being the abettor and aider of the persecution by the Company's officers of his own highly respectable and closely connected female relations. After mal-administering Oudh for another sixteen years Asaf-ud-daulah died in 1797.

Asanga—a renowned Buddhist scholar, saint and author, flourished in the Gupta period (4th century A.D.). He was the brother of the more famous Vasubandhu, teacher and minister of the second Gupta Emperor Samudragupta (*c.* A.D. 330-60) and was the author of the *Yogacharya bhumi Shastra* which is rightly regarded as one of the basic texts of the Mahayana.

Asawal—old site of the city of Ahmadabad, was the nucleus out of which developed the Muslim kingdom of Gujarat (*q.v.*) in the 15th century.

Ashtapradhan—was the collective name of the Council of Eight Ministers created by Shivaji, the founder of the Maratha kingdom, in order to help him in running the administration. It was an advisory body and was in no sense a responsible cabinet. The eight ministers were:—(1) the Peshwa or the Prime Minister who was to look after the general welfare and interests of the kingdom; (2) the *Amátya* who was in charge of the Finance Department; (3) the *Mantri* who preserved daily records of the king's acts and of the proceedings of the royal court; (4) the *Sachiva* who superintended all royal correspondence; (5) the *Sámanta* who was in charge of Foreign Affairs; (6) the *Senápati* or the Commander-in-Chief; (7) the *Pandit Rao* and *Dandádhyaksha* was the Royal Chaplain and Almoner and (8) the *Nyáyádhisa* or *Shástri* who was the Chief Justice and interpreted the Hindu Law. All the eight ministers except the *Pandit Rao* and the *Shástri* held military commands and the civil work of administering their different departments at the capital was performed by deputies.

Ashti, battle of—was fought on the 20th February, 1818 between the East India Company and the Peshwa Baji Rao II in the course of the Third Anglo-Maratha War (1817-18). The Peshwa's army was defeated and his able general Gokhale was killed. This defeat led to the surrender of the Peshwa in June 1818.

Asiatic Society of Bengal—an association of learned men especially interested in Oriental studies, was founded in Calcutta in 1784 by Sir William Jones supported by Warren Hastings who was then the Governor-General. It has promoted research on varied subjects connected not only with India but also with Asia. It maintains a fine library of printed books and manuscripts, publishes a learned Journal and has saved from oblivion by reprinting hundreds of books which would have been otherwise lost and by translating many books into English and has published many rare Sanskrit and Persian manuscripts. After the Sepoy Mutiny and transfer of power from the Company to the Crown of England it came to be known as the Royal Asiatic Society of Bengal. Since the attainment of independence by India in 1947 it came again to be known by its old name of Asiatic Society of Bengal.

Asikini, the—river mentioned in the *Rig-Veda*. *See* under Akisines.

Asirgarh—a strong fortress on the Tapti in Khandesh, was believed to be impregnable but it passed hands several times. Originally it belonged to the Hindu Rajas of Malwa from whom it passed under the Muslim sultans of Delhi. After the death of Muhammad Tughluq it came into the possession of the Faruqi dynasty of Khandesh from whose control Emperor Akbar captured it in 1601. With the growth of the Maratha power it became a part of the Maratha kingdom and was held by the Sindhia. Finally in 1803 after the victory of the East India Company over the combined armies of Sindhia and Bhonsla at the battle of Assaye it was captured by the Company and became a part of the British Indian Empire. In modern times it has lost its strategic importance.

Askari—the fourth and youngest son of the first Mughul Emperor Babur (1526-30), was given by his eldest brother Humayun (*q.v.*) (1530-56) the fief of Sambhal. Later on he accompanied Humayun in his campaign against Gujarat in 1534 where he plunged in feasting and revelry after its easy conquest. He retired safely with Humayun to Delhi. He, however, did not accompany Humayun in his Bengal campaign in 1539 and thus did not share the latter's defeat at the battle of Buxar. During Humayun's absence in Bengal Askari tried to seize the throne for himself but was frustrated by the return of the vanquished Humayun to Delhi. Askari rendered little or no help to Humayun during the years (1540-54) of his distress and exile following his defeat at the battle of Kanauj. Askari saved himself by making humble submission to Sher Shah. On Humayun's restoration to the throne of Delhi Askari was pardoned but he had to proceed to Mecca where he eventually died.

Asoka—the third Emperor (*c.* 273 B.C. - 232 B.C.) of the Maurya dynasty of Magadha founded by his grandfather Chandragupta Maurya (*c.* 322 B.C. - 298 B.C.), succeeded his father King Bindusara (*c.* 298 B.C. - 273 B.C.). According to tradition as preserved in the Ceylonese Chronicles Asoka was one of the many sons of his father King Bindusara and was the Viceroy at Ujjain in Malwa at the time of his father's death. He then won a bloody succession war in the course of which ninety-nine of his brothers were killed and he ascended his father's throne. There is nothing, however, in any of the many inscriptions that Asoka himself has left to indicate the occurrence of such a fratricidal war. On the other hand one inscription, viz. Rock Edict V, shows that Asoka was very much interested in the welfare of the families of his brothers and sisters. The story of the fratricidal war preceding the accession of Asoka would not therefore be accepted as true by some historians. His coronation, however, did not take place until four years after his accession. This delay has been considered as an evidence in support of the idea that his accession was disputed.

Asoka was a contemporary of Antiochus II of Syria (261 b.c.- 246 b.c.) and some other Hellenistic kings whom he has mentioned in his Rock Edict XIII and this circumstance suggests that he ruled in the latter half of the third century b.c.; but the exact date of his accession has not yet been ascertained. He ruled for forty years and must have been a young man at the time of his accession.

Asoka's full name was Asokavardhana. In his inscriptions he is always called *Devanampiya* (Beloved of the Gods) and *Piyadarshin* (One who looks to the welfare of his subjects) except in the Maski version of his Minor Rock Edict I where alone he is designated *Devanampiya* Asoka.

Nothing definite is known about the first twelve years of Asoka's reign except that during this period he was, like his predecessors, fond of convivial parties, hunting excursions, meat diet and tours of pleasure. But the thirteenth year of his reign proved a turning point in his career. In that year, eight years after his coronation, he embarked on a war with Kalinga which lay along the coast of the Bay of Bengal from the Mahanadi to the Godavari, for reasons which are not known. Kalinga was conquered and annexed to Asoka's dominions, but the war had been extremely bloody in the course of which one lakh of persons were killed, one and a half lakhs were made captives and many lakhs of persons perished from famines, pestilence and other calamities that inevitably follow wars. Such widespread human suffering struck the conscience of Asoka who considered it very much painful and deplorable. Immediately afterwards Asoka began the study of what he calls in his edicts *dhama* (*dharma*) which has been identified with Buddhism and which he soon afterwards embraced. After his conversion to Buddhism Asoka became a changed man. In Rock Edict XIII, which was probably issued four years after the conquest of Kalinga, Asoka declared that the loss of "even the hundredth part or the thousandth part of all those people who were slain, who died, and who were deported at the time in Kalinga, would now be considered very deplorable" by himself. He also declared that "even to one who should wrong him, what can be forgiven is to be forgiven." He forswore war and never again did he fight a war during the long period of thirty-one years which intervened between his conversion and his death. He also called upon his descendants to give up "conquest by arms" and to concentrate their energies on conquest by *dhama*. Asoka now gave up his old habits of joining in convivial parties and going on hunting excursions and his attachment to predominantly non-vegetarian diet. Instead he went on tours of pilgrimage to Buddhist holy places visiting Bodh-Gaya in the fourteenth year and Lumbini-grama, where the Buddha had been born, in the twenty-fourth year of his reign. During the course of these visits he deliberately contacted the ordinary people to whom he expounded the *dhama*. For the purpose of permanently recording the doctrines of the *dhama* he inscribed them on rocks and pillars and issued them for the edification of the people from the sixteenth year of his reign till at least the thirty-second year of it. He also held public shows of edifying objects for the promotion of *dhama* and ordered his officers to go on tours looking not only after the administration but also after the propagation of the *dhama*. He appointed in the seventeenth year of his reign a special class of officers called *Dhama-Mahamatras* for propagating *dhama* and for promoting its practice all through his dominions. He called upon his officers to remember that all his subjects were like his own children to the king (*sarve munisha paja mama*) and should be treated by them as they would treat the royal children. He also called upon his officers to exert themselves and to render impartial justice softened with mercy. He exhorted his subjects to be tolerant in their views and practices and he encouraged the holding of concourses (i.e. meetings) where the essence of all religions would be discussed and which would thus broaden their outlooks. He also sent missionaries not only to the different parts of his vast empire but also outside it, to the independent kingdoms of southern India, to the Hellenistic monarchies of Syria, Egypt, Cyrene, Macedonia and Epirus, and to Ceylon, and possibly also to Burma. His missions embraced the three continents of Asia, Africa and Europe. Asoka thus started Buddhism on that career of conquest which turned it into a world religion. He also promoted the welfare of men and beasts by planting trees and digging wells by the roadside and by establishing hospitals for men and beasts not only throughout his vast empire but also in the neighbouring Hellenistic kingdoms where he also sent medicines and planted medicinal plants. Indeed Asoka was cosmopolitan in his benefactions which were not allowed to be limited by considerations of race or language or religion. Asoka is a unique figure in history who devoted himself deliberately to the welfare of mankind and deserves the title of "the Great" much better than war-lords like Alexander of Macedon, Julius Caesar of Rome and Napoleon of France.

Asoka's dominions extended from the Hindu-kush in the north-west to Bengal in the east and from the foot of the Himalayas in the north to the river Pennar in the south. He left his inscriptions scattered all over his vast empire and these have been found at such distant places as Qandahar and Jalalabad in Afghanistan and Maski in Mysore, Girnar in Kathiawar and Tosali in Orissa. His inscriptions were meant for the education of the common people and were, therefore, written in scripts known to them. Thus Greek and Aramaic were used in his Qandahar and Jalalabad inscriptions, Kharosthi in his inscriptions at Shahbaz-garhi and Manshera in the north-western frontier and Brahmi in all his inscriptions on rocks and pillars lying scattered all over the rest of India. The language used was *ardha-Magadhi* which was very much like the Pali language and was evidently read and understood by the mass of the Indian people.

Asoka left his inscriptions engraved on rocks, pillars of stone and in caves. His inscriptions are thus naturally divided into three classes, namely rock, pillar and cave inscriptions. Those on rocks and pillars are again sub-divided into two classes. Fourteen inscriptions on rocks form a serially arranged set and are known as the Fourteen Rock Inscriptions. These have been found at Shahbazgarhi, Mansehra, Kalsi, Girnar, Sopara, Dhauli and Jaugada. Some detached inscriptions on rocks have also been found and are known, presumably on account of their comparative brevity, as Minor Rock Edicts. Versions of the first of these have been found at Rupnath, Sasaram, Bairat, Maski, Siddapura, Jatinga Rameswara and Brahmagiri. Versions of the second Minor Rock Edict have been found at Bairat (also called Bhabru), Yerragudi and Kopbal. Two other Minor Rock Edicts have recently been found in Afghanistan—one in Jalalabad and the other near Qandahar. Again, seven inscrip-tions on stone pillars form a set and these are therefore known as the Seven Pillar Edicts. These are found at Delhi, Allahabad, Lauriya-Araraj, Lauriya-Nandangarh and Rampurva. Some pillars again contain single inscriptions relating to matters different from those of the Seven Pillar Edicts. These are therefore called Minor Pillar Edicts. There are three of them which have been found at Sarnath, Sanchi, Rummindei and Nigliva. Lastly three Edicts have been found inscribed in the caves of Barabar Hills and are known as the Cave Inscriptions.

Asoka is reported to have built a thousand *stupas* none of which except probably one at Bhilsa has survived. His palace at Pataliputra which Fa-Hien (*q.v.*) saw in the fourth century A.D., had disappeared by the time of Hiuen-Tsang's visit in the seventh century. His palace looked so impressive even in the fourth century A.D. that Fa-Hien believed that it was executed by spirits in the service of Asoka. Some of his pillars, however, have withstood the ravages of time and have extorted the admiration of all connoisseurs of art and sculpture. These extant pillars are all monolithic and are marvels of technical execution. "They show that the art of polishing hard stone was carried to such perfection that it has become a lost art beyond modern powers." A high degree of knowledge of engineering was displayed in cutting these huge blocks of stone and removing them hundreds of miles from the quarry, and sometimes to the top of a hill. At the top of every pillar there was a capital consisting of one or more animal figures in the round, resting on an abacus below which there is an inverted lotus. The artistic merit of these capitals, especially of the Sarnath Capital (*q.v.*), has been highly praised and, according to Sir John Marshall, "stands unsurpassed by anything of their kind in the ancient world."

Very little is known about the family life of Asoka. According to tradition as preserved in later literature he had several queens. Inscriptions, however, tell us of only two, the second of whom was named Kaluvaki or Charuvaki who was the mother of Tivara. Similarly very little is known about the sons of Asoka. Tivara was certainly one but who the other sons were and how many of them he had are not known. According to Ceylonese Chronicles Mahendra who propagated Buddhism in Ceylon, was a son of Asoka who sent him there as a missionary. In that case Mahendra's sister and helper, Sanghamitra, was a daughter of Asoka, but inscriptions make no mention of either of them. Literary tradition preserves the names of two other sons, namely Kunala and Jalauka. But Asoka was succeeded by no son of his. His empire passed to his two grandsons, Dasaratha and Samprati, who divided it between themselves.

It is not known how or where or when Asoka passed away from his strenuous life. According to a Tibetan tradition he died at Taxila. According to his inscriptions one of his last acts was to condemn schisms in the Buddhist Church. This condemnation of schisms followed perhaps the meeting of the Third Buddhist Council, which, according to Ceylonese Chronicles, was held at Pataliputra during Asoka's reign.

Asoka's personal religion, after the conquest of Kalinga, was Buddhism, as is proved by his reference to himself as a Buddha-Sakya in the Maski version of the Minor Rock Edict I, by his confession of faith in and reference to the Buddhist Trinity in the Bhabru edict, by the circumstance that he went on pilgrimage exclusively to Buddhist holy places and by his anxiety for the maintenance of the integrity of the Buddhist Church (*Samgha*) as is clear from the Sarnath Pillar Edict.

But the circumstance that in none of his inscriptions is there any reference to the fundamental principles of Buddhism like the Four Noble Truths, the Noble Eightfold Path and to *Nirvana* coupled with the fact that in his inscriptions Asoka also held up, contrary to orthodox Buddhism, the attainment of *svarga* (heaven) as a very desirable goal for which *dhama* is to be practised, has led some scholars to hold that the *dhama* (religion) that Asoka preached was not Buddhism but a Universal Religion. This view is not tenable. All through his inscriptions Asoka uses the same term *dhama* to denote his personal religion as well as the religion that he preached. If therefore the former is held to be Buddhism the latter also must be held to have been the same. Sanctity of animal life, obedience and reverence to parents and teachers, truthfulness and courtesy to all, which are repeatedly emphasized in Asoka's edicts, are certainly virtues common to all religions, but no religion has put so much emphasis on them, to the exclusion of all creeds and doctrines, as Buddhism has done and in many Buddhist sacred books these virtues and practices are particularly recommended for practice by the Buddhist laity. The *dhama* that Asoka preached in his inscriptions was for the benefit of the laity, the common householder, and has therefore been rightly regarded as Buddhism. (Hultzsch, *C.I.I.*, I; Bhandarkar, *Asoka*; Mukherjee, *Asoka*; Smith, *E.H.I.*; Wells, *History of the World*; Bhattacharya, *Select Asokan Epigraphs*)

Aspasians, the—a tribal people who lived in the valley of the Kunar or Chitral river to the north-west of the Indian frontier at the time of the invasion of India by Alexander the Great, offered very stout resistance to the Greek invader and Alexander had to fight two battles with them before they were finally reduced to submission.

Assakenois, the—a tribal people who occupied at the time of the invasion of India by Alexander the Great a portion of the Swat valley near the Malakand Pass, had a large army and the seat of their government was at a fortified place called Massaga. It was a formidable fortress protected by nature and human art. The Assakenois offered very stout resistance and on one occasion succeeded in wounding Alexander with an arrow. But in the end Alexander triumphed, the fort of Massaga was captured and the Assakenois were reduced to submission after a severe slaughter.

Assam—is the modern name of the state situated in the north-eastern part of India. It extends at present from the river Sankosh in the west to Sadiya in the east. It is pre-eminently the gift of the Brahmaputra which flowing between the eastern portion of the Himalayas on the north and the Assam Range on the south, has created the alluvial plain now known as Assam. It is called Pragjyotisha in the Epics and Kamarupa in the Puranas. The Muhammadan historians called it Kamrud and it came to be known by its modern name of Assam some time after the Ahoms (*q.v.*) had overcome and occupied the land. It is easy of access from all directions and has therefore attracted the hungry and the adventurous from all the neighbouring areas in all ages. It has therefore a very much mixed population consisting of tribes of Austric, Mongolian and Dravidian origins as well as of peoples of Aryan stock. The modern population of Assam is as composite as that of the rest of India and speaks a variety of languages and dialects of which Assamese and Bengali alone have their own scripts and literatures. The other dialects and languages are written in Roman scripts and have no literature of their own.

The history of Assam may be broadly divided into four periods, viz. the legendary period, the early period, the Ahom period and the modern period. During the legendary period Assam was ruled, first, by non-Aryan peoples called Danavas and Asuras, yet it was during this period that the Aryans also came into the country overland from the north-west. The early period begins in the fourth century A.D. and the earliest epigraphic reference to Assam (Kamarupa) is found in the Allahabad inscription of the second Gupta Emperor, Samudragupta (*c.* A.D. 330-80). The early period may be said to have continued till the thirteenth century when Assam began to be invaded from the east by the Ahoms and from the west by the Muhammadans. The Muhammadan invasions were resisted and practically speaking there is no Muslim period in the history of Assam. The Ahoms, however, conquered the country which they ruled for about six hundred years at the end of which Assam was first conquered and held by the Burmese for a very short period and then was annexed to the British Indian Empire in 1826. It was then that the modern period began in the history of Assam which now for the first time became politically and administratively an integral part of India, though culturally it had always been a part of Hindu India.

The most renowned king of the legendary period of Assam was Narakásura who, however, is said to have come to rule over Pragjyotisha from Mithila in Bihar. His rule, therefore, may be considered as marking the beginning of the Aryanisation of Assam. Naraka's name is associated with much of ancient Assam, especially the cult of the Goddess Kamakhya and the construction of her temple at its present site on a hillock called Nilachala near Gauhati. His son Bhagadatta is referred to in the *Mahabharata* as a great warrior who took part on behalf of the Kurus in the battle of Kurukshetra where he was killed. His successor Vajradatta and his successors are said to have ruled over Kamarupa for three thousand years, which is obviously an exaggeration, before the country came to be ruled by King Pushyavarman about the 4th century A.D. Pushyavarman is definitely a historical figure and is mentioned in the Nidhanpur Grant of Bhaskaravarman (A.D. 604-649) (*q.v.*) as the founder of a dynasty of thirteen kings namely Samudravarman, Balavarman, Kalyanavarman, Ganapativarman, Mahendravarman, Narayanavarman, Mahabhutivarman or Bhutivarman, Chandramukhavarman, Sthitavarman, Sushthitavarman, Supratisthitavarman and Bhaskaravarman. Pushyavarman is believed to have been the king of Kamarupa who, according to the Allahabad inscription, submitted to the second Gupta Emperor, Samudragupta (*c.* A.D. 330-80), and Bhaskaravarman was certainly the contemporary of Emperor Harshavardhana, as is known from Bana's *Harsha-Charita* and the *Travels* of Hiuen-Tsang. Bhaskaravarman (*q.v.*) died in about A.D. 649, a couple of years after Harsha's death. Kamarupa then passed under the rule of a new dynasty founded by a Mleccha chief named Salastambha in about the middle of the seventh century. He transferred the capital from Pragjyotisapura (Gauhati) to Haruppesvara on the bank of the Brahmaputra, near modern Tezpur. This dynasty had thirteen kings *viz.* Vijaya, Palaka, Kumara, Vajradatta, Harsha, Balavarman, Chakra, Pralambha,

Harjjara, Vanamala, Jayamala, Balavarman and Tyagasingh. It ruled over Kamarupa from the middle of the seventh century to the middle of the tenth century A.D. Tyagasingh having died without any issue, one Brahmapala who traced his descent from Naraka, was elected king of Kamarupa in the latter part of the tenth century A.D. Brahmapala founded the third dynasty of Hindu kings in Kamarupa. This Pala dynasty, which must be distinguished from the Pala dynasty of Bengal, ruled the country from the latter part of the tenth century to the early part of the 12th century and had six kings, *viz.* Ratnapala, Indrapala, Gopala, Harsapala, Dharmapala and Jayapala. The last king Jayapala was overthrown by Ramapala of Bengal who established in Kamarupa a vassal-king named Tingyadeva. But he soon rebelled against Ramapala and was superseded by Vaidyadeva, a general of the Bengal king Kumarapala. But Vaidyadeva also soon rebelled and a period of confusion ensued in the history of Kamarupa which lasted for more than a century. During this period of confusion a Sena king of Bengal might have defeated one or other of the kings of Kamarupa. But the Sena Dynasty of Bengal was itself overthrown by Iktiaruddin, popularly known as Baktiyar Khalji, who led the first Muhammadan invasion into Bengal in A.D. 1198 and who after his conquest of Bengal led an expedition into Assam in A.D. 1205. A two lined Sanskrit inscription on a boulder in the village of Kanai-barsi-ber on the Brahmaputra just opposite Gauhati, records that the Turks who had invaded Kamarupa were destroyed in battle on the 13th day of the month of Chaitra (March-April) in the Saka year 1127 (A.D. 1205). The record, however, does not mention the name of the national hero of Kamarupa who had the honour of having repulsed the first Muhammadan invasion of Kamarupa. This gap in our knowledge is due to the fact that darkness began to descend on Kamarupa in the thirteenth century. If the Muhammadans invaded it, though unsuccessfully, from the west in A.D. 1205 the Ahoms invaded it with great success from the east in A.D. 1228. Under the pressure of these two invading hosts the unity and integrity of the Kamarupa kingdom was broken and Kamarupa became divided into a number of states. In the extreme west was Kamta-pur extending from the Karatoya to the Sankosh; and to the east of it was Kamarupa on the north bank of the Brahmaputra from the Barnadi upto the Subanasiri ruled by a number of petty chiefs called Bhuiyás or Bára Bhuiyás (Twelve Landlords). East of the Subanasiri the country on the north bank of the

Brahmaputra formed the kingdom of the Chutiyas while the opposite region on the south bank formed a kingdom ruled by the Kacharies. To the south-west of this lay the Jaintia kingdom of the Khasis. This division of the country into so many petty states facilitated its conquest by the invading hosts of the Muhammadans and the Ahoms who came practically simultaneously from the west and the east respectively. In the west the kings of Kamtapur and Kamarupa held back the Muhammadan invaders till 1498 when Husain Shah of Bengal conquered the kingdoms of Kamtapur and Kamarupa upto the Barnadi and established his son at Hajo as the governor of the newly conquered territories. But early in the 16th century a new Hindu kingdom soon came to be founded by one Bisva Singh, the leader of the Koches, in the western part of modern Assam. He subdued the Bára Bhuiyás, established his capital at Cooch-Behar, drove the Muhammadans beyond the Karatoya and thus re-established Hindu rule in the westernmost part of modern Assam including the districts of Goalpara, Kamarupa and Darrang. The Koch kings waged long wars with the Muhammadan invaders who came from Bengal until at last they were obliged to make peace by accepting the protection of the Mughul Emperor Akbar in 1596. Thus not only the district of Goalpara but also a large portion of the district of Kamarupa passed under Muhammadan control. But the district of Kamarupa was recovered from the Muhammadans by the Ahom kings who had in the meantime established their rule over the whole of the eastern part of Assam. The first Ahom king Sukapha who invaded Assam in 1228 occupied the district of Sibsagar and founded the dynasty which ruled over the Brahmaputra valley up to the district of Kamarupa for the next six centuries (1228 to 1824). There were thirty-nine Ahom kings of whom the seventeenth king Susengpha was the first to assume a Sanskritic name, viz. Pratap Singh. His successors followed his example. The more prominent amongst them were Jayadhvaj Singh, Chakradvaja Singh, Udayaditya Singh, Ramadhavaja Singh, Gadadhar Singh, Rudra Singh, Sib Singh, Pramatta Singh, Rajeswar Singh, Laksmi Singh, Gourinath Singh, Kamaleswar Singh, Chandra Kant Singh, Purandar Singh and Jogeshwar Singh. Internal dissensions amongst the ruling section of the Ahoms, especially between Purnanand, the *Burha Gohain* (Prime Minister) and Badan Chandra, the *Bar Phukan* (governor) at Gauhati led the latter to approach the Burmese Government to send an army for conquering

Assam and the first Burmese army entered into Assam in 1816. It was, however, not till 1819 that the Burmese conquered the country over which they ruled till 1824 with great harshness and cruelty. The Ahom nobles were soon disgruntled and the British in India also did not like this expansion of Burmese rule in a territory so adjacent to their dominions. Chandra Kant, the reigning Ahom king, made repeated efforts to drive out the Burmese, but all his efforts failed and eventually he became a prisoner in the hands of the Burmese who however soon became engaged in a war with the British Indian Government. In this war which was fought not only in Assam but also in Burma, the Burmese were ultimately defeated and had to make peace with the British by the treaty of Yandabo (1826) (*q.v.*) by which the Burmese withdrew from Assam and the neighbouring districts of Cachar and Manipur. Lower Assam comprising the districts of Kamarupa, Darrang and Nowgong were straightaway annexed to the British dominions, made an appendage of Bengal and placed under the administration of David Scott who was then in charge of the Bengal districts of Goalpara and Garo Hills. Thus it was that these two Bengal districts came to be joined with Assam. Upper Assam comprising the modern districts of Sibsagar and Lakhimpur but excluding Sadiya and Matak was restored to Purandar Singh, a descendant of the old Ahom royal dynasty. But Purandar Singh proved a failure as a ruler and his dominions, that is to say—the districts of Sibsagar and Lakhimpur were joined with Lower Assam and placed under the direct rule of the British Indian Government in 1839. Sadiya and Matak which were at first placed in charge of two Ahom officials were also brought under direct British rule by 1843 and were incorporated with the district of Lakhimpur. Assam continued to be administered as an appendage of the province of Bengal till 1874 when for improving its administration Assam was separated from the Bengal province and placed under a Chief Commissioner. It was at this time that the districts of Sylhet, Cachar, Goalpara as well as the northern part of the district of Garo Hills were tagged with the province of Assam and a large number of Bengali-speaking people were made citizens of Assam. Since then (1874) the term Assam, which had originally been applied to the tract of country ruled by the Ahoms, i.e. the five districts of Kamarup, Darrang, Nowgong, Sibsagar and Lakhimpur has been given a wider signification and came to be used as the designation of the whole country from Sadiya to Goalpara including the hill districts of the Khasi and Jaintia Hills, the Surma valley comprising the two districts of Sylhet and Cachar and last, but not the least, the Bengal districts of Garo Hills and Goalpara. Thus the population of Assam which was already composite, was now made much more so by the incorporation within it of a large body of comparatively backward hill people and of a larger and much more advanced Bengali-speaking people; and seeds were laid for the serious linguistic troubles which had disturbed Assam in recent years. In 1905 Assam was amalgamated with the districts of the Dacca, Chittagong and Rajshahi Divisions of Bengal, formed into a new province known as Eastern Bengal and Assam and placed under a Lieutenant-Governor. Six years later this set-up was again altered; the partition of Bengal was undone; Eastern Bengal was re-united with Western Bengal, and Assam again became a Chief Commissionership but was allowed to retain not only the Khasi and Jaintia Hill districts but also the Bengal districts of Sylhet, Cachar, Garo Hills and Goalpara. In 1912 Assam was constituted into a Governor's province with an Executive Council and a Legislature. This status of a Governor's province, now called a State, has been retained by Assam after the attainment of Independence, but as the result of the Partition which accompanied it, the district of Sylhet except the sub-division of Karimganj has been lost by Assam to Pakistan. The origin of much of the modern linguistic troubles of Assam is thus to be traced to the haphazard way in which the province was formed by the British rulers in India on the plea of administrative convenience or expediency and which it is now hard, if not impossible, to change. (*Kalika Purana; Yogini Tantra;* Kakati, *Mother Goddess Kamakhya* and *Assamese, Its Formation and Development*; Barua, K. L., *History of Kamarupa;* Bhattacharya, P., *Kamarupasasanavali;* Barua B. K., *Cultural History of Assam;* Bhattacharya, S., *Date of the Nidhanpur Copper-Plate, Journal of Indian History,* Vol. XXXI, Aug., 1953, pp. 111-17; Gait, Sir Edward, *History of Assam;* Barua, Golap Chandra, *Ahom Buranji*; Bhuiyan, S. K., *Buranjis* and *Anglo-Assamese Relations*)

Assaye, the battle of—was fought in the course of the Second Anglo-Maratha War (1803-05). In this battle the English army led by Sir Arthur Wellesley completely defeated the combined larger army of Sindhia and Bhonsla on September 23, 1803. Sindhia's army that took part in this battle had been trained by European officers after the European method, but was utterly defeated by a smaller English army.

Asvaghosha—a Buddhist saint and scholar who flourished in the second century of the Christian era, was born in Magadha but later on moved to the court of Kanishka (*q.v.*), the Great Kushan king of North India and lived at Peshawar. He was a poet, musician, scholar, philosopher, dramatist, religious controversialist, zealous Buddhist monk, orthodox in creed and strict in the observance of discipline. Amongst his dramas *Rastrapala* and *Sariputra Prakasha* are the better known. He also wrote a lyric named *Sutralankara*. His great work the *Buddhacharita* is an epic like the *Ramayana* and dealt with the life and work of Gautama Buddha. He attended the Buddhist Church Council which Kanishka held at Peshawar and took a leading part in it. In his *Awakening of the Faith* he gave a clear exposition of the doctrine of unreality and developed the doctrine of *Tri-kayas*, namely the *Dharma-kaya*, *Sambhoga kaya* and the *Nirmana kaya*. He held that in order to attain the ideal of enlightenment it is necessary for the Buddhist to believe in any of these three aspects of Buddha's personality. The later development of *Mahayanism* was to a certain extent due to his speculations. (*E.R.E.*)

Asvalayana—an ancient author whose *Grihya-Sutra* is a storehouse of information about religious rituals and social customs of the early Brahmanical Hindus. The earliest reference to the *Mahabharata* is found in his *Grihya-Sutra*. Its date is uncertain.

Asvamedha—was a rite performed by a victorious king to celebrate his imperial sovereignty over the whole country. An *asva*, i.e. a horse, was set free to roam abroad at pleasure under the guardianship of the victorious king or his sons who were all fully armed. The horse was allowed to roam about for a particular period of time and if it returned safe at the end of the period it signalised the undisputed power of its royal master who then sacrificed the horse. This rite was said to have been performed by many kings mentioned in the Epics. In historical times Pushyamitra Sunga (187 B.C. - 151 B.C.) was the first king who celebrated it twice. Samudragupta, the second Gupta Emperor (A.D. 330-75), also celebrated it and issued coins in its commemoration. (*See poste* Horse sacrifice)

Atala Masjid—built at Jaunpur by Ibrahim Shah (1402-38) of the Sharqi dynasty in 1408, stands as a brilliant specimen of the Jaunpur style of architecture. It is a mosque without minarets of the usual type. (Fuhrer, A., *Sharqi Architecture of Jaunpur*)

Atisha—a renowned Buddhist monk and preacher, was born in about A.D. 981 in a well-to-do family of landlords in Eastern India in Sa-hor or Za-hor which has been placed by some in Bengal. His father was Kalyana Sree and his mother was Padmaprabha. He was one of many sons and was named Chandragarbha by his parents. In his early life he was a householder devoted to the worship of Goddess Tara and it was only after he had fairly reached his youth that he took up Buddhistic studies. Soon, however, he acquired such a profound knowledge in Buddhistic lore that Acharya Shilabhadra of the *Vihara* of Odantapuri, where Atisha was studying, conferred on him the title of Dipankara Sree Jnana. Later on the Tibetans called him Atisha. People soon came to forget the original name, Chandragarbha, and he became immortal under the name of Atisha Dipankara Sree Jnana. He entered the Order at the age of 31 and spent the next twelve years of his life in studying and practising *Yoga* in and outside India and visited Pegu and Ceylon. On his return from his studies abroad he was persuaded by the Pala king Nyayapala to accept the post of the Principal of the Vikramasila *Vihara*. The reputation of his learning and piety soon spread far and wide and he was persistently invited by the king of Tibet to come to Tibet and to restore Buddhism there in all its perfection. Atisha was then sixty years old, but so earnest and insistent was the request of the Tibetan king that he could not refuse it. Accompanied by two Tibetan monks he made the perilous and hazardous journey from Vikramasila to Tibet through Nepal and was received in Tibet with royal honours. The monastery at Thalong was specially set apart for him and there he drew a large number of Tibetans to him. He lived and preached in Tibet for twelve years, learnt Tibetan to perfection and composed more than a hundred books on Buddhism in Sanskrit and Tibetan. His teachings removed many of the abuses that had crept into Buddhism in Tibet and created amongst the Tibetans many Buddhist monks who upheld the religion in Tibet for many years afterwards. Atisha travelled over many parts of Tibet where at last he laid his bones in A.D. 1054 at the age of seventy three. The Tibetans buried his body with royal honours in the monastery of Ne-Thang where his remains still rest. He is remembered even now by the Tibetans with very great reverence and his image is actually worshipped as a *Bodhisattva*. (Das, S. C., *Indian Pundits in the Land of Snow;* Sumpa Khan, *Pag-Sam Jon Zenk* ed. by Das, pp. 185-87; Roerich, G. N., *The Blue*

Annals, pp. 240-60; Ray, Nihar Ranjan, *Banglar Itihasa*, pp. 716-17)

Attlee, Clement Richard (1883-   )—Prime Minister of Great Britain (1945-50 & 1950-51), educated at Oxford, and a member of the Inner Temple, became a socialist in 1907. He served as a soldier in the First World War and attained the rank of a Major. He was elected to the Parliament in 1922 and continued to be a member of the House of Commons till his promotion to the peerage. In 1935 he became the leader of the Labour Party. He held Cabinet posts in the War Cabinet of Winston Churchill (*q.v.*) whom he succeeded as Prime Minister in 1945 when the Conservative party was defeated in the General Election after the War. His administration was made memorable by the grant by the British Parliament of independence to India in August, 1947, on the basis of the partition of India into India and Pakistan. In 1951 the Labour Party was defeated in the General Election. Attlee was raised to the peerage and continues to take an active part in Parliamentary affairs.

Auchmuty, Sir Samuel—was appointed Commander-in-Chief of the Company's army in Madras by Lord Minto I (1807-13) early in his administration following a mutiny of the army officers in Madras. Auchmuty soon restored order and was rewarded by being placed in supreme direction of the British Expedition to Java (1810-11) which led to the conquest of Java in 1811.

Auckland, Lord—was Governor-General of India for six years (1836-42). His administration had little merit. It is true that he took certain steps for the promotion of education and the study of western medical science by the Indians. He gave effect to the orders of the Directors for abolishing the tax on pilgrims and ending all official control over religious endowments. But he failed to take adequate measures to ameliorate the sufferings of the people caused by the Great Famine that overtook northern India in 1837-38 and caused the death of at least eight lakhs of persons. He suppressed a rebellion made by the Padshah Begum of Oudh in 1837 and tried to force on Nasir-ud-din Haidar, the new king of Oudh, a new treaty requiring him to pay a heavier subsidy. The treaty was disallowed by the Court of Directors but Lord Auckland did not communicate to the king of Oudh the fact of his discomfiture. He deposed the Raja of Satara for having entered into treasonable intrigues with the Portuguese and placed on the *gadi* the brother of the deposed Raja. He also deposed the Nawab of Karnul for an attempt to wage war against the Company and annexed his state to the British Indian empire. The last and most notorious act of Lord Auckland was to enter into the first Anglo-Afghan War (1838-42) (*q.v.*) for the purpose of deposing Dost Mohammad (*q.v.*), the reigning Amir of Afghanistan who was supposed to be in favour of Russia, and replacing him with Shah Shuja, (*q.v.*) who was expected to be in favour of the British. The war was unjustifiable; it involved a callous breach of a recently made treaty with the Amirs of Sind and was so inefficiently conducted that it resulted in a great tragedy. Lord Auckland was recalled and succeeded by Lord Ellenborough.

Aungier, Gerald—Governor of Bombay (1669-1707), was the real founder of the city of Bombay who foresaw its future greatness. He may be regarded as one of the early founders of the British Indian empire. He lies buried in a nameless grave in Surat. (Malabari, *Bombay in the Making*)

Aurangzeb—the sixth Mughul Emperor (1659-1707) of India, was the third son of Shah Jahan (1627-59) (*q.v.*). As a Prince he had held important administrative and military posts, having been his father's viceroy twice in the Deccan and once in Afghanistan. In these capacities he had shown ability, courage and assiduity—virtues which he certainly possessed in abundance and which marked his administration as the Emperor of India. In 1657 when his father Emperor Shah Jahan fell ill he was the viceroy in the Deccan and his eldest brother, Dara Shukoh, Shah Jahan's favourite and choice for the imperial throne, was with the Emperor in Delhi; his second brother Shuja was the viceroy in Bengal and his fourth and youngest brother Murad was the viceroy in Gujarat. As soon as the news of Shah Jahan's illness was known Shuja declared himself to be the Emperor in Bengal and Murad followed suit in Gujarat. In the circumstances Aurangzeb also decided to strike for the throne, entered into an alliance with Murad on condition of partitioning the Empire with him and thus there began a fratricidal succession war amongst the four sons of Shah Jahan. The combined armies of Aurangzeb and Murad defeated the imperial armies at the battles of Dharmat, near Ujjain, in April, 1658, and of Samugarh in May, 1658. Prince Dara, who was personally present at the battle of Samugrah, practically lost the war as the result of this defeat and fled to Agra. There he was hotly pursued by the victorious brothers who soon pressed on to Agra and received the surrender of the Fort with all its treasures (June 8, 1658). Emperor Shah Jahan was made a prisoner for life. Murad was soon afterwards executed by Aurangzeb's orders on a charge of the murder of his Diwan in Gujarat in 1657. In the meantime Shuja who had already been defeated by Dara's son, Sulaiman, in February 1658 at Bahadurpur near Benares, had recovered some power. Aurangzeb, therefore, personally led an army into Bengal against Shuja whom he defeated at the battle of Khajwah. Shuja was hotly pursued by Aurangzeb's general Mir Jumla, was driven across Bengal to the Deccan and thence to Arakan (May, 1660), where he eventually perished with his whole family. Lastly, Dara who had fled from Agra on its occupation by Aurangzeb and had become a fugitive, was finally defeated by Aurangzeb's army at the battle of Deorai in April, 1659, betrayed in June to Aurangzeb, who subjected him to great public humiliation, had him tried and condemned on a charge of apostasy and got him executed on August 30, 1659. Thus Aurangzeb alone survived amongst his brothers. He had already been informally crowned on July 21, 1658, when Emperor Shah Jahan was made a prisoner for life, and, now he was formally enthroned in June, 1659 and assumed the title of Alamgir (Conqueror of the World).

Aurangzeb's chief wife was Dilras Bano Begum. He was the father of five sons, namely Muhammad who was privately executed in 1676, Muazzam who succeeded him, Ajam who was killed in the Succession War following the death of Aurangzeb, Akbar who revolted against his father and was exiled to Persia where he died in 1704, and Kam Baksh who was killed in the Succession War in 1709.

Like his predecessors Aurangzeb took pains to extend the bounds of the Mughul Empire in India. In 1661 Palamau was conquered and annexed. Next year his General Mir Jumla carried for the first time the victorious arms of the Mughuls into Assam upto Garhgaon, the capital of the Ahom kings and forced the Ahom king to make peace by ceding to the Mughuls a large part of the modern district of Darrang, by paying a large indemnity and by agreeing to pay an annual tribute. The island of Sandwip in the Bay of Bengal and Chitta-gong were conquered in 1666. The risings of the Afghans in the north-west frontier which had begun in 1667, were all suppressed by 1675. Embassies came to him from foreign Muslim powers such as the Sharif of Mecca and the kings of Persia, Balkh, Bokhara, Kashgar, Khiva and even from distant Abys-sinia. The Rajput War which had begun in 1679 and in which the Rana of Mewar had joined with the ruler of Marwar to fight against the Mughuls was brought to an end by a peace between Delhi and Mewar in 1681. Bijapur was conquered and annexed in 1686 and Golkunda in 1689. Shivaji's son and successor, Shambhuji was captured and executed in 1689, his capital Raigarh was occupied and his son and heir, the young Shahu, was also made a captive and retained in the Mughul court. In 1691 the victorious Aurangzeb levied tribute for the first time on the Hindu kings of Tanjore and Trichinopoly and thus extended the Mughul Empire to its furthest boundaries in the South.

Notwithstanding all these successes Emperor Aurangzeb proved to be the last of the Great Mughuls and the symptoms of the disintegration of the Mughul Empire appeared even before the Emperor breathed his last at Burhanpur in the Deccan in 1707. The Mughul Empire which had been vast enough at the accession of Aurangzeb became, as the result of his further conquests and annexations, "too vast to be governed by one man and from one centre." As Sir Jadunath observes, "Like the boa constrictor it had swallowed more than it could digest." Already the Afghan Wars of 1667-75 had been ruinous financially and extremely harmful politically for it made impossible the employment of the Afghans in the wars that soon followed with the Rajputs and prevented the Emperor from concentrating the full resources of the Mughul Empire against Shivaji (1627-80) who was building up an independent Maratha kingdom in the Deccan. The Jats in Mathura and its neighbourhood had risen in rebellion in 1669. They were followed by the Bundelas in Bundelkhand and Malwa in 1671, the Satnámis in Narnol in the Patiala State and the Mewatis in the Alwar region in 1672. All these rebellions were forcibly suppressed, but they illustrated the prevailing widespread hostility to the Mughul Empire. In the Panjab the Sikhs were being gradually forged into a united and strong people but their Guru Teg Bahadur was executed by Aurangzeb's orders for his refusal to accept Islam and this bloody act inspired the Sikhs with feelings of revenge and hostility against the Mughul Empire. In Assam the Ahoms disavowed the treaty imposed upon them in 1663 and recovered their lost territories by 1671. The execution of Shambhuji and the captivity of his son Shahu did not destroy the nationalism of the Marathas who found a new leader first in Shambhuji's brother, Raja Ram and then on the latter's death, in his widow Tara Bai, continued relentlessly the war against the Mughuls and recovered much of their lost territories even before the death of Aurangzeb. They showed that Aurangzeb had failed to crush the Marathas who were very much alive. The Deccan campaign which kept Aurangzeb engaged from 1681 to his death in 1707 was financially ruinous and was as disastrous to him as the Spanish campaign proved to Napoleon. Lastly, the Rajput War of 1679-80 which was also no doubt won in a way by Aurangzeb, clearly revealed that he had completely forfeited the support of the Hindu Rajputs, which Emperor Akbar in his wisdom had made the mainstay of his empire. Indeed Aurangzeb strayed far away from the wise policy of his great-grandfather. Unlike Akbar he deliberately subordinated the state to religion and decided to wield his imperial powers not for his own individual benefit, not for the benefit of his dynasty, not for the benefit of his subjects, but for the benefit of Islam. He was a zealous Sunni Muhammadan and tried to live and rule strictly in the spirit of the Quranic law. He had the courage of his conviction and he spared neither himself nor the interests of his dynasty in his determination to act upto his faith. He imposed upon himself all those restrictions of food, drink and dress which the Quranic laws demanded of a good Mussulman and also decided to administer the Empire to which he had succeeded, for the purpose of converting it into a realm of Islam (*dar-ul-Islam*). This determination led him to embark on a policy of intolerance and persecution of the Hindus on whom he reimposed in 1679 the *Jizya* which Akbar had abolished in 1564. He forbade the employment of Hindus to high offices, increased the taxes payable by them, forbade the construction of new Hindu temples, destroyed many old Hindu temples including the Kesava Deva's temple at Mathura and Viswanath's temple at Benares, tried to forcibly seize and then convert to Islam the minor child of Raja Jasvant Singh of Marwar and harassed the Hindus by issuing many other insulting regulations and by burying under the steps of mosques the Hindu images that were brought from their temples destroyed by his orders. Lastly, though he ruled for half a century (1658-1707) during which the strength and power of the Europeans who had already settled in various parts of India, was steadily increasing, he failed not only to appreciate the latent danger in the presence and growth of the power of these foreigners but also to appreciate the need for developing an Indian navy strong enough to prevent the coming of the Europeans from across the seas. No wonder that half a century after his death one such

European power, clever and adroit enough to exploit the disaffection of the Hindus, the disloyal ambition of the Muhammadan vassals of the Mughul Emperor as well as the internal dissensions amongst the Indians, succeeded in bringing about the downfall of the dynasty of the Great Mughuls of whom Aurangzeb was the last and the establishment in its place of the British rule in India. (Sarkar, J. N., *History of Aurangzeb*, Vols. I-V and *Anecdotes of Aurangzeb*; Edwardes & Garret, *Mughul Rule in India*; Khafi Khan, *Muntakhab-ul Lubab* in Elliot & Dawson, Vol. VII, pp. 211-533)

Austrian Succession, the War of—broke out in Europe in 1740 and was continued till 1748 when it was concluded by the treaty of Aix-la-Chapelle. In this war England and France took opposite sides and the English East India Company and the French East India Company fought against each other in the Carnatic in India. The French interests were upheld by Dupleix, the French Governor at Pondicherry. He captured the English settlement of Madras, held the city against a large relieving Indian army sent by Anwaruddin (*q.v.*), the Nawab of the Carnatic, within whose territories Madras and Pondicherry were situated and defeated another army of the Nawab at the battle of St. Thome. The war in Europe was concluded by the treaty of Aix-la-Chapelle which re-established peace on the basis of mutual restitution of territories between England and France. Madras had, therefore, to be restored to the English but the War of Austrian Succession which had resulted in the first great Anglo-French War on Indian soil (it is also called the Carnatic War) had great significance in Indian history. First, it showed the weakness of the Nawab of the Carnatic as well as of his sovereign, the Nizam of Hyderabad, who could not compel foreigners settled within their dominions to respect their sovereignty and to maintain peace. Secondly, the two defeats of the larger armies of the Nawab of the Carnatic at the hands of smaller French armies composed of French men and of Indians showed the superiority of regular armies trained and armed after the European method over the irregular levies which constituted the armies of the Indian princes. Thirdly, in this war the French and the English both had recruited Indian nationals to their armies and the French had even employed with impunity Indian nationals in their military service in fighting against Indian states. This lesson was thoroughly utilised by the English who later on conquered India with the active assistance of Indians themselves.

Avamukta—a state mentioned in the Allahabad Pillar inscription of Samudragupta (*q.v.*) whose king Nilaraja is said to have been defeated but restored to his dominions by the Gupta Emperor. Avamukta was a state in the Deccan, but its exact position is uncertain.

Avanti—an important state in ancient India. Its capital was Ujjaini in modern Malwa. It was one of the sixteen states (*sodasa janapada*) into which, according to early Buddhist texts, India was divided shortly before the rise of Buddhism in the fifth century of the pre-Christian era. Later on it absorbed the neighbouring small states and became one of the four great Indian states—the other three being Vatsa (Allahabad region), Koshala (Oudh) and Magadha (South Bihar). Its king Pradyota was a comtemporary of Bimbisara and Ajatasatru of Magadha. In the fourth century B.C. Chandragupta Maurya conquered and annexed Avanti to his dominions.

Avantivarman—a king of Kanauj of the Maukhari dynasty, was a contemporary of king Prabhakaravardhana (*q.v.*) of the Pushyabhuti family of Thaneswar. His son Grahavarman married Rajyasri, the daughter of Prabhakarvardhana.

Avantivarman of Kashmir—founded in A.D. 855 in Kashmir the Utpala dynasty after overthrowing the Karkata dynasty. He is famous for the irrigation works that were executed by his orders in Kashmir.

Avataras—are incarnations of the Supreme Being in some living form on the earth. Orthodox Hindus believe that whenever virtue (*dharma*) declines and sins (*adharma*) prosper the Supreme Being incarnates himself on some living form for the purpose of saving the virtuous, destroying the sinful and thus re-establishing virtue (*dharma*). Such living forms of the Supreme Being are called the *Avataras* and orthodox Hindus believe that there have been already nine such *Avataras* since the creation and the tenth one, Kalki, is to come. The nine past *Avataras* were the Fish, the Tortoise, the Boar, the Man-Lion (Nri-Sinha), Vamana, Parsurama, Shri Ramachandra, Valarama and the Buddha. (*Bhagavat Gita*, IV, 7 & 8).

Avitabile, General—was a Neopolitan soldier of fortune who came to India and was one of the European officers whom Ranjit Singh of the Panjab engaged for organising the Sikh army on the European model.

Ayodhya—an ancient city on the bank of the Saraju, near modern Fyzabad, was the capital of the kingdom of Koshala (Oudh). According to the *Ramayana* it was the capital of King Dasaratha, the father of Shri Ramachandra. It is considered to be one of seven sacred cities in India. In historical times it was probably the second capital of the Gupta Emperors from the time of Samudragupta to the time of Puragupta (A.D. 330-472).

Ayub Khan—was the son of Amir Sher Ali (*q.v*) of Afghanistan. During the second Anglo-Afghan War (1878-80) Ayub Khan defeated a large British army at the battle of Maiwand (July, 1880), but later on he was defeated before Qandahar by Lord Roberts. He recovered Qandahar for a time but was eventually defeated by the new Amir Abdur Rahman (*q.v.*) who drove him out of Qandahar and of Afghanistan.

Ayub Khan—a General of the Pakistan army, has made himself by a *coup* the military dictator of Pakistan and has overthrown the parliamentary form of Govt. there. He has been re-elected to be the President of Pakistan for a five years' term from 1965 and plunged in a war with India which has been stopped at the time of writing by an 'uneasy cease-fire' imposed by the U.N.O.

Azam, Prince—the third son of the sixth Mughul Emperor Aurangzeb (1658-1707) embarked on the death of his father on a war of succession against his elder brother Prince Muazzam and was defeated and killed in the battle of Jajau near Agra on June 10, 1707.

Azari, Shaikh—a poet who came from Khorasan to the court of the ninth Bahmani sultan Ahmad (1422-33), was rewarded by the Sultan with a large sum of money for having composed two verses in eulogy of the Sultan's palace in his new capital at Bidar.

Azes I—an Indo-Parthian prince, ruled over the Panjab. He was originally the viceroy of Arachosia and Sistan and was then transferred to Taxila in about 58 B.C. in succession to Maues. He at first governed the province as a subordinate of the Parthian king Mithradates. He was a powerful prince and ruled for about forty years and it is probable that during the closing years of his long reign he made himself independent of Parthia. Many coins bearing his name have been found in the Panjab. Some hold that the Vikrama era which dated from 58-57 B.C. was started by him. (*E.H.I.*, Chap. x)

Azes II—the grandson of Azes I, succeeded to his grandfather's throne after his father Azilises (*q.v.*) and ruled till about A.D. 20. The name of Azes II is also known from coins in some of which his name is associated with that of *strategos* Aspavarman showing the close co-operation that had come to be established between the Parthians and the Indians. (*P.H.A.I.*, p. 123)

Azilises—was the son and successor of Azes I. His coins have been considered to be the finest ever struck by the Indo-Parthian princes and were later on imitated by an Indian prince. (*P.H.A.I.*, p. 441)

Azim-ud-daulah—was made in 1801 the titular Nawab of the Carnatic by Lord Wellesley, Governor-General (1798-1805) and was granted a pension. The entire civil and military administration of the Carnatic was taken over by the Company and the Carnatic was annexed to the British Indian Empire.

Azim-ullah Khan—a retainer of Nana Shaheb (*q.v.*), the son of Peshwa Baji Rao II (1796-1818), played a mysterious part in bringing about the Sepoy Mutiny in 1857. He was actively engaged in promoting anti-British feelings amongst the Indians and is believed to have paid a visit to Europe during the Crimean War in order to effect an alliance between his master and the Russians. His efforts failed, but he brought back stories about the vulnerability of the British power which had so long been considered invincible by the Indians and the mutineers were to a certain extent encouraged by his reports in their hopes of success against the British.

Azim-us-shan, Prince—the second son of the seventh Mughul Emperor Bahadur Shah I (1707-12), was killed in the course of the war of succession that followed his father's death in 1712. A year later his son Farruksiyar (1713-19) became the Emperor.

Aziz-ud-din—was the original name of the sixteenth Mughul Emperor Alamgir II (*q.v.*) (1754-59).

B

Babur—the first Mughul Emperor (1526-30) of Delhi, descended on his father's side from Timur better known as Tamerlane (*q.v.*) and on his mother's side from Chingiz Khan (*q.v.*) was born in 1483. At the age of eleven he inherited from his father the small principality of Farghana, now in Chinese Turkestan. His early life was full of hardships but he was ambitious and daring. Though he was soon dispossessed of Farghana he succeeded in occupying Kabul in 1504 when he was just twenty-one years of age. Babur next made a futile attempt to conquer Samarqand which had been the capital of his ancestor Timur. Henceforward he decided to try his luck in the south-east in

India. Political condition in India favoured his designs. The Delhi sultanate had lost much of its old territories and was on the point of disintegration. The Deccan had long been independent of Delhi. In northern India also Kashmir, Malwa, Gujarat and Bengal were practically independent under different Afghan rulers. Rajput chiefs were also practically independent in Rajputana where Rana Sangram Singh of Mewar was thinking of re-establishing Hindu rule in northern India. The Panjab was held by a disaffected noble named Daulat Khan and the very title of the reigning sultan Ibrahim Lodi (1517-26) to the Delhi throne was disputed by his uncle Alam Khan. Thus on the eve of Babur's invasion there was no Indian Empire. There was a congeries of warring states whose internal dissensions helped Babur materially. Daulat Khan and Alam Khan even went to the extent of inviting Babur to invade India in the hope that Babur, like Timur, would deal a crushing blow at the Delhi sultanate and thus leave the throne of Delhi to be occupied by either of them. Accordingly Babur entered into the Panjab in 1524, occupied Lahore and showed every intention of staying on in India. This upset the plans of Daulat Khan and Alam Khan who therefore deserted Babur. Thus deprived of the support of his Indian confederates Babur was obliged to go back to Kabul. But he came back next year with a larger army, subdued Daulat Khan and defeated and killed Sultan Ibrahim Lodi in the first battle of Panipat on April 21, 1526. This victory made Babur the ruler of Delhi and Agra. His authority was not readily accepted by either the Afghan chiefs ruling in different parts of India or by Rana Sangram Singh of Mewar. But the Rajputs and the Afghans could not combine and Babur was therefore able to meet them separately. He defeated the Rana in the battle of Khanua on March 16, 1527. He then crossed the Jumna and stormed the fortress of Chanderi. The Rajput opposition was thus effectively overcome. Two years later Babur defeated the recalcitrant Afghan chiefs of Bihar and Bengal in the battle of the Gogra (May 6, 1529) near the junction of that river with the Ganges above Patna. These three victories made Babur the master of a kingdom extending from Afghanisthan to the Bengal border and from the foot of the Himalayas to Gwalior. Babur thus founded the Mughul Empire in India. But he died too soon on December 26, 1530 and had no time to weld his empire into a strong unit by devising for it an adequate administrative machinery as was done later on by his grandson, Akbar (1556-1605). Babur was not simply a soldier of fortune who after many vicissitudes of life raised himself to the imperial throne of Delhi, but he was also a man of fine literary taste which is proved by his *Memoirs* which he wrote in Turki and which was later on translated into Persian under the direction of Akbar. (*Memoirs* translated into English by Leyden and Erskine; Lane-Poole, *Babur*)

Bactria—was the name of the region between the Hindu Kush and the Oxus. It was a part of the Seleukidian empire of Syria but about 202 B.C. it became an independent Hellenistic kingdom under Euthydemos. His successor, Demetrios, conquered Afghanistan and a part of the Panjab and became known as a 'King of the Indians'. Close contact was thus established between the Hellenistic people of Bactria and the north-western part of India which soon came to be parcelled into many states ruled by various Indo-Bactrian princes of whom Menander (*q.v.*) was one of the best known. This contact of Bactria with India led to the expansion of Hellenistic influence on Indian art and sculpture leading to the development of the Gandhara school of sculpture.

Badal—a Rajput hero of Mewar, along with Gora, at the head of a small band of Rajputs resisted the much larger forces of Sultan Alauddin Khalji when he invaded Chitor. Badal was ultimately overwhelmed and killed in battle, and Chitor was stormed by the Sultan. The ladies within, including the famous Padmini whose beauty is said to have lured Alauddin on to this expedition, perished in flames rather than fall into the hands of the Muhammadan invaders.

Badan Chandra—*Bar Phukan* (*i.e.* governor) at Gauhati (1810-20), was very oppressive in his treatment to the people and was also guilty of gross exactions. At last things came to such a pass that the *Burha Gohain* (Prime Minister) Purnananda whose son had married Badan Chandra's daughter, decided to remove him. Men were sent to Gauhati to arrest him, but having been previously informed by his daughter Badan Chandra left Gauhati just before the soldiers who were sent to arrest him, arrived there. Badan Chandra was determined on revenge. He escaped to Bengal, went to Calcutta and there he first tried to persuade the Governor-General, Lord Minto, to send an expedition to Assam. But Lord Minto refused to interfere. Badan Chandra then proceeded to the court of the king of Burma and succeeded in persuading the king of Burma to send an expedition to Assam. Accordingly a Brumese army invaded Assam in 1816, advanced up to Jorhat and restored

Badan Chandra to the post of the governor of Gauhati. Purnananda had died in the meantime and Badan Chandra succeeded
in persuading the Burmese army to evacuate Assam by paying
them a heavy indemnity. At this success Badan Chandra became
very insolent and alienated the king's mother and many other
Ahom nobles. At their instigation Badan Chandra was soon
afterwards assassinated. He had laid down a course of policy
and action which culminated in the conquest and occupation
of Assam by the Burmese in 1819.

Badami—is the modern name of the old city of Vatapi in the Bijapur
district. It was the capital of the Chalukyas (*q.v.*). In its
neighbourhood there is a number of cave-temples as well as
stone temples containing fine images and excellent sculptures.

Badan Singh—son of Bhau Singh, established by his military
skill, cunning and marriage policy a Jat State comprising the
districts of Agra and Mathura. The date of his birth is not known.
He died in 1756.

Badarayana—an ancient Brahmanical author of uncertain date. His
work *Brahma Sutra* was one of the fundamental books on which
Sankaracharya (*q.v.*) based his Vedantic philosophy of *Advaitavada*
(monism).

Badaoni—Abdul Kadir Al Badaoni—was a reputed contemporary
historian of Akbar's court. He was an orthodox sunni. His work,
the *Muntakhabu-t-Tawarik* contains an account of Akbar's
reign from the point of view of an orthodox sunni Muhammadan who could not appreciate the liberalism of Akbar.
It is available in English translation and sometimes serves as a
corrective to Abul Fazl's extremely eulogistic *Akbarnama*.

Baden-Powell, Lord—founded the worldwide organisation.
known as the Boy Scouts Movement. Indians were at first refused admission into this organisation. The colour-bar was
removed by the efforts of Lord Baden-Powell after he had paid
a visit to India.

Badr-i-Chach—was a contemporary historian of the time of
Muhammad Tughluq (1325-51).

Badrinath—on the snowy heights of the Himalayas in the Kumaon
district of the Uttar Pradesh, is an important place of pilgrimage
of the Hindus. It contains a Shiva temple and a monastery, the
foundation of which is attributed to the great Sankaracharya
(*q.v.*). It attracts large bodies of pilgrims every year.

Badshah-namah—is a dependable historical work written in
the reign of Aurangzeb by Abdul Hamid.

Bagh—in Central India near Gwalior, has some fresco paintings of high merit in some of its cave-temples. The paintings are of the Ajanta type and style, but are not so well known on account of inaccessibility of the place.

Baghat—a cis-Sutlej hill state, was annexed by Lord Dalhousie in 1850 by the application of the principles of the Doctrine of Lapse(*q.v.*). This decision was reversed by Dalhousie's successor, Lord Canning, who restored the State to its original ruler.

Bahadurpur, the battle of—was fought in February 1658 between Sulaiman, the eldest son of Prince Dara Shukoh and Prince Shuja, the second son of Emperor Shah Jahan who had set himself up as an independent ruler of Bengal as soon as Shah Jahan fell ill. Prince Shuja was defeated and obliged to retire to Bengal.

Bahadur Shah I—the seventh Mughul Emperor (1707-12) of Delhi, was the second son of Emperor Aurangzeb whom he succeeded on his death in 1707 after a war of succession in the course of which his surviving brothers, Azam and Kam Baksh were defeated and killed. As a prince his name was Muazzam and he was also known as Shah Alam. After his accession he assumed the title of Bahadur Shah and he was also often called by his older title of Shah Alam or Alam Shah. He had not been very generously treated by his father during his life-time and indeed for some years he had been kept imprisoned by his father. This prolonged repression destroyed his spirit and he was hardly the man to save and strengthen the Mughul empire at the critical time when he ascended the throne. Yet during his short reign of five years he made an effort to restore the strength of the Mughul empire which was threatened at that time by three main enemies, viz. the Rajputs, the Marathas and the Sikhs. He conciliated the Rajputs by wise concessions. He neutralised the Maratha hostility by releasing Shambhuji's son, Shahu, whom Aurangzeb had kept a captive in his court since 1689 and by sending him back to Maharashtra where his return created dissensions amongst the Marathas and thus prevented them for some time from troubling the Mughul Government at Delhi. But against the Sikhs he assumed a strict attitude, inflicted a defeat on them and their leader Banda and effectively subdued them for the time. But Bahadur Shah I died soon afterwards in 1712.

Bahadur Shah II—was the nineteenth and the last Mughul Emperor (1837-58) of Delhi. Like his father and predecessor Akbar II, Bahadur Shah continued to be a pensioner of the East India Company and could not improve upon his position in any way.

On the outbreak of the Sepoy Mutiny in 1857 Bahadur Shah, who was then 82 years of age and was too old either to think or act for himself, was set up as the Emperor of liberated India by the mutinous sepoys and thus incurred the intense displeasure and hostility of the British. After the recapture of Delhi by the British in September, 1857, Emperor Bahadur Shah II was arrested by the British, put on a trial and condemned to exile in Rangoon where he died in 1862 at the age of 87 years. On the day of his arrest his two sons and a grandson had also been arrested and shot dead. Thus perished the last of the descendants of Emperor Akbar.

Bahadur Shah—the sultan of Gujarat (1526-37), defeated the sultan of Malwa and annexed his territories in 1531. He also overran Mewar and stormed Chitor in 1534. But next year he was utterly defeated by the Mughul Emperor Humayun. Bahadur Shah saved himself by a flight to Goa. Shortly afterwards Humayun left Gujarat and Bahadur Shah easily recovered his kingdom. Under the pressure of Mughul invasion Bahadur Shah had purchased peace with the Portuguese by surrendering to them Bassein. After the recovery of his kingdom differences arose between him and the Portuguese as to the extent of the concessions made by Bahadur Shah. Negotiations were opened for the settlement of the differences and Bahadur Shah was persuaded by the Portuguese to visit the Portuguese Governor Nuno da Cunah on board his ship in February, 1537, but he was treacherously drowned by the Portuguese who also murdered all his companions.

Bahadur Shah—the ruler of Khandesh towards the close of the 16th century, held the fort of Asirgarh when Emperor Akbar besieged it in 1600. Bahadur Shah defended the fort very ably for six months, but was later on inveigled by Akbar to the Mughul camp to negotiate for a treaty of peace on a promise of personal safety. But Akbar broke his word of honour and Bahadur Shah was detained and forced to write a letter asking the garrison to surrender the fort which was eventually captured by Akbar.

Bahar Khan Lohani—the independent Afghan ruler of Bihar in the first quarter of 16th century, appointed Farid Khan, later on famous as Sher Shah, in his service in 1522. It was Bahar Khan who conferred upon Farid the tittle of Sher Khan for the latter's bravery in killing a tiger single-handed. Bahar Khan also appointed Sher Khan as his Deputy and also as a tutor of his minor son Jalal Khan and thus started Sher Khan on his future career of power and greatness.

Baha-ud-din Gurshasp—was the son of a sister of Sultan Ghiyas-ud-din Tughluq (1320-25). At the accession of Sultan Muhammad Tughluq in 1325 Baha-ud-din who held the fief of Sagar in the Deccan, refused to accept Muhammad Tughluq as his sovereign and rose in revolt against him in 1326-27. He was defeated, captured and sent as a prisoner to Delhi where he was flayed alive and his dead body was paraded round the city as a warning to all possible traitors and rebels.

Bahaism—was the religion founded by Baha-ullah (1817-92) a Persian by birth, but an exile by the Shah's orders. The funda-mental principles of Bahaism are: God is unknowable except through his manifestation, the Prophet: divine revelations are continuous and progressive; prophets are born every 1000 years; the divine command for this age is to unify humanity with one faith and one order. The headship of this religious sect was at first vested in its founder, Baha-ullah and after his death it became hereditary in his family. Bahaism is looked upon as a heretical creed by the orthodox Muslims, but it flourishes in 40 countries including India and Pakistan. It has an organ called *The Bahai World.*

Bahlol (also spelt Bahlul or Buhlul) Lodi—was the sultan of Delhi from 1451-89. He belonged to the Lodi tribe of the Afghans. He was the governor of Lahore and Sirhind in 1451 when Sultan Alam Shah of the Sayyid dynasty abdicated the throne. Bahlol Lodi with the support of his minister Hamid Khan immediately occupied the throne of Delhi. He was the first Afghan sultan of Delhi and the founder of the Lodi dynasty (*q.v.*). At the time of his accession the Delhi sultanate was a mere shadow of the old empire. Bahlol Lodi was a brave, warlike and ambitious person. He reduced to submission Jaunpur, Mewat, Sambhal, Rewari and the chiefs of the Doab. He also captured Gwalior. He thus recovered much of the old territories of the Delhi sultanate and restored its old strength to a great extent. He was kind to the poor and a patron of scholars.

Bahmani kingdom and dynasty—was founded in the Deccan in 1347 by Hasan, entitled Zafar Khan, an officer of Sultan Muhammad Tughluq (1325-51) of Delhi. He raised himself to the throne by taking advantage of the disaffection created amongst the Muhammadan nobles of the Deccan by the tyrannic-al and whimsical administration of Muhammad Tughluq. Hassan claimed descent from the Persian hero Bahman, and, accordingly the dynasty founded by him came to be known as the Bahmani Dynasty. After his accession Hassan took the title of Alauddin Bahman Shah (*q.v.*) and established his capital at Kulbarga or Gulbarga. He ruled for eleven years (1347-58). At his death the Bahmani kingdom extended from the Penganga river in the north to the Krishna river in the south and from Goa in the west to Bhongir in the east.

The Bahmani dynasty comprised fourteen kings including the founder. Hassan's thirteen successors were (i) Muhammad I (1358-73); (ii) Mujahid (1373-77); (iii) Daud (1378); (iv) Muhammad II (1378-97); (v) Ghiyasuddin (1397); (vi) Samsuddin (1397); (vii) Firoz (1397-1422); (viii) Ahmad II (1422-35); (ix) Alauddin (1435-57); (x) Humayun (1457-61); (xi) Nizam (1461-63); (xii) Muhammad III (1463-82) and (xiii) Mahmud (1482-1518).

The most outstanding feature of the history of the Bahmani kingdom was its chronic hostility with the neighbouring Hindu kingdom of Vijayanagar (*q.v.*) which lay in the lower Deccan and extended south-wards from the Tungabhadra. The Raichur Doab between the Tungabhadra on the south and the Krishna on the north was coveted equally by the Bahmani and the Vijayanagar kingdoms, as it contained the two strong forts of Mudgal and Raichur. Further, religion separated the Muslim Bahmani kingdom from the Hindu Vijayanagar kingdom. As a result wars began between the two kingdoms soon after their foundations and continued with varied fortunes as long as the Bahmani kingdom lasted. But all the efforts of the Bahmani sultans to destroy their Hindu neighbour failed. In the wars, however, the Bahmani sultans had generally the greater success and they were more often in possession of the Raichur Doab than the Vijayanagar kings.

The Bahmani sultans were a violent lot. Four of them were murdered, two others were deposed and blinded and only five out of the fourteen sultans died natural deaths. The ninth sultan, Ahmad, transferred the capital from Kulbarga to Bidar which was soon beautified with many fine buildings.

The Muhammadans were a small minority in the Bahmani kingdom and the sultans therefore always encouraged Muhammadans from outside to come and settle within the kingdom. This resulted in a large influx of foreign Muhammadans who were mostly shias and many of whom came to occupy important positions in the state. This increasing importance of the foreign Muhammadans in the Bahmani kingdom soon inspired the hostile jealousy of the Deccanee Muhammadans and of the Abyssinians who were mostly sunnis. From the reign of the tenth sultan Alauddin II (1435-57) this quarrel between the Deccanee and the foreign Muhammadans began to grow very acute. It culminated in 1481 during the reign of the thirteenth sultan Muhammad III in the execution of Muhammad Gawan (*q.v.*) who had been the chief minister of the kingdom since the time of the eleventh sultan Humayun and had rendered great services to the state. The death of Muhammad Gawan marked the beginning of the end of the Bahmani kingdom, and it was during the reign of the next and last sultan, Mahmud that the Bahmani kingdom broke up into five independent states, viz. Berar, Bidar, Ahmadnagar, Golkunda and Bijapur where the provincial governors set themselves up as independent sovereigns. These five states maintained their independent existences until these were all annexed to the Mughul Empire in the 17th century.

The story of the Bahmani kingdom is not attractive. It hardly conferred any definite benefit on India. Some of the Bahmani sultans no doubt gave some encouragement to Muslim learning and constructed some irrigation works in the eastern part of the kingdom. But their wars, massacres and burnings did immeasurable harm to the people. The condition of the common people was very miserable, as was observed by the Russian merchant, Athanasius Nikitin, who travelled through the Bahmani kingdom for four years (1470-74). He observes: "The land was overstocked with people; but those in the country are very miserable, while the nobles were extremely opulent and delighted in luxury. They were wont to be carried on their silver beds preceded and followed by large retinues of soldiers, on horse and foot, torch-bearers and musicians." The Bahmani sultans built strong forts at Gawailgarh and Narnala and some mosques in Kulbarga and Bidar. The history of the Bahmani sultans illustrates the futility of any attempt to convert the Hindu population *en masse* into Islam even by force. (Meadows Taylor, *Manual of Indian History;* King, *History of the Bahmani Kingdom &* Nikitin, *India in the Fifteenth Century*)

Bahram Aiba—surnamed Kishlu Khan, was in charge of the fiefs of Uch, Sind and Multan in the reign of Sultan Muhammad Tughluq (1325-51). In 1329 Bahram Aiba revolted against the Sultan who was then in Devagiri from where the Sultan marched to Multan, defeated and captured Bahram whom he beheaded. His head was hung up in the gate of the city of Multan as a warning to all intending rebels.

Bahram Khan—a foster-brother of Sultan Muhammad Tughluq, was appointed by the Sultan as a co-governor with Ghiyasuddin

Bahadur Shah in East Bengal. When Ghiyasuddin revolted against the Sultan, Bahram Khan defeated and killed him. Bahram then became the sole governor of East Bengal. He died in 1336 and soon afterwards East Bengal seceded from the Delhi sultanate.

Baille, Colonel—was an officer in the service of the East India Company. During the course of the Second Anglo-Mysore War Col. Baille with 3720 soldiers was completely overwhelmed near Conjeeveram by Tipu, son of Haidar Ali, king of Mysore. Most of his soldiers were killed and Baille himself was made a captive. Later on he was released, but he was not given any other important military post after this disaster.

Bairam Khan—a companion of Emperor Humayun, was appointed by him as the guardian of his minor son, Akbar. On the death of Humayun in 1556 Bairam Khan took the initiative and the necessary measures for proclaiming Akbar as the successor of Humayun on the throne of Delhi. But Delhi was soon lost and it was the energy and generalship of Bairam Khan which enabled Akbar to win the second battle of Panipat in 1556 and to recover the throne of Delhi. For the next four years Bairam Khan acted as the Regent of the minor king, and during these four years the Mughul armies conquered under his direction Gwalior, Ajmer and Jaunpur. Bairam also began arrangements for the conquest of Malwa. But Bairam had been exercising his powers rather sternly and thus irritated not only many Mughuls of high position but even also Akbar. The young Emperor who was then only 18 years of age, decided to take up the administration in his own hands. He therefore dismissed Bairam in 1560 from his post of Regent and Protector. Bairam at first peacefully submitted and started for Mecca but, on second thoughts, he rose in rebellion. Bairam was defeated and was leniently treated by Akbar who allowed him again to proceed to Mecca. But on his way to Mecca he was murdered by a private enemy at Patan in Gujarat in 1561. His minor son Abdur Rahman later on rose high in the service of Akbar.

Baird, Sir David—held a high military command in India under the East India Company during the administration of Lord Wellesley (1798-1805). In 1801 Baird led an expedition to the Red Sea in order to help in driving out the French from Egypt. The French at Alexandria had capitulated before Baird arrived at Cairo; but Baird had successfully commanded the expedition and was knighted.

Baiza Bai, Maharani—was the consort of Daulat Rao Sindhia (*q.v.*). On the death of Daulat Rao in 1827 she became the Regent of his minor successor, Jankoji Rao. She was very ambitious and wanted to completely control the whole administration. This led to much intrigue and confusion and culminated in her expulsion from the state in 1833.

Baji Rao I—the second Peshwa (1720-40), was appointed to the office in succession to his father Balaji Viswanath (*q.v.*) by Raja Shahu (*q.v.*). The Raja generally kept himself in the background and the administration of the Maratha dominion was actually carried on by the Peshwa Baji Rao I. A great statesman and an able general, he appreciated that the Mughul empire was disintegrating and he thought of utilising this circumstance to enhance the power of the Marathas with the sympathy and support of the Hindu chiefs outside the Maratha country. In other words Baji Rao I thought of establishing a Hindu empire (*Hindu-pad-Padshahi*) in place of the Muslim Mughul empire. He therefore decided to carry the victorious arms of the Marathas into northern India so that they might "strike at the trunk of the withering tree". He invaded Malwa in 1723 and conquered Gujarat with the help of the local Hindus in 1724. But his policy of expansion in northern India was opposed by a section of the Marathas who found a leader in Trimbak Rao Dhabade, the *Senapati* or Commander-in-Chief of the Maratha kingdom. Baji Rao defeated and killed Dhabaḍe in the battle of Dhaboi. He also made an agreement with the Nizam in 1731 by which the Peshwa was to be free to extend his power in north and the Nizam in south India. Baji Rao I was now without any rival at home and the control that Raja Shahu exercised over him was only nominal. In the circumstances Baji Rao I easily made the Peshwaship hereditary in his family and resumed his plans for expansion in northern India. He allied himself with the Rajput ruler of Amber as well as with the Bundelas, and, in 1737 he marched at the head of a victorious Maratha army to the vicinity of Delhi. Emperor Muhammad Shah (1719-48) in alarm called in the Nizam of Hyderabad who, in violation of the treaty made in 1731, sent an army to north India to resist the further advance of Baji Rao I. The Peshwa defeated the Nizam's army in a battle near Bhopal and forced him to make peace by a treaty which left to the Marathas not only Malwa but also the territory lying between the Narmada and Chambal. This treaty was confirmed by the Emperor and the Maratha supremacy was thus established over a large part of Hindusthan. In 1739

Baji Rao I captured Salsette and Bassein from the Portuguese. But Baji Rao I had to confront constant opposition from the Marathas many of whom, especially those belonging to the Kshatriya caste, were jealous of the power of the Brahman Peshwa. In order therefore to counter-balance the influence of this hereditary nobility Baji Rao I created a new nobility from amongst his own supporters and invested them with the ad-ministration of large parts of the newly conquered Maratha dominions. Thus was founded the Maratha confederacy con-sisting of the Sindhia of Gwalior, the Gwaikar of Baroda, the Holkar of Indore and the Bhonsla of Nagpur, all of whom held large territories. They also upheld the power of Baji Rao I and contributed much to the expansion of the Maratha power. But they also formed the nucleus of a feudal body which was ultimately sure to bring division and disintegration amongst the Marathas. If Baji Rao I had lived for some years more he might have taken remedial measures. But he died in 1740 at the age of 42. His death was, as events proved, a sad blow to the cause of Hindu independence. (Duff, Grant, *History of the Marathas;* Sinha, H. N., *Rise of the Peshwas*)

Baji Rao II—was the eighth and last Peshwa (1796-1818). Son of Raghoba who had tried to secure the Peshwaship with the assistance of the English purchased by surrendering Maratha territories, Baji Rao II proved a most selfish and worthless ruler. He was ambitious and jealous of the power of Nana Faḍnavis (*q.v.*) who was the Peshwa's chief Minister at the time of his accession. Nana died in 1800 and Peshwa Baji Rao now became anxious to be his own master. But he was devoid of military qualities, was personally a coward who believed that he could get his object by mere intrigues which actually brought him and the Marathas to great grief. Imme-diately after the death of Nana rivalry began between Daulat Rao Sindhia (*q.v.*) and Jaswant Rao Holkar (*q.v.*) for the office and the power vacated by Nana's death. Baji Rao II made matters worse by incessant intrigues. He wanted to avoid the control of both alike, but Sindhia and Holkar began a battle before the very gates of Poona in order to settle which of them should control the Peshwa. Baji Rao II sided with Sindhia but their combined armies were defeated by Holkar. In sheer fright Peshwa Baji Rao II immediately fled to the English at Bassein (1801) and there, on board a British ship, he signed the treaty of Bassein (December 31, 1802) by which he entered into a subsidiary alliance with the East India Company.

By this treaty the Company's Government agreed to re-establish Baji Rao II at his capital in Poona and to maintain an adequate force in the Peshwa's territory in order to protect him against all enemies including his own subjects. The Peshwa, in return, agreed to surrender to the Company Maratha territories yielding revenue enough to maintain the British army, to refrain from appointing in his service any European hostile to the English and lastly to subject his relations with the other states to the control of the Company's Government. Thus Peshwa Baji Rao II sacrificed his independence as the price of protection. The treaty of Bassein was naturally resented by the other Maratha chiefs who found that the cowardly Peshwa had sold away the liberty of all of them. Accordingly they prepared to fight for undoing this cursed treaty. The result was the Second Anglo-Maratha War (*q.v.*) (1803-6) which ended in British triumph and in upholding British suzerainty over the Marathas. Peshwa Baji Rao II soon showed that he was not only a coward but a traitor too. He could not long remain faithful to the British alliance. He resented the restraints that it imposed upon him. He soon began to exploit the discontent of the other Maratha chiefs and to organise a second combined Maratha rising against the English. In November, 1870 Baji Rao II at the head of an army sacked and burnt the British Residency at Poona and attacked the British army stationed at Kirki. But he was defeated. He fought two more battles at Koregaon in January 1818 and a month later at Ashti but was defeated in both the battles. He tried to escape but was obliged to surrender to the English on June 3, 1818. The English now abolished the Peshwaship, deposed Baji Rao II and sent him as a British pensioner to live at Bithur near Cawnpore where he died in 1853. He was mainly responsible for the loss of independence by the Marathas.

Bajpai, Shri Ram—was a member of the Servants of India Society founded by G. K. Gokhale (*q.v.*) in 1905. Shri Ram founded in 1914 the Seva Samiti Boy Scouts Association on the line of the Boy Scouts Association organised by Lord Baden-Powell in England. The Seva Samity aimed at the complete indianisation of the Boy Scouts movement in India and succeeded in his task.

Bakht Khan—a leader of the mutinous sepoys at Delhi in 1857, played a prominent part in Delhi during the Mutiny.

Bakhtiyar Khalji—was the father of Ikhtiyar-ud-din Muhammad who drove away Lakshmana Sen from Nadia and thus laid the foundation of Muslim rule in Bengal.

Baladitya I—*see* Narasimha Gupta.

Baladitya II—was the surname of the Gupta king Bhanu Gupta (*q.v.*).

Balaji Baji Rao—the third Peshwa (1740-61), succeeded his father Baji Rao 1 to the Peshwaship in 1740. The situation at the time of his accession was very favourable for the establishment of a Hindu empire in India in place of the Mughul empire. India had been invaded and Delhi had been cruelly sacked by Nadir Shah (*q.v.*) in 1739 and never before did the Mughul empire stand more discredited. It was further weakened in the succeeding years by the repeated invasions of Ahmad Shah Abdali who actually conquered and occupied the Panjab, sacked Delhi and left there as his agent Najib-ud-daulah who practically became the dictator over the Mughul Emperor. It thus became apparent that if only the Hindus of India could unite they could deal a death blow to the Mughul empire. Peshwa Balaji Baji Rao however could not rise to the occasion. He was so much carried away by the idea of Maratha predominance that he deliberately gave up his father's plan of establishing a Hindu empire in place of the Mughul empire and thought of establishing a Maratha empire instead. The Maratha imperialism thus ceased to be Hindu nationalism and Balaji Baji Rao never thought of organising all the Hindu resources in India against the Muslims in India or outside it. As the Marathas were too few for so gigantic a task Peshwa Balaji Baji Rao adopted the policy of strengthening his army by recruiting to it non-Maratha mercenaries. Thus his army ceased to be national in its composition and was inspired by no higher motive than plunder and loot. Balaji Baji Rao also largely modified the old Maratha method of fighting with light-armed mobile infantry and depended more than ever on heavily armed cavalry and heavy artillery. The Peshwa himself was further guilty of encouraging his subordinates to make cruel plundering raids on the neighbouring territories of the Rajput princes and thus entirely forfeited their support which had been of much help to his father, Baji Rao 1. Balaji Baji Rao made the further mistake of fighting at the same time on two fronts—in the south against the Nizam and in the north against Ahmad Shah Abdali. At first he had some successes. He defeated the Nizam at the battle of Udgir in 1760 and forced him to make peace by ceding the whole province of Bijapur and large parts of Aurangabad and Bidar. The Marathas proceeded further south, defeated the Hindu king of Mysore and invaded Bednore. But their progress in this direction was stopped by Haidar Ali, the Muslim general of Mysore who eventually displaced the Hindu Raja there. In the north Balaji Baji Rao had at first much success. His armies plundered the Rajput states at pleasure, overran the Doab which they occupied, entered into an alliance with the Mughul Emperor, were admitted into Delhi, drove away Abdali's agent, Nazib-ud-daulah, advanced into the Panjab and expelled from the province Abdali's son, Timur. The Maratha power appeared to have been extended up to Attock. But the triumph was short-lived. Abdali again invaded India in 1759, defeated the Marathas at the battle of Barari Ghat in January, 1760, recovered the Panjab and proceeded towards Delhi. In the meantime the plundering raids of the Marathas had alienated not only the Muhammadan Ruhellas and the Nawab of Oudh who actually co-operated with Abdali but also the Rajputs, the Jats and the Sikhs who preferred to remain neutral. In the circumstances Abdali's march towards Delhi became a positive danger as much to Emperor Shah Alam II as to the Marathas who, therefore, made an alliance. The Peshwa Balaji Baji Rao accordingly sent a large army—indeed the largest ever sent by the Peshwa— to north India under the command of Sadasiva Rao Bhao. The Marathas captured Delhi which however proved to be a Dead Sea apple as it had no resources of food and supplies adequate for the large Maratha army. The Marathas therefore soon moved from Delhi to Panipat where they met Abdali in the grim third battle of Panipat on January 14, 1761. The Marathas were utterly routed. The Peshwa's young son Viswas Rao, who was in nominal command, the Bhao, who was in actual command and many other leading Maratha generals fell fighting. Thousands of their cavalry and infantry were also killed. In fact the third battle of Panipat was a nation-wide disaster and Peshwa Balaji Baji Rao who had already developed a wasting disease from sheer dissipation, died of a broken heart on June 23, 1761. (Duff, G., *History of the Marathas;* Sarkar, J. N., *Fall of the Mughul Empire*)

Balaji Viswanath—the first Peshwa (1713-20), was born of a poor family and began his career as the *carcon* or Revenue clerk under the Commander-in-Chief of Raja Shahu (*q.v.*). His ability both as a civil administrator and military organiser soon attracted the attention of Raja Shahu who appointed him as Peshwa in 1713. In theory the Peshwa was then only one of the eight ministers of the Raja and was certainly below the *Pratinidhi* (*q.v.*) but by dint of his abilities Balaji Viswanath soon made the Peshwa the real head of the Maratha administration. He also greatly increased the strength and prestige of the Maratha state. In 1714 he made a treaty with the Mughul Emperor by which in return of a promise to pay to the Emperor an annual tribute of ten lakhs of rupees, to maintain 15,000 cavalry for imperial service and to preserve peace and order in the Deccan he recovered for the Marathas not only all those territories that had once belonged to Shivaji (*q.v.*) but had been later on conquered by the Mughuls but also secured for the Marathas the district of Khandesh, Gondowana, Berar and some parts of Hyderabad and Karnatak. He also got for the Maratha Government the right of collecting *Chauth* (*q.v.*) and *Sardeshmukhi* (*q.v.*) from the six subas (provinces) into which the Mughul empire in the Deccan was then divided. Later on at the request of the Government of Delhi he sent a large Maratha army to the Mughul capital where it upheld the power of the Sayyid Brothers, the king-makers (*q.v.*). Thus Peshwa Balaji Vishwanath by a nominal recognition of the supremacy of the Mughul Emperor not only largely added to the territories directly under the rule of the Maratha king and secured for him an undefined and indefinite claim of collecting two taxes from all over the Deccan but also made the Marathas "co-partners in the revenues of the imperial provinces, and, as a corollary, in political power". The grateful Raja Shahu rewarded Balaji Viswanath by appointing his son Baji Rao I to the Peshwaship on Balaji Viswanath's death in 1720. (Duff, G., *History of the Marathas* & Sarkar, J. N., *Fall of the Mughul Empire*.)

Balaputradeva—a king of the Sailendra dynasty of Suvarnadvipa (*q.v.*), built a monastery at Nalanda and sent an embassy to King Devapala (*c.* A.D. 839-78) of Magadha and Bengal asking for the grant of five villages for the maintenance of his monastery at Nalanda. (*H. B.*, Vol. I.)

Balaram Seth—was the Minister of Jaswant Rao Holkar (1798-1811). On the death of Jaswant Rao, Balaram Seth supported the Holkar's favourite mistress, Tulsi Bai, and kept her in power until the outbreak of the third Anglo-Maratha War (1817-18), after which he passed into oblivion.

Balasri, Queen—was the mother of the Satavahana king Gautamiputra (*c.* A.D. 102). Queen Balasri executed an inscription at Nasik which records the conquests of her son Gautamiputra. (*P.H.A.I.* p. 490)

Balavarman—was the king of a state of Aryavarta who, according to the Allahabad inscription, was violently exterminated by

Samudragupta (c.A.D. 330-80). Neither Balavarman nor his kingdom has yet been identified.

Balban, Sultan Ghiyas-ud-din—was the ninth sultan (1266-87) of the Slave dynasty (q.v.). Balban was originally a Turki Slave of Sultan Iltutmish (q.v.). By dint of merit and ability Balban gradually rose to higher rank and positions. His daughter was married to Sultan Nasir-ud-din (1246-66) who appointed him as his Minister and Deputy. In the latter capacity Balban practically administered the Delhi sultanate in the name of his son-in-law till his death in 1266 when Balban himself ascended the throne and assumed the name of Sultan Ghiyas-ud-din. He ruled with great ability, restored peace and order within the state by suppressing the rebellious Turkish nobility, by severely punishing robbers like the Mewaties, by dispensing even-handed justice which was no respector of persons and by organising a most efficient system of espionage which kept him informed of all that happened all over his vast dominions. He raised the prestige of the Sultan by insisting on the maintenance of decorum and decency in the Court and by keeping the nobles in their places. He ruthlessly suppressed the Hindus of the Doab for having attempted a rebellion against him. He defeated and killed Tughril Khan, the governor of Bengal, for having risen in revolt and hanged by the side of the main street of Lakhnauti, the capital of Bengal, the more prominent supporters of Tughril. He then appointed his son Boghra Khan as the governor of Bengal and left him with the warning that the fate of Tughril Khan would overtake him and his adherents if any revolt was attempted.

Balban concentrated his attention on the maintenance of the safety of the sultanate which was then threatened by the presence of the Mongols on the other side of the north-western frontier from where they might at any moment invade India. Balban therefore strengthened the defences of the north-western frontier, appointed his own beloved elder son Muhammad Khan as the governor of Multan and he himself generally stayed near about the frontier. His dread was not unfounded. The Mongols attempted an invasion of India in 1279, and were beaten back by Prince Muhammad Khan. But they repeated the invasion in 1285, advanced up to Multan where Prince Muhammad was killed in an ambush. This was a terrible bereavement to the Sultan who had dearly loved his son and expected him to succeed to the sultanate. Balban was then 80 years old and his son's death hastened his own which followed two years later in 1287. He was one of the strongest sultans of Delhi. (Barni, *Tarikh-i-Firoz Shahi*)

Baldwin, Stanley—(1867-1947)—was the Prime Minister of England from 1923-29 and again from 1935-37. He appointed in 1928 the Simon Commission of seven members, all Britishers, to enquire into the working of the Govt. of India Act 1919 in India. The exclusion of all Indians from this Royal Commission to enquire into Indian affairs caused intense dissatisfaction and resentment in India.

Balhara—is the Arabic transliteration of the Sanskrit word *Vallabharaja* which was applied by the Arab writers to the Rashtrakuta kings of Manyakheta or Malkhed. The title perhaps referred particularly to the Rashtrakuta king Amoghavarsha I (*q.v.*) who reigned for about 62 years (A.D. 815-77).

bali—is a tax, an extra impost, in addition to the *bhaga* or one-sixth of the produce. It was a land tax collected by the Maurya kings (*q.v.*).

Bali—an island in the Malaya Archipelago, is one of the places in south-eastern Asia where Hindu civilization, culture and religion were taken by Hindu colonists in the early centuries of the Christian era. Hinduism is still the religion of the island of Bali. (Majumdar, R. C., *Hindu Colonies in the Far East*)

Ballal Sen—was a prominent king (*c.* A.D. 1158-79) of the Sen dynasty of Bengal. He conquered north Bengal and probably made a campaign against the Palas of Magadha. In any case he finally destroyed the Pala rule in Bengal. He was a learned scholar and a renowned author who wrote in Sanskrit. Two of his works, *Danasagara* and *Adbhutasagara,* have come down to modern times. He revived orthodox Hindu rites in Bengal and he is traditionally regarded as the founder of *kulinism* or a system of nobility, amongst the Brahmanas and Kayasthas of Bengal. (*H. B.,* Vol. I.)

Balochpur, the battle of—was fought in 1623 between the imperial troops of Jahangir and his son Shah Jahan who had risen in revolt against the Emperor. Shah Jahan was defeated and was obliged to flee to the Deccan.

Baluchistan—lies to the north-west of India beyond the Kirthur range. Geographically it lies outside India, but politically it has often been a part of the Indian empire. It was overrun by Alexander the Great, ceded by Seleucos to Chandragupta Maurya (322 B.C. - 298 B.C.) and became a part of the Maurya empire. Thereafter for a long period it remained outside any Indian empire. In 1595 it was conquered by Akbar and became

a part of the Mughul empire. Late in the 18th century it became
a dependency of Afghanistan. In 1839 a British Indian army
first marched through it in order to invade Afghanistan and
by 1843 it came under the control of the British Indian empire.
Its capital Quetta was formally annexed in 1847. In 1947 after
the Partition of India Baluchistan formed a part of West Pakistan.

Ban Pal, Rana—of the small state of Santur, gave shelter to Qutlagh
Khan of Bayana who had risen in revolt against Sultan Nasir-
uddin (1246-66) but was defeated and put to flight by the
Sultan's Deputy, Balban.

Bana—was the court-poet of King Harshavardhana (A.D. 606-47)
(*q.v.*) of the Pushyabhuti dynasty of Thaneswar and Kanauj.
His work, *Harsha-charita*, written about A.D. 620, is a contemporary account of the deeds of Harsha during the earlier
years of his reign. His other work *Kadambari* is a famous classic
of Sanskrit literature.

Banaras—*see* Baranasi.

Banda—became the leader of the Sikhs after the assassination in
1708 of the tenth guru Govind Singh (*q.v.*) (1664-1708). Banda
was not the spiritual leader of the Sikhs, but he was certainly
their political leader from 1708 till his cruel execution in 1715.
The children of Guru Govind had been most cruelly killed by
Wazir Khan, the *faujdar* of Sirhind, and taking vengeance on
Wazir Khan was considered by Banda as his bounden duty.
This he performed swiftly and completely. He organised a
large number of the Sikhs and with their help captured Sirhind
and killed the *faujdar* Wazir Khan. He brought under his control
the country between the Sutlej and the Jumna and built the
strong fort of Lohgarh (or Blood and Iron Fort) at Mukhishpur,
assumed regal state and issued coins in his name. But Emperor
Bahadur Shah I (1707-12) soon besieged and captured the
fort of Lohgarh and Banda with many of his followers were
forced to remain in hiding till after the death of Bahadur Shah I
Banda then recovered the fort of Lohgarh and again plundered
the province of Sirhind. But in 1715 the Mughuls besieged
the fort of Gurudashpur where Banda then happened to be.
The fort was captured and this time Banda, along with many
of his followers, were also captured. Banda was sent as a prisoner
to Delhi where he was put to inhuman tortures. His son was
killed before his eyes and he himself "was tormented to death
under the feet of an elephant" in 1715. Banda was a martyr
whose example inspired the Sikhs in the succeeding years.

Bandhupalita—was, according to the *Vayu Purana*, a son of Kunala (*q.v.*) and a grandson of Asoka Maurya. He is said to have succeeded his father, Kunala, but nothing is known of him from epigraphic or other sources.

Bandhuvarman—was the viceroy or feudatory of the Gupta emperor, Kumara Gupta I (A.D. 415-55), at Dasapura in western Malwa. He is mentioned in the Mandasor inscription of A.D. 437-38.

Bandula or Maha Bandula—the Burmese general led, on the outbreak of the first Anglo-Burmese War (*q.v.*) (1824-26), a Burmese army into Bengal in 1824. He was so sure of success that he brought with him golden fetters for the Governor-General, Lord Amherst. Bandula defeated a British regiment at Ramu near Chittagong frontier, but the British in the meantime had sent a naval expedition to Rangoon which was captured by the British in May, 1824. Bandula was now re-called to meet the British invaders in Burma. Back to Burma, Bandula showed there great skill as a general, but he was defeated in a battle near Rangoon in December, 1824, retreated to Donabew, where he built a stockade and held out bravely till he was suddenly killed by a rocket on April 2, 1825. After his death his army abandoned the stockade and dispersed. The first Anglo-Burmese War thus ended in the defeat of Burma.

Banerjee, Hemchandra—a Bengalee poet (1838-1903), introduced in his poetical works like *Vritrasamhar* (1875-77) a nationalistic spirit. His famous poem *Bharat-Sangeeta* (1870) called upon the people to strive for realising the independence of India. This poem certainly made an intense appeal to its readers.

Banerjee, Rangalal—a Bengalee poet (1827-87) tried to spread the spirit of nationalism and the desire for freedom amongst his countrymen through his writings. As early as 1859 he published a poetical work named *Padmini* which contained the famous piece beginning with '*Swadhinata hinataya ke vachite chayre, ke vachite chay*' ("Who wants to live in a state where there is no freedom").

Banerjee, Krishnamohan—one of the early students of Derozio (1809-31) was a prominent example of the Young Bengal produced by the Hindu College. Born of a Brahman family of Calcutta he was so much attracted by the rationalism of the West that he left his paternal religion, was converted to Christianity and late in life joined the Order and became a clergyman. He was an educationist and journalist who also took part in the political movements of the time. He was the first Secretary of the Indian Association (*q.v.*) and was also one of the earliest Fellows of the Senate of Calcutta University.

Banerjee, Sir Gurudas (1844-1918)—a Puisne Judge of the Calcutta High Court, began his career as a Professor in a college in Bengal, soon took to the practice of law, earned the D.L. degree in 1876 and was raised to the bench in 1888 from which he retired in 1904. He always maintained keen interest in the development and expansion of education and was Vice-Chancellor of Calcutta University for two terms. He was an orthodox Hindu and wrote several books on Hindu religion. Chief amongst his works were *Jnana O Karma* (Knowledge and Rituals) in Bengali and *Few Thoughts on Education*.

Banerjee, Sir Surendranath—born in 1848 of a Brahman family of Calcutta, graduated from the Calcutta University, passed the I.C.S. Examination in 1869, joined the Indian Civil Service in 1871, was posted as Assistant Magistrate and Collector at Sylhet but was before long dismissed from the service on account of what was considered an irregular manner of trying a case. He then tried to be enrolled as a Barrister but he was refused enrolment as he had been dismissed from the Indian Civil Service. This was a heavy blow and he felt that he had suffered simply because he was an Indian. This incident influenced his subsequent career. On his return to India in 1875, after his failure to be a Barrister, he became a Professor first at the Metropolitan Institution (now called Vidyasagar College) and then the Principal and Professor at Ripon College (now Surendranath College) which he founded. As a teacher he infused in his students patriotic feelings and public spirit and his extra-curricular lectures on subjects like the Life of Mazzini and Indian Unity roused great enthusiasm amongst the students. He also took to politics and played a prominent part in founding the Indian Association (*q.v.*) in 1876 and in holding the first All-India National Conference in Calcutta in 1883. It marked the first stage in India's efforts towards the establishment of a National organisation in India. After the foundation of the Indian National Congress in 1885 he took a leading part in merging the All-India National Conference with the Indian National Congress and became henceforth one of the strongest supporters of the Congress movement in India. He presided over the eleventh session of the Indian National Congress held at Poona in 1895 and also over the eighteenth session held at Ahmedabad in 1902. He toured over India addressing large assemblies on the need of national solidarity and the right of the Indians to a larger share in the administration of the country. He also became a journalist and was the editor and proprietor of *The Bengalee* which wielded a great deal of influence on public opinion up to the first decade of the twentieth century. He had led the opposition to the Vernacular Press Act of 1878 and had taken a prominent part in supporting the Ilbert Bill. He was a member of the Bengal Legislative Council from 1893 to 1901 and very strongly opposed Lord Curzon's Calcutta Corporation Act which aimed at officialising the Corporation and he refused to sit in the body when the Act was passed. He strongly opposed the Partition of Bengal effected by Lord Curzon in 1905 and led such a strong and popular agitation against it that he came to be recognised as the undisputed leader of Bengal, indeed "as the uncrowned king" of Bengal. The Partition of Bengal was modified in 1911 and it was a great triumph for Surendranath. But opposition had already begun to grow amongst a section of his countrymen who thought that the constitutional agitation which the Indian National Congress had so long been carrying on had proved a failure and who demanded a more effective policy aiming at the establishment of self-government in India. This section, known as the Extremists, was not afraid of resorting to violent methods, even if this led to a revolution. But Surendranath who had been reared up on the English literature of the 18th century, especially on Burke, would have nothing to do with Revolution or revolutionary methods and could not think of a separation between India and England. Thus Surendranath, who had once been considered a fire-brand extremist by the English administrators, now came to be looked upon as a moderate by many of his own countrymen. He succeeded after the Surat Congress (1907) in preventing the Extremists from dominating the Congress but ere long the organisation passed under the control of the Extremists with the result that when the Govt. of India Act of 1919 (*q.v.*) was passed on the basis of the Montagu-Chelmsford Report Surendranath accepted it as fulfilling to a large extent the demand that the Congress had made in its earlier days but the Congress itself refused to accept it. Thus a definite breach took place between the Indian National Congress and Surendranath who along with other older leaders of the Congress formed a new organisation called the Liberal Federation which, however, failed to secure much popular support. Surendranath, however, was elected to the new Bengal Legislative Council, was knighted in 1921 and became a Minister of the Bengal Government, piloted through the Legislature the Calcutta Municipal Bill of 1923 which undid the work of Lord Curzon's earlier Act on the organistion and established complete popular control over the Calcutta Corporation. Surendranath had no faith in the non-co-operation movement started in 1920. Notwithstanding therefore his important Legislative achievement in the realm of local Self-Government his countrymen ceased to regard him, as before, as their accredited leader. He was defeated in the election in 1923 and was henceforward practically excluded from public life till his death in 1925. The Indian Nationalist movement which Surendranath had initiated as far back as 1876, had immensely developed during the succeeding years and his countrymen refused to be satisfied with a mere increased share in the legislation and administration of the country for which Surendranath had fought for over half a century. They demanded more. Indeed they demanded independence which was much beyond Surendranath's vision. He therefore did not die in a blaze of glory, but there is no doubt that he had been one of the makers of modern Indian nationalism of which independent India is the product. (Banerjee S. N., *A Nation in Making*)

Banerjee, W. C. (1844-1906)—the first President of the Indian National Congress, was a prominent lawyer of the Calcutta Bar, who gathered a roaring practice in Calcutta High Court and was so typical an anglicised person that he anglicised his family name Banerjee into Bonnerjee and gave the English name of Shelley to his son. But at heart he was a true Indian and was the President of the *first* session of the Indian National Congress held at Bombay in 1885. He continued to be a Congress man and was made its President a second time at its Allahabad session in 1892. In 1902 he settled in England where also he continued to promote the cause of the Indian National Congress till his death there in 1906.

Bhandi—a prominent statesman at the court of Thaneswar at the accession in A.D. 606 of Harshavardhana (*q.v.*) which he supported.

Bapa—was the founder of the *Guhilot* Rajput dynasty of Chitor from whom were descended the famous Ranas of Mewar including Rana Sangram Singh and Rana Pratap Singh.

Bankideva-Alupendra—was one of the petty Hindu kings who were ruling in the extreme southern part of India on the eve of the invasion of the region by Sultan Alauddin Khalji's (*q.v.*) general, Malik Kafur. In one of Kafur's raids he was defeated and overthrown.

Banswara—a Rajput state on the border of Rajputana and Gujarat, was ruled by a branch of the Ranas of Udaipur. It submitted to the East India Company and secured British protection by entering into a subsidiary alliance in December, 1818.

Barabar Hills—stand about 15 miles north of Gaya. There are seven caves in the hills, four of which are associated with the name of Asoka Maurya. The remaining three, known as the Nagarjuni group, contain inscriptions of Asoka's grandson Dasaratha. The hills were known as Khalatika Hills in the time of Asoka. In Kharavela's time these hills came to be called Gorathagiri Hills. Later on, these were known as Pravaragiri Hills. In modern times that part of the hills in which are the caves containing Asokan inscriptions, is known as the Barabar Hills and the other part as the Nagarjuni Hills.

Bar Barua—was the official designation of the administrator who was placed in charge of the area east of Kaliabar in upper Assam by the Ahom King Pratap Singh (*q.v.*) (1603-41). The first incumbent of this post was Momai Tamuli, the uncle of the king.

Barabudur, the—the most famous Buddhist shrine in Java, was built by a king of the Sailendra dynasty (*q.v.*) of Java (*c.* A.D. 750-850). The name of the royal builder is not known nor is the date of its construction known. It is a *stupa*. The Barabudur stands to this day as the living monument of the grandeur and magnificence of the Sailendra kings and it may be considered as the eighth wonder of the world. It unmistakably bears traces of Indian influence both in its architectural scheme and in its sculpture. It stands on the top of a hill, consists of a series of nine successive terraces, each smaller than the one beneath it, and the topmost terrace is crowned with a bell-shaped *stupa*. It is of large dimensions, the lowest terrace having a length of 131 yards. There are lots of Buddha images and the galleries are covered with sculptures, illustrating scenes from Buddha's life, some of which were taken from the *Lalitavistara* (*q.v.*). It is a magnificent monument to the grandeur of the architectural conception and skill of the kings of Indian origin who ruled over Java and the neighbouring islands. (Majumdar, R. C., *Suvarnadvipa*, Vol. II. and Coomarswamy, A. K., *History of Indian and Indonesian Art*)

Bar Gohain—was the official designation of one of the two highest officials of the Ahom kings of Assam who exercised powers second only to those of the king himself. The other high officer was called the *Burha Gohain*. The post was held exclusively by a member of one of the fifteen Ahom families who formed the Ahom aristocracy. It was generally hereditary but the king had the right to select any member of the prescribed family that he liked and he could also, if he so desired, dismiss a *Bar Gohain*. The administration of a part of the Ahom kingdom was vested in the *Bar Gohain* who exercised high executive, military and judicial powers. (Gait, E. *History of Assam*)

Baranasi (also spelt Varanasi)—is modern Benares. Situated on the northern bank of the Ganges between its two tributaries, the Varuna and the Ashi, it runs along a crescentlike bend of the river. It is first mentioned in the *Atharva Veda* as the capital of the kingdom of Kashi and is generally called Kashi by the orthodox Hindus. At any rate it is under this name that it has been known from time immemorial as one of the seven sacred cities of the Hindus. Kashi as a state soon merged in the larger kingdom of Koshala, but Kashi or Baranasi as a city continues to flourish throughout the course of Indian history both as a sacred city and a very important seat of learning. In the days of Gautama Buddha Baranasi was so important a seat of religion, culture and learning that it was there that Gautama Buddha delivered his first sermon, the famous *Dharma-chakra-pravartana-Sutra*. The Jains also regard it as a very important place of learning and claim that the founder of their religion Parsva was the son of a king of Baranasi. In the beginning of the medieval period Baranasi passed under the control of the Gahaḍvala kings of Kanauj and on the conquest of Kanauj by the Muhammadans Baranasi also passed under Muhammadan control and became a part of the dominions of the rulers of Delhi. Later on, it formed a part of the dominions of the Nawab of Oudh until 1775 when the ruling local Hindu Raja, Chait Singh, (*q.v.*) entered into a treaty with the East India Company and placed himself under the overlordship of the Company. In 1781 Raja Chait Singh was deposed by Warren Hastings, the Governor-General and Baranasi became an integral part of the British Indian Empire.

As a place of pilgrimage the main attraction of Baranasi is the temple of Viswanath (Siva). It is not known who was the first founder of this deity and how the original temple looked. In 1669 Emperor Aurangzeb demolished the original temple and built on its site a mosque with the materials of the destroyed temple. The modern temple of Viswanath was built later on. Baranasi is not only the city of temples it is also a seat of industries. Its cotton fabrics were known for their excellence in the age of the *Arthasastra* (*c.* 3rd century B.C.) (*q.v.*). Baranasi is still famous for its silk brocades, metal works and cotton fabrics. Baranasi, long recognised as a seat of ancient Indian culture and religious life, still occupies a high place on the educational map of India and boasts of many modern educational institutions of which the Benares Hindu University is the most important. Baranasi has not been very prominent in the political field in recent times, but it was at Baranasi that at the twenty-first session of the Indian National Congress held under the President-ship of Gopal Krishna Gokhale (*q.v.*) the extremist party which later on demanded absolute freedom for India, first appeared.

Barani, Ziauddin—a Muslim historian, flourished in the reign of Sultan Firoz Shah Tughluq (1351-88). His *Tarikh-i-Firoz Shahi* is an authentic contemporary account of the reign of Firoz Shah Tughluq and is also very informative about the reigns of the preceding sultans of Delhi.

Barari Ghat, the battle of—was fought on January 9, 1760. The place is situated ten miles north of Delhi and here Ahmad Shah Abdali (*q.v.*) defeated the Maratha general, Dattaji Sindhia who was killed. The Maratha army fled and thus left the way to Delhi open to Abdali. This defeat of the Marathas was a prelude to their greater defeat in the third battle of Panipat which followed a year later.

Barbak Shah of Bengal—was the son of Nasiruddin Mahmud, the independent king of Bengal (1442-60). His original name was Rukun-ud-din. He ruled over Bengal for 14 years from 1460-74. His power was upheld by a large number of Abyssinian slaves some of whom he appointed to high places. He was a sagacious ruler who administered the country according to the Islamic laws.

Barbak Shah—was originally an Abyssinian slave in the service of King Jalaluddin Fath Shah (1481-86) of Bengal. He rose against King Jalaluddin and put himself at the head of the discontented Abyssinian slaves, defeated and murdered his master and himself ascended the throne of Bengal in 1486 with the title of Barbak Shah and also Sultan Shahzada. But soon after his accession he was murdered by another Abyssinian slave named Indil Khan who then ascended the throne of Bengal.

Barbak Shah—the elder son of Sultan Bahlol Lodi (*q.v.*), was appointed as his viceroy in Jaunpur in 1486. He was passed over on his father's death in 1489 and the throne of Delhi came to be occupied by his younger brother Sikandar Lodi (*q.v.*) who, three years later, expelled Barbak Shah from Jaunpur where the latter had tried to set himself up as an independent ruler.

Barbosa, Edoardo—a Jesuit traveller, came to India in 1560 and stayed for a few years. He visited Vijayanagar and travelled into northern India as well visiting Bengal in 1518. He was much impressed by the economic prosperity of Vijayanagar and the excellence of the goods manufactured in Bengal. (Maclagan, *Jesuit Missions*)

Barhut (**also spelt Bharhut**)—in Central India, is famous for its early Buddhist sculptures of the Sunga period (*c.* 185 B.C. - 73 B.C.).

Barid, Amir—the son and successor of Kasim Barid, the founder of the Barid Shahi dynasty of Bidar, assumed royal title in 1526.

Barid Shahi dynasty, of Bidar—was founded by Kasim Barid in 1492 after the Bahmani kingdom had split up into five off-shoots. The dynasty ruled over Bidar and its neighbourhood till 1619 when it was overthrown by the Sultan of Bijapur who annexed its dominions.

Barkar, Sir Robert—was in the employment of the East India Company during the administration of Warren Hastings and later on rose to be the Commander-in-Chief of the Company's army. It was in his presence that on June 17, 1772 a treaty was signed between Shuja-ud-daulah, the Nawab of Oudh and Hafiz Rahamat Khan, the leader of the Ruhellas. This treaty laid down that if the Marathas invaded Rohilkhand, the Nawab of Oudh would help the Ruhellas in expelling the Marathas and the Ruhellas would in return pay him forty lakhs of rupees. Sir Robert Barkar only witnessed the signing of the treaty and gave no assurance on behalf of the East India Company or of Warren Hastings of enforcing the treaty. Later on, the treaty was violated and the English sent an army into Rohilkhand to enforce it.

Barlow, Sir George—came out to India as a civil servant in the employment of the East India Company. He rose to be a member of the Council during the administration of Lord Wellesley (1798-1805) and was the senior member of the Council at the time of the death of Lord Cornwallis in October, 1805. He was then appointed to act as Governor-General and held the office till 1807. He followed the policy of non-intervention which had been adopted by his predecessor, Lord Cornwallis. He thus left the Rajput Princes at the mercy of the Marathas who raided and plundered Rajputana at their pleasure. The prestige of the Company's Government was thus greatly reduced. During his administration the sepoys at Vellore rose in a mutiny which was suppressed by force. His policy of non-intervention reduced expenditure and resulted in an annual surplus. This pleased the Directors at home but his weakness provoked so much resentment amongst the English both in India and England that he was not confirmed as Governor-General and was replaced by Lord Minto I.

Barnett, Commodore Curtis—was in charge of the East India Company's fleet in the Indian waters at the outbreak of the war of Austrian Succession in 1740. Barnett captured the French ships in the Indian Ocean, but on the arrival of a French fleet under La Bourdonnais off the Madras coast Barnett avoided an engagement with the French navy and sailed to Hooghly. The lack of enterprise on the part of Barnett enabled the French to besiege and capture Madras.

Baroda—an important city of Gujarat, was first raided by the Marathas in 1706. In 1732 Pilaji Gaikwar, an adherent and follower of Peshwa Baji Rao I (*q.v.*) established his authority in Gujarat and made Baroda his headquarters there. Baroda rose into prominence during the administration of Pilaji's son and successor, Damaji II (1732-68) from whose time it became the capital of the Gaikwars who beautified it with many buildings and endowed it with many institutions. It is now the seat of a University.

Barrackpore, mutiny at—broke out twice, first in 1824 and, secondly, in 1857. Barrackpore was the country seat of the Governor-General on the Hooghly, fifteen miles above Calcutta. It was also a sort of cantonment area where some regiments of the Company's troops were stationed. In 1824 an expeditionary force of the Indian army was to be sent to Burma to fight the first Anglo-Burmese War (1824-26). The sepoys of the Indian army that was to constitute the expeditionary force were required under the rules then in force to provide themselves with land-transport which was extremely difficult, if not impossible, to secure. This was a genuine grievance which should have been removed, but nothing was done to remedy it. Further, a sea-voyage was then dreaded by the Hindu sepoys as it was believed to involve the loss of the caste. Naturally the Indian sepoys, particularly the Hindus amongst them, were very much aggrieved and as nothing was done to remove their grievances the 47th Native Infantry and few other troops stationed at Barrackpore, when assembled for a parade, refused to obey orders and remained sullenly, but passively, defiant. A battery of European artillery, supported by two British regiments, opened fire on the sepoys and turned the parade ground into a shambles. It was a most high-handed and characteristic way in which the Indian section of the Indo-British army was treated by the English and left bitter memories in the minds of the Indian soldiers under the East India Company.

The second mutinous outbreak of the sepoys took place at Barrackpore on March 29, 1857 when a Brahman sepoy named Mangal Pande who belonged to the 34th Native Infantry, attacked and cut down the European Adjutant of his regiment on the parade ground in the presence and full view of the comrades of his regiment who looked on without stirring. Immediately British soldiers were called in and the mutineers were either killed or otherwise severely punished. But the rising produced great excitement amongst the sepoys at Barrackpore and eventually proved to be an early symptom of the great Sepoy Mutiny that soon racked the British Indian Empire.

Barthema, L. di—a foreign traveller, visited India between 1503 and 1508 and travelled from Gujarat to Bengal. He highly praised the excellence of goods manufactured in Bengal which he considered to be the richest country in the world for cotton, sugar, grain and flesh of every kind.

Bartoli, F.—a Jesuit priest and author, visited India during the reign of Emperor Akbar (1556-1605) and left an account of what he saw in India. His view of the *Din Ilahi* religion preached by Akbar is interesting. According to him it was a new religion compounded out of various elements, taken partly from the Quran of Muhammad, partly from the scriptures of the Brahmans and to a certain extent, as far as suited his purpose, from the Bible.

Barua—was a designation of a class of officials of Ahom kings of Assam. They were next in rank to the *Phukans* (*q.v.*). Originally there were about twenty such officials who were recruited from amongst the high Ahom families only. They were in charge of different branches of administration. Later on the appointments were given to non-Ahom subjects of the Ahom kings and Barua practically came to be a family title irrespective of race or the religion of the holders. It is adopted by all any of whose predecessors had at one time or other in the past held the office. Even certain Muhammadan families of Assam bear the title of Barua.

Barwell, Richard—was in the service of the East India Company in Bengal from 1758. In 1773 he was appointed by the Regulating Act as a Member of the Governor-General's Council. He supported Warren Hastings as against the three other Members of the Council and continued to be a supporter of Warren Hastings throughout the latter's administration as Governor-General.

Basarah—*see* Vaisali.

Barygaza—was the ancient Greek name of the modern coastal town Broach. Its Sanskrit name was *Bhrigucachha*. In old days it was a

busy port from which trade was carried on westward to Madagascar and eastward to the Indian Archipelago.

Basava—was the Brahman Minister of Bijjala Kalachurya, king of
Kalyani, who abdicated his throne in A.D. 1167. Basava was the
founder of the Lingayet or Vira Saiva Sect.

Bassein—a port on the western coast of India near Bombay, was
occupied by the Portuguese early in the 16th century. The
Marathas recovered the port from the Portuguese in about 1770.
The East India Company which was in possession of Bombay
coveted it. With the object of acquiring Bassein the Bombay
Government began to intervene in the domestic politics of the
Marathas after the death of Peshwa Narayan Rao in 1772.
This eventually led to the first Anglo-Maratha War (1775-82)
which left Bassein in the possession of the Marathas.

Bassein, the treaty of—was concluded on December 31, 1802.
between Peshwa Baji Rao II and the British by which the
Peshwa agreed to enter into a subsidiary alliance with the East
India Company. The treaty purported to be a general defensive
alliance for the purpose of the reciprocal protection of the territories of the East India Company in India and of the Peshwa.
The Company undertook to station in the Peshwa's dominions a
force of not less than six battalions and to protect the Peshwa
against all his enemies. In return the Peshwa agreed to pay to
the Company an annual subsidy of 26 lakhs of rupees, to exclude
from his service all Europeans belonging to nations hostile to
the English, to give up all his claims to Surat, to abstain from
any relation with any foreign powers except in consultation with
the British Indian Government and to accept the arbitration of
that Government in disputes with the Nizam and the Gaekwar.
Soon after the conclusion of this treaty of Bassein a British
Indian army restored Peshwa Baji Rao II to his throne at Poona.
But the Treaty of Bassein really meant that the Peshwa Baji
Rao II had sacrificed his independence as well as that of the
Marathas as the price of British protection. The Marathas,
especially Sindhia and Holkar, resented this treaty very much
and their opposition to it as well as the intention of the Peshwa
Baji Rao II himself to evade the treaty as early as possible led to
the outbreak of the Second Maratha War (1803-05) and ultimately led to the establishment of the British paramountcy over
the Marathas.

Bassein—a port in the north-west corner of the Irrawaddy river in
Burma, was captured by the British Indian army from the

Burmese in May, 1852, during the course of the Second Burmese War.

batta—is a technical term meaning 'field allowance' or extra pay granted to the officers of the East India Company in Bengal. The amount of it was doubled by Mir Jafar on his installation for the second time as the Nawab of Bengal, but in 1766 the Directors of the East India Company decided to stop it. When Clive who was then the Governor of Bengal, enforced the decision stopping the *batta*, the junior English officers of the Company's armies in India tried to prevent the enforcement of the order by combining to throw up their commissions simultaneously. This was practically an act of mutiny; but Clive handled the situation very tactfully and the officers submitted. The *batta* was restored in 1795 when the European officers unitedly insisted on its restoration; it was however finally withdrawn during the administration of Lord William Bentinck (1828-35) by the order of the Directors.

Bayazid—the son of Sulaiman Karnani, king of Bengal (1569-72), succeeded his father but soon lost Bengal to the Mughul Emperor Akbar and retired to Orissa where he died soon afterwards.

Bayazid Shah—was the titular ruler of Bengal (1412-14) who was probably overthrown by Raja Ganesh.

Bayley, Butterworth—the Senior Member of the Governor-General's Council during the administration of Lord Amherst (1823-28), acted on the resignation of Lord Amherst in March, 1828, as the Governor-General till July, 1828 when Lord William Bentinck took charge as the Governor-General. Nothing specially worthy of record took place during the short period of his administration.

Baz Bahadur—the ruler of Malwa, was defeated by Akbar's generals, Adham Khan and Pir Muhammad in A.D. 1561-62. Baz Bahadur, however, soon recovered Malwa and waged with the Mughuls a war for some time more but was eventually again defeated and driven out of Malwa. He then found shelter for some time with the Rana of Mewar. But on the fall of Chitor in February, 1568, he surrendered to Emperor Akbar. His love for Rupamati has passed into legend. He was a man of taste and constructed some fine buildings at Mandu, the capital of Malwa. He later on entered into the service of Emperor Akbar and won great reputation as a musician.

Bebadal Khan—a famous and excellent jeweller of Agra, superintended the making of the Peacock Throne by the order of Emperor Shah Jahan.

Becher, Richard—an officer employed by the East India Company in Bengal in the late sixties of the eighteenth century, sent on 24 May, 1764 a report to the Secret Committee of the Court of Directors in London which revealed the sad state of things that prevailed in Bengal on the eve of the outbreak of the terrible famine of 1770. He wrote to say that since the accession of the Company to the Diwani the condition of the people had undoubtedly become worse than it had been before and that Bengal which had flourished under the most despotic and arbitrary government, was verging on ruin. The report was practically ignored.

Bedara (Biderra), battle of—was fought in November, 1759. The Dutch who had a settlement at Chinsurah, several miles up the Ganges from Calcutta, wanted to supplant the English, entered into intrigues with Nawab Mir Jafar and made some efforts to import fresh military supplies from their settlements in Java. Robert Clive who was then the Governor of Bengal anticipated the Dutch and defeated them at the battle of Bedara near Chinsurah. The battle destroyed all prospects of Dutch supremacy in Bengal and left the English without any European rival in Bengal.

Begums of Oudh, the—were the mother and grandmother of Nawab Asaf-ud-daulah of Oudh who ascended the throne of Oudh in 1775. Soon after his accession he entered into the treaty of Faizabad with the East India Company by which he agreed to pay a large subsidy to the Company for the maintenance of a British army in Oudh. The administration of Oudh was corrupt and inefficient and the Nawab soon fell into arrears and by 1781 these became very large exactly at a time when the Company, pressed by the wars with Mysore, the Marathas and Chait Singh, urgently required large sums of money. Warren Hastings, who was then the Governor-General, called upon the Nawab of Oudh to clear the arrears but the Nawab pleaded his inability to pay unless he was put in possession of the large estate and wealth that were in possession of his widowed mother and grandmother, commonly known as the Begums of Oudh. In 1775 on the representations of Middleton, the British Resident in Oudh, the Begums gave to Nawab Asaf-ud-daulah £ 300,000, in addition to £ 250,000 already paid to him and the Council in Calcutta gave the Begums an assurance that no further demand should be made on them in future. Warren Hastings opposed this guarantee but was outvoted. Then in 1780 there was the affair of Chait

Singh (*q.v.*) of Benares. Hastings was hostile to the Begums because they had in 1775 the support of his opponents in the Council. So when in 1781 the Nawab of Oudh pleaded his inability to pay up the arrears in his subsidies unless he was placed in possession of the wealth of the Begums of Oudh Warren Hastings readily agreed to the request and ordered the British Resident Middleton to put the necessary pressure on the ladies to make them pay. As the Resident, Middleton, was not sufficiently energetic in applying coercion he was replaced by Bristow who imprisoned the ministers of the Begums, put them in irons, deprived them of food and even perhaps flogged them. So severe were the punishments inflicted and so acute was the hardship to which the Begums were consequently subjected that even the Nawab began to waver, but Warren Hastings would not relent and forbade any negotiations or forbearance until at last the Begums were obliged to surrender in December, 1782 the treasure in the possession of which they had been formally guaranteed by the Council in Calcutta in 1775. The whole affair was undoubtedly sordid, shabby and unjustifiable even on the ground of the necessities of the State. Hastings' later argument that the Begums had forfeited their claim to British protection and to the enjoyment of treasures guaranteed to them by the Calcutta Council on account of their complicity in the affair of Chait Singh lacks any proof in its support and was an afterthought. Warren Hastings acted under malice and it is astonishing that the Lords acquitted him of the charge of high-handedness against the Begums of Oudh of which he was undoubtedly guilty, though the proceeds of the high-handed action were utilised in the service of the Company. (Roberts, P. E., *History of the British Rule in India*; & Lyall, Sir Alfred, *Warren Hastings*)

Benares—*see* under Baranasi of which it is the modern name.

Benares, the treaty of—w·s concluded in 1773 between Nawab Suja-ud-daula of Oudh and the East India Company. By this treaty the districts of Kora and Allahabad which had been given to Emperor Shah Alam II in 1765, were taken away from him and given to the Nawab of Oudh in return for fifty lakhs of rupees and an annual subsidy on condition that the Company should maintain within Oudh a garrison of Company's troops for the protection of the Nawab.

Benares, the treaty of—was made in 1775 between Chait Singh, the Raja of Benares and the East India Company. By this treaty Chait Singh who was originally a feudatory of the Nawab of Oudh, placed himself under the overlordship of the East India Company on condition that the Raja would pay to the Company an annual tribute of 22½ lakhs of rupees. The treaty further laid down that "no demand shall be made upon him (Chait Singh) by the Hon'ble Company of any kind, or on any pretence whatsoever, nor shall any person be allowed to interfere with his authority or to disturb the peace of the country". Notwithstanding this definite undertaking Warren Hastings came upon Raja Chait Singh with demands for additional payments in the years 1778-80 and thus brought about what is known as the Chait Singh affair (*q.v.*).

Benares, Hindu University of—was established by the untiring zeal and efforts of Pandit Madan Mohan Malaviya in 1915. It is now one of the largest residential Universities in India.

Benfield, Paul—was one of the unscrupulous English usurers who lent large sums of money on exorbitant rates of interest to the Nawab of the Carnatic during the early years of the East India Company's control over the Nawab. Benfield wielded a great deal of parliamentary influence on William Dundas, the President of the Board of Control. Dundas influenced Sir John Macpherson during his acting Governor-Generalship (1785-86) to insist on the repayment out of the revenues of the Carnatic of the alleged debts of the Nawab of the Carnatic to Paul Benfield and others amounting to five million sterling without examination. It was an instance of scandalous jobbery committed by the order of Dundas.

Bengal—is the name given to the region lying between Bihar on the west and Assam and the Bay of Bengal on the east and the foot of the Himalayas on the north to Orissa on the south. It is a riparian region watered mainly by the Ganges and the Brahmaputra with their numerous tributaries. Its alluvial soil makes agriculture comparatively easy and its rich and varied resources have in all ages attracted to it the peoples of the neighbouring states. Bengal is the anglicised form of the term Bangla which is again the Bengali form of the Sanskrit term 'Vanga' which denoted Eastern and Central Bengal in the age of the *Dharmasutras*. It is also used in the epics. Western and north-western Bengal was then known as Gauḍa. Vanga and Gauḍa were both included in the empires of the Mauryas (*q.v.*) and of the Guptas (*q.v.*). After the fall of the Imperial Guptas local princes like Dharmaditya, Gopachandra and Samacharadeva asserted their independence. In the middle of the sixth century A.D. Gauḍa became quite a powerful state which found early in the next century a very astute and war-like king in Sasanka (*q.v.*), the great rival of Harshavardhana (*q.v.*). It was only after the death of Sasanka that Bengal became a part of the empire of Harshavardhana after whose death it passed under the rule of Bhaskaravarman (*q.v.*) of Kamarupa. How and when Bengal was freed from the rule of Kamarupa is not known. At any rate it did not last long, for early in the eighth century Bengal was overrun by Yasovarman of Kanauj. This raid plunged the country into confusion. If popular tradition as preserved in geneological works is to be trusted then it was about this time that there ruled in Bengal a king named Adisura (*q.v.*) who is said to have invited to Bengal five Brahmanas with five non-Brahmana attendants from Mithila for the purpose of restoring the purity of Hindu cult and rites in Bengal. At any rate peace and order seem to have been restored to Bengal with the election to the throne of Bengal of one Gopala by the people of Bengal. Gopala founded the famous Pala dynasty (*q.v.*) of kings under whom Bengal attained great prosperity and power, became an important centre of Buddhistic culture sending her monks, e.g. Dharmapala and Atisa (*q.v.*) to distant lands like China and Tibet and developing her own school of art and architecture of which the great Dhiman (*q.v.*) and Vitapal (*q.v.*) were the chief exponents. By the middle of the twelfth century the Pala dynasty declined in power and Bengal passed under the rule of the Sena dynasty (*q.v.*) which held sway over Bengal until western Bengal was conquered some time between 1198 and 1201 by Malik Ikhtiyar-ud-din Muhammad Khalji (*q.v.*). Fifty years later eastern Bengal also was conquered by the Muhammadans and Bengal became a part of the Delhi sultanate. But this tie did not last long. In about 1336 Fakhr-ud-din Mubarak Shah (*q.v.*) started a rebellion in eastern Bengal, which eventually spread over the whole province and brought about a complete separation from the sultanate of Delhi. From 1345 to 1490 Bengal was ruled by the Iliyas Shahi dynasty (*q.v.*) with a short interregnum of four years (*c.* 1414-18) during which four Hindu kings, namely Raja Ganesh, his son Jadu, Danuja-mardana and Mahendra held temporary sway. In 1490 Alauddin Hussain Shah (*q.v.*) started in Bengal the dynasty of Sayyid kings of Bengal which ruled till 1538 when Emperor Humayun conquered Bengal only to be dispossessed of it a year later by Sher Shah (*q.v.*) whose descendants ruled over Bengal till 1564 when Sulaiman Karnani (*q.v.*) established a new dynasty of kings, the last of whom, Daud Khan, was defeated by Emperor Akbar in 1576 and Bengal again passed under the sway of Delhi. A period of peaceful prosperity followed and Bengal so prospered in trade and commerce that her wealth secured the admiration of foreign travellers and also attracted European trading companies to establish factories. First came the Portuguese but they took more to piracy and to trading in slaves than to peaceful commerce and became a terror in deltaic Bengal until they were forcibly suppressed by the Mughul Governor Kasim Ali Khan in 1632. Then came the Dutch, the Danes, the French and the English in quick succession and established themselves respectively in Chinsurah, Serampore, Chandernagore and Calcutta, all on the banks of the Hooghly. So long as the Mughul Emperors were capable, their governors in Bengal were also strong enough to keep these European traders in their places and they dared not disturb the peace of the land. The jurisdiction of the province of Bengal was also expanded by governor Murshid Quli Khan (*q.v.*) who added Bihar and by his successor Shuja-ud-din (1727-38) who conquered Orissa. But Shuja's son and successor Sarfaraz Khan proved incapable and was overthrown in 1740 by Alivardi Khan, his deputy in Bihar. Nawab Alivardi Khan (*q.v.*) ruled in practical independence of Delhi till his death in 1756. His grandson and successor Nawab Siraj-ud-daula (*q.v.*) was too young to rule prudently and public morality amongst the people, Hindus as well as Muhammadans, was very low with the result that Siraj not only failed to prevent the English from waging a war against the French in Bengal in complete violation of his sovereignty but even fell a victim to a conspiracy hatched by the English with the Nawab's disaffected officers leading to the battle of Plassey (*q.v.*) in June 1757, where Siraj was defeated. He fled from the battle-field to Murshidabad, and, failing to organise any resistance to the victors, fled again. The victorious English installed Mir Jafar, one of the chief conspirators and a close relation of Siraj, as the Nawab on 28th June, 1757. Four days later Siraj was executed. Thus fell ingloriously Muhammadan rule in Bengal, for Mir Jafar (*q.v.*) soon found himself no better than a toy in the hands of the English who soon deposed him, put on his throne his son-in-law Mir Kasim, (*q.v.*) with whom also they soon fought a war which ended in his defeat at Buxar in 1764. Mir Kasim passed into oblivion and Mir Jafar, who had been re-installed as Nawab, died in 1765. The same year the English got the grant of the *Diwani* of Bengal, Bihar and Orissa from the Emperor of Delhi. Robert Clive, the victor of Plassey, was now appointed Company's governor in Bengal. Two years later he left for England, and for the next five years Bengal came to be most misgoverned. The Nawab was a puppet in the hands of the local officers of the Company and nobody was responsible for the welfare of the people. The result was a terrible famine in 1770 which carried away one-third of the population of Bengal. In 1772 Warren Hastings was appointed by the Company as its governor in Bengal. Next year the Regulating Act was passed which made Warren Hastings the Governor-General and placed the Presidencies of Bombay and Madras under the Governor-General in Bengal. Thus Bengal came not only to be connected with the growing British Empire in India but also became its nervecentre as Calcutta in Bengal soon became the capital of the Indo-British Empire.

Administratively Bengal underwent several changes. In the beginning of British administration Bengal with Bihar and Orissa as its adjuncts was governed by the Governor-General in Council. In 1854 it was placed in charge of a Lieutenant-Governor. In 1905 the province was partitioned by Lord Curzon into two—West Bengal, Bihar and Orissa forming one unit under a Lieutenant-Governor and Eastern Bengal with Assam forming another under another Lieutenant-Governor. This partition of Bengal (*q.v.*) was strongly resented by the people of Bengal, especially by the Hindus, who started against it a great popular agitation under the leadership of Surendranath Banerjee (*q.v.*). Bengal resorted to *swadeshi* or use of indigenous manufactures and boycott of British goods. The attempt that the British Government made to suppress this agitation by force drove discontent underground and terrorism raised its head in Bengal under the leadership of Arabinda Ghose (*q.v.*) leading to his trial in the famous Alipore Bomb case. The trial ended in his acquittal, though many of his associates were sentenced to imprisonment for life. The agitation still continued and at last the British Government annulled the partition in 1911 and West Bengal, separated from Bihar and Orissa, was united with East Bengal, separated from Assam, and the reunited province of Bengal was placed under a Governor-in-Council. In 1947, as the price of India's independence, Bengal was again partitioned into two parts— the West Bengal districts with some districts of north Bengal constituting the state of West Bengal in India, and the East Bengal districts forming what is now called East Pakistan. This unnatural partition, though made with the consent of the Indian National Congress, has resulted in uprooting millions of people, mostly Hindus of East Bengal, and has caused immense suffering to them. The truncated state of West Bengal is only one-third of its old self and is confronted with many problems of which the resettlement of the Hindus who are seeking refuge in West Bengal, is the most tremendous and at the same time the most baffling.

If Bengal was the first Indian province to have welcomed British rule it has also been the first province in India to absorb British political ideas of parliamentary rule and of democracy, to preach Indian nationalism and to hold the first Indian National Conference (*q.v.*) and thus to show the way to the inauguration of the Indian National Congress (*q.v.*) to which again it supplied the first President and which ultimately won for India independence. "What Bengal thinks today India thinks to-morrow" is not an undeserved compliment that Gopal Krishna Gokhale so warmly paid her.

Bentinck, Lord William Cavendish—was the last of the Governors-General of Bengal (1828-33) and the first of the Governors-General of India (1833-35). He first came to India as a governor of Madras but was re-called on the outbreak of the mutiny of the sepoys at Vellore in 1806. Twenty-one years later on the resignation of Lord Amherst he was appointed as the Governor-General and took over charge in July, 1828. His administration which lasted seven years, was unique. It saw no war and was marked entirely by peaceful activities. Bentinck made no territorial annexation by war though Cachar was annexed in 1830 for failure of heirs, Coorg in 1834 for gross misgovernment by its ruler and Jaintia Parganas in Assam in 1835 on account of the refusal of the local chief to surrender men who had kidnapped British subjects and sacrificed them to the goddess Kali. Generally speaking, Lord William Bentinck followed a policy of non-interference in the affairs of the Indian States, but in 1831 continued misgovernment by the Raja of Mysore induced him to place the State under British administration. Bentinck believed in personal knowledge of the various parts of the Indian Empire and travelled much. In 1829 he visited the Malay Peninsula and transferred its capital from Penang to Singapore. Under the direction of the Government of England he concluded commercial treaties with the Amirs of Sind opening up the Indus to navigation by the British and then in 1831 he concluded the treaty with Maharaja Ranjit Singh of the Panjab by which perpetual friendship was established between the English and the Maharaja who also agreed to encourage trade along the Sutlej and the Upper Indus. Shah Shuja, the exiled pretender to the throne of Afghanistan, was encouraged to make a futile bid for recovering the Afghan throne from the reigning Amir, Dost Muhammad. Thus was initiated the ill-conceived policy which brought about the tragedy of the First Afghan War (1838-42) and to the annexation of Sind.

The importance of the administration of Bentinck lies in the series of reforms, administrative and social, which he effected and which, on account of the liberal spirit underlying them, endeared him immensely to the people of India. He began by effecting economies in the army as well as in the civil service, increased the revenue especially from the opium monopoly and soon turned the annual deficits into surpluses. He abolished flogging as a punishment in the Indian army, encouraged the introduction of steam navigation on Indian rivers, effected a land revenue settlement in the Agra area which increased the revenue, made a fair assessment of the rent payable by the cultivators and provided them with records of rights. Bentinck reversed the erroneous policy of Lord Cornwallis of excluding Indians from any but inferior posts under the Company, appointed Indians to higher offices like those of subordinate judges, combined the office of the District Magistrate with that of District Collector, abolished the provincial courts, appointed Indians to executive posts like those of Deputy Magistrates on comparatively decent salaries, introduced the posts of Divisional Commissioners and thus gave to the Indian administrative machinery its modern form. The social reforms of Lord William Bentinck were no less remarkable. In 1829 he abolished the *Sati* or the burning of Hindu widows on the funeral pyres of their dead husbands. With the active support of Col. Sleeman he suppressed the Thugs or bands of robbers who formed a secret society extending over the whole country, travelled over the country, murdered unsuspecting persons by strangling them with handkerchiefs or scarfs and then robbed the victims. In 1832 all disabilities due to the change of religion were abolished. In 1833 the Company's Charter was renewed for another twenty years and the Company, deprived of its monopoly of the China trade, became an exclusively administrative body. The new Charter Act effected certain important changes. It changed the title of the Governor-General of Bengal to the Governor-General of India; it added a fourth member to the Governor-General's Council and laid down the important principle that no Indian shall be excluded, by reason only of his religion, birth or colour, from any office under the Company for which he may be otherwise fitted. Another provision of the Charter Act of 1832 required that steps should be taken for spreading education amongst the Indians and Lord William Bentinck decided that henceforth English should be the medium of instruction in the schools maintained by the Government and more money should be spent on spreading Western education amongst the Indians. Lord William Bentinck established the Calcutta Medical College in 1835. In March of the same year Lord William Bentinck retired from his high post. The liberalism and sympathy that had marked his administration won him greater popularity with the Indians than any of his predecessors. (Thornton, *History of India;* Marshman, *History of India;* Boulger. D., *Life of Lord William Bentinck*)

Berar—is the modern name of the ancient state of Vidarbha, situated in the valley of the Varada or Warda river. It was a part of the Magadhan empire of the Mauryas (*q.v.*) and made a futile attempt to secede during the rule of Agnimitra, son of Pushyamitra Sunga (*q.v.*). Latet on it passed under the rule of the Chalukyas from whom it was conquered by Alauddin Khalji and was a part of the dominion of Muhammad Tughluq. With the establishment of the Bahmani kingdom, Berar formed a part of of it and continued to be so till 1484 when it was set up as an independent kingdom by Imadul Mulk who founded the Imad Shahi dynasty which lasted until 1574 when Berar was absorbed by Ahmadnagar. In 1596 it was ceded to Emperor Akbar who constituted it into a *subah*. By the treaty of 1714 between Sayyid Hussain Ali, one of the two king-makers, and Peshwa Balaji Viswanath Berar passed under the control of the Marathas. Berar was soon afterwards bestowed as a jaigir on Raghuji Bhonsla, who was related by marriage to Raja Shahu. As time passed on and the Maratha dominion extended Raghuji Bhonsla added further territories to his jaigir and by the time of the third Peshwa Balaji Baji Rao, Berar became the centre of the Bhonsla State. In the second Anglo-Maratha War the Bhonsla Raja was defeated in the battle of Argaon and by the treaty of Deogaon (December, 1803) Berar was ceded by the Bhonsla Raja and was given as a reward to the Nizam of Hyderabad. The Nizam who had already entered into a subsidiary alliance with the English and had undertaken to pay an annual subsidy for the maintenance of a British contingent in his dominions, fell into arrears and assigned to the Indo-British Government the revenue of Berar as a security for the due payment of the annual subsidy. But this arrangement did not work satisfactorily and in 1902 Berar was assigned by the Nizam in perpetual lease to the Government of India and became a part of British India.

Bernier, Francois—a learned French physician, visited India from 1656 to 1668, travelled over the country and has left an interesting account of what he saw in the country during the later years of the reign of Shah Jahan and the earlier years of the reign of Aurangzeb. He entered into the service of Danishmand Khan, an important nobleman of the Mughul Court. He was present in Delhi when Prince Dara was brought there as a captive and paraded through the streets of the metropolis. He witnessed the procession and noticed that the crowds wailed in sympathy for the fallen Prince, but "Not a single movement was made, no one offered to draw his sword with a view to delivering the beloved and compassionate Dara." Bernier, though a foreigner, thus touched upon the characteristic passivity and helplessness of the Indian mob. Bernier has left character-sketches of Shah Jahan as well of Aurangzeb. He was much impressed by the prosperity of Bengal but was much depressed by the sight of the general poverty of the mass of the people who were excessively taxed for the maintenance of a large splendid Court and a very large army which was maintained to keep down the people. (*Travels of Bernier*, ed. V. A. Smith).

Besant, Mrs. Annie (1847-1933)—English theosophist, born in London in October, 1847, was a daughter of Mr. William Page Wood and married at the age of twenty Rev. Frank Besant; but the marriage did not prove happy and Mrs. Besant obtained a separation from her husband in 1873. She now became an ardent free-thinker and for the next eleven years she worked in close association with Charles Bradlaugh, both in politics and in free-thought propaganda as a lecturer and writer under the pen-name of Ajax. She however gradually became a revolutionary socialist and this led to a breach between her and Charles Bradlaugh in 1889. Henceforth she became an ardent theosophist, was closely attached to Helena Blavatsky and threw in her lot very largely with India. She founded the Central Hindu College at Benares, and was elected President of the Theosophical Society in 1907. In 1916 she founded the Indian Home Rule League and became its first

President and in 1917 she was the President of the Indian Nationl Congress at its Calcutta session. Though later on she dissociated herself from the extreme wing of the Indian National-ist Party she was looked upon as a dangerous person by the British Indian Government and was kept in internment for some time in 1917. While the Montague reforms were in pre-paration Mrs. Besant at first supported the Government, but after a brief spell of constitutionalism she strongly supported the extreme nationalist position. In the meantime she set up her *protégé*, J. Krishnamurti, as the coming world teacher and founded the new Order of the Star. In 1926-27 Mrs. Besant travelled widely in England and America with Krishnamurti and eloquently urged his claims to be the new Messiah. On her return to India she became involved in a law-suit with the father of the boy Krishnamurti and this incident largely reduced her prestige. She died in India in 1933. She possessed great gifts as an orator and organiser and these coupled with her love of freedom enabled her to win the position, unique for an English lady, of a leader in the Indian nationalist movement. She was a voluminous writer and wrote much on free-thought and theosophy. She published an *Autobiography* in 1893 and the *Religious Problem in India*, published in 1902, was her last great literary work. In her *How India Wrought for Freedom* she called India her 'motherland'.

Besnagar—modern name of the ancient city of Vidisa in Eastern Malwa, was an important city during the reign of the Sungas (*q.v.*) (*c.* 187-75 B.C.) and continued to be the seat of local princes for many years afterwards. Its princes maintained diplomatic relations with the Greek princes of the north-western frontier region of India. Here stands a monolithic column raised in honour of god Vasudeva by Heliodoros, the Greek ambassador of the Greek king Antialkidas of Taxila in about 135 B.C.

Best, Captain—was the commander of the English ship *Dragon*. In November, 1612, assisted by only one small ship, the *Osiander*, he defeated in a naval battle fought in the Indian Ocean a Portuguese fleet comprising four large and twenty-five small ships and thus marked the entrance of the British fleet into Indian politics, for the news of this battle convinced the Mughul Emperor Jahangir that the old notion that amongst the Euro-peans the Portuguese were the most powerful, was found wrong.

Bethune, John Elliot Drinkwater (1806-62)—was Law Member of the Supreme Council of India. He took a keen interest in the

promotion of education amongst the Indians, particularly
amongst Indian women. He founded the Bethune School in
Calcutta for promoting western education amongst the Indian
girls of the higher classes. Later on the institution was raised
in standard and is now a well-known girls' college in Calcutta.

Bhadrabahu—last of the Jain saints known as the *shrutakevalins*,
was a contemporary of the Maurya king Chandragupta Maurya
(*c.* 322-298 B.C.). When at the close of the reign of Chandragupta
Maurya a twelve years' famine overwhelmed the empire
Chandragupta Maurya abdicated the throne and saint Bhadrabahu led him, along with other Jain adherents, to southern
India where they settled at Sravana Belgola in Mysore. In the
fullness of time Bhadrabahu starved himself to death in the
approved Jain manner. He had effected the introduction of
Jainism to southern India. He is mentioned in two inscriptions
dated about A.D. 900 found near Seringapatam and the present
head of the Jain temple at Sravana Belgola, who is recognised
as the head of all the Jains of southern India, claims to be the
successor of Bhadrabahu. (Jacobi, *Sacred Books of the East.*,
Vol. XXII)

Bhadraka—was the fifth king of the Sunga dynasty (*q.v.*). He has
been identified with king Udaka or Odraka of the Pabhosa
inscription. But this is not certain. Nothing else is known of him.
(*P.H.A.I.,* pp. 393-94)

Bhadrasala—the general of the last Nanda king, was defeated with
great slaughter by Chandragupta Maurya on the eve of his
accession to the throne of Pataliputra.

Bhadrayasas—an Indian leader, played an important part in
destroying the Bactrian Greek kingdom of the eastern Panjab.
(*P.H.A.I.,* p. 429)

Bhagadatta—mythical king of Kamarupa, is mentioned in the *Mahabharata*. In later historical times the kings of Kamarupa belonging to the dynasty of Pushyavarman (*c.* A.D. 330-646) claimed to
be his direct descendants and even still later kings like Harsha
ruling in the 8th century A.D. who gave his daughter Rajyamati
in marriage to a king of Nepal, was referred to in a Nepal inscription as a descendant of Bhagadatta. (*I.A.,* ix, p. 179)

Bhagavad-Gita—forms a part of the sixth book of the *Mahabharata*
(*q.v.*). Orthodox Hindus believe that this contains the very
words of Sri Krishna, a divine incarnation, to his disciple and
friend, the Pandava hero, Arjuna. Its date has not yet been
precisely fixed. Swami Vivekananda held that it was composed
before the time of Buddha. Western scholars assign it to the

4th century A.D. At any rate it is an epitome of the Hindu system of thought emphasizing the doctrines of *nishkama karma* (work done without seeking any reward) and *bhakti* (loving faith) in a God of Grace.

Bharat—was the name borne by several Vedic kings as well as by a younger brother of Rama, the hero of the *Ramayana*. The country lying north of the ocean and south of the snowy mountains, the Himalayas, came to be called Bháratavarsha, for "there dwell the descendants of Bharata". (*Vishnu Purana*, II. 3.1)

Bhagawan Das—Raja of Amber or Jaipur, was the son of Raja Behari Mall (*q.v.*) who voluntarily submitted to the Mughul Emperor Akbar and entered into a marriage alliance with him. Bhagwan Das rose high in the service of Akbar and led the Mughul invasion into Kashmir which was conquered and annexed to the Mughul empire. Raja Bhagwan Das was also a reputed Hindi poet.

bhaga—was the land-tax representing the king's share of the agricultural produce of land and was generally fixed at one-sixth of the produce. It was, however, variable, according to conditions, e.g. Asoka reduced it to one-eighth for Lumbini-grama in honour of the Buddha who was born there.

Bhagabhadra, Kashiputra—a king of Vidisa, received in the fourteenth year of his reign Heliodoros as an ambassador to his court from Antialkidas, the Greek king of Taxila. (*E.H.I.*, p. 238 *n* 3: *P.H.A.I*, p. 394)

Bhagavata—was a king of Vidisa in the twelfth year of whose reign a Garuḍa Pillar was raised at Vidisa or Besnagar. He is to be distinguished from king Bhagabhadra of Besnagar referred to by Heliodoros (*q.v.*) in the Garuḍa Pillar that he raised at Besnagar. (*P.H.A.I.*, p. 394)

Bhagavatas, the—a religious sect devoted to the worship of Lord Vishnu, also called Vasudeva and Krishna. The origin of the belief of this sect has been traced to the late Vedic period. It progressed as time went on, making converts even amongst the Greeks who settled in India, the most historical of whom was Heliodoros, the Greek ambassador of the Greek king Antialkidas of Taxila, who visited Besnagar or Vidisa between 140 and 130 B.C. and raised there a Garuḍa Pillar in which he proudly declared himself as an ardent Bhagavata (*parama bhágavata*). They were also known as Vaishnavas and insisted on the efficacy of *bhakti* or loving devotion to the Lord Vasudeva as a means of getting grace and escaping even the fruits of *karma*. The sect grew greatly in importance under the Gupta rulers some of whom were themselves Bhagavatas. Some of the Chalukya kings also professed Bhagavatism and the famous bas-reliefs at Badami prove the prevalence of the cult in the sixth century in the Deccan. The theology and philosophy of the sect were developed and systematised by a succession of teachers called *Acharyas*, the most famous amongst whom was Ramanuja. In the later ages Sri Chaitanya was the most important exponent of the cult in Bengal and eastern India. (Roy Choudhury, *Early History of the Vaishnava Sect*)

Bhandi—was the chief statesman in Kanauj at the time of the death of Rajyavardhana (*q.v.*) and played a prominent part in placing Harsha (*q.v.*) on the throne.

Bhanudeva—a king of the Ganga dynasty, ruled over Orissa on the eve of Alauddin's invasion of the Deccan. He was swept away by the onrush of the Muslim conquest in about A.D. 1294.

Bhanugupta—one of the latest of the early Imperial Guptas, has been assigned to about A.D. 510 and has been identified with the Gupta Emperor Baladitya who, according to Hiuen Tsang, defeated the Hunas under Mihirakula (*q.v.*). (*P.H.A.S.*, p. 596)

Bhao Shaheb—*see* Sadasiva Rao.

Bharatavarsha—is the name of the land in which dwell the children of king Bharata (*q.v.*). It extends from the Himalayas in the north to the sea on the south. (*Vishnu Purana*, II. 3.1.) Its modern name is Bhárat or India.

Bharatpur—is a town and kingdom founded in the first half of the eighteenth century by the Jat chief Badan Singh. During the rule of his adopted son and successor Suraj Mal the authority of the Bharatpur kingdom was extended over the districts of Agra, Dholpur, Mainpuri, Hathras, Aligarh, Etawah, Gurgaon and Muttra. It thus became a considerable and powerful kingdom in central India and a very strong fort was built at Bharatpur. It did not side with the Marathas in the third battle of Panipat (1761) and thus remained a powerful state at the death of Suraj Mal in 1763. Its reputation was further enhanced when in 1805, during the course of the second Anglo-Maratha war it repulsed a British army led by Lord Lake and frustrated the attempt to capture the fort. Thus Bharatpur came to be considered as impregnable. The Raja of Bharatpur, however, concluded a treaty of subsidiary alliance with the British and remained on friendly terms with the British Indian Government until 1824 when, encouraged by the reverses that the British arms had suffered in the course of the first Anglo-Burmese war, Durjan Sal, a claimant to the throne of Bharatpur, disputed with arms the decision of the British Indian Government conferring the throne on his minor cousin, the son of the late Raja. But a British army led by Lord Combermere easily stormed the fortress of Bharatpur in 1826. Durjan Sal was deported and the British nominee was put on the throne. Bharatpur remained ever since a faithful subordinate state within the British Indian Empire until it was merged in the Republic of India after the attainment of her independence.

Bhargas, the—a tribal republican people, flourished in the region of Sumsumara Hill in pre-Mauryan times.

Bharhut (or Barhut) Stupa—is the oldest monument of the Sunga period (*c.* 185-73 B.C.), in the opinion of Sir John Marshall. Bharhut is in the Rewa State, not far from modern Bikaner. The *stupa* was built at a place where the roads from Magadha and Allahabad joined with the roads to Malwa and the Deccan. It was constructed of brick and stone and had an elaborately carved circular railing around it, with four gateways. On two of the gates inscriptions have been found which enumerated three generations of the kings of Dahala who were the feudatories of the Sungas (*q.v.*). The *stupa* was dismantled by the neighbouring villagers after the disappearance of Buddhism. The remains were found by Cunningham at whose instance portions of the eastern gateway and of the railings which had yet survived were brought to Calcutta and housed in the Indian Museum. The eastern gateway was twenty-three feet high, and the pillars as well as the cross-bars and architrave of the *stupa* are decorated with mumerous bas-reliefs representing scenes from the life of Buddha or those illustrative of his previous births. (*C.H.I.*, I, 624-25)

Bhartridaman—the Great Satrap of Ujjaini from A.D. 289-95, was the son of the Great Satrap Rudrasen (died 274) and succeeded his elder brother Visvasimha (died A.D. 288). His son Visvasura was only a *satrap* and the Great Satrapship appears to have been temporarily suspended after the death of Bhartridaman. This was perhaps due to the invasion and occupation of the northwestern parts of India by the Sassanian emperors (*c.* A.D. 293-350).

Bhartrihari—a famous Sanskrit poet, flourished in the seventh century of the Christian era. His most famous book, *Bhattikavyam*, which he wrote primarily for the purpose of teaching Sanskrit grammar, shows that Bhartrihari was, as Macdonell observes, a poet, grammarian and philosopher. (Macdonell, *Hist. of Sanskrit Literature*)

Bhas—an early Sanskrit dramatist anterior to Kautilya, the author of the *Arthashastra* (*q.v.*), is believed to have composed thirteen dramas like *Charudatta, Pratima* and *Swapna Vasavadatta*, the last of which refers to king Darsaka (*c.* 467 B.C.) of the Saisunaga dynasty (*q.v.*). His dramas which had been completely forgotten in later ages, were discovered early in the twentieth century by Ganapati Shastri. (Shastri, Ganapati, *The Dramas of Bhasa & Ind. Ant.,* 1916, pp. 189-95)

Bhaskaracharya—the most celebrated Indian astronomer and mathematician, was born in A.D. 1114 at Bijapur at the foot of the Sahyadri range in the Deccan. His father Chuḍamani Maheswar was an astrologer from whom he learnt astrology. At the early age of 36 he wrote his famous work *Siddhanta Shiromani.* The book is divided into two parts—Arithmetic and Algebra, also called *Lilavati.* It is written in verses and shows the extent of the contribution of the Hindus to the science of Mathematics. (Banerjee, H., *Lilavati* & Dutt, B. B., *Contributions of the Hindus to Mathematics*)

Bhaskar Pandit—a general of the Maratha chief, Raghuji Bhonsla, raided Bengal in 1743-45 during the reign of Nawab Alivardi Khan (1740-56). Unable to check him by open fighting the Nawab inveigled Bhaskar Pandit to a private conference at Mankarah near Cossimbazar and had him assassinated. But Bhaskar's assassination did not stop the raids of the Marathas from whom the Nawab had to purchase peace in 1751 by ceding Orissa to them and by agreeing to pay an annual *chauth* of twelve lakhs of rupees. Bhaskar's raids had roused most lively fears amongst the people of Bengal and the depredations of his soldiers, called *Bargirs*, are still remembered in Bengal (Sarkar, *Hist. of Bengal*, II. pp. 455-61)

Bhaskaravarman—the most famous of the early kings of Kamarupa (Assam), ruled from about A.D. 600 to A.D. 650 and was the last but the greatest monarch of the dynasty established by Pushyavarman in the fourth century A.D. He is mentioned in Bana's *Harshacharita* and in Hiuen Tsang's *Travels* and *Life* and is commemorated in his Nidhanpur Copper-plate Grant which is undated but was probably issued some time after the death of Harshavardhana in 646 A.D. Early in his reign Bhaskaravarman, referred to as Kumara by Bana as well as by Hiuen Tsang, entered into an alliance with Harshavardhana, presumably for the purpose of checking the power of their common enemy, king Sasanka (*q.v.*) of Bengal. But there is no record to show that the allies ever made a combined attack on Sasanka. The fact that the Nidhanpur Grant was issued by Bhaskaravarman from his victorious camp at Karnasuvarna which has been identified with Rangamati in Murshidabad district, certainly proves that some time during his reign Bhaskaravarman, the king of Kamarupa, extended his dominions into Bengal as far as the district of Murshidabad. He was a patron of learning and though he was personally an orthodox Brahmanical Hindu he invited to his court the Buddhist Chinese pilgrim Hiuen Tsang and received him with great honour. Later on at the command of Emperor Harshavardhana, Bhaskaravarman escorted the Chinese pilgrim to the camp of Harshavardhana near Rajmahal and then accompanied his imperial ally to his assemblies at Kanauj and Prayag. Bhaskaravarman outlived Harsha by several years, and, according to the Chinese annals, after Harsha's death (A.D. 648) he became the supreme master of eastern India and later on helped with abundant supplies the Chinese ambassador Wang-heuen-tse (*q.v.*) in his punitive campaign against Harsha's erstwhile minister Arjuna who, on his master's death, had usurped his throne. Bhaskaravarman died childless and on his death (*c.* A.D. 650) his kingdom of Kamarupa passed to the new Salastambha dynasty (*q.v.*). (Barua, K., *Early History of Kamarupa*, Bhattacharya, P., *Kamarupa-Sasanavali* and Bhattacharya, S., *Date of Nidhanpur Grant*, *J.I.H.*, Vol. XXXI, August, 1953, pp. 112-17)

Bhat family—produced Balaji Viswanath Bhat who, as one of the eight ministers of Raja Shahu, occupied the position of the Peshwa the status of which post he raised to that of the chief minister of the Maratha state and made it hereditary in his family to which belonged all the Peshwas.

Bhavabhuti—Sanskrit poet and dramatist and author of *Uttaracharita* and *Malatimadhava*, was the court-poet of king Yasovarman of Kanauj who ruled early in the 8th century.

Bhava Naga—a sovereign of the Bharasivas, has been mentioned in several inscriptions of the Vakatakas. He flourished before the rise of the Gupta empire and founded a family which in later times extended its sway up to the Ganges and performed ten *Asvamedha* sacrifices. (*P.H.A.I.*, p. 480)

Bhils, the—are a primitive tribal people of India. They are referred to as Nishadas in the Vedic literature. They speak a kind of Austric language.

Bhilsa—is the modern name of the ancient town of Vidisa. Near it stand the ruins of some *stupas* which tradition ascribes to Asoka. It was a flourishing place in Muslim times. It had a fort which gave it great strategic importance in Malwa. It was captured in 1234 by Sultan Iltutmish and it was its occupation by Alauddin in 1292 that whetted his ambition and made feasible his first raid into the Deccan in 1293.

Bhima or Bhimasena—is a famous name in Indian mythology. The second of the Pandava (*q.v.*) princes, who was considered physically the strongest of the five sons of Pandu, bore this name and his many exploits are related in the *Mahabharata*.

Bhima I—was the Chalukya or Solanki king of Gujarat. During his rule Sultan Mahmud of Ghazni made a raid on the Siva temple of Somnath. King Bhima I failed to prevent the raid and to protect the temple which was destroyed by Sultan Mahmud in A.D. 1025. On the retirement of the Sultan king Bhima began to build at Somnath a temple of stone in place of the old temple built of brick and wood.

Bhima—belonged to the caste of the Kaivartas and was the nephew and successor of Divvoka, or Divya (*q.v.*). He led a revolt against the Pala king, Mahipala II, of Bengal and established an independent kingdom in north Bengal. Bhima's rule was short-lived, for he was overthrown by Mahipala's youngest brother, Ramapala in A.D. 1084.

Bhima—the fourth king of the Hindu Shahiya dynasty of Udbandhapura. His daughter's daugher was the celebrated queen Didda of Kashmir. During his reign the kingdom of Ghazni rose into power under Sabuktigin (A.D. 977-97) whose progress Bhima's successor, Jaipal, tried to check in vain.

Bhimdeva II—a later king of the Solanki or Chalukya dynasty of Gujarat, had the great distinction of repulsing in A.D. 1178 a raid by Shihabuddin Muhammad Ghuri with heavy losses. The victory protected Gujarat as a whole from Muslim conquest and occupation for more than a century, though Bhimdeva's capital Anhilwara was raided and plundered by Qutb-ud-din in 1197. Bhimdeva II was one of the few Hindu princes who succeeded in checking for a time at least Muslim progress in India.

Bhimsen—a Hindu historian, flourished in the reign of Aurangzeb (1656-1707) and wrote in Persian a historical work named *Nushka-i-Dilkusha*. He was born at Burhanpur in the Deccan and is therefore known as Bhimsen Burhanpuri. He gives much information about the economic condition of the country.

Bhinmal—old name of Broach and the region round it, was the home district of the Gurjara-Pratiharas (*q.v.*).

Bhitargaon—in Cawnpore district, U.P., has a stone temple of the

Gupta age. It has been ascribed to the reign of Chandragupta II (*q.v.*) and is remarkable for its vigorous and well-designed sculpture in terra-cotta and is one of the few examples of the excellence of the art and architecture in the Gupta Age.

Bhitari—is in the Ghazipur district to the east of Benares. Here a pillar surmounted by a statue of Vishnu was raised by the fifth Gupta emperor Skandagupta (*q.v.*) (*c.* A.D. 455-67). The statue has disappeared but the pillar still stands and it contains an elaborate inscription in Sanskrit written by the order of Skandagupta. It contains the geneology of Skandagupta and also an account of his fight with the Pushyamitras and the Hunas. According to this inscription Skandagupta was the son and successor of Kumaragupta I (*c.* A.D. 413-55). In 1889 a seal of Kumaragupta II was discovered at Bhitari. This seal completely ignores Skandagupta and represents Puragupta as the son and successor of Kumaragupta I. This apparent contradiction between the testimony of the inscription and the seal, both found at Bhitari, has been attempted to be reconciled by the assumption that Puragupta was a step-brother of Skandagupta and succeeded the latter after his death. (Fleet, *Gupta Inscriptions* No. 13; Banerji, *Chronology of the Late Imperial Guptas* in the Annals of Bhandarkar Research Institute, Vol I, Pt. I, 1919 and *P.H.A.I.*, pp. 572-85)

Bhogavarman—a Maukhari chief of Kanauj, married a daughter of the later Gupta emperor Adityasena (*c.* A.D. 772-73) and was a subordinate ally of his royal father-in-law. (*P.H.A.I.*, p. 610)

Bhogas, the—a tribal people who were members of the Vrijian confederacy which had its chief centre at Vaisali (*q.v.*), are mentioned in Buddhist tradition. (*Sacred Books of the East*, XLV, 71*n*)

Bhoi dynasty—ruled in Orissa from 1542-59. It was founded by Govinda, formerly a minister of the earlier Orissan king Prataparudra (1497-1540). Govinda belonged to the Bhoi or writer class and his dynasty accordingly came to be known as Bhoi dynasty. It comprised only three kings. viz. Govinda, his son and grandson and lasted only for eighteen years.

Bhoja—is used in ancient literature in three senses: first, as the royal designation applicable to the consecrated monarchs of the southern region; secondly, as a tribal name, as in R.E. XIII of Asoka, of a people living perhaps in Berar; and thirdly as a proper name borne by several princes of Kanauj and Malwa.

Bhoja I—a Gurjara-Pratihara king of Kanauj, ruled for 50 years (*c.* 840-900). His original name was Mihira and Bhoja was his

cognomen. He was a very powerful monarch and his dominions
which extended from the foot of the Himalayas in the north to
the Narmada in the south and from Bengal in the east to the
Sutlej in the west, may easily be described as an empire.
Bhoja I was especially devoted to the worship of Vishnu in the
Boar incarnation and placed on his coins the legend *Adi
Varaha*. He was a valiant warrior who not only held in check
the Arabs in Sind but also waged many wars with Sankaravarman, the king of Kashmir, the Rashtrakuta king Dhruva of
Broach and with the Pala kings of Bengal. Emperor Bhoja I
was a great patron of learning. The Arab traveller, Sulaiman,
who visited his dominions, tells us that Emperor Bhoja I maintained a powerful army, including the best cavalry in India
and a large force of camels, that he was extremely rich and that
no country in India was safer from robbers. This shows that
Bhoja I maintained an efficient internal administration. (Majumdar, R. C., *Age of Imperial Kanouj;* Tripathy, *History of Kanouj*)

Bhoja II—a grandson of Bhoja I, ruled over the Pratihara kingdom
for the short period of two or three years (*c.* A.D. 908-10).

Bhoja of Malwa—a king of the Paramara or Pawar dynasty of
Malwa, ruled from *c.* A.D. 1018-60. His capital was at Dhara.
He assumed the title of Navashahasanka, i.e. New Vikramaditya.
He claimed victories over the Turushkas or Turks. He was a
great patron of learning and wrote in Sanskrit books on numerous subjects including poetics, rhetoric, astronomy and architecture. He built the great Bhojpur Lake covering an area of
more than 250 sq. miles which lasted till the fifteenth century
when the embankments were cut by the local rulers. His reign,
however, ended in a disaster. He was defeated by an allied army
of Gujarat and Chedi in about A.D. 1060 and died soon afterwards.

Bhonsla—was the name of the family to which Shivaji belonged.
A branch of this family later on established itself at Nagpur,
and became known as the Bhonsla Raj family.

Bhopal—in Central India was created by Akbar (*q.v.*) into a fief out
of the dominions of Rani Durgavati of Gondwana. It was held
by a Nawab who became a semi-independent ruler after 1761,
but was obliged to enter into a subsidiary alliance with the
British in 1817. In 1948 the state was merged into the Republic
of India.

Bhotiyas, the—are one of the social groups like the Gujars into
which the rank and file of the Hinduised foreign invaders of the
seventh and eighth centuries were assimilated.

bhottavisti—was a kind of forced labour which had to be rendered under the Guptas in lands on the borders of Tibet.

Bhrigu—is the name of a sage to whom tradition ascribed the composition of the *Manava-dharma-shastra* or the Institutes of Manu. He has been ascribed to the period from 200 B.C. to A.D. 200.

Bhrigu-kachha—an important and busy port in pre-Mauryan times and for many years later on, is represented by modern Broach.

Bhuiyas, the—a title assumed by petty landlords in eastern Bengal as well as in Assam. Their number is said to have been twelve. They were not a caste, but a body of landlords or zamindars who had grown rich and powerful enough to exercise semi-independent powers. Each was independent of the others with his own domain. In eastern Bengal they occupied large parts of the districts of Dacca, Mymensingh, Faridpur, Barisal and Comilla. In Assam their territories lay along both banks of the Brahmaputra between the Kamta kingdom on the west and the Chutiya kingdom on the east. In Bengal they were all suppressed in the 16th century by Akbar. In Assam they were first subdued by king Nara Narayan (1540-84) of Cooch-Behar and later on their territories merged into the dominions of the Ahom kings. The term Bhuiya in Assam, and less frequently in Bengal, has since become a common family designation, held irrespective of caste and religious considerations. (Sarkar, J. N., *History of Bengal*, Part II & Gait, *History of Assam*)

bhukti—indicated an administrative unit of the Gupta empire. It was usually applied to indicate a province. A *Bhukti* was sub-divided into a number of *Vishayas* or *Mandalas*. The officer administering a *Bhukti* was called an Uparika.

Bhumaka—was the founder of the Kshaharata or Great Satrap family of Maharashtra with his capital at Nasik. He is known only from his coins. His exact date is not known. He has been assigned to the early years of the first century A.D.

Bhutan—is an independent state in the eastern Himalayas lying between Tibet and India with the latter of which its boundaries march for about 200 miles. It is bounded on the east by the lands of the Abors and the Mishmis and on the west by Sikkim. It is a mountainous country which is naturally divided into three tracts: the southern which is contiguous to India is mountainous and has got heavy rainfall; the central which is the region of valleys where rainfall is moderate and cultivation is possible, and where dwell the main body of the inhabitants;

and the northern which is full of mountains, some rising to 24,000 ft. and is neither cultivated nor populated. Bhutan is drained by many rivers of which the Manas, the Torsa and the Sankosh are well known to the Indians. It is rich in valuable timber and is the home of wild animals like elephant, rhino, tiger, leopard and bison.

The name Bhutan is a contraction of the Indian term *Bhotanta* meaning the end of Bhot, i.e. Tibet. The majority of the people called Bhotias are of Tibetan origin and they profess a form of Buddhism which is largely similar to the Lamaism of Tibet. As in Tibet the priests in Bhutan are called Lamas, are believed to possess supernatural powers and are looked upon by the people with dread and reverence. Bhutan has a feudalistic society, all temporal power being in the possession of nine chiefs (*penlops*) who live in forty-five residences called *Jongs* and maintain armed retainers. There is a Maharaja at the head of the state who was in theory elected by a Council but was in practice merely the nominee of the most powerful of the *penlops*. In 1907 kingship in Bhutan became hereditary in the family of the *penlop* of west Bhutan.

Little is known about the early history of Bhutan. Some princes of Indian origin are said to have ruled in Bhutan till the 9th century A.D. when they were driven out by the Tibetans. No Indo-Muslim sovereign is known to have ruled over Bhutan. Its relations with British India began in 1772 when a Bhutanese army invaded Cooch-Behar and took the Raja away as a captive. Warren Hastings, who was then the Governor-General, sent a force which drove away the invaders and a treaty of peace was made in 1774. Warren Hastings sent George Bogle in 1774 and Samuel Torner shortly afterwards as emissaries to Bhutan for promoting mutual commerce. But both of them failed. After the annexation of Assam in 1826 closer contact came to be established. Capt. Robert Pemberton's mission having failed to persuade Bhutan to surrender the Duars in Darrang district which Bhutan had illegally occupied, the Assam Duars were annexed in 1841 and the British Government agreed to pay Bhutan an annual subsidy of Rs. 1000 so long as the peace was kept. But Bhutanese raids continued and in 1863 the Bhutan Government treated very badly Sir Ashley Eden who had gone to Bhutan as a British envoy. Consequently a British army invaded Bhutan in 1865 and though it was at first defeated by the Bhutanese at the battle of Dewangiri it ultimately defeated the Bhutanese and compelled them to make peace by ceding all the Duars of Bengal and Assam and to maintain peace in consideration of an annual subsidy. Henceforth relations between Bhutan and India grew closer and in 1910 it was further agreed that the Bhutan Government would be guided by the advice of the British Indian Government in regard to its external relations, while the latter would not interfere in the internal administration of Bhutan. The annual allowance was raised to Rs. 100,000. Soon after the conclusion of this treaty the Chinese Government formally claimed Bhutan as a feudatory, but the Indo-British Government informed China that Bhutan was independent of China and that its external relations were under the Indo-British Government, which would not tolerate any interference in Bhutan by China. After India attained independence, she entered into a fresh treaty with Bhutan by which her annual subsidy was raised to Rs. 500,000, and the territory known as Dewangiri was ceded to Bhutan which in its turn continued to agree to allow its foreign relations to be guided by the advice of India. (Ronaldshay, *Lands of the Thunderbolt* & Ball, Sir Charles, *Tibet, Past and Present*)

Bhutivarman—also called Mahabhutivarman or Bhutavarman, an early king of Kamarupa belonging to the dynasty founded by Pushyavarman, ruled in the middle of the 6th century A.D., and, according to the Baḍaganga Rock Inscription which is said to bear a date in the Gupta era corresponding to A.D. 554, he performed the *Asvamedha* sacrifice. This shows that he discarded the earlier suzerainty of the Guptas. He also made land grants to a large number of Brahmans in the Chandrapuri Visaya, near the river Kausiki, which were later on renewed by his illustrious successor, King Bhaskaravarman. (*J.R.A.S.*, VIII, pp. 138-39 & X, pp. 64-67; Bhattacharya, *Kamarupa-Shasanavali*, p. 27)

Bhubaneswara—ancient city in Orissa, and now its capital, contains some excellant specimens of early Orissan art, e.g. the Lingaraja and the Rajarani temples built by the kings of Kara or Kesari dynasty. (Banerji, R. D., *History of Orissa*, Vol. I)

Beas, the—is a tributary of the Indus. Its Sanskrit name is Bipasa from which is derived 'Beas'. The classical writers called it Hypasis. It merges itself into the Sutlej or Satadru near Lahore. It marked the furthest easternmost point of the advance into India of Alexander the Great.

Bibigarh—was a building at Cawnpur where during the course of the Sepoy Mutiny in 1857 two hundred and eleven British women and children who had surrendered on the 27th June, were kept confined and were put to death on the 15th July by orders of Nana Shahib (*q.v.*) and Tantia Topi, and their bodies were flung into a nearby well. It was an act of reprisal for the earlier repressive measures taken by the British at Benares and Allahabad and led in its turn to the British armies perpetrating barbarous atrocities on the Indians.

Bidar—an old city in the Deccan, not far from the modern city of Hyderabad, was within the ancient Hindu kingdom of Warangal. It was first overrun by Ala-ud-din Khalji and later on annexed to the Delhi sultanate by Juna Khan during the reign of his father, Sultan Ghiyas-ud-din Tughluq. With the formation of the Bahmani kingdom in 1347 Bidar formed a part of the Bahmani kingdom and became its capital during the reign of the ninth Sultan Ahmad Shah (1422-35) and continued to be so until the disintegration and dissolution of the Bahmani kingdom in 1492 when it became the headquarters of the kingdom bearing the same name, founded by Kasim Barid. In 1565 it joined in a coalition with Bijapur, Ahmadnagar and Golkunda against Vijayanagar and shared in the great victory of Talikota. But in 1619 it was itself annexed to Bijapur and ceased to have an independent existence. Ruins of some noteworthy buildings erected by the Barid Shahi sultans are still to be found at Bidar. (Meadows Taylor, *Manual of Indian History*)

Bihar—is the modern name of the state situated between West Bengal on the east and Uttar Pradesh on the west. It comprises the area included in the ancient kingdoms of Anga (Bhagalpur division in east Bihar), Vriji (Tirhut division in north Bihar), and Magadha (Patna and Gaya districts in south Bihar). In course of time Anga and Vriji were merged in Magadha (*q. v.*) which continued to be the name of the modern state of Bihar until the close of the twelfth century when Magadha was overrun by the Muhammadans and annexed to the Delhi sultanate by Ikhtiyar-ud-din Muhammad, son of Bakhtiyar Khalji. The invading Muhammadans took for forts the Buddhist *viharas* (monasteries) with which the province was then studded and came to call it by the new name of Bihar. It formed a *subah* or province in Akbar's empire. It was, however, annexed to the *subah* of Bengal in about 1719 when Murshid Kuli Khan was the subadar of Bengal. Thus began the administrative union of Bihar with Bengal which lasted till 1911 when Bihar with Orissa was constituted into a separate province to be administered by a Governor. It continues to be a separate important state within the Indian Union, though Orissa has been recently separated from it. It is an important state, having an area of 70,368 square miles and a population of 4,02,18,916 according to the census of 1951. It has many towns of which its capital Patna carries the memories of the ancient city of Pataliputra and Jamshedpur-Tatanagar is the home of the modern steel and iron industry. The Ganges flows through it, dividing it into two parts. It is rich in agricultural products like rice, wheat, maize, sugar-cane, tobacco and oil-seeds as well as in minerals like coal, iron and mica. As industrialisation progresses in India Bihar is sure to make great advance as it has rich supplies of coal and iron and more power will be available as the result of the harnessing of its many rivers for the double purpose of flood control and the supply of electricity. Bihar which was the home of Asoka (*q.v.*), the greatest of the ancient Indian emperors, is also the home of Rajendra Prasad (*q.v.*), the first President of the Independent Republic of India. (*Imperial Gazetteer, Bihar*)

Bihari Lal—next to Tulasi Das, the most eminent Hindi poet of the seventeenth century, completed his *Satsai* in 1662.

Bihari Mall—Raja of Amber, was a realist in politics. He was one of the earliest of the Rajput rulers of Rajputana to appreciate the futility of the policy of opposition to the Mughuls and he submitted to Babur and, on his death, to his son Humayun. In 1555 he was presented to Akbar and was well received. In 1561 Raja Bihari Mall was attacked by the *jaigirdar* of Ajmer and reduced to great straits and his son was taken as a hostage. To escape complete destruction Bihari Mall submitted to Emperor Akbar and cemented the friendship by giving a daughter in marriage to Akbar. This marriage proved very happy and the princess became the mother of Akbar's eldest son, Jahangir. Raja Bihari Mall with his son Bhagwan Das and his grandson, by adoption, Raja Man Singh, entered into the service of Emperor Akbar and were all given high ranks in the army. Raja Bihari Mall's policy thus saved Amber (Jaipur) from the loss and depredations that antagonism to the Mughuls would have involved and made Jaipur the richest state in Rajaputana.

Bijapur—is the name of a kingdom as well as of its capital city. It was the most important of the five sultanates into which the Bahmani kingdom broke up towards the close of the fifteenth century. It was the southernmost of the five sultanates and the city stood in the doab between the Bhima and the Krishna not far from the fort of Raichur. The sultanate was founded by Yusuf Adil Shah, who was originally a slave but had risen by his merit to be the governor of Bijapur under the Bahmani sultans, but who in 1489 declared his independence and started

Bijapur on its career as a separate state under the Adil Shahi dynasty. It had nine kings, viz. Yusuf (1490-1510), Ismail (1510-34), Mallu (1534-35), Ibrahim I (1535-57), Ali (1557-80), Ibrahim II (1580-1626), Muhammad (1626-56), Ali II (1656-73) and Sikandar (1673-88). It had to fight at first with its neighbours, expecially with the Hindu kingdom of Vijayanagar. The port of Goa which was situated within the kingdom of Bijapur passed into Portuguese possession in 1510. In 1536 Bidar, Ahmadnagar and Golkunda made a combined attack on Bijapur but were repulsed. As a retaliatory measure in 1558 Bijapur entered into an alliance with Vijayanagar and the combined armies plundered Ahmadnagar. But six years later Bijapur combined with Bidar, Ahmadnagar and Golkunda against Vijayanagar and decisively defeated the latter in the battle of Talikota (1565) which led to the destruction of Vijayanagar. Thus the Hindu rival was eliminated, but the efforts of the Bijapur sultan who was helped by Ahmadnagar, the Zamorin of Calicut and the Raja of Achin to recover Goa by driving out the Portuguese from it in 1570 failed. In the seventeenth century Bijapur confronted two enemies—the Mughul emperor who advanced from the north and the rising power of the Marathas under Shivaji (*q.v.*). The seventh sultan purchased peace with Emperor Shah Jahan by agreeing to pay him an annual tribute (1636), but neither he nor his successor could suppress Shivaji whose growth and advancement largely weakened Bijapur. Finally in 1686 under the ninth Adil Shahi sultan Sikandar (1673-81) Bijapur was forced to surrender to the Mughul Emperor Aurangzeb after a siege of eighteen months. Sultan Sikandar was made a captive and sent to prison where he died fifteen years later. With his fall the independent existence of Bijapur also ended.

The founder of the Bijapur sultanate publicly professed shiaism which continued to be the state form of worship till the reign of the fourth sultan Ibrahim I (1535-57) who returned to sunnism. But his son and successor Ali (1557-80) resumed the shia creed. The Adil Shahi sultans were generally tolerant. Yusuf Adil Shah married a Maratha lady who became the mother of his son and successor, Ismail Adil Shah. Hindus were appointed to offices of trust and Marathi was used for keeping state accounts and internal correspondence. The Adil Shahi sultans were patrons of art and literature. The famous historian, Muhammad Qasim, surnamed Firishta, lived and wrote under the patronage of the sixth sultan Ibrahim II (1580-1626).

Bijapur had also a fine library of books some of which are still to be found in the British Museum. Bijapur also developed a fine school of art and architecture which was marked by a grandeur of conception and boldness in construction unequalled by any edifices erected in India. Sultans Yusuf, Ali, Ibrahim II and Muhammad Shah were all great builders. The gigantic walls of the city, six and a quarter miles in circumference, the principal mosque at Bijapur which can accommodate 5000 worshippers, the audience hall known as the Gagan Mahall, the tomb of Ibrahim II and the mausoleum of Muhammad Shah which has the second largest dome in the world, are some of the surviving monuments of the past grandeur of Bijapur. (Sewell, *A Forgotten Empire;* Meadows Taylor, *Manual of the History of India;* Henry Cousins, *Bijapur and its Architectural Remains, with an Historical Outline of the Adil Shahi Dynasty*)

Bijjala Kalachurya—a rebel against the Chalukya kings of Kalyani, succeeded, with the help of his sons, to oust the Chalukya dynasty and to occupy the throne of Kalyani in south India from 1156 to 1167 when he abdicated. Bijjala founded the Kalachurya dynasty and was a patron of Jainism. His Brahman minister, Vasava, founded the Lingayet or Vira Saiva sect.

Bikaner—is a town and state in Rajputana. It is now a part of the Rajasthan Union of the Republic of India. It was established by a Rathor Chief named 'Bika', is only 250 miles from Delhi and is on the precincts of the Thar desert. It submitted to the Mughul Emperor Akbar in 1570 and continued to be a part of the Mughul empire till 1818 when it entered into a subordinate alliance with the British Indian Government. Bikaner is famous for its camels and during the first World War the Maharaja of Bikaner organised the Bikaner Camel Corps which rendered important service in Somaliland. The Maharaja of Bikaner was rewarded with the status of an Indian representative in the League of Nations, and was an important member of the Chamber of Princes when it was formed. After independence Bikaner merged with the Indian Union.

Bilgrami, Syed Hussain—was the Director of Public Instruction in the Nizam's Dominions. He was one of the only two Indian members (the other being Sir Gurudas Banerjee) of the Education Commission appointed by Lord Curzon in 1902. He was also one of the first two Indians (the other being Sir K. G. Gupta) to be appointed as Members of the India Council by the Secretary of State, Lord Morley.

Bilhana—was born in Kashmir. He became the court poet of the

Chalukya king Vikramaditya VI (1076-1127) of Kalyan and commemorated the exploits of his patron in war and chas in his *Vikramanka-charita*. The book was discovered by Buhle in a Jain library and was edited by him.

Bilhapur, battle of—was fought on 1st April, 1731, between Peshwa Baji Rao I and his rival Trimbak Rao Dhabade, th hereditary *senapati* or commander-in-chief of the Marath kingdom. Dhabade, who was backed by the Kolhapur Raj an by the Nizam-ul-Mulk, was defeated and killed in this battle This victory of Baji Rao I left him without a rival in the Marath state and thus made the Peshwa its practical ruler.

Bimbisara—was the king of Magadha and was the founder of th greatness of Magadha which he started on its victorious caree by conquering and annexing Anga (east Bihar), by enterin into matrimonial alliances with Koshala and Vaisali and b building a new capital at Rajagriha, the modern Rajgir in th Patna district. Under him Magadha became a flourishin kingdom. Both Vardhamana Mahavira, the last apostle of th Jains, and Gautama Buddha, the founder of Buddhism, wer his contemporaries. According to a Ceylonese tradition Bimbisar was anointed king sixty years before the death of Gautam Buddha which is believed by many to have taken place in 486 B.C According to this reckoning Bimbisara ascended the throne i about 546 B.C. Tradition affirms that in his old age he wa murdered by his son and successor, Ajatasatru. According t the Puranas Bimbisara was the fifth king of the Saisunag dynasty (*q.v.*) but according to the Ceylonese chronicles an the testimony of Asvaghosha, Bimbisara belonged to an earlie dynasty known as the Haryanka dynasty (*q.v.*). At any rat Bimbisara was the first great king of Magadha. (*P.H.A.I* pp. 115 ff; *O.H.*, p. 72)

Bindusara—the second Maurya emperor (*c*. 300 B.C. - 273 B.C. was the son and successor of Chandragupta Maurya, the founde of the Maurya dynasty. Very little is known about his activitie The fact that he bore the title of *Amitraghata* suggests that h slayed many enemies and that the Deccan, excluding Kaling: was perhaps added to the Maurya empire during his reign. H maintained friendly relations with the Hellenic kingdoms to th west of his empire and received a Greek ambassador name Deimachos. He was succeeded by his famous son Asoka.

Bir Narayan—was the king of Gondwana. At the time of Akbar invasion of the country Bir Narayan was a minor and th invaders were first opposed by his valiant mother Rani Durga vati. After her defeat and death in war Bir Narayan, though a minor, continued the war against the Mughul invaders till he lost his life in battle.

Bir Singh Bundela—the chief of the Bundelas, murdered at the instigation of Prince Salim in 1602 Akbar's trusted friend and councillor Abul Fazl, whom the Prince hated and feared. Later on, after Salim's accession to the throne as Emperor Jahangir, Bir Singh got as his reward a mansabdari of 3000 horse. Later on Bir Singh built the magnificent temple of Kesava Deva at Mathura at a cost of 33 lakhs of rupees. He was succeeded to his estate by his son Jujhar Singh, but his temple at Mathura which was so high that its top could be seen from the imperial fort at Agra, roused the fanatical hostility of Aurangzeb by whose order it was levelled to the ground in 1670.

Birbal, Raja—a Rajput chief, voluntarily entered into the service of Emperor Akbar (1556-1605), rose high in his favour and was given the title of Raja. But Birbal was more a poet who wrote in Hindi than a general and was honoured by Akbar with the title of Kavi Priya. He was defeated and killed in 1586 when leading a Mughul army against the Yusufzi tribe on the north-western frontier.

Bird, R. M.—an officer in the employment of the British Indian Government, was placed in charge of the land-revenue settlement of the North-West Provinces during the administration of Lord William Bentinck. He took ten years (1830-40) to complete the work and gave the province a semi-permanent settlement known as the *mahalwari* system, as opposed to the permanent zamindari settlement (*q.v.*) introduced in Bengal during the administration of Lord Cornwallis.

Birkenhead, Lord—(1872-1930) was a very successful English lawyer and statesman. He was a member of the Parliament from 1906-19 when he was raised to the peerage. He was Attorney-General from 1915-19, Lord Chancellor from 1919-22 and Secretary of State for India from 1924-28. He was a politician of liberal views, but he incurred much obloquy with the Indians by appointing the all British Simon Commission (*q.v.*) in 1927 to enquire into the working of the Government of India Act, 1919.

Bishan Das—a Hindu painter of repute, enjoyed the patronage of Emperor Jahangir (1603-27).

Bishannath, temple of—*see* Viswanath.

Bisnaga—is the name applied to Vijayanagar by the Portuguese traveller, Fernao Nuniz who visited the kingdom in 1535.

Biswa Singh—was the founder of the Koch kingdom with moder॒ Cooch Behar as his capital in about 1515. The line of king॒ founded by him in Cooch Behar lasted till modern times. (Gait *History of Assam,* Ch. iv)

Bithal Das—son of the famous Vaishnava saint, Vallabhacharyॱ (born 1479) was not only his father's successor to the headshiॿ of the sect founded by him, but was also a reputed Hindi autho॒ who wrote the *Chaurasi Vaishnava ki-varta.*

Bithur—a small township near Cawnpur in Uttara Pradesh wherॱ the last Peshwa Baji Rao II retired after his defeat at the hand of the English in 1818 on a pension of eight lakhs of rupees ॱ year and where he lived till his death in 1853. Thereafteॸ Bithur continued to be the residence of Nana Shahib, the son oॸ Peshwa Baji Rao II and it was at Bithur that, on the outbreaॿ of the Mutiny in 1857, Nana Shahib (*q.v.*) proclaimeॸ himself as Peshwa and held his court till his defeat anॸ escape.

Bitikchi, the—was the official in charge of the accounts of a *subah* o province during the Mughul administration.

Bittiga or Bittideva—*see* under Vishnuvardhana.

Biyana—in Central India, not very far from Agra, was the seat of ॱ Muslim feudatory and had a fort which made its possession aॸ important acquisition in the medieval struggles for the thronॱ of Delhi. The neighbouring country produced the best quality of indigo and therefore attracted the early attention of thॱ English traders in India.

Black Hole—was the name of a small room, 18 feet by 14 feeॸ 10 inches, in the old Fort William in Calcutta. On June 20ॸ 1756, Nawab Siraj-ud-daulah (*q.v.*) captured the Fort. ॱ number of English was made prisoners. According to V. Z Holwell, who had been in charge of the defence of the Fort, thॸ number of English prisoners was 146 who were all kept confineॿ during the night in the Black Hole of the Fort and as a resuॿ of suffocation 123 of the prisoners died during the night. I was considered an act of horrible atrocity for which Nawaॿ Siraj-ud-daula was held responsible. The truth of this storॺ has been doubted on good grounds and it might not have takeॸ place at all. At any rate Siraj-ud-daula was not in any waॺ responsible for it. (Mill, *Hist. of India*, with Wilson's notes, Voॿ III, ed 1858: Maitra, A. K., *Siraj-ud-daulah* in Bengali; Littlॱ C., *The Black Hole Tragedy*)

Blackett, Sir Basil—was the Finance Member of the Viceroyॺ Executive Council during the administration of Lord Irwiॸ

(1926-31). Sir Basil stabilsed the Indian rupee at 1s.6d. and thus earned much odium with the Indian people.

Blavatsky, Madame Helena Petravna—(1831-91) was a Russian lady of very great talents. She developed a great admiration for the ancient spiritualism of India and founded in 1875 the Theosophical Society. In 1879 she came to India and set up the Society's headquarters at Adyar near Madras. The more important of her publications are *Isis Unveiled, Secret Doctrine* and *The Voice of Silence.* (Cleather, A. P., *H. P. Blavatsky—herself*)

Board of Control, the—was formed as a measure for increasing the control of the British Crown on the administration of the East India Company in India by Pitt's India Act of 1784. It consisted of six unpaid Privy Councillors, one of whom was the President with a casting vote. The Board had no patronage and did not interfere in commercial matters, but it had power to superintend, direct and control all acts relating to the civil or military Government or the revenues of India. Despatches from the Court of Directors to the East India Company's officers in India were subject to the approval of the Board which also could send its own orders without the consent of the Directors. The first President of the Board of Control was Henry Dundas, a friend of Pitt and a member of his Cabinet. The diligence and intelligence of Dundas soon transformed the post of the President virtually to that of the Secretary of State for India, and, as years passed, the extent of the authority exercised by the Board of Control over the administration of India greatly increased. After the Mutiny when the Government of India was transferred to the British Crown by the Government of India Act, 1858, the Board of Control as such was abolished. Its President became the Secretary of State for India and the Board was merged in the India Council of the Secretary of State for India. Lord Ellenborough was the last President of the Board of Control. (Ilbert, Sir C., *Government of India*; Keith, B., *Constitutional History of India*)

Board of Revenue, the—was set up in Calcutta by Warren Hastings in 1772 when the East India Company stood forth as the *Diwan* and the posts of the two Deputy Naib Diwans were abolished. At first the Governor and his Council acted as the Board of Revenue, but in 1787 it was reconstituted with a member of the Council as the President and some senior officers of the Company as members. Lord Cornwallis appointed Sir John Shore as the President of the Board of Revenue and entrusted it with the task of reporting on the advisability of introducing a long-term system of land revenue settlement in Bengal. Though Shore was opposed to a permanent settlement Lord Cornwallis introduced the Permanent System of Land Revenue in Bengal. This step increased the work of the Board of Revenue in Calcutta and it continued to function with a very senior official as its head. He came to bear the designation of Member and was next in importance to an Executive Councillor of the Provincial Government. The Board of Revenue still continues to function with a senior official as its head and is mainly concerned with revenue matters.

Board of Trade, the—was a body consisting of the senior officers of the East India Company who controlled, along with the administration of the country, the commercial transactions of the East India Company. They were all interested in private trade and it was with their direct or indrect support that all the employees of the East India Company joined in private trade to the great economic loss of the country as well as of the East India Company. One of the first tasks of Lord Cornwallis was to purify it. This he did first by removing from it the corrupt members and then by reconstituting it with men who were not to have any share in the administration. Thus the Board of Trade only looked after the commercial transactions of the East India Company. It gradually lost its importance as the trading rights of the Company were limited and was ultimately abolished with the abolition of the East India Company as a trading body in 1833.

Bodawpaya—king of Burma (1779-1819), added to his dominions Arakan in 1785 and Manipur in 1813 and overran Assam in 1816. Then Bodawpaya demanded that the British Indian Government should surrender to him Chittagong, Dacca and Murshidabad. But a defeat at the hands of the Siamese chastened the Burmese king who himself died in 1819. Lord Hastings who was then the Governor-General returned the letter to the Burmese king with the comment that it was perhaps a forgery. Thus the Anglo-Burmese conflict was averted for the time being.

Bodh-Gaya—six miles to the south of the modern city of Gaya in Bihar, stands on the Nairanjana. Here under the famous Bo-tree Gautama is said to have received *buddhi* or enlightenment and thus became the Buddha. It is a holy place of the Buddhists. According to Rock Edict VIII Asoka visited the place in the tenth year after his coronation and thus began to substitute *dharma-yatras* (tours of piety) for the *vihara-yatras* (tours of pleasure) of which the previous kings were fond. Asoka also built a monastery at Bodh Gaya which became a place of pilgrimage for the Buddhists and attracted them even from outside India. During the reign of Samudragupta (*c.* A.D. 335-75) a monastery was built at Bodh-Gaya by Meghavarna, the king of Ceylon, with the permission of the Gupta Emperor. But early in the fifth century Fa-hien who visited India during the years A.D. 405-11, found the place surrounded by jungles. Further disaster overtook the place early in the seventh century when Sasanka, the king of Gauḍa or central Bengal urged by his animosity to the Buddhists, dug up and burnt the holy Bodhi tree which had been receiving the veneration of the Buddhists for centuries. The tree was later on re-planted, according to Hiuen-Tsang, by Purnavarman, a local Raja of Magadha who is described as the last descendant of Asoka. The place is now well-preserved, has got a good rest-house and still continues to attract pilgrims from all over the Buddhist world (*E.H.I.*, pp. 303, 316, 367)

Bodhi-sattva—is a conception of the Mahayana school of the Buddhists. Buddhist *arhats* or saints who have qualified themselves to attain Buddhahood in this life, voluntarily forego that state in order to help all their fellowmen to attain that happy state. Such persons are called Bodhi-sattvas and came to receive the same kind of veneration, respect and worship as the Buddha himself. (Elliott, Sir C., *Hinduism and Buddhism*)

Boghaz Kaui—is a site in Asia Minor, where important archaeological finds have been made. Inscriptions found at Boghaz Kaui which have been assigned to the fourteenth century B.C. contain references to kings who bore Aryan names (e.g. Dasaratha, Artatama) and invoked Aryan gods (e.g. Indra, Varuna and the Nasatyas) to witness and safeguard treaties. Boghaz Kaui, therefore, helps in suggesting the routes of the migrations of the Aryans. (Hall, *Hist. of Egypt*)

Bogle, George—an officer under the East India Company in Bengal, was sent in 1774 by Warren Hastings, the Governor-General, on what was the first English mission to Tibet for obtaining trade facilities. He had little success.

Boigne, Benoit de—a Savoyard soldier of fortune, was employed by Mahadaji Sindhia for the purpose of reorganising Sindhia's army on European methods. Benoit de Boigne did it so effectively that Sindhia's army became superior to the armies of his Indian rivals and under his leadership it severely defeated Holkar's army in the battle of Lakheri near Ajmer in

1793. Soon after Mahadaji Sindhia died (February, 1794) and de Boigne retired from his service.

Bolan Pass, the—connects the plains of Sind with the plateaus of Kalat and Qandahar in Afghanistan. Its control and possession was one of the many considerations that influenced Anglo-Afghan relations in the nineteenth century.

Bombay—is the name of an Indian state as well as of its capital. The city port is situated at 18.53 N. lat. and 72.54 E. long. on the Arabian Sea and has a magnificent natural harbour, but before the English occupation and development it was of no importance as it was cut off from the interior of India by creeks, swamps and mountains. The site of the present city and port along with adjacent territories were occupied by the Portuguese general Albuquerque in 1510. In 1661 it was ceded by the Portuguese to the English as part of the dowry of the Portuguese Princess, Catharine of Braganza, on the occasion of her marriage with Charles II of England. It continued to be so unpromising a possession that in 1668 King Charles II transferred it to the East India Company at an annual rental of £ 10 only. Due to the efforts of Gerald Aungier who was its Governor from 1669 to 1677, Bombay began to develop and soon became so prosperous that in 1687 it superseded Surat as the chief settlement of the English in the East. The Regulating Act (*q.v.*) (1773) placed the Bombay Presidency under the general control of the Governor-General and Council of Bengal and Bombay never became the seat of the Central Government in India. But its importance grew with the expansion of British dominions and the Presidency of Bombay came to include the upper part of the whole of the western coast of India including Sind as well as Malwa and Gujarat. The city's wealth increased; the port was developed and new docks were built. With the construction of the Bombay-Baroda and Central India Railway line in 1864 and the opening of the Suez Canal in 1869 it became the first calling station in India for ships coming from Europe to the East and earned the title of being the 'Gateway to India'. It also became an important manufacturing centre, especially for textiles. It became the home of the rich Parsee community which has contributed much to its wealth and prosperity. The first session of the Indian National Congress met in Bombay in 1885 and Bombay played an important part in the Indian national struggle for independence. Sind was separated from it in 1935. Very recently the state of Bombay was divided into two states on linguistic grounds, one being Maharashtra with

Bombay as its capital and the other being Saurashtra with Ahamedabad as the capital. (Hunter, Sir W., *Imp. Gazetteer*, Vol. VII; Edwardes, S. M., *The Rise of Bombay* & Sheppard, *Bombay, 1932*)

Bombay-Burma Trading Corporation—an English trading Company, did timber business in Upper Assam. In 1884 the Company was accused by the Government of Burma, then ruled by king Thibaw, of various charges and condemned to pay a fine of £ 230,000. Relations between the British Indian Government and Burma were already strained and the rejection by the Burma Government of the demand of the British Government that the matter of the Bombay-Burma Trading Corporation should be submitted to the arbitration of the Viceroy, was made an ostensible cause of the third Burmese War (1885-86) leading to the annexation of Upper Burma.

Bombay Plague Crisis, the—took place in 1897 when there was a serious outbreak of bubonic plague in the cities of Bombay and Poona. The terrified Government took unnecessary and ex-extremely stringent measures for segregating not only persons attacked with the plague, but also persons who were suspected of having been infected. These measures were most harshly applied by Mr. W. C. Rand, the Plague Commissioner, and his Assistant, Mr. Lewis. Their conduct came in for severe condemnation by Bal Gangadhar Tilak in his journal *Kesari*, who praised the Government efforts for checking the epidemic but asked for abandoning all harshness in their application. Soon afterwards Mr. Rand and his companion Lieut. Ayerst were shot dead by unknown assailants. Tilak was prosecuted on a charge of creating disaffection, condemned and sentenced to a term of imprisonment. The Bombay Plague Crisis thus brought Tilak into prominence.

Bonnerjea, W. C.—*see* under Banerjea, W. C.

Boonc, Charles—Governor of Bombay (1715-22), built a wall round the city of Bombay and increased the number of the armed ships of the Company stationed at the port in order to strengthen the defences of its factories and trade.

Bopadeva—a famous Sanskrit grammarian, flourished under the later Yadavas of Devagiri (*q.v.*). His work known as *Mugdhabodha* is considered to be a standard work on Sanskrit grammar.

Boscawen, Admiral Edward—came with a large squadron of fleet in June 1748 to avenge the capture of Madras by the French. Boscawen besieged Pondicherry, but conducted the operations with so little skill that Pondicherry resisted the besiegers till the arrival of the monsoon when he was compelled to raise the siege. On the conclusion of the war by the treaty of Aix-la-Chapelle in 1748 Boscawen sailed back with his fleet to England.

Bose, Ananda Mohan (1847-1906)—was a prominent Indian public man in his times. Born of a middle-class Hindu Bengali family in the district of Mymensingh he was educated at Presidency College, Calcutta, graduating with a First Class First in Mathematics in 1867, won the Premchand Roychand Scholarship and was the first Indian to be a Wrangler of Cambridge University in 1873. In 1874 he was called to the Bar and on his return to India he devoted his versatile genius to the service of his country till the end of his life as a politician, educationist and religious reformer. He was the first founder-Secretary of the Indian Association which was established in Calcutta in 1876 and took a prominent part in convening the first session of the Indian National Conference in Calcutta in 1883 and thus showed the way to the organisation of the Indian National Congress which had its first session in 1885. He was a prominent Congressman all his life and presided over its fourteenth session held in Madras in 1898. He was closely associated with the Anti-Partition movement in Bengal and was one of the earliest to suggest the *Swadeshi* movement which aimed at developing and promoting indigenous industries to the exclusion of foreign products. His last public act was the laying of the foundation stone of the Federation Hall in Calcutta on October 16, 1905, just a few months before his death. He encouraged the expansion of education in his country and City College in Calcutta and Ananda Mohan College at Mymensingh still bear witness to his work as an educationist. He was supremely religious minded and was a rationalist in his outlook. Early in his life he accepted Brahmaism, took a prominent part in the development of the Brahma movement in Bengal and was the first President of the Sadharan Brahma Samaj which owes its democratic organisation to him. (Sarkar, H. C., *A Life of Ananda Mohan Bose*)

Bose, Sir Jagadish Chandra (1858-1937)—renowned Indian scientist, plant physiologist and physicist, was born in the district of Dacca in Bengal, was educated at St. Xavier's College, Calcutta and Cambridge University, where he gained high honours in 1884. He was awarded D. Sc. of Cambridge University in 1896, was Professor of Physical Sciences at Presidency College, Calcutta, from 1885 to 1915 and founded in 1917 the

Bose Research Institute in Calcutta of which he was the Director till his death in 1937.

He was a pioneer amongst the Indian scientists and had to work against great odds. He made great contributions to physical science by his work on electrical radiation and still more important contributions in the field of animal and plant physiology. He introduced new experimental methods and devised new apparatus for demonstrating the effects of sleep, air, food and drugs on plants and showed how there is a parallelism between the responses of plant and animal tissues. He was a voluminous writer and the more important of his works are: *Response in the Living and the Non-Living* (1902); *Plant Responses* (1906) and *Motor Mechanism of Plants* (1928). (Geddes, P., *The Life and Work of Sir Jagdis C. Bose* and *Sir J. C. Bose*)

Bose, Subhas Chandra—popularly known as Netaji, was born on January 23, 1897, at Cuttack in Orissa of respectable middle-class Bengali parents. He passed the B.A. Examination in 1919, went to England, competed in the Indian Civil Service Examination in 1920, standing fourth in order of merit, but resigned from the I.C.S. and on his return to India in 1921 joined the Indian National Congress under the inspiration of Chitta Ranjan Das (*q.v.*) and Mahatma Gandhi. Thereafter began his political career in India which was one of prolonged fight with the British for the freedom of India. He was first put into prison for six months in December, 1921, and, thereafter, he was imprisoned eleven times. He showed great organising capacity as the Executive Officer of the Calcutta Corporation in 1924. From October, 1924 to May 16, 1927 he was detained in Mandalay under the new Bengal Ordinance. He was opposed to the moderates of the Congress and as early as 1928 he opposed in the Subjects Committee of the Congress held in Calcutta the Dominion Status resolution. He was vehemently opposed to the continuance of British rule in India in any form and the British Government incarcerated him in many ways all his life. In 1938 he was the President of the Indian National Congress at its Haripura session and in 1939 he was elected President of the Tripuri session of the Indian National Congress in spite of the open opposition of Mahatma Gandhi. He presided over the session and in his Presidential Address he suggested that the national demand for independence should be submitted to the British Government with a time-limit and failure of the latter to comply should be met with sanctions like Civil Disobedience and *Satyagraha*. But the persistent opposition of the majority of the members of the Working Committee who were staunch supporters of Mahatma Gandhi, obliged him to resign the office of the Congress President in April, 1939. Thereafter he became engaged in a twofold conflict with the British Indian Government which he wanted to overthrow by all means on the one hand and with the 'non-violence' party of Mahatma Gandhi to which he refused to be wedded as a principle, and not as a means. The Second World War was then in full swing and Subhas Chandra believed that India should take the fullest advantage of the international situation and secure the armed help of the enemies of England on terms honourable to India. Naturally the British Government looked upon him as "most dangerous" and placed him under orders of detention in his own home under strict police guard. But Subhas Chandra jumped his home-internment on January 26, 1941, made his way overland to Kabul and then to Germany. Next year a conference of Indians in South East Asia invited him to take charge of the Indian National Army and of the Indian Independence League which were then being organised there. Accordingly in 1943, Subhas Chandra went by a submarine from Germany to Singapore which had been in the meantime vacated by the English army. He immediately organised the Indian troops that had been left in the Malay Peninsula by the retreating English, into what came to be known as the Indian National Army. On October 21, 1943 he issued his famous proclamation constituting the Provisional Government of India and soon afterwards led the I.N.A. on the Burma front to recover the independence of India by attacking the British India Government from the eastern side. He advanced as far as Kohima in Manipur, but deficiency of supplies in arms and ammunitions, especially the lack of aeroplanes, obliged him to withdraw from the Manipur front in 1944. In the meantime Japan had been defeated and was no longer in a position to help Subhas Chandra in any way. He was, therefore, obliged to take a plane from Singapore to Japan but his plane crashed at Thaihoku and Subhas Chandra, whom his followers and admiring countrymen had come to call by the honoured name of Netaji, perished on August 18, 1945. His stormy life had not been in vain; he had enthused his countrymen with a desire and determination for driving out the English from India and for recovering India's independence which they did in 1947. (Bose, Subhas Chandra, *Autobiography*; Saggi, P. D., *Life and Work of Netaji Subhas Chandra Bose*)

Brahma—a Hindu deity, forms along with Vishnu and Siva, the Hindu Trinity. He is the creator and is mentioned in the Vedas as *Vidhatri* (the Ordainer), *Hiranyagarbha* (the Germ of Gold) and *Prajapati* (the Lord of creatures). He is to be distinguished from the Brahman (*q.v.*).

Brahman, the—also called Paramatman, is the name given by Brahmanical philosophers to the Universal Soul or the Absolute "that dwelleth in every thing, that guideth all beings within, the Inward Guide Immortal". The conception of the *Brahman* is discussed in the *Upanishadas* (*q.v.*) and in the *Vedanta* (*q.v.*) and amplified in the works of Sankaracharya (*q.v.*).

Brahmapala—the founder of the Pala dynasty of kings of Kamarupa, flourished about A.D. 1000. On the extinction of the Salastambha dynasty Brahmapala, who was related to the Salastambha dynasty, was chosen by the people on account of his fitness as the king of Kamarupa. There were eight kings of his dynasty, all bearing names ending with the suffix 'Pala'. They should be distinguished from the contemporary Pala kings of Bengal. The dynasty of Brahmapala came to an end in the first half of the twelfth century A.D. (Barua, B. K., *A Cultural History of Assam*, pp. 33-35)

Brahmajit Gaur—was a Hindu general in the service of Sher Shah (1530-45).

Brahma Movement—had its origin in the Brahma Sabha (*q.v.*) started by Raja Ram Mohan Roy in 1828. It organised the Brahma movement which stood for monotheism on a non-sectarian basis and various social reforms like the abolition of caste, introduction of inter-caste marriages and emancipation and education of women. The departure of Raja Ram Mohan Roy for England and his subsequent death there led to the decline of the Brahma Sabha but a new life was infused into it by Maharshi Devendranath Tagore (1817-1905) who took up the reins of the organisation in 1843 and propagated its principles through the *Tattva Bodhini Patrika*. It was then a movement for preaching the pure monotheistic form of Hinduism and its followers looked upon the Vedas as divine revelation and therefore as infallible and was opposed to social reforms like the abolition of caste and introduction of inter-caste marriages. But the younger section of the Brahmas led at first by Akshoya Kumar Datta and later on by Keshab Chandra Sen questioned the infallibility of the Vedas and insisted on the abolition of caste restrictions amongst the Brahmas and on other social reforms. But Devendra Nath Tagore would not accept those demands and dismissed in 1865 Keshab Chandra and his followers from all offices of trust and responsibility. Thus there took place a great schism in the Brahma movement. Devendra Nath and his followers constituted the Adi Brahma Samaj which stood for the pure monotheistic form of Hinduism and was opposed to social reforms. The younger section under Keshab Chandra Sen formed the Brahma Samaj of India which had a prosperous career till 1878 when, on account of certain differences of principles between Keshab Chandra and his followers which were heightened by the marriage, according to Hindu rites, of Keshab's minor daughter with the Maharaja of Cooch Behar, the younger Brahmas again became divided and the seceders formed the *Sadharan Brahma Samaj* while Keshab and his group formed a new church called the *Nava-Vidhana*. Thus the Brahmas are at present divided under three churches—the *Adi Brahma Samaj*, the *Sadharan Brahma Samaj* and the *Nava-Vidhana*, each with its own shrine.

The Brahma movement which started in Calcutta soon spread throughout Bengal and outside it to Uttar Pradesh, the Panjab and Madras. The provincial samajas are all affiliated to the Sadharan Brahma Samaj. In Maharashtra also the movement spread under the name of *Prarthana Samaj*.

The Brahma movement subsequently lost much of its vigour. But it had rendered useful services to the country. It largely helped the removal of the *purdah* system, the introduction of widow remarriage, the legalisation of inter-caste marriages, the removal of caste rigidity, the cessation of the tendency amongst the Hindus to conversion to Christianity, and the promotion of higher education, specially amongst women. It has had, however, little success in persuading Hindu society to accept its fundamental ideas of monotheism and the abolition of the worship of images (Sastri, Sibnath, *History of the Brahmo Samaj*, Vols. I-II)

Brahma Sabha—was a theistic organisation founded by Raja Ram Mohan Roy in Calcutta in 1828. It was meant to be an assembly of all who believed in the unity of God and discarded the worship of images. At first it was housed in a rented building and its first secretary was Tarachand Chakrabarty. It held weekly meetings on Saturdays in which the Vedas were recited by Brahmins. It soon attracted a large number of people and in 1830 Raja Ram Mohan Roy purchased with subscriptions collected from its supporters, a house for it on the Chitpur Road and handed it over to a body of trustees. The starting of the

Brahma Sabha is now regarded as marking the foundation of the Brahma Samaj, though essential differences existed between the two bodies. For example, the members of the Brahma Sabha unlike those of the Brahma Samaj, declared themselves to be Hindus and maintained caste restrictions in matters of religious worship and marriages.

Brahmana, the caste of—is considered as the first and highest of the castes which prevail amongst the Hindus. The orthodox view is that the Brahmana orginated from the mouth of *Purusha* or Primeval Man and as such is of divine origin and is entitled to the highest place in the hierarchy of castes amongst the Hindus. The other view that regards the castes as occupational groups, holds that the priestly class who generally devoted themselves to studies and intellectual pursuits, came to form the Brahmana caste and was originally the second in order of precedence amongst the castes, the highest place being occupied by the Kshatriyas or fighting class to which belonged the early rulers. In any case as time passed on the primacy of the Brahamanas as a caste came to be recognised by the orthodox section of the Hindus. (*see* under Caste System)

Brahmanapal—a grandson of King Jaipal and son of Anandapal of the Hindu Shahiya dynasty of Udbhandapur (Waihand) in the north-western frontier of India, led in A.D. 1008 the army of his father against Sultan Mahmud of Ghazni at the battle of Waihand but was defeated in the battle and perished.

Brahmanas, **the Vedic**—are supplements of the *Vedas*. These are written in prose, as opposed to the *Samhitas* which are all in verse, and are considered as revelations. These treatises contain observations on sacrifices, rituals, cosmogonic myths, old legends and *gathas* or verses narrating the exploits of ancient Vedic kings. (Macdonnell & Keith, *Vedic Index*)

Brahmanaspati—is a Rig Vedic deity who is the Lord of Prayer. (*Vedic Index*)

Brahmanism—is the name given to the earlier phase of Hinduism as it was practised before the secession of the dissident faiths like Buddhism and Jainism in the 6th century of the pre-Christian era.

Brahmaputra, the—a great river flowing from Tibet where it is known as the Tsangpo to India, is 1800 miles in length. Running through the state of Assam, from the east to the west, and then from the north to the south it meets the Ganges in Bengal. The ancient city of Pragjyotishapura (modern Gauhati), capital of the kingdom of Kamarupa, was situated on the bank of the Brahmaputra.

Brahmarshi-desha—(or the land of the sages) is the name given by Manu to the region about Thaneswar, eastern Rajasthan, the Doab between the Ganges and the Jumna and the Mathura district.

Brahmavarta—(or the land of the Gods) denoted the area lying between the rivers Saraswati and Drishadvati, both of which are now lost and cannot be precisely identified.

Brahmi, script—is the ancient form of the modern Devanagari characters used in writing Sanskrit and the allied languages of northern and western India. The inscriptions of Asoka excepting those in the north-western frontier region, are written in the Brahmi script.

Barhuis, the—form a small people in Baluchistan. They speak the Dravidian language and their present existence and residence suggest that the Dravidian people who are now mainly confined to the Deccan, once inhabited the whole of India and left a small remnant in Baluchistan on their way presumably to Mesopotamia.

Braithwaite, Col.—a British military officer, was defeated by the army of Haidar Ali, King of Mysore, in a battle during the Second Anglo-Mysore war in 1781.

Brajabhasa—a variety of Hindi dialects, was used and made popular by the disciples of Vallabhacharya collectively known as *Astachap,* the most prominent of whom was Surdas, the author of *Sursagar* in which the sports of Krishna's early life are described in poems. The famous Meera Bai sang in *Brajasbhasa.*

Brajabhumi—is the name given to the Jumna valley in which stand the holy cities of Mathura and Vrindaban associated by the Vaishnava devotees with the life of Krishna and Radha.

Brasyer, Captain—a military officer in the service of the East India Company, showed great bravery and resources in holding with a small force of the Sikhs the fort of Allahabad against the mutinous sepoys in May-June, 1857 till he was relieved on the 11th June by a British force led by Neill.

Brihadratha—was the founder of the earliest dynasty of Magadhan kings. He was the father of Jarasandha and his dynasty ruled in Magadha till the sixth century B.C. (*P.H.A.I.,* pp. 113-14)

Brihadratha—the last king of the Maurya dynasty (*q.v.*) of Magadha, was deposed in about 185 B.C. by his Brahman commander-in-chief, Pushyamitra (*q.v.*). With his deposition the Maurya dynasty came to an end.

Brihaspati—an ancient lawgiver of India. His work, the *Brihaspati-Smriti,* is assigned to the Gupta age.

Brihaspatimitra—is supposed to be the Sanskritised form of the name Bahapati-mita or Bahasatimita found in the Hathigumpha inscription of a king of Kharavela (*q.v.*) of Kalinga. Brihaspati-mitra is described in the inscription as a king of Rajagriha and has been identified by many with the Magadhan king Pushyamitra (*q.v.*) who founded the Sunga dynasty in about 185 B.C. But the identification is not free from doubt. (*P.H.A.I.*, pp. 373 ff. & 418 ff.)

Brindavana—*see* Vrindavana.

Brindavan Das—*see* Vrindavan Das.

British Administration—in India was an institution of slow growth and falls into two periods, the first from 1773 to 1858 and the second from 1858 to 1947. Its nucleus lay in the Regulating Act of 1773 and its culmination in the present administration of independent India. Previous to the passing of the Regulating Act the East India Company had in India three separate centres in Calcutta, Madras and Bombay, each under a President independent of the other two. The battle of Plassey (1757) and the events that followed during the next few years led to the acquisition of the kingdom of Bengal and Bihar by the East India Company. Institutions which had been created for carrying on the administration of a commercial and trading concern were rightly felt to be inadequate for running the administration of a kingdom which was expected to expand. The Parliament of England, therefore, passed in 1773, the Regulating Act (*q.v.*) which left the administration in the hands of the East India Company but also provided for Parliamentary supervision over the Company's administration in Indian territories and laid down the basis of a unitary system of administration over the Company's possessions in India by vesting the administration of Bengal in a Governor-General and a Council of four Members and by bestowing upon them the rights of supervision and control in matters relating to war and peace over Madras and Bombay, each of which was also placed under a Governor with a Council. As the Governor-General and the Members of his Council were all named in the Act, were all appointed for the same term of five years, and were re-callable by the same authority and as all decisions were to be arrived at by a majority of votes, the setting-up of one man's despotic rule was precluded from the beginning and a system of administration based on the principles of consultation and agreement was started. Further, the Regulating Act established in Calcutta a Supreme Court with a Chief Justice and three puisne Judges, all liberally paid, all appointed by the Crown, with jurisdiction over all British citizens of Calcutta including all the officials of the East India Company in Calcutta. It thus envisaged the establishment of the sovereignty of law in the territories administered by the East India Company. The Regulating Act was, however, defective in several respects, as was revealed during 1773-84 when it was being worked by Warren Hastings, the first Governor-General and his Council of four Members. The control of the Parliament over the Company's affairs in India could not be effectively exercised; in the absence of the power to over-rule the Council the Governor-General became a victim of a partisan opposition in the Council and the right of supervision vested in the Governor-General and the Council over distant Madras and Bombay was so vague that each of these two provinces embarked on wars without the previous sanction of the Governor-General and the Council. Lastly the Supreme Court's right to try even the highest officials encouraged litigation against them and tended to set up the judiciary as a rival to the executive. To meet these difficulties Pitt's India Act was passed in 1784. It vested the Government jointly in the Crown and the Company. It tightened the control of the Parliament over the administration of the Company's territories in India by setting up in England a Board of Control (*q.v.*) consisting of six unpaid Privy Councillors, one of whom was to be the President with a casting vote. The Board had no patronage nor any control over commercial matters, both of which were left to the Court of Directors (*q.v.*) of the East India Company, but it had power to superintend, direct and control everything connected with the civil, military and fiscal administration of the British territorial possessions in the East Indies.

No dispatches were to be sent to the Company's officers in India without the approval of the Board of Control which also had the right to issue any orders it thought proper without the consent of the Board of Directors. Henry John Dundas was the first President of the Board of Control and under his masterful and diligent guidance the Board of Control became the real ruling authority. In India the Governor-General's position vis-à-vis the Council was strengthened by reducing the number of Councillors from four to three of whom the Commander-in-Chief was to be one. The control of the Governor-General and the Council over the administrations of Bombay and Madras in matters of war, revenue and diplomacy was tightened. Two years later a supplementary Act authorised the Governor-General to over-rule in special cases the majority of the Council. The administration of the British territories in India now came to be vested in the Governor-General in Council, a change which was emphasized in 1834 by changing the title from the Governor-General of Fort William in Bengal to that of the Governor-General of India.

The dual system of control over the Indian adminstration, exercised by the Parliament of England through the Board of Control and by the East India Company through the Court of Directors, lasted until the Mutiny in 1857. In practice, however, the Parliament tended to be the more effective partner. This was mainly due to the diligence and skill of Dundas, the first President of the Board of Control, who, during his long term of office, firmly established the Board of Control as the final arbiter of political decisions, and, by concentrating all powers of the Board in his own hands virtually made the President of the Board the Cabinet Minister for India.

By passing these two acts the Parliament of England implicitly undertook a moral responsibility for the administration of India. Advantage was, therefore, taken of the circumstance that the Charter of the East India Company had to be periodically renewed every twenty years to make such alterations in the administrative system of British India as were necessitated by the needs of the time. Thus by the Charter Act of 1813 the Indian trade was partially thrown open to the public in England and the East India Company began to cease to be mainly a commercial concern. By the Charter Act of 1833 the Company lost the Indian trade altogether and became the political agent of the Crown of England for the administration of India. This Act also added a fourth member to the Governor-General's Council which was also given rights to legislate. The Commander-in-Chief continued to be an extraordinary member. It also appointed a Law Commission which eventually introduced in India a common public law for civil and criminal matters. Finally the Charter Act of 1853 introduced the system of open competition for entry into the Indian Civil Service and thus prepared the way for the eventual Indianisation of the Civil Service in India which had so long been a preserve of the British people. This Act also laid down that for legislative purposes the Governor-General's Council was to be extended by the addition of six members. The six members who were eventually appointed were no doubt all Europeans, but their inclusion in the Council for legislative purposes marked the modest beginning of a liberal legislative system in India.

Four years after the passing of the Charter Act of 1853 the Company's rule in India was shaken to its foundations by the outbreak of the Sepoy Mutiny which was suppressed by the Company's troops but which so clearly exposed the weakness of the Company's administration in India that by the Act for the Better Government of India which the British Parliament passed in 1858 the control of the administration of India was vested in the Crown of England. The Act provided that India shall be governed by and in the name of the British Sovereign through one of the principal Secretaries of State, assisted by a Council of fifteen members. The Governor-General was given the new title of Viceroy, the Court of Directors (*q.v.*) ceased to function, the Board of Control (*q.v.*) was changed into the Council of India and its President became the Secretary of State for India. The change in the system of administration was announced in the Queen's Proclamation (*q.v.*) issued on the 1st November, 1858, which confirmed the treaties and engagements made by the East India Company with the Indian princes, granted a general amnesty and declared that "all persons of whatever race or creed, may be freely and impartially admitted to offices in the Crown's service, the duties of which they may be qualified, by their education, ability and integrity, duly to discharge."

The next important change in the administrative system was effected by the Indian Councils Act of 1861. By this Act a fifth ordinary non-official (European) member was added to the Viceroy's Executive Council, Viceroy's powers were considerably increased and he was empowered to make rules for the transaction of business by the Executive Council. By using this authority Canning, who was then the Viceroy, introduced the portfolio system by which each member of the Executive Council was placed in charge of certain Departments. He could dispose of on his own authority minor matters relating to his Departments and matters of greater importance in consultation with the Viceroy. Questions of general policy or those relating to other Departments were referred to the Executive Council for decision. This Departmental system which saved much time, continued not only throughout the whole period of British rule in India but has been adopted with some changes in independent India.

The Indian Councils Act of 1861 also made important changes in the legislative system of India. The Indian Mutiny had emphasized the need for a machinery through which Indian public opinion could be ascertained. The Act of 1861, therefore, provided that for the purposes of legislation the Viceroy's Council was to be enlarged by the addition of six to twelve members of whom at least one half must be non-officials. The rights of legislation were hedged round by various limitations, but the principle that the non-official Indians should have a part in the making of the laws which governed them, was conceded and three Indians, namely, the Maharaja of Patiala, the Raja of Benares and Sir Dinkar Rao of Gwalior were nominated to the Viceroy's Legislative Council.

The Indian Councils Act of 1861 also restored to the Governments of Bombay and Madras the right to legislate, within certain limitations, for the peace and good government of the Presidencies and for this purpose of legislation the provincial Executive Councils were to be enlarged by the addition of four to eight members of whom at least one-half should be non-officials.

The Act of 1861 further authorised the Governor-General-in-Council to create similar Legislative Councils not only in the remaining three existing provinces of Bengal, the North-Western Provinces (later on the United Provinces) and the Panjab but also in any new province that may be constituted later on in pursuance of this Act. Legislative Councils came to be established in Bengal in 1862, in the N.-W. Provinces in 1886 and in the Panjab in 1898. Though the Act of 1861 had conceded the right of the non-official Indians to be consulted in matters of legislation there was no intention to weaken the hold of the Government on the country and the people. Rather the tendency was in the opposite direction as was shown by the Indian Councils Act of 1870 which not only empowered the Governor-General in-Council to pass regulations without reference to the Legislative Council but also conferred on the Viceroy the right to over-ride the decisions of the majority of his Executive Council when the Viceroy considered it necessary to do so for the safety, the tranquillity or interests of the British Empire in India. The Viceroy thus tended to be the Great Mughul. In 1874 the Viceroy's Executive Council was enlarged by the addition of a sixth ordinary member who was to be placed in charge of Public Works.

All this while public opinion in India was growing bolder and finding expression in the press and on the platform on account of the spread of Western education which was greatly promoted by the ·foundation of Universities in Calcutta, Madras and

Bombay during the regime of Lord Canning. The opening of the Suez Canal in 1869 and the establishment of a direct telegraph line between England and India in 1870 reduced the distance between the two countries and a larger number of Indians visited England and returned to their mother country, bringing back with them much of the spirit of liberalism which then prevailed in England. The result was the foundation of the Indian National Congress (*q.v.*) which held its first session in Bombay in 1885. Educated Indians stood forth, as they had never done before, as one people and demanded not only a larger share in the services of the country but also an expansion of the strength and powers of Legislative Councils by the addition of an adequate number of elected representatives of the people and by the acquisition of the rights of discussing the annual Budget and of eliciting information by means of interpellations.

As a result of the pressure exercised by this enlightened public opinion the Parliament passed in 1892 an Indian Councils Act which increased the strength of the Legislative Council of the Governor-General as well as of the Provincial Governors by increasing the numbers of additional non-official members some of whom continued to be nominated by the Government but some of whom were also to be elected, though indirectly. It also granted to the Legislative Councils the rights of discussing the Budgets and putting interpellations. By conceding the principle of election and by giving the Legislative Councils some control over the Executive, the Indian Councils Act of 1892 paved the way for further reforms in India.

Indian public opinion continued to press for further liberalisation of the system of administration and the next important change in it was effected by the Government of India Act of 1909 embodying what are popularly known as the Morley-Minto Reforms. This Act provided for the association of qualified Indians with the Government to a greater extent than before and led to the appointment of one Indian (Sir Satyendra Prasanna Sinha, later on Lord Sinha of Raipur) to the Viceroy's Executive Council and of Raja Kisorilal Goswami to the Executive Council of Bengal and of other Indians to the Executive Councils of Madras and Bombay. The Act of 1909 also introduced important changes in the composition and functions of the Legislative Councils. In the Central Legislature the number of members was raised to sixty and in the Provincial Legislatures of the major provinces to fifty, and in all the legislatures the proportions of the non-official elected members were strengthened, though the nominated official and non-official members still continued to form the majority. The election of members continued to be by an indirect process and was further based on communal representation, but the constituencies were more broadened than before. The legislatures were allowed to discuss the Budget and to move resolutions on it as well as on other matters of general interest except in matters concerning the Army, Foreign Affairs and Indian States. The resolutions were, however, of the character of recommendations and were not binding on the Government. Thus the Act of 1909 which certainly marked an important step in the introduction of representative Government in India, did not give India a system of responsible Government and the Indian administration continued to be carried on with absolute responsibility to the British Parliament.

The Reforms of 1909 did not, therefore, satisfy Indian political aspirations and discontent continued unabated. Then came the First World War during which India stood loyally by England and demanded a larger share in the control of the policy of her Government. To satisfy this insistent Indian demand the British Government declared on August 20, 1917 through Mr. Edwin Montague, the Secretary of State for India, that "the policy of His Majesty's Government was that of the increasing association of Indians in every branch of the administration and the gradual development of self-governing institutions with a view to the progressive realisation of responsible Government in India as an integral part of the British Empire". This was an epoch-making declaration which promised India a Parliamentary system of Government. In pursuance of this policy the Government of India Act, 1919, was passed and came into operation in 1921.

The Government of India Act, 1919, did not make any effective change in the relation between the Secretary of State for India and the Indian administration. Appointments of Indians to the Secretary of State's Council were made feasible, but the Council remained subordinate to the Secretary of State who retained for all practical purposes as complete a control over the Indian administration as before except in connection with the administration of 'transferred departments' in the provinces. He was, however, relieved of the agency work on behalf of the Central and Provincial Governments of India the discharge of which was vested in a new officer called the High Commissioner to be appointed by the Government of India.

Further, the salaries of the Secretary of State and of his Under-Secretaries as well as the expenses of his department which had been heretofore paid from the Indian revenues, were to be henceforward paid out of the moneys provided in the budget of Great Britain by the British Parliament. Thus the control of the British Parliament over India was strengthened.

The Act of 1919 made important changes in the administrative set-up of India. The Viceroy and Governor-General remained, as before, responsible to the Secretary of State and the Parliament, but his Executive Council was enlarged and the practice came to be established that three of its members were to be Indians who thus were placed in a better position for influencing the Indian administration. The functions of the Central and Provincial Governments were clearly divided as far as possible and the sources of their incomes were also delimited.

The Central Legislature also was thoroughly remodelled. It was made bicameral, being divided into the two houses of the Council of State and the Legislative Assembly. The members of the Executive Council could be nominated by the Governor-General to one or the other houses of the legislature. Though communal representation was retained the principle of direct election was recognised and in both the houses the elected representatives of the people were given a majority. The franchise was based on a property qualification, which was higher for the Council of State, but was not unduly restrictive.

The powers of the Central Legislature, though limited to a certain extent by the powers of certification and promulgation of ordinances that were given to the Governor-General, were also largely extended in the spheres of finance as well as legislation. The powers of the two houses were co-ordinate, but demands for grants were to be submitted to the lower house. Thus India came to have for the first time in her history an elected parliament with powers to influence largely her administration.

In the sphere of Provincial Government also the Act of 1919 made extensive changes. All the ten provinces into which the British Indian Empire was then divided, were made Governors' Provinces with Executive Councils some of whose members were to be non-official Indians. The Governor who was to be appointed by the Crown, had enormous powers and privileges and remained the real authority over the Provincial Government. The Act, however, introduced dyarchy (*q.v.*) or dual governments in the Provincial Executive. The administrative departments were divided into 'Reserved subjects' like police, justice, land revenue etc. and 'Transferred subjects' like Local Self-Government, education, public health, excise etc. The Reserved subjects were to be administered by the Governor on the advice and with the help of an Executive Council which was responsible, as before, to the Governor-General and the Secretary of State while the Transferred subjects were to be administered by the Governor acting with his Ministers who were to be appointed by him from amongst the elected members of the Provincial Legislature. The Ministers were to hold office during the pleasure of the Governor, but were to retain the confidence of the legislature and were to be dismissed on an adverse vote.

The legislatures in the provinces were also largely strengthened and the majority of the members were to be directly elected non-officials. Communal representation was retained as well as the practice of nomination. The powers of the Provincial Legislatures were also extended. They could entertain a bill on any provincial subject; and though a bill concerning a Reserved subject could be enacted into a law, in spite of an adverse vote of the legislature, if the Governor 'certified' that it was necessary for the safety and tranquillity of the province, but bills concerning Transferred subjects could be passed only with the consent of the legislature. Similarly, the entire Budget of a province was to be placed and discussed by the legislature whose assent was essential for all demands regarding the Transferred subjects while those regarding the Reserved subjects, if refused by the legislature, could be restored on the Governor's Certificate. Thus both in matters of law-making and finance the authority of the Provincial Legislatures, though restricted within certain limits as regards the Reserved subjects, was much more extended than before. The introduction of direct election on a wide franchise both for the Central and Provincial Legislatures and the wider rights of discussion and decision that were conferred on them mark the Act of 1919, in spite of its limitations, as an important landmark in the development of the British administration in India which was placed by it definitely on the road to a democratic parliamentary form of Government.

But the Government of India Act 1919, which came into operation in 1921, failed to satisfy Indian aspirations. The Moderates amongst the Indians accepted the Reforms and tried to work them. But the Indian National Congress considered them so inadequate that it refused to accept them. Mahatma Gandhi who had by that time come to be the recognised leader of the Congress, joined with Khilafatists (*q.v.*) and started the non-co-operation movement (*q.v.*) and a great agitation raged over the country. But by 1924 the Khilafatists seceded from the Congress and the British Government also succeeded in subduing the non-co-operation movement by force. But the Congress, far from being repressed, declared at its Madras session in 1927 independence as the goal of India and re-iterated the declaration in more definite terms at its Lahore session in 1929 and in 1930 Mahatma Gandhi started the Civil Disobedience movement (*q.v.*). Again, the British Indian Government adopted a policy of severe repression, imprisoned the Congress leaders including Mahatma Gandhi and sent thousands of persons to jail. As a result, the Civil Disobedience movement petered out but the country remained sullen. In expectation of satisfying disaffected India the British Parliament passed in 1935 a new Government of India Act which effected important changes in the British administrative system in India.

The Government of India Act of 1935 retained the old subor-dination of the Government of India to the British Parliament through the Secretary of State to whom the Viceroy and Gover-nor-General continued to be responsible. It also retained all the existing features of the Indian constitution, namely popular representation in the legislatures, dyarchy, ministerial res-ponsibility, provincial autonomy, communal representations and safeguards. In addition to these the Act introduced two new features, namely, federation at the Centre and popular res-ponsible government in the provinces which were to have autonomy.

Two new provinces were formed, namely Sind and Orissa and these along with the North-West Frontier Province were all made Governor's provinces. But Burma was separated from British India which now came to consist of eleven Governor's provinces, the four Chief Commissionerships of Delhi, Ajmer-Merwar, Coorg, the Andaman and Nicobar islands and the agency of British Baluchistan.

The most striking feature of the Act of 1935 was the federal principle. All the Indian provinces and all the separate Princely states in India were to be integrated into one federated unit with a bicameral legislature under a Governor-General with a dyarchical Executive Council consisting of two Councillors nominated by the Governor-General to be in charge of the reserved departments of defence and foreign affairs and a body of ministers appointed by the Governor-General but responsible to the legislature for the administration of all other departments which were transferred under popular control. The Governor-General retained the powers of certifying legislation in spite of adverse popular votes in the federal legislature and also of issuing ordinances with the force of law for six months at a time. Both the chambers of the federal legislature were to have a majority of members directly elected by voters with certain property qualifications, but the federating Indian Princes were to nominate one-third of the representatives of the Lower Federal Chamber and two-fifths of the Upper. Thus the whole of India would come to be represented in one assembly, as she had never been previously.

The Act of 1935 abolished 'dyarchy' in the provinces where popular governments were established. Administration in all the departments was to be carried on by Ministers to be appointed by the Governors and were to be responsible to the popularly elected legislative assemblies. Communal representation was retained, and six of the provinces were given bicameral legislatures. The Lower House in each province, however, consisted entirely of members elected on a popular basis, the suffrage being given to all adult men and women with a small property qualification.

The Act of 1935 marked a major step towards bestowing 'dominion status' on India, but the system as established by it fell short of dominion status in certain important respects. First, the existence of 'dyarchy' at the centre left a part of the Executive irremovable by the people of India and responsible to the British Parliament. Secondly, the special powers of the Viceroy of certification and legislation by ordinances were inconsistent with real 'dominion status' and clearly showed India's continuing dependence on England. Thirdly, the provision that all legislation by the Indian Federal Legislature was 'subject to refusal of assent or reservation by the Governor-General and to disallowance by the Crown under the Secretary of State's advice' was a serious impediment to the full enjoyment of 'dominion status' by India.

In these circumstances the Indian National Congress was critical in its attitude to the Act of 1935. The implementation of the Federal portion of the Act depended on the co-operation of the Indian princes, and as it was not readily received, only the provincial part of the Act was enforced in 1937. All the parties took part in the elections and popular governments were established in all the provinces while at the Centre the old system of an irresponsible Executive and partly popular legislature as established by the Act of 1919 continued to function Two years later the Second World War broke out and produced a tremendous impact on the Indian situation. The initial British reverses followed by stubborn resistance, the Japanese invasion and American intervention in the War coupled with the acute differences between the National Congress and the Muslim League created an extremely tense political situation in India. Some thought that Britain's dangers afforded opportunities to India for pressing her claims for independence, but Mahatma Gandhi declared that "We do not seek our independence out of British ruin". In the circumstances the British Government expanded the Viceroy's Executive Council to a total of fifteen, of whom eleven were Indians who were thus given a great deal of control over the Indian administration and sent out Sir Stafford Cripps on a mission to India for finding a solution to the Indian political problem yet the Indian National Congress continued to agitate for immediate grant of full dominion status. As the British Government did not readily concede the demand, the Congress under the leadership of Mahatma Gandhi demanded that the British should immediately 'quit India' and started in 1942 a countrywide Civil disobedience movement which was attended, in spite of Mahatma Gandhi's insistence on non-violence, with much violence. The British Government succeeded in suppressing the movement by force, and ultimately also won the war. But the rising of 1942 and the naval mutiny of 1946 had shown that Britain could no longer continue her sovereignty over India with the willing consent of the majority of the Indian people. The failure of the Cabinet Mission (*q.v.*) which was sent to India in April, 1946 followed by communal riots all over India, further strengthened the above conviction. This coupled with the exhaustion which had crippled victorious Great Britain in the recent fatal war, convinced her that India could no longer he held by sheer force and that unless independence was immediately granted to her Great Britain would not only lose India as a dominion but would also fail to maintain with her friendly commercial relations on which the economy and finanical solvency of Great Britain vitally depended. In the circumstances British statesmanship rose to an unprecedented height, took courage in both hands and granted India independence on August 15, 1947, on the basis of a partition of the country between India and Pakistan which had become inevitable as the result of the unbridgeable gulf that had come to separate the Hindus and Muhammadans in India as the result of the British policy of 'divide and rule'. Thus the British Indian administration that was first attempted to be reduced to a system by the Regulating Act of 1773 came to a culmination by the grant of independence to India in 1947. (Ilbert, Sir C., *The Government of India* & Keith, A. B., *Constitutional Hist. of India*)

Brown, the Rev. David—was one of the earliest Christian missionaries from Britain to come to Bengal. At that time Christian missionaries were not allowed to carry on their evangelical work within the Company's Indian territories. So David Brown became the East India Company's chaplain in Calcutta where he worked as a priest.

Brydon, Dr.—was a surgeon attached to the British army that invaded Afghanistan during the First Afghan War (1839-42) (*q.v.*). His regiment was utterly routed and he was the only survivor who reached Jalalabad, severely wounded and utterly exhausted, on January 13, 1942, to tell the British garrison there the painful story of the British defeat at the hands of the Afghans.

Bubuji Khanam—was the name assumed by the Maratha wife of Sultan Yusuf Adil Shah (1489-1510) of Bijapur. She was the sister of a Maratha chieftain named Mukund Rao who was defeated by Yusuf Adil Shah early in his reign and given in marriage to him. She became the mother of the second Adil Shahi Sultan Ismail and of three princesses who were married to members of the royal families of the neighbouring Muslim states.

Buckingham, John Silk—the editor of the *Calcutta Journal*, criticised the public officials rather freely and was therefore expelled from India by John Adams, the officiating Governor-General in 1823.

Buddewal—was the scene of a skirmish on 21st January, 1846, in which a British army led by Sir Harry Smith was defeated by the Sikhs, just a week before the latter's defeat at Aliwal (*q.v.*).

Buddha, Gautama—the renowned founder of Buddhism, was born in a princely Kshatriya family of Kapilavastu in the Nepalese Tarai to the north of the Basti district in Uttara Pradesha. His father's name was Suddhodhana and his mother was Maya. She died in childbirth and her son who was given the name of Siddhartha was brought up by his aunt and step-mother, Prajapati Gautami. His family name was Gautama. After the name of the Sakya tribe to which his father belonged he was also called Sakya-Sinha, or lion amongst the Sakyas, and later on, Sakya-Muni or sage amongst the Sakyas. At the age of sixteen he was married to a lady named Yasodhara (also called Bhadda Kachchaná, Subhadraká, Bimbá or Gopá). For the next thirteen years Siddhartha lived a luxurious life in his father's palace till at last the vision of old age, disease and death made him realise the hollowness of worldly pleasures and its attractions so intensely that the very night on which a son was born to him he felt the fetters of earthly life growing stronger than before and left his father's comfortable home, his beloved young and beautiful wife as well as his newborn son and assumed the life of a wandering monk determined to find out a way of escape from the sufferings of disease, old age and death to which all persons were prey. At the time of this Great Renunciation Gautama was only twenty-nine years of age. For one year he studied Indian philosophy, but it gave him no solution. Then for the next five years he practised severe austerities hoping thereby to find the way to salvation. But all proved futile. Then one day as he sat immersed in deep meditation under the famous Bo-tree of modern Bodh-Gaya on the bank of the Nairanjana enlightenment came to him and he realised the truth. Henceforth he came to be known as the Buddha or the Enlightened and decided to spend the rest of his life in preaching the truth as he saw it. He delivered his first sermon at the Deer Park at Sarnath near Benares where five disciples joined him. From that time for the next forty-five years Buddha moved about the Gangetic valley in Uttara Pradesha and Bihar preaching and teaching, visiting and converting princes as well as peasants, irrespective of caste, organising his disciples in the great Buddhist *Sangha* or Order, endowing it with rules and discipline and converting hundreds and thousands to his faith which came to be known as Buddhism (*q.v.*). He died at the age of eighty at Kusinagara which has been identified by many archaeologists with Kasia in the Gorakhpur district. The date of his *Parinirvana* or decease, like the date of his birth, has not yet been decided with accuracy, though it is admitted by all that he was contemporary with kings Bimbisara and Ajatasatru of Magadha and died in the reign of the latter. According to a Cantonese tradition Buddha passed away in 486 B.C. He was, then, born eighty years earlier, in 566 B.C.

Gautama Buddha is a unique figure amongst the founders of religions. First, he is definitely a historical person. Secondly, he claimed no divinity for himself and discouraged any idea of being worshipped. He only claimed that he had attained 'knowledge' which again he held could be attained by any other person provided he made the necessary effort. Thirdly, he was the first founder of a religion who organised a brotherhood of monks and started evangelization in an organised manner by peaceful means alone carrying the message of equality, peace, mercy. Lastly, he put reason above everything and exhorted his followers to accept nothing as true unless it stood the test of reasoning. He not only preached the brotherhood of man but also practised it all through his life as a religious teacher accepting as his disciples all who cared to listen to him without any consideration of caste and race and thus founding a religion which eventually passed beyond the limits of India and became one of the world's greatest religions. (Oldenberg, *Buddha;* Thomas, E. J., *Life of Buddha*; Arnold, Edwin, *Light of Asia*)

Buddhism—is the religion founded by Gautama Buddha in the latter half of the sixth century B.C. It started with the basic principles of rebirth and *karma* which were then accepted by Indian philosophers as truths which required no proof. The *karma* doctrine means that the merits and demerits of a being in his past existences determine his condition in the present life. The doctrine of rebirth implies that at death the body perishes, but the soul which is immortal, takes new births until it attains salvation. But according to the Buddhist view the connecting link between a former existence and a later one is not to be found in the soul, the existence and immortality of which are assumed by Hindu philosophers but denied by Buddhism. On the death of a person the only thing that survives is not the soul, as the Hindus hold, but the result of his action, speech and thought, that is to say, his *karma* (doings) which does not die with the body. Buddhism thus came to be based on what was claimed to be the four Noble Truths: (1) There is suffering in life. (2) This suffering has a cause. (3) Suffering must be caused to cease. (4) Suffering can cease if one knows the right way. Buddhism holds that the suffering inseparably connected with existence is mainly due to desire, to a craving thirst (Sans. *trishna*: Pali *tanha*) for satisfying the senses. Therefore the extinction of desire will lead to the cessation of existence by rebirth and of consequent suffering. Desire can be extinguished if one followed the Noble Eightfold Path which consists of the following: (1) right views or beliefs meaning simply a knowledge of the Four Noble Truths and of the doctrine of rebirth and *karma* implied in them. (2) Right aims implying the determination to renounce pleasures, to bear no malice and do no harm. (3) Right speech implying abstention from falsehood, slandering, harsh words and foolish talk. (4) Right conduct or action involving abstention from taking life, from stealing and from immorality. (5) Right means of livelihood implying occupations which do not hurt or endanger any living being. (6) Right endeavour involving active benevolence and love towards all beings as well as effort to prevent the growth of evil thoughts in the mind. (7) Right mindfulness meaning complete self-mastery by means of self-knowledge. (8) Right meditation which is to be practised in a quiet place sitting with body erect and intelligence alert and thought concentrated on the Four Noble Truths.

This Noble Eightfold Path is also called the Middle Path, for it avoided extremes of luxury as well as of austerity. By the pursuit of it persons will attain *Nirvana* which is the highest goal of a Buddhist.

Buddhism repudiates the authority of the Vedas, denies the spiritual efficacy of Vedic rites and sacrifices, denies the efficacy of prayers and practically ignores the existence of a Supreme Being or God. It holds that the acceptance of the Four Noble Truths and the pursuit of the Noble Eightfold Path which is open to all, irrespective of caste and sex, laymen as well as monks and nuns, will lead to the extinction of desire and this will lead to *Nirvana* which it is possible to attain even in this life and will free a person from the curse of re-birth. It holds that it is easier for a monk living a secluded life to attain *Nirvana* but it is also open to lay Buddhists to attain the same. The Buddhist monks are not priests and they can pray neither for themselves nor for others who may wish to employ them. They are an intellectual aristocracy like the Brahmans and are to be maintained by pious Buddhists. Buddhism requires no church or temple, but it recognises congregational discourses where the teachings of Gautama Buddha are recited and explained. The founder of Buddhism, Gautama Buddha, himself is to be recognised as a supremely wise person who has known the truth, but not as God to whom prayers can be addressed. It was spread by Gautama Buddha during his lifetime in the Gangetic valley of Uttara Pradesha and of Bihar. About 250 years after the decease of Gautama Buddha Emperor Asoka embraced the religion, sent Buddhist missionaries throughout India as well as to many countries outside India and thus started Buddhism on its victorious career which gradually turned it into a world religion. But it eventually disappeared from the land of its birth for a variety of causes. The wealth of the monasteries and the easy life there which soon attracted many undesirable and unworthy inmates, the preponderance of the monks over the laity, the gradual replacement of the earlier ethical idealism of Buddhism by the ritualism of the Mahayana (*q.v.*), the support that later Buddhism gave to Tantricism (*q.v.*) which was marked by various vicious and immoral practices, the reorganisation and re-vitaltzation of Hinduism by Sankara (*q.v.*) and Kumarila (*q.v.*) and finally the Muhammadan invasions of India—all combined to bring about the decline and fall of Buddhism in India, though it still counts one-third of the world's population as its followers. (Radhakrishnan, S., *Hist. of Indian Philosophy*, Vol. I; Rhys Davids, *Buddhism*; Thomas, *Hist. of Buddhist Thought*; Eliot, Sir Charles, *Hinduism and Buddhism*, 3 vols; Couze, E, *Buddhism, its Essence and Development*, 1953)

Buddhist Councils—were held four times. The First Council met at Rajagriha (modern Rajgir) in Bihar soon after the death of Gautama Buddha. It was attended by the Buddhist elders (*Theras*) and was presided over by one of Buddha's prominent Brahman disciples, named Mahakassapa. As Buddha had left none of his teachings in writing so at this Council three of his disciples, Kasyapa, the most learned, Upali, the oldest and Ananda, the most favoured of Buddha's disciples, recited his teachings which were at first learnt orally and transmitted by teachers to disciples and were much later on put down in writing. A century later a Second Council of the Buddhist elders met at Vaisali to settle a dispute that had arisen by that time amongst the Buddhist monks on certain questions of discipline. The Council decided in favour of rigid discipline and revised the Buddhist scriptures which were still unwritten. A Third Council met, according to tradition, 236 years after the death of Buddha, under the patronage of King Asoka Maurya. It was presided over by monk Tissa Moggaliputta, the author of the *Kathavattu*, a sacred Buddhist text. This Council is believed to have drawn up the Buddhist canon in the final form of the *Tripitaka* (*q.v.*) or the Three Baskets, and gave its decisions on all disputed points. If the Sarnath Pillar Edict of Asoka is correctly believed to have been issued after the session of this Third Council it can be rightly held that its decisions were not accepted by so many Buddhist monks and nuns that King Asoka found it necessary to threaten the schismatics with dire punishment. The Fourth and last Council of the Buddhist elders met during the reign of Kanishka, the Kushana king (*c.* A.D. 120-144). It drew up authentic commentaries on the canon and these were engraved on copper-plates which were encased in a stone-coffer and kept for safety in the Kundalavana monastery. These have not yet been found. (Kern, *Manual of Buddhism;* Rhys Davids, *Buddhism; I.H.Q.*, March, 1959)

Buddhist scriptures—have all grown after the death of Gautama Buddha who left nothing in writing. The scriptures known as the *Tripitaka* are believed to have been first recited by Ananda Upali and Kasyapa, three close disciples of Gautama Buddha at the session of the First Council of the Buddhist elders which met at Rajagriha soon after Buddha's death. For many centuries these were learnt orally, being transmitted by teachers to their disciples and it was not till 80 B.C. that these were put down in writing in Ceylon in the reign of king Vattagamani. The *Tripitaka* consists of the *Sutta*, the *Vinaya* and the *Abhidhamma*. The *Sutta* contains stories and parables related by Buddha during his preaching tours; the *Vinaya* lays down the laws and rules of discipline and the *Abhidhamma* contains the doctrines and metaphysical views of Buddhism. The *Sutta* is subdivided into five *Nikayas* of varying length, one of which contains the *Dhammapada*, *Thera* and *Therigathas* and the *Jatakas*; the *Vinaya* has three sub-divisions, while the *Abhidhamma* has seven sub-divisions of which the celebrated *Dhammasangini* is the first. There are now four versions of the *Tripitaka*, namely the Pali version which is followed in Ceylon, Burma and Siam; the Sanskrit version which is current in Nepal and among the Buddhists in Central Asia; the Chinese version which is a rendering in Chinese of the Sanskrit version and the Tibetan version which is a translation made between the ninth and the eleventh centuries of the Christian era. The whole forms a massive body of literature. The Japanese version of it runs into one hundred bound volumes of one thousand pages each.

Besides the *Tripitaka*, the *Milindapanha* by Nagasena (*c.* 140 B.C.) and the *Visuddhimagga* by Buddhaghosha are also important as religious literature of the Buddhists. (Takakusu, *Essentials of Buddhist Philosophy*)

Buddhist sects—arose as a result of the circumstance that none of the teachings of Gautama Buddha was written down during his lifetime. Differences on questions of discipline for the monks and nuns as well as on the significance of what he had taught arose amongst his followers soon after his death and within a century of the *Parinirvana* the Buddhists became split up into several sects of which the two most important came eventually to be known as the Hinayanists (i.e., followers of the Lower Vehicle) and the Mahayanists (i.e., the followers of the Higher Vehicle). The scriptures of the *Hinayana* are written in Pali while those of the *Mahayana* in Sanskrit. Consequently the *Hinayana* is often known as the Pali school and the *Mahayana* as the Sanskrit school of Buddhism. Again, the *Hinayana* prevails mainly in Ceylon and Burma and is consequently often called the Southern Buddhism while the *Mahayana* which mainly prevails in Nepal, China, Tibet, Mongolia, Korea and Japan is called the Northern Buddhism. As all Buddhist canonical literature wherever it might have extended, arose in northern India and the two schools possess traces of mutual influence so the division of the Buddhist Church into Northern and Southern Schools is more or less unjustified. As the two schools represent only different aspects of the same religious system so the use of terms lower and higher is not also justifiable. Indeed many prefer to call the *Hinayana* as *Theravada*, that is to say, the opinion of the Theras or older monks.

When exactly this division of the Buddhist Church took place, is not definitely known. Mahayanism was not a sudden development; it developed slowly and gradually in the course of some centuries. The origin of the Mahayana thought has been traced by some to the *Mahásánghika* and *Sarvástivádin* sects of Buddhism which existed as far back as 350 B.C. The inscriptions of Asoka (*c.* 273-231 B.C.) practically show no sign of Mahayanism which also did not have the controlling voice even at the fourth and last Buddhist Council which met in the reign of Kanishka (acc. *c.* A.D. 120), though Nagarjuna who was a contemporary and *protégé* of Kanishka exposed in his *Karika* the hollowness of the Hinayana thought. When, however, Fa-Hien came to India in the fourth century A.D. he found Mahayanist monasteries existing side by side with those of the Hinayanists in all the places that he visited in India. It was, therefore, between the second and the fourth centuries of the Christian era that Mahayanism fully developed in India. It was also during this period that many non-Indians were converted to Buddhism. This circumstance has led to the theory that Mahayanism was developed in order to meet their requirements. There are, however, reasons for holding that Mahayanism grew up in order to meet the religious and philosophical needs of the Indian Buddhists themselves though in later times it grew more popular outside India.

The differences between the two schools are wide. According

to the Hinayana Gautama is the Buddha, the sole Buddha, who now reposes in *Nirvana*, the absence of desire and striving, having left to mankind a simple rule by which they also may attain a like bliss, either in this existence or at a later. This creed knows no prayers, invocations or offerings and worships no images, for Buddha is not God, but a man who has attained perfection and thrown off the *karma* which dooms mankind to successive existences in the world of pain and sorrow. Each is to work for himself and attain *Nirvana* by overcoming all thirst or attachment by living a good life as indicated by the Noble Eightfold Path. According to the Mahayana, Gautama is merely one re-incarnation in a vast series of Buddhas stretching from an illimitable past into an equally infinite future. Not only in this world but in other worlds numerous as the sands of the Ganges, Buddhas have lived and preached at intervals separated by myriads of years from a time past human calcula tion. This world is but a speck in space and an instant in time; it will pass away and Maitreya will be the Buddha of the next period. Past Buddhas and Buddhas to come are gods of trans cendant power, hearkening to the prayers of mankind, res ponding to invocations and delighting in offerings and incense. Ultimately in China Amida or Amitabha Buddha, a personage unknown to early Buddhist scriptures, became the object of almost exclusive devotion and his pure paradise, called the Western Heaven, the goal to which the pious should aspire; *Nirvana* and Gautama Buddha were almost forgotten. The *Mahayana* holds that the ultimate aim of the life of a Buddhist is not the attainment of individual liberation. A person who acquires enlightenment should not remain satisfied with his own *Nirvana*, but should work for the good of his fellowmen. Such a person is called *Bodhi-sattva* (wisdom being). Thus Buddhas and Bodhi-sattvas came to be worshipped and their images were made and installed in temples where these were worshipped with various rituals and incantations. Every inci dent of Buddha's life as well as of his previous births familiarised by the Jataka stories and by later biographical sketches like the *Lalitavistara* came to be depicted in Buddhist sculptures. Using Sanskrit in its rituals and scriptures and worshipping images of Buddhas and Bodhi-sattvas Mahayanism tended to shorten the breach that separated Buddhism from Hinduism within the wide folds of which it was ultimately assimilated. In spite of the differences that exist between the *Hinayana* and the *Mahayana* there are not two Buddhisms. They are really one and the spirit of the founder of Buddhism prevails in both. Each has developed in its own way, according to the differences in environments in which each has thriven and grown. (Eliot, *Hinduism and Buddhism;* Smith, V. A., *Ox. Hist of India;* Mc-Gregor, *Introduction to Mahayana Philosophy;* Suzuki, *Devt. of Mahayana Buddhism;* Dutt, N., *Aspects of Mahayana Buddhism*)

Buddha Gupta—the last emperor (*c.* A.D. 476-95) of the main line of the Guptas, maintained some semblance of the unity of the Gupta empire which was broken up into pieces after his death as the result of the invasions by the Hunas under Toraman (*q.v.*) and his son Mihiragula (*q.v.*).

Buddharaja—a prince of the Kalachuri family, is supposed to have been a contemporary of Rajyavardhana who reduced him to submission. Little is known of him (*P.H.A.I.*, p. 607 n.)

Buddhavarman—a Pallava king of Kanchi, defeated the Cholas. His name is mentioned in inscriptions and he is believed to have been the sixth in succession after Vishnugopa who was the contemporary of Samudragupta (*q.v.*). Nothing else is known of him. (*P.H.A.I.*, p. 501)

Buhlul (Bahlul) Lodi—*see* Bahlol Lodi.

Bukka I—was a son of Sangama and co-operated with his brother Harihara I, in founding the city of Vijayanagar in 1336. Later on after the death of Harihar I he ruled as the sole king from 1354 till his death in 1377. Most of his life was spent in waging wars against the Bahmani kings in the midst of which he also managed to send an embassy to China.

Bukka II—was a grandson of Bukka I. His succession was disputed by a brother named Virupaksha and his rule occupied a very short period of two years. (1404-06).

Bulwand Darwaza—or Lofty Portal, was built by Akbar at Fathpur Sikri in 1575-76, probably as a triumphal arch to commemorate his conquest of Gujarat. Built of marble and sandstone it leads to the great mosque at Fathpur Sikri.

Bundellas, the—a clan of Rajputs of indigenous origin, who in the middle of the fourteenth century became prominent in the region lying to the south of the Jumna and north of the Vindhyas which was previously known as Jejakabhukti over which the Chandellas ruled. The Bundellas were a warlike people who gave their name to the land which they ruled and which came to be known as Bundelkhand. The Bundellas were reduced to submission by Akbar, but later on, in the reign of Aurangzeb, the Bundella chief Chhatrasal succeeded in carving out an independent principality for himself in eastern Malwa with his

capital at Panna. Still later on the state accepted British supremacy and its chief became one of the Indian princes within the
British empire.

Bundelkhand—is the name of the region between the Jumna on the
north and the Vindhyas on the south and between the Betwa on
the east and the Tons or Tamasa on the west. The name is
derived from the Bundellas who established their rule there in
the fourteenth century. Previously it was known as Jijhoti or
Jejakabhukti and was ruled by the Chandellas from the ninth
to the fourteenth centuries. The principal towns of the kingdom
were Khajuraho in Chhatarpur District, Mahoba in Hamirpur
District and Kalanjar in the Banda District of U. P. Khajuraho
still contains many beautiful architectural monuments while
Kalanjar had a strong fortress which strengthened the defences
of the state. Sher Shah was killed in 1545 when he was directing
the siege of Kalanjar. Bundelkhand is now a part of Vindhya
Pradesh which lies between Uttara Pradesh and Madhya
Pradesh within both of which some parts of the old Bundelkhand have been merged.

Bundi—is a small Rajput state not far from Mewar. Its prince
maintained independence for long years, but submitted to
Akbar and it thus became a part of the Mughul Empire. On the
decline of the Mughul Empire it passed for a time under the
control of the Maratha chief, Holkar, which ended with Holkar's
defeat in the Second Maratha War (1803-06). But the fear of the
Marathas still continued and in 1818 Bundi sought peace and
security by entering into a defensive alliance with the East
India Company. It thus became a part of the British Indian
Empire as a protected state and continued to be such a state
until its merger with the Indian Republic in 1947-48.

Buran—a leader of the Pindaries, played a prominent part in
their depredations from 1812 till their suppression in 1818. He
was killed in action during the campaign against the Pindaries
organised by Lord Hastings in 1817-18.

Burgoyne, Col.—was a member of the British Parliament who led
in May, 1773 a parliamentary attack on Robert Clive (*q.v.*).
On his motion resolutions were passed declaring that the
appropriation of any territories or funds acquired in India by
the armies of the East India Company to the private emoluments
of any person in the employment of the Company was illegal
and that Robert Clive did obtain and possess himself of the sum of
£ 234,000. A rider was added that Robert Clive at the same time
rendered great and meritorious services to his country. Clive

resented Col. Burgoyne's resolution and committed suicide in 1774.

Burha Gohain—was one of the two highest officers under the Ahom kings of Assam, the other being the *Bar Gohain* (*q.v.*). The officer was selected by the Ahom kings from amongst the members of a particular family and succession was practically hereditary. (Gait, *Hist. of Assam*, 235-36)

Burhan-i-Maasir, the—is a chronicle of the sultans of the Bahmani kingdom. It is a more authoritative account than Firishta's history. It was written by Sayyid Ali Tabá-tabá. The author was in the service of Burhan Nizam Shah II, sultan of Ahmadnagar, after whom the book is named. He took six years (1591-96) to complete writing the book. It deals with the history of the Bahmani dynasty as well as of the sultans of Ahmadnagar.

Burhan Nizam Shah I—was the second king of the Nizam Shahi dynasty of Ahmadnagar. During his long reign of forty-five years (1508-53) he was mainly engaged in wars with the neighbouring states, especially the Hindu kingdom of Vijayanagar. In 1550 he made a new departure by entering into an alliance with the Hindu kingdom of Vijayanagar against the Muhammadan state of Bijapur, but the alliance did not last long. Burhan was originally a sunni but late in life he adopted the shia form of Islam.

Burke, Edmund (1729-97)—was a prominent public man of England. He made his mark in literature and in political thinking and was acknowledged as the philosopher of British conservatism of the age. He entered the Parliament where he soon made his mark. It was as a member of the Parliament that he took a prominent part in the impeachment of Warren Hastings, Governor-General in India from 1774-85, and showed his innate liberalism and opposition to persecution of the people by men in authority, even though they belonged to his own country and his own race. His main works are *On Conciliation with America; French Revolution & The Sublime and the Beautiful.*

Burma—is a vast country lying to the east of India from which it is separated by the Patkoi range, by dense jungles, and the Bay of Bengal. No political relations appear to have existed between India and Burma in the earlier times, though the latter was influenced, first, by Hindu culture to such an extent that many parts of it bore Sanskritised names like Ayuthia or Ayodha. Later on from the time of Asoka Buddhist religion and culture began to spread in Burma to so large an extent that the majority of the Burmese are still Buddhists. India under Muhammadan

rule lost all contact with Burma which was also militarily not
very strong as it was divided into small states. But in 1757 a
new dynasty was founded in Burma by king Alompra. He and
his successors not only joined Upper and Lower Burma into one
kingdom but also extended their sway over Siam, Tennasserim,
Arakan and Manipur. These conquests, especially that of Assam
in 1816, brought the Burmese territories in dangerously close
proximity to the expansive British Indian Empire and made
inevitable a trial of strength between them. This led to three
successive Burmese wars (*q.v.*) leading to the annexation of the
whole of Burma to the British Indian Empire in 1886. Thus
Burma came to be united with India under British rule, but the
union was constitutionally terminated by the Government of
India Act, 1935. Since 1947 India and Burma have been
two friendly independent neighbours.

Burmese wars—were three in number. The *First Burmese War*
lasted two years (1824-26). It was caused by the expansion of
Burmese authority over Assam and its threatened expansion
in the region of Chittagong in lower Bengal. The Government
of Lord Amherst which declared the war, at first badly mismanaged it while the Burmese General Bandula (*q.v.*) showed
great efficiency. The British expelled the Burmese army from
Assam, sent a naval expedition to Rangoon which captured
and defeated Bandula in the battle of Donabew in which he
was killed by a chance shot. The British then occupied Prome,
the capital of Lower Burma, and soon forced the Burmese Government to make peace by the treaty of Yandabo (1826) by which
they agreed to pay to the British an indemnity of one crore of
rupees, to surrender to them the provinces of Arakan and
Tennasserim, to recognise Manipur as an independent state
and to abstain from any interference in Assam, Cachar and
Jaintia, to admit a British Resident at Ava and to conclude
a commercial treaty with the British which gave them some indefinite rights of trade and commerce in Burma.

The political and commercial claims arising out of the treaty
of Yandabo led to the *Second Burmese War* in 1852. The masterful Lord Dalhousie who was then the Governor-General,
insisted on a complete fulfilment of all the terms of the treaty by
the king of Burma who held that the British were demanding
more than what was stipulated. To enforce the acceptance of
the British demands by a particular date Lord Dalhousie sent a
frigate under Commodore Lambert to Rangoon and the um-
brageous temper of the British naval officer led to an exchange

of fire between the British frigate and a Burmese ship. Lord Dalhousie immediately sent an ultimatum and a British naval expedition under Admiral Austen soon invaded Lower Burma. Rangoon, Martaban, Bassein, Prome and Pegu were quickly captured. Lord Dalhousie personally visited Rangoon in September, 1852, and as the king of Burma still refused to come to terms and as the Governor-General did not consider it prudent to proceed immediately to Upper Burma he on his own initiative brought the war to a close by declaring that Lower Burma was annexed to the British Indian Empire. The annexation of Pegu or Lower Burma established the British control over the whole of the eastern coast of the Bay of Bengal.

The *Third Burmese War* followed 38 years later in 1885. Thibaw was then the king of Upper Burma with his capital at Mandalay and Lord Dufferin was the Governor-General of India. The Burmese king resented the forced loss of Lower Burma while the British Resident and officials at Mandalay resented the medieval formalities that they were required to follow in interviews with king Thibaw Full of resentment at the defeat of 1852, Thibaw began to look for support and help from the French who had in the meantime established a fairly large colonial empire in Cochin-China and Tonkin to the east of Upper Burma. These Burmese approaches to the French, coupled with the imposition by Thibaw's Government of a very heavy fine on an English firm engaged in timber business in Upper Burma, led the British Indian Government to declare the Third Burmese War in 1885. The British preparations were made with great thoroughness while Thibaw's expectations of receiving help from the French in Indo-China proved illusory. The war was declared on 9th November, 1885, and, within twenty days Mandalay was captured and king Thibaw was made a prisoner. He was deposed; Upper Burma was now annexed to the British Indian Empire and along with Lower Burma formed the new province of Burma with its headquarters at Rangoon. The British Indian Empire thus reached its furthest extent in the north-east. (Phayre, Sir A., *Hist. of Burma;* Harvey, G. E., *Hist. of Burma*)

Burnes, Sir Alexander (1805-41)—entered the Company's military service at the age of 16, learnt Persian, made his mark as a diplomat when in 1830 he was sent on a mission to Ranjit Singh (*q.v.*) at Lahore and was later on sent to travel through Afghanistan, Bokhara and Persia. In 1830 he went on a nominally commercial but in reality a political mission to Kabul when he

discovered the presence of a Russian agent. On his return to
India he advised support to Amir Dost Muhammad but his
advice was rejected. The policy that was adopted by Lord
Lytton I led to the Second Afghan War (*q.v.*) in the course of
which Burnes was appointed Political Agent at Kabul under
Sir W. H. Macnaghten (*q.v.*) in 1839, but on November 2, 1840
the Afghan mob rose and Burnes was assassinated in Kabul, thus
paying the penalty for an aggressive policy for which others
were responsible.

Burnes, James (1801-62)—elder brother of Sir Alexander Burnes,
came to India in 1821 and was a surgeon in the Company's
army till 1849. He was a scholarly type of man and wrote a
History of Kutch.

Burney, Major Henry—was the first British Resident appointed
in the Court of Ava in 1830.

Burn, Colonel—was the British commanding officer at Khirki
when the British garrison there was suddenly attacked by
Peshwa Baji Rao II in 1816. Col. Burn completely defeated the
Peshwa and thus frustrated his plan.

Buses, Father—a Christian missionary, came to India and became
very intimate with Prince Dara Shukoh (*q.v.*), the eldest son of
Emperor Shah Jahan.

Bussy, Marquis de—a prominent French general, played an
important part in the Anglo-French wars (*q.v.*) that were
fought in the Carnatic. His full name was Charles Joseph
Patissier, Marquis de Bussy. In 1751 he escorted as per the
order of Dupleix the new Nizam Muzaffar Jang to his capital at
Aurangabad. On the death of Muzaffar Jang and the accession
of Salabat Jang Bussy became the adviser and guide of the new
Nizam whose government he directed for seven years with
great skill. In 1753 Bussy persuaded Nizam Salabat Jang to
assign to him the revenue of the Northern Circars for the payment of his troops who upheld the French influence in the
Nizam's Court and the Nizam's authority against all
his enemies. Soon after the outbreak of the Third Anglo-
French War (1756-63) Bussy was recalled from the Nizam's
dominions by Count de Lally (*q.v.*) in 1758. With his recall the
French influence in the Nizam's Court was destroyed. The
Northern Circars were also occupied by the English army which
under Sir Eyre Coote defeated the French in 1760 at the battle of
Wandiwash (*q.v.*) where Bussy was made a prisoner. Later on he
was released and went back to France. He was sent again to
India in 1783 to help Haidar Ali (*q.v.*) in his move against the

English. But Bussy was then an old sickly man and Haidar Ali died before Bussy's arrival. In the circumstances Bussy could not influence the progress of events and finally retired to France to enjoy the wealth that he had earned as the adviser of Nizam Salabat Jang.

Butler, Dr Fanny—the first English female physician to come to India and to practise medicine, arrived in 1860 and set up a new ideal of service which could be rendered by women.

Butler, Sir Harcourt—was a member of the Viceroy's Executive Council and, later on, became in succession the Governor of the United Provinces and of Burma. He was known as a capable administrator and was appointed in 1927 the Chairman of the Indian States Committee that was set up by the Secretary of State for investigating the relationship between the Paramount Power and the Indian states. The Committee submitted the Report (q.v.) in 1929.

Butler Committee Report—was submitted in 1929. After investigating the relationship that existed between the Paramount Power in India and the Indian states the Report made recommendations for the adjustment of financial and economic relations between British India and the Indian states. Its fundamental recommendation was that "in view of the historical nature of the relationship between the Paramount Power and the princes, the latter should not be transferred without their own agreement to a relationship with a new Government responsible to an Indian legislature". The Report reflected the fears of the Indian princes of losing their powers in a popularly governed India, but it was looked upon as retrograde by the general public opinion in India.

Buxar, the battle of—was fought on the 22nd October, 1764. In this battle the Company's army led by Major Hector Munro defeated the combined armies of Emperor Shah Alam II, Nawab Shuja-ud-daulah of Oudh and Mir Kasim, the fugitive Nawab of Bengal. The victory of the Company at Buxar greatly increased its prestige in India, consolidated its supremacy over Bengal and led to an arrangement between the Company and the Emperor of Delhi according to which the Emperor granted to the Company the Diwani of Bengal, Bihar and Orissa in return for the districts of Allahabad and Kora taken from the Nawab of Oudh and an annual tribute of 26 lakhs of rupees from the revenues of Bengal, Bihar and Orissa. Thus the position of the East India Company was legalised in Bengal, Bihar and Orissa.

C

Cabinet Mission—was sent out to India in 1946 by the Ministry of Attlee (*q.v.*). The Mission had Lord Pethick-Lawrence as the Chairman and Sir Stafford Cripps and Mr. (later on Viscount) A. V. Alexander as members. The Mission, which arrived in India in April, at first tried to effect a compromise between the Indian National Congress and Muslim League over the constitutional problem that faced the country. But as the efforts at mediation failed the Cabinet Mission made its own proposals for constitutional progress. These were: (i) formation of a Federal Union of the British Indian provinces with powers to control defence, foreign affairs and communications; (ii) inclusion of the princely states within the federal union after negotiation; (iii) formation of subordinate unions of their own by individual provinces at their option with rights to decide for themselves the powers that they would exercise outside the range of federal subjects; (iv) the convention, on the basis of the three above-mentioned provisions, of a Constituent Assembly representing all parties for drawing up an agreed constitution for India; and (v) the formation, in the meanwhile, of an Interim National Government to run the administration. The Cabinet Mission proposals fell through over the communal allotment of seats in the Interim Government (*q.v.*).

Cabral, Antonio—came to the court of Emperor Akbar in 1573 as the envoy of the Portuguese viceroy at Goa and negotiated terms of peace between the Mughul Emperor and the Portuguese. Cabral visited Akbar in his capital a second time in 1578 and was asked by the Emperor to arrange to send to the court qualified Christian theologians from whom Akbar might get accurate information about the Christian religion and theology. On receipt of this request the Portuguese Government at Goa sent to Akbar's court Father Aquaviva and Father Monserrate who were received courteously by Akbar and imparted to him correct information on Christianity.

Cabral, Father John—a Portuguese Jesuit missionary, was in Bengal in 1632 when the Portuguese settlement at Hughli was invaded and captured by the order of Emperor Shah Jahan. Cabral who was an eye-witness, wrote an account of the incident in 1633.

Cabral, Pedro Alvares—was the second Portuguese admiral who arrived in India in 1500, just one year after the departure of Vasco da Gama with a large Portuguese fleet. He established a factory or agency at Calicut, obtained good cargoes from Cannanore and Cochin and returned to Portugal after a successful voyage.

Cachar—now a district with its headquarters at Silchar within the modern state of Assam, has a long history which can be traced many centuries back and it had a line of kings who claimed descent from Bhima, the second of the five Pandavas. In historical times it was more often than not a subordinate and protected state under the Ahom kings of Assam. It was overrun by the Burmese in 1819 with the connivance of the reigning king Govinda Chandra, but the Burmese were soon expelled from Cachar by the British who by the treaty of Badarpur (March, 1824) reinstated Govinda Chandra as the Raja of Cachar on his agreeing to acknowledge the suzerainty of the East India Company and to pay an annual tribute of Rs. 10,000. But Govinda Chandra mismanaged the administration, failed to suppress local rebels, oppressed his subjects with heavy taxation and was at last killed by an assassin in 1830. He had left no heir and the state of Cachar was annexed to the British Empire by a proclamation in August, 1832 and has since been a part of the Indian Empire. (Gait, *History of Assam*)

Cactus line or hedge—2500 miles in length, was raised in the earlier part of the British Rule in India in order to prevent the free transit of bulk articles from province to province, particularly the smuggling of salt into the Indian states. 12,000 men were needed to watch it. With the progress of free trading principles in India the first 1000 miles of it were abolished during the administration of Lord Northbrook and the rest under Lord Lytton (1876 to 1880).

Caillaud, Colonel John—was the commander of the Company's troops in Bengal in 1760. He entered into the intrigue of Vansittart for replacing Nawab Mir Jafar with Mir Kasim, and, acting under the orders of Vansittart, entered Murshidabad with an army, occupied the Nawab's palace and thus practically forced Nawab Mir Jafar to abdicate. Thereafter Mir Kasim was declared Nawab of Bengal.

Calcutta—was founded by Job Charnock, the English agent of the East India Company, in 1690. He established an English factory at Sutanati on the Hughli, 15 miles down from the modern town of Hughli. Sutanati was surrounded by swamps and did not at first appear to be a very promising site. But it was navigable and better suited to be the headquarters of a sea-power than both Chinsurah where the Dutch had settled and Chandernagore where the French had already established themselves, for the ships of neither could reach their factories without passing by Sutanati. In 1696 the rebellion of Sobha Singh gave the English an excuse for fortifying their factory at Sutanati. Two years later, in 1698, the English acquired Zamindari rights over the three adjacent villages of Sutanati, Kalikata and Govindapur by paying Rs. 1,200/- only to the previous proprietors and the three together formed one unit which later on came to be known as Calcutta which was an anglicised form of the older Bengali name Kalikata. In 1700 it became the seat of a Presidency under the name of Fort William in Bengal with Sir Charles Eyre as the first President. In 1716 the construction of Fort William was completed. As a result of Surman's embassy to the Court of Emperor Farruksiyar the Company got in 1717 the right of free trade in Bengal, subject to an annual payment of Rs. 3,000/- only. This greatly promoted the trade of the Company in Bengal and increased the prosperity of Calcutta which came to have a population of 100,000 by 1735 and its shipping amounted to ten thousand tons a year by 1727. In 1742 the alarm of a Maratha incursion led to the beginning of the Maratha Ditch, now represented by the Circular Road. On the death of Nawab Ali Vardi in April 1756 his grandson Siraj-ud-daula became the Nawab of Bengal. An Anglo-French war was in the offing and the English and the French both began to fortify their settlements. Siraj disliked this and ordered them to stop the constructions. The French desisted but the English not only prevaricated but also gave asylum in Calcutta to a political fugitive. This infuriated Siraj who attacked Calcutta and invested it on the 16th June, 1756. After only a four days' siege Calcutta surrendered to the Nawab who soon afterwards left it without taking adequate steps for following up his victory and preventing the re-capture of Calcutta by the English. Taking advantage of this negligence of the Nawab an English army under Clive and Watson recovered Calcutta in January, 1757 and the Nawab recognised the restoration of the Company's power in Calcutta by a treaty concluded in February, 1757. Soon a conspiracy was started between the Company's officers in Calcutta and the disaffected nobles at the Court of the Nawab culminating in the battle of Plassey on the 23rd June, 1757, the defeat and execution of Nawab Siraj-ud-daula and installation of Mir Jafar as the Nawab of Bengal in Murshidabad. These and subsequent events largely enhanced the prestige of the Company in Bengal which now practically passed under the rule of the English with the result that Calcutta, rather than the Nawab's capital at Murshidabad, became the real centre of administration in Bengal. Subsequent political changes still further increased the importance of Calcutta to which the Board of Revenue, so long stationed at Murshidabad, was transferred in 1772, and next year the Regulating Act made the Governor of Bengal in the person of Warren Hastings the Governor-General over the British possessions in India. Calcutta thus became the official capital of the British Indian Empire, a distinction which it continued to enjoy until 1912, when the headquarters of the Government of India were transferred to Delhi. Calcutta is now the headquarters of the state of West Bengal.

Calcutta, like the other two Presidency towns of Madras and Bombay, has enjoyed some special rights of local self-government. At the close of the eighteenth century the maintenance of the sanitation of the city as well as its police were entrusted to a number of Justices of the Peace appointed by the Government. In 1856 three Commissioners were appointed to look after the conservancy of the city, its general improvement and the assessment and collection of rates. But as this arrangement did not work satisfactorily a Chairman was appointed to supervise the work of the Justices of the Peace and the Chairman was also made the Commissioner of Police of the city. Under the Chairmanship of Sir Stuart Hogg foundations were laid for a proper system of drainage by the construction of sewers and of water-supply. Other improvements were also made and Calcutta began to develop into the city of palaces that it is now. But there were constant bickerings between the Justices of the Peace and the Chairman, so in 1876 the Corporation of Calcutta was reconstituted and was vested in a Chairman and a body of seventy-two members of whom two-thirds were elected. In 1882 the number of elected members was raised to fifty and the jurisdiction of the Corporation was extended by the addition of some suburban areas. But in 1899, by an Act passed at the instance of Lord Curzon, the number of elected members was reduced to a half of the total strength and the Chairman, who was to be an official appointed by the Government, was vested with large independent powers. This Act was deeply resented by the Indian public and was strenuously opposed in the local legislature by the Indian members led by Surendranath Banerjee (*q.v*). But the Act was passed in spite of their protest. So when it came to be enforced twenty-eight Indian members of the

Calcutta Corporation, led by Surendranath Banerjee, resigned their seats in the Corporation. This may be considered as the earliest instance of the practice of non-co-operation in India. Twenty-four years later Surendranath Banerjee, then the Minister of Local Self-Government in Bengal, passed a new Act which entirely changed the constitution of the Corporation of Calcutta by abolishing the office of the official Chairman, by giving the Corporation an entirely elected body of Councillors, a Mayor elected by the Councillors and an Executive officer appointed by and responsible to the Corporation. Calcutta thus came to control its own civic administration.

Calcutta Journal, the—was printed and published by an English journalist, named John Silk Buckingham. He was expelled from the country by the government of John Adams, the officiating Governor-General in 1823 and the *Calcutta Journal* ceased publication.

Calcutta Madrassa—founded in 1781 by Warren Hastings who was then the Governor-General, has since been a very important centre of Oriental (Persian and Arabic) studies in India.

Calcutta Medical College—founded in March, 1835, by Lord William Bentinck who was then the Governor-General, marked the beginning of the study and practice of the western medical science in India. It has produced a large number of eminent Indian physicians and surgeons one of whom was Bidhan Chandra Roy, the Chief Minister of Bengal, in recent years and another was Upendranath Brahmachari who invented a specific for *Kalazar*.

Calcutta University, the—was founded in 1857 during the administration of Lord Canning. It was started as an affiliating and examining body with a nominated Vice-Chancellor, who held the office on an honorary basis, and was to act with the advice and consent of a Senate and a Syndicate. The earlier Vice-Chancellors were all Europeans and the first Indian to be appointed as Vice-Chancellor was Sir Gurudas Banerjee. In 1904 Lord Curzon passed the Indian Universities Act with the main intention of tightening Government control over the Universities and restricting their territorial jurisdiction, especially of the Calcutta University which at that time extended to such distant parts as Burma and Ceylon. The Act limited the number of Senators, the majority of whom were to be nominated by the Government, laid down stringent conditions for the affiliation of new colleges, prescribed systematic inspection of the affiliated colleges by the Universities and authorised the Universities to

make provisions for teaching by appointing Professors and
Lecturers and by equipping laboratories and museums. This Act
of 1904 which was at first fashioned to restrict the expansion of
education in Bengal, was utilised by Sir Asutosh Mookerjee
during his Vice-Chancellorship to open the teaching section of
the Calcutta University, which has done work which has been
useful not only to Bengal but also to the rest of India. The
jurisdiction of Calcutta University is now much less than before,
but it still continues to be the premier University in India and
its contribution to the advancement of learning which has always
been its aim, still continues to be larger than that of any other
Indian University. The constitution of the Calcutta University
was recently changed and it has now got a whole-time paid
Vice-Chancellor and a Treasurer at the top of its executive.

Calicut—was in the 15th century the most important port on the
Malabar coast. On 27th May, 1498, the Portuguese explorer and
admiral Vasco da Gama arrived at this port with three ships
and was kindly received by its Hindu ruler who bore the title
of Zamorin. This incident revolutionized Indian history by
opening up the country to adventurers coming by sea, and thus
prepared the way for the eventual establishment of the British
Empire in India.

Cambodia—*see* Kambuja.

Camac, General—led an English army during the First Maratha
War (1775-82) and won a battle against the Sindhia at Sipri on
16th February, 1781.

Campbell, Sir Archibald—was the Commander-in-Chief of the
British expeditionary force that was sent to Burma during the
First Burmese War (1824-26). He committed many mistakes in
organising and executing the campaign which was therefore
needlessly prolonged and subjected the expeditionary forces to
many avoidable hardships. But in spite of these mistakes Campbell
captured Rangoon in May, 1824, defeated the large relieving
army brought up by the Burmese General Bandula, who was
soon afterwards killed in action, occupied Prome, marched
up to Yandabo within 60 miles of the Burmese capital and thus
forced the king of Burma to purchase peace by the treaty of
Yandabo (1826) which Campbell dictated.

Campbell, Sir Colin (afterwards Lord Clyde)—came to India
in the midst of the Sepoy Mutiny (*q.v.*) as the Commander-in-
Chief of the British Indian army. He played an important part
in suppressing the Mutiny (1857-58). He organised a well-
thought-out plan of campaign, secured the help of Jang Bahadur

of Nepal, relieved Lucknow in the middle of November, 1857, recovered Cawnpore from the mutinous Gwalior army in December, suppressed the risings in Oudh and Rohilkhand, relentlessly pursued the Rani of Jhansi and Tantia Topi until the first was killed in action and the second was made a prisoner and hanged. Campbell thus largely contributed to the suppression of the Mutiny and the triumph of the British Raj.

Campbell, John—a civilian employed in the Company's service, was between 1847 and 1854 in charge of the Orissa administration and took a leading part under the direction of Lord Hardinge I, Governor-General of India, in stamping out the custom of human sacrifice which was till then rampant in Orissa.

Canning, Captain—was sent by the British Indian Government as an envoy to the Court of Bodawpaya, King of Burma (1779-1819) on three successive occasions in 1803, 1809 and 1811. Like the envoys sent earlier Canning was not treated well and failed to conclude an agreement on the frontier between India and Burma.

Canning, Viscount (Earl)—was the Governor-General of India from 1856 to 1862. He was the first Viceroy in India. The most outstanding event in the earlier part of his administration was the outbreak of the Sepoy Mutiny (1857-58) which at one time threatened the existence of the British rule in India. By his organising ability and the latent support of the vast majority of the civil population of India Lord Canning succeeded in suppressing the Mutiny. The suppression of the Mutiny was followed by the passing in 1858 by the Parliament of an Act for the Better Government of India which transferred the administration of India from the East India Company to the Crown of England and made the Governor-General of India the Viceroy. The passing of the Act was soon followed by the publication of the Queen's Proclamation (*q.v.*) and, thus Lord Canning, who became the first Viceroy, started a new system of administration in India. Lord Canning tried to put a curb on the revengeful temper of the triumphant British community in India and was dubbed by them with the title of 'Clemency Canning'. The commercial British community of Calcutta even went to the length of submitting to the Queen a petition asking for the recall of Lord Canning. But the petition was rejected and Lord Canning continued to be in charge of the administration of India. He reorganised the army of India and restored stability to her finances by introducing the income tax, a uniform tariff of ten per cent and a convertible paper currency. He passed a Rent

Act in 1859 to give greater security to the tenants under the Bengal system of land-tenure. The Indian Penal Code was enacted in 1860 and the Criminal Procedure Code appeared in 1861. In 1862 the old Supreme Courts and the Company's *Adalats* were replaced by Chartered High Courts in Calcutta, Madras and Bombay. Lord Canning appointed a Commission to enquire into the grievances of the tenants in Bengal and Bihar against the European Indigo-planters and on the strength of its Report the oppression by the Indigo-planters was greatly limited. Lord Canning founded the three Universities of Calcutta, Bombay and Madras in 1857 and started a new period of enlightenment in India. The last important event in the administration of Lord Canning was the passing of the Indian Councils Act of 1861 which effected important improvements in the administrative machinery and facilitated the introduction of a non-official Indian element in the legislature of India (*q.v.*).

Careri, Dr. Gemelli—an Italian traveller, visited India during the reign of Aurangzeb. In 1695 he was actually in the camp of Aurangzeb at Galgala on the northern bank of the Krishna. He has left a very interesting account of the camp of Aurangzeb, his appearance and the method of his living and work.

Carey, William—originally a shoe-maker by profession, became a Baptist Missionary, came to Calcutta in 1793, settled, along with other Baptist Missionaries, at Serampore and devoted himself to the propagation of Christianity amongst the people of Bengal. He learnt Bengali and with the help of his Munshi Ramram Bose translated the Bible into Bengali, published other books in Bengali prose of which the best known was *Kathopakathan* and helped in the publication of two Bengali journals namely, *Digdarshan* and *Samachar Darpan*. Carey thus can be called the creator of Bengali prose. In 1801 Carey became the Professor of Sanskrit and Bengali at the Fort William College in Calcutta and held the post until his death in 1831. In this capacity also he encouraged the writing in Bengali of several books on History, Philosophy as well as legends and stories. As an educationist Carey advocated the teaching of the Western sciences and English literature amongst the Indians and his views largely implemented the decision of Lord William Bentinck in favour of the expansion of Western education in India. Carey was also a prominent social reformer and it was at his instance that in 1802 Lord Wellesley prohibited the custom of throwing children at the confluence of the Ganges and the sea. *Sati* or the immolation of widows on the funeral pyres of their husbands was also strongly condemned by Carey who played an important part in moulding public opinion even amongst the Hindus to such an extent that Lord William Bentinck prohibited it in 1829. An educationist and a social reformer Carey is still remembered by the Indians. (Smith, George, *Life of William Carey*)

Carmichael, Lord—was the first Governor of Bengal (1912-16) after it was constituted into a Governor's province separated from Bihar as well as Assam.

Carnac, Colonel—was a General in the Company's army and was in charge of Bihar in 1765 when he was promoted to the Bengal Council and helped Lord Clive in administering the Company's affairs in Bengal from 1765 to 1767. Later on he accompanied a British army sent against the Marathas during the First Maratha War and disgraced himself by signing the Convention of Wargaon (13 January, 1719) by which it was agreed that some English officers would be handed over to the Marathas as hostages for the restoration to the Marathas of all territories acquired by the Company since 1773. The Convention was repudiated by Warren Hastings and Carnac was dismissed by order of the Directors.

Carnatic Wars, the—were fought between the English and the French in the second half of the eighteenth century on Indian soil. The wars were fought to decide the rivalry between the English and French and were directly concerned with their rivalry in Europe. These were really part of the great Anglo-French Wars of the eighteenth century and are called Carnatic Wars because the theatre of these wars in India lay mainly in the Carnatic.

The *First Carnatic War* was the result of Anglo-French hostility in the War of Austrian Succession (1740-48) and began in India in 1746 when Madras was captured by the French. Anwar-ud-din, Nawab of the Carnatic, was prevailed upon by the English to send a large Indian army for the purpose of driving the French out of Madras, but this large army of the Nawab was defeated by the French at the battle of St. Thome. The English attack on Pondicherry was repulsed by the French who, under the leadership of Dupleix, remained in possession of Madras. The war came to an end by the Treaty of Aix-la-Chapelle (1748) on the basis of mutual restitution of conquests. Madras was therefore restored to the English and territorially the English and the French position remained unaltered. But the First Carnatic War left the important lesson that a small army of Europeans aided by Indian troops trained and armed after the European fashion could easily defeat much larger Indian armies.

This lesson was exploited by Dupleix in order to secure political advantages by intervening in the affairs of Hyderabad where Asaf Jah, the Nizam, died in 1748 and of the Carnatic where Nawab Anwar-ud-din died in 1749. The succession to both of them were disputed and Dupleix pledged French support to Chanda Shaheb to the throne of the Carnatic as against the late Nawab's illegitimate son Muhammad Ali and to the late Nizam's grandson, Muzaffar Jang, as against the Nizam's second son, Nazir Jang, to the throne of Hyderabad. Naturally therefore the English in India supported Nazir Jang for the throne of the Nizam and Muhammad Ali for the Nawabship of the Carnatic. Thus began the second phase of the Anglo-French War which is known as the *Second Carnatic War* (1751-54). It was an unofficial war fought between the English and the French in India at a time when there was peace between them in Europe. At first the French under the direction of Dupleix carried everything before them. Their *protégé* Chanda Shaheb obtained possession of the Carnatic and forced his rival Muhammad Ali to take refuge in the fort of Trichinopoly under the protection of the English troops. In Hyderabad Muzaffar Jung was installed as the Nizam and he rewarded the French by recognizing them as the sovereign of southern India from the Krishna to Cape Comorin. In 1751 Muzaffar Jung was killed, but the French succeeded in putting on the throne of the Nizam another *protégé* named Salabat Jung who continued to allow the French to enjoy the rights and privileges that had been bestowed on them by Muzaffar Jung. It now only seemed a question of time which would complete the French triumph by the capture of Trichinopoly where Muhammad Ali was besieged by Chanda Shaheb with French support. If Trichinopoly would fall English power in the Carnatic and in the Deccan would be ruined. At this critical stage the English at the suggestion of Robert Clive, a young Captain, decided to make a diversion by attacking Arcot, the capital of Chanda Shaheb. The plan proved a great success. Clive and his small army of 200 European and 300 Indian soldiers easily captured the fort at Arcot. Immediately Chanda Shaheb moved large forces from before Trichinopoly and besieged Arcot in a supreme effort at its capture. But Clive and his small army stood the siege for 53 days and then so successfully repulsed an attempt of Chanda Shaheb to storm the place that Chanda Shaheb with his army withdrew from before Arcot.

The triumphant army of Clive then came out of the fort and strengthened by fresh relieving armies sent by the English and their Indian allies, defeated Chanda Shaheb at several important battles including one fought at Kaveripak. The French now resigned all claims to the Carnatic and their *protégé* Chanda Shaheb who had surrendered, was executed. The French influence was still upheld at the Nizam's Court by Bussy whom Dupleix had sent there. But the failure of the French in the Carnatic acted as a damper on the Government of France which had been opposed to the unofficial war on which Dupleix had embarked and was determined to restore peace. So it recalled Dupleix to France in 1754 and the Second Carnatic War came to an end. It left the French predominant in the Nizam's Court and the English in the Carnatic.

A *Third Carnatic War* followed just two years later in 1756 when the Seven Years' War broke out in Europe. Again England and France were at war and consequently their agents in India began a war amongst themselves. This time the war passed beyond the limits of the Carnatic into Bengal where the English captured the French possession of Chandernagore in 1757. But the most decisive battles of the war were fought in the Carnatic. France sent to Pondicherry a new Governor, named Count de Lally. He began well, captured Fort. St. David and other small English possessions in the region, but failed to take Madras. He also committed the mistake of recalling Bussy from the Nizam's Court where the French influence at once collapsed. An English army under Col. Forde, sent from Bengal, occupied in 1758 the Northern Sarkars, so long held by the French. The war still continued but in 1760 an English army under Sir Eyre Coote defeated the French under Lally at the battle of Wandiwash. Lally retreated to Pondicherry which was soon besieged by the English and was forced to surrender in 1761.

The war ended in 1763 with the Peace of Paris which restored to France Pondicherry and her other Indian possessions to be held as mere trading centres without any fortifications and armies. Thus the Third Carnatic War ended in the complete triumph of the English over their French rivals in India and cleared the way for the establishment of the British Empire in India, unhampered by any European rival. (Orme, R., *Hist. of Military Transactions etc.*, Wilks, M., *Sketches of South India.*, Roberts, P. E., *Hist. of India to the End of the East India Company*)

Caron, Francois—was the founder of the first French factory in India. Sent by the French East India Company he came to the

Indian coast with a small French fleet in 1667 and founded a factory at Surat.

Cartier, John—an employee in the service of the East India Company, rose to the position of the Governor of Bengal which he held from 1769 to 1772. His administration was marked by much corruption and carelessness for the interests of the children of the soil and was rendered infamous by the outbreak of the famine of 1770 which carried away one-third of the population of Bengal and Bihar.

Cartridges, greased—had to be used for the Enfield rifle which was introduced in the British Indian army in 1856. The cartridges were smeared with grease and had to be bitten off before insertion into the rifle. As no animal grease was taboo with the English manufacturers of the rifle it came to be believed that the cartridges were deliberately introduced for polluting the Hindu as well as the Muslim sepoy. The authorities at first denied the use of any grease at all, but later enquiries revealed that at the Woolwich arsenal where the cartridges were manufactured, animal fat had been used. So the official denial only made the position more intriguing and gave to the attempt at the introduction of greased cartridges the appearance of a deliberate conspiracy on the part of a Christian Government to defile the Hindu as well as the Muslim. The cartridges were later on withdrawn, but this came too late and was considered to be only a sign of weakness on the part of the Government. The protestations of the Government were disbelieved and the introduction of the greased cartridges set the spark that enkindled the embers of the prevalent discontent amongst the sepoys and largely contributed to the Mutiny in 1857.

Caste System, the—is the most characteristic institution in the social life of the Hindus and therefore of their country, India. It dominates their manners, morals and thought. How old it is poses a difficult question. Orthodox Hindus consider it to be of divine origin and trace it to the Rig-Veda. But modern opinion regards it as a man-made institution which was not created all at once by any single person, but was developed as a result of conditions prevailing at different times. Orthodox texts hold that the people are divinely divided into four castes, viz. the Brahmanas, the Kshatriyas, the Vaishyas and the Sudras and each caste is separated from the others by its own *dharma* or obligatory rules and inter-dining and inter-marriages are prohibited. In reality, however, there are several thousands of castes and sub-castes and the prohibitions regarding inter-dining and inter-marriages have differed in different ages and in different parts of India. At present the prohibitions about inter-dining have practically ceased, especially in urban areas, and restrictions as to inter-marriages have also been much relaxed. Yet the caste system continues to be a live institution even amongst educated Indians and is still the one system that distinguishes Hindu social life from that of the followers of other religions.

Historically speaking the caste system is found to have existed in the early Vedic age only in a nebulous form. In the later Vedic age, in the era of the *Sutras*, it became hereditary and represented occupational groups. Those who specialised in the study of the Vedas and took charge of religious ceremonies were called Brahmanas. Those who devoted themselves to political and military activities were called Kshatriyas. The general mass of the Aryan people were known as Vaishyas whose principal occupations were trade and commerce. The rest of the people, whose occupation was service, was known as the Sudras. In the historical period the Mauryas were believed to be Sudras while Megasthenes who came to India during the reign of Chandragupta Maurya, noticed the people divided into seven castes which were really occupational groups, rather than hereditary groups or castes. We are told that, except for the philosophers who occupied the highest rung of the ladder, inter-marriages as well as change of occupations were prohibited. In still later times foreigners who came to India either as conquerors or as immigrants and settled in the country were embraced within the fold of Hinduism and placed in castes suiting their occupations. The fighting peoples were placed in the caste of the Kshatriyas and came to be known as Rajputs. Similarly indigenous tribal peoples like the Gonds who raised themselves in the political sphere, were also recognised as Kshatriyas. Thus the caste system was still a dynamic force in Indian society up to the invasion and conquest of the country by the Muhammadans. This cataclysm tightened the bonds of the caste. The Hindus, unable to resist the Muhammadans in the field, defended themselves passively by increased rigidity of the caste restrictions and thus saved themselves and Hinduism during the many centuries of Muslim rule in India. The rigidity of the caste system has been greatly relaxed in modern times as the result of the spreading of modern ideas and knowledge amongst the Hindus and the policy of the independent Republic of India is to work gradually for the extinction of the caste divisions and restrictions. (Ketkar, S. V.,

Hist. of Caste in India; Senart, E., *Caste in India;* Hutton, J. H., *Caste in India,* (1946)

Cavagnari, Sir Pierre—was the envoy of the British Indian Government who was stationed at Kabul after the treaty of Kurram (1879) which closed the earlier phase of the Second Afghan War (1878-80). He arrived at Kabul in July 1879 but was murdered by the mutinous Afghan troops of the Amir six weeks later in September, 1879. His murder led to a revival of hostilities and the continuation of the Second Afghan War for another year.

Cave architecture—is a very interesting feature of ancient Indian architecture. Caves came to be used for housing purposes as early as the reign of Asoka and at Barabar (*q.v.*) near Gaya are still to be found several caves which Emperor Asoka turned into habitable places and bestowed on the Ajivikas for residential purposes. The Asokan caves were plain chambers, but in later times pillars and sculptures were introduced to make the caves beautiful places of residence and worship, especially by the Buddhists. Hundreds of such caves lie scattered in different parts of India. The caves used as monasteries or residences of monks were plain and consisted of a central hall with small cells on the sides. Caves used for purposes of worship were called *Chaityas*. These were fine works of art. A *Chaitya* had a long rectangular hall with an apsidal end. Two long rows of pillars divided the hall into a nave and two side aisles. Near the apsidal end there was a small *stupa*. The front wall was decorated with elaborate sculptures. Three small doorways led to the nave and the aisles. The *stupa* at the other end was lighted by a horse-shoe shaped window at the top of the central doorway. Many such caves have been found at Nasik, Bhaja, Bedsa, Karle and many other places in the Bombay Presidency. The Karle cave is considered the finest of them all which were built in the period between *c.* 200 B.C. and A.D. 320. (Smith, *Hist. of Fine Art in India and Ceylon*).

Cawnpore—is an old city situated on the bank of the Ganges in Uttar Pradesh. It was a garrison town from the early days of British rule in India. It played a prominent part during the Sepoy Mutiny. Nana Shaheb, the son of the ex-Peshwa Baji Rao II, was living at Bithur near Cawnpore when the Sepoy Mutiny broke out. He declared himself the Peshwa and took the leadership of the mutinous sepoys stationed at Cawnpore. The British entrenchments were invested on the 8th June, 1857 and the British community within was compelled to surrender on the 27th, having been assured of safe-conduct to Allahabad.

But as the garrison prepared to leave the place by boats a murderous fire was opened on them and all but four soldiers were killed. Of the civilian English community 211 women and children were at first kept confined in a building, known as the Bibigarh, where, on the 15th July, they were all mercilessly put to death by orders of Nana Shaheb and his friend Tantia Topi and their dead bodies were flung into a well. This massacre roused intense feelings of revenge in the minds of the English and an English army led by Neill and Havelock recovered Cawnpore a day after the massacre and perpetrated acts of extreme cruelty against the Indians. The city was occupied by the mutinous Gwalior contingent late in November, 1857, but was recovered by Sir Colin Campbell early in December, 1857. Cawnpore is now a busy industrial centre. In 1931 it was the scene of bitter communal riots in which the Muhammadans had the worst and which a section of them later on turned into an excuse for not joining the Indian National Congress in its struggle against British imperialism.

Census—was known in ancient India. Megasthenes records that one of the duties of the Municipal Board in charge of the administration of the city of Pataliputra in the reign of Chandragupta Maurya (*c.* 325 B.C. - 298 B.C.) was to register births and deaths amongst the citizens. The *Arthasastra* (*q.v.*) also refers to a permanent census. But the practice fell into disuse in later times, and was revived in modern times by the British Indian Government and continues now to be a regular feature in the administration of the country. A census is taken every ten years.

Ceylon—geologically a fragment detached from the Indian peninsula in relatively recent times, has had close cultural ties with India but a distinct political existence. It has been known in Indian literature by various names in different ages. The Pali Texts and the Asokan inscriptions refer to it as Tamraparni, the classical writers call it Taprobane, the *Ramayana* calls it Lanka ruled by Ravana, the King of the Rakhasas, and the modern Europeans call it Ceylon. Its Sanskritised name is Singhala, and, according to a tradition preserved in Bengal, this name came to be given to it after a fugitive Bengali prince named Vijaya Singha who conquered the island. Sober history knows of no such incident. Close commercial connection has always existed between Ceylon and India and very close cultural connection came to be established between the two countries in the third century B.C. when Devanampiya Tissa, the King of Ceylon, along with his whole family, was converted to Buddhism by Mahendra, a son or brother of King Asoka Maurya of Magadha. From that time onward Ceylon became a centre of Buddhism where the Buddhist scriptures (*Tripitaka*) were first put down in writing in 80 B.C. during the reign of the Ceylonese king Vattagamani and Anuradhapura came to be the centre from which Buddhism spread not only over the whole of Ceylon but also over large parts of South East Asia and even Indian Buddhist scholars visited Ceylon to complete their studies there. In the political tussle fortunes varied. In the fourth century A.D. the Ceylonese king Meghavarna maintained courteous relations with his illustrious contemporary Gupta monarch, Samudragupta, and got from him permission for building a monastery at Bodh Gaya for Ceylonese pilgrims coming on pilgrimage there. In the sixth century the early Pallava kings Simhavishnu and his grandson Narsimhavarman ruled over Ceylon. Again in the tenth-eleventh centuries the Chola kings Rajaraja and Rajendra I ruled over Ceylon but the island soon recovered its independence which was soon afterwards threatened by an invasion by the Sailendras of Sri Vijaya (*q.v.*) but Ceylon repulsed the invasion successfully. Ceylon never passed under Muslim rule, though early in the fifteenth century it appears to have passed under the control of the Vijayanagar king Deva Raya II (1425-47). Ceylon soon reassumed her independence but by the middle of the sixteenth century the major portion of coastal Ceylon passed under the control of the Portuguese who had established themselves at Goa in 1510. In 1658 the Portuguese were, however, pushed out of Ceylon by the Dutch who in their turn were driven out of the island by the British during the Napoleonic Wars. By the treaty of Vienna Ceylon definitely became a part of the British Empire and was more or less subordinate to India. In 1947 when independence came to India Ceylon continued to be a part of the British Empire but to it also practical independence has since come as a Dominion within the British Empire.

Chach—was the founder of a dynasty of Brahman kings which was ruling in Sind when the state was invaded by the Arabs in A.D. 711 when his son and successor Dahir was (*q.v.*) on the throne of Sind.

Chagatai—was the second son of Chingiz Khan, the famous Mongol leader, who in the latter half of the twelfth century established a vast empire comprising Central and western Asia. Chagatai's descendants are known as Chagatai Mughuls. Emperor Babur belonged to the line of Chagatai on his mother's side.

Chain of Justice, the—bearing sixty bells, was set up by Emperor
Jahangir immediately after his accession to the throne in 1605.
It was set up between the Shahburji in the fort of Agra and a
stone pillar which was set up on the bank of the Jumna. It could
be shaken by any one of his subjects, however humble the person
might have been, to bring his grievances direct to the notice of
Emperor Jahangir. It was an indication of Jahangir's love of,
and determination for, doing justice to his people.

Chait Singh—was the Raja of Benares. He was at first a feudatory of
the Nawab of Oudh but transferred his allegiance to the Company by a treaty by which he agreed to pay to the Company an
annual tribute of 22½ lakhs of rupees (£ 250,000), and the Company in its turn agreed that the demand would not be increased
on any pretence whatsoever and that nobody should be allowed
to interfere with his authority, or to disturb the peace of his
country. In 1778 when the Company was engaged in a war
with the French in India and were also involved in entangle-
ments with Mysore and the Marathas, Hastings demanded
from Chait Singh a special contribution of a sum of rupees
five lakhs which the Raja paid. The demand was repeated in
1779 and enforced by a threat of military action. In 1780 the
demand was renewed for the third successive year. This time
Chait Singh sent 2 lakhs of rupees to Hastings as a personal
gift to the latter in the hope that it, if accepted, would mollify
Hastings. The latter took the money, which he used for the
Company's forces, but far from relaxing his demand he required
the Raja to furnish 2,000 horsemen, which were reduced to
1,000 on the Raja's humble representations. But the Raja could
collect only 500 horsemen and 500 matchlockmen and informed
Hastings that they were ready for serving the Company. No
reply was sent to him and Hastings determined to exact from
him a fine of 50 lakhs of rupees. To carry out his plans Hastings
went in person to Benares and placed the Raja under arrest in
his own palace in Benares. The Raja submitted quietly, but his
soldiers were infuriated by the indignity inflicted on him and
massacred the small British force with only which Hastings had
foolishly come to Benares. Hastings had to retire quickly for
his personal safety to Chunar, brought up reinforcements,
recovered Benares, and occupied the Raja's palace which was
allowed to be looted by the Company's troops, but failed to
capture Chait Singh who made good his escape to Gwalior.
Hastings confiscated his kingdom, conferred it upon his nephew
on condition of the payment of an increased annual tribute of

40 lakhs of rupees the pressure of which affected very adversely the economic condition of the state. The British Prime Minister Pitt felt convinced that Hastings' conduct in the Chait Singh affair was cruel, unjust and oppressive and it was one of the counts on which he agreed to his impeachment. (Lyall, Sir Alfred, *Warren Hastings*; Roberts, P. E., *Hist. of British India*)

Chaitanya Deva—was the founder of Vaishnavism in Bengal. He was born in a learned Brahmana family of Nabadwipa in Bengal in 1485. He soon distinguished himself by wonderful literary knowledge and might have made his career as a great Sanskrit scholar. But at the age of twenty-four he renounced domestic life and leaving behind his old mother and young beautiful wife, adopted the life of a *sannyasin* and spent the rest of his short life of 48 years in preaching his message of love and devotion—eighteen years in Orissa and six years in the Deccan, Vrindavan, Gaur and other places. He came to be regarded by his followers as an incarnation of Lord Vishnu. He was opposed to priestly ritualism and preached faith in Hari. He believed that through love and devotion the personal presence of God can be realised. His gospel was meant for all, irrespective of caste and creed, and Hindus even of low castes as well as Muhammadans, flocked to be his disciples. The cult of *bhakti* or devotion was re-emphasized by him. His doctrine exercised a profound influence on the masses of the people, especially in Bengal and tended to bridge the gulf not only between the high castes and low castes but also between the Hindus and the Muhammadans. A large body of literature has grown up round the life and teachings of Chaitanya and the *kirtan* to the accompaniment of the Indian musical instrument known as the *khol* which Chaitanya started, still continues to be very popular in Bengal as well as amongst the Vaishnavas outside Bengal, especially in Manipur. ((Kaviraj, Krishnadas, *Chaitanya-Charitamrita*)

Chaitanya Bhagavata—is a biographical account of Chaitanya's life containing a discussion also of his creed. It was written in Bengali by Brindavan Das (born in A.D. 1507). It is a store- house of information on the social life of Bengal in the time of Chaitanya.

Chaitanya-Charitamrita—is the most important biography of Chaitanya. It was written by Krishnadas Kaviraj who was born in the district of Burdwan (Bengal) in 1517.

Chaitanya Mangal—is the title of two books on the life of Chaitanya. One of these was written by Jayananda who was born in 1513 and the other by Trilochan Das who was born in 1523 in the

district of Burdwan. Trilochan Das's book is the more popular of
the two.

Chaitya Caves—*see* Cave architecture.

Chakks, the—were a tribal people who ruled over Kashmir from
1555 to 1586 when their rule was overthrown by the Mughul
Emperor Akbar.

Chakrapani—a renowned Sanskrit scholar, specialised in medicinal
literature. He flourished in Bengal in the eleventh century
A.D. and wrote illuminating commentaries on Charaka and
Susruta—the first is called *Ayurveda-dipika* and the second
Bhanumati. His other work *Chikitsa-Samgraha* is a compendium of
therapeutics. (*Hist. of Bengal,* Vol. I, pp. 316-318)

Chakravarti Raja—is a Sanskrit term conveying the conception of
the universal sovereign ruling over the whole of India. It runs
through Sanskrit literature and is also mentioned in various inscriptions. The achievement of the status conveyed by this title
was the aim of all powerful ancient Indian sovereigns, though
few only attained it. At any rate its use in literature and epi-
graphy suggests the fundamental political unity of India.

Chakrayudha—was a *protégé* of king Dharmapala of Bengal (*c.* A.D.
770-800) and was installed by the latter as the king of Kanauj in
place of Indrayudha or Indraraja who was defeated by Dharmapala. Nothing is known of his origin or of his activities as the
ruler of Kanauj. Epigraphic evidences suggest that he was a
feudatory of king Dharmapala and his fortunes followed those
of his patron. In any case Chakrayudha's rule over Kanauj did
not last long, as he and his patron were defeated by the Gurjara-
Pratihara king Nagabhata who annexed Kanauj to his growing
dominions. Whether on the defeat of Nagabhata by the Rastrakuta king, Govinda III, Chakrayudha was restored to the throne
of Kanauj is not definitely known. At any rate Chakrayudha
founded no dynasty of kings ruling in Kanauj.

Chalukyas, the—came into prominence in southern India in about
the middle of the sixth century A.D. Their origin is not definitely
known. They claimed to be a race of Rajputs who had their
origin in Ayodhya and were descended from the lunar dynasty.
From the occurrence of the name of the Chalukya king
Pulakeshin in an inscription of the Chapas who formed a branch
of the Gurjaras it has been inferred by some modern writers that
the Chalukyas, also known as Solankis, were connected with
the Gurjaras and came from Rajputana to the Deccan. At
any rate this is definite that in about A.D. 550 the Chalukya chief
Pulakeshin I established a kingdom with Vatapi, the modern

Badami in Bijapur district, as his capital and performed the *asvamedha* sacrifice in order to proclaim his paramountcy. His dynasty, known as that of the early Chalukyas, ruled, with a short interregnum of thirteen years (642-55) from A.D. 550 to A.D. 757 with Vatapi as the capital. The kings of this dynasty were Pulakeshin I (A.D. 550-66), Kirttivarman I (*c.* 566-97), Mangalesa (*c.* 597-608), Pulakeshin II (*c.* 609-42), interregnum (*c* 642-55), Vikramaditya I (655-80), Vinayaditya (680-96), Vijayaditya (696-733), Vikramaditya II (733-46) and Kirtti-varman II (746-57). Amongst these nine early Chalukya kings the fourth king Pulakeshin II was the most pre-eminent. His rule lasted for 34 years (A.D. 608-42) and his dominions extended from the Narmáda in the north to the Kaveri in the south. But in 642 he was defeated and presumably killed by the Pallava king, Narasimhavarman, and for the next thirteen years the Chalukya power was in abeyance. It was restored in A.D. 655 by Pulakeshin's son Vikramaditya. I. The conflict with the Pallavas continued and in about, A.D. 740 the Chalukya king Vikramaditya II sacked the Pallava capital Kanchi, but his son and successor Kirttivarman II was overthrown by the Rastrakuta chief Dantidurga in about A.D. 753 and the Chalukya power suffered its second eclipse. But Phoenix-like it rose from its ashes two centuries later when Taila or Tailappa, who traced his descent from the seventh Chalukya king Vijayaditya overthrew the Rastrakuta king Kakka II in A.D. 973 and founded a new Chalukya dynasty with its capital at Kalyani. This dynasty held sway from A.D. 973 to 1200 and produced twelve kings, namely, (i) Taila or Tailappa (973-97), (ii) Satyasraya (997-1008), (iii) Vikramaditya V (1008-14), (iv) Ayyana II (1015), (v) Jaiyasimha (1015-42), (vi) Somesvara I (1042-68), (vii) Somesvara II (1068-76), (viii) Vikramaditya VI (1076-1127), (ix) Somesvara III (1127-38), (x) Jagadekamalla (1138-51), (xi) Tailappa III (1151-56) and (xii) Somesvara IV (1184-1200). The most prominent feature of the rule of the Chalukya dynasty of Kalyani was a prolonged conflict with the Chola kings of Tanjore. The second king Satyasraya was defeated by the Chola king Rajaraja who overran the Chalukya king-dom, but the sixth king Somesvara I more than avenged the earlier humiliation by inflicting on the Chola king Rajadhiraja a signal defeat in the battle of Koppam where the Chola king lost his life. The seventh king Vikramaditya VI, also known as Vikramanka, captured Kanchi and patronised the poet Bilhana who recorded the life of his royal patron in the celebrated

Vikramanka-Charita. The power of the Chalukyas of Kalyani declined after the death of Vikramaditya VI. During the reign of the eleventh king Tailappa III the greater portion of the kingdom was usurped by his commander-in-chief, Bijjala Kalachurya, and the dynasty was so weakened that by 1200 at the end of the rule of the twelfth king, Somesvara IV, his kingdom was absorbed by the Yadavas of Devagiri on the west and the Hoysalas of Dvarasamudra on the south. The early Chalukya kings of Vatapi as well as the later Chalukya kings of Kalyani were ardent Hindus, but Buddhism and Jainism were both tolerated and allowed to flourish. The sacrificial form of the Hindu religion received the special attention of the Chalukya kings who built many ordinary and cave-temples to the Hindu gods. The celebrated jurist Vijnanesvara, author of the *Mitakshara*, the chief authority of Hindu law outside Bengal, lived in the Chalukya capital, Kalyani. (Smith, V. A., *E.H.I.*)

Chalukya-Cholas—were the descendants of Rajendra the Third, the twenty-eighth king of the Chalukya dynasty of Vengi who united the Eastern Chalukya and Chola crowns by right of inheritance. He assumed the title of Kulottunga Chola and reigned from 1070-1122. The dynasty ruled over the Chola kingdom till A.D. 1527 when with the death of Kulottunga Chola III the dynasty sank into insignificance and its territories were overran by the Muhammadan troops of Alauddin Khalji.

Chalukyas of Kalyani—*see* under Chalukyas.

Chalukyas of Vatapi—*see* under Chalukyas.

Chalukyas of Vengi—also known as the Eastern Chalukyas, were a branch of the Chalukyas of Vatapi. The founder of the line was Kubja Vishnuvardhana, a brother of king Pulakeshin II (*q.v.*) and was installed in A.D. 611 by the latter as a feudatory king on the throne of Vengi between the Krishna and the Godavari. He had his capital at Pishtapura, modern Pithapuram. In about A.D. 615 Vishnuvardhana set himself up as an independent king and thus set up the dynasty of the Chalukyas of Vengi or Eastern Chalukyas. He had a line of tweny-seven descendants, viz. Jayasinha I, Indra, Vishnuvardhana II, Mangi, Jayasinha II, Kokkili, Vishnuvardhana III, Vijayaditya I, Vishnuvardhana IV, Vijayaditya II, Vishnuvardhana V, Vijayaditya III, Bhima I, Vijayaditya IV, Vishnuvardhana VI, Vijayaditya V, Tarapa or Tala I, Vikramaditya II, Bhima II, Yuddhamalla, Bhima III, Badapa, Danarnava, Saktivarman, Vimaladitya, Rajaraja and Rajendra. The penultimate king Rajaraja married the daughter of Rajendra Chola I and their son Rajendra who married a daughter of the Chola king Rajendra IV united by inheritance the crowns of Vengi and Chola and thus merged the line of the Chalukyas of Vengi or the Eastern Chalukyas in that of the Chalukya-Cholas.

Chamber of Princes, the—was set up, in pursuance to a recommendation made in the Montague-Chelmsford Report, by a Royal Proclamation on the 8th February, 1921. It consisted of the representatives of the different classes of Indian States, with the Viceroy as its President and a Chancellor and Pro-Chancellor elected annually from amongst its princely members. It was a consultative body and had no executive power. The Viceroy could consult it in all matters which concerned British India and the States in common. It could not interfere in the internal affairs of the States or their rulers, or their relations with the Crown, or the existing rights or engagements of the States, or restrict their freedom of action. The creation of the Chamber of Princes was an attempt to bring the States more closely in touch with the British Indian Government and with the new national trends. It did not prove a very effective institution and its only usefulness lies in the circumstance that it partly cleared the way to the establishment of a federal type of government for the whole of India as it exists at present.

Chamberlain, Sir Neville—was the British envoy that was sent by Lord Lytton I, the Viceroy, in 1878 to Afghanistan to counterbalance at the Court of Kabul the influence of the Russian envoy whom Amir Sher Ali had received. But the Amir refused to receive Sir Neville who had to return from Ali Masjid. This repulse of the British envoy led to the Second Afghan War (1878-80).

Chamo Rajendra, Sir Raja—the ruler of Mysore from 1868 to 1896, was one of the earliest of the Indian princes who infused a spirit of liberalism in the administration which had been previously marked by autocracy.

Champa, city of—was the capital of the ancient kingdom of Anga which lay to the east of Magadha and west of the Rajmahal Hills. It comprised the modern Bhagalpur area of Bihar. The city was situated at the confluence of the rivers Champa and the Ganges and was noted for its wealth and commerce. It has been identified with the villages of Champanagara and Champapura near the city of Bhagalpur. (*P.H.A.I.*, p. 107)

Champa, kingdom of—was an ancient Hindu kingdom founded by Indian emigrants in the second century A.D. in that part of

Indo-China which is known as Annam, now Vietnam. Its
capital was also called Champa. The kingdom of Champa
existed for about thirteen centuries (c. A.D. 150-1471) and
had a glorious record of successes in wars against Kambuja
and Annam, and even against the great Mongol chief,
Kublai Khan. It maintained diplomatic relations with China.
The people were mainly Hindu in religion and erected many
temples to the Hindu gods Brahma, Vishnu and Siva. Buddhism
also had many followers. The language used in inscriptions is
Sanskrit written in *devanagari* script. In the sixteenth century the
Hindu kingdom of Champa was overrun and extinguished by
the Annamese of Mongolian origin. (Majumdar, R. C., *Champa*)

Champat Rai—a chief of the Bundelas, imposed his control over
them and rose against Aurangzeb in the early part of his reign
(1658-1707), but he was so hard pressed by the Mughul Emperor
that defeat and capture seemed imminent. He committed
suicide to escape imprisonment and left to his son Chhatrasal
(*q.v.*) the task of carrying on the war against Aurangzeb.

Champion, 'Col. Alexander—a military officer in the service of the
East India Company in Bengal, was sent by Warren Hastings
as the commander of a British army to help the Nawab of Oudh
against the Ruhellas. The combined armies defeated the Ruhellas
in the battle of Miranpur Katra on 23 April, 1774.

Chamunda Raja—was a minister of a king of the Ganga dynasty
(*q.v.*) who ruled over Mysore. By his order was built a colossal
statue of Gomata, 56½ feet in height, wrought out of a block of
gneiss on the top of a hill at Sravana Belgola. The statue is
unrivalled in the world for its daring conception and gigantic
dimensions.

Chanakya—*see* Kautilya.

Chand Bardai—was the court-poet of the Chauhan king Prithviraj
(*q.v.*) of Delhi and Ajmer (c. A.D. 1170-92). He wrote an epic
called the *Chand Raisa* or *Prithviraja Raso* dealing mainly with the
deeds of Prithviraj, his marriage and his battles with the
Muhammadans.

Chand Bibi—was a daughter of Husain Nizam Shah, the third
sovereign of Ahmadnagar and was married to Ali Adil Shah
(1557-80), the fifth sultan of Bijapur. Her husband having died
in 1580, she became the guardian of her minor son Ibrahim
Adil Shah II, the sixth sultan of Bijapur. The administration of
Bijapur was carried on by the ministers. But in 1584 Chand
Bibi left Bijapur and returned to her native city of Ahmadnagar
and never visited Bijapur again. Ahmadnagar was invaded by

the armies of the Mughul Emperor Akbar in 1593 and the city was besieged by the Mughuls in 1596. At this crisis Chand Bibi took the leadership in Ahmadnagar and made a gallant and successful resistance to the Mughul army led by Akbar's son Prince Murad. But the odds were so much against the limited resources of Ahmadnagar that she had to make peace by ceding Berar to the Mughuls. The war soon broke out again but so efficient was the defensive organisation set up by Chand Bibi that the Mughuls could not capture the city so long as she was alive. She, however, soon perished at the hands of the mob and Ahmadnagar also fell to the Mughuls.

Chand Raisa—is a celebrated epic written in Hindi by Chand Bardai, the court poet of Prithviraj, the Chauhan king of Delhi and Ajmer. Much was added to it by later reciters and the book now comprises about 125,000 verses. It is practically the sole Indian source of our knowledge about Prithviraj, his rivalry with Jaychand, the Rathor king of Kanauj, his marriage, his wars with the Muhammadans and his death.

Chanda Pradyota Mahasena—*see* Pradyota of Avanti.

Chanda Shaheb—was the son-in-law of Nawab Dost Ali of the Carnatic. In 1741 the Marathas invaded the Carnatic, killed Nawab Dost Ali and carried off his son-in-law, Chanda Shaheb, as a prisoner. Seven years later, in 1748, Chanda Shaheb was set free by the Marathas. In the meantime the First Carnatic or Anglo-French war had been fought and the French under Dupleix had earned a great reputation for military skill. Chanda Shaheb, therefore, entered into an alliance with Dupleix for deposing Anwar-ud-din who had been appointed Nawab of the Carnatic by the Nizam in 1743, from the governorship of the Carnatic. Their combined armies defeated and killed Anwar-ud-din in the battle of Ambur in August 1749 and drove his son and prospective successor Muhammad Ali to flee to the fort of Trichinopoly. Chanda Shaheb was declared the Nawab of the Carnatic with his capital at Arcot. He and his French allies soon besieged Muhammad Ali in Trichinopoly but the siege was not efficiently conducted and was allowed to drag on. Thus valuable time was lost which was utilised by Muhammad Ali in securing the help of the ruler of Mysore and Tanjore. Lastly, the delay enabled the English in Madras to interfere energetically on behalf of Muhammad Ali. Young Robert Clive (*q.v.*) with an army of two hundred Europeans and three hundred Indians surprised the fort of Arcot. Chanda Shaheb at once sent a large army to recapture Arcot, but he not only failed in

this attempt but was also defeated in a pitched battle, obliged
to surrender and was beheaded by the order of the Raja of
Tanjore (1752).

Chandellas, the—a Rajput clan, claimed descent from a Kshatriya.
But most modern scholars think that they sprang from the
aboriginal Gonds and/or Bhars and were promoted to the rank
of Kshatriyas on the assumption of royal powers by their leaders.
They flourished in what is now known as Bundelkhand lying
between the Jumna on the north and the Vindhyas on the south
in the modern state of Vindhya Pradesh. It was then known as
Jejakabhukti or Jajhoti. Khajuraho with its magnificent temples, Kalanjar with its strong fortress, Ajaygarh with its palace
and Mahoba with its natural beauty were the centres of the
culture and achievements of the Chandellas. The Chandellas
were Hindus and devout worshippers of Shiva and Krishna but
Buddhism and Jainism also had many followers. They developed
a magnificent school of architecture, examples of which are still
found at Khajuraho where the main temple dedicated to Siva
called Mahadeva, is 109 ft. in length, 60 ft. in breadth and $116\frac{1}{2}$
ft. in height and contains excellent sculptures. The Chandellas
had a monarchical form of government and the succession not
only to the throne but also to the office of the ministers was
hereditary. The Chandellas had an opportunity of seizing the
control of northern India after the decline of the Pratihara
power towards the close of the tenth century, but they proved
unequal to the task. (Bose, N. S., *Hist. of the Candellas*; Mitra,
S. K., *The Early Rulers of Khajuraho*)

Chandellas, the dynasty of—was founded early in the ninth
century A.D. by one Nannuka Chandella who overthrew a
Pratihara chieftain and became lord of the southern part of
Jejakabhukti, or modern Bundelkhand. From Nannuka sprang
a dynasty of twenty kings, the earlier of whom were probably
feudatories of the Gurjara-Pratiharas. It was the seventh king
Yasovarman who occupied the fortress of Kalanjar and forced
the contemporary Pratihara king Devapala to surrender a
valuable image of Vishnu, who was the first practically
independent ruler in the dynasty. His son Dhanga (*c.* A.D.
950-1008), the eighth in the line of succession, was the most
notable Chandella king. He extended his dominion over the
whole of Jejakabhukti and took an active part in the Indian
politics of the time. In A.D. 989 or 990 he joined the league
formed by Jaipal, king of the Panjab, to resist Sabuktigin of
Afghanistan and shared in his defeat. Dhanga attained the

age of one hundred years and then gave up his life by drowning himself at Prayaga. Dhanga's son Ganda shared in the defeat of Anandapal, king of the Panjab, at the hands of Sultan Mahmud. The tenth king Vijayapala (*c.* 1030-50) attacked Kanauj and defeated and killed its king Rajyapal, for having submitted to Sultan Mahmud, but he himself in his turn was defeated soon afterwards by Sultan Mahmud. Though Sultan Mahmud did not retain his conquest the defeat of Vijayapala so compromised the position of the dynasty that none of the later twelve kings could play any important part in contemporary politics and the dynasty gradually declined in power. The twelfth king Kirttivarman (*c.* 1060–1100) was the patron of the author of the celebrated mystical drama *Prabodha Chandrodaya.* The last Chandella king to play any considerable part upon the stage of history was Paramardi, the seventeenth king (*c.* 1165-1202) who was first defeated by Prithviraj, the Chauhan king of Ajmer and then by Kutubuddin Ibak who captured the fort of Kalanjar. Chandella Rajas lingered on in Bundelkhand as purely local chiefs until the beginning of the 14th century when with the death of the last king Hammiravarman the dynasty came to an end. (Bose, N. S., *Hist. of the Candellas*)

Chandernagore—was the site of a factory in Bengal established by the French East India Company. The site was granted to the French by Nawab Shaista Khan in 1674 and the factory was built in 1690-92. It was captured by the English led by Clive and Watson in 1757 and was restored to the French in 1763 to be held as a mere trading centre. It continued to be a French possession till 1950 when it was merged with the Republic of India.

Chandidas, Ananta Badu—famous Vaishnava poet, was born, probably towards the end of the fourteenth century, in the village of Nannur in the district of Birbhum in West Bengal. He sang about the love of Krishna and Radha and his lyrics still continue to be very popular. The *Sree-Krishna-Kirtan* is attributed to him.

Chandra, Raja—mentioned in the Meherauli Iron Pillar inscription, is said to have defeated his enemies in Vanga on one side and on the other the Vahlikas at the mouths of the Indus. The identity of the king is not definitely settled. A king named Chandra is also mentioned in the Susunia inscription. (*P.H.A.I.*, p. 535 n)

Chandradeva—founded the Gahadvala dynasty with his capital at Kanauj in the closing decade of the eleventh century. His dynasty ruled over the country till the beginning of the thirteenth century.

Chandragiri—became the capital of the later Rajas of Vijaya-nagar in about 1585. In 1639 a Naik, subordinate to the Raja of Chandragiri, granted the site of Madras to Mr. Day, an English factor. In 1645 Ranga II, the Raja of Chandragiri, confirmed the grant. There the Fort of St. David came to be built and round the fort the city of Madras developed.

Chandragupta I—was the first king and founder of the Imperial dynasty of the Guptas. He was a local chief ruling over parts of Magadha but he largely increased his power and territories by marrying a Lichchhavi princess named Kumara Devi. He set up his capital at Pataliputra, assumed the title of Maharajadhi-raja, issued gold coins in the joint names of himself, his queen and the Lichchhavis, extended his dominions beyond Magadha as far as Allahabad, and founded an era known as the Gupta Era which runs from February 26, A.D. 320, the date probably of his coronation. His reign was short, having ended in about A.D. 330. Before his death he nominated as his successor his son Samudragupta (*q.v.*) born of queen Kumara Devi. From his loins sprang the line of the Imperial Guptas who held sway over Magadha till the end of the fifth century of the Christian era.

Chandragupta II—the third sovereign of the line of the Imperial Guptas, was a son and successor of Samudragupta (*q.v.*). His reign extended probably from A.D. 375 to A.D. 413. He con-quered Malwa, Gujarat and Kathiawar, overthrew the Saka Satraps of Ujjain and annexed their dominions to the Gupta Empire. In celebration of his victorious conquests he assumed the title of Vikramaditya and was probably the king round whom gathered all the exploits of the Vikramaditya (*q.v.*) of Indian legends and tradition. At any rate he was a very powerful king during whose reign art, architecture and sculpture all flourished and the cultural development of India reached its climax. He was probably the patron of Kalidas, the great Sanskrit poet and dramatist. During his reign India was visited by the Chinese pilgrim, Fa-Hien, who spent in his dominions six year (A.D. 405-11) but never visited the Emperor or his court and never even mentioned his name. He has left a very pleasing picture of the state of the country which was well governed and in which the people lived peaceful and prosperous lives. Though the Emperor lived generally either at Ayodhya or at Kausamb Pataliputra still continued to be an important city, the pros perity and grandeur of which immensely impressed the pilgrim. The Emperor maintained public works of general utility like free hospitals for men and free rest-houses for travellers on high roads. Chandragupta II was, like his predecessors, a devout Hindu and a worshipper of Vishnu, but he also tolerated Buddhism as well as Jainism.

Chandragupta Maurya—was the founder of the Maurya dynasty. The names of his parents are not definitely known, though according to the Puranas he was the illegitimate son of a Nanda king of Magadha born of a maid-servant named Mura from whom his family name Maurya came to be derived. But Buddhist and Jain sources suggest that Chandragupta Maurya was born of the Kshatriya family of the Moriyas of Pippalivana. At any rate, he became an adventurer early in his life and while still a lad met Alexander the Great in one of his camps in the Panjab. But he offended the king by the boldness of his speech and saved his life, which was declared forfeit, by speedy flight. In the place of his refuge he is said to have been joined by a Taxilian Brahman named Chanakya or Kautilya, who found him resources for recruiting an army of mercenaries and helped him in overthrowing the last king of the Nanda dynasty and thus in establishing his rule in Magadha. In the meantime Alexander the Great had not only gone back from India, but had also died, and taking advantage of the situation which thus arose in the Panjab, Chandragupta Maurya overthrew the Greek rule in the Panjab. The definite date by which these developments took place is not yet ascertained, but it must have been some time between 324 B.C. and 321 B.C. Chandragupta maintained a large army consisting of 30,000 cavalry, 9,000 elephants, 600,000 infantry and a very large number of chariots. With this force he overran and conquered the whole of northern India including Malwa, Gujarat and Saurashtra and extended his dominions to the Narmada, if not beyond it. His power was challenged in 305 B.C. by the Greek general Seleucos who had become the sovereign of all the eastern dominions of Alexander the Great. The Indian and the Greek sovereigns met in battle and though the details of the campaign are not known it is certain that Seleucos was defeated and forced to conclude a humiliating peace by which he surrendered to Chandragupta Maurya the satrapies of Kabul, Herat, Qandahar and Baluchistan, entered into a matrimonial alliance with the Maurya Emperor and received in return 500 elephants only. Thus Chandragupta Maurya extended his dominions in the north-west up to the Hindu Kush mountains, and reached what has been called the 'scientific frontier' of India. This treaty, which has been dated 303 B.C., marked the culmination of the achievements of Chandragupta Maurya. In the course of eighteen short years he had not only raised himself to the throne of Magadha but had also expelled the Macedonian garrisons from the Panjab and Sind, repulsed and humbled Seleucos and established himself as the emperor of the whole of north India as far as the Hindu Kush mountains. "These achievements entitle him to rank among the greatest and most successful kings known to history."

A Greek ambassador named Megasthenes (*q.v.*) was sent to his court. His account *Indica* (*q.v.*) as well as the *Arthashastra*, (*q.v.*) a treatise on administration, written by his prime minister Chanakya or Kautilya (*q.v.*) give some idea of the system of administration by which Chandragupta Maurya held together his vast empire over which he ruled for twenty-four years (*c.* 322 B.C. to 298 B.C.) with great success. His palace at Pataliputra which in Megasthenes' opinion excelled in splendour and magnificence the palaces of Susa and Ecbatana, has disappeared and the city itself which stood at the confluence of the Ganges and the Sone near modern Dinapore has also been buried under the sands of the river, but the memory of their illustrious builder will shine for ever., (E.H.I., Ch. v.; *P.H.A.I.*, Chap. iv & McCrindle, *Ancient India*)

Chandragupta—was the third king of the Karkota dynasty which was established in Kashmir in the seventh century A.D.

Chandra Sena Jadav—son of Dhanaji Jadav, was the Commander-in-Chief of the Maratha king Sahu. Chandra Sena had under him Balaji Viswanath as an agent in charge of the army but was gradually eclipsed by the rising power and position of Balaji who eventually became the Peshwa in 1713.

Chandras, the—were local chieftains who ruled for a time over parts of Eastern Bengal after the power of the Pala dynasty had begun to decline in the eleventh century.

Chandravarman—was a name borne by two kings. One was a king of the Kambojas mentioned in the epics. Secondly, the Allahabad inscription of Samudragupta mentions that, amongst the kings of northern India 'uprooted' and deposed by the Gupta Emperor, was one named Chandravarman. He has been identified with the king of the same name mentioned in the Susunia inscription. He was the ruler of Pokarna or Pushkarana on the Damodar river in the Bankura district of West Bengal. (*P.H.A.I.*, pp. 534-53)

Chandwar, the battle of—was fought in 1194 between Shihab-ud-din Muhammad Ghori and Jaychand, the Raja of Benares and Kanauj. Jaychand was defeated and killed and Kanauj and Benares passed under Muhammadan rule.

Charaka—was a celebrated physician who wrote a very authoritative book called after his own name, on pathology and medicine. Charaka is believed to have been a contemporary of the Kushana king, Kanishka, whose royal patronage he enjoyed. Some, therefore, hold that he flourished in the second century of the Christian era, but Dr. P. C. Ray in his *History of Hindu Chemistry* has tried to prove that Charaka belonged to the pre-Buddhistic period.

Charles II—king of England (1660-85) got from the king of Portugal the site of modern Bombay as a dowry on the occasion of his marriage with Princess Catherine of Braganza and leased out the site to the East India Company in 1668 at an annual rental of £ 10 only. This laid the foundation of the prosperity of Bombay which in 1687 superseded Surat as the chief settlement of the English on the west coast. In various other ways also Charles II helped the development of the East India Company in India.

Charnock, Job—was the chief of the East India Company's settlement on the Hughli. On the invitation of Nawab Ibrahim Khan, who succeeded Shaista Khan as the Subadar of Bengal, Job Charnock chose the site of modern Calcutta and there laid its humble foundation on 24 August, 1690. Next year he got from the Nawab a *firman* granting the English exemption from the payment of customs duties in return for a payment of Rs. 3000 a year. Thus Job Charnock started Calcutta and the East India Company on their magnificent careers in Bengal and India. (Wilson, C. R., *Old Fort William in Bengal*, 2 vols.)

Charter Acts, the—were passed in 1793, 1813, 1833 and 1853. The East India Company was started by a Charter granted by Queen Elizabeth I on the last day of 1600 with the monopoly of trading in the East Indies. By 1793 as a result of a series of strange political events in India the Company came to be vested, along with its trading and commercial rights, with the duty of administering large territories in India. In the midst of these circumstances the existing Charter of the Company fell due to run out in 1794. Therefore, after some discussions and enquiries into the activities of the Company a fresh Charter Act was passed in 1793 extending the life and rights of the Company for another twenty years. Thereafter it became the custom to pass a Charter Act at the end of every twenty years until 1858 when the East India Company was abolished and its powers, rights and territories were taken over by the Crown. The Charter Act of 1793 made no important change and left the Company in full enjoyment of its commercial monopoly as well as of its rights to govern the Company's dominions in India. The Charter Act of 1813 took away the Company's monopolistic right of trading with India and partially threw open the Indian trade, commerce and industries to the private enterprise of Englishmen, but it left to the Company the monopoly of its trade with China. It allowed Christian missionaries admission into the Company's Indian territories and added one ecclesiastical department to the administrative system of India. It also laid down that it was the duty of England to promote the interests and happiness of the Indians by adopting such measures as would lead to the introduction amongst them of useful knowledge and to their religious and moral improvement. Nothing came immediately out of this declaration which remained a pious wish. The Charter Act of 1833 ended the life of the Company as a commercial agency and turned it completely into a political agency of the Crown of England for the administration of India. A Law Member was added to the Governor-General's Council and a Law Commission was established which eventually led to the promulgation of the Indian Penal Code and the Indian Civil and Criminal Procedure Codes. Thus the Charter Act of 1833 marked the starting point for the development of the existing public law in India. The Governor-General and his Council, sitting together, were also given the right of making laws. The Act of 1833 further laid down the principle that no Indian was to be excluded from holding office under the Government for which he was educationally and otherwise fit, simply by reason of religion and colour. This declaration also long remained an expression of a pious wish, but it was not without ultimate significance. The Charter Act of 1853 was the fourth and last of the series. It continued the Company as a Government agency. It arranged for the completion of the Law Commission's work. It provided that for the purposes of legislation six members were to be added to the Governor-General's Council. The Act further introduced the system of open competition for entry into the Indian Civil Service which had so long been an exclusive field of patronage for the Directors of the East India Company and threw it open to the best talents of the British and, later on, of the Indians.

Charvaka—was the exponent of the materialistic school (*lokayata*) of Indian philosophy. Unlike the orthodox school of Hindu philosophers, he discarded the authority of the Vedas, denied the existence of an imperishable soul outside the body, refused to accept the doctrine of rebirth and expounded a system of philosophy which asked men to eat, drink and be merry in this life, for the body once cremated can never be formed again. (Shastri, D. R. *The Lokayata School of Philosophy*)

Charumati—was a daughter of the Maurya Emperor Asoka (*c* 272 B.C. - 232 B.C.). She had married Devapala Kshatriya, but later on adopted a religious life and became a nun. She accompanied her royal father on his visit to Nepal in 250 or 249 B.C. She remained in Nepal after her father's departure, founded a town called Devapatana after her deceased husband and settled as a nun in a convent which she built to the north of Pasupatinath and which still bears her name.

Chastana—was the founder of the line of the Great Satraps of Malwa who had their capital at Ujjain in the later part of the first century of the Christian era. He issued a large number of coins in silver and gold, many of which have been found.

Chatfield Committee—was appointed during the administration of Lord Linlithgow (1936-41) to report on the modernisation of the Indian army. Lord Chatfield was the President of the Committee which submitted its Report in 1939. In accordance with the Report the Government of the United Kingdom provided a large sum of money for the necessary reforms. The strength of the British army in India was to be reduced by 25 per cent and the army in India was to be re-distributed into four groups, viz. frontier defence, internal security, coast defence and general reserve. Light tanks, armoured cars and motor transport were to be provided for the Indian army. Bomber squadrons were to be added to the Indian Air Force which was to co-operate with the land army and the navy for coastal defence. The Royal Indian Navy was also to be strengthened by the acquisition of men-of-war of the latest model and steps were to be taken for increasing the production of munitions by the reconstruction and expansion of ordnance factories.

Chatter Singh—was a leading Sikh Sardar on the eve of the outbreak of the Second Sikh War in 1848. He and his son Sher Singh played leading parts in the war against the English, but submitted to the English after the defeat of the Sikhs in the battle of Gujarat (*q.v.*) (1849).

Chauhans, the—also called the Chahamanas, were a clan of Rajputs who claimed to have originated, like the Pawars, the

Pratiharas and the Solankis, from a sacrificial fire-pit at Mount Abu in southern Rajputana. Some modern scholars hold that the Chauhans, like the Pawars, Pratiharas and Solankis were really descended from foreign immigrants like the Gurjaras and other tribes of White Huns who entered India in the fifth and sixth centuries of the Christian era, settled here, were Hinduised, and were classed as Kshatriyas on account of their military occupation and rank as rulers. (*E.H.I.*, pp. 428-29)

Chauhans, the dynasty of the—ruled in Sambhar (Sakambhari) in Rajputana with Ajmer as their capital for several centuries. Theirs was a long line of kings and many names have been left recorded in inscriptions. Two of them deserve notice. The first is Vigraha-raja who ruled in the middle of the twelfth century. He extended his dominions considerably and conquered Delhi and its neighbourhood. He was himself a poet who wrote the *Hara Kali Nataka* and was also a patron of literature. The *Lalita-Vigraha-Nataka* was composed in his honour during his reign and has come down, like his own work, inscribed on marble slabs found at Ajmer. The second most noteworthy king of this dynasty was his nephew Prithviraja II or Rai Pithora (*q.v.*). The Chauhan dynasty of Ajmer and Delhi fell with the defeat and death of Prithviraja II in the second battle of Tarain in 1192.

A dynasty of Chauhan kings ruled in Malwa in succession to the Tomaras. The Chauhans of Malwa were defeated and dispossessed by the Muhammadans in 1401. (*E.H.I.*, pp. 400-404)

Chaunsa, the battle of—was fought in June, 1539 between Humayun, the second Mughul Emperor and Sher Shah (*q.v.*). Emperor Humayun was utterly defeated, threw himself into the Ganges, was saved by a water-carrier and fled to Agra leaving Sher Shah practically in independent possession of Bihar and Bengal. Chaunsa was situated on the bank of the Ganges near Buxar and the battle of Chaunsa is, therefore, sometimes referred to as the battle of Buxar also.

Chauri-chaura—in Bihar, was in 1922 the seat of a violent outbreak of popular upheaval against the British rule in India. It was an incident in connection with the non-co-operation movement started in 1920 by the Indian National Congress under the leadership of Mahatma Gandhi who insisted that the movement should be non-violent. The violence of the demonstration shocked Gandhi so much that he admitted that he had committed a serious blunder and at once ordered, to the chagrin and disappointment of many Congressmen, the stoppage of the non-co-operation movement on a mass scale. Lord Reading, the Viceroy, took advantage of the outbreak to arrest Gandhi himself for his alleged responsibility for promoting violence. Gandhi was put on trial and sentenced to six years' imprisonment. It seemed that as a result of the Chauri-chaura incident the non-co-operation movement suffered a great set-back.

Chauth—was a levy amounting to one-fourth of the revenue assessment of the area on which it was imposed. It was a forced contribution exacted by a military leader from a territory which he was strong enough to overrun but could not bring under his direct rule. It was first collected by the Raja of Ramnagar from the Portuguese subjects in Daman. Shivaji turned it into an essential part of the revenue of his state and collected it in 1670 from Khandesh which lay within the Mughul Empire. Thereafter it became a regular feature of his financial resources and continued to be levied by his successors in later times. Opinions differ as to whether it was blackmail which involved no responsibility on the power which collected it or "a payment in lieu of protection". In practice, however, it was nothing but a forced military contribution. (Ranade, *The Rise of the Maratha Power;* Sen, S. N., *Administrative System of the Marathas*)

Chedi—was the name of the region lying between the Jumna and the Narmada. It was one of the sixteen great states (*Mahajanapadas*) mentoned in early Buddhist texts. In later times it was ruled by the Kalachuris (*q.v.*).

Chelmsford, Lord—was the Viceroy and Governor-General of India from 1916 to 1921. He was nearly fifty years of age at the time of his appointment and had not much administrative experience. He played a rather passive part in the dynamic politics of India of the times. His administration began under the shadow of the defeat of the British arms in Mesopotamia and India was discontented as Britain had made no positive response to the spontaneous loyalty that India had displayed to her since the beginning of the First World War in 1914. Lord Chelmsford had little initiative of his own and he had little influence on the framing of the Indo-British policy which led to the famous announcement made on August 20, 1917, in the House of Commons by Mr. Edwin Montague, the Secretary of State for India, stating that the ultimate aim of the British Government in India was "the progressive realisation of responsible government in India". Later on when Mr. Montague came to India in 1917 Lord Chelmsford accompanied him on his extensive tours over the whole of India and his name was also associated with that of Montague as the author of the Report on the Indian Constitutional Reforms published in 1918. Lord Chelmsford had also little to do with the framing of the Government of India Act, 1919, which was based on the Montague-Chelmsford Report and which came into operation before Lord Chelmsford's term of office expired. Lord Chelmsford very clumsily handled the prevailing political situation in India. The war ended in 1918, but in 1919 Lord Chelmsford's Government passed laws based on the recommendations of the Rowlatt Committee (*q.v.*) which empowered judges to try political cases without the aid of juries and gave provincial governments large powers of internment. These laws were passed though all the non-official members of the Imperial Legislative Council voted against them. The passing of such punitive laws led to great public agitation and, under the direction of Mahatma Gandhi, hartals were organised and public meetings were held all over the country in protest against the Acts. One such meeting was to be held, in spite of official prohibition, at Jallianwala Bagh at Amritsar, but it was broken up without warning by a body of troops acting under General Dyer who ordered them to open fire on an unarmed crowd which had assembled within an enclosed space, the only exit from which was occupied by the British army. Hundreds of persons, men women and children, were killed and wounded. This was a massacre. It was further followed by the proclamation of martial law, severe punitive measures and humiliating penalties like public flogging and crawling imposed upon unoffending persons. Lord Chelmsford who was aware of all these enormities, did little to stop these barbarities and to assuage public feeling and very tardily agreed to the appointment of a Committee known as the Hunter Committee (*q.v.*) to enquire into the Jallianwala Bagh incident. Before, however, the Committee began its work the Viceroy passed an Indemnity Act giving immunity to all military and civilian officers for all their atrocious acts. The Committee censured General Dyer and criticised the administration of martial law. Lord Chelmsford failed to repress effectively and immediately the official criminals, especially in the Panjab and thus alienated Indo-British feelings more deeply than any other Viceroy since the Sepoy Mutiny. His administration, however, escaped an Indian revolt mainly on account of the influence over the Indians exercised by Mahatma Gandhi who remained steady in the pursuit of his policy of non-violence and kept Indian opposition to the British rule wedded to a policy of non-violence.

Chera—*see* Kerala.

Chhatrapati—a royal title assumed by Shivaji on the occasion of his coronation as an independent king in June, 1674.

Chhatrasal—was the son and successor of the Bundela chief Champat Rai. Chhatrasal had accompanied Emperor Aurangzeb's armies in their campaign against Shivaji, but he was inspired by the example of the Maratha leader to take to a life of adventure with the hope of establishing an independent kingdom for himself. On his return from the Deccan campaign he championed the cause of the discontented Hindus of Bundelkhand and Malwa. He gained several victories over the Mughuls and carved out an independent kingdom for himself in eastern Malwa by 1671. He established his capital at Panna and ruled till his death in 1731.

Child, Sir John—was the President of the East India Company's factory at Surat. Acting under instructions from England he refused to recognise Aurangzeb's authority on the western coast, but was defeated by the Mughuls who seized the Company's factory at Surat. The Emperor later on ordered the expulsion of all Englishmen from his dominions, but ultimately the English submitted and were permitted to return to Surat.

Child, Sir Josiah—was the Chairman or Governor of the East India Company. Unlike the other Directors of the Company, Sir Josiah Child was ambitious and aimed at laying the foundation of an English dominion in India. In 1685 he succeeded in persuading King James II to dispatch an expedition of ten or twelve ships for the purpose of seizing and fortifying Chittagong. The expedition failed miserably and led to the expulsion of the English from Bengal in 1688. Sir Josiah's dream thus did not come true during his lifetime, but he had not dreamt a vain dream, as later events showed.

Chillianwalla, the battle of—was fought on the 13th January, 1849, between the Sikhs and the Indo-British army under Lord Gough in the course of the Second Sikh War (*q.v.*). It was a terrible battle in which the Sikhs of all arms fought with desperate courage and contested the field. They inflicted upon the British heavy casualties, amounting to 2357 men and 89 officers killed and wounded and captured the colours of three regiments and four of their guns. The Sikhs also lost many soldiers and twelve guns. It was really a defeat of the British army, but as the Sikhs left their entrenched position at night and moved away in good order 3 miles from the battlefield, the British claimed it to be a drawn battle.

Chin Qilich Khan—*see* Asaf Jah.

China—has a long, though often interrupted, connection with India. The earliest relations were commercial, as is suggested by the references to Chinese silk in Kautilya's *Arthashastra* (*q.v.*). Asoka's missionaries are not known to have visited China. Towards the close of the first century of the Christian era when a large part of India was within the dominion of the Kushana king Kadphises II (*c.* A.D. 78-110) there was a military clash between the armies of the Kushana king and of the Chinese Emperor Ho-ti (A.D. 89-105) in which the Kushana king Kadphises II was defeated. But the defeat was avenged by his successor, the famous king Kaniskha, (*c.* A.D. 120-162) (*q.v.*) who defeated the Chinese and recovered those trans-Indian dominions that had been ceded to the Chinese by Kadphises II. But already the seeds of a more peaceful and a more effective connection between China and India had begun to be sown. In 2 B.C. a Chinese ambassador of Emperor Ai to the Bactrian court accepted Buddhism. A few years later, in about A.D. 67, two Indian Buddhist monks, named Kasyapa Matanga and Dharma-raksha, reached the court of the Chinese Emperor Ming-ti (A.D. 58-75) who was much impressed by the teachings of the Buddhist monks for whose residence and worship he built in his capital a new temple known as the Temple of the White Horse. Kasyapa and Dharma-raksha began to translate Buddhist texts into Chinese and also made many converts. Thus began a process of the expansion of the Indian religion of Buddhism in China. Many Indian Buddhist monks went to China both by the north-western land-route and the north-eastern sea-route and there met with great success in the work of evangelisation. In the fourth century the Chinese Emperor Wu-ti embraced Buddhism which soon spread, in spite of occasional set-backs, all over China and came to be recognised as much a religion of China as Confucianism and Taoism. Indeed the number of Chinese Buddhists soon exceeded that of the followers of other creeds. For one thousand years there was brisk intercourse between China and India—Indian Buddhist monks going to China, settling there, translating hundreds of sacred Buddhist texts into Chinese and Chinese Buddhist pilgrims visiting India in order to study the religion in the land of its founder and to collect and carry back to China Buddhist sacred books from India. The more famous of the Indian monks who visited China were Kumarajiva, Bodhidharma, Gunavarman and Amoghovajra while Fa-Hien who visited India in the 4th century A.D. and Hiuen Tsang who visited India early in the seventh century, were the more famous amongst the Chinese pilgrims who visited India. Thousands of Sanskrit texts embracing not only Buddhist religion and philosophy but many other branches of Indian knowledge were thus carried from India to China and were translated into Chinese and read by the Chinese. Buddhism in the form of the *Mahayana* (*q.v.*) became especially popular with the Chinese who gave to it a new content. Gautama Buddha's exhortation for the extinguishing of all desires (*trishna*) as the main means for attaining *Nirvana* which was regarded as the *summum bonum* of human existence, was ignored and in its place the cult of *Bodhisattwas*, especially of Amitabha, was developed and it was held that, apart from pursuing the Noble Eightfold Path as laid down by Gautama the mere repetition of the name of Amitabha would secure for the Buddhist, not *Nirvana* for which he did not care, but bliss in the next life in the Western Heaven. Thus China made her contribution to the development of Buddhism. The religious and cultural contact with India which began in the first century of the Christian era and continued for the next one thousand years also materially influenced Chinese art, sculpture and architecture, as shown by the rock-cut caves at Tun-huang, Yan-kang and Long-men, colossal images of Buddha, 60 to 70 feet in height, fresco-paintings on the walls of the caves and Chinese temples with super-imposed storeys built in the Sung period. Indian music, Indian astronomy, Indian mathematics and Indian medicine were also studied in China and largely influenced Chinese culture.

With the establishment of Muhammadan rule in India as well as in the regions to the north-west of India contact between China and India practically ceased for several centuries only to be resumed after the establishment in India of the rule of the East India Company which had trading relations with China. But in the new set-up Indo-Chinese relations were controlled by the commercial and imperial interests of Britain. It was only after the establishment of the independent Republic of India in 1947 that what may be truly called Indo-Chinese contact was re-established. At first it was very friendly and exchanges of embassies between the two Republics of China and India took place, cultural contacts were promoted, the Prime Ministers of the two countries paid friendly visits and an agreement based on *Panchashila* was effected between China represented by her Prime Minister, Chou En-lai, and India by Jawaharlal Nehru. India also supported China's claims for inclusion in the U.N.O. from which she was kept excluded by the Western Powers. Notwithstanding all this show of friendship China suddenly invaded India in 1962, claiming large portions of her territories in the two areas of Ladakh and the North-Eastern Frontier. India was completely taken by surprise and though her troops fought bravely they were defeated on the North-Eastern Frontier where China advanced up to the frontier of Assam proper but then suddenly stopped on her victorious march and imposed a cease-fire followed by cessation of fighting which, however, may be resumed at any time. Indo-Chinese relations thus stand alarmingly embittered. In 1965 when India was engaged in a war with Pakistan, China who had entered into an alliance with Pakistan, laid false charges of aggression against India and even issued an ultimatum. Later on China withdrew the ultimatum, but her hostility to India continues and may develop into an armed conflict at any moment.

Chinese pilgrims—were Buddhists who visited India, the Holy Land of Buddhism, in search of Buddha's relics and Buddhist texts which they could take back to their country as well as to pay their reverential respect to all those holy places in India which were associated with Gautama Buddha and his chief adherents. The earliest of the Chinese pilgrims to India was Fa-Hien or Fa-Hsian who visited India during the reign of Chandragupta II (A.D. 375-413) and stayed in India from A.D. 401 to 410. Between that date and A.D. 700 many other Chinese pilgrims visited India of whom more than sixty have left valuable accounts of their travels. They crowded into the Buddhist Universities of Taxila, Vallabhi, Nalanda and Vikrama-sila. The most famous of these later Chinese pilgrims were I-tsing (*q.v.*) and Hiuen Tsang or Yuan Chwang (*q.v.*).

Chingiz Khan—was born in 1162. His original name was Tamu-chin. He was a Mongol chief who became famous under his official Chinese name of Chingiz Khan. He was a great general and conqueror who in the course of a few years conquered a large portion of China and all the famous kingdoms of Central Asia including Balkh, Bokhara and Samarqand as well as Herat and Ghazni. He defeated Jalaluddin, the king of Khiva who fled before him to the Panjab and sought shelter from the reigning Delhi Sultan, Il-tutmish (1211-36) but was refused asylum by the Delhi Sultan. This wise restraint of Sultan Il-tutmish dissuaded Chingiz Khan who had actually advanced as far as the Indus, from advancing further into India. Chingiz Khan then turned his victorious arms towards south-eastern Europe and extended his conquest up to the Dnieper before his death in 1227. Chingiz Khan was not merely a soldier and conqueror but he was also an organiser of no mean ability and gave laws and institutions to the vast empire that he created. His descendants later on embraced Islam and it was from the Muhammadan line of his descendants that Babur, the founder of the Mughul Empire in India, claimed descent on the mother's side.

Chinsura, the Dutch settlement at—was established in 1653 by the Dutch East India Company. It was a rich trading centre from which the Dutch exported raw silk, textiles and saltpetre. The Dutch at Chinsura were naturally enough jealous of the English success in Bengal after the battle of Plassey and entered into an alliance with Mir Jafar, the Nawab of Bengal, against the English. But the vigilance of Robert Clive frustrated the scheme. Before the Dutch could bring fresh military forces Clive attacked the Dutch, defeated them in the battle of Biderra (*q.v.*) in November, 1769 and compelled the Dutch to sue for peace on terms which left Chinsura as only a trading station to be used by the Dutch. They retained the place until 1825 when it was ceded to the British Government in exchange for certain places in Sumatra.

Chittu—the most daring leader of the Pindaries, (*q.v.*) led many of their depredations. But in course of the British action against the Pindaries he was chased from place to place and fled to the forest near Asirgarh where he fell victim to a tiger.

Chitor—was the fortified capital of the Ranas of Mewar. Its strength was renowned all over Rajputana and the fortifications which were a source of glory and pride to Mewar enabled the Ranas to hold back the Muhammadan invaders through many centuries. It, however, fell before Alauddin Khalji in 1303 and was held by him till 1311 when the Rajputs recovered it. In 1534 it was stormed by Sultan Bahadur Shah of Gujarat, but was again recovered by the Rana. Akbar captured the fort in 1568 after it had stood a siege for four months under the capable leadership of Jai Mal and Patta. Every time Chitor fell the female inmates including the queens and the other ladies-in-attendance threw themselves into a huge fire-pit which was enkindled within the fortress and thus immolated themselves to their great honour and to the disgrace of their male folk. Akbar took away from Chitor the gates of the fortress, the huge kettle-drums which used to announce for miles around the exit and entrance of the princes and the massive candelabra which lighted the shrine of the great Mother, the presiding deity of the fortress and removed

them all to Agra. Chitor was left desolate and its walls, which
were later on rebuilt by Rana Jagat Singh, were again demolished by the order of Shah Jahan in 1654. The result was that in
the eighteenth century Chitor became a haunt of tigers and
other wild beasts. In the late nineteenth century it partially
recovered. There is a small town with a railway station at the
foot of the precipice at the top of which the old fort stands and
attracts thousands of visitors.

Chitral—a valley lying between Afghanistan and India, passed
under British-Indian rule in 1893 as the result of the acceptance
of the Durand line (*q.v.*) as the boundary between Afghanistan
and the British Indian Empire. When the Indo-British Government
proceeded to assert its authority over the Chitral valley the
tribes inhabiting it resisted and necessitated the Chitral Campaign in 1895 which reduced the valley to submission for the
time.

Chittagong, the district of—was ceded to the Mughul Emperor
Aurangzeb in 1666 by the king of Arakan. In 1760 the district
was assigned to the East India Company by Mir Kasim. In
1905 it, along with other districts of East Bengal, was added to the
newly created province of East Bengal and Assam. It returned
to the province of Bengal in 1912 when the partition of Bengal
was modified, but as a consequence of the partition of India
into India and Pakistan in 1941 the district of Chittagong has
become a part of East Pakistan. Its headquarters, the town of
Chittagong on the Karnaphuli, not far from the sea, is now
developing into a very large and rich port with many modern
facilities.

Cholas, the—were one of the three prominent peoples—the other
two being the Pandyas and the Cheras or Keralas—who inhabited the southernmost parts of India in ancient times. The
land of the Cholas or *Cholamandalam*, extended along the Coromandel coast from Nellore to Pudukottai. It is mentioned in the
Asokan inscriptions as an independent kingdom to which the
Maurya Emperor sent Buddhist missionaries. The people speak
Tamil and developed a rich literature of which the *Kural* of
Tiruvallur is a fine example. The earliest Chola king definitely
known to history was Karikkal (*c*. A.D. 100) who laid the foundation of Puhar or Pukar, fought a long war with Ceylon, built
with the labour of Ceylonese captives a hundred mile long
embankment along the Kaveri river and transferred the capital
from Uraiyur to Kaviripaddinam. How and when his dynasty
came to an end is not known; but it appears that the Chola

kingdom declined both in extent and in power in the early centuries of the Christian era on account of the rise of the Pallavas (*q.v.*) in the north and of the Pandyas (*q.v.*) in the south. At any rate in the first half of the seventh century when Hiuen Tsang visited the region, the Chola kingdom had come to be restricted to the Cuddapah district alone and its ruler was subordinate to the great Pallava king Narasimhavarman (*q.v.*).But the defeat of the Pallavas in A.D. 740 at the hands of the Chalukya king Vikramaditya who sacked the Pallava capital, Kanchi, weakened the Pallavas and gave the Cholas their chance. About the middle of the ninth century the Chola king Vijayalaya ruled for thirty-four years. His son and successor Aditya (*c.* A.D. 880-907) defeated the Pallava king Aparajita and thus facilitated the rise of the Cholas. Aditya's son Parantaka I completely overthrew the power of the Pallavas, captured Madura, the Pandya capital and invaded Ceylon. He thus founded the Chola dynasty which ruled over the country till the close of the thirteenth century. The Chola kings were Rajaditya I (947-49), Gandaraditya (949-57), Arinjaya (957), Parantaka II (957-73), Madurantaka Uttama (973-85), Rajaraja I (985-1016),Rajendra I (1016-44), Rajadhiraja I (1044-54),Rajendradeva II (1054-64), Virarajendra (1064-69), Adhi-rajendra (1069-70), Rajendra III, Kulottunga I (1070-1122), Vikramachola (1122-35), Kulottanga II (1135-50), Rajaraja II (1150-73), Rajadhiraja II (1173-79), Kulottanga III (1179-1218), Rajaraja III (218-46) and Rajendra IV (1246-79). The Chola kings had the custom of accepting the heir-apparent as a colleague during their lifetime. Rajaraja I (985-1016) made himself the paramount sovereign of southern India bringing under his sway the whole of the Madras Presidency, Mysore, Coorg and even the island of Ceylon. He built the Great Temple at his capital Tanjore which bears to this day eloquent testimony to his greatness. His son and successor, Rajendra I (1016-44), maintained a strong navy by which he conquered Pegu, Martaban, the Nicobar and Andaman islands, fought a war with Mahipal, the king of Bengal and Bihar by leading an expedition to the banks of the Ganges and assumed the title of Gongaikonda. His son and successor Rajadhiraja (1044-54) was defeated and killed in the battle of Koppam by the Chalukyas who were, however, defeated at the battle of Kudal-Sangamam by Virarajendra (1064-69) who thus retrieved the Chola power. But a succession war soon followed at the end of which the Chola throne passed to Rajendra Kulottanga I (1070-1122) whose mother was a Chola princess and father a Chalukya prince. He thus founded a new dynasty of Chalukya-Cholas. He ruled for more than forty years and reconquered Kalinga. His successors for four generations carried on the traditional wars with their neighbours which weakened them greatly and predominance in the south passed, for a time, to the Pandya kings. Then in 1310 the Muhammadans under Malik Kafur overran all the Hindu kingdoms of the south which by the end of the fourteenth century came to be absorbed in the kingdom of Vijayanagar.

Chola administration—was highly systematized. It was based upon a union of villages (*kurram* or *kottam*). Each such union managed its local affairs through an assembly the members of which were elected by an elaborate system of casting lots for one year at a time. The assembly possessed large powers and had its own local treasury. A certain number of *kurrams* constituted a district (*nadu*) and a group of districts formed a province (*mandala*) of which there were six in the kingdom. Each such group enjoyed large autonomy, but there was no central assembly for controlling the administration by the king. The land revenue was one-sixth of the produce and could be paid either in kind or in gold which was the medium of currency, the unit being the *Kasu* which weighed about 28 grams troy. Besides a large army a strong fleet was also maintained. Irrigation works of vast dimensions were constructed and roads were carefully maintained. The Chola administrative system was efficient and left much of the local administration to the people. (Aiyangar, S. K., *Ancient India*; Shastri, N. K., *The Cholas*).

Chola art—was purely Indian and Hindu. It bore no trace of any foreign influence. The best example of Chola art is the great Siva temple at Tanjore which was built by the Chola king Rajaraja the Great (*c.* A.D. 985-1016). Other examples are found at Gongaikonda-Cholapuram which had, beside the massive main building, a magnificent palace, a vast artificial lake with a fifteen mile long embankment. All these are now in ruins. Later examples of Chola art are to be found at Madura, Srirangam, Rameswaram and many other places on the Coromandel coast. As Fergusson observes, the Chola artists conceived like giants and finished like jewellers. The Chola temples are marked by a massive grandeur. They have several characteristics. First, they are built in a large number of ever-receding terraces or storeys which are collectively known as the *shikhara*. The *shikhara* of the Siva temple at Tanjore consists of fourteen storeys, rising to a height of 190 feet and is crowned by a single block of stone

25 sq. ft. and weighing 80 tons. Secondly, the temples are covered from the base to the top with endless sculptures and decorative mouldings. Thirdly, to every temple there is a huge gateway, called a *Gopurama*, leading to the enclosure of the temple. Some of these *Gopuramas* as, for example, the *Gopurama* at Kumbhakonam, are gigantic in size and splendid in execution. Fourthly, successive enclosures, long courts studded with subsidiary temples and buildings, thousand-pillared halls and long covered colonnades decorate most of the temples left by the Cholas or built in later times on the model of the earlier Chola temples. (Fergusson, J., *Hist. of Indian and Eastern Architecture;* Coomarswamy, A. K., *Hist. of Indian and Indonesian Art*)

Christian missions—have been a great influence on modern India. The presence from very early times of a large number of Syrian Christians in the Far South of India suggests that the earliest Christian mission came to India not from Europe but from Syria. At any rate the tradition that associates St. Thomas with king Gondophernes (*q.v.*) (*c.* A.D. 28 to A.D. 48) indicates that a Christian mission probably came to India even in the first century of the Christian era. It is, however, definitely known that Christian missionaries began to work in India from the time of St. Francis Xavier in the sixteenth century, whose name continues to be associated even up to the present time with several colleges in India. Forcible conversion to Christianity had begun earlier with the coming of the Portuguese to India and their settlement in Goa. The earlier Christian missions were all sponsored by the Roman Catholic Church and were sporadic. Systematic Christian missionary work did not begin until the commencement of the nineteenth century when it was taken up by the Anglican Protestant Church. The East India Company did not permit Christian missionaries to live within the Company's dominions lest their teachings should rouse popular feelings amongst the Indians. Consequently, the first British Protestant missionaries like William Carey had to live at Serampore outside the Company's jurisdiction or to serve as the Company's Chaplains as did David Brown and Henry Martyn. In 1813 the ban on the entry of Christian missionaries was raised and within a few years various Christian missions coming from England, Germany and America settled in India and began to preach Christianity amongst the Indians. The Christian missions did not confine themselves long to pure evangelical work. They engaged in educational and philanthropic (especially medical) work and established and conducted colleges in the greater

cities in India. In this respect Alexander Duff, a Scottish Presbyterian missionary, was a pioneer and the General Assembly's
Institution which he founded in Calcutta in 1830 was followed
by the foundation of other missionary colleges in Calcutta and
outside Bengal. The popular demand for a knowledge of English
attracted to the missionary colleges large numbers of Indian
youths who soon proved to be an important channel by
which Western knowledge and Western values were poured into
the conservative Hindu and Muslim societies alike. Christian
missions and missionaries influenced the Indian mind on the
intellectual side and through their philanthropic activities
presented to the Indians European and Christian ethics in
action. Thus the Christian missionaries exercised a profound
influence on the development of the new India. The Christian
missionaries often made unwarranted and uninformed criticism
of the Indian religion and thus created some bitterness, but
they also rendered unquestioned services to the social improvement amongst the Indians by drawing pointed attention to the
unenlightened condition of the women in India as well as to the
social abuses like the burning of a Hindu widow on the funeral
pyre of her husband, infanticide, child marriage, polygamy
and the evils of the caste system. The complete or partial removal
of these evils is largely due to the efforts of the Christian missions
working in India.

Churaman Jat—organised the Jats of the Mathura district into a
strong military power and offered armed resistance against the
Mughuls after the death of Emperor Aurangzeb. But in 1721
his stronghold of Thun was captured by Sawai Jay Singh II and
Churaman committed suicide. He had not, however, lived
entirely in vain. By his efforts and sacrifice he facilitated the
work of building up a Jat state comprising the district of Mathura
and a part of the Agra district by his nephew Badan Singh (*q.v.*).

Churchill, the Rt. Hon'ble Sir Winston—was the Prime Minister
of Great Britain who won the Second World War. Journalist,
littérateur, historian and descendant of the family of the Duke of
Marlborough, he held many high offices until at last in one of the
darkest hours in the history of Great Britain he became her
Prime Minister on May 10, 1940 and carried the heavy
burden of the office till July 7, 1945. During this short but
exacting period he steered Great Britain to victory through the
Second World War. He fought the war as the leader of a Coalition Ministry, but he was really a die-hard Tory and had very
little sympathy with the nationalistic movement in India. He

was a stern imperialist who on one occasion declared "Sooner or later you will have to crush Gandhi, the Indian Congress and all they stand for". He disparagingly referred to Gandhi as the 'naked Indian *Fakir*' and on another occasion made a pompous display of his Olympian conceit by announcing that "he had not accepted the Prime Ministership in order to preside over the liquidation of His Majesty's Empire". But circumstances proved too strong for him for within a couple of years after the termination of his premiership, Great Britain had to recognise the independence of India. Sir Winston who died recently must have been ruefully conscious of the failure of the policy of repression and suppression which he had followed in respect of India.

Chuti Khan—son of Paragal Khan, the general of Husain Shah, king of Bengal (1493-1518), was the governor of Chittagong. Like the king whom he served, he was a patron of Bengali literature and it was under his patronage that the *Asvamedha Parva* of the *Mahabharata* was translated into Bengali by Srikara Nandi.

Chutiyas, the—a tribal people of Upper Assam, are now found chiefly at Lakhimpur and the adjacent part of Sibsagar. Their language is Bodo. They had in earlier times a considerable infusion of Shan blood and later on intermarried and intermingled with the Ahoms who conquered them in the sixteenth century after fighting with them from the thirteenth century onward. Sadiya was their headquarters. They had their own priests called *Deoris* with whose help they worshipped various forms of the goddess Kali to whom they offered human sacrifices in her great copper temple at Sadiya. (Gait, *Hist. of Assam*, pp. 41-42).

Chutu dynasty—was a branch of the Satavahanas which some time about A.D. 225 ruled over a part of the Satavahana dominions with its headquarters at Vanavasi on the Upper Tungabhadra in south Bombay. It reigned until towards the end of the third century. Inscriptions mention two kings Vishnukada and his daughter's son, Skandanaga. The Chutu dynasty was followed by the Kadambas (*q.v.*). (*P.H.A.I.*, pp. 503-504)

Cis-Sutlej states—or the Sikh states situated between the Sutlej and the Jumna, were constantly engaged in feuds with one another and taking advantage of their divisions and weakness the Marathas under Mahadaji Sindhia first established a sort of control over them after 1785. But the English soon drove out Sindhia and established an informal protectoral right over the Cis-Sutlej Sikh states. Ranjit Singh who was then fast rising to power and wanted to unite the whole of the Panjab under his rule sent, at the request of some of the Cis-Sutlej Sikh chiefs, expeditions into the area in 1806 and 1807 and occupied Ludhiana. But this extension of Ranjit Singh's power was opposed by some of the Sikh states and was also looked upon with apprehension by the English in India. So in 1809 the English sent a body of troops under David Ochterlony into the Cis-Sutlej states and Ranjit Singh, in his anxiety to avoid an armed conflict with the English, who would probably have been helped by some of the Cis-Sutlej Sikh states, made peace with the English by the treaty of Amritsar in 1809 by which he withdrew from the Cis-Sutlej states which now passed definitely under protection of the British Government of India which soon stationed an army at Ludhiana. The Sikhs thus became divided—some under Ranjit Singh and some under the English.

Civil Disobedience Movement—was an episode in the struggle of the Indian National Congress against British imperialism. By 1929 India had grown sceptical about Britain's intentions to implement her declaration regarding the grant of Dominion Status to India and the Indian National Congress at its Lahore session, 1929 declared that its goal was "the attainment of complete independence for India". To enforce this demand Mahatma Gandhi started on 6th April, 1930, the Civil Disobedience Movement which aimed at paralysing the British Government in India by the mass performance of specific illegal acts. This policy of deliberately breaking laws was formally put into action when Mahatma Gandhi, accompanied by a chosen band of followers, marched from his Sabarmati Ashrama to Dandi on the sea-shore and there broke the current Salt Act by distilling salt. The Indian Liberals and a large section of the Indian Muslims stood aloof from the movement, but it caught the imagination of the common man and woman in India. Thousands joined in breaking such laws as they found convenient to do and the whole country plunged into a serious agitation. The Government, on its part, took stringent measures to suppress the movement and Gandhi and the Congress leaders and thousands of their followers were put into prison. Serious clashes between the supporters of the movement and the forces of the Government took place. Industrial riots at places like Sholapur and communal riots at places like Cawnpore also broke out. This outbreak of violence alarmed Gandhi who was absolutely convinced of the necessity of running the agitation on non-violent lines. The Government also showed a desire for an accommodation by releasing from prison Gandhi and other Congress leaders and arranging direct talks between the Viceroy Lord Irwin and Gandhi which resulted in the Gandhi-Irwin pact or truce by the terms of which the Civil Disobedience Movement was called off, persons imprisoned in that connection, except those who were convicted of crimes of violence, were released and the Congress agreed to join the second session of the Round Table Conference (1931). But the session ended in the disappointment of Indian hopes and Gandhi was arrested and put into prison within three weeks after his return from England and the Congress was proscribed. This led to a renewal of the Civil Disobedience Movement in 1932. Thousands joined it but again brute force prevailed and the second phase of the Civil Disobedience Movement petered out. But the spirit behind the movement remained alive and it was revived for the third time in 1940 when Gandhi demanded that either the British should 'quit India' or the Civil Disobedience Movement would be revived. Again the British Government resorted to force and interned Gandhi and all the members of the Congress Working Committee. Riots broke out, shootings by the Government followed and hundreds of lives were lost and property worth a million pounds was damaged. The Civil Disobedience Movement was again suppressed, but it had not been in vain. It demonstrated how difficult a task it was for the British to hold on to India with the vast mass of her people prone to disobey and to thwart British authority in India. Just seven years after Gandhi had first voiced the Indian demand that Britain must quit India Britain had to quit.

Civil Service, *see* Indian Civil Service.

Clavering, General Sir John—was named in the Regulating Act of 1773 as a member of the Governor-General's Council and served in that capacity from his arrival in Calcutta in October, 1774 till his death there in August, 1777. He was an honest man with moderate talents and during his tenure of office he always sided with his colleague, Philip Francis, in opposing Warren Hastings. He was looked upon by Nanda Kumar as a patron, but he did nothing to save Nanda Kumar from the gallows. Early in 1777 on the reported resignation of Warren Hastings Sir John Clavering was appointed to succeed him, but Hastings disowned the reported resignation and would not allow Clavering to assume charge. A reference was made to the Supreme Court which upheld Hastings. This incident caused great bitterness in the midst of which Clavering died.

Clive, Robert, Lord—born in 1725, came out to India when he was a young boy and was at first employed as a writer (clerk) in the service of the East Company in Madras. Later on he was permitted to join the Company's military service and had worked his way to the rank of a Captain in 1751 when he was twenty-six years of age. At that time the Second Anglo-French War in the Carnatic (*q.v.*) was going on. The French *protégé* Chanda Shaheb was besieging the English *protégé* Muhammad Ali in Trichinopoly and the Company's officers in Madras did not know how to relieve their *protégé*. At this stage young Captain Robert Clive suggested a diversion by making a sudden attack on Arcot, the capital of the Carnatic, and carried it out with complete success. Later on he stood a siege for 53 days against a large force that Chanda Shaheb sent for recapturing Arcot. This turned the tide of the war definitely in favour of the English Company and brought Clive into prominence.

Clive went on leave to England in 1753 and returned two years later along with a squadron under the command of Admiral Watson. On their arrival at Bombay they were sent on an expedition against the pirate-infested port of Gheria which was conquered and was later on handed over to the Marathas in exchange for Bankot with nine villages on the mainland of western India.

Clive and Watson then sailed to Madras and were soon afterwards sent to Bengal where in the meantime Calcutta had been captured by Siraj-ud-daula, Nawab of Bengal. They recovered Calcutta in January, 1757 meeting with practically no opposition from the Nawab. From this time Clive was virtually in charge of the Company's affairs in Bengal. In February he made peace with the Nawab by the treaty of Alinagar (*q.v.*) by which the Company promised to respect the authority of the Nawab over Bengal. But only a month later Clive attacked the French possession of Chandernagore which was captured and destroyed. Having thus eliminated French rivalry in Bengal, Clive, on behalf of the East India Company, entered into a conspiracy with the disaffected courtiers of Nawab Siraj for the purpose of deposing him and installing in his place Mir Jafar as the Nawab of Bengal. A formal treaty to the effect was drawn up in June, 1757. Aminchand (*q.v.*), a banker of Calcutta, who knew of the treaty threatened to divulge it unless he was promised a share of the expected loot and Clive had no hesitation in deceiving him with a forged copy of the treaty in order to make him keep the treaty a secret. In pursuance of this treaty Clive without any formal declaration of war led an expedition against Nawab Siraj-ud-daula and defeated his army on June 23, 1757, at the battle of Plassey. Siraj fled and Clive with his army marched on to Murshidabad which was captured without any resistance. Here he now installed Mir Jafar as the Nawab of Bengal. All the higher employees of the Company in Bengal received large rewards and Robert Clive got as his share the gigantic sum of £234,100 as well as an assignment of the revenue of £30,000 a year which the Company was to pay to Nawab Mir Jafar for the Zamindari of 24 Parganas which the Nawab had recently conferred on the Company. Thus Robert Clive became the landlord of his own employers. Clive was also made the Governor of Bengal. He defeated the Dutch at the battle of Biderra (*q.v.*) near Chinsura and thus destroyed their power in Bengal. He sent Col. Forde to the Northern Circars which had so long been under French control and brought it within the dominions of the East India Company. Clive then proceeded on leave to England where he spent five years (1760-65) and was made Baron Clive of Plassey in the Irish peerage and was hailed by the Earl of Chatham as "the heaven-born general". During his absence in England important changes had taken place in Bengal where Nawab Mir Jafar was deposed by a corrupt Council and replaced by Nawab Mir Kasim (*q.v.*) who in his turn soon incurred so much displeasure of the Calcutta Council that a war broke out between him and the Company in which Mir Kasim was defeated. He fled to Oudh where he made an alliance with Nawab Suja-ud-daula and Emperor Shah Alam II. All these incidents alarmed the Directors at home and Robert Clive, now Lord Clive, was sent to Bengal as Governor and Commander-in-Chief. He arrived on May 3, 1765 but already Mir Kasim and his allies had been defeated in the battle of Buxar and it fell to Lord Clive to come to a political arrangement with the vanquished enemies. Mir Kasim after his defeat at Buxar fled away a fugitive and the vacant throne of Bengal was given to a grandson of Mir Jafar. Oudh was restored to Nawab Suja-ud-daula who ceded the districts of Kora and Allahabad which were given to Emperor Shah Alam II who conferred on the East India Company the *Dewani*, i.e. the authority to administer civil government and collect the revenues of Bengal, Bihar and Orissa on condition that the Company would pay him an annual revenue of 26 lakhs of rupees. This was the basis of the double government of the Emperor and the Company that Lord Clive established in Bengal, Bihar and Orissa. Having made this political arrangement Lord Clive took up the more difficult task of internal reforms. At the time of his appointment in 1765, Lord Clive was specially directed to uproot the prevailing corrupt practices amongst the Company's officers in Bengal and to stop the evil of private trade in which they engaged to the loss of the Company's revenue as well as of the Nawab's. Lord Clive enforced the signing by the Company's officers of covenants by which they promised to refrain from taking bribes. He also effected economies by reducing the field-allowances of the officers and manfully suppressed them when they attempted a White Mutiny. But in the matter of stopping private trade he ignored his instructions and organised the Trading Society with the Company's senior officers as its members and allowed it the monopoly of private trade in salt and some other articles. He himself held five shares in the Society which he later on sold for more than three lakhs of rupees. Lord Clive then finally retired in 1767. On his return to England he was attacked by the numerous personal enemies that his administration in Bengal had created as well as by some noble-spirited public men of England who really wanted to free the Company's administration from corruption and venality. One such person was Col. Burgoyne at whose instance Clive's administration in Bengal was subjected to a severe parliamentary enquiry resulting in the passing, on Col. Burgoyne's motion, resolutions condemning the malpractices that had been current in Bengal, declaring as illegal the appropriation of acquisitions made in Bengal with the Company's army to private purposes and declaring further that Robert Clive had illegally appropriated the gigantic sum of £234,000 with the rider that Robert Clive had at the same time rendered great and meritorious services to his country. Lord Clive took this veiled condemnation too much to heart and committed suicide by cutting his own throat on November 22, 1774.

Close, Sir Barry (1756-1813)—came to India in 1771 as an officer in the Company's Madras army, fought in the war against Haidar Ali in 1780 and was present at the siege of Seringapatam in 1792 and again in 1799 and was appointed the first British Resident in Mysore in 1799. He proved to be a sympathetic guide to the new Raja. He was next appointed as Resident at Poona in 1801 and remained there for 10 years. He negotiated with Peshwa Baji Rao II the treaty of Bassein (*q.v.*) in December, 1802. He retired from service in 1811, was created a Baronet and died in 1813.

Clyde, Colin Campbell, Lord (1792-1863)—a veteran military

officer who had seen action in the Peninsular and Napoleonic
Wars in Europe and in the China War of 1842, joined the
British Indian army in 1846. He fought in the Second Sikh War
(*q.v.*) as a Brigadier and won distinction. He went back to
England soon afterwards, but came back to India on a day's
notice in July, 1856, as the Commander-in-Chief of the British
army during the Sepoy Mutiny. He quickly reorganised the
British plan of campaign, hurried up reinforcements to Cawnpore, relieved Lucknow, defeated the rebels at Cawnpore,
besieged and took Lucknow in March, 1858 and soon reduced to
submission the rebels in northern India. He was made a General
and raised to the peerage in 1858. His victories in India made
him a hero to the British public and on his death in 1863 he
was buried in Westminister Abbey.

Cochin—is on the Malabar coast. It was a Hindu kingdom but
it was on unfriendly terms with the neighbouring Hindu state
of Calicut at the beginning of the 16th century. It gave shelter
to the Portuguese adventurer Cabral and thus established trading
relations with the Portuguese who soon established a factory at
Cochin. Before long the Hindu Raja was reduced to a cipher by
the Portuguese who in their turn were driven out of Cochin by
the Dutch in 1662. In the 18th century it became a feudatory of
Haidar Ali (*q.v.*) of Mysore. On the fall of Tipu Sultan (*q.v.*)
of Mysore it passed under British control and became one of the
protected states in India.

Cockburn, Col. James—was in the Bombay army of the East
India Company. During the First Maratha War (*q.v.*) he was
confronted by a Maratha army, got alarmed, decided to retreat,
reached Wadgaon and found that further retreat was not
possible. So he made peace with the Marathas by the Convention of Wadgaon (*q.v.*). The treaty was considered humiliating and was disavowed by the Company. Cockburn was subsequently dismissed from the service.

Coimbatore, the district of—was a part of the Mysore kingdom
during the rule of Tipu Sultan (*q.v.*). On his defeat and death in
the last Mysore War (*q.v.*), Coimbatore was annexed to the
British Indian Empire in 1799.

Coinage—has a long history in India. The earliest Indian coins were
punch-marked silver or copper pieces, very commonly square or
rectangular in shape. Such coins belong to at least the 4th
century B.C. and remained current for several centuries later.
From the second century B.C. Greek influence came to modify
the Indian coinage and the Indo-Bactrian princes issued a

finer type of coinage with legends in Greek and also in Prakrit.
From the first century A.D. the Kushana kings (*q.v.*) issued gold
and copper coins bearing on the obverse the effigy of the king
offering a sacrifice and on the reverse deities of all religions of
the time. This type of coins remained the general type of north-
Indian coinage for many centuries onwards. The Gupta Emperors in the fourth century A.D. issued coins of an improved
standard. They struck an extensive coinage with legends in
Sanskrit giving the names of the issuing kings and showing them
in various postures. Such, for example, are the gold coins of
Samudragupta (*q.v.*) showing him sitting on a couch and playing
on a lyre or performing the horse-sacrifice. The western Satraps
issued silver coins which bear the name and the bust of the
issuing ruler. The Huna invasions in the 6th century led to a
debasement of the coinage but a revival followed in the 10th
century when a neat silver coinage was issued by the Shahi
kings of Gandhara. This type of coinage was later on imitated
by the Muhammadan conquerors of India. The Delhi sultans
issued a varied and extensive coinage, mainly gold and silver
tankas (rupees) of 178 grains. They are large and thick pieces
with the *kalima* or profession of faith on one side and the names
of the issuing king and mint and date on the other. Muhammad
bin Tughluq (*q.v.*) made an effort to replace the gold coinage
with token copper currency in order to tide over a financial
crisis. The experiment proved a sad failure and token currency
was not tried by any other Muhammadan ruler in India. But
coinage continued to be debased until at last Sher Shah (*q.v.*)
stabilised it by issuing a good silver coinage of *tanka* or *rupeya*
(from which the term Rupee is derived) and fixing the ratio
between the silver rupee and the copper pice at 1:64. This silver
rupee continued to be the standard of coinage in India during
the whole of the Mughul rule with one important change.
Aurangzeb (*q.v.*) replaced the *kalima* by the name of the mint
and the date of issue. This continued to be the practice with his
successors. The British continued to coin on Mughul lines and
their coinage up to 1835 purported to have been issued in the
nineteenth regnal year of Emperor Shah Alam II. It was only
in that year that a new coinage was issued by the British in which
the old legends were replaced by the English monarch's effigy
and superscription. Silver and copper coins of different denominations were issued and elaborate steps were taken to prevent
counterfeiting. Under the pressure of World War I gold coins
ceased to be issued and World War II led to the debasement

of the silver rupee as well as of the coins of lesser denomination. Token paper currency of Rupee one came to take the place of the silver rupee and became legal tender. Since India gained her independence she has been issuing a new coinage, not of gold nor of silver nor even of copper but of base mixed metals of various denominations from one rupee downwards to one *paisa*, the ratio being 1:100 with new legends appropriate to her new status and has also been continuing the practice of issuing paper currency of various denominations from one rupee upwards. (Cunningham. A., *Coins of An. Ind., & Coins of Med. Ind.*, Smith, V. A., *Cat. of Ind. Coins;* Allan. J., *Coins of the Guptas*)

Collector, the—is the official designation of an officer placed in charge of the collection of the revenue of a district since the establishment of British rule in India. The post was first created in 1772 when the revenue administration of Bengal, Bihar and Orissa was taken over by the Governor-in-Council from the hands of the Indian Naib-Diwans who had so long been in charge of the collection of the revenue, and placed in the hands of the Collectors. The incumbents were all Britishers and each district was placed in charge of a Collector. Abolished in 1773 and recreated in 1781, the Collector had little to do till 1786 when he was made responsible for settling and collecting the revenue of the district with the advice and sanction of the Board of Revenue (*q.v.*). The Collector was also in charge of the civil justice in the district, was vested with powers of a Magistrate and could try criminal cases. The Collector thus became the sole representative of British authority in a district and was burdened with multifarious duties. The Cornwallis Code of 1793 divested the Collector of all judicial and magisterial powers which were vested in the District Judge. Some time later magisterial duties were vested in the District Magistrate whose office was separated from that of the District Collector. Still later the Collector was vested with the duties of the Magistrate and the district came to be administered by the District Magistrate and Collector. Indians were made eligible to the office when entrance to the Indian Civil Service was thrown open to a competitive examination in 1853. The District Magistrate and Collector was a very important part of the Indian administrative machinery during British rule. In Republican India with popular control over the executive, the power and importance of the District Magistrate and Collector have been much reduced, but he still continues to be a very important limb of the administrative system. (O'Malley L. S. S., *Indian Civil Service;* Joshi, G. N., *Ind. Admn.*)

Colvin, John (1797-57)—the son of a Calcutta merchant and born in Calcutta, entered the Indian Civil Service in 1826 and rose to be the Private Secretary to the Governor-General Lord Auckland (*q.v.*) whose Afghan policy he largely influenced. He was the Lt.-Governor of N. W. P. (modern Uttar Pradesh) from 1853 till his death in September 1857 when the country was racked by the Sepoy Mutiny which he least expected. His handling of the situation left much to be desired. He was worn out by the anxieties and labours imposed on him by the Mutiny and died.

Combermere, Stapleton Cotton, First Viscount (1773-1865)— came out to India as a Lt.-Col. in the army in 1799 and took part in the war against Tipu Sultan (*q.v.*). In 1822 he became the Commander-in-Chief of the Indian army and had the distinction of capturing the fort of Bharatpur in 1826. He retired from the Company's service in 1830 and died in 1865.

Commissioner—is the designation of the officer placed in charge of a division comprising several districts in a province of British India. The office was created in 1829. Originally the Divisional Commissioner was vested with judicial and police duties in addition to the duty of supervising the work of the Collectors Magistrates and Judges of the districts placed under him. But so many duties soon proved too heavy for one person and the Divisional Commissioner was relieved of his judicial and police duties, and remained as a supervisor of the District Collectors under him with some judicial work in connection with revenue matters. (References as under Collector).

Communal Award—was made by Ramsay Macdonald, the British Prime Minister, on the 4th August, 1932, as a preliminary and essential part of the Government of India Act which was then under discussion at the Round Table Conference held in London and which was subsequently passed in 1935. The Award was based on the principle of communal representation which was embodied in the Government of India Act, 1909. When in 1906 it became clear to the Indian public that changes in the existing constitution would be soon effected with a view to giving the people a larger share in the administration of the country a deputation of some leading Muslims of India was deliberately got up by some official Europeans in India with the connivance of the Viceroy Lord Minto II. It requested the Viceroy to grant representation of Muslim interests through special Muslim constituencies. The reason adduced by them was that on account of the greater poverty of the Indian Muslims they would be under-represented in any general electoral roll based on a property qualification. The Viceroy who was anxious for having some means for counterbalancing the growing nationalism in India, particularly in Bengal, thought that it would be useful for the Government to introduce a wedge between the Hindus and the Muslims of India. So the Government of Lord Minto II readily accepted the Muslim demand and in the Government of India Act of 1909 six special Muslim landholders constituencies were created for the Imperial Legislative Council and other similar constituencies in the provinces. This measure had very sinister significance and has been correctly described as the official germ of Pakistan. Muslim demands for separate communal representation grew with the passing of the years and with the feeling that these had the secret support of the British. So in later years, the principle had to be conceded and on the eve of the further grant of constitutional reforms in the thirties demands for special representations on communal bases were advanced not only on behalf of the Muslims but also on behalf of all other major communities like the Sikhs, Christians, Jains, Parsis and the tribal peoples. The division that was characteristic of Indian population stood nakedly exposed. The Indians, as ever before, failed to come to an agreement amongst themselves, either by their discussions on the soil of India or by their debates in the three successive Round Table Conferences held in London in the thirties. The British Prime Minister, Ramsay Macdonald, therefore, had an excellent opportunity for putting into action the principle of 'divide and rule' and gave his Communal Award on the 4th August, 1932. It was more of an imposition than an award, for the Congress had never asked for it. It not only recognised the divisions amongst the Indians on a religious basis but also the divisions amongst the Hindus on the basis of castes and gave separate representation to the depressed classes amongst the Hindus. This last provision was a most mischievous measure to divide the Hindus for all time to come and it was only as a result of a fast unto death undertaken by Mahatma Gandhi that it was modified by the Poona Pact on the 24th September, 1932, which kept the depressed classes as an integral part of the Hindu population of India and yet gave them general as well as special representation in the legislative bodies of the country. While the Communal Award had given the depressed classes 71 seats in the various State-legislatures the Poona Pact gave them 148 as well as eighteen per cent of the general seats in the Central legislature. The Muslim share remained unaltered and the Indian population was thus definitely divided into two unreconciled communities leading eventually to the partition of India in 1947. (Morley, J., *Recollections;* Das, M. N., *India under Morley and Minto*, Ch. v)

Company, the Dutch East India—or, more precisely, the United East India Company of the Netherlands was founded in 1602. It had large financial resources and also the backing of the State. The Dutch, like the English, were at first opposed by the Portuguese whose claim to a monopoly of trade in the East the Dutch contested in co-operation with the English East India Company and won their rights to trade. The Dutch Company, however, concentrated on settling in and trading with the Spice Islands from which they succeeded in excluding the English by the massacre of Amboyna in 1623. In India, however, the Dutch Company had not equal success. Its factories in Pulicut and Masulipatam never rivalled Madras and its settlement at Chinsura in Bengal was soon eclipsed by the English settlement in Calcutta. Finally in 1759 the Dutch of Chinsura were defeated by the English at the battle of Biderra (*q.v.*) and made peace with the English by giving up all pretensions to political power in Bengal as well as in the rest of India, though the Dutch East India Company continued to maintain a prosperous trade with India. It also founded a large empire in the Malay Archipelago which continued to be in the possession of the Dutch till 1952, when the Dutch had to recognise the independence of Indonesia.

Company, the East India—was formed on the last day of 1600 by virtue of a Charter granted by Queen Elizabeth I to "the Governor and Company of Merchants of London trading into the East Indies" which vested them with exclusive trading rights. The East India Company, which was thus formed, traded at first with the Spice Islands and it was only in 1608 that one of their trading vessels first reached Surat, but Portuguese hostility prevented the Company from starting trade with India immediately. The English got the support of the Dutch East India Company against the Portuguese, with whom the two fought long and bitterly. In 1612 an English fleet led by Captain Best repulsed the Portuguese attacks and the English Company began trading at Surat. In 1613 the Company was granted an imperial *farman* and its trading rights at Surat became secure. It 1622 the English captured Ormuz and this acquisition secured them against any effective opposition by the Portuguese. Earlier, in 1615-18 Sir Thomas Roe as an ambassador of King James I to Emperor Jahangir, secured some privileges for the East India Company. Soon afterwards the Company established factories at Masulipatam and Armagaon on the Bay of Bengal, but their first important achievement came in March, 1640, when they acquired from the Raja of Chandragiri, representative of the old kings of Vijayanagar, the site of modern Madras where they quickly built the Fort St. George. In 1661 King Charles II got Bombay from Portugal as a part of the dowry given to his Portuguese Queen and in 1668 transferred it to the East India Company for an annual rent of £10 only. Then between 1669 and 1677 the Company's Governor, Gerald Aungier, laid the beginnings of the modern city of Bombay to which the head-quarters of the East India Company in western India were transferred from Surat in 1687. Lastly, in 1690 Job Charnock, 'a faithful servant' of the East India Company, at the invitation of Nawab Ibrahim Khan of Bengal, laid the foundation of Calcutta in swampy land on the Bhagirathi comprising the village of Sutanuti to which were added in 1698 the two adjoining villages of Kalikata and Govindapur. Thus after overcoming the strenuous resistance of the Portuguese, the East India Company was within ninety years of its foundation in possession of three excellent harbours at Bombay, Madras and Calcutta, each with a fort of its own. These were called Presidencies and each was under the administration of a Governor appointed by the Court of Directors (*q.v.*) and Court of Proprietors (*q.v.*) who managed from London with their offices at Leadon Hall Street the affairs of the East India Company across the seas.

In 1691 the East India Company was granted by a *farman* issued by Nawab Ibrahim Khan (*q.v.*) the privilege of being exempted from the payment of customs duties in Bengal in return for an annual payment of Rs. 3000 only, whereas the other European companies trading in Bengal had to pay 3 per cent duties. This right was later on confirmed by imperial *farmans* granted by Emperor Farruksiyar in 1715 in recognition of the medical services that were rendered to him by the Company's surgeon Hamilton, who had accompanied the embassy that the Company had sent to the Mughul Court. The monopoly of trading rights possessed by the East India Company was resented by many English merchants who formed, towards the close of the seventeenth century, a rival body named 'The English Company Trading to the East Indies'. Fierce rivalry ensued between the old and the new companies and the older one was threatened with extinction. But after much bitter and undignified quarrelling in England as well as in India a compromise was effected in 1708 which combined the two rival bodies into one concern to be called 'the United Company of the Merchants of England Trading to the East Indies'. This United Company continued to be known as the East India Company which in the course of the succeeding one hundred and fifty years passed from a trading corporation into a body claiming sovereignty over the whole of India.

The acquisition of the sovereignty over India was not suddenly effected. It was a prolonged process covering over a century and necessitating eliminating wars with the French and the Dutch companies which had also come out to the East for trading with India and also numerous wars with the Indians. Fortunately for the East India Company, the central Mughul Government which claimed *de jure* right to the sovereignty over India grew weaker and weaker as the eighteenth century advanced in years and India became divided into a number of Muslim and Hindu states with no unity amongst themselves. Not only were the Muslims opposed to the Hindus with whom they fought, but there was no love lost even amongst the Muslim states nor did they feel any loyalty to the Muslim Emperor ruling in Delhi. This division worked in favour of the East India Company. It eliminated the French East India Company by its victory at the battle of Wandiwash (*q.v.*) (1761). Already its victory at the battle of Plassey (*q.v.*) (1757) had given it practical sovereignty over Bengal, Bihar and Orissa. The Mughul Emperor Shah Alam II looked on helplessly as the Company's armies went on conquering and annexing the Muslim state of Mysore, receiving the submission of the Muslim Nizam of Hyderabad and could have little counterbalancing consolation on the reduction of the Hindu Marathas by the Company. The brave Rajputs, divided as always, practically submitted without striking a single blow in self-defence. With the submission of the Marathas during the administration of Lord Hastings (1813-23) (*q.v.*) the Mughul Emperor virtually became a pensioner of the Company. Assam passed under Company's rule in 1829, Sind in 1843, the Panjab in 1849 and Lower Burma in 1852. Indeed the Company's sway was now supreme from Burma to Peshawar. Already the East India Company had been divested of its trading rights and monopolies and was now acting as the administrative agency of the Crown of Great Britain. All seemed quiet, when the storm of the Sepoy Mutiny burst over the land in 1857. It was suppressed by the Company with Indian assistance with which indeed it had been possible for it to have built up its sovereignty over India, but the display of resistance and disaffection by some section of the Indians tolled the death-knell of the East India Company which was liquidated in 1858 when the monarch of Great Britain assumed sovereignty over India.

Company, the French East India—was formed at the instance of Colbert in A.D. 1664. It was created by the French Government which also financed it, but it was not efficiently·managed and frittered away its energies during the first four years of its existence in fruitless attempts at colonising Madras. When it attempted to start trading with India it met with resistance alike from the English and the Dutch Companies which had already entered into trade with India and established factories there. In spite of this resistance the French succeeded in establishing their first Indian factory at Surat in 1668 and secured in 1673 the site of modern Pondicherry, 85 miles south of Madras. It was placed in charge of Francois Martin in 1674 and was soon developed by him into an important place to become the headquarters of the French East India Company in India. The French Company also got in 1674 from Nawab Shaista Khan of Bengal a site on the Bhagirathi where during the years 1690-92 they built their factory of Chandernagore, a few miles above Calcutta, where the English Company established their settlement in 1690. Thus the French in Pondicherry and Chandernagore became the neighbours and rivals of the English in Madras and Calcutta. But the business of the French Company declined in the first two decades of the eighteenth century and its factory at Surat was closed. Prosperity, however, came during the next two decades and the French Company acquired Mauritius in 1721, Mahe on the Malabar coast in 1725 and Karikal on the Coromandel coast in 1739. So long the French Company had concentrated practically entirely on trading with India, but a change came over its policy and aims with the appointment of Dupleix (*q.v.*) as the Governor of Pondicherry in 1742. The War of the Austrian Succession (1740-48) was then going on in Europe and France was at war with England. Taking advantage of the absence of any English fleet on the Coromandel coast and the presence of a French fleet there the French attacked and captured Madras in September, 1746. On an appeal made by the English Company's officers driven from Madras Anwar-ud-din, the Nawab of the Carnatic within whose dominions Madras was situated, sent a large Indian army to recover Madras from the French. A tiny force of Frenchmen won a complete victory over the much larger army of the Nawab at the battle of Mylapore or St. Thome and held Madras for the French. Two years later the European war between the English and the French was brought to a close by the treaty of Aix-la-Chapelle by the terms of which Madras was restored to the English Company. But the war, particularly the French victory over the Nawab's army at the battle of Mylapore, had revealed how a large old-fashioned Indian army could be defeated by a small disciplined army of Europeans supported by Indians. This lesson deeply influenced the policy of Dupleix who so long had no political ambitions, but who now thought of taking part in Indian politics with his superior army and thus make political and territorial gains in India. On his initiative the French Company took part in the succession disputes that arose for the thrones of the Carnatic and Hyderabad in 1748 and had at first spectacular successes. A French Company's *protégé* sat on the throne of the Nizam under the control of the French general Bussy and the revenue of the Northern Circars was assigned by the Nizam to the French for the maintenance of their army. But Dupleix failed to achieve his great aim of expelling the English Company from India. All this time England and France were at peace in Europe and the Government of France decided to end the unofficial war with England that Dupleix had begun in India. So in 1754 Dupleix was recalled to France and his dream was left unrealised. Two years after the recall of Dupleix the Seven Years' War broke out in Europe and the English and the French Companies were again at war in India. In 1757 the English first captured the French settlement at Chandernagore in Bengal and soon afterwards got control over the resources of Bengal by defeating Nawab Siraj-ud-daula of Bengal at the battle of Plassey and installing their *protégé* Mir Jafar as the Nawab of Bengal (1757). In 1758 the French were deprived of the Northern Circars by an English army led by Col. Forde and in 1760 the French suffered a decisive defeat at the hands of the English General Sir Eyre Coote in the battle of Wandiwash (*q.v.*). Next year the English captured Pondicherry and thus the French East India Company lost all they had held in India. The Peace of Paris which brought the Seven Years' War to a close in 1763 marked the fall of the French East India Company as a political power in India and by returning to the French the possession of Pondicherry, Chandernagore, Mahe and Karikal to be held as unfortified trading centres only obliged the French East India Company to continue in India merely as a body of traders. These French possessions in India were surrendered to the Republic of India in 1950.

Congress—*see* Indian National Congress.

Connaught, the Duke of—son of Queen Victoria and the premier nobleman of England belonging to the royal family, came to India in March, 1921 and inaugurated the new constitution introduced in India by the Government of India Act, 1919. In spite of this royal touch at its inauguration the Act did not satisfy the Indian demands and relations between India and England were not much smoothened.

Constituent Assembly—*see* the Indian Constituent Assembly.

Constitution of India Act, the—was passed by the Constituent Assembly (*q.v.*) on the 26th November, 1949 and became effective with effect from the 26th January, 1950. It is a voluminous document comprising 395 articles divided into 22 Parts, besides nine Schedules. It gave India a written but partly flexible constitution and established in India a sovereign, federal, democratic, secular and parliamentary Republic. It begins with a Preamble which asserts "We, the people of India, having solemnly resolved to constitute India into a sovereign democratic Republic and to secure to all citizens Justice, social, economic and political; Liberty of thought, expression, belief, faith and worship; Equality of status and of opportunity; and to promote among them all Fraternity assuring the dignity of the individual and the unity of the Nation, do hereby adopt, enact and give to ourselves this constitution." It provides that India shall be a Union of States as enumerated in one of the schedules and confers citizenship upon all persons who are born in India, or either of whose parents was born in India or who have been ordinarily residents of India for not less than five years preceding the commencement of the Constitution. It enunciates certain *fundamental rights*, namely, equality, untouchability, freedom of speech and expression, of peaceful un-armed assembly, of forming associations, of movement and residence in any part of India, of acquiring and holding property and of practising any profession or carrying on any occupation, trade and business and makes these fundamental rights *justiciable*. It lays down certain *directive principles* which, though not justiciable, are to guide the Union and the component States

in their administrative work with a view to the development
of a welfare state in India. The Act provides for separate administrative bodies for the Union and the component States.
The executive administration of the Union is vested in an
elected President who shall hold office for five years, is eligible
for re-election, shall draw a salary of Rs. 10,000 per month
with additional allowances, an elected Vice-President and
a Council of Ministers with a Prime Minister at its head.
The President is to appoint the Prime Minister and the other
Ministers on the advice of the Prime Minister. The Act vests
in the President very large executive and legislative powers
but these are all to be exercised, following the British system,
on the advice and with the consent of the Ministers, who hold
office during the pleasure of the President but are really responsible to the Union Legislature. The President can be
impeached and removed from office by a vote of the Union
Legislature. The legislative organ of the Union is a Parliament
of two houses, namely the Council of States (*Rajya Sabha*)
and the House of the People (*Lok Sabha*). The Council shall
consist of 238 representatives of whom 12 are to be nominated
by the President and the rest are to be elected by the elected
representatives of the legislatures of the component States
in proportion to their population. The House of the People
shall consist of five hundred members all elected for a term
of 5 years on the basis of universal adult suffrage. The two
houses of the Parliament have co-ordinate powers except in
the case of Money-bills which can be initiated only in the
House of the People and to which the Council of State can
suggest amendments which the House of the People is free to
accept or reject. The Judiciary of the Union is vested in the
Supreme Court with a Chief Justice and 13 other judges to
be appointed by the President and holding office till the completion of the age of 65 years. It has both original and appellate
jurisdictions and can decide the constitutionality of a law,
but not its propriety. For the component States the Act provides for an Executive consisting of the Governor to be
appointed by the President for a term of five years drawing
a salary of Rs. 5,500 per month, a Council of Ministers with
a Chief Minister to be appointed by the Governor and responsible to the Legislature and for a Legislature consisting of
two chambers, namely an indirectly elected Council and an
entirely directly elected Assembly in the cases of Andhra,
Bihar, Madhya Pradesh, Madras, Maharashtra, Mysore,

Panjab, Uttar Pradesh and West Bengal and of an entirely elected Assembly alone in the cases of the other States. The State Judiciary is vested in the State High Court with a Chief Justice and a number of judges who are appointed by the President and are to hold office till the completion of 62 years. Seventeen Acts amending the Constitution have since been passed and others are likely to follow as necessity may arise. The Constitution of India Act has thus more than fulfilled the aspirations of the Indian National Congress by establishing in India a government of the people, for the people and by the people. (Govt. of India: *The Constitution of India;* Basu, B. D., *The Constitution of India*).

Conti, Nicolo de—an Italian traveller, visited India early in the fifteenth century and was at Vijayanagar in 1420 when the kingdom was being ruled by king Devaraya II (*q.v.*). He has left a very interesting account of the city, the circumference of which he estimated to be sixty miles and the fortifications of which he considered to be very impressive. The city was densely populated and within it there were ninety thousand men fit to bear arms. The king married many wives and the practice of *Sati* (*q.v.*) prevailed, even amongst the queens.

Convention of Wadgaon—was signed in January, 1779 by Col. Carnac on behalf of the Company's Government in India in course of the First Maratha War (*q.v.*) (1776-82). An English army led by Col. Cockburn with Col. Carnac as the Civil Commissioner with the force, began a march on Poona but was confronted on its way by a large Maratha army at Telegaon in the Western Ghats, suffered reverses and found itself practically surrounded by the Marathas. In the circumstances, Carnac lost courage and it was on his insistence that Col. Cockburn, the commanding officer, signed the Convention of Wadgaon. By it all territories acquired by the Bombay Government since 1773 were to be surrendered for which British hostages were to be handed over to the Marathas and the pretender Raghoba (*q.v.*) on whose behalf the English had begun the war, was also to be surrendered, the relieving English army that was coming from Bengal was to be withdrawn and Mahadaji Sindhia was to be paid by the English a share of the revenue received by the English from Broach. The military situation did not justify the Convention and it was soon disavowed by the Governor-General. The officers concerned were dismissed from the service. Raghoba saved himself and the English by taking refuge with Sindhia whom the English thought it wise to pay the stipulated

share of the revenue of Broach and thus to establish good terms
with him.

Cooch-Behar (also spelt Kuch Behar)—is a town and district in
West Bengal, India. The town is on the Torsa river and the
Tista and the Sankosh also pass through the district before they
fall into the Brahmaputra. The name is derived from that of a
tribal people called the Koches. In later times they, especially
their kings, came to be considered as Kshatriyas. The district
lay within the dominions of the early Hindu kings of Kamarupa
(Assam) which extended under Bhaskaravarman (*c.* A.D. 600-
650) up to the Karotoya. But it got separated from Kamarupa
and early in the sixteenth century the town became the capital of
a new kingdom called Cooch-Behar founded by a local Koch chief
named Biswa Singha. The greatest monarch of the dynasty was
Nara Narayan (1540-84), the son and successor of Biswa Singha,
who extended his power over a large part of Assam and south-
ward over a part of the modern Rangpur district. He was a great
patron of Hinduism as well as of arts and letters. He rebuilt the
temple of the goddess Kamakhya near Gauhati which had been
destroyed by a Muslim raid led by Kala Pahar and was also the
patron of Sankara Deva (*q.v.*), the great founder of Vaishnavism
in Assam. On his death a struggle ensued between his son and
nephew for the succession to his dominions and his son made
himself a tributary of the Mughul Emperor Akbar in order to
protect himself against his cousin. The state remained tributary
to the Mughuls, but later on in 1772 it was invaded by the
Bhutanese and the reigning Raja appealed for assistance to
Warren Hastings, then Governor of Bengal. A detachment of
the Company's sepoys was accordingly sent by Warren Hastings
and the Bhutanese were expelled and compelled to sue for peace.
A treaty was then drawn up between the Company and the
Raja of Cooch-Behar by which the Raja acknowledged the
supremacy of the East India Company over his dominions and
agreed to pay an annual revenue in return for British protection.
It was subject to the agency of the Governor of Bengal till 1938
when it was transferred to the control of the Eastern States
Agency. In 1950 it was merged with the Republic of India, its
ruler was granted a privy-purse and it became a district of West
Bengal. (Aman-ullah, *Kuchbeharer Itihasa*)

Co-operative Movement in India—was started at the suggestion
of Frederick Nicholson, a Madras civilian, who recommended it
to the notice of the Madras Government in 1892. A committee
was appointed in 1901 to explore the possibilities and feasibility

of the co-operative system in India and an Act was passed in
1904 providing for the starting of rural as well as urban credit
societies for helping the people in getting money at reasonable
rates of interests and thus escaping the clutches of usurious money-
lenders. The co-operative movement which was thus started in
India in 1904 at first made remarkable progress in every Indian
province and its progress was further facilitated in 1912 when an
Amending Act was passed which granted recognition to non-
credit societies, central financing societies and unions. Under the
Government of India Act, 1919, co-operation became a provincial transferred subject and was placed under the administration
of Indian Ministers. The co-operative movement gradually came
to establish and run agricultural credit societies, central financing agencies and Provincial Banks. It has also led to the establishment of Land Mortgage Banks in some of the provinces with a
view to enabling the agriculturists to repay their old debts through
long-term credit obtainable on the security of their lands. The
co-operative movement in India passed through a crisis when
the prices of agricultural products fell after 1925; but even
after prices rose after the Second World War the co-operative
movement did not make in India as much progress as it might
be expected to have done. There is, however, much scope for
it in India for marketing goods, especially agricultural products, and enabling the middle-class people to build houses of
their own. (Neogi, J. P. *Hist. of the Co-operative Movement in India*)

Coorg—is now a district in the state of Mysore. It lies in the south
of the peninsula on the plateau of the Western Ghats, sloping
inland towards Mysore. The district capital is Mercara and the
official language is now Kannada (Kanarese). It grows rice and
coffee in abundance and it is the latter product that particularly
attracted the English to it. The district has taken its name from
the tribe of the Coorg who form the most numerous section of the
tribal peoples who were the original inhabitants of this district.
Its history cannot be traced beyond the 9th and 10th centuries of
the Christian era when it was ruled over by the Ganga kings
(*q.v.*). On the overthrow of the line of the Gangas in the 11th
century it passed successively under the rule of the Cholas, and
the Hoysalas and then became a part of the Vijayanagar empire.
On the fall of Vijayanagar a prince of the family established his
sway over the territory and his descendants continued to rule
over it until its annexation to the British Indian Empire in 1834.
Haidar Ali of Mysore and his son Tipu Sultan claimed sovereignty over it, though the Coorgs repeatedly rebelled against the Mus-

lim rule. In 1788, when Lord Cornwallis embarked on a war with
Tipu Sultan he made a treaty with Vira Raja who claimed to
be the king of Coorg and later on by the treaty of peace that was
made between the Company and Tipu Sultan in March 1792,
Tipu ceded Coorg to the Company and the Company recognised
Vira Raja as an independent ruler of Coorg. Vira Raja died in
1809. Vira Raja II who succeeded to the throne in 1820, proved
a monster of cruelty and sensuality and was therefore deposed in
1834 by Lord William Bentinck, Governor-General of India
and Coorg was annexed to the British Indian Empire. So long
as British rule lasted in India Coorg was administered as a
separate state by a Chief Commissioner. In 1951 it was integrated
into the Indian Republic and is now a district in the state of
Mysore. (Muttanna, P. M., *Coorg and the Coorgs*)

Coote, Sir Eyre (1726-1783)—came out to India as a Captain
attached to the first British regiment (the 39th) that was sent to
India in 1754. He accompanied Clive to Bengal in 1756 and
was present both at the recapture of Calcutta and the battle of
Plassey. After the battle of Plassey he pursued a fugitive French
army for 400 miles and was rewarded with the rank of
Lt.-Colonel. He was then sent to Madras where he first captured
the district of the Northern Circars which had been for the past
few years under the control of the French and in January 22, 1760,
he led the British army to their decisive victory over the French
at the battle of Wandiwash. He also participated in the capture of
Pondicherry in 1761. In 1779 he became a member of the Governor-General's Council after the death of Clavering. In 1780 he
was despatched to Madras to lead the English against Haidar
Ali, but though he won a victory over Haidar Ali at the battle
of Porto Novo in June, 1781, his achievement in this campaign
was not in keeping with his reputation as the victor of Wandiwash. Moreover, in a subsequent battle with Haidar Ali at
Palilur Coote lost one of his legs. This accident robbed him of
his old enterprising spirit and after 1782 till his death at Madras
in 1793 he did little in keeping with his earlier reputation.
(Wylly. S. C., *Life of Sir Eyre Coote*)

Cornwallis, Charles, First Marquis (1738-1805)—had been
during the American War of Independence, in charge of York-
town where he was obliged to surrender in October, 1781. With
him fell the English cause in America. Five years later he was
appointed Governor-General of India and Commander-in-Chief
of Bengal which posts he held for seven years (1786-93). He
had a second term of the said office from July 1805 till his death

three months later on October 5, 1805, at Ghazipur, India. During his first administration he fought the Third Mysore War (*q.v.*) (1790-92) in which he, in alliance with the Nizam of Hyderabad and the Marathas, personally led two campaigns against Tipu Sultan of Mysore, advanced up to Seringapatam and forced Tipu Sultan to make peace by the treaty of Seringapatam (*q.v.*) (1792) by which Tipu ceded one half of his territories to the victorious allies. The share of the English comprised Malabar, Coorg, Dindigul and Baramahal. Coorg was maintained as a protected state while the other territories were directly annexed to the British Indian Empire.

The importance of the administration of Lord Cornwallis lay in his internal reforms. He first reformed the commercial administration of the Company in Bengal by reducing the number of the members of the Board of Trade from eleven to five and by arranging that contracts for supplies to the Company should be not, as before, with the Company's officers, but with merchants. This enabled the Company to purchase goods at lower rates. He took away from the Nawab the power of administering criminal justice and transferred the *Sadr Nizamat Adalat* to Calcutta where the *Sadr Dewani Adalat* had already been transferred by Warren Hastings. The *Sadr Nizamat Adalat* was to be presided over by the Governor-General and Council aided by the Chief *Qazi* and *Muftis*. Four courts of circuit were established, each under two British judges aided by *Qazis* and *Muftis*. They were to make tours twice a year throughout the districts and to administer criminal justice. Four Provincial Courts of Appeal were established at Calcutta, Patna, Dacca and Murshidabad to decide more important civil disputes and to hear appeals from the lower civil courts presided over by *Munsiffs*. Appeals from the Provincial courts lay to the *Sadr Dewani Adalat*. For administrative purposes Bengal was divided into a number of districts in each of which the Collector was in charge of the collection of revenue and the District Judge was to perform magisterial duties as well as to dispense justice. Each district was also to have a Superintendent of Police who, acting under the Judge, was to help in the maintenance of law and order within the district. Each district was again divided into a number of *Thanas*, each under the charge of a *Daroga* (Sub-Inspector of Police) who controlled the local police and relieved the Zamindars of the police duties which they had so long been performing. All officers above the *Daroga* were to be appointed exclusively from Europeans and Indians were deliberately debarred from holding any but very petty offices in the state. It was on this basis of excluding Indians from the services in their own land and paying very high salaries to the European officers of all ranks that Cornwallis based the civil service in Bengal. It was imitated with the necessary changes in the other provinces. The system broke down eventually on account of its expensiveness. All these reforms were embodied in the Cornwallis Code (*q.v.*).

The most important reform introduced by Lord Cornwallis was the introduction of the Permanent Settlement of land revenue in Bengal. It recognised the *Zamindars* as the proprietors of the land which they held and which they were now permitted to hold in perpetuity on condition of paying ninety per cent of the estimated revenue to the Company's treasury by the sunset of a particular day each year. Failure to pay the revenue due on the fixed date would be punished with forfeiture and the sale of the land of the defaulting *Zamindar* by auction to the highest bidder. This system assured the Company of a certain income from land revenue every year and created in Bengal a class of landowners who found their interests closely bound up with those of the Company. But it deprived the provincial government of any share of the increase in land revenue that would result from increased prices of agricultural products, better administration and general economic improvement and it left the ryot, the man behind the plough, absolutely at the mercy of the *Zamindar*. In spite of its recognised defects the Permanent Settlement of land revenue which was introduced in Bengal, Bihar and Orissa in 1793 lasted throughout the British rule in India. (Seton-Karr, W. S., *The Marquis of Cornwallis;* Ascoli, F. D., *Early Rev. Hist. of Bengal*)

Cornwallis Code—was promulgated in May, 1793. It was drawn up by Mr. George Barlow, afterwards Governor-General. It defined the changes in internal administration effected during the regime of Lord Cornwallis (1786-93) and formed the basis of the Civil Service in Bengal and later on in India. Its fundamental defect was the complete exclusion of Indians from all high offices in the Company's higher services which were completely Europeanised and thus made too expensive for a poor country like India and too under-manned in view of the vastness of the country.

Cossijura Case—arose out of an attempt of the Supreme Court (*q.v.*) in Calcutta to exercise its jurisdiction over the *Zamindar* (entitled Raja) of Cossijura against whom the court entertained a suit brought by a private person for the recovery of a personal debt. The Supreme Court issued a writ against the *Zamindar* calling upon him to appear before it and stand trial. But on the representation of the *Zamindar* that he being neither a servant of the Company nor a resident of Calcutta the Supreme Court had no jurisdiction over him, the Supreme Council, i.e. the Governor-General-in-Council, asked the Supreme Court to refrain from proceeding further with the matter. But the Supreme Court was then out to expand its jurisdiction and sent its officers to arrest the *Zamindar*. The Supreme Council at once sent sepoys to arrest the officers sent by the Supreme Court to arrest the *Zamindar*. Thus a piquant situation arose and the conflict between the Executive and Judiciary, both creations of the Regulating Act, (*q.v.*) stood out in all its ugly nakedness. A final catastrophe was averted and the conflict was settled for the time by the appointment of Sir Elijah Impey, the Chief Justice of the Supreme Court as also the Chief Justice of the *Sadr Dewani Adalat* on a handsome allowance. The acceptance of this post by Impey was considered very improper and formed one of the counts for which he was later on impeached. (Banerjee, I. B., *The Supreme Court in Conflict*)

Cosmas Indikopleustes—was a Greek merchant who later on became a monk. He travelled widely from A.D. 535 to 547 in the Mediterranean, Red Sea and Persian Gulf regions as well as in Ceylon and India and left a record of his travel-impressions and experiences in his book *Christian Topography*. His book contains much valuable information regarding the trading relations between India and Ceylon and other countries on the western sea-coasts. (M'Crindle, J. W., *Ancient India*)

Cossimbazar (**also spelt Kasimbazar**)—is on the Bhagirathi in Murshidabad district, West Bengal. Its proximity to the town of Murshidabad which was the capital of the Nawabs of Bengal in the eighteenth century, attracted to it European traders and the British, the French and the Dutch all established their factories at Cossimbazar. The English factory at Cossimbazar was first seized by the Nawab of Bengal in 1686, but was restored in 1690. It was again captured by Nawab Siraj-ud-daula in 1756 and the resident and his assistant (Warren Hastings) were taken as prisoners to Murshidabad. It was recovered by the Company after the battle of Plassey and continued to be a flourishing place until the great famine of 1770, which greatly reduced the area of the cultivated land in the neighbourhood. Finally by 1813 the Bhagirathi changed its course and moved three miles

away from Cossimbazar which, as a result, lost all its old importance as a trading centre.

Cotton, Sir Arthur Thomas (1803-99)—was a distinguished
English engineer in the Company's service in Madras. He was a
specialist in irrigation works in southern India. He constructed
irrigation works on the Kaveri, Coleroon, Godavari and Krishna
rivers and thereby improved the irrigation in the Tanjore,
Trichinopoly and South Arcot districts. He also constructed an
anicut (dam) on the Godavari in the Godavari district. He was
the founder of the modern school of Indian Hydraulic Engineering. He was knighted in 1861, retired in 1862 and died in 1899.
His book on *Public Works in India* is a standard text on the subject.

Cotton, Sir Henry John Stedman (1845-1915)—entered the
Indian Civil Service in 1867, rose to be the Chief Secretary in
Bengal in 1891, the Home Secretary to the Government of India
in 1896 and the Chief Commissioner of Assam which post he held
from 1896 till his retirement in 1902. He was a most liberal
Civilian and became a leading champion of Indian nationalism.
He was elected to be the President of the 20th session of the
Indian National Congress held in Bombay in 1904. It was in his
Presidential address delivered at this session of the Congress
that he visualized for the first time the ideal of "a Federation of
free and separate states, the United States of India" (Sitaramaya, P., *Hist. of the Ind. National Congress*, Vol. I).

Cotton, Sir Willioughby (1783-1860)—came out to India in 1821
as a military officer, took part in the First Burmese War (*q.v.*)
(1825-26) and in the First Afghan War (*q.v.*) (1838-39), left
Kabul prior to the great disaster of 1841 and rose to be the
Commander-in-Chief of the Bombay army (1841-50).

Cotton, Sir Sydney (1792-1874)—came out to India as a military
officer in 1810 and served in Madras, Bengal and Bombay Presidencies and took part in the Pindari War (*q.v.*) in 1817-18, in
the Burmese War (*q.v.*) in 1828 and in the war with Sind (*q.v.*)
in 1842-43. He was in command of the British army in the N. W.
Frontier in 1853, was, at the outbreak of the Sepoy Mutiny,
Brigadier-General at Peshawar and prevented by his foresight,
tact and decision any outbreak of disturbances there. This
enabled the Panjab Government to denude the Panjab of
most of the British army and send them on to take part in
suppressing the Mutiny at Delhi. His works, *Nine Years on the
North Western Frontier* and the *Central Asian Question* are valuable
contributions on the subjects.

Council of India, the (also called the India Council)—was

created by the Government of India Act of 1858 which transferred the administration of India from the East India Company
to the Crown. The act abolished the Board of Control along
with its President and established in its place the Council of
India with a Secretary of State for India at its head. The Council
consisted of fifteen members, appointed at first for life but later
on for periods of between ten and fifteen years. It consisted of
fifteen members with Indian experience and was expected to
advise and to control the Secretary of State. It was, therefore,
given specific powers and its consent was necessary for the appropriation and expenditure of the Indian revenue and for the
appointment of the ordinary members of the Viceroy's Council.
By the Act of 1869 the tenure of office of each member was reduced to ten years, renewable at the option of the Secretary of
State and the Council was reduced to an advisory body. It was
a preserve for Britishers throughout the nineteenth century and
two Indians, Sir Krishna Govinda Gupta and Sayyed Hussain
Bilgrami, were for the first time appointed as members of the
Council of India in 1907. By the Act of 1919 the number of
members was reduced to a maximum of twelve and the term
of office was reduced to five years. It became more than
before subordinate to the Secretary of State. As provided by the
Government of India Act of 1935, the Council of India was
abolished from April, 1937. It had been throughout all its existence looked upon by Indians as a reactionary body determined
to uphold British interests in India at the cost of the Indians.

Council of State, the—was created by the Government of India
Act of 1919 which established in British India a bi-cameral legislature. The Council of State was the Upper House of this bi-
cameral legislature. It had a membership of 61 of whom 34 were
to be elected, 10 officials and the rest nominated non-officials.
The franchise was conferred on voters with a very high property
qualification. The Council had a President nominated by the
Governor-General from amongst its members. It had co-ordinate powers with the Lower House called the Legislative Assembly, but demands for grants, were to be initiated in the Lower
House. The Council of State was expected to act as a curb on
the possible liberal and democratic tendencies of the Legislative
Assembly. It fulfilled these expectations to a large extent.
Accordingly the Government of India Act of 1935 enlarged its
membership and importance. It was to consist of 156 members
for British India and not more than 104 members for the federating Indian States. Thus the total membership was raised to 260.

Six of the 156 members for British India were to be nominated by the Governor-General so as to secure due representation of the minority communities, depressed classes and women and the remaining 150 were to be elected on a high franchise by communal electorates. All the 104 members for the federating Indian States were to be appointed by the rulers of the respective States. Thus in a house of 260 members as many as 110 were to be nominees of the Central and States Governments. The Council of State was to be a permanent body not subject to dissolution, though one-third of the members was to retire every three years and the term of no member should exceed nine years. The Council was to have co-ordinate powers with the Legislative Assembly, even in financial matters. Thus the Council of State, as formed by the Government of India Act, 1935, was sure to prove to be a serious obstacle to the growth of a really responsible government at the centre. But this part of the Act of 1935 was not fully put into force before India gained her independence. Under the new constitution that India adopted after her independence the Council of State was transformed into the Rajya Sabha (*q.v.*) with a different constitution and a different status.

Court, General Claude Auguste—a French military officer, joined service under Ranjit Singh (*q.v.*) of the Panjab in 1827. In collaboration with Avitabile (*q.v.*) he reorganised and greatly improved Ranjit Singh's artillery. But after Ranjit Singh's death the Sikh troops, for reasons not known, lost confidence in him and attacked him. Court was, however, saved by his French colleague, Ventura, and retired from Lahore to France where he sank into oblivion.

Court of Directors—*see* Court of Proprietors.

Court of Proprietors, the—was the name by which the shareholders of the East India Company were known. This body elected annually a body or Court of twenty-four Directors who managed the affairs of the Company. Originally the Court of Proprietors had the right of reviewing the acts of omission and commission by the Court of Directors and its meetings were tumultuous and its actions were controlled only by considerations of profit and loss. Rival factions made and unmade Directors at the annual elections and shares were bought and split in order to obtain and increase voting power. This led to a great deal of jobbery. Accordingly the Regulating Act of 1773 raised the qualification for a vote in the meeting of the Court of Proprietors from £500 to £1000 and limited its right of electing Directors to six a year for a four-year term. Yet the Court of Proprietors which was merely a body of merchants interested in trade and commerce continued to influence the decisions of the Court of Directors which had been in the meantime vested with the duty of controlling the administration of the growing British dominions in India. So Pitt's India Act (*q.v.*) set up a Board of Control for supervising the work of the Court of Directors. The Court of Proprietors henceforth lost the power of modifying or rescinding any proceedings of the Court of Directors which had received the approval of the Board of Control. Thus the Court of Proprietors lost all opportunities for influencing politics in India. The Court of Directors, however, continued to be the administrative agency of the British Crown in India, though as the years passed its administration came to be controlled more and more by the President of the Board of Control. Yet the Directors were strong enough to secure the recall of Lord Wellesley and of Lord Ellenborough before the termination of their terms of office. The assumption of the administration of India by the Crown of Great Britain in 1858 led to the abolition of the East India Company along with its executive body, namely the Court of Directors.

Covenanted Civil Service (later Indian Civil Service), the—was the bureaucratic administrative machinery that the East India Company developed in India for running its administration. It began in a humble way. The East India Company as a body of traders employed in their service young Britishers as 'writers'. They were generally the nominees of the Directors and chosen for their relationship with the Company's shareholders. Their age was below 20, they had little or no school education and their salaries were low. When after the battle of Plassey (*q.v.*) (1757) the East India Company found themselves in possession of large Indian dominions the Company put their 'writers' or clerks in charge of administration of the newly acquired territories. As these officers were soon found to be guilty of gross corruption and dishonesty so the Company required them to sign 'covenants' or contracts promising to serve the Company with honesty and integrity. It was during the second administration of Lord Clive in Bengal that the Company first began to insist on the acceptance of such covenants by their officers who in their turn resented this new requisition. But they had all ultimately to submit and during the administration of Lord Cornwallis (*q.v.*) the Covenanted Civil Service became a regular part of the Company's administrative machinery in India. Lord Cornwallis filled the service entirely with Britishers and substantially raised their salaries and emoluments. They were appointed to all the important civil posts under the Company and monopolised the offices of District Collectors, District Magistrates and District Judges. They also filled the posts of Departmental Secretaries when these posts were created later on and of Diplomatic Agents. Lord Wellesley tried to improve the intellectual attainments of the members of the Covenanted Civil Service by requiring them to go through a period of training in the College of Fort William which he established in Calcutta. But the College had to be closed down in 1805 as the Company resented the cost of its maintenance and during the following fifty years the recruits to the Covenanted Civil Service were trained in the Haileybury College in London. Some of such recruits proved indeed to be great and successful administrators, but generally speaking much was lacking in an average member of the Covenanted Civil Service which still continued to be a preserve for the nominees of the Directors of the Company who had little general education that was essential to make them competent administrators. Demands arose in England itself that the best and most talented British young men should be encouraged to go out to India as administrators and consequently the admission to the Covenanted Civil Service, which now came to be called the Indian Civil Service, was thrown open in 1853 to competition through a public examination to be held in London in 1855 under the supervision of the Board of Control. From 1858 it was run under the supervision of the Civil Service Commissioners. Entry into the Indian Civil Service which was thus thrown open to all talented Britishers, continued, however, to be practically denied to Indians, in spite of the liberal declarations made in the Charter Act of 1832 (*q.v.*) and the Queen's Proclamation of 1858 (*q.v.*) and it was not till 1864 that an Indian (Satyendra Nath Tagore, elder brother of the Poet Rabindranath) succeeded in competing in the Indian Civil Service examination held in London and won a place in the Indian Civil Service. But admission of Indians to the Indian Civil Service continued to be extremely meagre and was made more difficult, if not impossible, in 1876 by the lowering of the maximum age of entry to 19 from 23. By this time Western education was spreading in India and the new products of Indian Universities naturally demanded more facilities for entering into the Indian Civil Service. Consequently, Indians began to demand that a simultaneous competitive examination should be held in India for admission into the

Indian Civil Service and the maximum age of entry should be raised to 23 years, as before. This demand was later on taken up by the Indian National Congress and reiterated practically in every one of its early sessions. But the demand was persistently ignored and in 1878 an attempt was made to evade the Indian demand by starting what was called the Statutory Civil Service to be filled up with Indian recruits. The members of this service were to hold only certain comparatively higher posts of less importance, mostly in the judicial line, and were to get only two-thirds of the salary that would be drawn by a member of the Indian Civil Service, if he had been appointèd to a similar post. The Statutory Civil Service did not, therefore, satisfy Indian demands and it was abolished in 1885. The age limit was raised to 23 years in 1889 but it was not till 1922 that simultaneous competitive examinations began to be held in India for entrance into the Indian Civil Service. Every effort was, however, still continued to be made by the Governments of Great Britain and India to keep the Indian Civil Service as a predominantly British preserve. Prime Minister Lloyd George in a speech delivered from his place in the House of Commons in August, 1922, referred to the British element in the Indian Civil Service as the "steel frame" of the Indian constitutional structure and prophesied that "you take the steel frame out, the structure will collapse". Twenty-five years later the structure collapsed even though the steel frame was still there to uphold it. The fact is that the British members of the Indian Civil Service did no doubt render great services in the development of India and even in the evolution of her political destiny, but they never became a part and parcel of India. They cost India too much in money and they generally treated the Indians as inferiors. Their last attempt to save themselves was extremely nefarious: they promoted the communal tension in India to such an extent that when at last in August, 1947 circumstances obliged them to leave the country they left it partitioned and bleeding. (Roy. N. C., *The Civil Service in India*)

Crewe, Lord—was the Secretary of State for India in 1911-12 when King George V visited India and held a Coronation Durbar in Delhi. At this Durbar the transfer of the capital from Calcutta to Delhi was announced. The other important changes announced were the modification of the partition of Bengal which was henceforth to be administered by a Governor-in-Council, the separation of Bihar and Orissa from Bengal and the creation of a new Lieutenant-Governorship for Bihar, Orissa and Chota

Nagpur and the reduction of Assam once more to a Chief-Commissionership. Thus Lord Crewe's name became associated with important changes in the administration of India.

Cripps, Sir Richard Stafford (1889-1952)—a British statesman and lawyer, was a distinguished member of the Labour Party, from which, however, he was expelled in 1939. But in 1940 Prime Minister Churchill appointed him ambassador to the U.S.S.R. where he concluded the Anglo-Soviet pact. In 1942 he was appointed Lord Privy Seal, leader of the House of Commons and a member of the war cabinet. He was known to be liberal in his views regarding the constitutional changes to be introduced in India and was sent twice, first in 1942 and again in 1946, to effect a peaceful settlement of the Indian political and constitutional problems. In 1942 Cripps made certain suggestions for constitutional development in India. These constituted the 'Cripps offer'. It reiterated the intention of the British Government to set up as soon as possible after the war an Indian Union with the status of a Dominion of the British Commonwealth. To achieve this end a constituent assembly elected by the provincial legislatures should negotiate a treaty with the British Government regarding the relation between them. India should have the option of secession from the Commonwealth, the Indian States the option of joining the Indian Union and any of the existing Indian provinces the right of contracting out of the proposed Indian Union and retaining its existing constitution. The offer had many merits and offered a real chance of establishing a united independent India. But the Cripps offer was rejected by the Indian National Congress as it did not promise the immediate grant of full Dominion Status to India. In 1946 Cripps, now a member of the Cabinet Mission (*q.v.*), was responsible for the Cabinet Mission Proposals which suggested the creation of a Federal Union of the British Indian provinces controlling defence, foreign affairs and communications. The States might join after negotiations. The individual provinces were to be at liberty to form subordinate unions of their own. Details were to be settled by a constituent assembly and pending the completion of the changes there was to be an interim National Government of all the parties at the centre. But the hostility between the Congress and the Muslim League proved insurmountable; the Cabinet Mission Proposals in the formulation of which Cripps had a large share, were rejected and the last effort to arrive at a solution of the Indian problem by peaceful methods failed. Cripps lived long enough to see

India win her independence through a blood-bath and a grievous partition.

Cromer, Evelyn Baring, Lord (1841-1917)—made his reputation as an expert in public finance as a member of an international financial board that was set up in 1877 in Egypt. In 1880 he came out to India as the Finance Member of the Viceroy's Executive Council, a post which he held for three years with success. He was raised to the peerage in 1892 and earned further laurels by his administration in Egypt.

Cultural and Colonial expansion of India in ancient times— constitutes a most interesting episode in the history of India. Contact between India and countries outside had existed in prehistoric times. In historical times, Indian culture was first started on a career of expansion outside India by the third Maurya Emperor Asoka (*c.* 273 B.C. - 232 B.C.) who sent Buddhist missionaries through Afghanistan to Persia, Syria, Egypt and Macedonia in the west and to Ceylon in the south. Asoka claimed in his inscriptions that as a result of his evangelical efforts many persons in all these countries adopted the Buddhist religion and that he established and maintained hospitals for men and beasts in all those countries. There are evidences which justify the declaration of Asoka. Classical sources record that in the early centuries of the Christian era Indian traders sailed from the various Indian ports in ships built and fitted by themselves, traded with western countries beyond the Arabian Sea, established a colony in Socotra and maintained a very rich trade with Rome and her Empire. About the same time, especially during the rule of the Kushanas, Buddhism from India became strongly established in Central Asia and many centres of Indian culture developed in that region, particularly at Taskhand, Khotan and Yarkand. Of these the Gomati Vihara and the city of Kucha or Kuchi were the most important. Sir Auriel Stein in the course of his explorations found ample evidence of the prevalance of Indian culture in Central Asia. Through Central Asia Indian Buddhism and Indian culture passed to China in the early centuries of the Christian era and for about one thousand years a close and intimate cultural contact was maintained between India and China. A large number of Indian Buddhist monks, well-versed in Sanskrit, the earliest of whom were Kashyapa Matanga and Dharma-raksha who went to China in A.D. 67, visited China, settled there, learnt Chinese and translated with the aid of Chinese scholars who learnt Sanskrit from the visiting Indian monks, hundreds of books not only on

Buddhism, but also on various other branches of Indian learning especially the humanities, art and medicine. The names of many such visiting Indian monks have been preserved in Chinese annals, the more prominent of whom were Kumara Jiva (A.D. 401-13), Bodhi-dharma (c. A.D. 520-9) Gunavarman (A.D. 424-60), and Amogha-vajra (A.D. 746-74). Similarly, a large number of Chinese monks visited India in search of sacred books on Buddhism and also in order to pay respect to the Buddhist holy places in India. They carried back with them hundreds of Sanskrit texts from India to China and got them translated into Chinese. The most famous of the visiting Chinese monks were Fa-Hien who came to India in the 5th century A.D. and Hiuen Tsang who came in the 7th century. As the result of this two-way traffic the Mahayana form of Buddhism came to be professed by so many persons in China that it practically came to be China's national religion. From China Buddhism and Indian culture passed to Korea and from Korea to Japan. Again, Buddhism came to be established in Nepal as well as in Tibet and Indian Buddhist monks of whom the names of Padmasambhava (*q.v.*) who visited Tibet in the middle of the 8th century and founded Lamaism there and of Atisha Deepankara Sreejnana (*q.v.*) (A.D. 1042-54) are still held in great veneration by the Tibetans. Along with her religion Tibet also received her script from India.

In Ceylon Asoka's missionary activities bore rich fruit. The island and the people were converted to Buddhism. Ceylon soon became a centre of Buddhist culture and it was in this island that the Buddhist *Tripitaka* was first put down in writing.

Beyond Ceylon Indian culture and Indian religions, Hinduism and Buddhism, travelled to Burma, the Malaya Peninsula, Sumatra, Java and the Malay Archipelago and northwards inland to Siam, Cambodia and Annam. In these countries Indians came not only as monks and traders but also as colonists who established Hindu kingdoms over which ruled princes who traced their descent from Kshatriya princes of India. Such were the kingdoms of Champa (*q.v.*) which comprised modern Annam and Indo-China, of Kambuja which has left its name to Cambodia and Sree-Vijaya with its capital at Prambanan in Sumatra. These Hindu kingdoms flourished from about the third century to the twelfth century of the Christian era. Their kings professed either Hinduism or Buddhism, inscribed their achievements in poetic Sanskrit, installed and venerated images of Shiva, Brahma and Buddha as well as of many other Brahmanical and Buddhist deities, built magnicent temples of which the *Barabudur* and *Pranatran* group of temples in Java and the *Angkor-Vat* in Cambodia have come down to modern times with practically all their glory to bear elequent testimony to the civilising achievements of the Hindu colonists in South-East Asia. The kingdom of Champa fell before the attacks of the Annamites (A.D. 1471), that of Kambuja declined at about the same time with the rise of Siam and the Hindu kingdom in the Malay Archipelago disappeared a century earlier as the result of the conversion of its last king to Islam. The fact is that with the conquest of India by the Muhammadans in the thirteenth century arrivals of fresh blood and enterprise from India to South-East Asia ceased; and as the contact between the two regions ended, South-East Asian countries were condemned to centuries of exploitation and oppression by the Portuguese, the French and the Dutch. (Majumdar, R. C., *Champa & Suvarnadvipa;* Chatterji, B. R., *Indian Influence on Combodge;* Hall, D. G. E., *Hist. of S. E. Asia*; Stein, Sir A., *Ancient Khotan, Innermost Asia, Ruins of Desert Cathay*)

Cunha, Nuno da—the Portuguese Governor at Diu in 1537, received on board his ship a visit from the contemporary Sultan of Gujarat, Bahadur Shah (1526-37) and arranged a treacherous attack on the Sultan when he was alighting from the ship. The Sultan jumped overboard in order to save himself, but was knocked on the head by a Portuguese sailor and killed.

Cunningham, Sir Alexander (1814-93)—came out to India as a cadet in 1833 and in 1836 became an A.D.C. to Lord Auckland, Governor-General. In 1836 he moved on to the Engineering branch of the service and was in the First Sikh War *(q.v.)* in 1846 as a field engineer. He also took part in the Second Sikh War, *(q.v.)* 1848-49, and was present at the battle of Chilianwalla. He was the Chief Engineer in Burma from 1856 to 1858 and then in the N. W. Province till his retirement in 1861. Immediately after his retirement he was made the first Archaeological Surveyor to the Government of India. In 1870 be became the Director of the department and held the post till his retirement from India in 1885. After his retirement he paid much attention to numismatics on which he had come to be considered an eminent authority before his death in 1893., His more important publications are the *Bhilsa Topes, The Ancient Geography of India, Corpus Inscriptionum Indicarum*, Vol. I, *The Stupa of Bharhut* and *The Book of Indian Eras*. His contributions on Indian archaeology largely promoted our knowledge of ancient Indian history, and

Sir Alexander Cunningham's works still continue to be of great value to students of ancient Indian History.

Cunningham, Joseph Davey, General (1812-51)—a brother of Sir Alexander Cunningham (*q.v.*), came out to India in 1834 as an officer in the Bengal Engineers. He was stationed at various places and in different capacities in the Panjab and was present at the interviews with Ranjit Singh and with Amir Dost Muhammad. He took part in the First Sikh War (*q.v.*) (1846) and saw action at Aliwal and Sobraon (*q.v.*). He thus had ample opportunities for knowing the Panjab and its people. He was liberal minded and a historian of no mean order. His *History of the Sikhs* is one of the most authoritative works on the subject, but its publication set a hornet's nest about him. His general sympathetic approach to the subject and his frank truthfulness (e.g. the statement that in the First Sikh War two of the Sikh generals were bought by the British) gave great offence to his superiors and brought about his relegation from special political appointment to ordinary duty. He died at Umbala in 1851.

Currie, Sir Frederick (1799-1875)—entered the Company's Covenanted Civil Service in 1820, rose to be the Foreign Secretary in 1842, was on the staff of the Governor-General and C-in-C during the First Sikh War (*q.v.*) (1845-46) and drew up the treaty of Lahore which closed the war. He was then appointed as the British Resident in Lahore on 6th April, 1848. When Mulraj, the dismissed Sikh Governor of Multan, raised trouble there and two young English officers were murdered on 20th April; Sir Frederick made some unsuccessful attempts to suppress the risings at Multan and to besiege the city. He sent Sher Singh, the Sikh Governor of Hazara district, to strengthen the besieging army, but Sher Singh went over to Mulraj and Sir Frederick's efforts completely failed. The Second Sikh War (*q.v.*) (1848-49) which soon followed ended in the complete collapse of the Sikh power and the annexation of the Panjab to the British Indian Empire. He retired from India in 1853, was elected a Director of the East India Company in 1854 and became its Chairman in 1857. Next year he saw the abolition of the Company and became one of the first members of the Council of India in 1858. He died in 1875.

Curtis, Lionel—was a reputed journalist. He was the founder and for many years the editor of the *Round Table*. He was a great supporter of the idea of the maintenance of the unity of the British Empire. It was at his suggestion that the principle of 'dyarchy' was first introduced in the Government of India Act,

1919, for the purpose of introducing partial responsibility in the administration of the provinces into which British India was then divided. The Government of India Act, 1935, provided for the introduction of the same principle in the Central Government of India, but it was ineffective.

Curzon, George Nathaniel, Marquis of Kedleston (1859-1925)— educated at Eton and Oxford, had already travelled much from Central Asia to Korea and published several books on his travels, before he was appointed Governor-General of India in 1899 which post he held till 1904 when he was reappointed for a second term but resigned in 1905 owing to want of support by the British Government on his difference of opinion with the Commander-in-Chief, Lord Kitchener, regarding the position of the Military Member of the Viceroy's Executive Council in India. Lord Curzon's administration was marked by many reforms. He inaugurated a new province called the North-West Frontier Province for keeping better control over the turbulent tribes that inhabited the area. Still he had to sanction the Waziri compaign in 1901. It ended in a British triumph. In 1903 he visited the Persian Gulf with a view to the prevention of any Russian encroachment on British interests as well as the promotion of British trade and British influence there. In order to check Russian influence in Tibet he sent a British mission to Tibet in 1903 but this led to a war with Tibet. An Anglo-Indian army marched into Lhasa and forced Tibet to make peace by the treaty of Lhasa (*q.v.*) in 1904. He probed into every branch of the administration and tried to introduce improvements as he thought necessary without caring much for public opinion. He reformed the four Chiefs' Colleges in India; he founded the Imperial Cadet Corps; he settled the question of Berar with the Nizam; he set on foot the construction of the Victoria Memorial Hall, Calcutta, for which he realised large donations from wealthy Indians; he held the Delhi Coronation Durbar in December, 1902; he administered Indian finances with ability, reducing the Salt Tax twice and removing the Income-tax on the lowest incomes; he passed some important legislative measures such as the Official Secrets Act, the Indian Mines Act, the Ancient Monuments Preservation Act and the Co-operative Credit Societies Act. But some of his measures like the Universities Act and the Partition of Bengal as well as contemptuous references in his public speeches to Indian character and to the Indian National Congress roused against him a great deal of popular 'resentment in India. He believed in a policy of suppressing all agitation in India for a more liberal system of government, but the main result of his policy was to rouse Indian nationalism more than ever before and to increase the popularity of the Indian National Congress.

After his retirement from India in 1905 Lord Curzon lived for another twenty years, holding very high posts in successive British cabinets, but the highest honour of being the Prime Minister of England which it was his life's ambition to secure, always eluded his grasp and he died a disappointed man in 1925. (Ronaldshay, Lord, *Life of Lord Curzon*)

Cyrus—was the king of Persia (558 B.C. - 530 B.C.). He is said to have led an expedition against India, through Gedrosia or Baluchistan, but his attempt failed. He is, however, said to have destroyed the ancient city of Kapisa which was situated in modern Afghanistan and received tribute from some Indian tribal peoples who at that time inhabited the valley of the Kabul river.

D

.d' Ache, Comte—was the French naval officer in charge of the French fleet that brought Count de Lally and a French army to India in 1758 when the last phase of the Anglo-French duel was being fought in the Carnatic. At first d'Ache had a great success and forced the British fleet under Pocock to leave the Madras coast. This enabled Lally to capture Fort St. David, but Pocock and his fleet soon returned and d'Ache was eventually defeated off Karikal (1758). This defeat of d'Ache very adversely affected French interests in the Fourth Carnatic War and d'Ache first retired to the Isle of France and then to France.

Dabo, battle of—was fought and won by the Indo-British army under Sir Charles Napier in March, 1843, against Muhammad, the most important Amir of Mirpur, Sind. This battle practically completed the conquest of Sind which was annexed to the British Indian Empire.

Dacca—is a city in lower Bengal and is situated on the river Buriganga which connects the Brahmaputra and the Ganges (called Padma). Dacca became the headquarters of the Mughul *suba* of Bengal in 1608 and was named Jahangirnagar in honour of the reigning Mughul Emperor. It was from Dacca that Mir

Jumla organised the first Mughul invasion of Assam which penetrated up to the Ahom capital in Upper Assam, but it was in Dacca that Mir Jumla died after his return from the Assam campaign. His successor Shaista Khan ruled Bengal from Dacca for thirty long years from 1663. The English East India Company established in Dacca a branch factory in order to deal in fine cotton fabrics especially muslin, for manufacturing which the Dacca weavers had won a great reputation. Murshid Kuli Khan, who became the Governor of Bengal in 1705, transferred the headquarters of the province from Dacca to Murshidabad and Dacca fell into a period of decline. But in 1905 it again became the headquarters of a province, namely Eastern Bengal and Assam; but the distinction was short-lived, for in 1912 the districts of Eastern Bengal were merged in the province of Bengal and Assam was separated to form a Chief Commissioner-ship. In 1920 Dacca became the seat of a University and in 1947, after partition and independence of India, Dacca again became the headquarters of a province, namely East Pakistan.

Dadabhai Naoroji (1825-1917)—a prominent business man of Bombay with trading connections with England, belonged to the Parsi community and was very rich. He was liberal in his outlook, took great interest in the public affairs of India and was elected President of the Indian National Congress at its second session held in Calcutta in 1886. He was the first Indian to be elected a member of the House of Commons in England on a ticket of the Liberal party. Twice again, in 1893 and in 1906, he was elected President of the Indian National Congress which he saw pass from the humble position of a subject peoples' organisation seeking redress of administrative grievances to that of a really National Assembly working for the object of attaining *swaraj* or self-government, a demand which was first made by the Indian National Congress at its 1906 session held in Calcutta under his presidentship. He died in 1917, full of years, and nine years later the Congress declared complete independence as its aim. (Masani, R. P., *Dadabhai Naoroji—the Grand Old Man of India*)

Dadaji Khonddev or Konadeo—a Maratha Brahmin, was the instructor and guardian of the great Maratha leader Shivaji (A.D. 1627-80) in his boyhood. He instilled into the mind of his young pupil a spirit of boldness and a love of adventure as well as an admiration for the achievements of the great Hindu heroes of ancient India and a veneration for the cow and the Brahmin which eventually led Shivaji to try to establish an independent Hindu Maratha kingdom in India. Dadaji Khond-dev also laid the basis of the future revenue system of Shivaji by managing Shivaji's small estate on sound principles. (Sarkar, J. N., *Shivaji*)

Daflas, the—a tribal people, inhabit the north-eastern frontier of Assam dominated by the Dafla hill range to the north of the modern Darang district.

Dadu—founded the sect known as the Dadupanthis. He was the son of a cotton-carder of Ahmedabad. He lived most of his life in Rajputana, was a contemporary of the Mughul Emperor Shah Jahan (1627-58) and composed many poems aiming at reconciling Hinduism and Islam. His followers wear no sectarian emblems and worship no images. They only recite the name of Rama and are generally peaceful, though one section of them joins the army.

Dahir—son of Chach, was the king of Sind when that kingdom was invaded by the Arabs in the first decade of the 8th century of the Christian era. Dahir repulsed the earlier Arab incursions, but in A.D. 712 he was defeated and killed at the battle of Raor by the Arabs led by Muhammad ibn-Kasim. His widowed queen perished in the defence of the fort of Raor which fell before the Arabs who then occupied Alor, the capital of Sind, which thus passed under the rule of the Muslim Arabs.

Dalai Lama—was till very recently the supreme spiritual and temporal power in Tibet and was the head of its theocratic government. The present Dalai Lama who is now a refugee in India as the result of Chinese aggression in Tibet, is the four-teenth in succession. The Dalai Lama is regarded by the Tibetan Buddhists as an incarnation of Bodhisattva Avolokitesvara. He is discovered by the united efforts of gods and men, according to a traditional system. At the time of his discovery he is generally a minor and his authority is then exercised through a Regent and a Council of Monks. When he attains majority he works through a Council of Monks chosen by him. (Morgan, *The Path of the Buddha*)

Dala'il-i Firuz Shahi—a very interesting book in Persian verses, was composed by the order of Sultan Firuz Shah Tughluq (A.D. 1351-88) by his court poet A'aaz-ud-din Khalid Khani and contains the translation of 300 volumes of Sanskrit books on various subjects which were found by the Sultan in the temple of Jwalamukhi near Nagarkot which was compelled to surrender to the Sultan after a siege of six months in A.D. 1337.

Dalhousie, Lord—was the Governor-General of India from 1848 to

1856. His administration was marked by large territorial annexations and expansion of the British Indian Empire as well as by the introduction of numerous reforms for the improvement of the country. He fought the Second Sikh War (1848-49) and annexed the Panjab; in 1850 he annexed a portion of Sikkim as a penalty for rough treatment of two Englishmen; and in 1853 he fought the Second Burmese War and annexed Lower Burma up to Prome. The British Indian Empire was thus extended from Peshawar to Burma including the whole of the coast of the Bay of Bengal. He held that British administration was more beneficial to the Indians than rule by their own princes. So he evolved the 'doctrine of lapse' (*q.v.*) according to which the right of an adopted son to inherit the dominion of his adoptive father, if he had been a ruler of a state created by the British in India, was to be ignored and the state was to be brought under the direct rule of the British Indian Government. By the application of this doctrine he annexed the states of Satara in 1848, Jaitpur and Sambalpur in 1849, Baghat in 1850, Udaipur in 1852, Jhansi in 1853, Nagpur in 1854 and Karauli in 1855. Baghat, Udaipur and Karauli were later on restored to the adopted heirs by order of the higher authorities. On the ground of want of any necessity Dalhousie abolished the titular sovereignties of the Carnatic and Tanjore and refused, on the death of the ex-Peshwa, Baji Rao II, in 1853, to continue to his adopted son Dundu Pant, better known as Nana Shaheb, the ex-Peshwa's huge pension of £80,000 a year. Lastly on the order of the Court of Directors, Lord Dalhousie annexed Oudh in 1856. Thus he had materially altered the political map of India within the eight short years of his administration.

In internal administration also Lord Dalhousie introduced a number of reforms. He placed the administration of Bengal in the hands of a Lieutenant-Governor (1854). He constituted the Public Works Department and vested it with the task of constructing and maintaining public works, like the Grand Trunk Road, on which more money began to be spent. Irrigation was given much greater attention than before and the Ganges Canal came to be constructed. A well-considered plan for laying down railways was drawn up and the first Indian Railway line from Bombay to Thana was opened in 1853 and that between Calcutta and Raniganj in 1854. The electric-telegraph system was introduced and an efficient postal system based on a uniform half-anna (three *naya paise*) postal rate all through India was introduced. Last, but not the least, he gave effect to the education despatch of 1854 for improving public education in India and took preliminary measures for the establishment of the Universities of Calcutta, Bombay and Madras.

Lord Dalhousie was a person with an autocratic bent of mind and did what he considered right and beneficial. He cared not for the feelings of others, especially of the Indian people and did certainly engender in the minds of the Indians, princes as well as commoners, a dread of things to be imposed by the British on them and thus created a feeling of uneasiness which no doubt contributed to the great upheaval of 1857 (Lee Warner, Sir, *Life of Dalhousie*)

Dalip Singh or (Dulip Singh)—was the youngest son of Ranjit Singh of the Panjab. He succeeded to his father's throne as a minor in 1843 with his mother, Rani Jindan as the Regent. His Government became involved in the First Sikh War (1845-46) in which the Sikh Government was defeated and compelled to purchase peace by surrendering all territories to the left of the Sutlej as well as the Jullundar Doab and by paying an indemnity of one and a half crores of rupees. The Regency was taken away from Rani Jindan and vested in a Council composed of several Sikh *sardars*. But the new Council of Regency involved the Government of Dalip Singh in a second war with the British Indian Government in 1848. The Sikhs were again defeated and the victorious British deposed Dalip Singh and annexed the Panjab. Dalip Singh was given a pension of five lakhs of rupees a year and was soon afterwards sent with his mother to England where he became a Christian and lived for some time as an English landowner in Norfolk, England. During his stay in England he made a visit to Russia and in 1887 made an abortive attempt at persuading the Tsarist Government to invade India Later on he returned to India and went back to his old faith to which he adhered till his death. (*Bengal Past and Present,* Vol. lxxiv, pp. 186ff.)

Damaji Gaekwad—son of Pilaji Gaekwad, was at first an adherent of the *Senapati* Trimbak Rao Dhabade of the Maratha kingdom On the defeat and death of Trimbak Rao in the battle of Bilhapur in 1731 where Damaji had shown great bravery and skill, the victorious Peshwa Baji Rao I took Damaji into his service and later on established him as the Peshwa's agent in Gujarat. Thus Damaji rose to power and prominence and established the Maratha feudatory house of the Gaekwads with his headquarters at Baroda. He continued to serve under the next Peshwa Balaji Baji Rao, was present at the third battle of Panipat in 1761, but was able to escape with his life. He succeeded in holding Gujarat after the disaster and died in 1768. (*Bombay Gazetteer*, Vol. vii.)

Damodara Gupta—was a reputed scholar who enjoyed the patronage of king Jayapida of Kashmir who ruled in the ninth century A.D.

Dane, Sir Louis—was sent in 1904 as the leader of a British Indian Mission to Afghanistan. This Mission remained in Kabul from December 1904 to March 1905 and succeeded in establishing better relations with the reigning Amir Habibullah Khan whose claim to the title of 'His Majesty' was recognised.

Dhanadhaksha—also known as the *Pandit Rao,* was one of Eight Chiefs in the administration of Shivaji. He was the Royal Chaplain and Almoner.

Danasagara—is a book written by king Vallala Sena (A.D. 1158-79) of Bengal. It contains seventy sections discussing the merits, nature, and the time of gifts and rites and procedures connected with the making of gifts.

Dandanayaka—was the title of the Commander-in-Chief of the army of the Hindu kings of Vijayanagara.

Dandin—flourished in the sixth century A.D. He was at once a poet, literary critic and prose writer of romances—all in Sanskrit. His *Kavyadarsa* is a poetical work on Sanskrit poetics and his *Dasakumaracharita* is one of the earliest and best known romances in Sanskrit literature.

Danish East India Company—was established in 1616 and founded its first factory at Tranquebar on the east coast of India in 1620. In 1755 it established a settlement at Serampore in Bengal. The Danish East India Company never prospered much and it sold its factories to the British Government in 1845.

Danishmand Khan—a courtier in the court of Delhi during the closing years of the reign of Shah Jahan and the early years of that of Aurangzeb, was the patron of Bernier who considered him the most learned man in Asia. (Bernier, *Travels*)

Daniyal, Prince—was the third and youngest son of the Mughul Emperor Akbar. He was born in 1572 and was in command of the Mughul army which received the surrender of Ahmadnagar. He was much beloved of Akbar, but he was too much addicted to wine and died of its effects in 1604.

Dantidurga—was the founder of the Rashtrakuta dynasty of kings in about the middle of the eighth century A.D. He defeated and overthrew Kirtivarman II, the last Chalukya king of Vatapi and

established the new line of kings who ruled in the Deccan from
A.D. 733 to 972.

Danujamardana Deva—was a king of Bengal whose coins bearing
Sanskrit legends in Bengali characters and issued from his mints
at such distantly separated places as Pandua (West Bengal),
Suvarnagrama (in Dacca district?) and Chittagong with Saka
dates, 1339 and 1340, have been found in many places in Bengal.
It is held that he was identical with Raja Ganesh who ruled in
Bengal early in the fifteenth century (*Dacca Hist. of Bengal*, Vol.
II, pp. 120-22)

Dara Shukoh, Prince—was the eldest son of Emperor Shah Jahan
(*q.v.*) born of his queen Mumtaz (*q.v.*). He was the governor of
the Panjab which he administered from the capital through
Deputies. He was the favourite of his father and generally lived
in the Court. He was personally brave and intellectually he had
inherited some of the characteristics of his great-grandfather,
Akbar. He was inclined to Sufism and belonged to the Hanafi
school of Islam. He was tolerant of all religious faiths and was
interested in Hindu philosophy as well as in Christianity. This
opened him to the charge of unorthodoxy in the estimate of
Muhammadan fanatics—a circumstance which was fully exploited against him by his third brother, Aurangzeb. He had
taken part in the third siege of Qandahar in 1653 and though he
had failed in the enterprise he continued to enjoy his father's
favour and was near him at Agra when Emperor Shah Jahan
fell ill in 1657. Dara was then 43 years of age and expected to
succeed to the throne of his father. But his claim to the throne
was resented by his three younger brothers, especially by Aurangzeb, and Dara had to fight with them a war of succession
(1657-58). Though backed by Shah Jahan from his sick-bed, his
army was first defeated at the battle of Dharmat on 15 April,
1658, by the combined armies of Aurangzeb and Murad. Dara
then personally led another imperial army against his rebellious brothers, but was again defeated at the battle of
Samugarh on 29 May, 1658. No retreat to Agra was possible
and Dara became a fugitive who after many hazardous journeys
through the Panjab, Kutch, Gujarat and Rajputana succeeded
in collecting a third army and met Aurangzeb's army for the
third and last time at the battle of Deorai where again he was
defeated after a three days' battle in April, 1659. Dara again
became a fugitive who fled for his life through Rajputana and
Kutch, reached Sind where he lost his beloved wife, Nadira
Begam and accepted the hospitality of Jiwan Khan, the Afghan

chief of Dadar. The latter proved a traitor and betrayed Dara to the troops of Aurangzeb who had been pursuing him all this time. Captive Dara was brought to Delhi where he was paraded through the streets by Aurangzeb's orders, clad like a beggar on the back of a small dirty female elephant. He was then subjected to a trial by Muslim Moulanas who sentenced him to death on a charge of apostasy. The order was carried out on 30th August, 1659, when Dara was beheaded. His elder son, Sulaiman, had already been a prisoner in the hands of Aurangzeb who had him murdered in his prison in 1662. Dara's second son, Sipihr Sukoh, was spared and was later on married to the third daughter of Aurangzeb. (Qanango, K. R., *Dara Shukhu*)

Darius—(*c*. 522 B.C.-486 B.C.) was the third emperor of the Achaemenian dynasty of Persia. In his Behistun or Bahistan inscription (*c*. 519 B.C.) the people of Gandhara are mentioned amongst his subject-peoples and his inscriptions found at Hamadan, Persepolis and Naqsh-i-Rustum also refer to the Indians as his subjects. According to Herodotus, Gandhara was included in the seventh satrapy and India, that is to say, the valley of the Indus (Sindhu) formed the twentieth satrapy of his empire. He derived a large revenue from his Indian dominions which were also required to supply recruits to his army. Contact was thus established between India and Persia with the result that communication between the two countries grew closer and many Persian words and ideas entered into the political phraseology of India and influenced her art to some extent. (*P.H.A.I.*, pp. 240ff.)

Daroga—is a Persian word meaning 'head'. In British times it became an official designation for the officer in charge of a *Thana* or police station. Its English version is Sub-Inspector of Police. The office was first created during the administration of Lord Cornwallis (1786-93) who divided each district into a number of *Thanas* or police stations over each of which was placed a *daroga*.

Darsaka—(*c*. 467 B.C. - 443 B.C.) was the son and successor of Ajatasatru, king of Magadha (*c*. 494 B.C. - 467 B.C.). He was probably the king Darsaka who is mentioned in the drama named *Swapna-Vasavadatta* by the poet Bhasa.

Dasabodha—is a book written by Ramdas, the famous *guru of* Shivaji, the founder of the Maratha kingdom in the seventeenth century.

Das, Chittaranjan—(1870-1925) an eminent lawyer practising in the High Court of Calcutta, first distinguished himself by successfully defending Aravinda Ghose (*q.v.*) in the famous Alipore Bomb Case. He then built up a very lucrative practice which he threw up in 1920 in order to join the non-co-operation movement started by Gandhi (*q.v.*) and devoted himself entirely to politics. He gave up his earlier luxurious life and toured over the countryside spreading the gospel of the Indian National Congress. He gave all his wealth and his palatial house in Calcutta to the national cause. He became the elected Mayor of Calcutta with Subhas Chandra Bose (*q.v.*) as the Chief Executive Officer of the Calcutta Corporation and thus freed that powerful institution from European control and devoted its resources, more than ever before, to the improvement of the portion of the city inhabited by Indians. He tried to solve the problem of Hindu-Muslim differences by concluding a pact with the Muhammadans which would give them a larger number of posts in the services than what was warranted by their number. He became the President of the Indian National Congress in 1922; but he was soon convinced of the futility of the policy of keeping out of the legislatures as expanded by the Government of India Act, 1919 and joined with Pandit Motilal Nehru (*q.v.*) in upper India and N. C. Kelkar in the Deccan to organise within the Indian National Congress a new party known as the *Swaraj* party which advocated entry into the legislatures and favoured the tactics of the Irish patriot Parnell with a view to "mending or ending" the constitution as established by the Act of 1919. It was to be a policy of responsive co-operation. The *Swaraj* party soon captured a large number of seats in the legislatures and in Bengal and Maharastra it was strong enough to prevent the formation of ministries under the dyarchical system. Under his leadership the *Swaraj* party created such fervour in the country that an understanding between Lord Birkenhead, the Secretary of State for India, and himself on the next stage of constitutional progress seemed imminent in 1925 when Chittaranjan, broken by his immense exertions and the rigours of the prison-life which his nationalist propaganda had brought upon him passed away on June 16, 1925. His death ended the talks of *rapprochement* between India and Britain and an opportunity for an early and peaceful solution of the problem posed by Indian nationalism was lost. The whole country mourned his death and came reverentially to call him *Desha bandhu* (friend of the country). Tagore mourned his loss in a couplet of intense grief and deep reverence:

> *Enechhile santhe kare mrityu-heen prán*
> *Marane táhái tumi kare gele dán.*

Das, Saratchandra—(1849-1917) was born of a poor family in Bengal and began life as a school-master. He had an innate love for adventure and knowledge and this led him as early as 1879 to visit Tibet, which was then a forbidden land to all non-Tibetans, long before Sir Francis Younghusband visited that country. Saratchandra thus was entitled to the credit of 'unveiling Lhasa' and Tibet. He visited Tibet a second time in 1881, Sikkim in 1884 and Pekin in 1885. He learnt Tibetan and translated for the first time into English the Tibetan chronicle, Sumpa Khan's *Pag Sam Jon Zang*. His work *Indian Pandits in the Land of Snow* first informed the English-speaking world of the services, evangelical and cultural, that had been rendered to Tibet by Indian Buddhist monks who visited Tibet and his *Tibetan-English Dictionary* (1902) is still a standard work.

Dasaratha—the king of Ayodhya or Oudh, was the father of Ramachandra, the hero of the great Indian Sanskrit epic *Ramayana* by Valmiki who is held to have been the first poet (*adi Kavi*) in India.

Dasaratha—was a grandson of Asoka Maurya whom he succeeded in *c.* 232 B.C. He bestowed on the Ajivikas some cave-dwellings at the Nagarjuni Hills in Bihar. The inscriptions on the walls of the caves show that he also, like his grandfather, bore the title of *devanampiya*. It is not known whether he also professed Buddhism. (*P.H.A.I.*, pp. 350-51).

Dasas, the—was a generic name applied in the Vedic literature to the people with whom the early Aryans had to fight in the Panjab. They are also called *Dasyus*. They are described as a dark-skinned, flat-nosed race who spoke a language which was not known to the Aryans. They possessed forts and herds of cattle which the Aryans coveted and they despised the sacrificial religion professed by the Aryans. The Dasas were probably connected with the people who developed the prehistoric civilisation in the lower Indus valley. In later times the term *Dasa* came to mean a servant, and even a slave and *Dasyu* to mean a robber. (Macdonell & Keith, *Vedic Index*)

Dastaks, the—were passports issued by the East India Company in Bengal authorising their agents to trade within the province without paying the usual customs duty of 2½ per cent as authorised by the *farman* granted in 1717 to the Company by Emperor Farruksiyar. Legally speaking this right of free-trade covered by the *dastaks* was to be enjoyed by the Company alone. But the concession was abused in two ways. First, the servants of the Company used the *dastaks* for carrying on their private trade.

Secondly, the Company sold the *dastaks* to their favoured Indian merchants to enable them to evade the customs duty. This abuse which was objected to in vain by Nawab Siraj-ud-daula (*q.v.*) became very rampant after the battle of Plassey (*q.v.*) (1757) when Nawab Mir Jafar (*q.v.*) was the nominal ruler. As a result, the Indian merchants suffered much and the Nawab also lost a large portion of his legitimate income. On the deposition of Mir Jafar and the installation of Mir Kasim (*q.v.*) as the Nawab of Bengal (1760-63) the evil increased to such an extent that in 1762 Nawab Mir Kasim vigorously protested to the Company against the misuse of the *dastaks* and demanded that it should be stopped. But as Mir Kasim's protests were unheeded he abolished the inland duties altogether so that all traders should be on an equal footing. This measure threatened the Company's servants with the loss of the large illegal incomes that they were making by private trade based on the abuse by them of the *dastaks* and they, especially Ellis, the Company's agent at Patna, tried to assert this illegal claim by arms. This eventually led to a war between the Company and Mir Kasim who was defeated and driven out of the country (1763). Clive (*q.v.*), who became the Governor of Bengal for the second time (1765-67), restricted to some extent the abuse of *dastaks* and private trade by the Company's servants, but it was not until the Governor-Generalship of Lord Cornwallis (1786-93) that the abuse was completely checked.

Dastan-i-Amir Hamzal, the—is an album or illustrated book which contains paintings that were drawn up by two famous Persian artists, Mir Sayyid Ali and Khwaja Abdus Samad whom Humayun took under his patronage, when he was a fugitive in Persia, brought to his court in Kabul and finally to Delhi. The models contained in this album laid the foundation of the Mughul school of painting.

Dasyus, the—*see* Dasas.

Dattaji Sindhia—a Maratha general, was placed in charge of the Panjab by the Peshwa Balaji Rao in 1759 when the province was recovered from the possession of Timur, son of Ahmad Shah Abdali (*q.v.*). Ahmad Shah Abdali got furious at the news of the expulsion of his son from the Panjab and before the year was out Abdali invaded India with a large army. Dattaji, who tried to check Abdali's advance, was first defeated by Abdali at Thaneswar in December 1759. He tried to fall back on Delhi but was defeated and killed on 9th January, 1760 by Abdali at the battle of Bararighat, about ten miles north of Delhi.

Daud Bahmani—was the fourth sultan of the Bahmani dynasty. He was the cousin of the third sultan, Mujahid Shah, whose murder he instigated and whose throne he usurped in 1378, but he could not reign long as he himself was murdered in the year of his accession at the instigation of the foster-sister of his murdered cousin, Mujahid Shah.

Daud Khan—was the son and successor of king Sulaiman Kàrarani of Bengal who died in 1572. Unlike his father, Daud claimed to be the independent ruler of Bengal. He even attacked the Mughul district of modern Ghazipur in U.P. The contemporary Mughul Emperor Akbar (*q.v.*) considered the existence of an independent Afghan kingdom in Bengal as a great threat to his security. So Akbar personally led a campaign against Daud in 1574 but he could do no better than drive him from Bihar. Daud retreated towards Orissa, and though defeated by the Mughul general Munim Khan at the battle of Tukaroi in March, 1575 he continued fighting against the Mughuls until his final defeat and death in a battle near Rajmahal in July, 1576. After the death of Daud Bengal became an integral part of the empire of Akbar.

Daud Khan—was the fourth king of the dynasty of independent Muslim kings of Gujarat founded by Zafar Khan in 1401. Daud ascended the throne in 1451 but he soon alienated the nobles of the kingdom by his evil ways and was deposed within a few days of his accession.

Daud Khan—was the sixth king of the Faruqi dynasty of Khandesh. He ruled for seven years (1501-1508). His was an uneventful reign.

Daulat Khan—was the Mughul governor of Qandahar when that fort was attacked by Shah Abbas, king of Persia, in December 1648. Daulat Khan proved unequal to the task and it was owing to his incapability that Qandahar fell before the Persian king in February, 1649.

Daulat Khan Lodi—was a premier Afghan nobleman in Delhi at the beginning of the fifteenth century when the power of the Tughluq dynasty came to an end with the death of Sultan Mahmud Tughluq (*q.v.*) in 1413. Daulat Khan Lodi was then placed on the throne of Delhi by the nobles of Delhi, but his sovereignty lasted only a few months, for in March, 1414 he was deposed by Khizr Khan (*q.v.*) who founded the Sayyid dynasty (*q.v.*) of the sultans of Delhi.

Daulat Khan Lodi—was the semi-independent governor of the Panjab early in the sixteenth century when the throne of Delhi was occupied by Ibrahim Lodi (1517-26). Daulat Khan Lodi

was an ambitious person who came to harbour a deep grievance
against Sultan Ibrahim Lodi who had treated Daulat Khan's
son, Dilwar Khan, with great harshness. So Daulat Khan contemplated the deposition of Sultan Ibrahim Lodi and in 1524 he
joined with the Sultan's uncle, Alam Khan, to send an invitation
to Babur, the Mughul prince, who had already made himself the
ruler of Afghanistan, expecting that Babur, like his ancestor,
Timur, would come, ravage Delhi, destroy the strength of the
Lodi Sultan and then would go back to his native land. Babur,
however, had other ideas. He accepted the invitation, entered
the Panjab and occupied Lahore in 1524. But as he showed no
sign of any intention of leaving India Daulat Khan Lodi and his
confederate, Alam Khan, withdrew their support and Babur was
obliged to retire to Kabul. But Babur renewed his invasion in
1525 and this time Daulat Khan Lodi was compelled to submit
to the future founder of the Mughul Empire in India.

Daulat Rao Sindhia—a grandson of Tukoji, brother of the great
Mahadaji Sindhia (*q.v.*) succeeded to the headship of the house
of Sindhia on the death of his uncle Mahadaji in 1794. Daulat
Rao was a young man at the time of his accession to power
which he held till his death in 1827. He inherited vast territories
spreading over large parts of northern and southern India and
a very large army, a part of which had been trained by a French
officer named de Boigne (*q.v.*) and was at the time under the
command of another French officer named Perron. Daulat
Rao's main ambition was to establish his authority over the
Peshwa in Poona. But he had a strong rival in Jaswant Rao
Holkar (*q.v.*) and he also found an insurmountable obstacle in
Nana Faḍnavis who was the chief minister of the Peshwa. But
Nana died in 1800. At once Daulat Rao began a deliberate effort
to obtain the upper hand at Poona, and, as he was opposed in his
endeavours by Jaswant Rao Holkar, the two weht to war. A
battle was fought outside the walls of Poona in October, 1802.
The terrified Peshwa Baji Rao II fled for safety to the English at
Bassein and there he signed a treaty with them by which the
English agreed to reinstate the Peshwa at Poona and he
entered into a subsidiary alliance with them. The English reinstated the Peshwa in May, 1803. But Daulat Rao Sindhia, along
with Bhonsla (*q.v.*) and Holkar, bitterly resented the treaty of
Bassein (*q.v.*) as it practically meant the surrender of the independence of the Marathas. This resentment led to the Second
Maratha War in 1803. In this war Daulat Rao's armies, in spite
of their European discipline, were badly defeated at the battles

of Assaye, Argaon and Laswari. Perron left his service. Daulat Rao was obliged to purchase peace by the treaty of Surji-Arjangaon by which he surrendered all his possessions in the Deccan as well as his claims over the Doab between the Ganges and the Jumna and claims to the cities of Delhi and Agra. Thus Daulat Rao lost much of what he had inherited, yet the territories that still remained under his control were vast. Daulat Rao resented his defeat as well as the restrictions put upon him by the treaty. So he was again up in arms against the English in 1805, and though he gained no military successes the English revised in November, 1805 some of the terms of the treaty of Surji-Arjangaon, freeing him from a defensive alliance and recognising the Chambal as the boundary between his and English dominions in northern India. Daulat Rao Sindhia still regretted the losses and extended his patronage to the Pindaris who plundered and terrorised parts of British territories lying on the frontiers. Consequently in 1817 Lord Hastings, on the eve of embarking on a campaign for destroying the Pindaris, forced upon him a new treaty by which Daulat Rao Sindhia promised not to give any help to the Pindaris and to recognise the right of the British to make treaties with the Rajput chieftains who now gladly accepted British protection. Daulat Rao Sindhia thus became incapable of doing any further harm to the British. He died in 1827, still ruling over a very large state with his headquarters in Gwalior.

Daulatabad—is the name given by Sultan Muhammad Tughluq to the city of Devagiri which was the capital of the kingdom of the Yadava dynasty (*q.v.*) in the Deccan. The city is situated in the upper valley of the Godavari and topographically occupies a central position in India. It has seen many ups and downs in Indian history. It continued to be the capital of the Yadava kings until the last of them, Harapala Deva, was defeated and killed in 1318 by the armies of Sultan Ala-ud-din Khalji who had earlier looted it in 1294. Sultan Muhammad Tughluq took a fancy to the city of Devagiri for its central position in his empire which then extended from the Panjab to Bengal and from the foot of the Himalayas to Cape Comorin. The Sultan renamed Devagiri as Daulatabad, beautified it with fine buildings and roads one of which connected it with Delhi. Then in 1327 the Sultan transferred his capital from Delhi to Daulatabad. But the people of Delhi never took kindly to the transfer and the Sultan's order to transfer all the people of Delhi to Daulatabad was a mistake. The transfer did not work and

Daulatabad could not remain the capital of the Indian empire. But it did not sink into complete insignificance. It became the headquarters of one of the four provinces into which the Bahmani kingdom (*q.v.*) was divided. Later on, when the Bahmani kingdom disintegrated, Daulatabad became a very important stronghold in the state of Ahmadnagar. Indeed the fort was so strongly built that it could be captured by Emperor Shah Jahan in 1631 only by bribing the governor, Fateh Khan. Under the Mughul rule Daulatabad continued to be a chief centre of imperial administration and it was from this city that Aurangzeb organised his Deccan campaigns and it was within the fort of Daulatabad that the last king of Golkunda, Abdul Hasan, was kept as a prisoner by Aurangzeb's order. It is again at Daulatabad that the body of Emperor Aurangzeb was buried after his death at Burhanpur in 1707. In 1760 Daulatabad passed into the hands of the Hindu Marathas, but it did not regain its older Hindu name of Devagiri and continues to be known at present as Daulatabad.

Davaka—is mentioned in the Allahabad inscription of Samudra-gupta (*c.* A.D. 330-80) as one of the states which, like Samatata (part of Eastern Bengal) and Kamarupa (Western Assam), paid tribute to the Gupta sovereign. Davaka has not yet been definitely identified. Probably it lay somewhere, either in Eastern Bengal or in Western Assam.

Dawar Baksh—was a son of Prince Khusrav or Khusru, (*q.v.*) the eldest son of Emperor Jahangir (1605-27), who had died in 1622. On the death of Jahangir in October 1627 Prince Dawar Baksh was installed on the Delhi throne by Asaf Khan, the father-in-law of Shah Jahan, as a stop-gap emperor so that the imperial throne might not be occupied by Jahangir's youngest son, Prince Shahryar, who was backed by the dowager Empress Nur Jahan. Shah Jahan arrived at Agra in February, 1628 and was proclaimed the Emperor of Delhi. Prince Dawar Baksh was quietly removed from the throne, kept as a prisoner for some years but was later on released and went to reside in Persia as a pensioner of the Shah of Persia.

Day, Francis—was the chief of the factory of the East India Company at Armagaon. In 1640 he secured from the local Hindu Raja the grant of a narrow strip of land about 230 miles south of Masulipatam with permission to build there a fortified factory which he named Fort St. George. The grant was later on confirmed by the Raja of Chandragiri who was the superior sovereign. Round the guns of Fort St. George there grew up within a few years the town of Madras which soon became the headquarters of the East India Company on the Coromandel coast. Francis Day was a very enterprising factor and had great foresight. It was his insistence that dissuaded the East India Company to abandon totally their factories on the Bay of Bengal. Later events justified the optimism of Francis Day.

Dayananda Saraswati, Swami (1824-83)—was the founder of the Arya Samaj (1875) which was a protest against the westernisation which had begun in India after the establishment of British rule, especially after the growth and expansion of western learning and Christianity amongst the Indians. Dayananda was a profoundly learned Sanskrit scholar, but he had no English education. He ardently believed in the Vedic scriptures and in the religious and philosophical ideas to be found in the Vedas on the basis of which he wanted to remould Hindu religion and society in India. 'Go back to the Vedas', was his motto. He disregarded the authority of the later scriptures like the Puranas, decried polytheism and the use of images, and believed in one God. He condemned caste-restrictions, child-marriage and prohibition against sea-voyages and encouraged female education and widow remarriage. In fact he wanted to remove the abuses that had crept into Hindu society during the period of Muslim predominance in India. Moreover, he held that anybody could be a Hindu and supported the *Shuddhi* movement, that is to say, the movement for re-converting non-Hindus to Hinduism. The *Shuddhi* movement was aimed at promoting the integrity and unity of the Indian people and had thus a political implication. Dayananda wrote several books to enunciate his principles, and the most important of his works was the *Satyartha Prakash*. He was also a great orator who preached directly to the masses, and secured many followers amongst them, especially in the Panjab and United Provinces where his doctrines took deep root. He avoided western science and what may be called the scientific views on sociology and religion, but his was a dynamic personality which stirred the Hindu society to its foundations and prepared the Hindu mind to meet the challenge of western learning and religion and to uphold the ancient, and what was considered the pure form of Hindu culture and religion. The Arya Samaj greatly stemmed the tide of conversion of the Hindus to other religions, reclaimed many non-Hindus to the fold of Hinduism and contributed to the eventual growth of Indian nationalism by teaching the Hindus that, irrespective of the divisions into castes and existence of different social practices, they were an integrated people. His

ideals are practised at the Gurukul founded at Hardwar which
was raised in 1907 to the status of a University teaching through
Sanskrit as the medium of instruction. Some of his followers
later on recognised also the utility of western education in
modern times and founded the Dayananda Anglo-Vedic College
in Lahore with the aim of propogating the ideas of the Arya
Samaj without discarding English. Dayananda was a great force
in the promotion of Indian nationalism in the nineteenth
century.

de Boigne, Benoit (1751-1830)—a Savoyard and a soldier of
fortune, who entered the East India Company's service at
Madras in 1778. But after some years he left the service of the
Company and entered that of Mahadaji Sindhia (*q.v.*). He drew a
very high salary in return for which he trained Sindhia's armies
after the European manner. With this army he helped Sindhia
in winning the battles of Patan in June, 1790 and Merta in
September, 1790 defeating mixed forces of Pathans, Rajputs and
Mughuls. He then became the commander-in-chief of Sindhia's
army and enabled him to defeat Holkar at the battle of Lakheri in
September, 1793. After the death of Mahadaji Sindhia in 1794
de Boigne continued to serve under his successor, Daulat Rao
Sindhia, but resigned his command in December, 1795 on
account of ill-health. Next year he left India and after residing for
some time in London he settled in France where he lived till his
death in 1830, leaving a property worth 20 million francs.

Deccan, the—is the English form of the Sanskrit term *Dakshina* or the
South. It is a term with a rather wide denotation. *Dakshina* or
Dakshinapatha was originally used to denote the whole of south
or peninsular India lying between the Vindhyas and the Narmada on the north and Cape Comorin on the south. In later
times it came to be applied to the region lying between the
Narmada on the north to the Krishna with its tributary the
Tungabhadra on the south, that is to say, to the Deccan plateau
proper, comprising the modern states of Madhya Pradesh,
Bombay and Andhra Pradesh. The land beyond the Krishna
and the Tungabhadra is sometimes called the Tamilakam or the
Land of the Tamils. For purposes of this note the Deccan is
taken to mean the Deccan plateau between the Narmada and
the Krishna. The Deccan plateau is rocky and, geologically
speaking, it is much older than the alluvial plains of north
India washed by the Ganges and the Indus. Archaeological
finds made in the Deccan are also of an older type than any
found in north India except the Himalayan area. The Deccan

practically rests on a mountainous triangle of which the Nilgiris represents the apex, the Western and Eastern Ghats the two sides and the Vindhya Hills the base. No river of north India flows into the south on account of the obstruction caused by the Vindhya Hills and the Western Ghats being higher than the Eastern the rivers of the Deccan below the Satpura Hills run from the west to the east and fall into the Bay of Bengal.

According to tradition as preserved in the *Ramayana* and the *Mahabharata*, the first Aryan immigrant to the Deccan was the sage Agastya who reclaimed the country from the hands of peoples who are called *Vanaras, Asuras* and *Rakshasas*, a motley host who are believed to have been Dravidians who had a higher material civilisation than their Aryan conquerors.

Historically speaking, our knowledge of the Deccan is more recent than of north India. It does not go beyond the times of the Nanda kings (*q.v.*) whose dominion included Kalinga and might have covered the whole of the Deccan, for though Kalinga was the one south Indian kingdom that Asoka conquered his empire extended up to the river Pennar and had on its extreme southern frontier the Tamil kingdoms of Chera, Chola, Pandya and Satiyaputra. After the decline and fall of the Maurya dynasty a large kingdom was built up in the Deccan by the Satavahanas (*q.v.*), also known as the Andhras, who ruled from about 50 B.C. to about A.D. 225. It was during this period that a branch of the Sakas (*q.v.*) occupied west Deccan. After the disappearance of the Satavahanas a number of lesser dynasties arose in different parts of the Deccan. The more important amongst them were the Gangas (*q.v.*), the Vakatakas (*q.v.*) and the Kadambas (*q.v.*). One branch of the Gangas ruled over the greater part of Mysore area from the second to the eleventh century and have left their memento in the colossal statue of Gomata, 56½ feet in height, wrought out of a block of gneiss on the top of a hill at Sravana Belgola. A second branch of the Gangas ruled in Orissa from the sixth to the sixteenth century and their memory lies enshrined in the temple of Jagannath at Puri built by Ananta-varman Choda Ganga (*q.v.*). The Kadambas ruled in south Kanara and western Mysore from the third to the sixth century while the Vakatakas ruled in Madhya Pradesh and west Deccan from the fourth to the sixth century. In the middle of the fourth century Samudragupta (*q.v.*), the second monarch of the Gupta dynasty, led an expedition into the Deccan and received the submission of many south Indian kings including the Pallava king, Vishnugopa, who had his capital at Kanchi, modern

Conjeeveram. The third Gupta Emperor Chandragupta II (*q.v.*) overthrew the Saka Satrap of Ujjaini and brought Malwa and Gujarat within his empire. After the fall of the Gupta empire the Deccan again separated from north India and a great kingdom came to be built up by the Chalukyas, who are believed to have belonged to a north Indian Rajput clan, with their capital at Batapi or Vatami, now in Bijapur district of Bombay. This dynasty ruled the Deccan for about 200 years. The greatest king of this dynasty was Pulakeshin II (*q.v.*) (608-42) who repulsed in 641 on the banks of the Narmada an invasion by the north Indian king Harshavardhana (*q.v.*) and thus preserved intact the traditional boundary line between the north and the south. Nearer home, however, he had very powerful rivals in the Pallava kings (*q.v.*) of Kanchi and it was the Pallava king Narasimhavarman (*q.v.*) who defeated and killed Pulakeshin II in a battle in A.D. 642. But thirty-two years later the Chalukya dynasty was overthrown by Dantidurga Rashtrakuta (*q.v.*) who established in the Deccan a new dynasty which ruled the plateau from its capital at Manyakheta, modern Malkhed. The greatest king of this dynasty was Amoghavarsha (*c.* 815-877) (*q.v.*) referred to by the Arab writers as Balhara or Vallabha Rai. In A.D. 973 the Rashtrakuta dynasty was overthrown by the second Chalukya dynasty which ruled the plateau until its fall in A.D. 1190. On the fall of the second Chalukya dynasty the sovereignty in the Deccan became divided amongst three dynasties, viz. the Yadavas ruling in west Deccan with Devagiri as their capital, the Hoysalas (*q.v.*) in Mysore with Dvarasamudra, modern Halebid as their capital and the Kakatiyas at Warangal or Talingana in the eastern side of the plateau. There was no love lost amongst these Hindu kingdoms of the Deccan and one by one they were all subdued by Sultan Ala-ud-din Khalji—the Yadavas between 1296 and 1312, the Kakatiyas in 1310 and the Hoysalas in 1311, though the last kingdom maintained a precarious existence until 1424-25 when it was annexed to the Bahmani kingdom. Thus ended Hindu rule in the Deccan in much the same way as in north India. Though politically speaking the Deccan during the Hindu rule had been, except for short periods under the Nandas, Mauryas and Guptas of Pataliputra, separate from north India, culturally and in religion it had always been an integral part of Hindu India. Though its people speak languages different from those spoken in the north, Sanskrit was their sacred and official language as of the Hindus in the north. Brahmanism, Buddhism and Jainism were all held in equal respect in the south as in the north. If the Deccan received much from north India it also gave to the north as much in Acharya Sankara who preached Vedantism, Acharya Ramanuja who founded Vaishnavism and the celebrated jurist Vijnaneswara, the author of the *Mitakshara* which controls the social life of all Hindu India except Bengal and Assam. In arts and architecture the Deccan has preserved the Hindu tradition and the achievements of the Hindus in the realms of art, architecture, sculpture and painting can be best studied only by visiting the many Hindu temples that still abound in the Deccan. These Hindu temples as well as the caves and temples at Elora and Ajanta bear eloquent testimony to the artistic skill and grandeur of the Hindus which nobody can correctly judge from the monuments extant in north India alone.

Later history of the Deccan:—Ala-ud-din Khalji who first compelled the submission of the Hindu kingdoms of Devagiri in 1310, Warrangal in 1310 and Dvarasamudra in 1311, later on sent his army under Kafur (*q.v.*) to the far south. Kafur captured Madura, the capital of the Pandya kingdom, advanced as far as Rameswaram and thus brought under Muslim sovereignty not only the Deccan plateau but the whole of the peninsula up to Cape Comorin. The rich booty of 612 elephants, 20,000 horses, 96,000 maunds of gold and many boxes of pearls and jewels that Kafur brought to Delhi indicates the immense wealth of the Deccan and the Far South. But the sovereignty of Delhi did not last long. As a reaction to the policy of Sultan Muhammad Tughluq, Ma'bar (Far South) revolted and became independent under Ahsan Shah (*q.v.*) in 1335 and within the next decade the Deccan plateau between the Narmada and the Krishna became independent under the rule of Ala-ud-din Hasan Bahmani (*q.v.*) in 1347 and the Hindu kingdom of Vijayanagar (*q.v.*) came to be established in the south of the Krishna at about the same time. Vijayanagar annexed the Muslim kingdom of Madura in 1377-78 and thereafter the sovereignty over the Deccan was divided between the Muslim Bahmani kingdom in the north and the Hindu Vijayanagar kingdom in the south. The Bahmani kingdom, however, disintegrated in the second decade of the sixteenth century and by 1526 when Babur established Mughul rule in Delhi the Deccan plateau proper had come to be parcelled out into the five Muslim states of Berar, Bidar, Bijapur, Ahmadnagar and Golkunda. The Hindu kings of Vijayanagar ruled over the tract south of the Krishna until 1565 when the city was destroyed by a combined attack by the

sultans of Bijapur, Ahmadnagar, Golkunda and Bidar following
their victory over the Vijayanagar army at the battle of Talikota. But their unity did not last long. Ahmadnagar which had
absorbed Berar in 1574, had to cede that territory to Emperor
Akbar in 1596 and was itself annexed to the Mughul empire in
1637. Bijapur which had absorbed Bidar in about 1619, was, in
its turn, annexed to the Mughul empire in 1686 and a year later
Golkunda was also annexed to the Mughul empire. Three years
later the independent Hindu kingdom that Shivaji had founded
in Maharashtra, that is to say, north-western Deccan was also
subjugated by Aurangzeb, the Mughul Emperor of Delhi. The
Deccan thus again became united with north India into one
empire. But this time also the union did not last long. Maharashtra regained her independence even before the death of
Aurangzeb in 1707 and his successor Bahadur Shah I (1707-12)
formally recognised the accomplished fact. In 1724 Chin Klich
Khan (*q.v.*) better known as Nizam-ul-Mulk Asaf Jah, who had
been the Mughul governor of the Deccan, set himself up as an
independent ruler. Thus the Deccan again became separate
from north India in the first quarter of the eighteenth century
and its sovereignty was soon divided between the Nizam of
Hyderabad and the Marathas with their capital at Poona. In
the meantime European traders had come to the Deccan and
had established themselves at various places on the eastern and
western coasts alike. The Portuguese were in Goa, Daman and
Diu; the English at Surat, Bombay and Madras and the French
at Pondicherry, Mahe and Karikal. The Portuguese were in
independent possession of Goa while the English had their
fortified settlements in Bombay and Madras and the French
at Pondicherry. At first these European traders were engaged in
rivalries amongst themselves and a combination of the English
and the French succeeded in outstripping the Portuguese in
trade and commerce to which they mainly devoted their energies. But Anglo-French hostilities in Europe were soon carried
overseas and between 1740 and 1763 the English and the
French fought on the soil of the Deccan with the aid of Deccanese
soldiers recruited by them into their armies with the passive
consent of the rulers of the Deccan, a series of wars known as the
Carnatic Wars (*q.v.*) which resulted in the destruction of the
political power of the French in the Deccan and the establishment of the English as a political power there. Important
political developments had in the meantime taken place in the
Deccan, particularly in Maharashtra where Shivaji's grandson,

king Sahu (1707-48) transferred in 1727 his power to his Peshwa Baji Rao I (*q.v.*) who ruled over Maharashtra until his death in 1740. He organised the Maratha confederacy, sent in 1737 a Maratha army for the first time to north India and appeared to be fairly striving for the establishment of a Hindu empire in succession to the Mughuls, but he died in 1740 after leaving his lieutenants, Bhonsla, Gaekwaḍ, Holkar and Sindhia in charge of areas around Nagpur, Baroda, Indore and Gwalior. His son and successor Balaji Baji Rao (*q.v.*) (1740-61) sent a Maratha army to the Panjab then under Timur, son of Ahmad Shah Abdali, and thus entered into hostilities with Ahmad Shah Abdali which culminated in the third battle of Panipat (*q.v.*) (1761) where the Maratha army was badly defeated. Balaji Baji Rao died of a broken heart and the unity of the Marathas was gone, leaving them much weaker than before. Moreover in 1761 a Muhammadan adventurer named Haidar Ali overthrew the Hindu Wodeyar dynasty (*q.v.*) which had been ruling in Mysore since the disintegration of the kingdom of Vijayanagar in 1565 and came to control the southern extremity of the peninsula. There was no love lost amongst the powers in the Deccan and not only did the Hindu Marathas try to extend their territories at the cost of the Muhammadan states of Hyderabad and Mysore, but the two Muslim states were also in conflict with each other. The serious implication of the rise of the English, who were foreigners, to political power in the Deccan was not fully and properly appreciated by the contending native powers in the Deccan. They continued to be engaged in despicable intrigues and unpatriotic ambition with the result that the rulers of the Deccan could make no combined effort to drive away the English. On the other hand, the English so cleverly manipulated the hostilities amongst the Indian rulers that they compelled the Nizam to accept their protection as a 'subsidiary ally' (*q.v.*) in 1798, defeated and killed Tipu Sultan, the king of Mysore, in the battle of Seringapatam in 1799, with the active help of the Nizam and the passive inactivity of the Marathas, annexed Tanjore and Surat also in 1799 and crowned their series of successes by the treaty of Bassein (*q.v.*) (1802) by which Peshwa Baji Rao II accepted the subsidiary alliance. This was deeply resented by the Marathas and led to the Second Maratha War (*q.v.*) (1803-05) in which members of the Maratha confederacy were defeated and obliged to enter into subsidiary alliances with the English. Thus sovereignty over the Deccan passed over to the English and the little show of power that was still retained by the Marathas perished in the Third Maratha War (*q.v.*) (1817-19) at the end of which Peshwa Baji Rao II was pensioned off and his post was abolished and all the Maratha chiefs including the Holkar frankly accepted the suzerainty of the British Indian Government. The Deccan thus lost its separate political existence outside the Indian empire and has since continued to be politically and culturally an integral part of India. Soon after India attained her independence in 1947 the states of the Indian princes in the Deccan, like those in north India, were integrated with the Republic of India which now comprises Hindusthan or north India and Dakshinapatha or the Deccan as inseparable units.

Deccan Education Society, the—was founded in 1884 under the inspiration of Justice M. G. Ranade of Maharashtra. Its headquarters were in Bombay and it started with the object of re-modelling the system of education of the young in the country so that they may be better fitted for the service of the country than young men trained in the ordinary educational institutions. The members of the society were required to serve for at least 20 years on a nominal salary starting with Rs. 75/ per month. Many self-sacrificing young men, amongst whom Gopal Krishna Gokhale and Sri Nivas Shastri later on became very renowned, joined the Deccan Education Society and succeeded by their selfless efforts to start the famous Fergusson College in Poona and the Willingdon College at Sangli.

Deedo Meer—a Muslim leader, had many followers in the district of Faridpur, now in East Pakistan. They created a sort of popular rising in 1847 and had to be suppressed by force.

Declarations, Parliamentary—mark important stages in the development of the Indian constitution leading to the ultimate independence of India. The first Parliamentary declaration was made on 20th August, 1917, by Mr. Edwin Montague, the Secretary of State for India. It made the important announcement that "the policy of His Majesty's Government, with which the Government of India are in complete accord, is that of the increasing association of Indians in every branch of the administration and the gradual development of self-governing institutions with a view to the progressive realisation of responsible government in India as an integral part of the British Empire". This declaration was followed by a visit of Mr. Montague to India in 1917-18 and by the passing of the Government of India Act, 1919, (see *supra, British Administration in India*) which introduced partial responsibility (dyarchy) over the executive and fully elected legislatures in the provinces and largely increased the elected element at the Central legislature and thus started India fairly on the way to a parliamentary form of government. The second important declaration was made in October, 1929 announcing that the natural issue of India's constitutional progress was the attainment of Dominion status. This declaration resulted in the passing of the Government of India Act, 1935 (see *supra, ibid.*) which envisaged the idea of a federal responsible government at the Centre and fully responsible governments in the provinces. The third and the final declaration was made on June 3, 1947, in the House of Commons by the British Prime Minister, Mr. Clement Attlee, announcing that His Majesty's Government had decided to transfer power to the people of India at the earliest possible moment. This declaration led to the enactment by the British Parliament of the Indian Independence Act, 1947, which came into force on the 15th August, 1947 and forms the legal basis of India's independence.

Defence of India Act, the—passed on the outbreak of the first World War in 1914, armed the Government of India with extensive powers of arrest, detention and restriction of individual freedom during the period of the war. Indians soon came to regard the measure as an extraordinary transgression of individual freedom and as an example of severe repression.

de la Haye—was a French admiral sent to protect French interests on the Coromandel coast. In 1672 the French had captured St. Thome near Madras; but next year their fleet stationed at Trincomali in Ceylon under Admiral de la Haye was driven out from the station by the Dutch who captured St. Thome in 1674.

de Lally—*see* Lally.

Deimachos—was a Greek ambassador sent by the king of Syria to the court of Bindusara (*q.v.*) (*c.* 300 B.C. - 273 B.C.), the second Maurya Emperor.

Delhi—is believed by many to stand on the site once occupied by the city of Indraprashtha which was the capital of the Pandavas, the heroes of the *Mahabharata*. The tradition of this ancient city is borne at present by the name of Indrapat where stands the fortress of Humayun and Sher Shah. It is also called Purana Kila (Old Fort). Historically the earliest builder of Delhi was Anangapal, the Tomara king, who ruled in the eleventh century A.D. He built a red fort where the Kutb Minar now stands, some three miles south of the present New Delhi. In the twelfth century it passed under the rule of the Chauhan dynasty of Ajmer, but in 1193 it was snatched from the hands of the last Chauhan king, Prithviraj, by Shihabuddin Muhammad Ghori. Thus ended Hindu rule in Delhi. Its Muhammadan conquerors retained it as their capital till the last of them, the Mughul Emperor Bahadur Shah (1837-57) was deposed in 1857. During this long period (1193-1857) various Muhammadan sovereigns at different times had built their residences at different parts of what may be called the Delhi area, but they never thought of deserting Delhi as their capital except for short periods under Babur, Akbar and Jahangir who shifted the capital to Agra. Thus Ala-ud-din Khalji (1296-1316) built Siri, about 3 miles north-east of Old Delhi, Ghiyasuddin Tughluq built Tughlukabad, 4 miles east of Old Delhi, his son and successor Muhammad Tughluq, who made in 1327 an abortive attempt to transfer the capital from Delhi to Daulatabad, built between Old Delhi and Siri the city of Jahanpannah and his successor Firoz Tughluq built Firozabad, about 8 miles north of Old Delhi. Indeed the Muhammadan sovereigns built as many as seven cities in the Delhi plain, but Old Delhi continued to be the centre. The Lodis made Àgra their capital which continued also to be the capital of Babur but Humayun brought back the capital to Old Delhi where he began building what is now known as the Purana Kila or Old Fort round which lay the capital of the Mughul emperors from the time of Shah Jahan who added to the old city a new adjunct known as Shah Jahanabad with its gorgeous palace. The Jumma Masjid is the most central edifice of Old Delhi. Delhi had more than its due share of sorrow and horror. It was occupied and sacked by Timur in 1398, by Nadir Shah in 1739 and by Ahmad Shah Abdali in 1757. Next year it narrowly escaped occupation by the Marathas. It was also spared spoliation after the third battle of Panipat (1761). The decline of the Mughul imperial power continued and Delhi was captured by the British in 1803 when Delhi lost its imperial glory as the sovereignty over India had by then definitely passed over to the English and Calcutta gradually tended to step into the place of Delhi. But as it still continued to be the residence of the Mughul Emperor popular imagination clung to it as the centre of imperial authority. Accordingly, on the outbreak of the Sepoy Mutiny its occupation became an object of great significance and Delhi was occupied by the mutinous sepoys in May and recaptured by the English in September, 1857. In January, 1858 the old Emperor Bahadur Shah, the last of the Mughul

Emperors, was formally deposed and sent into exile to live as a British pensioner in Rangoon. From that time Delhi lost all its imperial glamour. But Phoenix-like, the city again rose from its ashes and in 1912 it again became the capital of the Indian Empire under the British Crown. Lord Hardinge (*q.v.*) was the first Viceroy to reside in Delhi where the British, like the earlier Muhammadan rulers, built for themselves, six miles from Old Delhi, a new city called New Delhi which continues to be the capital of the independent Republic of India.

Delhi Durbars—were imperial assemblages held in Delhi in 1877, 1903 and 1911. The first was held in 1877 by Lord Lytton to announce publicly the assumption by Queen Victoria of the title of 'Empress of India'. It was attended with much pageantry and pomp and involved the Government of India in very heavy expenditure at a time when it was not spending enough to save the people of the Deccan from the terrible famine that raged there from 1876 to 1878 and took thousands of lives. Naturally the heavy expenditure incurred in holding the Durbar was considered by the Indian public as waste of public funds.

The second Durbar in Delhi was held by Lord Curzon, the Viceroy, in 1903 to proclaim the coronation of King Edward VII. This Durbar was attended with greater pomp and pageantry and was therefore more expensive than the Durbar held in 1877. No useful purpose was served by either of these two Durbars except satisfying the craze for pomp and grandeur that was inherent in the characters of their two sponsors, Lord Lytton and Lord Curzon.

The third Durbar in Delhi was held in 1911 during the administration of Lord Hardinge (*q.v.*). King-Emperor George V and his Queen came on a royal visit to India on the occasion and held a Durbar in Delhi to celebrate their coronation. On this occasion a royal declaration was made modifying the Partition of Bengal (*q.v.*) and transferring the capital of the British Empire in India from Calcutta to Delhi.

Delhi pact—was concluded on the 5th March, 1931, between Lord Irwin, the Viceroy (1926-31) and Mahatma Gandhi, the leader of the Indian National Congress, by which the Civil Disobedience Movement that had been started in April, 1930, was called off by the Congress which agreed to participate in the Round Table Conference in London for settling the political issue between Great Britain and India and the repressive ordinances which had been passed since 1930, were withdrawn and the political prisoners made in connection with the Civil

Disobedience Movement were released by the Government of
India.

Delhi Sultanate—covers the period from 1206 when Qutb-ud-din
became the first Muhammadan sultan of Delhi ruling over the
whole of northern India to 1526 when the last sultan, Ibrahim
Lodi, was defeated and killed in the battle of Panipat by Babur
who founded the dynasty of Mughul emperors. During this long
period (1206-1526) of three hundred and twenty years the
sultans of Delhi were recognised as the sovereigns of India
though the degree of their authority and the extent of their
dominions varied from time to time, covering the whole of India
from the Himalayas to Cape Comorin for some years during the
reign of Muhammad Tughluq (1325-51) and shrinking to the
area round Delhi and the Panjab on the eve of the first battle of
Panipat in 1526.

The Delhi sultans were divided into five separate dynasties,
each unconnected with the others. These were the Slaves
(1206-90), the Khaljis (1290-1320), the Tughluqs (1320-1413),
the Sayyids (1414-51) and the Lodis (1451-1526). The sultans of
the Slave dynasty were (i) Qutb-ud-din, 1206-10, (ii) Aram,
1211, (iii) Iltutmish, 1211-36, (iv) Rukn-ud-din, 1236, (v)
Raziya, 1236-40, (vi) Bahram, 1240-42, (vii) Masud, 1242-46,
(viii) Nasir-ud-din, 1246-66, (ix) Ghiyas-ud-din Balban, 1266-87,
and (x) Kaiqubad, 1287-90. Most of these sultans were at the
beginnings of their careers slaves and so they are said to constitute the Slave dynasty. They were of Turkish birth, like the
other succeeding dynasties, except the Lodis who were Afghans.
The fifth sovereign, Sultana Raziya, was a daughter of the third
sultan, Iltutmish, and occupies a unique place in Indo-Muslim
history, as the only female who ever sat by her own right on the
throne of Delhi. The Khalji dynasty produced six sultans,
namely (i) Jalal-ud-din, 1290-96, (ii) Rukn-ud-din, 1296, (iii)
Ala-ud-din, 1296-1316, (iv) Shihab-ud-din Umar, 1316, (v)
Mubarak, 1316-20 and (vi) Khusrav, 1320. Ala-ud-din was the
most outstanding sovereign amongst the sultans of Delhi. He
brought not only the whole of north India including Rajputana
under his control but carried his victorious arms all over the
Deccan extending his dominions to Cape Comorin. He held the
vast empire under his sway with the aid of a large army and an
organised system of espionage. Severe punishments were meted
out to all who attempted opposition to his rule; salaries of soldiers
were fixed and prices also were controlled and fixed. But his successors proved weak and nine years after his death the sultanate

passed to the Tughluq dynasty. The house of Tughluq gave nine sultans, namely, (i) Ghiyas-ud-din, 1320-25, (ii) Muhammad, 1325-51, (iii) Firuz, 1351-88, (iv) Ghiyas-ud-din II, 1389, (v) Abu Bakr, 1389-90, (vi) Nasir-ud-din, 1390-94, (vii) Ala-ud-din, 1394, (viii) Nusrat Shah, 1395-98 and (ix) Mahmud, 1399-1413. It was during the reign of the second Tughluq sultan, Muhammad, that the Delhi sultanate reached its greatest extent, but it was also during his reign that the process of the disintegration of the sultanate began with the revolts of Bengal and Ma'bar in 1338 and the secession of the Bahmani kingdom in the Deccan and the foundation of the Hindu kingdom of Vijayanagar further to the south in about 1347. His reign is, however, memorable for an attempt at the transfer of the capital from Delhi to Devagiri (renamed Daulatabad) in 1327 and the introduction of a system of token currency in 1329-32. Both the experiments failed and earned the Sultan a great deal of unpopularity. None of his successors was strong enough to recover the lost provinces and the *coup de grâce* to the dynasty was given by Timur, the Mongol leader, who invaded India in 1398, occupied and sacked Delhi before his departure. On the death of Mahmud Tughluq in 1413 the Delhi throne was occupied by Khizr Khan who founded the Sayyid dynasty which ruled from 1414-51. It gave four sultans, viz., (i) Khizr Khan, 1414-21, (ii) Mubarak, 1421-34, (iii) Muhammad, 1434-45 and (iv) Alam Shah, 1445-53. None of them was strong enough to recover the old power of the sultanate and during the rule of Alam Shah (1445-53) its dominions came to consist only of the city of Delhi and its neighbouring villages. Easily enough he was pushed down from the throne which now passed to the Lodi dynasty founded by Buhlol Lodi which ruled from 1453-1526 and produced three sultans, viz., (i) Buhlol, 1453-89, (ii) Sikandar, 1489-1517 and (iii) Ibrahim, 1517-26. Sikandar was a strong ruler who recovered Jaunpur, re-established his authority in Bihar and also over some parts of Rajputana and developed Agra into a city in order to enforce his sovereignty over the neighbouring states. His son and successor Ibrahim Lodi displeased by his haughtiness the leading Afghan nobles, two of whom Daulat Khan, the governor of the Panjab and Alam Khan, the Sultan's uncle and a pretender to the throne of Delhi, invited Babur, the Mughul leader who had already made himself the king of Afghanistan, to invade India. Encouraged by this invitation Babur invaded India in 1526, defeated and killed Ibrahim Lodi in the first battle of Panipat in 1526, occupied the throne of Delhi and put an end to the Delhi sultanate.

The Delhi sultans ruled by the sword and established an administration which aimed at keeping down the people with the assistance of a large number of nobles. It was an autocratic system of government in which the common man, Hindu as well as Muslim, had neither any right nor any power. The Hindus suffered grievously; they were assessed in a poll tax called the *Jizya* and a pilgrim's tax in addition to the heavy land and other taxes which were imposed at the pleasure of the sultans. The administrative system was incapable of further progress and was entirely sectarian. There was a regular hierarchy of officers, but the officers were all responsible to the sultan alone, were appointed and liable to dismissal at his pleasure, and were really agents for carrying out the will of the sultan who was the commander-in-chief, the chief law-giver and the final court of appeal. The administration involved no care of the Hindus, though they formed the majority of the people of the land. Not even the mildest sultan is known to have taken any step whatsoever for the benefit of the Hindu subjects. It is indicative of the inertness of the Hindus that even when the sultanate so declined in power as to enable the provincial governors who were all Muslims, to set up independent states for themselves, the Hindus as a body could not avail themselves of the opportunity to throw off the Muslim yoke except in Vijaya-nagar.

Hindu culture and civilisation which had absorbed the earlier invaders like the Greeks, Sakas and Huns, failed to assimilate the Muhammadan invaders and their religion and culture. On the contrary thousands of the conquered Hindus were converted, either by force or by conviction to Muhammadanism which thus became a permanent feature in India. Islam too failed, in spite of all the resources that the sovereignty of India placed at the disposal of its followers, not only to eradicate Hinduism from the soil of India but also to convert even the major portion of the Hindu population and continued to be the religion of a minority in India. Thus Muhammadans were condemned to live side by side with the Hindus who, having failed in the battle-field, tried to save themselves by following a policy of avoiding, as far as possible, contact with their ruthless conquerors. Caste rules were stiffened; women were placed behind the purdah, and untouchability was made a part of Hinduism. But some contact was unavoidable and this led to the development of a new language, viz. *Urdu*, in order to maintain communication between the conquering

Muhammadans who spoke Turki and used Persian for official purposes and Arabic for religious ceremonies, and the conquered Hindus who spoke a variety of languages and used Sanskrit for divine worship. Gradually the sacred books of the two religious bodies came to be studied by the more liberal members of the two sects and a religious reconciliation was attempted by the *Sufis* who were professedly Muhammadans and by Hindu religious reformers like Ramananda, Chaitanya, Kabir and Nanak, who placed devotion to God above sectarian rituals, but the gulf between the Hindus and the Muhammadans remained unbridged.

Some of the sultans were great builders who constructed magnificent mosques and palaces. None of the palaces built by them has come down intact to modern times, but many mosques still bear testimony to their taste and love for art and architecture. They built mostly with the aid of Indian (Hindu) artisans and architects and with the materials which they got from the Hindu temples which they destroyed and over the ruins of which they built their mosques. Thus art and architecture of the Delhi sultanate came to represent a mingling of Indian (Hindu) and foreign (Persian, Turkish) Islamic ideas and led to the development of a new school of architecture in India which has been called the Indo-Saracenic type. But different styles of architecture developed in different parts of the dominions of the sultans, as these came to be independent of Delhi. Thus Jaunpur, Bengal, Gujarat, Malwa and the Deccan all developed different styles, each of which has distinctive features of its own. The more celebrated edifices built by the Delhi sultans are the Qutb Minar with its Alai Darwaja, the Quwwat-ul-Islam Mosque, the Dargah of Nizamudin Auliya with its mosque and tomb of Feroz Shah Tughluq all in Delhi. (*C.H.I.*, Vol. III; Prasad, I., *Medieval India;* Thomas, *Chronicles of the Pathan Kings of Delhi;* Ashraf, K. M., *Life and Condition of the People of Hindusthan;* Fergusson, *Hist. of Indian Architecture;* Havell, *Indian Architecture;* Smith V. A., *Hist. of Fine Arts in India*)

Delhi University—was founded in 1922 and re-organised in 1952. It is a teaching University composed of federated colleges and as such exemplified a new type of Universities in India.

Demetrios—son of Euthydemos, was the king of Bactria. He married a daughter of Antiochus the Great of Syria (*c.* 223 B.C. - 187 B.C.). He conquered some portion of northern India which perhaps included Kabul, the Panjab and Sind in about 190 B.C. By virtue of these conquests he became known as the "King of the Indians" but eventually he was defeated and dispossessed of his dominions by Eukratides (*q.v.*).

Deogaon, the treaty of—was concluded on 17th December, 1803, between Raghuji Bhonsla II and the English after the former's defeat at Argaon in the previous November during the course of the Second Maratha War (*q.v.*) (1803-04). By this treaty the Bhonsla Raja of Berar ceded to the English the province of Cuttuck which included Balasore as well as the whole of his territory west of the river Warda. He was to maintain a British Resident at his capital at Nagpur, to accept the arbitration of the English in any dispute with the Nizam and the Peshwa and was not to appoint any European or American or even any British subject without the previous consent of the British. In short, by this treaty the Bhonsla Raja practically became a subsidiary ally of the English in India.

Deogarh—in Jhansi district in Uttar Pradesh, is the site of one of the rare extant monuments of the Gupta period (A.D. 300-450). The images of Siva, Vishnu and other Hindu Gods are excellently delineated in the panels of the temple of Deogarh which excaped the vandalism of the Muhammadans.

Deogiri—or Devagiri *see ante* Daulatabad.

Deorai, the battle of—was the last battle that Prince Dara (*q.v.*) fought against the armies of Aurangzeb. The battle took place in a mountain pass to the south of Ajmer and lasted for three days, 12-14 April, 1659. The battle ended in the complete defeat of Prince Dara who was forced to seek safety in flight. This defeat destroyed all his chances of success and eventually he became a captive in the hands of Aurangzeb who had him executed after a show of a trial on a charge of heresy.

Derozio, Henry Louis Vivian—was born in Calcutta in 1809 in a Portuguese-Indian family. He began his life as a clerk in his father's office, but soon adopted the profession of a teacher and journalist. In 1826 he was appointed a teacher in the Hindu College in Calcutta and occupied that post till his forced resignation in April, 1831. During this short spell of five years he exercised an immense influence on his students of the Hindu College and through them over a very large number of Bengali youths who were students and thus created a group of free-thinkers known as Young Bengal. They were radical in their views, openly attacked all that they considered unreasonable in Hindu society and religion and thus created a great stir in the country. The attacks that Young Bengal made on Hinduism were bitterly resented by the orthodox community and their opposition to his continuance as a teacher obliged Derozio to resign. He lived but a short time after his resignation, but he had left his mark on the history of modern Bengal, and through it, of modern India by creating a body of young men who were radicals in thought and whose opposition to authority in religion was soon to be directed against authority in administration also. Seldom has a teacher exercised such a great influence on his students within so short a time. (Edwardes, T., *Life of Derozio*)

Devabhuti (or Devabhumi)—the last king of the Sunga dynasty (*q.v.*) (*c.* 185 B.C. - 73 B.C.) of Magadha, was a person of licentious habits and his death was brought about in *c.* 73 B.C. by his Brahman minister, Vasudeva, who established the Kanva dynasty.

Devadatta—a cousin of Gautama Buddha, the founder of Buddhism, broke away from Buddhism and founded a rival sect which existed even in the times of the Guptas in the fourth century of the Christian era.

Devagiri—*see ante* Daulatabad.

Devagupta—was the name borne by three kings of three different dynasties. First, it was one of the names of Chandragupta II, son of Samudragupta, the third emperor of the Gupta dynasty (*c.* A.D. 320-590). He has been called Devagupta I. Secondly, it was the name of a Gupta king of Malwa who defeated and killed Harshavardhana's brother-in-law, the Maukhari king Grahavarman (*q.v.*) in about A.D. 606. This Gupta king of Malwa has been called Devagupta II. Thirdly, the son and successor of Adityasena who founded in Magadha the line of the later Guptas some time after the death of Harshavardhana in A.D. 646 was a Devagupta who has been called Devagupta III. He was probably the ruler of the whole of north India. He was defeated by the Chalukya king Vinayaditya who ruled from A.D. 680-96. (*P.H.A.I.*, pp. 554, 607 & 610)

Devanampiya Piyadasi—is the title by which the third Maurya Emperor Asoka (*q.v.*) is referred to in his numerous inscriptions, except the one at Maski which refers to him as Devanampiya Asoka and thus settles the question of the identity of the Devanampiya Piyadasi of the inscriptions with the third Maurya Emperor Asoka. The expression means Beloved of the Gods who looks after the welfare (of all). (Bhattacharya. S., *Select Asokan Epigraphs*)

Devanampiya Tissa—was the king of Ceylon and a contemporary of Asoka (*q.v.*). He received at his court the Buddhist mission that Asoka sent to Ceylon under the leadership of his brother or son Mahendra (*q.v.*) and was converted to Buddhism.

Devapala—(*c.* A.D. 810-50)—son of king Dharmapal, was the third king of the Pala dynasty (*q.v.*) which ruled over Bengal and Bihar. He ruled for at least 35 years and under him the Pala dynasty reached the zenith of its power. His suzerainty was acknowledged over the whole of northern India from Assam to the borders of Kashmir and from the foot of the Himalayas to the Vindhyas. He received an embassy from Balaputradeva, a king of the Sailendra dynasty of Java, and granted at his request five villages for the maintenance of a monastery at Nalanda which the Sailendra king patronised. King Devapala was a great patron of Buddhism and took a very keen interest in the affairs of Nalanda monastery which was a centre of Buddhistic studies. (*Dacca Hist. of Bengal.* Vol. I, pp. 116ff.)

Devapala—the Pratihara king of Kanauj, ruled from *c.* A.D. 940-55. During his reign the Pratihara power began to decline. He was defeated by the Chandella king Yasovarman and obliged to surrender a much-prized image of Vishnu which Yasovarman enshrined in one of the finest temples at Khajuraho.

Devarashtra—is a territory whose king Kubera is stated to have been captured and then set free by king Samudragupta (*q.v.*) (*c.* A.D. 330-75) in the course of his victorious campaign in the Deccan. Smith identified Devarashtra with the Maratha country, but the recent view is to place it in the Vizagapatam district on the eastern coast of India. (*E.H.I.*, p. 301 & *A.H.D.*, p. 160.

Deva Raya I—(*c.* A.D. 1406-22)—was the third king of the first dynasty of the kings of Vijayanagar (*q.v.*). His accession to the throne was disputed and this weakened his power so much that the Bahmani sultan, Firoze (*q.v.*) attacked Vijayanagar and occupied the capital for some time. Devaraya I was obliged to purchase peace by agreeing to pay a tribute and by giving a daughter in marriage to the Sultan.

Deva Raya II (A.D. 1425-46)—the sixth king of the first dynasty in Vijayanagar (*q.v.*), re-extended the northern boundary of his kingdom up to the Krishna and established his supremacy over Kerala. During his reign the kingdom suffered terribly as the result of an invasion by the contemporary Bahmani sultan, Ahmad (*q.v.*) who cruelly ravaged the country. But prosperity appears to have soon returned, for the Italian traveller, Nicolo Conti, who visited the country in 1420 and the Persian traveller, Abdur Razzak, who came in 1443, have left very glowing accounts of the wealth and prosperity of the kingdom.

Devichandraguptam—is a recently discovered fragmentary play attributed to Visakhadatta (*q.v.*). It centres round the murder of Rudra Sinha, the last of the Saka satraps, by Chandragupta II during the reign of his weaker elder brother Ramagupta whom he later on killed and whose wife he married. It is on the strength of this much later literary evidence that the existence of a Ramagupta between Samudragupta (*q.v.*) and Chandragupta II (*q.v.*) has been inferred. (*Ind. Ant.* 1923, p. 181 ff.)

Dhana Nanda—was the last of the Nanda kings who ruled in Magadha when Alexander the Great invaded India. He is the Agrammes or Xandrames of classical writers. According to classical writers he possessed vast wealth, his territories extended up to the Beas in the Panjab and he maintained a huge army of 20,000 cavalry, 200,000 infantry, 2000 chariots and 3,000 elephants. It was the fear of meeting this vast host that was probably responsible for the refusal of the army of Alexander to pass beyond the Beas and the retreat of Alexander the Great. But Dhana Nanda was an oppressive king who was, therefore, detested by his subjects. Chandragupta Maurya (*q.v.*) with the assistance of a Taxilian Brahmin named Chanakya cleverly exploited this popular disaffection against king Dhana Nanda whom he defeated and killed, and established on the throne of Magadha with its capital at Pataliputra the Maurya dynasty (*c.* 322 B.C.).

Dhananjaya—was the king of Kusthalapura in North Arcot district who, according to the Allahabad inscription, was one of the kings of the Deccan whom Samudragupta, the second Gupta Emperor, defeated and then set free during his south Indian campaign.

Dhanga (*c.* A.D. 950-99)—was the most powerful king of the Chandella dynasty. He extended his dominions in all directions and ruled over a fairly large kingdom in central India. He built some of the grander temples at Khajuraho. He also took an active part in the politics of his time. In A.D. 989 or 990 he joined the confederacy of Indian princes formed by Jaipal, (*q.v.*), king of the Panjab, to resist Sabuktigin (*q.v.*) and shared with them the defeat which was inflicted on the Hindu princes in a battle near the Kurram valley. He lived for a hundred years, on the completion of which he died by drowning himself in the holy waters of the Ganges at Allahabad (Basu, N. S., *Hist. of the Chandellas*)

Dhanaji Jadav—was a Maratha leader who contributed much by his energy and dash to the continuance of the Maratha opposition to the Mughuls after the defeat and death of Sambhuji (*q.v.*) in 1689. He swept on from one area to another, caused great loss and confusion to the Mughuls and thus kept up Maratha

resistance and continued the struggle for Maratha independence. On Shahu's release in 1707 Dhanaji Jadava was appointed
as his commander-in-chief, and was succeeded on his death to
that office by his son, Chandra Sena Jadav.

Dharasena—was a name borne by four kings of the Maitraka
dynasty (*q.v.*) of Vallabhi which attained royal power after
the decline of the Guptas (*q.v.*). Dharasena I bore the title of
Senapati, but the three later Dharasenas all bore royal titles.
Dharasena IV who was the son of the daughter of Harshavardhana (*q.v.*), ruled for four years (A.D. 645-49), assumed the
imperial title of *Paramabattaraka Parameswara Chakravartin*. But
he could never make good his claim to the succession to his
maternal grandfather's imperial legacy and nothing is known
in detail of his activities.

Dharmapal—the second king of the Pala dynasty (*q.v.*) of Bengal
and Bihar, had a long reign (*c* A.D. 752-94) and was the real
founder of the greatness of the Pala dynasty. He was in fact one
of the greatest kings that ever ruled in Bengal. Pataliputra was
his capital and from there he carried his victorious arms beyond
the limits of Bengal and Bihar. He made himself, for some years
at least, the master of most of northern India, deposed Indraraja
the reigning king of Kanauj and installed in his place his *protégé*
Chakrayudha. He had to wage wars on two fronts—with the
Rastrakutas (*q.v.*) of the Deccan who forced him to retire from
the doab between the Ganges and the Jumna and with the
Pratiharas (*q.v.*) who drove from Kanauj his *protégé*, Chakra
yudha. King Dharmapala was a zealous Buddhist and founded
the famous monastery and college at Vikramasila in modern
Bhagalpur district and also the Somapura-vihara near Paharpur
in Rajshahi district. (*Dacca Hist. of Bengal*, Vol. I.)

Dharmapala—the seventh king of the dynasty founded by Brahma
pala in Kamarupa, modern Assam, in the later part of the 10th
century of the Christian era, reigned in the 12th century, but
the exact period of his reign has not yet been fixed. There are
three land-grants which record Dharmapala's gifts of lands to
Brahmanas. He was a pious king who expatiated in his land
grants on the merits of *dharma* and was probably a worshipper
of Vishnu. (Barua, B. K., *Cul. Hist. of Assam*)

Dharmaratna—an Indian monk residing in Central Asia, went along
with Kasyapa Matanga (*q.v.*) to China in A.D. 65 and under the
patronage of the Han Emperor Ming-ti, established the White
House monastery at Lo-yang and thus started Buddhism on a
proselytising enterprise in China.

Dharmasastras, the—are the sacred texts of the orthodox Hindus next in importance to the Vedas. Along with the Vedic *Dharma sutras* which treat of social and legal usages the *Dharmasastras* include the *Smritis* like the *Manusamhita* (Institutes of Manu) and other similar sacred literature.

Dharmat, the battle of—was fought on the 15th April, 1658, fourteen miles from Ujjain, between Shah Jahan's imperial army led by Raja Jaswant Singh and Qasim Ali Khan and the army led by his two rebellious sons, Aurangzeb and Murad, who combined to oppose the claim of their eldest brother, Dara, to the throne, after Shah Jahan had fallen seriously ill a few months earlier. The imperial army was utterly defeated by the two rebellious brothers who continued to march towards Delhi, crossed the Chambal and reached Samugarh (*q.v.*), eight miles to the east of the Agra Fort, where their further advance was once again opposed by an imperial army led by Prince Dara personally who was again defeated.

Dhauli—in the Puri district in Orissa, is the site where one version of the Fourteen Rock Edicts of Asoka has been found. At Dhauli Rock Edicts Nos. XI, XII and XIII are replaced by two separate Edicts, as in Jaugada, which are known as the separate Kalinga Edicts I & II.

Dhiman—a celebrated artist and sculptor, flourished in the ninth century in Bengal when the Palas (*q.v.*) were reigning. He and his son, Vitopal, are mentioned by the Tibetan historian Taranath as founders of a school of sculpture, bronze-casting and painting in Bengal.

Dhritarastra—was the father of the Kauravas whose war with their cousins, the Pandavas, is the theme of the great Indian epic, the *Mahabharata*. He was born blind and so on his father's death the throne of Hastinapura passed to his younger brother, Pandu. On the death of Pandu leaving behind him five sons of whom Yudhisthira was the eldest, the succession to the throne was disputed by Dhritarastra's sons of whom Duryodhana was the eldest. This dispute culminated in the battle of Kurukshetra in which Duryodhana and the Kauravas were defeated and the Pandavas victorious.

Dhoyi—was a court poet of king Laksmana Sena (A.D. 1179-1205) of Bengal. His work *Pavanadutam*, composed on the model of the *Meghadutam* of Kalidas, describes an adventure of Laksmana Sena, as the prince.

Dhruva—the fourth king (*c.* A.D. 780-93) of the Rashtrakuta dynasty of Manyakheta, was a stout warrior who defeated Vatsaraja, the Gurjara king of Bhinmal and took from him two white umbrellas which the Gurjara king had previously taken from the king of Gauda. King Dhruva also inflicted a defeat on the Pallavas (*q.v.*) in about A.D. 775.

Dhruvabhata—the king of Vallabhi, married the daughter of Harshavardhana of Kanauj (A.D. 606-47) and on the latter's death his son, Dharasena IV (*q.v.*) assumed imperial titles.

Dhruva Devi—the queen of Chandragupta II, Vikramaditya (*q.v.*) (A.D. 380-415), was the mother of the next Gupta sovereign, Kumaragupta I(A.D. 415-55).

Diaz de Novaes, Bartholomeo—was the Portuguese navigator who first rounded the Cape of Good Hope in 1487 and thus made feasible the opening of the direct sea-route between Europe and India.

Didda—was the queen of Khema Gupta, king of Kashmir who administered the kingdom towards the close of the tenth century, first, in the name of her husband, who was a mere puppet in her hands, and later on, after her husband's death, seized the crown herself. In A.D. 1003 she passed on the crown to her nephew, Sangramaraja, who founded the Lohara dynasty of the kings of Kashmir.

Dig, the battle of—was fought in November, 1804, during the Second Maratha War *(q.v.)*. In this battle an army of the Maratha chief Holkar was defeated by the English.

Digambara Jains—is the naked sect amongst the Jains (*q.v.*). They go about nude as opposed to the Svetamvara Jains who dress themselves in white.

Dignaga—was an Acharya or great teacher. He was a celebrated Buddhist sage who flourished in the fourth century A.D., probably during the reign of Chandragupta II, Vikramaditya (A.D. 380-415.)

Digby, John—was the Collector of Rangpur under whom Ram Mohan Roy (*q.v.*), then a young man of about 20 years of age, became employed as a *Sheristadar* in 1809 at Rangpur. Digby was at Rangpur till 1814 and it was during this period that Ram Mohan Roy learnt English and began to make himself well posted in international affairs by reading the English journals that came to Digby.

Dilawar Khan Ghuri—who claimed descent from Shihab-ud-din Muhammad Ghuri, was appointed governor of Malwa in 1392. He took advantage of the confusion created by Timur's invasion in 1398 and set himself up practically as an independent ruler of Malwa in 1401. He ruled only for five years and was succeeded in 1406 by his son, Alp Khan, who assumed royal titles. The dynasty founded by Dilawar Khan Ghuri was overthrown in 1439, but Malwa continued to be an independent state until its conquest and annexation by Akbar in 1561.

Dilawar Khan Lodi—son of Daulat Khan Lodi, semi-independent governor of Lahore, under Sultan Ibrahim Lodi (1517-26), the last of the Delhi sultans, was treated very harshly and unsympathetically by the Sultan. Such treatment to the son deeply enraged his father who, in his anger, invited Babur to invade India.

Dilir Khan—was a Mughul noble who was sent by Emperor Aurangzeb as one of the two commanders—the other being Raja Jay Singh of Amber—against the Maratha leader, Shivaji. He shared with the Raja the glory of forcing Shivaji to accept the treaty of Purandar in June, 1665, by which peace was made between the Mughuls and the Maratha leader. But war between the two was renewed in 1670 when Dilir Khan was sent to fight as a lieutenant of Prince Shah Alam who was placed in supreme command of the Mughul army against Shivaji. But this time Dilir Khan had little success and Shivaji who recovered many of the forts surrendered by the treaty of Purandar, assumed royal title in 1674.

Dilras Bano Begum—a daughter of Shah Nawaz Khan, a Persian nobleman employed as a Mughul officer, was married to Prince Aurangzeb in 1637. On his succession to the throne of Delhi in 1658 she became the Empress.

Din-Ilahi—or Divine Faith, was promulgated by Emperor Akbar in 1582. It was an eclectic religion compounded out of various elements taken from the scriptures of the Muhammadans, Hindus, Buddhists, Jains, Parsis and Christians. It was based on monotheism with a tinge of pantheism. Its great object was the establishment of universal toleration which in a land like India, torn by religious dissensions, was a national requisite. It was based on rationalism. It gained many adherents during Akbar's life-time. But it disappeared after his death. (Ray Chowdhury, M. L., *Din-i-Ilahi*)

Rao, Sir Dinkar—was the Diwan of the Maharaja Sindhia in the middle of the nineteenth century. He kept Sindhia and his army steadily loyal to the British Indian government during the period of the Sepoy Mutiny and was thus of great help to the British.

Diodoros—a classical historian, wrote an account of Alexander's invasion of India based on the account of Megasthenes.

Dionysios—a Greek envoy, was sent by Ptolemy Philadelphos, king of Egypt (*c.* 285-47 B.C.) to the court of Pataliputra during the reign either of Bindusara or of Asoka who referred to Ptolemy in his Rock Inscription XIII.

Dipavamsa—a chronicle of the ancient history of Ceylon, was composed in the fourth or fifth century A.D. It not only corroborates but also amplifies the fact of the despatch by Asoka Maurya of Buddhist missions to countries outside India. It also mentions the names of the missionaries employed by Asoka and thus throws very interesting light on his evangelical activities.

Disraeli, Benjamin, Earl of Beaconsfield—English statesman and novelist, entered Parliament in 1837, became the leader of the anti-Peel section of the Conservatives, but had only short spells of office before his term as Prime Minister in 1868 and again from 1874-80. His second term of office left distinct marks on the history of India. By purchasing the Suez Canal shares in 1874 he helped in establishing a shorter route between England and India; by conferring on Queen Victoria the title, Empress of India, in 1877 he emphasized the imperial dignity of the Crown of England and its paramount supremacy over India, and by supporting the 'forward policy' of Viceroy Lord Lytton (*q.v.*) (1876-80) he brought about the Second Afghan War (*q.v.*) (1878-79).

Diu—is an important trading centre and sea-port on the coast of Gujarat. In 1535 when Gujarat was conquered by Emperor Humayun, Sultan Bahadur Shah of Gujarat (*q.v.*) (1526-37) was forced to take refuge in Malwa and to seek the help of the Portuguese who took advantage of the distress of Bahadur Shah to occupy Diu in 1535. Diu continued to be in possession of the Portuguese till the recovery of the Portuguese possessions in India by the independent republic of India in 1961.

Divakara—a poet, flourished during the reign of Harshavardhana (*q.v.*) (A.D. 606-47) and enjoyed his patronage.

Divodasa—was a famous king mentioned in the Rigveda who fought against Sambara, the non-Aryan king of the Dasas.

Divoka or Divya—a Kaivarta leader, set up for a time an independent state in North Bengal during the reign of Mahipala II (*c.* A.D. 1070-75) whom he defeated and killed.

Diwan—was the highest officer in the Mughul system of administration. He was in sole charge of revenues and finance. A *Diwan* functioned not only in the Central government but also in the provincial governments where he occupied a post next in importance to the *Subadar* or provincial governor. The provincial *Diwan* was appointed directly by the Emperor to whom alone he was responsible. The provincial *Diwan* thus was a check on the provincial governor.

Diwani Adalat—court of civil justice.

Diwan-i—was a term used in the sense of a department. Thus:

Diwan-i-'Am or the Emperor's office.

Diwan-i-Amir Kohi or Department of Agriculture.

Diwan-i-'Arz or Military Department.

Diwan-i-Bandagan or the Department of slaves.

Diwan-i-Insha or Department of Correspondence.

Diwan-i-Istihqaq or Department of Pensions.

Diwan-i-Khairat or Department of charity.

Diwan-i-Khas or Hall of Private audience.

Diwan-i-Mustakhraj or Department of collection of arrears due from collectors.

Diwan-i-Qazi-i-Mamalik or Department of Justice, Intelligence and Posts.

Diwan-i-Risalat or the Department of appeals.

Diwan-i-Riyasat or the Department of the superintendent of markets.

These terms suggest that some sort of a departmental arrangement existed in the administrative system set up by the emperors of Delhi.

Diwani of Bengal—was granted by Emperor Shah Alam II in 1765 to the East India Company in consideration of the cession to him of Allahabad and the surrounding area by the East India Company who had secured the territories from the Nawab of Oudh after the latter's defeat in the battle of Buxar in 1764. It meant that the East India Company got the right of collecting revenue due to the Mughul Emperor from Bengal, Bihar and Orissa on condition of paying to the Emperor Shah Alam an annual revenue of twenty-six lakhs of rupees and to pay to the Nawab of Murshidabad fifty-three lakhs (later on reduced to thirty-two lakhs) of rupees yearly for the expense of the general administration of the province and to keep the balance to their gain. The grant of the *Diwani* gave to the Company for the first time a legal status in the administration of the province which they had practically acquired as the result of a conspiracy leading to their victory in the battle of Plassey in 1757. The East India Company, however, did not "stand forth as the *Diwan*" and take up actually the task of collecting the revenue of the province until 1772. By taking up the task of collection of revenue the East India Company practically took up the province's civil administration as it was too closely connected with revenue to be treated separately. Though the East India Company had become the *de facto* rulers of Bengal after the battle of Plassey in 1757 their legal status in Bengal continued, strictly speaking, to be that of the *Diwan* until the assumption of the title of the Empress of India by Queen Victoria in 1877.

Doabs, the—between the Ganges and the Jamuna in north India and between the Krishna and the Tungabhadra in south India, are two of the most fertile regions in India. Their possession had always been coveted by the neighbouring princes. The sultans of Delhi were always most eager to enforce their authority over the doab between the Ganges and Jamuna which generally formed a part of the dominions of the sovereign ruling with Delhi as his capital. The Marathas led by Sindhia were for a short time in possession of it, but it passed under the control of the British Indian Government in 1803. The doab between the Krishna and Tungabhadra, known as the Raichur doab, formed throughout the existence of the Bahmani kingdom a bone of serious contention between it and the Hindu kingdom of Vijaya-nagar. The Raichur doab was strengthened by the two forts of Raichur and Mudgal. After the destruction of the city of Vijaya-nagar in 1565 the Raichur doab passed into the possession of the sultan of Bijapur from whom it passed to the Mughul emperors and from them to the Indo-British Government.

Doctrine of Lapse, the—was the principle that in dependent states or in those which owed their existence to the British power the sovereignty 'lapsed' or passed back to the supreme power, that is to say, to the Indo-British Government, if and when such a state lacked a natural heir and no right of adoption was to be recognised. In other words, according to this principle an adopted son could inherit the personal properties of his adoptive father, but not the sovereignty over his state. The principle was first enunciated in 1834, but it was Lord Dalhousie (*q.v.*) who during his administration (1848-56) applied it with the utmost rigour, ignoring the alarm and commotion that it caused amongst the Indian Hindu princes with whom, on the failure of a natural heir, the adoption of a son was a religious requirement. By the application of this doctrine of lapse Dalhousie annexed to the British Indian Empire the states of Satara in 1848, Jaitpur and Sambalpur in 1849, Baghat in 1850, Udaipur in 1852, Jhansi in 1855 and Nagpur in 1854 and sold the jewels and furniture of the Nagpur Raj in a public auction. He also wanted to annex the Rajput state of Karauli. The Home Government annulled the annexation of Udaipur in the Central Provinces and of Baghat which was a cis-Sutlej state and disallowed the proposed annexation of Karauli. The annexation of Satara and Nagpur greatly promoted the imperial interests of the Indo-British Government by removing all semi-independent territories on the direct routes between Calcutta and Bombay as well as between Madras and Bombay. But these annexations filled the minds of the Indian princes with great anxiety as to the security of their hold on their states and contributed much to the commotion that burst into the Sepoy Mutiny of 1857.

Dominion status—was first demanded by the Indian National Congress in 1908. At that time it meant no more than the right of self-government in internal affairs as was enjoyed by the dominion of Canada under the British Crown. But the Indo-British Government would not concede the demand and twenty-one valuable years were missed until on October 31, 1929, Lord Irwin, the Viceroy, made an announcement that the natural issue of the constitutional progress in India was the attainment of dominion status. But as no attempt was made to define clearly the content of the 'dominion status', thus promised, the Indian National Congress refused to be satisfied with this vague and late announcement and proceeded towards the end of the year at its session at Lahore to declare that independence was the goal of Indian nationalism. Thus the tragedy of the Indo-British relations continued. A concession which, if made 20 years earlier, would have satisfied the Indian aspirations came too late to be accepted by a resurgent India pulsating with the kaleidoscopic changes which were taking place in the international situation on account of World War II. Even then nothing was done to hasten the implementation of the promised 'dominion status' for six long years and when at last it took shape in the Government of India Act, 1935, it fell short of 'dominion status' in several important respects. Thus, there was to be dyarchy at the centre depriving the elected legislature of all control over important departments like foreign affairs and defence. Secondly, the Act provided for several safeguards vesting in the Viceroy large autocratic powers. Thirdly, the legislation passed by the Indian legislature continued to be subject to the approval of the Crown of England which was empowered to refuse such approval. These restrictions showed that the 'dominion status' as envisaged by the Act of 1935 was to be of a brand, distinct from, and inferior

to, its definition in the Statute of Westminister, 1931, which recognised the sovereignty of a Dominion in its internal affairs and
gave it full autonomy in external affairs with unfettered powers
to sign treaties with foreign countries. This implied the rights of
neutrality and secession for each dominion. As none of these
important rights associated with dominion status was conceded
to India by the Government of India Act, 1935 it failed to satisfy
the Indian nationalist demand. The Act further so developed
and applied the principle of communal respresentation that a
division of India into a Hindu Hindusthan and a Muslim
Pakistan was clearly in the offing. In this situation the re-
iteration of the offer for dominion status made by Sir Stafford
Cripps on March 11, 1942, failed to raise enthusiasm amongst
the Indian nationalists. At last under the pressure of the losses in
men and resources inflicted on Great Britain in the course of the
Second World War as well as the strength of the nationalist
demand Great Britain had to concede independence to India
and Pakistan as full-fledged dominions as defined in the Statute of
Westminister, 1931. This position was further clarified in 1949
when India was recognised as a sovereign independent Republic
which preferred, on account of her own reasons, to continue as a
member of the Commonwealth of Nations, committed to the
policy of pursuing peace, liberty and progress of which the
sovereign of England was a symbolical head with full option to
secede, if and when India may consider such secession as necessary for her own interests. (Joshi. G. N., *Constn. of India*, 1956)

Donabew, the battle of—was fought in April, 1824, during the
First Burmese War (*q.v.*) between the English and the Burmans.
In this battle the Burmese General Bandula was defeated and
killed.

Dorasamudra (or Dvarasamudra)—modern Halebid, was the
capital of the Hoysala kingdom founded in the modern Mysore
area by Bittiga (*q.v.*), later on famous as Vishnuvardhana in
about A.D. 1111-41. It became the centre of Vaishnava religion
as preached by Ramanuja who enjoyed the royal patronage of
Vishnuvardhana who built many temples including one specially
magnificent temple dedicated to Vishnu at Dorasumudra which
developed a distinct style of art and sculpture. At one time the
sway of Dorasamudra extended up to Devagiri (*q.v.*), but the
city was sacked and destroyed by a Muslim force sent by Sultan
Muhammad Tughluq in 1326.

Dorijieff—a Mongolian and by birth a Russian subject, rose high
in the service of the Grand Lama in Tibet. Between 1898 and

1901 he made several visits to Russia and in 1901 was even received in audience by the Russian Tsar. The ostensible object of his repeated visits was the collection of subscriptions from the Russian Buddhists for Buddhist temples in Tibet. Though the Russian Government assured the British ambassador in St. Petersburg that Dorijieff's visits had no political significance yet the Government of India, then administered by the prancing Pro-Consul Lord Curzon, dished up various charges against the Government of Tibet and sent into that country an expedition led by Sir Francis Younghusband (*q.v.*) in 1904.

Dost Ali—was the Nawab of the Carnatic which province be held under the suzerainty of the Nizam of Hyderabad. In 1743 the Carnatic was invaded by the Marathas who defeated and killed Dost Ali and carried away as a captive his son-in-law, Chanda Shaheb (*q.v.*), who was destined to play an important role in the later history of the Carnatic.

Dost Muhammad Khan—was the Amir of Afghanistan (1826-63). In 1836 when Herat was being threatened with an invasion by Persia backed by Russia Amir Dost Muhammad sought an alliance with the British Indian Government on condition that he should be helped by the British Indian Government to recover Peshawar which had been recently seized by Ranjit Singh, the king of the Panjab. As the British Indian Government refused to enter into an alliance with the Amir on such a condition the Amir received in his court a Russian embassy in 1837. This was bitterly resented by Lord Auckland (*q.v.*), the Governor-General of India, and led him to embark on a policy which culminated in the First Anglo-Afghan War .(*q.v.*) (1838-42). During the course of the War Dost Muhammad surrendered himself in 1840 and was sent as a prisoner to Calcutta. But by 1842 the British Indian army had to evacuate Afghanistan after losing 20,000 lives and wasting fifteen crores of rupees. Dost Muhammad was soon afterwards released and, making his way back into Afghanistan, he re-established himself there as the Amir and ruled the country as an independent king until his death in 1863. In 1855 and in 1857 he entered into two treaties of alliance with the British Indian Government and remained true to these engagements even during the days of the Sepoy Mutiny (1857-58) and thus rendered great indirect assistance to the British Indian Government in suppressing the Mutiny.

Drake, Roger—was the Governor of the East India Company's Fort in Calcutta in June, 1756, when Calcutta was invaded by Nawab Siraj-ud-daula (*q.v.*). Without making any serious effort for defending the Fort, Drake, along with the English women and children, fled on board a ship waiting on the river and sailed downstream leaving the garrison to its fate. Drake was a most incompetent person, but lucky enough to be restored to his post when Calcutta was recovered by Watson and Clive in January 1757. Thereafter he sank into oblivion.

Draupadi—the daughter of the king of Panchala, was won by Arjuna, the third Pandava brother, by dint of his superior skill in archery. She was eventually married to all the five Pandava brothers and is the heroine of the great epic the *Mahabharata*.

Dravida—is the older name for the modern Tamil land, that is to say, southern India from near Madras in the north to Cape Comorin in the south.

Dravidians, the—are believed by some authorities to have been one of the earliest races inhabiting all over India, south as well as north. They gradually migrated from north India to Mesopotamia leaving on their route small bodies, like the Brahuis in Baluchistan, who still speak a Dravidian dialect. The Dravidians were pressed out of northern India by the Aryans who brought with them an inferior culture and civilisation, but who proved to be better warriors and had succeeded in establishing their authority over northern India. The Dravidians retained their predominance in south India for long centuries after the Aryanisation of north India and the Dravidians are still represented by the peoples who speak Tamil, Telegu, Malayalam and Kanarese which languages, unlike those spoken in north India, do not owe their origin to Sanskrit, the language of the Aryans. In course of time there followed a mingling of Dravidian and Aryan blood and at the present time the distinction between the two races has been entirely obliterated and there has been a mutual give and take between the cultures, cilivisations and religions of the two peoples. Dravidian gods and goddesses have entered into the Vedic pantheon and receive equal veneration with the latter. (Haddon, *Races of Man*)

Dual system, the, of Clive—was established in Bengal, Bihar and Orissa as the result of the treaty of Allahabad (*q.v.*) (1765) which formally brought to an end the war between the East India Company on one side and Nawab Mir Kasim of Bengal, Nawab Shuja-ud-daula of Oudh and Emperor Shah Alam II on the other. By this treaty the Emperor conferred upon the East India Company the *Diwani* (*q.v.*) i.e. the post of the *Diwan* or Finance Minister and Collector of Revenue of Bengal while Mir Jafar's son continued to be the Nawab of Bengal. The Company undertook to collect from the province the revenue due to the Emperor on condition of paying to the Emperor an annual revenue of 26 lakhs of rupees, to the Nawab of Bengal a sum of 52 lakhs of rupees yearly to meet the cost of the administration and to keep the balance to their own gain. Thus was inaugurated in the province of Bengal, Bihar and Orissa a dual or double system of government according to which the Company became responsible for the collection of the revenue and the Nawab of Bengal for its civil and criminal administration, both under the Mughul Emperor who became entitled to a revenue from a province which had been lost to the Empire for some years past. The Dual System regularised to a certain extent the anomalous position of the Company in the province, but it did nothing to improve the administration. On the other hand, by taking away the control of finance from the Nawab and leaving him saddled with the duty of maintaining peace and order and of checking the grabbing tendency of the Company's officers who were really his masters, it prepared the way for a complete break-down of the administrative machinery in the province and left the common man a helpless prey to the rapacity of the Company's as well as of the Nawab's officials. This led to the outbreak of the terrible famine of 1769-70 which carried off one-third of the population of the province. This tragedy, more than any other circumstance, exposed the defects of the dual system of government which was abolished in 1772.

Duff, Revd. Alexander—a Scottish Presbyterian missionary was in Calcutta from 1830 to 1863. He was sent by the Church of Scotland presumably in pursuance to a request made to it by Raja Ram Mohan Roy in 1823 for sending out to India competent teachers to spread English education. He was warmly welcomed by the Raja and it was with his help that he started an English School known as the General Assembly's Institution soon after his arrival in Calcutta in 1830. In course of time the school developed into a college which for some years was known as the Duff College and is now known as the Scottish Churches College. Dr. Duff was a learned missionary who did much to promote education and social reform in Bengal. He played an important part in persuading the Government to establish Universities in India and was one of the earliest Members of the administrative body of the Calcutta University. He was also for several years from 1859 the President of the Bethune Society, a cultural organisation where Europeans and Indians met and contributed much to the promotion of culture and mutual respect among them. But Dr. Duff was above all a Christian missionary, determined to spread Christianity amongst the people of Bengal and in his work, *India and Indian Missions*, he went to the length of declaring that "of all the systems of false religion ever fabricated by the perverse ingenuity of fallen man, Hinduism is surely the most stupendous". Naturally enough such an attack raised bitter criticisms from Indian scholars, especially from the Brahmas whom Dr. Duff considered rather strong opponents. The Brahmas led by Devendranath Tagore and later on by Kesabchandra Sen proved more than a match for the Christian missionary in Dr. Duff who succeeded in making very few converts amongst the educated section of the people of Bengal and must have been a disappointed man when he finally left Bengal in 1863. He died in 1878. (Smith, George, *Life of Alexander Duff*)

Dufferin, Frederick Temple Hamilton-Temple Blackwood, Marquis of—was the Viceroy and Governor-General of India from 1884 to 1888 when he voluntarily retired. His administration was generally speaking peaceful, though it saw the Third Burmese War (*q.v.*) (1885-86) which led to the annexation of upper Burma to the British Indian Empire. Henceforth 'Ava' was added to Dufferin in his title. A war with Russia was threatened over the occupation by the Russians of Panjdeh on the Russo-Afghan frontier, but was avoided by the calmness of Amir Abdur Rahman (*q.v.*) (1880-1901) and the moderation and sanity of Lord Dufferin. It was during his administration that the Bengal Tenancy Act of 1885 was passed giving the ryot greater security of tenure at judicial rents and restricted the landlord's right of eviction. Similar land acts were also passed for the benefit of ryots in Oudh as well as the Panjab. The most outstanding internal event in Lord Dufferin's administration was, however, the holding of the first session of the Indian National Congress in Bombay in 1885. The significance of this event could not be fully appreciated at the time, but it was this organisation which won the independence of India only sixty-two years later in 1947 and has since been running the administration of the Republic of India. (Lyall, Sir Alfred, *Life of Marquis of Dufferin and Ava*)

Dufferin, Lady Harriet Georgiana—was married to Lord Dufferin in 1862. When in India as the Vicereine she established the National Association for supplying female medical aid according to Western medical science to the women of India. The

Association started the Countess of Dufferin Fund out of which the Lady Dufferin Hospital was later on established in Calcutta.

Dumas, General—was the governor of the French possession at Pondicherry and greatly promoted its development. He was succeeded in 1744 by Dupleix whose greater fame eclipsed the achievement of Dumas.

Duncan, Jonathan (1756-1811)—came to India in the East India Company's service in 1772. He became the Resident and Superintendent at Benares in 1778 where he improved the administration and suppressed infanticide. Later on, as Governor of Bombay from 1795 to 1811 he suppressed infanticide in Kathiawar as well. He thus took the initiative in effecting an important social reform. As the Governor of Bombay he played a prominent part in the Fourth Mysore War (*q.v.*) (1799), in the Second Maratha War (*q.v.*) (1803-05), in organising Baird's expedition to Egypt in 1801 and in the pacification of Gujarat and Kathiawar. He was, as his epitaph records,' a good man and just'.

Dundas, Henry—was the first President of the Board of Control (*q.v.*) set up by Pitt's India Act of 1784. In 1786 he defended in Parliament the Rohilla War fought by Warren Hastings, but later on supported his impeachment, especially in connection with the affairs of Chait Singh and the Begums of Oudh. In 1802 Henry Dundas was elevated to the peerage and became the first Lord Melville, but in 1806 he was himself impeached on a charge of malversation, was found guilty of negligence but was acquitted. As the President of the Board of Control he showed great ability and administrative skill which enabled him to turn the Board practically into a Government Department and to make the President the virtual Minister to the British Government in respect of India.

Dupleix, Joseph Francois—came out to India in the commercial service of the French East India Company and rose to be the Governor of Chandernagore in 1731. He was promoted to be the Governor-General at Pondicherry in 1741 and continued in that position until his recall in 1754. Dupleix was no soldier, but he was a politician and statesman who divined, when none else could do so, that a change in the balance of political forces was taking place in south India in the early forties of the eighteenth century and appreciated the inherent weakness of the political system in south India in his time and the consequent decisive importance that a tiny European force with long-range guns, quick-firing muskets and steady soldiers could acquire in south Indian politics. At that time France was at war with England and Dupleix's first aim was to cripple the power of the English in India by capturing Madras. With this object in view he financed the French Admiral, La Bourdonnais, to fit up the fleet which enabled him to capture Madras from the English in September, 1746. But La Bourdonnais wanted to make a huge personal profit by returning Madras to the English and it took all the skill and authority of Dupleix to prevent La Bourdonnais from completing this transaction until at last the arrival of the monsoons in October obliged La Bourdonnais to withdraw with his fleet to the Isles of France. Dupleix took advantage of his absence to seize Madras. He then made an attempt to take the neighbouring English fort of St. David, but failed. He had, however, important and significant success elsewhere. A large army sent by Nawab Anwar-ud-din of the Carnatic to recover Madras from the French was twice defeated by a much smaller Indo-French army at the battles of Kaveripack and St. Thome. The Anglo-French war in Europe was, however, brought to a close in 1748 by the treaty of Aix-la-Chapelle by the terms of which Madras had to be restored to the English and Dupleix found himself deprived of the prize for which he had worked so hard. But the war had not been fought without any gain. It had shown the superiority of a small Indo-French army, trained and armed after the European manner, over much larger Indian armies. Dupleix now proceeded to utilise this knowledge by interfering in the internal affairs of the south Indian states which, he felt, looked outwardly magnificent and strong but were really weak on account of internal dissensions and military inefficiency. So he availed himself of the disputed succession at Hyderabad that arose on the death of the Nizam in 1748, and took up the cause of his grandson Muzaffar Jang against the Nizam's son, Nasir Jang. At the same time he also backed the claims of Chanda Shaheb to the throne of the Carnatic against the reigning Nawab, Anwar-ud-din. On this occasion also success favoured Dupleix in the beginning. Nawab Anwar-ud-din was defeated and killed in the battle of Ambur in 1749, and his son Muhammad Ali was obliged to flee to Trichinopoly where he was soon besieged by the combined army of Chanda Shaheb and the French. Soon afterwards Nasir Jang was also killed (1750) and Muzaffar Jang, the *protégé* of the French, proceeded to Hyderabad with a French army led by General Bussy and was installed as the Nizam. Dupleix was appointed by the grateful new Nizam as the Governor of all the Mughul territories south of the Krishna. The new Nizam also ceded to the French territories near Pondicherry as well as on the Orissa coast including the port of Masulipatam. Dupleix thus appeared to have nearly realised his dream of creating a French empire in India. But fortune now turned against him and the incompetence of the French generals on whom he had to depend also contributed to the failure of his scheme. First, the siege of Trichinopoly was suffered to drag on until the English in Madras could send help there. Secondly, an Anglo-Indian army led by Robert Clive (q.v.) who had so long been a clerk in Madras but now took up a military career, surprised the fort at Arcot, the capital of the Carnatic, held it against superior forces for fifty days and then came out to receive large relieving forces with whose aid he defeated the armies of Chanda Shaheb who was captured and killed. About this time Nizam Muzaffar Jang died, but his successor Salabat Jang remained attached to Dupleix and the French cause. In the circumstances, Dupleix with unrelenting steadfastness continued his exertions to capture Trichinopoly. He succeeded in securing the neutrality of the Raja of Tanjore and the active support of the Maratha leader Morari Rao as well as of the ruler of Mysore to his side and renewed the siege of Trichinopoly on December 31, 1752. The siege continued throughout 1753 and the first half of 1754. In the midst of this campaign the French Government who had never understood the full implications of Dupleix's policy and were greatly worried over the cost it had involved, recalled Dupleix who had to make over charge to the new Governor-General, Godehu on August, 1, 1754. Godehu soon opened negotiations with the English with whom a treaty was concluded in 1755 by which both parties agreed to desist from interference in the affairs of the Indian rulers and to retain the territories which each of the two powers occupied at that time. Thus Dupleix's policy was undone, except in the court of the Nizam where the French influence still continued to be upheld by General Bussy who had under him an Indo-French army at the Nizam's capital at Hyderabad. Dupleix returned to France where he died in 1763 in comparative poverty. In spite of his final failure Dupleix is a striking and brilliant figure in Indian history. The English made use of and benefited by his daring and imaginative political conceptions and though Dupleix's dream of a Franco-Indian empire was not achieved, an Anglo-Indian Empire was built up largely on the ruins of the vision of Dupleix. (Cultru, P., *Dupleix;* Dodwell, H. H., *Dupleix and Clive*)

Durand Line—is the boundary line drawn up in 1893 by the Afghan Boundary Commission of which Sir Mortimer Durand (*q.v.*) was the chief. It divided the tribal region lying between Afghanistan and the British Indian Empire into two zones—the northern to be controlled by Afghanistan and the southern by the British Indian Government. The British zone contained the Afridis of the Khyber region, the Mahsuds, the Waziris, the Swat tribes and the chiefships of Chitral and Gilgit.

Durand, Sir Henry Mortimer—entered the Indian Civil Service in 1873, at the age of 23. He was the son of Sir Henry Marian Durand who came out to India as an officer in the Bengal Engineers and rose to be Governor of the Panjab in 1870, but died as the result of an accident in 1871. Sir Henry Mortimer Durand was the political Secretary to Sir Frederick Roberts (*q.v.*) in the Kabul campaign of 1879 and rose to be the Foreign Secretary to the Government of India in 1884. He held this post till 1894 and in this capacity he conducted a mission to the Amir Abdur Rahman (*q.v.*) of Afghanistan in 1893. He showed great ability and skill in the negotiations which led to the appointment of a boundary commission under his own chairmanship. This commission drew up the famous Durand Line (*q.v.*) to mark the Indo-Afghan boundaries. Pakistan still insists on the maintenance of this Durand Line as marking the boundary between herself and Afghanistan.

Durgadas—was a famous leader of the Rathors of Marwar. He was a son of Askaran, minister of Raja Jaswant Singh of Marwar. The Raja died in the service of the Mughul Emperor at Jamrud in Afghanistan on December 10, 1678. At the time of his death he left no sons, but two months later two posthumous sons were born to him. One of them died soon after his birth, but the other named Ajit Singh survived and was the Raja's legal heir. He was brought along with his mother to Delhi by the chief adherents of his late father. Durgadas was the most prominent of these Rathor leaders who requested Emperor Aurangzeb to recognise the infant Ajit Singh as the heir and successor to Raja Jaswant Singh on the throne of Marwar. But Emperor Aurangzeb who planned to take advantage of the situation for bringing Marwar under his direct rule, refused to do so unless Ajit Singh was converted to Islam. A Mughul force was sent by the Emperor's orders to the residence of the widowed Ranies with whom Ajit Singh was living, to seize them. It was the courage and skill of Durgadas that frustrated this sinister effort of the Emperor. While a band of Rathor soldiers rushed upon the imperial troops Durgadas led the Ranies and the infant by forced rides to safety in Jodhpur. Durgadas then succeeded in organising an alliance with the Rana of Mewar against the invading army sent by Aurangzeb. In the war that now followed in 1680 Durgadas led the Rathors with great skill and valour and the war in the course of which Aurangzeb's son, Prince Akbar, defected to the Rajputs, might have taken a very serious turn against the Mughuls but for the fact that the clever Aurangzeb succeeded by a ruse to separate the Rajputs from Prince Akbar. When the fraud was detected Durgadas very chivalrously escorted Prince Akbar through Khandesh and Baglana to the court of the Maratha king, Shambhuji; but he could not make that indolent Maratha king rise to the occasion and lead a joint Rajput-Maratha-Muslim expedition against Aurangzeb. Durgadas then came back to Marwar in 1687 and though Mewar had made peace with the Mughul Emperor, he conducted, on behalf of Marwar, a prolonged war with the Mughuls who were ultimately forced to recognise Ajit Singh as the Rana of Marwar in 1709.

Durgavati, Rani—of Gondwana, was one of the most illustrious female rulers in the history of India. She was a daughter of Kirat Rai, the Chandella king of Mahoba and Kalanjar who was killed when Sher Shah besieged the fort of Kalanjar in 1545. Durgavati was married to Raja Dalpat Sa of Garha Mandala (Gondwana) in about 1545 but became a widow with a minor son, named Bir Narayan. She carried on the administration of the kingdom on behalf of her minor son and maintained its integrity against both Baj Bahadur of Malwa and the Afghans of Bengal. In 1564 Akbar sent his general Asaf Khan to make an entirely unprovoked invasion of Rani Durgavati's kingdom. The Rani, accompanied by her son Bir Narayan, opposed the Mughul army of 50,000 men and fought with them a two days' battle at Narhi near the capital. On the second day of the battle her son was wounded and had to be escorted out of the battle-field to safety by a body of the Rani's troops. The withdrawal of this escort so weakened the Rani's army that it was soon overpowered. The Rani herself was wounded by two arrows, stabbed herself to death and thus escaped the disgrace of capture. Her death was immediately followed by the advance of the Mughuls upon her capital at Chauragarh where her gallant son, Bir Narayan, though wounded, offered a stout resistance, but was defeated and killed in battle and the kingdom passed under the control of Akbar. The rich spoils in the form of jewels, gold and silver, coined and uncoined, and one thousand elephants taken by Asaf Khan, the victorious Mughul general, bore testimony to the efficiency of Rani Durgavati as a ruler.

Durjan Sal—occupied the throne of Bharatpur in 1824 in opposition to the claims of the minor son of the lately deceased Raja who was backed by the Indo-British Government. The latter refused to recognise the claim of Durjan Sal and an expedition sent under the command of Lord Combermere easily stormed the fort of Bharatpur in January 1826. The vanquished Durjan Sal was deported.

Durlabha, Rai—was a treacherous general of Nawab Siraj-ud-daula (*q.v.*) of Bengal who, along with Mir Jafar (*q.v.*), joined in a conspiracy with the English by a treaty on June 10, 1757, against his own master, the Nawab, and contributed to his defeat at the battle of Plassey (June 23, 1757) by refraining from taking any part in the fighting.

Durlabhavardhana—founded the Karkota dynasty of kings in Kashmir in the seventh century A.D. His dynasty ruled over Kashmir till A.D. 855 when it was supplanted by the Utpala dynasty. The more famous kings of the dynasty founded by Durlabharvardhana were Lalitaditya (*q.v.*) and Jayapida Vinayaditya (*q.v.*).

Durrani—is the name by which the Abdali clan to which Ahmed Shah, king of Afghanistan (1747-73) belonged, came to be known after the title of *Durr-i-Durran* (the pearl of the age) which Abdali assumed on his succession to the throne of Afghanistan after the assassination of Nadir Shah.

Duryodhana—was the eldest of the Kaurava brothers who fought against the Pandavas (*q.v.*) a great battle, as described in the famous Indian epic, the *Mahabharata*.

Dutch, the, East India Company—*see* Company, the Dutch East India.

Dutt, Narendranath—*See* Swami Vivekananda.

Dutt, Ramesh Chandra—born in 1848, belonged to the Dutt family of Rambagan in Calcutta. He played a very important role in the Indianisation of the Civil Service and in promoting the causes of social reforms and nationalism in India. He passed, along with Surendranath Banerjee and Behari Lal Gupta, the Indian Civil Service Examination held in London in 1869 and joined the Indian Civil Service in 1871. His promotion to higher office was long delayed on account of his Indian nationality and it was not till 1894 that he was appointed to be the Commissioner of a Division (Orissa). Three years later he retired. Later on he served as the *Diwan* in the Gaekwaḍ's state of Baroda and introduced there many reforms for modernising and liberalising the administration of the state. He also took a prominent part in the Indian national movement and presided over the session of the Indian National Congress held at Lucknow in 1899. He wrote in Bengali a series of historical and social novels like *Maharastra Jivan Pravat, Rajput Jivan Sandhya, Vanga Vijeta, Madhavi Kankan,* and *Samsar* with the object of promoting the spirit of Indian nationalism and the cause of social reform. He also translated the *Rig-Veda* in Bengali and the *Ramayana* and the *Mahabharata* in English verse. His *Civilisation in Ancient India* was a pioneer work on the subject and his *Economic History of British India* (1757-1900) in two volumes was the first authoritative and scholarly exposition of the economic exploitation of India under British rule. (Dutt, A., *Life of Ramesh Chandra Dutt*).

Dyarchy—is a feature of the constitutional arrangement of a country. It was first suggested by Lionel Curtis, for many years the editor of the *Round Table*, and was incorporated in the Government of India Act, 1919 in respect of the administrative set-up in the British Indian provinces. According to this dyarchical system certain departments like education, local self-government, public health, public works, agriculture and co-operative societies were 'transferred' for administration to Ministers who were to be elected members of the provincial legislatures and to which they were to be responsible, while the departments of land revenue, law, justice, the police, irrigation, labour and finance were reserved for administration by Executive Councillors responsible to the Provincial governors but not to the legislatures. This dyarchical system was meant to teach the Indians the art of administration by stages and it was certainly a reflection on their capacity to rule themselves. Moreover, the transferred departments were all spending branches of the administration while the reserved departments were the revenue-making ones. Such an allocation naturally put the Ministers at a great disadvantage in comparison with the Councillors whose co-operation became essential for them. In fact the whole system smacked of a probationary nature and never became popular with the Indians. But the British Government found it a very convenient method of keeping the control of the more important departments in the hands of Councillors appointed by and responsible only to the

British Government. So in spite of its unpopularity and the difficulty of working it, the principle of dyarchy was subsequently incorporated in the Government of India Act, 1935, and extended to the Central Executive. But that Act was never fully implemented and dyarchy at the centre was not enforced. It was buried when independent India drew up her own constitution.

Dyer, General—was a military officer in the service of the Indo-British Government. He was stationed at Amritsar in the Panjab in April, 1919. Early that year a severely repressive law, popularly known as the Rowlatt Act, was passed by the British Indian Government against the votes of all the non-official members of the Imperial Legislative Council. Such flagrant and utter disregard for Indian public opinion roused the greatest indignation amongst the children of the soil and demonstrations against the new repressive measure took place in Delhi, Gujarat and the Panjab. On April 10 the people of Amritsar broke into a violent anti-British demonstration in the course of which four Europeans were killed, a lady missionary was severely beaten and some banks and Government buildings were burnt. The Panjab Government at once decided on revengeful repression, issued a proclamation prohibiting all public meetings at Amritsar and handed over the control of the city to the military under General Dyer. But a large number of unarmed Indians assembled in a semi-enclosed space known as the Jallianwalla Bagh. It had only one entrance and no exit. Hearing of this assemblage General Dyer, the officer in command of the military who had taken over the control of the city, marched with a company of ninety well-armed soldiers to the Bagh, occupied with his troops the only exit from it and without giving any warning to the assembled people who were all unarmed and amongst whom there were many women and children, ordered his soldiers to shoot straight and to shoot to kill. The firing continued for ten minutes killing, according to the official report, 379 persons and wounding 1208. No step was taken to supply hospital facilities or any treatment to the dying and the wounded and General Dyer marched back to his headquarters with the conviction that he had done a good day's work. Even then the General did not consider that enough had been done for avenging the death of some Europeans. He, therefore, proceeded to impose martial law on the city, to resort to severe punitive measures and to issue humiliating orders like public flogging and requiring Indians who happened to pass by the place, where the European lady missionary had been maltreated, to crawl along the road. All these measures formed a sickening demonstration of brute force by the threat of which Englishmen like General Dyer thought of keeping down the Indians. The whole country rang in protest. Rabindranath Tagore renounced in disgust and contempt the knighthood that the British Government had conferred on him. But the British Indian Government at first paid no heed to this general protest by the Indians and the Lieutenant-Governor of the Panjab and the higher military authorities all approved of Dyer's action and even conferred on him a higher command in Afghanistan. But there were still some Englishmen in England who were horrified at the enormity of General Dyer's crime. Mr. Asquith described the incident as "one of the worst outrages in the whole of our history". Pressed by such enlightened public opinion in England as well as by the universal demand from the Indians the Government of India appointed in October, 1919 a Committee of Enquiry under the chairmanship of Lord Hunter, a Scottish Judge, to hold an enquiry into the conduct of General Dyer at Jallianwalla Bagh. The Committee reported adversely on General Dyer's action. The Government approved of the Report, censured General Dyer and required him to resign. But General Dyer had many admirers amongst the aggressive British people who soon raised a handsome subscription on his behalf and gave the amount to him. (*Report of Hunter's Committee;* Sitaramaya, P. *Hist. of the Ind. Nat. Congress,* Vol. I, pp. 165 ff.)

E

East India College at Haileybury—was established in 1805 by the East India Company for giving a training to the young persons who were given nomination by the Company for entering as cadets in the Company's Civil Service in India. Every young recruit was required to spend two years at the East India College at Haileybury where his general education was continued and increased and where he was to learn something of Indian languages, laws and history. On completion of the course of two years' studies the young cadets were sent to India for entering into their work as Civil Servants. The cadets were all nominated young persons and the East India College aimed not at screening them but at adding to their knowledge as much as they were capable of assimilation. The College developed amongst its students a spirit of comradeship and emulation, but did not add much to their intellectual attainments. The College functioned for fifty years (1805-55) and was abolished soon after the introduction of the competitive system for appointment to the Indian Civil Service. (Roy, N. C., *Civil Service*)

East India Company—*see* Company.

East Indies, the Dutch—comprised the Spice Islands, Java and the Moluccas. The Dutch established trading centres there early in the seventeenth century and practically expelled the English traders who went to that region by the massacre of the English at Amboyna in 1623. The Dutch established their headquarters at Batavia in Java and from there ruled over a large part of the Malay Archipelago which came to be known as the Dutch East Indies. In 1807 when Lord Minto I assumed the Governor-Generalship, the Dutch East Indies were practically under the control of Napoleon who dominated Holland in Europe. Lord Minto, therefore, decided to capture the Dutch East Indies. Careful preparations were made. Amboyna and the Spice Islands were conquered in 1810 and next year a formidable fleet, carrying 12,000 troops under Sir Samuel Auchmuty as Commander-in-Chief, first assembled in Malacca. Lord Minto himself accompanied the expedition which easily occupied Batavia and then, after a bloody encounter, stormed the neighbouring fort of Cornelis from the French General Jansens, whom Napoleon had placed in charge of the fort. As a result of this victory the whole of the Dutch East Indies passed under British control. Lord Minto entrusted the administration of the newly acquired islands to Mr. (later on Sir) Stamford Raffles and returned to India. But on the restoration of peace in Europe in 1815 the Dutch East Indies were restored to Holland in 1816. They now constitute the independent republic of Eastern Indonesia.

Eastern Bengal—comprising the fifteen districts contained in the three Divisions of Dacca, Rajshahi and Chittagong, was separated from the rest of Bengal and joined with Assam by Lord Curzon, the Viceroy, in 1905 and formed into the new province of Eastern Bengal and Assam. Lord Curzon justified the measure on the ground of administrative necessity, but the people of Bengal, specially the Hindus considered it as amounting to a partition of their province for the deliberate purpose of weakening and strangling the growing nationalism of the renascent Bengalee people. Curzon remained adamant in his resolution. Reasoned protests grew into heated popular agitation under the leadership of Surendranath Banerjee (*q.v.*); monster meetings were held and to put pressure on England foreign goods, particularly cloth, were boycotted and the *Swadeshi* movement was started. As popular protests still continued to be ignored ardent spirits amongst the Bengalees resorted to acts of terrorism. The Government replied by a policy of severe repression on the one hand and on the other by a policy of divide and rule by showing definite inclination to support the Muhammadans who formed a majority in Eastern Bengal as against the Hindus who formed a minority there. But nothing availed, and at last in 1912 the partition was revoked and the fifteen districts of Eastern Bengal were re-joined with the rest of Bengal to form a Governor's province. Assam was formed into a separate Chief Commissionership. Eastern Bengal was again separated from West Bengal after the partition of India in 1947 and is now known as Eastern Pakistan.

Eastern Gangas, the dynasty of—was founded by Rajaraja I, son of Vajrahasta, in the middle of the eleventh century in Kalinga (Orissa) to the north of the delta of the Godavari. The dynasty ruled over Kalinga from the middle of the eleventh century to 1402 when it was overthrown by the Muhammadans. The dynasty comprised fifteen kings, viz. Rajaraja I, Anantavarman Choḍaganga (1078-1142), Kamarnava, Raghava, Rajaraja II, Anangabhima I, Rajaraja III, Anangabhima II, Narasinha I, Bhanudeva I, Narasinha II, Bhanudeva II, Narasinha III, Bhanudeva III and Narasinha IV (1384-1402). The second king, Anantavarma Choḍaganga who built the present temple of Jagannatha at Puri, was the most famous. The Eastern Gangas were great patrons of art and literature and under their patronage Orissa developed a separate school of art and architecture and temples were built on a scale unsurpassed anywhere in India. Politically, however, the Eastern Gangas maintained a selfish existence and failed to take any action against the aggressions of the Muhammadans, first, in Bengal and then on their own frontiers during the sixty years covered by the four immediate successors of king Anantavarman. But later Eastern Ganga kings, who ruled in the thirteenth century, repelled Muhammadan inroads for many years until at last the dynasty was overthrown by the Muhammadans in 1402. (*H.O.*, Vol. I; *D.H.N.I.*, Vol. I; *P.A. & H.I.*, p. 315)

Edward VII—King of England and Emperor of India from 1903 to 1911. His accession was proclaimed in a Durbar held in

Delhi by Lord Curzon, the Viceroy. As the constitutional king of England Edward VII had to act, in matters relating to India, on the advice given to him by the Secretary of State for India. In 1908 on the fiftieth anniversary of the assumption of the Government of India by the Crown of England, Edward VII issued a proclamation to the princes and peoples of India which proudly referred to Great Britain's services to India during the previous fifty years and concluded by promising the extended application of representative institutions in India. This royal proclamation was implemented by the passing in 1909 of the India Councils Act based on reform proposals sponsored by Lord Morley, the Secretary of State for India and Lord Minto II, the Viceroy and Governor-General. Personally King Edward VII was opposed to the 'reforms', but he had the good sense to approve of the policy and action of his responsible Minister.

Edward, Prince of Wales—later on King Edward VIII of England, visited India in 1921. The non-co-operation movement started by Mahatma Gandhi in protest against the unsatisfactory nature of the Government of India Act, 1919, was then in full swing and the Prince of Wales found on his landing at Bombay in November as well as on his subsequent arrival in Calcutta deserted streets and no Indian crowd to receive and acclaim the Prince, as India observed hartals on these occasions and completely boycotted the show. His subsequent reign as King-Emperor was of too short a duration to leave any impression on India, though his abdication in order to marry a thrice divorced woman with whom he fell deeply in love, created a stir in India.

Edwardes, Sir Herbert (1819-68)—came out to India in the Company's service in 1841 and was posted to the Panjab. He was a civilian who saw action at the batttles of Mudki and Sabraon fought in the course of the First Sikh War (*q.v.*) (1845-46). In 1848 he happened to be at Multan when two Britishers, Agnew and Anderson, were murdered and the Sikh governor Mulraj rose in rebellion. He collected a force, defeated Mulraj and his associates in two battles and held out at Multan for several months until it was relieved. His services were recognised by the British Parliament. As the Commissioner in Peshawar he played an important part in the conclusion of two treaties in 1855 and 1857 with Amir Dost Muhammad of Afghanistan which kept the Amir quiet and friendly to the British during the Mutiny of 1857. He retired from India in 1865 for reasons of health. He had literary aptitude, and wrote the *Brahmani Bull's*

letters in India to his cousin John Bull in England early in his career
and later on *A year on the Panjab Frontier* in 1848-49.

Edwards, William—an ambassador from King James I of
England to the court of Emperor Jahangir, arrived at the court
of the Mughul Emperor in 1615, was kindly received but could
get no concession from the Emperor.

Ekanath—a Maratha religious reformer and saint, flourished in
the later part of the sixteenth century. He was born at Paithan
and was a Brahman by caste. He was also a poet. He preached
the doctrine of devotion to God, condemned the caste system
and went to the extent of dining with a low caste Mahar. He
died in 1608. By his poems and exhortations he contributed
much to the rise of the Marathas under the leadership of Shivaji.

Elara—an ancient Chola king, in the second century B.C., is said to
have conquered Ceylon and demonstrated a great sense of
justice in administration.

Elephanta caves—near Bombay, are renowned for a number of
large and remarkably well executed images of Brahmanical
gods.

Elgin, the Earl of, and Kincardine—commonly called
Lord Elgin I, succeeded Lord Canning as Viceroy and Governor-
General in March, 1862, but he died after a short spell of office in
November, 1863, of heart disease and lies buried at Dharmsala
in the Panjab. The only noticeable event that took place during
his brief term of office was a campaign known as 'Umbeyla Campaign' in the north-western frontier to suppress a tribal rising
there.

Elgin, the Earl of, II—the Viceroy and Governor-General of India
from 1894 to 1899 had, unlike his father Elgin I, held no important office before his appointment as the Viceroy in India nor
did he possess any conspicuous personal ability. Moreover, fate
was against him and during his administration India suffered
from two terrible visitations, viz. the outbreak of bubonic plague
in Bombay in 1896 and a severe country-wide famine in
1896-97. The administration of Lord Elgin II failed to take
effective preventive as well as ameliorative measures against
either of the two scourges which carried off, between them,
about a million persons in British India alone. Further, the
outbreak of the plague in Bombay filled the Britishers in India
with so much alarm that the Government tried to enforce, with
the aid of the army, stringent preventive and precautionary
measures which violated even the privacy of Indian homes.
This created great bitterness amongst Indian citizens and

at Poona two British officers, one civilian and the other military, engaged in plague work there, were assassinated. This incident tended to give a political colouring to the whole affair. The administration of Lord Elgin II also exposed how the fiscal policy of India was manipulated in the interests of English manufactures. To avoid an apprehended deficit in the budget in 1895 a duty of five per cent was imposed on all imports with the sole exception of cotton goods which came from Lancashire to India. This invidious favouritism was deeply resented by the Indians who made strong protests. As a result of these protests cotton goods imported into India were included in the tariff in the next budget which, however, imposed a corresponding counter-vailing excise duty on Indian-made cotton textiles. It was thus quite clear that the Indo-British Government was opposed to the development of the cotton textile industry in India. The administration of Lord Elgin II also involved itself in prolonged and expensive campaigns in the north-western frontier as the result of an uncalled for British interference in 1895 on the question of succession to the state of Chitral to the west of Gilgit and south of the Hindukush. British Indian arms ulti-mately triumphed and a military road was constructed from the Indo-Afghan frontier to Chitral. But the Indo-British Government's interference in Chitral affairs was resented by the neighbouring tribes of the Mohmands and the Afridis who rose in revolt against the British in 1897. Two hard fought campaigns had to be undertaken and an army, 35,000 strong, had to be deployed before the tribes could be compelled to submit in 1898. It was the severest test to which the British army in India was subjected since the Mutiny. Earlier during his administration an important military administrative reform was effected by placing the whole of the Indian army under the Commander-in-Chief under whom there were four Lieutenant-Generals for the forces in Bengal, Bombay, Madras and the North-West Provinces with the Panjab. This is the only solid reform effected during the Governor-Generalship of Lord Elgin II.

Ellenborough, Lord—the Governor-General of India (1842-44) in succession to Lord Auckland (*q.v.*), had been the President of the Board of Control three times before his appointment as the Governor-General of India. The Indo-British Government was then engaged in the First Afghan War (*q.v.*) (1839-42). Lord Ellenborough withdrew the British Indian expeditionary force from Afghanistan without letting it appear that the war had virtually ended in British discomfiture. He next sent unjustifiably an expeditionary force into Sind, where the Amirs were defeated by Sir Charles Napier (*q.v.*) and Sind was annexed to the British Indian Empire in 1843. Lord Ellenborough then intervened in the affairs of Sindhia's state, basing his action on the long forgotten and dead treaty of 1804 and sent a British expeditionary force into Sindhia's territories which defeated Sindhia's armies at the battles of Maharajapur and Paniar. Ellenborough did not directly annex Sindhia's state, but definitely made it a protected territory. The ruler was a minor, so the administration was put into the hands of a Council of Regency consisting of Indians who were required to follow the advice of the British Resident at Gwalior. The native army was reduced to a force of 9,000 while a British contingent of 10,000 was stationed within the State which was thus practically brought under British administration. These activities of Lord Ellenborough were not exactly to the liking of the Court of Directors who exercised in 1844 for the first time their right of recalling a Governor-General and Lord Ellenborough had to leave. Even after his return to England he continued to be interested in Indian affairs and strenuously opposed in 1853 the proposed introduction of the system of recruitment to the Indian Civil Service through open competitive examinations. But his opposition proved futile.

Ellis, William—was the chief of the English factory at Patna in 1762 when Mir Kasim (*q.v.*) who had been made the Nawab of Bengal in 1760, abolished all transit dues or tolls payable by all traders throughout the province of Bengal, Bihar and Orissa and thus ended the illegal preferential treatment that the East India Company and all its employees had been enjoying for the past few years. The Company's officers whose claim to preferential treatment was wholly illegal, protested against the Nawab's orders. William Ellis was most violent in asserting these unjustifiable rights and privileges and made an attempt to seize the city of Patna. The Nawab's troops resisted and Ellis with his garrison was defeated and killed. But the events led to the outbreak of a war between the East India Company and Nawab Mir Kasim in 1763.

Ellora—in Maharashtra, is famous for its rock-cut temples. These are divided into three separate groups, each belonging to a separate religion. The right side contains Buddhist Chaitya-halls and the extreme left is occupied by Jain caves. In between the two, the centre is occupied by Hindu temples, the largest of which is the Kailasha temple (*q.v.*) built by order of the Rastrakuta king

Krishna (*c.* A.D. 760-75). It is a unique monument cut out of a single rock, remarkable not only for its very large size but also for the excellence of the decorations. (*C.T.I.*)

Elphinstone, John, Baron (1807-60)—was Governor of Madras from 1837 to 1842 during an uneventful period and of Bombay from 1853 to 1860 during the hectic days of the Mutiny. By his tact, sobriety and moderation he kept the Bombay Presidency quiet during that difficult time and spared troops from Bombay to help in the fight to suppress the mutineers in the disaffected parts of central India.

Elphinstone, Mountstuart (1779-1859)—came out as a writer in the service of the East India Company in 1795. He rose quickly in service and in 1801 became Assistant to the British Resident at the Court of Peshwa Baji Rao II. He saw action at the battles of Assaye and Argaon where he showed great gallantry. He was British Resident at Nagpur from 1804 to 1808 and became the British Resident at Poona in 1811 in which capacity he showed great diplomatic skill. Later on he showed great courage and organising ability when the Third Maratha War (*q.v.*) (1817-19) broke out. His house was raided, his library was destroyed, but he held out and defeated Peshwa Baji Rao II in the battle of Kirki (1817). On the conclusion of the war he was appointed Governor of Bombay which he administered till his retirement from India in 1827. As Governor he instituted many reforms in the Presidency and promoted popular education. The Elphinstone College in Bombay was founded in his honour. His *History of India* which he wrote in 1841, is a masterpiece.

Elphinstone, General, William George Keith (1782-1872)—entered the British army in 1804. He had seen action at various places including Waterloo. He was in command of the Benares Division of the British Indian army in 1839 and joined the Afghan expedition. Towards the close of 1841 be became the Commander-in-Chief of the British expeditionary forces in Kabul, but, on the murder of Sir W. Macnaghten by the Afghans on December 23, 1841 he failed entirely through old age and ill-health to take measures for the safety of the force. During the disastrous retreat of the British army from Kabul he surrendered himself, along with other British officers, as hostages to Akbar Khan and thus brought shame and disgrace to the British. He died at Tezira on his way back to India in April, 1842.

English Company Trading to the East Indies—was a rival of the East India Company (*q.v.*), was founded in 1698 and entered into competition with the older Company which was brought to the brink of ruin. But the Directors of the East India Company were full of fight and declared that two East India Companies in England trading with the East Indies would destroy each other. After much bitter quarrelling, an agreement was arranged in 1702 and eventually the two companies were combined in a single body styled the United Company of Merchants of England trading to the East Indies, which came commonly to be known as the East India Company (*q.v.*).).

Empress of India—was the imperial title that was conferred by the British Parliament on Queen Victoria of England in 1876 in order to emphasize the enhanced prestige and position of the Crown of England in relation to the people and princes of India as a consequence of the assumption of the administration of India by the Crown of England in 1858.

Enfield rifle—was a new type of rifle introduced in the Indian army in 1856 in which greased cartridges (*q.v.*) had to be used. The cartridges had to be bitten off before insertion into the rifle. The sepoys believed that the animal fat used in the cartridges was of cow and pig and its use would pollute the religion of the Hindu as well as of the Muhammadan sepoy. It thus created great consternation in the Indian army and its introduction has been considered to have been one of the causes of the Mutiny of 1857.

Epthalites or White Huns—a section of the Huns who settled in the Oxus Valley in about the middle of the fifth century A.D., made a raid on the Gupta empire in A.D. 455, but were repulsed by the reigning Gupta Emperor Skandagupta. In A.D. 484 they succeeded in overrunning Persia and in the succeeding years they overran the kingdoms of Kabul and Gandhara, penetrated into the heart of the Gangetic provinces and under the leadership of Toramana and his son Mihiragula (*q.v.*) overthrew the Gupta Empire early in the 6th century and established their rule over the lower portion of northern India which they administered from their Indian headquarters at Sakala or Sialkot in the Panjab. Theirs was a cruel and barbarous rule which was ended in about A.D. 528 when their leader Mihiragula was defeated by a confederacy of Indian princes led by Yasodharman (*q.v.*), king of Malwa and Baladitya, a scion of the imperial Gupta dynasty. The loss of the Indian dominions weakened the Epthalites and some time between A.D. 563 and 567 their power was destroyed by the Persian king, Khusru Anushirvan.

Eras, ancient Indian—are numerous. No one era, however,

prevailed all over India at any period in ancient times. Various eras were started by kings who considered their accessions important enough to be commemorated. No uniform system was followed in this matter and sometimes it cannot be traced why and by whom exactly an era was started. As a result, the determination of fixed chronological points becomes possible only when a synchronism is established between a date given in an Indian era and one in the Christian era. More than a score of eras are known to have been prevalent in ancient India. The more important of these eras are—(i) the *Kaliyuga* or Yudhisthira era dating from 3102 B.C. This date is prehistoric and its use is limited to literary tradition. (2) *Vikrama era* also called *Sa-nanda Vikrama Samvat* or *Samvat Vikrama* or *Sri-Nripa Vikrama Samvat* or *Malava era* dates from 58 B.C. The name of the founder as well as the occasion which is commemorated by its foundation are uncertain. (3) *Aanada Vikrama era* dates from A.D. 33. Founder is uncertain. (4) *Saka era* dates from A.D. 78 and was founded probably by the Kushan king Kanishka I. (5) *Lichchavi era* dating from A.D. 111. Founder is unknown, (6) *Chedi* or *Traikutaka Kalachuri era* dates from A.D. 248. (7) *Gupta era* dating from A.D. 319-20 was founded by Chandragupta I, the founder of the line of the imperial Guptas to commemorate his accession. (8) *Huna era* dating from A.D. 448, was used by Toramana (*q.v.*) in his coins. (9) *Harsha era* dating from A.D. 606 commemorates the accession of king Harshavardhana (*q.v.*) of Thaneswar. (10) *Kallam* or *Malabar era* dating from A.D. 824 used by the Chera or Kerala kings. (11) *Nepalese era* dating from A.D. 879. (12) *Vikramanka-Chalukya era* dating from A.D. 1076 started by the Chalukya king Vikramanka (*q.v.*) to celebrate his accession. (13) *Laksmana Sena era* dating from 1190, was started by king Laksmana Sena of Bengal. (Cunningham, *Book of Indian Eras*; *J.R.A.S.*, 1913, p. 627 *ff*; Kielhorn in *Ind. Ant.* XX (1891) & *P.H.A.I.*, pp. 465-72)

Eudemos—was the Greek officer who was appointed to command a Thracian garrison in the Western Panjab in succession to Philippos whom Alexander the Great had appointed to the command but who was killed by the Indians in 324 B.C. Eudemos maintained himself in the lower Indus valley up to 317 B.C., though the upper Indus valley was freed from Greek rule in about 322 B.C. by Chandragupta Maurya (*q.v.*). On his return from India Eudemos became involved in the wars amongst the generals of Alexander the Great and had no further dealings with India.

Eukratides—a Bactrian Greek, who made himself the master of

Bactria in about 175 B.C., defeated Demetrios who had assumed the title of 'king of the Indians' after a prolonged conflict during the years *c.* 160-156 B.C. and extended his rule over some portions of western India, but he was killed by hs son, probably Apollodotos, on his way from India to Bactria in 156 B.C. His Indian conquests, however, led to the parcelling out of northwestern India amongst a number of Indo-Bactrian princelings, the most famous of whom was Menander (*q.v.*).

European travellers, early—who left accounts of what they saw in the country, are to be distinguished from the Greeks who came to India following the invasion of the country by Alexander the Great, king of Macedon, in 327 B.C. and who never called themselves Europeans. The earliest of European travellers to India was the Venetian Marco Polo who came in 1288 and 1293. Then after a long interval came the Italian traveller Nicolo Conti who visited Vijayanagar in 1420. Fifty years later the Russian traveller Athanasius Nikitin travelled through the Bahmani kingdom from 1470 to 1474. In 1522 the Portuguese traveller Domingos Paes visited Vijayanagar. Thirteen years later came another Portuguese traveller named Fernao Nuniz who also visited Vijayanagar. The first Englishman who lived on the mainland of India was Thomas Stephens who became the Rector of a Jesuit College in Goa. His letters written to his parents in England roused great interest there. In 1583 came the English merchant, Fitch, along with two other companions. He stayed in this country for seven years and on his return to England in 1592 published accounts of what he had seen in India and this roused great interest for India in England. In 1599 the English traveller John Midnal or Mildenhall reached India by the overland route and spent here seven years during which he visited the court of Emperor Akbar at Agra. Already the direct sea-route via the Cape of Good Hope had been opened and lots of Europeans began to come to this country. Of these later travellers interesting accounts have been left by Captain William Hawkins who was in India from 1608 to 1614, Sir Thomas Roe and his Chaplain Rev. Edward Terry who were in India from 1615 to 1619, Francois Bernier and Jean Baptiste Tavernier, both of whom visited India towards the close of Shah Jahan's reign (1627-60).

Euthydemos—was the third king of Bactria. He was succeeded by his son Demetrios who probably led an expedition into India in about 175 B.C. and was repulsed by the Sunga king Pushyamitra (*q.v.*) (*c.* 185 B.C.).

Eyre, Sir Charles—was the first President of Fort William which came to control all the English factories in Bengal from 1700. His administration appears to have been uneventful.

Eyre, Major Vincent (1811-81)—came out to India in 1828 as an officer in the Bengal Artillery. He joined the Kabul expedition of 1839-42 and on his return to India was transferred to Burma. When he was on his way there the Mutiny broke out and he was recalled to India. On his way up country he heard at Buxar that the mutineers led by Kumar Singh of Jagadishpur had besieged Arrah. On his own responsibility he collected whatever troops he could, confronted Kumar Singh's army and defeated him. He then proceeded to Lucknow and helped in its capture by the British in 1858. He retired in 1863.

F

Fa-Hien (**also spelt Fa-Hsein**)—was a Chinese pilgrim who visited India from A.D. 401 to 410. He came to India with the object of securing authentic texts of the *Vinaya-pitaka* (*q.v.*). Starting from Western China he followed the route to the south of the Gobi desert through Lop-nor to Khotan where he found that Buddhism of the Mahayana school was generally prevalent. He then crossed the Pamirs overcoming infinite difficulties and made his way to Udyanor (Swat) and then to Taxila and Purushapur or Peshawar. He travelled all over northern India spending three years at Pataliputra and two at Tamralipti, modern Tamluk, in the Midnapore district of West Bengal. In A.D. 410 he sailed from Tamluk which was at that time an important port, on his return journey by sea, visiting Ceylon and Java on the way, to China where he arrived in A.D. 414. Fa-Hien has left a very interesting account of what he saw in India. He was particularly attracted by the Gangetic plain which he calls Mid-India then under the rule of the third Gupta Emperor, Chandragupta II (*c.* A.D. 380-415) whom, however, the pilgrim never mentions and whose court he seems never to have visited. But he was much impressed by the efficiency and mildness of the administration of the country where the people were free to come and go as they liked without being required to be registered or to obtain passes. Crimes were ordinarily punished with fines only; the capital punishment was not inflicted and obstinate rebels alone were punished with mutilation. The revenue was derived from the rent of the crown lands and royal officers were all paid regular salaries. He was much pleased with the towns of Magadha, especially Pataliputra where he spent three years in studying the Sanskrit language and Buddhist scriptures. The people were rich and prosperous; charitable institutions were numerous; rest-houses for travellers were provided on the highways and there was an excellent free hospital. The palace of Asoka, which was still standing, impressed the pilgrim so deeply with its massiveness and grandeur that it seemed to him to be the work of spirits, beyond the capacity of human craftsmen. Fa-Hien found the cities of Gaya, Bodh-Gaya, Sravasti, Kapilavastu and Kusinagara—all holy places to the Buddhists—either empty or very sparsely populated. Throughout the country, he declares, no one kills any living thing, or drinks wine, or eats onions or garlic. This shows that the people were very temperate in their habits and accustomed to vegetarian diet. There is one noteworthy omission in Fa-Hien's observations. He does not mention Nalanda Monastery and University which must have been, therefore, founded after Fa-Hien had left India. (Legge, *Travels*)

Faizi—son of Shaikh Mubarak and elder brother of Abul Fazl, was a poet and littérateur who first met Akbar in 1567. The Emperor who had already heard of his reputation for learning, received him with kindness and gave him an honoured place amongst his courtiers. It was Faizi who composed the *Khutba* which Emperor Akbar recited when he ascended the pulpit for the first time on June 27, 1579, and thus started his new religious policy which culminated in the propagation of *Din-Ilahi* (*q.v.*). Faizi was sent by the Emperor as his envoy to Khandesh and Ahmadnagar in 1591. He succeeded in securing the submission of Khandesh, but Ahmadnagar refused to yield. Thus Faizi had partial success as a diplomat. He died in 1595.

Faizulla Khan—was the son of Ali Muhammad Ruhela, one of the founders of the Rohilkhand state. After the defeat and death of Hafiz Rahamat Khan in 1774, Faizulla Khan was given a part of Rohilkhand including Rampura and was set up as a ruler there subordinate to the Company's Government.

Fakhr-ud-din—was the *Kotwal* of Delhi during the reign of Sultan Balban. He lived a luxurious life, wearing a new dress every day of the year. When Balban in pursuance of his policy of curbing the power of the nobles tried to regulate the tenure of lands in the Doab enjoyed by 2000 *shamsi* horsemen and resume the old grants on the ground that the grantees had ceased to perform the military services on condition of which the lands had been granted to them, the threatened land-owners found a protector and spokesman in Fakhr-ud-din. One day he approached the Sultan with a thoughtful and dejected face; and when the Sultan enquired about the cause of his dejection, he said that the resumption of the grant of land of the *shamsi* horsemen had made him much worried about his own future because he too had become old. He further added that if old men were to be rejected on the day of judgment and were to find no place in heaven what would happen to him. This clever speech moved the Sultan to compassion and the orders for the resumption of the lands were rescinded. Later on Fakhr-ud-din played an important part, first, in the installation of Kaiqubad on the throne of Delhi after the death of Sultan Balban in A.D. 1287, and later on, in 1290, in the deposition of Sultan Kaiqubad in favour of Jalal-ud-din Khalji. The whole family of Fakhr-ud-din was later on killed and destroyed by Sultan Ala-ud-din Khalji on suspicion that they had instigated the rebellion of Haji Maula in A.D. 1301.

Fakhr-ud-din Abdul Aziz Kufi—was the Qazi of Nishapur who purchased a boy slave, and provided for his religious and military training along with his sons. This boy slave was Qutb-ud-din Aibak who became the first Muslim Sultan of Delhi. Fakhr-ud-din's sons later on sold the boy slave to a merchant who re-sold him at Ghazni.

Fakhr-ud-din Mubarak Shah—was the armour bearer of Bahram Khan (also called Tatar Khan) who was the governor of Sonargaon in Bengal during the early part of the reign of Sultan Muhammad Tughluq (A.D. 1325-51). On the death of Bahram Khan in 1336, Fakhr-ud-din immediately proclaimed himself as the ruler of Sonargaon and assumed the title of Fakhr-ud-din Mubarak Shah. He thus set up an independent kingdom in Bengal over which he ruled for about ten years (1336-46) (*I.S.B.*, p. 15)

Fakhr-ud-din Muhammad Jauna Khan—*see* Muhammad Tughluq.

Famines—have been unfortunately a much too familiar feature of the economic life in India. The well-known observation of Megasthenes (*q.v.*) that famine was unknown to India (*c.* 4th century B.C.) is not corroborated by historical evidence. Indeed in a country like India where agriculture largely depends on the unpredictable monsoons, famines have been of frequent occur rence. Detailed records of famines that overtook the country before the beginning of the British rule are not available. It is, however, known that between the battle of Plassey in 1757 and the end of the British rule in India in 1947, that is to say, during the short period of 190 years there had been nine serious famines in the country. These were the famines of

(i) 1769-70—which carried away one-third of the population of Bengal, Bihar and Orissa;

(ii) 1837-38—which visited northern India and led to the deaths of 800,000 persons;

(iii) 1861—in northern India: the number of casualties was very large;

(iv) 1866—in Orissa causing the deaths of one million persons;

(v) 1868-69—in Rajputana and Bundelkhand: the casualties were comparatively limited, but they ran to six figures;

(vi) 1873-74—in Bengal and Bihar—large number of deaths;

(vii) 1876-78—affected the whole of India and carried away five million persons in British India alone;

(viii) 1896-1900—raged in south, central and northern India killing at least 750,000 persons, and

(ix) 1943—man-made famine in Bengal resulting from the scorched-earth policy of the British Indian Government, the cupidity and greed of the merchants and the dishonesty and corruption in the administration.

Famine Code—was drawn up in 1883 on the lines of the recommendations made by the Famine Commission of 1880. The Code laid down the procedure for detecting the symptoms of food shortage, for declaring first a state of scarcity and then of famine. The principles were that, as soon as a state of scarcity was declared, measures were to be adopted for bringing into the affected area by railways or shipping grain from unaffected areas or overseas, for supplying relief on a regulated basis and for providing for able-bodied persons remunerative work of a productive kind. The Famine Code, it has been observed, could not prevent famines, but by using the new resources of science and planning it succeeded in decreasing the havoc of famines.

Famine Commission—was appointed in 1880 by Lord Lytton, Viceroy of India (1876-81), with Sir Richard Strachey as the Chairman. It was on the basis of the report of the Famine Commission that the Famine Code (*q.v.*) was drawn up. A second Famine Commission was appointed in 1897 by Lord Elgin, Viceroy (1894-99), with Sir James Lyall as the Chairman.

It fully approved of the principles recommended by the earlier Famine Commission of 1880 and suggested some alterations in the detailed working of the scheme. A third Famine Commission was appointed in 1900 by Lord Curzon, Viceroy (*q.v.*) with Sir Antony Macdonnell as the Chairman. It also endorsed the principles laid down by the Famine Commission of 1880 and recommended the appointment of a Famine Commissioner in a province where relief operations were to be adopted on a large scale, distribution of relief by providing employment in local works of public utility in preference to large public works at a distance, larger employment of non-official agencies for distribution of relief, establishment of agricultural banks, introduction of improved methods of cultivation and wide extension of irrigation work. These recommendations were accepted and were acted upon by the Government.

Famine Relief and Insurance Fund—was started in pursuance of the recommendations made in the Famine Report of 1880 (*q.v.*).

Famine Report of 1880—was submitted by the Famine Commission of 1880 presided over by Sir Richard Strachey. The Report laid down, first, the fundamental principle that it is the duty of the State to provide relief to the needy in times of famine. The relief was to be administered in the shape of providing work for able-bodied persons and distributing food or money to the aged and infirm. For the first, schemes of relief work should be prepared in advance, so that relief may be available to the needy as soon as a famine breaks out. The relief work undertaken should be of permanent utility and should be extensive enough to provide employment for all who may seek it. Persons who were not fit to be sent out to a distant place to work on larger schemes, should be provided with local work like excavation of ponds or raising embankments. Relief to be effective must be promptly organised and given and work should be provided before the affected people lose their physical fitness as the result of starvation. Additional and general relief was to be provided by suspension and remission of land-revenue and rents and by the advancement of loans for purchasing seeds and agricultural implements. In order to avoid waste and extravagance in the grant of relief the main share of the cost was to be borne by the local government of the affected province and the Central Government should only supplement the local resources and the distribution should be done through non-official representatives bodies. The report further recommended that a sum of Rs. 15,000,000 should be annually set apart to create the 'Famine Relief and Insurance Fund' out of which the unforeseen expenditure on famines was to be met.

Faraidhi (pronounced Faraizi) movement—was started by Haji Shariat-ullah of Faridpur, now in Eastern Pakistan. It was a Muslim revivalist movement which aimed at purifying Islam. It attracted a large number of adherents amongst the Muslim cultivators of the district of Faridpur and the adjacent area. It was peaceful in its activities but it soon developed into an agrarian agitation and gradually declined.

Farid Khan—*see* Sher Shah.

Farruksiyar—was the ninth Mughul Emperor (1713-19). Son of Azim-us-Shan who had been killed in 1712 in the course of the war of succession following the death of his father, Emperor Shah Alam I (1707-12), Farruksiyar secured the support of the Chief Minister Zulfiqar Khan, deposed his uncle, Emperor Jahandar Shah (1712-13), who was strangled to death and ascended the throne of Delhi. Soon after his accession Emperor Farruksiyar had Zulfiqar Khan executed and placed his chief reliance on the two Sayyid brothers, Husain Ali and Abdullah, and made the former the Commander-in-Chief and the latter the *Wazir*. The short reign of Farruksiyar had one inglorious success. The Sikh leader Banda with about 1,000 followers were captured and executed in 1715. The East India Company in India derived great benefit from Farruksiyar. In 1715 an English embassy including a surgeon named William Hamilton, waited upon the Emperor. This English surgeon cured the Emperor's daughter of a 'malignant distemper' and the grateful Emperor rewarded his masters, the East India Company, by granting them valuable trade concessions and exemption from customs duties in Bengal. Farruksiyar was weak in mind but wanted to free himself from the control of the Sayyid brothers who having come to know of the Emperor's intrigues, anticipated his action by deposing, blinding and killing him in 1719.

Faruqi dynasty—was established in Khandesh in 1388 by Malik Raja Faruqi, a personal attendant of Sultan Firoz Shah Tughluq (1351-88) whom the Sultan had entrusted with the administration of the province. He ruled for eleven years (1388-99) and was succeeded by his son Malik Nasir (A.D. 1399-1438). He captured the fortress of Asirgarh from its Hindu Raja but was defeated by the neighbouring Muslim king of Gujarat and the

Bahmani Sultan, Ala-ud-din Ahmad, who had married his
daughter. The third king Adil Khan I (A.D. 1438-41) and the
fourth king Mubarak Khan I (A.D. 1441-57) had uneventful
reigns. But the fifth king Adil Khan II (A.D. 1457-1508) was an
able and vigorous ruler who extended his sovereignty over
Gondwana. Adil Khan II had no son and was succeeded by his
brother Daud (A.D. 1501-08) whose son and successor, Ghazni
Khan, was poisoned within ten days of his accession. The Faruqi
dynasty now became involved in a factious fight which was
fomented by the sultans of Ahmadnagar and Gujarat. This
internal strife greatly weakened the Faruqi dynasty and Bahadur
Faruqi, the last ruler, submitted to Emperor Akbar in 1601.
The kings of the Faruqi dynasty beautified their capital, Burhanpur, as well as the city of Thalner, by building beautiful mosques
and tombs. The remains of their palace built on a commanding
situation above the Tapti river at Burhanpur bear testimony to
their artistic and architectural tastes. (*C.H.I.* IV.)

Fath Khan—was the eldest son of Sultan Firoz Shah Tughluq
(A.D. 1351-88) whom he predeceased. His elder son, Ghiyasuddin Tughluq, succeeded his father Sultan Firoz Shah
immediately after the latter's death but was deposed and killed
only a few months later. His second son, Nusrat Shah, was the
penultimate sultan of the Tughluq dynasty and ruled from
1395-99.

Fath Khan—was a son of Malik Ambar, (*q.v.*) the Chief Minister for
years of the Nizam Shahi kings of Ahmadnagar. Fath Khan had
not the loyalty of his father. He was the Chief Minister of Murtaza
Nizam Shah II, the penultimate king of Ahmadnagar, whom
however, he killed in 1630 and proclaimed his young son, Husain
the king of Ahmadnagar. In 1631 he gallantly defended against
Shah Jahan's armies the fort of Daulatabad which had been
very strongly fortified by his father, but in 1633 the Mughul
Emperor offered him most generous terms and Fath Khan
surrendered the fort to the Mughul Emperor who sent Husain
the last Nizam Shahi king of Ahmadnagar, to life-long imprisonment in the fort of Gwalior. Fath Khan was taken into the
imperial service in which he continued till his death (*C.H.I.*
IV, p.265)

Fathpur-Sikri—is situated 23 miles west of Agra. It is a rocky place
where the famous Muslim saint Shaikh Salim Chishti resided
Emperor Akbar who pined for sons, visited this saint for favour
of his blessings and when in 1596 his first Hindu queen
Jodh Bai, gave birth at Sikri to a son, the future Emperor

Jahangir, the grateful Emperor named him Salim in honour of the saint and presently decided to build at Sikri a royal town so that the Emperor himself might reside there. The construction began in 1570 and the whole city with its numerous magnificent buildings was built within a very few years. It was from Sikri that Akbar started on his Gujarat campaign in 1573 and in celebration of the victorious termination of the campaign named the city Fathpur or Victory town. Henceforth Sikri became known as Fathpur Sikri. It continued to be Akbar's capital for about fifteen years, but within this short period it was decorated with many edifices, all built generally of red sand-stone, the more important of which were—the Jami Masjid, tomb of Salim Chishti, the Bulwand Darwaja, Jodh Bai's palace, Hawa Khana, Dewani Khas, Birbal's residence, the houses of Miriam and Turkish sultanas and the *Ibadat-Khana* or House of Worship. All the buildings, except the last, are still extant and bear eloquent testimony to the fine artistic taste of Emperor Akbar. (*H.I.E.A.*, II, 297)

Fathullah—a Hindu convert to Islam, was the governor of Berar during the reign of the fourteenth Bahmani sultan Mahmud (A.D.1482-1518). Taking advantage of the minority of the Sultan and the disorganisation that followed the execution of Mahmud Gawan (*q.v.*) Fathullah set himself up as an independent ruler in Berar in A.D. 1484 and assumed the title of Imad-ul-Mulk. The Imad Shahi dynasty, which was thus started, ruled in Berar till A.D. 1574 when Berar was absorbed by Ahmadnagar.

Faujdar, **the**—was an officer in Mughul India who was in charge of the maintenance of law and order in a district, then called a *Sarkar*. He was the commander of the military force stationed in the district and was to put down smaller rebellions, disperse or arrest gangs of robbers, take cognizance of all violent crimes, and make demonstrations of force to overawe opposition to the revenue authorities, or the criminal judge, or the censor. He generally resided in the headquarters of the district.

Faujdari Adalat, **the**—is a court with jurisdiction to try criminal cases. At the beginning of British rule in Bengal there was a *Faujdari Adalat* in every district and appeals from them lay to the *Sadar Nizamat Adalat*. The *Faujdari Adalat* dispensing justice in criminal cases, is to be distinguished from the *Dewani Adalat* which tries civil and revenue cases.

Fazl-ul-Huq, Abul Kasem (1873-1962)—was the Governor of East Pakistan. Born in Barisal, now in East Pakistan, he began his career as a deputy magistrate, but soon took to the practice of law as a vakil in the Calcutta High Court and also to politics. He had a chequered and rather strange career. He joined the Indian National Congress in 1904 and became its secretary for a term. But he soon left it and joined the Muslim League (*q.v.*) which he represented in the first and second sessions of the Round Table Conference (*q.v.*), and of which he was the President. He was the Chief Minister in undivided Bengal from 1937 to 1943 and founded the Krishak-Praja Party. After the Partition he went to East Pakistan where he was the Chief Minister for a short time and then Governor for a longer period. He was a rather benevolent person who enjoyed great popularity with the masses.

Federal Court of India, the—was created by the Government of India Act, 1935 and began to function from 1937 with Sir Maurice Gwyer (*q.v.*) as the first Chief Justice of India. It exercised exclusive original jurisdiction in any dispute between the Federation, the Provinces and the Federated States. It exercised a limited appellate jurisdiction and appeals lay from its decisions to the Privy Council in England. It merged into the Supreme Court of India in January, 1950 (*Govt. of India Act.* 1935).

Female sepoys—were recruited by the Nizam of Hyderabad in the last quarter of the eighteenth century. They are said to have taken part in the battle of Kurdla (*q.v.*) which the Nizam fought with the Marathas in 1795. They are said to have behaved no worse than the male part of the Nizam's army. (*Bengal: Past and Present*, 1933)

Ferozeshah, the battle of—was fought on 21 and 22 December, 1845, between the British and the Sikhs in the course of the First Sikh War (1845-46). The battle lasted for two days and the position of the British force was extremely critical on the night of December 21, when the British troops had to bivouac on the open ground. The fighting was renewed at dawn, but it ended rather suddenly as the Sikh general Tej Singh betrayed his brave soldiers by ordering a retreat for reasons of his own. The Sikhs lost the battle but the British had to pay heavily for the victory. The British casualties numbered 2,415 including 103 officers, amongst whom were five aides-de-camp of the Governor-General, who were killed and another four wounded. The battle, however, did not end the war which was concluded two months later by the British victory at Sobraon (*q.v.*) in February, 1846. (Cunningham, J. D., *Hist. of the Sikhs*)

Firishta, Muhammad Kasim (*c* 1570-1612)—was a famous historian who wrote in Persian. Born at Astrabad on the shores of the Caspian Sea in Persia he came as a young boy with his father to Ahmadnagar where he lived till 1589 when he moved on to Bijapur. There he got the patronage of Sultan Ibrahim Adil Shah II who engaged him to write a history of India. He lived in Bijapur and completed his work known as *Tarikh-i-Firishta* in 1609. According to Briggs, who has translated his work under the title of *The History of the Rise of the Muhammadan Power in India*, Firishta died in 1612 in Bijapur. He is known to be one of the most trustworthy of oriental historians and his monumental work still maintains a high place as an authority on the Muhammadan rule in India.

Firuz Khan—was the only son of Islam (or Salim) Shah, the only son and successor of Sher Shah (1540-45). On the death of Islam Shah (1545-54) his minor son, Firuz Khan, was murdered in 1554 by his maternal uncle Mubariz Khan who became king under the title of Muhammad Adil Shah (1554-56).

Firuz Shah—was a relation of the Mughul Emperor Bahadur Shah II (1837-58). He played a prominent part in fomenting anti-British feelings in the pre-Mutiny days.

Firuz Shah Bahmani (1397-1422)—was the eighth sultan of the Bahmani dynasty (*q.v.*) in whose reign the dynasty attained, according to the historian Firishta, the greatest splendour. Firuz led practically annual expeditions against the neighbouring Hindu kingdom of Vijayanagar. In 1406 Firuz actually entered into the city and obliged Deva Raya I, the king of Vijayanagar (1406-12) to make peace by giving his daughter in marriage to the Muslim invader. But in 1420 Sultan Firuz suffered a severe defeat at the hands of the Hindus in the battle of Pangal, to the north of the Krishna and returned home a broken-down man. The remaining two years of his life he spent in works of piety, leaving the administration in the hands of two Turki slaves. Sultan Firuz was a lover of buildings and adorned his capital Kulbarga with many edifices including the principal mosque built on the model of the mosque of Cordova in Spain. He also built a fortified palace at Firozabad on the Bhima to the south of the capital.

Firuz Shah Khalji—*see* Jalal-ud-din Firuz Shah Khalji

Firuz Shah Tughluq—the first cousin and successor of Muhammad Tughluq, the second sultan of the Tughluq dynasty, ruled from March 1351 till his death in September, 1388. His father Rajab was the younger brother of Sultan Ghiyasuddin Tughluq (1320-25). He was a peace-loving monarch whose first task was to bring back safely the Delhi army that was in Tatha (Sind) at the time of the sudden death of his predecessor, Muhammad Tughluq, who had gone there to suppress a revolt. Years later, in 1361-63 Firuz made an effort to reduce Sind and after a prolonged campaign he succeeded in obliging its rebellious ruler, Jam Babaniya, to submit and promise the payment of an annual tribute to the Delhi sultanate. But Sultan Firuz failed in his attempts in 1353 as well as in 1359 to reconquer Bengal. Nor did he make any attempt to reconquer the Deccan where the Muslim Bahmani sultans and the Hindu kings of Vijayanagar had thrown off the yoke of Delhi during the closing years of the reign of his predecessor, Muhammad Tughluq (1325-51). Thus Firuz failed to stem the disintegration of the Delhi sultanate which had commenced during the reign of his predecessor. The only great military success of Firuz was the reduction of Jajnagar (Orissa) in 1360. Sultan Firuz was an orthodox Muslim and tried to administer the country according to Islamic theocratic principles. Such an attempt naturally imposed much hardship on the majority of his subjects who were Hindus whose fairs and public worship he forbade. He was a benevolent sovereign within the restrictions of his religion. He abolished many vexatious and unjust taxes, though he extended the *Jizya* to the Brahmins who had so long been exempt from it. He encouraged irrigation works, founded cities including Jaunpur on the Gumti, planted many gardens and orchards, built numerous mosques, abolished cruel punishments like mutilation, and founded one charitable hospital where medicines and diet were supplied at the cost of the state. The administration was mild, prices were from natural causes very low and people generally lived in peace. But Firuz's mildness was cruelty to posterity. He organised the army on a feudal basis, generally paid the officers with *jagirs* and the soldiers with land-grants, and, out of his kindness for the old, he made service in the army hereditary. Thus the army of the Delhi sultanate was weakened and could be easily routed by Timur when he invaded Delhi in 1398, only ten years after the death of Sultan Firuz. The Sultan, however, had an inquisitive mind and this led him to bring, with infinite care and skill, to Delhi and install there two inscribed Asokan pillars —one from Topra and the other from Meerut. He was also the patron of two Muhammadan historians—Zia-ud-din Barani (*q.v.*) and Sams-i-Siraj Afif (*q.v.*).

Firuzabad—is the name of a town founded by Sultan Firuz Shah Tughluq (1351-88) at a distance of ten miles from his capital at Delhi. This was also the name that the same Sultan gave to the city of Pandua in Bengal during his campaign there in 1353-54.

Fitch, Ralph—was an English merchant who came overland to India in 1583. He travelled through Upper India, Bengal, Burma, Malacca and Ceylon and returned safely to England in 1591. The report prepared by him on his travels was one of the records on which the East India Company relied in their earlier trading ventures.

Foote—an English dramatist, wrote in 1770 a drama named *The Nabob* in caricature of the servants of the East India Company who returned home from Bengal after having amassed immense riches there, scandalized English society by their ostentation and created jealousy by their wealth. His drama did much to draw public attention in England to the source of the wealth of the Company's retired officers who came to be derisively known as the 'Nabobs'.

Forbes, James (1749-1819)—was one of those rare early Englishmen in India who found much merit in the ancient civilisation and way of life of the Hindus of India. He came out to India in 1765 as a civil servant in the East India Company's service. In 1778 on the eve of the First Maratha War (*q.v.*) he became the Private Secretary of Col. Keating and continued in the Company's service till 1784 when he retired and left India. At the time of his final departure from India he took with him 154 volumes of materials on Indian subjects like literature, philosophy, art and architecture. He published his *Oriental Memoirs* in four volumes in 1813-15.

Forde, Colonel—an officer employed in the Bengal army of the East India Company, was sent early in 1759 by Robert Clive to strike a blow at the French in south India. He made a successful march along the coast and captured Masulipatam and thus ended French control over the Northern Circars which now passed under English control. Later in the same year he defeated the Dutch, who had their headquarters at Chinsurah in Bengal, in the battle of Biderra which ended Dutch pretensions in Bengal. Colonel Forde, however, had an unfortunate end. In 1769 he was sent, along with Vansittart and Scrafton, by the Court of Directors in London as 'Supervisors' with powers to investigate every branch of the administration in India. But the ship in which Col. Forde and his two colleagues sailed was never heard of again after leaving the Cape of Good Hope and was presumably wrecked.

Fort St. David—was built by the East India Company early in the eighteenth century. It was situated on the Coromandel coast, a little to the south of Pondicherry. In 1747-48 it stood an eighteen months' siege by the French. It was captured by the French under Count de Lally after a month's siege in 1758, but it was recovered by the English after the battle of Wandiwash (*q.v.*) in 1760.

Fort St. George—was built in 1640 by Francis Day, a member of the East India Company's council at Masulipatam, on a narrow strip of land on the Coromandel coast of which he got a lease from the neighbouring Hindu Raja of Chandragiri. Round the guns of this Fort grew up the town of Madras, which soon displaced Masulipatam as the chief English settlement on the Coromandel coast and was eventually made the seat of a Presidency.

Fort William—was built in Calcutta during the years 1696-1715 and gave protection to the city. It was captured by Nawab Siraj-ud-daula in 1756 but was recovered by the English in 1757. The original site of Fort William was later on vacated and is now occupied by more modern buildings like the Customs House and General Post Office and the site where the Fort now stands was chosen later on.

Forth, Dr.—was an English physician attached to the East India Company's factory at Cossimbazar, near Murshidabad which was the capital of Bengal at that time. One day, late in March, 1756 when Nawab Alivardi Khan (*q.v.*) was lying seriously ill, Dr. Forth came to see him. When Dr. Forth was talking to the ailing Nawab his grandson and heir-presumptive, Siraj-ud-daula came in, and reported to the Nawab that the English had agreed to help Ghasiti Begum (*q.v.*) who was intriguing against Siraj. On being asked by the dying Nawab whether the information was correct Dr. Forth not only denied the charge but disavowed on behalf of the East India Company any intention to interfere in Bengal politics. But this disavowal had no effect on Siraj-ud-daula. Forth's conduct showed how English employees of the Company would prevaricate in order to promote the Company's interests.

Fowler, Sir Henry—was the Secretary of State for India in 1894. In 1898 he presided over a Committee which recommended that both sovereigns (gold) and rupees (silver) should be made unlimited legal tender at the rate of 1s. 4d. to the rupee and the mints were to be opened to the free coinage of gold only. These recommendations were accepted and adopted in 1899.

Fox, Charles James (1749-1806)—was a leading English politician and parliamentarian. In 1783 he formed the coalition ministry in England with Lord North as his colleague and in the same year he brought forward his India Bill which proposed to supersede both the Court of Proprietors and the Board of Directors of the East India Company and to transfer for four years all political and military powers to seven Directors or Commissioners, to be appointed at first by the Parliament and afterwards by the Crown. The Bill was passed by the House of Commons by ample majorities, but was thrown out by the House of Lords as the result of personal canvassing by King George III through Lord Temple. On the rejection of the Bill by the House of Lords George III dismissed the ministry of Fox and North, but Fox, with his genuine liberalism, continued to take an earnest interest in Indian affairs and in 1788 he became one of the chief managers of the impeachment of Warren Hastings (*q.v.*).

Francis, Sir Philip (1740-1818)—was named in the Regulating Act (1773) (*q.v.*) as a member of the Council of the Governor-General of Fort William in Bengal on an annual salary of £10,000. He arrived in Calcutta in October, 1774. Soon after his arrival he joined with his two colleagues, Monson and Clavering, in opposing Governor-General Warren Hastings on his whole policy and method of government. Thus a tussle began between Francis and Warren Hastings which eventually ended in the discomfiture of Francis. Ultimately Francis fought a duel with Hastings in 1780, was disabled and went back to England where he took a prominent part in organising and conducting the impeachment of Warren Hastings. Sir Philip was the first Englishman in authority to suggest the introduction of a permanent settlement of land-revenue in Bengal. He was disappointed at the acquittal of Warren Hastings in 1795, retired from public life in 1807 and died in 1810.

French East India Company, the—*see ante* under Company.

Frere, Sir Henry Bartle Edward (1815-84)—an eminent British administrator, came to India as a civil servant in 1834 and was posted in Bombay. In 1846 he was appointed as Resident at Satara and became, on its annexation, which he had opposed, its Commissioner in 1848. In 1850 he became the Commissioner of Sind which he administered for nine years (1850-59) with great success. From 1859 to 1862 he was a member of the Viceroy's Executive Council and helped in the restoration of India's financial equilibrium. From 1862 to 1867 he was the Governor of Bombay where he advanced education, built colleges (e.g. Deccan College), pushed on railways, established the Bombay Municipality and promoted female education, but incurred adverse criticism for the failure of the Bank of Bombay and retired from India. Back in England he became

a member of the India Council (1867-77). He advocated a
'forward policy' in Afghanistan and was a staunch advocate of
the paternalism of the British administration in India. His
greatest service to England was, however, rendered in Africa
where he was from 1877 to 1880; but his aggressive policy there
brought about the Zulu War and he was recalled. He died in
1889.

Friend of India, the—was a journal started by the Serampore missionaries under the guidance of John Marshman in 1818. It
struck a Christian and reforming note and supported the abolition of social abuses like the *sati* or burning of widows on the
funeral pyres of their husbands. Later on the journal was incorporated with the *Statesman* of Calcutta.

Fryer, Dr. John—was a British traveller who visited India, in the
seventies of the seventeenth century, travelled mainly over
southern India and left an account of what he saw. (*A New
Account*, edn. Crook)

Fullarton, Colonel William—an officer in the East India Company's army during the Second Mysore War (*q.v.*) (1779-84)
captured Coimbatore in November, 1783, and was about to
attack Seringapatam when he was recalled by the Madras
Government in their anxiety to make peace with Tipu
Sultan. On his retirement which he spent in England he lived
an active life becoming an F.R.S. and an M.P. and wrote *A
View of English Interests in India*. He died in 1808.

Fuller, Sir J. Bamfylde—was the first Lieutenant-Governor of the
province of Eastern Bengal and Assam created in 1905 by Lord
Curzon, Viceroy (1899-1905). Fuller had risen from the Indian
Civil Service and was opposed to Indian nationalistic aspirations.
In administering the new province he deliberately adopted an
anti-Hindu attitude and openly declared "the favourite wife"
principle in order to wean the Muhammadans from the agitation against the Partition of Bengal (*q.v.*). But this did not
suppress the agitation which found the largest number of supporters amongst the school students. To check this student
agitation Fuller issued a circular order to the schools threatening
them with forfeiture of Government aids as well as with disaffiliation in case their students would take part in political
agitation. Two schools were considered guilty of violating the
circular and Fuller wanted to disaffiliate them. But the Government of India, acting in agreement with the Secretary of State,
Lord Morley, requested Fuller to withdraw his suggestion for
the disaffiliation of the two offending schools. Fuller was very

much chagrined and in a fit of pique offered his resignation which was readily accepted. Fuller then sank into oblivion.

Fu-nan—was the earlier Chinese name of the kingdom of Kambuja (*q.v.*), modern Cambodia, where a Hindu kingdom was founded by an Indian Brahman named Kaundinya probably in the first century of the Christian era. From the sixth century onwards, Fu-nan became completely merged in Kambujadesa.

Fytche, General (1820-92)—was an officer in the British Indian army who took part in the Second Burmese War (*q.v.*) (1852). On the victorious termination of the war he was of much help to the newly appointed Commissioner, Major (afterwards Sir) Arthur Phayre, in introducing necessary administrative reforms in the newly annexed province of Burma. His work on *Burma, Past and Present* was published in 1878.

G

Gadadhar Singh—was the twenty-ninth Ahom king who ruled over Assam for fifteen years (1681-96). His first act was to recover in 1682 Gauhati from the Mughul occupation and to compel Emperor Aurangzeb to recognise as the boundary between the Mughul and Ahom dominions the river Monas which flows between the modern districts of Goalpara and Kamrup. Gadadhar Singh was a very strong king who put down all internal intrigues and disturbances, raised high the fallen prestige of the monarch in Assam, suppressed Miri and Naga revolts, and broke the power of the Ahom nobles. Gadadhar Singh was a *Sakta* (worshipper of the goddess of strength) severely persecuted the Vaishnavas and broke the powers of the Vaishnava *Gosains*. He built the temple of Umananda on an island in the Brahmaputra just opposite the *Kutcheri* ghat at Gauhati. He made landgrants to Brahmanas and to Hindu temples, built several high roads, constructed two stone bridges, excavated tanks and started a detailed survey of land-holdings in Assam. (Gait, Sir Edward, *Hist. of Assam*)

Gadai, Shaikh—was a *shiah* whom Bairam Khan, the guardian of Emperor Akbar, appointed as the *Sadr-us-Sudur* or the chief law officer and ecclesiastic in the state, having control over all grants, endorsements and allowances. The appointment to such a high post of Gadai who had no special qualification for and who was moreover a *shiah*, was resented by the orthodox *sunni* Muslims and strengthened the opposition to Bairam Khan.

Gaekwad—is the family name of a Maratha chieftain who rose to power during the Peshwaship of Baji Rao I (1720-40). Little is known of Damaji I, the founder of the family which began to come into prominence during the life-time of his nephew Pilaji (1721-32) who began his career as an adherent of Khande Rao Dabade, the *Senapati* of King Shahu and built himself a fort at Songarh, fifty miles east of Surat, in 1720. He fought on the side of Trimbak Rao Dabade, son and successor of Khande Rao, in the battle of Bilhapur or Balapur in 1731 and on the defeat and death of Dabade in that battle he made his peace with Peshwa Baji Rao I and was placed in charge of the Maratha interests in Gujarat. The Gaekwad now set up his headquarters in Baroda. Pilaji was assassinated in 1732 and was succeeded by his son Damaji II who was present at the battle of Panipat in 1761, made good his escape but died in 1768. Damaji II left behind him a pretty large number of sons who carried on a sporadic succession war from 1768 to 1800 when Anand Rao, the son of Govinda Rao, the eldest son of Damaji II, got the throne. He ruled from 1800 to 1819 and during his rule the House of Gaekwad, which had always maintained peaceful treaty relations with the English, entered, without any fighting, into a subsidiary alliance with the English in 1805. To this alliance the House of Gaekwad remained loyal and thus escaped the horror and loss in men and money caused to the other Maratha leaders by the Second and Third Anglo-Maratha Wars. Ananda Rao was succeeded by his brother Sayaji II (1819-47) and he was succeeded, one after the other, by his three sons Ganpat Rao (1847-56), Khande Rao (1856-70) and Malhar Rao (1870-75). Malhar Rao was accused of gross misgovernment as well as of an attempt to kill by poisoning the British Resident, Col. Phayre. He was arrested and tried by a Commission appointed by Lord Northbrook, the Viceroy. The Commission was divided in their opinion as to the guilt of Malhar Rao who was, thereupon, acquitted of the charge of attempted murder but was deposed for his "notorious misconduct and gross misgovernment". As he had no son the Government of India installed on the throne a boy named Sayaji Rao who was distantly connected with the Gaekwad family and placed the administration of the state during the minority of the new ruler in the hands of Sir T. Madhava Rao. Sayaji Rao III who thus became the Gaekwad in 1875 lived up to 1939, proved to be one of the most enlightened of the Indian princes and made Baroda one of the most progressive of the Indian states.

Gahadvala (also pronounced Gaharwar), dynasty, the—was founded by a Rajput prince named Chandradeva in the last decade of the eleventh century. His grandson, Govinda Chandra, who reigned as crown prince from 1104 to 1114 and thereafter as king up to 1154, ruled over a vast kingdom comprising the greater part of the modern United Provinces and Bihar. He successfully defended holy places like Jetavana and Benares against the inroads of the Muslim Turks. He restored to some extent the glory of Kanauj which was his capital. His grandson was Raja Jaychandra, popularly known as Raja Jaichand,whose beautiful daughter was carried off by Prithviraj, the Chauhan king of Ajmer. This created such deep hostility between the two princes that Jaychandra did not lend any assistance to Prithviraj when the latter's kingdom was invaded by the Muslims who defeated and killed him in the second battle of Tarain in 1192. Two years later, in 1194, Jaychandra himself was defeated and killed by Shihabuddin Muhammad Ghuri in the battle of Chandwar on the Jumna. His capital Kanauj was sacked and destroyed by the Muhammadans and the Gahadvala dynasty came to an end.

Gajabahu—an ancient king of Ceylon, ruled between *c*. A.D. 173 and 191. This dating is significant inasmuch as it helps in fixing the dates of the early Pandya, Chera and Chola kings who were his contemporaries.

Gajapati Prataparudra—the king of Orissa, was defeated by the Vijayanagar king, Krishnadeva Raya (1510-30) to whom he lost the fortress of Udayagiri

Gakkars, the—were a tribal people who were subdued by Shihab-uddin Muhammad Ghuri in 1204 and again by Sher Shah in 1533 who built a fort at Rohtas in the Panjab for holding them down.

Gama, Vasco da—was the first Portuguese, and for the matter of that, the first European sailor who doubled the Cape of Good Hope and reached Calicut in May 1498. He was kindly received by the local Hindu Raja, known as the Zamorin, though the Muhammadan Arab traders tried to hamper him as much as they could. But Vasco da Gama succeeded in visiting Cochin and Cannanore and then safely made his return voyage, reaching Lisbon in August, 1499. He thus opened the direct sea route between Europe and India.

Ganda—the son and successor (A.D. 999-1025) of the Chandella king,

Dhanga, joined the confederacy of Hindu princes organised by king Anandapal of the Panjab in 1008-9, and shared in his defeat. Ten years later his son Vidyadhara attacked and killed Rajyapala, the king of Kanauj because he had made terms with Sultan Mahmud. The enraged Sultan invaded Ganda's kingdom and forced him to purchase peace by surrendering the fortress of Kalanjar. (*E.H.I.*, p. 407)

Gandamak, the treaty of—concluded in May 1879, marked a stage in the Second Afghan War (*q.v.*) (1878-80). It was concluded between the British Indian Government of which Lord Lytton was then at the head, and Yakub Khan, the eldest son of Sher Ali, the deposed Amir of Afghanistan. By this treaty Yakub Khan, who was recognised as the Amir, agreed to subordinate his foreign relations to British guidance, to accept a British Resident at his capital in Kabul and to assign to British control the Kurram Pass and the districts of Pishin and Sibi which lie near the Bolan Pass. The treaty of Gandamak marked the apogee of Lord Lytton's Afghan policy (*q.v.*) and gave to British India what was declared by Lord Beaconsfield, then the Prime Minister of England, to be "a scientific and adequate frontier". But the triumph was short-lived. On September 2, 1879, only four months after the conclusion of the treaty of Gandamak, there was a popular rising amongst the Afghans who killed the British Resident and thus turned the treaty of Gandamak into a worthless piece of paper. The war in Afghanistan flared up again and could be ended by surrendering not only their *protégé* Yakub Khan but also the idea of keeping a British Resident at Kabul and most of the territorial gains effected by the treaty.

Gandhara—is the name by which the land on both sides of the Indus embracing the modern Rawalpindi and Peshawar districts of West Pakistan was known in ancient times. It contained the two great cities of Taxila and Pushkaravati. Its people were also known as the Gandharas and are referred to in Asokan inscriptions. The land was included within the dominions of the Persian Emperor Darius as is proved by his Bahistan inscription (*q.v.*) (*c.* 520-518 B.C.). The kingdom at some time even included Kashmir. It was certainly a part of the empire of Asoka. It maintained close relations with India and a princess of Gandhara was the queen of the Kaurava king Dhritarashtra and the mother of Duryodhana, as related in the *Mahabharata*. After the decline and fall of the Maurya dynasty, Gandhara came to be parcelled out amongst the Indo-Bactrian princes and still later on it formed a part of the Kushan dominions. It thus became a meeting place of eastern and western cultures and gave birth to a school of art which bears its name.

Gandhi, Mohandas Karamchand—better known as Mahatma Gandhi, was born on October 2, 1869 at Porbandar in Western India. His parents were orthodox Hindus. His father Karamchand was the prime minister, first, to the ruler of Porbandar and later on to that of Rajkot in Kathiawar, and still later on to that of Wankaner. At the age of thirteen when he was still a school student Gandhi married Kasturbai, the daughter of a Porbandar merchant. The bride was of practically the same age as the bridegroom, and the marriage lasted till the death of Kasturbai in a British prison sixty-two years later. At the age of eighteen Gandhi became the father of a son and next year he left for England where he stayed for three years (1888-91) and qualified himself as a barrister-at-law. On his return to India he practised law at Rajkot and in Bombay but he had little success.

So when in 1892 an offer of a brief came from an Indian Muhammadan firm which had business in South Africa Gandhi readily accepted it and went to South Africa in 1893. Ere long he had the bitter experience of the humiliating treatment to which Indians were then subjected in South Africa. He was travelling with a first class ticket by railway from Durban to Pretoria. On the way at Maritzburg a white man entered the compartment in which Gandhi was travelling and had him ejected from the compartment with the help of the local police, for in South Africa no Indian, however rich and respectable, was to be allowed to travel in the first class along with white passengers. The Maritzburg incident had a profound influence in shaping Gandhi's career. As he himself wrote, "I was pushed out of the train by a police constable at Maritzburg, and the train having left, was sitting in the waiting room, shivering in the cold. I did not know where my luggage was nor did I dare to enquire of anybody, lest I might be insulted and assaulted once again. Sleep was out of the question. Doubt took possession of my mind. Late at night I came to the conclusion that to run back to India would be cowardly. I must accomplish what I had undertaken." The Maritzburg incident marked the dawn in his mind of the determination of dedicating himself for the emancipation of the Indians from the insulting life to which they had been so long condemned in South Africa. So for the next twenty years (1893-1914) Gandhi stayed, with short breaks, in South Africa where he soon took the leadership in a movement for removing the disabilities under which the Indians there were suffering. In pursuit of this movement he gave up the lucrative legal practice that he had soon acquired in South Africa, devoted himself to a drastic course of *brahmacharya* or self-discipline and lived with his family and friends in a self-supporting colony which he called Tolstoy Farm. He read deeply the *Bhagavatgita* (*q.v.*) on which he later on published a commentary as well as Ruskin and Tolstoy from all of which he drew his ideas and inspiration. He became convinced that a life to be useful must be full of activities unselfishly done for the good of the community and that a good life was the life lived near the soil, with a minimum dependence on machines. He formed the Natal Indian Congress in 1894 and in the course of the long South African agitation he, his wife and companions suffered arrest and imprisonment. Gandhi himself was assaulted personally on one occasion by Europeans who hated his presence in South Africa and on another occasion by some Indian Pathans because he supported a compromise with the South African leader, General Smuts who, however, proved untrue to his own pledged words. During the South African War of 1899-1902 and the Zulu rebellion of 1906 he organised with Indians an ambulance corps to nurse the wounded British soldiers, for he considered that it was the duty of the Indians to assist the British Empire in times of stress, as it was essentially beneficent. But the British imperialists were not touched. On the other hand, on the heels of a series of repressive measures an act was passed requiring every Indian living in the Transvaal to register himself along with every member of his family each of whom was to carry on his person an identity card. Against this humiliating law Gandhi organised a mighty movement of resistance amongst the Indians in South Africa based on the policy of **non-violent civil disobedience.** Under his leadership bands of Indians refused to register themselves and repeatedly crossed the Transvaal frontier in violation of the law and were put into prison until at last more than 2000 Indians followed Gandhi, non-violently disobeyed the law, crossed the frontier and were put into prison. The voluntary sufferings of these civil resisters at last forced the South African Government to repeal in 1914 most of the obnoxious acts and Gandhi and his creed of non-violent civil disobedience had their first great success.

In 1914 Gandhi returned to India and was received with great admiration by his countrymen who henceforth preferred to call him *Mahatma.* He spent the next four years in studying the

Indian situation and in preparing himself and those who wanted to follow him for *Satyagraha* or the application of soul force based on truth for the removal of the social and political inequities then prevalent in India. But he was no inactive observer. In 1917 he went to Champaran in north Bihar and by means of civil disobedience put a new courage and faith in the hearts of the down-trodden peasants and thus ended the long standing exploitation of the peasants by the European indigo-planters and Indian landlords. Soon afterwards he lent his leadership to the mill-hands at Ahmedabad who were badly underpaid, organised a strike by them which lasted 21 days and ended with the acceptance of the principle of arbitration by the employers and the labourers. Finally after the passing of the Rowlatt Acts (*q.v.*) in March, 1919 in the face of the united opposition of all Indian members of the Central Legislature and the Jalianwala Bagh massacre (*q.v.*) which followed in April, 1919, and which showed the utter contempt in which the Britishers held Indian lives, Gandhi declared the British Government in India to be 'satanic' and called upon all Indians to non-co-operate with it by withdrawing from all Government posts and offices and institutions, and even from schools and colleges and thus passively paralyse the British Government in India. At his call a *hartal* was observed in Bombay and all other important cities in India on March 30, 1919, by way of protest against the Rowlatt Acts and in the villages on April 6, 1919. Cities were all paralysed, all business was at a standstill and the British were helpless spectators. This showed the strength of the principle and practice of non-violent non-co-operation. In 1920 Gandhi became the leader of the Congress and under his direction and inspiration thousands of Indians gave up their connection, often very lucrative, with the British Government. Thousands of the non-co-operators were put into British prisons and many more thousands were extremely cruelly dealt with by the Government officials. In the face of such provocation the people could not remain non-violent and they broke out into violent acts in several places. Such outbreaks of violence were utterly distasteful to Gandhi who confessed that in asking the people to non-co-operate without first disciplining them in non-violence, he had committed a 'Himalayan miscalculation' and he called off the movement. The 'swaraj' that he had promised would come within a year as a result of non-violent non-co-operation, did not come and people were not wanting to point out the failure of the movement. But non-violent non-co-operation had really been a tremendous success; it had effectively shaken the corner-stone of the British empire in India by instilling in the minds of the conquered Indians the priceless virtue of fearlessness, by removing from the minds of thousands of Indians the fear of British guns, British bayonets and British prisons. Hence-forth the end of British rule in India was only a question of time. But the struggle was hard and long. In 1922 Gandhi was arrested on a charge of sedition, tried and sentenced by a sweet-tongued British judge to six years' imprisonment. In 1924 following an attack of appendicitis he was released.

Gandhi believed that India's future political progress depended on Hindu-Muslim unity and from 1918 he was busily engaged in its pursuit. He supported the demand of the Indian Muslims for the preservation of the Turkish Khilafat as a symbol of the unity of Islam; but his efforts failed to produce any permanent effect. In September, 1924, therefore, he undertook a three weeks' fast at Delhi in the house of the Muslim leader, Muhammad Ali, hoping thereby to bring about a complete understanding between the Hindus and the Muslims. For a time it seemed that his rigorous fast had attained its object, but the two communities soon drifted away from each other as a result of their mutual distrust and clashing interests which were encouraged by the Anglo-Indian Government. Gandhi called upon the Hindus to refrain from being agitated over the slaughter of cows by the Muhammadans and from the practice of taking processions with music in front of mosques in times of prayer. But these exhortations in their favour would not and did not mollify the Muhammadans; for their difference with the Hindus lay in causes deeper than objection to cow-slaughter and music before mosques. They apprehended that with the passing of power from the British to Indian hands the Muhammadans who were in a minority in India, would be placed under the rule of the Hindus who formed the vast majority of the population of India. This apprehension which was encouraged by the British rulers and the reality of which had been recognised by them by the introduction of communal representation in the Indian and provincial legislatures by the Government of India Acts of 1909 and 1919 could not be allayed by Gandhi and the Indian National Congress. Nor could any means be devised by which the Muhammadans could be assured of an equal share in the administration of a country where they were a minority. Herein lay the failure of Gandhi and of the Indian National Congress which he led and the genesis of Pakistan.

In 1925 being out of sympathy with the desire of most Congressmen to enter the legislatures set up by the Government of India Act, 1919, Gandhi retired for a time from active politics and during the next three years he devoted himself to the uplifting of the Indian villages by popularising amongst them hand-spinning with the *charkha* (spinning wheel) as a remedy for their dire poverty and on the removal of untouchability amongst the Hindus. This he called his 'constructive programme' and by it he came, more than any other Indian leader, closer to the villagers who formed 90% of the population of India. He moved from village to village visiting every part of India, dressed like a common villager and speaking to them in an Indian language. Thus he made the teeming millions of Indian villagers politically more conscious than ever before and changed the demand for national government from the level of the middle class agitation that it had so long been to a popular mass movement which soon became irresistible. In 1927 Gandhi resumed his political activities, as he saw that owing to the slow progress of the constitutional development the country was on the verge of plunging into a movement for violence. The Congress had already declared that full independence was its goal. Under Gandhi's leadership it was soon resolved that as the Government would not make any promise of the immediate grant of dominion status, the Congress would launch a new campaign of non-violent civil disobedience and Gandhi took charge of it. Accordingly, in 1930 Gandhi with some of his chosen followers walked all the way from Sabarmati Ashram near Ahmedabad to the sea at Dandi, and there he and his followers made salt from the sea-water which, under the existing laws, was illegal and punishable. This Salt March from Sabarmati to Dandi amounted to an active step of disobedience, defiance and revolution. It had an extraordinary effect on the country and before long many thousands of Indians all over the land followed his lead, broke such laws as they found convenient to do and the country was again plunged into a great agitation. The British Government at first tried its old remedy of severe repression and persecution, clapping thousands into the prisons. Gandhi himself was again imprisoned.

The British Government also opened political talks and in 1931 and 1932 Gandhi attended as the sole representative of the Indian National Congress the second and third Round Table Conferences (*q.v.*) held in London where he appeared dressed in 'dhoti and chaddar' like an ordinary Indian which provoked the derision of Sir Winston Churchill who called him an 'Indian Fakir' (beggar). Gandhi was received in audience by the King-Emperor, but he was disappointed with the result of the Conferences. On his way back he declared his intention to resume the Civil Disobedience Movement on his return to India. He was, therefore, arrested as soon as he landed in India. He was in prison when the British Prime Minister, Ramsay Macdonald, issued his infamous communal award (*q.v.*) in which separate representation was given not only to the Muham-madans and Christians but also to the scheduled castes amongst the Hindus. This was an attempt to drive a permanent wedge between them and the Caste Hindus. Gandhi appreciated the danger inherent in this new proposal and, in protest, started a fast unto death. He could not tolerate the idea of the perpetual separation of the untouchables from the rest of the Hindus. As a result of his fast a compromise was effected by the Poona Pact (*q.v.*) which provided for joint constituencies with reserved seats for the depressed classes for some years to come. The integrity and unity of Hindu society were thus preserved.

Gandhi was released in 1933 and for the next few years he concentrated his main attention to work for the untouchables, for the promotion of which he started a journal called the *Harijan* or *Children of God*. This weekly paper he continued to edit and publish during the rest of his life.

When the Second World War broke out, Gandhi was prepared to give his moral support to Great Britain and would do nothing that would embarrass Great Britain in a time of stress. He, therefore, would not support Netaji Subhas Bose in his attempts to promote the cause of Indian independence by securing the military aid of Germany or of Japan, but he agreed with other Congress leaders that India would fully co-operate with Great Britain if only the latter would give definite assurance of granting full freedom to India after the War. But as no such promise came he started in 1940 what was called 'Individual Civil Disobedience' to be undertaken by himself and his chosen followers. But as this movement did not sufficiently impress the British Government, Gandhi in August, 1942 called upon the British to 'quit India' and immediately transfer power to the Indians. The 'quit India' cry was taken up by thousands all over the country. Even the navy was affected. The British were again confronted with a mighty popular agitation; thousands were arrested and imprisoned and Gandhi himself was imprisoned, along with all Congress leaders, in 1943. Gandhi's wife, Kasturba, was also arrested and the British Government suffered her to die in detention in 1944.

Gandhi was soon afterwards released. The British and their allies won the war, but the British felt that in the face of the mighty popular demand for India's freedom they could no longer retain India, and they decided to transfer power to the Indians. But the question was whether free India should be one united country or divided into two on a communal basis. Self-interested leaders of both the communities plunged the country into a terrible communal riot in 1946. Gandhi was opposed to the division of the country as well as to the communal riots. He moved from village to village in Bengal, Bihar and the Panjab trying to instil into the popular mind the desirability and benefit of communal amity and national unity. But his efforts were unavailing. His comrades in the Congress accepted independence on the basis of a partition of the country into India and Pakistan and Gandhi had to fall in line with them. India got her independence on the 15th August, 1947. Horrible communal riots soon broke out and unspeakable horrors were committed against the minority communities on both sides of the western frontier. Delhi itself was badly affected by the communal riots and in the middle of January, 1948, Gandhi in Delhi again undertook a fast to allay communal discord. Within a few days a compromise was effected and communal amity was restored in the capital. Through Gandhi's intervention the newly established Government of India paid the Pakistan Government a very large sum of money to which many Hindus thought the Pakistan Government were not legally entitled. Gandhi thus came to be considered by some Hindus as an obstacle to the establishment of a Hindu Raj in India. On January 30, 1948, ten days after his last fast, Gandhi was fatally shot by one such Hindu fanatic when Gandhi was walking to his daily prayer meeting at the house where he was residing in Delhi.

The profound grief and sorrow with which the country heard of the demise of their great leader was voiced by Pandit Jawaharlal Nehru, the Prime Minister of India, who, in announcing the sad news of the murder of Gandhi said, "The light has gone out of our lives and there is darkness everywhere and I do not quite know what to tell you and how to say it. Our beloved leader, Bapu, as we call him, the father of our nation, is no more." Indeed Mahatma Gandhi was the father of the Indian nation which he had led within the short span of only twenty-seven years from the darkness of the centuries' old thraldom to the dawn of an age of independence. But Gandhi's contribution was not confined to the narrow boundaries of India alone. He exercised profound influence on humanity as a whole. As Arnold Toynbee observes, "The generation into which I happen to have been born has not only been Hitler's generation in the West and Stalin's in Russia: it has also been Gandhi's in India; and it can already be forecast with some confidence that Gandhi's effect on human history is going to be greater and more lasting than Stalin's or Hitler's." (Gandhi, M. K., *Autobiography;* Tendulkar, D. G., *Mahatma;* Fisher, L., *Life of Gandhi;* Mukherjee, H., *Gandhiji;* Toynbee. A., *Study of History,* Vol. xii)

Ganesh, Raja—was originally a powerful baron of Dinajpur in North Bengal. His ability, experience, wealth and other resources made him the foremost person at the court of Sultan Ghiyas-ud-din Azam (*c.* 1393-1410) of Bengal. On the death of the Sultan in A.D. 1410 a succession struggle ensued amongst his young sons and confusion prevailed in the country. Taking advantage of this confused condition Ganesh assumed the crown of Bengal in 817 A.H.=A.D. 1414. He also assumed the title of *Danuja-mardana-Deva.* He ruled for four years during which his kingdom was invaded by an army of Sultan Ibrahim Shah of Jaunpur. Raja Ganesh bought off the invaders, ruled efficiently and died peacefully in his old age in 821 A.H.=A.D. 1418. Raja Ganesh left behind him two sons, the elder, Jadu, who accepted Islam and the name of Jalal-ud-din and the younger Mahendra who remained true to his father's religion, Hinduism. After a futile attempt on the part of some persons to set up Mahendra on the throne lying vacant on his father's death the crown of Bengal was assumed by Ganesh's elder son Jadu or Jalal-ud-din who ruled over Bengal from 1418 to 1431. His son and successor Shams-ud-din Ahmad turned into a foolish tyrant and was murdered by two of his slaves in *c.* A.D. 1442. With his death the line of Raja Ganesh became extinct. (*H.B.*, II. pp. 120-129)

Ganga Bai—was the wife of Peshwa Narayan Rao (1772-73) who was murdered at the instigation of his uncle Raghoba in August, 1773. Next year Ganga Bai, the Peshwa's widowed wife, gave birth to a posthumous child who was named Madhav Rao Narayan who was the Peshwa from 1774 to 1796.

Gangadhar Shastri—the chief minister of the Gaekwaḍ of Baroda, was friendly towards the English and thereby incurred the displeasure of Peshwa Baji Rao II (1796-1818). In order to settle some outstanding disputes between the Peshwa and the

Gaekwaḍ, Gangadhar Shastri arrived in 1814 on a visit at Poona. The Peshwa conducted him to Nasik where Gangadhar was murdered at the instigation of the Peshwa's favourite, Trimbakji. The murder of Gangadhar Shastri was considered as an unfriendly act by the British Indian Government and indirectly contributed to the outbreak of the Third Maratha War (*q.v.*).

Gangaikonda—was the title assumed by the Chola king Rajendra Choladeva I (1018-35) in celebration of his victory either over Mahipala, the king of Bengal or over the Gangas. He also founded a new city called Gangaikonda Cholapuram in celebration of the victory. (*E.H.I.*, 487)

Gangaraja—was the minister of King Vishnuvardhana (*c*. 1110-41) of Dvarasamudra. The King was an ardent Vishnu-worshipper while his minister, Gangaraja, was a Jain who built many Jain temples.

Gangas, the dynasty of the—ruled over the greater part of Mysore from the second to the eleventh century of the Christian era. The first ruler, Konganivarma, distinguished himself in many battles and carved out a large kingdom for himself. His successors played an important part in the wars amongst the southern Indian kings and were sometimes under the suzerainty of the Pallavas. The Ganga kings of the tenth century were zealous patrons of Jainism. In A.D. 983 was executed the colossal statue of Gomata, $56\frac{1}{2}$ feet high, made to the order of Chamunda Rai, minister of the Ganga king Rasamalla IV, at Sravana Belgola. The power of the Gangas was destroyed by Vishnuvardhana (*c*. A.D. 1110-41) in the battle of Talaked. (*A.H.D.*)

Gangas, the Eastern—a branch of the Gangas of Mysore, ruled over Kalinga or Orissa. The founder of the dynasty was Vajrahasta whose son and successor Rajaraja I married Rajasundari, a daughter of Rajendra Choladeva II (A.D. 1070-1118). This union greatly added to the strength of the dynasty and enabled Anantavarman Choḍaganga (1078-1148) (*q.v.*), the son of Rajaraja I, to extend his kingdom northwards. He ruled for seventy years and his kingdom included part of the Northern Circars of Madras. He had a strong navy and repeatedly attacked the southern frontier of Bengal. Anantavarman was succeeded by his four sons who, one after another, ruled for a total period of sixty years. During this period the Muhammadans began their aggressions which the Eastern Ganga kings could not check. Nine generations of kings followed the four sons of Anantavarman until at last the last of them,

Narasimha IV, who ruled from 1384 to 1402, was overthrown by the Muhammadans. The Eastern Gangas were great patrons of art. The present temple of Jagannath at Puri (Orissa) and the temple of Rajarajeswara at Mukhalingam (Orissa) are the two most remarkable extant monuments of the Eastern Gangas who designed their temples on a grand scale that has remained unsurpassed anywhere else in India. (*P.A. & H.I.*, pp. 270 ff.; *E.H.I.*, p. 498)

Ganga Singh, Sir, Maharaja—ruled over Bikaner in Rajputana from 1887 to 1934. He was a progressive Indian prince. He was the first Chancellor of the Chamber of Princes (1921-25) and General Secretary of the Princes' Conference held in Delhi, 1916-20. On the outbreak of the First World War in 1914 he placed all his resources at the disposal of the British Government and offered his personal services. He was appointed to the staff of Sir John French, the British Commander-in-Chief in France.

Ganges, the—is the most sacred river of the Hindus. On its banks stand numerous cities, the most ancient and sacred of which is Benares (*q.v.*). Lower down the river stood the imperial city of Pataliputra at the confluence of the Ganges and the Son. In modern times the city of Calcutta has been built up on one of the branches of the Ganges which continues to be a great highway of commerce and to fertilize with its rich alluvial deposits the major portion of north India. The basin of the Ganges has been and still is the heart of India. The Doab lying between the Ganges and the Jumna is the most fertile part of India and has witnessed the rise and fall of numerous dynasties in India.

Gangeyadeva Kalachuri—the king (*c.* 1015-40) of Chedi (*q.v.*) lying between the Jumna and the Narmada rivers, was an able and ambitious prince who assumed the title of Vikramaditya and tried to attain with some success the position of the paramount sovereign in upper India. In 1019 his suzerainty was recognised in distant Tirhut (modern Bihar). Allahabad and Benares were protected by him against invaders from the northwest as well as against the Pala kings of Bengal. He was succeeded by his son, Karna or Laksmi-Karna (*c.* 1040-70 A.D.)

Gangu—was, according to Firishta, a Brahman astrologer of Delhi, who was the master of Hasan and foretold the future greatness of the founder of the Bahmani kingdom. This story is not corroborated by other chronicles or by the evidence of coins and inscriptions.

Ganjam—a town in Orissa, was in A.D. 619 under the control of the Bengal king Sasanka, contemporary and rival of Emperor Harshavardhana of Kanauj (A.D. 606-47). It was invaded by Harsha in A.D. 643 when it passed under his control. It is now an important town.

Garah Katanga—in Gondwana, roughly corresponded to the northern districts of the modern state of Madhya Pradesh (Central Provinces). In 1564 when it was being administered by Rani Durgavati on behalf of her minor son, Bir Narayan, it was invaded by Akbar (1556-1605) in pursuit of a policy of wanton aggression and was conquered and annexed to the latter's dominions.

Gardner, Col. Alexander Houghton (1785-1877)—an English adventurer and soldier of fortune, came overland to Afghanistan where he took service under Habibullah Khan and fought in his wars against his uncle Amir Dost Muhammad. In 1826 Gardner left Afghanistan and passed into the Panjab where he joined Ranjit Singh's service as a Colonel and helped in the training of his artillery. He helped the Sikhs in their war against the Afghans in 1835. He also took part in the succession war that followed the death of Ranjit Singh, was at Lahore during the First Sikh War (*q.v.*) but was given no active part in it. In 1846 he entered the service of Raja Gulab Singh in Jammu and Kashmir and remained there till his death in 1847.

Garhgaon—was the capital of Assam during the rule of the Ahom kings (A.D. 1228-1824). It stood on the river Dikhu in the modern Sibsagar district. The city was attacked and occupied in 1662-63 by Muslims under Mir Jumla, the general of Emperor Aurangzeb (1658-1707). Shihab-ud-din, who wrote a detailed account of the expedition, was much impressed by the grandeur and strength of the city of Garhgaon which had four gates of stone set in mud, each of which led to the royal palace three *kos* (two miles) away. Around the city, in the place of a wall, there was an encampassing bamboo plantation running continuously, two *kos* or more in width. Round the palace there was a moat, deeper than a man's height and full of water. The palace stood on 66 pillars, each four cubits round, The pillars were extremely smooth and the woodwork in the palace was so grand and fine that Shihab-ud-din believed that nowhere else in the world could wooden houses be built with such decoration and figure-carving as by the people of this country. Assam threw off the Mughul yoke in 1667 and Garhgaon continued to be the capital of the Ahom kings until the British conquest of Assam in 1824. (*H.A.*, p. 149)

Gauhati—the largest town in Assam, stands on the left or southern
bank of the Brahmaputra. It traces its history back to a very
ancient period when it was the capital of the kingdom of Kamarupa and bore the name Pragjyotishapura. Not very far from
the modern city of Gauhati is situated the temple of Goddess
Kamakhya on the Nilachala hill. When exactly the town dropped
the old name of Pragjyotishapura and came to be called Gauhati
is uncertain. Probably the new name replaced the old some
time after the decline and fall of the ancient Hindu kingdom
of Kamarupa in the middle of the twelfth century and the
conquest of the region by the Muhammadans early in the
sixteenth century. At any rate, the town had definitely come to
be known as Guva-hati or Gauhati by 1637 when it was made
the headquarters of the Mughul administrator in lower Assam.
Thirty years later the town was recovered by the Ahom king
Chakradvaj Singh (1663-69) who established a viceroy (*Bar
Phukan*) in the city. It was again conquered by Mir Jumla for the
Mughuls in 1679 but recovered in 1682 by the Ahom king
Gadadhar Singh (*q.v.*) (1681-96). In 1786 the Ahom king, Gauri-
nath Singh (1780-94), made it his capital. In 1793 Captain
Welsh, who led a British relieving army into the town, found it
an extensive and populous place situated on both banks of the
mighty Brahmaputra. It lost its metropolitan status soon after
the occupation of Assam by the British who fixed the new capital
at Shillong. Gauhati at present is the emporium of Assam's
trade, the seat of a University and the centre of the throbbing
life of a new Assam.

Gauda, city of—in the modern district of Maldah in West Bengal,
was the capital of Bengal during the rule of the Sena kings
(eleventh and twelfth centuries). It was captured by Malik
Iktyar-ud-din Muhammad Bakhtiyar in A.D. 1203. It was made
the capital of Bengal by Ghyas-ud-din Iwaz in 1220. It was
plundered and burnt by Sher Shah in 1538. Emperor Humayun
restored and reconstructed the city. In 1570 Gauda was occupied
by an expeditionary force of Emperor Akbar. This occupation
was followed by a violent outbreak of an epidemic which depo-
pulated the city and a change in the course of the nearby Ganges
completed its downfall. It is now a heap of ruins, almost
overgrown with forests. The city in its days of prosperity
was $7\frac{1}{2}$ miles in length and about 2 miles in breadth and was
surrounded by strong ramparts. Gauda developed its own
architectural style, the principal characteristic being heavy
short pillars of stone supporting pointed arches and vaults in

brick. The finest ruins at Gauḍa are the Great Golden Mosque (1526), the Small Golden Mosque, the Loton Mosque with the unique glazed tiles and the Kadam Rasul Mosque (1530) which is still in good condition.

Gauḍa—is referred to both as a country and as a people in early literature like the *sutras* of Panini, Kautilya's *Arthasastra* and some of the Puranas. It denoted Western and North-Western Bengal as well as the people of the region. It was distinct from Vanga which comprised Eastern and Central Bengal. The Allahabad inscription of Samudragupta (c. A.D. 330-80) which shows that Bengal was within the Gupta Empire, does not, however, specifically mention Gauḍa. The state of Gauḍa came into prominence after the fall of the Imperial Guptas under several local rulers of whom Gopachandra and Samacharadeva were more prominent who turned Gauḍa into a great military power. In the seventh century the Gauḍa king, Sasanka, who had his capital at Karnasuvarna (usually placed in the Murshidabad district), waged a long war against the Pushyabhuti dynasty of Thaneswar killing its second king, Rajyavardhana (*q.v.*) and resisting the war of revenge on which Rajyavardhana's brother and successor, Harshavardhana (*q.v.*), embarked in alliance with Kumar Bhaskaravarman of Kamarupa (Assam) till at least A.D. 619. After Sasanka's death his capital Karnasuvarna passed, at least for some time, under the rule of Bhaskaravarman. How long his rule lasted is not known. The hundred years from the middle of the seventh to the middle of the eighth century were a period of turmoil, foreign invasions and anarchy in Gauda which came to an end with the enthronement of the Pala dynasty (c. A.D. 750) the kings of which assumed the title of Gauḍesvara. Gauḍa became a most prominent power in northern India during the reigns of the second Pala king, Dharmapala (c. A.D. 752-810) and his son Devapala (c. A.D. 810-49). Thereafter with the decline of the Pala power Gauḍa also declined until at last in about (c. A.D. 1158) it passed under the rule of the new dynasty of the Senas from whom it was conquered by Malik Ikhtiyar-ud-din Muhammad, son of Bakhtiyar Khalji, towards the close of the twelfth century. With its conquest by the Muhammadans Gauḍa ceased to have a separate existence as a state, though the city (*q.v.*) bearing its name continued to have the honour of being a provincial capital for another three centuries. (*H. B.*, Vol. I.)

Gautama, the Buddha—*see* Buddha.

Gautami Balasri—a dowager-queen of the Satavahana dynasty,

is mentioned in an inscription found at Nasik where she is
described as a lady who delighted in truth, charity, patience
and respect for life, who was bent on penance, self-control,
restraint and abstinence. She was an ideal *rajarshibadhu* (a royal
sage's wife) and was the mother of the famous Satavahana king,
Gautamiputra Satakarni.

Gautamiputra Satakarni—a famous king of the Satavahana
dynasty, ruled in the first quarter of the second century of the
Christian era. He extirpated the Kshaharata dynasty which had
been established by Bhumaka and annexed their dominions to
his kingdom which comprised Malwa, Kathiawar, Gujarat,
North Konkan, Berar and the whole country watered by the
Godavari. He was a champion of Hinduism and claimed to
have destroyed the Sakas, Yavanas (Greeks) and Pahlavas
(Parthians). He made liberal donations to Brahmans and Buddhists and prided himself on having re-established the practice
of caste rules. At any rate he restored the glory of the Satavahana dynasty.

Gawilgarh—a strong fortress in Berar, was built by the Bahmani
sultans and later on passed under the control of the Marathas.
In the course of the Second Maratha War (1804-6) the fortress
was captured by the English on the 15th December, 1803 from
the Bhonsla Raja of Berar.

Gawspur—a small state in modern Uttara Pradesh, was given to
the Pindari leader, Karim Khan, after he had surrendered to the
British in 1818. His descendants ruled the state till modern times.

Gaya—a town in Bihar, is a place of pilgrimage for the Hindus
who consider it a sacred duty to offer oblations to their forefathers at a particular spot of this town which is believed to
contain the footprints of *Vishnu*. Within a few miles of Gaya
is Bodh-Gaya where Gautama Buddha attained enlightenment. Bodh-Gaya is a holy place to the Buddhists. Gaya
attracts a very large number of pilgrims every year, especially
during the fortnight known as *Pitripaksha* (i.e. fortnight
sacred to the forefathers) when Hindus from far and near
crowd into the city and offer their oblations with the waters
and sand of the river Phalgu which flows by the city. Gaya is
now the seat of the University of Magadha.

Gedrosia—the name by which Baluchistan was known to the Greeks,
was conquered by Alexander the Great in the course of his
Indian expedition, but was later on surrendered by Seleukos
Nicator (*q.v.*) to Chandragupta Maurya (*c.* 323 B.C. - 298 B.C.)
and became included in the Indian empire of the Mauryas.

Gamelli-Careri, Dr.—a learned Italian lawyer, visited India during the closing years of the reign of Emperor Aurangzeb (1658-1707). He had the honour of an audience with the Emperor in his camp at Galgala on the Krishna near the town of Mudhol in 1695. He has left a very interesting account of the appearance and habits of the aged Emperor as well as of his camp which had a circumference of thirty miles, a population of half a million and 250 separate markets where every class of goods including the most costly articles were offered for sale.

General Society—*see* Company, East India.

Ghafur Khan—was the son-in-law of Amir Khan, predatory Afghan mercenary leader, who was recognised by the Company as the Nawab of Tonk in 1817. Ghafur Khan was similarly recognised as the Nawab of Jaora which was ceded to the British by Holkar by the treaty of Mandasor in 1819.

Ghairwajh—a technical term, denoted the irregular troops in the army of Sultan Firuz Shah Tughluq (1351-88). They were paid their salaries direct from the royal treasury.

Ghalib Khan—a feudatory Pathan chief, set himself up as an independent ruler in the fief of Samana soon after the invasion of India by Timur in 1398-99.

Ghasiti Begum—was the eldest daughter of Alivardi Khan, Nawab of Bengal (1740-56). She was married to Nawazis Muhammad, a son of the elder brother of Nawab Alivardi Khan. Nawazis was made governor at Dacca, where he died. His widowed wife, Ghasiti Begum, returned to Murshidabad. Her financial affairs were looked after by Diwan Rajballabh while Husain Quli Khan became her trusted agent on her return to Murshidabad. Ghasiti who was the elder aunt of Siraj-ud-daula would not support his succession to the throne after Alivardi Khan. She professed the claims of Shaukat Jang, the son of her second sister and governor of Purnia. Siraj was inflamed by hearing rumours of improper intimacy between Ghasiti Begum and Husain Quli Khan and murdered the latter in broad daylight in a public street in the city of Murshidabad. This widened the breach between Ghasiti Begum and Siraj. Accordingly, when there was no hope of the recovery of Alivardi Khan from the illness into which he had fallen early in 1756, Ghasiti Begum, acting on the advice of Rajballabh, left the Nawab's palace at Murshidabad and took up her residence with a guard of 10,000 men at Moti Jhil, a garden house two miles south of the city, and became the centre of a conspiracy against Siraj-ud-daula. But soon after his accession Siraj succeeded by a masterly stroke in quietly removing Ghasiti Begum from her residence at Moti Jhil to the Nawab's palace in Murshidabad. Rajballabh fled with her wealth to the English, but Ghasiti Begum was effectively prevented from taking any further part in the conspiracy against Siraj-ud-daula. Her sister's son, Shaukat Jang, was defeated and killed in battle by Siraj-ud-daula later in the year 1756. Ghasiti Begum henceforward ceased to influence Bengal politics and died in oblivion. Moti Jhil now stands as a ruin.

Ghazi—is a title meaning 'holy warrior'. Amongst others Emperor Aurangzeb assumed this title.

Ghazi Malik—*see* Ghiyas-ud-din Tughluq.

Ghazi-ud-din Firuz Jang—a Persian, came to India during the reign of Aurangzeb and rose to fame by holding several posts in the Mughul imperial service. He was present at the siege of Bijapur in 1685 and of Golconda in 1687 and exhibited courage and skill. He lost his eye-sight as the result of an attack of bubonic plague in 1688, but continued to be an influential member of the Mughul court till his death. His son was Mir Qamar-ud-din Chin Qilich Khan who became the first Nizam of Hyderabad in 1713.

Ghazi-ud-din Imad-ul-Mulk—son of Ghazi-ud-din Khan, the eldest son of the first Nizam of Hyderabad. When his father was poisoned to death in 1752 at Aurangabad at the instance of his step-mother Ghazi-ud-din was in Delhi, and with the help of Safdar Jang, an influential nobleman, who was the governor of Oudh, became the Paymaster-General. Almost immediately he turned against his patron Safdar Jang and called in the Marathas with whose help he deposed the reigning Emperor Ahmad Shah (1748-54). Young, wicked and faithless Ghazi-ud-din had vaulting ambition, but he lacked sufficient military skill and the power for organisation. He could do nothing to stop the aggression of Ahmad Shah Abdali who invaded and sacked Delhi in 1756 and occupied the Panjab. Ghazi-ud-din intrigued with the Marathas after Abdali's departure and connived at the occupation of the Panjab by the Marathas in 1758. But in 1759 Abdali again invaded India and recovered the Panjab and Ghazi-ud-din, who was in essence a bully, secured pardon of Abdali. But as soon as Abdali went back Ghazi-ud-din resumed his bullying tactics and murdered Emperor Alamgir II in 1759 and set up a grandson of Kam Baksh, the youngest son of Emperor Aurangzeb, as Emperor Shah Jahan III. But Abdali soon reappeared and Ghazi-ud-din took shelter with the Jat ruler Suraj Mall in the hope of organising with Maratha help a successful opposition to Abdali. But the latter's decisive victory over the Marathas in the third battle of Panipat (1761) crushed the Marathas and ended the intrigues and political activities of Ghazi-ud-din who died in 1800.

Ghazni—a fortified mountain town in Afghanistan, 78 miles south west of Kabul, is a great trading centre. It sprang into fame in the tenth century when it became the capital of a kingdom set up by a Turk named Alptigin who died in A.D. 963. The city was adorned with many buildings, wide roads, museums etc., by Alptigin's grandson, Sultan Mahmud (997-1030), but it was burnt to ashes in 1151 by Ala-ud-din Husain of Ghur who received on this account the title of Jahan-soz (world burner). Later on it was partially restored when it became the headquarters of the kingdom ruled over by Shihabuddin Muhammad Ghuri, the first Muslim conqueror of Hindusthan and has continued till modern times to be a place of great strategic importance, though its fortifications were all destroyed by the British General, Nott, in the course of the First Afghan War (*q.v.*).

Ghaznavids—were the rulers of Ghazni starting with Alptigin who died in A.D. 963. They ruled till 1173 and the more important amongst them were Amir Subuktigin (977-97), Sultan Mahmud (997-1030), and Bahram Shah during whose rule Ghazni was burnt in 1151 by Ala-ud-din Hussain of Ghur. His son, Khusru Shah left Ghazni and retired to the Panjab making Lahore his headquarters in 1160. The last of the Ghaznavids was Khusru Malik, son and successor of Khusru Shah, who was deposed by Shihabuddin Muhammad Ghuri in 1186. With him ended the line of the Ghaznavids.

Ghazni Khan—the seventh sultan of Khandesh, was the son and successor of the sixth sultan, Daud. He was poisoned to death within ten days of his accession in 1508.

Ghilzais, the—an Afghan tribe, took advantage of the insecurity of the British expeditionary force in Afghanistan in 1840 and rose in revolt. Though suppressed for the time being they rose in revolt again in 1841 and contributed much to the disasters that befell the retreating British army on its way from Kabul to Jelalabad in 1841-42.

Ghiyas-ud-din of Ghur—the sultan of Ghur, wrested in 1173 Ghazni from the Turkmans who had held the city and its neighbourhood since 1151. He made over this region to his brother Shihabuddin or Muizuddin Muhammad Sam, better known as Muhammad Ghuri. Ghiyas-ud-din died in 1203 leaving his throne to his brother Shihabuddin who had already conquered Delhi.

Ghiyas-ud-din Balban—*see ante* Balban.

Ghiyas-ud-din Bahadur—was one of the five sons of Shams-ud-din Firoz Shah, the governor of Bengal. On the death of Shams-ud-din in 1318 Ghiyas-ud-din Bahadur who had been ruling over Eastern Bengal since 1310 as an independent sovereign, contested with his brothers for the throne of Bengal. He was defeated and made a captive by Sultan Ghiyas-ud-din Tughluq, (*q.v.*) in 1324 and ended his life as a prisoner in Delhi.

Ghiyas-ud-din Bahmani—the sixth sultan of the Bahmani dynasty, ruled only for a few months in 1397. He was blinded and deposed.

Ghiyas-ud-din Khilji—the second sultan of the Khilji dynasty of Malwa, ruled from 1469 to 1501 peacefully leaving his crown to his elder son whom he had enthroned in 1500, when he was still alive.

Ghiyas-ud-din Mahmud Shah—was the last king of the Husain Shahi dynasty which ruled in Bengal from 1493 to 1538. He came to the throne of Bengal in 1533 but was expelled from Bengal after a short reign of five years by Sher Khan Sur (*q.v.*).

Ghiyas-ud-din Tughluq (**also called Tughluq Shah**)—was a sultan of Delhi (1320-25) and the founder of the Tughluq dynasty. His father was a Turkish slave of Sultan Balban (1266-86) (*q.v.*) who was manumitted by the Sultan and married a Jat lady. His earlier name was Ghazi Malik and he rose by dint of his merit and valour. He was appointed to the important post of the Warden of the Marches by Sultan Ala-ud-din Khalji (1296-1316) and successfully defended the north-western frontiers against the Mongols. He took a leading part in defeating, and dethroning Khusrav (*q.v.*) who had usurped the throne of the Delhi sultans in 1320 and was acclaimed as the sultan of Delhi by the nobles of the court in September, 1320. He now assumed the title of Ghiyas-ud-din Tughluq. His rule lasted only for five years but during this short period he re-established the military might of the Delhi sultanate, subdued the Kakatiya king, Prataparudradeva II of Warangal and Ghiyas-ud-din Bahadur, the rebellious ruler of Bengal, and also improved the administration by resuming unlawful land grants, by appointing capable and upright persons as governors of provinces, by restraining official rapacity and extortion in respect of land revenue, by promoting agriculture, by constructing irrigation works, by improving the administration of justice and police, by devising a system of poor relief, and by developing the postal system. He also patronised men of letters amongst whom Amir Khusrav, the poet, was the most prominent. Ghiyas-ud-din's rule was cut short by an accident which, according to some, was premeditated by his son and successor, Jauna Khan (*q.v.*).

Ghosh, Aravinda (1872-1950)—an ardent nationalist who later on became a saint, was educated in England and competed for the Indian Civil Service. But he was disqualified in the riding test and began his career in India as the Vice-Principal of Baroda College. There he soon began to take a lively interest in Indian politics by publishing a series of articles in the *Induprakash*. His very first article published on August 7, 1893, showed that he stood for a fundamental change in the attitude of the Indians to politics. In these articles he declared that the Indian National Congress by its moderate principles, had failed to give the country the proper leadership and he emphasized the need for making the Congress a really popular body by holding up before the nation a nobler and more inspiring patriotism and also the need for purification by blood and fire. His views were readily accepted by Lala Lajpat Rai of the Panjab and Bal Gangadhar Tilak of Maharashtra and led to the formation within the Congress of an extremist school which would not hesitate to resort to force for achieving their political aims. In 1902 Aravinda sent an agent from Baroda to Bengal to organise secret societies for terroristic activities. He also soon afterwards personally came to Bengal where he became the Principal of the National College and began to propagate his ideas through journals like the *Bandemataram* and *Karmayogin* which he edited with great credit and ability. All this propaganda led to several terroristic outrages in Bengal resulting in the prosecution of Aravinda, along with many young Bengalees, in the celebrated Alipore Bomb case. After a prolonged trial Aravinda was acquitted, but the British Government looked upon him as an irreconcilable opponent of British rule in India and contemplated his arrest and detention. In the meantime a change had come over Aravinda's thoughts and ideas. He decided to cease to take an active part in politics, and retired in 1909 to Pondicherry which was then a French possession. There he founded an *ashrama* which aimed at inspiring men to live a higher life, the essential ideas of which he set forth in his great work, the *Divine Life*. He passed away in 1950, leaving behind him a great tradition of intrepid courage, high patriotism and of a higher and purer life dedicated to the illumination of mankind and has been called 'a poet of patriotism, prophet of nationalism and lover of humanity'. and reverentially named Sree Aravinda. (Purani, *Life of Sri Aravinda*)

Ghose, Lalmohan (1849-1909)—was a Barrister-at-law, practising in the Calcutta High Court. When in 1877 the reduction of the maximum limit of age for the open competitive examination for the Indian Civil Service from 21 to 19 was first proposed for the purpose of making it more difficult for Indian nationals to sit for it, the Indian Association in Calcutta drew up an All-India Memorial on this question and sent under the leadership of Lalmohan Ghose a deputation to the House of Commons in 1879-80. Lalmohan Ghose presented the Indian case admirably and his eloquence made a profound impression on the English mind. The statutory Civil Service (*q.v.*) was instituted by the British Government in response to this representation. Encouraged by this success Lalmohan went to England again and stood for election to the British Parliament as a Liberal party candidate. He failed to win the election, but his effort encouraged the national movement in India. Lalmohan was a thorough constitutionalist and thoroughly loyal to the British connection. He was the greatest Indian orator of his time and his adherence to it added much strength to the Indian National Congress.

Ghose, Rashbehari—was a leading *vakil* of the Calcutta High Court. He was elected President of the Surat session of the Indian National Congress in 1907 in which the Moderates and Extremists came to a serious clash leading to the break-up of the session. Next year he presided over the Madras session of the Indian National Congress. Rashbehari Ghose was a person of great munificence and it was his princely donations to the Calcutta University that enabled that University to take up Post-Graduate teaching, especially in scientific subjects.

Ghosha—was one of the few eminent Indian ladies of the Vedic age. Some of the hymns of the Vedas are attributed to her.

Ghulam Husain Khan Tabataba, Syed—a famous historian, was a Muhammadan nobleman related as a cousin to Nawab Alivardi Khan (*q.v.*) of Bengal. He was the Mir Munshi of the Mughul Emperor and was posted at the court of the Nawab of Bengal at Murshidabad. Later on he represented for some time Nawab Mir Kasim (*q.v.*) at Calcutta and entered the service of the East India Company on the fall of Nawab Mir Kasim. He was a historian of great merit and his *Siyar-al-Muta-kharin* is a very authoritative and reliable account of the decay of the Mughul Empire and of Muhammadan domination in India during the reigns of the last seven Mughul emperors of India. It also traces the progress of the English in Bengal up to A.D. 1780.

Ghulam Qadir— a grandson of the Rohilla chief, Najib-ud-daula (*q.v.*), practically ruled Delhi from 1761 to 1770 as the deputy of Ahmad Shah Abdali as well as of the Mughul Emperor Shah Alam II (1759-1806). In 1787 Ghulam Qadir seized Delhi in the expectation of getting rich plunder. But Delhi had been recently bled white by Abdali's raids and plunder and Qadir did not find in the palace the treasure he had expected. In a fit of frenzied frustration he blinded Emperor Shah Alam II. Qadir was soon afterwards defeated and executed by Mahadaji Sindhia who then became the practical protector of the Mughul Emperor.

Ghur, the sultans of—were of eastern Persian extraction and were originally feudatories of the sultans of Ghazni. Taking advantage of the weakness of the later Ghaznavids (*q.v.*) the chiefs of Ghur entered into a prolonged contest with them for supremacy until at last in A.D. 1151 the Ghuri chief Ala-ud-din Husain sacked the city of Ghazni and burnt it completely. He thus liberated Ghur from subordination to Ghazni and assumed the title and dignity of the sultan. Though his son and successor, Saif-ud-din Muhammad, was killed soon after his accession in a battle with the Ghazz Turkmans his cousin and successor, Ghiyas-ud-din Muhammad, proved a very successful ruler. He occupied Ghazni in 1173 and appointed as its governor his younger brother, Shihabuddin, also known as Muizuddin Muhammad bin Sam and popularly called Muhammad of Ghuri (*q.v.*). It was from his base at Ghazni that Shihabuddin started on his Indian campaigns beginning with an attack on Multan in A.D. 1175 and culminating in his great victory in the second battle of Tarain over the Chouhan king, Prithvi Raj of Delhi and Ajmer, in A.D. 1192 leading to the establishment of Muslim rule over northern India. In A.D. 1203 Sultan Ghiyas-ud-din Muhammad died and Shihabuddin became the ruler of Ghur, Ghazni and northern India. His rule was short, as he was killed by Khokar rebels in A.D. 1206. He left behind no male heirs to succeed him and with his death the line of the sultans of Ghur became practically extinct.

Gilgit—is the name of a river and of the valley through which it runs. The Gilgit is a tributary of the Indus and running along the Gilgit valley it flows into Kashmir. The headquarters of the district which lies to the extreme north-west of Kashmir is also

Gilgit. It is strategically very important, for it gives direct communication with Chitral and through Chitral it opens the road to Afghanistan. Consequently, the Government of India during the regime of Lord Lytton I (*q.v.*) became very anxious for establishing direct control over this district which was within the territories of the Maharaja of Kashmir. Fear of Russian aggression in the region added strength to the expansionist policy of the Government of India. By a confidential arrangement with the Maharaja of Kashmir, Lord Lytton I established a British agency in Gilgit and in 1889 a British officer was sent to Gilgit. These activities of the Indo-British Government caused irritation to Amir Abdur Rahman of Afghanistan who feared not unreasonably that the presence of a British agent at Gilgit presaged British aggressive designs on Afghanistan. Thus Gilgit continued to be a sore point in Indo-Afghan relations. Recently the district has been occupied by the so-called Azad Kashmir Government sponsored by Pakistan and is thus practically under the control of Pakistan.

Gillespie, General Sir R. R.—won a great reputation by defeating the French in Java in 1811 but was defeated and killed in the Gurkha War (1814-15) by the Gurkhas while he was trying to storm the mountain fortress of Kalanga. It was a major reverse and tended to lower British prestige.

Gingee—a strong fortress in the Carnatic, lay within the dominions of the sultan of Golkonda. In 1677 the Maratha king Shivaji captured the fortress which along with the surrounding district formed a part of his dominions at the time of his death in 1680. Shivaji's second son, Raja Ram, who became king after the capture and execution by the Mughuls of his elder brother, Shambhuji, in 1689, had to escape from the Maratha capital Raigarh which the Mughuls captured and fled to Gingee which was soon turned into the centre of Maratha enterprise on the east coast. The rock fortress of Gingee consists of three fortified hillocks connected by strong walls and forms a triangle nearly 3 miles in circumference. These hills are steep and rocky and covered with enormous boulders. Emperor Aurangzeb felt that the capture of this strongly fortified place was essential for the reduction of Raja Ram. Accordingly the fortress was besieged by a Mughul army in 1690, but so strong were its defences that the fort stood a brave siege, repulsed the Mughuls several times and could be captured only after eight years of military effort in 1698. But Raja Ram escaped unhurt and the Mughul victory proved ineffective.

Giria—near Rajmahal in Bihar, was the scene of two battles. The first was fought in A.D. 1740 between Alivardi Khan (*q.v.*) who claimed to be the Nawab of Bengal, against his rival Sarfaraz Khan who was defeated and killed. This victory enabled Alivardi Khan to occupy the *masnad* of Bengal. The second battle at Giria was fought in 1763 between Nawab Mir Kasim (*q.v.*) of Bengal and the East India Company. Mir Kasim was defeated in this and three other successive battles and obliged to flee to Patna, eventually losing the *masnad* of Bengal.

Girivraja—is the ancient name of the modern town of Rajgir in Patna district. King Bimbisara (*c.* 550 B.C.) built the city, named it Rajagriha, or the king's house and made it his capital. A later king of his dynasty who was named Kalasoka transferred the capital from Girivraja or Rajagriha to Pataliputra. It was at Rajagriha that the first Buddhist Church Council was held shortly after the death of Buddha in 486 B.C. and the *Dharma* (*Abhidharma*) and *Vinaya* Pitakas were drawn up. Girivraja or Rajagriha long continued to be an important place variously associated with Buddhism. Rajgir in modern times is patronised as a health-resort on account of its hot springs.

Girnar—is situated near Junagarh, in the Kathiawar peninsula. A version of the Fourteen Rock Inscriptions of Asoka Maurya (*c.* 273 B.C. - 232 B.C.) is incised on a rock here and on another side of the same rock is incised an inscription of the Saka Satrap Rudradaman (*c.* A.D. 150) which refers to the construction there of a lake named *Sudarshana* by the order of the first Maurya Emperor Chandragupta (*c.* 322 B.C. - 298 B.C.). Besides these two most important historical records, Girnar also contains a large number of magnificent temples built by the Chalukya kings of Gujarat. (*R.A.S.W.I.* II; & *E.I.* viii, 36)

Gita Govinda—is a book of the sweetest Sanskrit lyrics. It was composed by Jayadeva, a Bengali poet, who graced the court of king Lakshmana Sena (*q.v.*) of Bengal (*c.* 1178-1203). The songs refer to the love of Govinda (Krishna) and Radha and express the intense yearning of the soul for the company of the Supreme Being called Govinda.

Gladstone, Rt. Hon. William Ewart, (1809-98)—was a famous British statesman and politician in the reign of Queen Victoria. He was the leader of the Liberal party in Britain and was the Prime Minister four times, from 1868-74, 1880-85, 1885 and 1892-94. He tried to breathe some degree of liberalism into the administration of India and was opposed to the expansionist policy of the Conservatives which led to the two

Afghan Wars. He appointed Lord Ripon as the Viceroy of India who held office from 1880 to 1884 and earned great popularity with the people. Gladstone concluded the Second Afghan War (1878-80) by recognising Abdur Rahman as the Amir of Afghanistan into the affairs of which he discouraged unnecessary British intervention. Gladstone's well-known liberal principles and his sympathy for Irish nationalism promoted liberalism amongst the educated section of the Indian people and led them to look upon him as a supporter of liberalism in India.

Glaukanikoi, the—a tribal people, occupied at the time of Alexander's invasion a part of the Panjab to the west of the Chinab and conterminous with the dominion of Poros(*q.v.*). They had a state with thirty-seven cities many of which had a population of more than 10,000. After the defeat of Poros, Alexander personally led an expedition into the territories occupied by the Glaukanikoi (also called the Glausi) and received their submission.

Goa—is an important island and port on the western coast of India, about 200 miles south of Bombay. It has always been an important entrepot for trade between India and the Western world. It was in the possession of the sultan of Bijapur in A.D. 1510 when it was stormed and occupied by the Portuguese under the leadership of Albuquerque. The efforts of the Mughul Emperors to recover Goa from the Portuguese failed, but in 1809 in the midst of the Napoleonic wars the British in India easily occupied Goa which was restored after the treaty of Vienna to Portugal which remained in possession of it until 1962 when it was freed by the Republic of India from Portuguese control and merged with India after more than four centuries of foreign domination.

Gobi desert—is in Central Asia, 1500 miles long, east to west and 500 to 700 miles broad, north to south. It is now a sandy desert, but flourishing Indian colonies once abounded in this area. The archaeological exploration of Sir Aurel Stein have resulted in the discovery of the bare ruins of numerous Buddhist stupas and monasteries, images of Buddhist and Brahmanical gods and many manuscripts and records written in Indian languages and Indian alphabets. Moving about in the excavated areas in this region Sir Aurel was so much impressed with the Indian characteristics of the archaeological finds that he felt he was in the familiar surroundings of an ancient Indian city of the Panjab. Hiuen Tsang who came to India and went back to China through Central Asia in the seventh century A.D. found that Buddhism and Indian culture dominated in this area. The expansion of the dreadful desert has driven under the sands all these centres of Indian culture in Central Asia.

Gobind, Guru—*see* Govinda Singh.

Gobind Pundit—*see* Govinda Pundit.

Godavari, the—is a large river, 800 miles in length, which flowing east across the Deccan, falls into the Bay of Bengal, a few miles above Masulipatam. It is one of the seven sacred rivers of India.

Goddard, Col., (1740-83)—began military service under Coote (*q.v.*) in Madras in 1759 and took part in the campaign leading to the fall of Pondicherry in 1761. He held various commands till 1778 when he made his name by leading, under the orders of Warren Hastings (*q.v.*), a contingent of British Indian troops from Bengal across India to help the British army in Bombay against the Marathas then engaged in their first war with the English. He took Mhow and Ahmadabad, defeated Mahadaji Sindhia, captured Bassein in 1780, threatened Poona but was then compelled to retreat. On the conclusion of the Maratha War by the treaty of Salbai in 1782 Goddard was promoted to be the Commander-in-Chief of the Bombay army, but he soon retired on account of ill-health and died at sea on his way back to England in1783.

Godehu, M.—was a Director of the French East India Company. He was sent to India by the French Company in 1754 to supersede Dupleix (*q.v.*) and to hold an enquiry into the state of affairs of the French in India. Soon after his arrival Godehu, to whom Dupleix made over charge peacefully, suspended hostilities with the English in India and made with them a provisional treaty in January 1755. By this treaty both nations agreed to cease interfering in the affairs of the Indian princes and to recognise certain territorial possessions of each of the two nations. The terms of the treaty which were subject to the approval of the two Companies could not be enforced, for in 1756 the Seven Years' War broke out and the English and the French were again at war in Europe and consequently in India too.

Godolphin, the Earl of—was from 1702 to 1708 the Chief Minister of Queen Anne of England (1702-14). He gave an award settling the differences between the old East India Company founded in 1600 and a New Society founded in 1698. On the basis of this award of Godolphin the two rival societies were united under the title of the "United Company of Merchants of

England Trading to the East Indies", popularly called the East
India Company.

Godwin, General Sir H. T.—an officer in the British Indian
army, rendered distinguished service during the First Burmese
War (1824-26). He was placed in command of the British land
army in the Second Burmese War (1852) which he brought to a
successful conclusion, even though he was seventy years old.

Gogunda, the battle of—was fought in 1576 between the armies
of the Mughul Emperor Akbar and Rana Pratap Singh (*q.v.*) of
Mewar. The Mughul army was led by Kunwar Man Singh of
Ambar and was much larger than the Rajput army of the Rana
who fought with great gallantry but was defeated. He, however,
succeeded in escaping death and kept up hostilities with Akbar
till his death in 1597. The battle was fought in the pass of
Haldighat near Gogunda and is often called the battle of
Haldighat.

Gokhale, General—was in the service of Peshwa Baji Rao II
(1796-1818). He led the Peshwa's army in the Third Maratha
War and was defeated and killed in the battle of Ashti in 1818.

Gokhale, Gopal Krishna (1866-1915)—a very prominent Indian
nationalist, was born of a Maratha Brahman family at Kolhapur.
He began his career as a Professor of History and Economics at
Fergusson College, Poona, and continued to be a member of its
teaching staff till he retired in 1902. Associated with the Indian
National Congress from its beginning he was its Joint Secretary
for some years and presided over its 1905 session. He became a
member of the Bombay Legislative Council in 1902 and was then
elected to represent its non-official members in the Viceregal
legislature. In 1905 he founded at Poona the Servants of India
Society whose members took vows of poverty and of life-long
service to their country in a religious spirit. In the enlarged
Viceregal legislature set up in 1910 Gokhale was the commanding
figure and became the most effective critic of the Government.
He specialised as a critic of Indian official finance and was
particularly brilliant in his handling of the annual budgets. He
sponsored a bill for compulsory primary education which was
rejected on account of the opposition of the Government of the
day. His last public duty was to serve as a Member of the Indian
Public Services Commission (1912-15) which recommended a
substantial increase of the Indian personnel in the Services.
His death in 1915 greatly weakened the constitutional party
in India. He was one of the best and the greatest of the old
school of Congress politicians before the age of non-co-operation

(Paranjpye, R. P., *Gopal Krishna Gokhale*; Shastri, S., *Life of Gopal Krishna Gokhale*)

Gokla—a leader of the Jats inhabiting the Mathura district of Uttara Pradesh, was a zamindar of Tilpat and had the hardihood and courage to lead the peasantry of the district in opposition to the might of the Mughul Emperor Aurangzeb. In 1669 Gokla took the lead in attacking the oppressive Mughul faujdar of Mathura who was killed. The whole district was thrown into disorder which was eventually suppressed by a strong imperial force sent against Gokla who was defeated and killed and the members of whose family were forcibly converted to Islam. But Gokla's life was not in vain; his example inspired the Jats to offer such a prolonged resistance to the intolerant policy of Aurangzeb as put a great strain even on his imperial resources. In 1691 the Jats plundered the sepulchre of Emperor Akbar, exhumed his bones which they burnt and thus retaliated Emperor Aurangzeb's persecution of the Hindus.

Golab Singh, Maharaja of Kashmir—began his career as a horseman in a cavalry troop of Maharaja Ranjit Singh (*q.v.*) of the Panjab who rewarded him for his services with the principality of Jammu. Golab Singh eventually extended his authority into Ladakh. After Ranjit Singh's death in 1839 Golab Singh was elected a minister of the Khalsa (*q.v.*) and after the battle of Sobraon (*q.v.*) in 1846 Golab Singh used his influence in favour of friendly relations with the victorious English and took a leading part in negotiating the treaty of Lahore (1846) which brought the war to an end. By one of the terms of this treaty Kashmir with its dependencies was ceded to the British. The latter in their turn handed Kashmir to Golab Singh for £ 1,000,000. Golab Singh was given the title of Maharaja and maintained very amicable relations with the British Government till his death in 1857. The dynasty founded by him ruled in Kashmir till its integration with India in 1948.

Golkonda (also spelt Gulkandah)—is a fort and ruined city near Hyderabad in South India. It was also the name of a kingdom lying between the lower courses of the Godavari and the Krishna rivers and extending to the coast of the Bay of Bengal. It was in ancient times a part of the Kakatiya kingdom of Barmangal (or Warangal) and was overrun by Sultan Ala-ud-din Khalji in A.D. 1310, but maintained an independent existence up to A.D. 1424-25 when it was annexed to the Bahmani kingdom (*q.v.*). The city of Warangal was made the headquarters of the eastern province of the Bahmani kingdom. In

A.D. 1518 a Turki officer named Sultan Quli Qutb Shah, who was the governor of this eastern province, set himself up as the independent sultan and transferred the capital to Golkonda. The kingdom maintained its independent existence till A.D. 1687, when it was conquered by Emperor Aurangzeb and annexed to the Mughul Empire. Golkonda was famous in the past for its diamonds. It is now reputed for the ruins of the many mosques and tombs built by its Qutb Shahi sultans.

Gollas—was the king of the White Huns mentioned by monk Cosmas Indikopleustes. Probably he was no other than the Huna king Mihiragula, son of Toramana, whose invasion in the second quarter of the sixth century A.D. shook the Gupta Empire to its foundations; but whose power was broken in about A.D. 533 by a combination of Narasimha Gupta Baladitya and Yasodharman (q.v.). (E. E. C. A. pp 416-17)

Gomata, image of—was constructed in about A.D. 983 by order of Chamunda Ray (q.v.), a minister of the Ganga king of Mysore. The statue stands on the top of a hillock at Sravana Belgola and is more than 56 feet in height. It is wrought out of a single block of black granite. In the boldness of conception and excellence in execution it stands unrivalled in the world as a piece of sculpture.

Gondophernes (**Gondophares**)—an Indo-Parthian king, ruled some time between A.D. 20 and A.D. 48 over an extensive kingdom including Qandahar, Kabul and Taxila. According to uncorroborated early ecclesiastical legends his kingdom was visited by the apostle St. Thomas who was martyred there.

Gonds, the—were a tribal people who lived in the modern Chhatarpur district of Madhya Pradesh. In course of time they gave up their predatory habits, took to fighting and became recognised as Rajputs. The Chandella kings (q.v.) of Jejakabhukti were probably originally Gonds.

Gondwana—or the kingdom of the Gonds, was equivalent to the northern portion of the present Madhya Pradesh. It was also called Garha-Katanga. It was conquered by Akbar in 1564 and annexed to his dominions. (see Durgavati, Rani.)

Gopachandra—was the earliest of three kings—the two other being Dharmaditya and Samacharadeva—who ruled over the independent kingdom of Vanga comprising parts of eastern, western and southern Bengal in about the second quarter of the sixth century A.D. when the Gupta Empire was declining. He is mentioned in some grants and his name has also been found on some gold coins. Nothing is known about his ancestors or about his successors. (H.B., I, 51-53)

Gopala I—was the founder of the Pala dynasty which ruled over Bengal and Bihar for about four centuries. His father's name was Vapyata and Dayitavishnu was his grandfather. Both of them appear to have been rather affluent commoners. In the middle of the eighth century A.D. when Bengal and Bihar were in the grip of a prolonged period of anarchy Gopala was chosen as king by common consent. He ruled probably from A.D. 750 to A.D. 770. The extent of his conquests is not known, but from his loins sprang the Pala dynasty of kings who were generally Buddhist in religion and who ruled over Bengal till the middle of the twelfth century, and over Bihar till it was conquered by the Muhammadans in 1119. (*H.B.*, I)

Gopala II—a later king of the Pala dynasty of Bengal, succeeded his father Rajyapala. He ruled probably from A.D. 940-57. The details of his activities are not known. (*Ibid.*)

Gopala III—a later Pala king, succeeded his father, Kumarapala, son and successor of king Ramapala (*q.v.*) but was deposed after a short reign by his uncle Madanapala in about A.D. 1145. Nothing is known about his activities. (*Ibid.*)

Gopuram—is a characteristic feature of South Indian temples, especially of temples built by the Chola (*q.v.*) kings. It means the gateway to the enclosure of a temple. In course of time the *gopurams* became huge structures, several storeys high with lavish and beautiful decorations. The *gopuram* at Kumbhakonam is a splendid piece of architectural work and still excites admiration.

Gora—a Rajput hero of Mewar, along with his comrade-in-arms, Badal, resisted the army of Ala-ud-din Khalji at the outer gate of Chitore when that fort was attacked by the Sultan's army. He would not yield but fell fighting.

Gosains—formed a religious sect who during the unsettled times that prevailed in the second quarter of the 19th century took up arms. Under the leadership of Himmat Bahadur they served in the army of Mahadaji Sindhia. The heads of the Vaishnava *satras* (hermitages) expecially those in Assam, are also called Gosains.

Gosala—a monk, was a contemporary of Buddha and of Mahavira. Gosala founded the Ajivika sect. (*q.v.*).

Gough, Hugh, First Viscount (1799-1869)—entered the British army in 1794, fought in the Peninsular War, came to India in 1857 as the Commander of the Mysore division of the Madras army, was away fighting in China from 1841 to 1843 and became on return the Commander-in-Chief of the British Indian army.

He defeated Sindhia's army in the battle of Maharajpur in 1843 and took command in person in the First Sikh War (1845-46), the Governor-General, Lord Hardinge, serving under him. He defeated the Sikhs in the battles of Mudki (1845), Firozshah (1846) and Sobroan (1846) and thus brought the war to a victorious end. He again commanded in the Second Sikh War (1848-49), won the battle of Ramnagar (1848), nearly lost the battle of Chilianwala (1849) but retrieved his reputation and won the war by decisively defeating the Sikhs in the battle of Gujarat. He retired in May, 1849, and died in 1869. He is said to have commanded in more general actions than any British officer, except the Duke of Wellington.

Government of India Acts—of 1858, 1909, 1919 and 1935—*see ante* under British Indian Administration.

Government of Burma Act—was passed by the British Parliament in 1932. It separated Burma from India and gave Burma a separate constitution on the lines of the Government of India Act, 1921.

Governor-General—was the highest dignitary in British India. The office was created by the Regulating Act (*q.v.*) passed in 1773 and Warren Hastings was the first incumbent to this high office which he held from 1774-86. The dignitary continued to be known as Governor-General of Fort William in Bengal up to 1834 when, after the passing of the Charter Act of 1833, he came to be called Governor-General of India. In 1858 when the administration of India was transferred from the Company to the Crown the Governor-General came also to be designated the Viceroy. So long as the British rule lasted in India no Indian national was appointed to this high office. The powers and functions of the Governor-General were first laid down in the Regulating Act of 1773 and was later on expanded by Pitt's India Act of 1784 and the supplementary Act of 1786. (*ante* British Indian Administration). The Governor-General was to administer the country generally with the advice and consent of his Council, but he could overrule the Council if and when he considered it essential. This practically made the Governor-General the supreme arbiter of Indian destiny, subject to the control of a Secretary of State and Parliament in far-off England.

The successive permanent Governors-General were— Warren Hastings, Lord Cornwallis, Sir John Shore, Lord Wellesley, Lord Cornwallis (second term), Lord Minto I, Lord Hastings, Lord Amherst, Lord William Bentinck, Lord Auckland, Lord Ellenborough, Lord Hardinge I, Lord

Dalhousie, Lord Canning, Lord Elgin I, Lord Lawrence, Lord Mayo, Lord Northbrook, Lord Lytton I, Lord Ripon, Lord Dufferin, Lord Lansdowne, Lord Elgin II, Lord Curzon, Lord Minto II, Lord Hardinge II, Lord Chelmsford, Lord Reading, Lord Irwin, Lord Willingdon, Lord Linlithgow, Lord Wavell, Lord Mountbatten and C. Rajagopalachari. Lord William Bentinck was the last Governor-General of Fort William in Bengal and the first Governor-General of India as per the Charter Act of 1833. Lord Canning was the first Viceroy as per the Government of India Act, 1858 and Lord Linlithgow was the last Viceroy and the first Crown Representative as per the Act of 1935. Lord Mountbatten was the last Crown Representative and C. Rajagopalachari was the last Governor-General of India (*For dates and details of each reference is to be made to the entry against the individual*).

Governor-General's Acts—were legislative measures which the Government of India Act, 1935, empowered the Governor-General to promulgate and were to have force of laws for six months at a time. These acts were intended to enable the Governor-General to pass such measures which he might consider necessary but which might not be approved of by the popular legislature.

Govinda Singh, Guru—the tenth *Guru* of the Sikhs, succeeded his father, the ninth Guru, Tegh Bahadur, in 1675 and occupied the position till his murder at Nander in the Deccan by an Afghan in 1708. He was the last *Guru* but was the real founder of the Sikh military power which he organised to oppose the Muhammadans. He instituted the ceremony of *pahul* or baptism consisting chiefly of partaking in a body of a drink made of consecrated flour, sugar and butter and intended to break the restrictions of caste. The brotherhood so constituted was called the *Khalsa* or Pure and every member of it bore the title of Singh. He also required the brotherhood to abjure tobacco and to wear the five *Ks* namely *Kesh* (long hair and beard), *Kungha* (hair-comb), *Kuchcha* (shorts), *Kara* (iron bangle) and *Kirpan* (sword). Guru Govind retained the old theology but altered the whole genius of the Sikh brotherhood and turned the Sikhs from a passive religious group into a dynamic socio-political body. He waged many wars against the local hill rajas as well as the local Mughul officers in which he lost his two sons who were executed by the Mughul governor of Sirhind. He supported Bahadur Shah in the war of succession and took service under him, but was murdered in 1708.

Govind Pundit—was a Maratha officer who was asked by Sadasiva Rao Bhao, the Maratha Commander-in-Chief, to operate on the lines of communication of Ahmad Shah Abdali on the eve of the third battle of Panipat. But Abdali made a bold and successful attack on the Pundit's army and dispersed it. This victory opened up Abdali's lines of communication and source of supply and delivered him from all danger of starvation. The freedom of movement thus secured eventually led to the third battle of Panipat (*q.v.*) fought a month later in January, 1761.

Govinda I—was the founder of the Bhoi dynasty which ruled in Orissa from A.D. 1542-59. He belonged to the Bhoi or writer caste and was formerly a minister of king Prataparudra (1497-1540) of Orissa. Govinda I ousted the line of Prataparudra (*q.v.*). He, his son and two grandsons reigned for 18 years. Little of interest is known of his three successors, except that the last of them was deposed in 1559 by Mukunda Harichandra.

Govinda I—was an ancestor of Dantidurga, the founder of the Rashtrakuta dynasty (*q.v.*) which ruled in the Deccan from A.D. 753 to 973. Nothing is known of him except his name.

Govinda II—was an early king of the Rashtrakuta dynasty (*q.v.*). He was the son and successor of king Krishna I and ruled from A.D. 775-79. He was deposed by his brother Dhruva.

Govinda III—the son and successor of king Dhruva (*q.v.*) was the most remarkable prince of the Rashtrakuta dynasty. He ruled from A.D. 793-815. He extended his power on the north beyond the Vindhya mountains into Malwa and on the south to Kanchi or Canjeeveram. He established his brother Indraraja as the Viceroy of Lata or Southern Gujarat, defeated the Pratihara king Vatsaraja and received the submission of king Dharmapala of Bengal and of his vassal, Chakrayudha, who held the throne of Kanauj.

Govinda IV—a later Rashtrakuta king, ruled from A.D. 918-34. The decline of the Rashtrakuta power which had already begun, continued in his reign and the dynasty came to an end about forty years after his death.

Govindachandra—a king of the Gahadvala or Gaharwar dynasty (*q.v.*) of Kanauj, was a grandson of the founder-king Chandradeva and ruled from A.D. 1114-54 over an extensive territory comprising the greater part of the modern states of Uttar Pradesh and Bihar. He was a benevolent ruler who made many land grants and issued many coins which have been found in various places of north India. The Muhammadans, however, had already begun their incursions into north India and one of Govindachandra's grants refers to a special levy called *Turushka danda* which was evidently collected for meeting the cost of resisting the Muhammadan raiders.

Govindapura—was one of the three adjacent villages—the other two being Sutanati and Kalikata—where the foundation of Calcutta was laid by Job Charnock in 1690 and the *Zamindari* right of which was granted to the East India Company in 1698.

Graeco-Bactrian monarchy, the—was established in about the middle of the third century B.C. when Diodotos, the Greek governor of Bactria, threw off the authority of the Greek king of Syria and assumed royal style. This Graeco-Bactrian dynasty ended in about 155 B.C. and comprised several kings of whom Demetrios (*c.* 200-190 B.C.) conquered a considerable portion of northern India, presumably including Kabul, the Panjab and Sind. But Demetrios was soon afterwards defeated and displaced by one Eukratides who was killed by his own son, Apollodotos, and the latter by his brother, Heliokles, with whose death the Graeco-Bactrian monarchy ended. Coins bearing nearly forty different names of Greek princelings have been found and ascribed to this period. This circumstance suggests that during this period the north-western borderland of India was parcelled out among a crowd of Greek princelings of whom Menander (*q.v.*) stands out conspicuously. He is believed to have embraced Buddhism and to have been the Milinda of the celebrated Buddhist theological work *Milindapanha* (*The Questions of Milinda*) (*q.v.*).

Graeco-Buddhist sculpture—is a name that is often applied to the Gandhara school of sculpture. In this style of sculpture the forms of Greek art have been applied to Buddhist subjects. Images of Buddha are made in the likeness of Apollo, of Yaksha Kuvera in that of the Phidian Zeus, and so on. The drapery follows the Hellenistic model and is generally transparent. Generally speaking, the dress and features of an Indian Buddhist monk were imposed on images of different Greek gods and goddessess who were given Buddhistic names. The Graeco-Buddhist or Gandhara sculpture is Graeco-Roman and based on the cosmopolitan art of Asia Minor and the Roman Empire as was current in the early centuries of the Christian era. The second century A.D. during which north and west India was ruled by the Kushan kings, Kanishka and Huvishka (*q.v.*), saw the best of the products of the Gandhara or Graeco-Buddhist school of sculpture.

Graham, General—was in command of the Indo-British army that repulsed a Tibetan invasion of Sikkim in 1887.

Grahavarman Maukhari—was the son of Avantivarman, the Maukhari king of Kanauj. He became king towards the close of the sixth century and married Rajyasri, daughter of Prabhakara-vardhan, king of Thaneswar. But in A.D. 605 he was attacked by the king of Malava, plausibly identified with Deva Gupta, and was defeated and killed. His queen Rajyasri was thrown into prison in his own capital and the dynasty of the Maukharis came to an end.

Grand Trunk Road, the—was constructed by Sher Shah (*q.v.*) (1540-45). It extended for 1500 *kos* from Sonargaon in Eastern Bengal to the Indus. It still exists and connects Calcutta with Upper India up to Amritsar in the Panjab.

Grant, Charles (1746-1823)—came out to India as a clerk in the E.I. Company's service in 1767 and rose in 1781 to be the Commercial Resident at Malda in Bengal. Lord Cornwallis was much impressed by his integrity and in 1787 Charles Grant became the Fourth Member of the Board of Trade. In India he was a strong patron of Christian missionary work. After retirement from India he entered Parliament in 1802 and became the Chairman of the Court of Directors in 1805 and again in 1809 and 1815. He took a leading part in the discussions of Indian affairs in the British Parliament and obtained parliamentary sanction for an annual grant for education in India, for the appointment of Bishops in India and for greater freedom for Christian missionary work in India.

Grant, James—was in the service of the E.I. Company in Bengal from 1784 to 1789. He superintended the management of revenues in the province and prepared in 1791 an elaborate report *On an Enquiry into the Nature of Zamindari Tenures in the Landed Property of Bengal* which still continues to be the best account of the revenue system then prevailing in Bengal.

Greased cartridges—were introduced in 1856 for use in the Indian army for the new Enfield rifle. The cartridges were smeared with animal grease and had to be bitten off before insertion into the rifle. It was rumoured and believed by the Indian soldiers that the cartridges were smeared with the fat of cows and pigs and were therefore abominable alike to the Hindu and the Muslim sepoy. The rumour spread like wild-fire and the Indian soldiers feared that a plot was afoot to destroy their religious purity. The presence of animal fat in the grease was first denied by the officers, but was later on found to be true and the cartridges were withdrawn. The order to bite was rescinded and the soldiers were allowed to provide their own grease. But these measures came too late and the sepoys, Hindus as well as Muslims, felt that their religions were threatened by the British and became very restive. This restiveness and disaffection no doubt contributed a great deal to the Sepoy Mutiny (*q.v.*).

Greeks, the—were an important factor in the history of India. Contact between Greece and India is now known to have been in existence centuries before the time of Alexander, the king of Macedon, who invaded India in 327-326 B.C. The philosophy of Pythagoras, the famous Greek philosopher, who lived towards the close of the sixth century of the pre-Christian era and who taught the doctrine of the transmigration of souls, was derived from the *Samkhya* system of Indian philosophy. There are records to show that an Indian philosopher met Socrates (469 B.C. - 399 B.C.) at Athens and had philosophical discussions with him. Plato (427 B.C. - 347 B.C.) was familiar with the characteristic Indian philosophical doctrine of *Karma*. These and numerous other coincidences that have been found to exist between Indian and Greek philosophy as expounded by the Eleatics and by Thales could have originated only in a close contact between Indian and Greek philosophers of the pre-Alexandrine period. The entirely unprovoked invasion of India by Alexander the Great which left behind it bloody scars of war, brought to India many more Greeks than had ever come before, and though Alexander's dominion in India fell away soon after his death in 323 B.C., the contact between the Greeks and India continued. In 305 B.C. Alexander's general, Seleucos Nikator, who had become after Alexander's death the ruler of his eastern dominions, invaded India, but was presumably defeated by the reigning Indian king, Chandragupta Maurya (*c.* 322 B.C. - 298 B.C.), entered into a matrimonial alliance with the latter and sent to his court Megasthenes as an Ambassador. Thus closer contact was established between the Greeks and the Indians. Bindusara who succeeded Chandragupta Maurya, maintained friendly relations with the Greek king of Syria whom he requested to send to his court a Greek sophist. Bindusara's son and successor, Asoka, maintained friendly relations with the Greek kings of Syria, Egypt, Macedonia and Epirus. He sent Buddhist missionaries to all these countries where also he established philanthropic institutions like hospitals and planted medicinal herbs and where, he claimed, many persons embraced

Buddhism. In his own employment in India there were many Greeks one of whom, named Tushaspa, was made the governor of Saurashtra. Indeed there were so many Greeks amongst his subjects in Afghanistan that Asoka issued for their edification a bilingual inscription in Greek and Aramaic which has been found near Qandahar. Some time after the death of Asoka the north-western part of his Indian empire passed into the hands of numerous Greek princelings who ruled in this area up to the establishment of the Kushan Empire in the first century of the Christian era. It was during this period that the Greeks in India came into close cultural contact with the Indians and as a result many of them were converted not only to Buddhism but also to the Brahmanical faith. If the famous Greek prince Menander became a Buddhist another highly placed Greek official, named Heliodoros, embraced the Vaishnava creed and erected at Besnagara a Garuḍa column in honour of Vasudeva. It was also during this period that the Gandhara school (*q.v.*) of sculpture developed and led to the immortalisation in stone of the stories of Buddha's life in Hellenic garb. The Greeks in India established a two-way traffic: they gave in art, coinage, literature and astronomy just as they took in philosophy, religion, mathematics and the other sciences. (Majumdar, R. C., *India's Influence on the Thought and Culture of the World; Swami Vivekananda Centenary Memorial Vol.*, 1963; Banerjee, G. D., *Hellenism in Ancient India*)

Griffin, Admiral—was in charge of a British fleet which frustrated the efforts of the French under the direction of Dupleix (*q.v.*) to capture Fort. St. David in 1747.

Gujar people—were the pastoral section of the larger group, the Gurjaras, who are believed to be a Hinduised people of foreign origin who came to India along with the Scythians or the Hunas.

Gujarat—is a state lying in the western part of India. In the widest sense it includes the whole compact area where the Gujarati language is spoken, i.e. Ahmadabad, Broach, Panch Mahal, Khaira and Surat districts in the old state of Bombay, the main territories of the former Baroda state and the states of Saurashtra and Cutch. It is comparatively a new state, as it finds no mention either in the Asokan inscription or in the inscription of Rudradaman. It acquired a name and distinction in the fifth century A.D. when the Huna raids began. The name is therefore held by many to be derived from the Gurjaras who entered into India from the north-west and settled in the region in the beginning of the fifth century A.D. In the course of the next two centuries they established a kingdom which comprised parts of Rajputana and spread to the south. The ancient Hindu capital was Anhilwaḍa and later on it was shifted to Bhilmal. Under the Gurjara-Pratiharas (*q.v.*) the kingdom came into great prominence but it declined and lost its prestige as the result of the invasion in A.D. 1024 by Sultan Mahmud who sacked on that occasion the temple of Somnath. The state, however, continued to be independent until A.D. 1297 when it was conquered and annexed to the sultanate of Delhi by Ala-ud-din Khalji (1294-1316). In 1401 the local Muslim governor, Zafar Khan, set himself up as an independent sovereign, assumed the title of Nasiruddin Muhammad Shah and founded a dynasty which ruled over Gujarat till 1572-73. The more important of the rulers of this dynasty were Ahmad Shah (1411-41), Sultan Mahmud Bigarha (1459-1511) and Bahadur Shah (1526-37). All of them added to the territories and glory of Gujarat. In 1537 Sultan Bahadur Shah was treacherously killed by the Portuguese when he was paying a visit to the Portuguese governor, de Cunha, on board his ship in the port of Diu. Confusion prevailed in Gujarat after the murder of Bahadur Shah and the kingdom was annexed to his empire by Akbar in 1572-73. It passed under the control of the Marathas during the administration of the second Peshwa Baji Rao I (1720-40) and was placed under the control of the Gaekwad family which established its capital at Baroda. The Gaekwads maintained friendly relations with the British and were given special protection by the Treaty of Bassein (*q.v.*), 1802. Ultimately after the Third Maratha War (1817-18) Gujarat became a part of the British Indian Empire, and a part of the Bombay Presidency. Very recently it has been separated from Bombay and constituted into a separate state with its capital at Ahmadabad. Gujarat has a wealth of architectural monuments built by its Hindu and Muhammadan rulers. Its capital Ahmadabad which is a very clean city, is the centre of the Indian textile industry. (Munshi, K. M., *The Glory That was Gurjarat*)

Gujarat, the battle of—was fought in the Panjab in 1849 between the Sikhs and the British army in the course of the Second Sikh War (1848-49). The artillery was so profusely used in this battle that it has been called the battle of the guns. Lord Gough, the British Commander-in-Chief, first carefully reconnoitred the ground and made such a tremendous bombardment on the Sikh batteries that these were all silenced. It was then that the British infantry attacked the Sikh army which was put to flight and a brilliant and relentless pursuit made the battle a decisive victory for the British and practically ended the Second Sikh War.

Gulab Singh—*see* Golab Singh.

Gulbadan Begum—was a daughter of the first Mughul Emperor, Babur (1525-30). She was a talented lady and wrote the *Humayun-namah*. It is an authoritative contemporary account of the times of Emperor Humayun (1530-56) and incidentally throws some light on the economic condition of contemporary India.

Gulbarga (also **spelt Kulbarga**)—was made the capital of the Bahmani kingdom by its founder Sultan Ala-ud-din Hasan Shah in 1347. He gave to the city the Muslim name of Ahsana-bad. It continued to be the capital of the Bahmani kingdom till about 1425 when during the reign of the ninth sultan, Ahmad Shah (1422-36), the capital was transferred to Bidar. The Bahmani sultans and their courtiers built many palaces and mosques at Gulbarga, but these buildings were heavy, gloomy and roughly constructed and can now be seen only in ruins.

Gunavarman—a prince born in the royal family of Kashmir, became a Buddhist monk and dedicated his life to the propaga-tion of the Buddhist religion in the Far East. He went to Ceylon and then to Java and finally to China. According to Chinese accounts he converted the Javanese to Buddhism and died in Nanking in China in A.D. 431.

Gupta dynasty, the—was founded by Chandragupta I in *c.* A.D. 320 and ruled in Northern India till about *c.* A.D. 510. Chandragupta I was the son of Ghatotkacha and grandson of Gupta, both of whom were local kings of Pataliputra. Chandragupta I married the Lichchhavi princess Kumaradevi and this marriage greatly strengthened his position. He not only became the king of the whole of Magadha but also extended his dominions up to Allaha-bad. His dominions included Tirhut, South Bihar and Oudh. He assumed the title of *Maharajadhiraj* and started a new era, known as the Gupta era, which dates from A.D. 320. From his loins sprang the Gupta dynasty comprising six great kings, namely, Samudragupta, Chandragupta II Vikramaditya, Kumaragupta I, Skandagupta, Narasimhagupta and Kumara-gupta II and a long line of later and weaker Gupta kings who became local rulers either in Magadha or in the seceding states like Malwa. The second Gupta Emperor, Samudragupta (*c.* A.D. 330-80) (*q.v.*), was a great conqueror who not only subdued almost the whole of northern India, but also led a victorious campaign into the Deccan resulting in the submission of such a distant potentate as Vishnugopa of Kanchi (Canjeeveram). The third Gupta Emperor, Chandragupta II (*c.* A.D. 380-415), conquered Saurashtra, overthrew the local dynasty of Saka rulers, patronised men of learning and assumed the titles of *Sakari* (*i.e.,* the foe of the Sakas) and Vikramaditya. He is believed to have been the Vikramaditya of legends who was the patron of the greatest Sanskrit poet and dramatist, Kalidasa. His son and successor Kumaragupta I (A.D. 415-55) repulsed an invasion by the Pushyamitras, a tribal people of uncertain origin and habitat, and maintained the integrity of the vast Gupta Empire. His son and successor, Skandagupta (A.D. 455-*c.*67) who had distinguished himself during his father's reign by taking the leading part in repulsing the Pushyamitras, encountered the more dangerous Huna invaders and though he decisively defeated them in a hard-fought battle early in his reign he could not stem the tide. Later on, the Hunas occupied Gandhara, or the north-western Panjab, advanced further into the heart of the Gupta Empire, and, when Skandagupta died in about A.D. 467, the Gupta Empire was tottering to its fall. His immediate successor was his brother, Puragupta, who ruled for a very short time (*c.* A.D. 467). His son and successor, Narasimhagupta Baladitya (A.D. 467-73) was, unlike his ancestors, an ardent Buddhist who built a magnificent brick-temple, 300 feet in height, in the celebrated Buddhist monastery at Nalanda in south Behar. He also waged a war against the Hunas whom he probably defeated. But his reign was short and came to an end in about A.D. 473 when the throne passed to his son, Kumaragupta II who also had a short reign (A.D. 473-76). Indeed the decline of the Gupta Empire had set in since the death of Skandagupta in A.D. 467 and the later history of the kings of the Gupta dynasty is confusing. Inscriptions mention various names of later Gupta kings whom it is not easy to fit in a regular line of succession. Plausibly a king named Buddha Gupta ruled from A.D. 476 to A.D. 495 during whose reign the Hunas under Toramana and his son, Mihiragula, pushed their conquests deep into the interior of northern India and the integrity of the Gupta Empire was destroyed. Though later on the Huna chief Mihiragula first received a check at the hands of a Gupta prince named Baladitya and was finally defeated and killed by Yasodharman, king of Mandasor, in about A.D. 533, the Gupta dynasty received no benefit from this victory. The imperial dynasty of the Guptas had already perished, though princes bearing the once-honoured Gupta surname continued to rule for some time more in such separated parts of India as Magadha and Malwa. (Majumdar, R. C., *The Classical Age.*)

Cultural achievements: The Gupta dynasty occupies a very important place in the cultural history of India. The imperial Guptas were all Brahmanical Hindus in religion and some of them, like Samudragupta and Kumaragupta I, celebrated the *asvamedha* sacrifice. They also tolerated other religions like Buddhism and Jainism. Fa-Hien, a Chinese pilgrim, who visited India during the reign of Chandragupta II Vikramaditya has left a record of what he saw in the country. His account shows that under the Guptas the country was very well governed and though punishments were light crimes were rare and the incidence of taxation was low. Sanskrit was the official language and it attained a high degree of excellence in all branches of literature. The great Sanskrit poets and dramatists like Kalidas, the author of the *Sakuntala* and the *Raghuvamsa*, Sudraka, the author of the *Mrichhakatika* (The Clay Cart), Visakhadatta, the author of the *Mudra Rakhsasa* (The Signet Ring) and Amara Singha, the lexicographer, have been generally assigned to the Gupta age. It is also believed that the great epics, the *Ramayana* and the *Mahabharata*, the *Puranas* especially the *Vayu Purana* and the *Manusamhita* (the Laws of Manu) all received their existing forms in the Gupta age. The celebrated mathematicians, Aryabhata (born in A.D. 476), Varahamihira (A.D. 505-87) and Brahmagupta (born in A.D. 598) contributed much to the sciences of Mathematics and Astronomy. It was during this period that the decimal system of notation was first devised in India from where it spread to Europe through Arab scholars. It is India's greatest legacy to the world in the sphere of practical knowledge. The arts of architecture, sculpture, painting and metallurgy were also all highly advanced, as is shown by the extant Gupta monuments found in the Jhansi and Cawnpore districts of Uttara Pradesh, numbers XVI and XVII of the Ajanta cave paintings, King Chandra's Iron Pillar found at Meherauli in Delhi and the eighty feet high copper image of Buddha erected at Nalanda as well as the $7\frac{1}{2}$ feet high Sultangunj Buddha statue in copper. Indeed so decisive and eloquent is the evidence of the extant examples of art, architecture, sculpture and metallurgy of the Gupta period that it has been well observed that Hindu art was at its best in the spacious and peaceful age of the Gupta dynasty. (Banerjee, R. D., *Age of the Imperial Guptas;* Dutta, *Hindu Contribution to*

Mathematical Science; Keith, A. B., *Hist. of Sanskrit Literature*; Majumdar, R. C., *The Classical Age*.)

Gupta—a perfumer by profession was the father of Upagupta who, according to tradition, converted Asoka to Buddhism and accompanied the Emperor on his tour to Rummindei, the birth-place of Gautama Buddha.

Gupta—a local chief in Magadha, was the grandfather of Chandra-gupta I, the founder of the Gupta dynasty (*q.v.*).

Gurjaras, the—were a people who are believed to have come to India in the train of the Hunas and began to play an important part in Indian history from the sixth century A.D. In the seventh century they are mentioned in Bana's *Harsha-charita*, Hiuen Tsang's works and the Aihole inscription of Pulakeshin. They established principalities in the Panjab, Marwar and Broach. They were divided into several septs, one of which was known as the Gurjara-Pratiharas who came into great prominence in Indian history in the eighth century A.D.

Gurjara-Pratihara dynasty—was founded in about A.D. 725 by a chief named Nagabhata who claimed descent from the Ksha-triya Laksmana of the Solar race who was the brother of Rama the hero of the *Ramayana* and belonged to the Pratihara or Parihara sept of the Rajputs. As it was in Gujarat that the dynasty had the nucleus of its power, it came to be known as the Gurjara-Pratihara dynasty. Western scholars are, however, of the opinion that the name of the dynasty originated from the circumstance that it belonged to the Pratihara (or Parihara) section of the Gurjaras who came to India along with the earlier bands of the Hunas. At any rate Nagabhata I was a successful ruler who held his own against the Arabs who had recently conquered Sind, as well as from the Chalukyas and the Rashtrakutas who were competing for the overlordship of the Deccan. Naga-bhata's grand-nephew, Vatsaraja, was the first ruler of the dynasty to assume the title of *Samrat* or Emperor, though he suffered a great defeat at the hands of the Rashtrakuta king, Dhruva. Vatsaraja's son and successor Nagabhata II in about A.D. 816 invaded the Gangetic valley, captured Kanauj, de-posed the reigning king and transferred his capital to the imperial city of Kanauj. Though Nagabhata II was himself soon after-wards defeated by the Rashtrakuta king, Govinda III (*q.v.*) his descendants continued to rule over Kanauj and the neigh-bouring territories until *c.* A.D. 1018-19 when Sultan Mahmud of Ghazni occupied Kanauj and forced the reigning Pratihara king to retire to Bari. The greatest king of the dynasty was

Bhoja I, also called Mihira Bhoja, the grandson of Nagabhata II. Bhoja I ruled for half a century (*c.* A.D. 836-86) and the Pratihara dominions which extended in the east to North Bengal and in the west to the Sutlej actually attained imperial dimensions. The Arab merchant Sulaiman who visited his empire spoke highly of its military strength and orderly administration. The next emperor, Mahendrapala, was a pupil and patron of the famous poet Rajasekhara, the author of *Karpura-manjuri.* Mahendra's son, Mahipala, was severely defeated by the Rashtrakuta king, Indra III (*q.v.*), who took Kanauj. Mahipala later on recovered Kanauj but his authority had been greatly weakened and the decline of the Gurjara-Pratihara empire began in his reign. The succeeding rulers, viz. Bhoja II, Vinayakapala, Mahendrapala, Devapala, Mahipala II and Vijayapala maintained a precarious hold on their dominions until A.D. 1019 when the reigning king, Rajyapal, fled before the invasion of Sultan Mahmud of Ghazni who captured and plundered Kanauj. The cowardly flight of Rajyapala angered the neighbouring princes who led by the Chandella king, Ganda, combined against him, defeated and killed him and replaced him by Trilochanapala who ruled not at Kanauj but at Bari and sank to the position of a local chief. Even from this reduced position the later Gujara-Pratihara rulers were swept away in the second quarter of the eleventh century with the rise of the Gahadvala or Rathor dynasty of Kanauj.

Little is known of the internal administrative system maintained by the Gurjara-Pratihara dynasty whose one great service to India was to have defended Hindusthan against the Arab invaders who had conquered Sind in A.D. 710 but were effectively prevented by the Gurjara-Pratihara kings from advancing further eastward into India.

Gurkhas, the—are a people with strong Mongolian features. They are beardless, yellow in complexion, snub-nosed, with flat faces and prominent cheek-bones. They lived on the slopes of the Himalaya mountain and were one of the peoples living in Nepal under its Kshatriya princes. But in A.D. 1768 they took advantage of the internal dissensions amongst the ruling clans of Nepal and imposed their rule on the country. They are a martial people and make very good soldiers. After their defeat in 1816 in their war with the Indo-British Government they enlisted in large numbers in the British Indian army and fought very effectively in expanding and upholding the British rule all over the British Empire.

Gurkha War, the—was fought in 1816 by the Indo-British Government when Lord Hastings was the Governor-General of India. In 1801 the Company occupied Gorakhpur district and this made their territories conterminous with those of the Gurkhas in the Nepalese Tarai, resulting in constant irritations to both. The Gurkhas who found their way to the north blocked by the empire of China sought expansion in the south towards India. In 1814 the Gurkhas attacked three police stations in Bhutwal which lay to the north of the Basti district of Uttara Pradesh and was under British occupation. This led to a declaration of war by the Indo-British Government. The first British campaign of 1814-15 was attended with reverses. British efforts to capture the capital of Nepal failed; General Gillespie was repulsed and killed while assaulting the mountain fortress of Kalanga, and another British army was defeated before the stronghold of Jaitak. But in 1815 the Indo-British armies had greater successes. They captured Almora and forced the surrender of the fort of Malon. The Gurkhas now felt that further resistance was hopeless and made peace by the treaty of Sagauli in November, 1815. But the Gurkhas delayed in ratifying the treaty and it was not before a fresh British campaign led by General Ochterlony had defeated the Gurkhas in the battle of Makwanpur in February, 1816 and advanced within fifty miles of the capital of Nepal that the Gurkhas finally acknowledged defeat and made peace by ceding to the British, according to the terms of the treaty of Sagauli, the districts of Garhwal and Kumaon and accepted a British Resident at their capital, Kathmandu. The Gurkhas remained true to the treaty and subsequently entered in large numbers into the Indo-British army which was greatly strengthened by their adhesion.

Gurudaspur—is a fortified place in the Panjab. In 1715 the Sikh leader, Banda (*q.v.*), was besieged by the Mughuls in the fort of Gurudaspur and was captured after a fierce battle. Banda and those of his followers who were captured alive, were later on sent as prisoners to Delhi where they were put to barbarous deaths.

Guru, the battle of—was fought between the Tibetans and the Indo-British forces in 1904. The Tibetans were easily defeated and the Indo-British expeditionary forces under Col. Francis Younghusband (*q.v.*) entered into Tibet which eventually submitted.

Guru Govinda Singh—*see* Govinda Singh.

Gurukul—is at Kangra near Hardwar in Uttara Pradesh. It is a seat of learning started by the Arya Samajists (*q.v.*) and aims at reviving the Vedic way of life in India. It imparts education through the medium of the Sanskrit language. It was founded in 1902 and now has the status of a University.

Gwalior—is the name of a city as well as of a former princely state in Central India. The city is now the winter capital of the state of Madhya Pradesh. It centres round the famous fort of Gwalior. It stands on an isolated sandstone-hill, 300 feet above the old town. The wall round the fort is also very high, and the fort which has an imposing appearance was long believed to be impregnable. When it was first built is uncertain but it was certainly built before A.D. 525. According to tradition it was founded by one Suraj who named it Gwalior after the sage Gwalipa who had cured him of leprosy. Epigraphic records, however, show that the fort was originally called Gopagiri or Gopadri from which Gwalior was later on derived. The first historical holders of the fort were the Huna chief, Toramana (*q.v.*) and his son, Mihiragula (*q.v.*) who flourished in the sixth century A.D. In the ninth century it belonged to the Gurjara-Pratihara king, Bhoja (*q.v.*) of Kanauj. It continued to be under the control of the Rajputs who held it against Sultan Mahmud in 1021. It was first taken by the Muhammadans under Kutb-ud-din (*q.v.*) in 1196, recovered by the Rajputs in 1210 but again lost to Sultan Iltutmish in 1232. It was recovered again by the Rajputs of the Tanwar tribe in 1398 and held by them till 1518. The most famous king of this dynasty was Raja Man Singh (1486-1517) who built the magnificent palace with its great gate and the patronage of whose consort Mrignaina (fawn-eyed) made Gwalior pre-eminent as the centre of Indian music, the greatest exponent of which Tan Sen was trained at Gwalior where he lies buried. In 1518 Gwalior fort was captured by Sultan Ibrahim Lodi (*q.v.*). Babur occupied it in 1526. It passed to Sher Shah (*q.v.*) in 1542 from whose descendants Akbar conquered it in 1558. The Mughul emperors used it as a prison for political prisoners. In 1751 the Marathas conquered it from the Mughuls and in 1771 the Sindhia family made it their capital. In 1781 a British army under Major Popham surprised it, but a few years later it passed to Sindhia again. Its garrison joined the Sepoy Mutiny in 1857 and Sindhia's rule was ended for the time being. But it was soon recovered by Sir Hugh Rose and remained in British possession till 1886 when it was returned to Sindhia in exchange for Jhansi district. It remained in Sindhia's possession till the integration of his state in the Union of the Indian Republic. The city and the state contain numerous historical monuments. Eight big tanks with perennial supply of water and six magnificent palaces are within the city. The ruins of ancient Ujjaini, of Bhilsa, Besnagar, Udayagiri and Bagh, famous for its rock-cut Buddhist Viharas, lie scattered within the state. Chanderi, Mandasor and Gohud, within the state, also contain numerous historical monuments.

Gwyer, Sir Maurice Linford—an eminent English jurist, was the President of the Federal Court of India (*q.v.*) and the First Chief Justice of India from 1937 to 1943 when he retired and became the Vice-Chancellor of Delhi University. In this capacity he remained in India till the passing of the Constitution of India Act, 1949, to the drafting of which he made significant contribution with his advice and vast legal knowledge.

Gyantse—is a town and mart in Tibet where an Indo-British trading mission was established as the result of an expedition sent by Lord Curzon into Tibet in 1904.

H

Habibullah Khan, the Amir—peacefully succeeded his father Amir Abdur Rahman on the latter's death in 1901 and ruled over Afghanistan till his assassination in 1919. He secured from the British Government the right of being addressed as His Majesty and thus emphasized his actual independence of the Indo-British Government. In 1906 he paid a visit to England and was much impressed. But when in 1907 the British and the Russian governments made a convention regarding their mutual relations with Afghanistan without prior consultation with Amir Habibullah Khan, the latter refused his formal approval to the convention. His policy was to maintain his independence, without subordinating himself to either Great Britain or Russia. During the First World War (1914-18) Amir Habibullah maintained a friendly neutrality and thus rendered significant services to the British Empire. On his assassination in 1919 he was succeeded by his son Amanullah Khan.

Hafiz Rahamat Khan—was the leader of a loose confederacy of Rohilla chiefs who ruled over Rohilkhand in the early seventies of the eighteenth century. Rahamat Khan had been the guardian (*hafiz*) of the sons of the late ruler, Ali Muhammad, and had ultimately usurped their rights. In 1772 being threatened by a Maratha invasion he entered into an alliance with Suja-ud-dullah, the Nawab of Oudh, by which the Rohillas agreed to pay him forty lakhs of rupees on his obliging the Marathas to retire from Rohilkhand either by peace or war. The treaty of alliance was due to the intervention of Sir Robert Barker, the British Commander-in-Chief and was signed in his presence. Almost before the treaty was signed the Marathas evacuated Rohilkhand in 1772, but they re-appeared on its frontiers in 1773, and entered the country by crossing the Ganges at Ramghat. The Nawab of Oudh with a British brigade in support under Sir Robert Barker, advanced to repel the Marathas who, however, evacuated Rohilkhand before any fighting had taken place. The Nawab of Oudh now claimed that the Rohillas should pay him forty lakhs of rupees as stipulated by the treaty of 1772. Hafiz Rahamat Khan refused the payment on the ground that the Nawab had done practically nothing in driving out the Marathas who were still in a position to return and invade Rohilkhand any time in the future. Hafiz Rahamat Khan was technically in the wrong and in 1774 the forces of Oudh backed by an Indo-British army under Col. Champion, whom Warren Hastings, then the Governor-General, commissioned to fight the Rohillas, marched into Rohilkhand and inflicted a decisive defeat on the Rohillas in the battle of Miranpur-Katra in the course of which Hafiz Rahamat Khan was killed fighting bravely at the head of the Rohilla army. He was an able, courageous and cultured ruler who had treated even his Hindu subjects with a great degree of consideration and under whose administration Rohilkhand had become a prosperous state.

Haidar Ali Khan (**also spelt Hyder Ali Khan**)—was a soldier of fortune who raised himself by his own innate ability to the throne of Mysore in the second half of the eighteenth century. He was the son of a soldier and began his career in the service of Nanraj the *Dalwai* or prime minister who had practically made himself the ruler of Mysore after reducing his master, the Hindu raja, to a mere titular head. Eventually Haidar Ali displaced the *Dalwai*, made the raja a prisoner in his own palace and himself became the ruler of Mysore in about 1761. He soon extended his dominions by conquering Bednore, Canara and the petty poligars of South India. He was unlettered but he proved himself to be a very efficient ruler and a very capable general. He had all the business of the state transacted in his own presence regularly and quickly. Easily accessible to all, he was the most tolerant of the Muhammadan princes of his time. His task was most difficult. He was simultaneously confronted with the hostilities of the Nizam of Hyderabad, the Marathas and the English, but he was never overwhelmed by the heavy odds against him. Thus in 1766 the Marathas, the Nizam and the English entered into a triple alliance against Haidar Ali but he soon bought off the Marathas and continued the war against the Nizam and the English with great vigour. He recovered Mangalore, defeated the Bombay army of the English, appeared within five miles of Madras in March, 1768 and dictated a peace in April, 1769 which provided for mutual restitution of conquests and secured from the English a promise to help Haidar Ali in case he was attacked by any other power. Thus ended Haidar Ali's first war with the English in India, leaving the honours to him. But the Company did not keep the terms of the treaty, for when the Marathas invaded Haidar's territories in 1771 the English failed to send him any assistance. Haidar Ali was, therefore, immensely offended with the English and in 1779 he joined in a confederacy with the Nizam and the Marathas in a war against the English who had given him further provocation by capturing the French settlement of Mahe, though it lay within Haidar's territories. In 1780 Haidar burst with a large army on the Carnatic 'like an avalanche', cut off an English detachment under Col. Baillie, seized Arcot and thus created a very critical situation for the English who, however, succeeded in detaching the Nizam and the Marathas from the alliance with Haidar who was eventually defeated by the English General, Sir Eyre Coote, at the battle of Porto Novo in 1781. The war still continued and Haidar had yet another victory over a British army under Col. Braithwaite. But Haidar Ali, who had been long suffering from cancer, died in the midst of the war on the 7th December, 1782, leaving to his only son and successor, Tipu Sultan, the task of bringing to a victorious close his second war with the British in India. Haidar Ali had more than held his own against the British though they were helped by his own co-religionists and countrymen. (Bowring, *Haidar Ali and Tipu Sultan*; Wilks, M., *Hist. Sketches of the South of India*)

Haidar Shah—was the second son and successor of Jain-ul-Abidin, king of Kashmir. He ruled from A.D. 1470 to 1472, did nothing worth recording and died as a result of a fall in a drunken fit in his own palace.

Haileybury College—in England, was founded in 1805. Young nominees to the Indian Civil Service were required to spend two years at this College in order to continue and strengthen their general education and to learn jurisprudence, political economy and one of the oriental languages. None could join the Indian Civil Service unless he passed from Haileybury College and for the next fifty years the members of the Indian Civil Service were all products of Haileybury College. The test was not severe and was easily passed, for the aim of the College was not to exclude but in rare cases. The College became noted for its corporate life and the excellent spirit of comradeship which bound the inmates of the institution together. It also promoted the sense of honesty and integrity amongst its members and went a long way in creating healthy traditions which none of its products could violate without bringing dishonour to the whole batch. But as the inmates of the College were all *nominees* of the Directors of the East India Company the Hailey-bury products did not represent the best of the intellectual elements of Britain. The College was abolished soon after the introduction in 1855 of the competitive examination for recruitment to the Indian Civil Service. John Lawrence, John Colvin, James Thomason and Richard Temple were eminent Indian Civil Servants who were products of Haileybury College (Roy, N. C., *The Civil Service in India*).

Haji Ahmad—was the brother of Nawab Alivardi Khan of Bengal (1740-56) (*q.v.*) whom he helped to defeat and kill Nawab Sarfaraz Khan (*q.v.*) of Bengal in the battle of Giria in 1740 and in becoming the Nawab of Bengal. His youngest daughter was the mother of Nawab Siraj-ud-daula (1756-57) of Bengal (*q.v.*).

Haji Ibrahim Sarhindi—was an eminent scholar who under the patronage of Emperor Akbar (1556-1605) translated into Persian the *Atharva-veda*.

Haji Iliyas—was the king of Bengal (*c.* 1345-57). He assumed the title of Shamsuddin Iliyas Shah. He annexed Eastern Bengal to his dominions, exacted tribute from Orissa and Tirhut and advanced as far as Benares. This brought upon him an expedition led by Sultan Firuz Shah Tughluq (A.D. 1357), but Iliyas organised his defence so well that Sultan Firuz had to return to Delhi without subduing Haji Iliyas who died at Pandua in A.D. 1357. His descendants ruled over Western Bengal till 1490.

Haji Maula—was a disgruntled officer in the service of Sultan Ala-ud-din Khalji (A.D. 1296-1316). He had been passed over in the selection of a *Kotwal* for Delhi and had been nursing a grievance. Taking advantage of the absence of the Sultan at Ranthambhor, Haji Maula organised a rebellion in Delhi, killed the *Kotwal*, occupied the Red Palace, broke into the treasury, distributed amongst his followers the money found there and declared a descendant of Sultan Iltutmish (A.D. 1211-36) as the Sultan of Delhi. But the rebellion lasted only four days at the end of which the supporters of Sultan Ala-ud-din re-asserted themselves, recovered the Red Palace and killed Haji Maula and his nominee to the throne of Delhi. The revolt had the effect of drawing Ala-ud-din's attention to the drawbacks in the administrative system and led him to adopt certain measures for preventing such outbreaks in the future. (*see* Ala-ud-din Khalji.)

Hakim, Prince Muhammad—was the second son of Emperor Humayun (1530-56) and the brother of Emperor Akbar (1556-1605). He was appointed by Akbar governor of the province of Afghanistan with his headquarters at Kabul. In 1581 he rose in revolt against Akbar but was reduced to submission. Akbar pardoned him and allowed him to continue to hold his post as governor of Afghanistan. Prince Hakim was a heavy drunkard and died in 1584 of a malady caused by strong drink.

Hakim Dawai—was a Persian scholar who acted as the teacher of Prince Khurram, later on Emperor Shah Jahan, in his boyhood and taught him Persian.

Hala—was the seventeenth king of the Satavahana dynasty (*q.v.*). Nothing is known of his political activities, but his name is associated with literature and the *Gatha Saptasati*, a collection of erotic poems, written in the ancient dialect of Maharastra, is attributed to him.

Haldighat, the battle of—*see* Gogunda, the battle of.

Halebid—was the capital of the Hoysala kings of Dvarasamudra. It contains the famous temple of Hoysalesvara which contains such remarkable sculptured work that it has been described as one of the most marvellous exhibitions of human labour to be found even in the patient East.

Halhed's *Hindu Law*—was prepared under the patronage of Warren Hastings, Governor-General. It was an English version of Hindu law based on a Persian translation of a Sanskrit version made by ten pundits.

Halliday, Sir F. J.—was the first Lieutenant-Governor of Bengal, Bihar, Orissa and Assam. The administration of these provinces which had been under the direct control of the Governor-

General and Council, was separated by the Charter Act of 1853 and placed in charge of a Lieutenant-Governor.

Halifax, Lord—*see* Lord Irwin.

Hamid Khan—was the Prime Minister under Alam Shah (A.D. 1445-53), the last Sultan of the Sayyid dynasty (*q.v.*). He helped Bahlul Lodi to occupy the throne of Delhi, but was thrown into prison by the latter soon after his accession, so that he might not be a thorn in the side of the new Sultan.

Hamida Banu Begum—was the consort of Emperor Humayun and mother of his great son Akbar. She exercised a great deal of influence on the administration during the early years of Akbar's reign.

Hamilton, William—was a surgeon in the employment of the East India Company in Calcutta. He accompanied John Surman's embassy to the Mughul court in 1715. Hamilton succeeded in curing the reigning Emperor Farruksiyar of a painful disease and the thankful Emperor issued in 1716, on Hamilton's request, *firmans* granting important trading and commercial facilities to the East India Company, the employers of William Hamilton.

Hamir—was a Rajput hero of Mewar and was connected with the royal family. In about 1316, towards the close of the reign of Sultan Ala-ud-din Khalji, he recovered Chitor from the Delhi sultanate. His reign was long and glorious. He recovered all the dominions of his ancestors before his death in 1364.

Hamir Deva—was the Chauhan king of Ranthambhor from A.D. 1282 until his death in 1301. Hamir began his career brilliantly, reduced to submission a part of Malwa and Garha Mandala. He extended his authority up to Ujjain in Malwa and to Mount Abu in Rajputana. So great was his strength and power that Sultan Jalal-ud-din Khalji abandoned in A.D. 1291 an attempt to capture Ranthambhor. Later on he defied the authority of Sultan Ala-ud-din Khalji by giving shelter to the leaders of the troops that had risen in mutiny against the Sultan and repulsed two invasions by the Sultan's armies but at last succumbed to the Muhammadans in 1301 when Sultan Ala-ud-din personally besieged and stormed Ranthambhor.

Hamza Shah, Saifuddin—was a king of Bengal who belonged to the Iliyas Shahi dynasty (*q.v.*). He ruled only for a year and some months (1410-12) and was displaced by Raja Ganesh (*q.v.*).

Har Dayal—was an educated Indian revolutionary. He belonged to Delhi, was a brilliant graduate of the Panjab University and later on studied at Oxford where he developed strong anti-British ideas, returned to India where he soon began to preach revolutionary doctrines. The Govt. of India thwarted his work and in 1908 he left India, travelled widely in Europe and eventually settled in the U.S.A. where he organised the *Ghadr* party. Expelled from the U.S.A. for his propaganda for Indo-German collaboration, he went to Europe and set up his headquarters in Berlin from where he tried to foment an anti-British rising in Afghanistan. But his efforts proved abortive. After the defeat of Germany he settled in Stockholm where he was appointed a Professor of Indian languages. He died in Central America where he had gone on a lecture-tour. He was a radical socialist and advocated organised rebellion against the British rule in India.

Hara Datta—was the Raja of Buran or Bulandshahr when it was invaded by Sultan Mahmud in 1018. He made peace with the Sultan by ready submission and acceptance of Islam.

Har Govind—was the sixth Guru (1606-45) of the Sikhs. He became the Guru after the execution of his father, the fifth Guru, Arjan by the order of Emperor Jahangir. He was not simply a religious teacher; he was also a great organiser and gave a military bent to his followers. He gathered a small army but was kept in prison for twelve years by Emperor Jahangir. On his release he rose against Shah Jahan and defeated an imperial army at Sangram near Amritsar in 1628. But he was eventually driven to the Kashmir hills where he died in 1645.

Har Kishan—was the eighth Guru (1661-64) of the Sikhs. He was the son and successor of Har Rai, the seventh Guru, and continued to encourage the military spirit introduced amongst the Sikhs by his grandfather, Guru Har Govind.

Har Rai—was the seventh Guru (1645-61). He continued the fiscal policy introduced by his grandfather, Guru Har Govind.

Harapala Deva—was the Yadava king of Devagiri. He was the son-in-law and successor of King Ramchandra Deva who had been forced to submit to Ala-ud-din Khalji in A.D. 1294 and later on compelled to agree to pay tribute. After the death of Sultan Ala-ud-din Khalji, Harapala Deva discontinued the payment of the tribute and practically asserted his independence. But he was defeated in A.D. 1317 by Sultan Mubarak (*q.v.*) who captured and executed him.

Harappa—is an ancient site of the Indus valley civilisation (*q.v.*). It is situated in the Montgomery district of the Panjab and is now in West Pakistan. It was a large city with a periphery of about three miles. Archaeological excavations carried on at the site have revealed ruins of a well planned city containing granaries, workmen's quarters, citadel with gates and terraces and cemeteries along with many seals which have not yet been deciphered and other objects bearing evidence to the existence there of an advanced type of civilisation. (Wheeler Mortimer, *The Indus Valley Civilisation*, 1953)

Haravijaya, the —is a considerable *kavya* (poetical work) running up to fifty cantos written by the Kashmirian poet Ratnakaran who flourished about the middle of the ninth century A.D. and was a contemporary of Avantivarman (*q.v.*), king of Kashmir.

Hardinge, Charles, Baron of Penshurst—was the Viceroy of India from 1910 to 1916. He was a grandson of Lord Hardinge, the Governor-General of India from 1844 to 1848. During his administration King-Emperor George V and his Queen visited India in December, 1911 and their coronation was formally proclaimed at a grand Durbar held in Delhi where the transference of the capital from Calcutta to Delhi was announced. The re-union of Eastern Bengal with Western Bengal to be administered by a Governor-in-Council, the creation of a new province of Bihar combined with Orissa under a Lieutenant-Governor and the reversion of Assam to a separate province administered by a Chief Commissioner, were also announced. In 1912 on the occasion of his formal entry in the new capital (New Delhi) a bomb was thrown at Lord Hardinge who was severely wounded. The Viceroy kept cool and did not launch on a policy of any retribution and revenge, as Lord Chelmsford (*q.v.*) did after the Amritsar riot in 1919. In 1913 Lord Hardinge in a public speech in Madras strongly criticised the anti-Indian Immigration Act passed by the South African Government as invidious and unjust, expressed his sympathy with the passive resistance movement that Gandhi (*q.v.*) had started in South Africa in protest against the Government's anti-Indian policy and demanded a Committee of Inquiry allowing Indians to take part in it. The South African Government had to yield and appointed a Commission as the result of whose report the Indian Immigration Act was so modified that Gandhi called it the *Magna Carta* of Indian liberty in South Africa. The most outstanding event during the administration of Lord Hardinge was the outbreak of the First World War in August, 1914 and India's participation in it. Lord Hardinge took courage in both hands and sent out of India practically every European soldier available in India and large contingents of Indian soldiers as well.

It speaks highly for his popularity as well as of India's trust in Great Britain that, in spite of the political upheaval and outbreak of terroristic activities that had marked the earlier part of Lord Hardinge's administration, India remained completely loyal to the British connection and contributed substantially to the British victory in 1919.

Hardinge, Henry, Viscount—was the Governor-General of India from 1844 to 1848. At the time of his appointment he was 59 years of age and had seen much fighting in the Peninsular War. During the first year and a half of his administration he took preliminary steps for the introduction of the railway system in India, made progress in the designs for the Ganges Canal and took effective measures for suppressing social evils like *Suttee* (*q.v.*), infanticide and human sacrifices, then prevalent in the Hill Tracts of Orissa. The most important event of his administration was the First Sikh War (*q.v.*) (1845-46) which was brought to a victorious close by the British victory at the battle of Sobraon followed by the treaty of Lahore according to which the Sikhs ceded all their lands on the British side of the Sutlej as well as the whole of the Jalandhar Doab lying between the Sutlej and the Beas rivers and agreed to pay an indemnity of one and a half million sterling or to cede Kashmir and pay a cash indemnity of half a million sterling. The Sikhs preferred to surrender Kashmir which was handed over to Gulab Singh, Raja of Jammu, for one million sterling. The Governor-General was rewarded with a Viscountship for his success in the First Sikh War. After his retirement from India in 1848 Lord Hardinge held high offices in Britain, first as the Master of Ordnance and then as Commander-in-Chief and made many improvements in the British army. He died in 1856.

Hardwar—in Uttar Pradesh, is one of the most sacred places of Hindu pilgrimage. The Ganges here first enters into the plain country and a bath in its holy water is considered as highly purifying. In its neighbourhood, at Kangra, the Gurukul University has been founded.

Hare, David (1775-1842)—was one of the few non-official liberal Englishmen resident in India who devoted their time and energy to the welfare of the Indians. He was specially interested in the spread of Western education in India. A watch-maker by profession and a Scott by birth, he came to Calcutta in 1800 and acquired a competence before he made over his business to a relative in1816 and devoted himself entirely to philanthropic work amongst the Indian population in Calcutta. He took a leading part in initiating the scheme of establishing an English School in Calcutta and it was largely due to his efforts that the Hindu College was opened on January 20, 1817. Next year he founded the School Book Society for printing and publishing English and Bengali books. He also worked hard for the repeal of the Regulations against the Press which bore fruit during the administration of Sir Charles Metcalfe in 1835 and to secure the introduction of the system of trial by jury in the Supreme Court which also was effected later on. He died of cholera in Calcutta in 1842. His philanthropy, benevolence and liberalism had so impressed the people of Calcutta that they erected by public subscription his life-size marble statue which is situated at a central place in Calcutta where he is also commemorated by a school which bears his name.

Hari Pant Phadke—was a Maratha general who led, under Nana Faḍnavis' orders, a Maratha army against Tipu Sultan of Mysore in December, 1785 and obliged Tipu to open peace negotiations which culminated in a treaty in 1787 by which Tipu agreed to pay the Marathas forty-five lakhs of rupees and to cede to them the three districts of Badami, Kithur and Nargund in return for the territories occupied by the Marathas.

Hari Singh Naola (Nalwa)—was the Sikh general of Maharaja Ranjit Singh of the Panjab who in May, 1834 captured the citadel of Peshawar which then passed under the control of Maharaja Ranjit Singh.

Hari Vijaya Suri—was a prominent Jain teacher who flourished during the reign of Emperor Akbar (1566-1605) and was invited by the Mughul Emperor to join in the religious discussions that were sponsored by the Emperor and held at the *Ibadat Khana* at Fatehpur Sikri.

Harihara I—was the son of Sangama. With the help and collaboration of his four brothers, of whom Bukka I was the most prominent, he founded in A.D. 1336 the city of Vijayanagar (*q.v.*) on the southern bank of the Tungabhadra and thus established a Hindu kingdom in the region. He was also helped by two saintly Brahmans named Mádhava Vidyáranya and his more celebrated brother Sáyana, the commentator on the Vedas. Harihara I died in 1354-55 after establishing his sovereignty over "the whole country between the eastern and the western oceans".

Harihara II—was the son and successor of Bukka I, the second king of Vijayanagar. Harihara II ruled from A.D. 1377-1404.

He extended and consolidated the dominion of Vijayanagar over the whole of south India as far as Trichinopoly.

Harinath—a reputed Hindi writer, enjoyed the patronage of Emperor Akbar (1566-1605).

Harishena—was the last king of the Vakataka dynasty (*q.v.*) which ruled over Madhya Pradesh from the fourth to the sixth centuries.

Harishena—was a general and the court-poet of the second Gupta Emperor Samudragupta (*c.* A.D. 330-80) and composed the Allahabad *Prasasti* (eulogium) commemorating the achievements of Samudragupta.

Harisinha—was a ruling chief of Tirhut. In A.D. 1321 he invaded Nepal, received the submission of the reigning king, Jayarudramalla and established his sovereignty over the whole valley. He established his headquarters at Bhatgaon and maintained diplomatic relations with China, but left the local rulers undisturbed. His descendants ruled over Nepal till A.D. 1418.

Haritiputras—*i.e.*, descendants of the sage Hariti. This family name was claimed by the Satakarnis (*q.v.*) and the Chalukyas.

Harris, Lord George—was a general in the service of the East India Company. During the Fourth Mysore War (1797) he routed Tipu Sultan at the battle of Malavalli in March, 1799 driving Tipu to take shelter within the walls of Seringapatam which General Harris carried by assault on May 4, 1799. He was rewarded in 1815 with a peerage for his success in this war.

Harsha—was a king of the Salastamva dynasty of Kamarupa. He ruled about the middle of the eighth century of the Christian era and gave his daughter, Rajyamati, in marriage to the Nepal king, Jayadeva.

Harsha—was a king of Kashmir from 1089 to 1101. He was a veritable tyrant and has been described as the Nero of Kashmir.

Harsha Charita, the or **The life of Harsha**—was written by Bana, the court-poet of Harshavardhana (*q.v.*). It is a biographical sketch of the early life of Harsha up to the recovery of his sister, Rajyasri. It also supplies vivid pictures of the army, of the life of the court and of social conditions in general.

Harsa era—dating from A.D. 606 was started in commemoration of the accession of King Harshavardhana (*q.v.*) of Thaneswar and Kanauj.

Harshavardhana—was the king of Kanauj and Thaneswar (A.D. 606-47). The second son of his father, Prabhakaravardhana, king of Thaneswar, he succeeded his elder brother Rajyavardhana on the latter's death in A.D. 606. The situation at the time of Harsha's accession was very critical. His brother had been killed by Sasanka, the king of Bengal, and his sister Rajyasri whose husband Grahavarman, the king of Kanauj, had been defeated and killed by the king of Malwa, had fled for safety nobody knew where. Harsha soon traced and recovered his fugitive sister, made an alliance with king Kumara Bhaskarvarman of Kamarupa and sent a large army against Sasanka, the king of Bengal. Though Sasanka could not be dethroned, for he certainly ruled till 1619 and probably lived for several years more, Harsha collected a large army, waged incessant warfare for six years following his accession and conquered the five Indies, as the contemporary Chinese pilgrim, Hiuen Tsang, states. What specific parts of India are meant by the term 'five Indies' is not clear, but there are records which show that though Harsha was repulsed in about A.D. 620 from the banks of the Narmada by the Chalukya king, Pulakeshin II (A.D. 609-42) he conquered Valabhi, Magadha, Kashmir, Gujarat and Sind. Indeed he fought all through his long reign and his last recorded campaign was against Ganjam in A.D. 643. He thus created a vast empire which extended from the snowy hills in the north to the Narmada on the south and from Ganjam in the east to Valabhi in the west. This vast empire with its capital at Kanauj was efficiently administered by Harsha who assumed the title of Maharajadhiraja. He maintained diplomatic relations with the Chinese Emperor. He was an eclectic in religion who distributed his devotions to Siva, the Sun and the Buddha, but in the later part of his life he became more devoted to the *Mahayana* Buddhism. Like Asoka, he established benevolent institutions for the benefit of travellers, the poor and the sick throughout his empire. He made large gifts and held quinquennial assemblies at the confluence of the Ganges and the Jumna at Prayag (Allahabad) in which he distributed all the treasures that he had accumulated during the previous four years. The Chinese pilgrim, Hiuen Tsang, attended in A.D. 643 the sixth of the series and has left an account of it which bears eloquent testimony to the wealth and charity of Harshavardhana. Himself a poet of no mean order who composed three Sanskrit literary gems, namely, the *Nagananda*, *Ratnavali* and *Priyadarsika*, Harsha was also a patron of men of letters and learning like Bana, the author of the *Kadambari* and the *Harshacharita*, Mayura, a lyric poet who wrote the *Subhasitabali* and last, but not the least, of the scholarly Chinese pilgrim, Hiuen Tsang (*q.v.*).

Hasan Ali Abdullah—was the elder of the Sayyid brothers (*q.v.*), the younger being Husain Ali (*q.v.*).

Hasan Khan—was the father of Emperor Sher Shah (1540-45). He came with his father, Ibrahim, from Peshawar, took service under a *jagirdar* in the Panjab where his son Farid, later on famous as Sher Shah, was born. Hasan later on got from the Governor of Jaunpur a *jagir* in Sasaram in Bihar. Under the influence of a wife who was not Sher Shah's mother, Hasan ill treated his young son who was thus turned into a soldier of fortune. Hasan had nothing to do with the building up of the great future of his famous son.

Hasan Ali Khan—a general in the service of Emperor Aurangzeb (1658-1707) was the faujdar of Mathura and suppressed the rising of the Jats under Gokla (*q.v.*) in 1669.

Hasan-i-Dihlavi—was the pen-name of poet Shaikh Nizam-ud-din Hasan. He flourished in the reign of Sultan Ala-ud-din Khalji (1296-1326) and his fame as a poet, writing in Persian, extended beyond India.

Hasan Khan Mewati—was an Afghan chief who supported the Lodi dynasty (*q.v.*) of the sultans of Delhi. He joined with Rana Sanga of Mewar against Babur and shared the defeat of the Rajput king at the battle of Khanua in 1527 at the hands of the first Mughul Emperor Babur (1526-30).

Hasan Zafar Khan—was the founder of the Bahmani kingdom and dynasty. (*see* Alauddin Hasan Bahman Shah.)

Hasan-un-Nizami—an early Muhammadan historian, wrote the *Taj-ul-Ma'asir* which is an authoritative account of the sultanate of Delhi (*q.v.*).

Hastings—Francis Rawdon, Earl of Moira, Marquess of Hastings, better known as Lord Hastings, was Governor-General from 1813 to 1823 in succession to Lord Minto I. He was fifty-nine years of age when he assumed office in India. His long administration, second in length only to that of Warren Hastings (1774-85), was remarkable for the expansion and consolidation of the British Empire in India from Cape Comorin in the south to the river Sutlej in the north-west, that is to say, over the whole of India except Assam in the east and Sind and the Panjab in the west. This was effected by his success in three major wars, viz. the Nepalese War (1814-16), the Pindari War (1817-19) and the Third Maratha War (1817-19). He had the advantage of being the Commander-in-Chief of the army in India in addition to being its highest administrative head. The campaigns were efficiently organised and led to great successes. The Nepalese

War (*q.v.*) which was concluded by the treaty of Sagauli, led to the annexation to the British Indian Empire of Simla and its neighbourhood and also to the establishment of friendly relations with Nepal which lasted throughout the continuance of the British rule in India. The Pindari War (*q.v.*) which developed into the Third Maratha War (*q.v.*) in which the Sindhia was isolated and neutralised, the Peshwa Baji Rao II (*q.v.*) was defeated at Kirkee in 1817 and at Ashti in 1818, the Bhonsla Raja Appa Shahib (*q.v.*) at Sitabaldi and Nagpur in 1817 and the Sindhia at Mahidpur in 1817 and the fort of Asirgarh was stormed in 1818, led to the destruction of the Pindari pests, to the abolition of the Peshwaship, to the installation of a descendant of Shivaji as the Raja of Satara and of a British nominee as the Bhonsla Raja and to the diminution of the dominions of Holkar and Sindhia who were further forbidden to interfere in the affairs of the Princes of Rajputana all of whom now readily accepted protective alliances with the British. These developments frankly marked the establishment and consolidation of British sovereignty over the whole of India to the east of the Sutlej and Sind. This significant change in the position of the British in India was clearly indicated when Lord Hastings stopped the presentation of *nazars* (or formal presents offered to a superior) which the Governors-General of India had so long been tendering to the titular Mughul Emperor at Delhi. Lord Hastings also suppressed the pirate chiefs who had so long infested the western coast of India as well as those of the Persian Gulf and the Red Sea. Lastly, in 1819 Lord Hastings acquired the island of Singapore at the extremity of the Malay Peninsula and thus secured for the British Empire an important strategical position in the Far East. Lord Hastings effected improvements in Calcutta, secured better water supply for Delhi, improved roads and bridges, encouraged education amongst the Indians, effected administrative reforms by ending the separation made by Lord Cornwallis (*q.v.*) between the offices of the magistrate and the collector and by increasing the number of courts, introduced the ryotwari system of land revenue collection in Madras, took measures to give greater security to the cultivators in Bengal where the establishment of the permanent system of land revenue practically placed the ryot at the absolute mercy of the landlord, and, lastly, abolished the censorship of the press imposed in 1799. The brilliant administration of Lord Hastings ended, however, in a cloud. He had shown great indulgence to the banking house of Palmer & Co., a partner of which was the husband of a ward of the Governor-General. Though he was cleared of any corrupt motive the home authorities passed a censure on him. Lord Hastings resigned and went back to England in 1823. He died in 1826.

Hastings, Warren (1732-1818)—was the first Governor-General of Bengal. Born of humble parents and educated through the generosity of an uncle, he entered into the service of the East India Company as a writer at the age of eighteen and landed in Calcutta in 1750. After three years of training in a small trading centre of the Company he was posted at Cossimbazar (*q.v.*), was imprisoned by Nawab Siraj-ud-daula (*q.v.*) when the latter captured Cossimbazar in 1756, was released and joined the English fugitives at Fulta, took part in the action that led to the recovery of Calcutta by Clive and Watson in 1757 and was appointed by Clive as Resident at the court at Murshidabad. In 1761 he was appointed a member of the Bengal Council under Vansittart. Hastings was generally opposed to the policy of private trading then practised by the Company's servants. He was also opposed to the policy that led to the war with Nawab Mir Kasim (*q.v.*), resigned after the battle of Buxar in 1764 and went back to England with some wealth which he had made by running through agents a large business in timber in Bengal. He came back to India in 1769 as second in the Council at Madras. On the voyage out to India Hastings, who was then a widower, made the acquaintance of Maria, wife of Baron Imhoff, who were fellow travellers and whom he later on married. In Madras Hastings worked efficiently and was appointed in 1772 as the President of the Bengal Council. Thus at the age of forty Warren Hastings became the Governor of Bengal. On the passing of the Regulating Act in 1773 Warren Hastings became the first Governor-General of the British dominions in India under the title of the Governor-General of Fort William in Bengal. On assuming the Governorship of Bengal in 1772 the first task of Warren Hastings was, as directed by the home authorities, to scrap the system of 'double government' (*q.v.*) which Clive had established in Bengal and to make the Company "stand forth as the Dewan", that is to say, to collect the revenue through their own agencies. Muhammad Reza Khan and Raja Shitab Ray, the Deputy Nawabs, who had so long been in charge of collection, were removed from their offices and put on trial, but they were acquitted. A Board of Revenue (*q.v.*) was set up in Calcutta in which the task of collection of revenue was now vested. The treasury was transferred from Murshidabad to Calcutta which thus tended to become the capital of British India. The allowance of the young Nawab of Bengal, a grandson of Nawab Mir Jafar (*q.v.*) was reduced to a half (16 lakhs of rupees) and Mani Begum was appointed as the guardian of the minor Nawab. As Emperor Shah Alam had become a dependant on the Marathas since 1771, the tribute of twenty-six lakhs of rupees that Clive had agreed to pay to the Emperor, was stopped and the districts of Kora and Allahabad, ceded to him by Clive, were also taken away and sold to the Nawab of Oudh for fifty lakhs of rupees. Hastings also embarked on a policy of friendship with the Nawab of Oudh which eventually involved him in the Rohilla war (*q.v.*) in 1774. The Rohillas were easily reduced, but the policy leading to the war and the subsequent conduct of the army in Rohilkhand came in for severe criticism and formed a count for the later attacks on Hastings in Parliament. He settled the land revenue in Bengal on a contract basis for five years which was later on turned into annual contracts. He placed the police and the military systems in Bengal on a new footing, appointed English officials, now first called Collectors, aided by Indian assistants, to superintend the district and to dispense civil justice. He set up two courts of appeal in Calcutta, namely, the *Sadar Dewani Adalat* presided over by the Governor-General and four members of the Council for dispensing civil justice and the *Sadar Nizamat Adalat* presided over by the Naib-Nazim to hear criminal appeals. Warren Hastings thus well and firmly laid the foundation of the system of civil administration on which the superstructure was raised later on by Lord Cornwallis (*q.v.*).

Soon after the Rohilla war the Regulating Act (*q.v.*) came into operation and Warren Hastings became the Governor-General with a Council of four members, three of whom, namely, General John Clavering, George Monson and Sir Philip Francis combined from the beginning into an opposition to the Governor-General, whose only supporter in the Council was the fourth member, Richard Barwell. As the majority decision was to prevail, Warren Hastings soon found himself embroiled in a struggle with his Council which continued for six years and made his task immensely difficult. Any other man but Hastings would have been hounded from office, but Hastings was a man of superhuman energy and endurance. Though often outvoted and obliged to bow down to decisions which he did not consider proper, Hastings stuck to his guns until two of his opponents, Monson and Clavering, died, and the third, Francis disabled in a duel with Hastings, left India in 1780. Then Hastings regained full control over the administration. The years of strain and struggle revealed at once the good and bad traits in the character of Hastings. All who like Maharaja Nandakumar, Raja Chait Singh of Benares and the Begums of Oudh had tried in some way or other to seek the favour of the hostile Council incurred his bitter hostility and were pursued with a vindictive vengeance. Nandakumar (*q.v.*) paid the penalty with his life; Raja Chait Singh (*q.v.*) was first punished with heavy, illegal and unjustifiable demands for men and money and finally harried out of his state; and the Begums of Oudh (*q.v.*) were insulted and unjustly made to pay large sums out of their private estates in order to escape complete ruin. All these incidents later on formed counts of charges against Hastings at his impeachment. Though he was acquitted on all the charges and his impeachment fell through, yet the circumstance that the British Government never conferred on Hastings the honour of a peerage which he greatly desired, suggests that the British conscience was never completely satisfied about the propriety of the conduct of Warren Hastings in connection with the incidents mentioned above. If, however, Warren Hastings was greedy and vindictive he was also a person of immense mental strength and unbounded resourcefulness—the two virtues which he brought to the service of the nascent British Empire in India the very existence of which came to be threatened during the years 1775-82. A war with the Marathas began in 1775; next year came the American War of Independence bringing in its train hostilities with France, Spain and Holland; and three years later, in 1779, the Nizam built up with Haidar Ali of Mysore and the Marathas a formidable anti-British confederacy on the soil of India. Disasters befell the Indo-British army. In 1779 the Marathas so cornered the army of Col. Camac that he had to sign the Convention of Waḍgaon (*q.v.*); next year Haidar Ali invaded the Carnatic, cut off a division of a British army led by Baillie, ruthlessly plundered the Carnatic and captured Arcot. The defeat of an army of Haidar Ali at Porto Novo in 1781 was robbed of its effect by the destruction in 1782 at Tanjore by Haidar's son, Tipu Sultan, of a considerable British force led by Braithwaite and the arrival in Indian waters of a French navy led by Admiral de Suffren. All these disasters which threatened the very existence of the British Empire, did not discourage Warren Hastings. He acted with great vigour. He sent an army under Goddard (*q.v.*) which marched across India and captured Bassein in 1780; while another army sent by him under Popham escaladed the fortress of Gwalior and restored British prestige; by skilful diplomacy Hastings also detached Bhonsla and Sindhia from the anti-British confederacy and concluded, through the good offices of the latter, the treaty of Salbai (*q.v.*) with the Marathas and thus ended the war with them and secured for the British the possession of Salsette. Hastings acted with equal energy in southern India. He suspended the Governor of Madras, sent the old veteran, Sir Eyre Coote, from Bengal with all available reinforcements to retrieve the past disgraces. He sent a second army under Pearce who made an overland march from Bengal to Madras. He had detached in 1780 the Nizam from the anti-British confederacy by surrendering to him Guntur and when he succeeded in 1782 in making peace with the Marathas by the treaty of Salbai, he had practically broken up the formidable anti-British confederacy that the Nizam had formed in 1779 and brought the war to be confined to hostilities with Mysore alone. Haidar died in 1782 and his successor, Tipu Sultan, carried on the war with the English till 1784 when peace was made by the treaty of Mangalore on the basis of mutual restitution of conquests. The treaty of Mangalore was not the work of Hastings and he did not approve of its terms, but he accepted them as the Madras Government which had taken the initiative in making the treaty, was very keen on the restoration of peace. In any case Hastings had won during the war diplomatic and military successes of which any administrator could be proud and which entitled him to be ranked as one of the greatest Governors-General of India.

After the passing of Pitt's India Act (1784) which Warren Hastings disliked, he resigned the Governor-Generalship in 1785 and retired to England. Three years later Warren Hastings was impeached on twenty charges, the chief of which were his treatment of Raja Chait Singh of Benares and of the Begums of Oudh and the acceptance of presents and bribes. The trial continued for seven years, at the end of which Warren Hastings was acquitted of all the charges. He died in England in 1818 at the ripe old age of 86 years (Lyall, Sir Alfred, *Warren Hastings;* Trotter, Lionel, *Warren Hastings*)

Hastivarman—was the king of Vengi. He was one of the kings of southern India who was defeated but restored to his dominions by the second Gupta Emperor, Samudragupta (*c.* A.D. 330-80). He is believed to have belonged to the Sálank-áyana dynasty which ruled at the time at Vegi or Pedda-Vegi, seven miles north of Ellore, between the Krishna and the Godavari. (*P.H.A.I.* p. 540)

Hathigumpha inscription of Kharavela—*see* Kharavela.

Havelock, General Sir Henry (1795-1857)—joined the army in 1816 and came to Calcutta in 1823. He fought in the Burma War in 1824 and published in 1828 his book on the campaigns in Ava. He was away in Afghanistan from 1838 to 1842 and fought in the First Sikh War (1845-46) under Sir Hugh Gough. He was fighting in 1856-57 in Persia from where he was sent straight in June, 1857, to fight the mutinous sepoys in Allahabad. He fought several actions, defeated Nana Shaheb and occupied Cawnpore in July, 1857. He then proceeded to relieve Lucknow in which task he succeeded, after three failures, in September, 1857. Two months later he died of illness while still in harness. A posthumous baronetcy and a pension were granted to him by the British Government.

Hawkins, Captain William—led the voyage of the ship *Hector* in the third voyage of the East India Company to the East. He arrived at Surat in 1608 bearing a letter from King James I of England to Emperor Jahangir. Hawkins travelled overland to the Mughul court, was received by Jahangir and was given a favourable reception. He lived at the Mughul court till 1611, was often received by the Emperor, was appointed to be a commander of 400 and was married, at the instance of the Emperor, to the daughter of an Armenian Christian. He persuaded the Emperor to grant some trading facilities to the English, but these could not be enforced on account of the strenuous opposition of the Portuguese. Hawkins left the Mughul court in 1611 and returned to England in 1612. He left records of his experiences in India. (Foster, *Early Travels in India*)

Heliodoros—was a son of Diya (Dion), a native of Taxila. He came to Vidisa as an ambassador of the Taxilian king Antialkidas (*c.* 140 - 130 B.C.), a Bactrian, to Rajan Kasiputra Bhagabhadra, the fifth Sunga king, in the fourteenth year of the latter's reign. Heliodoros, though a Greek, professed the Bhagavata religion, and set up a monolithic pillar (*Garuda-dhvaja*) in honour of Vasudeva (Krishna), the god of gods. All this is found recorded on the pillar which also shows that Heliodoros was well versed in the *Mahabharata*. The inscription is important as it shows that Greeks embraced Hinduism in the second

century of the pre-Christian era and marks a stage in the growth
of the cult of Vaishnavism.

Heliokles—was the last Greek king of Bactria and has been assigned
to *c.* 140 - 130 B.C.

Hemachandra—was a Jain author (A.D. 1088-1172) whose
enormous work, the *Trisastichhalakapurasacharitra*, deals with the
lives of one hundred and twenty-six Jain saints. It has a supplement known as the *Parishista Parvan* to which some historical
value has been sometimes assigned.

Hemadri—a famous jurist, flourished in southern India and enjoyed
the patronage of the Yadava kings of Warangal. Some time
between A.D. 1260 and 1309 he wrote his famous work
Chaturvargachintamani in which he sets out in great detail rules
of vows, offerings, pilgrimages, the attainment of release and
offerings to the dead.

Hemanta Sena—the second king of the Sena dynasty of Bengal,
ruled in the last quarter of the eleventh century A.D. He bore
the title of *Maharajadhiraja*, but he was not as powerful as the
title would suggest. Little is known of his activities.

Hemu—later on Raja Bikramajit—born of a Bania family of
Rewari in Mewat, raised himself by dint of his own ability
to be the chief minister of Adil Shah (1554-56), the third ruler
of the Sur dynasty, founded by Sher Shah. At the time of the
recovery of Delhi by Humayun in 1555 Adil Shah was in
Chunar and left his interests in northern India to Hemu. On
the death of Humayun in 1555 Hemu, advancing through
Gwalior, occupied Agra and Delhi. These successes inspired his
ambition and he practically declared himself to be an independent sovereign with the name of Raja Bikramajit. He thus
became the most formidable rival of Akbar whom he opposed
in the second battle of Panipat fought on the 5th November,
1556. Hemu showed great bravery and good generalship, but
an accident gave the victory to Akbar. Hemu was hit in the
eye by a stray arrow and became unconscious. At once his
army which was a motley host of Afghans, Pathans and Hindus
and was held together only by his leadership and money, broke
up and Hemu was captured and taken a prisoner to young
Akbar who, under the instruction of his guardian Bairam Khan,
struck him on the neck with his sword and killed him.

Herat—is a city which was the capital of a province which the
Greeks called Aria. The area lies just to the east of the Hindu
Kush and is of great strategical importance. Indeed it has
been considered as marking the scientific frontier of India on the

north-west. In the sixth century B.C. it was a part of the Persian empire. In the fourth century B.C. it was ceded by Seleucos to Chandragupta Maurya and continued to be a part of the Indian Empire of the Mauryas until their fall. It then passed under the rule of the Indo-Bactrian and Indo-Parthian princes amongst whom Afghanistan came to be parcelled in the early centuries of the Christian era. Never again in later times did Herat become a part of the Indian Empire. It became a bone of contention between Persia and Afghanistan of which it finally became a part in 1863 when Amir Dost Muhammed annexed it to his dominions. The 'forward school' of Indo-British politicians and strategists have always pined for it and this aspiration lay at the bottom of the policy that led to the First and Second Afghan Wars (*q.v.*), but all was in vain. The 'scientific frontier' on the north-west ever eluded its exponents.

Hermaios—was the last Indo-Greek king to rule over the north-western frontier territory of India. He ruled in the first century of the Christian era when he was overthrown by Kadphises I, the founder of the Kushan dynasty in India.

Herschell Committee—was appointed in 1892 to consider the current currency system in British India. On the strength of its recommendations the Government of India closed the free coinage in Indian mints of gold and silver to the public. Gold, however, was received in mints in exchange for rupees at the ratio of 1s. 4d. to the rupee and sovereigns were received in payment of public dues at the rate of Rs. 15/- per sovereign. As a result of these measures gold became the standard of value, though not yet made legal tender.

Hewitt, General—was the commanding officer of the Indo-British troops stationed at Meerut in May, 1857, when the Mutiny broke out. Though he had 2,200 European troops under him he took no steps to suppress the mutineers who were thus suffered to gallop to Delhi and bring it under their control.

Hickey, Thomas—was a portrait-painter who came to India and published in Calcutta in 1788 *The Hist. of Painting and Sculpture from the Earliest Account*, printed historical pictures at Seringapatam in 1799 and by 1822 he had painted many pictures which are in the Government House in Calcutta.

Hicky, James Augustus—was the editor of the *Bengal Gazette*, the first newspaper in India. It appeared in 1780 but was suppressed by Warren Hastings in 1782 on account of its persistent attacks on the Government and its personnel. (Busteed, *Echoes from Old Calcutta*)

High Courts in India—were established by the Indian High Courts Act passed in 1861. Heretofore there were in each Presidency two high courts of appeal, namely, the Supreme Court which represented the authority of the British Crown and the *Sadar* courts which represented the Company. This dual authority in judicial matters was cumbrous and in 1861 a High Court was established in their places in each of the three Presidency towns of Calcutta, Bombay and Madras. Later on a High Court was established at Allahabad and a Chief Court in the Panjab in 1866. These courts dispensed justice according to a uniform system of Civil Procedure Code, Criminal Procedure Code and Penal Code which were all promulgated between 1859 and 1861. There are now High Courts at the headquarters of all the major states in India.

Hijra era—is the Muslim era dating from A.D. 622 when Muhammad was obliged to quit Mecca and flee for safety to Medina. Hijra means 'flight'. It is a lunar era of about 354 days, and so is 11 days shorter than the solar year.

Himalayas, the—is the name applied to the portion of the mountain region between India and Tibet and enclosed between the arms of the Indus in the west and the Brahmaputra in the east, 1500 miles in length and from 100 to 150 miles in width. The highest peak is Mount Everest. Portions of it are snow-clad all through the year. It is the source of many rivers, the chief of which are the Indus, the Sutlej, the Ganges, the Jamuna, the Brahmaputra, the Kosi, the Gandak and the Subansiri. Climate varies from extreme heat to extreme cold and the flora and the fauna native to the region are immensely varied and rich. It has profoundly influenced the politics, philosophy and religion of India. It has provided a practically insurmountable defence to India in the north. Its sombreness, dignity and magnitude led the Hindu mind to consider it as the abode of the gods and deeply oriented Hindu philosophy and religion and coloured Hindu literature in all ages.

Himmat Bahadur—was the leader of an armed sect of religious ascetics known as the Gosains who served Mahadaji Sindhia.

Himu—*see ante* Hemu.

Hinaynana or **the Lesser Vehicle,**—is the name applied to primitive Buddhism as opposed to the *Mahayana* or Great Vehicle which was a later development of Buddhism. According to the *Hinayana* Gautama Buddha, the founder of Buddhism, was only a saint to whom respect and reverence are to be paid but who is not to be worshipped as a god, as the *Mahayana* held.

Further with the *Hinayana* the attainment of *Nirvana* is the highest ideal for a Buddhist monk and is to be striven after by following the Noble Eightfold Path and believing in the Four Noble Truths. (*See* also under Buddhism.)

Hindal Mirza—was one of the three younger brothers of the Mughul Emperor Humayun (1530-55). Though treated with kind generosity by Humayun he often proved disloyal to him. When Humayun was campaigning in Bengal, Hindal was put in charge of the line of communications, but he failed in his duty and thus contributed to Humayun's defeat at the battle of Chausa in 1539. Humayun, however, forgave him, but Hindal did not stand by Humayun in the years of his distress. He even joined his elder brother Kamran and declined to help Humayun. With Kamran also he soon quarrelled and came over to Humayun, but was killed by an Afghan in a night assault before Humayun could recover the throne of Delhi.

Hindi—has been declared by the constitution of the Republic of India to be the national language of India. It is based on Sanskrit and is written, like Sanskrit, in Devanagari script, which, however, differs in actual practice in the different Hindi-speaking parts of India. It is the spoken language of the whole of northern India, excepting Bengal and Assam. In southern India it is not the popular language, but it is fast extending there. It has got a large literature and the most popular book in Hindi is the *Ramacharitamanasa* by Tulsidas who flourished in the sixteenth century and was a contemporary of Emperor Akbar (1556-1605). Premchand (1880-1936) is the most prolific of Hindi writers. He wrote many novels. Hindi is divided into two branches, viz., the eastern as spoken in Oudh and Baghalkhand and the western as current in the middle and upper Gangetic Doab. It is the language spoken by the largest linguistic group in India, but it is not the language of the majority of the people of India.

Hindu—means one who professes Hinduism (*q.v.*) as his religion. He is not required to believe in any particular creed and the only outward symbol in social life is the acceptance of the caste system, but even this is rapidly weakening. (*see* Hinduism.)

Hinduism—is a unique religion. It is *apauresheya*, that is to say, not founded by any particular human being and it is also *sanatana*, that is to say, eternal. It insists on no creed to be believed by its adherents. It believes in one supreme being who rules the creation, but does not exclude from its fold those who believe in many gods and goddesses as well as those who hold that

God does not exist. It holds that the supreme being is formless, yet it recognises the worship of images. It believes in the existence of the soul and that the soul transmigrates from birth to birth which is caused by the *karma* or action of a being. It believes that *moksha* or *mukti*, that is to say, freedom from rebirth and from all the sorrows that human flesh and blood is heir to, can be secured by both *jnana* (knowledge) and good *karma* and that *moksha* means merging of an individual soul into the Supreme Soul (*paramatma*). It holds that sacrifices (*jajna*) are efficacious in propitiating the divine beings, but considers these as inferior to knowledge and devotion. It is bold enough to declare that man is God (*soham*) but at the same time it recognises the duality between man and his creator to whom devotion can be rendered. Its outward symbol is adherence to the caste system and the recognition of the Vedas as the sacred scripture, though modern Hinduism differs much from the ancient Vedic religion. The prevalent idea that Hinduism is not a proselytizing religion is historically incorrect. Epigraphic and literary evidence shows that in the past many Greeks and the Sakas, Gurjaras and Hunas who invaded India and settled here, were embraced within the fold of Hinduism. In more recent times the Ahoms who entered into India towards the beginning of the thirteenth century and settled in Assam which they conquered, were converted *en masse* to Hinduism in the sixteenth century. It is also historically equally incorrect to hold that Hinduism has always been confined to India. Unimpeachable evidence shows that Hinduism spread, before the advent of Islam, to Madagascar in the west and in the east to the Malay Peninsula, Java, Sumatra, Champa (Annam) and Cambodia where Indian colonists carried their rule, their religion, their philosophy, their sacred language, Sanskrit, and their arts and architecture of which splendid monuments are still to be found from Java to Cambodia. Hinduism has within its fold many sects, the chief amongst which are the *Saivas* (worshippers of Siva), the *Saktas* (worshippers of Sakti) and *Vaishnavas* (worshippers of Vishnu), but they all agree in upholding the authority of the Vedas. The philosophy of Hinduism is contained in the *Upanishadas* (*q.v.*) of which the *Bhagavat Gita* is a symposium and is elaborated in the *Sadadarshana* or Six Systems (*q.v.*) of Philosophy. The two great epics, the *Ramayana* and the *Mahabharata*, contain religious and social ideas and ideals which are highly esteemed by the Hindu. Last, but not the least, an important feature of Hinduism is its spirit of toleration. It tolerates every form of religious dissent and its spirit is completely alien to the bloody feuds that marked the relation between Roman Catholicism and Protestantism in Christian countries and between Islam and the other religions with which it came into contact. Many temples have been erected all over India to Hindu gods and goddesses, but a temple is not a necessity, for the Hindu form of worship is individualistic, though congregational worship is also recognised. Indeed Hinduism permits its followers a greater deal of freedom in the matter, form and place of worship and prayer.

Hindusthan—means the land of the Hindus. It is a term that is used to indicate northern India from Peshawar to Assam and came into use after the conquest of northern India by the Muhammadans. Sometimes it is used in a wider sense to denote the whole of India.

Hindu College—was established in Calcutta in 1816 by the efforts of men like Raja Ram Mohan Roy and David Hare for the purpose of propagating English education amongst the children of the soil. Though Lord Hastings who was then the Governor-General agreed to be its patron it was in the beginning a purely private enterprise. Later on it was taken over by the Government and developed into Presidency College, Calcutta.

Hindu Kush—is a large and high mountain range continuing west of the Himalayas. Beyond it lie the plains of Central Asia. It has been, therefore, often considered as marking the scientific frontier of India, but except for a short period in the fourth-third centuries B.C. it has never been included within the Indian Empire.

Hindu Pad Padshahi, **the**—was the aim and slogan of the second Peshwa Baji Rao I (1720-40). It meant a combination of all the Hindu rulers of India for overthrowing the Muhammadan rule over India. Its application involved friendly, kindly and equal treatment to the different Hindu rulers then existing in India by the rising power of the Marathas so that all the Hindus might share in the recovery of independence from Muhammadan rule. The third Peshwa Balaji Baji Rao (1740-61) deliberately gave up this policy and aimed at establishing the supremacy of the Marathas alone over the Hindus and the Muhammadans alike and plundered and harried the Hindu Princes and their Hindu subjects as mercilessly as he treated the Muhammadans and thus destroyed the idea of *Hindu Pad Padshahi.*

Hindu University, Benares—was founded by the efforts of Pandit
Madan Mohan Malaviya in 1915, using as a nucleus the Central
Hindu College founded some years earlier by Mrs. Annie
Besant. Malaviya toured all over India and secured the financial
support of the Indian Princes and thus established the first
non-official and denominational university in India. It is now
maintained by the Republic of India.

Hislop, Sir Thomas—came to India as the Commander-in-Chief
of the Madras army (1814-20) and commanded the British
forces in the Deccan in the war against the Pindaris (1817-18)
who were suppressed. He also defeated Holkar in the battle
of Mahidpur (1817). He wanted to secure for the Deccan army
the entire booty taken by it during the war. This led to litigation which obliged him to share the booty with the army of
Upper India.

Hiuen Tsang or Yuan Chwang (A.D. 600-64)—was a Chinese
Buddhist monk and scholar who came to India in A.D. 630 in
search of sacred Buddhist literature. He travelled from China to
Kabul at the gates of India covering a distance of 3000 miles
along the most difficult route that lay to the north of the Gobi
desert and returned by the southern route crossing the Pamirs
and passing through Kashgar, Yarkand, Khotan and Lop-nor.
It was a very dangerous journey and it bears eloquent testimony
to his courage, endurance and determination. He was in India
from A.D. 630 to 643. He travelled all over India and visited
almost every state in it. He spent eight years (635-43) within the
dominions of Harshavardhana (*q.v.*) who was then the supreme
ruler over northern India. He was very warmly received by
Harsha who treated him with very great honour and took him
in the royal train from near Rajmahal, where the Chinese
pilgrim first met him, to Kanauj and then to Allahabad. In
both the places Hiuen Tsang witnessed large religious assemblies, the one at Allahabad being the sixth of the quinquennial
assemblies that it was the practice of Emperor Harshavardhana
to hold. Hiuen Tsang was a Mahayanist Buddhist and an
erudite scholar. He has left in his *Travels* or *Records of Western
Lands*, comprising twelve *chuans* or books, detailed records of
all that he observed during his long journey through India and
his book is a very important source of information on the political, social, religious and economic condition of India during
the first half of the seventh century. Hiuen Tsang attended the
Nalanda University as a student for several years and has left
an interesting account of the academic life there. Supplied by

Harshavardhana on a lavish scale with funds for his return journey and also with adequate escorts, Hiuen Tsang returned to China in A.D. 645 bringing back with him from India 150 particles of Buddha's bodily relics, a large number of Buddha's images in gold, silver and sandalwood and 657 distinct volumes of manuscripts requiring twenty horses for their carriage. The rest of his life in China he devoted to the work of translating these texts into Chinese and completed the translation of 74 books before his death in about A.D. 664. (Watters, *On Yuan Chwang;* Beal, *Life of Hiuen Tsang*)

Hodgson, Brian Houghton, (1800-94)—was a product of Hailey-bury College and joined the Indian Civil Service in 1818. He spent most of his service period in Nepal where he was Assistant Resident from 1820 to 1833 and then was made Resident which post he held till 1844. He became an earnest enquirer into the religion, literature and language of Nepal as well as its ethnology, zoology and geography. He discovered in Nepal the literature of Northern Buddhism and made such important contributions to its study that the great French Orientalist, Burnouf, called him 'the founder of the true study of Buddhsim'.

Hodson, Major William Stephen Raikes (1821-58)—a Cambridge graduate, entered the Company's service in 1845. He saw action during the First Sikh War (1845) and was appointed Assistant Commissioner in the Panjab after its annexation in 1849. He was soon afterwards removed from service on charges of dishonesty, but was later on exonerated and reinstated in service. On the outbreak of the Sepoy Mutiny he was given a commission and raised an irregular army of cavalry which came to be known as Hodson's Horse at the head of which he was present at the siege of Delhi. After its capture Hodson rode to Humayun's tomb where he made a prisoner of the aged Emperor Bahadur Shah and made a show of British power and irresponsibility by shooting to death the Mughul Princes as soon as the latter were captured at the same place. He then took part in the fighting before Cawnpore, but was killed on March 12, 1858 when engaged in the recovery of Lucknow. He made himself notorious for his revengeful treatment of Indians during the Mutiny.

Hogg, Sir Stuart Saunders—entered the Indian Civil Service at the age of twenty in 1853. He was employed in the political department in the old North Western Province and rendered efficient service in the Panjab during the Sepoy Mutiny. Later on he was transferred to Bengal where he became the Commissioner of Police in Calcutta and Chairman of the Calcutta Municipality which post he held from 1863 to 1877. He started the policy of improving civic amenities in Calcutta and is commemorated by the Hogg Market near Chowringhee in Calcutta.

Holkar, the family and the state of—was founded by Malhar Rao who served with distinction under the second Peshwa Baji Rao I (1720-40). The south-western part of Malwa fell to his control and he established his headquarters at Indore. He died in 1764 and his only son Khande Rao having predeceased him ten years ago, the state first passed to a grandson, named Malle Rao (1764-66) but he proved very incompetent and from 1765 the administration passed into the hands of Khande Rao's widow, Ahalya Bai (*q.v.*) who administered the state with great success from 1765 to 1795. On her death in 1795 the state passed to Tukoji Holkar, a distant relation, whom Ahalya Bai had appointed as the Commander-in-Chief in 1767. Tukoji ruled only for two years and on his death was succeeded by his third son Jaswant Rao I who ruled from 1798 to 1811. On account of his rivalry with Daulat Rao Sindhia, Jaswant Rao Holkar at first kept himself aloof from the Second Maratha War, but was unwise enough to declare war against the English in April, 1804, after the Peshwa and the Sindhia had already been defeated. After an initial victory over an English army under Col. Monson, Jaswant Rao failed in his attempt to capture Delhi; his army was defeated at the battle of Dig and he himself also was defeated four days later. But the failure of the English to storm the fort of Bharatpur followed by the recall of Lord Wellesley, enabled Jaswant Rao to make peace with the English on very favourable terms which practically left him an independent ruler with no territorial loss. Jaswant Rao, however, soon afterwards became insane and died in 1811. His son and successor Malhar Rao Holkar II (1811-33) joined in the Third Maratha War (1817), was defeated by the English at the battle of Mahidpur in December, 1817 and forced to make peace by the treaty of Mandasor (January, 1818) by which he agreed to maintain a subsidiary force within his territories, to accept a permanent British Resident at his capital, Indore, to give up all claims on the Rajput states, and to cede to the English all his territories south of the Narmada. Thus the Holkars became subsidiary princes without any trace of independence. The later Holkars who ruled at Indore were generally immersed in personal pleasures and cared little for the welfare of the people. One of them became implicated in an infamous murder and was forced to abdicate. The family, however, continued to rule or misrule until the merger of the State within the Republic of India in 1948.

Holwell, John Zephaniah, (1711-98)—came out to Calcutta as a mate to the surgeon in one of the E.I. Company's ships in 1732 and was employed as a surgeon in the Company's ships successively at Patna, Dacca and Calcutta where at last he became the principal surgeon. He was the seventh member in the Council when the fort at Calcutta was attacked by Nawab Siraj-ud-daulah of Bengal on June 18, 1756 and was called upon to take charge of the defences of the fort when Governor Drake and all the other senior members of the Council fled from Calcutta and sought safety lower down the Ganges at Fulta. Holwell could hold out only for a day and the fort was captured by the Nawab on June 20, 1756. According to Holwell's own account, known as the *Narrative of the Black Hole*, 146 English prisoners, men and women, and including his own self, were put on the night of June 20-21 in a very small prison room within the fort and after a desperate struggle for air and water, both of which were denied, only 23 prisoners including Holwell survived next morning. Holwell was then sent as a prisoner to Murshidabad, but was set at liberty on July 17, 1756. In the following February he went on leave to England to return a short time later to Bengal as a member of the Council. From January 28 to July 27, 1760 he also acted as Governor and was succeeded by Vansittart. He then retired from service but was later on dismissed by the Court of Directors in 1761 for having signed a despatch remonstrating against the appointment of Vansittart as the Governor. Holwell had a gift for writing but the veracity of his account of the Black Hole Tragedy has been seriously questioned. (*see* Black Hole Tragedy.)

Home Rule League—was founded by Bala Gangadhar Tilak (*q.v.*) at Poona in April, 1916. In the following September another association bearing the same title was started in Calcutta by Mrs. Annie Besant (*q.v.*). Both the leagues worked in co-operation for securing home rule for the Indians, on the basis of the League-Congress scheme (*q.v.*) formulated at Lucknow in 1916. The Home Rule League, however, proved short-lived, as its leaders were really supporters of the Indian National Congress and their organisations were eventually merged with that body when it made the immediate grant of Home Rule its objective.

Horse sacrifice, the *(asvamedha)*—is prescribed in the *Rigveda* for the celebration of the conquests of a victorious king in order to signify his paramountcy. A sacrificial horse was let loose and allowed to roam at large at his pleasure for a year accompanied by an army led either by the sacrificing king or his agent. When the horse entered a foreign country the ruler of that country was bound either to fight or to submit. If the liberator of the horse succeeded in obtaining or enforcing the submission of all the countries over which it passed, he returned in triumph with all the vanquished kings in his train and celebrated a great festival at which the horse was sacrificed. In the sacrifice, a priest recited the *pariplava ákhyána* (circling narrative) and tales of ancient kings, while a Kshatriya lute-player sang to the lute extempore verses delineating the victories of the sacrificer. Buddha strongly deprecated the practice of narrating tales of wars and terror and condemned the horse-sacrifice and for a time it fell into disuse. But it was revived by Pushyamitra Sunga (*c.* 185 B.C. - 150 B.C.) who performed the horse sacrifice, as mentioned in Kalidasa's drama *Malavikagni-mitra*, in celebration of his victories over the Greeks who had come up to the banks of the Indus. It was also performed in the fourth century A.D. by the second Gupta Emperor, Samudragupta (*q.v.*), in celebration of his great victories. In the fifth century it was celebrated by Mahendravarman, the sixth king of the Pushyavarman dynasty of Kamarupa. In the seventh century it was celebrated by a later Gupta king named Adityasena. In southern India several Chalukya kings claimed to have celebrated it.

Hoshang Shah (also spelt **Hushang Shah**)—was the Sultan of Malwa (1406-35). His original name was Alp Khan (*q.v.*). He constructed many beautiful buildings at his capital, Mandu.

House of Worship, the or *Ibadat Khana*—was an edifice built by Emperor Akbar in 1575 at Fatehpur Sikri. It was used as a debating hall for holding discussions on religion and theology. From 1575-78 the discussions were confined to Muhammadan theology only, and from 1579 to 1582 discussions were thrown open to all religious persuasions. The discussions ceased to be held from 1583 after Akbar had proclaimed the *Din Ilahi* (*q.v.*).

Hoysala dynasty, the—was founded by Bittiga or Bittideva in about A.D. 1111 in Mysore territory. He assumed the name of Vishnuvardhana (*q.v.*) and ruled till A.D. 1141. He established his capital at Dvarasamudra (the modern Halebid). He was at first a Jain, but was later on converted to Vaishnavism. He made extensive conquests and built magnificent temples at Halebid. His grandson, Vira Ballala (A.D. 1173-1220) defeated the Yadavas of Devagiri and made the Hoysalas the dominant power in southern India. The dynasty continued to be powerful until A.D. 1310 when the Muhammadans under Malik Kafur, the general of Sultan Ala-ud-din Khalji (*q.v.*) invaded the country, sacked the capital and captured the reigning king. The dynasty was finally overthrown by the Sultan in A.D. 1326.

Hügel, Baron Carl von—was a German traveller who visited the court of Ranjit Singh (*q.v.*) of the Panjab in 1835. He considered Ranjit Singh to have been a strong ruler with absolute control over his government who wantonly shed no blood.

Hughes, Admiral Sir Edward (1720-94)—entered the British navy and was the chief in command of the British navy off the eastern coast of India from 1773 to 1777 and again from 1779 to 1783. He destroyed the navy of Haidar Ali of Mysore at Mangalore in 1780; in 1781 he helped to take Nagapatam from the Dutch and in 1782 he crowned his successes by taking Trincomale also from the Dutch. But he had not equal success against the French. In 1782-83 he fought between Madras and Trincomale five times with the French fleet of Admiral M.de Suffren, without any decisive results. He then returned to England with a large fortune which he had made in India, but was given no further command.

Hughli, the—is a river connecting the Ganges with the Bay of Bengal. It is also called the Bhagirathi. On its banks are important cities like Calcutta, Hughli, Chinsurah. It is now studded on both banks with many industrial concerns, especially jute mills.

Hughli— is a town on the river Hughli, a few miles above Calcutta. A short distance above it was Satgaon (Saptagram) which was the mart of the trade in Bengal in the 16th century. The Portuguese settled at Hughli in about 1579. The Portuguese settlement at Hughli was besieged and captured by the Mughuls in 1632 and the city thereafter began to decline. It was in its neighbourhood that later on the Danes settled at Serampore, the Dutch at Chinsurah and the French at Chandernagore.

Hulagu, the Mongol—was at first welcomed by Sultan Muhammad Tughluq (1325-51) and was settled in a *jagir* at Lahore in the Panjab. He revolted against the Sultan during the latter's absence from Delhi in 1335 and declared his independence. He slew the governor of the Panjab, but was soon afterwards defeated by the Sultan's army led by his minister, Khwaja Jahan. Hulagu fled from the country and his supporters were ruthlessly slain, but his revolt was a signal of the decline of the power of the Sultan.

Human sacrifice—was an evil that prevailed amongst some of the tribal people in Orissa. Its suppression was taken up during the administration of Lord Hardinge I (1844-48) and was completed under the lead of John Campbell between 1847 and 1854.

Humayun, Bahmani—was the eleventh sultan of the Bahmani dynasty (*q.v.*). He ruled from 1457 to 1461. He was such a cruel ruler that he earned the epithet of *Zalim* (tyrant).

Humayun, the Emperor—was the son and successor of Babur, the founder of the Mughul dynasty. Humayun ruled from 1530 to 1540 and again from 1555 to 1556. He was not strong and resolute enough to consolidate the conquests in India made by his father. He began well by conquering Malwa and Gujarat as the result of a campaign led by him personally in 1535, but he was foolish enough to refuse the proffered alliance of the Rajputs of Mewar and then to hurry back to the pleasures of Agra before the new conquests were consolidated with the result that Malwa and Gujarat were lost next year. In the meantime an Afghan soldier of fortune named Sher Khan (*q.v.*) had risen in Bihar and Bengal and in 1537 Humayun moved against him. He was completely outgeneralled and outmanœuvred by Sher Khan and was defeated by him in 1539 at the battle of Chausa on the Ganges and lost Bihar and Bengal. In 1540 Humayun made his second effort at reducing Sher Khan but was again defeated by the latter in the battle of Kanauj, lost his capital and throne and became a fugitive, pursued by the victorious Sher Khan who now became the Emperor of Delhi. He was a homeless wanderer, seeking support first in Sind, then in Marwar and lastly in Sind again. It was during this period of misery that Humayun married Hamida Banu Begum who bore him his famous son, Akbar, at Umarkot in 1542. With great difficulty Humayun reached Persia in 1544 where King Shah Tahmasp granted him asylum. Humayun then declared himself a Shiah (*q.v.*) and was granted by Shah Tahmasp military aid with which Humayun conquered Qandahar and Kabul from his own disloyal brother Kamran in 1545. He thus recovered the sovereignty over Afghanistan

where he waited till 1555 when, availing himself of the civil
wars amongst the descendants of Sher Shah, he swooped down
upon India, captured Lahore in February and after defeating
Sikandar Sur, the rebel Afghan governor of the Panjab, at
the battle of Sirhind, recovered Delhi and Agra in July of the
same year. But he died in January, 1556, as the result of an
accidental fall from the staircase of his library at Delhi. (Prasad.
I., *Life and Times of Humayun*)

Hume, Allan Octavian, (1829-1912)—educated at Haileybury,
entered the Indian Civil Service in Bengal in 1849 and rose to
be the Member of the Board of Revenue in N.W.P. He had been
the Magistrate in the district of Etawah at the time of the
Sepoy Mutiny. He retired from the Indian Civil Service in
1882 but continued to be interested in Indian affairs. He took
the initiative in organising the Indian National Congress
and was one of the convenors of the first session of the Congress
which was held at Bombay in 1885, and continued to take,
all through his life, an ardent interest in the Indian National
Congress of which he is rightly regarded as one of the founders.
He was the General Secretary of the Indian National Congress
for the first twenty-two years (1885-1908) of its existence,
and was declared by its twenty-third session as "the father and
founder of the Indian National Congress". He was an ardent
ornithologist and wrote several books on ornithology. (Wedderburn, W., *Life of Allan Octavian Hume*)

Hunas (or **Huns**), **the**—were nomads from Central Asia who
began their inroads into India in the fifth century A.D. Their
first considerable attack on India was in the middle of the
fifth century and was beaten back by the reigning sovereign
Skandagupta (A.D. 455-67), in A.D. 455, but the Huns raided
in larger numbers in later years and put the Gupta emperor
to such straits as compelled him to debase the coinage. But
still they came in irresistible numbers and their leader Toramana (*q.v.*) established himself as an independent ruler in
Malwa in about A.D. 500. His son and successor, Mihiragula,
was a viciously terrible general. He established his capital at
Sakala or Sialkot in the Panjab and roused universal terror
and hatred in India. At last he was defeated in about A.D. 528
by the combined efforts of Yasodharman, king of Malwa, and
Baladitya, usually identified with Narasimha, the Gupta king
of Magadha. The vanquished Hunas settled in India and
were Indianised and Hinduised. Many of the Rajput tribes
who came into prominence in the eighth century and later

on, are believed to have been Huns in origin. (*E.E.C.A.* pp. 109 ff.)

Hunter, Sir William Wilson (1840-1900)—educated at Glasgow, Paris and Bonn, entered the Indian Civil Service in 1862 and was posted in Bengal. He had a facile pen and made his name as an author and statesman by publishing the *Annals of Rural Bengal* in 1868. Four years later he gave further proof of his erudition by publishing a *Comparative Dictionary of Non-Aryan Languages of India*. He organised the Statistical Survey of India and published in 1875-77 the *Statistical Account of Bengal* in 20 volumes. He also prepared the *Imperial Gazetteer of India* in 23 volumes which testify to his learning and diligence. He presided over the Education Commission (*q.v.*) in 1882-83 and his Report largely influenced the later educational development in the country. After his retirement in 1887 he edited the *Rulers of India* series and he himself wrote on *Dalhousie* and *Mayo*. He wrote a fine style and his books, which were at once immensely informative and pleasant-reading, made India better known to the English-speaking world.

Hunter Education Commission—was appointed in 1882 during the administration of Lord Ripon (1880-84). This body reviewed the progress of education so far achieved in India, endorsed fully the policy adopted in 1854 of expanding Western education in the country, but recommended that special steps should be taken for the extension and improvement of elementary education of the masses. It also suggested the reorganisation of the Educational Service with a view to attracting better men to it. It also approved of the system of grants-in-aid to educational institutions and recommended that education in all its stages should be increasingly left to private enterprise supported by Government grants. The Report was accepted by the Government and the result was a steady increase in the number of educational institutions in the country.

Husain Ali, Barha Sayyid—was the younger of the two Sayyid brothers, the elder being Hasan Ali Abdullah. They helped Emperor Farrukhsiyar (1713-19) to defeat his uncle Jahandar Shah (1712-13) and to get the imperial crown. The two brothers soon became the power behind the throne in Delhi. Husain Ali became the Paymaster, suppressed a revolt in Marwar, and was appointed viceroy of the Deccan. But he returned to the capital in 1718 hearing that the Emperor was plotting his and his brother's destruction. The brothers then blinded and deposed Farrukhsiyar (1719). Then in the course of the next seven months he and his brother placed on the throne of Delhi as many as four puppet sovereigns only to depose and kill them after a short while. Thus they became the 'king-makers'. But at last Husain Ali found a master in their fifth nominee, Muhammad Shah, whom he put on the throne in 1719. He was murdered with the connivance of the new Emperor in 1720.

Husain, Amir—was the commander of an Egyptian fleet that came to assist Sultan Mahmud Bigarha (1459-1511) of Gujarat against the Portuguese. Acting in combination with the Sultan's fleet Amir Husain defeated a Portuguese fleet at Chaul in 1508. But next year he was defeated and his fleet was destroyed by the Portuguese in a battle fought off Diu.

Husain Nizam Shah of Ahmadnagar—was the third sovereign of the Nizam Shahi dynasty (*q.v.*) of Ahmadnagar. He ruled from 1553 to 1565. He joined in a confederacy with the sultans of Golconda and Bijapur against Vijayanagar and shared in the great Muslim victory over the Hindu kingdom at the battle of Talikota in 1565. But he died in the same year and could not reap any benefit from the great triumph.

Husain Shah, Prince of Ahmadnagar—was placed on the throne of Ahmadnagar in 1630 by Fath Khan, the treacherous minister. But in 1631 the Mughuls occupied Ahmadnagar which was then annexed to the Mughul Empire. Prince Husain Shah was consigned to life-long imprisonment at Gwalior and with his fall the existence of Ahmadnagar as an independent state came to an end.

Husain Shah—was the king of Bengal from A.D. 1493-1519. He was at first the chief minister of Sultan Shams-ud-din (*q.v.*) of Bengal who on account of his unbearable tyranny, was deposed and killed by the nobles who then raised Husain Shah to the throne of Bengal. He assumed the name of Sultan *Ala-ud-din* Husain Shah (*q.v.*). He founded the Husain Shahi dynasty which ruled in Bengal from 1493 to 1539.

Husain Shah—was the last king (1457-76) of the Sharqi dynasty of Jaunpur. He commenced his reign with the conclusion of a treaty of peace with Sultan Bahalol Lodi (*q.v.*) of Delhi. He then suppressed the zamindars of Tirhut, led a plundering raid into Orissa and even led an expedition against Raja Man Singh of Gwalior whom he made pay a heavy indemnity. But in 1476 Husain Shah was defeated and expelled from Jaunpur by Sultan Bahalol Lodi. He spent his last days as a refugee at Colgong in Bihar near Bhagalpur under the hospitable protection of King Husain Shah of Bengal, dying in A.D. 1500.

Huvishka (or **Huska**)—was the son and successor of the Kushan king, Kanishka (*c*. A.D. 120-62). He ruled from *c*. A.D. 162 to 180. He issued a large and varied coinage which suggests that he ruled over the extensive empire built by Kanishka. His coins exhibit Greek, Iranian and Indian deities which imply that he was an eclectic in religion. No details of the events of his reign are known.

Hydaspes, the battle of the—was fought between Puru (*q.v.*) whose kingdom lay between the Hydaspes (Jhelum) and the Akesines (Chinab), and Alexander, the King of Macedon, who wantonly invaded the former's territory, probably in July, 325 B.C. Puru had an initial reverse inasmuch as the Greeks stole a passage and crossed the river unnoticed and unchallenged. Puru depended mainly on a large body of elephants backed by 30,000 infantry, 400 cavalry and 300 chariots whereas Alexander relied more on cavalry and mounted archers. The greater mobility of the Greek army gave the victory to Alexander, though Puru had fought very bravely. He was wounded and made a captive. But he was treated with honour by the victorious Greek king and was restored to his dominions. Puru later on helped Alexander in his further conquests in the Panjab.

Hyder Ali Khan—*see* Haidar Ali Khan.

Hyderabad—is the name of a city which is now the capital of the State of Andhra Pradesh and was also the capital of the former State of the Nizam, the premier Muhammadan Indian ruler. The city was founded in 1589 by Muhammad Kuli, the fifth of the Kutb Shahi sultans. Situated on the right bank of the riv ˉ Musi, a tributary of the Krishna, the city occupies a fine site and has many imposing buildings including the Nizam's Palaces, the Residency and the Mecca Mosque. It is also the seat of the Osmania University which was founded in 1918 and was the first to start teaching in an Indian language, namely Urdu, in preference to English which is taught as a second language. The state was founded by Asaf Jah in 1713 who came to Hyderabad as the *Subadar* of the Deccan but made himself its independent ruler in about 1740. On his death in 1748 his dominions fell prey to a succession of troubles in which the English and the French in India tried to fish. The Nizam's hold was much weakened, and, faced with the hostility of Haidar Ali in the south and of the Marathas in the west and the north and ruling precariously over a Hindu majority population, the Nizam was the first of the Indian princes to enter in 1798 into the system of subsidiary alliance during the administration of Lord Wellesley (1798-1805) and thus parted with his independence. After India attained her independence the Nizam tried for a time to maintain himself as an independent ruler, but he failed in his attempt. The state was merged in the Indian Republic in 1948 and popular government was set up in 1952, the Nizam remaining as the *Rajpramukh* with a very fat allowance.

Hyderabad—is a city and cantonment in Sind, now in West Pakistan. The city was founded in 1768 and was the capital of Sind until 1843 and again from 1948 to 1955. It is now the headquarters of a division bearing the same name. It is an important centre of industries and has an old fort and a modern University.

I

Ibadat Khana—*see* House of Worship.

Ibn Batuta—was a scholarly African traveller who came to India in 1333 during the reign of Sultan Muhammad Tughluq (1325-51), was received hospitably and appointed by him as the Chief Qazi at Delhi, which post he occupied till he was sent by the Sultan as his ambassador to China in 1342. He has left a valuable account of his Indian experiences which forms an important source of information about the life and times of Sultan Muhammad Tughluq. His account is generally trustworthy, though it is not free from exaggeration. His account of the reasons for which the Sultan ordered the transfer of his capital from Delhi to Daulatabad and the thoroughness with which the evacuation of Delhi was carried out, may be cited as an example.

Ibrahim—the third king of the Qutb Shahi dynasty of Golconda, ruled from 1550 to 1580. In 1565 he joined in an alliance with the sultans of Bijapur, Berar and Ahmadnagar against Vijayanagar and shared in the victory over it at the battle of Talikota (1556) and the subsequent destruction of Vijayanagar. Ibrahim was, however, a liberal ruler within his own dominions where he freely admitted his Hindu subjects to high offices of state.

Ibrahim—was the last of the four titular Mughul emperors of Delhi whom the Sayyid brothers set up on the throne of Delhi in 1719. He was a son of Rafi-us-shan, the third son of Bahadur Shah I (1707-12). A short while after his installation he was deposed and killed by the 'king-makers', as the Sayyid brothers were called.

Ibrahim Adil Shah I—the fourth Sultan (1534-57) of the Adil Shahi dynasty of Bijapur, rejected the Shiah faith which the founder of the dynasty had adopted and favoured the Deccani nobles as against the Persians. He had a very able minister in Asad Khan. He made a state visit to Vijayanagar for a week and returned with many valuable presents. He also repulsed a combined attack on his state by the sultans of Bidar, Ahmadnagar and Golconda. His reign was full of intrigues and late in his life, he gave himself up to too much drinking of which he died.

Ibrahim Adil Shah II—the sixth sultan of the Adil Shahi dynasty of Bijapur, ruled from 1580 to 1626. His mother was Chand Bibi, the famous princess of Ahmadnagar. Ibrahim Adil Shah II was a minor at the time of his accession and was looked after by his mother till 1584 when she returned to Ahmadnagar. In 1595 Ibrahim Adil Shah II defeated and killed the sultan of Ahmadnagar, but both the states soon faced the dread of Mughul conquest. Ibrahim Adil Shah II was a very liberal and tolerant monarch who allowed complete freedom of worship to his non-Muhammadan subjects, Hindus as well as Christians. He improved civil administration, systematised the land settlements, maintained friendly relations with the Portuguese at Goa, extended his dominions up to the borders of Mysore, beautified Bijapur with fine buildings, and, last but not the least, was the patron of the famous historian, Muhammad Qusim, surnamed Firishta.

Ibrahim Khan—the Mughul viceroy in Bengal from 1689-97, was an old man of mild disposition and friendly to the English who had been driven out of the province by the preceding viceroy, Shaista Khan (*q.v.*). Ibrahim called back the English to Bengal and permitted Job Charnock (*q.v.*) to settle in what later on developed into the city of Calcutta. Ibrahim's negligence of public affairs made possible the outbreak of a rebellion under Shova Singh, a zamindar in Midnapore district, which he failed to suppress immediately. He made matters worse by permitting the English, the French and the Dutch to fortify their settlements in Bengal so that they might oppose

Shova Singh. Such a policy of weakness displeased Emperor Aurangzeb who dismissed Ibrahim Khan from the viceroyalty of Bengal in 1697.

Ibrahim Khan Gardi—a soldier of fortune, was trained by Bussy (*q.v.*) himself and became the chief of his artillery. He joined the service of the Nizam in 1757 but went over to the Peshwa's service in 1758. He contributed much to the victory of the Marathas over the Nizam in the battle of Udgir (*q.v.*) in 1760. He fought on the side of the Marathas at the head of 9000 sepoys with forty pieces of cannon at the third battle of Panipat (*q.v.*). Though he had some initial successes he shared in the great defeat, was taken captive and slaughtered by the triumphant Afghans.

Ibrahim Lodi—the third Sultan (1517-26) of the Lodi dynasty (*q.v.*) of Delhi, captured Gwalior early in his reign from the Rajputs. But his policy of keeping the Afghan nobles under strict control and his harsh treatment of some of them drove the Afghan nobles into opposition to him. One of these disaffected nobles, namely Daulat Khan Lodi, governor of the Panjab, invited Babur who had already made himself the king of Afghanistan to come and overthrow Ibrahim. Babur accepted the invitation and Ibrahim Lodi was defeated and killed by him in the first battle of Panipat (*q.v.*) on April 21, 1526. Ibrahim Lodi was the last of the sultans of Delhi.

Ibrahim Shah Sharqi—the king of Jaunpur (1402-36), was the ablest ruler of the Sharqi dynasty (*q.v.*). He was intolerant of Hinduism, but was a man of culture and a patron of art and literature. He made Jaunpur an important centre of Muslim learning and beautified the city by constructing many impressive buildings of which the Atala mosque, completed in 1408, was the most prominent.

Ibrahim Sur—the fourth king of the Sur dynasty (*q.v.*), ruled only for a short time in 1555. On the restoration of Mughul rule over Delhi by Humayun, Ibrahim Sur fled to Orissa where he was killed in about 1567.

Ikhtiyar-ud-din Altuniya—was the governor of Bhatinda in the early part of the reign of Sultana Raziya (1236-40) (*q.v.*). He rose in revolt against Raziya, defeated and imprisoned her in 1240. But he did not get from Bahram who was now declared sultan, adequate rewards. He, therefore, released Raziya from prison, married her and marched with a large army to Delhi with a view to restore his newly wedded wife to the throne. But he was defeated in the battle of Kaithal and he and Raziya were murdered on the day following their defeat.

Ikhtiyar-ud-din Gazi Shah—was the son and successor of Fakhr-ud-din Mubarak Shah, the first independent king of Eastern Bengal. He ruled from 1329 to 1352 when he was overthrown by Shams-ud-din Iliyas Shah (*q.v.*), the king of Western Bengal.

Ikhtiyar-ud-din Muhammad—the son of Bakhtiyar Khalji, was the first Muhammadan conqueror of Bengal. He is popularly known as Bakhtiyar Khalji. Within an unprepossessing appearance he harboured great courage and ambition. He began by making raids into Bihar, took its capital Odantapuri, put to death the Buddhist monks dwelling in the great monastery there and conquered the province in 1192. Soon afterwards, probably in 1193, at any rate not later than 1202, he surprised Nadiya which was then the capital of the last Sena king, Laksmana Sen, who fled to Eastern Bengal, established himself at Gaur (*q.v.*) as the governor of Bengal under Shihab-ud-din Muhammad Ghuri (*q.v.*). This success increased his ambition and in 1205 he led a large Muhammadan army against Tibet through Kamrup (Assam). In what direction he marched after leaving his base in Bengal or what exactly was his objective is uncertain. But after fifteen days' march he was confronted by an opposing army of the invaded territory and was defeated with severe losses. On his way back the remnant of his army perished and Ikhtiyar-ud-din succeeded in returning to his capital with only one hundred out of the ten thousand horsemen who had accompanied him on the expedition. This disaster broke his spirit and he died of grief and mortification in A.D. 1206.

Ikshvaku—was a famous Vedic hero from whom Dasaratha, the king of Koshala and father of Rama, the hero of the *Ramayana*, claimed his descent.

Ilahi **era, the**—or the Divine era, was started by Emperor Akbar in 1584. It was a solar year and dated from 11 March, 1556, the date of the first Nauraz festival after Akbar's accession. Its use was discouraged and abolished from the coinage by Emperor Shah Jahan and was entirely discontinued by Emperor Aurangzeb soon after his accession in 1658.

Ilbert, Sir Courtney Persegrime—an Oxford graduate and a barrister-at-law, came out to India as the Law Member of the Viceroy's Executive Council in 1882 and stayed in India till 1886. In his capacity as the Law Member he sponsored the

Ilbert Bill (*q.v.*) which he steered with fundamental modifications through the legislature. He was the Vice-Chancellor of Calcutta University from 1885 to 1887 and his work on the *Government of India,* published in 1898, is an authoritative book on the subject.

Ilbert Bill—was sponsored by the Viceroy's Law Member, Sir C. P. Ilbert, in 1883. It proposed to remove racial distinctions amongst the services and the peoples of India by enabling judges and magistrates, who were Indians by birth, to try Europeans, contrary to the provisions of the Criminal Procedure Code of 1873 which had enacted that Europeans could be tried only by European magistrates and judges, except in Presidency towns where the latter could be tried by Indian magistrates and judges. In spite of the fact that no evil had resulted from Europeans appearing before Indian magistrates and judges in Presidency towns the Europeans in India whipped up a great agitation against the Ilbert Bill, treated the Viceroy, Lord Ripon, with something very like insult and all non-official Europeans practically subjected him to a boycott. Indian opinion, on the other hand, enthusiastically supported the Bill. But so great a commotion was caused by the anti-Ilbert Bill agitation started by the Anglo-Indian community that the Government bowed before it and altered the Ilbert Bill to provide that whenever a European was brought for trial before an Indian magistrate or a sessions judge he could claim to be tried by a jury, one half of which was to be European. Thus the racial distinction that the Government wanted to remove not only continued but was extended to Presidency towns and the Anglo-Indians considered it a great triumph. The agitation, however, produced important consequences. It demonstrated to the Indians the value of combination, organisation and public agitation and there were amongst the Indians men like Surendranath Banerjee (*q.v.*), on whom the lesson was not lost. Within a year a National Fund was created under Surendranath's leadership and the Indian National Conference with representatives from all parts of India, met in Calcutta in 1883. Two years later was born the Indian National Congress. It was India's reply to Anglo-Indian chauvinism.

Iliyas Shah—(also called Haji or Malik Iliyas) was a foster-brother of Ala-ud-din Ali Shah, the independent king of Western Bengal from A.D. 1339 to 1345, whom he succeeded to the throne of Western Bengal in about 1345. He assumed the title of Shams-ud-din Iliyas Shah and ruled till 1357. He conquered

Eastern Bengal in 1352, exacted tributes from Orissa and Tirhut and even threatened Benares. This roused the hostility of the reigning Delhi sultan, Firuz Shah Tughluq (1351-88), who invaded Bengal. Iliyas retired before him from his capital at Pandua to Ikdala in Eastern Bengal and succeeded in repulsing the invasion. His reign was prosperous; he issued a new coinage and he beautified his capital with many mosques and buildings. He died in his capital at Pandua in 1357 and left behind him a long line of descendants known as the Iliyas Shahi dynasty of Bengal who ruled in Bengal till A.D. 1490.

Iltutmish—was the sultan of Delhi (A.D. 1211-36). He began his career as a slave in the service of Qutb-ud-din Aibak, the first sultan of Delhi (A.D. 1206-10). By dint of his abilities he endeared himself to his master who manumitted him, gave him one of his daughters in marriage and made him the governor of Badaun. A year after the death of Qutb-ud-din he ascended the throne of Delhi after defeating Qutb-ud-din's immediate successor, Aram. Iltutmish proved a very capable ruler. He suppressed a rebellion of the disaffected Muhammadan nobles. He also defeated three powerful rivals, namely, Yildiz in the Panjab, Qabacha in Sind and Ali Mardan Khan in Bengal. He reconquered from the Hindus Ranthambhor and Gwalior which they had recovered during the weak rule of Sultan Aram (q.v.). He also conquered Malwa including Bhilsa and Ujjaini. During his reign Chingiz Khan, the terrible leader of the Mongols, arrived on the frontiers of India in pursuit of Jalal-ud-din, the Shah of Khiva, and threatened to invade India. Iltutmish escaped the terror by a politic refusal of asylum which the fugitive Shah requested. Iltutmish also received from the Caliph of Baghdad a patent of investiture and thus strengthened the authority of the Delhi sultanate with a religious sanction. He issued a good system of silver coinage which supplied a model to the later sultans. Last but not the least, he built at Delhi the famous Qutb Minar in 1232 in honour of the Muhammadan saint Khwaja Qutb-ud-din. An intrepid warrior and an efficient administrator, Iltutmish stands out as the greatest of the early sultans of Delhi.

Imad Shahi dynasty—was founded in Berar in about 1490 by Fatullah (q.v.) entitled Imad-ul-Mulk who seceded from the Bahmani kingdom (q.v.) and set himself up as an independent ruler. This dynasty lasted four generations, from 1490 to 1574, when it ceased on the annexation of Berar by Ahmadnagar (q.v.).

Imad-ul-Mulk—was a very high title during the Mughul regime. It was conferred upon Firuz Jang Gazi-ud-din, the eldest son of Nizam-ul-Mulk and also, on his death, on his son and successor, Sihab-ud-din, also called Gazi-ud-din, in 1753 when the latter was appointed Wazir of the Emperor. (*See* Gazi-ud-din.)

Immadi Narasimha—the second and last king of the Saluva dynasty (1486-1503) of Vijayanagar (*q.v.*), ruled probably from A.D. 1492 till his murder by Vira Narasimha in about 1503. Nothing is known of his activities.

Imperial Cadet Corps, the—was founded in 1901 by Viceroy Lord Curzon. It consisted of young men of princely and noble families and gave them elementary training in military service.

Imperial Conferences—held in 1921, 1923 and 1926 in London, were participated in by representatives of India.

Imperial Legislative Council, the—was constituted by the Indian Councils Act of 1861. It was then only the Viceroy's Executive Council enlarged by the addition of six to twelve nominated members of whom at least one half was to be non-officials. The Maharaja of Patiala, the Raja of Benares and Sir Dinkar Rao of Gwalior were the first three non-official Indian members of the Imperial Legislative Council. Its rights of legislation were also very limited. The membership of the Imperial Legislative Council was increased by the Indian Councils Act of 1892—the number of additional members was increased from twelve to sixteen of whom not more than six were to be nominated officials and of the ten non-official members four were to be elected by the provincial legislatures and one by the Calcutta Chamber of Commerce, while the remaining five were to be nominated by the Governor-General. The functions of the Imperial Legislative Council were also widened, it being given the rights of discussing the budget and of interpellations. A further change was effected by the Government of India Act, 1909, which increased the number of its members to sixty of whom twenty-eight were to be nominated officials, five nominated non-officials and twenty-seven non-officials elected by provincial legislatures, by land-holders, by Muhammadans and Chambers of Commerce in varying numbers. The functions of the Imperial Legislative Council were also enlarged, it being given the right of moving resolutions on the budget and on certain matters of general interest. The resolutions which were to be expressed as recommendations had, however, no binding effect on the Government and could be disallowed by the Governor-General who acted as the President of the Assembly at his pleasure. The next change came in 1919 when the Government of India Act based on the Montague-Chelmsford Report (*q.v.*) thoroughly remodelled the Imperial Legislature which now became bi-cameral and the Imperial Legislative Council became merged in the popular Chamber of the Indian Legislative Assembly with a membership of 145 of whom 105 were to be directly elected and with much larger powers of legislation and control. (*See under* British Administration.)

Imperial Library, the (now called **the National Library**)— was founded by Lord Curzon during his administration as Viceroy (1899-1905). It is located in Calcutta and is now housed at the Belvedere which was originally the official residence of the Lieutenant-Governor of Bengal. It is a free library open to the public and has a very large stock of books.

Imperial Service Corps—was instituted during the administration of Lord Dufferin (1884-88). Under this scheme troops were raised by Indian princes and officered by Indians. They were made available for imperial service when required. They participated in both World Wars and rendered valuable services.

Impey, Sir Elijah (1732-1809)—educated at Westminster where he was a fellow student of Warren Hastings, Governor-General (*q.v.*), a King's scholar and barrister-at-law, was appointed as the Chief Justice of the Supreme Court in Calcutta by the Regulating Act of 1773 and arrived in Calcutta in 1774. In 1775 he presided over the trial of Nandakumar (*q.v.*) and passed on him the sentence of death on a charge of forgery. Impey's conduct at the trial has been considered by many to have been influenced by his intimacy with Warren Hastings. In 1777 he also decided in favour of Warren Hastings on the question of his reported resignation. He also sentenced Sir Philip Francis, the opponent of Warren Hastings, to pay damages of Rs. 50,000 in the Grand case. Under his leadership the Supreme Court entered in 1779 into a most disreputable quarrel with the Council over the question of its jurisdiction. But the impasse ended as soon as he was appointed by Warren Hastings as the President of the *Sadar Dewani Adalat* on a salary of £ 6,000 a year in addition to his salary of £ 8,000 as Chief Justice. The Parliament considered the whole transaction as highly irregular, recalled Impey in 1782 and there was even an attempt at impeaching him. He defended himself at the bar of the House and the impeachment was abandoned. He was elected to the Parliament in 1790 and remained an M.P. till 1796.

Indentured system of labour supply, the—was started in the thirties of the nineteenth century. Under this system an individual or a group of Indian labourers bound himself or themselves to serve on a plantation for a term of years (usually five or seven) at the end of which time the labourer was free to return to India with a free passage or settle in the colony as a free labourer. There were variations of this general plan and there were also abuses of the terms of contracts made by educated and unscrupulous contractors who had ample funds, with ignorant, needy and unorganised Indian labourers. But the system prospered and large numbers of Indian labourers under the indentured system went to and settled in Mauritius and Fiji in the Indian and the Pacific Oceans, the Malay Peninsula and Archipelago, Ceylon, Kenya, Tanganayika, Uganda, South Africa, Trinidad, Jamaica and British Guiana. Many of these Indian labourers preferred to settle in the countries of their adoption at the end of the period of indenture and make their living there working either as free labourers for whose services there was a good demand or as small traders for whom there was scope. Thus large settlements of Indians sprang up in the British colonies mentioned above and as the Indian settlers grew in number as well as in wealth they provoked the jealous hostility of the European colonists who had once invited their forbears to their countries and had derived much benefit from services of the indentured Indian labourers who had contributed as much as the colonists to the development and prosperity of the colonies but who were no longer willing to slave for their white masters. Thus new problems, mainly based on racial hostility, have developed out of the indentured system of labour supply and still remain unsolved.

India—is the middle and the largest of the three peninsulas which form the southern coast of Asia. It is triangular in form, the Himalayan range being the base and Cape Comorin the apex. Situated between the Himalayas in the north and the Indian Ocean in the south and cut off by high mountains from Afghanistan in the North-West and Burma in the North-East it forms a geographical unit with an area of 1,709,500 sq. miles and a population of 446,866,300 according to the census of 1951. It is naturally divided into three well-defined tracts, viz., the Himalayan region; the northern plains washed by the Indus, the Ganges and the Brahmaputra; and the Deccan separated from the northern plains by the Vindhyas. Its vast population speak different languages numbering more than two hundred and profess all the principal religions of the world. The name India is derived through the Greeks from the Persianised form of the Sanskrit '*sindhu*' meaning river, particularly the Indus. The original name of the country is Bhárat-Varsha, from Bharata, a legendary monarch of prehistoric days. It has now been shortened and the peninsula minus the two small parts known as West Pakistan and East Pakistan is now officially called Bhárata. The term Hindusthan is properly applicable only to the upper basin of the Ganges where Hindi is the spoken language and may not be used as a correct designation of Bhárata or India.

India or Bhárata has a fundamental unity based on culture and civilisation all its own, the most obvious symbol of which is the prevalence of Hinduism as the religion all over the country, the recognition of Sanskrit as the sacred language, the cults of sacred rivers which include the Indus in the Panjab and the Kaveri in the Deccan and of sacred cities including Hardwar in the U.P. as well as Kanchi in the Far South and the aspirations of all its sovereigns to rule over the whole of it. But such a vast country, actually a sub-continent equal in area to the whole of Europe without European Russia, can hardly be consolidated into one political unit and, as a matter of fact, the whole of India was never united into one empire except for very brief periods before the middle of the nineteenth century when British rule was established all over its vast length with a uniform system of administration and a common language, namely English, as the medium of administration as well as of education. Even this unity perished in less than a century when India won her independence in 1947 at the cost of a partition which wrested from her Sind, the North-West Frontier, Western Panjab (now called West Pakistan) and Eastern and Northern Bengal which constitute East Pakistan.

The history of India goes back to the prehistoric period. Between 3000 B.C. and 1500 B.C. a very advanced civilisation flourished in the Indus Valley (*q.v.*), monuments of which have been found in Mohenjodaro and Harappa (*q.v.*). Later on the Aryans are believed to have entered into the country where they found a pre-Aryan population in occupation with a civilisation in no way inferior, if not in many ways superior, to that of the Aryans. The largest section of this pre-Aryan population is known as the Dravidians (*q.v.*) who were gradually pushed back by the Aryans from the north to south India which they long maintained as their preserve. Later on they submitted to the Aryans with whom they intermarried and now form the great nation of the Indians. Besides the Dravidians there were other indigenous peoples some of whom are at present represented by primitive tribes like the Mundas, Koles, Bhils and others who speak dialects belonging to the Mon-Khmer group. The earliest literature of the Indo-Aryans as well as a picture of their civilisation are to be found in the Vedas (*q.v.*), especially the Rig-Veda (*q.v.*) which has been assigned by some to three millennium B.C. The Aryans, however, did not bring to the land any political unity, though they gave it a profound system of philosophy and a system of religion popularly called Hinduism (*q.v.*) which has stood the test of at least four thousand years.

The ancient Indians preserved no dated history. The earliest definite date known is, therefore, 326 B.C. when India was invaded by Alexander, the King of Macedon. By a system of back reckoning from this date and by making use of historical traditions as recorded in literature the political history of India has been traced back to the seventh century B.C. when India from the Kabul Valley to the Godavari was divided into sixteen states (*soḍasajanapada*), namely, Anga (East Bihar), Magadha (South Bihar), Kashi (Benares), Koshala (Oudh), Vriji (North Bihar), Malla (Gorakhpur), Chedi (Bundelkhand), Vatsa (Allahabad), Kuru (Thaneswar and Delhi region), Panchala (Bareilly and Badaun area), Matsya (Jaipur), Surasena (Mathura), Asmaka (on the Godavari), Avanti (Malwa), Gandhara (Peshawar region) and Kamboja (Kashmir and Afghanistan). There were constant strifes amongst these states until at last in about the middle of the sixth century B.C. Magadha under its kings, Bimbisara (*q.v.*) and Ajatasatru (*q.v.*) started on a career of expansion by acquiring Kashi and Koshala. It was, again, during the reign of those two Magadhan kings that Vardhamana Mahavira (*q.v.*) preached Jainism and Gautama Buddha (*q.v.*) promulgated Buddhism. The expansion of Magadha continued in the succeeding years and towards the close of the fourth century B.C. Magadha under the kings of the Nanda dynasty (*q.v.*) extended her sway over the whole of northern India from Bengal to the Bias in the Panjab. The people, called the Prasii (*q.v.*) by the classical historians, were so powerful that Alexander's forces would not cross the Bias and penetrate into the land of the Prasii and obliged Alexander who had invaded the Panjab in 326 B.C., to retrace his steps and he returned down the Indus. Shortly afterwards Magadha passed under the rule of the Maurya dynasty (*q.v.*) whose founder, Chandragupta Maurya (*c.* 322 B.C. - 298 B.C.), drove out from the Panjab the officers left there by Alexander, subsequently defeated in battle Alexander's general Seleucos who made peace by surrendering all the territories up to the Hindu Kush and extended his sway over the whole of northern India and probably also conquered the Deccan. He ruled over this vast empire from his capital at Pataliputra (*q.v.*) which in its grandeur and wealth surpassed Susa and Ecbatana. His grandson was the great Asoka (*q.v.*) who added Kalinga (Orissa) to his dominions which extended from the foot of the Himalayas to the river Pennar in the south and from the Hindu Kush in the north-west to the Assam border in the north-east. Asoka earned undying fame by devoting all the resources of his vast empire to the promotion of the welfare of men and beasts and to the expansion of Buddhism for preaching which he sent missionaries and established benevolent institutions in far-off lands like Egypt, Macedonia and Corinth. His efforts turned Buddhism into a world religion but his peaceful unwarlike policy weakened his dynasty which was overthrown, about half a century later, by Pushyamitra (*q.v.*) who established the Sunga dynasty (*c.* 185 B.C. - 73 B.C.) which in its turn was overthrown by the Kanva dynasty (*c.* 73 B.C. - 28 B.C.). The sway of Magadha began to decline after the fall of the Mauryas and the Deccan seceded from its rule under the leadership of the Satavahanas (*q.v.*) also called the Andhras (*q.v.*) who ruled from 50 B.C. to A.D. 225. Taking advantage of the absence of a strong central government in India the Bactrians and the Parthians began to raid northern India under many chiefs of whom Menander (*q.v.*) is the best known. The Sakas (*q.v.*) soon followed in the wake of the Indo-Bactrians and set up subordinate states (*satrapies*) in Maharashtra, Surashtra and Mathura. The unity of history which was thus broken was, however, restored in the first century A.D. with the establishment of the Kushan dynasty (*q.v.*) by Kadphises I (*q.v.*). The most renowned king of this dynasty which ruled over northern India till the middle of the third century A.D., was Kanishka (*c.* A.D. 120-144) (*q.v.*) who had his capital at Purushapura or Peshawar, embraced Buddhism as his religion and patronised Indian scholars and scientists like Asvaghosha (*q.v.*), Nagarjuna (*q.v.*) and Charaka (*q.v.*). The Kushan dynasty declined and fell about the middle of the third century A.D. for reasons unknown. Darkness which covers Indian history during the second half of the third century was lifted early in the fourth century with the establishment in about A.D. 320 by Chandragupta of the Gupta dynasty (*q.v.*) which again made Pataliputra the capital, produced four generations of great and powerful kings who ruled over the whole of northern India, received also the submission of many south Indian states, made Hinduism the state religion, tolerated Buddhism and Jainism, promoted learning, science, art, architecture and painting. It was the age of Kalidas (*q.v.*), Aryabhata (*q.v.*) and Varahamihir (*q.v.*) and it was during this age that the Epics and the Puranas and the *Manusamhita* derived their present forms. The Chinese pilgrim, Fa-Hien, who visited India from A.D. 401 to 410, has left a very interesting account of the country which he considered to be extremely well-governed. Naturally enough the period has been called the golden age in Indian history and has been compared with the Periclean age of Athens. Internal disintegration and invasions by the Huns brought about the downfall of the Gupta empire in the sixth century, but early in the seventh century another great empire was built up by Harshavardhana (*q.v.*) who ruled with his capital at Kanauj over an empire that included the whole of northern India and extended to the Narmada in the south where he was successfully resisted by the Chalukya king, Pulakeshin II. The Chinese pilgrim, Hiuen Tsang (*q.v.*) visited India during the reign of Harshavardhana whose power and prosperity have been left recorded in his *Travels*. The death of Harshavardhana in A.D. 647 without any male successor again threw north India into a condition of turmoil out of which emerged several warlike dynasties of kings who called themselves Rajputs (*q.v.*). Such were the Hindu Sahiya kings of the Panjab, the Gurjara-Pratihara kings (*q.v.*) of Gujarat, the Chauhans (*q.v.*) of Ajmer, the Gahadvalas (*q.v.*) of Kanauj, the Palas (*q.v.*) of Magadha and Bengal. In the Deccan also a similar disintegration had taken place after the fall of the Satavahanas. The Gangas (*q.v.*) in Orissa who built the famous Jagannath temple at Puri, the Chalukyas (*q.v.*) of Vatapi who were responsible for some of the cave paintings at Ajanta (*q.v.*) and the Pallavas (*q.v.*) of Kanchi whose memory is borne by the famous temples there, parcelled out the Deccan amongst themselves and fought one another to destruction. Then arose the Rashtrakutas (*q.v.*)

of Manyakheta or Malkhed to be ousted by a new branch of the older Chalukyas who established their capital at Kalyani (*q.v.*). They in their turn were overthrown by the Yadavas (*q.v.*) of Devagiri and the Hoysalas (*q.v.*) of Dvarasamudra. Further to the south arose the kingdom of the Cheras (*q.v.*) Pandyas (*q.v.*) and the Cholas (*q.v.*) the last of whom proved most successful and ruled from A.D. 900 to 1300. Thus disunity prevailed all over India.

Already in A.D. 712 a new element had entered into Indian life with the invasion and conquest of Sind from its Brahman king, Dahir, by the Muhammadan Arabs led by Muhammad bin Kasim. Islam thus got its first foothold on the soil of India from which the Hindus during the succeeding centuries failed to dislodge them. But Arab rule in Sind was essentially weak and was easily overthrown by Shihab-ud-din Muhammad Ghuri (*q.v.*) in 1176. Earlier Muhammadan raids led by Sabuktigin (*q.v.*) in A.D. 918 had led to the conquest of the Panjab by the Muhammadans and by Sultan Mahmud (*q.v.*) of Ghazni from A.D. 997 to 1030 who led seventeen expeditions into India, to the demoralisation of Indian Hindu opposition. Yet the strength and persistence of Hindu opposition is not to be minimised. Unlike Persia and the other kingdoms of western Asia, India which easily lost Sind to the Muhammadan Arabs, held them at bay there for over four centuries and the Muhammadan raiders from the north-west for over three centuries. Even the first attempt of Shihab-ud-din Muhammad Ghuri to conquer Delhi was frustrated by Prithviraj (*q.v.*) at the first battle of Tarain in 1191 and it was only in his second effort that he succeeded in defeating Prithviraj in the second battle of Tarain in 1193. This victory was followed by other conquests by Shihab-ud-din and his generals in northern India where Muhammadan rule was established at the beginning of the thirteenth century and unity was again established in northern India under the Delhi sultanate. The Deccan retained its independence for another century and was not conquered by the Delhi sultanate until the reign of Sultan Ala-ud-din Khalji (*q.v.*) and in the fourteenth century the whole of India came to be governed for a time from one centre. But disintegration soon began in the Delhi sultanate and a large Hindu kingdom was established in the Deccan with Vijayanagar as its capital in 1336 and independent Muhammadan kingdoms were founded in Bengal (1338), Jaunpur (1393), Gujarat and in the upper Deccan known as the Bahmani kingdom

(1347). Further in 1398 Timur (*q.v.*) invaded India, occupied Delhi which he sacked and left the Delhi sultanate bleeding. Lastly the Delhi sultanate was essentially weak as it did never attempt to broadbase itself on the affections of the conquered Hindus. On the contrary, the sultans were horrible fanatics who tried to convert by force the conquered Hindus to Islam and thereby completely alienated their sympathies. The result was that in 1526 the Delhi sultanate was easily overthrown by Babur (*q.v.*) who defeated the last Sultan, Ibrahim Lodi, at the first battle of Panipat and established the Mughul dynasty (*q.v.*) which ruled over India from 1526 to 1858. The third Mughul Emperor, Akbar (*q.v.*) was a sovereign of exceptional merit and insight who tried to win the love and affection of the conquered Hindus, especially of the war-like Rajput princes, by a policy of religious toleration and conciliation, by abolishing sectional taxes and by throwing careers open to merit. With the support of the Rajputs and of the Mughuls he extended his dominions from Qandahar to the Assam frontier and from the foot of the Himalayas to Ahmadnagar in the Deccan. The territorial expansion of the Mughul Empire continued during the reigns of his son Jahangir (*q.v.*), and grandson Shah Jahan (*q.v.*) who built the Taj (*q.v.*) but lost Qandahar, and under his great-grandson Aurangzeb (*q.v.*) the Mughul Empire reached its greatest expansion and covered the whole of India for a time. But Aurangzeb deliberately gave up Akbar's policy of religious toleration and thus alienated the Hindus, wanted to rule India for the benefit of Islam and embarked on futile efforts to force the Hindus to embrace Islam. This roused Hindu opposition in Rajputana, Bundelkhand and the Panjab while in Maharashtra Shivaji (*q.v.*) built up an independent Hindu kingdom even before the death in 1707 of Aurangzeb, who proved to be the last of the Great Mughuls. His successors were weak and inefficient; their ministers were treacherous and a fatal blow was struck at their power by Nadir Shah (*q.v.*) of Persia, who invaded India in 1739, occupied Delhi which he cruelly sacked and left the Mughul Empire utterly demoralised. This hastened the disintegration of the Mughul Empire. Oudh, Bengal and the Deccan—all under Muhammadan governors—seceded and became practically independent; the Rajput Princes became semi-independent while the Marathas (*q.v.*) under the Peshwa Baji Rao I (*q.v.*) boldly struck for establishing a Hindu Empire on the ruins of the Mughul Empire.

But that was not to be. Already European adventurers had arrived in India from across the seas. The Mughul emperors from Akbar to Aurangzeb failed to appreciate the significance of the opening of this new route to India. None of them could foresee the political ambition of these newcomers and appreciate the need for building up an Indian navy to meet them on their own element. Thus without any Indian opposition the Portuguese first came to India and were soon followed by the Dutch, the English and the French. Throughout the sixteenth century these European intruders fought amongst themselves mostly on the seas and the first to be eliminated were the Portuguese by a combination of the Dutch and the English; then the Dutch found the trade with the Spice Islands more profitable than that with India where the English and the French were thus left to confront each other. At the beginning of the eighteenth century the English East India Company (*q.v.*) occupied Bombay, Madras and Calcutta while the French East India Company occupied Mahe, Pondicherry and Chandernagore. They were also allowed to recruit Indians to their respective armies and employ such Indian military personnel in their services in their wars not only between themselves but also against the Indian princes whose rivalries and weakness roused their political ambition and enabled them to secure the alliance of some of them against others. As early as 1744-49 they fought between themselves the First Carnatic War (*q.v.*) in complete disregard of the Mughul sovereignty and a year later began the Second Carnatic War (*q.v.*) in which the French governor Dupleix (*q.v.*) availed himself of the lessons of the earlier war and struck for securing for France the political control over the administration not only of the Carnatic but also of the Nizam's dominions; but his aspirations were frustrated by the success of the English in Bengal where in 1757, just fifty years after the death of Emperor Aurangzeb, the English led by Robert Clive (*q.v.*) entered into a treacherous and treasonable conspiracy against Nawab Siraj-ud-daula (*q.v.*), won the battle of Plassey (*q.v.*) and practically became the masters of Bengal on the throne of which they placed their *protégé* Mirjafar as the puppet Nawab. Other events followed in quick succession. Ahmad Shah Abdali (*q.v.*) invaded India several times between 1748 and 1760, dealt the *coup de grâce* to the Mughul Empire by his great victory at the third battle of Panipat (*q.v.*) in 1761 and occupied Delhi which was again sacked. The brunt of the losses of the third battle of Panipat fell on the Marathas who were laid low for the moment and lost the chance of stepping into the shoes of the Mughul emperors; but the battle really marked the fall of the Mughul Empire and facilitated the foundation in its place of the British Empire in India. Neither Abdali nor any of his Indian Muhammadan allies could derive any benefit from Abdali's great victory the real beneficiaries of which proved to be the English Company which henceforth marched from one triumph to another. Strengthened with the resources of Bengal, the English defeated the French at the battle of Wandiwash in 1760, captured Pondicherry in 1762 and thus completely destroyed the political power of the French in India. In 1764 the English defeated the combined armies of Emperor Bahadur Shah (*q.v.*) and the Nawab of Oudh in the battle of Buxar and got from the Emperor in 1765 the grant of the *Diwani* (*q.v.*) which for the first time gave to the East India Company a legal status in the administration of Bengal, Bihar and Orissa and is regarded by some historians as marking the beginning of the British rule in India. In 1773 the British Parliament tried to give a system to the British administration in India by passing the Regulating Act (*q.v.*) which vested the administration of the Company's territories in India in a Governor-General with a Council of Four, raised the Governor of Bengal to be the Governor-General and also established a Supreme Court in Calcutta. Warren Hastings who was then the Governor of Bengal, was made the first Governor-General in 1773.

The period from 1773 to 1947 when British rule in India ended in the establishment of Indian independence, may be divided into two parts—the first one of the Company's rule up to 1858 and the second from 1858 to 1947 when India was under the direct rule of the British Crown.

During the Company's rule India was administered by a succession of twenty-two Governors-General (*q.v.*) and the most outstanding feature of Indian history of the period was the steady extension of the Company's dominions in India effected by wars and diplomacy. Four wars with Mysore (*q.v.*), three with the Marathas (*q.v.*), two each with Burma (*q.v.*) and the Sikhs (*q.v.*), and one each with the Amirs of Sind (*q.v.*), the Gurkhas (*q.v.*) and Afghanistan (*q.v.*) in each of which the Company was helped by one or the other of the Indian Princes and fought with armies the major portions of whose personnel consisted of Indian sepoys and the cost of which was entirely borne by the Indian tax-payer, established by 1857 the Company's sovereignty over the whole of India of which about two-thirds were brought under the direct rule of the Company and the remaining one-third was left to be administered by the Indian Princes who accepted the suzerainty of the Company and ruled as subordinate and protected allies. During this period some social reforms like the abolition of *sati* (*q.v.*) were effected; the beginnings were laid for the introduction of Western learning through the medium of English which was made the official language of the country; and uniform codes of civil and criminal procedures were introduced all over India promoting a sense of unity throughout the country. But the administration was autocratic and was run entirely by the Britishers, Indians being excluded from all high posts, contrary to the policy laid down in the Charter Act of 1833 (*q.v.*). Introduction of steamships and railways, aggressive missionary efforts of the Christian Church, the annexations of some old princely states by Lord Dalhousie (*q.v.*) either by the application of the Doctrine of Lapse (*q.v.*) or on the ground of misgovernment coupled with undeniable grievances of the Indian sepoys in the British Indian army combined to create wide-spread consternation all over India which burst forth in the Sepoy Mutiny (*q.v.*) in 1857-58. Materially assisted by the loyalty of practically all the Indian Princes and of the vast majority of the civil population of India the Company succeeded in suppressing the Mutiny by force; but its rule over India was terminated by the British Parliament which now transferred the administration of India to the Crown of England and Queen Victoria issued a Proclamation (*q.v.*) assuring to her Indian subjects certain rights and liberties.

Thus began the second period (1858-1947) of British rule in India which was carried on by a succession of thirty-one Viceroys (*q.v.*), as the Governors-General were henceforth designated, the first Viceroy and Governor-General being Lord Canning (*q.v.*). The most outstanding feature of Indian history during this period is the growth of Indian nationalism and its ultimate triumph in the grant of independence to India in 1947. The expansion of education as the result of the foundation in 1857 of Universities in Calcutta, Madras and Bombay, and close contact with England and Europe as the result of the opening of the Suez Canal in 1869 led to the growth in India of a new middle class which, inspired by

Western ideas of philosophy, politics and economics, deeply resented the position of inferiority to which Indians had so long been subjected. The *Pax Britannica* made them feel that India was one country and the Indians one people and the Parliamentary system of Government as prevailing in Great Britain which attracted them strongly, became their objective. They began to feel the need of an organisation representing the entire Indian nation and the consequence was the foundation of the Indian National Congress in 1885 in Bombay with only 71 representatives from all parts of India. The second session of the Congress which met in Calcutta in 1886 was attended by 434 duly elected delegates from all over India and boldly demanded that the legislative bodies in India should be enlarged and one-half of its members should be 'elected' Indians. Year after year the Congress persisted in its demands, survived the ridicule of Lord Dufferin (*q.v.*) who called it a 'microscopic minority', the complete indifference of Lord Lansdowne (*q.v.*), the open derision of Lord Curzon (*q.v.*) and the sinister efforts of Lord Minto II (*q.v.*) at its disruption by bribing the Muhammadans with the sop of unjustifiably excessive communal representation in the legislative bodies as created by the Indian Councils Act of 1909 and had the first modicum of success in 1909 when two Indians were for the first time appointed as members of the India Council and one Indian was for the first time appointed as a member of the Viceroy's Executive Council and the Indian Council's Act was passed which enlarged the legislative bodies to which elected Indian representatives were to be admitted in a larger proportion than before. Though Lord Morley (*q.v.*), the sponsor of these reforms, disavowed any intention of introducing any Parliamentary institutions in India, the Act could have but that one end. In 1911 the Partition of Bengal effected by Lord Curzon in 1905 was modified and the capital of the British Empire in India which had so long been situated in Calcutta, was transferred to Delhi in 1912. Two years later came the First World War (*q.v.*)) and though India stood loyally by Great Britain and helped her with large supplies of men, money and materials to win the war she also expected to be considered in the sharing of the benefits of the War. For once the Indian Muhammadans joined with their Hindu countrymen to demand self-government for India and in August, 1917, the British Government declared that the aim of British administration in India was "the increasing association of Indians in every branch of administration and the gradual development of self-governing institutions with a view to the progressive realisation of responsible government in India as an integral part of the British Empire". In consonance with this declaration the Government of India Act was passed in 1919 which enlarged the legislatures the majority of the members of which were to be the elected representatives of the people of India, and divided the functions of the Central and Provincial Governments in the latter of which the Executive was made partially responsible to the legislature by introducing the method of dyarchy. The Act no doubt marked a distinct advance: it gave to the Indians an institution where the elected representatives of the people of British India could for the first time in her history meet on an official basis, where they formed a majority and were free to criticise Government measures with impunity. This satisfied the older Congressmen but the younger section which found a new leader in M. K. Gandhi (*q.v.*) considered inadequate the reforms which left the Executive at the Centre irresponsible and armed the Viceroy with too large powers, and rejected them. That these fears were not unjustified was soon proved by the enactment of new repressive laws known as the Rowlatt Acts (*q.v.*) and severe repressive measures like the Jallianwala Bagh massacre (*q.v.*) and the Congress at its Nagpur session held in 1920 declared that its goal was the attainment of *Purna Swaraj* or complete self-rule and adopted the policy of non-violent non-co-operation to enforce its demands. As the British Government would not yield and succeeded in suppressing the non-co-operation movement by a policy of repression the Congress at its Lahore session held in December, 1929, resolved that its goal was the attainment of complete independence and in order to implement its demand it started in 1930 the Civil Disobedience movement (*q.v.*). The Government, as in the past, tried a mixture of severe repression and conciliation and passed in 1935 a Government of India Act (*q.v.*) which envisaged a Federal administration for British and Princely India, introduced a sort of dyarchy at the Centre and conceded autonomy to the provinces. The provincial part of the Act was enforced and provincial autonomy was inaugurated in April, 1937; but before the Federal Part of the Act could be enforced the Second World War broke out in September, 1939, and continued till 1945. It was a global war and extremely strained the resources of Great Britain. India stood loyally by her and the exploitation of her vast resources in men and money as well as the help of the U.S.A. enabled Great Britain to emerge victorious out of the war. Though the immense influence of Gandhiji over his countrymen and his profound faith in non-violence had kept India loyal to the British connection there was enough to show that India was not any longer willing to remain a subordinate part of the British Empire. The last sinister effort that was made by some Anglo-Indian officers to prevent the Congress from attaining its goal of independence was to prop up the Muslim demand for a Pakistan to be carved out of India. It resulted only in the outbreak of bitter and. bloody communal riots all over the country in August, 1946 which the Viceroy Lord Wavell (*q.v.*) with all his military experience and resources, failed to prevent. Continuance of the administration of India by a Government which was predominantly British in its composition was felt to be impossible and Lord Wavell formed in September, 1946, an Interim Government consisting of Indian leaders with Pandit Jawaharlal Nehru as its leader. The pampered Muslim League joined the Interim Government after keeping away from it for a month and an Indian Constituent Assembly was convened to draw up a Constitution for India. Lord Mountbatten who succeeded Lord Wavell as Viceroy early in 1947, was confronted with severe communal riots in the Panjab engineered by some Anglo-Indian officers there. He succeeded in convincing the Government in Great Britain then headed by Attlee as the Prime Minister, that nothing but the grant of independence to India on the basis of the partition of the country into India and Pakistan would restore peace in India and enable Great Britain to preserve her vast commercial interests in India and on June 3, 1947 announced on the authority of the Government of Great Britain that independence would be granted to India on the basis of the partition of the country into India and Pakistan. The Parliament of Great Britain passed on August 15, 1947 the Independence of India Act and thus India, shorn of the predominantly Muslim provinces of the North Western Frontier, Baluchistan, Sind, Western Panjab and East and part of North Bengal, started on a new career of independence after more than seven centuries of foreign domination.

The task that confronted independent India was of no little difficulty. Communal passions which had been roused to a frenzy, had to be calmed and India deliberately preferred to be a secular state assuring full citizenship to those of the Indian Muhammadans who preferred to stay in India to migrating to Pakistan, though Pakistan equally deliberately followed the policy of driving out the Hindus or assigning practically second class citizenship to those Hindus who preferred to stay on in Pakistan. Lord Mountbatten was retained to be the first Governor-General of independent India and Pandit Jawaharlal Nehru and his Congress colleagues in the Interim Government with some changes formed the first Indian Ministry which included Sardar Patel, Maulana Abul Kalam Azad but dropped Saratchandra Bose, Netaji's elder brother. Mahatma Gandhi whom the people of India acclaimed as the father of the nation, was murdered by a Hindu fanatic on January 30, 1948, but the country which deeply mourned his death, escaped any breach of the peace. Nine months later Mr. Jinnah, who had become the first Governor-General of Pakistan also died. Before the year was out Lord Mountbatten retired and was succeeded by Mr C. Rajagopalachari to be the first Indian and the last Governor-General of India. Most of the Indian Princes who had been given an option of joining with either of the two States of India and Pakistan acceded to India, but Kashmir and Hyderabad held out. Pakistan attempted to take forcible possession of Kashmir but the Raja acceded to India in October, 1947 and Indian troops had to be flown to the state only in time to hold Kashmir valley with Srinagar and Jammu. The Pakistani raiders remained in possession of the northern half of the state and a war with Pakistan began. At this point India referred the matter to the U.N.O. which imposed a peace on the basis of the existing territorial occupations subject to a final decision which has not yet been reached. The Nizam of Hyderabad intrigued for acquiring and maintaining the status of an independent state but was forced by the police action of the Government of India to merge in India in 1948. On January 26, 1950 the Constitution of India Act (*q.v.*), as passed by the Indian Constituent Assembly on November 26, 1949, was enforced and gave India a Federal Republican Constitution under which Dr. Rajendra Prasad was elected the first President and Pandit Jawaharlal Nehru, as the leader of the majority party, assumed the office of the Prime Minister which he retained till his death on May 27, 1964. His long tenure of office was of great assistance to the young Republic of India, as it gave a continuity to its administration and policy at home and abroad. Nehru adopted the policy

of non-alignment in India's foreign relations, established diplomatic relations with China, secured the peaceful cession of
Chandernagore in 1951 from France who also peacefully
ceded to India in 1956 all her other Indian possessions (Pondicherry, Karikal, Mahe and Yunnan). The refusal of Portugal
to follow the example of France and to hand over amicably
her Indian possessions (Goa, Daman and Diu) to India obliged
the latter to take forcible possession of those territories in 1961.
Thus the integration of India was completed. Nehru started
India in 1951 on a scheme of planned economy and industrialisation with the First Five Year Plan with a total outlay of
Rs. 2,069 crores. India adopted universal adult suffrage and
peacefully held her First General Election on this basis in
1952. In 1953 Andhra was separated from Madras and formed
into a new state on the linguistic basis and on the same basis
truncated Panjab is being divided into two states at the time
of writing. In June, 1954 Chou En-lai, the Prime Minister of
China, visited India. In the following October Nehru paid a
return visit to China and Indo-Chinese relations reached the
highest point of amity with the signature of what was called
the *Pancha Shila* agreement. In 1955 India made further advance in international politics by playing a leading part in
the Bandung Conference which met in April. In the following
June Nehru visited the U.S.S.R. where he received a very
warm welcome. The Russian leaders, Khrushchev and Bulganin,
paid a return visit to India in November and were received
with uproarious popular ovations. In 1956 India started her
Second Five Year Plan with a proposed outlay of Rs. 4,800
crores and joined with Burma, Ceylon and Indonesia
in demanding the withdrawal of British troops from Egypt
which under Nasser had taken up the control of the Suez Canal
and India's prestige stood high in international politics. In
1957 the Republic of India held her Second General Election
on the basis of adult suffrage and the Congress party under the
leadership of Nehru was again returned with majorities at
the Centre as well as in all the States except Kerala where a
Communist-led ministry was established, but the Centre under
Nehru maintained its control over it. In 1958 India marked
her progress in large industries by the incorporation of the
Indian Refineries Ltd. and her advance in the sphere of science
by erecting the first Atomic Reactor. India, however, refused
to make atom bombs and declared her determination to use
her atomic resources and knowledge for peaceful purposes

only. In 1959 China invaded Tibet and Nehru's Government remained passive spectators. The Dalai Lama and thousands of Tibetan refugees sought asylum in India which Nehru's Government readily gave. This was regarded as an unfriendly act by China which soon revealed her real aggressive designs against India by forcibly occupying the Indian territories of Longju in the North-Eastern Frontier area and Ladakh in the Himalayan region in 1959. Three years later China without any provocation and without any previous notice launched an aggressive massive attack on the northern and eastern frontiers of India. The Indian Army which was not prepared for such an attack by what was considered to be a friendly power, somehow held its own in the north but on the north-eastern front the Indian army could offer little or no resistance and the Chinese advanced within striking distance of Assam. This was a great humiliation for India and a greater one was dealt by China when she unilaterally declared in 1963 a cease-fire, stopped fighting and remained in occupation of such Indian territories as she thought fit. This was a serious disillusionment for Nehru who had been following a very friendly policy towards China since 1950 and hastened his death in 1964. Further, Pakistan continued to cause great concern to India. Ever since her first attempt at sending Pakistani soldiers as infiltrators into Kashmir in 1947 Pakistan had kept up the Kashmir issue as a cause of contention with India and this developed into a Three Weeks' War with India in September, 1965. The war was ended on the intervention of the U.N.O. and the U.S.S.R. which arranged for a conference at Tashkent between President Ayub Khan of Pakistan and Prime Minister Lal Bahadur Shastri (*q.v.*) of India. The heads of the two States issued a joint declaration announcing their agreement to try to decide all outstanding issues by peaceful methods and to withdraw their respective armies to positions before the outbreak of the war. Lal Bahadur Shastri breathed his last at Tashkent a few short hours after he had signed the Tashkent Declaration (*q.v.*) on January 11, 1966. Nehru's daughter Srimati Indira Gandhi succeeded him and is the Prime Minister of India at the time of writing.

India Act, Pitt's—was sponsored by William Pitt, the younger, who was then the Prime Minister of England and was passed in 1784 with the main object of removing some of the obvious defects of the Regulating Act (*q.v.*) passed in 1773. It set up a joint government of the Company and the Crown of England over the British possessions in India. The Court of Directors (*q.v.*) was left in control of commerce and patronage but the Court of Proprietors (*q.v.*) was deprived of all powers except that of electing the Court of Directors. A Board of Control was set up. It consisted of six unpaid privy councillors, one of whom was the president with a casting vote. No despatch was to be sent by the Court of Directors to India without the previous approval of the Board and all despatches from India were also to be placed before the Board. It could also insist on its own orders being sent to India without the consent of the Court of Directors. The Crown also could recall the Governor-General who continued to be appointed by the Court of Directors. The number of the members of the Governor-General's Council was reduced from four to three of whom the Commander-in-Chief was to be one. The Governor-General-in-Council was given fuller control over the Presidencies of Bombay and Madras in matters of war, revenue and diplomacy. The Councils of Bombay and Madras were also reduced from four to three members. The Governor-General-in-Council was also forbidden to declare war or to enter into any aggressive design without the explicit authority of the Court or of its Secret Committee acting in agreement with the Board of Control. An amending act passed a little later gave the Governor-General the right to overrule his Council, when he thought it essential.

Indian Association, the—was founded in Calcutta in July, 1876 for the creation of a strong body of public opinion in India and for unification of Indian races and peoples upon the basis of common political interests and aspirations. From its inception it tried to organise and express Indian public opinion on political questions that confronted the country. Started by Surendranath Banerjee (*q.v.*) who was then considered a radical, it remained an organisation of the moderates and still continues as such.

Indian Association for the Cultivation of Science, the—was established in Calcutta in 1876 by the munificence of Dr. Mahendralal Sarkar, an eminent Homeopath of Calcutta. It was the first institute to offer facilities to Indians for scientific researches. Sir C. V. Raman carried on much of his famous researches at this institute.

Indian Council—*see* Council of India.

Indian Civil Service, the—*see* Covenanted Civil Service.

Indian Colonial and Cultural Expansion—*see* Cultural and Colonial Expansion of India.

Indian Constituent Assembly—was conceded by the British Parliament in the Cabinet Mission's (*q.v.*) plan of May 16, 1946. Under this plan a Constituent Assembly was formed, consisting of 381 members representing all the Provinces and the Indian States and met in New Delhi in December, 1946. But the Muslim League abstained from attending it and the Indian Constituent Assembly which met in December, 1946, did not function. On the passing by the British Parliament of the Indian Independence Act 1947, on the basis of the partition of India into two independent dominions of Pakistan and India, the Constituent Assembly was also partitioned, the members representing the areas included in Pakistan formed the Constituent Assembly for Pakistan, and the remaining members the Constituent Assembly of India. After prolonged discussions the Indian Constituent Assembly with Dr. Rajendra Prasad (*q.v.*) as the President, adopted the Constitution of India Act on November 26, 1949, which laid down that India should be a sovereign Democratic Republic comprising within it the territories which had hitherto been Governor's provinces, the Indian States and Chief Commissioners' Provinces. The Constituent Assembly in its capacity as the Indian Legislative Assembly also decided to remain a member of the British Commonwealth. The Constitution drawn up by the Indian Constituent Assembly which made India a Federal Democratic Republic with an elected President was adopted by a proclamation made on January 26, 1950 and came into force from that date which is now annually celebrated as the Republic Day in India.

Indian Constitutional Reforms, Report on—embodied the recommendations made by Edwin Montague, Secretary of State for India, and Lord Chelmsford, Viceroy in 1917-18. The Report was published in July, 1918. The Government of India Act, 1919, was based on this Report. It enlarged the legislatures both at the centre and in the provinces, and introduced partial responsibility in the administration of the provinces by adopting the device of 'dyarchy' (*q.v.*).

Indian Councils Act, the—was passed, first, in 1861. The second came in 1892 and the third in 1909. These acts marked stages in the gradual progress of the development of an administrative system in India in which the children of the soil would have some voice. The Indian Councils Act of 1861 added a fifth member to the Viceroy's Executive Council and introduced the portfolio system by which each member of the Executive

Council was placed in charge of specific departments and remodelled the Legislative Council by providing that the number of additional members was to be twelve in place of six and one half of these twelve was to be non-officials. The Indian Councils Act of 1892 raised the number of members of the Imperial Legislative Council from twelve to sixteen who were to be nominated in such a way as to be representatives of different classes and interests. Thus though an official majority was retained in the Legislature the representative, if not the elective, principle was introduced in the legislative bodies which were also given the larger powers of discussing the annual budget and of asking questions. The Indian Councils Act of 1909 was based on what are known as the Morley-Minto reforms (*q.v.*). This Act increased the number of members of the Imperial Legislative Council as well as of the provincial legislatures. It also increased the number of the non-official members of the legislatures a portion of whom were to be indirectly elected. Last, but not the least, it introduced the principle of communal representation for the Muhammadans and thus laid the seeds of the partition of India.

Indian Law Commission, the—was appointed in 1833 with Lord Macaulay as the President. It laboured for many years and on the basis of its work the Indian Penal Code was enacted in 1860 and the Codes of Civil and Criminal Procedure in 1861. Thus British India came to possess uniform codes of laws.

Indian Mutiny—*see* Sepoy Mutiny.

Indian National Conference, the—was held in Calcutta under the auspices of the Indian Association of Calcutta on December 28, 29 and 30, 1883. It was the first assembly where non-official representatives from all over India met for discussing public affairs that touched them all and may be said to have set the model on which the Indian National Congress was built up two years later. It discussed questions relating to industrial and technical education, wider employment of Indians in the Civil Service, separation of the judicial from executive functions, representative government and the Arms Act. The second session of the Indian National Conference was also held in Calcutta in 1885. It was more representative than the first and it also discussed the political questions of the day. After 1885 the Indian National Conference merged with the Indian National Congress which held its first session in 1885. (Majumdar, R. C., *Glimpses of Bengal in the 19th Century*).

Indian National Congress, the—the largest political organisation of Indians, was founded on 28 December, 1885. It held its first session in Bombay with Mr. W. C. Bonnerji, an eminent Barrister of the Calcutta High Court, as the President. At its origin it is said to have received the indirect support of Lord Dufferin, the Viceroy (1884-88) and it is true that the initiative at its foundation was taken by a retired English civilian named Allan Octavian Hume whom, on his death in 1912, the Congress designated as its "father and founder" and none but whom, according to Gokhale, could have founded the Congress in 1885. The fact, however, is, as C. Y. Chintamani observes, the idea of a national assemblage for definitely political ends was conceived by a number of persons and materialized in 1885. During the early years of its existence its protagonists openly declared that it would strengthen the foundation of the British Empire in India. It was, therefore, at first looked upon with some favour by the Government and the Viceroy, Lord Dufferin, even met at a garden party the delegates of the second Indian National Congress which was held in Calcutta in 1886 and the Governor of Madras extended the same courtesy to the members of the third session of the Congress which met in Madras in 1887. But already the Indian National Congress had begun to show unmistakably that it was going to develop not on lines expected by Lord Dufferin but on really national lines and to stand for rights and principles which the Congress considered would be conducive to the political development of the Indian nation. The Indian National Congress thus soon lost grace with the Government but it endeared itself increasingly to the Indian people and soon became the organiser and the voice of the Indian nation which it led to independence only sixty-two years after its foundation. It is an achievement of which any organisation can justly be proud. But before the attainment of this magnificent result the Indian National Congress had to pass through various strains and stresses. The number of delegates (then called representatives) which was only 71 at the first session and rose to 436 at the second session held in Calcutta, increased to 1889 at the fifth session held in Bombay and it was felt necessary to restrict it at 1000 to be elected by different political public associations all over the country. The number of visitors also continued to increase and the provision for the boarding and lodging of the delegates and for the sitting accommodation of the delegates and the visitors proved a great problem which it was not easy to tackle satisfactorily. The increasing numbers of the delegates as well as of the visitors left no doubt about the national character of the Congress, though the Muhammadans generally kept aloof from it. The aims and methods of the Congress also changed with the passing years. The first Congress passed only nine resolutions urging (i) an enquiry into the working of the Indian administration by a Royal Commission in which India should be adequately represented, (ii) the abolition of the India Council, (iii) the expansion of the Supreme and the Local Legislative Councils by the admission of a 'considerable proportion' of elected members with the rights of considering the annual budgets and of interpellations, (iv) holding of the Indian Civil Service Examination simultaneously in England and India and raising of the maximum age of the entrants to 23 years from 19, (v) reduction of military expenditure, (vi) the re-imposition of customs duties and the extension of the licence tax to meet the increased military expenditure, if it could not be reduced, (vii) separation of Burma, the annexation of which was deprecated, (viii) circulation of the above resolutions to all political associations in all provinces for pressing for their implementation and (ix) the re-assemblage of the Indian National Congress next year in Calcutta in the Christmas week.

Agreeable to the last resolution the Indian National Congress met for its second session in Calcutta in the Christmas week of 1886 and thereafter for long succeeding years it met annually during the Christmas week in one or other of the important towns of India until 1937 when it met for the first time in a village (Faizpore). It is to be observed that for the implementation of its resolutions the Indian National Congress at first relied entirely on the sense of justice of the British Government to whom these were presented as requests in the form of petitions. Indeed an implicit faith in Great Britain and genuine admiration for her political principles and institutions were the foundation on which the Indian National Congress was built and for long years its sponsors believed that the British were so fair-minded a people that Indian grievances were sure to be removed if these could only be brought to their notice. Acting on such beliefs other reforms like the extension of the trial by jury, the separation of judicial and executive functions in the administration of criminal justice, the abolition of the Arms Act, expansion of education, both general and technical, and, above all, the development of self-government in India by the expansion of the Central and Provincial Legislatures with the admission into these bodies of a larger number of popularly elected Indian representatives with enlarged powers over the financial and general administration of the country, were urged by the method popularly known as 'constitutional agitation'. Arrangements were also made to inform the public in Great Britain itself by establishing in London in 1888 a paid agency and later on by organising there the British Committee of the Indian National Congress which published a weekly paper called *India*. All these efforts, however, proved unavailing and no reforms except the halting Indian Councils Act of 1892 (*q.v.*) was conceded by the British Government which simply ignored the Congress and its resolutions. This bred a feeling of despondency amongst the followers of the Congress whose number was annually increasing as a result of the Congress propaganda in the country and a spirit of opposition against the British Government began to grow. A section of the Congressmen lost faith in the 'constitutional method' of agitation of the Congress and ridiculed the practice of sending humble petitions, year after year, to the Government which unceremoniously rejected them. This section, led by B. G. Tilak, Aravinda Ghose, Bepin Pal and Lala Lajpat Rai openly declared that reforms would not be secured by mere talk, but action was essential. They also declared that the country could not be satisfied with a mere expansion of self-governing institutions, but wanted a real control over its administration. They preached self-help and the necessity of rousing the masses. In the meantime the Government of India took many retrograde measures like closing of the mints to the free coinage of silver, the Exchange Compensation allowance grant, the Indian Universities Act (*q.v.*) and the Partition of Bengal (*q.v.*) (1905) combined with unwise Viceregal utterances like "India was conquered by the sword and by the sword it shall be held" (Lord Elgin) and "India has no regard for truth, and indeed truth has never been an Indian ideal" (Lord Curzon) profoundly displeased Indians, especially the new and young section of the Congressmen. The differences between the two sections of the Congressmen, the old and the young, the Moderates and the Extremists, the Constitutionalists and the Radical Nationalists, revealed themselves first at the Congress session held in Benares in 1905 with G. K. Gokhale (*q.v.*) as the President when in opposition to the official request for "further expansion and reform of the Indian Legislatures" the younger section demanded that India should have a Government which should be "autonomous and absolutely free of British control". The official resolution was passed and the divergence extended to the next session held in Calcutta in 1906 where a compromise was attempted to be effected by the President, Mr. Dadabhai Naoroji (*q.v.*), who in his Presidential address declared that India should have "*swaraj*, like that of the United Kingdom or the Colonies". But the accord proved illusory and at the next Congress session held at Surat in 1907 the Moderates and the Radicals came to an open clash and the session ended in disorder. Next year (1908) at its Allahabad session the Indian National Congress drew up a constitution, the first Article of which declared that "the attainment of a system of government similar to that enjoyed by the self-governing members of the British Empire by constitutional means" was the object of the Congress. None was to be permitted to be a delegate to a Congress session unless he would subscribe in writing to the above formula which was accepted as the creed of the Congress. The Morley-Minto Reforms as embodied in the Indian Councils Act of 1909 (*q.v.*) and the modification of the Partition of Bengal (*q.v.*) in 1911 strengthened the Moderates and enabled them to control the Congress till 1916. But the limitations of the Morley-Minto Reforms soon proved irksome and already internal developments and pressure of international events were leading to the emergence of a section amongst the Indian Muhammadans who had so long generally held themselves aloof from the nationalistic movement led by the Congress, to feel the urge for self-government and who, in spite of the sop of communal representation granted to them by the Indian Councils Act of 1909, made the Muslim League declare in 1913 the attainment of self-government as its object. In 1916 a joint scheme of reforms was actually formulated by the Indian National Congress and the Muslim League which met practically simultaneously at Lucknow. To meet this joint demand and pressed also by the exigencies of the First World War (*q.v.*) Great Britain announced in 1918 the Montague-Chelmsford Reforms (*q.v.*) which were embodied soon afterwards in the Government of India Act of 1919 (*q.v.*) which frankly extended the principle of direct popular representations in the legislatures and established partial provincial autonomy. The Congress became divided on the question of the acceptance of these reforms. The Moderates led by veteran Congressmen like

Surendranath Banerjee and Tej Bahadur Sapru accepted the Reforms and decided to work them, but the Nationalists who now predominated in the Congress, considered the Reforms as inadequate and the Congress rejected the Reforms in its 1918 session. The Moderates now left the Congress which they had built up through long years of labour and sacrifice. About this time the Congress found a new leader in M. K. Gandhi (*q.v.*) and under his direction declared at its Nagpur session in 1920 that the goal of the Indian National Congress was the attainment of *Purna Swaraj* or complete self-rule by all justifiable and peaceful means and also decided to adopt a policy of non-violent non-co-operation with the Government of India as a means for the implementation of its demands. Thus a great change came over both the aim and methods of the Congress. It came to attract to itself more popular support than ever before and had also found a real sanction which it could enforce for the implementation of its demands. In 1921 the Congress under the leadership of Gandhiji joined its forces with those of the Khilafat movement (*q.v.*) of the Muhammadans and started the non-co-operation movement (*q.v.*) promising Swaraj within a year. The visit of the Prince of Wales was completely boycotted and there was a unique demonstration showing how joint Hindu-Muslim non-co-operation could very nearly paralyse the Government. The Government resorted to severe repressive measures and the movement could not remain non-violent, as Gandhiji insisted it to be. Further owing to developments in Turkey itself the Khilafat movement also frittered away and the non-co-operation movement was stopped. But the Congress agitation continued and in 1929 the Congress at its Lahore session declared that the attainment of complete independence was its goal and started in April, 1930 the Civil Disobedience Movement (*q.v.*) for enforcing its demand. The Muslim League refused to co-operate in Civil Disobedience and the Government also resorted to severe repressive measures putting Gandhiji with many other leaders of the Congress into prison and the Congress was again thwarted. But the urge for independence could not be suppressed by repression and the outbreak of the Second World War in 1939 exposed Britain's utter dependence for her victory on the resources of India. The Indian National Congress under the guidance of Gandhiji definitely declined to side openly with Great Britain's enemies and still preferred to wait for the dawning of generous good sense on Great Britain which would voluntarily concede to India her political demands. One section of the Congressmen, however, under the leadership of Subhas Chandra Bose (*q.v.*) was for an actual military alliance with the enemies of Great Britain. Netaji, as Subhas Chandra Bose now came to be known, actually jumped his home internment in Calcutta, went overland to Germany and then, after strange adventures, arrived at Singapore where in 1942-43 he organised the Indian troops, 90,000 strong, whom the British had left prisoners in the hands of Japan at the time when the British evacuated Burma, into the Indian National Army, established there a Provisional National Government of India with himself as its head and started on a military campaign for the forcible recovery of India from the east with Japanese support. But his efforts ended in a failure in 1944. So also had Gandhiji's call to Great Britain to 'quit India' which he had issued in 1942. By 1945 Great Britain was again victorious and appeared to be set in for another spell of imperialism. But the War had actually left her sorely wounded, bleeding and paralysed in men and money. The Indian National Congress, though apparently suppressed, had inspired the country with such anti-British feelings and activities that it became clear to Great Britain that she could hold India only on the terms laid down by the Congress which at its Meerut session held in 1946 reiterated its demand for independence, which it ultimately won in August, 1947 at the heavy price of the partition of India into India and Pakistan (*q.v.*). The Indian National Congress thus attained much more than what it had set before it as its aim at its foundation sixty-two years ago. It now forms the Government of India which has adopted a Federal Democratic Republican constitution and has taken upon itself the difficult task of freeing this very vast land of ours of the curses of poverty, ignorance and social and economical inequalities bequeathed to India by long centuries of foreign domination. The Indian National Congress now continues as the predominant political party in India.

The Indian National Congress is a democratic body which works through a graded organisation covering the whole country. Any person of the age of 18 or above can be a primary member of the Congress by paying an annual subscription of 25 *paisa*; and any such primary member above the age of 20 fulfilling certain conditions as to wearing *khadi* (hand-spun cloth) can be a full and active member. At the base there is a village or *mahalla* Committee, over a number of which there is a District Congress Committee. Each State has its own State Congress Committee to supervise and control the work of all the District Congress Committees within it. All the State Congress Committees are under the All-India Congress Committee with a large elected membership representing all the states. The work of the Indian National Congress is carried on throughout the year and a central direction is given to it by the Working Committee which has now a whole-time elected President holding office for a term of two years. The organisation appears at first sight to be loose and decentralised but it is capable, as events have already proved, of strong centralised action in times of need.

The list below of the venues and Presidents of the Indian National Congress from its first session in 1885 to its session in 1947 illustrates its national and all-India character:

1885 — Bombay — W. C. Bonnerji.
1886 — Calcutta — Dadabhai Naoroji.
1887 — Madras — Syed Badruddin Tyabji.
1888 — Allahabad — George Yule.
1889 — Bombay — Sir William Wedderburn.
1890 — Calcutta — Sir Phirozeshah Mehta.
1891 — Nagpur — Ananda Charlu.
1892 — Allahabad — W. C. Bonnerji.
1893 — Lahore — Dadabhai Naoroji.
1894 — Madras — A. Webb.
1895 — Poona — Surendranath Banerji.
1896 — Calcutta — M. Rahimtullah Sayani.
1897 — Amraoti — C. Sankaran Nair.
1898 — Madras — Ananda Mohan Bose.
1899 — Lucknow — Rameshchandra Dutt.
1900 — Lahore — N. G. Chandravarkar.
1901 — Calcutta — E. D. Wacha.
1902 — Ahmedabad — Surendranath Banerji.
1903 — Madras — Lalmohan Ghose.
1904 — Bombay — Sir Henry Cotton.
1905 — Benares — G. K. Gokhale.
1906 — Calcutta — Dadabhai Naoroji.
1907 — Surat — Rashbehari Ghose. (broken up)
1908 — Madras — Rashbehari Ghose.
1909 — Lahore — Madan Mohan Malviya.
1910 — Allahabad — Sir William Wedderburn.

1911 — Calcutta — Bishan Narayan Dhar.
1912 — Patna — R. N. Mudholkar.
1913 — Karachi — Nawab Syed Mahomed Bahadur.
1914 — Madras — Bhupendranath Bose.
1915 — Bombay —Sir S. P. Sinha.
1916 — Lucknow — A. C. Majumdar.
1917 — Calcutta — Mrs. Annie Besant.
1918 — Bombay (*Special*) — Syed Hasan Imam.
1918 — Delhi — Madan Mohan Malviya.
1919 — Amritsar — Pt. Matilal Nehru.
1920 — Calcutta (*Special*) — Lala Lajpat Rai.
1920 — Nagpur — C. Vijaya Raghavachariyar.
1921 — Ahmedabad — Hakim Ajmal Khan.
1922 — Gaya — C. R. Das.
1923 — Coconada — Maulana Mahammad Ali.
1923 — Delhi (*special*) — Abul Kalam Azad.
1924 — Belgaon — M. K. Gandhi.
1925 — Cawnpore — Mrs Sarojini Naidu.
1926 — Gauhati — Srinivas Ayengar.
1927 — Madras — M. A. Ansari.
1928 — Calcutta — Pt. Matilal Nehru.
1929 — Lahore — Pt. Jawaharlal Nehru.
1930 — No session.
1931 — Karachi — Vallabhbhai Patel.
1932 — Delhi — Seth Ranchhorlal Dass Amritlal.
1933 — Calcutta — Mrs Nellie Sengupta.
1934 — Bombay — Rajendra Prasad.
1935 — No session.
1936 — Lucknow — Pt. Jawaharlal Nehru.
1937 — Faizpur — Pt. Jawaharlal Nehru.
1938 — Haripura — Subhaschandra Bose.
1939 — Tripuri — Subhaschandra Bose.
1940 — Ramgarh — Maulana Abul Kalam Azad.
1941 — 1945— No session.
1946 — . . . . — Pt. Jawaharlal Nehru.
1946 — Meerut — Acharya J. B. Kripalani.
1947 — . . . . — Rajendra Prasad.

After independence the Congress met in 1948 at Jaipur under
the Presidentship of P. Sitaramaiya, in 1950 at Nasik under
P. D. Tandon, in 1951 at New Delhi under Pt. J. Nehru who
also presided over the Hyderabad (1953) and Kalyani (1954)
sessions, in 1955 at Avadi under U. N. Dhebar who also presided

over the Amritsar (1956) and Gauhati (1958) sessions, in 1959
at Nagpur under Srimati Indira Gandhi, in 1960 at Bangalore
and in 1961 at Gujarat under N. Sanjiva Reddy, in 1962 at
Bhubaneswar and in 1963 at Patna under D. Sanjivaya and
in 1964 at Bhubaneswar and in 1965 at Durgapur under K.
Kamaraj. At the Avadi session (1955) the Congress adopted the
policy of establishing in India a socialistic state on a democratic
basis which it reiterated at the Bhubaneswar session (1965).
(Sitaramaiya, P., *Hist. of the Ind. Nat. Congress*, Vols. I & II.

Indo-Aryans, the—were the section of the Aryans (*q.v.*) who are
supposed to have entered into India from the north-west at
an uncertain date about two thousand years before the beginning of the Christian era. They were a nomadic people who
first settled in the Panjab and then advanced further within
northern India along the Gangetic basin, after prolonged
fighting with the indigenous population whom they called
Dasas or *Dasyus*, even though the latter had a more advanced
civilisation. The Aryans eventually triumphed, reduced the
indigenous people to submission and evolved a religion which
found expression in their literature known as the *Vedas* (*q.v.*)
which throw much light on their political and social organisation. They were divided into tribes which were generally ruled
by kings and which fought amongst themselves, uniting, however, against their non-Aryan foes. The king was hereditary
and derived his income from tributes paid by the conquered
tribes and gifts made by the subjects. His chief functionaries
were the *senani* (leader of the army), the *gramani* (village
chief) and the *purohita* (priest). The people in general were
associated with the monarchy through a popular assembly
called the *samiti* and a council of elders called the *sabha*.
Society was patriarchal and the father was the head of the
family. Monogamy was the prevalent form of marriage, but
polygamy was not unknown. The status of women was high;
they normally controlled the household and some of them
even composed sacred hymns. The caste system in its modern
form was not in existence, but the division of the people into
Brahmans representing holy power, the Kshatriyas representing the royal power and the Vis or the commonalty was
nascent. Inter-dining and inter-marriages were prevalent. The
Indo-Aryans were a rural people who had no cities and towns
and who lived a pastoral life in villages. Cattle rearing was
the chief source of income and agriculture was their principal

occupation. Industries like tanning and carpentry were practised and trade was carried on through the medium of oxen and
gold ornaments. Their chief food consisted of butter, vegetables
and fruits, but meat, especially of animals like cows and bullocks
slaughtered at the sacrifices, were partaken. Intoxicating drinks
like *soma* and *sura* were frequently taken. Dicing and chariot-
racing were common amusements. The Indo-Aryans assimilated
within their fold the conquered non-Aryans whom they later
on classed as *Sudras*. The religion of the early Indo-Aryans may
be described as the worship of Nature leading up to Nature's
God. Natural phenomena like the sky, thunder and the sun
were personified as gods named Varuna, Indra and Surya
and worshipped. The number of deities known to the Indo-
Aryans was indefinite and numerous and elaborate rituals requiring the services of a large number of persons specially
trained in them, were required. The belief that God is one,
although He bears many names, was also shared by the Indo-
Aryans who were a dynamic people whose ideas and institutions went on developing as years passed and enabled them
to develop the great Hindu civilisation and culture. (*C.H.I.* I.
chs. IV & V; Majumdar, R. C., *The Vedic Age*)

Indo-Greeks, the dynasty of the—came to be established in
Afghanistan and the north-west frontier region some time
after the death of Asoka (*c.* 232 B.C.). Antiochus the Great of
Syria crossed the Hindu Kush in about 206 B.C., defeated an
Indian prince named Subhagasena, the ruler of the Kabul
valley and returned home after extorting a large indemnity in
cash and elephants. Shortly afterwards another Greek Bactrian
king named Demetrios (*q.v.*) conquered a considerable portion
of the Panjab. He might have been the *Yavana* prince who
invaded upper India during the reign of Pushyamitra Sunga
(*q.v.*). Though Demetrios was soon deprived of Bactria by
another Greek prince named Eukratides the north-western
frontier of India soon came to be parcelled into numerous
states ruled over by petty Greek princes who issued numerous
types of coins and are remembered by these alone. The most
prominent of them was Menander who advanced far into the
interior of India, became a convert to Buddhism and has been
identified with king Milinda mentioned in the Buddhist work
Milinda Panha (*Dialogues of Milinda*). Another such Indo-Greek
king was Antialkidas, who ruled at Taxila, and sent an ambassador named Heliodoros (*q.v.*) to the court of the Sunga king,
Bhagabhadra, at Besnagar, where he erected a pillar in honour

of Vasudeva, whose worshipper he professed himself to be. The last of the Indo-Greek kings was Hermaios who was overthrown by the Kushana king, Kadphises I (*q.v.*) in the first century of the Christian era.

Indore—was the capital of the state founded by Mulhar Rao Holkar (*q.v.*) during the second quarter of the eighteenth century.

Indra—is the name of a Vedic deity who was the God of thunder. In the Vedic pantheon his rank was the highest.

Indra—was the name borne by four kings of the Rashtrakuta dynasty (*q.v.*). Very little is known about Indra I and Indra II except their names. Indra III (A.D. 915-17) ruled for a short time, but signalised his reign by an invasion and temporary occupation of Kanauj. His death soon afterwards was followed by the loss of Kanauj. Indra IV who died in A.D. 982 was the last of the Rastrakuta kings.

Indraprastha—was the capital of the Pandavas whose war with the Kurus is the central theme of the epic *Mahabharata*. It has been identified with the village of Indrapat in the vicinity of modern Delhi.

Indus, the—is the chief river of the Panjab. It rises in the Tibetan Himalayas, flows through Kashmir and the Panjab receiving the waters of many tributaries of which the Jhelum, the Chinab, the Ravi, the Vipasa and the Sutlej are the most important and then running through Sind it falls into the sea. It is 18,000 miles in length and is one of the seven sacred rivers of the Hindus. The Sanskritic form of the name is Sindhu. Its valley was the home of a civilisation that flourished from 2500 B.C. to 1500 B.C. if not earlier still.

Indus valley civilisation, the—has been revealed as the result of excavations recently carried out in various places in the Indus valley, particularly at Mohenjo-Daro in the Larkana district of Sind and at Harappa in the Montgomery district of the Panjab. It is provisionally believed to have flourished between 2500 B.C. and 1500 B.C. and might have been older. It was an urban civilisation and the people who developed it enjoyed many civic amenities like broad roads, well-laid-out drainage systems and public baths. They had also communion meeting halls and large places of worship. They had brick-built houses some of which were two-storied with regular supplies of water and internal drainage systems. They worshipped images including the phallic emblem of Siva. They knew the use of copper, bronze, silver, lead and gold, the last being used for making elaborate jewellery. They used woven cotton fabrics as well as woollen clothes, fine clay pottery which was often decorated, drank milk and ate wheat, barley, fruits as well as flesh of various animals. They had a system of writing but their script which has been found on the numerous seals that have been discovered, has not yet been deciphered. It is, therefore, impossible to make any guess as to the nature of their language. They disposed of their dead by burial as well as by cremation. Their civilisation is believed to have had close similarity with that of the Euphrates valley and is believed to have flourished earlier than the Vedic civilisation of the Indo-Aryans who probably entered into India after the fall of the Indus valley civilisation the cause of the decline and fall of which is not known. (Mackay, *The Indus Civilisation*; Wheeler, Mortimer, *The Indus Civilisation*)

Infallibility Decree, the—was issued by Emperor Akbar in 1579 authorising the Emperor to give the final decision on any question concerning the Muhammadan religion "for the glory of God and propagation of Islam". It made the Mughul Emperor the final arbiter on all theological questions of Muhammadanism and largely increased his authority.

Infanticide, suppression of—was effected in British India by the Bengal Regulation of 1795 which prohibited and made penal the killing of female children at births in order to avoid the difficulties of getting them married and by Regulation VI of 1802 which similarly forbade and made penal the throwing at the mouths of the Ganges of a first-born child by a barren mother if and when she got, after years of married life, more than one child. The evils, specially the first one, continued to prevail particularly in the Indian states and were finally suppressed during the administration of Lord Hardinge I (1844-48).

Institutes of Manu—*see* Laws of Manu.

Iqbal, Sir Muhammad (1876-1938)—was a modern Indian Muhammadan poet who wrote mainly in Persian and produced only one work, namely *Six Lectures on the Reconstruction of Religious Thought*. He held that Islam stood for a dynamic spirit of struggle for spiritual freedom and was the root and branch of all religious experience. It is a living principle of action which could give purpose and remake worlds. Europe was motivated by the need for wealth and lust for power. Islam alone could create true values and assert man's mastery of nature by constant struggle. His works infused in Muhammadan youths in India the sense of a separate destiny. It was again Iqbal's suggestion made in

1930 for the union of the North-Western Frontier Province, Baluchistan, Sind and Kashmir as a Muhammadan, state within an Indian federation that gave birth to Pakistan, though the term was actually coined not by him but by Choudhri Rahamat Ali in 1933. Iqbal was knighted by the British Government in recognition of his poetic genius.

Irwin, Lord, Edward Frederick Lindley Wood—son of the second Viscount Halifax, was born in 1881. Educated at Eton he was a Member of Parliament from 1910 to 1925 during which period he held various ministerial posts in the British Cabinet. In 1925 he was appointed Viceroy and Governor-General of India which post he held till 1931. His Viceroyalty in India was a period of great storm and stress. The non-co-operation movement (*q.v.*) started in 1920 was still active while Indian public opinion was further estranged by the appointment of the Simon Commission (*q.v.*) consisting exclusively of Britishers, to assess the working of the Act of 1919 (*q.v.*). The exclusion of Indians from the Commission caused widespread political unrest all over India which Lord Irwin attempted to remove by announcing on October 31, 1929, in consultation with, and the approval of, the British Government, that the attainment of dominion status was the natural issue of the constitutional progress in India and that after the submission of a report by the Simon Commission a Round Table Conference of all the Indian political parties would be held in London prior to the submission of a new Indian Constitution Bill before the Parliament. But as the British authorities soon hastened to water down the definition of dominion status as meaning the constitution of a dependency enjoying autonomous government not equal in status with dominions like Canada, Lord Irwin's proclamation failed to satisfy the Indian National Congress which at its Lahore session held at the end of 1929 declared that the goal of the Indian Congress was complete national independence. The Congress further started in April, 1930, the Civil Disobedience Movement under the leadership of Mahatma Gandhi who himself with some followers made a spectacular march to Dandi and deliberately broke the Salt ban of the Government and then started a movement which soon spread all over the country which was filled with turmoil. Lord Irwin tried to meet the situation with tact. While he applied all the resources of the state for upholding law and order and imprisoned all the members of the Working Committee of the Congress he carried on negotiations with Mahatma Gandhi and met him in several interviews at the end of which the Gandhi-Irwin Pact was made by which the Congress agreed to recall the Civil Disobedience Movement and to send Mahatma Gandhi as its sole representative to the second session of the Round Table Conference whose first session it had boycotted and the Government released all political prisoners except those condemned for violent outrages. A month after the conclusion of the Gandhi-Irwin Pact Lord Irwin retired from the Viceroyalty of India, leaving to his successor, Lord Willingdon, the task of doing or undoing his policy. After his retirement from India Lord Irwin served as the British Ambassador to the U.S.A. from 1940 to 1946 and was created the Earl of Halifax in 1944.

Isa Khan—was one of twelve *Bhuiyans* (landlords) who controlled Eastern Bengal in the third quarter of the sixteenth century. Isa Khan held power over east and central Dacca district and much of Mymensingh district. He, in co-operation with his neighbouring Hindu leader, Kedar Rai of Vikrampur (Dacca), resisted successfully for some time the power of Emperor Akbar, but eventually they fell out and Isa Khan was overthrown by the Mughul Emperor.

Isanavarman—was the fourth king of the Maukhari dynasty of Kanauj. He ruled in about A.D. 554, claimed victories over the Andhras and the Gaudas and was the first Maukhari king to assume the title of *Maharajadhiraja.*

Islam—*see* Muhammadanism.

Islam Khan—was the Mughul governor of Bengal appointed by Emperor Jahangir. He defeated the rebellious Afghan chief Usman Khan who died of a wound inflicted in course of a battle and put an end to Afghan power in Bengal.

Islam Khan Lodi—whose original name was Sultan Shah Lodi, was the governor of Sirhind. His claim to fame rests on the circumstance that he was the uncle of Bahlol Lodi (*q.v.*), the founder of the Lodi dynasty of the sultans of Delhi.

Islam Shah Sur—was the son and successor of Sher Shah, the Emperor of Delhi from A.D. 1540 to 1545. Islam Shah (whose original name was Jalal Khan and who was also known as Salim Shah) ruled from 1545 to 1554. He suppressed the rebellious nobles, crushed the Ghakkars and strengthened his hold on Kashmir by completing the construction of the fortress of Mankot. He maintained the efficiency of the army and preserved many of the reforms introduced by his father. But he died young and soon afterwards the Sur dynasty was overthrown by Emperor Humayun (*q.v.*).

Islington Commission—was appointed in 1912 with Lord Islington as the Chairman' with Indian and British public men as members for investigating the problem of the recruitment of Indians to the higher public services, particularly the Indian Civil Service. It recommended that in addition to the Indians who might succeed in entering the Civil Service by competing in the public examination held in London, 25 per cent of the posts in the Indian Civil Service should be filled with Indians partly by direct recruitment and partly by promotion from the Provincial Civil Service. It also recommended the holding of an examination in India for the recruitment of Indians to the Indian Civil Service. The Report which was published in 1917 thus conceded a demand which the Indian National Congress had been making for more than thirty years. But the large additional emoluments that it recommended for the I.C.S. caused great resentment amongst the Indians.

Ismail Mukh—was an elderly Afghan noble in the service of Sultan Muhammad Tughluq and held a high post in the Deccan. In about 1345 he was set up as the independent ruler of the Deccan by the rebellious Afghan nobles there. He assumed the name of Nasir-ud-din Shah, but feeling himself unequal to the onerous duties of the ruler of a new kingdom, he voluntarily abdicated his power in 1347 in favour of Hasan who established the famous Bahmani kingdom and dynasty (*q.v.*).

Ismail Shah—the second king of the Adil Shahi (*q.v.*) dynasty of Bijapur, ruled from 1510 to 1534. He ascended the throne as a minor but on attaining majority he fought many wars and conquered from Vijayanagar the Raichur doab lying between the Krishna and the Tungabhadra. He also received an embassy from the Shah of Persia and was so pleased that he became very much well disposed towards Shiahism which was professed by the Shah of Persia.

Isvara—is one of the names by which the Supreme Being, the Creator and Preserver, was known to the Hindus in the early Magadhan period. It was believed that His grace which could be secured by the devotion (*bhakti*) of the worshipper, could change the effects of one's deeds (*karma*) which were otherwise inexorable.

Isvaradeva—is a name given by Hiuen Tsang (*q.v.*) to the image of Siva which, along with those of Buddha and the Sun, Emperor Harsha worshipped at the quinquennial festival held at Prayag (Allahabad) in A.D. 643 and which Hiuen Tsang personally attended.

Isvarasena—was the Abhira king who, towards the close of the second century A.D., overthrew the rule of the Satavahanas in North Western Maharashtra. The Traikutaka era dating from A.D. 248 has been attributed to the dynasty founded by him. (*P.H.A.I.*, pp. 498-99)

Isvaravarman—the third king of the Maukhari dynasty of Kanauj, ruled in the second quarter of the sixth century A.D., bore the title of Maharaja and probably married a Gupta princess, named Upaguptá. His son and successor was the more famous Isanavarman (*q.v.*). (*P.H.A.I.*, p. 604)

I'timad-ud-daula—was a title bestowed by Emperor Jahangir soon after his accession on Mirja Ghiyas Beg, a Persian gentleman who had come to the court of Akbar and served him well. He was the father of the famous Nur Jahan, whom Emperor Jahangir married in A.D. 1611. He and his son, Asaf Khan, held high offices under Jahangir. He died in 1622 and over his grave in Agra his loving daughter, the Empress Nur Jahan, built a magnificent tomb of white marble. It also is known as I'timad-ud-daula. "There is no other building like it in the entire range of Mughul architecture, the delicacy of treatment and the chaste quality of its decoration placing it in a class by itself." (Fergusson)

I-tsing—a Chinese monk and pilgrim, visited India in A.D. 675 by the sea-route via Sumatra. He stayed at the University of Nalanda for the next ten years, studied under the greatest professors of the day and became a sound scholar in Sanskrit and Buddhist learning. In A.D. 691 he composed his famous work, *A Record of the Buddhist Religion as practised in India and the Malay Archipelago*, which contributes little to our knowledge of the political history of India but is invaluable for the history of Buddhism and Sanskrit literature.

Izid Baksh—was the son of Prince Murad, the fourth son of Shah Jahan. His life was spared by Aurangzeb who later on married him to his fifth daughter.

J

Jackson, Coverly—was the Chief Commissioner of Oudh on the eve of the outbreak of the Sepoy Mutiny in 1857. He was a man of imperious temper, lacking in tact and moderation. He disbanded the army of the dispossessed Nawab of Oudh and created great discontent among the soldiers who thus lost the means of their livelihood. He also started inquiries into the titles of the *taluqdars* of Oudh and thus filled that influential section of the people of Oudh with consternation and alarm. The disbanded soldiers and the alarmed *taluqdars* played an important role in the Sepoy Mutiny. Jackson was replaced by Henry Lawrence in 1854, too late to prevent the outbreak of the Mutiny in Oudh.

Jacob, John, (1812-58)—entered E. I. Company's Bombay Artillery in 1828. He took part in the First Afghan War (*q.v.*) and in the battle of Miami (*q.v.*) in 1843 in Sind where he was appointed Political Superintendent in 1847. He was an efficient administrator and enforced peace on the Sind frontier by his personality and military measures. He was also an acute observer and in 1853 he warned the Government of India of the danger of mutiny amongst the sepoys, but was rebuked by Lord Dalhousie as an alarmist. He died of brain fever in Sind in 1858 and is remembered by the town of Jacobabad named after him.

Jacobabad, the treaty of—was concluded between the British Indian Government and the Khan of Kalat in 1876. By this treaty Quetta was secured by the British Indian Government as a military base.

Jacquemont, Victor—was a French Botanist who visited the court of Ranjit Singh (*q.v.*) of the Panjab in about 1830 and put down his impressions about the 'lion of the Panjab' in his *Letters from India*. He was deeply impressed by the inquisitiveness of Ranjit whom he considered 'an extraordinary man—a Bonaparte in miniature'. His works contain important information on the flora of the Himalayan region as well as the social condition of India in those days.

Jafar Khan—*see* Murshid Kuli Khan.

Jagadishpur—in Bihar was made famous by the exploits of its Zamindar, Kunwar Singh (*q.v.*) during the Sepoy Mutiny.

Jagannath, the temple of—is at Puri in Orissa. It was built by the Orissan king, Anantavarman Choda Ganga (*c.* A.D. 1076-1148). It is a marvellous architectural monument which has survived the ravages of time through many centuries, is still visited by thousands of pious Hindu pilgrims from all over India and also attracts tourists from abroad.

Jagat Seth—a title meaning 'the banker of the world', was conferred on Fatehchand, nephew and adopted son of Manickchand, a very rich banker in Bengal, by the Emperor of Delhi in about 1723. The house of Jagat Seth had branches in the cities of Dacca and Patna and its headquarters in Murshidabad. References to the wealth of this family are numerous in contemporary political writings and speeches of English statesmen like Clive and Burke who declared that the transactions of the house of Jagat Seth were "similar to those of the Bank of England". Indeed not only were its financial transactions extensive but it also performed for the Government of Bengal many of the functions which the Bank of England rendered to the British Government in the eighteenth century. It controlled the purchase of bullion in Bengal, helped in the establishment of a mint at Murshidabad, received on behalf of the provincial government the land-revenue paid by the Zamindars, remitted to Delhi the annual revenue payable to the Imperial treasury and regulated the rate of exchange on all moneys that came to Bengal by way of trade and commerce. The second Jagat Seth was Fatehchand's grandson, Mahatabchand, who succeeded to the title in 1744. He and his cousin and partner, Maharaja Swarupchand, enjoyed great influence during the reign of Nawab Alivardi Khan (*q.v.*), were insulted and alienated by Alivardi's successor, Nawab Siraj-ud-daula (*q.v.*), joined in a conspiracy against him with the English, helped them very materially with large funds before and after the battle of Plassey (*q.v.*), continued to enjoy power and prestige during the Nawabship of Mir Jafar (*q.v.*), but incurred the intense displeasure of Nawab Mir Kasim (*q.v.*) who justly suspected their loyalty to him and were killed by his order in 1763. This disaster followed by the transfer of the administration of Bengal from the hands of the Nawab to those of the English, who knew not Joseph, and who most unscrupulously disowned large parts of the debts which the E. I. Company owed to the Seths, led to the rapid decline and fall of the house early in the nineteenth century, though the proud title of Jagat Seth continued to be borne by six generations of the successors of Mahatabchand. The later Jagat Seths were, however, no better than petty pensioners of the British Indian Government. The last of them bearing the famous name of Jagat Seth Fatehchand inherited the title in 1912. With his death the title ceased to be renewed. (Bhattacharya, S., *The East India Company and the Economy of Bengal*; Kanishka, *Jagat Sether Kahini*)

Jagat Seth Fatehchand—was the nephew and adopted son of Manikchand, the founder of the banking house of Jagat Seth. The title of Jagat Seth was conferred on him by the Mughul Emperor Muhammad Shah in 1723-24. It was during his time that the house of Jagat Seth reached the zenith of prestige and wealth. Fatehchand Jagat Seth was the head of the family from 1714 to 1744 and wielded great influence over Nawab Murshid Kuli Khan and after his death over Nawab Alivardi Khan (1740-56).

Jagat Singh, Rana of Mewar—was the grandson of Rana Pratap of Mewar and the son of Rana Amar Singh. He was a contemporary of Emperor Jahangir during whose reign he reconstructed the fortifications of Chitor. He refused to obey the orders of Emperor Shah Jahan (1628-58) and had the mortification of seeing the demolition in 1654 of the reconstructed fort by the orders of Shah Jahan.

Jagat Singh—was the son of Man Singh of Amber who held many high offices under Emperor Akbar. He was his father's deputy when the latter was the Governor of Bengal, but he died in October, 1599.

Jagir **system, the**—was introduced in India by the early sultans of Delhi. According to this system an officer was paid not in cash but with the right of administering and collecting the revenue of a landed property called a *jagir*. It was feudalistic in character and tended to weaken the central government. It was, therefore, checked by Sultan Ghiyas-ud-din Balban (*q.v.*), abolished by Sultan Ala-ud-din Khalji (*q.v.*), but was reintroduced by Sultan Firuz Shah Tughluq (*q.v.*) and continued in later times. Sher Shah and Akbar were both opposed to it and wanted its abolition and substitution by a system of payment to officers in cash. But the system was revived under the later Mughul Emperors and contributed much to their weakness and decline.

Jahan Khan—an able Afghan general, was appointed by Ahmad Shah Abdali (*q.v.*) as the wazir of his son, Timur Shah, who was left as Abdali's viceroy at Lahore in 1757. He could not restore peace and order in the Panjab and Timur's viceroyalty was overthrown by the Maratha occupation of the Panjab in 1758.

Jahan Shah—the fourth son of Emperor Bahadur Shah I (1707-12), took part and was defeated and killed in the succession war that followed his father's death in 1712.

Jahanara, Begum—the elder of the two daughters of Emperor

Shah Jahan, was a very cultured and spirited lady. In 1644 she accidentally received severe burns and was cured, not by Dr. Boughton as is generally held, but with a medicine prepared by a slave named Arif. In the succession war amongst her brothers she supported Dara (*q.v.*) and after the succession of Aurangzeb (*q.v.*) she voluntarily devoted herself to the service of her imprisoned father. She died a spinster and was buried in a simple grave within the grounds of the mosque of Nizamuddin Auliya. She was a poet and herself composed the Persian couplet that is inscribed on her tomb.

Jahandar Shah—the eldest son of Emperor Bahadur Shah (*q.v.*), whom he succeeded in 1712. But his rule was very short (1712-13). He was defeated and killed by his nephew Farruksiyar (*q.v.*) in 1713.

Jahangir, Emperor—the eldest son of Emperor Akbar (*q.v.*) whom he succeeded on his death in 1605. He ruled till his death in 1627. As a prince his name was Salim and was in rebellion against his imperial father from 1601 to 1604, but was pardoned. He was born in 1569 of a Rajput mother and began his rule with a promise to uphold Muhammadanism. He had, however, imbibed some of his father's liberalism and spirit of toleration and maintained his system of government. At the very outset of his reign he was confronted with the rebellion of his eldest son, Khusru, who had been fancied for the throne towards the close of Akbar's reign. Jahangir showed great energy, pursued the rebellious Prince to the Panjab where the Prince was defeated, captured and brought back to the capital and kept in prison where he died in 1622. Emperor Jahangir was not much of a general, yet he added to the vast empire that he had inherited from his father Ahmadnagar in 1616 and Kangra in 1620. He also completely reduced to submission in 1612 the Afghans who under Usman Khan had maintained independence in Bengal and received in 1614 the submission of Rana Amar Singh of Mewar. But he lost Qandahar (*q.v.*) to the Shah of Persia in 1622. He received at his court Captain Hawkins (*q.v.*) in 1608-11 and Sir Thomas Roe (*q.v.*) in 1615-18. He like his father failed to appreciate the growing need of a strong navy for the Mughul Empire and depended in his quarrels with the Portuguese on the naval assistance of their European rivals who were crowding into India seeking commercial facilities. The most significant event of his reign was his marriage with Nur Jahan (*q.v.*), the widowed wife of Sher Afghan (*q.v.*) in 1611 after

which the administration gradually fell more and more under
her control, and her name was even minted on the coins. His
third son, Prince Khurram (Shah Jahan) revolted against
him in 1622 but was reduced to submission with the aid of
his general, Mahabat Khan (*q.v.*) in 1625. But next year
Mahabat Khan himself revolted and succeeded for a time in
seizing Jahangir himself. But soon afterwards the Emperor was
released by the skill and stratagem of Empress Nur Jahan and
Mahabat Khan was obliged to submit. His second son, Parviz,
died in 1626 and a year later Emperor Jahangir himself died.
Emperor Jahangir was a connoisseur of the arts of drawing and
painting and extended his patronage to Abul Hasan and
Mansur, the two great Muhammadan artists of his time. He
had a strong sense of justice and his anxiety for dispensing
the same was shown immediately after his accession by hanging
before the gate of his palace in the capital a bell which could
be rung by any seeker of justice at any time. His religion is not
easy to define. Certainly he was a Muhammadan in public
profession but for long years he kept on such intimate terms
with the Christian priests as led them to hope to be able to
convert him to Christianity. But he disappointed them. He,
however, did not deviate from his father's policy of toleration.
(Beni Prasad, *Hist. of Jahangir*)

Jahansuz, the—meaning 'world-burner' was an epithet that was
applied to Ala-ud-din Husain of Ghur who in A.D. 1151 sacked
the city of Ghazni and gave it up to the flames for seven days
and nights burning everything in the city excepting the tomb
of Sultan Mahmud (*q.v.*).

Jahaz Mahall—or 'Ship Palace' was an edifice of remarkable
architectural beauty built at Mandu, the capital of the Khalji
kings of Malwa. Standing between two lakes with its fine arched
halls, its roof-pavilions and boldly designed reservoirs it is
one of the most conspicuous landmarks in Mandu. Very likely
it was built by Sultan Mahmud Khalji (1436-69) (*q.v.*).

Jahazpur, the fort of—guarding the pass from Mewar to Bundi,
is ascribed to Samprati, a grandson of Asoka, (*q.v.*) who,
according to a tradition, succeeded to the western part of his
grandfather's dominions.

Jai Chand (or Jaychandra)—was the king of Kanauj and
Benares in the closing years of the twelfth century. He was a
contemporary and rival of Prithviraj, the king of Ajmer and
Delhi. According to the *Chand Raisa* (*q.v.*) his daughter Sanjukta
was taken away by Prithviraj and Jai Chand in his anger and

vindictiveness helped Shihab-ud-din Muhammad Ghuri (*q.v.*) in his war with Prithviraj who was defeated and killed by Ghuri in the second battle of Tarain in 1192. But next year his own kingdom was invaded by the Muhammadans under Ghuri and his lieutenant Qutb-ud-din who defeated and killed King Jai Chand at the battle of Chandwar, now Firuzabad, on the Jumna between Agra and Etawah. With his death his dynasty ended and Kanauj passed under Muhammadan rule.

Jaidev—was an eminent poet who was a contemporary of Laksmana Sena, king of Bengal (*c.* A.D. 1180-1202). He was the author of the famous lyric *Gita Govinda* which continues to enjoy great popularity even now.

Jaimall—was a valiant Rajput hero of Mewar. He was left in charge of the fort of Chitor when the reigning Rana Udai Singh left it to its fate before the besieging army of Emperor Akbar. Jaimall heroically defended the fort for four months (20 October, 1567 to 23 February, 1568). On the last date Jaimall was killed by a musket-shot fired by Emperor Akbar himself. The death of Jaimall was soon followed by the fall of Chitor.

Jai Singh—the Maharana of Mewar (1680-98) succeeded his father, Raj Singh. He confronted the army of Emperor Aurangzeb and made peace with him towards the end of 1681 by the terms of which he ceded to the Mughul Emperor three parganas in lieu of the *jizya* (*q.v.*) and secured the withdrawal from Mewar of the invading Mughul army.

Jai Singh—the chief of Amber (Jaipur), played a prominent part late in the reign of Shah Jahan and early in the reign of Aurangzeb. When Shah Jahan fell ill and a war of succession broke out amongst his sons, Jai Singh was sent against Prince Shuja whom he defeated and pursued to the borders of Bengal. He was later on sent against Prince Dara after the latter's defeat at the battle of Deorai (*q.v.*) and pursued him all the way to Sind. He was next employed by Aurangzeb in the Deccan where he carried on from 1665 to 1666 a campaign against Bijapur which he failed to capture, but he was more successful against Shivaji (*q.v.*) whom he pressed so hard and whose capital Purandhar he so threatened that Shivaji was obliged to conclude with him in 1665 the treaty of Purandhar by which he made peace with the Mughul Emperor, ceding to him 23 forts and agreed to acknowledge the suzerainty of the Emperor. He also persuaded Shivaji to go to Agra to visit the Mughul court in 1666. But his failure to capture Bijapur displeased Aurangzeb and he was recalled. He died on his way back to Delhi in 1667.

Jai Singh Sawai—Raja of Amber, was a valiant warrior and astute diplomat. He made his mark during the troubled times that followed the death of Emperor Aurangzeb. He revolted against Bahadur Shah I, but was pardoned. He became the Mughul viceroy in Malwa and later on in Agra itself. He maintained friendly relations with Peshwa Baji Rao I (*q.v.*) and was attracted by his principle of *Hindu Pád Pádshahi* (*q.v.*), i.e. re-establishment of Hindu independence on the ruins of the Mughuls. But he died in 1743 after ruling over Amber for 44 years.

Jainism—is a religion founded in the sixth century B.C. by Vardhamana Mahavira (*q.v.*) on the basis of principles taught by Parsvanath who had flourished earlier. Parsvanath and Mahavira were both born in princely families, both renounced the world and became stern ascetics. Mahavira attained the supreme knowledge (*kaivalya*) and became a *Jina* (conqueror of passions) and *Nirgrantha* (free from worldly bondage). Hence his followers are called *Jains* as well as *Nirgranthas*. Jainism accepts the Brahmanical doctrines of *Karma* (*q.v.*) and rebirth but rejects the authority of the Vedas, the caste system and the practice of animal sacrifice. It also denies the existence of God, the creator, and holds that God is 'the highest, the noblest and fullest manifestation of all the powers that lie latent in the soul of man'. The aim of a Jain is the attainment of salvation meaning complete deliverance of the soul from rebirth and reaching the pure and blissful abode which the Jains call *Siddha Sila*. This can be attained only through what is called *Tri-ratna* or Three Jewels, viz. right faith, right knowledge, and right conduct. The pursuit of the Three Jewels can be effective by following the principles of non-injury (*ahimsa*), truthfulness, non-stealing, non-attachment and chastity. Jainism carries the principle of non-injury (*ahimsa*) much further than Buddhism, believing that everything, animate as well as inanimate, is imbued with *jiva* (or soul) and is capable of feeling pain. The Jain, therefore, would abstain from hurting anything in any way. Jainism recommends strict and austere asceticism as a necessary means for attaining salvation and in its insistence on renunciation it would even support nudism. But on this point the Jains differ, some of them insisting on the need for wearing clothes which are to be all white. Thus the Jains came to be divided into two sects namely, the *Digambaras* who would go naked and the *Svetambaras* who would wear white clothes. Jains employ Brahmins as priests and, though they do not believe in God, the creator, they worship some of the Hindu gods. In their temples images of the Jina Mahavira as well as of the earlier *Tirthankaras* (path-finders) are installed and worshipped. The Jains consider themselves as Hindus, differing from them only in certain philosophical and theological principles. Jainism gave the laity a prominent place; it never organised a *Sangha* or brotherhood of monks and never spread outside the boundaries of India, the southern and western parts of which were formerly strongholds of Jainism. It also developed a large canonical literature consisting of fourteen *Purvas* written originally in the popular language known as Ardha Magadhi and containing the teachings of Mahavira, twelve *Angas* and sundry *Upanga*, *Mula Sutra* etc. They have also a vast non-canonical literature comprising epics, novels, dramas, philosophy, logic, grammar, lexicography, poetics, mathematics, astronomy, astrology, political science and education. By the variety and depth of their literary contribution the Jains added much to the development of Indian thought and culture. (Stevenson, Mrs Sinclair, *The Heart of Jainism*)

Jaintia, the kingdom of—comprised the Jaintia hills tract now in Assam and the plain country lying between these hills and the Barak river. The inhabitants belong to the same type as the Khasis (*q.v.*) and speak the same language. They were a matriarchal people amongst whom property descends through the female. A line of Hindu kings bearing Sanskritic names came to be established in Jaintia in about A.D. 1500 by Parbat Ray and had its capital at Jaintiapur which is believed to have been one of the places in which a sacred limb of Sati, Shiva's consort, fell and is therefore regarded as a sacred place. Between A.D. 1548 and 1564 Jaintia was conquered by Nara Narayan, the king of Cooch Behar. Later on early in the seventeenth century the Jaintia king Dhan Manik was defeated and deposed by the Kachari Raja. Dhan Manik's son and successor Jasa Manik (*c.* 1605-25) recovered his independence by securing the alliance of the Ahom king Pratap Singh (A.D. 1603-41) to whom he gave his daughter in marriage. Laksmi Narayan (1669-97), the sixth king after Jasa Manik, built a palace at Jaintiapur, the ruins of which still exist. His successor Ram Singh (1697-1708) became involved in a war with the Ahom king Rudra Singh (1696-1714) and lost his life in 1708, but the kingdom preserved its independence which, however, it lost in 1824 when the Burmese invaded and conquered Assam. Two years later the British drove away the Burmese and restored Jaintia to King Ram Singh who had been dispossessed by the Burmese. Ram Singh's nephew and successor, Rajendra Singh, gave great offence to the British Indian Government by his persistent refusal to hand over to the latter his subjects who had seized and immolated four British subjects and was therefore deposed in 1835 and Jaintia was annexed to the British Indian Empire. (Gait, Sir Edward, *Hist. of Assam*)

Jaipal (also spelt Jayapala)—was a king of the Hindu Shahiya dynasty of Waihand (Udabhandapur) whose dominions extended from Kangra in Uttar Pradesh to Laghman in Afghanistan. His contemporary on the throne of Ghazni was Amir Sabuktigin (A.D. 977-97). Hearing that Sabuktigin was making encroachments on his dominions in Afghanistan he determined to stop his depredations and advanced up to Ghuzuk lying between Ghazni and Laghman, but a snow-storm suddenly burst out and Jaipal was obliged to make a humiliating peace. He, however, soon broke its terms and war again broke out with Sabuktigin who died in A.D. 997. His son and successor Sultan Mahmud renewed the war and Jaipal received in A.D. 1001 a crushing defeat at his hands near Peshawar. He was too proud and patriotic to live and reign after this defeat. So he burnt himself on a funeral pyre, hoping that his son and successor Anandapal would be able to defend the country with greater success. Jaipal was the only Hindu king who tried to take the aggressive against the Muhammadan invaders who threatened the country from the north-west, and who by his immolation set an example of self-sacrifice worthy of emulation.

Jaipur—is the name of a city and a former princely state in Rajputana. The city was founded in 1728 by Maharaja Jai Singh II and is now the capital of the Union of Rajasthan. It is a well laid out beautiful city with regular main roads which divide it into six rectangular blocks and with coloured buildings. The state was founded in about A.D. 1128 by Dulha Rai, a Kachwaha Rajput, who came from Gwalior. In the sixteenth century its ruler, Raja Bihari Mall, voluntarily submitted to Emperor Akbar to whom he gave his daughter in marriage. She became the mother of Jahangir. Amongst the descendants of Bihari Mall, Raja Man Singh (*q.v.*) in the reign of Akbar and Mirza Raja Jai Singh II in the reign of Aurangzeb, won particular fame as generals. Jai Singh II was also a famous mathematician and astronomer who built observatories at Delhi and Jaipur. Towards the close of the eighteenth century the state was in great confusion on account of rivalry with Jodhpur (*q.v.*) and the depredations of the Pindaris (*q.v.*) under Amir Khan (*q.v.*). In these circumstances the state of Jaipur secured British protection by the treaty of Jaipur (*q.v.*) on condition of paying a fixed annual tribute. The state merged in the Union of Rajasthan on 30 March, 1949 and the ruling Prince, Maharaja Sawai Man Singh, was chosen as Rajpramukh of the Union.

Jaipur, the treaty of—was made between the state of Jaipur and the British Indian Government in 1817 during the Governor-Generalship of Lord Hastings. By this treaty the state of Jaipur accepted British protection.

Jaitpur—was a small Indian princely state that was annexed to the Indo-British Empire by Lord Dalhousie (*q.v.*) by the application of the doctrine of lapse in 1850.

Jajau, the battle of—was fought in 1707 between Prince Muazzam (afterwards Emperor Bahadur Shah I) and his younger brother, Prince Azam. The latter was defeated and killed and thus the way for the accession of his elder brother was paved.

Jajnagar—was the name by which Orissa was indicated by the Muhammadans.

Jalal Khan Lodi—a brother of Sultan Ibrahim Lodi (1517-26), was installed as the ruler of Jaunpur in 1517. But this partition of the empire was not acceptable to many and Jalal Khan soon rose in rebellion against Delhi. Pursued by the armies sent against him by the Sultan, Jalal fled for shelter to Gwalior where he was given protection by the Rajput king, Vikramajit. This roused the hostility of Sultan Ibrahim who invaded Gwalior and compelled the Raja to surrender. Jalal Khan was killed in action.

Jalal Khan Lohani—was the Afghan ruler in Bihar in whose service Sher Shah entered in 1527. But he was defeated at the battle of Surajgarh and ousted from his possessions by Sher Shah in about 1533.

Jalal Khan Sur—the son and successor of Sher Shah (*q.v.*) to the throne of Delhi, assumed on his accession the title of Sultan Islam Shah (*q.v.*). He ruled for nine years (1545-54).

Jalal-ud-din—was a title borne by Sultana Raziya (1236-40) (*q.v.*).

Jalal-ud-din Khalji—sultan of Delhi (1290-96), was the founder of the Khalji dynasty of the Delhi sultans. His original name was Firuz Shah Khalji who, on his installation as the Sultan by

488 Jalal-ud-din Mangbarni

the Delhi nobles in 1290 after the murder of Sultan Qaiqabad (*q.v.*), assumed the title of Jalal-ud-din. He was an old man of seventy years of age at his accession and was too mild to act boldly. He had one achievement to his credit: he repulsed a large Mongol invasion in 1292. But he created a new problem by allowing a large number of the Mongol fugitives to embrace Islam and settle in the neighbourhood of Delhi. The old Sultan had two sons but his nephew and son-in-law, Ala-ud-din (*q.v.*), was his favourite and it was this favourite who treacherously murdered him in 1296, ascended the throne and became his successor.

Jalal-ud-din Mangbarni—the sultan of Khiva, fled before the invading host of Chengiz Khan (*q.v.*) and sought shelter at the court of Delhi in 1221. The reigning sultan, Iltutmish, turned down his request and Mangbarni retired to Persia after plundering Sind and northern Gujarat on his way.

Jalal-ud-din Rumi—was a Persian mystic and poet whose ideas greatly influenced Emperor Akbar and his prominent courtier Abul-Fazl, the historian (*q.v.*).

Jalandhar—is a doab lying between the Bias and the Sutlej in the Panjab. It was included within the kingdom of Maharaja Ranjit Singh but was surrendered and annexed to the British Indian dominion by the treaty of Lahore (9 March, 1846) which concluded the first Anglo-Sikh war.

Jalauka—was, according to the *Chronicles of Kashmir* (*q.v.*), the son of Asoka (*q.v.*), and succeeded him in the sovereignty of Kashmir. He is also said to have been, along with his consort Isanadevi, a worshipper of Siva and not a Buddhist like his great imperial father. He is also credited with the expulsion of a number of foreigners (*mlechchas*) from Kashmir. He is not mentioned in any inscription of his father nor has he himself left any behind him. Belief in his existence and activities as recorded in the *Chronicles of Kashmir* would show how shallow was the hold of Buddhism on Asoka's own family.

Jama Masjid (also spelt Jami Masjid)—means the great place for congregational prayers by the Muhammadans. The construction of such a big mosque was a special feature of Mughul architecture and there are Jama Masjids at Sambhal built by Emperor Babur in 1526, at Fathpur-Sikri by Emperor Akbar, at Delhi by Emperor Shah Jahan who built a second Jama Masjid at Agra, at Bijapur built in 1565 by Sultan Ali Adil Shah I (*q.v.*) and at Burhanpur in 1588 by King Ali Khan of the Faruqi dynasty of Khandesh. The Jama Masjid at Delhi is the largest and most imposing of these edifices. It took fourteen years (1644-58) in building and was the central point of the Mughul metropolis.

James I—king of England (1603-25), sent Sir Thomas Roe as his ambassador to the court of Emperor Jahangir (*q.v.*) in 1615. James I was thus the first king of England to establish direct contact with India.

Jamrud, the battle of—was fought between Maharaja Ranjit Singh (*q.v.*) of the Panjab and Dost Muhammad (*q.v.*), Amir of Afghanistan, in 1803. The Amir was defeated and forced to surrender Peshawar to Ranjit Singh.

Jamshedpur—is the 'steel-town' of India. It is named after Sir Jamshedji Tata, who formed the idea of founding a steel plant in Bihar at the site now occupied by Jamshedpur and Tatanagar. It has the largest single steel works in the world, producing about a million tons annually.

Jamshed—a famous Persian artist, enjoyed the patronage of Emperor Akbar (*q.v.*).

Jamshid—the second sultan of the Qutb Shahi dynasty (*q.v.*) of Golconda, got his father Quli Qutb Shah, the founder of the dynasty, murdered in 1543 and reigned till his death in 1550.

Jamshid—the son and successor of Shah Mirza (*q.v.*) who founded a Muhammadan dynasty of kings in Kashmir in about 1340, ruled for about ten years. Little is known about his activities.

Jaoli (also spelt Javli)—was a small principality in Maharashtra in the middle of the seventeenth century. Its chief, Chandra Rao, refused to join Shivaji in his efforts at attaining independence and was done to death by an agent of Shivaji. The principality was brought under Shivaji's control in 1655.

Jaswant Rao Holkar—son and the successor of Tukoji Rao Holkar, was the ruler of the Holkar's state from 1798 to 1811. (*see* under Holkar.)

Jaswant Singh—the Raja of Marwar with his capital at Jodhpur, was in the service of Emperor Shah Jahan and held high commands. When Shah Jahan fell ill and a succession war broke out amongst his sons Jaswant Singh who was then in the capital, was sent against Aurangzeb in order to prevent him from passing from the Deccan into North India. But Jaswant was defeated at the battle of Dharmat (*q.v.*) near Ujjain in 1658. Later on he continued under the service of Emperor Aurangzeb (*q.v.*) and after the death of Raja Jai Singh (*q.v.*) he became the premier Rajput prince in the Mughul service. He was then sent, along with Prince Muazzam, (*q.v.*) to fight against Shivaji (*q.v.*) but failed to attain any success. He was, therefore, sent as the commandant of Jamrud at the mouth of the Khyber Pass where he died in 1678. His death was considered a good riddance by Emperor Aurangzeb who schemed to confiscate his territories and convert his posthumous son, Ajit Singh, to Islam. This plan failed and led to a prolonged war with the Rajputs which adversely affected the Mughul Empire.

Jatakas, the—are the birth-stories of the Buddha in previous existences. They form a vast literature, written in Pali, and afford an interesting account of the social and political condition of India about the times of Gautama Buddha. At any rate they were composed before the third century B.C., as the bas reliefs in the stupas of Barhut and Sanchi which have been assigned to that period, illustrate many of the *Jataka* stories. The name of the composer or composers is not known, but the stories profoundly influenced Buddhist religion, literature and art. (Rhys Davids, *Buddhist India*, Ch. XI)

Jats, the—are a sturdy people inhabiting the region round Agra and Mathura. Some ethnologists attribute to them a foreign origin like that of the Rajputs. Unlike the Rajputs, however, they formed no state before the eighteenth century. But they were a freedom-loving people who deeply resented the anti-Hindu policy of Aurangzeb (*q.v.*), rose in revolt against it in 1681, plundered the tomb of Akbar, dragging out from the grave his bones which they burnt and put the Mughul administration to no small trouble. They found later on a leader in Churaman Singh who built a fort at Thun and dreamt of attaining independence, but he was reduced to submission in 1721. Churaman's nephew, Badan Singh, achieved before his death in 1756 the seemingly impossible task of uniting the scattered Jat people and gave them a state which under his successor, Suraj Mal, came to be known as Bharatpur comprising the districts of Agra, Dholpur, Mainpuri, Hathras, Aligarh, Etawah, Meerut, Rohtak, Furruknagar, Mewat, Rewari, Gurgaon and Muthra. Indeed the Jats under Suraj Mal (1756-63) came to be so powerful that their assistance was eagerly sought by the Marathas in their struggle with Ahmad Shah Abdali. The Jats, however, were offended by the vanity of the Maratha leader Sadasiva Rao Bhao (*q.v.*) and abstained from taking any part in the third battle of Panipat (*q.v.*). But danger came from the east. The expanding British Indian Government during the administration of Lord Wellesley (*q.v.*) attempted to capture the fort of Bharatpur but failed (1805). The respite, however, proved short. In 1826 the fort was easily captured by the British and the Jats ceased to be an independent people.

Jaunpur—is the name of a town as well as of a kingdom in modern Uttar Pradesh. The city was founded by Sultan Firuz Shah Tughluq (*q.v.*) and named in honour of his predecessor Muhammad Tughluq (*q.v.*), also called Jauna Khan. On the eve of Timur's invasion it was being governed by Khwaja Jahan who had rendered valuable services to the Delhi sultanate. During the confusion caused by Timur's invasion Khwaja Jahan set himself up as an independent ruler and established the Sharqi dynasty (*q.v.*) of Jaunpur which maintained its independence for eighty-five years at the end of which it was overthrown by Sultan Bahlul Lodi (*q.v.*). Under the Sharqi dynasty Jaunpur developed into a great centre of art and culture. It also developed a special type of architecture to the grandeur of which the *Atala Masjid*, completed by the third sultan, Ibrahim, in A.D. 1408, still bears eloquent testimony.

Java—an island in the Malay Archipelago, had contact with India from very ancient times. It is mentioned in the *Ramayana* as Java-dvipa. In historical times Hindu colonists from India settled in the island which formed a part of the Sailendra empire (8th to the 11th centuries) on the decline and fall of which another Hindu state was founded with Majapahit as its capital. Java abounds in many Hindu and Buddhist monuments, the most imposing of which is the *Barabudur* (*q.v.*). The Hindu rule in Majapahit was overthrown in the fifteenth century as the result of the conversion of the reigning dynasty to Islam followed by Muslim occupation of the island. Connection of Java with India thus closed for a time. It was revived in the seventeenth century as the result of the coming of the European trading companies of which the East India Company tried to have commerce with India as well as Java. But the English were gradually excluded by the Dutch from Java, especially after the massacre of Amboyna in 1623 and its connection with India again ceased. But in 1811, during the height of the Napoleonic Wars, Lord Minto, Governor-General of India, led an expedition against the Dutch in Java and conquered the island. It was, however, restored to the Dutch by the Congress of Vienna in 1815 and continued to be under Dutch rule till recent times, when, after the Second World War, the Dutch had to withdraw and Java along with the neighbouring islands formed into the independent state of Indonesia with the moral and political support of the independent Republic of India.

Javid Khan—a eunuch, became the leader of the court party in Delhi in the reign of Emperor Ahmad Shah (1748-54), but was assassinated at the instigation of the Wazir, Safdar Jang (*q.v.*) whose authority and power he had threatened.

Jay Singh—*see* Jai Singh.

Jay Singh Suri—a Sanskrit dramatist, flourished early in the thirteenth century and wrote a drama called *Hammir-mada-mardana* some time between A.D. 1219 and 1229.

Jaya-Sthitamalla—a relation of the kings of Tirhut, married a daughter of the king of Nepal, seized the throne of Nepal in 1376 and brought the whole country under his rule. He founded a new line of kings who ruled over undivided Nepal till 1476.

Jayachandra—*see* Jai Chand.

Jayadeva—*see* Jaidev.

Jayadvaja Singh—was the Ahom king (1648-63) of Kamarupa (Assam) during whose reign the Mughul general, Mir Jumla, (*q.v.*) led an expedition into Assam. All the efforts of Jayadvaja Singh to repulse him failed; he left his capital, retired to Namrup and had the mortification of seeing his capital occupied by Mir Jumla in 1662 and to purchase peace by making a treaty with the invader in January, 1663 by which he agreed to pay a heavy indemnity and to cede Lower Assam to the Mughul Emperor. Jayadvaja Singh then returned to his capital only to die there a few months later in November, 1663.

Jayaji Rao Sindhia—(1843-86)—became the head of the Sindhia family when he was a minor. Intrigues followed over the appointment of a Regent during his minority and these led the Government of Lord Ellenborough (*q.v.*) to send an expedition against the State. Sindhia's army was defeated at the battles of Maharajpur and Paniar and Sindhia was reduced to the status of a protected prince. Jayaji Rao remained loyal to the British during the Mutiny, though his army sided with the mutineers. Jayaji was later on rewarded with the restoration of Gwalior which the British had captured in 1858 from his mutinous army. (*see* under Gwalior.)

Jayapida Vinayaditya—was a grandson of Lalitaditya, the famous king of Kashmir (A.D. 724-760) whom he succeeded. He defeated the kings of Gauda and Kanauj. He was also a patron of learning and men of learning like Kshirasvamin (*q.v.*) enjoyed his patronage.

Jayarudra Malla—the king of Nepal, was reduced to submission in A.D. 1342 by Harisimha of Tirhut. He and his descendants continued to rule over the regions of Patan and Kathmandu till the middle of the fifteenth century.

Jayastambha, Rana Kumbha's—also called *Krittistambha* (Tower of Fame), was raised in about the middle of the fifteenth century at Chitor by Rana Kumbha (A.D. 1431-69) in celebration of his victory against the Muhammadan ruler either of Malwa or of Gujarat.

Jejakabhukti—lay between the Jumna and the Narmada rivers. It is now known as Bundelkhand. It was ruled over by the Chandellas (*q.v.*). It is now included partly in Uttar Pradesh and partly in Madhya Pradesh. Its chief towns, Mahoba, Kalanjar and Khajuraho contain many magnificent temples and lovely lakes which were formed by the construction of massive dams across the openings between the hills.

Jenkins, Sir Richard (1785-1853)—joined the East India Company's Civil Service in 1800 and was transferred to the Political Department in 1804. He was the British Resident at Nagpur from 1810 to 1827. After the deposition of Appa Shaheb (*q.v.*) in 1818 he was also placed in charge of the administration of the Nagpur state during the minority of the next ruler. He retired from the E. I. Company's service in 1828 and was a Member of Parliament from 1837-1841. In 1839 he also became the Chairman of the E. I. Company's Court of Directors.

Jesuits—or members of the Society of Jesus, first came to India and to the Portuguese settlement in Goa in 1542. The first Jesuit priests to visit Emperor Akbar were Father Rodolfo Aquaviva and Father Antonio Monserrate (*q.v.*) who met the Emperor at Fathpur-Sikri in 1580. A second Jesuit mission came to the Emperor's court in 1590 and a third in 1595. The Jesuit missionaries were listened to and treated with such courtesy by the Emperor that they at one time hoped to be able to convert the Emperor to Christianity. They also acted as unofficial agents of the Portuguese Company trading in India for whom they tried to secure political and commercial advantages. But all their efforts failed and Akbar did not embrace Christianity. Jesuit missionaries were also active in Jahangir's court who allowed them to have a church of their own and a residence for the priests at Lahore and also to make converts amongst the Indian subjects of the Emperor. But Jahangir also disappointed the Jesuit hope that he would embrace Christianity and political considerations led him later in his reign to declare a war against the Portuguese and as a consequence to close the Jesuit Church and to forbid them to make converts. The Jesuit missionaries who lost all political influence after the reign of Jahangir continued, however, their evangelical work in India, made many converts and established educational institutions like the St. Xavier's College in Calcutta.

Jhansi—a state in Bundelkhand, was a dependency of the Peshwa Baji Rao II on whose defeat in the Third Maratha War (*q.v.*) it passed in 1819 under the protection of the British Indian Government. In 1853 during the administration of Lord Dalhousie the doctrine of lapse was applied to the state which was annexed to the British Indian Empire. This was very much resented by the dowager Rani Laksmi Bai (*q.v.*) and led her to join the mutineers in 1858.

Jijhoti—is another name for Jejakabhukti (*q.v.*).

Jhelum, the—is one of the five important rivers of the Panjab. The Greeks called it the Hydaspes to the east of which lay the kingdom of Puru (or Poros) (*q.v.*), the first Indian king to offer stout resistance to Alexander, the king of Macedon when he invaded India in 326 B.C.

Jhindan, Rani—the fifth wife of Maharaja Ranjit Singh (*q.v.*) of the Panjab and the mother of his youngest son, Dalip Singh, became the Regent on the accession of Dalip Singh in 1843 as he was a minor. She proved unequal to the task and suffered the First Sikh War (*q.v.*) to break out in 1845, but was left to continue as the Regent by the treaty of Lahore (*q.v.*) which concluded the war (1846). But her conduct soon roused the suspicion of the British Government which removed her in 1848 from Lahore on a charge of conspiracy. Her removal was one of the circumstances that led to the Second Sikh War (1849) in which also the Sikhs were defeated. At the end of the war Dalip Singh was deposed and sent to England along with Rani Jhindan who later on died in London.

Jihad—means 'holy war' which the Muhammadans fought against non-Muhammadans. It is even now at times a favourite war-cry of bellicose Muhammadan leaders.

Jija Bai (or Jiji Bai)—was the mother of Shivaji (*q.v.*), the creator of the Maratha kingdom. She was neglected by her husband and remained as the guardian of her son whose character, hopes and ideals she shaped to a very great extent, and her influence was a factor of prime importance in the making of Shivaji's career.

Jinji (also spelt Gingee)—A fort in the Karnatak, was conquered by Shivaji in 1677 and it was to this fort that Shivaji's younger son, Rajaram, who became the leader of the Maratha resistance after the defeat and execution of his elder brother, Shambhuji, in 1689 fled. It then became the centre of Maratha opposition to the Mughuls and defied Mughul arms for eight years (1690-98) at the end of which it was stormed by the Mughuls. Later on it passed under the control of the French who had to surrender it to the English soon after the fall of Pondicherry in 1761.

Jinnah, Mohammed Ali (1876-1948)—the maker of Pakistan, was an Indian Muhammadan born in Karachi, studied law and built up a good practice as a barrister in Bombay. He joined Indian politics as a follower of moderate Congress leaders like Dadabhai Naoroji (*q.v.*) and G. K. Gokhale (*q.v.*). He was elected to the Central Legislative Council from a Muhammadan constituency in Bombay in 1910. In 1913 he joined the Moslem League and in 1916 he became the President of the League. In this capacity he sponsored a joint Congress-League scheme of constitutional reforms, a part of which, known as the Lucknow Pact, provided for separate Moslem electorates and weighted representations for them in those provinces where they were in a minority. Jinnah, who had so long supported the Indian National Congress, strongly disapproved of Gandhi's non-co-operation movement and broke with the Indian National Congress on this issue. Henceforth Jinnah became obsessed with Hinduphobia, holding that if and when the British would transfer power they must not do it to the Hindus, though they formed the majority of the population, as such a transfer would only mean to the Indian Muhammadans subordination to the Hindus. Jinnah now stood more for Moslem rights than for the rights of the Indians to self-government. He generally got the tacit support of the British and was thus encouraged to stand out finally as the leader of the Muhammadan community in India. He reorganised the League, became known as the *Qaid-i-Azam* (the Great Leader) and in 1940 he demanded the partition of India on a religious basis and establishment of Pakistan consisting of the Moslem majority provinces. He, therefore, rejected the Cripps' offer (*q.v.*), Gandhi's advances in 1944 offering him a blank cheque and the Cabinet Mission plan in 1946. He was the person who was most instrumental in partitioning India and in creating Pakistan in 1947 of which he became the first Governor-General. He organised Pakistan into a Moslem State, witnessed the Panjab riots and mass migrations and created the Kashmir dispute between India and Pakistan. He died at Karachi on 11, September 1948. (Symonds, Richard., *The Making of Pakistan*)

Jivita Gupta I—one of the earlier of the later Gupta kings, was the son and successor of Harsha Gupta and flourished in the second quarter of the sixth century A.D. He ruled over the territory lying between the eastern Himalayas and the Bay of Bengal. Little else is known of him.

Jivita Gupta II—the last of the later Gupta kings, reigned in the sixties of the eighth century of the Christian era. The Deo-Barnak inscription records the grant of a piece of land during his reign. Nothing else is known about him.

Jiwan Khan—was the Afghan chief of Dadar near the Bolan pass with whom the fugitive Prince Dara, the eldest son of Shah Jahan, took shelter in 1659. Prince Dara had previously saved Jiwan Khan from a sentence of death passed on him by Shah Jahan. But Jiwan Khan proved ungrateful and handed over Dara with his two daughters and a son to Aurangzeb's general Bahadur Khan who brought them as captives to Delhi where Dara was soon afterwards executed.

Jizya—a poll-tax which was legally payable by the Jews and Christians, was levied on the Hindus also by the Muhammadan conquerors. It was first imposed by Muhammad bin Kasim who conquered Sind in A.D. 712. The conquered Hindus were required to pay this tax which was graded according to the wealth of the assessees. With the extension of the Muhammadan rule over India the *jizya* was imposed on the Hindus all over India. The Brahmans were originally exempted from the obligation to pay it and were first required to pay it during the sultanate of Firuz Shah Tughluq (1351-88) (*q.v.*). Emperor Abkar earned the good-will of the Hindus by abolishing it in 1564, but it was reimposed by Aurangzeb in 1679. This act of intolerance caused widespread discontent amongst the Hindus and led to a prolonged war between Aurangzeb and the Rajputs as the result of which its collection had to be dropped by Aurangzeb only so far as Mewar was concerned. It was, however, abolished by Emperor Farruksiyar on his accession in 1713 but was reimposed by him in 1717. Thereafter, its levy continued to be theoretically legal but in practice its collection was discontinued from the time of Emperor Muhammad Shah (1719-48). The total yield under this tax was substantial when the control of Delhi was effective, but in the days of the later Mughuls this must have considerably decreased. In any case it was an invidious tax and the obligation to pay it was always resented by the Hindus.

Jodhpur—is the name of a city and state in Rajputana. The state is popularly known as Marwar and its rich commercial community of businessmen are known as Marwaris. The city was founded in 1459 by Rao Jodha, who was a descendant of Raja Jai Chand (*q.v.*) of Kanauj. The state was founded much earlier by Rao Chand, the twelfth in succession from Jai Chand. In 1561 Jodhpur was forced to submit to Emperor Akbar and enter into matrimonial alliances with the Mughuls. On the death of Raja Jaswant Singh (*q.v.*) in 1678 Aurangzeb schemed the conversion of his infant son to Islam and the annexation of Jodhpur. This led to the conclusion of an alliance among Jodhpur, Jaipur and Udaipur with the object of throwing off the Mughul yoke, and culminated in the Rajput War which ended with the grant of certain concessions to the Rajput states by the Mughuls. But troubles arose later on from one of the conditions of the triple alliance which provided that the chiefs of Jaipur and Jodhpur should regain the privilege of marriage with the Udaipur Rana family, which they had forfeited for having contracted marriages with the Mughul emperors, on the understanding that the offsprings of Udaipur princesses married into the families of Jaipur and Jodhpur should succeed to the states of their husbands in preference to all other children by other wives. This stipulation led to many succession disputes throughout the succeeding generations, led rival aspirants to invite help from the Marathas culminating in the eventual subjection and sacking of the Rajput states by the Marathas. At last in 1818 Jodhpur secured peace and safety by accepting British protection. It remained loyal to the British during the Sepoy Mutiny and it was merged in the Union of Rajasthan on 30 March, 1949.

Jones, Sir Harford—was the leader of an embassy sent in 1809 from England to the court of the Shah of Persia to forestall the expansion of French and Russian influence over Persia. Sir Harford concluded a treaty by which Persia undertook to deny any European power a passage to India through Persia and to help British India, if attacked by a foreign power. Britain on her part undertook to help Persia in the event of an attack by a European power either with troops or with a subsidy and a loan of officers. It was hoped that this treaty would turn Persia into a sort of a buffer between the Franco-

Russian menace and India. But events soon showed that England and India were both too distant and too weak to render to Persia the degree of help that she needed for her protection against Russia and the treaty of 1809 proved ineffective.

Jones, Sir William (1746-94)—was a famous British Orientalist and jurist. Born of English parents in England and educated at Oxford he learnt Arabic, Persian, Hebrew and Chinese in addition to various European languages. As early as 1770 he translated into French a life of Nadir Shah written in Persian. He was called to the bar in 1774 and attracted notice by his works on certain aspects of the law in England. In 1783 he was appointed a judge at the Supreme Court in Calcutta and was knighted. Soon after his arrival in Bengal he founded in January, 1784, the Bengal Asiatic Society of which he remained the President till his death in Calcutta in 1794. As a judge of the Supreme Court he was soon convinced of the importance of consulting Hindu legal authorities in the original for the proper dispensation of justice amongst the Hindus. He, therefore, began to study Sanskrit and soon learnt it well enough to be able to translate into English Kalidasa's *Sakuntala* in 1789. He also translated into English the *Manusamhita* (*q.v.*) under the name of *Institutes of Hindu Law* which was published in 1794, the *Hitopodesha* (*q.v.*) and the *Gita Govinda* (*q.v.*). He also wrote a *Grammar of Persian Langauge* (1771), the *Muhammadan Law of Succession* and the *Muhammadan Law of Inheritance* (1782). There were many amongst the Englishmen in India who were good Persian scholars, but Sir William Jones was one of the earliest of the Anglo-Indians who learnt Sanskrit and rendered the language and literature of the ancient Hindus accessible to European scholars and thus practically started the study of Comparative Philology.

Jujhar Singh—was the son and successor of Raja Bir Singh Bundela (*q.v.*) who had murdered Abul Fazl at the instigation of Jahangir (then Prince Salim) in 1602 and had been richly rewarded by Jahangir on his accession in 1605. On the accession of Shah Jahan there was a talk of holding an enquiry into the acquisitions of his father and Jujhar Singh rose in revolt, but was forced to submit and to pay a heavy indemnity in money and lands. Jujhar Singh then entered into the imperial service and for several years served with distinction in the Deccan. He was rewarded with a high rank and the title of raja. These favours roused his ambition and he dared to attack and kill, despite Shah Jahan's orders to desist, the chief of the neighbouring state of Chauragarh. He was thereupon attacked by an imperial force which soon defeated him and pursued him into the neighbouring jungles where he was killed by the Gonds.

Juna Khan (also spelt Jauna Khan)—*see* Muhammad Tughluq.

K

Kabir—was a saint who preached to foster harmony between man and man, between Hinduism and Muhammadanism. The dates of his birth and death are uncertain, very probably he lived towards the close of the fourteenth and the beginning of the fifteenth centuries. He is believed to have been a disciple of the famous Vaishnava saint Ramananda, though he was a weaver brought up in a Muhammadan family. With Hinduism as the background of his thought and influenced greatly by Muhammadan Sufi saints and poets, Kabir preached a religion of love which would promote unity amongst all classes and creeds. To him "Hindu and Turk were pots of the same clay: Allah and Rama were but different names." Kabir did not believe in the efficacy of rituals or external formalities, common to Hinduism and Islam. He held that *Bhajan* or devotional worship together with abstention from all sham, insincerity, hypocrisy and cruelty would lead to God which was the same to the Hindus and the Muhammadans.

Kabul—is the name of a city as well as of the river on which the city stands. The city is the capital of modern Afghanistan and the river, known in ancient times as the Kophen, falls into the Indus. Kabul was a part of the Indian Empire during the reign of the Mauryas (*q.v.*) on whose decline and fall it passed under several Indo-Greek kings. It formed a part of the Indian Empire of the Kushans (*q.v.*) but later on India lost control over it until Babur, who was on the throne of Kabul, conquered Delhi in 1526. From that time onwards it remained a part of the Indian Empire until Nadir Shah (*q.v.*) conquered Afghanistan which on his death passed to Ahmad Shah Abdali (*q.v.*) and has since continued to be an independent state.

Kacha—is the name of a prince borne on some of the coins of the

Gupta period. He was probably identical with the second Gupta Emperor, Samudragupta (*q.v.*).

Kacharis, the—were a tribal people who are believed to have been the earliest known inhabitants of the Brahmaputra valley and gave their name to the modern district of Cachar in Assam. In the thirteenth century they ruled over a kingdom extending along the south bank of the Brahmaputra, comprising much of the modern district of Nowgong and some part of Cachar district. Their capital was at Dimapur on the Dhansiri river, forty-five miles south of the modern town of Golaghat. The Ahoms (*q.v.*) conquered their country in 1536 and the Kacharis deserted Dimapur which now lies in ruins. The vanquished Kacharis established a new kingdom with Maibong as their capital, but even then they had to be in frequent conflicts with the Ahom kings who claimed that their country was a 'protected state'. The last king, Gobinda Chandra, was defeated in 1818 by a chieftain of Manipur (*q.v.*) and in 1821 his kingdom was also overrun by the Burmese. On the expulsion of the Burmese in 1826 by the British Indian Government, Gobinda Chandra was restored to the throne, but he died at the hands of a Manipuri assassin in 1830. He had no descendants and the state was annexed to the British Indian Empire in 1832. (Gait, E., *Hist. of Assam*, p. 304)

Kadambas, the—were a clan or family which came into royal power in north and south Kanara and in western Mysore in the third century A.D. Their capital was Vanavasi or Vaijayanti. They were Brahmans by caste and came to be regarded as Kshatriyas on account of their occupation. Their first ruler Mayurasarman flourished in the fourth century. Very little is known of his successors who gradually declined into mere local chiefs and held subordinate positions. The Rayas of Vijayanagar might have had Kadamba connections.

Kadphises I—whose full name was Kujala-Kara-Kadphises, was the first king of the Kushan dynasty. He probably came to the throne in 40 A.D., ruled for about 37 years and extended his dominions beyond Bactria over Afghanistan and the north-western frontier region of India beyond the Indus.

Kadphises II—the son and successor of Kadphises I (*q.v.*), extended the Kushan dominions all over northern India, and is believed by many to have started the Saka era (*q.v.*) which dates from 78 A.D. in celebration of his accession in that year. Benares in the east and the Narmada in the south marked the extent of his Indian dominions which also included Malwa and western India where the Saka satraps (*q.v.*) recognised him as their overlord. In A.D. 87 he claimed equality with the Chinese Emperor by demanding a Chinese princess in marriage. When that demand was rejected Kadphises II sent a vast expedition into China across the Pamirs. But his army was defeated and Kadphises II had to make peace by agreeing to pay tribute to China. Kadphises II issued coins of various types in large numbers and this fact suggests that he had a long reign which probably came to an end in about A.D. 110.

Kafur—was originally a Hindu eunuch who was purchased as a slave for one thousand *dinars* and thus came to be called '*Hazardinari*'. He was brought to Sultan Ala-ud-din Khalji as one of the trophies from conquered Gujarat in 1297. He soon attracted the notice of the Sultan who conferred upon him high offices and made him in 1307 *Malik Naib* (lieutenant) of the kingdom. Kafur proved himself to be a very capable general and brought under the Sultan's rule the kingdoms of Devagiri, Warangal, Dorasamudra, Ma'bar and Madura and thus extended the Sultan's dominion to Rameswaram. All these successes raised his prestige and he became the most trusted official of Sultan Ala-ud-din Khalji and influenced all his actions. All this power and influence increased Kafur's ambition and on the death of Sultan Ala-ud-din Khalji in 1316 he set up one of his minor sons on the throne with all powers in his own hands. He even began to think of securing the throne for himself; he blinded the elder sons of the late Sultan, imprisoned the queen-mother and also sought to remove all nobles and slaves attached to the family of the late Sultan. The threatened persons combined and murdered him after he had ruled for barely thirty-five days.

Kailash, the temple of—is at Ellora in Andhra state. This rock-cut temple was constructed by the Rashtrakuta king Krishna I (acc. *c.* A.D. 760). It is one of the most marvellous works of architecture in the world. The whole temple is hewn out of the side of a hill and is enriched with endless ornaments. The polishing of the stones is so excellent that even at this distance of time they throw clear reflections of all who enter into the temple.

Kaiquabad—was a grandson of Sultan Balban (*q.v.*) and son of his eldest son Bughra Khan. On the death of Sultan Balban in A.D. 1287 and the refusal of Bughra Khan to accept the burden of the sultanship, Kaiquabad, a young man of seventeen or eighteen years, was installed as the sultan of Delhi. But he soon became so much addicted to wine and women that he became a physical wreck who could not run the administration. He was murdered in his own palace in A.D. 1290. With his death ended the so-called Slave dynasty of the Delhi sultans.

Kaithal, the battle of—was fought in A.D. 1240 in which Sultana Raziya (*q.v.*) and her husband Altuniya were defeated and captured by her brother, Bahram. The day after the battle Raziya and her husband were killed and Bahram became the sultan.

Kakatiyas, the—rose to power in the twelfth century after the fall of the Chalukya dynasty of Kalyani. They founded the kingdom of Warangal. At one time its power extended up to Kanchi in the south. Its king, Prataparudradeva II, was defeated in 1310 by the armies of Sultan Ala-ud-din Khalji who extorted from him a heavy indemnity and a promise of annual tribute. The kingdom was finally subdued and annexed to the Delhi sultanate during the reign of Sultan Ghiyas-ud-din Tughluq (1320-25).

Kakka—a Pratihara (*q.v.*) chieftain, gained in A.D. 837 renown by fighting with the Gauḍas at Monghyr.

Kakka II—the last king of the Rashtrakuta dynasty (*q.v.*), was overthrown by Taila Chalukya (*q.v.*) in A.D. 973.

Kala-Chakra—is the name of a school of Buddhist philosophy with monotheistic tendencies. It was popular with the people of Tibet as well as in Orissa. (Vasu, N. N. & Shastri H. P., *Modern Buddhism and its Followers in Orissa*)

Kalachuris, the—lived in Malwa and northern Maharastra. They are also known as the Haihayas. Their kingdom was called Chedi comprising a large part of the modern Madhya Pradesh. The most famous kings of the Kalachuri dynasty were Gangeyadeva Kalachuri (*c.* A.D. 1015-40) and his son and successor Karnadeva (*c.* A.D. 1040-70). The latter crushed Bhoja (*q.v.*) the king of Malwa, in about A.D. 1060, but he was later on defeated by Kirtivarman Chandella (*q.v.*) who ruled from 1049 to 1100. This defeat weakened the Kalachuris and by A.D. 1181 their dynasty ceased to exist for reasons which are not known. The Kalachuri kings used the Traikutaka era (*q.v.*) which was started in A.D. 248-49. (Cunningham, *Reports*, Vols. IX, X, XXI)

Kalanjar (also spelt Kalinjar)—in the Banda district of Uttar Pradesh, has a fortress which was considered extremely strong and whose possession was coveted by the neighbouring Hindu kings. In 1203 it was compelled to capitulate to

Shihab-ud-din Muhammad Ghuri, but was later on recovered by the Rajputs from whom Sher Shah Sur captured it in 1545, dying as the result of an explosion of gunpowder when the siege was proceeding. Soon afterwards the fort was recovered by the Rajputs from whom Emperor Akbar conquered it in 1569. It thus became definitely a part of the Mughul Empire on the fall of which it came under British control.

Kalapahar (alias Raju)—a Brahman who had been converted to Muhammadanism, was a very good general and served under Sulaiman Karnani (*q.v.*) (1565-72) of Bengal with distinction. In 1568 he led an expedition into Orissa, defeated the reigning king and plundered the temple of Jagannath at Puri. He next defeated the Koch army led by Chila Rai, brother of king Nara Narayan (*q.v.*), advanced into Assam as far as Tezpur and demolished the temple of Kamakhya near Gauhati. But in 1583 he was defeated and killed in a naval battle with the army of Emperor Akbar near Rajmahal. (*H. B.*, vol. II.)

Kalasoka (also called Kakavarna)—was the successor of Sisunāga, king of Magadha (*q.v.*). He transferred his capital from Girivraja to Pataliputra. It was during his reign that the second Buddhist Council was held, a hundred years after the death of Gautama Buddha (*c.* 486 B.C.). For reasons not known he was murdered.

Kalat (also spelt Kelat)—is a state in Baluchistan now in Pakistan. Its ruler bearing the title of Khan entered into a treaty with the Indo-British Government by which he gave the latter the right to occupy Quetta (*q.v.*) which commanded the Bolan Pass. In 1892 the Khan executed his Wazir along with the latter's father and son. For this crime the British Government forced him to abdicate and installed his son as the Khan. Kalat continued to be a protected dependency of India till the creation of Pakistan of which it is now a dependency.

Kalhana—the author of the *Rajatarangini* (*q.v.*) which is a chronicle in Sanskrit of the kings of Kashmir, lived in the twelfth century A.D.

Kalidas—was the 'prince of Sanskrit poets and dramatists'. His works are the *Raghuvamsa* (an epic), *Sakuntala* (a drama), *Malavikagnimitra* (a drama), *Meghadutam* (a lyric) and *Ritusamhara* (a lyric). His date has been the subject of much discussion. Tradition makes him the court-poet of king Vikramaditya who has been identified with King Chandragupta II (*c.* A.D. 375-413) and the traditional date (close of the fourth and beginning of the fifth centuries) is probably

correct. (Shastri, H. P., *J.B.O.R.S.*, Vol. I, pp. 197-212 & Vol·
II, pp. 179-189 & Keith, *Hist. of Sans. Lit.* and *J.R.A.S.*, 1909,
pp. 433-39).

Kalikata (or Kalighata)—*see* Calcutta.

Kalimulla—was the last nominal sultan of the Bahmani dynasty
who fled in 1526 to Bijapur to escape death at the hands of
Kasim Barid, the *de facto* ruler. He retired later on to Ahmadnagar where he died.

Kalinga—was the name of the eastern coastal region lying between
the Mahanadi and the Godavari. It thus comprised the modern
state of Orissa. It was conquered by Asoka Maurya (*q.v.*) in
the eighth year of his reign (*c.* 273-232 B.C.). The Kalinga people
offered such stout resistance that 100,000 persons were slain,
150,000 were made captives and many times that number
perished. The sight of all this human misery and the knowledge
that his ambition had caused it smote the conscience of Asoka
and caused him such profound sorrow and grief that he foreswore war and soon afterwards embraced Buddhism. (*See* also
Orissa.)

Kalsi—is a small place now in the Dehra Dun district of Uttar
Pradesh. A set of the Fourteen Rock inscriptions of Asoka
incised in the Brahmi script, has been found at Kalsi.

Kalusha—was the Brahman minister of Shambhuji (1680-89),
son and successor of Shivaji, the Maratha king. Kalusha was
captured by the Mughuls along with Shambhuji and was
executed with cruel barbarity.

Kalyani—now in Andhra Pradesh, was the capital of the Chalukyas
(*q.v.*) for about two centuries (A.D. 973-1190).

Kam Buksh—the fifth son of Emperor Aurangzeb, (*q.v.*), was
killed in battle in 1707 in the war of succession that followed
Aurangzeb's death.

Kamala Devi—was the queen of King Karnadeva II (*q.v.*) of
Gujarat. In 1297 her husband was defeated by the army of
Ala-ud-din Khalji, so they fled with their daughter, Devala
Devi, but Kamala Devi was captured by the Muhammadans,
and taken to Delhi where she became a favourite wife of the
Sultan.

Kamakhya, the temple of—is situated on a hillock called Nilachal
near Gauhati in Assam. The temple is believed to contain the
genitive organ of Siva's consort, Sati, which fell on that hillock
when her dead body was cut into pieces by Vishnu in order to
unburden the disconsolate Siva of the corpse of his consort. It
is a centre of Sákta worship and is visited by orthodox Hindus

from all over India. The present temple was built by the Koch king, Nara Narayan (1540-84) (*q.v.*).

Kamandaka—was a Hindu writer on polity. His work *Nitisara* is considered an authoritative book on the subject.

Kamarupa—*see* Assam.

Kamata—was a variant name by which Kamarupa (*q.v.*) was known.

Kamatapur—was situated a few miles to the south of modern Cooch Behar. During the declining period of the kingdom of Kamarupa a tribal people called the Khens established a kingdom with Kamatapur as their capital. They ruled over the kingdom for about 75 years but their last ruler Nilambar was overthrown by Ala-ud-din Husain Shah (*q.v.*) of Bengal in about A.D. 1498.

Kamboja—lay in south-west Kashmir and included parts of Kafiristan. Its people, also called Kambojas, are referred to in Asoka's inscriptions as his subjects amongst whom Buddhism was preached by the Emperor.

Kambuja Desha—was the name of the Hindu kingdom that was established by Indian colonists in modern Cambodia. Tradition assigns its origin to the enterprise of an Indian Brahman named Kaundinya who married Soma, the daughter of the local Naga ruler, and founded a dynasty in Kambuja in about the second century of the Christian era. The kingdom was called Fu-nan by the Chinese. Hundreds of Brahmans are said to have come from India, settled in Fu-nan and intermarried with the local people. It sent ambassadors to India as well as to China. In the sixth century the name Fu-nan gave place to the new name of Kambuja Desha from which is derived the modern name of Cambodia. Its kings who had Indian blood in their veins, ruled in great pomp and splendour for nine centuries. In the fifteenth century the Hindu kingdom of Kambuja Desha was overrun by the Annamites and the Siamese and reduced to the petty principality of Cambodia which was till recently under the protectorate of France. Amongst the great kings of Kambuja Desha four deserve special mention. These were Jayavarman I and II, Yasovarman who founded the great city of Yasodharapura now known as Angkor Thom and has left several diagraphic inscriptions recording his victorious achievements in Sanskrit as well as in the local language, and Suryavarman II who built the magnificent temple of Angkor Vat which on account of its dimensions as well as architectural beauties is considered a

wonder of the world. Hinduism and Buddhism prevailed in
Kambuja Desha, though later on Buddhism became more
predominant and continues to be the religion of modern Cambodia. (Chatterji, B. R., *Indian Cultural Influence in Cambodia*)

Kamran, Prince—the second son of Babur (1526-30), the founder
of the Mughul dynasty in Delhi, was, on the death of his father,
treated very generously by his elder brother, Emperor
Humayun (*q.v.*), who gave him the province of Afghanistan
to govern. But Kamran proved ungrateful; he did not stand
by Humayun during his war with Sher Shah (*q.v.*). He even
refused him shelter when he fled from India. Humayun could
win back the Delhi throne only after he had defeated, deposed
and killed Kamran in battle with the help of Persia.

Kanara—is a small tract of territory in the West of Mysore separating it from the sea. It was annexed to the Indo-British Empire
in 1799.

Kanauj—is a very ancient and famous city in north India. Its
original name was Kánya Kubja and it was a centre of
Brahmanical influence though it is now only a petty town
inhabited mostly by Muhammadans. It is frequently referred
to in the *Mahabharata* and is alluded to by Patanjali (*q.v.*) who
flourished in the second century B.C. When the Chinese pilgrim
Fa-Hien (*q.v.*) visited it in about A.D. 405 it had only two
Buddhist monasteries and was not much of the big city that it
had become by the time when Hiuen Tsang (*q.v.*) visited it in
A.D. 636. He stayed there for seven years. It then had a teeming
population, hundreds of Hindu and Buddhist temples and
monasteries, extended along the east bank of the Ganges for
about four miles, had lovely gardens and beautiful tanks and
was strongly fortified. This great change had been brought
about by Emperor Harshavardhana (A.D. 606-647) who made
it his capital. Its grandeur and prosperity made it earn the
name of 'Mahodaya Sree' and its possession became the aim
of the Hindu dynasties that came into power after the death
of Harshavardhana. Indeed the Pratihara kings (A.D. 816-1090)
made it their capital and Kanauj once again became the
premier city of northern India. King Dharmapala (*q.v.*) of
Bengal felt very proud of its acquisition, though only for a
very short time. Misfortunes, however, began to fall upon it
when Sultan Mahmud first raided it in A.D. 1018 and the ruling
Pratihara king moved his headquarters from Kanauj to Bari
on the other bank of the Ganges. The last Pratihara king,
Rajyapal (*q.v.*) was soon afterwards deposed by the neighbour-

ing Chandella king, Ganda, and Kanauj passed under the rule of the Gaharwar Rajputs popularly called Rathors in the twelfth century. The last Rathor king of Kanauj was Jai Chand (*q.v.*) who was defeated and killed by Shihab-ud-din Muhammad Ghuri in A.D. 1194. Henceforth, Kanauj sank into insignificance and was finally destroyed by Sher Shah Sur (*q.v.*) soon after he had won his decisive victory over Humayun in the battle fought against the Mughul Emperor in the vicinity of the city in 1540. Nothing but heaps of ruins now remain of its ancient buildings. (Smith, V. A., *A Hist. of the City of Kanauj* and Tripathi, R. S., *Hist. of Kanauj*)

Kanchi—is one of the seven sacred cities of the Hindus in India. The first historical record that mentions it is the Allahabad inscription of Samudragupta (*c* A.D. 335-80) which records the submission of its king Vishnugopa to the Gupta Emperor. Kanchi, now called Conjeeveram, was the capital of the Pallavas (*q.v.*). It was visited by Hiuen Tsang (*q.v.*) in about A.D. 640 when the Pallava power reached its zenith during the rule of Narasimhavarman. He found Kanchi a large city 5 or 6 miles in circumference in which Hindu, Buddhist and Jain temples abounded. Kanchi was the birth-place of the famous Buddhist metaphysician Dharmapala as well as the place where the famous Hindu philosopher, Ramanuja, received his education and lived for many years. Kanchi suffered a great deal on account of the perennial conflict between the Pallavas and the Chalukyas, who, however, beautified it with many temples of which the most famous is the temple of Kailashanatha.

Kandahar—*see* Qandahar.

Kandarpanarayan—was one of the twelve landlords (*Bhuiyans*) of Bengal who ruled over the province in the sixteenth century. His territory was called Chandradvipa which was equivalent to the modern district of Bakharganj, now in East Pakistan. After long resistance he had to acknowledge the suzerainty of Emperor Akbar.

Kangra—a fortified place near modern Hardwar in Uttar Pradesh, formed the eastern boundary of the kingdom of Jaipal (*q.v.*) of Bathindah. It was sacked by Timur in 1399 but continued to be ruled by the Hindus until it was conquered by Emperor Jahangir in 1620 and became a part of the empire of the Mughuls under whose patronage a school of painters developed at Kangra. In 1811 it passed under the control of Ranjit Singh and became a part of his kingdom on the annexation of which in 1848 it became a part of the British Empire in India.

Kanhoji Angira—a renowned Maratha sea-captain or pirate chief, controlled the two forts of Gheria and Suvarnadrug from which he dominated the coast between Bombay and Goa.

Kanishka—was the most famous king of the Kushan (*q.v.*) dynasty founded by Kadphises I (*q.v.*). The date of Kanishka has been the subject of much controversy. According to some his reign began in A.D. 78 from which year the Saka era (*q.v.*) dates. According to the other view he ascended the throne in about A.D. 120, ten years after the death of the second Kushan king Kadphises II with whom his relationship is unknown. His father's name was Vajheshka who, however, did not become the king. Kanishka's capital was at Purushapur or Peshawar which he beautified with many buildings. His dominions included Gandhara (eastern Afghanistan), Kashmir, and the basins of the Indus and the Ganges. He sent an expedition across the Pamirs into Chinese Turkistan and subdued the chiefs of Khotan, Yarkand and Kashgar who had so long been dependants of the Chinese Emperor and some of whom were now obliged to send hostages to the court of Kanishka. His rule was long covering probably 24 years from A.D. 120 to 144. His name is recorded in many inscriptions and he issued a large variety of coins which bear a mixed assortment of Zoroastrian, Greek, Mithraic and Indian deities like Siva and Buddha. This circumstance suggests that Kanishka was rather eclectic in his religious ideas. Buddhist tradition, however, claims that he was an earnest and ardent Buddhist who convened the Fourth Buddhist Council which adopted authorized commentaries on the Buddhist canon. These were recorded on copper-sheets, deposited in a stone coffer and placed for security in the Kundalavana monastery in Kashmir where the Council had met. The council was attended mainly by the followers of *Hinayana* (*q.v.*) but the *Mahayana* (*q.v.*) had already grown very numerous and claimed amongst its followers eminent Buddhist authors like Aswaghosha, Nagarjuna and Vasumitra all of whom enjoyed the patronage of Kanishka. Indeed Kanishka was a great patron of learning. Charaka, the celebrated Indian authority on the science of medicine, was his court physician. Kanishka was also a great builder and lover of art and architecture. He built a 400 feet high tower at Peshawar over the relics of Buddha, added the Sir Sukh section to the town of Taxila, built a city called after his own name in Kashmir, adorned Mathura with numerous fine buildings with artistic sculpture and was probably the sponsor of the Gandhara school of art (*q.v.*). His royal patronage was extended to artists beyond Gandhara and significant schools of art and sculpture developed at Sarnath and Mathura, both within his empire, as well as in Amaravati on the Krishna in the Deccan. Indeed so great and impressive were Kanishka's contributions to Indian art, culture and civilisation that he stands out, in spite of his foreign origin, as one of the greatest of the kings of ancient India.

Kanva (or Kanvayana), the dynasty of—succeeded the Sunga dynasty (*q.v.*) in about 73 B.C. in Magadha. It was founded by Vasudeva, the Brahman minister of Devabhuti, the last king of the Sunga dynasty. The Kanva dynasty comprising four reigns including that of the founder, covered forty-five years and its last king Susarman was overthrown in about 28 B.C. by Simuka, the founder of the Andhra dynasty (*q.v.*).

Kapaya Nayaka—was the leader of the Hindus of Telingana. By 1336 he built up a kingdom on the east coast of southern India. Later on he collaborated with the brothers, Harihara and Bukka (*q.v.*), the founders of the Vijayanagar state, in throwing off the Muslim yoke and in establishing the Hindu kingdom.

Kapilavastu—is in the Nepal Tarai to the north of the Basti district of Uttar Pradesh. Literally the word means 'Kapila's Abode'. It is, however, not known whether it had any connection with the great Hindu philosopher, Kapila, the propounder of the Sankhya (*q.v.*) school of Indian philosophy. Kapilavastu is historically famous as the birth-place of Gautama Buddha, (*q.v.*) the founder of Buddhism.

Kapilendra (or Kapileswara)—a king who overthrew the Ganga dynasty (*q.v.*) of Orissa in about 1453, ruled till 1470. He was a very able and vigorous person who restored the prestige of Orissa by suppressing the rebels within the state and by extending his dominions from the Ganges to the Kaveri. He thus founded a new dynasty of kings in Orissa, the more prominent of whom were Purushottama (*q.v.*) (A.D. 1470-97) and his son Prataparudra (*q.v.*) (1497-1540). In about A.D. 1541 the dynasty of Kapilendra was overthrown by the Bhoi dynasty (*q.v.*).

Kapur Singh—a Sikh leader of Fyzallapur in the Panjab, flourished in the middle of the eighteenth century. After the execution of Banda (*q.v.*) he started amongst the Sikhs an organisation which later on developed into the *Dal Khalsa* of the theocracy of the Sikhs and contributed much to the preservation of the Sikhs as a sect in the Panjab.

Kara—was a town in Allahabad district. Here Sultan Jalal-ud-din Khalji (*q.v.*) was murdered by his nephew and son-in-law Ala-ud-din Khalji (*q.v.*) in 1296.

Kara-jal—was a territory lying between India and China. Sultan Muhammad Tughluq sent an army for its conquest and miserably failed. Earlier historians mistook it for China and wrongly held that the Sultan in his unbalanced state of mind sent a disastrous expedition to China.

Karan Singh—was the son of Rana Amar Singh (*q.v.*) of Mewar and a grandson of Rana Pratap Singh. In 1614 Rana Amar Singh submitted to the Mughuls and he and his son Karan Singh recognised the suzerainty of Emperor Jahangir. A statue of Karan Singh along with one of his father's was set up at the Agra Palace by order of Jahangir who felt very proud of the submission of Mewar. Karan Singh had to accept the rank of a commander of 5000 and ruled, after his father's death, as a dependent of the Mughuls.

Karan Singh—was the last Maharaja of Kashmir. His father had acceded to the Indian Union and he is now the *Rajpramukh* in Kashmir. He is a scholarly type of person and has written a book on Gandhiji.

Karauli, the state of—was proposed by Lord Dalhousie to be annexed to the British Indian Empire in accordance with the 'doctrine of lapse' (*q.v.*). But the authorities in England refused approval to the proposal on the ground that Karauli was not 'a dependent state' in regard to which the doctrine was applicable but a 'protected ally'.

Karikkal (also spelt Karikal)—the earliest known Chola king, has been assigned to A.D. 100. He is said to have founded the city of Puhar or Pukar and constructed along the Kaveri river an embankment one hundred miles in length.

Karim Khan—was a leader of the Pindaris (*q.v.*). He was compelled to surrender to the British in 1818 as a result of the campaign that Lord Hastings, Governor-General of India (1813-23), started against the Pindaris. He was given the small state of Gawspur in Uttar Pradesh where he lived on as a peaceful landlord.

Karkota, the dynasty of—was founded in Kashmir in the seventh century by Durlabhavardhana. It ruled over Kashmir up to A.D. 855 when it was overthrown by the Utpala dynasty. Chandrapida (*q.v.*), Muktapida Lalitaditya (*q.v.*) and Jayapida Vinayaditya (*q.v.*) were the three most famous kings of this dynasty.

Karnadeva—was the king of Gujarat when the kingdom was invaded by Sultan Ala-ud-din Khalji's generals in 1297. He was defeated and his consort, Kamala Devi, was captured and sent to the harem of the Sultan while he himself could effect an escape to Devagiri whose king, Ramachandra Deva (*q.v.*), gave him shelter. But the hostility of Sultan Ala-ud-din still pursued him to Nandurbar in the Deccan where he had set up a small principality and he was overthrown after a stout resistance.

Karnal, the battle of—was fought in A.D. 1739 between Nadir Shah (*q.v.*) who had invaded India and advanced without any resistance up to Karnal, in dangerous proximity to Delhi, and the army of the Mughul Emperor, Muhammad Shah (1719-48) (*q.v.*). The Mughuls were decisively defeated, Emperor Muhammad Shah was made a captive and Nadir entered into Delhi which he later on cruelly sacked.

Karnasuvarna—was the capital of the kingdom of Gauḍa (Bengal) (*q.v.*) when Sasanka (*q.v.*) was its king. After the death of Sasanka as well as of his great imperial contemporary, Harshavardhana, Karnasuvarna was for a time at least conquered and occupied by king Bhaskaravarman (*q.v.*) of Kamarup (Assam) who issued his Nidhanpur grant from his victorious camp at Karnasuvarna. It has been plausibly identified with Murshidabad on the Bhagirathi in Bengal.

Karnatic—*see* Carnatic.

Karnavati—the Rani of Mewar, was a very heroic lady and organised the defence of Chitor when the fort was threatened in 1535 by Bahadur Shah, king of Gujarat. Exactly at that time Emperor Humayun was on his way from Delhi in a campaign against Bahadur Shah. Rani Karnavati offered to enter into an alliance with the Mughul Emperor against the common enemy, Bahadur Shah. But Humayun foolishly rejected the proffered alliance. Rani Karnavati failed to save Chitor, but Humayun was no gainer by this Muslim victory over the Hindus, for he himself was soon afterwards obliged by Bahadur Shah to leave Gujarat.

Karnul—was a small state in Madras ruled by a Muhammadan chief bearing the title of Nawab. During the administration of Lord Auckland (1836-42) the state was annexed to the British Indian Empire on suspicion of the hostile designs of its ruler.

Karpura-Manjuri, **the**—is a drama written wholly in Prakrit by Rajasekhara, a poet from the Deccan, who was the teacher of King Mahendrapala (*q.v.*), a Gurjara-Pratihara king (*c.* A.D. 890-910).

Kartripura—is a state mentioned in the Allahabad inscription of Samudragupta (*c.* A.D. 330-380) as one of the frontier kingdoms whose kings paid tribute and rendered homage to Samudragupta. The state probably occupied the modern districts of Kumaon and Garhwal.

Karuvaki (or Kaluvaki)—was the second queen of Asoka Maurya and the mother of Tivala or Tivara. She is the only queen of Asoka who has the distinction of being mentioned in his inscriptions. The Sanskritic form of the name is Charuvaki.

Karve—was a distinguished Professor of Sanskrit who founded the Women's University at Poona, a unique institution marking great progress in female education in India in modern times.

Kashgar—a state in Central Turkistan, was under Chinese control before it was subdued by the Kushan Emperor, Kanishka (*c.* A.D. 120-44) (*q.v.*). In the seventh century it became permeated with Indian Buddhist influence as recorded by the Chinese pilgrim Hiuen Tsang (*q.v.*). Archaeological researches have revealed incontestable evidence of the prevalence of Indian culture in this region.

Kashmir—is on the north-western frontier of India. It is bounded on the north-west by Afghanistan, on the north-east by the Sin-Kiang province of China and on the east by Tibet. Famed for its natural beauty and healthy climate it is also strategically important as guarding one of the approaches to India on the north-west. On its frontiers meet Afghanistan, Turkistan and China. Its history up to A.D. 1006 is found in Kalhan's (*q.v.*) *Rajatarangini*, from 1006 to 1420 in Jonaraja's continuation of the work, from 1420 to 1489 in Sri Vasa's continuation and from 1489 to 1586 in *Rajabalipataka* by Prajna Bhatta— all written in Sanskrit. According to tradition, Kashmir was originally a lake which was drained by the sage Kasyapa who settled Brahmans in the valley. The *Mahabharata* mentions the Kashmir people (*the Kasmiras*) as Kshatriyas. Buddhism was introduced into the country by missionaries sent by Asoka and continued to flourish in the country when it was under Kushan rule in the second century A.D. But Hinduism continued to be the predominant religion and in the seventh century A.D. the Karkota dynasty (*q.v.*) was founded by Durlabhavardhana. In A.D. 855 the Karkota dynasty was supplanted by the Utpala dynasty. Later on the *Tantrins*, and the dynasties of Yasaskara and Parva Gupta ruled in succession. Didda, the widowed queen of a later Gupta king named Kshema Gupta, ruled till A.D. 1003 when Kashmir passed to the Lohara dynasty. It escaped an invasion by Sultan Mahmud but in A.D. 1346 the last Hindu king, Udiana Deva, was murdered by his Muhammadan minister, Amir Shah, who ascended the throne under the name of Sams-ud-din. His dynasty ruled in Kashmir till 1586 when it was conquered and annexed to his dominions by Emperor Akbar. In 1757 it was conquered by Ahmad Shah Durrani and remained a part of the kingdom of Afghanistan till 1819 when it was re-covered by Ranjit Singh and annexed to his dominions. As the result of the defeat of the Sikhs in the First Sikh War (1846) Kashmir was sold to Raja Gulab Singh of Jammu for the sum of one crore of rupees which went to the payment of an indemnity of one crore and a half by the defeated Sikh Government to the victorious British. Gulab Singh entered also into a separate treaty with the British Indian Government which recognised him as an independent ruler of Kashmir and Jammu. Gulab Singh who also conquered Ladakh, died in 1857. His successors were Ranbir Singh (1857-85), Partab Singh (1885-1925) and Hari Singh (1925-49). After the partition of India in 1947 Kashmir at first wanted to stay out of both India and Pakistan, but on 20 October, 1947 Pakistani tribesmen from the north-western frontiers, with the connivance and support of the newly established Government of Pakistan, invaded Kashmir and threatened its capital Srinagar. The ruling king, Maharaja Sir Hari Singh, found that the resources of Kashmir and Jammu were not adequate to repulse the raiders and uphold the independence and integrity of his king-dom. Acting on the advice of Shaikh Muhammad Abdullah he, therefore, asked for military aid from India, and executed an Instrument of Accession to the Indian Union which, therefore, rushed airborne troops into Kashmir just in time to save Srinagar. But the raiders had already occupied one-half of Kashmir and could be ousted only by a bloody war between India and Pakistan. In their anxiety to avoid such a fratricidal war and to get the dispute settled by peaceful methods the Government of India placed the matter before the United Nations Security Council on 6 January, 1948 and the Security Council imposed a cease-fire in the same month. But Kashmir now became a pawn in the power-politics of the Western nations and the U.N.O. has not yet succeeded in settling the issue with the result that one-half of Kashmir, euphemistically called 'Azad Kashmir' (Free Kashmir) is in the illegal occupation of Pakistan and the other half along with Jammu is within the Union of India.

Kasi—*see* Benares.

Kasi Raj Pandit—was a Maratha scribe who accompanied the Maratha army led by Sadasiva Rao Bhao in Northern India culminating in the third Battle of Panipat in 1761. He made careful enquiries and sent his reports to the Court at Poona. These despatches included also an *Account of the Battle of Panipat* which has been published under the same title by the Oxford University Press. He was a careful observer.

Kasimbazar—*see* Cossimbazar.

Kasiram Das—a poet born in Bengal, composed the Bengali version of the *Mahabharata* in the sixteenth century. His name is a household word in Bengal and his *Mahabharata* is one of the most popular and revered books in Bengali literature.

Kassijura case—*see* Cossijura case.

Kasyapa-Matanga—was the first Indian monk to go to China and to introduce Buddhism there in about A.D. 67. He was born in Magadha and was residing in Gandhara when he went to China on the invitation of a Chinese mission sent by Emperor Ming (A.D. 58-75).

Katachuris—*see* Kalachuris.

Kathaioi—was the name of the tribe that inhabited the tract lying between the Chinab and the Ravi in the Panjab. Their capital was Sangala which was probably situated in the modern Gurudaspur district. Alexander, the king of Macedon, overcame them during his invasion in 326 B.C.

Kathasaritsagara, **the**—or the 'Ocean of Stories', is a book of romantic stories written by Somadeva some time between A.D. 1063 and 1081. It frequently refers to the adventurous voyages of Indian merchants across the seas in south-eastern Asia.

Kathavatthu, **the**—is an important Buddhist treatise in Pali. Prof. Rhys Davids ascribed its composition to the time of Asoka. (*c.* 273 - 232 B.C.).

Kathiawar (also called Saurashtra)—lies in the western part of India. It was included within the Maurya Empire after the fall of which it passed under the rule of Saka satraps who recognised the suzerainty of the Kushan kings. Later on Kathiawar became a part of the Gupta Empire and was also under the domination of Harshavardhana (A.D. 606-47). It then passed under local Hindu rajas but was overrun by the Arabs under Muhammad bin Kasim in about A.D. 712. It, however, still continued to be a centre of Hindu pilgrimage, particularly its Siva temple at Somnath drew many Hindu worshippers. In A.D. 1026 the famous temple of Somnath was captured and destroyed by Sultan Mahmud and Kathiawar gradually passed under Muhammadan control. It became a part of the British Indian Empire after the Third Maratha War (*q.v.*)

Kathmandu—is the capital of Nepal. A British attack on it in 1815 was beaten back by the Gurkhas.

Kaundinya—was, according to tradition as preserved in Cambodia, an Indian Brahman who established the kingdom of Kambuja Desha (*q.v.*), now Cambodia.

Kauffmann, General—was appointed by Russia as her Governor-General in Turkestan in 1867. He soon opened a correspondence with Amir Sher Ali of Afghanistan which the latter forwarded to the British Indian Government. This correspondence roused apprehension about Russian intentions with regard to Afghanistan. But no good came out of it. On the outbreak of the Second Afghan War in 1878 Sher Ali's appeals to Russia for help were ineffective and he was even discouraged from seeking shelter in Russia. General Kauffmann's intrigues only led Sher Ali to his doom.

Kautilya (also called Chanakya or Vishnu Gupta)—was a Taxilian Brahman who, according to tradition as recorded in the drama *Mudrarakshasa* (*q.v.*), came to Pataliputra (*q.v.*) where he was insulted by the reigning Nanda king (*q.v.*). In order to be avenged he joined Chandragupta Maurya, helped him to defeat and kill the Nanda king and installed him as the king of Magadha. He then became his Chief Minister and helped him to consolidate and administer his kingdom. Where and when he died is not known. Kautilya was the author of the *Arthasastra*, the most famous book in Sanskrit on polity. Though Kautilya (or Chanakya or Vishnugupta), the minister of Chandragupta Maurya (*c.* 322-298 B.C.) and the author of the Kautilyan *Arthasastra* are believed to be identical it is difficult to put the *Arthasastra* as early as the fourth century B.C. The reference in the *Arthasastra* to China, the use of Sanskrit as the official language and the absence in the Asokan inscriptions of any use of the designations (like *Samadhatri* etc.) used in the *Arthasastra* are reasons for holding that the *Arthasastra* was a work later than the age of the early Mauryas. But its influence on ancient Indian polity is undeniable. (*P.H.A.I.*, pp 9-10; Sham Shastri, *Arthasastra*)

Kayal—a city on the Tamraparni river in South India, was visited twice by the Venetian traveller, Marco Polo, in 1288 and 1299. He found it a great and noble city where much business was done. It was a busy and wealthy port which was frequented by traders from the west as well as from the east as far as China.

Kayastha—is a high caste Hindu. In Bengal he is next in rank to the Brahman in the hierarchy of caste. Many hold that the Kayasthas in Bengal were originally Kshatriyas who came to be known as Kayasthas as they changed the sword for the pen and became practically a caste of writers or clerks. But Raja Pratapaditya of Jessore, Raja Kandarpanarayan of Chandradvipa as well as Kedar Rai of Vikrampur (Dacca) all of whom offered stout resistance to Akbar and delayed the Mughul conquest of Bengal for several years, were all Kayasthas.

Kennedy, Vans (1784-1846)—was the agent of the British Indian Government for the Simla Hill States which came under British rule in 1816. He first discovered the salubrious and practically European climate of Simla, built the first permanent home at Simla in 1822 and thus started Simla on its career as a favourite hill-station, and later on as the summer capital of the Government of India. He was also an efficient linguist who wrote two interesting books, namely, *Ancient Hindu Mythology* and *Vedanta Philosophy of the Hindus*.

Keralaputras, the—were a people who, as mentioned in Rock Edict II of Asoka, lived on the southern frontier of the Asokan empire. Their country was included in the modern Travancore region.

Kesava Deva temple of Mathura—was built by Raja Bir Singh Bundela (*q.v.*) and dedicated to the worship of Kesava (i.e. Vishnu) during the reign of Emperor Jahangir (A.D. 1605-27). This magnificent temple was destroyed in 1670 by the order of Emperor Aurangzeb, a mosque was built on its site and its richly jewelled images were brought to Agra and placed beneath the steps of Jahanara's mosque.

Keshub Chandra Sen—*see* Sen, Keshavchandra.

Khafi Khan—was the pen-name under which Muhammad Hashim of Kwaf in Khurasan wrote his famous historical work *Muntakhab-ul-Lubab*. He enjoyed the patronage of the Mughul court and wrote his book during the reign of Emperor Muhammad Shah (1719-48). He was a singularly impartial Muhammadan historian who was liberal and truthful enough to record in his work the victory of the Maratha king, Shivaji, and to appreciate some of his merits. His work is the most authoritative and a semi-contemporary account of the reign of Emperor Aurangzeb (A.D. 1659-1707).

Khairpur, the city of—in Sind, was the seat of one of the three Amirs or Mirs of the Talpura tribe who ruled over Sind (*q.v.*) on the eve of its conquest in 1843 by the British Indian Government.

Khajuraho—the religious capital of the Chandellas (*q.v.*), is situated 27 miles to the east of Chatarpur in Bundelkhand (*q.v.*) and abounds in temples bearing testimony to the grandeur of the Chandellas and their patronage of art, sculpture and architecture. These constitute one of the finest groups of Hindu temples in northern India, built in the 10th and 11th centuries A.D. The Kandarya Mahadeva temple is the grandest and most magnificent of the Khajuraho monuments. (Dharma, B. L. and Chandra, S. C., *Khajuraho*)

Khajwah, the battle of—was fought in 1659 between Prince Shuja (*q.v.*) and Prince Aurangzeb, (*q.v.*), the second and third sons of Shah Jahan. Shuja was defeated, put to flight and hunted out of Bengal to perish in Arakan.

Khalaf Hasan Basri—a foreign merchant, came to the Bahmani kingdom in the fifteenth century and helped Prince Ahmad, brother of the eighth Bahmani sultan, Firuz, (*q.v.*), to depose and murder Firuz in 1422. He then became the chief minister of the new sultan, Ahmad (1422-35) but was murdered during the reign of the next sultan Ala-ud-din (1435-57), in the course of a riot between the Deccanese and foreigners in the Bahmani kingdom.

Khalilullah Khan—was a general in the army with which Prince Dara (*q.v.*), the eldest son of Emperor Shah Jahan, fought against his third and fourth brothers, Princes Aurangzeb and Murad, at Samugarh, 8 miles to the east of the Agra Fort in 1658. It was on the treacherous advice of Khalilullah Khan that at a critical moment in the battle Prince Dara dismounted from the elephant on which he had been riding since the commencement of the battle and preferred to ride on a horse. The sight of the vacant *howdah* (seat) on his elephant's back led his soldiers to think that Dara was killed and they ran away. Dara lost the battle and along with it the imperial crown of Mughul India.

Khaljis, the—a tribe, Turkish in origin, came to settle in India after the conquest of northern India by the Muhammadans. Jalal-ud-din who overthrew the last of the sultans of the Slave dynasty (*q.v.*), established the Khalji dynasty of the sultans of

Delhi which ruled from A.D. 1290 to 1320. Ala-ud-din (1296-1316) (*q.v.*) was the most famous and the ablest of the Khalji sultans of Delhi.

Khalsa—means 'crown-land'. It was a term used in connection with the land revenue system under the Delhi sultanate.

Khalsa, the—means the military theocracy of the Sikhs. It came into existence after the execution of Banda (*q.v.*) in 1716 and was initiated by Kapur Singh (*q.v.*). As years passed it indicated the whole military might of the Sikhs. But the *Khalsa* was not a united body for many years after its inception. It was divided into twelve *misls* or confederacies which had their own internal feuds and jealousies. These quarrelling *misls* were organised into a compact body by Maharaja Ranjit Singh (1798-1839) (*q.v.*) who styled himself and his people collectively the *Khalsa* or commonwealth of Guru Govind. The *Khalsa* was defeated in the First Sikh War (*q.v.*) and dissolved after its defeat in the Second Sikh War (1848-49).

Kham, the—was a source of the revenue in the Indo-Muslim state system. It amounted to one-fifth of the spoils of war and of the produce of mines.

Khan-i-Dauran—a provincial governor during the reign of Shah Jahan (1627-59), was notorious for his pitiless exactions from the *ryots* and his death was hailed as a divine deliverance.

Khan Jahan—originally a Hindu resident of Telingana, embraced Islam and rose by dint of his merit to be a very high officer under Sultan Firuz Tughluq (1351-88). Indeed he was in charge of the internal administration of the sultanate till his death in 1370.

Khan Jahan (the younger)—the son of Khan Jahan (senior) whom he succeeded on his death in 1370 as the minister of Sultan Firuz Tughluq (1351-88). He tried to alienate Sultan Firuz from his eldest surviving son, Muhammad Khan, but the Prince was astute enough to expose the whole conspiracy to the Sultan. Khan Jahan thus lost all favour with the Sultan and was dismissed and killed in 1387.

Khan Jahan Bahadur—an officer under Emperor Aurangzeb (1659-1707) whom he served very loyally in his iconoclastic mission, destroyed many Hindu temples in Jodhpur in 1679 and sent so many cartloads of idols from Jodhpur to Agra that he received warm praise from Aurangzeb.

Khan Jahan Lodi—an Afghan who was the governor of the Deccan at the time of the accession of Emperor Shah Jahan (1627-59), supported the Pretender, Dawar Baksh (*q.v.*), was pardoned by Shah Jahan on his accession and was allowed to retain his post in the Deccan. But on his failure to recover Balaghat which he had sold earlier to the Nizam Shah, he was recalled to Delhi. He, however, was afraid of further punishment which he tried to escape by fleeing to Ahmadnagar, but was hunted by imperial troops and killed in a battle in 1631.

Khan Zaman—an Uzbeg chief who disliked the Persianized ways of Akbar (1556-1605), rose in revolt against the Emperor in 1567. The rebellion was soon subdued, though it had delayed Akbar's expedition against Chitor.

Khanua, the battle of—was fought not very far from Agra in 1527 between Emperor Babur (1525-30) and Rana Sangram Singha of Mewar who was decisively defeated. This battle consolidated the infant Mughul Empire so far as Rajputana was concerned.

Kharak Singh—the son and successor of Maharaja Ranjit Singh (*q.v.*), he was not only slow-witted but also lacked strength enough to control the rude Sikhs. He was murdered in 1840 only a year after his accession.

Kharavela—was an early king of Kalinga (Orissa) and the neighbouring region. All information about him is derived from a single inscription, namely, the Hathigumpha inscription, the reading of which again has not been definitely established. Two expressions in particular supposed to indicate a date still require a final interpretation acceptable to all reasonable persons. In any case the location of the inscription in a Jain cave in the Udaygiri Hills in the district of Puri establishes the fact that Kharavela was a king of Kalinga and a Jain by religion. He was a great warrior who extended his conquests all over eastern India from the realm of the Pandyas in the Far South to Magadha in the north where he defeated a king named Bahapati-mitam who has been identified with King Pushyamitra (*q.v.*) who established the Sunga dynasty in about 185 B.C. He is also said to have fought with a Yavana king of Mathura as well as with a Satakarni king (of the Satavahana family) (*q.v.*). He also attended to public works and reclaimed within his original kingdom a canal which had been first constructed by a Nanda king three hundred years ago. Nothing is known about the length of his own reign and his successors never attained much stature. (*P.H.A.I.* pp. 373-78)

Kharda (or Kurdla), the battle of—was fought in 1795 between the Nizam of Hyderabad and the Marathas in which the Nizam was badly defeated and compelled to make peace on very unfavourable terms. This defeat was one of the main reasons which led the Nizam to enter into a subsidiary alliance with the English in India in 1798 and thus save himself by bartering away his independence.

Kharosthi—is the name of an ancient Indian script which is written, unlike the *Brahmi* script, from the right to the left. It was used by Asoka in the Mansera and Shahbazghari versions of his Fourteen Rock Edicts, suggesting that this script, rather than the *Brahmi*, was used in the north-western frontier regions of India as early as the third century B.C.

Kher, B. G.—was the first Congress Chief Minister in the Bombay Presidency who took office in 1937 and carried on the administration with efficiency and success.

Khilafat Movement—aimed at the preservation of the power and integrity of Turkey under Muhammadan rule and the continuance of the Sultan of Turkey as the *Caliph* of the Muhammadan world. The growing weakness and fast decline of Turkey before 1914 and her losses during the First World War (1914-18) threatening her with complete extinction roused the liveliest interests of the Indian Muhammadans and a movement was started in about 1920 for exercising pressure on England so that she might not join in the destruction of Turkey and the Caliphate. This movement amongst the Indian Muhammadans is known as the *Khilafat* movement. It threw up two leaders in the brothers, Shaukat Ali and Muhammad Ali, both of whom were well-educated and good orators. They joined with the Indian National Congress which, under the leadership of Mahatma Gandhi, started the Non-co-operation movement in 1920. Thus the *Khilafat* movement led to an unprecedented union between the Indian Muhammadans and the Hindus and greatly strengthened the cause of Indian Nationalism. The *Khilafat* movement combined with the idea of non-co-operation led to an attempted migration (*hijrat*) of a large number of Indian Muhammadans to Afghanistan. But it proved a disaster, for the Afghans, though Muhammadans, were definitely cold towards their Indian brothers-in-faith. Further, Kemal Ataturk emerged in Turkey and succeeded in reviving the Turks. Finally the Sultan was deposed in 1923, the office of the Caliph was abolished in 1924 and Turkey was declared to be a secular state by the Turks themselves. The ground was thus completely cut from beneath the feet of the movement which soon collapsed.

Khilji—*see* Khalji.

Khiva—is in Uzbegistan, now within the U.S.S.R. On the eve of the First Afghan War it was a dependency of Afghanistan and coveted by Russia which, however, failed completely in her attack on Khiva in 1839. The weakness of Russia at this distance from her capital was thus exposed. But years later, in 1873, Russia succeeded in capturing Khiva. This Russian advance filled Sher Ali, the Amir of Afghanistan, with apprehension and he approached the British Indian Government with a request for a definitive offensive and defensive treaty which was refused by the British Indian Government at that time only to insist on imposing on an unwilling Afghanistan a similar treaty in 1878 leading to the Second Afghan War (1878-81).

Khizr Khan—the eldest son of Sultan Ala-ud-din Khalji (1296-1316), was appointed in 1303 as the governor of the recently conquered kingdom of Mewar with its capital at Chitor and held the post till 1311. He married Devala Devi, the daughter of Rai Karnadeva (*q.v.*), the vanquished king of Gujarat, in 1307 and their love was sung by the poet Amir Khusru (*q.v.*). He was naturally looked upon as his father's prospective successor. But on the death of Sultan Ala-ud-din in 1316 he was prevented from ascending the throne by Malik Kafur (*q.v.*) who blinded him.

Khizr Khan Sayyid—the governor of Multan on behalf of Timur, marched in 1414 against the last of the Tughluq sultans of Delhi, imprisoned him and occupied the capital. He thus became the founder of a new dynasty—the Sayyid—of the sultans of Delhi. His sovereignty was confined to Delhi and its neighbourhood over which he ruled for seven years (1414-21).

Khokhara Khurda—was the diamond area on the Orissa frontier. It was conquered and annexed to the Mughul Empire by Emperor Jahangir (1605-27) and passed under British control after the battle of Plassey in 1757.

Khurrum, Prince—*see* Shah Jahan.

Khusrav, Prince—was the eldest son of Salim (Jahangir) and a grandson of Emperor Akbar. On the eve of Akbar's death in 1605 there was an attempt to install Prince Khusrav on the throne in preference to his father, Salim. The scheme failed in spite of the support of Raja Man Singh who was his maternal uncle. Salim on his accession pardoned his son but kept him in practical confinement at Agra. But he soon escaped and rose in revolt against his father, Emperor Jahangir, but was easily reduced to submission and again pardoned. But soon afterwards another plot was hatched in favour of Prince Khusrav but it failed, and the Prince was now blinded. He was popular and for a Mughul was a very loyal husband, refusing to marry as his second wife even the daughter of Empress Nur Jahan (*q.v.*) by her first husband. The Prince was never completely reconciled to his father and was constantly envied and hated by his younger brother Khurram (Shah Jahan). In 1620 Jahangir handed over Khusrav to the custody of Shah Jahan who kept him at Burhanpur where he died in 1622. The cause of his death is not definitely known, but many believed it was due in some way to Shah Jahan's hostility.

Khusrav Khan—a low-caste convert from Gujarat, became a great favourite of Sultan Mubarak Khalji (1316-20) and became his chief minister. He was base enough to get his master murdered in 1320 and bold enough to usurp his throne. On his accession he assumed the title of Sultan Nasir-ud-din Khusrav Shah. He squandered the wealth of the state on either bribing the nobles whom he feared or on rewarding his relatives and tribesmen. He also put to death the members of the family of the late Sultan and massacred his adherents. But his rule proved short, lasting from April to September, 1320 when he was defeated and killed by a combination of the Muhammadan nobles in Delhi.

Khusrav Malik—the son and successor of Khusrav Shah (*q.v.*), was the last Ghaznavid to rule over the Panjab. He was defeated by Shihab-ud-din Muhammad Ghuri in 1186. With him the Ghaznavid dynasty came to an end.

Khusrav Shah—the son and successor of the Ghaznavid king, Bahram Shah, was forced by an invasion of Ghuzz Turkomans to leave Ghazni and to retire to the Panjab in 1160 where he ruled till his death. He was succeeded by his son, Khusrav Malik.

Khwaja Haji—was a renowned and loyal general of Sultan Ala-ud-din Khalji (1296-1316) who in co-operation with Kafur (*q.v.*) led several expeditions into, and conquered, southern India and established Ala-ud-din's sovereignty there.

Khawaja Jahan—whose original name was Ahmad, was an inspector of buildings in the reign of Sultan Ghiyas-ud-din Tughluq (1320-25). He was employed by the Sultan's son, Jauna Khan, in the construction of a pavilion at Tughluqabad which fell on the Sultan causing his death. The throne being thus vacant, Jauna Khan ascended the throne with the name of Sultan Muhammad Tughluq (1325-51). Ahmad was awarded by the Sultan the title of Khwaja Jahan and was made his minister. Khwaja Jahan served the Sultan during his reign of twenty-six years and won many campaigns for him. But on the death of the Sultan in 1351 he set up a rival to his nephew, Firuz Tughluq, was frustrated in his design, pardoned by the new Sultan and permitted to retire to a peaceful life at Samana, but was killed on his way there by the military escort that was sent to accompany him.

Khwaja Jahan—was the title conferred on Malik Sarvar, an eunuch, whom the sixth Tughluq Sultan Nasir-ud-din (1390-94) appointed in 1394 as Lord of the East (*Malik-ush-Sharq*) with his headquarters at Jaunpur. He soon extended his authority over the whole of the Gangetic Doab and practically ruled as an independent king till his death in 1399. His adopted son and successor Mubarak assumed the royal style and founded the Sharqi dynasty of rulers at Jaunpur (*q.v.*).

Khwaja Jahan—was for many years the minister of the Bahmani sultans, but as he aimed at monopolizing all power in the state he was put to death in 1463 and his office and title were conferred on Muhammad Gawan (*q.v.*).

Khwarizm—is an alternate name of Khiva (*q.v.*).

Khyber Pass—is the main but difficult mountain pass between India including West Pakistan and Afghanistan. At its Indian end are Peshawar and Landi Kotal from where it leads to Kabul, the capital of Afghanistan. Most of the invaders who came into India from the north-west entered India by this pass. It now connects western Panjab in Western Pakistan with Afghanistan. The early Hindu rulers could not protect it against foreign raiders; during the Muhammadan regime it was traversed by Timur, Babur, Humayun, Nadir Shah and Ahmad Shah Abdali. It was only after the Panjab had passed under British rule that the Khyber Pass was efficiently protected and since then no incursion has taken place through it into India.

Kile Gul Muhammad—is a small place near Quetta. Archaeological researches have revealed here the existence in prehistoric times of a lithic village culture without pottery. (Piggott, Stuart, *Prehistoric India*)

Kilpatrick, Col. John—was in the service of the East India Company and stationed in Madras. On receipt of the news of the Black Hole tragedy (*q.v.*) Kilpatrick was sent with 230 soldiers and brought the first relieving British army to the English refugees at Fulta in Bengal, lower down the Hughly from

Calcutta. Later on after the arrival of Clive (*q.v.*) and Watson (*q.v.*) he took part in recovering Calcutta. He is reported to have voted in the council of war that Clive held immediately before the battle of Plassey, against an advance, a decision which Clive at first accepted but which he later on rejected. Kilpatrick died in 1787.

Ki-pin—has been identified with Kashmir and also with Gandhara (*q.v.*). The latter identification appears to be more reasonable. In any case it was a territory lying between Afghanistan and the Panjab and included within itself Taxila. It was occupied by the Sakas (*q.v.*) from whom it passed under the control of the Kushan king, Kadphises I (*c.* A.D. 40-78).

Kirat Sagar—a fine lake near Mahoba in Bundelkhand, was constructed by the Chandella king, Kirtivarman (*c.* 1049-1100). It was eleven miles in circumference and had many temples on its banks.

Kirat Singh—the Raja of Kalanjar in Bundelkhand, incurred the displeasure of Sher Shah Sur (1540-45) by giving shelter to Bir Singh (or Bir Bhan) the Baghela Raja of Rewah, and offered him stout resistance when he tried to storm the fort of Kalanjar in 1545. Sher Shah took the fort but was mortally wounded. Later on Kirat Singh was killed by Sher Shah's son, Islam Shah.

Kirat Singh—a son of Raja Jay Singh (*q.v.*) of Amber, was reported to have killed his father in 1667 by poisoning at the instigation of Emperor Aurangzeb who considered the Raja's death as a good riddance.

Kirki, the battle of—marked the beginning of the Third Maratha War in 1817. Peshwa Baji Rao II attacked the British force stationed at Poona, but the latter was well led by Elphinstone (*q.v.*) and defeated the Peshwa in the battle of Kirki.

Kirtivarman—the Chandella king who ruled over Bundelkhand (*c.* A.D. 1049-1100), was a vigorous ruler who defeated Karnadeva (*q.v.*), the king of Chedi (Madhya Pradesh) and widely extended his dominions. He was also known for his public works of which the artificial lake Kirat Sagar (*q.v.*) was one He was also a patron of men of learning and Sri Krishna Misra, the author of the drama *Probodhachandrodaya* enjoyed his patronage.

Kishlu Khan—the governor of Multan and Sind, rose in rebellion against Sultan Muhammad Tughluq (1325-51) in 1328 but was defeated and slain in battle.

Kistna (or Krishna), the—is a river in south India. It rises in

the Western Ghats and flows eastward until it falls into the
Bay of Bengal near Guntur in Andhra Pradesh. Its tributary,
the Tungabhadra, merges into it near Raichur and creates
a doab which was for many years a bone of contention between
the Vijayanagar and Bahmani kingdoms. On its bank stood
the ancient city of Amaravati which developed its own style
of art and sculpture rivalling the Gandhara school. Its valley
is a most thickly populated and most fertile region.

Kitchener, Horatio Hubert, Earl, (1850-1916)—became the
Commander-in-Chief in India in 1902 after he had already
made his mark as a general in the Egypt and Sudan campaigns
(1896-99) and in the South African War in 1900. As the Commander-in-Chief in India, he carried out many administrative
reforms and re-organized the strategical re-distribution of
British and Indian troops in India. Lord Kitchener was no
liberal and opposed the appointment of an Indian to the
Viceroy's Executive Council. The most outstanding incident of
his regime in India was a serious controversy with the Viceroy,
Lord Curzon (*q.v.*) on the question of military administration.
The matter at issue was whether in the Viceroy's Executive
Council there should be an Army Member in addition to the
Commander-in-Chief. The Army Member was a military man,
but was necessarily junior in rank and inferior in military ex-
perience to the C.-in-C. Lord Kitchener wanted the abolition
of the post of the Army Member and the continuance of the
C.-in-C. as the sole military authority in the Executive Council.
Lord Curzon was definitely opposed to the proposal of Lord
Kitchener. The Secretary of State to whom the dispute was
referred for a final settlement, attempted a compromise which
Lord Kitchener accepted but was unacceptable to Lord
Curzon who resigned. Lord Kitchener thus retired from India
with a feather in his cap. On the outbreak of the First World
War in August, 1914 Lord Kitchener was placed in charge of
the War Office in England and made a great success in that
post. He died in harness as the result of the destruction of the
Hampshire which struck a mine in June, 1916, while on his voyage from Scapa Flow to Russia on an important military and
diplomatic mission.

Kleophis—was, according to the classical historians, the queen of
the Assakenoi (*q.v.*). She is reported to have borne a son to
Alexander, the king of Macedon.

Koh-i-noor, the—is the world-famous diamond. It adorned the
crown of the Mughul emperors, but was taken away by Nadir

Shah. On his death it passed to Ahmad Shah Abdali (*q.v.*) from whose descendant, Shah Shuja, it passed to Maharaja Ranjit Singh from whose successor it was taken by the British Indian Government which passed it on to Queen Victoria. It now adorns the crown of England.

Kolhapur—is the name of a city as well as of the state over which the second son of Shivaji ruled. It came under British protection after the Third Maratha war and continued to be a small subsidiary protected state till its merger with the Union of India in 1948.

Kollam—is the older name of the city of Quilon in Travancore. The Kollam era which dates from A.D. 824-25 and was often used in inscriptions found in the ancient Chera Kingdom, is supposed to mark the foundation of the city of Kollam.

Komaroff—a Russian general, drove an Afghan outpost from Panjdeh, a village and district a hundred miles south of Merv in 1885 and thus created a critical situation. Panjdeh was claimed by Russia as lying within the area which had passed into Russian control after the capture of Merv by Russia in 1884 but the British Government considered it a part of Afghanistan and its occupation by Russia as a threat to the integrity of Afghanistan. Thus Komaroff's action led to what is known as the Panjdeh incident (*q.v.*).

Konagamana, the stupa of—was situated near the village of Nigliva in the Basti district, U.P. It was visited by Emperor Asoka twice—once in the fourteenth year and the second time in the twentieth year of his reign. During his first visit he enlarged the stupa to double of its original size and during the second visit he added a stone pillar to the stupa. (*S.A.E.*, p. 55)

Kondapalli—a fortified place within the kingdom of Vijayanagar, was captured by the Bahmani sultan, Muhammad Shah III, in 1481, who killed with his own hands some Brahmans whom he found officiating as priests in a temple within the fort and thus earned the title of *Ghazi* of which he felt very proud.

Konkon, the—is a maritime tract extending from Daman on the north to Kanara on the south, the Western Ghats on the east and the Arabian Sea on the west. Violent monsoon rains and the rugged coast lines made piracy comparatively easy along the Konkan coast. Piracy was, however, extinguished by 1812.

Koppam, the battle of—was fought in A.D. 1152 or 1153 between Someswara (*q.v.*), the Chalukya king of Kalyani, and Rajadhiraja (*q.v.*), the Chola king. The latter was defeated and killed. It was an incident in the long-drawn Chalukya-Chola rivalry.

Kora, the district of—lying near Allahabad, was taken by the East India Company from the Nawab of Oudh after the battle of Buxar (1764) and was handed over to Emperor Shah Alam in 1765 along with Allahabad and a promise of an annual tribute of 26 lakhs of rupees in return for the grant by the Emperor to the Company of the Dewani of Bengal. Soon afterwards Shah Alam handed over Kora along with Allahabad to the Marathas from whom it was later on recovered and annexed to the British Indian Empire.

Korigaon, the battle of—was fought in the course of the Third Maratha War (*q.v.*) in 1818 between Peshwa Baji Rao II and the English. The Peshwa was defeated and eventually surrendered to Sir John Malcolm.

Korkai—an important port on the Tinnevelly coast in the early centuries of the Christian era, was the principal seat of the pearl trade. It has long been turned into an inland place on account of the change in the coast line. It has many Jain temples.

Koshala—is the name of two ancient kingdoms—one in north India comprising northern Oudh with its capital at Ayodhya and the other in south India in the Upper Mahanadi valley. Mahendra, the king of Koshala, in the south is mentioned in the Allahabad Pillar inscription of Samudragupta (*c.* A.D. 330-80) to whom he submitted. This Koshala in the south comprised the modern Bilaspur, Raipur and Sambalpur districts with its capital at Sripura, the modern Sripur in Raipur district. It did not play any prominent part in Indian history. But the Koshala of the north occupied a very important place in ancient Indian tradition and history. Its glory is recorded in the great epic the *Ramayana* of Valmiki who sings the praises of its king, Dasaratha and of his son, Rama. In historical times Koshala was a pretty large kingdom. It was one of the sixteen big states (*Mahajanapadas*) into which India was divided in about the sixth century B.C. It contained three great cities, namely, Ayodhya, Saketa and Sravasti. It was ruled by kings who traced their descent from Ikshvaku, some of whose descendants are mentioned in the Vedas. The first definitely historical king of Koshala was Prasenajit who was a contemporary of king Bimbisara of Magadha. Both of them were again contemporaries of Gautama Buddha. There was a keen competition between Koshala and Magadha for supremacy which ended in the absorption of Koshala in the kingdom of

Magadha during the reign of the latter's king, Ajatasatru (*c.* 494-467 B.C.).

Kotah, the battle of—was fought between the East India Company's army under Col. Monson and the Holkar's army in 1804. Col. Monson was defeated and forced to retreat to Agra. It was one of the reverses that broke the spell of the victories hitherto won by Lord Wellesley.

Kotah, the city and state of—is in Rajputana on the right bank of the Chambal, 250 miles from Delhi. The state was created in 1625 by Emperor Shah Jahan who made a gift of it to a younger son of the Raja of Bundi in recognition of services rendered by the Prince when Shah Jahan was in rebellion against his father, Jahangir. The state was merged in the Union of Rajasthan in March, 1948.

Krateros—one of the most faithful and capable Greek generals who accompanied Alexander on his expedition into the Panjab, whom Alexander valued "equally with himself", took part in the battle of the Karri plain where Poros (*q.v.*) was defeated. Later on he led the Greek army down the Indus along its right bank through the lower Panjab and Sind. Finally he led back the victorious Greek army by way of Qandahar and Sistan to Babylon.

Krishna—is the name of a Hindu *avatar* who is worshipped all over India. His exploits are related in the *Mahabharata* and in the *Bhagavata*.

Krishna I—the second Rashtrakuta (*q.v.*) king (A.D. 768-72), completed the establishment of Rashtrakuta supremacy over the Chalukyas (*q.v.*) and built the Kailasha monolithic temple (*q.v.*) at Ellora which has been described as the most marvellous architectural monument of ancient India.

Krishna II—was a later Rashtrakuta king who ruled from A.D. 877-913.

Krishna III—the last great king of the Rashtrakuta dynasty, ruled from A.D. 939-68, and was succeeded by three nominal rulers.

Krishna—was the second king of the Satavahana (*q.v.*) dynasty. His probable date is 235 B.C. He extended the Satavahana dominions up to Nasik in the west.

Krishna, the—*see* Kistna, the.

Krishna Raja—son and successor of Sir Chamo Rajendra of Mysore, ascended the throne in 1896, was a liberal ruler and introduced many reforms in the administration of his kingdom which he made an advanced state in the British Empire in India.

Krishnadeva Raya—the king of Vijayanagar from 1509 to 1529, was one of the greatest monarchs of Vijayanagar. He repulsed an attack of the Sultan of Bidar, defeated and killed in battle Yusuf Adil Shah (*q.v.*), Sultan of Bijapur, and later on recovered from Bijapur the fortress of Raichur over which there had been a prolonged contest. He even temporarily occupied Bijapur and destroyed the fortress of Kulbarga. He also defeated Raja Prataprudra of Orissa and extended his dominions up to the Krishna, and later on through Telingana to beyond the Godavari into Orissa. In the south he extended his dominions up to Sriringapattanam (Seringapatam) in Mysore. Thus during his rule the Vijayanagar kingdom came to cover the whole of the Presidency of Madras with a large part of Orissa in the north and the whole of Mysore in the south. Krishnadeva Raya was a brave and chivalrous king who deeply impressed all who came in contact with him including foreign travellers like Nuniz (*q.v.*) and Paes (*q.v.*) who happened to visit his kingdom. Himself a poet and author, Krishnadeva Raya was also a liberal patron of men of letters and made large endowments on temples and learned Brahmans and the famous Telugu poet, Alasani Peddana, was his court poet. (Aiyangar, S. K., *Krishnadeva Raya of Vijayanagar*)

Kirttivasa—a famous Bengali poet, born in A.D. 1346, made a free translation of the Sanskrit *Ramayana* into Bengali. It has been called the Bible of Bengal.

Kshatriyas, the—formed the second of the four *varnas* into which Indo-Aryan society was divided at a very early age. They formed the fighting and the ruling class. Etymologically the term means one who saves (others) from injury. According to the Brahmanical texts the Kshatriyas formed the second of the four *varnas*, but several Buddhist texts place them above the Brahmans and make them the highest caste. Gautama Buddha and Mahavira both belonged to the Kshatriya caste and this circumstance lends support to the theory that Buddhism and Jainism represented as much the resentment of the Kshatriyas at the Brahmanical claim to supremacy as the desire for a separate philosophy of life. In any case, in later times the Kshatriyas definitely formed the second of the four higher castes amongst the Hindus.

Kshemadharma—the third king of the Saisunaga dynasty (*q.v.*), ruled in the second half of the seventh century B.C. Nothing is known about his reign.

Kshemajit (or Kshatraujas)—was the fourth king of the

Saisunaga dynasty and the immediate predecessor of king Bimbisara (*q.v.*) (*c.* 522 - 494 B.C.). Nothing but his name is known.

Kshudrakas, the—were the tribal people whom the classical historians called the Oxydrakoi, who occupied the part of the Panjab below the confluence of the Jhelum and the Chinab. They submitted to Alexander when he invaded their country and sent as tribute a number of chariots and bucklers, 100 talents of steel and a great store of linen showing that they had an advanced civilisation.

Kubera—was a king of Devarashtra who, according to the Allahabad Pillar inscription, was captured in battle and then set free by Samudragupta (*q.v.*). Devarashtra has been located in the modern Vizagapatam district in Andhra Pradesh.

Kuberanaga—was one of the queens of Chandragupta II (*c.* A.D. 380-413).

Kubja Vishnuvardhana—a younger brother of the Chalukya king, Pulakeshin II (*c.* A.D. 609-42), was appointed in 611 by his royal brother as the Governor of the kingdom of Vengi lying between the Krishna and the Godavari with his capital at Pishtapura, modern Pithapuram. In about A.D. 615 Kubja Vishnuvardhana set himself up as an independent king at Vengi and founded the line of the Eastern Chalukyas (*q.v.*) which ruled till A.D. 1070.

Kucha or Kuchi—was a town in Turkistan. It was a great centre of Indian culture and civilisation and of Buddhism in the early centuries of the Christian era. It was from this town that the famous Buddhist monk, Kumarajiva (*q.v.*) was taken as a prisoner to China where he devoted himself to the preaching of Buddhism.

Kujula Kadphises—*see* Kadphises I.

Kulinism—is a system of nobility that was introduced amongst the Brahmans of Bengal by Vallalasena (*c.* A.D. 1158-79), the second Sena king of Bengal. Later on it was extended by his son and successor, Lakshmanasena (*c.* A.D. 1179-1206). Its original purpose is uncertain, but in later times it became a source of great social tyranny limiting marriages within certain groups resulting in an excess of unmarried girls amongst the Kulins and in the marriages by Kulins of a large number of women whom they did not support. This led to much social abuse and the system was seriously challenged by the Western-educated Bengalees in the nineteenth century. Though in recent times it has lost much of its old strictness it still persists amongst the higher castes of Hindus in Bengal.

Kulluka—a Sanskrit scholar born in Bengal but domiciled at Benares, flourished about the middle of the fourteenth century, was the author of a commentary on *Manu-Samhita* (Institutes of Manu) (*q.v.*) which greatly influenced Hindu society in Bengal.

Kulottunga I—was the son of Ammangadevi, a daughter of the Chola king, Rajendra I (*q.v.*) (A.D. 1012-44) and of the Eastern Chalukya king Rajaraja Narendra I (A.D. 1022-63). On the death of the Chola king, Adhirajendra (A.D. 1067-70) he succeeded to the Chola throne and thus started the new Chalukya-Chola dynasty. He ruled from A.D. 1070 to 1122. His dynasty ruled over the Chola kingdom from A.D. 1070 till its extinction in A.D. 1279. He was a capable king who conquered Kalinga and effected in A.D. 1086 (the year of the survey of the Domesday Book) an elaborate revision of the revenue survey of the Chola kingdom. During his rule Ramanuja (*q.v.*) who had left the Chola country during the reign of his predecessor Adhirajendra on account of his policy of religious intolerance, returned to and settled again at Srirangam, the Chola capital.

Kulottunga Chola II—the third king of the Chalukya-Chola dynasty, ruled from A.D. 1133 to 1150. (Shastri, N. K., *Hist. of S. India*)

Kulottunga Chola III—the last great king of the Chalukya-Chola dynasty, reigned from A.D. 1178 to 1218. He led several campaigns into the Pandya country which submitted to him for some time. He is also said to have led in A.D. 1208 an expedition against Vengi (*q.v.*). But in A.D. 1216 he suffered a severe reverse at the hands of the Pandya king and could get back his throne only by accepting the suzerainty of the Pandya king, Sundara. The Chalukya-Chola dynasty never recovered from this blow. (Shastri, N. K., *Hist. of S. India*)

Kumara—*see* Bhaskaravarman.

Kumara Devi—a Lichchavi princess, was married to Chandragupta I (*c.* A.D. 320-30) and was the mother of the famous Samudragupta (*c.* A.D. 330-380). This marriage is believed to have largely helped in the progress of Chandragupta I and was proudly mentioned in the inscription of her son.

Kumaragupta I—the son and successor of Chandragupta II Vikramaditya (*c.* A.D. 375-413), ruled from *c.* A.D. 413 to 453, maintained the integrity of the vast empire that he inherited and probably also extended it as he, like his grandfather Samudragupta, celebrated the horse-sacrifice; but threatening clouds began to gather over the Gupta Empire even during his reign. First, a people called the Pushyamitras, hitherto unknown, invaded the empire. Their repulse was followed by raids by the Hunas which were stopped after some hard fighting under the leadership of Kumaragupta's son, Skandagupta. Kumaragupta I, however, died in the midst of these troubles.

Kumaragupta II—a great-grandson of Kumaragupta I, succeeded his father, Narasimhagupta Baladitya, in about A.D. 473 and ruled till 474. His dominions were restricted to the eastern provinces of his ancestral empire and his rule was short. He was the last of the Gupta rulers in the direct line.

Kumaraghosha—a celebrated Buddhist monk of Bengal, became the Guru or preceptor of the Sailendra kings (*q.v.*) of Java. At his bidding a Sailendra king built in Java the beautiful temple of Tara.

Kumarajiva—born in A.D. 344 of an Indian father named Kumara or Kumarayana and of Princess Jiva, sister of the king of Kucha in Central Asia, epitomised the story of the expansion of Indian culture in general and of Buddhism in particular outside India. Educated first at Kucha and then in Kashmir and ordained as a Buddhist monk at the age of 20 Kumarajiva settled in Kucha to teach the *Mahayana* form of Buddhism. Taken as a captive to China Kumarajiva was commissioned by the Chinese Emperor, Yao Hhin, in A.D. 401 to propagate Buddhism in his dominions. He then settled in the Chinese capital Chang-an where he lived till his death in A.D. 413. During these last twelve years of his life Kumarajiva, with the help of a band of Chinese scholars whose services were placed at his disposal by the Chinese Emperor, translated as many as ninety-eight Sanskrit Buddhist works into Chinese including the *Prajnaparamita*, the *Vimalakirtinirdesha* and the *Saddharma-Pundarikasutra*—all fundamental texts of the *Mahayana* school. He also made many disciples amongst the Chinese, the most famous of whom was Fa-Hien who, at his instance, visited India during the years A.D. 405-11. Kumarajiva thus started the *Mahayana* form of Buddhism on that career of conquest which soon passed over from China to Korea and then to Japan. Greater India fulfilled herself in Kumarajiva and the numerous other Indian Buddhist monks who followed in his footsteps.

Kumaramatya—was an official designation borne by high officials in the Gupta Empire. Poet Harishena who composed the Allahabad Pillar inscription of Samudragupta (*q.v.*) bore this title in addition to other designations like *Mahadandanayaka* meaning a military officer. A *Kumaramatya* was attached either directly to the sovereign or to a prince royal or to a provincial governor.

Kumarapala—a Chalukya prince, was selected by the nobles for the throne of Gujarat, ruled from A.D. 1143 to 1172 with Anhilwara as his capital, and was an ardent Jain and patron of the famous Jain *Acharya* Hemachandra. In his zeal for non-violence he ruthlessly inflicted the capital punishment on all persons guilty of violating the *ahimsa* doctrine by killing any living being on any pretext. He also built many Jain temples.

Kumarapala—a later king of the Pala dynasty of Bengal, was the son of Ramapala whom he succeeded in *c.* A.D. 1120. His reign was short covering only 5 years during which the decline of the Pala power began with the establishment of an independent state in Kamarupa by Kumarapala's favourite and minister, Vidyadeva.

Kumarila Bhatta—was an erudite commentator on the Sutras and the philosophical works of the orthodox Hindus, upheld the doctrine of the immortality of the individual soul and was a severe critic of Buddhist doctrines and philosophy. He was a native of southern India and flourished in about A.D. 700.

Kumbha—the Rana of Mewar (A.D. 1431-69), was one of the greatest rulers of Mewar who fought against the Muslim rulers of Malwa and Gujarat and held his own against their superior resources. He was also a great builder and built thirty-two out of the eighty-four fortresses that defended Mewar. Amongst these edifices the fortress of Kumbhalgarh is a masterpiece of military architecture and his *Jayastambha* (also called *Kirttistambha*) bears eloquent testimony to the genius of this versatile king who was a poet, a man of letters and an accomplished musician in addition to being a great administrator and warrior. (Todd, *Annals of Rajasthan*)

Kumrahar—is a village near Bankipore in Bihar. It is the site of the ancient city of Pataliputra (*q.v.*).

Kuna (also called Sundara Nedumaran)—a Pandya king, ruled in about the middle of the seventh century A.D., was originally a Jain by religion, but later on embraced Saivaism. He signalised his conversion by atrocious outrages on the Jains, 8000 of whom he is said to have impaled.

Kunala—was a son of Asoka. He is not mentioned in any inscription of Asoka or of his descendants. According to the Puranas, however, he succeeded his father Asoka to the throne of Magadha. He is also the centre of legends which arouse great pathos. He is said to have incurred the anger of his stepmother Tishyarakshita, who is also not mentioned in any Asokan inscription. She got him blinded and deposed from his governorship of Taxila by order of Asoka. Later on, however, Asoka found out his mistake and had the consolation of seeing the eyesight of his beloved son restored by the application, on his blinded eyes, of the tears that rolled down the cheeks of hundreds of pious monks who wept on hearing a sermon on Buddha delivered by the pious monk Ghosha.

Kunika—a name of Ajatasatru (*q.v.*).

Kunwar Singh—a Rajput landlord of Jagadishpur in the district of Arrah in Bihar, was deprived of his estates by the Board of Revenue of Bengal some time before the Sepoy Mutiny and had begun to conspire against the Company's rule before 1857. The Sepoy Mutiny offered him a golden opportunity and he joined it with great energy. He killed several Europeans on whom he could lay his hands, but was eventually suppressed by William Taylor, the Commissioner of Patna Division, who was helped by Major Vincent Eyre (*q.v.*) of the Bengal Artillery

Kural, the—is an important poetical work in Tamil. It was written in the early centuries of the Christian era. It is the most venerated and popular book south of the Godavari. It has been described as the mouthpiece of the Tamil people giving expression to their moral ideals and ethical doctrines.

Kurala—was a state in the Deccan mentioned in Samudragupta's (*q.v.*) Allahabad inscription. Its king Mantaraja was defeated and then reinstated in his throne by the Gupta Emperor Kurala has not yet been definitely identified.

Kurram (**also called** *Kottam*)—was a territorial and administrative unit in the Chola kingdom (*q.v.*). It comprised a group of villages which managed local affairs through the agency of an assembly called *mahasabha* which was elected annually by an elaborate system. It exercised extensive powers of local self-government, subject to the royal control, imposed local taxes, had its own local treasury and enjoyed full control over the lands of the Union. It also looked, through committees of its own, after tanks, gardens, maintenance of peace and dispensation of justice within its locality.

Kurdla—*see* Kharda.

Kurukshetra—was the famous battlefield where, according to the *Mahabharata*, the Kurus and the Pandavas fought a great battle lasting eighteen days to decide who between them should rule over north India. The battle ended in the victory of the

Pandavas. The site of the battle has been located near Delhi, not very far from Panipat, where the fate of India was decided thrice. The historicity of the battle has been questioned by Western scholars but is accepted by all orthodox Hindus.

Kurus, the—were the sons of Dhritarashtra, the king of Indraprastha which was situated near the modern village of Indrapat, adjacent to Delhi. Their rivalry and war with their cousins, the Pandavas (or sons of Pandu) (*q.v.*) form the central theme of the great Sanskrit epic, the *Mahabharata*.

Kushans, the—were a section of the Yueh-chi horde who were a nomadic people who settled in Bactria where they shed their nomadic habits. In the first century of the pre-Christian era they began to make raids into India. They were divided into several sections of which the Kushans were one who under Kujula Kara Kadphises (*q.v.*) eventually established their predominance over the other four sections. This chieftain later on established the Kushan dynasty of kings in India and came to be known in Indian history as Kadphises I (*q.v.*). The Kushans established a vast empire in India over which they ruled probably from *c*. A.D. 48 to 220. Kadphises I, Kadphises II, Kanishka, Huvishka and Vasudeva were the more important Kushan kings of India. The foundation of the *Saka* era dating from A.D. 78 has been generally attributed to the Kushans.

Kusinagara—is modern Kasia in the Gorakhpur district of Uttar Pradesh. Here Gautama Buddha died.

Kusthalapura—was one of the South Indian states whose king Dhananjaya was dethroned but reinstated by Samudragupta (*q.v.*). It was possibly situated in North Arcot.

Kusumpura—was an alternative name of the city of Pataliputra (*q.v.*).

Kutb Minar—*see* Qutb Minar.

Kutbu-ud-din Ibak—*see* Qutb-ud-din Aibak.

Kuveranaga—*see* Kuberanaga.

L

La Bourdonnais, M.—was the French Governor of Mauritius on the eve of the outbreak of the First Anglo-French War (*q.v.*) in India. He was a leader of genius who, in the absence of a French fleet in Indian waters, improvised a fleet of French merchant ships and country craft, sailed to the Coromandel coast, forced the British fleet under Peyton (*q.v.*) to retire to the Bay of Bengal and captured Madras in September, 1746. This was a signal triumph for the French but La Bourdonnais soon quarrelled with Dupleix and his fleet was also dispersed by a storm. Madras, however, remained in French possession until the war was concluded by the treaty of Aix-la-Chapelle in 1748 when Madras was restored to the English. After his retirement he published his *Memoirs* in 1750.

Lad Malika—was the widowed wife of Taj Khan, the Lord of Chunar, who on the murder of her husband by her step-son in about 1528, married Sher Khan (later on Sher Shah) and gave him the possession of the fortress of Chunar with its large treasure. She thus started Sher Shah on his victorious career which culminated in his accession to the throne of Delhi in 1540.

Laghman (also spelt Lamghan)—is on the north bank of the Kabul river, a little above Jalalabad in Afghanistan. Near it, at Pul-i-Duranta an Asokan inscription in Aramaic has been found, proving that Laghman was included in the Asokan empire. More than a thousand years later, it was included within the kingdom of Jaipal (*q.v.*) who lost it to Amir Sabuktigin in about A.D. 990. Henceforth it has been a part of the kingdom of Afghanistan.

Lahore—is on the left bank of the Ravi in the Punjab of which it is the capital. It is an ancient city which, according to Hindu tradition, was founded by Lava, son of Rama, the hero of the *Ramayana*. It was perhaps founded in the early centuries of the Christian era and in the seventh century was important enough to be mentioned by the Chinese pilgrim, Hiuen Tsang (*q.v.*). It fell successively to the rulers of Ghazni and of Ghur and of the sultans of Delhi. Under the Mughuls it rose in importance because it became a place of royal residence where Akbar Jahangir and Shah Jahan all liked to stay. It developed into a magnificent city with its fort, palaces, mosques, and above all, its gardens of which the Shahdara was planted by Jahangir and the Shalimar by Shah Jahan. From 1707 till 1799 when it was captured by Ranjit Singh (*q.v.*) it suffered repeated invasions and conquests by Nadir Shah (*q.v.*) and Ahmad Shah Abdali (*q.v.*). It became a possession of the Sikhs in 1768. Ranjit Singh made it the capital of his kingdom. In 1849 at the end of the Second Sikh War (*q.v.*) it was annexed to the British Indian Empire and continued to be the capital of the Panjab till 1947 when it became the capital of West Pakistan. From this distinction it has been recently deprived in favour of Rawalpindi.

Laing, Samuel, (1810-97)—was a British author on Economics and an expert Railway administrator. He was Finance Member of the Viceroy's Executive Council from 1860 to 1862. Following up the measures of his predecessor, James Wilson, Laing restored equilibrium to Indian finances badly affected by the Mutiny by enforcing drastic economies, by increasing the salt tax, by imposing a uniform tariff of 10 per cent, and by instituting an income tax on non-agricultural incomes.

Lake, Lord Gerard (1744-1808)—was a renowned British general who fought in the Second Maratha War (*q.v.*). After several years of efficient service as an officer in the British army in France and Ireland he was appointed Commander-in-Chief of the E. I. Company's army in India in 1800. He reached Calcutta in 1802 and had hardly time enough to introduce certain reforms in the army when on the outbreak of the Second Maratha War (*q.v.*) he took charge of the British army in North India where his principal enemy was the Sindhia whom he defeated at Coel, then stormed Alighar, took Delhi and Agra and then completely broke his power by his great victory at Laswari (*q.v.*) (1803) which obliged Sindhia to make peace with the British. Lake then engaged Holkar (*q.v.*) whom he defeated at Furukabad in 1804; but he failed to capture the fort of Bharatpur in 1805 and had to make peace with the Raja by leaving him in independent possession of his fort and territories. Lake, however, pursued Holkar into the Panjab and compelled him to make peace. For his brilliant achievements in the war Lake was honoured with a peerage which, however, he did not live long to enjoy.

Lakha—was the Rana of Mewar from 1382 to 1418.

Lakhsmaniya, Rai—*see* Lakshmana Sena.

Lakhnauti—*see* Gour.

Lakshmana—was a younger brother of Rama, the hero of the *Ramayana*, who accompanied his eldest brother, Rama in his exile for fourteen years and stood by him loyally all through his life. The Pratihara (*q.v.*) kings claimed descent from him.

Lakshmana Sena—was the son and successor of King Ballal Sena of Bengal. He ascended the throne either in A.D. 1184-85 or a few years earlier in A.D. 1178-79. In the earlier part of his reign he reduced Kamarupa (Assam) to subjection and defeated the Gahadvala king of Benares. He was also a patron of learning and his court was adorned by two great poets, namely, Jayadeva, the author of the famous lyric *Gita Govinda* and Dhoyi, the author of the *Pavanaduta* and also by the great Hindu jurist, Halayudha. But later in his life he lost all energy and suffered himself to be surprised in his capital city of Nadiah, when he was taking his mid-day meal, by Malik Iktiyar-ud-din Muhammad Khalji (*q.v.*) either in 1199 or 1202. According to the Muhammadan historian, the Khalji chief had brought with him only eighteen troopers with whom he succeeded in effecting a complete surprise. Lakshmana Sena, called Rai Lakshmaniya by the Muhammadan historians, fled from his palace by a back-door and retired to East Bengal where his descendants maintained their independence for the next fifty years. (*H.B.*, Vol. I)

Lakhsmi Bai—the dowager Rani of Jhansi (*q.v.*), deeply and intensely resented the annexation of her husband's state in 1853 by the application of the Doctrine of Lapse by Lord Dalhousie. So on the outbreak of the Sepoy Mutiny she joined the mutineers and gallantly defended Jhansi against the English army under Sir Hugh Rose. When Jhansi was stormed by the English, Lakshmi Bai left the fort and continued her hostility from Kalpi. On the fall of Kalpi Rani Lakshmi Bai, acting in co-operation with Tantia Topi (*q.v.*), attacked Gwalior, the capital of Sindhia, who with his personal army had been standing loyally by the Company. Lakshmi Bai forced Sindhia to escape for safety to the English at Agra and her courage won over the Sindhia's army to the side of the mutineers. The Rani and her associates there proclaimed Nana Shaheb (*q.v.*) as the Peshwa, threatened to march into the Maratha country and thus spread the Mutiny amongst the Marathas. At this critical juncture Sir Hugh Rose and his army made supreme efforts to stop the further success of the Rani. They recovered Gwalior and inflicted two severe defeats on the Rani's army at the battles of Marar and Kotah. The Rani, dressed in male attire as a sowar, was killed in one of these battles on the 17th June, 1858. She was the best and bravest military leader of the mutinous sepoys and with her death the back of the Mutiny was broken in Central India.

Lakshmi Karna—the son and successor of the Kalachuri king, Gangeyadeva (*q.v.*) of Chedi or Bundelkhand, ruled from *c*. A.D. 1040-1070. Lakshmi Karna completed the conquest of the Southern Doab, made an alliance with the Pala king of Bengal and extended his conquests up to Kalinga. But he was defeated and killed in the battle fought against a combination of the rulers of Gujarat, Malwa and the Deccan.

Lakshmanavati—*see* Gour.

Lala Lajpat Rai (1856-1928)—born in the Punjab, was a lawyer by profession and an Arya Samajist in religion. He took a most prominent part in the Congress affairs and along with Tilak (*q.v.*) and Bepin Pal (*q.v.*) took a prominent part in changing the Congress method from one of petition to that of application of direct sanction. He, therefore, incurred the displeasure of the British Government and was deported under Regulation III to Burma in 1907. He was President of the Calcutta session of the Indian National Congress in 1919. He joined the non-co-operation movement and took a leading part in organising the boycott movement against the Simon Commission in 1928; but he died on 27 November, the same year as a result of a severe assault by the police on the 30th of the preceding month. He wrote several books of which *Unhappy India* was a severe condemnation of British administration in India. He was a political leader of great eminence and a national hero loved and admired by millions of his countrymen. A suburb of New Delhi has been named Lajpat Nagar after him.

Lalitaditya—a king of Kashmir belonging to the Karkota dynasty (*q.v.*), ruled from A.D. 724 to 760 and is credited with many victories. He certainly defeated Yasovarman (*q.v.*) of Kanauj and had victories over the Tibetans and the Turks on the Indus and over a king of Bengal. He built many edifices of which the Martand temple dedicated to the Sun-god is the most famous.

Lally, Comte de—was a French general of Irish parentage who was sent by the Government of France to succeed Dupleix (*q.v.*). He arrived at Pondicherry in 1758 and signalised his arrival by capturing Fort St. David from the English. But he had no more success in India. He was brave and incorruptible and no mean tactician, but was hot-headed and intolerant of advice. He failed in an attack on the Raja of Tanjore to compel him to clear up a debt and thus lowered French prestige in India. He then attempted to besiege and capture Madras and recalled Bussy (*q.v.*) from the Nizam's court at Hyderabad. The siege of Madras failed. On Bussy's recall, French influence at Hyderabad ended and the English also captured the Northern Circars of which the French had so long been in possession. Finally he was defeated by the English at the battle of Wandiwash (*q.v.*) in 1760 and forced to surrender Pondicherry in 1761 to the English who made him a prisoner of war and sent him to England. In the meantime serious charges had been brought against him in France and Lally returned on parole to France where he was pronounced guilty, condemned to death and executed in 1763.

Lall Singh—a Sikh leader, became in 1843 the minister of Rani Jhindan, (*q.v.*), the mother and Regent of Maharaja Dalip Singh (*q.v.*) of the Panjab. Two years later on the outbreak of the First Sikh War (*q.v.*) which was due to a certain extent to his crooked policy, he took command of the Sikh army and lost through his supineness the battles of Mudki (1845) and Ferozshah and finally the battle of Sabraon (1846) which practically brought to a close the First Sikh War. In the treaty of Lahore (1846), which restored peace, Lall Singh retained his position as the chief minister, but he was suspected of connivance in an attack on the British *protégé*, Raja Golab Singh (*q.v.*) of Kashmir and was dismissed from office.

Lalsont, the battle of—was fought between Mahadaji Sindhia and the Mughul army in 1787 in which Sindhia was defeated. This reverse checked Sindhia's progress for a time.

Lambert, Commodore—was sent by Lord Dalhousie in command of a frigate to Pagan, the king of Burma, to demand compensation for the losses that English merchants had suffered at the hands of the Government of Burma. Lambert who was of a 'combustible temperament', took serious offence at the refusal of the Burmese Governor of Rangoon to receive a deputation of some of his naval officials, declared Rangoon to be in a state of blockade and seized a ship of the king of Burma. This led the Burmese to open fire on the English frigate which, under Lambert's order, returned the fire. Lord Dalhousie made this a pretext for demanding heavy compensation. As the Burmese Government did not agree the Second Burmese War (*q.v.*) broke out.

Land Revenue—has been since ancient times the mainstay of the finance of governments in India. That the government of the day is entitled to a share of the produce of the land has always been an accepted principle in India. Under the rule of Hindu princes, like the Mauryas and the Guptas, the government was entitled to one-sixth of the gross produce of the land. During the Muhammadan period it was often arbitrarily raised, but Akbar fixed it at one-third of the produce and that continued to be recognised as the legal rate throughout the rest of the Mughul rule. In practice, however, there existed infinite diversity both in the amount of the incidence as well as in the manner of its collection. The British, who adopted the Mughul system with necessary alterations, practically followed the principle of taking no less than one-third of the produce and continued to recognise land revenue as one of the main sources of Governmental revenue. They, however, took more elaborate measures than the Mughuls to survey periodically the land which had been first done in the sixteenth century by Sher Shah Sur (*q.v.*) to settle the gross produce and the money value of it and to collect rigorously all that may be considered as the Government share. Nothing, however, was done to diminish the incidence of land revenue. The present Republican Government of India so far has been practically carrying on the British system, though it has begun to try to abolish the middleman variously called zamindar, talukdar and jotdar between the Government and the man behind the plough and thus turn the *ryot* into the owner of the land that he cultivates.

Land Tenure, systems of—are varied in different parts of India. The exact conditions on which land was held by the cultivators when India was ruled by Indian kings, is difficult to determine. During the Muslim period the method was haphazard until Akbar introduced a system according to which the revenue payable by the cultivator was collected directly by the officers of the state and could be paid either in cash or in kind, though cash payments were encouraged. Thus the ryot held his land directly from the Crown. But in the eighteenth century, with the growing decline of the power of the Mughul Emperor, the tax collectors tended to be hereditary and the right of collection of revenue from the cultivator which was a duty, came to be considered as a right and a possession and the collector of revenue came to be looked upon as the owner or zamindar of the land the revenue of which he collected. He thus came to assume a position which had never been his before. The British successors of the Mughuls, especially in Bengal, Bihar and Orissa, after some disastrous experiments, came to recognise the Zamindars as the proprietors of the land and established in Bengal, Bihar and Orissa what is known as the Permanent Settlement by which the Zamindar was recognised as the proprietor of the land on condition that he paid to the Government by a fixed date of the year the annual rent which amounted to ninety per cent of the estimated revenue that he received from the ryots who held land at his pleasure. Later legislation attempted to give the ryot protection against rack-renting and unjust eviction, but he continued to be without any proprietory right on the land he tilled unless he had purchased it by paying the Zamindar a special additional fee and price. This Zamindari system which was established in Bengal, Bihar and Orissa in 1793 continued till after the attainment of independence by India and has only been recently abolished and measures are still to be taken to give the proprietorship of the land to only the man who ploughs it. Secondly, the *Ryotwari* system of land tenure was introduced early in the nineteenth century in Madras and Bombay. Under this system the settlement is made by the Government direct with the ryot or cultivator who thus becomes the proprietor, but only for a period of time which was later on fixed for thirty years after which there was to be a re-assessment and re-settlement on new terms. The Government share was fixed at one-half of the produce. Thus the cultivator was only partially benefited; he got security of tenure for a period of time, but was subject not only to heavy but also to over-assessment. A third system of land tenure known as the *Mahalwari* system was established in Uttar Pradesh. According to it the settlement was made with village communities or *mahals* and the whole community was recognised as owners of land and liable to pay the revenue for it. The village elders apportioned the demand amongst the cultivators according to the areas of their respective holdings which were carefully measured. Side by side with the *Mahalwari* system there existed in Uttar Pradesh the *Talukdari* system which recognised the *Talukdar* as the proprietor and gave him full control over the ryot. It differed from the Zamindari or Permanent system of Bengal only in as much as it was not permanent. A fifth system of land tenure that prevailed in Gujarat and the Deccan is known as the *Mamlatdari* system under which local officers called *Mamlatdars* settled by bargaining with the *Desari* and *Patels* of each village the sum of money payable by the village as land-revenue and left to them the task of raising the agreed sums in their own way without interference. Gradually the *Ryotwari* system replaced the *Mamlatdari* system throughout the Bombay Presidency. The essence of the different systems of land tenure prevalent in the British Indian Empire was the maintenance of a set of middlemen called by different names in different parts of the vast country, who acted as intermediaries between the Government and the cultivators and formed a sort of a feudal aristocracy on whose support the Government could count. After the attainment of independence, the Republic of India has set before itself the ideal of setting up a socialistic pattern of society which involves the liquidation of all traces of feudalism. But so far little has been done to distribute land, especially agricultural land, on a socialistic basis so that the arable land will be the property only of the man behind the plough.

Lansdowne, Marquess of—was the Viceroy and Governor-General of India from 1888 to 1894. His administration was marked by peace within India except for a short rising in the independent state of Manipur (*q.v.*) for which Tikendrajit, the Commander-in-Chief of the state, was held responsible. The rising was suppressed and Tikendrajit was executed. The price of silver was falling for some time past and during Lord Lansdowne's administration it reached such a pass that in 1893 the Indian mints were closed to the unrestricted coinage of silver and gold coins or bullion were to be accepted in exchange for rupees at the rate of fifteen for a sovereign in place of the earlier rate of ten for a sovereign. This led ultimately to the fixation of the exchange at 1*s*. 4*d*. per rupee to the considerable loss of India. Lord Lansdowne upheld to a certain extent the 'forward policy' on the frontiers of India in the north-east as well as in the north-west. The British conquest of Burma was recognised by China. The independent kingdom of Sikkim was brought under British protection in 1888 and its boundary with Tibet was demarcated. The Lushais who inhabit the hill country north-east of Chittagong, the Chins a little further east and the Shan states beyond the Irrawady were all brought within the sphere of British influence. In the north-west a strategic railway line was constructed from Quetta to the Bolan Pass making easier an advance on Qandahar. Two small states, Hunza and Nagar, on the Afghan frontier near Gilgit were annexed in 1892 and Kalat leading to the Chitral valley was brought under British protection the same year. All this expansion of British rule in the north-west caused some uneasiness to the reigning Amir, Abdur Rahman, who suspected the intentions of the British. Ultimately in 1892, Lord Lansdowne succeeded in persuading the Amir to accept Sir Mortimer Durand as the British envoy to Afghanistan where he went without any British escort, established cordial relations with the Amir, came to an agreement with him over certain disputed territories and finally succeeded in drawing up the famous Durand line marking the boundary, where possible, between Afghanistan and India.

Lausena (also spelt **Lavanasena**)—a general of king Devapala (*c.* A.D. 810-850) of Bengal, is said to have conquered Assam and Kalinga. (*E.H.I.*, p. 414; 1924)

Laswari, the battle of—was fought in 1803 in the course of the Second Maratha War (*q.v.*). In this battle the British army under Lord Lake severely defeated the Maratha army led by the Sindhia.

Law, Jean—a French adventurer, was in India in the middle of the eighteenth century. He came to be acquainted with Shahjada, later on Emperor Shah Alam II (1759-1806) and has left his impressions about the Prince in his *Memoirs*.

Lawrence, Sir Henry Montgomery (1806-57)—was a famous British soldier and statesman who contributed much to the consolidation of the British rule, particularly in the Panjab. Born in Ceylon, he joined the Bengal Artillery in 1823 and took part in the First Burmese War (*q.v.*), in the First Afghan War (*q.v.*) and in the First Sikh War (*q.v.*). He was opposed to the policy of the annexation of the Panjab and supported the policy of reconstruction there. He was appointed British Resident at Lahore and President of the Council of Regency till Maharaja Dalip Singh (*q.v.*) would come of age. In 1849 after the Second Sikh War (*q.v.*) which led to the annexation of the Panjab he was made the President of the Board of Administration of the annexed province with charge of the political duties while his brother, John Lawrence, six years his junior, was placed in charge of the financial administration of the province. Henry was for treating the Sikh aristocracy with generosity by granting them life-pensions and large estates, but John was for improvement of the condition of the common man by reducing the revenue and controlling the rights of the landlords. Lord Dalhousie, who was then the Governor-General, thought John's policy better and Henry was transferred to Rajputana as the British Resident. While in Rajputana he wrote on the necessity of Army Reforms in India and warned against a possible mutiny, but was unheeded. In March, 1857, he was placed in charge at Lucknow, and two months later in May, 1857 the Mutiny broke out. Lucknow became a centre of attack by the mutineers and Henry Lawrence organised the defence of the Residency which was besieged on 29 June. On 2 July, he was struck by a shell and died of the wound two days later.

Lawrence, Lord John (1811-79)—was the Viceroy and Governor-General of India from 1864 to 1869. He was a younger brother of Sir Henry Lawrence (*q.v.*) and came to Calcutta in 1830 in the Company's Civil Service. He started as Assistant Collector at Delhi in which region he served as Magistrate and Collector for nineteen years (1830-49). During this period he paid much attention to the system of land revenue and was in favour of a permanent settlement. He was opposed to the oppression by the *Talukdars* on the peasantry whose condition he wanted to improve. He showed great energy in sending supplies from the Delhi region to the Indo-British army fighting in the Panjab in the First Sikh War (*q.v.*) and was rewarded with promotion to the Commissionership of the Jullandar Doab when he was only 35. In 1853 he was appointed to be the Chief Commissioner of the Panjab where he organised the administration by dividing the province into 32 districts and 36 tributary states, created a police force, made inter-district roads, constructed canals, enforced justice and reduced crimes. On the outbreak of the Mutiny he disarmed the Hindusthani sepoys there with the help of a Panjabi army whose strength he raised from 12,000 to 59,000, kept the Panjab loyal to the British and sent the Sikh army to relieve Delhi which fell on 20 September, 1858. For his work in connection with the Mutiny he was rewarded with a baronetcy and a life-pension. Further recognition came in 1864 when he was appointed Viceroy and Governor-General of India which he administered very successfully for the next five years. He promoted the interest of the common man and took interest in the expansion of education amongst the Indians. He was opposed to the forward policy in the north-western frontier and followed a policy of non-interference in the succession dispute in Afghanistan after the death of Amir Dost Mohammad (*q.v.*) in 1863 and thus avoided an entanglement in the affairs of Afghanistan. A departure from his policy in later years led to the Second Afghan War (*q.v.*) involving heavy losses in men and money and justified his policy of non-interference.

Lawrence, Col. Stringer—(1697-1775)—was a renowned English general who joined the Company's military service in India in 1748. He foiled a French attack on Cuddalore, but was later on captured by the French and was released after the peace of Aix-la-Chappelle (*q.v.*). In 1749 when he captured Devicote he had Robert Clive as a subordinate officer under him. The two became life-long friends and Stringer Lawrence greatly helped Robert Clive in his career. In 1752 Lawrence was in command of the army sent to relieve Trichinopoly and he again had Clive as an officer under him. He gave Clive every encouragement and at the end of the campaign gave Clive more than due credit. He remained in the south while Clive was sent to Bengal, shared in the British victory of Wandiwash (*q.v.*) and was in charge of Fort St. George in 1758-59 when it was besieged by Count de Lally (*q.v.*), the French governor of Pondicherry, whom he repulsed. He retired in 1766. He was an energetic and chivalrous officer who contributed much to the victory of the English in the Carnatic Wars (*q.v.*).

Laws of Manu (or Institute of Manu)—is the most important of the *Dharma Shastras* of the Hindus. It is the English version of the Sanskrit *Manusamhita* by Sir William Jones. It deals with all domestic duties, religious and ethical, of the orthodox Hindu who considers it as a very ancient work written by the sage Manu. It is held to belong to "the time of the Christian era or before it than later". (*C.H.I.*, Vol. I, p. 249)

Lee Commission, the—was appointed by the Secretary of State in 1929 to enquire into the question of pay and emoluments of the Superior Civil Services and also the question of their further Indianisation. It was presided over by Lord Lee and amongst its members there were three Indians. The Commission submitted its Report in March, 1924. Without recommending much alteration in the basic pay of the Indian Civil Service the Lee Commission recommended a considerable addition to the Overseas Pay, liberal conditions of furlough with free first class passages to and from England for the members of the Indian Civil Service. The Commission's recommendations involved a twelve per cent increase in the pay of the members of the Indian Civil Service. On the question of Indianisation the Lee Commission recommended that with a view to the attainment within the next fifteen years of a proportion of 50 per cent Europeans and 50 per cent Indians, 20 per cent of the superior posts were to be filled by promotion from the Provincial Civil Services, and of the direct recruits, one-half was to be Indians and the other half Europeans. The Lee Commission's Report was accepted by the Government in spite of the opposition to it expressed in the Imperial Legislative Assembly. As a result the salaries and emoluments of the members of the Superior Civil Services were considerably enhanced, but the progress of Indianisation of the services proved very slow. (Roy, N. C., *Civil Service in India*)

Leedes—an Englishman, a jeweller by profession, travelled overland to India along with Fitch (*q.v.*) in 1583 and entered into the service of the Mughul Government.

Legislative Assembly, the—was created by the Government of India Act, 1919, for the Central Government in India. It constituted along with the Council of State the Indian legislature which thus became bi-cameral. The Legislative Assembly had 106 elected and 40 nominated members, of whom 25 were officials. The franchise was wider than for the Council of State and the life of an Assembly was for three years. The Assembly had general control over finance and over legislation. But the Governor-General could at his discretion authorize any expenditure and pass any legislative measure which he considered essential for the safety or tranquillity of British India, in spite of the opposition of the Legislative Assembly. (*See ante* under British Admn. in India).

Legislative Council, the—was the name applied to the legislatures of the Supreme Government as well as of the Provincial Governments that were created by the Indian Councils Act of 1861. The designation continued to be used till 1919 when, by the Government of India Act, the Legislative Council of the Governor-General was made bi-cameral of which the Upper House came to be called the Council of State and the Lower the Legislative Assembly and the appellation of the Legislative Council became confined to the legislatures of the Provinces. Under the constitution of the Republic of India the term Legislative Council came to be applied to the Upper House of a state with a bi-cameral legislature. (*See ante* under British Admn. in India).

Lenoir—the French Governor of Pondicherry from 1720 for several years, contributed much to the development of Pondicherry as a trading centre. He had no political ambitions or ideas of conquest.

Leslie, Colonel Bradford—an English Civil Engineer employed in Bengal, designed and built the first bridge over the Hughli between Calcutta and Howrah in 1874 and also the Jubilee Bridge over the Hughli at Naihati in 1881.

Lespinay, Bellanger de—was a French volunteer who came to India in 1672 with the French fleet co-operated with Francois Martin (*q.v.*) to obtain the site of Pondicherry in 1673 from the Muslim Governor of Valikondapuram and thus in laying the foundation of Pondicherry.

Lhasa—the capital of Tibet, was founded in A.D. 639 by king

Srong-tsan Gampo (A.D. 629-698) by filling up a lake with stones. It lay on the route from China to India and was visited, on Tibetan invitation, by many Indian Buddhist monks, the most famous of whom was Atisa (*q.v.*). In later times the Tibetans did not like Britishers to go to Lhasa but in 1904 a British army under Sir Francis Younghusband (*q.v.*) forced an entrance into it and opened up the city to European eyes.

Lhasa, the treaty of—was imposed in 1904 on Tibet by Sir Francis Younghusband who led an expeditionary British army into Tibet. It provided that (i) for the promotion and encouragement of commerce between India and Tibet trade-markets were to be established at Yatung, Gyantse and Gartok; (ii) a British commercial agent was to be stationed at Gyantse with the right to proceed to Lhasa; (iii) Tibet was to pay an annual indemnity of a lakh of rupees for 75 years; (iv) the occupation by British troops of the Chumbi valley till the whole indemnity was paid off; (v) no portion of Tibetan territory was to be alienated to any foreign power, and (vi) no concessions for railways, roads, telegraphs or mining rights were to be granted to any foreign state or the subjects thereof unless similar rights were granted to the British. The terms of the treaty were very harsh and roused opposition. So the indemnity was reduced from 75 lakhs to 25 lakhs, the occupation of the Chumbi valley was reduced to three years and the right of the British commercial agent to go to Lhasa at his discretion was dropped. Chinese assent to this treaty was secured in 1906 with the result that China and England both agreed to respect the integrity of Tibet.

Liaquat Ali Khan—belonged to Uttar Pradesh. He was a leader of the Muslim League and a trusted lieutenant of Jinnah (*q.v.*). He became the Finance Minister in the Interim Government formed in 1946. When India was partitioned and Pakistan was created in 1947 he became the first Prime Minister of Pakistan and entered into a pact with Nehru regarding the treatment of minorities in India and Pakistan. He was soon afterwards murdered when addressing a public meeting by an assailant who was killed on the spot and the cause of his murder and the identity of the murderer could not be definitely known.

Liaquat Hossain—an earnest Muhammadan nationalist, played a prominent part in the agitation against the partition of Bengal (1906-1912) (*q.v.*).

Lichchhavis, the clan of the—was settled in the Muzzaffarpur district of Bihar to the north of the Ganges. Their capital Vaisali (near modern Basarh) was a large city, ten or twelve miles in circuit and had many notable edifices. The Lichchhavis had an aristocratic republican form of government in which every (noble) man had an equal part. They occupied an important social position at the time of Gautama Buddha who is believed to have drawn up the constitution of the Buddhist Sangha on the model of the republican constitution of the Lichchhavis. The Brahmanical sources represent them as degraded Kshatriyas; in reality they were probably a hill tribe or clan which was gradually assimilated into the Aryan society. The Lichchhavis continued to enjoy a position of power and prestige from the sixth century B.C. to the fourth century A.D. when the marriage of the Lichchhavi princess, Kumara Devi, with Chandragupta I of Magadha enabled the latter to lay the foundation of the Gupta Empire. The second Gupta Emperor, Samudragupta, took pride in declaring himself the daughter's son of the Lichchhavi. The Lichchhavis faded into oblivion after the growth of the Gupta Empire in the fourth century A.D.

Lilavati—is a treatise on arithmetic and algebra ⸲written by Bhaskaracharya (*q.v.*) in A.D. 1150. It is a part of his bigger mathematical work *Siddhanta-Shiromani*. *Lilavati* was translated into Persian by Akbar's courtier, Faizi (*q.v.*).

Lieutenant-Governorship of Bengal—was created by Lord Dalhousie in 1854. So long as Bengal was under the direct administration of the Governor-General it was often neglected on account of the increasing burden of work placed on the Governor-General as a result of the expansion of the British Empire in India. The Lieutenant-Governorship of Bengal was abolished in 1912 on the reversal of the partition of Bengal (*q.v.*) which has since been a Governor's province or state.

Lingayet (or Vira-Saiva) Sect, the—was founded by Basava, a Brahman, who was a minister of Vijjala Kalachurya (*q.v.*) in the first half of the twelfth century. The Lingayet sect is so called because its members worship Siva in his phallic (*lingam*) form. They reject the authority of the Vedas, discard the doctrine of rebirth, object to child-marriage, approve of the remarriage of widows and are intensely averse to Brahmanical claims to superiority. The Lingayet sect is still very powerful in the Kanarese country.

Linlithgow, Lord—was the Viceroy and Governor-General of India from 1936 to 1943. He assumed office immediately after the passing of the Government of India Act, 1936 (*q.v.*) which provided for the establishment of a federation of autonomous provincial governments in British India and of the autonomous Princely states which had so far been individually connected by direct ties with the Crown. Lord Linlithgow set out to enforce the whole Act by bringing about the proposed federation at the centre and autonomy with responsible government in the provinces. The provincial elections were held in 1937, the Indian National Congress securing clear majorities in five out of the eleven provinces and were also in a position to form governments in two other provinces. In these circumstances the provincial part of the new constitution was inaugurated, but much time was lost in carrying on negotiations with the Princely states regarding their accession to the proposed federation and then the Second World War broke out in 1939 and the in-auguration of the federal part of the constitution was post-poned. On the outbreak of the Second World War Lord Linlithgow was confronted with the double task of managing public opinion in India which became very restive and of organising the war effort in India in favour of Britain. His difficulty was immensely increased when Japan joined the war against England and began her invasion of Malayasia and captured Singapore in 1941. In the face of these adverse circumstances Lord Linlithgow not only turned India into a base for the supply of essential war materials but also increased the strength of the British Indian army from 175,000 to more than two millions and despatched these armed forces to the south-eastern and middle Asian centres of war who gradually turned a British débâcle into a British victory. But the war effort involving mounting expenditure and the pursuit of the policy of the scorched earth in Bengal culminated in the out-break of a severe famine there in 1943 which the adminis-tration of Lord Linlithgow failed to tackle and he was soon relieved by his successor, Lord Wavell (*q.v.*) who brought his military experience and push to bear on the situation. Lord Linlithgow's attempt at maintaining internal peace in India by tactfully managing the restive public opinion had a qualified success. By announcing in October, 1939, that the attainment of Dominion Status was the goal of constitutional development of India, by playing on the rival claims of the Indian National Congress and of the Muslim League and by bringing in 1942 Sir Stafford Cripps (*q.v.*) on a mission to India to persuade her to accept what came to be known as the Cripps' offer (*q.v.* under Cripps), Lord Linlithgow succeeded in preventing an open outbreak in India. Yet the persistent refusal of the British Government to make a categorical declaration anouncing the grant of independence to India by a certain date led Mahatma Gandhi to start the 'Quit India' movement demanding the immediate abdication by Britain of sovereignty over India which was supported by the Indian National Congress. Lord Linlithgow replied by imprisoning Mahatma Gandhi and interning the whole Working Committee of the Indian National Congress on the eve of his retirement from the office of Viceroy in 1943. Four years later the independence of India had to be conceded, showing how unavailing were the efforts of Lord Linlithgow to uphold by force the British suzerainty over India.

Lloyd George, David—(1863-1945)—was the British statesman who led his country to victory in the First World War (1914-1918). He was the Prime Minister of Britain for six years (1916-22) and was raised to the peerage in 1944. He was a Liberal and as Chancellor of the Exchequer laid the foundation of the welfare state in Great Britain and as Prime Minister led England to victory in 1918. For sixteen years (1906-22) he dominated British politics and was the one man who more than any other person shaped British fortunes in peace and war in the first quarter of the 20th century. His contribution to the development of India was also very significant. It was during his premiership that the famous declaration was made in August, 1917, stating that the progressive realisation of Self-Government was the aim of British rule in India. He followed up this declaration by passing the Government of India Act, 1919, and thus started India definitely on the road to a parliamentary responsible Government.

Local Self-Government in India—in some form or other was prevalent in all ages. In ancient times in the villages and towns which were small states in miniature, popular bodies looked after sanitation, communication, justice and maintenance of peace. The system worked with particular efficiency in the Chola kingdom. During the turmoil that prevailed in the eighteenth century much of this perished and all powers and duties came to belong to the Government. At first the Government adopted no definite system for the administration of local affairs in rural areas. Money was raised for the maintenance of ferries and construction of roads and bridges and the funds so raised were administered by the District Magistrate on the advice of local committees. The first systematic effort was made in Bombay where in 1869 an Act was passed authorizing the imposition of a small cess on the land revenue and authorizing its expenditure by committees working separately for a district as a whole and for its subdivisions. Stimulated by the success of the system in Bombay similar committees were set up for districts in other provinces in 1870. These committees did much for the improvement of local amenities, but they were entirely dominated by the officials and their areas covering whole districts were too large to be efficiently looked after. In 1882 Lord Ripon (*q.v.*) who wanted to make the local bodies centres for instructing the people in self-government, issued instructions for forming local bodies for each subdivision of a district with a large majority of elected non-official members presided over by a non-official Chairman. A real beginning was thus made in local self-government, though bureaucratic opposition to the liberal principles laid down by Lord Ripon delayed their practical application for many years. It was only after 1921 when local self-government became a transferred subject and was placed in charge of a responsible Minister that the district and local boards came to be completely controlled by elected non-official representatives of the people.

It was also due to the initiative of Lord Ripon that municipal administration in the towns and cities which had been under control of the District Magistrate was vested in municpal bodies consisting of elected representatives of the inhabitants to be called municipal councillors who were to elect their own Chairmen who might be non-officials. The municipalities were to look after sanitation, provision of light and of drinking water, construction of roads and other social amenities including education. Here also bureaucratic opposition delayed the full implementation of the system till 1921.

The municipal administration of the three Presidency towns of Calcutta, Bombay and Madras developed apart from that in the rural areas. Up to the middle of the nineteenth century the municipal administration of these three towns was vested in bodies of justices of the peace appointed by the Governor-General. They were to provide for sanitation and police and were authorized to raise the necessary funds by levying rates on owners and occupiers of the houses within the cities. In 1856, three commissioners were appointed in each of the three cities for the maintenance of the conservancy and improvements of the towns. Special provisions were made for introducing gas-lighting and construction of sewers in Calcutta. This system having proved ineffective in Calcutta, the Corporation of Calcutta was reconstituted in 1876 with 72 members of whom 48 were to be elected representatives of the ratepayers but the Chairman was to be nominated by the Government. In 1882 the number of elected members was raised to 50, but in 1899 the number of elected representatives was reduced to one-half of the total strength of the Corporation and large powers were given to the Chairman who was to be nominated by the Government. This restriction was vehemently opposed by the Calcutta public and as a protest twenty-eight members of the Calcutta Corporation led by Surendranath Banerjee resigned. Twenty-four years later it was given to Surendra-nath Banerjee, then Minister for Local Self-Government in Bengal, to repeal the reactionary act of 1899 and to pass a new law which gave Calcutta a Corporation consisting practically entirely of elected representatives of the ratepayers with the right of electing the Mayor and of appointing the executive officers of the Corporation. In Bombay, the Corporation was given a new constitution in 1872 which changed its official nature and made it a popular body with sixty-four members of whom one-fourth was nominated by the Government with an official Chairman, called the Commissioner, appointed by the Government. This constitution with changes to make it more popular has since been in force. Similarly, in Madras the elective principle was introduced in the Corporation in 1884 with a salaried official Chairman appointed by the Government.

Lodi dynasty—founded in Delhi by Bahlol Lodi in A.D. 1451, ruled over the Delhi sultanate from 1451 to 1526 and had three sultans, namely Bahlol Lodi (1451-1489), Sikandar Lodi (1489-1517) and Ibrahim Lodi (1517-26). The dynasty was overthrown by Babur who defeated and killed Ibrahim Lodi at the first battle of Panipat in 1526.

Lohani, the—was an Afghan tribe, who under the leadership of Dariya Khan Lohani, settled in Bihar. During the sultanate of Ibrahim Lodi (1517-26) (*q.v.*) they were so harshly treated that they rose in revolt against Delhi and set up an independent state in Bihar. They were subsequently reduced to submission by Babur (1526-30) as the result of his victory in the battle of the Gogra in 1529.

Lohara dynasty, the—was founded in Kashmir in A.D. 1003 by Sangramaraja who received the crown of Kashmir from his aunt Queen Didda (*q.v.*). It was so much weakened by internal conflicts that it could do nothing to stop the Muhammadan conquest of northern India and was ultimately overthrown in 1339 by a Muhammadan adventurer named Shah Mirza (*q.v.*) who had entered the service of the last Lohara king of Kashmir in A.D. 1315.

Lucknow—is a city on the Gumti in Uttar Pradesh. It was the capital of the Nawabs of Oudh who built here many beautiful palaces and mosques. It played an important part in the Sepoy Mutiny (*q.v.*) and was occupied for a time by the mutinous sepoys but was recovered later on by the British army led by Sir Colin Campbell in November, 1857. It is now the seat of a teaching University.

Lucknow Pact, the—was an agreement effected in 1916 between the Indian National Congress and the Muslim League by which the League agreed to work with the Indian National Congress for securing self-government for India on the basis of separate electorates and an equitable distribution of offices between the two communities. (Banerjee, A. C., *Indian Constl. Documents*, Vol II, pp. 289 ff.)

Lumbini Grama—is a village near Kapilavastu (*q.v.*) where Gautama Buddha (*q.v.*) was born about the year 566 B.C. The place was visited by Asoka (*q.v.*) in the twentieth year of his reign and marked by a stone-pillar that Asoka set up at the site of the nativity. The place, now called Rummindei, is in the Nepalese Terai where the pillar still stands. In honour of the sanctity associated with the place Asoka made it free of all religious cesses (*bali*) and reduced the land revenue to only one-eighth of the produce in place of the normal rate of one-sixth.

Lutf-un-nisa—the consort of Nawab Siraj-ud-daulah (*q.v.*) of Bengal (1756-57), accompanied him on his flight from Murshidabad after the battle of Plassey (1757) and lived to mourn his murder.

Lytton, Lord, the First—was the Viceroy and Governor-General of India from 1876 to 1880. He was a man of letters and had a distinguished appearance, but his administrative record in India was anything but bright. His administration began under the shadow of a severe famine which stalked over the whole of southern India for two years from 1876 to 1878, spreading over Central India and the Panjab in the second year and carried off five millions of the people. The Government's measures to save life proved most inadequate yet the Viceroy held a Darbar of unsurpassed magnificence in Delhi in 1877 to proclaim the assumption by Queen Victoria of the title of

Empress of India. Later on the Viceroy appointed a Famine Commission with General Richard Strachey as the President to conduct an enquiry into the whole question of the causes and relief of famine. On the strength of its Report a Famine Code was drawn up which laid down some sound principles for combating famines in the future. During his administration the Salt tax was made uniform in British and Indian India, stopping thereby the prevalent smuggling of it and making possible the removal of the customs line of cactus hedge extending from Attock on the Indus to the Mahanadi in the Deccan, a distance of 2,500 miles. In the interest really of the Lancashire textile mills, but in the name of Free Trade, Lord Lytton abolished, overriding his Executive Council, the duty of 5% import duty hitherto imposed on imported textiles and thus obstructed the expansion of the growing textile industry of India. In 1878 he passed the Vernacular Press Act (*q.v.*) in order to suppress adverse criticism of governmental measures by the Indians in their Press—a retrograde measure which was abolished four years later by his successor, Lord Ripon. The most calamitous and unjustifiable act of Lord Lytton was his declaration of war on Afghanistan in 1878 in pursuit of a spirited foreign policy and imperialistic aims which were to be achieved by a subtle and provocative diplomacy. This Second Afghan War (1878-88) (*q.v.*) was a dismal failure which cost many lives and involved a very heavy expenditure the major portion of which was borne by the Indian taxpayer and darkened the close of Lord Lytton's administration.

Lytton, Lord, the Second—came to India as the Governor of Bengal in 1922 and it fell to him to officiate as the Viceroy from the 10th April to the 7th August, 1925 and thus to hold the distinguished office that had been held several years earlier by his father. He reverted to the Governorship of Bengal from which office he retired in 1927. His administration in Bengal was marked by an undignified epistolary controversy with Sir Asuthosh Mukherjee in which the latter had the better of it over the question of Government's control over Calcutta University.

M

Maasir-i-Alamgiri—written by Muhammad Saqi, is practically a contemporary historical work on the time and career of Emperor Aurangzeb (1658-1707).

Ma'bar—was the name given by Muhammadan historians to the Coromandel coast. It was conquered by Alauddin Khalji (*q.v.*) but revolted and became an independent kingdom under Ahsan Shah in 1334.

Macao (also spelt **Macau**)—was a Portuguese station in China which the East India Company seized in 1809.

Macartney, Lord—came to India in 1781 as the Governor of Madras. He was an energetic man of considerable force of character and was incorruptible. He effected considerable improvement in the internal administration of Madras. He was very much anxious for restoring peace and brought the Second Mysore War to a close by concluding in 1784 the treaty of Mangalore on the basis of *uti possidetis*. He resigned in 1785 over a difference regarding the method of collection of revenue from the Carnatic assigned by the Nawab to the Company. He was passed over for the post of the Governor-General on the retirement of Warren Hastings in 1785 and did not return to India.

Macaulay, Thomas Babington, Baron (1800-59)—was a renowned English poet, essayist, historian and politician. He was called to the Bar in 1826 but preferred public life to the practice of law. He became a Member of Parliament in 1830 and came out to India in 1834 as the first Law Member of the Governor-General's Executive Council. In India he tried to apply sound liberal principles to an administration which had till then been "jealous, close and repressive". He supported the liberty of the Press in India, maintained the equality of Europeans and Indians before the law, inaugurated the system of liberal education on Western lines through the medium of English and drafted the Penal Code which later on became the basis of the Indian Criminal Code. He continued to take interest in Indian affairs even after his retirement from India and in 1855 spoke in Parliament in defence of the introduction of the competitive examination system for admission into the Indian Civil Service. He was a life-long scholar, was created a peer in 1857 and died two years later in 1859. His more important works were the *Armada* (1833), *Lays of Ancient Rome* (1842), *Essays* (1825-43) and *History of England* in four volumes (1848-1858). The last work had a huge sale and brought him an income of £20,000 and was translated into different European languages.

Macdonald, James Ramsay (1866-1937)—was the Prime Minister of England twice, first in 1924 and then from 1929 to 1935. His father was a labourer. James Ramsay Macdonald began his career at the age of 18 as a clerk on 12/6 d. a week and worked his way up to the premiership. He joined the Labour party in 1894 and was first elected to the Parliament in 1906 and practically created the Parliamentary Labour Party of which he became the leader in 1911. He refused his support to the War-policy of Britain in 1914, incurred great public odium, lost his parliamentary seat in 1918 and was in the wilderness until 1922 when he was re-elected to the Parliament and the Labour Party in England agreed to work for socialism not through violence, as had been done in Russia, but through Parliament. In other words, he stood for Parliamentary and Democratic socialism. In the post-war years he worked for peace in Europe and in 1924 he played an important part in the settlement of the long-standing dispute over reparations. His first ministry formed in January, 1924, lasted barely eleven months. His second ministry, had a longer life from 1929 till 1931 when it was turned into a National Government. He was always keenly interested in India which he twice visited in 1910 and 1913-14. In 1911 he published his first work on India—*The Awakening of India.* which was highly appreciated by the nationalist Indians. Eight years later he wrote his second book on India, viz. *The Government of India.* He presided over the Round Table Conference (*q.v.*) held in England for settling the problem of the constitutional development in India with which was closely associated the problem of communal representation. As the two major Indian communities could not come to an agreement on this issue he made a communal award at the end of the Third Round Table Conference which extended the principle of communal representation to what was called the 'Depressed Classes' amongst the Hindus. This led to a fast of protest by Gandhiji and had to be modified by the Poona Pact (*q.v.*). The approval of the Poona Pact was the last act of Ramsay Macdonald in regard to India.

Macdonnell, Sir Anthony—was the Chairman of the Famine Commission appointed by Lord Curzon, Viceroy, in 1900. (*See ante* Famine Commission.)

MacMahon, Sir Henry—born in 1862, joined the Indian Staff Corps in 1885 and was transferred to the Political Department in 1890. In 1893 he accompanied the Durand mission to Kabul and later on demarcated the boundary between Baluchistan and Afghanistan, and also took part in settling the Perso-Afghan boundary in 1903. His most famous work was the settlement of the boundary between India and Tibet cum China along the north-eastern frontier of India.

Macmahon line—is the boundary line that marks off the North-Eastern Frontier Agency from the Tibet and China frontiers. It was drawn up by Sir Henry MacMahon (*q.v.*).

Macnaghten, Sir William Hay (1793-1841)—entered the Company's military service in 1809, picked up several oriental languages and was made Secretary in the Political Department in 1833. He made the tripartite treaty with Ranjit Singh and Shah Shuja in June 1838, was appointed British envoy at the Afghan court of Shah Shuja, accompanied the British expeditionary force from India via Qandahar and Ghazni to Kabul and saw Shah Shuja reinstated. Macnaghten was rewarded with a baronetcy in 1840, but troubles soon ensued. The Afghans rose in revolt and murdered Burnes (*q.v.*) on 2 November, 1841; yet on 11 December Macnaghten was foolish enough to enter into terms with the Afghans and to surrender hostages. This policy of appeasement emboldened the Afghans who under the leadership of Dost Mahommad's son, Akbar Khan, rose against the British and at an interview Macnaghten was killed by Akbar himself on 23 December, 1841. Macnaghten was largely responsible for the whole policy of the Afghan War (1839-42) and paid the penalty for his mistake with his own life.

Macpherson, Sir John (1745-1821)—was Governor-General of India from February, 1785 to September, 1786. He came to India in 1767 as the purser of a ship and entered the Company's service as a clerk in Madras in 1770, but was dismissed from the service in 1777. He was, however, reinstated by the Court of Directors and rose to be the Governor-General, though only for about twenty months. His administration was corrupt.

Madan Mohan Malviya—*see* Malviya, Madan Mohan.

Madhava, Achariya—was the brother of Sayana, the celebrated Vedic commentator. Madhava was also a very learned man who wrote several commentaries. He served as the Minister of Bukka (acc. A.D. 1354), the second king of Vijayanagar (*q.v.*).

Madhavacharya—was a Bengali poet of Triveni in the district of Hooghly. He was a contemporary of Emperor Akbar and was the author of the popular work *Chandi-mangal*. He appears to have received some patronage from the Mughul Emperor.

Madhava Rao (also called **Madhu Rao**)—was the second son

of Peshwa Balaji Baji Rao whom he succeeded to the Peshwaship in 1761. He was only 17 years of age when he assumed
the Peshwaship soon after the great defeat of the Marathas
in the third battle of Panipat. At first his uncle Raghunath
Rao was the Regent but the young Peshwa soon asserted himself. Gradually he recovered much of the power and prestige
lost by the Peshwa as the result of the defeat at Panipat. The
Nizam was twice defeated and frustrated in his attempt to
destroy the Peshwa's power. Haidar Ali (*q.v.*) of Mysore who
had begun to encroach on Maratha territories in the south,
was also twice defeated and the Bhonsla Raja of Berar, who
was in league with the Nizam and Haidar Ali against the
Peshwa, was reduced to submission. The greatest achievement
of Peshwa Madhava Rao was in North India where in 1771-72
his army reoccupied Malwa and Bundelkhand, exacted tribute
from the Rajput chiefs, crushed the Jats and the Rohilas, reoccupied Delhi and restored to the imperial throne of Delhi
the fugitive Mughul Emperor, Shah Alam II (1769-1806),
who had so long been a pensioner of the East India Company
at Allahabad. It seemed the losses inflicted on the Maratha
power by the third battle of Panipat (*q.v.*) were almost made
up when suddenly the great Peshwa Madhava Rao died in
1772. As Grant Duff observes, "The plains of Panipat were
not more fatal to the Maratha Empire than the early end of
this excellent prince."

Madhava Rao Narayan (also called **Madhava II**)—was the
posthumous son of Peshwa Narayan Rao (*q.v.*) whom he
succeeded in 1774. As he was a mere child a Council of Regency
was formed with Nana Faḍnavis as its chief. The intrigues of
his father's uncle, Raghoba, for gaining the Peshwaship with
the help of the East India Company involved the child Peshwa
in the First Maratha War (1775-82) which was concluded by
the treaty of Salbai (1782) and left the Peshwa's dominions
intact. The Peshwa's childhood encouraged a rivalry for power
between Mahadaji Sindhia and Nana Faḍnavis which greatly
weakened the Peshwa's authority until the death of the former
in 1794. Next year (1795) the Marathas defeated the Nizam
at the battle of Kharda (*q.v.*). But the young Peshwa Madhava
Rao Narayan grew tired of the stringency of Nana's guardianship and ended his life by committing suicide in 1795.

Madhu Rao Sindhia—was the ruler of the Gwalior state (*q.v.*)
from 1886 to 1925. He was a liberal ruler and effected some
improvements in the administration of the state.

Madhya Bharat—is the region lying between the Chambal on the north, the Narmada on the south, Gujarat on the west and Bundelkhand on the east. It was the seat of many famous Hindu kingdoms in the past containing the famous city of Ujjayini (*q.v.*). It was in a very prosperous condition early in the fifth century A.D. when it was visited by the Chinese pilgrim Fa-Hien (A.D. 401-10). Its later history is merged with that of the Gurjara-Pratiharas (*q.v.*).

Madhya Pradesh—is the present name of the region which was known as Central Provinces and Berar during the British rule. In the Hindu period this region formed the kingdom of Jejaka-bhukti or Jijhoti (*q.v.*). The ancient cities of Khajuraho, Mahoba and Kalanjar are situated within this region and the architectural monuments that are still found in these cities bear testimony to the great power of the Chandella kings (*q.v.*) who ruled over this region.

Madhyamika—was an ancient town near Chitor in Rajasthan. It is now called Nagari. It was besieged by a 'viciously valiant Yavana' conqueror who was probably the Greek king, Menander (*q.v.*). It was a place of much importance in the third century B.C. and amongst its ruins traces of a Maurya building and two inscriptions of the Sunga period have been found. These record the performance of *asvamedha* and *vajapeya* sacrifices.

Madras—is a city created by the English in India. In 1640 Francis Day (*q.v.*) of the East India Company procured from the local Hindu chief the site of the present city of Madras with permission to build a fort there. The grant was subsequently confirmed by the Raja of Chandragiri and by the Sultan of Golconda. The fort that was built on the site was named Fort St. George. In 1642 Madras displaced Masulipatam as the chief settlement of the East India Company on the Coromandel coast and in 1653 it became an independent agency and later on a Presidency. It maintained good relations with the Nizam of Hyderabad as well as with the Nawab of the Carnatic and prospered as a trading centre. A municipal administration was set up in Madras in 1688. A mayor's court was established in 1726 for dispensing civil justice. During the first Anglo-French War in India Madras was captured by the French in 1746, but was restored to the East India Company in 1748 by the treaty of Aix-la-Chapelle. After the capture of Calcutta by Nawab Siraj-ud-daula (*q.v.*) a body of the Company's troops was sent from Madras under Clive and Watson in 1756 which easily recovered Calcutta. In 1773 the Regulating Act placed the Madras territories of the Company under a rather loose control of the Bengal Government. Pitt's India Act (*q.v.*) made Madras completely subordinate to the Governor-General of Fort William in Bengal. With the extension of British territories in the Deccan the area of the Presidency of which Madras was the capital, expanded until at last it came to comprise the whole of the eastern coast of India from the Orissa frontier to Cape Comorin. A University was established in Madras in 1857. Madras recognised the greatness of Swami Vivekananda earlier than any other place in India. Madras also played an important part in the history of the Indian National Congress which held its third session in Madras in 1887. In later years the Congress met there on several occasions. Madras gave India her first Indian Governor-General in Chakravarti Rajagopalachari. Recently the Presidency of Madras has been divided into the two states of Andhra and Madras on a linguistic basis. Thus Madras Presidency has been deprived of its large Telugu-speaking northern area and has been confined to the Tamil-speaking south.

Madrasa, the Calcutta—was founded in 1781 by Warren Hastings (*q.v.*) for the study of Arabic and Persian. Many eminent orientalists like Sir Denison Ross had been on the staff of the Calcutta Madrasa.

Madura—is a very ancient city. It was the capital of the Pandya kingdom in the first century of the Christian era. The *Arthasastra* of Kautilya mentions its fine textile products and its pearls. That it was a very rich city is borne out by the fact that when in 1311 it was captured and plundered by the Muhammadan army of Sultan Alauddin Khalji (*q.v.*), the victorious general, captured booty which consisted of 512 elephants, five thousand horses and five hundred maunds of jewels like diamonds, pearls, emeralds and rubies. Later on it became a part of the Vijayanagar empire. On the fall of the latter it became the seat of the kingdom of the Nayaks (*q.v.*). It has many magnificent temples of which the most prominent is the double temple of Sundaresvara and Minakshi. Madura still enjoys her reputation for cotton fabrics.

Magadha—comprised the districts of Patna and Gaya in South Bihar. It is a very ancient kingdom and is referred to in the Vedas. In historical times it was being ruled by a dynasty of kings to which belonged Bimbisara (*q.v.*) who was a contemporary of both Vardhamana Mahavira, the founder of Jainism, and Gautama Buddha, the founder of Buddhism. Bimbisara honoured them both and at the same time extended the limits of his kingdom of Magadha by annexing Anga or East Bihar (Bhagalpur district) and entering into marriage relations with the kings of Koshala and Vaisali. Bimbisara's son and successor Ajatasatru annexed Vaisali (Tirhut), humbled Koshala and built a fortress at Pataligrama, which stood at the confluence of the Ganges and the Son. Round this fort was built the city of Pataliputra or Kusumapura by a later king of Bimbisara's dynasty where a still later king transferred the capital from Girivraja. Magadha and Pataliputra thus became closely associated. From this new capital King Mahapadma Nanda who overthrew the line of Bimbisara, extended the sway of Magadha from Kalinga (Orissa) on the east to the Beas in the Panjab on the west. It was the dread of meeting the armed forces of the king of the Prasii (as the classical historians called the Magadhan king) that led the army of Alexander the Great to refuse to advance beyond the Beas and forced his retreat. It was, however, the Maurya king, Chandragupta (*q.v.*), who overthrew the Nandas and raised Magadha to the imperial position in the closing years of the fourth century B.C. The Magadhan sway was extended from the Hindu Kush on the west to Kalinga on the east and probably extended over the Deccan as well. Chandragupta's grandson, Asoka (*q.v.*), conquered and annexed Kalinga and then turned a Buddhist and employed all the resources of his vast empire to the amelioration of the sufferings of mankind and the propagation of Buddhism. Magadha thus came to stand for new ideals and gave to Indian history a unity which it had previously lacked. Its capital Pataliputra was so magnificent a city that it extorted the praise not only of the contemporary Greek ambassador, Megasthenes, but also of the Chinese pilgrim, Fa-Hien (*q.v.*) in the beginning of the fifth century of the Christian era. In the meanwhile, Magadha had suffered an eclipse under the Sungas and Kanvas but recovered its glory in the beginning of the fourth century A.D. with the establishment of the Gupta dynasty (*q.v.*) under which its sway again extended over the whole of northern India and was also acknowledged by south Indian kings ruling as far down as Kanchi. With the fall of the Gupta dynasty towards the close of the sixth century Magadha lost its primacy to recover it, though only for a short while, in the ninth century A.D. under King Dharmapala (*q.v.*). Towards the close of the twelfth century Magadha was conquered by the Muhammadans who reduced it to a mere province changing its name into Bihar from the large number of *Viharas* or monasteries which abounded in the country.

Magas—is referred to by Asoka (*q.v.*) in his inscriptions as Maka whose dominions lay beyond the territories of Antiochus. Magas was the king of Cyrene from 300 to 250 B.C. Asoka also claims in his edicts that he made many 'conquests by Dharma', that is to say, converts to Buddhism in the kingdom of Magas.

Mahabat Khan—was a Mughul title. It was bestowed on different persons at different times. The one person who raised the title to great fame and honour was a capable soldier named Zamana Beg on whom Emperor Jahangir (*q.v.*) conferred the title in 1605 soon after his accession to the throne. At first, he proved a very loyal and capable officer and was sent to Mewar to fight against Rana Amar Singh whom he defeated in several pitched battles. On his return from Mewar he was sent to the Deccan to bring back to the capital the recalcitrant governor, Khan Khanan, a task which he completed with great tact and success. But as Nur Jahan's influence on Jahangir increased Mahabat Khan, who was opposed by her father and brother, gradually lost the favour of Emperor Jahangir and got no important charge for twelve years. This created in him a sense of frustration, yet when Prince Khurram re-volted against Jahangir, Mahabat Khan led the imperial forces against the rebellious prince whom he defeated at Bilochpur in the Deccan and then again at Damdama near Allahabad. But these victories only increased the hostility of Empress Nur Jahan against him and he was transferred from the governorship of Kabul to Bengal. This exasperated Mahabat Khan so much that he attempted in 1626 a *coup d'état* and succeeded in getting for a time the control over the person of Emperor Jahangir when he was on his way to Kabul. But Empress Nur Jahan, who was much more intelligent than Mahabat Khan, soon succeeded in recovering control and Mahabat Khan's influence faded. In desperation he joined Prince Khurram in his rebellion in 1626. But no actual fighting took place before Jahangir died in 1627. On the accession of Shah Jahan whose succession he had supported, Mahabat Khan was appointed to high offices and made the Khan Khanan. He reduced a rebellion in Bundelkhand, besieged and captured Daulatabad and thus completed the reduction of Ahmadnagar. But this was practically the last success of this great Mughul general. His attempt to conquer Bijapur failed and he was censured by the Emperor. This humiliation he took very much to heart and he died a broken man in 1634.

Mahabharata, **the**—is the second great Sanskrit epic and is attributed to the sage Vyasa. It is a very big work containing one lakh of verses. The complete *Mahabharata* is mentioned for the first time in an inscription of the Gupta period (4th - 5th centuries A.D.) but its kernel must be older, for it was known to Panini who belonged to the pre-Christian era. The main theme of the *Mahabharata* is the contest between the cousins, the Kurus who were the sons of Dhritarashtra of Hastinapur (probably situated in Meerut district) and the Pandavas, who were the sons of Dhritarashtra's younger brother, Pandu, and who were the rulers of Indraprastha near modern Delhi. The Pandavas were allied through marriages with the Panchalas and the Yadavas. Their claim to be paramount rulers was strongly resented by the Kurus and out of this rivalry sprang a war in which all the kings of India took part as allies of either the Kurus or of the Pandavas. A great battle lasting eighteen days was fought in the plain of Kurukshetra near the field of Panipat where in historical times the fate of India was thrice decided. The Kurus were defeated and the triumphant Pandavas gained the victory and with it the suzerainty over India. But with the characteristic Hindu spirit of non-attachment they abdicated the throne which was inherited by their descendant, Parikshit. In addition to this main theme the *Mahabharata* contains many charming and edifying stories of noble kings and their consorts, of great sages and the great religious poem known as the *Bhagavad Gita*, which is the bed-rock of Hindu theism. The *Mahabharata* is, therefore, looked upon as the national epic of Hindu India, has been translated into all the Indian languages and has been carried by the Hindu immigrants to their overseas homes in distant Java and Cambodia.

Maharaja Sindhia—*see* Sindhia.

Mahalwari system—*see* Land Tenure systems.

Maham Anaga—was the chief nurse of Emperor Akbar (*q.v.*) in his infancy and was the mother of Adham Khan. She joined the 'harem party' which was opposed to the domination of Bairam Khan (*q.v.*) and played an important part in persuading Akbar to sever himself from his guardian, Bairam Khan, whom he left at Agra and joined his widowed mother at Delhi in 1560. She had great influence with Akbar during the next two years and protected her son, Adham Khan, from the wrath of Akbar in 1561. But next year when Adham Khan killed Atga Khan, the chief minister, she could no longer protect him. Adham was thrown over the ramparts and killed and out of grief for her son Maham Anaga died. With her death Akbar freed himself from the heavy control of the 'harem party'.

Mahanandin—the last king of the Sisunaga dynasty, ruled towards the close of the fifth century B.C. or the first half of the fourth century B.C. No events of his reign are recorded.

Mahapadma—was the founder o the Nanda dynasty of Magadha. According to the Puranas he was the son of Mahanandin, the last king of the Sisunaga dynasty by a Sudra wife. In spite of his humble origin, Mahapadma, who usurped the throne after murdering the rightful king, proved a vigorous ruler. He extended his conquests from Kalinga on the east to the Beas in the Panjab on the west. These vast dominions he appeared to have ruled well and efficiently. The exact date of his accession as well as the total period of his reign are uncertain, but the vastness of his dominions suggest a long reign of about thirty years in the first half of the 4th century B.C.

Maharashtra—is the name of the region of the Western Ghats between the Warda on the east and the sea on the west. It comprises three regional divisions, namely *Konkan* lying between the Western Ghats and the sea, *Maval* only 20 miles in breadth lying to the east of the Ghats, and *Desh* lying further to the east of Maval. The hilltops which are well supplied with water, afford natural facilities for fortifications. The people are simple, active and self-reliant who lack the chivalry of the Rajputs but surpass them in resourcefulness and intelligence and care more for the end than for the means for attaining it. In the early centuries of the Christian era a dynasty of Saka Satraps founded by Bhumaka ruled over this region. In the fifth century A.D. it was brought within the Gupta Empire as the result of the destruction of the Saka rule in Saurashtra by Chandragupta II (*q.v.*). In the seventh century it was a part of the dominions of the Chalukya king, Pulakeshin II (608-42) (*q.v.*) and was visited by the Chinese pilgrim Hiuen Tsang who found travelling very difficult in the country. It then passed successively under the rule of the Rashtrakutas (*q.v.*) and of the Yadavas (*q.v.*) of Devagiri from whom it passed under the rule of the Delhi sultanate (*q.v.*). Later on, it formed a part of the Bahmani kingdom on the disintegration of which it became divided between the states of Ahmadnagar and Bijapur and practically ceased to have a separate entity or history. But in the middle of the seventeenth century it apparently suddenly sprang into life and to prominence at the touch of one man of genius. That person was Shivaji who, born in 1627, instilled in the people of Maharashtra a sense of national unity and a spirit of independence and established before his death in 1680 an independent Hindu kingdom in Maharashtra which withstood all the resources of the Mughul Empire and maintained its independent existence for about a century and a half. Shivaji's direct line ended with the death of his grandson Shahu in 1749, but the administration of the Maharashtra kingdom had already passed into the hands of the Peshwas (*q.v.*). The Peshwas ruled over Maharashtra with their capital at Poona till the defeat of the last Peshwa, Baji Rao II, at the hands of the English in 1818 and his deposition. But the Marathas still continued to be an important factor in Indian politics. The Maratha chieftains, namely, the Gaekwar of Baroda, Sindhia of Gwalior, Holkar of Indore and the Bhonsla at Nagpur shared amongst themselves the right to rule large portions of central and southern India as protected princes under the suzerainty of the British Indian Government directly and the Crown of England indirectly. All these princely states merged with the Republic of India in 1948-49.

Mahatma Gandhi—*see* Gandhi, M. K.

Mahavamsa, **the**—or the 'Great Chronicle' is a history of Ceylon. It was written during the reign of the Ceylonese king, Mahanama, who ruled from A.D. 458 to 480. In tracing the history of Ceylon in ancient times it makes frequent references to India and her history. As a matter of fact much of the detailed information about Asoka and the introduction and expansion of Buddhism in Ceylon is derived from the *Mahavamsa.*

Mahavira—or Vardhamana Mahavira, to give his full name, was the founder of Jainism. He was born of a noble Kshatriya family related to the ruling families of Vaisali and Magadha and was named Vardhamana. The exact dates of his birth and decease are not known, but this much is certain that he was born in the reign of Bimbisara (*q.v.*) and died in the reign of the latter's son and successor, Ajatasatru (*q.v.*), a few years before the passing away of Gautama Buddha. He lived for some years the life of a pious householder. At the age of thirty, however, he renounced the world, turned into a nude wandering monk, practising severe penances for twelve years at the end of which he attained the highest spiritual knowledge called *Kevala-jnana*. Henceforth he became known as *Kevalin* (Omniscient), *Nirgrantha* (Free from fetters), *Jina* (Conqueror) and *Mahavira* (The Great Hero). During the next thirty years he moved about the country, preaching a new religion called Jainism (*q.v.*) and died at the age of seventy-two at Pava in Patna district of Bihar some time during the reign of King Ajatasatru. But the date is uncertain. (Jacobi. H., *On Mahavira and his Predecessors, Ind. Ant.* ix, 158 ff)

Mahendra, Prince (also spelt **Mahindra**)—was either a son or a brother of Asoka (*q.v.*). He along with his sister Sanghamitra went in *c.* 251 B.C. to Ceylon where they propagated Buddhism, converting King Tissa and the members of the royal family as well as many of the common people. His name is not mentioned in any of the inscriptions of Asoka, but the reality of his existence and the greatness of his achievement are amply proved by the Ceylonese Chronicles, *Dipavamsa* and *Mahavamsa* as well as by the monuments which the Sinhalese raised in his honour at Anuradhapura in Ceylon where he died in about 204 B.C. (Saunders, K. S., *The Story of Buddhism*)

Mahendrapala—(c. 890 - 910)—the son and successor of the Gurjara-Pratihara king, Mihira Bhoja (*q.v.*), not only maintained intact his father's vast empire extending from Saurashtra to Oudh, but also drove the Pala kings from Magadha and advanced into western Bengal where he left an inscription. He was also a patron of men of letters and the celebrated poet Rajasekhara, the author of the drama *Karpura-manjuri*, was his teacher as well as an honoured member of his court.

Mahendravarman I (c. A.D. 600 - 25)—was the son and successor of the Pallava king, Simhavishnu of Kanchi. His reign was famous for the numerous public works like rock-cut temples and caves, the establishment of the new town of Mahendravadi between Arcot and Arconam and the construction, near the new city, of a great reservoir. He was, however, defeated by the Chalukya king, Pulakeshin II (*q.v.*), in about A.D. 610 and obliged to surrender Vengi to the Chalukya conqueror. He was originally a Jain by religion but later on became a worshipper of Siva.

Mahendravarman II—a grandson of the Pallava king, Mahendravarman I (*q.v.*) and son and successor of Narasimhavarman I (*q.v.*), ascended the throne in *c.* A.D. 668 and ruled only for six years. He was defeated by his Chalukya contemporary, King Vikramaditya.

Mahindra, Prince—*see* Mahendra.

Mahipala I (*c.* A.D. 978-1030)—was the ninth king of the Pala dynasty of Bengal. During his rule the disintegration of the Pala kingdom began. South-west Bengal passed under the rule of the Senas and Eastern Bengal under that of the Chandras. Finally in A.D. 1023 the Chola king, Rajendra, led an expedition into Bengal and penetrated up to the very bank of the Ganges. He also fought a losing campaign against the Kalachuri king, Gangayedeva. He was, however, the greatest Pala king after Devapala and his name is associated with many public works in Benares, Nalanda and in North and West Bengal.

Mahipala II—was a great-grandson of the Pala king, Mahipala I (*q.v.*). He was the eldest of the three sons of King Vigrahapala (*q.v.*), whom he succeeded. But his rule was short (*c.* 1070-75 A.D.), his administration was weak and he was defeated and killed in a battle with the rebel, Divya, one of his high officials who was a Kaivarta by caste.

Mahmud—was a sultan of Bidar (*q.v.*) who invaded Vijayanagar immediately after the accession of Krishnadevaraya (*q.v.*) and was beaten back and wounded by the Vijayanagar king.

Mahmud, king of Jaunpur—the third king of the Sharqi dynasty, ruled from 1436 to 1458. He was a successful ruler who built some beautiful mosques at Jaunpur.

Mahmud, Sultan of Ghazni—was the son of Amir Sabuktigin whom he succeeded to the throne of Ghazni in A.D. 986-87. He assumed the title of Sultan to signify his independence and ruled till his death in A.D. 1030. During this period he made frequent raids (generally computed to be seventeen in number) into India. His first attack was in 1001 on Jaipal (*q.v.*) whom he defeated near Peshawar. Seven years later he defeated Jaipal's son and successor, Anandapal. These successes practically made him the master of the Panjab. In the following years he raided Thaneswar, Mathura and Kanauj and received also the submission of Gwalior and Kalanjar. In 1026 he led an expedition into Kathiawar (or Saurashtra) and sacked the temple of Somnath, broke the *lingam* within the temple which he defiled and destroyed and plundered all the accumulated wealth within the temple and the city. His last Indian expedition was made in 1027 against Multan. Sultan Mahmud, who was a very capable general, was also a patron of learning and lover of art and architecture. He adorned his capital Ghazni with many beautiful edifices and useful public works like aqueducts and libraries. He annexed to his dominions the Panjab and left the rest of India bleeding and demoralised.

Mahmud Begara (or Bigarha)—was the sixth sultan of Gujarat. Ascending the throne at the age of thirteen he ruled prosperously for fifty-two years (A.D. 1459 - 1511) and turned out to be the most eminent sovereign of his dynasty. He conquered Champaner near Baroda, Junagarh and Oudh and defeated the sultan of Ahmadnagar. He also fought against the Portuguese in the Indian waters and defeated a Portuguese fleet at the battle of Chaul in 1508, and, though his fleet was destroyed by the Portuguese in 1509, he prevented them from getting possession of Diu during his life-time. He grew a magnificent pair of moustaches and was so good an eater that many fanciful stories about him became circulated all over the country and were recorded by the Italian traveller, Ludovico di Varthema, who visited his kingdom.

Mahmud Gawan, Khwaja—was a Persian who entered into the service of the eleventh Bahmani sultan, Humayun (1457-61) and rose high. During the rule of Humayun's minor son, Nizam (1461-63) Mahmud Gawan rose further and was one of the two chief advisers of the queen-mother who was the Regent. Nizam dying suddenly in 1413 the throne passed to his brother Muhammad who ruled from 1436 to 1482. During his reign Mahmud Gawan was the chief minister. He showed equal ability as a general and statesman and largely contributed to the expansion of the Bahmani kingdom. He was also a patron of learning and lover of arts and architecture and established at Bidar which was then the capital of the Bahmani kingdom, a college and a library. He, however, incurred the hostility of the Deccani Muhammadan nobles who after years of effort succeeded by producing a forged letter in persuading Sultan Muhammad Shah to believe that Gawan was in treasonable correspondence with the king of Vijayanagar and in bringing about his execution by the Sultan's order in 1481. His unjust execution led to the loss of all cohesion and power of the Bahmani sultanate.

Mahmud Ghuri (1432-36)—the third and last king of the Ghuri dynasty of Malwa, was a worthless ruler, too much addicted to drinking and was poisoned to death by his minister in 1436.

Mahmud Khilji—the minister of Mahmud Ghuri, king of Malwa (1432-36) (*q.v.*), poisoned his master to death and usurped his throne in 1436. He ruled from 1436 till his death in 1469 and established the Khilji dynasty of Malwa. He spent his life in fighting with his neighbours including the sultan of Gujarat, Rana Kumbha of Mewar and Nizam Shah Bahmani and extended the boundaries of his kingdom. He was famous for his sense of justice and built several fine edifices including a seven-storied tower at his capital at Mandu.

Mahmud II (1512-31)—was the last king of the Khilji dynasty of Malwa. He was defeated by King Bahadur Shah (*q.v.*) of Gujarat (1526-37) who annexed his kingdom.

Mahmud Shah Bahmani (1482-1518)—was the son and successor of the penultimate Bahmani sultan, Muhammad III. He was a boy of twelve at the time of his accession and during the twenty-six years of his rule he possessed little power and witnessed the general disintegration of the Bahmani sultanate as the result of the secession of Bijapur, Golconda, Berar and Ahmadnagar. Only Bidar acknowledged his nominal sway at the time of his death in 1518.

Mahmud Tughluq (1394-1413)—was the last sultan of the Tughluq dynasty of Delhi. His reign was one of struggle and misery, the earlier part of which was spent in a succession dispute which continued till 1399 when his rival, Sultan Nusrat Shah, was defeated and killed. In the latter part of his reign the disintegration of the Delhi empire began. Jaunpur, Gujarat, Malwa and Khandesh all became independent Muslim states while a Hindu principality was established in Gwalior and the Hindus of the Doab were constantly in revolt. In the midst of such circumstances Timur (*q.v.*) invaded India in 1398. So disorganised was the administration of Sultan Mahmud Tughluq that no resistance could be offered to the invader until he reached the outskirts of Delhi where the Sultan's army was decisively defeated and Mahmud was forced to flee to Gujarat. Victorious Timur then entered Delhi which he cruelly ransacked for fifteen days and then departed leaving India in the grip of a terrible famine and pestilence and the Delhi sultanate a mere carcass of its old self. Sultan Mahmud Tughluq who returned to Delhi after the departure of Timur could do nothing to stop the ruin and with his death in 1413 the Tughluq dynasty came to an end.

Mahoba—an old town in the Hamirpur district of Uttar Pradesh, was the capital of the kings of Chandel dynasty (*q.v.*) who ruled over the region then called Jejaka-bhukti or Jijhoti (*q.v.*) from the ninth to the beginning of the thirteenth century Mohoba was beautified with many fine temples built by the

Chandel kings and their ruins bear testimony to the excellence of its architecture and sculpture.

Mahsuds, the—are a frontier tribe of Afghans who were placed on the Indian side of the Durand line (*q.v.*). They are a warlike and troublesome people and required to be frequently chastised by the British Indian Government in order to be forced to remain quiet and peaceful.

Mailapur—is modern Mylapore near Madras. According to some old Christian tradition the apostle St. Thomas was martyred at Mailapur. There is no historical evidence in support of the tradition.

Maitraka, the—was the name of a clan of Rajputs. Its chief, Bhatarka, established a dynasty of rulers towards the close of the fifth century A.D. at Valabhi (*q.v.*) in eastern Saurashtra. A branch of the Maitraka family established itself in Mo-la-po or western Malwa in the second half of the sixth century and made extensive conquests in the Vindhya region. In the seventh century the Maitraka king, Dhruvasena II (also called Dhruvabhata) (*q.v.*) married a daughter of Emperor Harsha of Kanauj. His son Dharasena IV (A.D. 645-49) assumed the imperial titles of *Paramabhattaraka Parameswara Chakravartin*. But in about A.D. 770 the Maitraka dynasty was overthrown by the Arabs who had conquered and occupied Sind in A.D. 712.

Malava—is the homeland of the Malavas, a very ancient clan. They were probably the people called the Malloi by the classical historians who occupied at the time of Alexander's invasion the right bank of the lower Hydraotes (Ravi) and had the distinction of inflicting a serious wound on the body of Alexander when he attacked their city. They were of course defeated by the Greek invader whose army killed many of the inoffensive members of the tribe. At some uncertain date they moved on to Avanti and gave their name to the region which came to be called Malava or Malwa with its capital at Ujjayini. They had at first a republican government which was later on turned into a monarchy. In the early centuries of the Christian era they passed under the rule of the Saka Satraps. In the fourth century they recognised the supremacy of Samudragupta whose son and successor, Chandragupta II, annexed their territory to the Gupta Empire. It was visited by Fa-Hien (*q.v.*) in the beginning of the fifth century and its prosperity, salubrious climate and good administration profoundly impressed the Chinese pilgrim. After the collapse of the Gupta Empire Malwa passed under the domination of the Hunas who again were defeated by King

Yasodharman (*q.v.*) in about A.D. 528 who then established his capital at Ujjayini, the famous and ancient city of the Malavas. It was not only a sacred city of the Hindus, but it was a centre of learning and is traditionally associated with the name of the great king, Vikramaditya (*q.v.*) and his famous court-poet, Kalidas. The tribal territory had in the meantime been turned into the settled well-governed state of Malwa which in later times formed a part, first, of the Chalukya dominions and later on of the Gurjara-Pratihara Empire. It was annexed to the Delhi sultanate in 1305 by Sultan Ala-ud-din Khalji, but seceded from it in 1401 when it was constituted into an independent Muhammadan kingdom. In 1531 it was annexed to the kingdom of Gujarat but forty-one years later it was conquered and annexed to the Mughul Empire by Akbar as the result of a lightning campaign in 1572-73. It passed under the control of the Marathas in 1738 and was eventually placed under the control of the Sindhia (*q.v.*) with whose subordination after the Third Maratha War (*q.v.*) it became a part of the British Indian Empire.

Malavikagnimitra, the—is a famous drama in Sanskrit written by the great poet, Kalidas (*q.v.*), probably in the fifth century A.D. It revolves round the careers of the first Sunga king Pushyamitra (*q.v.*) and his son Agnimitra and the latter's love for Malavika. It is a drama with some historical importance as a source-book.

Malaya—indicating the modern Malay Peninsula, has had long connection with India. Its name, Malaya, suggests some connection with the Malavas (*q.v.*), a well-known Indian clan, though the connection is not now easily traceable. Buddhist *Jataka* stories as well as Ptolemy's geography show that it was known to the Indians as *Suvarnadvipa* or *Suvarnabhumi* and a brisk trade existed between Malaya and India. Inscriptions written in correct Sanskrit dating from the early fifth century A.D. have been found in the Malay Peninsula as well as further to the west in Annam and Cambodia. Malaya was included in the great empire founded in south-eastern Asia by the Sailendras (*q.v.*) who had close association with Bengal and India. The cultural connection of Malaya with India was cut off in the thirteenth century A.D. when India passed under Muslim domination. (Majumdar, R. C. *Suvarnadvipa*).

Malcolm, Sir John (1769-1833)—an eminent officer in the Company's service, which he joined in 1782, came to India in

1783 and served in India till his retirement in 1830. He was present at the siege of Seringapatam in 1792 as well as at its capture in 1799. He held high political offices till the outbreak of the Second Maratha War (*q.v.*) in 1803 in which he played an important part and drew up the treaty of Surji-Arjangaon (*q.v.*) with the defeated Sindhia. He then served under Lord Lake in the war against Holkar (*q.v.*). He also played a prominent part in the Third Maratha War (*q.v.*) (1817-18), won the battle of Mahidpur (*q.v.*) and obliged Peshwa Baji Rao II to abdicate and granted him a generous pension for life. He was then placed in charge of the administration of Central India including Malwa and was made Governor of Bombay in 1827 from which post he retired in 1830. He was great as a soldier and greater as a diplomat. He was also an author and wrote several historical works amongst which his *Sketch of the Sikhs* and *Central India* are the more noteworthy.

Malhar Rao Holkar—the founder of the Holkar family of Indore, rose into prominence by rendering efficient and loyal service to Peshwa Baji Rao I (1720-40) and was rewarded with large territories in Central India which were held by his successors till their merger in the Republic of India in 1948.

Malik Ahmad—the founder of the Nizam Shahi dynasty of Ahmadnagar, had been the governor of Junnar near Poona under the Bahmani sultan, Mahmud (*q.v.*), for some years before he revolted and set himself up as an independent sovereign in 1490. He assumed the title of Ahmad Nizam Shah and established his capital at Ahmadnagar. He conquered Deogiri or Daulatabad in 1499 and thus consolidated his kingdom. He died in 1508 and his dynasty known as the Nizam Shahi ruled at Ahmadnagar till 1637 when the kingdom was finally annexed to the Mughul Empire.

Malik Amber—was an Abyssinian slave who rose to be the chief minister of Ahmadnagar and was in charge of its administration for many years. He first rose into prominence in 1601 by defeating in south-eastern Berar a Mughul army which attempted to conquer Daulatabad where the capital of the Ahmadnagar sultanate had been transferred after the surrender of the city in 1601. He was distinguished alike as a general and as a statesman and it was his efforts that foiled all the efforts of Emperor Jahangir to conquer Ahmadnagar. He gave to the state of Ahmadnagar not only a good and efficient system of administration but a very sound system of land revenue based on the classification of all arable land into four classes according to fertility, fixation of a permanent rent payable in cash and collection by the state officials directly from the village headman or patel. Malik Amber died at an advanced age in 1626 and it was only after his death that the Ahmadnagar kingdom could be annexed to the Mughul Empire.

Malik Ayaz—was the admiral of the fleet of Sultan Mahmud Bigarha (*q.v.*) (1459-1511) of Gujarat. In combination and co-operation with an Egyptian fleet commanded by Amir Husain he defeated the Portuguese at the naval battle of Chaul in 1508. But next year he was defeated and his fleet was destroyed by the Portuguese in a battle off Diu.

Malik Ghazi Shahna—was the chief architect of Sultan Firuz Tughluq (1351-88) who was an indefatigable builder. Under his patronage Malik Ghazi Shahna built new cities like Firuzabad and Jaunpur, 120 rest-houses for Muslim travellers, and works of public utility like canals of which one, known as the old Jumna canal, is still in use and bears testimony to the skill of Malik Ghazi Shahna.

Malik Hasan—was originally a Brahman who became a convert to Islam and was given the name of Malik Hasan. He was the governor of Telingana during the rule of the Bahmani sultan, Muhammad III (1463-82). He was a leading member of the party of the Muhammadan nobles of the Deccan and was opposed to the supremacy of Mahmud Gawan (*q.v.*), the leader of the party of foreigners. He took a leading part in the conspiracy that culminated in the execution of Mahmud Gawan in 1481.

Malik Kafur—*see* Kafur

Malik Maqbul—was the governor of Warangal during the sultanate of Muhammad Tughluq (1325-51). Malik Maqbul was driven out of Warangal by the brothers Harihara and Bukka in about 1340; and the latter then established the kingdom of Vijayanagar (*q.v.*).

Malik Muhammad—a contemporary of Emperor Humayun (1530-56), was one of those rare Muhammadan men of letters who wrote his books in Hindi.

Malik Shahu Lodi—an Afghan chief of Multan, revolted towards the later part of the reign of Sultan Muhammad Tughluq (1325-31) but was defeated and forced to escape to Afghanistan.

Malkhed—*see* Manyakheta.

Mallas, the—were a tribal people who resided at Pava and Kusinagara in the time of Gautama Buddha (*q.v.*). They are often mentioned in Buddhist legends.

Mallikarjuna—the son and successor of King Devaraya II (*q.v.*) of Vijayanagar, ruled from A.D. 1447 to 1465. Unable to control his nobles at home and pressed by invasions from without by the Bahmani sultan, Ala-ud-din and the Orissan king, Kapileswara, Mallikarjuna had the mortification of seeing the beginning of the decline of his dynasty which was shortly afterwards overthrown by Narasimha Saluva (*q.v.*) of Chandragiri whose successful career begun in the reign of Mallikarjuna.

Mallu—the third sultan of Bijapur, ruled only for six months in 1534 and was blinded and deposed for his viciousness.

Malviya, Madan Mohan, Pandit (1861-1946)—was a leading nationalist leader, prominent educationist and social reformer. Born in Allahabad, he began his career in 1885 as a school teacher but he soon passed over to the legal profession and in 1893 enrolled himself as a Vakil in the Allahabad High Court. He also tried his hand at journalism and between 1885 and 1907 he edited three journals named *Hindustan*, *Indian Union* and *Abhyudaya*. He took to politics early in life and joined the second session of the Indian National Congress held in 1886 and twice became its President in 1909 and 1918. He was also elected a member of the Legislative Council of the U.P. in 1902 and later on of the Legislative Assembly. He was a fearless critic of the British Government and severely criticised its repressive policy in the Panjab culminating in the horrible Jalianwala Bagh massacre (*q.v.*). He was an orthodox Hindu but he believed in *Suddhi* (reconversion to Hinduism of Hindus who had been converted to other faiths) and the removal of untouchability. He was thrice elected as the President of the Hindu Mahasabha. His greatest achievement was, however, the foundation in 1915 in Benares of the Hindu University by raising the necessary funds from the Princes and peoples of India.

Malwa—*see* Malava.

Mamallapuram—was a city founded by the Pallava king, Narasimhavarman (*c.* A.D. 625-45). It is now called Mahabalipuram. This place contains the wonderful *Rathas* or 'seven Pagodas', each of which is cut out from a great rock-boulder and is decorated with remarkable relief sculptures. Some of the buildings in south-east Asian countries like Champa (*q.v.*) and Cambodia (*q.v.*) probably borrowed their architectural ideas from the monuments at Mamallapuram.

Mamulanar—an ancient Tamil Brahman poet, flourished four centuries after the Mauryas (*q.v.*). He makes in his works frequent references to the power of the Mauryas in the Deccan.

Mandasor—is an ancient town in Malwa and is not far from the more famous royal city of Ujjayini. It was probably the home of the great poet, Kalidas (*q.v.*). Certainly it was the capital of King Yasodharman (*c.* A.D. 530) who finally subjugated the Huna king, Mihirakula (*q.v.*) and extended his conquests up to Assam.

Mandu—a city in Malwa (*q.v.*) was made its capital by Sultan Hoshang Shah (A.D. 1405-35) of the Ghuri dynasty ,of Malwa. It was a fortified city standing on the extensive summit of a commanding hill, protected by walls about 25 miles in length. It contains ruins of many massive and beautiful edifices including the Jami Mosque, the Hindola Mahal, the Jahaz Mahal, the palaces of Baz Bahadur and Rupamati, built of sandstone and marble. The city was fancied by Emperor Jahangir (1605-27) who stayed there in 1617 and renovated some of its buildings.

Mangalore, the treaty of—was concluded between the East India Company and Tipu Sultan (*q.v.*) of Mysore in 1784. It marked the close of the Second Mysore War (*q.v.*) which had begun in 1781, on the basis of mutual restitution of all conquests.

Manimekalai, **the**—is an epic written in Tamil by Sattanar, a grain merchant of Madura. This is a Buddhist poem relating to the life-story, mainly of religious interest, of the heroine Manimekalai. Its date is uncertain but is probably the fifth century A.D.

Manipur—is a small state in the north-eastern part of India, lying to the south of Assam. Its capital is Imphal. Its total area is 8,620 sq. miles and it has a population of about 6 lakhs. Tradition connects the name with a state mentioned in the *Mahabharata* and the royal family with the third Pandava brother, Arjuna. But the Manipur mentioned in the *Mahabharata* was situated near Kalinga and its identification with the modern Manipur is not justifiable. Its history also is not traceable beyond 1714 when its rule was assumed by a local chieftain named Gharib Nawaz or 'patron of the poor'. He was a Hindu and proved to be an able king and ruled well. But his descendants became involved in wars with the Burmese who invaded the country frequently and at last occupied it in 1825. But Burmese expansion in this region brought about the Anglo-Burmese War (*q.v.*) which was concluded by the treaty of Yandabo (*q.v*) (1826) which restored Manipur to its king, Gambhir Singh.

Manipur was now treated by the Indo-British Government as a semi-independent protected state governed by its own king. But in 1890 the reigning king of Manipur was deposed at the instigation of his brother, Tikendrajit, who was also the Commander-in-Chief of the state army. A new ruler was set up. The British Government recognised the new ruler but decided to banish Tikendrajit. But Mr. Quinton, the Chief Commissioner of Assam, who went to Manipur to execute the order of banishment, was treacherously attacked and killed. An Indo-British force now marched into the state, overran it easily, captured and executed Tikendrajit as well as his *protégé* the new king, and set up a new Raja. As the new Raja was a minor, the administration of the state was carried on during his minority by the Political Agent. Manipur continued to be one of the subordinate princely states of India until its merger with the Republic of India in 1948-49.

Manrique, Sebastian—a Spanish friar, was in India in the thirties of the seventeenth century, wrote a full account of the siege and capture of the Portuguese factory of Hughli by Shah Jahan's army in 1632.

Man Singh—was the most famous king of the Tonwar dynasty of the Rajputs of Gwalior. He ruled from 1486 to 1517. He was great as a soldier as well as a builder. So long as he lived he more than held his own against the Muhammadan rulers of Jaunpur and Malwa as well as against the sultans of Delhi and maintained the independence of Gwalior. He and his beloved consort, Mrignayaná, developed at Gwalior a great centre of fine arts like music attracting the best musical talent from all over India. Man Singh also built at Gwalior the magnificent palace with its great gate on the eastern face of the rock, whose strength and grace best illustrated the personality of their builder.

Man Singh, Kunwar and Raja—was the grandson by adoption of Raja Bihari Mall (*q.v.*) of Amber. He entered into the service of Emperor Akbar in 1562 when Raja Bihari Mall made his submission to the Emperor and gave him a daughter in marriage. Man Singh served the Mughul Empire until his death in the Deccan in 1614. He was a great general and contributed considerably to the success of the Mughul arms in different parts of the empire. He was appointed to hold charge of important provinces like Kabul and Bengal where he reduced the Afghans to subjection. He was one of the main Hindu supporters of Mughul imperialism.

Mansabdar —was one who held a *mansab* or official appointment in Mughul India from the time of Emperor Akbar. The *mansabdar* held an office of rank and profit and, as such, was to supply a number of troops for the military service of the state. The *mansabdars* formed the Mughul bureaucracy on military lines. Akbar introduced and systematised the organisation. All officers, civil as well as military, were classified into thirty-three grades, ranging from commanders of ten to commanders of 10,000, with salaries which varied according to the strength of the 'command.' The highest grades of commanders of 7000, 8000 and 10,000 were reserved for the royal princes. The *mansabdars* were directly recruited, promoted, suspended and dismissed by the Emperor. A definite rate of pay was fixed for each grade and out of this remuneration each *mansabdar* was required to maintain a certain number of troopers, elephants and beasts of burden. But the *mansabdars* rarely fulfilled this condition. In order to check fraudulent practices Akbar used to brand their horses and introduced in the eleventh year of his reign a double system of ranking, viz. *zat* and *sowar*, the first denoting the personal rank of the *mansabdar* and the second indicating the actual number of effective soldiers that he must maintain. The *mansabdari* dignity was not hereditary nor did it depend on specialisation. The *mansabdars* were highly paid and it has been estimated that, after deducting all expenses for maintaining the required number of troops, a *mansabdar* of 500 got a net monthly income of Rs. 1000/- which was as high as Rs. 18,000/- in case of a *mansabdar* of 10,000. Akbar preferred to pay the *mansabdars* in cash, but the system of paying them with *jagirs* with incomes equivalent to their rank-pay, came to be introduced in later times. This development tended to weaken the Mughul system of government.

Mansel, Charles G.—was a member of the Board of the Panjab administration set up by Lord Dalhousie after the annexation of the province in 1849. He served on the Board till 1851.

Mansur Ali Khan (1829-84)—was the last Nawab *Nazim* of Bengal. The honours and emoluments previously attached to the Nawab of Murshidabad like the salute of 19 guns and exemption from attendance in civil courts were taken away from him and his pension was also reduced. He went personally to England and submitted his appeal to the House of Commons which rejected it. In protest he resigned his position and titles in 1880.

Mansur, Khwaja Shah—was the first finance minister of Emperor Akbar and was much trusted by him. But Mansur intrigued against Akbar with his brother, Prince Hakim, and was hanged by Akbar's order in 1581.

Manu—was a famous sage and law-giver of the Hindus. His book the *Manu-Samhita* (or the Laws of Manu) deals with all aspects of the domestic life of an orthodox Hindu. (*see Laws of Manu*).

Manucci, Niccolo—was an Italian traveller who visited India in the seventeenth century and was in India during practically the whole of the reign of Aurangzeb (1659-1707). He recorded his varied experiences and observations in his large work *Storia do Mogor* which runs into four volumes.

Manyakheta—modern Malkhed in the present Andhra Pradesh, was made the capital of the Rashtrakuta kingdom (*q.v.*) by king Amoghavarsha (*c.* A.D. 815-77). The city has several Jain temples.

Marathas, the—*see* Maharashtra.

Maratha administrative and military system, the—was a mixture of Hindu and Muhammadan institutions. It was founded by Shivaji (*q.v.*) who created the independent Maratha state. The king was the head of the administration in which he was helped by Eight Pradhans or chiefs who were all appointed by the king and removable at his pleasure. Of the Eight Pradhans, the *Peshwa* was the Prime Minister and the other seven held departmental charges such as finance, record-keeping, correspondence, foreign affairs, army, religious questions and charities and justice. All the eight ministers except the two in charge of religious questions and justice also held military commands. During their absence on military work their administrative duties were performed by deputies. The ministers could not appoint their subordinates who were all appointed by the king. In revenue matters collection was made by the king's officers called *Patels* directly from the tenants who were required to pay rent at the rate of one-third of the gross produce. The land was carefully surveyed and divided into four classes according to the fertility of the soil. Lands under alien or Mughul control were subjected to the payment of two taxes, known as the *sardeshmukhi* amounting to one-tenth of the assessed revenue and the *chauth* amounting to one-fourth of the revenue assessment. The latter was a fee for non-molestation and gave to the Maratha administrative system a predatory character in the eyes of all states lying outside Maharashtra proper. This was an evil which grew in extent with the expansion of the Maratha domination and was one of the factors that prevented the establishment of the Maratha rule over the country on the basis of either Hindu or Indian Nationalism.

Closely connected with the Maratha administrative system was the military organisation set up by Shivaji. The army consisted mainly of light infantry and light cavalry, admirably well adopted for guerilla warfare and fighting in the mountainous region. Every soldier was individually selected after a personal examination by the king himself and was paid a fixed salary in cash or by assignment on the district administration. Shivaji did not pay by *jagirs*. Strict discipline was enforced in the army and no one was allowed to keep a woman in the camp. The booty taken by the soldiers was to be handed entirely over to the state. The army was not to be encumbered with heavy arms or costly camp equipage. Shivaji's cavalry was divided into two classes, namely, the *Bargirs* who were equipped with horses and arms by the state and the *Silahdars* who supplied their own equipment. The army was controlled by a regular gradation of officers called *naiks, havaldars, jumladars, hazaris* and *panjhazaris* with one *surnobat* for the cavalry and another for the infantry. Over the army as a whole there was a *Senapati* or Commander-in-Chief. In hilly Maharashtra forts were very important and Shivaji established a fort at every important pass in his territory and devised an elaborate system for garrisoning them and providing them with necessaries. The efficiency of the whole organisation, civil and military, depended on the direct supervision by the king which imposed upon him a burden which later Maratha rulers could not bear efficiently and adequately, leading to the introduction of laxity in the system and its failure when pitted against the modern British armies.

Maratha Confederacy—originated during the administration of the second Peshwa, Baji Rao I (1720-40). Forced partly by the opposition of the Kshatriya section of the Marathas led by the Senapati Dabade and partly by the rapid expansion of Maratha domination in north as well as in south India, Peshwa Baji Rao I had to depend on the loyal support of his adherents with proven military capacity. He thus put large areas under the control of his lieutenants of whom the chiefs were Raghuji Bhonsla, Ranoji Sindhia, Malhar Rao Holkar and Damaji Gaekwar. These leaders formed the Maratha Confederacy which during the administration of Baji Rao I (1720-40) and his son, Balaji Baji Rao (1740-61) was held in strict control by the Peshwa and carried his victorious arms to Delhi and even into the Panjab. But the severe defeat of the Peshwa's army in the third battle of Panipat in 1761 followed soon after by the death of Peshwa Balaji Baji Rao himself and the succession disputes that followed, weakened the Peshwa's hold on the ambitious members of the Maratha Confederacy which then became a serious disintegrating element in the Maratha state. The conflicts amongst its members, their jealousies and their rivalries, especially between the Holkar and the Sindhia, made united action amongst them impossible and contributed much to the decline and fall of the Maratha Empire and independence.

Maratha Wars—were fought with the British in India in 1775-82, 1803-05 and 1817-19. The *First Maratha War* (1775-82) was brought about by the intrigues of Raghoba, the uncle of Peshwa Narayan Rao (*q.v.*) (1772-73) who wanted to dispossess from the Peshwaship Narayan Rao's posthumous son and successor, Madhav Rao Narayan (*q.v.*) (1774-96) and sought British support by promising to cede to the Company Salsette and Bassein and the unscrupulous greed of the Company for profiting out of the succession dispute amongst the Marathas. It was a long and inglorious war during the course of which a British army under Col. Camac surrendered at Wargaon (1779) and made a Convention by which the British undertook to surrender Raghoba. But the Convention was repudiated by Warren Hastings (*q.v.*) who was then the Governor-General and the war was resumed. In spite of a spectacular march of an Indo-British army under Leslie and Goddard from Bengal right across India to Surat in 1779 and the capture of Gwalior by Major Popham in 1780 the British could not gain any decisive victory nor could the Marathas inflict any decisive defeat on the Company. In the circumstances, the British sought the mediation of Mahadaji Sindhia (*q.v.*) and concluded the war by the treaty of Salbai (*q.v.*) (1782) which secured a pension for their *protégé* Raghoba and a mutual restitution of territories except Salsette which was ceded to the Company. The Marathas and the English thus got a taste of their respective strength and weakness and remained at peace for the next twenty years. The internal jealousies and the rivalries amongst the Maratha chiefs continued and in October 25, 1802, Sindhia and Holkar fought a battle outside Poona in order to secure control over the reigning Peshwa Baji Rao II (*q.v.*) (1796-1818). Baji Rao II was a coward and intriguer without any thought for the welfare of his state. In his anxiety for escaping the control of the contending Maratha chiefs, he fled, when the battle of Poona was still being waged, to the English at Bassein and there he concluded on December 31, 1802, the ignoble treaty of Bassein (*q.v.*), by which he entered into a subsidiary alliance with the British on condition of his restoration to the Peshwaship. Baji Rao II thus bartered away the freedom and independence of the Marathas and was reinstalled by the British at Poona. But the Maratha chiefs, especially Sindhia, Bhonsla and Holkar, were not prepared to accept this arrangement and embarked on the *Second Maratha War* (*q.v.*) (1803-05). Again the Marathas could not unite. The Gaekwar sided with the English. Though Sindhia and Bhonsla combined yet Holkar would not join with them, though he was as much opposed to the treaty of Bassein as Sindhia and Bhonsla. The result was that even at this crisis the entire Maratha resources could not be employed against the British. Further, the Marathas produced no great general and strategist. As a consequence, in the Deccan the British army, led by Sir Arthur Wellesley (the future Duke of Wellington) after defeating a combined army of the Sindhia and Bhonsla at the battle of Assaye in September, 1803, so decisively vanquished Bhonsla at the battle of Argaon in the following November that next month Bhonsla made peace with the British by the treaty of Deogaon by which he ceded Cuttuck to the British and practically accepted the subsidiary alliance and British protection. In the meantime in northern India the British army under Lord Lake captured Aligarh and Delhi and finally so decisively defeated Sindhia at the battle of Laswari that Sindhia who had also shared the defeat at Argaon, was obliged to make peace by the treaty of Surji Arjangaon on 30th December, 1803, by which he surrendered to the British all his territories between the Ganges and the Jumna, renounced all his claims on the Mughul Emperor, the Peshwa and the Nizam, agreed not to appoint any European in his service without the consent of the British and thus practically became a subsidiary protected prince under the British. The Holkar, who had stood aloof so long in order to see the destruction of his rival the Sindhia at the hands of the British, was foolish enough to begin fighting in 1804 on his sole account against the British. He had some initial successes against the British in Rajputana, but he failed in his attack on Delhi in October and was defeated at the battle of Deeg in November, 1804.

The success, however, of his ally, the Raja of Bharatpur in repulsing a British attack led by Lord Lake on his fort created in England a reaction against the continuance of the war, and led to the recall of Lord Wellesley (*q.v.*) in 1805. His successor made peace with the Holkar on more favourable terms than the latter could have expected. He surrendered all claims to territories north of the Chambal and got back the greater part of his dominions (1806).

None of the Maratha chiefs including the Peshwa was satisfied with the result of the Second Anglo-Maratha War. They all regretted the loss of their power and prestige and the inveterate intriguer, Peshwa Baji Rao II, took the lead in organising a combination of the Maratha chieftains against the British in 1817 and in beginning the *Third Maratha War* (1817-19) in the hope of regaining what he had so thoughtlessly surrendered. But the British in India then under the Governor-Generalship of Lord Hastings proved too strong. The Sindhia was strategically so isolated at the beginning of hostilities that he could take no part in the war. The Bhonsla was defeated at the battles of Sitabaldi and Nagpur in 1817 and the Holkar at Mahidpur the same year. The Peshwa who had begun the war, was defeated, first at Kirki in 1817, and then, again, at the battles of Koregaon in January, 1818 and of Ashti a month later. This last defeat compelled the Peshwa to surrender to the British in June, 1818. The Third Maratha War thus ended in complete triumph for the British. They now abolished the Peshwaship and allowed Baji Rao II to retire to Bithur near Cawnpur on a large pension and his dominions all passed under British control. All the territories of the Bhonsla lying to the north of the Narmada were annexed by the British and over the rest a minor grandson of Raghuji Bhonsla II (*q.v.*) was installed as a subsidiary prince. Similarly the Holkar ceded to the British the districts south of the Narmada, gave up all claims on the Rajput states, accepted a subsidiary force within his territories and became a subordinate chief, ruling on sufferance of the British who thus became the dominant power all over India outside the Panjab and Sind.

Marshman, John—an English Christian missionary who was a member of the Baptist Mission, settled at Serampore which was then a Dutch possession. He conducted a journal named *The Friend of India*, in which he struck a Christian and reforming note. He was also an advocate for the expansion of education in India and supported the idea of establishing a University in Calcutta.

Martand temple, the—in Kashmir, was built by King Lalitaditya (*q.v.*) who ruled in Kashmir from A.D. 724 to 760.

Martyn, the Revd. Henry—was one of the earliest of the British Christian missionaries to have arrived in India. At the time of his arrival the E. I. Company did not grant licences to Christian missionaries to reside within the Company's territories for fear of the adverse effect that their religious teachings might produce amongst the Indians. So Henry Martyn became a chaplain under the E. I. Company in Bengal and carried on his missionary work within the restricted limits permitted by his appointment. The ban on the Christian missionaries was raised in 1813.

Marudvridha, the—is one of the ten streams mentioned in the hymn *In praise of the Rivers* in the Rig Veda. It has been identified with the Maruwardhan which flows through the Maru valley of the Kashmir-Jammu state and falls into the Chinab. The other nine rivers are the Ganges, Jumna, Saraswati, Satadru (Sutlej), Parushni (Ravi), Asikini (Chinab), Vitasta (Jhelum), the Arjikiya (Kanshi) and the Sushoma (Sohan), both in the Rawalpindi district. The reference to the Marudvridha shows the intimate knowledge of the Rig Vedic Aryans with the interior of Kashmir and Jammu.

Marwar—*see* Jodhpur.

Maski—is now a small place in the Raichur district of Andhra Pradesh. A version of the first Minor Rock Edict of Emperor Asoka (*q.v.*) was discovered at Maski in 1919. This Maski edict of Asoka is unique because it is the only inscription of Asoka in which the royal author is not called, as in other edicts, simply *Devanampriya*, but also Asoka. This edict thus finally confirmed the identification of King *Devanampriya Priyadarshin* with Asoka, the third Maurya Emperor, made simply on speculative evidence by George Turnour as far back as 1837.

Masson, Charles—saw Maharaja Ranjit Singh of the Panjab in the twenties of the nineteenth century. He has left a very interesting account of the personal appearance and habits of the Maharaja. He gives no dates and sometimes supplies fanciful accounts.

Masud—the son of Sultan Mahmud (*q.v.*) of Ghazni, was the patron of the famous scholar and historian, Abu-Rihan Muhammad, commonly called Al-Beruni (*q.v.*).

Masulipatam—is a town and port on the Bay of Bengal on the eastern coast. The East India Company established a factory there in 1611. The French East India Company also founded a factory at Masulipatam in 1669. The city was captured by the French during the First Carnatic War (*q.v.*), but was stormed by Col. Forde (*q.v.*) during the Third Carnatic War (*q.v.*) and ceded to the English in 1759.

Masulipatam, the treaty of—was concluded in 1768 between the English and the Nizam of Hyderabad by which the English recognised the Nizam as the ruler of Balaghat, a district over which the English recognised the sovereignty of Mysore by a treaty made in 1769 and also by the treaty of Mangalore (*q.v.*) in 1784. This was an example of double-crossing in diplomacy committed by the East India Company in India and the attempt of Lord Cornwallis in 1788-89 to evade the Company's pledges given to Mysore in 1769 and 1784 led to the Third Mysore War (*q.v.*) (1790-92).

Mathura (or Muttra)—is an ancient city on the Jumna in Uttar Pradesh. It is esteemed by the orthodox Hindus as a very holy city, as it is closely interwoven with the Krishna cult and is believed to have been the place where Krishna, an *avatar*, was born. It became in the early centuries of the Christian era a very important and prolific centre of art, sculpture and image-making. It was also very much favoured by Jains and Buddhists and the Chinese pilgrim, Fa-Hien (*q.v.*) who visited India early in the fifth century, found at Mathura and its neighbourhood twenty Buddhist monasteries. It was beautified with many fine and rich buildings, the wealth of which roused the greed of Sultan Mahmud who sacked the city, destroyed the temples and plundered its wealth in about A.D. 1020. But Hindu piety later on rebuilt much of what was destroyed and the most magnificent edifice was built by the Bundela chief, Bir Singh (*q.v.*) in the reign of Jahangir. The temple was so high that it could be seen from the imperial capital of the Mughuls and was destroyed by the order of Emperor Aurangzeb in 1670. In the eighteenth century Mathura became the capital of the Jat chief, Suraj Mal. It was sacked by Ahmad Shah Abdali in 1757, but a severe outbreak of cholera in Abdali's army stationed at Mathura filled Abdali's soldiers with such horror that when, after the third battle of Panipat in 1761, they were ordered to proceed to sack Mathura they definitely refused to do so and thus forced Abdali to retire from India without reaping fully the fruits of his great victory. It was annexed to the Indo-British Empire after the Third Maratha War.

Matsya—was the name of an ancient Indian kingdom which lay in the eastern part of modern Rajputana. Its capital was

Viratanagara or Bairat in the modern Jaipur state. It is referred to in the Vedas and it occupies an important place in the *Mahabharata* story of the war between the Kurus and the Pandavas. In historical times it was absorbed into the Magadhan empire and its capital, Bairat, has yielded some of the most famous inscriptions of Asoka (*q.v.*).

***Matsya Purana,* the**—is one of the eighteen *Puranas* (*q.v.*) of the ancient Hindus. Its kernel is very old and was known in the fourth century B.C., though it might have taken its present form much later. It contains dynastic lists of ancient Indian kings which modern researches have proved to be largely authentic.

Maues—was either a Saka or an Indo-Parthian king who ruled over Arachosia and the Panjab in about 90 B.C. His name is known from coins.

Maukhari dynasty, the—was founded in or about A.D. 554 by Isanavarman who defeated a later Gupta king and assumed the imperial title of *Maharajadhiraja*. His territories covered the eastern part of Uttar Pradesh as well as the Gaya region of Magadha. For the next quarter of a century the Maukhari dynasty was the strongest power in the Upper Gangetic valley. Isanavarman was succeeded by Suvavarman, Avantivarman and Grahavarman who was the last king of this dynasty. He married Rajya-sri, the daughter of Prabhakaravardhana of Thaneswar. His capital was at Kanauj. But Grahavarman was defeated and killed in about A.D. 606 by Devagupta, king of Malwa. As he was childless the dynasty ended with him and Kanauj passed to his brother-in-law, Harshavardhana (A.D. 606-47).

Maurya dynasty, the—was founded in about 322 B.C. soon after the death of Alexander, the king of Macedon, in 323 B.C. by Chandragupta Maurya (*q.v.*) who overthrew the last of the Nanda kings of Magadha with the assistance of a Taxilian Brahman named Chanakya. His capital was at Pataliputra and he ruled till about 298 B.C. During the course of these few years he drove the Greeks out of the Panjab and Taxila, extended his dominions all over northern India including Saurashtra in the west. In about 305 B.C. he repulsed an invasion by Seleukos who had inherited the eastern dominions of Alexander and obliged him to make peace by surrendering all his eastern territories beyond the Hindu Kush. Seleukos also entered into a matrimonial alliance with Chandragupta to whose court at Pataliputra he also sent an ambassador named Magasthenes (*q.v.*) who has left an interesting and illuminating account of India as he found her. The dynasty founded by Chandragupta came to be known as the Maurya dynasty after his mother named Mura. Chandragupta's son and successor Bindusara (*q.v.*) ruled from about 298 B.C. to 273 B.C. He bore the title of *Amitraghata* (Slayer of Enemies) and probably conquered the Deccan. The third Maurya emperor was Bindusara's son, Asoka (*q.v.*) who ruled from about 273 B.C. to 232 B.C. Asoka's succession was probably disputed, as his coronation took place four years after his accession. Eight years after his accession he conquered Kalinga after a bloody battle which so deeply affected his mind and filled him with such profound sorrow that soon afterwards he became a Buddhist and foreswore war. During the years that he lived after his conversion he devoted all the resources of his vast empire to the propagation of Buddhism in and outside India and to the amelioration of the sufferings of men and beasts by establishing benevolent institutions. He left all over India many inscriptions on rocks and pillars calling upon his subjects to cultivate the virtues of charity, truthfulness, kindness, obedience to parents and teachers, non-violence and toleration. He also sent Buddhist missionaries to Ceylon as well as the countries on the west with the result that Buddhism now became a world religion. Asoka did not leave behind him any competent successor, and on his death his empire was probably divided between a son named Jalauka and a grandson named Dasaratha. Neither of them appears to have shared Asoka's love for Buddhism which appears to have lost the royal patronage soon after Asoka's death. In any case the successors of Asoka were weak princes and the last of them, named Brihadratha, was killed in about 185 B.C. by his Brahman Commander-in-Chief, Pushyamitra, who established the Sunga dynasty.

Mawalis, the—are the indigenous hill-people of the Western Ghats, who, in Shivaji's (*q.v.*) time, looked uncouth and were backward. They proved hardy, brave and intensely loyal to the new leader. They knew every path and rock in their native mountainous country and it was by keeping company with them in his early youth that Shivaji also came to be intimately familiar with the topography of the land.

Mayo, Lord—was the Viceroy and Governor-General of India from 1869 to 1872. He had great geniality and diplomatic skill which enabled him to secure the goodwill and admiration of Amir Sher Ali (*q.v.*) who met him at Ambala in 1869, though he did not agree to the latter's request for a definite treaty and the recognition of his son, Abdulla Jan, as his prospective successor. Lord Mayo was confronted with a bad financial condition in India with deficit budgets and unreliable estimates. During his short administration Lord Mayo greatly improved the finances of the country by increasing the salt-tax, by enforcing economy in public administration and by introducing a new system of division of funds between the Central and Provincial Governments. As a result the deficit budget was turned into a surplus budget. It was during his administration that the first general census of India was taken in 1870. He organised a statistical survey of the country and created a department of commerce and agriculture. In 1872 when on a visit to Port Blair in the Andaman Islands he was assassinated by a Pathan convict.

Mayurasarman—the founder of the Kadamba dynasty (*q.v.*) which ruled in Mysore, was a Brahman by caste but a warrior by profession who, probably in the fourth century A.D., revolted against the Pallavas of Kanchi and established the Kadamba dynasty (*q.v.*). He made extensive conquests in the Deccan.

Mecca—in Arabia is the birth-place of Muhammad, the Prophet of Islam. It is a holy place of pilgrimage for the Muhammadans of India and is visited every year by hundreds of them.

Medina—is the second important city in Arabia. In A.D. 622 Muhammad fled from Mecca to Medina and it is from that year that the Muhammadan era of Hijra dates.

Medini Rao—was a loyal vassal of Rana Sangrama Singh (*q.v.*) of Mewar. He was in charge of the fort of Chanderi when it was invaded by Babur (*q.v.*) in 1528. Medini Rao was killed and the fort was stormed by the Mughuls.

Medows, General Sir William—led the British army during the Third Mysore War (*q.v.*) against Tipu Sultan in 1790. He succeeded in occupying some of Tipu's possessions like Dindigul. Coimbatore and Palghat, but his success was far from decisive. So in 1791 Cornwallis himself took the chief command, and General Medows served under him.

Meerut—is a town in Uttar Pradesh. It was a garrison-town in 1857 and it was in this town that the sepoys first broke out in open revolt on the 10th May, 1857. They swarmed into the military prisons, released their imprisoned comrades, murdered the European officers and galloped next day to Delhi and thus began the Sepoy Mutiny.

Megasthenes—was the Greek ambassador who was sent by Seleukos Nikator (*q.v.*) to the court of Chandragupta Maurya (*q.v.*) at Pataliputra in about 302 B.C. He travelled all over north India from the north-western frontier to Pataliputra in Magadha and wrote an account, called *Indica*, of what he saw and heard in India. The original of this account has been lost, but fragments of it have been preserved by later classical historians like Arrian and Diodoras and have been collected by M'Crindle in modern times. Megasthenes' account is a very important source of our knowledge of Maurya India, as it is the first dated account of the times. It has its defects no doubt, but yet its value is immense. (M'Crindle, *Indica*).

Meghaduta, the—is a lyric poem by Kalidas (*q.v.*) in Sanskrit. Here a Yaksa, banished at Ramgiri as a result of Siva's anger, is reminded by the approach of the rainy season of his wife, lamenting her separation in their abode Alaka, and begs a passing cloud to bear to his beloved the news of his welfare and the assurance of his devotion. The brilliance of the description of the cloud's progress from the eastern end of India to the western end and the pathos of the picture of the sorrowful wife are exquisite. The poem has, accordingly, been ranked as the best among Kalidas's works for brevity of expression, richness of content and the power to elicit sentiment.

Meghavarna—was the contemporary king (*c.* A.D. 352-79) of Ceylon when Samudragupta, the second Gupta emperor, was ruling (*c.* A.D. 330-80) in India. King Meghavarna sent to Emperor Samudragupta an embassy with presents and obtained his permission to build a splendid monastery to the north of Bodh Gaya (*q.v.*) for the use of Ceylonese pilgrims. In the Allahabad inscription Samudragupta records to have received 'acts of respectful service' from the Sinhalese amongst others.

Menander—was a Greek dramatist. Some European scholars like Windisch hold that the Greek plays written by Menander and other dramatists of his school influenced Indian classical dramas as suggested by the unmistakable resemblances between them. This is a debatable issue.

Menander (Milinda)—was the most remarkable Indo-Greek king who reigned in the Panjab from about 160 B.C. to 140 B.C. His coins which were abundant and issued in various types, have been found over an extensive part of northern India, even to the south of the Jumna. He might have been the 'viciously valiant *yavana*' prince who, according to the *Gargi*

Samhita, occupied Allahabad and threatened Kusumapura, that is to say, Pataliputra. According to Buddhist tradition, he embraced Buddhism and the famous Buddhist text, *Milindapanha* (*q.v.*) (Dialogues with Milinda) records his discussions with the famous Buddhist monk, Nagasena.

Mendosa, Dom Andreas de—was the Portuguese viceroy at Goa for about five months in 1609. He had the temerity to oppose the concessions that Emperor Jahangir (*q.v.*) had granted to the English E. I. Company on the representation of Captain William Hawkins. Jahangir revoked the concessions granted to the English Company, but hostilities broke out between the Portuguese and the Mughuls which were ended through the mediation of the Portuguese missionary Father Pinheiro, but led to the recall of Mendosa.

Meos, the—were a tribal people who lived to the south of Delhi. They were Hindus and naturally created trouble for the recently established Muhammadan sultanate of Delhi. Consequently in 1260 Balban (*q.v.*) who was then administering the country on behalf of his son-in-law, Sultan Nasir-ud-din (*q.v.*) led a campaign against them, slaughtering the people and pillaging their country. Two hundred and fifty of their leaders were carried as captives to Delhi where many of them were cast under the feet of elephants and killed, and many were flayed alive and their skins, stuffed with straw, were hung over every gate of Delhi. The brave Meos were not cowed down even by such barbarous treatment and continued their hostilities to the Muhammadan intruders. So Balban led a second campaign against them towards the close of 1260. This time he fell upon them unawares, captured them all, to the number of 12,000 men, women and children, who were all put to the sword. The Meos were the brave victims of Muhammadan barbarity.

Merv—is a town about 150 miles northwards from the north-western frontier of Afghanistan. In 1884 it was captured by Russia. The fall of Merv, to which a fictitious strategic importance had been attached by some people in England, roused in English minds the dread of Russian designs on Afghanistan, and directly and indirectly on India. This threatened an Anglo-Russian War which was avoided by the moderation of Amir Abdur Rahman (*q.v.*) and the diplomatic skill of English and Russian statesmen. (*See* also Panjdeh incident.)

Mesopotamia, operations in—were consequential to the outbreak of the First World War (1914-18) during which Turkey joined with the Central Powers. Mesopotamia was then under Turkish rule. An Anglo-Indian expeditionary force was therefore sent to operate in 1915 with the limited objects of (i) protecting the Anglo-Persian oil installations, (2) occupying Basra and its neighbourhood round the head of the Persian Gulf and (3) impressing the Arabs of the region. The expeditionary force which was organised and sent by the British Indian Government at first had great success. It marched up the country, occupied Kut in September, 1915, and decided to march on to Baghdad, but it was beaten back from Ctesiphon to Kut where it was soon besieged. The siege lasted from 8 December, 1915 to 24 April, 1916, when Kut fell and the garrison of 9000 British and Indian troops with General Townshend, surrendered. The campaign had caused 24,000 casualties. This disaster was followed by the appointment of a Royal Commission to enquire into the causes of it. In accordance with its recommendations increased military preparations were made, new generals were put in command and a fresh campaign began in December, 1916. Kut was reoccupied on 26 February, 1917 and Baghdad was captured on 11 March, 1917. The victorious General Maud died of cholera in November, 1917, but his successor, General Sir William Marshall, carried on the expedition with vigour, broke the Turkish resistance at Kirkuk and captured Mosul just when the war was brought to a close by the Armistice in 1918. Thus the long-drawn operations in Mesopotamia ended in an Anglo-Indian victory. (Moberley, F. J., *The Mesopotamian Campaign*)

Metcalfe, Sir Charles, afterwards Lord, (1985-1846)—was acting Governor-General of India from March, 1835 to March 1836. He was born in Calcutta, being a son of Major Thomson Metcalfe who was a military officer in the Company's service in India. He was educated at Eton and came out to Calcutta as a writer in the Company's service in 1801. He held various political appointments up to 1808 when he was sent on a special mission to Maharaja Ranjit Singh at Lahore and had his first great diplomatic success in concluding with him in 1809 the treaty of Amritsar (*q.v.*) by which all Sikh states east of the Sutlej were recognised by Ranjit Singh to be under British protection. He was Resident in Gwalior in 1810, in Delhi from 1811 to 1819, in Hyderabad from 1820 to 1822 and Member of the Governor-General's Council from 1827 to 1834 when he became the Governor of Agra. He acted as Governor-General of India from 1834 to 1835 and liberated the Press by abolishing all the existing restrictions on the Press in India. This estranged the Directors and they refused to confirm him as Governor-General. He was, instead, appointed as Lt.-Governor of the North-West Province (modern Uttar Pradesh) which he administered from 1836 to 1838. But he was disappointed of the Governorship of Madras and resigned. After his retirement to England he held successively the Governorship of Jamaica and Canada, was created a peer in 1845 and died in 1846. He was a statesman tried in many high posts and equal to all. His liberation of the Press made him very popular with the Indians and they raised the Metcalfe Hall in Calcutta in his honour.

Mewar—*see* Udaipur.

Miani, the battle of—was fought in 1843 between a British Indian army led by Sir Charles Napier (*q.v.*) and the Amirs of Sind. The Amirs were badly defeated and Sind was annexed to the British Indian Empire.

Midnapur—is the name of a town and district in West Bengal. It is partly a coastal district abutting on the Bay of Bengal. The ancient port of Tamralipti from which the Chinese pilgrim Fa-Hien (*q.v.*) sailed on his way back to China, is now represented by the town of Tamluk, 60 miles from the sea, in the Midnapur district. In 1760 the district of Midnapur, along with Burdwan and Chittagong, was ceded to the East India Company by Nawab Mir Kasim (1760-63) as a price of his installation as the Nawab of Bengal.

Mihiragula (also spelt Mihirakula)—was the son and successor of the Huna king, Toramana (*q.v.*) who ruled over an extensive dominion comprising a large part of the western frontiers of the Gupta Empire and central Malwa in the last quarter of the fifth century A.D. Mihiragula ascended the throne in about A.D. 500. His dominions extended beyond India into Afghanistan. He was very tyrannical and a cruel persecutor of Buddhism. His capital was Sakala or Sialkot in the Panjab. He was defeated and driven from his kingdom in about A.D. 528 by a combination of Baladitya, king of Magadha, and Yasovarman, king of Mandasor. After the defeat Mihiragula fled to Kàshmir where he eventually seized the throne, but died after a short reign.

Mildenhall, John—was an English merchant-adventurer who came to India overland in 1599. He spent seven years in the East. He visited Emperor Akbar in the last years of his life and "spoke with Akbar face to face". He, however, failed to secure from either Akbar or his son, Jahangir, any trading facilities for the English. He died in 1614. He was a "dishonest scoundrel but a pioneer of Anglo-Indian enterprise".

Milinda—*see ante* Menander.

Ming-ti—was an emperor (A.D. 58-75) of the earlier Han dynasty of China. Having seen Buddha in a dream in A.D. 62 he sent ambassadors to India to enquire into his doctrines. The Chinese ambassadors who came to India returned to China in about A.D. 67 taking back with them some Buddhist holy texts and statues, and two Indian Buddhist monks, named Kasyapa Matanga (*q.v.*) and Gobharana (*q.v.*). The two Indian monks settled in China, translated some Buddhist books into Chinese and converted some Chinese to Buddhism. Thus Emperor Ming-ti came to have the distinction of having introduced Buddhism in China for the first time.

Minhaj-i-Siraj—(full name Minhaj-ud-din) was a famous historian. He held high office under Sultan Nasir-ud-din (*q.v.*) (1246-66) and named his work *Tabaqat-i-Nasiri* after his royal patron. He was practically a contemporary historian for the early period of the sultanate of Delhi and is considered fairly reliable. His *Tabaqat* has been translated into English by Raverty.

Minto, Earl, I (1751-1814)—was the Governor-General of India from 1807-1813. He was wedded to the policy of Non-Intervention and succeeded in avoiding any major war in India. But he had several diplomatic triumphs. By a show of force he prevented the Pindari leader, Amir Khan, from interfering in Berar in 1809. A greater triumph was the conclusion of the treaty of Amritsar (*q.v.*) in 1809 with Ranjit Singh of the Panjab by which the Sutlej was recognised as the boundary between the Sikh state in the Panjab and the British Indian territories. In order to forestall a combined Franco-Russian invasion of India, Lord Minto sent Sir John Malcolm on a mission to Persia in 1808 and Mountstuart Elphinstone to Shah Shuja, Amir of Afghanistan, the same year. Understandings were arrived at with both the kingdoms on measures that were to be taken for arresting the Franco-Russian menace which was removed by the rupture between France and Russia in 1810. But the fear of French aggression still continued and Lord Minto I conquered the French islands of Bourbon and Mauritius in the west, the Dutch possessions of Amboyna and the Spice Islands in the east in 1810 and the island of Java in 1811. Lord Minto I thus effectively checked France and her subordinate states in the East Indies.

Minto, Earl, II (1845-1914)—was the Viceroy and Governor-General of India from 1905 to 1910, in succession to Lord Curzon (*q.v.*). He was the great-grandson of Lord Minto I (*q.v.*). He showed great tact in facing the critical situation in which Lord Curzon left India as well as in working with amity with Lord Morley who was the Secretary of State for India at the time. He healed the breach with Lord Kitchener (*q.v.*), the Commander-in-Chief with whom Lord Curzon had quarrelled and he considerably improved relations with the Amir of Afghanistan, who paid him a visit in Calcutta. But the most important task that confronted Lord Minto II was the conciliation of the tide of nationalism coupled with terrorism that had begun to rise in India since the ill-advised Partition of Bengal (*q.v.*) ordered by Lord Curzon. He took strong steps to suppress terrorism and to uphold law and order by muzzling the Press, by deporting nationalist leaders under Regulation III and by detaining persons in prison without trial. At the same time he took some measures to conciliate moderate opinion in India by agreeing to two Indians being appointed for the first time to the Council of the Secretary of State for India and also to an Indian for the first time to the Viceroy's Executive Council. Last but not the least of his reforms was the enactment of the Government of India Act, 1909 (generally called the Morley-Minto Reforms Act) which laid the foundation of the policy of gradual extension of self-government in India by introducing the system of direct election to the legislatures as well as by increasing the numbers of elected representatives in the provincial as well as the Central legislatures. Lord Minto II deliberately encouraged the Muslims in India to counterbalance the importance of the Hindus, gave legal recognition to communal representation in the country's legislative bodies, encouraged the foundation of the Muslim League in 1906 and thus sowed the seeds of future trouble. (Das, M. C., *India under Morley and Minto*)

Mir Fath Ali Khan Talpura—overthrew the control of the descendants of Ahmad Shah Abdali over Sind in 1783 and practically made Sind an independent state. He died in 1802 and his descendants who ruled over central Sind became divided into four families settled at Shahadadpur. They were all known as the Amirs of Sind like their kinsmen who were settled in Mirpur and Khairpur.

Mir Jafar—was the Nawab of Bengal from 1757 to 1760 and again from 1763 to 1765. He was a brother-in-law of Nawab Alivardi

Khan (*q.v.*) of Bengal and was the most powerful noble in the court of Murshidabad. Alivardi's grandson and successor Nawab Siraj-ud-daulah (*q.v.*) suspected his loyalty and dismissed him from the office of the *bakshi* (*q.v.*). This estranged Mir Jafar further and he entered into a conspiracy with other disaffected elements including the rich banker Jagat Seth (*q.v.*) of Murshidabad for deposing Siraj and securing the Nawabship for himself. Mir Jafar as the leader of the conspirators entered on the 10th June, 1757 into a treaty with the English in Calcutta by which Mir Jafar promised that in the event of his being made the Nawab of Bengal with the help of the English he would confirm all the privileges allowed them by Siraj-ud-daulah by the treaty of Alinagar (9th February, 1757), would make an offensive and defensive alliance with the English, would exclude the French from Bengal, would pay to the E. I. Company a million sterling as compensation for the loss of Calcutta in 1756, and pay a half of that amount in addition to the European inhabitants. By a private arrangement Mir Jafar also promised large gratuities to the English army and navy and members of the Council in Calcutta. Accordingly on 23 June, 1757 in the battle of Plassey Mir Jafar and his fellow-conspirators took no active part in the battle which the English easily won. Siraj who fled from the battle-field, was soon made a captive and killed by Miran, the son of Mir Jafar who was then installed as the Nawab of Bengal. On his accession he not only gave to the English all that he had stipulated to grant by the treaty of 10 June, 1757, but also granted to the Company the Zamindari of 24 Parganas. Further by a fresh treaty which he made with the Company on the 15th July, 1757, he agreed to two new clauses which laid down that (i) "The enemies of the English are my enemies, whether they be Indians or Europeans", and (ii) "Whenever I demand the English assistance I will be at the charge of the maintenance of them". Mir Jafar thus started his inglorious Nawabship of Bengal by practically agreeing to the English political and military ascendancy in Bengal. Further Mir Jafar condemned his state to bankruptcy by paying Rs. 1,77,00,000 in compensation to those who had suffered at the capture of Calcutta in 1756, Rs. 1,12,50,000 (including Rs. 23,40,000 paid to Clive alone) to the English army, navy and officials besides assignment of the revenue of 24 Parganas payable by the Company to the Nawab. Naturally all these heavy payments emptied the Nawab's treasury and the salaries of his own army

fell into arrears. Mir Jafar thus became more and more dependent on the English and soon began to feel ill at ease with his
new masters. He, therefore, entered into an intrigue with the
Dutch against the English who, however, anticipated his hostility by defeating the Dutch at Biderra (*q.v.*). His patron Clive
went to England in 1760 and soon afterwards his son and
prospective successor, Miran, was killed by lightning. This
raised the question of succession to Mir Jafar. The successors
of Clive in office in Bengal took a leaf from Clive's book
and deposed Clive's *protégé* Mir Jafar in 1760 in favour of his
son-in-law, Mir Kasim (*q.v.*). Without offering any resistance
Mir Jafar retired from the inglorious Nawabship in 1760, but
was reinstated in 1763 on the outbreak of a war between the
English and Nawab Mir Kasim, after Mir Jafar had entered
into a fresh treaty with the English by which he agreed to
limit the number of troops to be maintained by himself, to
receive a permanent British Resident at his capital at Murshidabad, to levy only a duty of 2 per cent on English trade in
salt, to pay to the Company 35 lakhs of rupees as cost of war,
$37\frac{1}{2}$ lakhs of rupees as presents to the English army and navy
personnel and also to pay due compensation to private individuals for their losses in the war with Mir Kasim. The
financial condition of Mir Jafar was, therefore, worse after his
restoration. His political power was practically annihilated.
Addicted to opium and suffering from leprosy he died an
inglorious death in 1765. He was the most outstanding of the
many Indian Muhammadans who were responsible for the
downfall of Muhammadan rule in Bengal.

Mir Jumla Mir Muhammad Said—was a Persian merchant-
adventurer who began his career in Golconda as a very successful diamond merchant, entered into the service of Sultan
Abdullah Qutb Shah (1626-72) of Golconda and rose to be
his chief minister. He was a great statesman and also great as
a general. His wealth, power and prestige made the Sultan of
Golconda envious and eager to chastise him. Mir Jumla entered
into a conspiracy with the Mughuls and with the support of
Prince Aurangzeb who was then leading the Mughul invasion
on Golconda, he entered into the service of Shah Jahan in the
Deccan in 1656. Soon afterwards he was appointed the chief
minister of Shah Jahan. On the outbreak of the war of succession amongst the sons of Shah Jahan (*q.v.*) Mir Jumla sided
with Aurangzeb, helped him materially in winning the battle
of Dharmat (*q.v.*) and was appointed by Aurangzeb in 1660 as

the Governor of Bengal where he drove Shuja (*q.v.*) out of the province. Later on he led an expedition against Assam, overran the country, drove the Ahom king from his capital and forced him to accept a treaty in 1662 by which the Ahom king agreed to pay a heavy indemnity and to cede to the Mughuls a large part of lower Assam. The return from the interior of Assam was a terrible process and imposed much hardship on the Mughul army and its general Mir Jumla who died of illness contracted during the arduous retreat on his way back to Dacca in January, 1663.

Mir Jumla, Shariyat-ullah Khan—was a Turani nobleman who was a judge at Dacca and Patna in the early part of the reign of Emperor Farruksiyar (1713-19). He was an intriguer who tried to set Farruksiyar against the Sayyid brothers (*q.v.*), but later on went over to the side of the Sayyid brothers and helped them in their nefarious activities.

Mir Kasim (also spelt Mir Qasim)—was installed by the English as the Nawab of Bengal in 1760 in place of his father-in-law, Mir Jafar, who was deposed. Mir Kasim purchased the office by ceding to the Company the three districts of Burdwan, Midnapur and Chittagong, by paying 20 lakhs of rupees in cash to the Calcutta Council and by agreeing to clear the outstanding debts of Mir Jafar. Mir Kasim was much more efficient than Mir Jafar and a much more determined man. He increased the rigour of his revenue system and almost doubled the old revenue of the state. He began to raise a force of disciplined troops, and to secure himself from the undue interference from Calcutta, he transferred his capital from Murshidabad to Monghyr. He then decided to stop the abuse of the right of free private trade which the Company's officers had been illegally exercising since the time of Mir Jafar (*q.v.*) (1757-60). He came to an agreement with Vansittart (*q.v.*), then President of the Calcutta Council, to the effect that an *ad valorem* duty of 9% should be levied by the Nawab on the private goods of European traders as against the duty of 40% for others. But the Calcutta Council rejected the arrangement and would not agree to the realisation of more than $2\frac{1}{2}$% on salt only. This most inequitable demand on the part of the Calcutta Council so exasperated Nawab Mir Kasim that he remitted all duties on Indian and European traders alike. Thus between the insistence of the Company's servants on the continued exercise of an illegal practice and the determination of Nawab Mir Kasim to be master in his own house, there could be no compromise, and war between the Nawab and the Company became inevitable. The first overt act was done by the Company's chief at Patna, Mr. Ellis, who tried to seize the city. He was foiled in his attempt and the war began. But Mir Kasim had no genius for war, nor had he in his employment any capable general. In the circumstances he was defeated by the Company's armies at the battles of Katwa, Gheria and Udhuanala, and, on the approach of the English army on his capital, Monghyr, he fled to Patna. There he killed all the English prisoners in his hands as well as his Indian opponents like Jagat Seth whom he could lay his hands upon. He then fled to Oudh where he entered into an alliance with Shuja-ud-daulah, the Nawab of Oudh and Shah Alam II, the fugitive Mughul Emperor, against the Company. But the allies were completely defeated by the English at the battle of Buxar on the 22nd October, 1764. Shuja-ud-daulah fled for safety to Rohilkhand, the Emperor went over to the English and Mir Kasim who became a fugitive, died in extreme poverty several years later in Delhi.

Miran—was the son and prospective heir of Nawab Mir Jafar (*q.v.*) (1757-60). He captured Nawab Siraj-ud-daulah (*q.v.*) who had fled after his defeat at the battle of Plassey, and brought him back to Murshidabad where he killed him in 1757. Soon afterwards Miran himself was killed by lightning.

Miran Bahadur Shah—the ruler of Khandesh in the valley of the Tapti, submitted to Emperor Akbar in 1590, but he soon repented of his submission and rose in revolt. But in 1599 Akbar personally marched to Khandesh, captured its chief fortress of Asirgarh and Miran Bahadur Shah was subdued. Khandesh was annexed to the Mughul Empire.

Miranpur Katra, the battle of—was fought between Nawab Shuja-ud-daulah of Oudh and the Rohillas in 1774. Shuja-ud-daulah, who was helped by a British brigade, defeated the Rohillas and annexed their dominions to his kingdom of Oudh.

Mirpur, family—was a branch of the Amirs of Sind. The family shared the defeat of the Amirs at the battle of Miani (*q.v.*) in 1843 and was dispossessed.

Mirza Abu Talib Khan—was one of the first Indian Muhammadans to go across the seas to England where he arrived in 1785.

Mirza Ghulam Ahmad (1839 - 1908)—was the founder of the Ahmadiya sect of Islam with its headquarters at Qadian in the Panjab.

Mirza Ghulam Hossain—was one of the latest Muhammadan historians of India. He lived and wrote in the second half of the eighteenth century and occupied important public offices. His work, the *Siyar-ul-Mutaqherin*, is a contemporary account of the closing years of the Mughul Empire and of the early years of the rise of the British Empire in India.

Mirza Haidar—was the king of Kashmir from 1540 to 1551. He was a Mughul and a relative of Emperor Humayun on whose behalf he claimed to govern the country. But his sub-ordination to Humayun was only nominal; in practice he was an independent king. He was overthrown by the Kashmiri nobles in 1551. Four years later the sovereignty of Kashmir passed to the Chakks from whom Emperor Akbar conquered it in 1586.

Mirza Muhammad—*see* Siraj-ud-daulah.

Mirza Najaf Khan—was a Persian adventurer who came to Delhi, entered into the Mughul service and rose to be the chief minister of Emperor Shah Alam II (1759 - 1806). He was appointed chief minister on Shah Alam's return to Delhi in 1772 and held the office till his own death in 1782. During this period he was the effective ruler of the Delhi empire. He repulsed the Sikhs, suppressed the Jats, recovered Agra and held the Marathas at arm's length. His was the last case of an immigrant Muhammadan rising to high office in Delhi.

Mirza (or Mir) Shah—the first Muhammadan sultan of Kashmir, came from Surat and rose by his ability to be the minister of the Hindu king of Kashmir. In 1346 he seized the throne, assumed the name of Sams-ud-din and founded a dynasty which ruled over Kashmir till 1541.

Mirzas, the—were the cousins of Akbar. They rose in revolt against him in Gujarat in 1572 and were suppressed by the Emperor next year.

Mitakshara, the—is a famous law-book in Sanskrit. It was written by the celebrated jurist Vijnaneswar who lived at Kalyani, the Chalukya capital in the Deccan, during the reign of Vikramaditya Chalukya (*q.v.*) (A.D. 1076-1126). The *Mitakshara* is the leading authority on Hindu law outside Bengal and Assam. In matters of succession it lays down the basic principle that the son is a co-sharer with the father of all ancestral pro-perties from which the son cannot be disinherited or other-wise deprived except with his own consent.

Mithridates I—was the king of Parthia (*c*. B.C. 171 - 136 B.C.). He annexed to his dominions the Indian kingdom of Taxila lying between the Indus and the Hydaspes (Jhelum).

Moggaliputta Tissa—meaning Tissa, the son of Moggali, is a Ceylonese monk who, according to the Ceylonese chronicle *Mahavamsa*, converted Asoka to Buddhism. According to Buddhist tradition as preserved in northern India the honour of being the preceptor of the Maurya Emperor belonged to Upagupta, son of Gupta, a perfumer of Benares. Some are of opinion that the two names indicate the same person.

Mohenjo-daro—is a site in the Larkana district of Sind, now in Pakistan. Many monuments of a prehistoric civilisation which flourished in the Indus valley from about 2500 B.C. to 1500 B.C. have been found at this site. (*See ante* Indus Valley Civilisation).

Moira, Lord—*see* Hastings, Lord.

Mongols (Mongolians), the—were a narrow-eyed, yellow-tinted beardless people. Bands of Mongols, or peoples of Mongolian origin, entered into India at various times and some of them settled in the land. Chengiz Khan (*q.v.*) who threatened to invade India in A.D. 1211 was a Mongol and so was Timur (*q.v.*) who invaded India in 1398. But Chengiz Khan and his followers were not Muhammadans whereas Timur and his hosts were Muhammadans. The term Mongol is applied to the non-Muslim peoples of the Mongolian type. These very people became known as Mughuls after their conversion to Muhammadanism. The Mongols made numerous incursions into India since Chengiz Khan's threatened raid in A.D. 1211 and to repel them was a task which imposed a heavy strain on such strong Delhi sultans as Balban (*q.v.*) and Ala-ud-din Khalji (*q.v.*). Timur's raid in 1398 shook the Delhi sultanate to its very foundation and prepared the way for the foundation in India of the Mughul dynasty which ruled the country till the establishment of the British rule in the eighteenth century.

Monserrate, Father Antonio—was a learned Jesuit monk who was sent by the Portuguese administration of Goa, at the invitation of Emperor Akbar, to the Mughul Court in 1580. Monserrate and his colleague, Father Aquaviva, were warmly received by Akbar who placed Monserrate in charge of the instruction of his second son, Prince Murad, in the Portuguese language. Monserrate spent several years in Akbar's court and wrote in Latin an excellent account of the Mission of which he was a member. This account is a very valuable and contemporary source of information for Akbar's reign.

Monson, Col. Sir George (1730-76)—came to India as a military officer in the Company's service in 1758 and was second in command at the siege of Pondicherry in 1760. He was appointed in 1774 under the Regulating Act (*q.v.*) as a Member of the Governor-General's Council. He generally sided with his two colleagues, Francis and Clavering (*q.v.*) against Warren Hastings (*q.v.*) who regarded him as a dangerous opponent. He, however, resigned in September, 1776 and died soon afterwards at Hughli (*q.v.*) in Bengal.

Montague, Edwin Samuel (1879-1924)—was the Secretary of State for India from 1917 to 1922 in Lloyd George's ministry. On August 20, 1917, he made from his place in the House of Commons the important declaration that the British Government's policy in India was "the progressive realisation of responsible government" in the country. With a view to the implementation of this policy he visited India in 1917-18, toured over the country in the company of Lord Chelmsford, the Viceroy and took the leading part in drawing up the Report on the Constitutional Reforms in India the main principles of which were embodied in the Government of India Act, 1919. His personal *Diary* published in 1930, six years after his death, throws a revealing light on the personalities at the back of the Report. He differed with the Prime Minister, Lloyd George, on the extent to which Indian public opinion should be allowed to influence the Turkish policy of the British Government and in 1922 he authorised without the consent of the Cabinet the publication of India's protest to the treaty of Sevres. Lloyd George considered this a breach of convention and demanded Montague's resignation. His political career ended when he lost his seat at the General election of 1922. He died in 1924.

Montague-Chelmsford Report—on the Indian Constitutional Reforms was drawn up in 1918 with a view to the fulfilment of the announcement made on the 20th August, 1917, by Edwin Montague, the Secretary of State for India, from his place in the House of Commons to the effect that the British Government had in view "the progressive realisation of responsible government in India". Montague came to India in November, 1917, made in the company of Lord Chelmsford, the Viceroy, an extensive tour all over India for ascertaining public opinion and then in April, 1918 published a Report on Indian Constitutional Reforms, commonly known as the Montague-Chelmsford Report. It formed the basis of the Government of India Act, 1919 (*see* under *British Administration in India*) which made a clear division between the functions of the Central and Provincial Governments, introduced the principle of direct election of representatives of the people who were to have majorities in all legislatures, enlarged the Viceroy's Executive Council to which more Indians soon came to be appointed and established dyarchy (*q.v.*) in the provinces.

Montgomery, Sir Robert (1809-87)—entered the Company's Civil Service in 1828. He served first in the North-West Province and then in the Panjab where he became after its annexation a member of the Board of Administration. On the outbreak of the Sepoy Mutiny he showed great initiative and disarmed several Hindustani regiments at Lahore and Mian Mir on his own responsibility. He sent warnings of the coming storm to Multan, Ferozepur and Kangra. He was Lieutenant-Governor of the Panjab from 1859 to 1865 and showed great ability in settling the province. On his retirement from India he became a member of the India Council in England which post he held till his death in 1887.

Moplahs, the—are a fanatical Muhammadan sect residing in Malabar. They are believed to be descendants of Arab immigrants who came to India in the ninth century A.D. and took Indian wives. They often rose up against their Hindu neighbours, as in 1925.

Morari Rao—a Maratha chief of Gooty in the Deccan, helped the English and Clive (*q.v.*) in the Carnatic War (*q.v.*) against Chanda Shahib (*q.v.*). He also helped Clive in relieving Trichinopoly in 1752 and in defeating Chanda Shahib the same year.

Morley, John (1838-1923)—was the Secretary of State for India from 1905 to 1910. He was a Gladstonian liberal. While he supported firmness against the terrorists in India in 1907 he tried to conciliate educated Indians by appointing two Indians to the Council of the Secretary of State in London and one Indian to the Viceroy's Executive Council. He disowned any intention to introduce parliamentary institutions in India but he largely remodelled the constitution of India by passing the Government of India Act, 1909 (*q.v.*), (popularly known as the Morley-Minto Reforms Act) which introduced more fully than ever before the representative element in the Indian constitution, allowed the legislatures the rights of interpellations, discussing the budget and moving resolutions. Along with Lord Minto II (*q.v.*) he was responsible for introducing communal representation in the Indian legislatures. Ten years later, when out of office, he considered the Montague-Chelmsford Reforms (*q.v.*) as premature. He was a pacifist and retired into private life on the outbreak of the First World

War in 1914. He was a renowned author and before his death in 1923 he had come to be recognised as the *doyen* of the English men of letters. His chief works are *Life of Gladstone* (1903), *Voltaire* (1872), *Rousseau* (1873), *Cobden* (1881), *Burke* (1879), *Walpole* (1889), *Cromwell* (1900) and his *Recollections* (2 vols.) in 1917.

Morley-Minto Reforms—*see ante* under British Administration in India.

Mornington, Lord, later **Marquess of Wellesley**—*see* Wellesley.

Mountbatten, Louis, Lord, of Burma—was born in 1900 at Windsor. He is the son of Prince Louis of Battenburg and of Princess Victoria of Hesse, a grand-daughter of Queen Victoria (*q.v.*). He entered the Royal Navy in 1913 and by his dash and ability he rose during the Second World War to high naval commands, becoming the Supreme Allied Commander in South-East Asia in 1943. He held the post till 1946 and successfully conducted the campaign against Japan that led to the recapture of Burma. He was appointed Viceroy in India in 1947 and in that capacity he showed great tact, dash and diplomatic skill in effecting the transfer of power from British hands to the peoples of India and Pakistan on the basis of the partition of India into India and Pakistan on 15 August, 1947. He was then appointed Governor-General of the new Indian state. In this capacity he played an important part in persuading the Indian Princes to merge their states either in the Union of India or in Pakistan. When Pakistan later on connived at the invasion of Kashmir by the frontier tribes he advised the Government of India to place the dispute before the Security Council of the United Nations Organisation and thus helped the creation and continuance of the Kashmir dispute between India and Pakistan. On his retirement in 1948 from the Governor-Generalship of India he held high offices in the British Navy. From 1955 to 1965 he was the First Sea Lord of Great Britain.

Mrichchhakatika, **the**—is a Sanskrit drama written by King Sudraka of whom little else is known. It affords a picture of the life in Ujjayini towards the close of the Gupta period and is believed to have been composed in the sixth century A.D. As a drama it occupies the highest rank amongst Sanskrit plays and can be easily placed on the same level as the drama of Shakespeare. It has been translated into English.

Muazzam, Prince—*see* Bahadur Shah I.

Mubarak Shah—was an Armenian Christian resident in Delhi and known to Emperor Jahangir. His daughter was given, at the instance of the Emperor, in marriage to Captain Hawkins (*q.v.*).

Mubarak Shah Sharqi—the first independent king of Jaunpur, ruled for only three years (1399-1402).

Mubarak Shaikh—*see* Shaikh Mubarak.

Mubarak-ud-daulah—was a minor Nawab of Bengal. Warren Hastings (*q.v.*) was accused in 1775 by Nanda Kumar (*q.v.*) of having accepted a large bribe from Munni Begam in return for her appointment as guardian of the minor Nawab. The charge was never completely investigated.

Muddiman Committee—was appointed by the Government of India in 1924. Its official designation was the Reforms Enquiry Committee, but it became popularly known as the Muddiman Committee after the name of its Chairman, Sir Alexander Muddiman, who was then the Home Member of the Government of India. The Committee included amongst its members some prominent non-officials like Sir Tej Bahadur Sapru. Its function was to enquire into the working and defects of the constitution as set up in 1921 in accordance with the Government of India Act, 1919. The Committee submitted in December, 1924, a divided report, the majority suggesting only minor changes while the minority consisting entirely of non-official Indians, roundly condemned dyarchy (*q.v.*) and recommended fundamental changes in the structure of the Act of 1919. No effect was given to the recommendation of the Committee.

Mudgal—a fortified town in the doab between the Krishna and the Tungabhadra in the Deccan, was a bone of contention between the Bahmani kingdom (*q.v.*) and Vijayanagar (*q.v.*) and often changed hands. It was finally lost by the Vijayanagara king, Achyuta Raya (*q.v.*) (1529-42) to the Bijapur sultan, Ismail Adil Shah (*q.v.*) (1510-34).

Mudki, the battle of—was fought between the English and the Sikhs in 1845. The Sikhs were defeated.

Mudrarakshasa, the—(or *the Signet of the Minister, Rakshasa*) is a Sanskrit drama written by Vishakadatta, whose precise date is unknown but who has been assigned to the later Gupta period. The drama refers to the historical incident of the deposition of the last Nanda king by the Maurya Chandragupta with the assistance of the Brahman Chanakya.

Mughul dynasty, the—was founded by Babur in 1526 as the result of his victory over the last Lodi sultan, Ibrahim, in the first battle of Panipat (*q.v.*) in 1526. This victory enabled Babur to occupy Delhi and Agra. Then in 1527 Babur defeated Rana Sanga of Mewar at the battle of Khanua and thus broke Rajput resistance. Lastly, in 1528 Babur inflicted a second defeat on the Afghans in the battle of the Ghagra and thus extended his rule over Bihar and Bengal. These three victories made Babur the Emperor of northern India and enabled him to found the Mughul dynasty which ruled in India from 1526 to 1858. The dynasty comprised nineteen sovereigns of whom the first six, namely Babur (1526-30), Humayun (1530-56, with a break from 1540 to 1555), Akbar (1556-1605), Jahangir (1605-27), Shah Jahan (1627-58) and Aurangzeb (1658-1707) are generally called the Great Mughuls. Akbar brought the whole of north India as well as Khandesh and Berar in the Deccan under his rule. The process of extension was continued by the next three rulers until at last in the reign of Aurangzeb the Mughul Empire came to comprise the whole of India from the foot of the Himalayas on the north to Cape Comorin on the south. But events soon showed that like the boa constrictor the Mughul Emperor had devoured more than he could digest. Further, Aurangzeb deliberately gave up the policy of religious toleration on which Akbar had based his imperialism and desired to turn India into an empire for the benefit of Islam. Naturally this radical change in policy led to Hindu revolts initiated, first, in Maharashtra by Shivaji (*q.v.*) and then spreading amongst the Sikhs in the Punjab, the Jats in Bundelkhand and in Rajputana amongst the Rajputs who had been since the time of Akbar loyal supporters of the Mughul Empire. Further complications were created by the presence in India of European traders from Portugal, Holland, England and France who hid ambitious political aspirations behind their apparently peaceful commercial activities, and who had better military equipment and organisation and completely outstripped the Mughuls in naval power. Lastly, wars of succession became a feature of Mughul dynastic rule from the end of Jahangir's reign and greatly weakened the Crown. As a result the last thirteen rulers of the Mughul dynasty, generally called the Later Mughul Emperors, were weak sovereigns whose dominions progressively declined throughout the eighteenth century—a process which was hastened by the invasions of Nadir Shah (*q.v.*) in 1739 and of Ahmad Shah Abdali (*q.v.*) from 1751 to 1767. The later Mughul sovereigns were Bahadur Shah I or Shah Alam I (1707-12), Jahandar Shah (1712-13),

Farruksiyar (1713-19), Rafid-ud-Darajat (1719), Rafi-ud-Daulat (1719), Nekusiyar (1719), Ibrahim (1719), Muhammad Shah (1719-48), Ahmad Shah (1748-54), Alamgir II (1754-59), Shah Alam II (1759-1806), Akbar II (1806-37) and Bahadur Shah II (1837-58). The Mughul dynasty which had been founded by Babur's victory at the first battle of Panipat (*q.v.*) in 1526 and confirmed by Akbar's victory at the second battle of Panipat (*q.v.*) in 1556, received its death blow at the third battle of Panipat (*q.v.*) in 1761 when Ahmad Shah Abdali helped by Shuja-ud-daulah, the Nawab of Oudh, defeated the Mughul Emperor, Shah Alam II, and his Maratha allies and protectors. Thereafter it dragged on a miserable existence not on account of any strength of its own but on account of the rivalries amongst its possible successors, namely the seceding Muslim states, the rebellious Hindus and the clever and steady English merchants, the last of whom defeated all their Muhammadan and Hindu competitors by exploiting their mutual, undying, suspicious jealousies and hostilities and succeeded in imposing their sovereignty in place of that of the Mughul dynasty. The last nominal Mughul Emperor, Bahadur Shah II, who had been a virtual pensioner of the English since his accession, was formally deposed in 1858 for his alleged complicity in the Sepoy Mutiny and exiled to Rangoon where he died in 1862. (*See* under different names of the Emperors.)

Mughul system of administration, the—was organised by the third Mughul Emperor, Akbar (1556-1605), his father and grandfather, Humayun and Babur, having had little time or talent for the work. The Mughul system of administration centred round the sovereign whose power was unlimited. His word was law, and his will none could dispute. He was the supreme authority in the state, the head of the Government, the supreme commander of the state forces, the fountain of justice, and the chief legislator. The efficient exercise of such large powers naturally imposed upon the sovereign a strenuous life which could be lived only by a physically strong and mentally alert person. But in a hereditary monarchical system, as the Mughul administration was, it was impossible to secure the succession of a long line of strong kings. And it was mainly on this rock that the Mughul administration was wrecked after a succession of six generations of strong kings. The Mughul emperor had no doubt a number of ministers of whom the four more important were the *Dewan* in charge of revenue and finance, the

Mir Bakshi at the head of the military department, the *Mir Saman* in charge of factories and stores, and the *Sadr-us-sadr* the head of the ecclesiastical and judicial department. Besides these four ministers, there were many other chief officers of the state who practically enjoyed the rank of ministers. But they never formed a cabinet and were entirely responsible to the sovereign who appointed them and dismissed them at his pleasure. Nor did the administrative machinery of the Mughuls provide for any institution which could legally and peacefully convey to the Mughul Emperor the feelings of the people, Muhammadans as well as Hindus. The Mughul administrative system thus lacked any corrective institution as was provided by the Parliament for the contemporary Tudor and Stuart sovereigns of England. Lacking thus in any corrective institution the working of the Mughul administrative machinery depended on the will of the sovereigns as long as they were strong minded persons; and later on when the Crown became weak it became a plaything at the hands of ambitious and unscrupulous ministers who made and unmade the Emperors at their pleasure.

The Mughul administrative system was bureaucratic without any separation between the civil and military departments. All superior officers were classified into thirty-three grades as *mansabdars* (*q.v.*) from those of 10 to those of 10,000. Every one of them held civil and military powers and functions and was to be paid a salary in cash, which in later times came to be paid either in the form of an assignment on the revenue of a district or of a *jagir*, or land-grant. The *mansabdari* system formed the foundation of the Mughul administration and regulated the pay and status of its officers. It was something like the Indian Civil and Military Services combined together with this essential difference that, unlike the members of the I.C.S. after 1853, the *mansabdars* were never recruited as the result of any public examination and their recruitment was mainly confined, even in the liberal days of Akbar, to Muhammadans, and to foreign Muhammadans in particular. Thus the Mughul central administrative system which was military in character and carried on by foreigners, never promoted any popular institutions and could, therefore, hardly count on the popular support of the children of the soil.

The Mughuls evolved a provincial system of administration which marked an improvement on the system previously maintained by the Delhi sultanate. Akbar divided his empire into

15 *Subas* or provinces, the number rising with the expansion of the empire to 17 in the reign of Jahangir, and to 21 during Aurangzeb's rule. Every *Suba* was again divided into a number of *Sarkars* (corresponding to the districts under the British system) and each *Sarkar* was subdivided into a number of *Parganas* or Unions of several villages. The Mughul provincial system of government was a replica of the central government with one important difference. The headship in provincial administration was practically divided between the Governor, called the *Nazim* or *Sipah salar* or *Subadar* who was the executive head of the administration and the *Dewan* who was in charge of the revenue administration of the province. Each one of them was appointed by the emperor and was responsible to him alone. Thus each acted as a check on the other and made provincial rebellion difficult, though not impossible. Besides the *Dewan*, the *Subadar* was helped also by the *Bakshi* or pay-master of the forces, and the *Qazi* and the *Sadr* who helped in the dispensation of justice. Over every *Sarkar* there was a *Faujdar* who was to maintain peace and order within his area, and was in charge of criminal justice and police and of the local military forces. In every important city there was one executive officer called the *Kotwal*. In every province, the Central Government also maintained a number of news-reporters, publicly as also secretly, whose duty was to report to the centre all that happened in the states. These reports were carefully attended to at the centre and were to be placed regularly before the emperor. This arrangement was a further check on the rebellious tendencies of provincial governors.

The main source of the income of the Mughul Empire was the land revenue, the other sources being customs, mintage, spoils of war and indemnities, presents, monopolies (the Mughul state was a great manufacturer making most of its military and other requirements) and poll-tax. The land revenue was fixed at one-third of the gross produce and collection was made by paid officials, appointed by the state, directly from the *ryot*. The land was divided into four classes according to fertility and elaborate measures were taken to find out the correct amount of production. The payment could be made both in kind and cash, though payment in cash was encouraged. The cash value of the product was carefully determined on the basis of prices prevailing during the previous three or ten years. A uniform system was not, however, prevalent all over the empire. In some parts like Lower Sind and Kashmir the state's share was decided by an actual division of the standing crop. In other and larger parts from Multan to Bihar prevailed the more elaborate system based on survey and measurement of land according to a uniform standard, classification according to the fertility of the soil, settlement of the average produce and the fixation of the cash value of its one-third. In Bengal again the state's share was fixed on *estimate* of the gross produce based on the reports prepared by revenue officers called Qanangos.

The Mughul army consisted of cavalry, infantry, artillery and navy. The cavalry was the most important of the four branches. The infantry, composed mainly of townsmen and peasantry recruited for the occasion, was rather insignificant. The artillery was equipped with guns either manufactured in India or imported from outside. The Mughul artillery, though superior to any that the contemporary Hindu states possessed, was inferior in range and precision to that possessed by the Europeans. The Mughul navy mainly consisted of boats, small and large, for guarding river traffic. It was no good for sailing on the high seas. As a matter of fact the Mughuls, not excluding Akbar and Aurangzeb, never appreciated the importance of the sea as a high road of commerce as well as of invasion and never built a navy which could fight with the Europeans on the high seas and prevent them from landing on the soil of India. They preferred to rely on the support of one European race of people against another and thus suffered themselves to be their victims. Again, the *mansabdari* system (*q.v.*) under which the Mughul army was organised, led to false musters and absence of any regular training and discipline. Further, the Mughul army on its march and even on the battlefield was attended with so much pomp and display and such heavy equipage that even in the time of Aurangzeb it ceased to be an effective fighting machinery against the nimble and fast-moving lightly equipped Maratha armies. It was defeated by Nadir Shah in 1739 and repeatedly by Ahmad Shah Abdali and thus moved on to its doom. Last but not the least, the Mughul army declined in strength and efficiency because it ignored the lessons of its own triumphs. It was their superiority in arms and equipment that had given victories to Babur at Panipat and Khanua and to Akbar at Haldighat; but in the eighteenth century that superiority passed to the English whom no Indian army could rival in arms and organisation. The failure of the Mughul military system has thus left a lesson which cannot be ignored by the Government of the Republic of India except at the risk of their own safety A state can survive only so long as it can modernise its arms and military equipment.

Muhammad, the Prophet of Islam—was born at Mecca in Arabia towards the close of the sixth century of the Christian era. He preached amongst his countrymen a new religion based on the principles of brotherhood of man, the unity of God and his own prophethood. The citizens of Mecca at first would not have anything of his new religion and became so hostile to him that in A.D. 622 he was obliged to quit his birthplace and take refuge in the neighbouring city of Medina. That event, renowned as 'the Flight', or *Hijra*, marks the beginning of the Muslim era of Hijra. Muhammad was not only an inspired religious teacher but also a supremely practical statesman. He made up his quarrel with his kinsmen of Mecca by accepting their shrine at Kaaba as the holy place of the new religion, returned to Mecca and with the united support of the people of Mecca and Medina soon succeeded in spreading his religion and in being accepted as its Prophet. He lived for ten years after his return to Mecca. During this short period the whole of Arabia accepted his religion and Muhammad combined in his person the religious and political headship of the Arabs whom he united into an inspired people who within the brief space of eighty years after his demise in A.D. 632, carried their victorious arms and imposed their new religion on Persia, Syria, Western Turkistan, Egypt, Southern Spain and Sind in India. A new religion and a new political force thus developed in India as the result of Muhammad's work in Arabia.

Muhammad Adil Shah (1626-56)—the seventh Adil Shahi sultan of Bijapur, saw during his long reign the beginning of the Maratha aggression in addition to more persistent Mughul invasion. He had at last to secure peace with Emperor Shah Jahan by becoming a tributary to him in 1636. He, however, ruled over a large realm across the Deccan peninsula extending from sea to sea, maintained a magnificent court and made his kingdom rich and powerful.

Muhammad Adil Shah (or Adali) Sur—the nephew of Sher Shah (*q.v.*) and the third king of the Sur dynasty of Delhi ruled only for two years (1554-56) and was killed at, Monghyr in 1556. He was the patron of Himu (*q.v.*) in whose hands he left the administration.

Muhammad Ali—an educated Indian Muhammadan who, along with his brother Shaukat Ali, led the Khilafat movement (*q.v.*) in 1920, and joined with Mahatma Gandhi and the Indian National Congress in the non-co-operation movement (*q.v.*). He presided over the Gaya session of the Indian National Congress and brought about an understanding between the followers of Gandhiji and the Swarajya party. Later on he moved away from the Congress, but remained a nationalist.

Muhammad Ali—was the natural son of Nawab Anwaruddin (*q.v.*) Nawab of the Carnatic. On the defeat and death of his father at the battle of Ambur (*q.v.*) in 1749 by the combined armies of Chanda Shahib (*q.v.*) Muzaffar Jang (*q.v.*) and the French, Muhammad Ali fled to the strong fort of Trichinopoly where he later on got the backing of the English with whose help his enemies were defeated and Muhammad Ali became the *de facto* Nawab of the Carnatic in 1752. His position on the throne of the Carnatic became dependent entirely on the support of the English in Madras. He, however, continued to rule as a British *protégé* in the Carnatic till his death.

Muhammad ibn-Kasim—was a young Arab general who was sent by Al-Hajjaj, the Arab governor of Irak, who was his uncle and father-in-law, to chastise Dahir, the king of Sind. Muhammad stormed Debal, captured Nerun, crossed the Indus and defeated and killed king Dahir at the battle of Raor in A.D. 712. He then stormed the fort of Raor, occupied Alor, the capital, as well as Multan. He thus established Arab rule over the whole of the lower Indus valley. He also showed skill as an administrator and gave to the newly conquered province a system of administration which assured peace in the state. But his career ended in tragedy. He incurred the displeasure of Khalif Sulaiman who dismissed him and had him tortured to death by his opponents.

Muhammad bin-Tughluq—was the sultan of Delhi from 1325 to 1351. He was the son and successor of Ghiyas-ud-din Tughluq, the founder of the Tughluq dynasty, whose accidental death was, according to some, contrived by Muhammad Tughluq himself. He was a man of complex personality. His innovations, his acts of cruelty and want of consideration for others have led many to brand him as a mad and bloodthirsty sultan. More learned and cultured than any other sultan of Delhi, a capable general who won more campaigns than he lost, eager to accumulate knowledge in all that affected humanity, bold enough to think of running the administration of a Muhammadan state ignoring the ecclesiastics and original enough to envisage schemes which in themselves were beneficial to the empire, he has been recognised by some as a versatile genius who was far in advance of his times and was an unfortunate victim of reaction. The truth perhaps lies in between the two. Muhammad Tughluq was neither a madman nor a genius, but was certainly a man of ideas who lacked in patience and had little sense of what was practical. In any case he was a 'transcendent failure'.

Muhammad Tughluq began his reign with triumphs. Two rebellions, one in the Deccan led by his own cousin in 1327 and the other in Multan led by the disaffected local governor in 1328, were suppressed. In the next few years Warangal, Ma'bar and Dvarasamudra were conquered and the Delhi sultanate was extended up to Madura. Revenue records of all the provinces were compiled; hospitals and almshouses were established in various places and learned persons including Ibn Batuta (*q.v.*) were honoured and amply patronised. But difficulties began to arise as the reign grew older. In 1327 the Sultan ordered the transfer of the capital from Delhi to the more centrally situated Devagiri which he re-named Daulatabad and took various measures for making comfortable the journey from the old to the new capital. But the scheme failed on account of the Sultan's insistence on the migration not only of the officials of Delhi but of the common people as well. Then in 1330 the Sultan decided to issue a token currency, as is now prevalent in every country of the world, and issued copper tokens in lieu of gold coins. But he failed to take steps for preventing counterfeiting the tokens which was absolutely essential for the success of the scheme which, therefore, failed and caused great confusion. Then in about 1332 he collected a vast army for an expedition against Persia., but the project had to be abandoned after a huge sum of money had already been spent on it. A second expedition was soon afterwards sent, not against China as Firishta says, but against Quarachal, that is to say, the Kumaon region. Though it led to the reduction of some of the hill-chiefs the expedition involved a disastrous loss of men and money. Pressed by financial needs the Sultan had already heavily enhanced the taxes, especially in the Doab, and when the people failed to pay up they were hunted like wild animals. Further, famines broke out in different parts of the Empire and the Sultan grew more tyrannical. Goaded by his tyranny Ma'bar first rose in revolt in 1334-35 and rebellion soon spread to other parts of the Deccan, then in north India, in Bengal, in Gujarat and in Sind, and Sultan Muhammad Tughluq died of fever when engaged in suppressing the rebellion in Sind in 1351.

Muhammad Ghuri (also called Shihab-ud-din and Muiz-ud-din)—was the founder of the Muslim rule in India and of the Delhi sultanate. He was a brother of Sultan Ghiyas-ud-din of Ghur who appointed him as the Sultan of the Ghaznavid territories which he conquered in 1773. Muhammad Ghuri was a great general and conqueror. He conquered Multan in 1175 and Uch next year. Repulsed from Gujarat by Bhim-dev II in 1178 Muhammad Ghuri compensated himself by conquering the Panjab from Khusru Malik (*q.v.*) in 1186 and thus came to occupy a position from which further advance into the fertile plains of north India was feasible. But his first effort ended in failure, as he was defeated in 1191 at the first battle of Tarain by a combined army of some of the northern Indian Rajput kings led by Prithviraj, the Chauhan king of Ajmer and Delhi. Muhammad Ghuri saved his life by fleeing from the battlefield, but he returned to the attack next year and fought a second battle with Prithviraj on the same field of Tarain. This time Muhammad Ghuri had strengthened his army by the addition of 10,000 mounted archers. This gave him superiority over the cumbrous Indian army of Prithviraj who was defeated and killed in the battle. This victory at the second battle of Tarain made him the master of all northern India to the gates of Delhi which was conquered in 1193 by his slave and lieutenant Qutb-ud-din. Next year Muhammad Ghuri defeated and killed Raja Jaichand of Kanauj in the battle of Chandwar. For the next few years Muhammad Ghuri remained more in his hilly kingdom of Ghazni than in India where, however, his victorious standard was carried by his lieutenant Qutb-ud-din (*q.v.*) and his subordinate Muhammad Khalji (*q.v.*) through the whole of the Gangetic valley into Bihar and Bengal. In 1203, on the death of Sultan Ghiyas-ud-din, Muhammad Ghuri became the ruler of Ghur, Ghazni and of northern India. But this position he could not enjoy long, for in 1206 he was stabbed to death on his way from Lahore to Ghazni by a band of rebellious Khokars. Muhammad Ghuri had done his work splendidly; he had established in India Muhammadan rule which lasted for the next six hundred years.

Muhammad Hakim, Mirza, Prince—the second son of Emperor

Humayun (*q.v.*) and the younger brother of Emperor Akbar, was eleven years of age at the death of his father and was recognised as the nominal ruler of Kabul province. As he grew up he became much addicted to drink, but he remained an orthodox Muhammadan. So when Akbar alienated orthodox Muslim opinion by his various reforms Hakim thought of exploiting the situation and invaded the Panjab in 1580. Akbar personally led a large army against him. Hakim fled before him and was soon reduced to submission. Hakim, however, was suffered to continue to rule over Kabul province until his death in 1585.

Muhammad Khalji, son of Bakhtiyar—*see ante* Ikhtiyar-ud-din Muhammad.

Muhammad, Prince—the eldest son and heir-apparent of Sultan Balban (*q.v.*) (1266-86), was the Governor of Multan when the Mongols invaded the Panjab in 1285. He was killed when engaged in fighting with the Mongols and earned the posthumous title of the *Shahid*, 'the Martyr'.

Muhammad Sultan, Prince—the eldest son of Emperor Aurangzeb, was appointed to various important posts by his imperial father and was rather popular with the Rajputs. On this account he incurred the suspicion of his father. He died in 1676, long before Aurangzeb's death.

Muhammad Quli—the fifth Qutb Shahi sultan of Golconda, had a long reign from 1580 to 1612. He spent his energies in fighting for the occupation of the Carnatic, Orissa and Bastar. He did not think of uniting his resources with those of the other sultans of the Deccan states to prevent the expansion of the Mughul rule. He left behind him a daughter named Hayat Baksh Begum who was married to his nephew and successor. Muhammad Qutb (*q.v.*).

Muhammad Qutb—the nephew and son-in-law of Muhammad Quli, fifth sultan of Golconda whom he succeeded in 1612, ruled till his death in 1626.

Muhammad Reza Khan—was appointed at the instance of the Calcutta Council of the East India Company to be the Deputy Nawab of Bengal on the death of Nawab Mir Jafar (*q.v.*) in 1765. It was stipulated at the accession of Mir Jafar's second son, Najm-ud-daulah in 1765, that the administration of Bengal should be carried on, not by the new Nawab but, by Muhammad Reza Khan who thus became the virtual administrator of Bengal nominally on behalf of the Nawab but, in reality, of the East India Company. His appointment, therefore, meant the practical end of Muhammadan rule in Bengal. Later on he was also appointed by the Company as the Deputy Dewan and was thus placed in control of the revenue administration of the province in addition to the administration of criminal justice and maintenance of peace and order. Thus through his agency the Company came to control the revenue as well as the general administration of Bengal. Reza Khan made large profits and did not care at all for the sufferings of the people who were extremely hard hit by the famine of 1769-70 which carried off one-third of the population of Bengal. In 1772 Muhammad Reza Khan was relieved of his duties of Deputy Dewan, as the revenue administration of the province was taken over by the Company. Muhammad Reza Khan was also prosecuted on charges of misappropriation, but he was acquitted. He continued to be the head of the *Sadar Nizamat Adalat* until he was relieved of that post during the administration of Lord Cornwallis (*q.v.*).

Muhammad Shah—the fourteenth Mughul Emperor of Delhi, ruled from 1719 to 1748. Installed on the throne of Delhi by the Sayyid brothers (*q.v.*) his first achievement was to get rid of them by murder and execution. He thus hoped to have recovered the control of the administration, but he could not stop the progressive disintegration of the Mughul empire caused by the rebellion of Chin Qlich Khan (*q.v.*) in the Deccan in 1724 followed by that of Bengal, Oudh and Rohilkhand during the next few years. He also had to cede Malwa to Peshwa Baji Rao I (*q.v.*) in 1737. These losses so weakened the Delhi empire that Muhammad Shah could offer no effective resistance to Nadir Shah (*q.v.*) when he invaded India in 1739, cruelly sacked Delhi and suffered Muhammad Shah to rule over a much truncated empire. He had, however, one success to his credit—that was the repulse in 1748 of the first invasion by Ahmad Shah Abdali (*q.v.*) in 1748, just a little time before his death.

Muhammad Shah I—the second Bahmani sultan, reigned from A.D. 1358 to 1573. His rule was chiefly occupied by wars against the Hindu kingdoms of Vijayanagar on the south and Warangal on the north. He was a stern ruler who put down brigandage within his own kingdom, gave it a system of government which was carried on with the help of eight ministers at the centre, re-organised the household guards and introduced the practice of annual royal tours in the provinces which were thus kept under effective control. He died as the result of heavy drinking.

Muhammad Shah II—the fifth Bahmani sultan, ruled from 1378 to 1397, was a lover of peace, was devoted to learning and fought no foreign wars. He built mosques, established free schools for orphans and patronised men of learning. Unlike most of the other Bahmani sultans, he died a natural death.

Muhammad Shah III—the thirteenth sultan (1463-82) of the Bahmani kingdom, was only nine years of age at his accession and the administration was carried on very efficiently by the minister, Muhammad Gawan (*q.v.*) who subdued the Hindu Rajas of Konkon as well as Goa. Muhammad III devastated Orissa in 1478 and sacked the distant city of Kanchi or Conjeeveram in 1481. His reign was thus one of military triumphs, but it had a tragic ending. Muhammad Shah III was addicted to much drinking, was persuaded to suspect the loyalty of Muhammad Gawan and to order his execution in 1481. The blunder was soon found out and the next year the Sultan died both of grief and the effects of drink.

Muin-ud-din Chishti—was a Muslim saint whose tomb at Ajmer Akbar and his son Jahangir frequently visited.

Mujahid—the third Bahmani sultan (1373-78), drank hard and was murdered by his cousin, Daud, who succeeded him only to be murdered within a year of his own accession by a slave.

Mukherjee, Asutosh (1864-1924)—eminent lawyer and educationist. Born of a middle class Bengali Brahman family in Calcutta, he had a distinguished academic record and began his career in 1888 as a Vakil practising in the Calcutta High Court. He was raised to the Bench in 1904, officiated as the Chief Justice of the Calcutta High Court in 1920 and retired from service in 1923. He took no part in politics, though he was a nominated member of the Bengal Legislative Council for a term from 1899, but he was certainly a maker of modern Bengal, if not of India, by virtue of his eminent services to the cause of education to which he practically dedicated all his life. At the early age of 25 he became a member of the Senate of the Calcutta University of which he became the Vice-Chancellor for four terms and with which he remained associated till the close of his life. He utilised the Indian Universities Act (*q.v.*) passed by Lord Curzon for throttling the progress of education in India, for the expansion of education in Bengal and for turning the Calcutta University from the mere examining body that it had so long been, into the greatest teaching University in India by inaugurating the Post-Graduate

Department and for making provision for imparting the highest Post-Graduate teaching not only in different branches of humanities but also in the practical and applied sciences for the teaching of which there had been so far no provision. He secured for the Calcutta University princely donations from the Maharaja of Darbhanga, Sir Tarak Nath Palit and Sir Rashbehari Ghosh, and utilised the money in constructing large buildings for the University Library and Science Colleges which were supplied with adequate laboratories. He thus gave a new turn to the education of the people. He also introduced the study of Bengali language for the highest degree examination of the M.A. and gave equal recognition to the other chief Indian languages. He was a true Indian in his dress and manners and was perhaps the first Indian who as a member of a Royal Commission (the Sadler Commission) travelled all over India dressed in dhoti and a coat. He had never been to England and showed in his life and activities how a true Indian could be catholic in his ideas, progresisve in his actions and internationalist in the selection of the staff of a University. Englishmen, Germans, and Americans, not to speak of Indians from all over India, were invited by him to occupy Chairs in the Calcutta University which he raised to the position of the leading University in the East.

Mukherjee, Dhan Gopal—a Bengali littérateur who settled in the U.S.A., wrote several books in English of which the *Portrait of my Brother* delineates the life and character of his elder brother, Jadu Gopal, a renowned terrorist leader of Bengal. His works won him great fame as a literary man.

Muktapida—*see* Lalitaditya.

Mukund Rao—was a Maratha chieftain who was defeated by the Bijapur sultan, Yusuf Adil Shah (*q.v.*) (1490-1510) and made peace with the sultan by giving in marriage to him his sister, who assumed the Muslim name of Bubuji Khanam and became the mother of the second sultan, Ismail (1510-34).

Mularaja—founded the Solanki (Chalukya) kingdom of Anhilwara in Gujarat about the middle of the tenth century. His reign extended from A.D. 942 to 997. He was probably a son of Mahipala (A.D. 910-40), the king of Kanauj, and acted on his own account. He was killed in battle by the Chauhan king, Vigraharaja II of Ajmer.

Müller, Max (1823-1900)—was the greatest orientalist of his days. Born in Germany of German parents he took up the study of Sanskrit at Leipsiz in 1841, became interested in Comparative

Philology as well as in Comparative Religion. In 1845 he began translating and editing the *Rig Veda* and came in that connection to England where he settled and later on became a naturalised English citizen. The Oxford University undertook the task of printing and publishing the *Rig Veda*. So he settled at Oxford where in 1868 he became the Professor of Comparative Philology, though on account of his foreign origin he had been earlier in 1860 denied the Professorship of Sanskrit. Besides the *Rig Veda* his essays, collected under the title of *Chips from a German Workshop, History of Sanskrit Literature* (1859), *Sacred Books of the East* in fifty-one volumes, *Science of Language* and *Introduction to the Science of Religion*, started the studies in Comparative Philology, established affinities between the Celtic languages and Aryan languages like Sanskrit and Persian and helped Europe to learn of the greatness of the literary and cultural achievements of the Indian Hindus.

Mulraj—a Sikh chieftain, was the governor of Multan in 1847. He was in financial trouble through a fall in the revenue-collection of his district. As the Lahore Darbar pressed for payment of his dues amounting to more than a crore of rupees he resigned in 1848. When his successor arrived in the company of two young British officers the latter were murdered probably at the instigation of Mulraj who soon rose in rebellion. This revolt of Mulraj in Multan culminated shortly in the Second Sikh War (*q.v.*). Multan was stormed by the English in 1849 and Mulraj was taken captive. He was tried by a military court and sentenced to transportation for life. He died in the place of his exile.

Multan—an important city in the western Panjab, now in Pakistan, on the river Chinab, is on the highroad from Sind to the Panjab and is strategically very important. It was conquered by Sultan Mahmud (*q.v.*) and annexed to his dominions. Later on it was captured by Shihabuddin Muhammad Ghuri (*q.v.*) from the Ghaznavids and long remained a part of the Delhi empire. It was annexed to Afghanistan by Ahmad Shah Abdali (*q.v.*) but was taken from the Afghans by Maharaja Ranjit Singh (*q.v.*) in 1818. Its Sikh Governor, Mulraj, raised a revolt against the English in 1848-49 which culminated in the Second Sikh War (*q.v.*) which ended in British triumph and in the annexation of Multan to the British dominions.

Mumtaz Mahal—was the daughter of Asaf Khan, brother of Nurjahan, and the richest and most powerful noble during the reign of Jahangir. Her original name was Arjumand Bano

Begum. She was married in 1612 to Jahangir's son Prince Khurram (later on Emperor Shah Jahan) and was given the name of Mumtaz Mahal (the ornament of the palace). The marriage proved very happy and Mumtaz bore to Shah Jahan fourteen children including his four sons Dara, Shuja, Aurangzeb and Murad. Mumtaz died in childbirth in 1631 at Burhanpur when she was only 39 years of age. Her body was removed to Agra and it was on her tomb that Shah Jahan built the unrivalled monument called the Taj Mahal (*q.v.*).

Mundy, Peter—a European traveller, was in India during the reign of Jahangir (*q.v.*) and has left an interesting account of what he saw in India. It throws much light on the social and economic conditions of India.

Munim Khan—a veteran officer in the service of Emperor Humayun, held a high command in Kabul early in the reign of Akbar. On the fall of Bairam Khan he was appointed Khan Khanan. He was in command of the Mughul expedition into Bengal in 1573, defeated its Afghan ruler Daud (*q.v.*) in 1575, received his submission but died soon afterwards of sickness.

Munim Khan—son of Sultan Beg, was the revenue minister of Prince Muazzam when he was the Governor of Afghanistan. In 1707 the Prince was at Jamrud when his father Emperor Aurangzeb died. Munim Khan, who had anticipated events, placed at the disposal of Prince Muazzam a large fund and helped him very energetically in securing transport and with an army. This enabled Prince Muazzam to reach Agra from Jamrud very quickly and to proclaim himself Emperor Bahadur Shah. Later on Munim Khan defeated Kam Baksh (*q.v.*) who was killed in battle, and also took a leading part in defeating Banda and the rebellious Sikhs in 1710. Munim Khan, to whom Emperor Bahadur Shah I owed much, did not, however, get the post of the Chief Minister and had to remain content with the post of the Revenue Minister of the Emperor.

Munni Begum—the widow of Nawab Mir Jafar (*q.v.*) of Bengal, was originally a dancing girl whom Mir Jafar later on married. She was placed by Warren Hastings (*q.v.*) in charge of the Nawab's household and was later on even appointed as the guardian of the young Nawab Mubarak-ud-daulah. In 1775 Nanda Kumar (*q.v.*) accused Warren Hastings of having accepted large sums of money as bribes from Munni Begum for the appointments conferred on her. But these charges were never investigated and Munni Begum continued to hold her assignments.

Munro, Sir Hector (1726-1805)—a general in the East India Company's service in India, won in 1764 great glory by winning the battle of Buxar (*q.v.*) but in 1780 he shamefully retreated before Haidar Ali, threw his artillery into a tank at Conjeeveram and retreated in panic to Madras. He retired in 1782.

Munro, Sir Thomas (1761-1827)—a distinguished officer in the service of the East India Company, rose from the rank of a district magistrate to be the Governor of Madras which Presidency he administered with great efficiency from 1820 to 1827. He organised the land revenue system in the province where he introduced the *ryotwari* system (*q.v.*). His reports, especially on the subsidiary system (*q.v.*) show his penetrating statesmanship.

Muqqarab Khan—whose original name was Shaikh Hasan, was a very trusted officer of Emperor Jahangir (*q.v.*) and was sent as the Emperor's ambassador to the Portuguese in Goa in 1607. Nothing came out of this embassy. Muqqarab Khan was later on appointed as governor of Surat where he encouraged the English to fight against the Portuguese who suffered defeat in a naval battle against the English but having no fleet of his own the Mughul governor had the mortification of being rebuffed by the Portuguese to whom he offered terms of peace.

Muqqarab Khan—whose original name was Shaikh Niam and who got the title of Khan Zaman, was an energetic military officer of Emperor Aurangzeb (*q.v.*). In 1689 having received information that the Maratha king Shambhuji, along with his minister, Kavi-Kalash, was on a pleasure trip at Sangameshwar, Muqqarab Khan, who was then at Kolhapur, made a forced march to Shambhuji's camp and surprised and captured the Maratha king along with his retinue including his chief minister, Kavi-Kalash.

Murad, Prince—the second son of Emperor Akbar (*q.v.*) born of Salima Begam (*q.v.*) in 1571, held important commands in Kabul and in the Deccan where he secured the cession of Berar from Ahmadnagar. He was given to too much drinking and died of its effects in 1599.

Murad Bakhsh—the fourth and youngest son of Emperor Shah Jahan (*q.v.*) was born in 1624 of Mumtaz Mahal and developed into a brave and warlike young man. He crushed a rebellion in Kangra and occupied Balkh from which, however, he withdrew. In 1657 when Shah Jahan fell ill Murad was the Mughul governor in Gujarat. He was impetuous and impatient and

being determined to exclude his eldest brother Dara from
the succession, he plundered Surat, proclaimed himself Emperor
and struck coins in his name. He was, however, soon persuaded
by his elder brother, Aurangzeb, to join with him on the basis
of the partition of the empire between Aurangzeb and himself.
He joined his forces with those of Aurangzeb and shared with
him the dangers and triumphs of the victories won by their
joint armies in the battles of Dharmat (*q.v.*) and Samugarh (*q.v.*).
Soon after the last battle the brothers marched on to Agra,
but there Murad began to suspect the *bona fides* of Aurangzeb
and began to take steps for strengthening himself against
Aurangzeb; but the crafty Aurangzeb invited Murad to his
camp where Murad was made a prisoner. He was sent away
to be detained in the fort of Gwalior where he was beheaded
in 1661 under a judicial sentence for the murder of his former
Diwan in Gujarat.

Murshid Quli Jafar Khan—was a Persian who entered the Mughul
service and was sent to the Deccan with Aurangzeb as *Diwan*
of the Highlands. In 1656 he was promoted to be the *Diwan*
of the whole of the Deccan. In this capacity he systematised
the revenue collection and land settlement in the Deccan
putting into practice, as far as possible, the principles of land
survey, measurement according to a uniform standard, assessment on the estimated produce and collection in kind or cash,
though the latter was favoured. His success in the Deccan
was so great that in 1701 he was appointed as the *Diwan* in
Bengal where, again, he administered the provincial finances so
well that he was made independent of the viceroy and was
allowed also to remove the revenue offices of the province from
the provincial capital at Dacca to a new place which came to
be called Murshidabad (*q.v.*) After the death of Aurangzeb he
was made the viceroy of Bengal, Bihar and Orissa which he
administered efficiently till his death in 1726.

Murshid Quli Khan—whose title was Rustam Jang, was the
deputy of Nawab Shuja-ud-din, the son-in-law and successor
of Murshid Quli Jafar Khan (*q.v.*) in Orissa. He held Orissa
in 1740 after Ali Vardi Khan had dispossessed the line of
Murshid Quli Jafar Khan from Bengal. He was defeated and
driven out of Orissa by Ali Vardi Khan in 1741.

Murshidabad—is a city on the Bhagirathi in Bengal. It was founded
by Murshid Quli Jafar Khan early in 1704 and was at first
only the headquarters of the *Diwan*. But as Murshid Quli Jafar
Khan advanced in life and rose from the *Diwan* to be the Nawab

of Bengal Murshidabad also rose to be the capital of Bengal. This honour it retained till 1773 when Calcutta robbed it of this distinction. The Nawab's palace, popularly known as the Hazar-duari (one thousand-doored) is a magnificent mansion which was built in 1837-40. The district of Murshidabad is separated from East Pakistan by the Padma while the Bhagirathi divides it into two parts viz. *Rarh* in the west which is high and has a Hindu majority and *Bagri*, the eastern half which is low and has a Muhammadan majority. It has no large industries but its mango orchards are numerous and famous.

Murtaza Ali—the Nawab of the Carnatic, was deposed in 1743 by the Nizam Asaf Jah (*q.v.*) who placed Anwar-ud-din (*q.v.*) on the throne of the Carnatic.

Muslim League—was founded in 1906 at the instance of Nawab Salim-ul-lah of Dacca, now in East Pakistan. Its formation was due to the encouragement that was extended to the Muhammadans by the Government of Lord Minto II (*q.v.*). It was from its inception an organisation for protecting, upholding and promoting the political interests of the Indian Muhammadans and always relied on the support of the British Indian Government which considered it a very useful counterpoise to the Indian National Congress in which the Hindus predominated. The Muslim League never made any demand for the political rights of Indians, except only once in 1916 when it agreed for the nonce with the Indian National Congress and accepted the Lucknow Pact (*q.v.*). But this union and co-operation soon ceased and the Muslim League reverted to its original principle of relying more on Government support for securing what it considered the Muslim interests in India. Its main bogey was that in a self-governing India with popularly elected democratic institutions the Muslims in India would be submerged by the Hindu majority. So, forgetting all lessons of the past history of the country and forgetting how the replacement of Muslim rule in India by the British Raj had been brought about more by Muslim help to the alien British than by Hindu opposition to the Muslim rule, the Muslim League consistently sided with the British against the Indian National Congress which stood for the political rights of the Indians, Hindus and Muslims alike. It developed, as years passed, such an anti-Hindu frenzy that in the thirties of the present century, when the gradually increasing weakness of the hold of the British Raj over India began to be exposed,

the Muslim League stood for the partition of India into a
Muslim part to be called Pakistan (*q.v.*) and a Hindu part to
be called Hindusthan. This short-sighted and absolutely communal demand was accepted by the British who at the hour
of their departure from India made a gift of Pakistan to the
Indian Muhammadan communalists and thus left India divided
and bleeding to the immense injury and suffering not only of
the Hindus but also of the Muhammadans. A divided and
weak India is the gift of the Muslim League to the Indians.

Murtaza Nizam Shah I—the fourth sultan of the Nizam Shahi
dynasty of Ahmadnagar, ruled from 1565 to 1586. During the
first six years of his reign he left the administration in the hands
of his mother. Later on he showed much energy, conquered
Berar, but failed in his efforts to capture Bidar. Still later on he
lost his reason and was killed by his own son, Husain, who
succeeded him.

Murtaza Nizam Shah II—the tenth sultan of Ahmadnagar,
ruled from 1603 to 1630. He was helped in administration by
Malik Ambar (*q.v.*) but lost the major portion of his territories
to the Mughuls. The war with the Mughuls continued and in
1630 Murtaza Nizam Shah II was put to death by his minister
Fath Khan (*q.v.*) who had succeeded his father Malik Ambar
in 1626.

Mutabar Khan—a military officer in the service of Emperor
Aurangzeb during the closing part of his reign, distinguished
himself by capturing many of the Maratha hill-forts in the
Nasik district, and then descended into the Konkon where he
took Kalyan and several other places and brought the western
coastal region under the Mughul rule. Mutabar lived at Kalyan
for many years and adorned the city with many beautiful
buildings.

Mutiny, Indian—*see* Sepoy Mutiny.

Muttra—*see ante* Mathura.

Muzaffar Jang—was the son of the daughter of Nizam-ul-Mulk
Chin Qilich Khan (*q.v.*). On the death of the Nizam in 1748 he
claimed the throne of Hyderabad in preference to his maternal
uncle, Nasir Jang. He secured the support of the French under
Dupleix. He also found an ally in Chanda Shahib (*q.v.*) who
claimed the throne of Arcot. At first the fortune of war
went against him, but Nasir Jang was assassinated in 1750, and
Muzaffar Jang got the Nizamship with the assistance of the
French in return for large grants. But Muzaffar Jang was, in
his turn, killed in a chance skirmish in 1751 and the throne of

Hyderabad passed to his third maternal uncle, Salabat Jang (*q.v*).

Mysore—is the name of a constituent state in the Republic of India as well as of a city which is its capital. The Mysore state is bounded on the north-west by Bombay, on the east by Andhra, on the south-east by Madras and on the south-west by Kerala. Its history goes far into the past. Its earliest rulers belonged to the Kadamba dynasty (*q.v.*) which has been mentioned by Ptolemy. The Kadambas had to fight against the Cheras, the Cholas, the Pallavas and the Chalukyas (*q.v.*), but it was not before the 12th century that Mysore passed entirely from the hands of the Kadambas into the hands of the Hoysalas who established their capital at Dvarasamudra (*q.v.*) modern Halebid. It was from the Hoysala king, Ramachandra, that Ala-ud-din Khalji (*q.v.*) conquered Mysore and annexed it to his dominions. Later on Mysore became incorporated within the Hindu kingdom of Vijayanagar on the fall of which Mysore passed under the rule of a local Hindu chief in 1610. The fourth successor of this line, Chikka Deva Raja, greatly increased the strength and power of Mysore. But in the middle of the 18th century his dynasty was overthrown by Haidar Ali (*q.v.*) who and whose son, Tipu Sultan (*q.v.*) ruled over it till 1799 when on the defeat and death of Tipu Sultan the victorious British placed Krishnaraja Wadyar, an infant of 5 years of age, on the throne of Mysore which became a protected state under the British. Krishnaraja eventually proved a very bad ruler and in 1831 the administration of Mysore was taken over by the British Government which, however, restored it to Chamarajendra, Krishna's successor, in 1867. The state which had since been well-governed, acceded to the Indian Union in 1947. Mysore is a beautiful city with a university which was established in 1916.

Mysore Wars, the—were fought between the English and Haidar Ali (*q.v.*) and his son, Tipu Sultan (*q.v.*) who were the rulers of Mysore. There were four wars fought during a period of thirty-two years (1767-99). The *First Mysore War* was fought from 1767 to 1769. It was caused by the aggressive designs of the English in Madras. In 1766 when Haidar Ali was engaged in a war with the Marathas, the English in Madras lent the Nizam a British detachment with which the Nizam invaded Mysore territory. This unprovoked enmity of the English made Haidar furious. He made up his quarrel with the Marathas and won over the fickle Nizam to his side and then

with the Nizam's assistance invaded the Carnatic which was
then under British control. Thus began the First Mysore (or
Anglo-Mysore) War. It lasted two years and was brought to
a close in 1769 when Haidar made a sudden dash and approached Madras. The Madras Council was panic-stricken and
accepted a treaty that Haidar dictated under the walls of
Madras. By this treaty conquests were mutually restored and
a defensive alliance was made between Haidar and the English.
The *Second Mysore War* (1780-84) was caused by the exaspera-
tion of Haidar Ali at the failure of the English to act according
to the treaty of 1769 and to render to Haidar the promised
help which he asked for in 1770 when he was attacked by the
Marathas. Such undependable conduct of the English thoroughly
disgusted Haidar who was further angered by the English
attack on, and occupation of, the French settlement at Mahe
though it was situated within Haidar Ali's territories.
Accordingly he joined in a tripartite alliance with the Marathas
and the Nizam in 1780 and the *Second Mysore War* began.
The English won over the Nizam to their side in 1780 and
ended their war with the Marathas in 1782 by the treaty of
Salbai (*q.v.*). Haidar was thus left alone to fight against the
English. But, nothing daunted, Haidar carried on the war,
entered with a large army the Carnatic which he ravaged,
created a circle of desolation round Madras, cut off a detachment of English troops under Baille but was defeated in 1781
by Sir Eyre Coote in the three battles of Porto Novo, Pollilore
and Sholinghur. Further, he did not get the expected assistance from the French. Yet he continued to hold his own and
his son compelled a British army under Col. Braithwaite to surrender in 1782 at Tanjore. In the midst of this war Haidar Ali
died, but the war was continued by his son and successor, Tipu
Sultan, who repulsed an English attack on Bednore and then
besieged Mangalore. The Madras Government felt that it was
unequal to carrying on the war any longer and made peace
with Tipu in 1784 by the treaty of Mangalore on the basis of
mutual restitution of conquests.

The *Third Mysore War* (1790-92) was caused by the double-
dealing of the British. In violation of the treaties made by
the British with Haidar Ali in 1769 and with Tipu Sultan as
recently as 1784 the British wrote to the Nizam in 1788 that
they would help him in recovering from Tipu Sultan certain
territories which they had expressedly recognised as lying
within the latter's kingdom. This double-dealing left in Tipu's

mind no doubt about the hostile intentions of the British and he anticipated their hostility by attacking in 1789 Travancore which was in alliance with the British and devastated the country in 1790. The British made this act of aggression a cause of war, entered into a league with the Peshwa and the Nizam in 1790 by which the two latter powers agreed to help the British with troops on condition of equal division of the conquests that would be made. The *Third Mysore War* which thus began lasted two years (1790-92). It fell into three campaigns. In 1790 three British armies marched on Mysore but though they occupied Dindigul, Coimbatore and Palghat, Tipu prevented them from achieving any substantial victory. This unsatisfactory character of the 1790 campaign led Lord Cornwallis, the Governor-General himself, to assume the command of the second campaign which began in December, 1790. Moving by Vellore and Ambur Cornwallis captured Bangalore in March, 1791 and advanced on Tipu's capital, Seringapatam, but Tipu's scorched-earth policy led to a famine in the British camp and obliged Cornwallis to spike his heavy guns and to retreat. The third campaign, late in the summer of 1791 proved more successful. Cornwallis, who again led the British army, captured the mountain fastnesses of Tipu and in January, 1792 besieged Seringapatam with an imposing army. When the outworks of the capital were captured Tipu made his submission and the war was concluded by the treaty of Seringapatam in March, 1792. By this treaty Tipu surrendered two of his sons as hostages, paid an indemnity of three crores of rupees to be equally divided amongst the allies and ceded one-half of his dominions of which the English kept Dindigul, Baramahal, Coorg and Malabar and thus cut off Tipu from any approach to the sea and deprived him of the control of the passes through which lay the access to the tableland of southern India. The Marathas got the territory between the Wardha and the Krishna and the Nizam the region lying between the Krishna and the Pennar rivers.

The *Fourth Mysore War* (March - May, 1799) was a sharp and short contest. It was caused by the refusal by Tipu Sultan of the British offer of continued peace on condition of the acceptance of a subsidiary alliance by Tipu with the British. Lord Wellesley, who was then the Governor-General, was convinced of the hostile intentions of Tipu who since his defeat in 1792 had tried to enter into alliances with France, Constantinople and Zaman Shah of Afghanistan for the purpose of driving out the English from India. He made Tipu's refusal of the offer of a subsidiary alliance the cause of war. He entered into a tripartite alliance with the Nizam and the Peshwa on the basis of equal distribution of the gains of the war. Three armies led by General Harris, General Stewart and the Governor-General's brother, Arthur Wellesley (the future Duke of Wellington) marched from three different directions on Tipu's dominions. Tipu was defeated in two pitched battles and driven within the walls of Seringapatam which was besieged on 17 April, and carried by assault on 4 May, 1799, Tipu dying sword in hand fighting bravely in defence of his fort. Tipu's son surrendered and the victorious English who did not wish to allow their allies to get an equal third share of Tipu's dominions, restored to the principal and central part of Mysore Krishnaraja, a descendant of the old Hindu Raja of Mysore who had been dispossessed by Haidar Ali years ago. Of the remaining parts of Tipu's dominions Kanara, Coimbatore and Seringapatam were annexed to the Company's dominions. The Marathas, who had taken no active part in the war, refused their share and the Nizam was given some portion of Tipu's territories to the north-east which, again, the Nizam surrendered to the British in 1800. Thus at the end of the *Fourth Mysore War* the entire kingdom of Mysore came under the control of the British in India.

N

Nabhapamti, the—a people mentioned in Rock Edict XIII of Asoka, have not yet been identified. They are also called Nabhakas and Nabhitis in some versions of the edict. Bhandarkar suggested that they lived somewhere between the North-West Frontier Province and the western coast of India (*Asoka*, p. 33).

Nadir Shah—ascended the throne of Persia in 1736. He captured Qandahar and Kabul in 1738 and then invaded India early in 1739. The reigning Mughul Emperor Muhammad Shah (*q.v.*) could not secure the services of the Rajputs and most of the Muhammadan nobles entered into treasonable correspondence with Nadir Shah. Consequently Nadir Shah advanced without any opposition up to Karnal where he easily defeated the Mughul army in February, 1739, marched on to Delhi which he entered on March 20 and where he was received by the vanquished Mughul emperor. At first he spared Delhi, but some sporadic attacks on his troops by some citizens of Delhi roused his anger and he ordered a general massacre of the citizens and gave up the city to plunder by his troops from eight in the morning until the evening when on the intercession of the Mughul Emperor he stopped the carnage and looting; but already 30,000 citizens of Delhi had been massacred and a great part of the city burnt. Nadir declared the province of Kabul and all territories west of the Indus annexed to his own dominions, suffered Muhammad Shah to continue to occupy the Delhi throne and started on his way back from Delhi on 16 May, 1739, leaving India "bleeding and prostrate" and carrying with him immense booty amounting to thirty crores of rupees in cash, besides jewels, pearls, diamonds including the Koh-i-nur (q.v.), the Peacock throne (q.v.), 1,000 elephants, 7,000 horses, 10,000 camels, a bevy of beautiful young girls from the Mughul harem, 200 builders, 100 masons and 200 carpenters. Indeed his loot was so rich and immense that he remitted all taxes throughout Persia for three years. This wealth, however, he was not destined to enjoy long. Eight years after his return from India he lost his reason and was stabbed to death in his own camp on the 2nd June, 1747.

Nadira Begum—was the wife of Prince Dara Sukhoh (q.v.), the eldest son of Emperor Shah Jahan. She accompanied Dara in his flight after the battle of Shamugarh (q.v.) and shared with him all his privations and hardships. She succumbed to the terrible strain and died on the way to Dadar in 1659. Her death was a terrible shock to Prince Dara.

Nagas, the—were the aboriginal people of the Narmada valley. One king named Ganapati Naga is mentioned in Samudra-gupta's Allahabad inscription.

Nagas, the—are a tribal people inhabiting the North-Eastern Frontier province. They were very ferocious and engaged in head-hunting. They now claim autonomy over the part of the territory occupied by them which is called Nagaland.

Nagabhata I—was the founder of the Gurjara-Pratihara dynasty. He is usually assigned to the eighth century A.D. He upheld the power of his family against the Arabs of Sind and the Chalukyas and Rashtrakutas of the Deccan.

Nagabhata II—an early king of the Gurjara-Pratihara dynasty, invaded the Gangetic region in about A.D. 816, captured Kanauj, deposed the reigning king and probably transferred his capital to Kanauj. But later on he was defeated by the Rashtrakuta king, Govinda III (*q.v.*).

Nagananda, **the**—is a drama in Sanskrit written by Harshavardhana (*q.v.*) in the 7th century A.D.

Nagarjuna—was a Buddhist author who flourished in the second century A.D. and probably enjoyed the patronage of king Kanishka (*q.v.*). His two important works were the *Suhrillekha* which summarises the Buddhist doctrines and the *Madhyama-káriká*, which is an important text of the *Mahayana* (*q.v.*).

Nagarjuna—was a renowned Hindu chemist who flourished in the seventh-eighth centuries of the Christian era. His work *Rasaratnákara* deals with the merits of metallic preparations of which quick silver ranks first in importance. The Arabs derived much of their knowledge in Chemistry from Nagarjuna's works. (Roy, P. C.—*Hist. of Hindu Chemistry*, ii)

Nagarkot—modern Kangra, in Uttar Pradesh, was captured by Sultan Muhammad Tughluq (*q.v.*) in 1337.

Nagpur—is the name of a city and of a former princely state in what was called the Central Provinces in the British days. Now it is within the state of Bombay. It was the capital of the Maratha chiefs belonging to the family founded by Raghuji Bhonsla during the Peshwaship of Baji Rao I (*q.v.*). The Bhonslas of Nagpur became practically independent after the death of Peshwa Balaji Baji Rao (*q.v.*) in 1761, but were defeated by the British during the Second Maratha War (*q.v.*) and compelled to accept the subsidiary alliance in 1803. It was annexed to the British Indian empire in 1854 by the application of the doctrine of lapse.

Nagasena—was a Buddhist sage or philosopher who is mentioned in the *Milindapanha* (*Dialogues of Menander*) as the learned person with whom Menander (*q.v.*) discussed the theories and principles of Buddhism.

Nagasena—was a king mentioned in the Allahabad inscription of Samudragupta (*q.v.*) who claimed to have defeated and deposed him and annexed his dominion which has since been identified with Padmavati lying between Gwalior and Jhansi.

Nahapana—a distinguished satrap of the Kshaharata family of the Sakas, ruled over Maharashtra with his capital at or near Nasik. His date has not yet been definitely settled but his coins and inscriptions have been taken to suggest that he ruled during the first quarter of the second century of the Christian era. His dominions included Poona, North Konkon, parts of Kathiawar, parts of Malwa and the district of Ajmer. He

has been credited also with the foundation of the Saka er
(*q.v.*).

Naidu, Mrs. Sarojini (1879-1949)—a most talented Indian lady
born of Bengali parents and married to a Maratha gentleman
was a poet and orator who took a prominent part in India:
politics. She presided over the Cawnpore session of the India:
National Congress in 1925 and was the first lady to occup
that exalted office. She was also the first lady to be appointee
a state Governor in the Republic of India. She held charg
of the difficult state of Uttar Pradesh from 1947 till her deat
in 1949. Her daughter, Srimati Padmaja Naidu, is the Governo
of the state of West Bengal at the time of writing.

Najaf Khan—*see ante* Mirza Najaf Khan.

Najm-ud-daulah—was the second son and successor of Nawab Mi
Jafar of Bengal. He was placed on the *masnad* (throne) i:
Bengal by the English on the death of Mir Jafar in 1766 i
preference to the son of his elder brother on condition tha
the government should be carried on by a *Deputy* selected b
the Calcutta Council. The Council chose Reza Khan as th
Deputy and Najm-ud-daulah became a mere nominal rulei
His allowance was reduced to 41 lakhs in 1766, to 32 lakhs i
1769 and to 15 lakhs in 1772 with a corresponding declin
in his status and power.

Nalanda—a famous seat of Buddhist learning in the seventh centur
of the Christian era, was situated near modern Rajgir i:
South Bihar and its ruins have· been located in the village c
Bargaon. Who exactly founded the monastery of Nalanda an
when is not known. It did not attract the notice of Fa-Hie
(*q.v.*) who visited Pataliputra early in the fifth century A.D.
but it received the unstinted admiration of the Chinese pilgrin
Hiuen-Tsang (*q.v.*) in the first half of the seventh century
So the Nalanda monastery came to earn its fame in the fifth an
sixth centuries. Indeed Hiuen-Tsang states that the Gupt.
Emperor, Narasimha Gupta Baladitya (*c.* A.D. 470) built a
Nalanda a fine temple and installed in it an 80 feet high Buddh
copper image which the Chinese pilgrim saw. When Hiuen
Tsang was at Nalanda a Bengali Buddhist monk named Shila
bhadra was its abbot. Later on early in the ninth centur
Viradeva, a Brahman from Jalalabad, became its abbot. I
was also about that time that the Sailendra king, Balaputradeva
built at Nalanda with the permission of Devapala, the reignin
king of Magadha, a monastery for the residence of Javanes
monks who might come for studies at Nalanda. Indeed th

monastery at Nalanda became a University enjoying international reputation where students and even elderly scholars crowded not only from all over India but even from distant Tibet, China and Java. Various branches of knowledge were studied, but special emphasis was laid on the study of the *Mahayana* (*q.v.*) system of Buddhism. It maintained a very large library of manuscripts housed in three large buildings of which one was nine-storeyed, a distinction which has not yet been attained by the library of any of the modern Indian Universities. Strict rules of discipline were enforced; time was carefully kept by a clepsydra (water clock); and free discussions were encouraged. When and how this great seat of learning was destroyed is not known, though the examination of the ruins suggests that it was gutted by a big fire. (Vapat, P. V., *2,500 Years of Buddhism*)

Nambudri Brahmans—who live in Malabar, have kept up Vedic rituals at very great personal sacrifice.

Nameless King', the—is supposed to have been the Kushan king who ruled in India from A.D. 110, when Kadphises II (*q.v.*) probably died, to A.D. 120 when Kanishka (*q.v.*) is believed to have ascended the Kushan throne. The 'Nameless King' probably issued the anonymous coins which bear the inscription of Soter Megas or Great Saviour.

Nana Fadnavis—a Maratha Brahman statesman, was in the Peshwa's service on the eve of the third battle of Panipat (*q.v.*) in which he was present but escaped death. Later on he led the party opposed to the pretensions of Raghaba (*q.v.*), the uncle of Peshwa Narayan Rao (*q.v.*) whose murder he procured in 1773. But Nana Fadnavis forestalled him by supporting the cause of Narayan Rao's posthumous son, Madhav Rao Narayan, who was installed as Peshwa in 1774. Nana Fadnavis became the chief minister of the minor Peshwa and practically ran the affairs of the Marathas from 1774 till his death in 1800. His position was not easy, as his authority was opposed by the Maratha chiefs, especially by Mahadaji Sindhia (*q.v.*) but he was clever enough to retain his power against all opponents. From 1775 to 1783 he carried on the first war of the Marathas against the English and concluded it by the treaty of Salbai (*q.v.*) by which Raghaba was pensioned off and the Marathas lost no territory except Salsette. In 1784 Nana Fadnavis fought a war against Tipu Sultan (*q.v.*) of Mysore and regained some territories that Tipu had forcibly taken. In 1789 he joined with the English and the Nizam in a war with Tipu Sultan and took part in the Third Mysore War (*q.v.*) as the result of which the Marathas got a portion of Tipu's territories. In 1794 the death of Mahadaji Sindhia removed his most powerful opponent and henceforth Nana Fadnavis administered Maratha affairs with undisputed authority. In 1795 he employed the united army of the Maratha confederacy (*q.v.*) in a war with the Nizam who was defeated at the battle of Kharda (*q.v.*) and obliged to cede important territories to the Marathas. But in 1796 the young Peshwa Madhav Rao Narayan grew impatient of the control of Nana Fadnavis and committed suicide. The next Peshwa, Baji Rao II (*q.v.*) was the son of Raghaba and was hostile to Nana Fadnavis from the beginning. A contest for power thus developed between the Brahman Peshwa and his Brahman Prime Minister. Neither of them possessed any military skill, but both were crafty and wily diplomats and their mutual intrigues divided the Marathas into hostile parties and weakened the power of the Peshwa, but so long as Nana Fadnavis lived he managed to hold together the Maratha confederacy. Nana Fadnavis died in 1800 and "with his death departed all the wisdom and moderation of the Maratha government."

Nana Sahib (**Dundu Pant**)—the adopted son of the last Peshwa Baji Rao II (*q.v.*). He lived with his exiled adoptive father at Bithur near Cawnpore and maintained very friendly terms with the English people of the locality. But when on the death of his father in 1853 Lord Dalhousie, who was then the Governor General, refused to renew to him his adoptive father's princely allowance Nana Sahib began to harbour bitter and hostile feelings to the English. What exact part he played in bringing about the Sepoy Mutiny is difficult to assess, but it is certain that he took a prominent part in organising it and that some of the mutineers thought of putting the crown on his head after overthrowing the power of the British. He was also responsible for the massacre of the English at Bibigarh near Cawnpore. Like his adoptive father he was no soldier and had no military talent. He could not give the mutinous sepoys the leadership that they wanted, though he had the satisfaction of being declared Peshwa in 1858 by Tantia Topi (*q.v.*) and his followers after the capture of Gwalior. After the defeat of Tantia Topi and the recapture of Gwalior by the British on 20 June, 1858, Nana Sahib escaped, frustrated all British efforts to capture him and died an unknown death.

Nanak—the founder of the Sikh religion, was born in 1469 in a

Khatri family of Talwandi (modern Nankana) near Lahore. He was a religious preacher of saintly disposition. He spent his whole life in preaching a religion based on all that was beneficial to man in Hinduism as well as in Islam. His mission was to put an end to religious conflicts and he, therefore, preached a gospel of universal toleration. He preached the unity of Godhead and condemned the formalism of religions. He considered all men as equals without caste restrictions, called upon his followers to be pure in the midst of the impurities of the world, to avoid extreme asceticism as well as extreme pleasure-seeking, to discard hypocrisy, selfishness and falsehood. He preached his religion to all and Muhammadans as well as Hindus were converted to his religion which came to be known as Sikhism. His sayings and sacred songs composed by him form the Sacred Book of the Sikhs and is known as the *Granth Shahib*. He died in 1539.

Nanda dynasty—was founded in about 362 B.C. by Mahapadma Nanda (*q.v.*) in Magadha. It comprised nine kings, namely, Mahapadma, the founder and his eight sons who ruled successively. Their rule lasted, according to different authorities, 100, 40 or 20 years. A period of one hundred years must be considered too long a period for two generations of kings, as the Nine Nandas constituted. A period of forty years which justifies the dating of the overthrow of the Nanda dynasty by Chandragupta (*q.v.*) in about 322 B.C., seems to be reasonable. The Nandas were of low origin, but they became very powerful and rich. The last king of the dynasty, called Dhanananda in the Puranas and Agrammes or Xandrames by the classical writers, possessed a vast treasure and commanded a huge army of 20,000 cavalry, 200,000 infantry, 2,000 chariots and 3,000 elephants. Classical writers refer to him as the king of the Prasii whose dominions extended on the west up to the Beas and the dread of whose power led the Greek soldiers of Alexander to refuse to proceed beyond the Beas and to force Alexander to retreat. But the last king of the Nanda dynasty was very much unpopular and was overthrown by Chandragupta Maurya (*q.v.*) with the assistance of a Brahman named Chanakya or Kautilya in about 322 B.C.

Nanda Kumar—was a Bengali Brahman holding the post of the *Faujdar* of Hughli in 1757 when the English under Clive and Watson attacked the French possession of Chandernagore in the vicinity of Hughli. Nanda Kumar had under him a large force of the Nawab's army which might have been used to

protect the French, but on the eve of the English attack Nanda
Kumar moved away with his army from Hughli and thus the
English were easily able to capture Chandernagore. "It i
almost certain that Nanda Kumar was bribed" to have acted
as he did. After Plassey he rose in the favour of Nawab Mir
Jafar and was honoured in 1764 by Emperor Shah Alam with
the title of Maharaja. In the same year he was appointed by
the East India Company as the Collector of Burdwan in place
of Warren Hastings who never forgave this replacement
Next year Nanda Kumar was appointed *Naib Subah* of Bengal
but was soon afterwards dismissed in favour of Muhammad
Reza Khan who, in his turn, was deposed in 1772 by Warren
Hastings, then the Governor-General, and was prosecuted
with the help of Nanda Kumar. But the prosecution failed
and estrangement began between Nanda Kumar and Warren
Hastings. In March, 1775 Nanda Kumar brought before the
Council grave charges of corruption against Warren Hastings
Next month Nanda Kumar was prosecuted by Barwell (*q.v.*)
on a charge of conspiracy. While these two cases were pending
a charge of forgery was brought against Nanda Kumar by one
Mohan Prasad. The trial of this case against Nanda Kumar
which began in May, 1775 was proceeded with great speed and
Nanda Kumar was found guilty, sentenced to death by hanging
by a bench of the Supreme Court, presided over by the Governor
General's friend, Chief Justice Sir Elijah Impey (*q.v.*) and
executed on 5 August, 1775. Nanda Kumar was no saintly
and selfless patriot but his execution on a charge of forgery
amounted to a denial of justice. (Beveridge, H.,—*Trial o*
Maharaja Nanda Kumar)

Nandivardhan—was the penultimate king of the Saisunaga
dynasty (*q.v.*) of Magadha. Nothing but his name is known.

Nao Nihal Singh—was a son of Kharak Singh (*q.v.*) son and
successor of Ranjit Singh (*q.v.*). He was accidentally killed a
day after the murder of his father, Kharak Singh, in March
1840.

Napier, Sir Charles James (1782-1853)—a British general and
statesman, was given, after a military career in Europe, the
command of the Indo-British army in Sind in 1842. He wa
very aggressive and imperialistic in temper. Immediately
after assuming the command he determined to conquer the
province without caring for the rights of the rulers and peoples o
Sind. He deliberately provoked a war with the Amirs (*q.v.*) by
his aggressive policy, won the battle of Miani (*q.v.*) in 184

and finally destroyed the army of the Amirs at the battle of Hyderabad (*q.v.*). He then administered the province autocratically but efficiently till 1847 when he went back to England with the reputation of being a very great general. After the battle of Chilianwala (*q.v.*) in which the Sikhs had nearly defeated the British army, Napier was called upon to be the Commander-in-Chief of the Company's army in India, but the Sikh War ended in British triumph before Napier arrived in India. He engaged himself in re-organising the army in India,˙ but was reprimanded by the Governor-General, Lord Dalhousie, for altering without his knowledge and consent certain regulations relating to allowances to Indian troops in the Company's army. As a protest he resigned and retired to England. He was a very great general but a most aggressive and unscrupulous diplomat and was much prone to be quarrelsome. He, however, had a premonition of the Mutiny of 1857. He wrote a book named *Defects, Civil and Military, of the Indian Government.*

Narasa Nayaka—was the regent during the reign of Immadi Narasimha, the minor king of Vijayanagar, the second and last king of the Saluva dynasty. He made the boy king a state prisoner and usurped real power so effectively that on his death in 1503 the regency passed to his son Vira Narasimha who assumed royal power in 1505.

Narasimha—was a king of the Gupta dynasty. His full name was Narasimhagupta Baladitya. He was the son and successor of Puragupta (*q.v.*) and ruled from *c.* A.D. 467 to 473. He was a devout Buddhist and built at Nalanda (*q.v.*) the principal seat of Buddhist learning in Northern India, a magnificently ornamented brick temple in which an eighty feet high copper image of Buddha was installed. He has been identified by some with the king Baladitya, the conqueror of the Huna king, Mihiragula, whose power was finally broken by A.D. 533-34. This identification is not consistent with the chronology mentioned above. (*P.H.A.I.*, p. 583).

Narasimha Varman—the son and successor of the Pallava king, Mahendravarman (*q.v.*) of Kanchi, also called Rajasimha, ruled from *c.* A.D. 625 to 645. He was the most successful and distinguished king of the Pallava dynasty. In A.D. 642 he defeated and killed the great Chalukya king Pulakeshin II and took Vatapi, the Chalukya capital. He thus made the Pallavas the dominant power in the Deccan. His capital, Kanchi (Conjeeveram) was visited in A.D. 640 by Hiuen-Tsang who was much impressed by the power and wealth of the king. The Dharmaraja Ratha at Mamallapuram and the noble temple of Kailashanath at Kanchi were built by him.

Narayan Rao—the fifth Peshwa who ruled for only nine months (1772-73), was a brother and successor of Peshwa Madhav Rao Narayan (1761-72) (*q.v.*) and was murdered nine months after his accession by the adherents of his uncle Raghunath Rao, commonly called Raghaba (*q.v.*).

Nasik—a town in Maharashtra, not far from Poona, is a holy city of the Hindus. It was probably the capital of the Saka Satrap Nahapana (*q.v.*) as well as of the Chalukya king, Pulakeshin II It was also the capital of the early Rashtrakuta (*q.v.*) kings and lost its metropolitan status during the reign of king Amogha varsha who transferred the capital from Nasik to Manyakheta now Malkhed. Nasik and its neighbourhood are rich in early Hindu, Buddhist and Jain monuments.

Nasir Jang—the second son and successor of Nizam-ul-Mulk Asaf Jah (*q.v.*) of the Deccan, became the Nizam in 1748, but his claim to the office was disputed by his sister's son, Muzaffar Jang (*q.v.*) who was backed by the French governor Dupleix (*q.v.*) and by Chanda Shahib (*q.v.*) a pretender to the throne of Arcot. Nasir Jang marched against them to the Carnatic defeated his enemies at the battle of Veludavur in March, 1750 and secured the abject surrender of Muzaffar Jang. But he was not destined to enjoy the fruits of his victory, for he was killed in a surprise attack on his camp in December, 1750.

Nasir-ud-din—was the sultan of Malwa from 1500 till his death in 1512. He was a parricide who poisoned his father in 1501, a year after his father had voluntarily handed over power to him. He proved to be a cruel tyrant.

Nasir-ud-din Mahmud—was the sultan of Delhi from 1246 to 1266. He was a younger son of Sultan Iltutmish (*q.v.*) (1211-36) Nasir-ud-din was more interested in studies and peaceful pursuits, lived an unostentatious life and left the work of administration to Ulugh Khan, better known as Ghiyasuddin Balban (*q.v.*) whose daughter the Sultan had married. Balban proved himself to be an able administrator who kept peace and order in the country by suppressing the rebellious Hindus in the Panjab as well as in the Doab and by successfully resisting Mughul inroads into the country. Nasir-ud-din was a patron of learning and Minhaj-ud-din Siraj, the author of the *Tabakat i-Nasiri* (*q.v.*) held a high post in his court.

Nasir-ud-din Muhammad Shah—was the royal name assumed

by Tatar Khan who in 1403 imprisoned his father Zafar Khan, the governor of Gujarat and made himself the independent ruler of the province. But a year later Nasir-ud-din was poisoned by his father who then ascended the throne of Gujarat.

Nasir-ud-din Qabacha—was a Turkish slave in the employment of Shihab-ud-din Muhammad Ghuri (*q.v.*). He rose by dint of his merit to be the Governor of Sind. He married the sister of Qutb-ud-din who also was, like him, a Turkish slave of the Ghuri chief. After the death of Shihab-ud-din when Qutb-ud-din became the Sultan of Delhi (A.D. 1206-10) Qabacha rose in revolt against the Sultan but was defeated and reduced to submission.

National Congress—*see* Indian National Congress.

Naval Mutiny—broke out in the Indian navy stationed in the port of Bombay in 1947. It was soon suppressed by force, but it showed that political disaffection had spread even amongst the Indian personnel of the navy and the British could no longer count on the unquestioning obedience and loyalty of this branch of their armed forces in India.

Nawab Wazir of Oudh—*see* Shuja-ud-daulah.

Nawaz Khan, Shah—was the Mughul governor of Ahmedabad in 1658-59. He gave shelter to Prince Dara (*q.v.*) when the Prince came to the city in the course of his flight after his defeat at the battle of Samugarh (*q.v.*). Nawaz Khan helped Prince Dara to occupy Surat and thus afforded him some sort of chance to recover his fortunes. But Dara left for Ajmer and the assistance given him by Nawaz Khan proved fruitless.

Nayapala—the tenth king of the Pala dynasty (*q.v.*) of Bengal and Bihar, was the son and successor of Mahipal (*q.v.*) and ruled from *c.* A.D. 1038 to 1055. His reign witnessed a long struggle with the Kalachuris (*q.v.*). The break-up of the Pala kingdom began in the reign of Nayapala who lost possession of the east, west and south Bengal. The one interesting fact in the reign of Nayapala was the mission of Atisa (*q.v.*) to Tibet on the invitation of the Tibetan Government.

Nearchos—the admiral of the fleet of Alexander, the king of Macedon (*q.v.*) commanded Alexander's fleet, first from the Jhelum to the mouth of the Indus and then to the Persian Gulf as far as the mouth of the Euphrates, and then turning back he sailed up the Tigris to Susa where he met Alexander who had in the meantime returned there by the overland route. Nearchos has also left an account of his observations during the long voyage.

Negapatam—is a town on the eastern coast of India. The Dutch established a settlement at Negapatam which was captured by the English in 1781.

Nehru, Pandit Jawaharlal (1889-1964)—was the first Prime Minister of independent India of which he was the fighter architect. He was born at Allahabad on 14 November, 1889, the only son of Pandit Matilal Nehru (*q.v.*) and Swaruprani Up to the age 15 when he was sent to Harrow, he was educated at home. From Harrow he went to Trinity College and graduated from Cambridge University taking his Natural Science Tripos in Chemistry, Geology and Botany. He was called to the Bar in 1912 when he returned to India and joined the Allahabad Bar. Law, however, did not attract him much and he soon began to take part in Indian politics. He joined as a delegate the Bankipore session of the Indian National Congress in 1912 and met Mahatma Gandhi for the first time at the Lucknow session of the Congress in 1916 in which year he also married Kamala Kaul who bore him a daughter, Indira, who is now the Prime Minister of India and a son who died soon after his birth. As years passed Nehru's part in Indian politics grew larger. He worked with C. R. Das and Mahatma Gandhi in connection with the enquiry started by the Congress in the Jalianwalla Bagh massacre (*q.v.*) and came into very close contact with Gandhiji during the non-co-operation movement in 1921. Their relations became deeper and deeper as the years passed and ceased only with the Mahatma's death. Nehru's prison term during that movement was the first of a series of nine totalling nine years. He took part in the demonstration at Lucknow against the Simon Commission and endured with the patience of a non-violent *Satyagrahi* a severe police lathi-charge. In 1928 he became the General Secretary of the Indian National Congress and in 1929 its President at its Lahore session which passed the Independence Resolution He became President of the Congress again in 1936, 1946 and in every session from 1951 to 1954. In 1958 he saw his daughter Indira, occupy the chair which both he and his father had filled. From 1929 Jawaharlal was constantly in the forefront of the Indian National struggle. In 1930 he was sent to prison for six months for his work in the civil disobedience movement Released in October he was re-arrested eight days later for a breach of an order under sec. 144 and was sent to prison for 30 months. A year later he was released. Twelve days after his release his father Pandit Matilal died (1931). Imprison-

ments and domestic bereavements crowded in quick succession.
His wife and mother were both ailing, one from tuberculosis
and the other from paralysis. His wife breathed her last in
Germany when he was undergoing his seventh term of
imprisonment and could be by her side only on Government's
permission. His mother died in 1938. He next visited Spain,
Czechoslovakia and Chungking. His political work in India
continued unremittingly. In 1939 he entered into a bitter
controversy with Netaji Subhas Chandra Bose on his re-election
as President of the Indian National Congress in spite of the
opposition of the Mahatma and resigned from Bose's Working
Committee. In 1940 he took part in the movement of civil
disobedience by individuals started by the Mahatma and was
sentenced to four years' imprisonment but was released a year
later. Then came the air-attack on Pearl Harbour which
signalled the entry of Japan and the U.S.A. into the Second
World War, which was then raging, bringing the hostilities near
to India's eastern frontier. The year 1941 and the early part of
1942 were periods of great mental anguish for Nehru who
wanted the defeat of the Axis but dreaded the consequences,
in respect of India, of the victory of the English and their allies.
He differed with the Mahatma on the approach to the question
of non-violence. While the Mahatma firmly believed in it as
a way of life Nehru looked upon it as merely a policy. But
ultimately he fell in with the Mahatma's views, and joined in
the 'Quit India' movement started by the Mahatma in August
1942. He was arrested along with other Indian leaders for his
ninth and longest prison term. He was released in June, 1945
and soon afterwards took part in discussions with the Muslim
League on the Cabinet Mission Plan (*q.v.*). These discussions
failed and on 2 September, 1946 Nehru, on the invitation of the
Viceroy, joined the Interim Government (*q.v.*) as its head. He
also succeeded in persuading the Muslim League to join the
Interim Government, but no real and sincere understanding
could be made with the League led by Jinnah (*q.v.*) and the
two bodies—the Congress which was predominantly Hindu
and the League which was exclusively Muhammadan, drifted
apart. The whole country, the Panjab and Bengal in particular,
became the scenes of bloody riots between the Hindus and the
Muhammadans. In the meantime Lord Mountbatten had
been appointed as the Viceroy and after some initial opposition Nehru agreed with the Viceroy that peace and independence of India could be secured only on the basis of the parti-

tion of India into Hindustan and Pakistan. On June 3, 1947
Nehru broadcast to the nation the acceptance of partition by
the Indian National Congress. On 15 August, 1947 he became
the first Prime Minister of independent India. He was then
just three months short of 58.

He remained head of the Government of India for the next
17 years and died in harness on 27 May, 1964. He soon rose
to the status of a world statesman, visited almost every country
in Europe and Asia and was received with frenzied demonstrations of good will in Russia and even in China which he
visited in 1954.

Inside the country Mr. Nehru's Government had no easy
time. Gandhiji's assassination subjected it to the first serious
shock. Then came the crises of Kashmir and Hyderabad and
the prolonged and heart-breaking refugee problem. Though
the French enclaves were amicably recovered, the Portuguese
ones had to be recovered in 1961 by the employment of military
force. Linguistic and other forms of sectarianism raised their
heads all over the country from the Deccan to the Nagaland,
and were sometimes accompanied with much violence. But
Nehru's Ministry managed to maintain general peace all
over the country and to maintain intact the democratic form
of government with which independent India had started on
her new career. His Ministry launched the most ambitious
schemes of industrial and social development India has ever
known—despite slender resources—in Three Five Year Plans.
The consequences are only to be realised after the lapse of
sufficient time. In foreign relations Nehru accepted and acted
upon the policy of non-alignment and would not join either
the Anglo-American or the Soviet bloc. He maintained friendly
relations with both and insisted on the settlement of all international disputes by peaceful methods of discussion and negotiation. He was often misunderstood and adversely criticised,
but he was generally regarded, in the words of a Mexican
Senator, "as a herald of peace and harmony". He tried his
best to maintain friendly relations with Pakistan and offered to
enter into a 'no-war pact' with that country, but emboldened by
her membership of the SEATO and the CENTO, especially
by the massive military help that the U.S.A. has voluntarily been
giving her over the years, Pakistan refused Nehru's offer.
Nehru's efforts at improving Indo-Pakistan relations thus
failed. His greatest disillusionment came in October, 1962
when China which had been earlier suffered to occupy Tibet

by force without any military opposition from India, made a massive invasion in the Ladakh and North-Eastern Frontier Agency areas over a long-standing border dispute. Nehru and India were both caught unawares and though the Indian army somehow held its own in the Ladakh area, in the North-Eastern Frontier the Chinese carried everything before them and were on the point of making an easy conquest of Assam; but in November the Chinese suddenly announced a unilateral cease-fire and started pulling out of NEFA. Though India did not accept the cease-fire, she found herself obliged to stop fighting. In the meantime the failure of India's military preparedness had roused much adverse comment in the country and Nehru had to drop his Defence Minister and reshuffle his cabinet. He also made earnest appeals for help to all the countries of the world and received prompt and sympathetic response from England, the U.S.A. as well as Russia. The Anglo-American bloc tried to exploit India's difficulty to force Nehru to an understanding with Pakistan on Anglo-American terms, but Nehru would not submit to intimidation and parting with territories that had become integral parts of India. Nehru was not a person to be cowed down by adversity. He, however, warned his countrymen that they would have to be prepared for a long-drawn war with China. In December, 1962 some Afro-Asian countries met at Colombo and drew up what came to be known as the Colombo proposals for solving what they chose to call India's border dispute with China. Though the proposals did less than justice to India yet so strong was Nehru's desire to solve the issue by means of peaceful negotiations rather than by force that he accepted them but China did not. And the stalemate continued throughout his lifetime.

In 1963 Nehru was the first Head of Government who hailed the signing of the partial test ban pact by Russia, England and the U.S.A.

Perturbed by some Parliamentary by-election reverses and advised by the Congress party to re-organise his Cabinet so that some of its prominent members might give all their time to party work Nehru reduced the size of his cabinet, accepted the resignation of some of his old comrades including Morarji Desai and S. K. Patil and formed a more compact cabinet. In January, 1964 when attending the Bhubaneswar session of the Congress he fell seriously ill; he recovered for the time being, but passed away on 27 May, 1964 in New Delhi.

Nehru was not only a great statesman and great orator, he was also a writer of distinction. His *Autobiography* published in 1936 created world-wide interest. His other works include *India and the World, Soviet Russia, Glimpses of World History, Unity of India* and *Independence and After*—the last two being collections of his speeches and writings.

Nehru as a fighter was the architect of the independent Republic of India, but he was no narrow nationalist. He had a love for liberty for all peoples of the world. He therefore expressed sympathy and support for all liberation movements in Africa, Asia and South America. He believed in the liberty of all without distinctions of class, creed and country. He was equally a staunch believer in World peace and was therefore an ardent advocate of the United Nations Organisation. On several international questions such as the Suez Canal, Korea, Laos, the Congo and Vietnam his was the voice of peace and his voice was always heard with respect.

Nehru, Pandit Matilal (also spelt Motilal) (1861-1931)—a renowned Indian patriot, was born on 6 May, 1861 in Delhi and was a Kashmiri Brahman. He began his career as a lawyer at the Allahabad High Court and soon gathered a roaring practice over the whole of north India. He joined the Indian National Congress movement after the inauguration of the 'Montford Reforms' (*q.v.*) and started a journal named *The Independent* to support the cause of Indian Nationalism. He joined the non-co-operation movement in 1920 and gave up his lucrative practice and his membership of the Indian Legislative Assembly. But he soon re-considered the situation and along with C. R. Das (*q.v.*) he formed the *Swarajist* party within the Congress. In 1923 he re-entered the Legislature and became the leader of the *Swarajist* party in the Assembly. He was a great orator and parliamentary tactician and led his party of minority with much success in the Assembly. He presided over the Indian National Congress twice—first in 1919 at Calcutta and again in 1928 at Amritsar. On behalf of the Indian National Congress he drew up in 1928 a report known as the Nehru Report on the future constitution of India. This Report recommended the immediate grant of 'Dominion Status' to India. But when the Government refused to concede the demand Matilal joined the civil disobedience movement in 1930 and was imprisoned. This incarceration broke his health and he died a year later. Himself a great son of India, he was the father of a greater son of India, Pandit Jawaharlal Nehru.

Neill, Brigadier-General, J.—was an officer in the army of the East India Company when the Mutiny (*q.v.*) broke out. On 11 June Neill by a bold and fortunate stroke secured the important fortress of Allahabad just when it was about to be captured by the mutineers. Soon afterwards he was joined by another British army led by General Havelock. Thus strengthened the British army under Neill and Havelock marched from Allahabad to relieve Cawnpore. All along the route Neill became responsible for an exhibition of a vulgar spirit of vengeance against the Indians by mercilessly putting to death all Indians, most of them unoffending, whom he came across. He thus gave to the Mutiny the character of a war of mutual revenge from which Indians and Britishers alike suffered. Before Neill with his contingent could take Cawnpore the tragedy of Bibigarh had already taken place. Neill and Havelock soon recovered Cawnpore where Neill stayed back wreaking a cruel vengeance on Indians whom he could get hold of and hanging them from branches of trees along the roads from Cawnpore to Lucknow where he was soon afterwards killed while fighting in its narrow streets.

Nekusiyar—a son of Prince Akbar, the fourth son of Emperor Aurangzeb (*q.v.*) was the third of the five puppet-emperors who were placed on the throne of Delhi by the "king-makers", the Sayyid brothers (*q.v.*) in the course of the year 1719. He was installed as Emperor only to be murdered a short while after his installation to make room for Muhammad Ibrahim (*q.v.*).

Nepal—is the kingdom running along the northern frontier of India for about 500 miles, from the Sutlej on the west to Sikkim on the east. Its capital is Kathmandu. It was a part of the empire of Asoka in the third century of the pre-Christian era and acknowledged the sovereignty of Samudragupta in the fourth century of the Christian era. In the seventh century it passed under the control of Tibet. Then followed a long period of internal struggle and strife accompanied with much bloodshed. In the eleventh century Nepal was ruled by the Thakuri dynasty. Then the dynasty of Nanyadeva of Mithila exercised a nominal sovereignty over Nepal which was actually ruled by the Malla dynasty of kings, the most renowned of whom was king Yakshamalla (*c.* A.D. 1426-75). Before his death he partitioned his kingdom amongst his sons and daughters. As a result of this partition Nepal became divided into the two rival principalities of Kathmandu and Bhatgaon. Their mutual quarrels facilitated the conquest of Nepal in 1768 by the Gurkhas, a tribe inhabiting the western Himalayas. They gradually built up a powerful state possessing considerable military strength. In the nineteenth century the gradual extension of their territories southwards made their frontier on the south conterminous with that of British India on the north. This proximity led to a war with the British in 1814-15. As a result of this Gurkha war (*q.v.*) which was concluded by the treaty of Sagauli (*q.v.*) Nepal ceded certain territories to the British and agreed to allow its foreign policy to be controlled by the British Indian Government. Nepal thus remained an independent country with certain limitations. The religion of the majority of the people of Nepal is Hinduism and a small minority follows a rather degraded form of Buddhism. Many important Sanskrit manuscripts have been found in Nepal. The present ruler, King Mahendra, is a much-travelled person and has given Nepal a constitution.

New Muslims—was the name applied to a band of Mongol raiders who in about 1292 embraced Islam and were allowed to settle at Kilokhri and other villages near Delhi. As Mongol raids still continued, the New Muslims were suspected and practically destroyed by a wholesale massacre in 1297 during the reign of Sultan Ala-ud-din Khalji (*q.v.*).

Nicholson, Brigadier-General, John (1821-57)—a brave soldier and a British hero in the Mutiny, came as an officer in the Company's service to Calcutta in 1839. He took part in the campaigns in Afghanistan in 1840-41, was made a prisoner but was released. He took part in the Sikh War of 1848-49 and won distinction. At the outbreak of the Mutiny in 1857 he was the Deputy Commissioner at Peshawar and was soon placed in command of a mobile column that was sent from the Panjab for the recovery of Delhi which he reached, after a strenuous march, on 14 August, 1857 and was in command of the main storming party on 14 September, when Delhi was recaptured by the British. But Nicholson was shot through the chest in the street-fighting that ensued, was mortally wounded and died on 23 September, 1857. By storming Delhi he had practically ended the Mutiny and saved the British empire in India.

Nikitin, Athanasius—a Russian merchant-traveller, visited the Bahmani kingdom during the years 1470-74. He has left an account of what he saw and this account throws much light on the condition of the common people who, we are told, lived a very miserable life, whilst the nobles were extremely rich and delighted in luxury.

Nil Prabhu Munshi—a Brahman adviser of Shivaji, was the author and writer of the letter addressed to Emperor Aurangzeb (*q.v.*) by Shivaji in protest against the re-imposition of the *jizya* (*q.v.*) on the Hindus by Aurangzeb in 1679.

Nivedita, Sister—a famous disciple of Swami Vivekananda (*q.v.*), was an Irish lady named Miss Margaret Noble. She met Swami Vivekananda in London and later on came over to India where she was formally initiated as a disciple of Swami Vivekananda and was attached to the Ramakrishna Mission. She devoted herself to social service, rendering exemplary service to the Indian community in Calcutta during the outbreak of the plague epidemic. She established a girls' school in north Calcutta in the midst of the most orthodox section of the city's Hindu population. She wrote several books in English popularising the ancient Hindu ideals and undertook lecturing tours all over India. She was an ardent supporter of India's claim to independence, was intimately associated with nationalists like Arabinda Ghose; and within a week of the death of Swami Vivekananda she cut off her connection with the Ramakrishna Mission in order to be free to devote herself entirely to the service of India. The *Cradle Tales of India* is one of her many works. (Pravarjika Atmaprana, *Sister Nivedita*)

Nizam Asaf Jah—*see* Asaf Jah.

Nizam Khan—*see* Sikandar Lodi.

Nizam Shah Bahmani—the twelfth sultan of the Bahmani kingdom (*q.v.*) was a minor when he succeeded his father Sultan Humayun (*q.v.*) in 1461. He died suddenly in 1463.

Nizam Shahi dynasty—was founded at Junnar by Malik Ahmad in 1490 as a result of a successful rebellion against Sultan Mahmud (1482-1518) (*q.v.*) of the Bahmani kingdom. He assumed the title of Nizam Shah, transferred his capital to Ahmadnagar and founded the Nizam Shahi dynasty which ruled over the kingdom of Ahmadnagar from A.D. 1490 till its annexation to the Mughul empire in 1637 during the reign of Shah Jahan. It absorbed Berar in 1574, but was obliged to cede it to Akbar in 1596. Its third ruler, Husain Shah, joined the confederacy of the Muhammadan states against Vijayanagar (*q.v.*), shared in the victory of Talikota (*q.v.*) in 1565 and took part in the sacking of the vanquished city. The gallant Chand Bibi (*q.v.*) was a daughter of the Nizam Shahi sultan, Husain Nizam Shah (1553-65). The principal monument left by the Nizam Shahi dynasty is the ruined Bhadr palace in white stone at Ahmadnagar.

Nizam-ud-din—the official historian of Akbar's times, wrote the *Tabakat-i-Akbari* which is an authentic and authoritative account of the reign of Akbar.

Nizam-ud-din Aulia—was a Sufi saint who settled in Delhi in Akbar's time. He was much respected and a magnificent mosque was built near his tomb in the suburb of Delhi.

Nizam-ul-Mulk—was a high title meaning 'Deputy for the Whole Empire". It was first conferred upon Chin Qilich Khan by Emperor Muhammad Shah (1719-48) and has since been hereditary in his family residing at Hyderabad the head of which is commonly called the Nizam.

Non-co-operation Movement—was inaugurated in India by Mahatma Gandhi (*q.v.*) in 1919-20 as a means for compelling the British Government to grant such constitutional reforms as were demanded by the Indian National Congress which then aimed only at Dominion Status. On account of the dissatisfaction caused amongst the Indian Muhammadans by the practical dissolution of the Turkish empire in Europe brought about by the First World War the non-co-operation movement got the support not only of the Indian Hindus but also of the Indian Muhammadans. It aimed at bringing down the Government by withdrawing all co-operation from it. The response was at first immense; hundreds and thousands refused to have to do anything with Government, resigned its offices, withdrew from its courts, abstained from attending the schools and colleges and boycotted the elections held under the Government of India Act, 1919. Mahatma Gandhi wanted the movement to be non-violent but such a country-wide movement against the Government inevitably led to occasional acts of violence which the Government tried to suppress by the application of force and by enforcing the punitive provisions of the law. Thousands were therefore thrown into prison and this in itself caused a difficult problem for the Government. The non-co-operation movement which was in full vigour till 1924, collapsed as the Indian Muslims gradually drifted away from it and internal dissension broke out amongst the Congressmen themselves. Some of them led by Pandit Matilal Nehru (*q.v.*) and Mr. C. R. Das (*q.v.*) formed the *Swarajist* party which wanted to contest the elections, enter the central and provincial legislatures as created by the Government of India Act, 1919 (*q.v.*) and fight the Government from within with a view to either mending or ending them. But the non-co-operation movement had not been in vain. The mass imprisonment of thousands of Indians from all ranks of society completely removed from the popular mind the sense of terror and ignominy that had been so long associated with imprisonment and the fear complex that had so long held down the millions of Indians under British rule vanished. This was no mean achievement for a popular movement.

Non-Regulation provinces, the—were the provinces within the British Indian Empire which were excluded from the rigorous application of the Cornwallis Code of Regulations of May, 1793. Such provinces were Delhi acquired in 1803, Assam, Arakan and Tenasserim in 1824, Saugar and Narmada territories in 1818 and the Panjab in 1849. The district collectors in these non-regulation provinces were called Deputy Commissioners and the provincial heads were called Chief Commissioners. Military officers could be employed in these provinces for performing civil duties.

North-West Frontier Province—was created in 1901 during the Viceroyalty of Lord Curzon (q.v.). The creation of such a frontier province was first suggested by Lord Lytton (1876-80) (q.v.) but he had suggested the inclusion within it of Sind and parts of the Panjab. The proposal was not then accepted. Lord Curzon excluded Sind and the Panjab from the new frontier province which he constituted with the whole of the Pathan tribal territory lying to the east of the Durand line (q.v.) together with the settled districts of Hazara, Peshawar, Kohat, Bannu and Dera Ismail Khan. It was to be administered by a Chief Commissioner directly under the control of the Viceroy, assisted by members of the Political Department. The creation of this North-West Frontier Province led to the changing of the name of the North-West Province into the United Provinces of Agra and Oudh, briefly called U.P. It became a Governor's Province in 1932 with its own legislature. After independence and partition of India it went to form a part of West Pakistan.

Northbrook, Earl of—was the Viceroy and Governor-General of India from 1872 to 1876. He was a liberal of the school of Gladstone and his policy in India was "to take off taxes, to stop unnecessary legislation and to give the land rest". He was a believer in free trade, but was unwilling to part with a revenue that could be easily collected by imposing some small duties on imports. He abolished all export duties except those on oil, rice, indigo and lac and reduced import duties from $7\frac{1}{2}$ per cent to 5 per cent. But the retention of

this small duty was resented by the Lancashire cotton indus-
trialists, and, in their interests on the specious plea of free
trade, the Conservative Government of Lord Disraeli and the
Secretary of State, Lord Salisbury, insisted on its abolition.
This created differences between Lord Northbrook and the
Secretary of State which widened on the question of the policy
to be followed in relation to Afghanistan. In 1873 when the
Russians captured Khiva (*q.v.*) Sher Ali, the Amir of
Afghanistan, asked for a closer alliance with the British Indian
Government against any possible aggression by Russia. Lord
Northbrook considered the request reasonable and asked the
British Government for permission to enter into such an agreement with Afghanistan. The British Government refused the
permission and asked him to give the Amir no more than a
general promise of help. But with the installation of the Government of Disraeli (*q.v.*) a change came over the policy of the
British Cabinet which then developed an inclination for what
was called 'forward policy' in preference to the policy of 'masterly
inactivity' that had been followed in relation to Afghanistan
up to 1873. Lord Salisbury, the new Secretary of State, ordered
Lord Northbrook in 1874 to ask Amir Sher Ali to admit a
British Resident within his kingdom. Lord Northbrook considered that such a demand, coming so soon after the refusal
by the British Indian Government of the Amir's offer for an
alliance, was unjustifiable and was bound to lead to dire consequences. But as Lord Salisbury insisted on the enforcement
of his policy Lord Northbrook who had already differed from
him on the question of the abolition of the import duty of
5%, though its continuance was essential for the stability of
Indian finance, resigned his office.

Nott, General Sir William (1782-1845)—came out as a military
officer in the Company's Bengal army in 1800. He rose quickly
and in 1839 was in command of the British army at Qandahar,
which, later on, he held against the Afghan attacks. After
the murder of Macnaghten (*q.v.*) he declined to retire to India
without express orders and when in July, 1842 he was allowed by
Lord Ellenborough (*q.v.*) a choice of routes, he deliberately chose
the longer route, marched via Ghazni to Kabul, where he arrived
on 17 September, 1842, re-asserted the supremacy of British arms,
returned to India *via* Jalalabad and thus turned the Afghan
war from a defeat into a sort of a victory. Later on he became
British Resident at Kabul and retired from India in 1844.

Nuniz, Fernao—a Portuguese traveller, visited Vijayanagar (*q.v.*)

in 1535. He travelled extensively over the kingdom and has left a very informative account of its history and the political, social and economic condition of the country.

Nurjahan—was the consort of Emperor Jahangir. Her original name was Mihr-un-nisa. She was born at Qandahar when her father, Mirza Ghiyas Beg, a Persian, was on his way to India with his family in search of fortune. Her father rose to high position in the court of Akbar and was appointed in the year of Jahangir's accession (1605) the revenue minister with the title of Itimad-ud-daula. At the age of seventeen Mihr-un-nisa was married to a Persian adventurer, named Ali Quli, who at the beginning of Jahangir's reign received the title of Sher Afghan and the *jagir* of Burdwan. In 1607 Sher Afghan was killed in a fight with the emissaries of the Mughul emperor, Jahangir, and the widowed Mihr-un-nisa was brought to the imperial harem in Delhi where she became an attendant on Salima Begum, a widow of Akbar. Jahangir was later on attracted by her exquisite beauty and married her in 1611. Her name was now changed, first into Nur Mahal (Light of the Palace) and then to Nur Jahan (Light of the World). Nur Jahan possessed, in addition to her uncommon beauty, a fine intellect, a versatile temper, sound common sense and a love for literature, poetry and arts. She was also a very good shot. In 1619 she killed a tiger at Fathpur Sikri with one shot. All these qualities soon enabled her to establish an unlimited ascendancy over her husband who practically left the administration to her. Her name was minted on coins and she gave audiences in her palace. Her father as well as her brother, Asaf Khan, held high offices in the Mughul court and her niece, the future Mumtaz, was married to Prince Khurram (*q.v.*). She gave her daughter by her first husband in marriage to Jahangir's youngest son, Prince Shahriyar, whom she wanted to succeed Jahangir to whom she bore no child. Her power and influence was opposed by Mahabat Khan (*q.v.*) and Prince Khurram, but she frustrated their efforts by her superior intelligence and tact. She continued to be all-powerful during the lifetime of Jahangir on whose death in 1627 she lost all her political power and lived a retired life in or near Lahore till her death in 1645. Her artistic taste is illustrated by the exquisitely beautiful tomb that she built at Agra over the remains of her father Itimad-ud-daula, which, it has been said, stands in a class by itself on account of the delicacy of treatment and the chaste quality of its decorations.

Nusrat Shah—the king of Bengal from 1518 to 1533, was the eldest son and successor of Husain Shah who left eighteen sons all of whom were treated well by Nusrat Shah. He conquered Tirhut. He was a patron of art, architecture and literature. He constructed in his capital at Gaur two famous mosques, namely, the Large Golden Mosque and *Kadam Rasul* (Foot of the Prophet) and had the *Mahabharata* translated from Sanskrit into Bengali.

Nusrat Shah—the eighth sultan of the Tughluq dynasty (*q.v.*), was a grandson of Sultan Firuz Tughluq (*q.v.*) and was set up as the sultan in January, 1395 only to be put to death after a brief nominal rule of three or four years. While he held his court at Firuzabad his rival and cousin Mahmud Tughluq ruled at Old Delhi. His death left Mahmud Tughluq the undisputed representative of the Tughluq dynasty.

O

Ochterlony, Sir David (1758-1825)—a distinguished British general in the service of the E.I. Company, won great credit by ably defending Delhi against the Holkar in 1804. Later on in the Gurkha War (1814-15) (*q.v.*) he led one of the three Indo-British armies that invaded Nepal; and while the other two generals failed, Ochterlony invading Nepal from the extreme west, succeeded in holding his own. This success led to his promotion to the supreme command of the Indo-British expeditionary army into Nepal and he justified his promotion by advancing, after hard fighting, to within fifty miles of Kathmandu, the capital, and thus obliging Nepal to make peace by the treaty of Sagauli (*q.v.*) in 1816. In the Pindari War (1817-18) he was in command of the Rajputana column and detached Amir Khan (*q.v.*) from the Pindaris and thus hastened the British victory. On the outbreak of the First Burmese War (1824-26) he started out to attack Bharatpur (*q.v.*) where a revolt against the infant Raja Balwant Singh was attempted by Durjan Sal but was promptly recalled by the Governor-General. Soon afterwards he died. He is commemorated by the Monument in Calcutta Maidan.

Omichand (also spelt Amin Chand)—was a rich but unscrupulous merchant and financier who resided in Calcutta in the middle of the eighteenth century. He conducted the negotiations between the English in Calcutta and the disaffected Indian nobles in Murshidabad for bringing about the deposition of Nawab Siraj-ud-daulah and the installation of Mir Jafar as the Nawab of Bengal. When the negotiations had sufficiently advanced and committed the English as partners in a conspiracy against Nawab Siraj-ud-daulah Omichand demanded a large commission on the money that was expected to be found in the Nawab's treasury at Murshidabad, and threatened that unless this was guaranteed to him he would divulge the whole plot to the Nawab. At the suggestion of Robert Clive two drafts of the treaty with Mir Jafar were drawn up, one authorized the payment of the commission demanded by Omichand and was shown to him, the other, the real document, did not. The fictitious treaty was signed by Clive and other members of the Calcutta Council with the exception of Admiral Watson whose signature was forged and put on the sham treaty by Clive. The deception was revealed to Omichand only after the battle of Plassey and he is said to have gone mad and died of disappointment.

Onesikritos—a classical historian, has left an account of Alexander's invasion of India. He accompanied Alexander to Taxila in 326 B.C. His account has been lost, but portions of it have survived in the writings of later classical historians.

Orissa—is now a State in the Republic of India. It lies along the eastern coast of India from Bengal on the north to Andhra on the south. In ancient times it was known as Kalinga (*q.v.*) and was a part of the dominions of Mahapadma Nanda (*q.v.*). It seems to have seceded from the Magadhan empire some time after the fall of the Nanda dynasty but was conquered and annexed to the Maurya empire by Asoka (*q.v.*) after a battle which was attended with so much slaughter and suffering that it profoundly affected the mind of Asoka and was the direct cause of his embracing Buddhism. After the fall of the Maurya dynasty Kalinga or Orissa again became an independent state under the Cheta (*q.v.*) dynasty and was raised to great power by King Kharavela (*q.v.*). In the fourth century A.D. it was a part of the Gupta empire and in the seventh century it was within the empire of Harshavardhana whose last recorded expedition was against Ganjam on its southern border in A.D. 642. Then follows a period of darkness which is partially lifted in the ninth century when Orissa passed under the Bhanja dynasty (*q.v.*). The most powerful king of this dynasty was

Ranabhanja who ruled for fifty years. In the middle of the eleventh century the Eastern Ganga dynasty established its rule in Orissa and continued to rule till 1434 when it was overthrown by Kapilendra (*q.v.*). The most famous king of the Eastern Ganga dynasty was Anantavarman Choḍaganga (*q.v.*) who ruled from A.D. 1076 to 1148 and built the present Jagannatha Temple at Puri. The Eastern Ganga kings upheld the independence of Orissa against the Muhammadan raids from northern India as well as against the attacks of the Bahmani sultans on the south. It submitted only temporarily to the Delhi sultanate under Ala-ud-din Khalji (*q.v.*). It was also invaded in A.D. 1359 by Sultan Firuz Tughluq who was satisfied with the gift of a large number of elephants and left Orissa, or *Jajnagar*, as the Muhammadan historians call it, to herself. But in 1568 it was conquered by Sulaiman Kararani, sultan of Bengal. It was annexed to the Mughul empire by Akbar in 1572 and formed a part of the *suba* of Bengal. In 1751 part of it was ceded by Nawab Alivardi Khan of Bengal to the Marathas under Raghuji Bhonsla and remained a part of the Maratha dominions till 1803 when it was ceded by the Bhonsla Raja to the East India Company by the treaty of Deogaon (*q.v.*). Already in 1765 that part of it which had been kept under the rule of the Nawab of Bengal had passed under the rule of the Company with the grant of the Diwani in 1765. Thus Orissa was tagged to the province of Bengal and was under the direct administration of the Governor-General until 1854 when along with Bengal and Bihar it was placed under the administration of a Lieutenant-Governor. In 1866-67 it was visited by a severe famine. In 1912 it was separated from Bengal but remained tagged to Bihar forming a separate province. In 1935 Orissa was finally constituted into a state by itself and continues to be so in the Republic of India.

Orme, Robert (1728-1801)—was an English soldier-historian in India. He was born in South India, his father having been a surgeon in the Company's service in India. He was appointed to a writership in Bengal in 1743 and when out on a voyage on leave to England he made a close friendship with Robert Clive (*q.v.*) which lasted long. From 1754 to 1758 he was a member of the Madras Council and largely influenced the appointment of Clive to lead an expedition for the recovery of Calcutta. His great work, A *History of the Military Transactions of the British Nation in Indostan from 1745*, was published in 3 volumes in 1763-78 and his *Historical Fragments* dealing with the earlier period in 1781. His works are characterised by minute details and his *History* which is one of the most authentic works on the period concerned, was largely used by Macaulay. He left a valuable collection of manuscripts, now preserved in the India Library.

Ostend Company—was a Belgian venture for trading with India. It was founded with international capital and was granted a charter by Emperor Charles VI of Austria in 1722. It aroused very strong objections and protests by the Dutch, the English and the French East India Companies backed by their respective Governments. So strong was the opposition that Emperor Charles VI agreed in 1731 to suppress the Company. The Ostend Company, however, did not become legally defunct before 1793.

Otantapuri—also known as Uddandapura, a town in Bihar, had a great monastery founded by Gopala, the founder of the Pala dynasty (*q.v.*) of Bengal and Bihar in the middle of the eighth century A.D. It became an important seat of learning, and was later on destroyed by the Muhammadan invaders under Muhammad, son of Bakhtyar (*q.v.*) in the beginning of the thirteenth century.

Oudh—is the modern name of the ancient kingdom of Koshala (*q.v.*) watered by the Saraju, a tributary of the Ganges, to the north-west of Allahabad. According to the *Ramayana*, it was the kingdom of Dasaratha, the father of the hero Rama and its capital was the sacred city of Ayodhya. In historical times Koshala or Oudh was one of the sixteen large states into which India was divided and its capital was Sravasti. In the sixth century B.C. its king, Prasenajit, was a contemporary and rival of the Magadhan kings, Bimbisara and Ajatasatru. Koshala was later on reduced by Magadha and became merged in the Magadhan empire of the Nandas and of the Mauryas. When exactly the name of the city of Ayodhya came to be applied to the whole state of Koshala and assumed its modern form of Oudh is not definitely known. In about *c.* 156 B.C. Oudh with its capital Saketa was over-run by "viciously valiant" Yavanas who have been identified with Menander (*q.v.*) and his Greek armies. Oudh was a part of the empire of the Guptas in the fourth century of the Christian era and Ayodhya probably was the alternate capital of the Guptas in the fifth century. In the seventh century it was included within the empire of Harshavardhana (*q.v.*) and from the ninth century it was a part of the Gurjara-Pratihara dominions. Oudh was conquered for the Delhi sultanate by Malik Hisam-ud-din A'ghul Bak, a lieutenant of Shihab-ud-din Muhammad Ghuri (*q.v.*), soon after the second battle of Tiraori (*q.v.*) (A.D. 1192). Its fertility and bracing climate proved attractive to the Muhammadan gentry many of whom gradually moved to and settled in Oudh especially during the rule of Sultan Muhammad Tughluq. In 1340 Ain-ul-Mulk who was the governor of Oudh and had administered it very efficiently, rose in revolt against Sultan Muhammad Tughluq who, however, suppressed the rebel and condemned him to imprisonment. Henceforth Oudh continued to be a part of the dominions of the Delhi sultanate, though a large slice of it was merged in the kingdom of Jaunpur (A.D. 1399-1476). On the fall of Jaunpur Oudh reverted entirely to the Delhi empire and passed under Mughul rule with Babur's victory over Ibrahim Lodi in 1526. It was one of the 15 *subas* into which Akbar divided his empire and continued to be an important province of the Mughul empire till A.D. 1724 when its Mughul governor, Saadat Khan, made himself practically independent and founded the line of the Nawabs of Oudh who ruled in independent possession of Oudh for three generations *viz.* (i) Saadat Khan (1724-39) (ii) Safdar Jang (1739-54) and (iii) Shuja-ud-daulah (1754-75) with the title of Nawab Wazir, i.e., First Minister of the Mughul empire. The defeat of the third Nawab Wazir, Shuja-ud-daulah (*q.v.*) at the hands of the English at the battle of Buxar in 1764 marked the beginning of the decline of the power of Oudh. Yet in 1774 Oudh incorporated, with British help, Rohilkhand and got the opportunity for misgoverning the newly acquired territories. During the rule of Shuja-ud-daulah's son and successor Asaf-ud-daulah (1775-97) Oudh came to be looked upon by the growing British power in India as a buffer state between it and the Maratha dominions. In 1797 on the death of Asaf-ud-daulah the throne of Oudh was first occupied for a short while by his illegitimate son Wazir Ali (1797-98) who was deposed by the English who now placed on the throne of Oudh Saadat Khan, a brother of Asaf-ud-daulah. The new Nawab who ruled from 1798 to 1814 made a treaty with the Company by which he agreed to cede to the Company the fort of Allahabad, to pay an annual subsidy of 76 lakhs of rupees and to hold no communication with any foreign state except the English in India in return for the Company's promise to undertake the entire defence of Oudh. Oudh thus practically became a protected feudatory state under the Company. This reduced status of

Oudh was further emphasized in 1801 when Oudh was forced by the Company to surrender to it Rohilkhand and the Lower Doab, that is to say, the territories lying between the Ganges and the Jumna, covering almost one-half of the territories of Oudh. The internal administration of the other half was left to the Nawab. Sa'adat Khan's son and successor, Ghazi-ud-din Haidar, (1814-27) was honoured with the title of King by Lord Hastings (*q.v.*), Governor-General, in 1819, but Oudh continued to be misgoverned by him and his successors, namely, Nasir-ud-din Haidar (1827-37), Ali Shah (1837-42), Amjad Ali Shah (1842-47) and Wazid Ali Shah (1847-56). The last was deposed on the ground of misgovernment in 1856 and Oudh was formally annexed to the British Indian empire. Lucknow, which was the capital of the Nawab of Oudh, was beautified by the Nawabs with mosques and palaces and developed into a seat of Muslim culture, music, pelf and immorality. The annexation of Oudh led to the disbandment of the Nawab's troops and to their unemployment resulting in a change in the financial condition of the large body of persons who had been hangers-on of the Nawab and caused great disaffection which was one of the contributory causes of the Sepoy Mutiny (*q.v.*).

Oudh, the Begums of—*see ante* under Begums of Oudh.

Oudh Tenancy Act—was passed in 1868 mainly owing to the support of the Governor-General, Sir John Lawrence. In Oudh a large and influential class of *Talukdars*, mostly Rajputs, had come into existence during the regime of the Nawabs, who badly exploited the peasants who were practically mere tenants-at-will. The Oudh Tenancy Act sought to improve the condition of the cultivators in Oudh by providing that cultivators who satisfied certain specified conditions were to be granted occupancy rights in the soil, that cultivators whose rents were raised should be compensated for unexhausted improvements, and that rent itself should be increased only after application to a court of law and equity. It was a very useful and beneficent piece of legislation.

Outram, Sir James (1803-63)—was one of the heroes of the English in the Sepoy Mutiny. He came to India as a cadet in 1819. His remarkable energy earned him a promotion the next year as an Adjutant at Poona. In 1825 he was sent to Khandesh where he profoundly impressed the Bhils and recruited from them a light infantry corps which was effectively employed in checking outrages and plunder by local robbers. From

1835 to 1838 he was Political Agent in Gujarat. In 1838 he was in the Afghan war in which he gained great fame by his personal bravery in capturing a banner of the enemy before the fortress of Ghazni. In 1839 he was appointed Political Agent in Sind where he showed his personality and love of justice by strongly opposing the policy of his superior, Sir Charles Napier, which led to a war with the Amirs of Sind (*q.v.*). But when war broke out he heroically defended the Residency at Hyderabad against 8000 Baluchis and earned from Sir Charles Napier the title of "the Bayard of India". In 1854 he was appointed Resident at Lucknow, carried out the annexation of Oudh in 1856 and became the first Chief Commissioner of the province. On the outbreak of the Mutiny he was away in Persia from where he was hurriedly recalled and placed in command of the Bengal army charged with the protection of the region from Calcutta to Cawnpore. He very materially helped Havelock (*q.v.*) in relieving Lucknow, then evacuated the Residency completely outwitting the sepoys and later on again helped Sir Colin Campbell in the final recovery of Lucknow. He fought in the Mutiny displaying the cunning of a fox combined with the courage of a tiger and earned from the Parliament thanks, a baronetcy and a pension. His equestrian statue in Calcutta was an excellent piece of sculpture. He retired in 1860 and died in England in 1863.

Oxenden, Sir George—was the President of the East India Company's factory at Surat and governor of Bombay from 1662 to 1669. He had the distinction of having gallantly defended Surat against Shivaji in 1664 and won the praise of Emperor Aurangzeb.

P

Padmabhusana —is the third highest honour conferrable by the Republic of India, the first being *Bharat-ratna* and the second *Padmavibhusana*.

Padmasambhava—a famous Indian monk, who flourished in the middle of the eighth century A.D., was said to have been a prince of Oddiyan who became a Buddhist monk. On the invitation of the Tibetan king Trisong-Detsen he went to Tibet where he preached a Tantrik form of Buddhism. He was credited by the Tibetans with supernatural powers by which he could effect miracles. He founded in Tibet a sect of the Buddhists who are called the Red Hat by Western scholars. He initiated many Tibetans including the king himself to his discipleship. He built a monastery at Samye which soon became a centre of learning. The religious system that he introduced in Tibet is known as Lamaism and the Tibetans look upon him with as much respect as on Buddha. (Snellgrove, D. C., *Buddhist Himalaya*).

Padma-sree—is the fourth honour conferrable by the Republic of India.

Padmini—the queen-consort of Rana Ratan Singh of Mewar, was exquisitely beautiful, and, according to Rajput tradition, Sultan Ala-ud-din Khalji was so infatuated for Padmini that he invaded Chitor in 1303 in order to take forcible possession of the queen. The Rajputs offered stout resistance, but failed in defending the fort of Chitor. When further resistance appeared to be impossible Padmini, along with the other ladies within the fort, performed the horrible rite, the *Jauhar*, by throwing themselves on funeral pyres that were kindled in the subterranean caves within the fort of Chitor.

Paes, Domingos—a Portuguese traveller, visited Vijayanagar in 1522 when Krishnadeva Raya (*q.v.*) was the ruling sovereign. Paes has left a very interesting account of the personal habits of the king as well as of the social and economic conditions of the people. He believed that the city of Vijayanagar was as large as Rome, was inhabited by a 'countless population' and was "the best provided city in the World". He saw that one room in the palace was "all of ivory" from the roof to the floor. The court ceremonial was extremely elaborate and the royal army was very large. (Sewell, *Forgotten Empire*)

Paithan—a city on the upper Godavari valley, earlier called Pratisthana, was the capital of the early Andhra kings (*q.v.*).

Pakistan—is a word coined in 1933 by Choudhri Rahmat Ali. In it 'P' stands for the Panjab, 'A' for Afghans (Frontier Province), 'K' for Kashmir and 'S' for Sind. The whole word means 'Land of the Pure'. It is to be observed that the four provinces included in the composition of the term were the provinces which had a Muhammadan majority in their populations. In 1930 Sir Muhammad Iqbal had suggested the Union of the N.W. Frontier Province, Baluchistan, Sind and Kashmir as a Muslim state within a federated India. In 1940 the establishment of Pakistan was adopted by the Muslim League as its official aim. As the impact of the transfer of power in India from British to Indian hands drew nearer the Muslims in India became apprehensive of being placed under the rule of a Hindu majority and under the leadership of M. A. Jinnah (*q.v.*) demanded the creation of what they called Pakistan which was to consist of the North-West Frontier Province, Panjab, Sind, Kashmir and Bengal by partitioning India into Hindustan and Pakistan. The demand was unhistorical and against the best interests of India and of her people as a whole, but in pursuit of their policy of divide and rule the British had supported the Muhammadan claim for separate communal electorates too long to refuse their demand for a separate state. Backed by some of the British officials, the Muhammadans began what they called 'direct action' leading to loot, arson, rape and murder all over the country, especially in the Muslim majority provinces of the Panjab, Sind and Bengal. The situation became anarchical and the Indian National Congress accepted independence on the condition of the division of the country and the creation of Pakistan in August, 1947. Pakistan came to consist of the North-West Frontier, Baluchistan, Sind, West Panjab and East Bengal; and it was thus not exactly the compact state that was demanded by the Muslim League, as Kashmir stayed out and later on opted for Hindustan and East Bengal (now called East Pakistan) was separated by more than a thousand miles from West Pakistan comprising the North-West Frontier, Sind and West Panjab. The first capital was at Karachi and its first Governor-General was Mr. Muhammad Ali Jinnah. It was organised into an Islamic state with a democratic parliamentary system of government based on representative institutions. But the constitution failed to work smoothly after the death of Jinnah in 1948. Many changes have since taken place, and Pakistan is now an Islamic theocratic state with a President who is a military man, (Ayub Khan) (1958) and holds office by indirect election in which only 80,000 persons have votes in a country inhabited by about 80,000,000 persons. In its foreign policy it is closely associated with the U.S.A. and is also a member of the SEATO and the CENTO. It has also recently entered into a strange alliance with Communist China with which the U.S.A. would have no dealings. In foreign policy its main principle seems to be opposition to India which earned its hostility especially on account of the accession of Kashmir to India. In the economic sphere it has been receiving large aids from the U.S.A. which has also given it vast military supplies which have turned Pakistan into a jingoistic state. At the moment of writing it is actually engaged in a war with the Republic of India which commenced on the 5th August, 1965.

Pala dynasty, the—was established in Bengal in about A.D. 750 by Gopala who was elected to the throne for the purpose of ending the anarchy from which the country had been suffering for some time past. As the names of all the eighteen kings of the dynasty founded by Gopala ended in the word 'pala' so the dynasty has been called the Pala dynasty. The dynasty ruled over Bengal from about A.D. 750 to about A.D. 1155 and over Bihar as well till the Muhammadan conquest in 1199. The chronology of the Palas, especially after the fourteenth king, Ramapala (c. A.D. 1077-1120), is confusing, but the following list may provisionally be accepted as correct: (i) Gopala (A.D. 750-70), (ii) Dharmapala (770-810), (iii) Devapala (810-50), (iv) Vigrahapala [or Surapala] (850-54), (v) Narayana-pala (854-908), (vi) Rajyapala (908-40), (vii) Gopala II (940-60), (viii) Vigrahapala II (960-88), (ix) Mahipala I (988-1038), (x) Nayapala (1038-55), (xi) Vigrahapala III (1055-70), (xii) Mahipala II (1070-75), (xiii) Surapala II (1075-77), (xiv) Ramapala (1077-1120), (xv) Kumarapala (1120-25), (xvi) Gopala III (1125-40), (xvii) Madanapala (1140-55) and (xviii) Govindapala (1155-59). The second king, Dharmapala (q.v.) was the greatest king of the dynasty who extended his conquests to Kanauj and held his own in a triangular contest with the Pratiharas and the Rashtrakutas. His son and successor, Devapala (q.v.) also won many military triumphs; he transferred his capital to Monghyr from Patali-putra and received an embassy from the Sumatran king, Balaputradeva. After Devapala (810-50) the decline of the power of the Palas began, mainly on account of the weakness of the succeeding kings and the aggression of the Gurjara-Pratihara kings. During the reign of the ninth king, Mahipala I, the Chola king Rajendra (q.v.) invaded the Gangetic basin in about A.D. 1023. There was a temporary revival of the power of the dynasty during the rule of Ramapala (1077-1120), but by the middle of the twelfth century the Palas lost Bengal to the Senas (q.v.) and later on in 1199 their power in Bihar also was overthrown by the Muhammadans under Iktiaruddin Muhammad, son of Bakhtiyar (q.v.). The Palas were Buddhists and were great patrons of Buddhist learning. The famous universities of Nalanda (q.v.) and Vikramasila (q.v.) received their munificent patronage. The famous Buddhist monk, Atisha (q.v.) lived in the reign of the tenth king, Nayapala, and went on invitation to Tibet. The Palas were great patrons of art and architecture and are known to have patronised the great artists, Dhiman (*q.v.*) and Vitapala (*q.v.*). No building of the Pala period appears to have survived but the interest that the Pala kings took in public works is remembered by many large tanks which they excavated, especially in the Dinajpur district. (Majumdar, R. C., *Hist. of Bengal*, Vol. I).

Pala dynasty of Kamarupa—is to be distinguished from the Pala dynasty of Bengal and Bihar. It was founded in Kamarupa in about A.D. 1000 by Brahmapala who is said to have been elected to the throne. From his loins sprang a dynasty of seven kings, namely, Ratnapala, Indrapala, Gopala, Harsapala, Dharmapala and Jayapala. These kings ruled over Kamarupa from the beginning of the eleventh century to the early part of the twelfth century. The second king Ratnapala enjoyed a long reign of more than 26 years, established a new capital at Durjaya which has not yet been identified and bore the title of *Parameswara Paramabhattaraka Maharajadhiraja*. The last king, Jayapala, was probably dethroned by the Bengal king, Ramapala (*q.v.*) who is credited with the conquest of Kamarupa. (Bhattacharya, P., *Kamarupa-Shasanavali*).

Pallava dynasty, the—ruled over the modern districts of north and south Arcot, Madras, Trichinopoly and Tanjore. At the height of their power their dominions extended along the eastern coast from the Orissa frontier on the north to the southern Pennar river on the south and penetrated deeply into the west over the Deccan and South India. When exactly the Pallava dynasty was founded and by whom is not definitely known. The earliest Pallava king referred to in a north Indian record was Vishnugopa of Kanchi who was captured and then liberated by Samudragupta (*q.v.*) about the middle of the fourth century A.D. The history of the dynasty becomes more definite from the reign of Simhavishnu who came to the throne in the latter half of the sixth century A.D. From his time for the next two centuries there was a long line of strong Pallava kings, namely, Mahendravarman I (*c.* A.D. 600-25), Narasimhavarman I (*c.* A.D. 625-45), Mahendravarman II, Parameshwaravarman I, Narasimhavarman II, Parameshwaravarman II, Mahendravarman III, Nandivarman I (*c.* 717-82), Dantivarman, Nandivarman II and Aparajita. The main feature of Pallava history was a perennial war with the Chalukyas of Vatapi in the earlier part and with the Rashtrakutas of Manyakheta in the latter part of the rule of the Pallava dynasty. Mahendravarman I was a great builder whose name is immortalized by many rock-cut temples and the Mahendra Tank which he excavated. He was defeated by his Chalukya contemporary Pulakeshin II (*q.v.*) in about A.D. 610 and was obliged to cede the province of Vengi to the Chalukya invader. Mahendra's son and successor, Narasimhavarman (*q.v.*) inflicted in A.D. 642 a crushing defeat on Pulakeshin II, took his capital, Vatapi, and killed him. But the Chalukyas had their revenge in A.D. 655 when the Pallava king Parameshwaravarman was defeated by the Chalukya Vikramaditya I who even captured the Pallava capital Kanchi. This marked the beginning of the decline of the Pallava power. In about A.D. 740 the reigning Pallava king, Nandivarman I, was decisively defeated by the Chalukya Vikramaditya II who again captured the Pallava capital, Kanchi. Nandivarman's successor Dantivarman was vanquished by the Rashtrakuta king Govinda III (*q.v.*). The next Pallava king tried to strengthen himself by marrying a daughter of the Rashtrakuta king, Amoghavarsha I. But even this alliance could not long support the Pallava dynasty whose last king, Aparajita Pallava, was vanquished by the Chola king Aditya I about the close of the ninth century A.D. and the Pallava dominions passed under the Chola kings. The earlier Pallava kings were great builders. They founded the town of Mamallapuram or Mahabalipuram, erected there the wonderful Rathas or terraced buildings, each of which is cut out from a great rock boulder. These were decorated with remarkable relief sculptures. Other Pallava monuments are to be found in the well-planned city of Kanchi which they turned into a city of temples. The Pallava kings were mostly Brahmanical Hindus, some being specially devoted to Vishnu and others to Siva.

Palmer, General Sir Arthur Power (1840-1904)—entered the Indian army as an officer in 1857, took part in suppressing the Sepoy Mutiny in 1857-58, in the campaign against the Mohmands in 1863-64, in the Dafla expedition in 1874-75, in the Afghan War of 1878-79 and in the Tirah campaign in 1897-98. He was the Commander-in-Chief in India from 1900 till his retirement in 1902. He introduced many improvements in the British Indian Army.

Palmer & Co., the affair of—attracted public notice. Palmer & Co. was a house of financiers who had a branch in the Nizam's capital at Hyderabad. Lady Rumbold, a partner in the firm, was the ward of Lord Hastings, Governor-General (1813-23) (*q.v.*). Though there was an Act of Parliament against the financial dealings of Europeans with Indian states Lord Hastings, through his affection for Lady Rumbold, permitted the firm to advance loans to the Nizam and failed to intervene even after irregularities had been exposed by the new Resident, Charles Metcalfe. The affair should have led to his recall, but he was permitted to continue in his high office through the intervention of King George IV, but it permanently damaged his relations with the Court of Directors.

Palmerston, Lord—a prominent British statesman, was the Foreign Secretary of England from 1830 to 1841. He re-acted sharply and strongly to the treaty of Unkiar-Skelessi which Russia concluded with Turkey in 1833 and which enabled Russia to acquire certain influence over Turkey which Palmerston considered might be used to the disadvantage of the British empire in India. Lord Palmerston was therefore anxious to turn Afghanistan into a sphere of influence of the British so that Afghanistan might be used for putting pressure on Russia. This anti-Russian policy of Lord Palmerston pushed Lord Auckland into the pursuit of a course of policy which culminated in the First Afghan War (1839-42) (*q.v.*).

Palpa, the battle of—was fought in the course of the Gurkha War (1814-16) between the British Indian army and the Gurkhas in which a British Indian army was defeated by the Gurkhas who were, however, ultimately, vanquished.

Palmyra—is a town in the Syrian desert. It was an important emporium of trade between India and the west in the Kushan period (*q.v.*).

Pamirs, the—25,000 ft. high mountain range, generally described as the 'roof of the world', separates India from the U.S.S.R. The Aryans are supposed to have migrated across it. In historical times the Kushan king Kanishka (*q.v.*) sent an army across it to invade China. In the fourth century A.D. Fa-Hien, the Chinese pilgrim, crossed it in order to pass into India. In the seventh century another Chinese pilgrim, Hiuen-Tsang, crossed it on his way back from India to China. In A.D. 657 a Chinese envoy named Wang-hiuen-tse, who came to India to offer robes at the Buddhist holy places, returned to China by the Pamir route. With the expansion of the Russian power in Central Asia, the Pamirs acquired a new strategic importance in the twentieth century. (*see* Panjdeh incident)

Panagal, Raja of—was the leader of the Justice or non-Brahman party and was appointed in 1921 as the Chief Minister in Madras in order to implement the constitution established by the Government of India Act, 1919. His ministry carried out some reforms in the spheres of education and management of temple endowments.

Pan Chao—was a Chinese general who some time between A.D. 73 and 102, advanced through Khotan, repulsed an invasion by Kadphises II and compelled him to pay tribute to the Chinese Emperor, Ho-ti (A.D. 89-105).

Pandavas, the—were the sons of Pandu and were five brothers. The great epic *Mahabharata* narrates the story of their rivalry and battle with the Kauravas.

Pandit, Vidyasagar—*see* Vidyasagar.

Pandit, Mrs. Vijaylakshmi—born in 1900, is a talented daughter of Pandit Matilal Nehru (*q.v.*) and the sister of Pandit Jawaharlal Nehru (*q.v.*). She took a prominent part in the nationalist and liberation movement in India and is a great orator. She has held many high offices since Indian independence including the post of India's High Commissioner in England (1955-61) and India's Ambassador to the U.S.S.R. (1947-49) as well as to the U.S.A. (1949-51). She was the President of the U.N. General Assembly in 1954. She was the Governor of Maharashtra from 1962 and resigned that office in October, 1964, in order to resume an active part in the country's politics. She is now a member of India's Parliament.

Pandita Ramabai (1858-1922)—was one of the few Indian ladies who availed themselves of Western education in the nineteenth century. She became a widow in her childhood, embraced Christianity, and opened a home for widows. She paid a lecturing visit to the U.S.A. where she tried to raise funds for establishing in India an institution for the education of Indian ladies, especially Hindu widows. She made a great impression on the Western world by her erudition and eloquence which had earned her the title of "Saraswati."

Pandit Rao—was one of the *astapradhan* (eight chiefs) who formed the Ministry of Shivaji (*q.v.*). He was the Royal chaplain and was in charge of the religious affairs of the Maratha state.

Pandyas, the—gave their name to the region between the Southern Vellaru river on the north and Cape Comorin on the south and the Coromandel coast on the east to the Achchankovil Pass leading to Travancore on the west. The Pandya kingdom was thus co-extensive with the modern districts of Madura and Tinnevelly and that part of Travancore in which Cape

Comorin is included. Its capital was Madura and it had extensive commercial relations with overseas countries which were carried on through its ports, Korkai, and, later on, Kayal. It was known to be a rich and flourishing country to Pliny in the first century of the Christian era, to the *Periplus* (*c*. A.D. 80) and to Ptolemy (*c*. A.D. 140). Megasthenes who visited India in the fourth century B.C., had heard of it and attributed its origin to the daughter of Heracles. That is of course a myth, but in the Pandya kingdom the matriarchal system prevailed. The Sanskrit grammarian, Katyayana, who flourished in the 4th century B.C., mentions the Pandyas. More definite information is supplied by Marco Polo (*q.v.*) who visited the Pandya kingdom twice, in A.D. 1288 and 1293, was much impressed by the wealth and magnificence of both the king and people of the realm. Though the Pandya kingdom occupied an important position in ancient Tamil literature not much definite information about its ancient history has yet been secured. The earliest Pandya king to whom a definite date (second century A.D.) can be assigned was Nedum-Cheliyan. The Pandya kingdom was at first a rival of the Pallavas (*q.v.*), but the latter appear to have gained the upper hand in the contest which lasted for centuries until at last the Pandya king was defeated by the Pallava king Aparajita in A.D. 862-63. But the Pallavas in their turn were subordinated by the Cholas whose supremacy the Pandya kings were also obliged to recognise from about the year A.D. 994 to the close of the thirteenth century. During this long period the Pandya kingdom had also to fight often with Ceylon. Whether independent or tributary, seventeen Pandya rajas are known to have ruled the country from A.D. 1100 to 1567, the most powerful of whom was Jatavarman Sundara who reigned from A.D. 1251 to 1271 and held sway over the whole of the eastern coast from Nellore to Cape Comorin. In 1310 the Pandya kingdom was over-run by the Muhammadans under Malik Kafur (*q.v.*), the general of Sultan Ala-ud-din Khalji. Thereafter the Pandya kings were reduced to the status of Polygars or local landlords. The Pandya kingdom, now called Ma'bar, remained under the Delhi sultanate till the reign of Muhammad Tughluq when its Muhammadan governor, Jalaluddin Ahsan Shah (*q.v.*), set himself up as an independent ruler in 1335. His dynasty ruled till 1378 when the country was absorbed into the Hindu kingdom of Vijayanagar.

Pangul, the battle of—was fought in A.D. 1420 between the

Bahmani sultan Firuz Shah and Deva Raya, the king of Vijayanagar. The Sultan was defeated and the Vijayanagar army occupied some of the eastern and southern districts of the Bahmani
kingdom. This defeat told so heavily on the Sultan's mind
and body that soon afterwards he retired from the administration and died.

Panini—the celebrated Sanskrit grammarian, flourished not later
than the fourth century B.C. He was the author of the *Astadhyayi*,
a most scientific grammar.

Panini—was a poet who is to be distinguished from the grammarian.
He was a Sanskrit poet of some merit and is remembered in
anthologies. (Keith, A. B., *History of Sanskrit Literature*).

Panipat—has been the scene of three decisive battles, each of
which profoundly influenced the course of Indian history. The
first battle of Panipat was fought on the 21st April, 1526 between Ibrahim Lodi (*q.v.*), the sultan of Delhi and Babur,
the Mughul invader. Ibrahim had an army of one lakh of
men while Babur had under him only 12,000 men and a large
park of artillery. Superior strategy and better generalship
combined with the effective use of the artillery enabled Babur
to win a decisive victory over Ibrahim Lodi who was killed
on the battlefield. The first battle of Panipat enabled Babur
to occupy Delhi and Agra and to establish the Mughul dynasty
in India. The second battle of Panipat was fought on the 5th
November, 1556, between Himu (*q.v.*), the capable Hindu
general and minister of the Afghan king, Adil Shah Sur (*q.v.*)
and Akbar who claimed the throne of his late father, Humayun
(*q.v.*). Himu had under him a much larger army than Akbar
and 1,500 elephants. Himu had initial success against the
Mughul army, but the day was decided by a chance arrow
which struck him in the eye. He lost conciousness and his army,
deprived of their leader, fled in confusion. Himu was captured,
taken to the presence of the young Akbar and was put to death.
The second battle of Panipat enabled Akbar to occupy Delhi
and Agra. It brought to a close the Mughul-Afghan contest
for the throne of Delhi in favour of the Mughuls who continued to hold that throne for the next three hundred years.
The third battle of Panipat was fought on the 14th January, 1761,
between the Afghan invader, Ahmad Shah Abdali (*q.v.*) and
the Marathas who came as protectors and auxiliaries of the
Mughul emperor, Shah Alam II (*q.v.*). The Maratha general,
Sadasiva Rao Bhao, was out-generalled by Abdali who, helped
by Shuja-ud-daulah, the Nawab of Oudh and Najib Khan,

an influential Indian Muhammadan leader, decisively defeated the Marathas after a hard-fought battle in the course of which Sadasiva Rao Bhao along with the Peshwa's young son and many other Maratha leaders were killed. It was a disaster for the Marathas. The Peshwa, Balaji Baji Rao, died of a broken heart only six months after the battle. The third battle of Panipat decided the fate of India which was then hanging in the balance. It marked the failure of the Mughul Emperor to save himself even with the assistance of the hated Marathas. It so discredited the Peshwa that he could no longer hold under his unified control the Maratha confederacy which lost its cohesion and consequently the chance of establishing Maratha rule on the dissolution of the Mughul empire. It proved to be a Pyrrhic victory to Ahmad Shah Abdali, as he was soon obliged, by a threatened mutiny amongst his victorious army, to return to Afghanistan without being able to establish himself on the throne of Delhi. Lastly, the losses suffered by the Marathas, the eclipse of the imperial power of the Mughuls and the ineptitude and want of cohesion amongst the Indian Muhammadans facilitated the growth of the British power in India.

Panjab, the (also spelt Punjab)—is the land of the five rivers, viz. the Jhelum, Chinab, Ravi, Beas and Sutlej—all tributaries of the Indus. It is a triangular tract of territory of which the Indus and the Sutlej form the two sides and the lower Himalayan range the base. It is connected with the trans-Himalayan countries on the north-west by four passes of which the chief is the Khyber. It has, therefore, received immigrants from the west in all ages and is a sort of an ethnological museum. Prior to the coming of the Europeans across the seas all the invaders who raided India entered this sub-continent through the Panjab and left some marks of themselves on its population. Civilisation flourished in the Panjab in the dim past, as has been shown by the recent finds of what is called the Indus-valley civilisation (*q.v.*). In historical times the Panjab was included within the Achaemenian empire of Darius I (*q.v.*) in the fifth century B.C. but by the time it was invaded by Alexander, the king of Macedon, in 326 B.C. the Panjab had come to be divided into a number of petty states which Alexander conquered. But his rule in the Panjab took no root and within a short time after his death the Panjab formed a part of the Maurya empire (*q.v.*). After the decline and fall of the Maurya empire the Panjab came to be successively raided and occupied by the Graeco-Bactrians, Sakas, Kushans and Hunas. Sultan Mahmud of Ghazni (A.D. 971-1030) (*q.v.*) was the first Moslem conqueror of the Panjab from whose descendants it was conquered by Shihab-ud-din Muhammad Ghuri in 1186. It formed a part of the Delhi sultanate from 1206 and continued to be a part of the Mughul empire till the middle of the eighteenth century when it became the theatre of a tripartite conflict amongst the Afghans, the Marathas and the Sikhs. The Maratha power was liquidated by the victory of the Afghan Ahmad Shah Abdali at the third battle of Panipat (*q.v.*) in 1761; and on the death of Ahmad Shah Abdali which followed soon, the Sikhs began to rise to power until Ranjit Singh (1790-1839) turned the Panjab into a strong and independent Sikh kingdom. But soon after his death disorder ensued in the state and as the result of two wars between the Sikhs and the British the Panjab was annexed to the British dominions in 1849. It continued to be a flourishing province of the British Indian Empire till 1947 when, following independence, the Panjab was divided into two parts—the predominantly Muslim west falling to the share of Pakistan (*q.v.*) and the predominantly Hindu east remaining a part of the parent state of India.

Panjab Land-Alienation Act—was passed in 1900 at the instance of the Viceroy, Lord Curzon. It provided for the protection of the cultivators of the soil from eviction by moneylenders to whom they might have mortgaged their lands. By laying down that lands of an hereditary cultivator cannot be henceforward sold in execution of a decree in a money-suit, it saved the cultivators of the Panjab from wholesale alienation of their lands.

Panjdeh—is a village and district a hundred miles due south from the important strategic city of Merv (*q.v.*). In 1884 the Russians occupied Merv, a town 150 miles from the frontier of Afghanistan, to which a fictitious importance had been attached by many English strategists and politicians. The occupation of Merv by Russia, therefore, caused much excitement in England which was further increased when in 1885 the Russians advanced further towards the Afghan frontier and drove off the Afghans from Panjdeh in March, 1885. England considered it a direct Russian threat to the integrity of Afghanistan, and, posing as the friend and protector of Afghanistan, but really in her own interest to check the advance of Russia towards India through Afghanistan, strongly resented the Russian action and an Anglo-Russian War over the question of the right to possess Panjdeh became imminent. The war was avoided by the shrewd common sense of Amir Abdur Rahman (*q.v.*) who correctly felt that an Anglo-Russian war over Panjdeh would necessarily turn Afghanistan into the theatre of war and he was determined to prevent this calamitous development. He declared that he was not sure whether Panjdeh really belonged to Afghanistan, that he did not particularly covet it and that he would be satisfied if the Zulfikar Pass, lying between Panjdeh and Afghanistan, was secured for him. This accommodating attitude of the Amir forced the hands of the British Government and on the recommendation of an Anglo-Russian Boundary Commission a boundary line was agreed upon in 1887 which left Panjdeh to the Russians and the Zulfikar Pass to Afghanistan. This left unchecked the Russian forward advance to the Pamirs.

Pant, Govinda Ballabh—was one of the leading members and leaders of the Indian National Congress. He became the Chief Minister in his native province of Uttar Pradesh after independence and conducted its administration very efficiently until he was taken into Nehru's Central Cabinet as the Home Minister. He proved himself to be a very great asset to the country and died in harness.

Pant Pratinidhi, **the**—was an office higher than that of the Peshwa (*q.v.*). The post was created by Raja Ram (*q.v.*), the second son of Shivaji, when he was a refugee at Gingee. The importance of the office of *Pant Pratinidhi* declined in the reign of Shahu (*q.v.*) as the Peshwa's position improved.

Pantaleon—was an Indo-Greek king who is remembered by the square coins that he issued. He has been assigned to *c*. 190-180 B.C.

Pan-Yang—a son of the Chinese general Pan-Chao (*q.v.*), was, like his father, the Chinese Governor of Turkistan. He was not only a general and administrator but also a historian. His statement that Khotan was lost to the Chinese empire in A.D. 152 is in agreement with the belief that Kanishka (*c*. A.D. 120-162) conquered Khotan and the neighbouring region between A.D. 125 and 160.

Paragal Khan—a general of Husain Shah, king of Bengal (A.D. 1493-1519), was a patron of Bengali literature and patronised the composition of a Bengali version of the *Mahabharata* by Parameswar who was the earliest translator of the *Mahabharata* into Bengali. (Sarkar, J. N., *Hist. of Bengal.* Vol. II).

Pargana, **the**—was an administrative unit into which a *Sarkar* (district) was sub-divided. It was introduced by Akbar.

Paramara (also called Pawar) dynasty, the—was founded in Malwa, the region north of the Narmada, anciently known as Avanti, by a chief named Upendra or Krishnaraja early in the ninth century. His capital was Dhara. The dynasty comprised eight kings of whom the seventh, named Munja, and the eighth, Bhoja (*q.v.*), the nephew of Munja, were the most famous. Munja carried on a long struggle with the Chalukyas of Kalyani and died in a battle with them in A.D. 995. His successor, Bhoja (A.D. 1018-60) perished in a battle with the combined armies of the kings of Gujarat and Chedi and with his death the Paramara dynasty lost its power and glory, though it lasted as a purely local power until the beginning of the thirteenth century when it was superseded by the Tomaras (*q.v.*). The Paramara kings, especially Raja Munja and Raja Bhoja, were both very learned persons and were ardent patrons of learning and men of letters.

Paramardi (or Parmal)—was the last Chandella king (*c.* A.D. 1166-1203) of Jejakabhukti (*q.v.*) to enjoy the position of an independent king of importance. He ascended the throne at the age of five and ruled the kingdom well until 1182 when he became involved in a war with the Chauhan king, Prithviraj (*q.v.*), who defeated him and sacked his capital. Before he could recover from the effects of this defeat, Paramardi was attacked by the Muhammadans under Qutb-ud-din (*q.v.*), the sultan of Delhi, stood a siege at Kalanjar which he was obliged to surrender and was very likely killed. With him fell the greatness of the Chandellas.

Paramartha—(A.D. 499-569) a famous Buddhist monk and scholar, wrote between A.D. 546 and 569 his famous book, *Life of Vasubandhu*, in which he has given an account of the Buddhist Council convoked by Kanishka (*q.v.*).

Parantaka I—the son and successor of the Chola king, Aditya (*q.v.*) ruled from A.D. 907 to 949. He was a mighty warrior and largely extended the boundaries of the Chola kingdom by capturing Madura, the capital of the Pandyas. He also invaded Ceylon.

Parantaka II—a grandson of Parantaka I (*q.v.*), was the Chola king from A.D. 956 to 973.

Parihara—*see* Pratihara.

Parinirvana—means the decease of Gautama Buddha (*q.v.*).

Parmal—*see* Paramardi.

Paropanisadai—was the name given by classical historians to that part of Afghanistan which lies round the city of Kabul which was its capital. This territory along with Aria (Herat region) and Arachosia (Qandahar region) and Gedrosia (Baluchistan) was surrendered by Seleucos Nikator to Chandragupta Maurya (*q.v.*).

Parsaji, Bhonsla—the son and successor of Raghuji Bhonsla (*q.v.*), was an imbecile and was murdered in 1817, a year after his accession by his cousin, Appa Shahib (*q.v.*).

Parsees, the—constitute a small community of Zoroastrian Persians who fled from Persia on the conquest of the country by the Muhammadan Arabs in the seventh century. Keen on the preservation of their religion and culture, this small community sought shelter in India, settled first at Sanjan on the Gujarat coast, moved later on to Bombay, have flourished there very much and are now one of the richest and most advanced minorities in India. Dadabhai Naoroji (*q.v.*), who was the first Indian to be elected to the British House of Commons, was a Parsee and so are the famous Tatas. The Parsees generally have great faith in astrology and in their marriage ceremonies the nuptial benediction is offered first in Zend and then in Sanskrit by their priests. (Karaka, D.F., *Hist. of the Parsees*).

Parsvanath—was the twenty-third *Tirthankara* (step-maker i.e., patriarch) of the Jains. He flourished about two centuries before Mahavira (*q.v.*) and was born in a princely family of Benares. He founded the Jain religion and enjoined on his disciples the four vows of non-injury, truthfulness, abstention from stealing and non-attachment. His religion was later on broadened by Mahavira (*q.v.*) in the sixth century B.C.

Partition of Bengal—was, first, effected in 1905 by the Viceroy Lord Curzon on the plea that the province of Bengal, as it was then constituted, inclusive of Bihar and Orissa, was too large to be administered by a Lieutenant-Governor and led to the neglect of the districts in Eastern Bengal where the Muhammadan population predominated. Therefore, fifteen districts of North and Eastern Bengal comprised in the Rajshahi, Dacca and Chittagong Divisions, were amalgamated with Assam and a new province called Eastern Bengal and Assam was created and separated from the old Bengal which continued to be, along with Bihar and Orissa, one administrative unit. This measure was greatly resented by the people of Bengal, especially by the Hindus, who held that it meant the partition of a nation, an attempt to divide a homogeneous people, a deliberate and sinister attack upon the tradition, history and language of the people, and as a means for keeping under check the political aspirations of the people. In spite of the province-wide agitation against it the measure was carried and enforced. The people of Bengal tried to prevent its implementation by insisting on the boycott of British goods, especially cotton textiles, and the observance of the 30th Asvin (17th Oct.), on which the partition was effected, as a day of national mourning and unity. The Government did not like this public demonstration of disaffection and tried to suppress it by an attempt to win over the Muhammadans by promising them special favour in the new province and by resorting to repression which was carried to the extent of punishing the shouting in public of the popular slogan *Vande-mataram* (Hail mother, i.e., Motherland). Repression drove discontent underground and terrorism took its birth in Bengal. Attempts were made on the lives of European officers as well as on those of the more ardent of their Indian supporters. The Government resorted to severe measures of repression. But all proved unavailing. The Bengalees could not be reconciled to the partition which was, therefore, modified in December, 1911 by a royal proclamation made at the Delhi Durbar. The 15 districts of Eastern Bengal were separated from Assam and reunited with those of Western Bengal which, again, was separated from Bihar and Orissa. United Bengal was created into a Governor's province—a solution for the alleged inefficiency in administration which had been suggested to Lord Curzon but rejected by him.

Bengal was partitioned a second time in 1947 as a sequence of the partition of India (*q.v.*) into Pakistan and India which was made a condition of the grant of independence to them. As a consequence of this partition all the Bengal districts of Dacca and Chittagong divisions along with some districts of Rajshahi and Presidency Divisions were separated from Bengal and constituted East Pakistan.

Partition of India—was effected in 1947 as a condition of the inauguration of the independence of India. On the insistent demand of the Muhammadans and in pursuit of the old British policy of divide and rule India was partitioned, with the consent of the leaders of the Indian National Congress and of the Muslim League, into Pakistan and India on the basis of the religion of the majority of the peoples inhabiting the different provinces of India. The North-West Frontier, West Punjab, Sind and East Bengal were joined together to form a new state, called Pakistan, which became an Islamic state and the rest of India constituted independent India which became a secular Federal Republic called India. The partition of India in 1947 has caused great hardship to many and is regretted by many more, but it has been accepted by the people at large as a necessity.

Parviz, Prince—was the second son of Emperor Jahangir. After his elder brother, Prince Khusru, was blinded Parviz was recognized as the heir-apparent. He held important commands against Mewar, in Allahabad and in the Deccan. He stood by his imperial father when his younger brother Prince Khurram (later on Shah Jahan) revolted against the Emperor and defeated Prince Khurram in 1624 at the battle of Damdama near Allahabad. Parviz was then appointed Governor of Gujarat but he died in 1626 from the results of overdrinking.

Pataliputra—was the famous capital of the kings of Magadha. It was situated at the confluence of the Son and the Ganges, near the modern cities of Patna and Bankipore. The fort at Pataliputra was built by king Ajatasatru (*c.* 494-467 B.C.) and his grandson, Udaya, (*c.* 443-418 B.C.) founded the city of Kusumapura on the Ganges under the protection of the fort at Pataliputra. The two sites soon merged together and developed under the Maurya king, Chandragupta, as the great metropolitan city of Pataliputra. The city was defended by a massive timber palisade with 570 towers and 64 gates. The palisade was protected by a deep moat filled with water from the Son. It contained the imperial palace, the ruins of which have been found near the modern village of Kumrahar. The palace was so grand that Megasthenes (*q.v.*) believed that it excelled the palaces of Susa and Ekbatana. It was built of timber and has practically perished. Asoka later on built within the city a stone palace which has also disappeared but which was still in existence in the first decade of the fifth century A.D. when Fa-Hien visited Pataliputra and looked so magnificent that the Chinese pilgrim believed that it could not have been built by mortal hands, and was executed by spirits. Pataliputra continued to be the capital of the Sungas (*q.v.*) and the Kanvas (*q.v.*), was invaded by the Orissan king Kharavela (*q.v.*) and also perhaps by the Indo-Greek king Menander (*q.v.*), but survived all these raids and was the capital of the Gupta emperors who ruled from A.D. 320 to 500 and was the centre of the culture and civilisation of the golden age in Indian history. The city declined in importance after the fall of the Gupta dynasty. It lost the position of primacy in the seventh century A.D. to Kanauj (*q.v.*). Later on the Palas (*q.v.*) transferred their capital to Mudgagiri (modern Monghyr) in the ninth century. After the Muhammadan conquest it declined further and the city of Patna (*q.v.*) which now stands very near the old site of Pataliputra, has since been only a provincial or State headquarters.

Patanjali—was the celebrated commentator on the Sanskrit grammar, the *Astadhyayi* of Panini (*q.v.*) on which he wrote the famous commentary known as the *Mahabhasya* (The Great Commentary). He is believed to have been a contemporary of King Pushyamitra Sunga (*q.v.*) and to have flourished in the second century B.C.

Patanjali—was a great Brahmanical philosopher who wrote in Sanskrit the celebrated work, the *Yoga Sutra*. His date is uncertain but he is to be distinguished from his equally celebrated grammarian namesake. (Keith, A. B., *Hist. of Sanskrit Lit.*. p 490)

Patel, Vallabhbhai, Sardar (1875-1950)—a renowned Indian patriot and politician, was born on the 31st October, 1875 in Gujarat and began his career as a lawyer in the small town of Podhara but later on went to England, became a Barrister-at-Law and began practising in Ahmedabad where he came into contact with Mahatma Gandhi. He soon joined the Indian National Congress, took a leading part in the Bardoli *Satyagraha* movement and was sent to prison. His success in organising the Bardoli peasants drew him much nearer Gandhiji who gave him the title of Sardar. Patel gradually became a very prominent leader amongst the Congressmen. In 1931 he became the President of the Congress, took a very prominent part in the 'Quit India' movement started by Mahatma Gandhi in 1942 and was imprisoned till 1945. He was detained again along with all the other members of the Congress Working Committee, but was released with them, joined the "Interim Government" set up in 1946 as the Home Member and tried in vain to stop the communal riots that had overtaken the country. His success was limited. He agreed to the partition of India as a condition of the inauguration of her independence and became the Home Minister and Deputy Prime Minister after independence and held the posts till his death on the 15th December, 1950. As Deputy Prime Minister and Home Minister of the Federal Republic of India he showed great strength of mind and determination which justified the title of 'iron man' popularly conferred on him. His great achievement was the peaceful integration of the states of the Indian princes with the Federal Republic of India. He also took a prominent part in enabling Kashmir to accede to India after it had been invaded by Pakistan in 1947. His last great achievement was the 'police action' against the Nizam of Hyderabad which forced the merger of that important state with the Indian republic and prevented the creation of a third independent state or at least of a Pakistani island in the Deccan. He showed his usual cool courage at the time of the murder of Mahatma Gandhi and prevented what might have burst out into a terrible civil war by declaring immediately after the murder the truth that the culprit was a Hindu and by taking adequate measures for maintaining public peace and order.

Patel, Vithaldas Javeri (1873-1933)—was a great fighter in the cause of Indian nationalism. Elder brother of Sardar Patel, he was born at Nadiad in Gujarat on the 27th September, 1873 and died in Vienna on the 22nd October, 1933. He was called to the Bar in 1905, began practising as an advocate, but soon gave more attention to the Indian political movement. He led a strong public agitation against the Rowlatt Acts (*q.v.*) was elected to the Indian Legislative Assembly, resigned his seat in accordance with the non-co-operation policy of the Congress but soon joined the Swarajist (*q.v.*) party and was re-elected to the Indian Legislative Assembly of which he became the first elected non-official President in which capacity he defeated the official Public Safety Bill by his casting vote and forbade the police to enter the Assembly Hall during the session. He resigned the Presidentship in 1930 by way of protest against the detention of the Congress leaders and was himself detained in prison. The imprisonment broke his health, and in order to recoup it he went to Europe. In Vienna he met Netaji Subhas Bose whom he implicitly trusted and he bequeathed to Netaji two lakhs of rupees to be spent at his discretion for national work. Soon afterwards he died in Vienna. On his death in 1933 his younger brother, Sardar Patel, in spite of his adherence to the principles of non-co-operation, filed a suit in a British court in India and got the bequest of his deceased elder brother nullified. V. J. Patel was a great patriot whom even the British in India feared in the hey-day of their power.

Pathans, the—represent the tribal peoples inhabiting the frontier region between India and Afghanistan. The term has sometimes been loosely used as in Thomas' *Chronicles of the Pathan Kings* where the term has been used to denote all the Muslim sultans of Delhi from Qutb-ud-din to Ibrahim Lodi. But most of the dynasties of the sultans of Delhi were of Turkish origin, the Lodis, and probably the Khaljis, being the exceptions. Sher Shah was of Afghan origin and his dynasty may be called Pathan. The Pathans on the frontier are divided into various tribes like the Waziris and the Afridis and continued till recent times to be more or less nomadic peoples who considered occasional raids on India as a legitimate means of livelihood. Many of them are astute money-lenders who come to India and thrive by lending money at exorbitant rates of interest.

Patiala—is the name of a city as well as of a former princely state, about 125 miles to the north-west of Delhi. The state was founded by a chief of the Phulkian *misl* of the Sikhs in 1763. Dreading the expansion of the dominions of Ranjit Singh (*q.v.*) the Patiala state sought and obtained British protection in 1809 and was a protected state till its merger with the Indian Federal Republic in July, 1948. It at first formed a part of the Patiala and East Panjab States Union (called PEPSU), but in 1956 by the Re-organisation of States Act it was merged in the Indian constituent state of the Panjab and is now known by its old name of Patiala. In the days of the British domination the Patiala chief, Maharaja Bhupindra Singh (1891-1938), greatly developed the State, promoted the inauguration of the Chamber of Princes and represented the Indian Princes at the League of Nations Assembly at Geneva in 1925.

Patna—is the capital of the state of Bihar in the Federal Republic of India. It is situated on the Ganges and occupies a site close to that of the famous ancient city, Pataliputra (*q.v.*). The East India Company established a factory at Patna and its chief Mr. Ellis took a most violent attitude towards Nawab Mir Qasim and attempted to capture Patna in 1763. His effort failed but it led to the outbreak of a war between the English and Nawab Mir Qasim. On the defeat of Mir Qasim and the granting of the *Dewani* to the East India Company Patna became the headquarters of the Patna division of Bihar. In 1912 it became the capital of the newly constituted province of Bihar and Orissa with its own High Court and University.

Pawar—*see* Paramara.

Pearce, Col. Hugh—a military officer in the employment of the East India Company, led overland an army of the

Company from Bengal to Madras during the First Mysore War (1767-69).

Penal Code, the Indian—was the fruit of the labours of the Law Commission appointed during the Governor-Generalship of Lord William Bentinck (1828-35) of which Lord Macaulay (*q.v.*) was the most prominent member. It was introduced in 1860 and established a uniform system of penal laws all over British India.

PEPSU—is the abbreviated form of the Patiala and East Panjab States Union which was formed by the combination of the Cis-Sutlej Sikh States which came under British protection by the treaty of Amritsar in 1809.

Pereira, Father Julian—was the vicar-general in Bengal. He came into contact with Emperor Akbar in 1576 and 1577 and gave him some knowledge about Christian religion.

Permanent Settlement—was introduced in Bengal, Bihar and Orissa by Lord Cornwallis (*q.v.*) in 1793. It was a system of land tenure and revenue collection (*q.v.*). According to it the Zamindar was recognised as the proprietor of the land on condition that he paid to the Government by a fixed date of the year the annual rent, which amounted to ninety per cent of the estimated annual revenue that he received from the ryots who held lands at his pleasure. Most diametrically opposite judgements have been passed on it. Some have considered it a brave, bold, and wise measure 'which was beneficial alike to the Government, the Zamindar and the people'; while others have called it 'a sad blunder' from which the tenants derived no benefit whatever. While it has to be admitted that the Permanent Settlement left the tenants largely at the mercy of the Zamindars and also sacrificed to them much future revenue, it gave popularity and stability to the British Government at a time when these were most needed. In view, however, of the unjustifiable advantage that it gave to the Zamindars and the hardship it caused to the cultivators it was abolished recently in Bengal on promise of payment of compensation to the Zamindars. It is as yet too early to decide whether the net State revenues have appreciably increased as the result of the abolition of the Permanent Settlement and whether the real cultivator has been benefited.

Perron, General (1755-1834)—a French soldier of fortune, first came to India in 1780 and in 1781 he entered the service of the Rana of Gohud and later on of the Bharatpur State. In 1790 he was taken by De Boigne (*q.v.*) into the service of

Mahadaji Sindhia and helped him in gaining several victories over his Indian rivals. In 1796, on the retirement of De Boigne, Perron succeeded him as the General of the Sindhia's army and subdued Rajputana. But in the Second Maratha War which broke out in 1803, Perron could not achieve any success against the Indo-British army and was even defeated at the battle of Aligarh and Koil. Daulat Rao Sindhia consequently lost confidence in Perron and superseded him by Ambaji. After the defeat of the Sindhia's army at Laswari (*q.v.*) Perron departed from Sindhia's service and reached Calcutta where he sought protection from the East India Company. The Company arranged for his safe return to France where he died in 1834.

Persia—has had long and ancient connection with India. The Aryans who settled in Persia are believed to have belonged to the same old stock of the Aryans to which the Indo-Aryans belonged. The language of the *Avesta* has such similarities with Sanskrit, the sacred and learned language of the Hindus, that these have been held to have belonged to the same linguistic group. Closer connection with India was established in the sixth century B.C. when the Persian Emperor, Cyrus (*c.* 558-530 B.C.) reduced to submission the territory between the Kabul river and the Indus then inhabited by Indian tribal peoples like the Asvakas (*q.v.*). Persian domination was further extended during the reign of Darius (*c.* 522-486 B.C.) over Gandhara and further eastward up to the Indus. The province to the east of Gandhara was called by the Persians 'the land of the Hindus' or India and constituted the twentieth satrapy of the Persian empire. Gandhara and 'India' continued to be under the rule of Darius's son and successor, Xerxes (486-465 B.C.) and sent contingents of troops to join the great invading host that Xerxes led against Greece. This early contact of Persia with India resulted in the introduction of the Kharosthi alphabet in north-western India and of the 'Persepolitan capital' in Indian architecture. Indian troops fought on the Persian side at the battle of Gaugamela where the Persian Emperor, Darius III (335 - 330 B.C.) was defeated by Alexander, the king of Macedon, in 331 B.C. This victory, followed soon afterwards by the death of Darius III, practically made Alexander the master of the Persian empire and led him to invade in 327 B.C. the Panjab and Sind over which the control of the Persian empire had already grown slack and which had been parcelled out into a number of tribal states.

Alexander's death which followed soon afterwards, broke the subordination of the Panjab to Persia, but commercial and cultural contact continued between Persia and India, and it was through Persia that Asoka sent Indian Buddhist monks to carry the message of Buddha to the countries further to the west. Those Buddhist monks influenced Manichaeism which was at that time a strong religious force in Persia. Diplomatic relations continued to be maintained as is suggested by the fresco painting in Cave No. 1 at Ajanta which represents the ceremonial attending the presentation to the Chalukya king, Pulakeshin II (A.D. 608-42), of their credentials by Persian envoys sent by king Khusru II in about A.D. 627. On the reduction and conversion of Persia by the Arabs in the middle of the seventh century an ardent band of Persians who prized their religion more than their lands and wealth, sought shelter in India which was generously extended and the descendants of these Persians, now known as the Parsees, continue to be a much respected and influential section of the Indian population. On the conquest of India by the Muhammadans, who were mostly Turkomans and Sunnis, connection with Persia where the people and the kings were Shias, tended to grow slack, but adventurous Persian Muhammadans often came to India in quest of fortune which they often found. One such example was Yusuf Adil Shah, the founder of the Adil Shahi dynasty in Bijapur (1490-1673). Another example of a different type was the famous Muhammadan historian Ferishta (q.v.) who wrote in Persian his history of the rise and growth of the Muhammadan power in India. Indeed Persian was used as the court language by the sultans of Delhi and continued to be used as such under the Mughuls as well. Persian language, Persian mode of dress and Persian etiquette were diligently followed in the courts of the Muhammadan rulers all over India. The second Mughul emperor, Humayun (q.v.) found shelter in the court of the Persian king, Shah Tahmasp, and it was with his assistance that he recovered the throne of Delhi. But Persia captured Qandahar in 1649 and turned to be a source of anxiety to Shah Jahan and Aurangzeb and foiled all their efforts to recover the place. The heaviest blow that Persia gave to India came in 1739 when the Persian king, Nadir Shah (q.v.) invaded India, mercilessly sacked Delhi and returned with immense booty including the Peacock Throne and the Koh-i-noor. He also declared all the territory west of the Indus annexed to the Persian empire. But Nadir's death in 1747 followed by the rise of Ahmad Shah Durrani, as the king of Afghanistan, broke the recently established political link that Persia had established with India. The worst mischief had, however, already been done. Nadir Shah's invasion left the Mughul empire bleeding and prostrate. The defeat of the Mughuls and of their allies, the Marathas, at the third battle of Panipat in 1761, followed by the growth of the British empire in India, was the fatal consequence of the blow struck by the tyrant of Persia. In the nineteenth century Persia became a bone of contention between Great Britain and Russia each of which was anxious to establish its protectorate over Persia and Persia's political relations with India became a matter of Anglo-Russian diplomacy which culminated in the Anglo-Russian Convention of 1907 by which the two contracting powers bound themselves to maintain the integrity of Persia but at the same time agreed that northern Persia should be recognised as a sphere of Russian influence and south-eastern Persia as a sphere of British influence. Russia further agreed that England had special interests in the Persian Gulf. Thus two civilized powers of Europe disposed of the heritage of an independent people with an annoying cynicism which exposed the real nature of the civilisation they represented. Persia has since grown into a strong modern state.

Peshawar—is an important town in the North-West Province of India and is its headquarters. It occupies an important strategic position as it is situated on the Indian side of the entrance of the Khyber pass through which invaders from the north-west have generally poured into India. Through it also runs the main trade-route between India and the countries on the north-west. Its earlier name was Purushapur and it was the capital of the Kushan empire in the early centuries of the Christian era. It passed under the control of Sultan Mahmud of Ghazni (*q.v.*) in the tenth century and continued thereafter to be a part of the kingdom of Afghanistan until 1834 when it was occupied by Ranjit Singh. It remained a part of the Sikh kingdom until 1848 when, on the outbreak of the Second Sikh War (*q.v.*) the Sikh government ceded it to Amir Dost Muhammad of Afghanistan in order to buy his aid against the English. With the annexation of the Panjab it passed within the British Indian empire. It is now in West Pakistan.

Peshwa, the—was originally one of the eight ministers of Shivaji. He was also called the *Mukhya Pradhan* or the Chief Minister whose duty was to look after the general welfare and interest of the people. It was during the reign of Shahu (*q.v.*) (1708-48) that the office was raised in power and dignity by Balaji Visvanath (*q.v.*) who was appointed Peshwa in 1713 and held the office till his death in 1720. His achievements in arms and diplomacy raised the status of the Peshwa much above the other Ministers and when on his death in 1720 his son, Baji Rao I (*q.v.*) was appointed to succeed him as the Peshwa the office practically became hereditary in the family of Balaji. Baji Rao I held the Peshwaship for twenty years (1720-40) and further improved the status and position of the Peshwa by his victory over the Nizam and his victorious march in northern India which led to the establishment of Maratha power in Malwa, Gujarat and Central India and the consolidation of the Maratha confederacy consisting of the Sindhia, Holkar, Gaekwar and Bhonsla. The succession on his death in 1740 of his son Balaji Baji Rao (*q.v.*) to the Peshwaship and the death of the childless Raja Shahu (*q.v.*) in 1749 made the Peshwaship not only hereditary but also the supreme office in the Maratha state. The Peshwa transferrred the Maratha capital from Satara, where it had been so long, to Poona and reduced the Maratha king to a mere puppet. Henceforth the history of the Marathas merged in the history of the Peshwas. Balaji Baji Rao ruled from 1740 to 1761 and became so powerful that first, the Mughul Emperor Alamgir II (*q.v.*) (1754-59) and later on, his successor, Emperor Shah Alam II (*q.v.*) (1759-1806) looked to him for protection against Ahmad Shah Abdali (*q.v.*). Unlike his father, Balaji aimed at establishing a Maratha empire in place of the Mughul and invaded and looted Hindus as much as the Muhammadans. Thus he alienated the sympathy of all outside the Maratha country. This was largely responsible for the disastrous defeat of his army by Ahmad Shah Abdali at the third battle of Panipat (*q.v.*) in 1761. The losses were so great and the consequences of this defeat were so profound that six months later Peshwa Balaji Baji Rao died of a broken heart. His death marked the beginning of the decline and fall of the power of the Peshwas which also involved the fall of the Marathas. His successor Madhava Rao I (*q.v.*) (1761-72) died too soon. The next Peshwa Narayana Rao (*q.v.*) (1772-73) was murdered at the instance of his uncle Raghaba (*q.v.*) who became the Peshwa only for a short time in 1773 but was obliged to make room for Narayan Rao's posthumous son, Madhav Rao Narayan (*q.v.*) who was the Peshwa from 1774 to 1796. But Raghaba was the evil genius of the Peshwas. By pursuing a selfish personal policy he got the Peshwa involved in the First Anglo-Maratha War which continued from 1775 to 1782 and further weakened the hold of the Peshwa on the Maratha confederacy. The astuteness and ability of Nana Faḍnavis (*q.v.*) who was the Peshwa's chief Minister, upheld during the following eighteen years the Peshwa's power in the Deccan, though all efforts at controlling northern India were given up. The death of Nana Faḍnavis in 1800 removed the wise counsel that had been guiding the Peshwa's conduct. In 1802 Peshwa Baji Rao II, who had succeeded to the Peshwaship in 1796, voluntarily entered with the English into the treaty of Bassein (*q.v.*) in order to escape domination by his feudatories, the Holkar and the Sindhia, and parted with his independence by accepting a subsidiary alliance with the English. The resentment that such cowardly conduct created amongst the Maratha chiefs led to the Second Maratha War (1803-5) which further riveted the British yoke on the Marathas. Soon afterwards Baji Rao II felt unhappy under the English yoke and his efforts to escape it led to the Third Maratha War (*q.v.*) (1817-19) in which the Peshwa was decisively defeated in various battles and was deposed. The Peshwaship was now abolished, though Baji Rao II was allowed to retire on an annual pension of 8 lakhs of rupees to Bithur near Cawnpore where he died in 1853. The English refused to continue his pension to his adopted son, Nana Sahib (*q.v.*) who, therefore, took a leading part in the Sepoy Mutiny and lost.

Pethwick-Lawrence, Lord—was the President of the Cabinet Mission (*q.v.*) which visited India in 1946. He was an ardent supporter of India's demands for constitutional reforms. As the Secretary of State for India (1945-47) in Attlee's Ministry he contributed much to the evolution of the British policy leading to the granting of independence to India in 1947.

Peyton, Admiral—was in command of an English squadron in Indian waters in 1746, who faced the French fleet under La Bourdannais (*q.v.*). Peyton retired before the French who were thus enabled to capture Madras (*q.v.*).

Phayre, Sir Arthur—a military officer (Major) in the Company's service in India, was placed, on the conquest of Burma, in charge of the administration of the newly conquered territory. He discharged his duties so well that he was appointed the first Chief Commissioner of Burma including British Burma, Tenasserim, Pegu and Arakan.

Phayre, Colonel—was the British Resident at the court of Mulhar Rao, the Gaekwar of Baroda, whom he charged with various acts of misgovernment. On enquiry by a Commission Mulhar Rao was given eighteen months to reform the administration under the direction of Phayre; but the period of probation passed without any improvement. Rather in 1875, Col. Phayre charged Mulhar Rao with an attempt to poison him. Mulhar Rao was put on trial which eventually led to his deposition.

Pigot, Lord—was the Governor of Madras (1775-78). He wanted to restrain, if not stop, the corrupt practices then prevalent amongst the Company's officers in Madras. But the guilty proved too strong for the honest and Lord Pigot had the most unhappy experience of being actually deposed and imprisoned by his subordinates. He died in prison in Madras.

Pindaris, the—were irregulars and skirmishers who followed the Maratha armies. They received no pay and subsisted on the plunder of the enemy's territory. Though some of the leading Pindaris were of Pathan origin, broken and desperate persons of all races joined their ranks. In the beginning of the nineteenth century they were patronised by the Sindhia who gave their leaders lands in Malwa in the Narmada valley from where they extended their raids far and wide in Central India, plundering and looting the rich and the poor alike. In 1812 they broke into Bundelkhand, in 1815 in the Nizam's dominions and in 1816 in the Northern Circars. Thus they seriously threatened peace and prosperity in the British Indian Empire. So in 1817 Governor-General Lord Hastings organised a very large army against them. Though the hunt for the Pindaris developed into the Third Marat a War (*q.v.*) the Pindaris were suppressed. Their Pathan leader Amir Khan was recognized as the Nawab of Tonk and submitted while the other important leader, Chittu, was hunted into the jungle where he was devoured by a tiger.

Pinheiro, Father Emmanuel—a Jesuit missionary, went along with Father Jerome Xavier, to the court of Emperor Akbar in 1595 and stayed there during the last few years of his reign. They succeeded in securing permission from the Emperor to make converts to Christianity, if they could. The letters that Pinheiro wrote home throw interesting light on the history of the times.

Pir Muhammad Khan—began his career as a servant of Bairam Khan (*q.v.*) and was sent, after the second battle of Panipat (*q.v.*) (1556) in pursuit of Himu's (*q.v.*) wife who had fled with the treasures of her husband. On return from the pursuit he joined the anti-Bairam faction. This provoked the hostility of Bairam Khan who deprived him of his honours and sent him to Gujarat. Pir Muhammad was considered a victim of Bairam's revenge, and, backed by the anti-Bairam party, soon returned to the court and was employed to watch the movements of Bairam. On the fall and assassination of Bairam in 1560 Pir Muhammad was sent as second in command to Adham Khan against Malwa which was conquered. Pir Muhammad disgraced himself by acts of cruelty and oppression against the Muhammadans who were taken captives. On the removal of Adham Khan, Pir Muhammad was elevated to the Governorship of Malwa. He then invaded Khandesh, was repulsed and was drowned when re-crossing the Narmada (1562).

Pir Muhammad—a grandson of Timur (*q.v.*), led the vanguard of Timur's invading army in 1397, conquered Kutch and Multan and thus prepared the way for the invasion by Timur.

Pitinikas, the—were a people mentioned in Asoka's Rock Edicts V and VIII as people living on the western border of his empire. (Bhattacharya, S., *Select Asokan Epigraphs*)

Pitt, William, the Younger—was the Prime Minister of Great Britain from 1783 to 1801. The main issue on which he won the election was the British administration in India. Further the decade that had elapsed since the passing of the Regulating Act in 1773 had exposed some of its defects and their removal was felt to be necessary. Accordingly one of the first important measures that Pitt took after his appointment as the Premier, was to pass the India Act (*q.v.*). It strengthened the control of the Parliament over the administration in India, set up the Board of Control and increased the power of the Governor-General and his Council in Bengal over the internal as well as external administration of the Presidencies of Bombay and Madras. On the passing of Pitt's India Act, Warren Hastings who was then the Governor-General in Bengal resigned office and soon afterwards a Parliamentary review of his Indian administration began. Pitt supported Warren Hastings on the question of Nanda Kumar (*q.v.*) and the Rohilla War (*q.v.*) but voted against him on the question of Chait Singh (*q.v.*) and the Begums of Oudh (*q.v.*). Hastings was, therefore, impeached in 1788 though after a trial lasting seven years he was acquitted. But Pitt never agreed to confer a peerage on him and thus showed his estimate of Warren Hastings. Pitt's

Premiership covered the Governor-Generalships of Lord Cornwallis (*q.v.*) (1786-93), Sir John Shore (*q.v.*) (1793-98) and Lord Wellesley (*q.v.*) (1798-1805). Pitt was on friendly terms with Lord Cornwallis and supported his proposal for the introduction of the Permanent Settlement of Land Revenue in Bengal. He also supported Lord Wellesley for the first few years of his administration, but as Lord Wellesley sprang from one war to another Pitt withdrew his support from the prancing proconsul who was recalled in 1805 and superseded by Lord Cornwallis. Pitt died in 1806.

Pitt's India Act—was passed in 1784. Its main object was to improve the administration of India by the East India Company by removing the defects that had been revealed by the working of the Regulating Act from 1773 to 1783. Pitt's India Act tried to improve the Indian administration by vesting all control over civil and military affairs of the Company in India in a body of six commissioners, popularly called the Board of Control (*q.v.*). The Directors were left in charge of the Company's commerce and of the appointments including that of the Governor-General, in the Company's service in India. But all directions by the Directors to the Company's officials in India were to be approved by the Board of Control before their despatch, and, once approved by the Board, no such directions could be altered or rescinded either by the Court of Directors or even by the Court of Proprietors which could only elect the Directors. The number of the members of the Council of the Governor-General was reduced from four to three, and by a supplementary Act the Governor-General was given the right of over-riding the majority of his Council at his discretion. The powers of the Governor-General of Bengal and his Council over the Presidencies of Bombay and Madras were increased, both in respect of their domestic administration and foreign relations, with the result that the two Presidencies were now made definitely subordinate to the Governor-General and Council of Bengal.

Plague, bubonic—broke out in Bombay in 1896 and led to the enforcement of stringent regulations for isolation and hospitalization which were enforced without due consideration being shown for the susceptibilities of the children of the soil. This generated much disaffection amongst the Indians and in 1897 two British officers engaged in plague work, were assassinated at Poona and in 1898 serious riots broke out in Bombay. These acts of terrorism led the Government to pass stringent repressive laws and to the trial and conviction of Bal Gangadhar Tilak (*q.v.*) on a charge of spreading disaffection against the Government. The plague spread to Calcutta in 1898 and created great havoc. This great calamity brought to public notice the Ramakrishna Mission (*q.v.*) and Sister Nivedita who devoted themselves to the nursing of the sick and the dying. Gradually the ravages of the plague waned, but it has not yet been completely eradicated from India.

Plassey, the battle of—was fought between the East India Company's army led by Robert Clive (*q.v.*) and the army of Nawab Siraj-ud-daulah of Bengal on the 23rd June, 1757. Owing to the treachery of the Nawab's leading general, Mir Jafar, and his comrades the battle which began in the morning was lost by mid-day. It was no more than a skirmish, but its results were very important. Nawab Siraj-ud-daulah who fled from the battlefield, was soon made a captive and then murdered. The victorious English with their *protégé*, the treacherous Mir Jafar, marched on to Murshidabad, which surrendered without any opposition. Mir Jafar was declared the Nawab of Bengal on promising such large rewards to Robert Clive and his English associates that the Nawab's treasury was emptied and he became absolutely dependent on the English who thus virtually became the masters of Bengal and got control over all its rich resources which contributed much to the victory of the English in their wars with the French in India, known as the Carnatic Wars.

Pliny—was an ancient classical geographer. His work, *Natural History*, believed to have been published in A.D. 77, contains much information about India in the first century of the Christian era.

Pocock, Admiral—led the English fleet in the Bay of Bengal against the French fleet under d' Ache and defeated the latter off Karikal in 1758. This victory facilitated the defence of Madras by the English against the French attack led by Lally.

Police, the Indian—was first established in British India by the Governor-General, Lord Cornwallis (1786-93). They worked under the supervision of four police Superintendents stationed in Calcutta, Dacca, Patna and Murshidabad. Gradually a Superintendent of Police was appointed in each district, under whom there are Deputy Superintendents of Police for each sub-division, inspectors of Police for a group of *thanas* called a circle, and sub-inspectors of Police in each thana. The sub-inspectors have constables under them. All these are paid by the state and are collectively responsible for the maintenance of peace and order within their respective areas. In villages there are *Chowkidars* or watchmen who are paid small sums of money by the Government, to keep watch on known bad characters and inform the *thana* officer of any criminal act within the village. In each of the three Presidency towns of Calcutta, Bombay and Madras there is a unified police force under the Police Commissioner who is directly under the State Minister in charge and is responsible for law and order and for departmental training. Though the Superintendents of police are now recruited, like the Indian Administrative Service personnel, mainly on the result of an All India Competitive Examination there is no Indian or All India police. The Police Act of 1861 made the police a provincial organisation, administered by the Government of the province concerned. At the head of the Police organisation in each province is the Inspector-General of Police who exercises general control over it. The greatest defect of the Police organisation all over India was a general lack of education amongst all ranks of the force and the prevalence of graft. In 1902 a Police Commission was appointed to investigate the state of police administration and on its recommendations steps for improving the police force and morale were taken. A Criminal Investigation Department was created and a Central Intelligence Bureau under the Home Department of the Central Government was organized to work for inter-provincial liaison. After the attainment of independence various measures like the improvement of pay-scales and grant of better amenities have been adopted to attract more educated persons to the police force and to imbue them with a new sense of service to the people but with only limited success.

Pollilore, the battle of—was fought in 1781 between Haidar Ali (*q.v.*) of Mysore and the Company's army led by Sir Eyre Coote and General Pearce. Haidar Ali was defeated and checked.

Pollock, General—was an able officer who was sent during the First Afghan War to Peshawar at the head of an army to relieve Jalalabad where an English army lay besieged late in 1841 Pollock showed great initiative, duly relieved Jalalabad, and then marching out of Jalalabad, defeated the Afghans at the two battles of Jagdalak and Tezin and entered Kabul at the head of a victorious army in September, 1842. After rescuing the European prisoners held in Kabul and setting ablaze the great Bazar of Kabul as an example of revengeful power, he safely evacuated Kabul in October, 1842 and thus brought to a close the First Afghan War (*q.v.*).

Polo, Marco—a Venetian traveller, visited India in A.D. 1288 and 1293 and left a very informative account of what he had seen and observed. He records the just and efficient administration of the Pandya kingdom, the wealth of its people and the busy trade that passed through its port, Kayal, which he described as "a great and noble city."

Pondicherry—is a port on the eastern coast of India, a few miles to the south of Madras. It was founded in 1674 by Francois Martin in the employ of the French East India Company. In 1693 the Dutch captured it and constructed there strong fortifications. It was restored to the French with defences intact in 1699. Martin developed it into a flourishing town and it became the capital of the French possessions in India consisting of Chandernagore in Bengal, Mahe in Malabar and Karikal on the Coromandel Coast. It was threatened in vain by the English in 1745 and again in 1747, and, finally captured by them in 1761. Its fall marked the end of the French dominion in India, and though it was restored to the French in 1763 its fortifications were demolished and the number of its garrison was strictly limited. It henceforward continued as the capital of the French commercial possessions in India. After the independence of India Pondicherry along with the other French possessions in India were peacefully merged by negotiations with the Federal Republic of India. It is still maintained as a centre of French culture in India and has been given its local government with an elected legislature. Pondicherry gave asylum to Arabinda Ghose (*q.v.*) who fled there from British rule and who later on founded at Pondicherry his *Ashram* which has attracted devotees from many parts of the world.

Poona—a town in Maharashtra, was the capital of Shivaji (*q.v.*) and of his son and successor, Shambhuji (*q.v.*). It was left by Shahu (*q.v.*) who made Satara his capital, but was made the capital of the Maharashtra dominions after the death of Shahu in 1749 by Peshwa Balaji Baji Rao (*q.v.*). It lost its primacy on the defeat and deposition of the last Peshwa, Baji Rao II. Poona still continues to be an important city with its own University. It was at Poona that Gandhiji went on his famous fast in 1932 and undid the communal award (*q.v.*) given by the British Prime Minister, Mr. Ramsay Macdonald.

Poona Pact—was the agreement reached at Poona on 24 September, 1932, by the sick-bed of Gandhiji who had undertaken a fast unto death in protest against the communal award (*q.v.*) of 1932 which gave separate representations not only to the Muhammadans but also to the Depressed Classes amongst the Hindus separating them from the main body of the Hindus. It secured the election of the representatives of the depressed classes through general constituencies in which all non-Muhammadans voted.

Poona, the treaty of—was concluded by Peshwa Baji Rao II (*q.v.*) with the British in 1817 in supersession of the treaty of Bassein (*q.v.*), concluded in 1802. By this treaty of Poona the Peshwa dismissed all foreign agents from his court, surrendered certain territories for the maintenance of a British contingent at Poona and renounced the headship of the Maratha Confederacy. Baji Rao II resented this treaty as an imposition and rose against the British in 1818 only to be defeated and obliged to surrender and to be deposed in 1818.

Poona Women's University—was founded by Professor Karve in 1916. It marked an important stage in the progress of female education in India.

Popham, Colonel—was an officer under the Company who, along with Goddard (*q.v.*), led an army overland from Bengal to Bombay in 1779 in the course of the First Maratha War (*q.v.*) (1775-82) and won great fame by storming the fort of Gwalior in 1780.

Poros—was, according to the classical historians, the name of the Indian king whose territory lay between the Jhelum and the Chinab when Alexander, the king of Macedon, invaded the Panjab in 326 B.C. Poros illustrated the chivalry and bravery as well as the conceit characteristic of Indian warrior-kings. Unlike his neighbour, Ambhi, the king of Taxila, on the west of the Jhelum, Poros did not submit to Alexander and decided to resist him with arms. But unlike Alexander who, having learnt that the strength of his Indian opponent depended on his elephants, took steps for teaching his Greek army how best to tackle the elephants, Poros does not appear to have taken any steps for finding out the secret of the strength of the Greek armies which lay in their mobile cavalry and mounted archers and for counteracting them. With the confidence in his fighting capacity and the strength of his elephants he first failed to resist the crossing of the Jhelum by Alexander and then met the mobile army of Alexander consisting mainly of cavalry and mounted archers in a battle in the Karri plain on the eastern bank of the Jhelum with his slow-moving infantry backed by elephants arranged in a dense square which made movement difficult and archers armed with long bows which must be securely planted on the earth in order to be used effectively. The battle was decided by the shock tactics of the more mobile army of Alexander, and Poros, who fought bravely and did not flee from the battlefield though he had received wounds, was made captive by the Greeks. Alexander had the wisdom to make a friend and ally of him by treating him as a king with due honour and by restoring him to his dominions and even perhaps by adding to them some parts of his conquest in the Panjab. What part Poros played after the departure of Alexander is not known. The liberation of the Panjab from the Greek yoke was the work of Chandragupta Maurya (q.v.).

Porto Novo, the battle of—was fought in 1781 between Haidar Ali of Mysore and the Company's armies led by Sir Eyre Coote. Haidar Ali was defeated with heavy losses and his victories were checked.

Portuguese, the—arrived in India on 20 May, 1498 in four ships under the leadership of Vasco da Gama. They were the first European traders to have reached India across the seas after doubling the Cape of Good Hope. They anchored near Calicut, were received kindly by the local Hindu raja who bore the title of Zamorin, visited Cochin and Cannanore and returned safely to Portugal. The Portuguese were fortunate in the time of their arrival. The Delhi sultanate in north India and the Bahmani kingdom in the Deccan were both disintegrating and none of the states into which India was then divided, possessed any navy, or thought of developing naval power. So the only opposition that stood in the way of the advancement of the Portuguese in India came from the Arab merchants who then controlled India's trade with the west. Vasco da Gama's second visit in 1502 led to a rupture with the Zamorin because he had refused to exclude the Arab merchants in favour of the Portuguese. But the Portuguese trade with India increased and in 1505 Dom Francisco de Almeida (q.v.) was appointed as the first Portuguese viceroy in India. In 1508 he defeated a combined Egyptian and Gujarati fleet in a naval battle in the Arabian sea and thus established Portuguese supremacy on the sea route. This advantage enabled the next Portuguese governor, Albuquerque, to secure bases covering all the entrances from the West into the Indian Ocean, to overcome the Arab shipping and to occupy the island of Goa in 1510 against the opposition of the sultan of Bijapur. Goa thus supplied the Portuguese with a base on the Indian soil. Albuquerque also occupied Malacca in 1511 and Ormuz in 1515, though he had earlier failed to capture Aden. Yet the successes attained coupled with the acquisition of two other Indian stations, Daman and Diu, on the western coast enabled the Portuguese to establish a sort of dominion in India over which they ruled till recent times. Their rule in their Indian dominions was marked with great unscrupulousness, terrible religious persecution, particularly of the Muhammadans, and the establishment of the Inquisition. Their small number was a handicap from the beginning which Albuquerque thought of overcoming by encouraging inter-marriage between the Portuguese sailors and the widows or the abducted wives and daughters of their Indian opponents. The half-castes that were thus created were expected to uphold Portuguese power in India, but they proved unequal to the task. Further, in the seventeenth century with the arrival of the Dutch and the English in India the Portuguese in India became involved on land as well as on the sea, in a prolonged contest in the course of which the Portuguese not only lost their monopoly of trade but also their supremacy on the sea. Their settlements in India, which defied the efforts at capturing them by the Mughul emperors as well as by the Marathas, would have certainly shared the fate of the French possessions in India and would have been absorbed within the British Indian empire but for the fact that in the Napoleonic wars Portugal was an ally of England. Thus, while in the beginning of the nineteenth century the French and the Dutch lost their territories in India and were suffered to retain them only as trading centres, Portugal continued to hold Goa, Daman and Diu in independent possession. Resurgent and independent India could not permit the continuance of the Portuguese domination over parts of her territories which were therefore forcibly freed in 1960, after all negotiations for a peaceful transfer of the territories had been obstinately rejected by Portugal.

Pottinger, Eldred—an English general in the service of the Company, defended Herat against a Persian attack in 1838.

Pottinger, Sir Henry—the first British Resident sent by the Company to Sind, negotiated a treaty with the Amirs of Sind (*q.v.*) in 1832 which threw open the lower Indus to commerce by the English.

Prabhakaravardhana—the king of Thaneswar, belonged to the Pushyabhuti dynasty (*q.v.*) and ruled towards the close of the sixth century. His mother was a Gupta princess, named Mahasenagupta, and he won considerable eminence by successful wars against his neighbours, the Malavas, the Hunas of the North-western Panjab and the Gurjaras. He gave his daughter, Rajyasri, in marriage to Grahavarman, the Maukhari king of Kanauj. He died in A.D. 604 and was succeeded by his elder son, Rajyavardhana.

Prabhabati Gupta—a daughter of Chandra Gupta II (*c.* A.D. 380-413) (*q.v.*), was married to the Vakataka (*q.v.*) king, Rudrasena II. Their descendants ruled in the Deccan for several centuries.

Prabodha-chandrodaya, **the**—is a Sanskrit allegorical play which gives in a dramatic form a clever exposition of the Vedanta system of philosophy. It was written under the patronage of the Chandella king, Kirtivarman (*q.v.*) who ruled in the second half of the eleventh century.

Pragjyotisha—the ancient name of the modern state of Assam, is mentioned in the *Mahabharata*. Its capital Pragjyotishapura has been identified by some with the modern town of Gauhati in the lower Assam valley.

Prakrit—a simpler and popular form of Sanskrit, is more allied to Pali and was the spoken language all over India in the days of Asoka Maurya who used it in all his inscriptions which he placed from Kalsi in the Dehra-Dun district to Mysore.

Prarthana Samaj, the—was founded in Maharashtra in 1867 under the guidance of the Bengali Brahma leader, Keshab Chandra Sen (*q.v.*). The adherents of the Prarthana Samaj considered themselves, unlike the earlier Brahmas, as Hindus. They were devoted theists and adhered to the great religious tradition of the Maratha saints like Tukaram (*q.v.*) and Ramdas. They devoted their chief attention to social reforms amongst the Hindus by encouraging inter-dining, inter-marriage, re-marriage of Hindu widows and improvement of depressed classes. The Prarthana Samaj attracted many followers and, due mainly to the support of Justice Mahadev Govinda Ranade (*q.v.*), started many benevolent institutions of which the famous Deccan Education Society (*q.v.*) was one.

Prasad, Rajendra—was the first President of the Republic of India. Born in Bihar in 1884, educated at Calcutta University, he began his career as an advocate and soon commanded a very large practice at Patna High Court. He came into contact with Mahatma Gandhi in 1917 in connection with the Champaran affair and eventually in 1920 gave up his lucrative legal practice and joined the non-co-operation movement. He was President of the Bihar Provincial Congress Committee for several years. He became the General Secretary of the Congress in 1922 and President of the Congress in 1934, 1939 and 1947. He was a staunch follower of Mahatma Gandhi and was for years a member of the Congress Working Committee. He became a Minister in Nehru's cabinet in 1947. From 1946 to 1949 he presided over the Indian Constituent Assembly and took an important part in shaping the constitution of India. His sobriety, patience and sterling merit led to his election in 1950 as the first President of the Republic of India and to his re-election in 1952 and again in 1957. He retired in 1962 but died soon afterwards at Patna.

Prasad, Rana—the ruler of Amarkot in Rajputana, gave shelter to the fugitive Mughul emperor, Humayun, and his newly wedded wife Hamida Banu. Their son, Akbar, was born at Amarkot under the protection of Rana Prasad in 1542.

Prasenajit—the king of Koshala in about the middle of the sixth century B.C., was a contemporary of Gautama Buddha (*q.v.*) and Vardhamana Mahavira (*q.v.*) both of whom paid visits to his kingdom. He married a sister of king Bimbisara (*q.v.*) of Magadha who had also married his sister. In spite of this marriage relation Prasenajit had to wage wars with Bimbisara and his son and successor, the parricide Ajatasatru, who forced him to surrender a Kasi village which had been promised to the Koshalan bride of Bimbisara and mother of Ajatasatru. Soon afterwards king Prasenajit died and the decline of Koshala began.

Pratapaditya—a valiant landlord in Jessore in Bengal, refused to pay tribute to Akbar, defeated a Mughul army but was ultimately defeated, made captive and sent to Delhi but died on the way.

Prataparudra—the Kakatiya (*q.v.*) king of Warangal, was defeated and overthrown in A.D. 1323 by Ulugh Khan, the general of Sultan Ghiyas-ud-din (*q.v.*) of Delhi.

Prataparudra—a king of Orissa, was defeated in about A.D. 1510 by the Vijayanagara king, Krishnadeva Raya (*q.v.*).

Pratap Sinha, Rana—the son and successor of Rana Uday Sinha of Mewar, ruled from A.D. 1572 till his death on 19 January, 1597. A great hero and a true patriot, he decided to stand against immense odds for the maintenance of the independence

of his native land, Mewar, against the much superior resources of Emperor Akbar who had already captured the
strategic fort of Chitor and was then "unmeasurably the
richest monarch on the face of the earth." Naturally Pratap's
refusal to submit to the Mughuls brought upon him a large
Mughul army led by Man Singh of Amber and Asaf Khan.
After a valiant battle at Haldighat (*q.v.*) in April, 1576 in
which Rana Pratap was defeated, he betook himself to the
hills. The Mughuls pursued him and captured many of his
strongholds. But Rana Pratap would not submit; hunted
from rock to rock and feeding his family on the fruits of his
native hills, he continued the war and had the satisfaction of
recovering some of his strongholds before his death in 1597. He
was the one Rajput king who had successfully resisted the
efforts of the great Mughul to conquer his country. He was
succeeded by his son, Amar Singh who in 1614 submitted to
Emperor Jahangir.

Pratihara (also called Parihara)—*see* Gurjara-Pratihara dynasty.

Praudha-devaraya (also called Padea Rao)—the last king of
the first dynasty of the kings of Vijayanagar, was deposed in
A.D. 1485 by Saluva Narasingha.

Pravarasena I—a king of the Vakataka dynasty (*q.v.*), ruled in
the fourth century A.D. He controlled Madhya Pradesh and
much of the western Deccan. Details are not known.

Pravarasena II—the son and successor of the Vakataka (*q.v.*) king,
Rudrasena II (*q.v.*) who had married Prabhavatigupta (*q.v.*),
ascended the throne in about A.D. 410 and gradually threw
off the Gupta domination.

Prince of Wales, the—Edward, Prince of Wales, visited India
in 1921. His visit was boycotted by the Indian National Congress.
The immense success of the peaceful boycott by the Indians of
all functions in connection with the Prince's visit indicated the
depth of Indian disaffection towards Britain, the strength of
the hold of the Indian National Congress over the people's
mind, and was an eye-opener to the British Government.

Prithviraj Chouhan (also called Rai Pithora)—was the king
of Sambhar, Ajmer and Delhi. His great Indian rival was
Raja Jaychandra (*q.v.*) of Kanauj whose daughter, Sanjukta,
chose him as her husband against her father's wish and was
forcibly abducted by Prithviraj in about A.D. 1175. Prithviraj
was a great soldier who defeated the Chandella king, Parmal,
and captured his capital, Mahoba, in 1182. He shouldered the
burden of resisting the invasion of Shihab-ud-din Muhammad

Ghuri and defeated him at the first battle of Tarain in 1192. But the next year he was defeated by Shihab-ud-din at the second battle of Tarain and killed. His deeds of love and valour are recorded by the famous bard Chand Bardai in his work called *Chand Raisa.*

Provincial autonomy—was an important feature of the constitutional changes introduced by the Government of India Act, 1933. (*see* under British Admn. in India.)

Ptolemy Philadelphos—the Greek king of Egypt (285 B.C.-247 B.C.) sent Dionysios as his envoy to the court of the Maurya king, Bindusara (*q.v.*) and is mentioned by Asoka (*q.v.*) in his Rock inscription XIII as one of the Greek kings in whose kingdom Buddhist evangelical work was carried on with success.

Public Works department, the—was set up by Lord Dalhousie during his Governor-Generalship (1848-56) and placed in charge of all construction work and maintenance of roads and bridges within the British Indian empire.

Pulakeshin I—the founder of the Chalukya dynasty (*q.v.*) of Vatapi or Badami in the Deccan, flourished in about the middle of the sixth century A.D.

Pulakeshin II—a grandson of Pulakeshin I and the fourth king of the Chalukya dynasty (*q.v.*), ruled from A.D. 609-42 and was the contemporary and rival of King Harshavardhana whose invasion into the Deccan he repulsed in A.D. 620. He was a great warrior-king and carried his conquests into Gujarat, Rajputana and Malwa. He conquered Vengi, lying between the Krishna and the Godavari, and established his brother, Kubja Vishnuvardhana (*q.v.*) as his viceroy there. His power was also made to be felt by the Choda, Pandya and Kerala kingdoms of south India as well as by the Pallavas with whom he waged a long war in the course of which he inflicted a severe defeat on their king, Mahendravarman, in about A.D. 609. His fame as a conqueror reached distant Persia whose king, Khusru II, received in A.D. 625-26 an embassy from Pulakeshin II and returned the compliment by sending soon afterwards an embassy to Pulakeshin II. In Ajanta Cave No. I a fresco painting vividly represents the ceremonial attending the reception of the Persian embassy by Pulakeshin II. His court and kingdom were also visited by the Chinese pilgrim, Hiuen Tsang, in A.D. 641 who was much impressed by the power of Pulakeshin II and the loyalty of his military vassals. But in A.D. 642 this very powerful monarch was defeated and killed in battle by the Pallava king, Narasimhavarman, who also captured his capital and put an end to his dynasty for the time being.

Puranas, **the**—are store-houses of Indian tradition and ancient history. They are eighteen in number of which five, namely, the *Vayu, Vishnu, Brahmmanda, Matsya* and *Bhagavata,* contain dynastic lists which are valuable. The age of the Puranas is difficult to determine. The oldest of them, the *Bhavishya,* the *Brahmmanda* and the *Matsya* are perhaps as old as the fourth century B.C. But additions went on in later times and the Puranas got their modern shape in the fourth and fifth centuries A.D. The other thirteen Puranas are the *Brahma, Padma, Naradiya, Markandeya, Agneya, Bhavishya, Brahmavaivarta, Lainga, Varaha, Skanda, Vamana, Kaurma* and *Goduda.* (Pargiter, F. E., *The Dynasties of the Kali Age*)

Purandhar, the treaty of—was concluded in March, 1776 between the Marathas and the Company represented by Col. Upton, the Company's agent sent from Calcutta for carrying on negotiations with the Marathas with whom a war had been started as the result of the treaty of Surat (*q.v.*) concluded by the Bombay Government with the pretender, Raghaba (*q.v.*) in 1775. By the treaty of Purandhar the English agreed to abandon the cause of Raghaba, on condition of being allowed to retain Salsette. The Court of Directors disapproved of the treaty and the war with the Marathas was renewed. It lasted till 1782 when it was concluded by the treaty of Salbai which restored peace between the Marathas and the English on practically the same terms as were agreed upon by the treaty of Purandhar.

Purchas, Samuel—was the author of the *Pilgrims,* which contained an account of the early European settlers in India. The Directors considered the book very necessary for study by the Company's employees in India for arriving at a mature understanding of the affairs of India, of the Dutch wiles and of former abuses amongst the English merchants in India. Copies of the book were sent by the Directors in 1686 to India for the illumination of their employees in India.

Puri—a sacred place of pilgrimage to the Hindus all over India, is on the sea coast in Orissa and contains the great temple of Jagannath built by the Orissan king, Anantavarman Chodaganga (*q.v.*) (A.D. 1076-1148).

Purnea—a Brahman by caste, belonged to Mysore where he rose by his ability to be the Dewan of Tipu Sultan (*q.v.*) (1782-99). On his defeat and death in 1799 Purnea was appointed by the victorious English as the Dewan of the minor Hindu prince installed by them as the king of a part of the old Mysore kingdom. Purnea proved to be a very capable administrator and efficiently ruled the state in the name of the boy king.

Purohita —literally means 'priest'. This was the designation applied to the royal chaplain who exercised considerable influence on the administration of orthodox Hindu rulers.

Puru—*see* Poros.

Purus, the—a tribal people mentioned in the Vedic literature, belonged to the Aryan race, but spoke 'a hostile tongue' and were often engaged in wars with other Aryan tribes with some of whom they dwelt on the banks of the river Saraswati. What connection Poros or Puru, who opposed Alexander (*q.v.*) on the bank of the Jhelum in 326 B.C. had with the tribal Purus, is not known.

Purushottama Gajapati—a king of Orissa (A.D. 1470-97) belonging to the Kapilendra dynasty (*q.v.*), had to fight against the king of Vijayanagar as well as against the Bahmani Sultan and lost to them, in the beginning of his reign, the southern part of his dominions from the Godavari southwards, but recovered before his death the doab between the Godavari and the Krishna and advanced as far as Kondavindu.

Purushottama—a Hindu philosopher, was invited by Emperor Akbar (*q.v.*) to take part in the discussions held at the *Ibadat Khana* at Fathpur Sikri in about A.D. 1580.

Purva Mimamsa—is a school of Hindu philosophy which emphasized the value of the performance of the Vedic rites. Its great exponents were Savarasvamin, Prabhakara and Kumarila who flourished in the fourth-fifth centuries A.D.

Purvananda—is a term which has been wrongly used to mean earlier Nandas. It is the name of a single individual and not of a line of kings (*P.H.A.I.*, pp. 222-24).

Purushapura—was the older name of modern Peshawar. It was the capital of Kanishka (*q.v.*), the great Kushan king.

Pushyabhuti dynasty, the—was founded in the sixth century A.D. at Thaneswar not far from Delhi, by Pushyabhuti who was a devoted worshipper of Siva. The dynasty was raised to greatness by Prabhakaravardhana (*q.v.*) and consisted of three kings, namely Prabhakaravardhana and his two sons, Rajyavardhana and Harshavardhana. On the death of Prabhakaravardhana the throne passed to his elder son, Rajyavardhana (*q.v.*) who, however, became engaged in a war immediately after his accession and was killed. He was succeeded by his illustrious brother, Harshavardhana (*q.v.*) (A.D. 606-47) who after a glorious reign of forty years died childless. With his death the Pushyabhuti dynasty came to an end.

Pushyagupta—a vaisya, was appointed by Chandragupta Maurya (*q.v.*) as the *rashtriya* (High Commissioner) in Surashtra where he constructed the famous Sudarsana Lake by damming a stream.

Pushyamitra Sunga—was the founder of the Sunga dynasty (*c.* 185 B.C.) on the deposition of the Maurya dynasty. He was a Brahman by caste and a soldier by profession who had risen to be the Commander-in-Chief of Brihadratha, the last of the Maurya kings whom he killed in the midst of a review of the army and ascended the throne. He ruled for 38 years. This was no easy task. The empire was invaded from the south-east by the Orissan king, Kharavela (*q.v.*) and from the north by the Indo-Greek king Menander (*q.v.*). Pushyamitra repulsed them both, held intact the vast empire and justly celebrated his triumph by performing, after a long abeyance, the *Asvamedha* sacrifice (*q.v.*) and thus declared the revival of orthodox Hinduism which had suffered an eclipse under Asoka. With the revival of Hinduism the Sanskrit language again came into court use. The celebrated grammarian Patanjali lived in his time and is supposed to have officiated as a priest in the celebration of the *Asvamedha* sacrifice. His son and successor Angimitra (*q.v.*) and his grandson Vasumitra (*q.v.*) were both great warriors. Pushyamitra is said to have been a zealous persecutor of Buddhism, but there is no confirmatory evidence.

Pushyamitras, the—a tribal people of unknown origin and habitat, raided the Gupta empire during the reign of Kumargupta I (*q.v.*) early in the fifth century. They were repulsed by the Crown Prince, Skandagupta (*q.v.*), but the fighting was so severe that one night the Crown Prince had to sleep on the bare earth with his arms as pillow. Their invasion was a remote cause of the decline of the Gupta power.

Q

Qabacha, Nasiruddin—was originally a slave who earned the goodwill and patronage of Shihab-ud-din Muhammad Ghuri and was appointed Governor of Sind by him. He was so powerful that Qutb-ud-din (*q.v.*), the first Sultan of Delhi, thought it wise to secure his friendship by giving him in marriage his own sister. On the death of Sultan Qutb-ud-din, Qabacha thought that he had good claims to the throne of Delhi and became a very strong rival of Sultan Iltutmish (*q.v.*), the son-in-law of Qutb-ud-din and his successor. Eventually Qabacha, after a prolonged conflict, was reduced to submission by Iltutmish.

Qadian—is a small town in the Panjab. It was the headquarters of Mirza Ghulam Ahmad (1838-1908) who started a reform movement amongst the Indian Muslims. His followers came to be called Qadians, after the name of this place. The Qadians are, however, looked upon as heretics by the orthodox Muhammadans as Mirza Ghulam Ahmad claimed prophethood.

Qaid-i-Azam—literally meaning 'a great leader', was a title popularly conferred on Muhammad Ali Jinnah (*q.v.*). Mahatma Gandhi was the first great public man who addressed Jinnah by this title.

Qaiqabad—the last sultan of the Slave Dynasty of Delhi, was a grandson and successor of Sultan Balban (*q.v.*) and ruled from A.D. 1286 to 1290. Coming to the throne at the age of only eighteen Qaiqabad disgraced himself by scandalous debauchery and was deposed and killed. The sultanate then passed to Jalal-ud-din Khalji in 1290 (*q.v.*).

Qamr-ud-din—the *Wazir* of Emperor Muhammad Shah (1719-48) (*q.v.*), was an able officer and materially helped the Emperor's son, Prince Ahmad, to repulse Ahmad Shah Abdali when Abdali invaded India for the first time in 1748. But Qamr-ud-din was killed at the battle of Sirhind on the Sutlej in the Panjab where Abdali was defeated.

Qandahar (**also spelt Kandahar**)—the second city in Afghanistan, has, besides its strategic importance for commanding the head of the railway line from India to Afghanistan, great commercial importance as the most important trading centre in Afghanistan through which passes the major portion of the overland trade between the East and the West. Qandahar has a unique system of sub-surface irrigation for supply of water by sinking shafts at intervals and connecting them by tunnels. Qandahar has a stormy history. It formed in the fifth century B.C. a part of the Persian Empire. It was conquered by Alexander, the king of Macedon, on his way to India in about 326 B.C. and passed after his death to his general Seleucos who in his turn had to cede it to Chandragupta Maurya (*q.v.*) a few years later. It was a part of the empire of Asoka one of whose inscriptions has been recently found in its neighbourhood. On the fall of the Mauryas it passed successively under the Bactrians, Parthians, Kushans and Sakas. In the tenth century it passed under the Afghans and became a Muslim state. In the eleventh century it was taken by Sultan Mahmud, in the thirteenth century by Chengiz Khan and in the fourteenth by Timur. In 1507 it was captured by Babur and remained in the possession of the Mughul emperors of Delhi till 1625 when it was captured by Shah Abbas of Persia. All efforts of Shah Jahan and Aurangzeb to recapture it failed and Qandahar remained a Persian possession, except for a short while (1708-37) till the death of Nadir Shah in 1747 when it was incorporated with Afghanistan by Ahmad Shah Abdali (*q.v.*). But after the death of his grandson, Zaman Shah (*q.v.*) Qandahar became separated from Kabul for a short time. In 1839 the British Indian Government, fighting on behalf of Shah Shuja (*q.v.*) occupied and kept it till 1842. It was again occupied by the British army in 1879 who had, however, to evacuate it in 1881. Since then it has remained a part of the kingdom of Afghanistan.

Qasim Barid—was the minister of the Bahmani Sultan Mahmud Shah (*q.v.*) (1482-1582). From 1492 Qasim Barid was practically the ruler of the residue of the Bahmani empire, consisting of the territory near the capital, left over after the secession of Bijapur, Berar, Golconda and Ahmadnagar. Qasim Barid is regarded as the founder of the Barid Shahi Dynasty which ruled in Bidar till 1619 when the territory was annexed by Bijapur.

Qasim Khan—a Mughul noble, was appointed by Emperor Shah Jahan (1627-59) as Governor of Bengal with orders to exterminate the Portuguese traders who had settled in Bengal but had been abusing the right of trade that had been granted to them. Qasim Khan captured Hughli in 1632 and the Portuguese in Bengal were sufficiently humbled. In 1658 Qasim Khan was sent as a colleague of Raja Jaswant Singh to stop the progress of the rebellious princes, Aurangzeb and Murad, from the Deccan into northern India, but at the battle of Dharmat (*q.v.*) where the Imperialists opposed the rebel Princes, Qasim Khan did little to help his master's cause and lost the battle.

Qazi, the—was the designation of the officer in charge of the dispensation of justice during the Muslim rule in India.

Queen Victoria—*see* Victoria.

Questions of Milinda, the—is the name of a book, the *Milinda-Panha*. It is a famous Buddhist text and contains an elaborate discussion on Buddhist philosophy and religion in the shape of a dialogue between a Yavana (Greek) king named Milinda who has been identified with the Indo-Greek ruler Menander, (*q.v.*) and a Buddhist sage called Nagasena (*q.v.*). Menander is believed to have embraced Buddhism. The work was written probably not later than the third century B.C.

Quli Qutb Shah—was a Turki officer who rose in the service of the Bahmani sultan, Muhammad III (*q.v.*) (1463-82) under the patronage of his minister, Muhammad Gawan (*q.v.*). He was the governor of the eastern part of the Bahmani kingdom, i.e., of Golconda. He withdrew from the Sultan's court at Bidar after the execution of his patron, Muhammad Gawan, in 1481 and declared himself as the independent ruler of Golconda in 1518. He ruled till 1543 when he was ninety years of age and was murdered by his own son Jamshid. The Qutb Shahi dynasty which he founded in Golconda, ruled there till its conquest and annexation by Aurangzeb (*q.v.*) in 1687.

Quran, **the**—is the sacred and holy book of the Muhammadans. It contains the sayings of the Prophet Muhammad and in it lies the foundation of Islamic theology as well as statecraft. The sayings of the Prophet are believed to have been revelations that God put into the Prophet's mouth.

Qutb Minar—is a 'minar' or turret. It is one of the most striking monuments of Muhammadan rule in Delhi and India. It was built, except the basement story, in about A.D. 1232 under the direction of Sultan Iltutmish and was so named probably after the saint from Ush who lies buried there, rather than after the first Sultan who built the basement story and the noble screen of arches. *(H.I.E.A. & A.M.A.I.)*

Qutb Shahi dynasty—was founded in 1518 by Quli Qutb Shah (*q.v.*) who was the governor of the eastern province of the Bahmani kingdom during the reign of Sultan Muhammad Shah III (*q.v.*) and his successor Mahmud Shah (*q.v.*) on whose death he set himself up as the independent ruler of Golconda where he founded the Qutb Shahi dynasty which ruled from 1518 to 1687. Its earlier sultans were Jamshid (1543-50), Ibrahim (1550-80) and Muhammad Quli (1580-1611). Jamshid was a parricide. Ibrahim was a good administrator who shared in the victory of Talikota (*q.v.*) in 1565 against Vijayanagar. The dynasty was overthrown in 1687 by Aurangzeb.

Qutb-ud-din Aibak—the first Muhammadan sultan of Delhi, was originally a native of Turkistan who was bought as a slave and attracted by his ability the notice and favour of his master, Shihab-ud-din Muhammad Ghuri (*q.v.*). After Shihab-ud-din's victory at the second battle of Tarain (*q.v.*) in 1192 Shihab-ud-din returned to Khurasan, leaving the conducting of the campaign in India in the hands of his trusted slave and lieutenant, Qutb-ud-din Aibak. Qutb-ud-din more than justified his master's confidence. In 1193 he occupied Delhi and advanced into the Doab and then during the next ten years (1193-1203) he helped his master in conquering Kanauj, Gwalior, Anhilwara, Ajmer and Kalanjar. In the meantime Qutb-ud-din's lieutenant, Muhammad, son of Baktiyar (*q.v.*), had conquered Bihar and Bengal. Thus at the death of Shihab-ud-din Muhammad Ghuri he had so securely established his reputation that he was easily recognised as the successor of Muhammad Ghuri in his Indian dominions. He is therefore reckoned as the first Sultan of Delhi. He ruled from 1206 till his death in 1210. Qutb-ud-din was a wise and prudent politician as well. He recognised that as he had no blood connection with Muhammad Ghuri so it was essential for him to create a band of supporters amongst the leading members of the entourage of Muhammad Ghuri. He, therefore, himself married the daughter of Taj-ud-din Yildiz, the governor of Kirman and gave his sister in marriage to Nasir-ud-din Qabacha (*q.v.*), the governor of Sind and his daughter to Iltutmish, the foremost of his slaves and the ablest of his generals. Qutb-ud-din ruled only for four years (1206-10) and died from the effects of an accident on the polo ground. He was a strong and ferocious conqueror and ruler, but he also had a fine sense of beauty which led him to begin the construction of the Qutb Minar (*q.v.*). *(F.M. & I.)*

Qutb-ud-din Koka—a foster brother of Emperor Jahangir (1605-27) was sent by the Emperor soon after his accession to arrest and bring to the court Sher Afghan (*q.v.*) who had married Mihr-un-Nisa (the future Empress Nur Jahan) (*q.v.*) and who was then holding a *jagir* at Burdwan in Bengal. Koka could not carry out the mission peacefully and became embroiled in a fight with Sher Afghan in the course of which both were killed.

Qutb-ud-din Mubarak—the last Sultan of the Khalji dynasty, was the son and successor of Sultan Ala-ud-din Khalji (*q.v.*) and ruled from 1316 to 1320. He began his reign with a military success against Harapal Dev, the Hindu king of Deogir, whom he defeated and flayed alive. The success turned his head and he became so much addicted to drinking and sexual pleasures that he was killed by his own favourite, Khusru Khan, in 1320. With his death the Khalji dynasty ended.

Qutlugh Khan—was appointed by Sultan Muhammad Tughluq (1325-51) as the governor of the Deccan. Distance from the capital as well as the disaffection caused by the whimsical administrative measures of the Sultan encouraged Qutlugh Khan to rise in revolt against the Sultan, but he was suppressed by the Sultan in 1344-45.

Qutlugh Khwaja—was a leader of the Mongols who made a raid on India in 1299 with the object of conquering the country. He was defeated in a battle outside Delhi by Zafar Khan, the great and brilliant general of Sultan Ala-ud-din Khalji (1296-1316) and withdrew from India. He had the satisfaction of knowing that his victorious rival Zafar Khan had been killed in the battle.

R

Races of Peoples in India—are divided into four broad classes, namely, the Indo-Aryans (*q.v.*), tall, fair-skinned, long-nosed, speaking languages derived from Sanskrit; the Dravidians (*q.v.*) who predominate in the Deccan and speak Tamil, Telugu, Kanarese and Malayalam which are different from Sanskrit; the primitive tribal peoples, short-statured, dark-skinned and snub-nosed like the Bhils, Kols and Mundas, speaking dialects which have no alphabets, nor any literature; and Mongoloid races, beardless, yellow in complexion and with prominent cheek-bones, like the Gurkhas, Bhutiyas and Khasis. The last two classes are descendants of the Neolithic peoples belonging to the Austric-speaking family of humanity. These four races have lived in India for so many centuries side by side that inter-marriages have often taken place amongst them, especially amongst the Indo-Aryans, the Dravidians and the Mongoloids, making the Indian peoples so mixed that it is now hardly possible to distinguish them. Indian races, like so many other Indian institutions, represent the assimilation and synthesis that have been going on in India for ages. (Risley, H. H., *The People of India*)

Radhakanta Deb, Raja, Sir (1794-1867)—was a well-known leader of the orthodox Hindu community in Bengal in the nineteenth century. He liberally patronised learning, Eastern as well as Western. He spent large sums of money in compiling the famous Sanskrit dictionary, *Sabda-Kalpa-druma*, to which his own contribution illustrated his own erudition and at the same time he co-operated with David Hare (*q.v.*) in founding the Hindu School in Calcutta for educating Indian boys in Western learning, specially in English, and in establishing the School Book Society so that there would be a cheap supply of good text-books which were essential for the expansion of education amongst the people. But he was opposed to social reforms, to the Brahma Samaj (*q.v.*) and even to the abolition of the *Sati* (*q.v.*), i.e. the burning of the Hindu widow on the funeral pyre of her dead husband and organised a mass petition to Parliament against it. He was an example of the conservative Hindu who would accept the utilitarian aspects of Western civilisation and yet retain his faith in the old social customs.

Radhakrishnan, Dr. Sarvapalli—is now the President of the Republic of India. Born in South India in 1888, he began his career as Professor of Philosophy in Presidency College, Madras, and soon won international reputation as a philosopher interpreting the Hindu view of life to the West. It was his association with the Calcutta University (1931-36) as King George V Professor of Philosophy that brought him to the forefront amongst Indian scholars and his appointment as Spalding Professor of Eastern Religions at the University of Oxford followed (1936-39). He then became the Vice-Chancellor of Benares Hindu University which post he held from 1939 to 1948. He had held many other high academic posts and received many academic honours before he took to public life and politics with his appointment as India's ambassador to the U.S.S.R. in 1949. He was the second incumbent to the post which he held till 1952, had the distinction of having been received with warm cordiality by Stalin in Moscow and inaugurated an era of mutual goodwill between the U.S.S.R. and India. On his return from the U.S.S.R., Dr. Radhakrishnan was elected Vice-President of the Republic of India which office he filled with such distinction and ability that he was elected in 1962 to be the President of the Republic of India. He has visited many countries of the world including China as well as the U.S.A. and everywhere has raised the prestige of India by his kindly manners, vast erudition and silver-tongued oratory. His latest visit was to Russia which resulted in strengthening Indo-Russian understanding and led to the public announcement by the U.S.S.R. of increased Russian military aid to India. He is the author of many well-known books of which *The History of Indian Philosophy* is the most noteworthy.

Radhiya Brahmans—are the descendants of Brahmans brought by King Adisura (*q.v.*) from Kanauj and settled in *Radha*, that is to say, western Bengal comprised in the districts of Burdwan, Hooghly and part of Birbhum.

Raffles, Sir Thomas Stamford (1781-1826)—was a famous English administrator who made his mark in the East and is still remembered as the founder of Singapore. Beginning his career as a clerk in the East India Company's office, he came out to Penang in 1805 as an Assistant Secretary and rose to be the Secretary in 1807. In 1808 he submitted a report on the importance of retaining Malacca which the Company had decided to abandon. The Report led to the reversal of the previous order. In 1810 he convinced Lord Minto I, Governor-General of India, of the imperative necessity of conquering Java which was then under French control and was sent to Malacca to prepare the way for the expedition. He did his work thoroughly well and was appointed Lieutenant-Governor of Java on its conquest in 1811. He administered Java for five years (1811-16) with conspicuous success, reducing the taxes but increasing the revenue eightfold. From 1818 to 1823 he administered Sumatra with equal success and it was during this period that with the approval of the British Indian Government he occupied the site of the present Singapore on 29 January, 1819, founded the city and fortified the port there. He greatly developed the place the occupation of which enabled England to control the shortest route from the Indian Ocean to the Pacific Ocean. Raffles was a man of letters and wrote his *History of Java* in 1817. He was also interested in the Biological Sciences, was an F.R.S., and LL.D. and helped in the foundation of the Zoological Society in London in 1825-26. (Boulger, D. C., *Life of Sir Stamford Raffles*)

Rafi-ud-darajat—the tenth Mughul Emperor of Delhi, was the second son of Rafi-us-Shan and a grandson of the seventh Mughul Emperor Bahadur Shah I (*q.v.*). Rafi-ud-darajat was a puppet king set up in 1719 by the Sayyid brothers, the 'king-makers', in succession to Emperor Farruksiyar (*q.v.*). Rafi-ud-darajat ruled for a few months only and was then deposed and killed by the 'king-makers'.

Rafi-ud-daulat—the eleventh Mughul Emperor, was set up by the king-makers, the Sayyid brothers (*q.v.*) in 1719 in succession to his younger brother, Rafi-ud-darajat (*q.v.*). He was, like his brother, a mere puppet in the hands of the Sayyid brothers who removed him shortly after his installation as the Emperor.

Raghaba—*see* Raghunath Rao.

Raghuji Bhonsla—was the founder of the Bhonsla family of Nagpur. He was a Maratha, Brahman by caste and related to Raja Shahu (*q.v.*) by marriage. He was a rival and co-adjutor to Peshwa Baji Rao I (*q.v.*) who practically left him free to establish and consolidate Maratha power in Berar. Raghuji was a great fighter and became an important member of the Maratha confederacy formed by Peshwa Baji Rao I. Raghuji extended his raids along the eastern coast of India into Orissa and Bengal and obliged Nawab Alivardi Khan (*q.v.*) of Bengal to make peace by ceding Orissa to him. His family ruled over Berar with its capital at Nagpur till 1853 when Berar was annexed to the British Indian dominion by Lord Dalhousie (*q.v.*) on the death of the childless Raghuji III.

Raghuji II—a grandson of Raghuji Bhonsla, was the head of the Bhonsla family from 1788 to 1816. He fought in the Second Maratha War (*q.v.*), was defeated at the battles of Assaye (August, 1803) and Argaon (November, 1803) and compelled to make peace with the English by the treaty of Deogaon in December, 1803. By this treaty he surrendered to the English the districts of Cuttuck and Balasore on the eastern coast of India and the whole of his territory west of the river Warda in Central India. Though he did not formally enter into a subsidiary alliance with the British he agreed to have his disputes with the Nizam as well as the Peshwa arbitrated by the British, to appoint no European in his service without the previous consent of the English and to receive a British Resident in his capital at Nagpur. Later on his territories were badly ravaged by the Pindaris, but he died in 1816 just before the outbreak of the Third Maratha War (*q.v.*). He was succeeded by his imbecile son, Parsoji (*q.v.*).

Raghuji Bhonsla III (1818-53)—was installed by the British on the throne of the Bhonslas at Nagpur frankly as a subsidiary prince. At his accession all his territories, north of the Narmada, were annexed by the British. He died childless in 1853 and his state was annexed to the Indo-British empire by the doctrine of lapse (*q.v.*) by Lord Dalhousie.

Raghunandan (also popularly called Smarta Bhattacharya)

—was a famous writer on *Dharmashastra*. He flourished probably
in the sixteenth century, was a contemporary of Chaitanya
Deva (*q.v.*) and was born at Nabadwip in Bengal. His father's
name was Harihara Bhattacharya. His works *Navya-Smriti*
and *Astavingshatitattva* moulded the social life and ritualistic
rites of the orthodox Hindu community of Bengal since his
time.

Raghunath Rao (**often called Raghaba**)—was the second son
of the second Peshwa, Baji Rao I (*q.v.*). He possessed some
military skill and during the Peshwaship of his elder brother,
Balaji Baji Rao (*q.v.*) he led a Maratha army into North India
and, acting in co-operation with the Holkar, he captured Sirhind
in 1758 from Timur Shah (*q.v.*), son of Ahmad Shah Abdali
(*q.v.*), occupied the Panjab, and carried the Hindu paramountcy
to Attock, though "the achievement was politically a hollow
show and financially barren". The expulsion of Timur Shah
from the Panjab brought about a fresh invasion of India by
Abdali in 1759, who not only undid Raghunath's work in the
Panjab but crushed the Maratha power in 1761 at the third
battle of Panipat from the carnage of which Raghunath Rao
escaped. Raghunath Rao, who was inordinately ambitious,
felt deeply chagrined at the accession of his nephew Madhav
Rao (*q.v.*) to the Peshwaship on the death of Balaji Baji Rao.
But his designs were checked by the young Peshwa who proved
to be very capable and intelligent. When, however, on the
untimely death of Madhav Rao in 1772 the Peshwaship passed
to his younger brother Narayan Rao (*q.v.*) Raghunath could
contain himself no longer. He organised a conspiracy against
his young nephew who was murdered before his eyes in 1773.
As Narayan Rao had left no son at the time of his death, Raghunath Rao now claimed the succession to the Peshwaship and
was actually declared Peshwa in 1773. But his accession was
opposed in Poona by a strong party led by Nana Faḍnavis.
This party was immensely strengthened in 1774 by the birth
of a posthumous son of Peshwa Narayan Rao. The infant
named Madhav Rao Narayan was at once declared as the
Peshwa by the opponents of Raghunath. They set up a Council
of Regency and took up the administration of the Maratha
dominions in the name of the infant Peshwa. Raghunath thus
found himself isolated and was even expelled from Maharashtra.
Foiled in his attempts Raghunath Rao proved dead to all
sense of patriotism, appealed to the English in Bombay for help
and eventually concluded with them in 1775 the treaty of

Surat. By this treaty the English agreed to help Raghunath Rao with a force of 2,500 men, the cost of which was to be borne by Raghunath; and, in return, Raghunath undertook to cede to the English Salsette and Bassein with a part of the revenue of Broach and Surat districts, to refrain from forming any alliance with the enemies of the Company and to include the English in any peace that he concluded with the Poona Government. On the basis of this treaty the English in Bombay took up the cause of Raghunath and thus began the First Maratha War which lasted from 1775 to 1783 when it was concluded by the treaty of Salbai. All that Raghunath got by his disgraceful conduct was a pension which he enjoyed in obscurity till his death.

Rahmat Ali Chawdhury—was an educated Indian Muhammadan who coined the term 'Pakistan' in 1933 in Cambridge. It was a development of Iqbal's conception of a Union of Indian provinces with a majority of Muhammadans in their population. These provinces were the North-Western Frontier Province, Baluchistan, Sind, Panjab and Kashmir. His idea was later on taken up by M. A. Jinnah (*q.v.*) who made Pakistan (*q.v.*) a reality in 1947.

Rahula—was the son of Buddha (*q.v.*). When quite a boy he was initiated by his father into the life of a Buddhist monk.

Rai Durlabh—was a Hindu general in the service of Nawab Siraj-ud-daulah (*q.v.*) of Bengal. Along with Mir Jafar, the other general of the Nawab, he joined in a conspiracy against the Nawab with the object of placing Mir Jafar on the throne of Bengal with the help of the English. The conspiracy eventually led to the battle of Plassey (*q.v.*) in which Rai Durlabh, like Mir Jafar, treacherously remained inactive and thus facilitated the English victory. Rai Durlabh was appointed to be the Dewan of Bengal after the installation of Mir Jafar as the Nawab, but he soon incurred the displeasure of the new Nawab and was saved from his wrath by the intervention of Robert Clive (*q.v.*). Rai Durlabh died later on in obscurity.

Raichur—is a fortified town between the Krishna and the Tunga-bhadra rivers. It had great strategic importance and its possession was for a long time a bone of contention between the Bahmani and Vijayanagar kingdoms. It was generally in possession of the Bahmani sultans, but in 1520 the Vijayanagar king, Krishnadeva Raya (*q.v.*) defeated Sultan Ismail Adil Shah of Bijapur and got possession of the fort which remained within the Vijayanagar kingdom until its fall in 1565.

Raigarh—a famous fortress in Maharashtra, was built by Shivaji. In 1674 he was ceremoniously crowned as an independent king in this fort. It was captured by Emperor Aurangzeb in 1689-90.

Railways in India—were first contemplated during the administration of Lord Hardinge I (1844-48), but were actually started in India in 1853 during the administration of Lord Dalhousie (1848-56) who took great pains to persuade the Home Government to agree. At first progress was slow and at the outbreak of the Mutiny only 200 miles of railway lines from Calcutta to Ranigunge in Bengal and from Bombay to Thanah in the Bombay Presidency had been laid. The utility of even these two short lines of railway was so amply proved during the Mutiny that the construction of 5,000 miles of track was sanctioned in 1859. The necessary capital was provided by private British companies who were guaranteed annual profit of about 5 per cent and any profit above that was to be shared between the companies and the Government which also undertook to meet the losses. In return for all these heavy financial liabilities the Government of India had the right to control the railway companies, to check their expenditure and operation, and to purchase the companies at the expiry of each twenty-five year period. Further, mails were to be carried free and troops at reduced rates. The system had many defects: it saddled the revenues of India with losses which the Government were not in a position to prevent and in avoidable waste of funds. But it had the merit of setting in motion on broad lines the whole mechanical transport project of India and made feasible the growth of a national network of railways owned and operated by the Government. Dalhousie had contemplated a uniform gauge all over India, but in practice three different systems— the broad, the metre and the narrow—came to be adopted. In the seventies the Government of India themselves began to take up the construction and operation of railways. Company management and ownership, state management and ownership and state ownership and company management—all these three types of organisations continued in the railways of India till the beginning of the twentieth century. Thereafter fresh company leases became rare and as leases expired the Government regularly purchased the railway lines. The necessity for a uniform system of control was increasingly felt and in 1905 a Railway Board was set up. After the First World War the Railway Board was re-organised, the state management of lines was hastened, and a separate railway budget was prepared from 1925-26. State ownership and state management were accelerated and the construction of new railway lines was encouraged with the result that on the eve of the partition of India there were 43,000 miles of railways in India. In the Federal Union of India there are now 35,395 miles of railways carrying daily four million passengers and 370,000 tons of goods all over the country. More than Rs. 1,200 crores have been invested and eleven lakhs of workers find employment in them. Indian railways have been making increasing contributions to the general revenues—36 crores in 1955-56, 56 crores in 1960-61, 76 crores in 1961-62 and 82 crores in 1962-63. Their economic effects have been great. They have made the tackling of famines easier, they have made the transportation of coal feasible and easier from the mines to the centres of industries, have promoted new industries like cotton, jute and sugar and secured better markets for agricultural products raised in remote parts of the country. In short, railways have hastened the industrialization of India. Their political effects have also been no less important. By making travelling and communication easier, cheaper and quicker they have materially contributed to the consciousness of the political unity of the country. (Knowles, L.C.A., *E.D.B.O.E.*)

Rai Pithora—*see* Prithviraj, Raja.

Raja Ram—was the second son of Shivaji (*q.v.*). After the capture and execution of his elder brother, Shambhuji (*q.v.*) and the capture of the latter's son, Shahu, in 1689 by Aurangzeb, Raja Ram retired to Jinji (also spelt Gingee) in the Karnatak and from there carried on Maratha resistance to Emperor Aurangzeb. He thus became the *de facto* Maratha king from 1689. He courageously stood against the Mughuls, defended Jinji for eight years, and, on its fall in 1698, he escaped to Satara where again he upheld Maratha kingship till his death in 1700.

Raja Ram—a rebellious leader of the Jats, rose against Aurangzeb's rule in 1685, plundered Akbar's tomb at Sikandra in 1688 but was defeated and slain by the Mughuls in 1691.

Raj Singh—was the Rana of Mewar. He gave protection to Ajit Singh, the infant son of Jaswant Singh (*q.v.*) of Mewar and to the latter's widowed wife. He thus incurred the hostility of Emperor Aurangzeb. He also protested against the reimposition of the *jizya* (*q.v.*) by Aurangzeb and started a war against him. This war lasted from 1679 to 1681 and Rana

Raj Singh conducted it with such success that Emperor Aurangzeb made peace with him by dropping the demand for the payment of the *jizya* in lieu of certain territories ceded by the Rana's son and successor, Jay Singh.

Raja Bikram—was a Hindu king who figures prominently in Indian legends as recorded in various story-books like the *Vatrish Simhasana*. But his identity as a historical person has not yet been definitely established. The popular legends about him were probably coloured by indistinct memories of the achievements of Chandragupta II (A.D. 380-415), the third Gupta Emperor.

Rajadhiraja I—the son and successor of the Chola king, Rajendra I (*q.v.*), was the *Yuvaraja* (Crown Prince) from *c.* A.D. 1018 to 1044 and king from 1044 to 1054. He continued the old war with the neighbouring powers, especially the Chalukyas and was defeated and killed by the Chalukya king, Someswara, at the battle of Koppam.

Rajadhiraja II—a later Chola king, ruled from 1163 to 1179.

Rajagopalachari, Chakravarti—a prominent Indian politician, was born in south India in 1879 and is still amongst us. He began his career as a lawyer in 1900, but soon gave up his profession, became an adherent of Mahatma Gandhi with whom he later on entered into matrimonial relations. He joined the non-co-operation movement and suffered imprisonment several times. He was the General Secretary of the Indian National Congress in 1921-22 and was a member of the Congress Working Committee. He is an astute politician and opposed the election of Netaji Subhas Bose as President of the Indian National Congress for the second successive term. He was the Chief Minister of Madras from 1937-39 and again from 1952-54. He supported the idea of the partition of India into India and Pakistan as the price of Indian independence. He became a Minister in the Interim Government in 1946-47 and the first Indian Governor of West Bengal after independence in 1947-48 and the first Indian Governor-General of India from 1948-50. On the inauguration of the new constitution of the Federal Republic of India he became Home Minister of India from 1950-51. Thereafter he ceased to be a member of the Nehru Cabinet, soon drifted away from the Indian National Congress and took a leading part in founding the Swatantra Party (*q.v.*) in 1959. He writes a fine style, is a polished speaker and a very astute statesman.

Rajagriha—the ancient name of the modern township of Rajgir in the Patna district in Bihar, was built by King Bimbisara (*q.v.*) who reigned in the middle of the sixth century B.C. The first Buddhist Council (*q.v.*) is said to have been held at Rajagriha soon after the demise of the Buddha. It is now famous for its hot springs. Near it lie the ruins of the ancient capital of the mythical King Jarasandha.

Rajanya —is a generic term meaning the fighting and princely caste, that is to say, the Kshatriyas. It is used several times in the Asokan edicts.

Rajaraja I—the Chola king (A.D. 985–1018), is entitled the Great. He began his career by the conquest of the Chera country and passing from victory to victory he became the Lord Paramount of Southern India and ruled over a kingdom which included not only the whole of the Madras Presidency and a large part of Mysore, but also Ceylon which he conquered in A.D. 1005 after protracted campaigns. He possessed a powerful navy which enabled him to conquer Kalinga and to acquire a large number of unspecified islands in the twenty-ninth year of his reign.

Rajaraja II—a later Chola king, was the son and successor of Kulottunga Chola II (*q.v.*) and ruled from A.D. 1146 to 1173. The decline of the Chola dynasty had already begun and he was the last Chola king in the direct line.

Rajasekhara—a poet and dramatist, was born in the Deccan but enjoyed the patronage of the Pratihara kings of Kanauj. He was the teacher of the Pratihara king, Mahendrapala (*c.* A.D. 890-910). Of his four extant dramas three are written in Sanskrit and one, named *Karpura-Manjuri*, in Prakrit. He also composed a work on the art of poetry.

Rajasimha—a later Pallava king (8th century), built many temples at Kanchi.

Rajasthan—is a name often applied to denote Rajputana.

Rajatarangini, **the**—is a history of Kashmir written in Sanskrit by Kalhana (*q.v.*) who flourished in the twelfth century A.D. It is a history of the kings of Kashmir in poetry. In addition to a large body of confused tradition about ancient history it contains a trustworthy record of local events in the twelfth century A.D. (*see* Kashmir.)

Rajballabh (A.D. 1698-1763)—was a prominent person in Bengal on the eve of the battle of Plassey (*q.v.*). Born in a Vaidya family with the family name of Sen in a village in the district of Faridpur, he rose by dint of his ability to be the Dewan of Ghasiti Begum (*q.v.*), aunt of Nawab Siraj-ud-daulah (*q.v.*) of

Bengal. He was honoured with the title of Raja by Nawab Alivardi Khan (*q.v.*) but with little scruple he went against Alivardi's grandson and successor, Siraj, and joined with Mir Jafar and other disaffected officers of Siraj in a conspiracy with the English against Siraj. His son, Krishnadas, who was in the service of the Nawab of Bengal, misappropriated a large sum of public money and fled from his post at Dacca to take shelter with the English in Calcutta. The protection that the English in Calcutta gave to Krishnadas, a fugitive from the Nawab's justice, was one of the reasons for which Siraj attacked and captured Calcutta in 1755. Father and son thus equally incurred the displeasure of Siraj, but their conspiracy succeeded. Siraj was defeated at Plassey by the English and Mir Jafar was installed as the Nawab. Rajballabh became one of the counsellors of Nawab Mir Jafar and was later on appointed as the Subadar at Monghyr. But Mir Jafar soon fell and his successor, Nawab Mir Kasim (*q.v.*), who was as hostile to the English as Nawab Siraj, suspected Rajballabh to be a pro-English conspirator and had him killed by drowning in the Ganges.

Rajendra I—the son and successor of the Chola king Rajaraja the Great, ruled from A.D. 1012 to 1044. He continued like his father, a career of conquests. His naval supremacy enabled him to conquer Lower Burma in A.D. 1025-27 and to annex the Andaman and Nicobar Islands. In A.D. 1023 he invaded Bengal, defeated its king, Mahipala (*q.v.*) and carried his victorious arms to the banks of the Ganges. This was a signal triumph and in celebration of it he personally assumed the title of Gongai-Konda and built a new capital city which he called Gangai-Konda-Cholapuram and which he beautified with a magnificent palace, a gigantic temple and a vast artificial lake, which also helped the irrigation of a large area.

Rajendra II—a younger son of the Chola king, Rajendra I (*q.v.*) ruled from A.D. 1052-1064. On the death of his elder brother Rajadhiraja (*q.v.*) while fighting in the battle of Koppam (*q.v.*) he was crowned king on the battlefield and retrieved the day. He maintained intact the power and dominions of the Chola dynasty.

Rajendra III (also called Kulottanga Chola I)—the son of Ammangadevi, a daughter of the Chola king, Rajendra I, who had been married to a Chalukya prince, succeeded to the Chola throne on the extinction of the direct male line with the death of Adhirajendra (*q.v.*) in A.D. 1070. Rajendra III ruled from A.D. 1070 to 1122 and was the most conspicuous of the

later Chalukya-Chola kings. His descendants ruled till
A.D. 1173.

Rajendra Prasad—*see* Prasad, Rajendra.

Rajputana—now called Rajasthan, lies in the north-western part
of India, on both sides of the Aravalli range. A large part of
it is desert-area. The rainfall is meagre and unequally distributed. It became known as Rajputana because it was politically
possessed by the Rajputs (*q.v.*). In the pre-Muhammadan days
it was ruled by a few powerful tribal dynasties of whom the
earliest were the Chalukyas and the Rashtrakutas. Then power
passed into the hands of the Rathors of Kanauj, the Chauhans
of Ajmer, the Solankis of Anhilwara, the Guhilots or Sesodiyas
in Mewar and the Kachchhwahas in Jaipur. These tribal dynasties
were weakened by internal feuds, and though most of them
fought strenuously against the Muhammadan invaders in the
twelfth century they had to yield to the Delhi sultanate whose
sovereignty had to be recognised, more or less, by the whole of
Rajputana. But the Muhammadan control was bitterly resented and attempts were made to throw it off, whenever the
sultanate of Delhi showed any signs of weakness. Thus, on the
eve of the Mughul invasion of India in 1520 by Babur,
Rajputana was again practically free and Sangram Singha
(*q.v.*), the Rana of Mewar, disputed Babur's claim to the Delhi
throne. He was, however, defeated by Babur in 1526 at the
battle of Khanua, and the Mughuls succeeded to the theoretical sovereignty of the Delhi sultans over Rajputana. But it
was Akbar's political sagacity that enabled him to win over
the willing support and loyalty of the Rajput states except
Mewar which also eventually submitted to Mughul sovereignty during the rule of Jahangir (*q.v.*). Rajputana remained
loyal to the Mughul connection till the time of Emperor
Aurangzeb whose policy of religious intolerance led to a war
with the Rajputs which was settled by a peace. Rajputana,
however, could derive no benefit from the decline of the power
of the Imperial Mughuls, for in about 1756 the Marathas
entered into Rajputana, which became so involved in the
general disorganisation of India in the late eighteenth century
and was so demoralised by the Maratha and Pindari plundering
raids that the various Rajputana states willingly accepted
British protection between 1717 and 1720. On the establishment of the Federal Republic of India the states of Rajputana
became merged in the Indian Union, partly in March, 1948
and partly a year later. It is now known as Rajasthan with

Jaipur as its capital, with a *Rajpramukh* and a state Assembly.
(*see* the Rajputs.)

Rajputs, the—were the people who played the most prominent
part in the history of India from the death of Harshavardhana
(*q.v.*) in the middle of the seventh century A.D. to the Muhammadan conquest of Hindusthan at the end of the twelfth
century A.D. They were divided into thirty-six clans, the m⌐st
prominent of which were the Gurjara-Pratiharas, the Chauhans
(or Chahamanas), the Solankis (or Chalukyas), the Paramaras,
the Chandellas, the Tomaras, the Kalachuris, the Gahadvalas
(or Rathors), the Rashtrakutas and the Guhilots (or Sisodias).
The Rajputs were brave, chivalrous, heroic, freedom-loving
and patriotic, but they were also extremely clannish and incapable of acting in unity for any length of time. They were,
however, in the age of Muhammadan aggression, the defenders of
the Hindu faith, patrons of Hindu culture and the protagonists
of Hindu traditions. The circumstance that the earlier princely
and fighting class of people in India was collectively called
Kshatriyas, and not Rajputs, has created a mystery round
the origin of the Rajputs who came into prominence only
after the first half of the seventh century A.D. According to
their own tradition, the Rajputs are the descendants of the
ancient Kshatriyas belonging to the Solar and Lunar dynasties
whose deeds are sung in the *Ramayana* and the *Mahabharata*.
But epigraphic evidence shows that the great clan of the
Sisodias or Guhilots to which belonged the Ranas of Udaipur
who claimed to be descendants of the Kshatriya Prince Rama,
the hero of the *Ramayana*, was founded by a Brahman. Again,
the Gurjara-Pratiharas who claimed descent from Rama's
younger brother, Laksmana, are described in an inscription
as sprung from the lineage of the Gurjaras who were a foreign
people and came to India about the time of the Huna
invasions. Further, epigraphic evidence also proves that
matrimonial relations were established between the Sakas and
the Hindus. The Sakas, the Hunas, the Gurjaras and other
foreign tribal peoples who poured into India during the fifth
and sixth centuries, were surely not exterminated by the
Hindus in India. They gradually merged themselves within
the Hindu society just as the Kushans and the Sakas had
done in an earlier age. Their position within the fold of Hindu
society was determined by their occupations. The fighting
and ruling families amongst them came to be regarded as
Kshatriyas and were given the name of Rajputs. Similarly,

some families amongst the aboriginal tribes, Gonds, Bhars, Kols and the like, raised themselves by their strong arms and carved out kingdoms or states for themselves. When they acquired power and took up princely duties appropriate to the Kshatriyas, they came to be recognised as Kshatriyas and were called Rajputs. Thus the Chandellas were closely connected with the Gonds, the Gaharwars with the Bhars and the Rathors with the Gaharwars. The fact is that castes in Hindu society were for long centuries hereditary as well as occupational groups. The Kshatriyas or Rajputs were more essentially an occupational group, composed of all clans following the Hindu rituals who actually undertook the work of government and military activities. Consequently people of most diverse races were lumped together as Rajputs.

The Rajputs fought long and strenuously against the Muhammadan invaders, and if their incapacity to unite in a common cause led to the final establishment of Muhammadan rule all over India, their determined opposition to Islam certainly delayed the Muhammadan conquest of India. But all their patriotism, valour and spirit of sacrifice seem to have been exhausted in the prolonged conflict with the Muhammadans. No important Rajput prince or state, ever waged any war to prevent the establishment of British rule in India. On the other hand, between 1817 and 1820 all the Rajput princes voluntarily accepted British protection and suzerainty. (Smith, V.A., *Early Hist. of India*; Ojha, G. H., *Hist. of the Rajputs* (Hindi) & Banerjee, A.C., *R.S.A.E.I.C.*)

Rajyamati—was a daughter of king Harshadeva (*c.* 8th century A.D.) of the Salastambha dynasty of Kamarupa (*q.v.*) who was given in marriage to King Jayadeva of Nepal in about A.D. 759.

Rajyapala—a later Pratihara (*q.v.*) king of Kanauj, was patriotic enough to join with King Jaipal (*q.v.*) of Bathindah in a battle with Amir Sabuktigin (*q.v.*) of Ghazni in A.D. 991 and shared the defeat of the confederate Indian army. Later on in A.D. 1019 his own kingdom was invaded by Sultan Mahmud (*q.v.*) and Rajyapal saved himself by timely submission. His conduct was considered cowardly by the neighbouring Hindu kings who soon afterwards, under the leadership of the Chandella king, Ganda, invaded his kingdom in the defence of which he was killed in battle.

Rajyasri—the daughter of Prabhakaravardhana (*q.v.*) king of Thaneswar and sister of Emperor Harshavardhana, was given in marriage to Grahavarman (*q.v.*) the Maukhari king of Kanauj. Soon after the death of her father, Grahavarman was killed by the king of Malwa who made Rajyasri a captive and kept her imprisoned at Kanauj. On the receipt of this news her elder brother, Rajyavardhana, set out to secure her release, but though he defeated the king of Malwa he was killed by the latter's ally, Sasanka (*q.v.*) the king of Bengal. In the midst of these troubles Rajyasri escaped from the prison and fled to the Vindhya forest for refuge. But his younger brother Harshavardhana who had succeeded Rajyavardhana, soon started in quest of her and found her just when she, despairing of all succour, was about to immolate herself. She was brought back to her husband's capital by her younger brother who treated her with very much respect and carried on the administration of Kanauj as well as of the rest of his vast dominions often in consultation with her.

Rakshasa—was, according to the Sanskrit drama, *Mudrarakshasa*, (*q.v.*) the Brahman minister of the last king of the Nanda dynasty who was overthrown by Chandragupta Maurya (*q.v.*).

Rakshasas, the—were, according to the *Ramayana*, the people of Lanka (Ceylon) over whom Ravana (*q.v.*) ruled. They had an advanced civilisation, as evinced by their well-built and beautiful capital city also called Lanka.

Ram Mohan Roy, Raja—*see* Roy, Ram Mohan.

Ram Raja—was a son of Shivaji III and a grandson of Raja Ram (*q.v.*) the second son of Shivaji I. Ram Raja was adopted as his son by Shahu (*q.v.*) and became on Shahu's death the king of Satara. He had little influence and power in Maratha politics.

Ram Raja (or Ram Raya)—was the *de facto* ruler of Vijayanagar kingdom (*q.v.*) during the rule of Sadasiva Rao (1542-65). He was an able statesman and was determined to restore the power of the Vijayanagar empire which had lately declined. He adopted the policy of interfering in the internal disputes among the five Deccan sultanates and allied himself with one or other of the five states against another. Thus, in 1558 he allied himself with Bijapur and Golconda and invaded and plundered Ahmadnagar. But the haughtiness with which he treated his Muhammadan allies so provoked them that in 1565 the Muhammadan sultans of the Deccan except that of Berar, all joined in a coalition against Vijayanagar, invaded the kingdom, defeated and killed Ram Raya in the battle of Talikota and effected the fall and destruction of Vijayanagar.

Ram Singh—the son of Raja Jai Singh (*q.v.*) of Amber, helped Shivaji I (*q.v.*)in his flight from Agra where Emperor Aurangzeb tried to keep the Maratha leader in confinement, contrary to the assurance of safe conduct given to him by Raja Jai Singh. Ram Singh with his Rajput contingent fought valiantly on behalf of Prince Dara (*q.v.*) in the battle of Samugarh and shared the Prince's defeat there. Later on in 1688 he led the Mughul army against the Ahom king, Gadadhar Singh (*q.v.*) of Assam, lost a naval battle near Gauhati and retreated.

Rama—is the hero of the epic the *Ramayana* (*q.v.*). He is considered by the orthodox Hindus as an incarnation of God on earth and is still worshipped by millions of them.

Ramachandra—the son and successor of the Vijayanagar king, Deva Raya II (*q.v.*), ruled only for a few months in A.D. 1422.

Ramachandra Deva—was a king of Devagiri in the Deccan and belonged to the Yadava dynasty. He ruled from 1271 to 1309. In 1292 his kingdom was invaded by a Muhammadan army led by Ala-ud-din Khalji four years before his accession as the sultan of Delhi. Ramachandra Deva was defeated and had to make peace by paying a heavy indemnity and agreeing to pay the revenue of Elichpur as annual tribute. Later on as he withheld the payment his kingdom was again invaded by a Muhammadan army of Sultan Ala-ud-din Khalji (1296-1316) under the command of his general Malik Kafur (*q.v.*) in 1307. Ramachandra Deva was again defeated, compelled to sue for peace and was sent to Delhi where the Sultan treated him kindly and restored him to his kingdom. During the next two years of his reign Ramachandra Deva ruled as a vassal of the Delhi sultanate, regularly remitted revenue to Delhi and even helped theDelhi sultan in his invasion in 1307 of Warangal (*q.v.*).

Ramacharita, **the**—is a Sanskrit *Kavya* (lyric) written by Sandhyakara Nandi, who composed it during the reign of king Madanapala (*q.v.*) (A.D. 1140-55) and whose father was the Minister of War and Peace of King Ramapala (*q.v.*) who ruled in Bengal and Bihar from A.D. 1077 to 1120. "It is a curious work. It is written throughout in double entendre... Read one way, it gives the connected story of the *Ramayana.* Read another way, it gives the history of Ramapaladeva of the Pala dynasty of Bengal." The manuscript of this unique work was discovered in Nepal in 1897 by the late Mahamahopadhyaya Pandit Haraprasad Shastri. (Shastri, H. P., *Memoirs of the Royal Asiatic Society of Bengal,* III, *No. I;* Majumdar, *Hist. of Bengal, Vol. I.*)

Ramacharitamanasa, **the (or the Pool of Rama's life)**—is the most famous work of Tulsidas (*q.v.*) (A.D. 1532-1623). It is written in Hindi and is so popular with all sections of the Hindus of northern India that it has been rightly called their Bible.

Ramagupta—was, according to some, a son and the immediate successor of Samudragupta (*q.v.*). He is said to have been a weak ruler who consented to surrender his wife, Dhruvadevi, to a Saka tyrant in order to save himself. The honour of the queen was saved by Chandragupta, the younger brother of Ramagupta, who killed the Saka, replaced his brother on the imperial throne and married Dhruvadevi. As no contemporary source, either epigraphic or literary, mentions the name of Ramagupta, his existence is considered most uncertain. (Altekar, J. *B.O.R.S.,* XVIII, 1, 1932, 17 ff. & *P.H.A.I.,* pp. 553-54).

Raman, Dr. Sir Chandrasekhara Venkata (1888-)—is an eminent Indian Physicist of international reputation who has raised the prestige of Indian scholarship in modern times. Born in southern India he began his career as an officer in the Indian Finance Department where he served from 1907 to 1917 when he was drafted to the academic world by Sir Asutosh Mukherjee as the Palit Professor of Physics in Calcutta University where he carried on his great researches in the molecular structure of light, leading ultimately to the discovery of a new optical effect, named after him (*Raman's Effect*) in 1928. In 1930 he was made a Fellow of the Royal Society and was awarded the Nobel prize for Physics. He was for years the Head of the Indian Association for the Cultivation of Science in Calcutta, and after retirement from Calcutta University he became the Director of the Indian Institute of Science, Bangalore, where he later on established the Raman Research Institute. He has been on invitation to various Universities in Europe and America as a Visiting Professor and was awarded the Metencai Medal by the Royal Society in 1930, the Franklin Medal of Merit by the Franklin Institute, U.S.A., in 1941 and the Lenin Prize for Peace in 1958. His achievements as a scientist when India was under British thraldom, considerably raised the prestige of India by showing that India could still make contributions to the world's knowledge in the realm of science.

Ramanand—one of the earliest teachers of the *Bhakti* cult, flourished in the fourteenth century A.D. Born at Allahabad in a Brahman family, he travelled through all the holy places of northern India and spent the later portion of his life in South India. He was a worshipper of Rama and preached the doctrine of *Bhakti* in Hindi to all without distinction of caste and sex. Amongst his twelve principal disciples were Padmavati, a lady, and, Kabir, a Muhammadan weaver.

Ramanuja—a celebrated philosopher and the most revered teacher of the Vaishnava Hindus of south India, flourished in the twelfth century A.D., was educated at Kanchi (*q.v.*) and resided at Srirangam near Trichinopoly within the kingdom of the Chola king, Adhirajendra (*q.v.*) but, owing to the hostility of the king, who was a Saivite, Ramanuja retired to Mysore where the Hoysala king, Bittiga (*q.v.*) who was a Jain by faith, was then ruling. Ramanuja converted Bittiga to Vaishnavism and Bittiga, who then assumed the name of Vishnuvardhana (*q.v.*) (A.D. 1111 to 1141), built at Belur and Halebid magnificent temples to Vishnu. Some time later, Ramanuja returned to Srirangam where he lived and preached till his decease. He was the leading opponent of the Absolute Monism (*Advaita*) taught by Sri Sankaracharya (*q.v.*). The system that he preached is known as *Visishtadvaita* or Qualified Monism.

Ramapala—was a Pala king of Bengal and Bihar who ruled for 42 years (*c.* A.D. 1077-1120) and was the fourteenth king of the dynasty. He was a brother of the preceding king, Mahipala II (*q.v.*) who lost his throne and life as the result of a popular revolt led by Divya or Divvoka (*q.v.*) the leader of the Kaivartas. Divya was later on succeeded by Bhima whom Ramapala overthrew, captured and executed along with all the members of the family. Ramapala then restored peace and order within his own kingdom which had been sadly distressed by the recent popular revolt. He also extended his victorious arms into Assam and Orissa and held in check the power of the Gahaḍvala king who ruled beyond Bihar. His achievements have been recorded by Sandhyakara Nandi in his *Ramacharita* (*q.v.*).

Rama's Bridge—is the English rendering of the Sanskrit name *Setubandha* given to the stone-blocks that lie sunk in sea-water between Rameswara on the Indian mainland and Ceylon. According to tradition, as preserved in the *Ramayana*, a stone-bridge was built connecting the mainland of India with Lanka (Ceylon) by the order of Rama, the self-exiled prince of Ayodhya, so that his invading army of *Vanaras* (monkeys) could easily pass from India to Lanka where Rama's consort,

Sita, was kept in confinement by Ravana, the Rakshasa king of Lanka.

Ramayana, the—is one of the two great Sanskrit epics, the other being the *Mahabharata*, which have come down from ancient times. It is attributed to Valmiki and is traditionally considered the earliest of poetic literature (*Adi-Kavya*). Modern historians consider that the *Ramayana* in its present form was a later work than the *Mahabharata* and was composed in the early centuries of the Christian era. The main theme is the story of Rama, the eldest son of King Dasaratha of Ayodhya, (*q.v.*) who, along with his devoted wife Sita and loyal younger brother Laksmana, voluntarily abdicated his right of succession to his father's throne and went into exile for fourteen years in order to enable his father to keep a promise that the latter had made to Rama's stepmother. The adventures of the banished prince, the abduction of Sita by Ravana, the king of Lanka, her recovery with the aid of Hanuman, the vindication of her honour and hundreds of other incidents showing the divine greatness of Rama and illustrating the ideas of the Hindus, are eloquently related in the epic. (Winternitz, *History of Sanskrit Literature*; Hopkins, *The Great Epic of India*; *P.H.A.I.*, pp. 3-4)

Ramdas Samarth—the guru or preceptor of Shivaji I (1627-80), exercised a great deal of influence in the shaping of Shivaji's career and character. He instilled into the mind of his devoted disciple the determination to unite the Marathas, to make religion live again by saving it from the persecution of the Muhammadans and to make the protection of gods, cows, Brahmans and the Hindu faith the objects of his life. Ramdas thus inspired Shivaji I (*q.v.*) to give a religious basis to the kingdom that he founded.

Ramkrishna Mission—was founded by Swami Vivekananda (*q.v.*) on 1 May, 1897, with the object of forming a brotherhood of monks believing in the gospels taught by Sri Ramkrishna Paramahamsa Deva (*q.v.*) dedicated to the preaching and teaching of the doctrines of Ramkrishna and to the selfless service of distressed humanity and thus giving a practical shape to the Vedanta philosophy which identified man with God. It is a progressive Order which accepts science and scientific thinking which it tries to combine with Indian spirituality so that India with her rich spiritual heritage may be as efficient as the West. The Ramkrishna Mission runs schools, colleges, hospitals; it teaches agriculture, arts, crafts;

it publishes magazines and books; it maintains branches (called *Ashramas*) all over India and in many countries outside India. It is now a very big organisation which has largely helped in spreading the message of India's Vedantic religion to the West and has also substantially contributed to the improvement and amelioration of the condition of the people of India. (Swami Tejasananda, *Ramkrishna Movement*)

Ramkrishna Paramahamsa (1834-86)—was a very great spiritual teacher of the Hindus in modern times; indeed he is looked upon by many as an incarnation of God himself. Born in a poor priestly family in a remote village in the district of Hooghly in Western Bengal he received practically no formal education, Eastern or Western, and became early in life attached to the temple of goddess Kali at Dakshineswar, near Calcutta, as a priest. By long years of *Sadhana* (meditation and prayer) he became a divinely inspired personage whose transcendent intellect, clear exposition of the most abstruse philosophical doctrines in the simplest language, his deep faith in the inherent truth of all religions, his broad catholicism, mysticism and spiritual fervour attracted to him men like Keshabchandra Sen (*q.v.*) a recognised leader of the Brahma Samaj, as well as a number of ardent young men of whom Narendranath Datta, the future Swami Vivekananda, was the most prominent. Ramkrishna preached that as different words in different languages denote the same substance, e.g., 'water', so Allah, Hari, Christ, Krishna etc. are but different names under which different peoples worship the same Great God who is both one and many, with and without forms, and may be conceived either as a great universal spirit or through different symbols. He further taught that an individual, however great, was too small to show to a fellow human being any compassion which was only a divine gift. All that a man can and should do is to try to *serve* a fellow man in a spirit of humility, for in serving a human being he serves God who is immanent in all beings, particularly in human beings. This doctrine of Ramkrishna that the best way of God-realization was through the selfless service of human beings as the essence of Hindu religion was carried on, after the passing away of the Master, by his favourite disciple, Swami Vivekananda (*q.v.*) throughout India as well as in America and England, and lies at the basis of the Ramkrishna Mission (*q.v.*) which has developed into an international organisation. (Rolland, Romain, *Life of Ramakrishna*; Swami Vivekananda, *My Master*)

Ramnagar, the battle of—was fought in 1848 between the English and the Sikhs during the course of the Second Sikh War (*q.v.*). It cost both sides heavily but was inconclusive.

Ramnarayan—was a prominent person in Bengal in the second half of the eighteenth century. He attracted the notice of Robert Clive (*q.v.*) after the battle of Plassey (*q.v.*) and secured his patronage. He was placed in charge of Bihar with his headquarters at Patna during the Nawabship of Mir Jafar (*q.v.*) and showed his ability by successfully holding Patna against an attack by Prince Ali Gauhar (later on Emperor Shah Alam II) (*q.v.*). But he lost the confidence of Nawab Mir Kasim (*q.v.*) who first dismissed him from his office and later on killed him in 1763 as a pro-British traitor.

Ramnarayan Tarkaratna (1822-86)—was the first modern Bengali dramatist. He was a good Sanskrit scholar and was a Professor of Sanskrit in Sanskrit College (*q.v.*), Calcutta, for twenty-seven years (1855-82) and wrote many Sanskrit and Bengali dramas. His *Kulin-Kula-Sarbbasva* which was published in 1854 is considered the earliest drama in Bengali. He was also a social reformer. His other works are '*Veni-Samhar*', *Ratnavali, Avijnana Sakuntala* and *Nava-Nataka*, all written in Bengali and *Arya-satakam* and *Daksha-Yajnam* in Sanskrit.

Ranade, Madhav Govinda (1852-1904)—was a prominent public man, reformer and scholar. Born in a Brahman family of Maharashtra, he had a brilliant academic career and started life as a lawyer. He was soon raised to the Bench and became a judge of the Bombay High Court. He was in the forefront of many public movements in the Bombay Presidency and was typical of the new generation of Indians that was growing up in the nineteenth century as the result of contact with Western culture and civilisation. He became a devoted and enthusiastic member of the *Prarthana Samaj* (*q.v.*) of Bombay and took a leading part in promoting its objects. He was one of the founders of the Widow Re-marriage Association in 1861 and of the Deccan Education Society. He also supported the foundation of the Indian National Congress (*q.v.*) which held its first session in Bombay in 1885 and in which he actually took part. He inaugurated the practice of holding a social conference along with the annual meeting of the Congress. He emphasized the interdependence of social, economical, political and religious development of men and insisted on a comprehensive reform movement aiming at the development on all spheres. He also emphasized that reforms to be successful should be constructive and not simply destructive and thus gave a new orientation to the reform movement in India. He was an erudite scholar and the more important of his works were *Widow-Remarriage, Land Revenue Act, Life of Raja Ram Mohan Roy, Rise of the Maratha Power,* and *Religious and Social Reform.* (Andrews, C. F., *Indian Renaissance*)

Ranga I—the second king of the fourth or Aravidu dynasty of Vijayanagar (*q.v.*), was the son and successor of Tirumala, brother of Ramraja, who lost his life at the battle of Talikota (*q.v.*), 1565. Ranga I ruled from *c.* 1573-85 over a kingdom which had shrunk much since 1565.

Ranga II—was practically the last king of the fourth dynasty of Vijayanagar (*q.v.*). He ruled from 1642 to 1646 when the dynasty was reduced to a family of local chiefs. His inscriptions continued till 1684, but little is known of his political activities.

Ranjit Singh, Maharaja (1780-1839)—was the founder of a Sikh kingdom in the Panjab. His father, Maha Singh, was the leader of the Sukerchakia *misl.* Ranjit was but a boy of twelve when his father died and Ranjit succeeded to the headship of a small confederacy of Sikh *misls* with a small territory and very limited military resources. But the repeated incursions into the Panjab by the Afghan ruler, Zaman Shah (*q.v.*) during the years 1793-98 created so much disorder in the province that young Ranjit, then in his eighteenth year, occupied Lahore in July 1799. Zaman Shah made virtue of a necessity, recognised Ranjit as the Governor of Lahore and conferred on him the title of Raja. Henceforward Ranjit followed a successful military career. He threw off the Afghan yoke, became the recognised leader of the trans-Sutlej *misls*, occupied Amritsar with its citadel and the famous gun *Zamzama* in 1805, and reduced Jammu to a tributary state. It was in 1805 that Jaswant Rao Holkar (*q.v.*) with Lord Lake (*q.v.*) in hot pursuit, entered the Panjab and Ranjit was threatened with a destructive war. But he got rid of both by clever diplomacy which culminated in a treaty with the British by which Holkar was to be excluded from the Panjab and the British recognised Ranjit's supremacy over all Panjab north of the Sutlej. Quarrels amongst the cis-Sutlej states and appeals by some of them for assistance combined with his natural desire for bringing all the Sikhs under his own unified control led Ranjit to send expeditions to the cis-Sutlej area and he occupied Ludhiana in 1807. But this extension of his power beyond the Sutlej was looked upon with great disfavour by some of the cis-Sutlej Sikh states as well as by the English who had already extended their power over Delhi. So a British mission under Sir Charles Metcalfe followed by the despatch of a British force under David Ochterlony met Ranjit Singh and the latter with his practical statesmanship entered into a 'perpetual friendship' with the British by the treaty of Amritsar (1809). According to this treaty Ranjit withdrew from Ludhiana, agreed to confine his conquests to the north and west of the Sutlej and to cease to interfere in the affairs of the cis-Sutlej states wihch passed definitely under British protection. But Ranjit's conquests continued in other directions. He captured Kangra in 1811, Attock in 1813, gave shelter to the fugitive Afghan king, Shah Shuja, and secured from him the celebrated Koh-i-noor (*q.v.*) in 1814, Multan in 1818, Kashmir in 1819, reduced Peshawar to a dependency in 1823 and captured its citadel in 1834. He also coveted Sind, but there he was forestalled by the British who looked with suspicious dread upon the expansion of Ranjit's dominions. His recognition of what was impossible led him to renew in 1831 the treaty of perpetual friendship with the English with whom he never measured swords and whom he never allowed to send any army into his dominions on any pretext whatsoever. When Ranjit died in his fifty-ninth year in 1839 he had created a compact Sikh kingdom extending from Peshawar to the Sutlej and from Kashmir to Sind. It is true that he did not endow his creation with suitable administrative institutions, nor did he succeed in instilling into the minds of the Sikhs a national fervour as Shivaji (*q.v.*) had done in Maharashtra with the result that his kingdom fell in a heap only ten years after his death. Yet what he did in the teeth of the opposition of the Afghans, of the English, and, last, but not the least, of many of his coreligionists was no mean achievement and entitles him to be regarded as one of the most important personalities in the history of India in the nineteenth century. (Sinha, N. K., *Ranjit Singh*; Griffin, Sir L., *Ranjit Singh*)

Ranoji Sindhia—*see* Sindhia.

Rashtrakuta dynasty, the—was founded by Dantidurga in A.D. 753 in the Deccan with Nasik (*q.v.*) as the capital. The dynasty ruled from A.D. 753 to 973 and produced fourteen kings, namely, Dantidurga (753-60), Krishna I (760-75), Govinda II (775-80), Dhruva (780-93), Govinda III (793-815), Amoghavarsa I (815-80), Krishna II (880-912), Indra III (912-16), Amoghavarsa II (916-17), Govinda IV

(917-35), Amoghavarsa III (935-40), Krishna III (940-65), Khattiga (965-72) and Kakka II (972-73). Dantidurga, the chieftain of the Rashtrakuta clan of the Rajputs, overthrew Kirtivarman II, the last Chalukya king of Vatapi, and established his rule over the Chalukya dominions in the Deccan. The second king, Krishna I, is memorable for the unique monolithic Kailasha temple at Ellora. The fourth king, Dhruva, defeated the Gurjara king, Vatsaraja. Govinda III, the fifth king, extended the Rashtrakuta dominions from Malwa in the north to Kanchi in the south. The sixth king, Amoghavarsha, was remarkable for his long rule of 65 years. He transferred the capital from Nasik to Manyakheta (modern Malkhed) and was so powerful and rich that the contemporary Arab merchant, Sulaiman, considered him to be one of the four great kings of the world. The seventh king, Indra III, ruled only for two years, but within this short period he successfully invaded Kanauj (*q.v.*) and dethroned for a time the Pratihara king, Mahipala (*q.v.*). In the reign of the twelfth king, Krishna III, began a prolonged war with the Cholas but the fall of the Rashtrakutas was brought about not by the Cholas but by a branch of the Chalukyas led by Taila or Tailapa in A.D. 973. The Rashtrakutas were Brahmanical Hindus who built many temples and liberally patronised Sanskrit literature. They, however, maintained friendly relations with the neighbouring Muhammadan state of Sind and their kings were known to the Arabs as 'Balhara' (i.e., Vallabha Rai).

Ravana—is the villain in the epic, *Ramayana* (*q.v.*). He was the Rakshasa king of Lanka (Ceylon) who stole Rama's wife, Sita, and by his unrighteous conduct brought ruin upon himself and his whole family.

Rawlinson, Sir Henry Creswicke (1810-95)—was an English soldier who came out to India in 1827 as a cadet in the Company's service. He developed into an eminent Orientalist, who deciphered in 1848 the cuneiform character of the Behistun inscription (*q.v.*). He is the author of many valuable works on the antiquities of Babylon and Assyria.

Rawlinson, Lord Henry Seymour (1864-1925)—was the Commander-in-Chief in India from 1920 to 1925. During his term of office a beginning was made in the Indianisation of the officers' cadre in the British Indian army. He died at Delhi in March, 1925.

Raymond—a distinguished French general, was appointed in

1795 by the Nizam of Hyderabad to re-organise his army. He carried out the work efficiently with the assistance of other French officers, but was discharged by the Nizam in 1798 as the result of the pressure exercised upon him by Governor-General, Lord Wellesley, who made the dismissal by the Nizam of his French officers a condition of the subsidiary alliance into which the Nizam entered for protecting himself against his Indian enemies.

Raziya, Sultana—was the only lady to occupy the throne of Delhi. She was a daughter of Sultan Iltutmish who, before his death, nominated her as his successor. The nobles, however, disliked the idea of a female ruling over them, set up her elder brother Rukn-ud-din (*q.v.*) as the Sultan in May, 1236, immediately after the death of Sultan Iltutmish. But Rukn-ud-din was deposed and killed a few months after his accession and his sister, Raziya, was installed on the throne of Delhi. She ruled for four years (1236-40). She took active part in politics as well as in wars, rode an elephant in the sight of the public and led the armies against Hindu and Muhammadan rebels alike. She possessed remarkable talents and kept intact the dominions of the Delhi sultanate extending from Sind to Bengal. But the Muhammadan nobles could not reconcile themselves to the rule of a woman. Further, the trust that she placed on an Abyssinian slave named Yaqut gave them an excuse for an open revolt in which the lead was taken by Altuniya (*q.v.*) the governor of Sind. The rebels deposed her, but Raziya tried to save her position by marrying the rebel-leader, Altuniya. This adroit move, however, could not reconcile the Muhammadan nobles who defeated and killed Raziya and her husband in October, 1240.

Reading, Lord Rufus Daniel Isaacs (1860-1935)—was the Viceroy and Governor-General of India from 1921 to 1925. He availed himself of the inherent Hindu-Muslim differences, arrested Gandhiji, saw the non-co-operation movement collapse, and made no positive contribution to the solution of the Indian constitutional problem.

Red Shirt Movement—was a militant anti-British movement started by Abdul Gaffar Khan (*q.v.*) in 1930 in the North-West Frontier Province. It was an amalgam of Pan-Islamism and Indian Nationalism. It professed to be non-violent, but violence was so much in the nature of the Frontier peoples that its profession of non-violence was always suspected. In any case it became for a while a strong force amongst the Frontier peoples and enabled the Congress party to win the elections to the provincial legislature and to be in power when independence and partition came in 1947. After the passing of the Frontier Province into Pakistan, the Red Shirt Movement adopted a new slogan of Pakhtoonistan which aimed at establishing a separate independent state consisting of the frontier districts inhabited by the tribal peoples. It was declared illegal and suppressed by the new Government of Pakistan.

Regulating Act, the—was passed in 1773 by the British Parliament with the object of effecting an improvement in the administration by the East India Company of the Indian territories that had already come under their control. It gave the Company a new constitution. The Directors were henceforth to be elected for four years, and one-fourth of their number was to retire every year, remaining at least one year out of office. The Directors were required to lay before the British Chancellor of the Exchequer all correspondence with India dealing with revenues, and before a Secretary of State everything dealing with civil and military affairs and administration in India. There was to be a Governor-General of Bengal, assisted and controlled by four Councillors and the opinion of the majority was to prevail. The Governor-General had a casting vote when there was an equal division of opinion. The Governor-General and Council were given power to superintend and check the Governments of the Presidencies of Bombay and Madras in their relations with the Indian powers. The first Governor-General and Councillors, Warren Hastings, Sir John Clavering, Colonel Monson, Philip Francis and Richard Barwell were all named in the Act. They were to hold office for five years, and future appointments were to be made by the Company. The Governor-General was granted a salary of £25,000 per year and each of the Councillors £10,000 annually. A Supreme Court was set up in Calcutta, consisting of a Chief Justice and three puisne judges. Sir Elijah Impey was appointed the first Chief Justice on an annual salary of £8,000. The Regulating Act which had the merit of being the first legal measure to prevent the growth of one man's rule in the Company's dominions in India, had many defects. First, though the Company had already become the *de facto* rulers of Bengal, the Act left the titular authority of the Nawab of Bengal intact. So the legal sovereignty lay with the Nawab and not with the Company or the British Crown. Secondly, a majority of the Council could over-rule the Governor-

General and create a deadlock in the executive administration. Thirdly, the control of the Governor-General and the Council over the Presidencies of Madras and Bombay was hemmed in by limitations which made it ineffective, and both the Presidencies became involved in wars with the neighbouring Indian states without obtaining the previous sanction of the Governor-General and Council. Lastly, the jurisdiction of the Supreme Court, the law it was to administer and its relations with the Council were not clearly and precisely stated, leading to disastrous consequences. (Ilbert, Sir C., *The Government of India*).

Regulation III of 1818, the—was a law authorising the British Government in India to put under detention for an indefinite period any person who may be suspected of committing or contemplating to commit any act injurious to the safety of the British Government in India. It was originally passed to check violent rebels, but was applied in the twentieth century to silence the supporters of the Indian National movement. Lala Lajpat Rai (*q.v.*) Krishna Kumar Mitra, Subhas Chandra Bose (*q.v.*) and many other patriotic Indians were detained and sent to exile in Burma under Regulation III of 1818.

Rennell, James (1742-1880)—was the Surveyor-General of Bengal from 1764 and produced the Bengal Atlas in 1779. He has been called the father of Indian Geography. Amongst his works are *Memoirs and Map of Hindustan, 1783,* and The *Marks of the British Army in the Peninsula of India.*

Reza Khan—*see* Muhammad Reza Khan.

Rig Veda, the—is the earliest and oldest of the four Vedas which are considered by orthodox Hindus as revelations by God to the various *Rishis* or sages with whose names the hymns are associated. The term is a combination of two words, namely, *rich* or hymns and *veda* or knowledge and its literal meaning is 'Hymns of Knowledge'. Like the other three Vedas the Rig Veda is divided into four parts, namely, *Samhita, Brahmana, Aranyaka* and *Upanishada*. The Rig Veda *Samhita* contains about 1,017 *shuktas* or hymns which are divided into 10 *mandalas* or books. Some of these hymns were sacrificial hymns while there are others in which the breath of genuine primeval religious poetry is felt. The *Aitareya* and *Kausitaki Brahmanas* as well as the *Aitareya* and *Kausitaki Aranyakas* also belong to the Rig Veda. The age of the Rig Veda has not yet been precisely fixed. Very probably its composition covered a long period of time extending from 2500 B.C. to 500 B.C.

Whatever may, however, be the date it is certain that the Rig Veda is the earliest literary record of the Indo-Aryans. It affords a picture of the religious, social, economic and political condition of the Indo-Aryans during the early period of their settlements in India. (*see* also *Vedas*). (*C.H.I.*, I., iv; Das, A. C., *Rigvedic India* & Kaegi, A., *The Rigveda*)

Ripon, Lord George Frederick Samuel Robinson (1827-1909)— was the Viceroy and Governor-General of India from 1880-84. He was a Gladstonian liberal in his political principles and endeared himself immensely to the Indians by his liberal administration. His first work in India was to bring to an end the second Afghan War (*q.v.*) by recognising Abdur Rahman (*q.v.*) as the Amir of Afghanistan and evacuating the Indo-British expeditionary forces from Afghanistan in 1881. Thereafter Lord Ripon devoted himself to the improvement and liberalisation of the internal administration of the country. He introduced complete free trade retaining small duties on a very few articles like wines, spirits, ammunition and arms, lowered the salt tax and tried unsuccessfully to persuade the British Government to give a pledge that in districts, which had once been surveyed, the land revenue should not be enhanced except on the sole ground of a rise in prices. He established in each *tahsil* or Sub-division a local board consisting of elected popular representatives with powers to administer such funds as the local governments may possibly place at their disposal for the management of local roads, of watch and ward arrangements and other local needs. Similarly popular bodies called District Boards were created and given charge of education, public works and other similar public duties. In towns and cities where municipal bodies existed the election of non-officials as Chairmen was permitted. He repealed the Vernacular Press Act which had been passed by Lord Lytton I (*q.v.*) in 1878 and thus allowed the newspapers published in the various Indian languages equal freedom with those published in the English language in India. He laid down regulations, in consonance with the Hunter Commission's Report (*q.v.*) for the improvement of primary and secondary schools in India. He carried out in 1881 the rendition of Mysore and handed over to the Raja the administration of Mysore, subject to the condition of good and efficient administration. In 1881 an Act was passed for the purpose of regulating and improving the condition of labour in Indian factories by restricting the age and hours of work of children below twelve years of age, by requiring that dangerous machinery should be properly fenced and by appointing inspectors. His last, but not the least, attempted reform was to abolish judicial disqualifications based on race distinctions by the Ilbert Bill (*q.v.*) in 1883. The bill provided that Indian judges should have the same rights as European judges to try and judge Europeans who might be charged with criminal offences. This bill provoked such an agitation amongst the Europeans and Anglo-Indians, non-official and even official, that the bill had to be substantially altered before it could be passed and racial distinctions continued to exist. But the very proposal to pass such a bill immensely increased the popularity of Lord Ripon with the Indians who presented him with hundreds of addresses on his retirement on resignation in 1884 and his journey from Simla to Bombay resembled a triumphal procession. (Lal, S., *India under Ripon*).

Rishis, **the**—are the sages in ancient India to whom the Vedic hymns are believed to have been revealed. They were the authors of the sacred literature of the Hindus. Vyasa was one such *rishi* to whom is attributed the authorship of the largest number of the sacred books. Some of them, like Agastya, were pioneers of Aryan civilisation in different parts of India. The Aryanisation of the Deccan is traditionally believed to have been started by *Rishi* Agastya.

Roberts, Lord Frederick Sleigh (1832-1914)—joined the Bengal Artillery in 1852. During the Mutiny (*q.v.*) he rendered distinguished service and won the V. C. for personal bravery. During the Second Afghan War (*q.v.*) he first commanded the Kuram Field Force in 1878, the Kabul Field Force in 1879, reached Kabul, received the submission of Yakub Khan (*q.v.*) and despatched him to India. After the British defeat at the battle of Maiwand (*q.v.*) in July 1880, Roberts made a historic march from Kabul to Qandahar covering 313 miles in 22 days and defeated Ayub Khan (*q.v.*) at Qandahar in September, 1880, and thus restored the prestige of British arms. He took part in the South African War in 1881 and was promoted C-in-C in Madras in 1881 and then C-in-C of India which office he held from 1885 to 1893. A peerage was conferred on him before he retired from India in 1893. Later on, Lord Roberts was made the C-in-C in the Boer War which he brought to a victorious close in 1900. He died in 1914 of pneumonia which he contracted while visiting the Indian troops who had been sent to France to take part in the First World War on behalf of Britain.

Roe, Sir Thomas—came to India in 1615 as an ambassador from King James I of England to Emperor Jahangir (*q.v.*) He landed at Surat and then proceeded to Jahangir's Court at Ajmer. Roe was an educated person, a polished courtier and a trained diplomat and was sent to India for the purpose of negotiating a treaty with the Mughul Emperor giving security to English trade. Roe won the favour of Jahangir and lived in his Court for three years at Ajmer, Mandu and Ahmedabad. He failed to procure a formal and definite treaty, but he obtained permission for the establishment by the English Company of factories at certain towns in the Mughul dominions and enhanced also the prestige of the English in the estimation of the Mughul administration. Roe disapproved of the military-commercial policies of the Portuguese and the Dutch and recommended that the English Company should confine their activities only to trade and commerce over the seas. He served the Company well and left India in 1619.

Rohilkhand (its people and Rohilla War)—is the name given to the fertile region lying to the north-west of Oudh between the Ganges on the south and the Kumaon hills on the north after its occupation by the Afghan tribe of Rohillas in about A.D. 1740. Its population was mainly Hindu, but its administration was run by the Muhammadan Rohillas. The Rohillas had sided with Ahmad Shah Abdali in the Third battle of Panipat (*q.v.*) in 1761. Ten years later when the Maratha power revived the Rohillas were threatened by the Marathas and in self-defence entered into an agreement with Nawab Shuja-ud-daulah of Oudh in 1772 by which they proposed to pay the Nawab 40 lakhs of rupees if the latter would assist them in repulsing the Maratha invasion. In 1773 the Marathas threatened Rohilkand with an invasion, but retired as they found that the Rohillas were backed by the Nawab of Oudh, supported by a British brigade. The Nawab demanded from the Rohillas the payment of 40 lakhs of rupees as agreed upon in 1772. The Rohillas evaded payment on the plea that the Marathas had retired for reasons of their own, and as the Nawab was not called upon to fight any battle so he was not entitled to the promised payment. In 1773 the Nawab of Oudh concluded with the British the treaty of Benares (*q.v.*) by which *inter alia* the British pledged to help the Nawab of Oudh with a British brigade in order to enable him to force the Rohillas to pay the Nawab the promised sum of 40 lakhs. In pursuance of this treaty the Nawab, helped by a British brigade, invaded

Rohilkand in 1774, defeated and killed its ruler, Hafiz Rahamat Khan, at the battle of Miranpur Katra and incorporated Rohilkhand, except for a small portion called Rampur, with Oudh. The British intervention in the war between the Nawab of Oudh and the Rohillas who had given no provocation to the British, was bitterly criticised in the British Parliament and it formed one of the charges against Warren Hastings who was responsible for it, at the time of his impeachment which, however, ended in his acquittal. The Nawab of Oudh, however, could not keep Rohilkhand long under his control, for he had to surrender it to the British in 1801 on a most inequitable demand made by Lord Wellesley (*q.v.*) who was then the Governor-General.

Ronaldshay, Earl of—was the Governor of Bengal from 1917 to 1922. (*see* Zetland, Lord.)

Rose, Sir Hugh—was a British general who was sent out to India to suppress the Sepoy Mutiny (*q.v.*). He landed in Bombay late in 1854, made Mhow his headquarters and carried on a brilliant campaign in Central India. He captured Aligarh early in 1858, relieved Saugor, invested Jhansi, defeated Tantia Topi (*q.v.*) at the battle of the Betwa, carried the fortress of Jhansi by storm and in May, 1858, he defeated a large sepoy army at the battle of Kunch. Thus when, in less than six months, he seemed to have ended the campaign and broken the Mutiny in central India the Rani of Jhansi (*q.v.*) and Tantia Topi (*q.v.*), both pursued by British troops, dashed on to Gwalior which they occupied, seized the arsenal, proclaimed Nana Shaheb as the Peshwa and thus re-vitalized the cause of the sepoys and threatened to spread the Mutiny to the Deccan. Rose by a supreme effort threw his tired army on Gwalior, defeated the rebels in two battles, in one of which the brave Rani of Jhansi, clad in male attire, met a soldier's death. Rose re-captured Gwalior in June, 1858 and thus brought to a victorious end a campaign which he had conducted very brilliantly.

Roshnara, Begum—was the younger and second daughter of Emperor Shah Jahan and his consort Mumtaz Mahal. During the succession war amongst her four brothers she supported Aurangzeb and helped his victory by supplying him secretly with all information about developments in her father's capital. She was a bitter opponent of her eldest brother, Dara, whose execution as a heretic she persistently demanded at his trial.

Round Table Conference—was held in London in 1930-32 in

consonance with the declaration made on the 31st August, 1929, by the Viceroy, Lord Irwin, that after the publication of the Report of the Simon Commission (*q.v.*) a Round Table Conference would be convened in London to draw up a new constitution for India. It was a measure to conciliate Indian public opinion which was very much estranged by the all-white composition of the Commission. The Indian National Congress at its 1929 session at Lahore with Pandit Jawaharlal Nehru as the President, declared that the attainment of complete independence was its goal and nothing was to be gained by the Congress taking part in the proposed Round Table Conference. On the 6th April, 1930, Mahatma Gandhi started the Civil Disobedience Movement. A month later the Report of the Simon Commission was published. Government issued new coercive ordinances and by resorting to various repressive measures including the arrest and detention of the Congress leaders, including Mahatma Gandhi, suppressed the outward manifestation of the Civil Disobedience Movement, but discontent continued to seethe beneath the surface. It was in order to allay this continued discontent that the Round Table Conference of the representatives of all the political parties in India as well as of England was called in London in November, 1931. Ramsay Macdonald, the Prime Minister, presided over the conference which held three sessions—the first from 16 November, 1930 to 19 January, 1931, the second from 1 September to 1 December, 1931 and the third from 17 November to 24 December, 1932. The Indian National Congress sent no representative to the first session of the Round Table Conference, yet it resulted in one signal advance, namely, the agreeement of the British Government to concede the responsibility of the executive to the legislature in India both in the provinces and at the Centre, provided the Central legislature was constituted on a basis of federation between British India and the Indian India ruled by the Princes. The second session was attended by Mahatma Gandhi as the sole representative of the Indian National Congress, and devoted its main efforts to settling the difficult question of the proportion of communal representation. This could not be settled by mutual agreement, as the Muhammadans were always led to believe that they would be getting more from the British than from an agreement with the Hindus. Making this stalemate an excuse, Mr. Ramsay Macdonald announced a Communal Award (*q.v.*) which gave separate representations not only to the recognised religious minorities but even to the depressed classes amongst the Hindus. This was deeply resented by Mahatma Gandhi who went on a fast unto death against it and led to the acceptance of the Poona Pact (*q.v.*) by the Congress and the British Government. The vexed problem of Communal Representation was thus settled in a way which was not very satisfactory, but which was accepted by all parties in the absence of a better one. The third session of the Round Table Conference agreed upon certain principles of constitutional development in India which were drawn up in a White Paper which was submitted to a Joint Select Committee of both Houses of Parliament and eventually formed the basis of the Government of India Act, 1933. (*Report of the First Round Table Conference*, 1931 & Lumby, E.W.R., *Transfer of Power in India*)

Rowlatt Acts—were passed by the Government of India in 1919 against the vote of every non-official Indian member of the Imperial Legislative Council. The two Acts, known as the Rowlatt Acts, were intended to implement the Report of the Rowlatt Committee submitted in 1917 which recommended strengthening the law in view of the evidence that it received on the existence of an extensive subversive movement. Of the two Acts one provided for greater and stricter control over the press, and the other provided for the trial of political offenders by judges without juries and legalising internment without trial by the Provincial Governments of persons suspected of subversive aims. The Rowlatt Acts created great discontent throughout the country leading to *hartals* all over the country, riots in many places culminating in the Jallianwala Bagh massacre (*q.v.*) and the starting of the non-co-operation movement in 1920. All these troubles were definitely the result of a very bad official miscalculation of the danger of sedition on which the laws were based, as was proved by the circumstance that the powers conferred on the Government by the two Acts were never required to be exercised.

Roy, Krishnachandra, Maharaja (1728-82)—of Nadia, a leading Hindu Zamindar of Bengal, was a great patron of Hindu religion and Sanskrit learning and made many gifts to *Pundits*, temples and *tols*. He advised the conspirators against Nawab Siraj-ud-daulah to seek the help of the English but he took no active part in the battle of Plassey (*q.v.*). His seventh descendant, Maharaja Kshaunishchandra, was a Member of the Executive Council in Bengal (1924-28).

Roy, Ram Mohan, Raja (1772-1833)—was the inaugurator of the Modern Age in India. He was born in a well-to-do Brahman family at Radhanagar in the Hughli district of West Bengal. He was educated at home, learnt Persian, Arabic and Sanskrit in his early youth and began the study of English at the age of twenty-two. He was a great linguist to the formation of whose religious ideas the sacred books of the Muhammadans, Hindus and Christians made considerable contribution. From about 1804 to 1814 he was employed in the Company's service of which the last five years (1809-14) were spent at Rangpur (now in East Pakistan) as the *Sheristadar* to the District Collector, Mr. Digby. In 1814 Ram Mohan retired from the Company's service and settled in Calcutta in 1815. Already in 1803 Ram Mohan had published a pamphlet in Persian in which he protested against the idolatry and superstitions of all creeds. It was during his stay at Rangpur that his religious ideas began to get clearer and more public expression and after his settlement in Calcutta in 1815 he began systematically and assiduously propagating his religious views which finally took the shape of Brahma-ism in 1828. He preached the unity of God, assailed the prevalent Hindu belief in many gods and in the elaborate ritualistic worship of their images and insisted that true Hinduism consisted, as was evident from the *Upanishadas* and the *Vedanta shastra*, in the recognition of one Formless True God to whom alone worship was to be rendered. Naturally this doctrine, though supported by the Hindu scriptures themselves, roused a storm of indignant opposition amongst the orthodox Hindu community and Ram Mohan was subjected to social ostracism and other sorts of persecution. His religious views which insisted on unqualified Unitarianism and discarded prophets and the Son of God as much as images, roused the hostile opposition of the Muhammadans as well as of the conventional Christians. But Ram Mohan, with the courage of conviction that was so characteristic of him, stuck to his faith and doctrine and refused to yield either to fear or to temptation neither of which was wanting. Ram Mohan, however, never denied that he was a Hindu. What he wanted to do was to reform Hinduism by remaining within its fold.

Ram Mohan was pre-eminently a rationalist and was against all social evils and wanted to end them. Thus he was opposed to caste distinctions, to polygamy, to the *Sati* (*q.v.*) or the system of burning widows on the funeral pyres of their dead husbands, to the degradation of women by keeping them in ignorance and forced widowhood of women who would like to re-marry and to the absence of a rational education amongst the common people. He was a sturdy supporter of removal of all these social evils and his efforts met with considerable success, especially in the field of education. Himself a profound scholar of Sanskrit, he was more than most of his contemporaries awake to the need of the expansion amongst the Indians of the knowledge of Western languages, philosophy and science so that a new Indian people might grow up drawing its strength from a synthesis of the best of Western and Eastern knowledge.

Ram Mohan was also a pioneer amongst the Indians in the field of politics. An uncompromising love of freedom and an unlimited faith in the capacity of his countrymen to run the administration of their own country were the basic principles of his politics. He laid down the lines for political agitation in a constitutional manner and may thus be said to have sown the seeds of the future Indian National Congress. He submitted strong written protests in the form of petitions against the Press regulations issued by the Governor-General, Lord Hastings (*q.v.*) against the Jury Act of 1827 which denied to Hindus and Muhammadans alike the right of sitting on the Grand Jury not only in the trial of Christians (European as well as Indian) but also of their co-religionists while it allowed Christians to sit as jurors in the trial of Hindus and Muhammadans, against the Government proposal to tax rent-free lands, and against the prolongation of the monopoly rights and other privileges enjoyed by the East India Company in India. He also wanted to ameliorate the condition of the peasants by reducing the incidence of land tax on them and to promote the industrialisation of India by stopping the annual heavy economic drain to England caused by England's industrial superiority and political supremacy over India.

Ram Mohan's love of freedom and liberty knew no limitation of race, religion or region. He was as much pained at the failure of the revolution in Naples in 1821 as he was jubilant over the successful Spanish American Revolution of 1823 and the Revolution in France in 1830. He watched with enthusiasm the progress of the Reform movement in England from 1830 and was much pleased with the passing of the First Reform Act in 1832 when he happened to be personally present in England where he had gone at the close of 1930 to represent to the British king and Parliament the grievances of the titular Mughul

Emperor Akbar II (*q.v.*) (1806-37) who invested him with the title of *Raja*. During his brief stay (1830-33) in England Raja Ram Mohan acted not only as the ambassador of the Mughul Emperor to the British king but also as the ambassador of a New India to England and the Western world. He interpreted India to England by his writings and public speeches. In his interviews with various persons of light and leading in England and France which he visited in 1832, he ably presented India's views and was warmly appreciated. All these exertions, however, proved too much for his health and he died at Bristol on the 27th September, 1833.

Ram Mohan was a prolific writer who wielded a facile pen in Persian, English and Bengali to the last of which his contributions were so important that he has been called the father of modern Bengali prose. His works include *Tuhfat-ul-Muwahhidin* (or A gift to Mono-theists) and *Manazarat-ul-Adiyan* (or Discussions on Various Religions), both in Persian, *Abridgement of the Vedanta, The Precepts of Jesus, Appeals to the Christian Public, Answer of a Hindu to the Question, Why do you frequent a Unitarian Place of Worship*, all in English, and *Vedanta Sutra, Isa, Kena, Katha, Mundaka and Mandukya Upanishads*, all in Bengali. (Collet, S. B., *Life and Letters of Raja Ram Mohan Ray*; Chatterjee, Ramananda, *Ram Mohan Ray and Modern India*)

Rudradaman I—the Saka Satrap of Surashtra with his capital at Ujjaini, the son of Jaydaman and grandson of Chastana, the founder of the dynasty, ruled probably from A.D. 128 to A.D. 150. He was the most powerful ruler of the dynasty, defeated the Andhra king, Pulamayi II (*q.v.*) who had married his daughter and extended his rule not only over Surashtra but also over Malwa, Cutch, Sind, Konkon and other districts—in short, over Western India. In about A.D. 150 he repaired, three times stronger, the embankments of Lake Sudarsana near Girnar which had been originally built by order of Chandragupta Maurya (*q.v.*) and repaired subsequently by his grandson, Asoka (*q.v.*).

Rudradaman II—was a later ruler amongst the Western Satraps (*q.v.*). His relation with the main line is uncertain. He ruled probably from A.D. 301 to A.D. 305. Nothing is known about him except his name.

Rudradeva—was a king somewhere in north India, who, according to the Allahabad inscription, was defeated and uprooted by Samudragupta (*q.v.*) in the beginning of the latter's career. Rudradeva and his kingdom have not yet been definitely identified.

Rudramma (or Rudramba) Devi—a daughter of the Kakatiya king, Ganapati (*q.v.*) of Warangal, ruled over her father's kingdom when Marco Polo (*q.v.*) visited it in the last decade of the thirteenth century. The Venetian traveller was much impressed by the efficient administration of the kingdom by Rudrammá.

Rudrasena I—a grandson of the Vakataka (*q.v.*) king Pravarasena whom he succeeded, ruled at the beginning of the fifth century A.D.

Rudrasena II—was the son and successor of the Vakataka king Prithivisena, the son and successor of Rudrasena I (*q.v.*) the Vakataka king. Rudrasena II must have been a ruler of considerable power as he married Pravabati Gupta, the daughter of Chandragupta II (*q.v.*). He ruled in the middle of the fourth century A.D. and appeared to have been a successful ruler.

Rudrasinha—was the last of the Western Satraps of Surashtra, belonging to the dynasty founded by Chastana (*q.v.*). He was over-libidinous and was defeated, dethroned and killed by the third Gupta Emperor, Chandragupta II, in about A.D. 388.

Rukn-ud-din—the son and immediate successor of Sultan Iltutmish (*q.v.*), was deposed after only a few months' rule in 1236 in favour of his sister Raziya who became the Sultan.

Rukn-ud-din Barbak—the ruler of Bengal (1460-1474), maintained a large number of Abyssinian slaves, some of whom were placed in high positions. He was said to have been a sagacious and law-abiding sovereign.

Rukn-ud-din Ibrahim—was a younger son of Sultan Jalal-ud-din Khalji (*q.v.*) and his consort Malika Jahan. Immediately after the murder of Sultan Jalal-ud-din at the instigation of his son-in-law and nephew Ala-ud-din, Rukn-ud-din was declared at the instance of his mother the sultan in July 1296. But he was defeated, captured, blinded and deposed by Ala-ud-din Khalji in the following November of the same year.

Rummindei—is a village in the Nepalese Terai. It is in the Bithri district of Nepal and not very far from the Basti district in Uttar Pradesh. In this village stands a pillar which Asoka (*q.v.*) raised in the twentieth year after his coronation to mark the spot where Gautama Buddha was born. Rummindei has been identified with Lumbini-grama where, according to tradition, Gautama Buddha was born. (*S.A.E.*, p. 53 ff.)

Rupa Goswami—was the Hindu minister of King Hussain Shah (*q.v.*) of Bengal (A.D. 1492-1518). Rupa Goswami is more renowned as a saintly scholar who composed twenty-five works in Sanskrit of which the *Vidagdha Madhava* and the *Lalita Madhava* were the most famous. (Sarkar, J. N., *Hist. of Bengal,* Vol. II)

Rupamati—was the mistress of king Baz Bahadur (*q.v.*) of Malwa (A.D. 1551-61). Their love figures prominently in Indo-Muslim tradition and two beautiful palaces still extant at Mandu are attributed to Rupamati and Baz Bahadur.

Ryot —means a cultivator holding land or homestead under a superior landlord.

Ryotwari system—*see* under Land tenure.

S

Sa'adat Ali—the Nawab of Oudh (1798-1814), was a brother of the earlier Nawab Asaf-ud-daula (1775-97) a year after whose death he was installed by the British on the throne of Oudh. Soon after his installation the Governor-General, Lord Wellesley, insisted on the pretext of Zaman Shah's (*q.v.*) threat to invade India, that the strength of the Indo-British subsidiary force in Oudh should be increased and deprived the Nawab of the belt of land between the Ganges and the Jumna and of Rohil-khand, amounting to one-half of his territories. Over the remaining and less prosperous half Sa'adat Ali was suffered to rule till his death in 1814. His son and successor Ghazi-ud-din Haidar (1814-27) assumed, with the approval of the Governor-General, Lord Hastings, the title of the King of Oudh in 1819, but enjoyed no increased power.

Sa'adat Khan—the Mughul Governor of Oudh, took advantage of the growing weakness of the imperial power, set himself up as the independent ruler of Oudh in 1724 and ruled over Oudh practically as an independent prince till his death in 1739.

Sabat Jang —a Persian honorific title meaning 'tried in battle', was procured for Robert Clive (*q.v.*) from the Mughul Emperor by Nawab Mir Jafar (*q.v.*) during the first term of his rule (1757-60).

Sachiva —is a Sanskrit term meaning a minister or adviser. It was made the official designation of the fourth of the eight ministers (*ashta pradhan*) of Shivaji I (*q.v.*). His duty was to supervise the king's correspondence and also to check the accounts of the *mahals* and *parganahs* into which the kingdom was divided.

Sadar Diwani Adalat—was set up in Calcutta in 1772 by Warren Hastings (*q.v.*) to hear appeals in civil cases from the lower Diwani or Civil courts of justice. It was presided over by the President and two Members of his Council in Bengal. To remove the friction that arose between it and the Supreme Court, established by the Regulating Act of 1773, Warren Hastings, the Governor-General, appointed Sir Elijah Impey, the Chief Justice of the Supreme Court, as the President of the *Sadar Diwani Adalat*. This arrangement was severely criticised and fell through. With the expansion of the Company's territories in north India a *Sadar Diwani Adalat* was established at Allahabad in 1831. In 1861 when High Courts were established in Calcutta, Madras and Bombay the *Sadar Diwani Adalat* of Calcutta was amalgamated, along with the Supreme Court, with the High Court of Calcutta.

Sadar Nizamat Adalat—was established in Calcutta by Warren Hastings (*q.v.*) in 1772 for the purpose of revising or confirming sentences passed in criminal cases by the lower district courts or lower officials. It was presided over by Indian judges, but some control over it was exercised by the President and Members of the Council. In 1775 the *Sadar Nizamat Adalat* was transferred from Calcutta to Murshidabad and placed in charge of the Deputy Nawab, but in 1790 it was re-transferred to Calcutta and came to be presided over, in the place of the Deputy Nawab, by the Governor-General and Council assisted by experts in Indian laws. A *Sadar Nizamat Adalat* was set up at Allahabad in 1831. In 1861 the *Sadar Nizamat Adalat* of Calcutta, like the *Sadar Dewani Adalat*, became merged in the High Court of Calcutta.

Sadasiva—the last king (1542-70) of the third dynasty of the kings of Vijayanagar, was a younger son of Krishnadeva Raya (*q.v.*) (1509-29) and, as he was a minor, power passed into the hands of Ramraja (*q.v.*). The latter's policy of promoting dissensions amongst the five Muslim sultanates of the Deccan led them to combine in an invasion of Vijayanagar which culminated in the battle of Talikota in 1565. Ramraja was defeated and killed in the battle and King Sadasiva fled from Vijayanagar under the protection of Ramraja's brother, Tirumala, to Penugonda where he was killed in about 1570 by Tirumala who usurped the throne.

Sadasiva Bhao—was a first cousin of Peshwa Balaji Baji Rao (*q.v.*) (1740-61). He had a sound training in the business of administration and practically controlled the administration of the Maratha kingdom, for the Peshwa left everything to him. He organised the large Maratha army more or less in the manner of the European armies, maintained a large train of artillery under the command of a Muslim general named Ibrahim Khan Gardi and secured a resounding victory over the Nizam, Salabat Jang (*q.v.*) at the battle of Udgir (*q.v.*) in 1760. This victory so much increased his prestige that he was soon afterwards sent to Northern India to destroy Ahmad Shah Abdali's (*q.v.*) power in the Panjab and then establish Maratha supremacy in Upper India. But Sadasiva failed in diplomacy as well as in battle. He alienated the Jats by his arrogance, could not do anything to secure the active assistance of the Rajputs and failed to win over Nawab Shuja-ud-daula (*q.v.*) to his side, though he was in theory acting on behalf of the Nawab's imperial overlord, the Emperor of Delhi. In strategy also he allowed the initiative to pass into the hands of Abdali who practically besieged Sadasiva with his large army and the larger entourage within the encampments that Sadasiva had built round his army at Panipat. On 15 January, 1761 Sadasiva Bhao with the entire Maratha army was completely routed at Panipat by Abdali. Sadasiva fought with great courage, but he lost the battle in the course of which he was killed.

Sadullah Khan—the Prime Minister of Emperor Shah Jahan (1627-58), conducted along with Prince Aurangzeb (*q.v.*) the first and second sieges of Qandahar, but failed to take the fort. He died in 1654.

Safdar Ali—was the son and successor of Dost Ali, the Nawab of the Carnatic who was killed by the Marathas in 1741. Safdar Ali's rule over the Carnatic was cut short in 1742 when he was murdered by his cousin, Murtaza Ali. Safdar's brother-in-law, Chanda Shaheb (*q.v.*) lived to fight in the Second Carnatic War (*q.v.*).

Safdar Jang—a son of the sister of Sa'adat Khan (*q.v.*), the first Nawab of Oudh, succeeded his maternal uncle as the Nawab of Oudh in 1739. Later on he was appointed by the Mughul Emperor as the Wazir, but he was ousted from that office by Ghazi-ud-din (*q.v.*) with Maratha assistance. Safdar Jang then returned to Oudh, but the enmity of Ghazi-ud-din pursued him and he was again defeated by Ghazi-ud-din in 1753. Next year he died.

Sadr —was the designation of the officer who was in Mughul times in charge of religious endowments and charities in a *parganah*.

Sadr-us-Sadr—was the chief officer in charge of religious endowments and charities all through the Mughul empire. His office was located in the Mughul capital and all the *Sadrs* outside the capital were under his control.

Sahu (also spelt Shahu)—was the grandson of the great Shivaji and son and successor of Shambhuji (*q.v.*) who was captured and killed by Aurangzeb in 1689. Sahu, whose real name was Shivaji and who was then a mere boy, was also captured, taken to the Mughul Court and was called by Aurangzeb *Sadhu* (or Honest) in contradistinction to Shivaji I, who, in Aurangzeb's estimate, was a knave. Sahu is the popular form of Sadhu and stuck. Soon after the death of Aurangzeb in 1707 Sahu was released by Emperor Bahadur Shah. On account of his long stay in the Mughul court Sahu was more a Mughul than a Maratha in outlook. His return to Maharashtra at once split the Marathas into two camps— one supporting him and the other his cousin, Shivaji III, son of his uncle, Rajaram (*q.v.*). Sahu found a very capable officer in Valaji Viswanath whom he appointed as the Peshwa. With his help Shivaji III was reduced to submission and Sahu came to be recognised as the undisputed king of the Marathas. His power was further extended in northern and southern India by the efforts of the second Peshwa, Baji Rao I, and the third Peshwa, Balaji Baji Rao, but Sahu had practically made the Peshwaship hereditary in the family of the first Peshwa, Balaji Viswanath, and gradually withdrew from the day-to-day administration which he left to the Peshwas. Thus as the result of his policy the Peshwa, rather than the Raja, tended to be the pivot of Maratha administration. Sahu died in 1749 and on his death the Peshwa became the practical ruler of the Maratha dominions. Sahu's adopted son, who was the grandson of Rajaram and Tarabai (*q.v.*) and was named Ram Raja, continued his line from his court at Satara, but he was no better than a puppet in the hands of the Peshwa.

Sailendra dynasty, the—was established in the eighth century A.D. and continued to rule till the thirteenth century. It was a dynasty of princes of Indian origin which ruled over the Malay Peninsula and over nearly the whole of the Malay Archipelago including the islands of Sumatra, Java, Bali and Borneo. Their wealth and power so profoundly impressed the Arab travellers, who frequented their dominions, that they styled the Sailendra rulers Maharajas. The Sailendra monarchs were Mahayanist Buddhists and their most impressive monument is the grand and magnificent Buddhist *stupa* known as the Barabudur (*q.v.*) situated in the island of Java. (Majumdar, R. C., *Suvarnadvipa*, Vols. I & II)

Saint Francis Xavier—was one of the founders of the Jesuit Order of Monks. He is believed to have visited India in the sixteenth century. His name is associated with various educational Institutions in India of which St. Xavier's College, Calcutta, is one.

Saint Thomas—was a Christian apostle who, according to ecclesiastical tradition, visited India, travelled from the dominions of Prince Gondopharnes in the north-western frontier of India to South India and was martyred at Mailapur (Mylapore) near Madras. The correctness of the tradition has been questioned by many competent scholars.

Saisunaga dynasty, the—was founded, according to the Puranas, by a king named Sisunaga who ruled over Magadha approximately about the middle of the seventh century before the Christian era. The dynasty comprised ten kings, namely, Sisunaga, Kakavarna, Kshemadharman, Kshemajit, Bimbisara or Srenika, Ajatasatru or Kunika, Darsaka, Udasin or Udaya, Nandivardhana and Mahanandin. No events are known about the reigns of the first four kings whose reigns probably covered the period from *c.* 650 B.C. to 522 B.C. It was the fifth king, Bimbisara (*c.* 522 B.C. to 494 B.C.) who brought glory and power to the Saisunaga dynasty. Bimbisara (*q.v.*), and, his son and successor, Ajatasatru (*q.v.*) raised the dynasty and Magadha to predominance in north India. The eighth king, Udasin or Udaya (*c.* 443 B.C. - 410 B.C.) built the city of Kusumapura which became the nucleus of the later famous city of Pataliputra. The tenth king, Mahanandin, was deposed and murdered in about 362 B.C. by Mahapadma who founded the Nanda dynasty of Magadha. Some Buddhist texts put Sisunaga and his three immediate successors, Kakavarna (or Kalasoka), Kshemadharman and Kshemajit after Bimbisara. In this view the Sisunaga dynasty comprised six kings, namely, Sisunaga (*c.* 413 B.C. to 395 B.C.), Kakavarna or Kalasoka, and sons of Kalasoka (*c.* 395 B.C. to 345 B.C.) during whose regime the *de facto* ruler of Magadha was Mahapadma Nanda who overthrew Kalasoka and brought the Saisunaga dynasty to an end. (*E.H.I.; P.H.A.I.*, pp. 115-17)

Sakas, the—were originally a nomadic people of Central Asia

from which they were displaced by the Yue-chis and forced
to migrate south in the second century B.C. They came in several
hordes to India and by the close of the first century B.C. had
established themselves in Gandhara, in the Panjab, at Mathura,
in Kathiawar and even so far down as Maharashtra. Their
leaders assumed the titles of Satraps (*q.v.*) or Great Satraps
and first recognised the supremacy of some Indo-Parthian (*q.v.*)
rulers and later on of the Kushanas (*q.v.*). They were at first
of course condemned by Indian writers as foreigners and classed
with the *Yavanas* (or Indo-Greeks) but later on they became
Indianised and Hinduised and were completely mixed up
with and absorbed in the Indian population. The last Saka
chief, who is known to have been a ruler, was Rudrasinha III,
the Great Satrap of Ujjaini, who was overthrown by Chandragupta II (*q.v.*) about A.D. 388. (*E.E.C.A.* & *E.H.I.*)

Saka Era, the—dates from A.D. 78. It is generally attributed to
the Kushan king, Kanishka I (*q.v.*), though other names have
also been suggested as its originator. In any case, it was the most
popularly used of ancient Indian eras (*q.v.*) and has been
accepted as the Indian national era by the Federal Republic
of India.

Sakuntala, **the**—the most famous work of Kalidas (*q.v.*), is a drama
written in Sanskrit and has been admired by eminent Western
savants like Goethe.

Sakya-Muni—literally meaning the sage of the Sakyas; was one
of the names by which Gautama Buddha (*q.v.*) was known.

Sakyas, the—were the tribal people who lived in the Nepalese
Terai in the sixth century B.C. Their chief, Suddhodhana of
Kapilavastu (*q.v.*) was the father of Gautama Buddha (*q.v.*).
They claimed to belong to the Solar race and the Ikshvaku
family.

Salabat Jang—the third son of Nizam-ul-Mulk, Asaf Jah (*q.v.*)
was installed as the Nizam of Hyderabad in 1751 by the
French and ruled for ten years. His power was at first upheld
by a French army under Bussy (*q.v.*) who resided in his capital
and was given the district of Northern Circars to meet the
expenses of his army. But when in 1758 Bussy was recalled
from Hyderabad and an English army under Forde (*q.v.*)
marched from Bengal along the eastern coast and captured
Masulipatam, Salabat Jang went over to the English side and
secured their support by ceding the Northern Circars to them.
But in spite of it, he was badly defeated by the Marathas at
the battle of Udgir (*q.v.*) in 1760 and had to make peace by

surrendering important territories. He was soon afterwards murdered by his brother, Nizam Ali, in 1761.

Salar Jang, Sir (1829-83)—was the Prime Minister of the Nizam of Hyderabad when the Sepoy Mutiny broke out in 1857 and kept the state loyal to the Indo-British Government. He was also a progressive administrator who did much to improve the administration in the Nizam's state.

Salbai, the treaty of—was concluded between the East India Company and Mahadaji Sindhia (*q.v.*) in May, 1782 and ratified by the Peshwa's Government in February, 1783. It brought to a close the First Maratha War (*q.v.*) which had begun in 1775. By this treaty the English retained Salsette but gave up the cause of Raghaba (*q.v.*) who was to be paid a pension by the Maratha Government. The English also recognised Madhav Rao Narayan (*q.v.*) as the Peshwa and returned to the Sindhia all his territories west of the Jumna. The peace which was thus established between the English and the Marathas lasted twenty years and left the former free to fight their other enemies like Tipu Sultan (*q.v.*).

Sale, General Sir Robert—a renowned English general, took part in the First Afghan War (*q.v.*). He was in command of an Indo-British army at Gandamak from where he was ordered to proceed to Kabul in November, 1841, but could not act up to the orders. He was even obliged to fall back upon Jalalabad where he was soon besieged by the Afghans. But he defended the place with great success and ultimately succeeded in repulsing the besiegers. Sale then took part in the First Sikh War (*q.v.*) and lost his life at the battle of Mudki in which the British defeated the Sikhs on 18 December, 1845.

Salim, Prince—was the eldest son and successor of Emperor Akbar and assumed the name of Jahangir (*q.v.*).

Salim Chishti, Shaikh—was a Muhammadan saint who dwelt among the rocks of Sikri, near Agra. Emperor Akbar showed him great respect and prayed to be blessed with a son. The saint promised him three sons. The prophecy was fulfilled and Akbar named his eldest son Salim in honour of the saint. Akbar further came to hold that the neighbourhood of the place where the saint lived, would be lucky for him and built there a magnificent mosque for the use of the Shaikh and later on a new city which he called Fathpur and made his capital.

Salima Begum—was the daughter of Babur's daughter and was thus a cousin of Emperor Akbar. She was first married to Bairam Khan in 1557-58 and after the latter's fall and death she was married by Emperor Akbar himself. She survived Akbar, dying in 1612. She was an accomplished lady and ranked as one of the most important ladies in Akbar's harem. She brought about a reconciliation between Akbar and his rebellious son, Prince Salim, in 1603.

Salisuka—was a later Maurya king who succeeded Asoka's grandson, Samprati (*q.v.*). He is said to have been an unrighteous and oppressive sovereign.

Salivahana—was a king who figures prominently in Indian folklore. His existence is not borne out by any epigraphic or numismatic evidence. The deeds of several kings of the Satavahana (*q.v.*) dynasty have been attributed to him.

Salsette—is a small island, 241 sq. miles north of Bombay with which it is now connected by a bridge and a causeway. It has old cave temples and antiquities. It was occupied by the British in 1775 on the outbreak of the First Maratha War (*q.v.*) and was ceded to them in 1783 by the treaty of Salbai (*q.v.*).

Saluva dynasty, the—was the second dynasty of the kings of Vijayanagar (*q.v.*) which ruled from A.D. 1486 to 1503. It was founded by Saluva Narasimha (*q.v.*) the chief of Chandragiri who deposed the worthless Praudhadeva, the last king of the First or Sangama dynasty, in about A.D. 1486. The dynasty had only one other king, named Immadi Narasimha, who was deposed in about A.D. 1505 by Vira Narasimha (*q.v.*), son of Narasa Nayaka, the chief of the Taluva country.

Saluva Narasimha—the founder and first king of the Saluva or second dynasty of the kings of Vijayanagar, came of the family of the feudatory chiefs of Chandragiri and held a high post under Praudhadeva, the Vijayanagar king. Finding that the king was incapable of defending the kingdom against the invading armies of the Bahmani Sultan (*q.v.*) as well as of the king of Orissa he deposed his worthless master, seized the throne for himself and justified his usurpation by recovering from the king of Orissa and the Bahmani Sultan some of the provinces of the Vijayanagar kingdom which they had occupied earlier. He died in A.D. 1490-91 leaving behind him two sons under the guidance of his trusted general, Narasa Nayaka (*q.v.*).

Saluva Timma—the minister and general of the Vijayanagar king, Krishnadeva Raya (*q.v.*) (1509-29), contributed much to the success of his royal master by his wise counsel and great generalship. He was the father of Rama Raja (*q.v.*) who was defeated and killed at the battle of Talikota (*q.v.*) in 1565.

Samatata—is mentioned, along with Davaka, in Samudragupta's (*q.v.*) Allahabad Pillar inscription as one of the *Pratyanta* (i.e. frontier) states, the king of which gratified his imperious command by paying all kinds of taxes, obeying his orders and coming to perform obeisance. It has been identified with the part of eastern Bengal bordering the sea. Its capital was probably Baḍ-Kamta near Comilla, now in East Pakistan.

Sama Veda, **the**—one of the four *Vedas* (*q.v.*), consists of 1,549 hymns, of which all but 75 are taken from the *Rig Veda Samhita* (*q.v.*). The hymns of the *Sama Veda* were meant to be chanted in connection with sacrifices. To the *Sama Veda* is attached *Chhandogya Upanishad* and the *Jaiminiya Brahmana* which again contains the *Kena Upanishad*.

Sambhuji (also spelt Shambhuji), Raja—the son and successor of Shivaji I (*q.v.*) ruled from 1680-89. He lacked his father's energy and determination and was a pleasure-loving young man. But he was brave and for nine years held back the mighty Mughul army the Emperor Aurangzeb had brought to the Deccan. He was, however, foolish enough to allow himself to be surprised along with his minister, Kulash (*q.v.*) by the Mughuls on 11 February, 1689 at Sangameshwar near Ratnagiri and was barbarously executed a month later by Aurangzeb's order.

Sambhuji Kavji—an attendant of Shivaji I, accompanied him at the time of his interview with Afzal Khan, (*q.v.*). He beheaded Afzal Khan after the Khan had already been severely wounded by Shivaji with a weapon called the 'tiger's claw.'

Samprati (also spelt Sampati)—was a son of Kunala and grandson of Asoka Maurya. Neither his father nor he himself is mentioned in any inscription, but according to tradition, he succeeded his grandfather and was a Jain by faith. Probably he ruled over the western part of Asoka's dominions where tradition associates his name with the foundation of many Jain temples.

Samugarh, the battle of—was fought between Prince Dara (*q.v.*), the eldest son of the ailing Emperor Shah Jahan (*q.v.*) and his two younger brothers, Princes Aurangzeb (*q.v.*) and Murad (*q.v.*), on 29 May, 1658. In this battle Prince Dara was decisively defeated and the victorious Princes, Aurangzeb and Murad, soon marched on to Agra which was eight miles away from the battlefield, seized the fort and thus practically destroyed the chances of Prince Dara succeeding to their father's throne.

Samudragupta—son and successor of Chandragupta I, was the second Emperor of the Gupta dynasty of Magadha. The exact period of his reign is not ascertained. It probably extended from A.D. 330 to 380. He was a great conqueror whose valiant deeds have been found recorded on the Allahabad Pillar of Asoka. He began his conquests by violently exterminating a number of kings ruling over Aryavarta or the Upper Ganges valley. He also reduced to vassalage the kings of Samatata (Eastern Bengal), Davaka (Nowgong in Assam), Kamarupa (Western Assam), Nepal, Kartripura (Garhwal and Jalandhar) and several tribal states of the eastern and central Panjab, Malwa and Western India as well as the chiefs of the Kushans and the Sakas. He led an expedition to the Deccan in the course of which he defeated, captured and reinstated to their dominions Mahendra, king of Koshala (Upper Mahanadi valley), Vyaghra-raja of Mahakantara, Mantaraja of Kaurala (unidentified), Mahendragiri of Pisthapur (Pithapuram), Svamidatta of Kotturu (in Madras Presidency), Damana of Erandapalla (probably in Madras Presidency), Vishnugopa of Kanchi, Nilaraja of Avamukta (not yet identified), Hastivarman of Vengi, Ugrasena of Palakka (Nellore district), Kubera of Devarashtra (Vizagapatam district) and Dhananjaya of Kushthalapura (possibly North Arcot). As a result of these brilliant conquests, the dominions under the direct rule of Samudragupta extended from the foot of the Himalayas on the north to the Narmada on the south and from the Brahmaputra on the east to the Jumna and the Chambal on the west. The acquisition of so vast an empire was a most remarkable feat and its acquisition was fittingly celebrated by the performance of the *Asvamedha* sacrifice by Samudragupta. His fame spread beyond the limits of India and Meghavarman, the king of Ceylon, sent an embassy to him with presents, requesting his permission to build a monastery at Bodh Gaya for the benefit of Ceylonese Buddhist pilgrims visiting the holy place. Samudragupta was not a mere soldier and conqueror. He was a versatile genius, generous to the vanquished, benevolent to the learned and the saintly of all creeds, highly intellectual, well-read in the scriptures, adept in music and a king amongst poets. He has been called the Indian Napoleon, but in fact he was much greater then Napoleon for he combined valour with culture. (*E.H.I.*; *Ind. Ant.* June, 1926)

Sangama—was the father of Harihara and Bukka, the two brothers who founded the kingdom of Vijayanagar in about A.D. 1336.

Sangha, **the**—means the brotherhood of the Buddhist monks. It forms one of the Buddhist Trinity—Buddha, Dharma and Sangha. In organising the Buddhist *Sangha* Gautama Buddha (*q.v.*) gave it a democratic constitution.

Sanghamitra—was a sister of Prince Mahendra (*q.v.*) who, according to Indian tradition, was a younger brother of Asoka, and who, according to the Ceylonese chronicle, led a Buddhist mission to Ceylon which he converted to Buddhism. Sanghamitra accompanied her brother, co-operated with him in his evangelical work and converted to Buddhism the ladies of the household of the Ceylonese king, Tissa, and many other ladies. She is still remembered in Ceylon.

Sangramasinha (**or Sanga**)—the Rana of Mewar from A.D. 1509 to 1529, succeeded his father Rayamalla and proved himself a great warrior. Indeed there was not a single ruler of the first rank in all the different kingdoms into which India was then divided, who was able to make headway against him. Rana Sangramsinha (popularly called Rana Sanga) had expected that Babur, like Timur (*q.v.*), would withdraw after sacking Delhi and breaking the power of the Delhi sultanate. But when the Rana found that after his victory at Panipat over Ibrahim Lodi (*q.v.*) in 1526 Babur settled at Delhi, he moved against the latter with a vast army composed of 120 chiefs, 80,000 horses and 500 war elephants and met Babur in a hotly contested battle of Khanua on 16 March, 1527. In spite of the desperate valour with which the Rajputs fought they were defeated by Babur. Sanga escaped from the battlefield but died broken-hearted two years later. His dream of establishing a Hindu Raj vanished.

Sankaracharya—one of the greatest Hindu philosophers and teachers of the post-Gupta period, was born in a Brahman family of Kaladi in South India in the eighth century A.D. He is famous for his commentaries on the classical *Upanishadas*, the *Bhagavad Gita* and the *Brahma Sutra* of Badrayana on which he based the doctrine of pure monism (*advaita*). He was an ardent Vedantist and travelled all over India explaining his doctrine. He was also a great organiser and established famous monasteries at Sringeri in Mysore, Dwaraka in Kathiawar, Puri in Orissa and Badrinath on the Himalayas. These monasteries are still functioning and inspire millions of Hindus. He died at an early age and is still held in great reverence by the Hindus.

Sankaradeva—was the son and successor of Ramachandradeva, the Yadava king of Devagiri. On his failure to continue payment of the annual tribute to Ala-ud-din Khalji his kingdom was invaded by the Sultan's army in 1312. Sankaradeva was defeated and killed and his kingdom was annexed to the Delhi sultanate.

Sankaradeva—the great Vaishnava reformer in Assam, was probably born in 1449 and died in 1579. He preached a purified Vaishnavism and inculcated the doctrine of salvation by faith rather than by sacrifices which were then very much popular in Assam. He received the patronage of King Nara Narayan (*q.v.*) of Cooch-Behar and made Barpeta his headquarters. He was a great preacher and his doctrines gradually became very popular in Assam. He was also a composer and dramatist of great merit and his songs and plays are still very popular in Assam.

Sanskrit—is the sacred language of the Hindus. It has a vast literature covering all branches of knowledge. It is based on a very scientific grammar. It was the official language of the ancient Indian kings, and though Asoka gave up its use in his inscriptions, Sanskrit soon came back into its own and was even used by many Indian rulers of foreign origin to record their achievements. It was a great unifying force in ancient India and still continues to be the sacred language of prayer, worship and sacrificial rites of the Hindus all over India. It is generally written in what is called the Devanagari script, but it is written and read in the various regional scripts of India as well. It was even carried across the seas by the Hindu colonists who settled in the Malay Peninsula, the Malaya Archipelago, Cambodia, and Annam where it was used in inscriptions recording the achievements of local kings.

Sanskrit Colleges—were established by the East India Company—one in Benares in 1794 and the second in Calcutta in 1820.

Sapru, Sir Tej Bahadur—was a distingushed leader of the Moderate party in India in the first half of the twentieth century. He was a lawyer by profession and served for a term as a Member of the Viceroy's Executive Council.

Sadadarshana, the—or the six systems of Hindu philosophy, are the *Nyaya*, the *Vaishesika*, the *Samkhya*, the *Patanjala* (or *Yoga*), the *Purva-Mimamsha* and the *Uttara-Mimamsha* or *Brahmasutra* by Gautama, Kanada, Kapila, Patanjali, Jaimini and Badarayana or Vyasa respectively. (Radhakrishnan, S., *History of Indian Philosophy*)

Sarda Act, the—was sponsored by Rai Shahib Harbilas Sarda and passed by the Indian Legislature in 1929. It raised the age of marriage and thus aimed at preventing child-marriages.

Sardar Vallabhbhai Patel—*see* Patel, V. B.

Sarfaraz Khan—the Nawab of Bengal (1739-40), was the son of a daughter of Nawab Murshid Quli Khan (*q.v.*). He was defeated and killed in 1740 by his subordinate, Alivardi Khan (*q.v.*) who then became the Nawab of Bengal.

Sargauli (or Sagauli), the treaty of—brought to a close the Gurkha or Nepalese War (*q.v.*) in 1816. By this treaty the Gurkhas accepted a British Resident at their capital Khatmandu and surrendered to the British the districts of Kumaon and Garhwal.

Sarkar, **the**—was an administrative territorial unit into which Sher Shah (*q.v.*) divided his empire. Emperor Akbar retained this territorial unit several of which were united by him to form a *Suba* or province. The *Sarkar* passed into the British administrative set-up and came to be known as the district.

Sarkar, Sir Jadunath, (1870-1961)—was a renowned historian. Born in Bengal and educated at Presidency College, Calcutta, Jadunath took to the profession of teaching and spent the major part of his life as Professor of History in Patna. He was the Vice-Chancellor of Calcutta University for a term from 1926. His works on *Shivaji, Life of Aurangzeb* (in 5 volumes) and *Fall of Mughul Empire* are recognised as authoritative. For his scholarship and erudition he was knighted by the British Government. He died in Calcutta.

Sarkars, (also spelt Circars), Northern—is the name of a district in the Carnatic. It was given by Nizam Salabat Jang (*q.v.*) to be controlled by the French, but was occupied by the British in 1758.

Sarnath—near Benares, is a holy place to the Buddhists because Gautama Buddha delivered his first sermon at Sarnath. Asoka (*q.v.*) later on built here a magnificent stone pillar surmounted by the famous lion-capital which is famous as a masterpiece of Asokan scuplture and has been adopted by the Government of India as its emblem. Sarnath abounds in Buddhist monuments many of which are now housed in a museum there.

Sarvasena—the second son of the Vakataka king, Pravarasena I (*q.v.*), was installed by his father as a feudatory king over Basim, or modern Berar. (*N.H.I.P.*, VI.)

Sasanka—was the first king of Bengal who extended his rule over territories outside Bengal. His origin is unknown and his connection with the Imperial Guptas is merely conjectural. Whatever, however, might have been his origin, it is certain that some time before A.D. 606 he became the king of Gauḍa (i.e. Bengal) with his capital at Karnasuvarna which has been identified with Rangamati in the district of Murshidabad in West Bengal. Whether southern and eastern Bengal were included within his dominions is uncertain, but in the west his rule extended over Magadha and in the south as far as the Chilka Lake in Orissa. The westward expansion of his dominions created hostilities with the Maukhari rulers of Kanauj and Sasanka entered into an alliance with Devagupta, the king of Malava and rival of the Maukharis. Devagupta defeated and killed his Maukhari rival, Grahavarman, and, Sasanka, coming to the aid of his ally, occupied the Maukhari capital Kanauj. This brought upon him an attack by Rajyavardhana (q.v.) who had just succeeded to the throne of Thaneswar and whose sister was the widow of the Maukhari king, Grahavarman. How exactly it happened is not known, but Rajyavardhana was killed by Sasanka or his attendants. At any rate, the death of Rajyavardhana prompted his brother and successor, Harshavardhana, to make an alliance with Bhaskaravarman, the king of Kamarupa, who dreaded the hostility of Sasanka and sought Harsha's support against him. Pressed on two fronts, Sasanka fell back on his capital and his enemies caused damage and destruction to his kingdom. But they soon had to retire and Sasanka remained in possession of his kingdom including Gauḍa, Magadha and Utkala up to the Chilka Lake until his death which took place some time after A.D. 619 but before A.D. 637. His coins show that he was a worshipper of Siva, but how far the stories of his persecution of Buddhism and Buddhists in Magadha, as related by Hiuen Tsang, are true is impossible to ascertain. (Majumdar, R. C., *Hist. of Bengal, Vol. I.*)

Sastri, Srinivasa (1869-1949)—was the leader of the Indian liberal party in the twenties of the present century. He began his career as a schoolmaster and joined the Servants of India Society in 1907. In 1913 he entered into Indian politics and became a member of the Madras Legislative Council. His silver-tongued oratory soon made him prominent amongst the Congressmen and he strongly protested against the Rowlatt Acts (q.v.). In 1920 he became a member of the Council of States and represented India at the Imperial Conference and at the League of Nations in 1921. He took great pains to solve the problem of Indian settlers in South Africa which he visited several times and where he was posted for some time as the

Agent-General of the Government of India. He was the Vice-Chancellor of Annamalai University from 1935 to 1940. He was a voluminous writer whose *Post-Puberty Marriage of Hindu Girls* is a well-known work and revealed the social reformer in him.

Satakarni I—the son and successor of Krishna (*q.v.*), the third king of the Satavahana dynasty (*q.v.*), ruled over the whole of the Deccan and also over Eastern Malwa. He celebrated the 'horse-sacrifice' (*q.v.*), though his power was once defied by Kharavela (*q.v.*). In any case he was so powerful a king that several of his successors added his name as an honorific to their names. (*P.H.A.I.*, p. 415)

Satakarni, Gautamiputra—a king of the Satavahana (*q.v.*) dynasty of the Deccan, ascended the throne in the beginning of the second century A.D. and ruled till A.D. 128. He extirpated the dynasty of the Saka Satraps (*q.v.*) of Maharashtra and annexed their dominions. He recalled their coins and re-issued them after re-stamping them with his name. His dominions included Berar, Malwa, Kathiawar, Gujarat and north Konkon. He was a great champion of Hinduism and prided himself on re-establishing society on the basis of the four *Varnas* (castes).

Satara—is a town and a former state in Bombay Presidency. It was the capital of the descendants of Sahu (*q.v.*) but was practically a dependency under the Peshwa. In 1818 after the defeat of Peshwa Baji Rao II, the state was restored by the British as a subsidiary state. In 1848 the state of Satara was annexed to the Indo-British empire by the application of the Doctrine of Lapse.

Satavahana dynasty, the—was founded by Simuka in about 60 B.C. in the valley lying between the Godavari and the Krishna, which is known as Andhra. The original home of Simuka was in the district of the Satavahanas lying in the neighbourhood of Bellary in Madras Presidency. The dynasty founded by Simuka is, therefore, known by two names, viz. the Andhra dynasty and the Satavahana dynasty. The era of its foundation, the total number of years covered by its regime as well as the total number of kings belonging to the Satavahana dynasty are very controversial issues. According to the Puranic account, which has been generally accepted, the Satavahana dynasty was founded by Simuka who over-threw the Sunga-Kanva yoke (*q.v.*). From him sprang a dynasty of thirty kings who ruled for about 400 years. Simuka's reign has been assigned to *c.* 60 B.C. to 37 B.C. He was succeeded

by his brother, Krishna and the latter by his son, Satakarni I.
This third king of the Satavahana dynasty was the real founder
of the power and might of the Satavahana family. He was a
contemporary of Kharavela (*q.v.*) who claimed to have defied
him. But this eclipse must have been only a temporary set-
back, for Satakarni I certainly celebrated the *Asvamedha* (*q.v.*)
(horse-sacrifice) and thus announced his overlordship over the
whole of the Deccan. His capital was Pratisthana, modern
Paithan, on the Godavari. He was so great a king that many
of his successors assumed his name as an honorific title. Some
time after the death of Satakarni I, the Satavahana power
appears to have declined under the pressure of Scythian
invasions resulting in the establishment of a Saka Satrapy in
Maharashtra, generally known as the Western Satraps (*q.v.*).
But the Satavahana king No. 23, Raja Gautamiputra Sri
Satakarni (*q.v.*), overthrew the power of the Western Satraps
and restored the prosperity, power and predominance of the
Satavahanas in the Deccan. His son and successor, Raja
Vasisthiputra Sri Pulamayi (*q.v.*) married a daughter of
Rudradaman I, the Saka Great Satrap of Ujjaini, but was
deprived by his father-in-law of the conquests that
Gautamiputra had made from the Western Satraps. The
Satavahana power was restored for the second time by the
twenty-seventh king Yajna Sri, who is believed to have recovered from the Satraps of Ujjaini some of the territories
snatched by them from king Pulamayi. Yajna Sri issued a
large variety of coins some of which bearing the figure of a
ship, suggest that his power extended even over the seas. At
any rate he was the last great king of the Satavahana dynasty.
The last three kings were Vijaya, Chanda Sri and Pulamayi.
Nothing is yet known as to the causes that brought about the
fall of the Satavahana dynasty. The kings of the dynasty were
orthodox Hindus who took pride in celebrating Vedic sacrifices, in upholding the social order based on the division into
castes and in resisting the Yavanas and foreigners like the
Sakas. But they were tolerant in religious matters and bestowed
endowments on Buddhist as well as Jain monasteries. Commerce, trade, agriculture and other industries all prospered
and gold, silver and copper currencies were in use. (Bhandarkar,
D. A., *Dekkan of the Satavahana period; C.H.I.,* I. xiv; *P.H.A.I.*
pp. 414 ff., & *E.H.I.* ch. viii)

Sati —meant a widowed wife who burnt herself on the funeral
pyre of her dead husband. The custom was unknown in the

Vedic age, but grew later on. It is mentioned as being practised in royal families in the Mahabharata and was found existent by the classical writers who came to India with Alexander the Great. It apparently spread from the kingly families to the common people and assumed huge proportions under the pressure of Muslim raids and conquests. Emperor Akbar tried to stop it, but failed. It was abolished in 1829 by the Governor-General, Lord William Bentinck, within British India but it persisted in the Panjab where it was suppressed only after the annexation of the province to British India in 1848.

Satiyaputra—a kingdom lying on the southern frontier of Asoka's dominions, is mentioned in Rock Edict II, along with Kerala-putra. It has not yet been definitely identified. It lay in the south no doubt and was probably adjacent to the Kerala or Chera (*q.v.*) kingdom.

Satraps (Kshatrapas), the—were designations of Saka (*q.v.*) chiefs who set up and ruled over several states in North India. They are divided into three main groups, namely, the Satraps of Kapisi in the Kabul valley, of Western Panjab or Taxila and of Mathura. Granavhryaka, Tiravharna and Sivasena were amongst the Satraps of Kapisi. The Panjab Satraps were a larger group to which belonged Laika and his son Patika, Manigul and his son Zeionises or Jihonika, and Indravarman and his son, Aspavarman and his nephew, Sasa. The Mathura group comprised Rajuvula or Rajula, his son Sudasa or Sodasa and his nephew Kharaosta. Very little is known of the acti-vities of those Saka satraps whose names have been found recorded on coins and in inscriptions which are only partially preserved. Their dates are still not precisely fixed though they are believed to have flourished before the Kushans (*q.v.*). (*P.A.H.I.*, pp. 443 ff.)

Satraps, the Great (Mahakshatrapas)—were divided into two branches viz. the Western satraps founded by Bhumaka in Maharashtra and the satraps of Ujjaini founded by Chastana. Both the founders were leaders of Saka hosts. The date of the establishment of the family of the Western Satraps (Kshatrapas) is not known. Their capital was probably Nasik and the names of only two rulers, Bhumaka, the founder, and Nahapana are known. The date of neither is definitely known. Bhumaka has been assigned to the early years of the first century A.D. and Nahapana to the beginning of the second century A.D. At any rate, Nahapana was the greatest of the Saka Satraps of

Western India. He is referred to in many inscriptions bearing dates of an unspecified era which has been supposed by many scholars to be the Saka era (*q.v.*) and they have assigned him to the period from A.D. 119 to 124. He began his career as a satrap but later on became a Great Satrap. He ruled over a considerable territory in western India and made many benefactions. But he was overthrown by the Satavahana king, Gautamiputra Sri Satakarni (*q.v.*) and the dynasty of the Western satraps ceased.

The Great Satraps of Ujjaini had a longer rule. The founder of the family was Chastana, son of Ysamotika whose name indicates that he was a Scythian, i.e., a Saka. His rule began in about A.D. 130 and his dynasty ruled till A.D. 388. The most important ruler of this dynasty was Chastana's grandson, Rudradaman I (A.D. 130-150) (*q.v.*). He ruled over an extensive dominion and his achievements have been left recorded in a Sanskrit inscription at Girnar which states that he reconstructed the embankment round the Sudarsana Lake which was first built in the reign of Chandragupta Maurya (*q.v.*). Rudradaman I was succeeded by his eldest son, Damaghsada I, who was succeeded, first, by his son Jivadaman and then by his brother, Rudra Sinha. The last was followed by his three sons namely, Rudrasena I, Sanghadaman, and Damasena, who was succeeded by his three sonss Yasodaman, Vijayasena and Damajada Sri. The later successor, were Rudrasena II, Visvamitra, Bhartridaman, Rudradaman II and Rudrasena III (A.D. 348-378). His successors were probably Simhasena, Rudrasena IV and Satya Sinha whose son and successor, Rudra Sinha III, was the last ruler of the dynasty. He was overthrown by Chandragupta II, Vikramaditya (*q.v.*). The history of the Great Satraps of Ujjaini is interesting as it illustrates how quickly a dynasty of foreign rulers was Indianised and Hinduised and adopted Sanskrit as their official language. (*P.H.A.I.*, pp. 503-12)

Satrunjaya—a town in Gujarat, contains several magnificent Jain temples, built during the rule of the Chalukya (*q.v.*) dynasty in Gujarat in the tenth and eleventh centuries.

Satyagraha movement, the—was initiated by Mahatma Gandhi (*q.v.*) first, in South Africa in 1894. It meant the application of soul-force based on truth and non-violence for the removal of a social or political grievance. In simple language it is a form of passive resistance which can be offered by a single individual as well as by a group of persons and aimed at changing the mind of the opponent by suffering. It was very successful in South Africa, extorted the respect of the South African Governor, General Smuts, and the admiring sympathy of the Indian Viceroy, Lord Hardinge, and eventually led to the amelioration of the more humiliating grievances of the Indians in South Africa. In 1920 it was applied to the nationalist agitation against the character of the British rule in India and took the form of non-violent non-co-operation and later on of the civil disobedience movement. It certainly spread widely amongst the Indians a determination to end the British rule in India and thus contributed very materially to the acquisition of independence by India.

Satyendranath Tagore—*see* Tagore, Satyendranath.

Saurashtra (also spelt Surashtra)—*see* Kathiawar.

Savarkar, Vinayak Damodar (1883-1966)—popularly called Vir (Brave) Savarkar, was a hero of India's fight for freedom from the British thraldom. In 1940 he founded at Poona a terroristic organisation called the *Abhinav Bharati* which aimed at wresting freedom by force, if necessary. While studying law in England he was arrested in 1910 on a charge of abetting murder in India, was sent on board a ship as an under-trial prisoner, effected an escape through a port-hole off Marseilles, was recaptured, brought back to India where he was tried by a Special Tribunal and sentenced to double transportation for life. He was released in 1937 but could not work in co-operation with the Indian National Congress and in 1948 was even suspected of complicity in Mahatma Gandhi's murder. He was acquitted and retired from politics. He was a voluminous writer and his more famous works are—*The War of Independence, My Transportation for Life* and *Echoes from the Andamans.*

Sayaji Rao I—was the Gaikwad of Baroda from 1771 to 1778. His claim to the throne was disputed by his brothers and his administration was much disturbed.

Sayaji Rao II—was the Gaikwad of Baroda from 1819 to 1847.

Sayaji Rao III—the Gaikwad of Baroda from 1875 to 1939, was installed on the throne by the British Government after the deposition of Malhar Rao Gaikwad in 1875 when he was a mere boy. During his minority the State was administered by Sir T. Madhava Rao. He assumed the administration in his own hands on attaining majority and proved to be one of the most enlightened of rulers amongst the Indian princes. Under his paternal guidance Baroda became the most progressive state in India. He requisitioned the services of eminent Indians including Ramesh Chandra Dutta, who was his Dewan for some years, and Aravinda Ghose who was the Principal of the Baroda College. He died in 1939.

Sayana—was the most famous Vedic commentator. He was also a statesman and was the minister of the Vijayanagar king, Harihara II (*q.v.*). Sayana lived in the fourteenth century, dying in A.D. 1387.

Sayyid Ahmed Khan, Sir (1815-98)—was a prominent leader of the Indian Muhammadans. Born in Delhi, he began his career in the service of the British in India in 1837 and rose to the rank of a subordinate judge. He retired from Government service in 1876 and devoted the remaining twenty-two years of his life to the service and uplift of the Muhammadans in India. He had remained loyal to the British during the Sepoy Mutiny and had a lively appreciation of the values of Western culture. He, therefore, devoted himself mainly to the task of propagating English education amongst the Indian Muslims and founded in 1875 the Muhammadan Anglo-Oriental College at Aligarh which aimed at securing a balance between Islamic and European learning. In 1920 the College was raised by the Government of India to the status of a University, called the Aligarh Muslim University. It has produced many talented young Muslim graduates of great ability and erudition. Sir Sayyid, however, was first a Muhammadan, and then only an Indian. He thought the Muslims of India were a people separate from the Hindus and must not be absorbed by them or united with them. He, therefore, asked the Indian Muslims to shun the Indian National Congress on account of the Hindu preponderance there. In fact, though Sir Sayyid did much to improve the condition of the Muhammadans in India, he did very little for India as a whole.

Sayyid brothers—were Hussain Ali and his brother Abdullah. They belonged to a high Muhammadan family of Oudh and both of them held high offices towards the close of the reign of Bahadur Shah I (*q.v.*). They were known as king-makers as they made and unmade Emperors of Delhi from 1713 to 1719. In 1713 they first helped Farruksiyar (*q.v.*) to the imperial throne, Abdullah becoming his Wazir and Hussain the Commander-in-Chief. The two brothers were thus in a position to control the imperial government. But as Farruksiyar intrigued against them they deposed and killed him in 1719. Then they decided to rule through imperial puppets, and in the course of the year 1719 they raised to the throne and then deposed and executed four Emperors, namely, Rafi-ud Darajat, Rafi-ud Daulat, Nekusiyar and Muhammad Ibrahim. The sixth Emperor set up by them was Muhammad Shah who proved more than a match for the two over-ambitious brothers. He rallied to his support the many enemies that the Sayyid brothers had created, especially Mir Qamar-ud-din, better known as Nizam-ul-Mulk Asaf Jah, and with their support Hussain Ali was removed by assassination while on his way to Malwa to chastise the Nizam and Abdullah was defeated and captured in a pitched battle in 1720 and killed by poisoning in 1722.

Sayyid dynasty, the—was founded in A.D. 1414 by Khizr Khan soon after the death of Sultan Mahmud (*q.v.*), the last of the Tughluq sultans of Delhi. The dynasty produced four sultans, namely Khizr Khan (1414-21), his son Mubarak (1421-34), his nephew Muhammad Shah (1434-45) and his son Alam Shah (1445-51). The last sultan was so weak and indolent that he made over the throne to Buhlol Lodi in 1451. The Sayyid dynasty did nothing memorable during its regime of 37 years.

School Book Society, the—was established in Calcutta in 1818 mainly by the efforts of David Hare. Its main object was to sell, print and publish English books in India at cheap prices.

Scott-Moncrieff Commission—was set up by the Viceroy, Lord Curzon (*q.v.*) in 1900 to plan irrigation work on an all-India scale. Its proposals providing irrigation facilities for six and a half million acres at a cost of £30,000,000 were sanctioned by Lord Curzon.

Scottish Church College—in Calcutta, commemorates the educational activities in India of Revd. Dr. Alexander Duff (*q.v.*). It was originally named Duff College and was founded in 1830. In the beginning of the twentieth century it dropped its old name and assumed the present one. It is one of the many proofs of the part that the Christian missions and missionaries had played in the expansion of Western education in India.

Scythians, the—were the people of Scythia in Central Asia. In Indian historical terminology it is used as a generic term denoting foreign tribes like the Sakas and Kushans who poured into India from the second century B.C. till the second century A.D. (*E.E.C.A.*)

Secretary of State for India, the—replaced the President of the Board of Control in London by the Government of India Act of 1858. The Secretary of State was a minister of the Crown and a member of the British Cabinet of Ministers and was responsible to the British Parliament for the administration of India which was transferred from the East India Company to the Crown of Great Britain in 1858. He was the fountain of authority as well as the director of policy in India. He was assisted by a Council of fifteen members some of whom were expected to help the Secretary of State with their local knowledge of India. At first this was a benefit both to Great Britain and India, but as years passed and India advanced politically most of the members of the Council were found to be re-actionaries and the Secretary of State's Council came to be considered by Indian politicians as unnecessary. The Secretary of State possessed very large powers of direction and control over the administration of India and he could also over-rule his Council. So a strong Secretary of State like Lord Morley or Edwin Montague could act very much like autocrats. His council was replaced by a body of advisers by the Government of India Act, 1935 (*q.v.*). Further to the extent to which the Act contemplated the introduction of responsibility in the Central Government in India it also limited the powers of the Secretary of State for India. The office was finally abolished with the grant of independence to India in 1947.

Seleucos Nikator—was a general of Alexander, the king of Macedon. On the death of Alexander, Seleucos succeeded to his eastern dominions and assumed the title of king in 306 B.C. In the meantime the Indian provinces conquered by Alexander had been freed from the Greek rule by Chandragupta Maurya (*q.v.*). Hoping to recover them Seleucos attempted an invasion of India some time before 302 B.C., but his attack was repulsed by Chandragupta and he was compelled to make peace by surrendering to Chandragupta all his territories to the east of the Hindu Kush as well as Gedrosia, modern Baluchistan, in return for 500 elephants. A matrimonial alliance was also made and Megasthenes (*q.v.*) was sent by Seleucos as his envoy to the court of Chandragupta at Pataliputra. The victory of Chandragupta Maurya secured India from all further Greek aggression.

Sena dynasty, the—ruled in Bengal from about A.D. 1095 to A.D. 1245. The dynasty traced its descent from a chief, named Samantasena, who originally belonged to Karnata (Mysore) but came to Bengal where he settled. Samantasena's son, Hemantasena, increased the power of the family and

Hemantasena's son, Vijayasena, was the first to assume distinctly the royal title. He ruled from A.D. 1095 to 1158 and brought West and North Bengal under his control. His son and successor, Vallalsena (*q.v.*) ruled from A.D. 1159 to 1179 when the throne passed to his son, Laksmanasena (*q.v.*) who ruled over the whole of Bengal and at one time extended his sway as far as Orissa on the south-east and Benares on the west. But in about A.D. 1202 he was suddenly attacked in his capital at Nadiya by a Muhammadan army under Iktiaruddin Muhammad, son of Bakhtyar Khilji (*q.v.*) and fled to East Bengal where he died soon afterwards. His sons, Visvarupasena and Kesavasena, continued to rule in East Bengal until about A.D. 1245 when East Bengal also passed under Muhammadan rule. The rule of the Sena dynasty is an important landmark in its history. The Sena kings made Bengal a united and powerful kingdom, promoted Sanskrit learning and were the patrons of poets like Jayadeva (*q.v.*) and jurists like Halayudha. (Majumdar, R. C., *Hist of Bengal*, Vol. I)

Sepoy Mutiny, the—broke out on 10 May, 1857 at Meerut, though earlier in the year signs of unrest had appeared amongst the sepoys stationed in Berhampore and Barrackpore where on 29 March, 1857, a sepoy named Mangal Pandey murdered a European officer in broad daylight and were suppressed. But the movement gradually gathered momentum and broke out in all its fury in the midsummer of the year. Its causes were political, social, religious and military. Dalhousie's policy of annexation (*q.v.*) by the application of the Doctrine of Lapse (*q.v.*) as well as on the ground of misgovernment filled the Indian Princes with uneasiness as to the security of their thrones, threw many of the dependents of the dispossessed rulers into unemployment and caused great distress and bitterness. Amongst the affected ruling chiefs, Nana Sahib (*q.v.*) the adopted son of the dispossessed Peshwa Baji Rao II, and Rani Lakshmi Bai of Jhansi (*q.v.*) took prominent part in organising the Mutiny and the latter even fought strenuously, till her death, against the British. The annexations and the new land-tenure system introduced in the annexed states, especially in Oudh, caused great social unrest amongst the landlords as well as amongst the common people, many of whom were disbanded soldiers who faced unemployment and disaffected the more educated Indians by contracting the areas of the country where they could find respectable employment. The public disparagement of Hindu mythology by English literary men like Macaulay, the open adverse criticism of the Hindu religion by the Christian missionaries, the prohibition of *Sati* and infanticide, the legalisation of re-marriage of Hindu widows, the prohibition of the disinheriting of a Hindu on his conversion to Christianity and the introduction of the telegraph and railways—all combined to fill the mind of the ordinary Hindu with the fear that his religion was in danger and insidious attempts were being made to force his conversion to Christianity. Lastly, the sepoy army which had contributed much to the building of the Indo-British empire was deeply dissatisfied. The salary and emoluments of an Indian sepoy were much less than those of an English soldier in the Indian army and his prospects of promotion were strictly restricted. The Indian sepoy was further expected to provide at his own cost for the carriage of his luggage even in distant theatres of war like Burma and Afghanistan, regions which were forbidden to the Hindu by his caste-rules and religious practices. The seniormost of the Indian sepoys had often to serve under very junior British officers. All these circumstances created bitterness in the Indian army of which the British portion formed only one-fifth (45,322 out of a total of 233, 000) enabling the sepoys to feel proud of their strength and importance in the maintenance of the Indo-British empire and resentful of the inferiority with which they were treated in comparison with the Britishers in the Indian army. The sepoy army which was thus discontented was driven to desperation when the Enfield rifle with the greased cartridges (*q.v.*) were imposed upon them, threatening the pollution of the religion of the Hindu as well as of the Muhammadan sepoys. It had been in an inflammable condition for some time past: the greased cartridge supplied the necessary spark and the fire of the Mutiny broke out.

At first the Mutineers had great success. Marching out from Meerut on 10 May, 1857 the Mutineers captured Delhi the next day and proclaimed Bahadur Shah II, who was then no more than a puppet, the Emperor of Delhi. The capture of Delhi immensely added to the prestige of the Mutineers and in the course of the next two months the Mutiny became general over Oudh and Rohilkhand, and the sepoys rose against the British at Nasirabad in Rajputana, at Nimach in Gwalior state, at Bareilly, Lucknow, Benares and Cawnpore in modern Uttar Pradesh, while the Rani of Jhansi headed the revolt in Bundelkhand, killing every European that fell into her hands. In almost every case the Mutineers after the outbreak started for Delhi, except those at Cawnpore who besieged the local British garrison and at Lucknow where the Residency was besieged. It was at Bithur, near Cawnpore, that Nana Sahib was declared the Peshwa. This incident exposed the lack of unity of purpose amongst the Mutineers. What was their aim? To restore Muhammadan rule in India under a restored Mughul Emperor, or to establish Hindu rule under a Brahman Peshwa? This conflict of aims persisted all through the Mutiny and weakened its strength. But at the beginning the cleavage did not appear to be very wide, and British rule in India was really threatened for a time. Delhi, Cawnpore, Lucknow and Bundelkhand became the storm centres. Gradually, with the help of the Sikhs, the Gurkhas and of the sepoys stationed in South India, the British power which seemed to have reeled under the first blow, re-established itself. Delhi was re-captured on 14 September, 1857, Cawnpore was relieved on 27 June, and Lucknow on 25 September, but was again lost only to be finally relieved on 5 November. In the meantime fresh regiments of British soldiers led by two generals of great experience, Sir Colin Campbell, Commander-in-Chief, and Sir Hugh Rose, had arrived. Campbell reduced Oudh and Rohilkhand to submission while Sir Hugh reduced Bundelkhand, defeated in successive engagements the Rani of Jhansi who fell fighting and Nana Sahib's general, Tantia Topi, who was captured and later on executed. On the fall of Delhi on 14 September, Emperor Bahadur Shah II was arrested and deported as a prisoner to Rangoon where he died and his two sons and grandsons were shot dead without any show of a trial by Colonel Hodson. Nana Sahib fled into the forests of Nepal and was never heard of again. On 8 July, 1858 Lord Canning, the Governor-General, proclaimed the end of the Mutiny and restoration of peace.

Horrible deeds of persecution had been perpetrated on both sides and their memories estranged for a long time, as never before, the feelings between the Europeans and the Indians. The Mutiny tolled the knell of the Company's rule in India and the administration of India was transferred from the Company to the Crown of England. Queen Victoria issued a Proclamation announcing this change and promising amnesty, religious toleration and recognition of the existing rights of the Princes of India and thus dropping the Doctrine of Lapse. The success of the British and the failure of the Mutineers were due to several causes. First, the Mutiny was parochial and sectional. It was a movement confined between the Panjab on the west and Bengal on the east and Oudh on the north and the Narmada on the south. It was confined to the sepoys; and the Princes and the common people of India generally stood aloof from it. Secondly, the Mutineers had no common objective, nor were they directed by a central intelligent leadership. Thirdly, they were ill-organised, each unit selecting its own leader and fighting on its own account. Fourthly, the Sikhs who foolishly attributed their recent defeat to the hostility of the sepoys, stood loyally by the English and it was mainly with their support that Delhi was re-captured and the back of the Mutiny was broken. Fifthly, the Mutineers often fought with great courage, but they did not develop from amongst themselves any great general while the British had a unified command and the services of a host of brilliant officers like Havelock, Nicholson, Outram and Lawrence. Lastly, the British victory over the Mutineers, who represented a very small section of the Indians, was secured with the active as well as the passive support of the vast majority of Indians who found nothing to enthuse over in the actions and activities of the mutinous sepoys. (There is a vast literature on the Sepoy Mutiny of which the more important are Holmes, T. R., *Hist. of the Indian Mutiny*; Malleson, *Hist. of the Sepoy War*; Sen, S. N., *1857*; Majumdar, R. C., *Hist. of the Freedom Movement*; I. vii Savarkar, V. D., *War of Indian Independence*)

Servants of India Society, the—was founded in 1905 by Gopal Krishna Gokhale (*q.v.*). Its object was "to train national missionaries for the service of India, and to promote, by all constitutional means, the true interests of the Indian people". It was a group of men who were to be trained and equipped for some form of unselfish service to India. Its first President, Gokhale, as well as his successor, Srinivasa Shastri, devoted themselves mainly to the furtherance of the political progress of India. A third distinguished member of the Society, Narayan Malhar Joshi, founded in 1911 the Social Service League in Bombay for spreading education and improving living conditions among the masses. Joshi also founded in 1920 the All-India Trade Union Congress, but as it leaned more and more towards communism Joshi had to leave the Servants of India Society. Pandit Hriday Nath Kunzru, a fourth member of the Servants of India Society, founded in 1914 the Seva Samiti at Allahabad. A fifth member, Sri Ram Bajpai, organised the Seva Samiti Boy Scouts Association in

1914 which aimed at the complete Indianisation of the Boy Scouts Movement in India. The activities of these five illustrious members of the Servants of India Society indicate the important part that the Society has played in moulding the national life of India.

Seths, the—is the name of the famous banking house of Murshidabad which controlled the finances of Bengal in the middle of the eighteenth century. (*see* Jagat Seth.)

Shah Nawaz Khan—was a Mughul noble whose daughter, Dilraj Bano Begum, was married to Prince Aurangzeb in 1637.

Shah Jahan—was the fifth Mughul Emperor of Delhi (1628-58). His original name was Prince Khurram and during the early years of the reign of his father, Jahangir, he was the Emperor's favourite, as his elder brother Khusrav (*q.v.*) had incurred the displeasure of Jahangir for having been put up as his rival for the throne of Delhi about the time of Akbar's death. Prince Khurram married in 1612 Arjumand Bano Begum (*q.v.*), daughter of Asaf Khan, the brother of Nurjahan (*q.v.*) who was the richest and most powerful noble in the Empire. But after the marriage of his youngest brother, Shahryar, with the daughter of Empress Nur Jahan by her first husband, Shah Jahan began to lose favour with the Empress who wanted the succession to go to Shahryar. An estrangement grew between Prince Khurram and Jahangir and the Prince was practically in rebellion and away in the Deccan when Emperor Jahangir died in October, 1627. His interests were upheld by his father-in-law, Asaf Khan, until Prince Khurram arrived at the capital and ascended the throne with the title of Shah Jahan in February, 1628. He ruled till his deposition by his rebellious son, Aurangzeb, in 1658. He died in captivity in 1668. Shah Jahan was the most magnificent of the Mughul Emperors. Soon after his accession he built for himself the Peacock throne (*q.v.*) at a cost of a crore of rupees. Later on, he built at Agra, which was his capital till 1648, the *Jumma Masjid*, the Red Fort containing the *Moti Masjid*, the *Dewan-i-Am* and the *Dewan-i-Khas* and the incomparable *Taj* which took 22 years (1632-53) in building. During his reign of thirty years he extended the Mughul dominions southwards into the Deccan by completely annexing Ahmadnagar and reducing Bijapur and Golconda to subjugation and recovered Qandahar in 1638. Qandahar was, however, again taken by Persia in 1649 and Shah Jahan's three attempts in 1649, 1652 and 1653 to reconquer the place ended in failure. In 1648 Shah Jahan transferred his capital from Agra to Delhi where he also built a gorgeous palace containing two halls of audience, the *Dewan-i-Am* and the *Dewan-i-khas,* the latter of which was so richly decorated that the proud declaration was recorded, "If on Earth be an Eden of Bliss, It is this, it is this, none but this". But Shah Jahan's last days were very miserable. In 1657 he fell ill and it was feared that he would not survive. At once a war of succession was begun amongst his four sons, Dara, Shuja, Aurangzeb and Murad. Dara had the support of Shah Jahan while Aurangzeb and Murad joined together on the basis of partitioning the Empire. Shuja fought alone and was first defeated by the Imperial army at the battle of Bahadurpur in February, 1658 and returned to Bengal where he was later on defeated again at the battle of Khajwah by Aurangzeb's army in January, 1659, became a fugitive and died in Arakan in 1660. The Imperial army sent against Aurangzeb and Murad was defeated by the Princes at the battle of Dharmat in April, 1658. Dara himself was next defeated at the battle of Samugarh in May, 1658, by Aurangzeb and Murad and became a fugitive. Aurangzeb then made a prisoner of Murad, marched on Agra which he easily captured, and practically imprisoned Shah Jahan in June, 1658. Next month he was informally enthroned as the Emperor of India. Dara was finally defeated by Aurangzeb at the battle of Deorai in April, 1659, betrayed as a captive and executed in 1659 after a trial on a charge of heresy. Aurangzeb was then formally enthroned as Emperor of Delhi with the title of Alamgir in June, 1659. The unfortunate Shah Jahan dragged on a pitiable existence as a prisoner in the hands of his own son until death released him in 1666.

Shahnama, the—is an immense epic in Persian written by Firdousi who enjoyed the patronage of Sultan Mahmud (*q.v.*).

Shahryar, Prince—was the youngest son of Emperor Jahangir. He married the daughter of Nur Jahan by her first husband, Sher Afghan (*q.v.*). Empress Nur Jahan, therefore, tried to secure for Shahryar the succession to the throne of Delhi after the death of Jahangir in 1627. But Shahryar had no ability of his own, and though on the death of Jahangir he was declared Emperor in Lahore, he was soon defeated, captured and blinded in the interest of Shah Jahan by the latter's father-in-law, Asaf Khan.

Shahu, Raja—*see* Sahu.

Shahji—was the father of the famous Shivaji I (*q.v.*) the founder of Maratha independence. He was a clever and astute person who began his career as a trooper in the army of the sultan of Ahmadnagar. By dint of his abilities he gradually rose to high distinction, and played the king-maker during the last years of the Nizam Shahi rule. After the annexation of Ahmadnagar by Shah Jahan he entered the service of the Bijapur state in 1636. Here also he earned considerable fame and was rewarded with an extensive fief in the Karnatak. When his son Shivaji began raiding the territories of Bijapur, Shahji was suspected of having abetted his son, was in consequence kept in confinement at Bijapur for four years and was released on the intervention of the Mughul Emperor Shah Jahan. Later on after 1659, he brought about a temporary understanding between Bijapur and Shivaji, which left the latter free to attack the Mughul dominions. That was all the service that he rendered to his son whose achievements had immortalised him.

Shah Shuja—was the Amir of Afghanistan from 1803 to 1809 when he was defeated and deposed. He was then kept as a prisoner in Kashmir. He was released from his captivity by Ranjit Singh (*q.v.*) in whose court he remained for two years (1813-15) and whose earnest help he sought to purchase by giving him the famous diamond, the Koh-i-noor. But finding that Ranjit Singh would not help him in getting back the Afghan throne, Shah Shuja fled from Lahore, reached Ludhiana where he placed himself under British protection in 1816 and received a pension from the British Government. In 1833 he sought an alliance with Ranjit Singh in an abortive attempt to recover his throne which enabled the Sikh monarch to occupy Peshawar. Four years later, in 1837, Lord Auckland (*q.v.*) the Governor-General of India, decided to utilise him for establishing British control over Afghanistan. So on his initiative Shah Shuja entered into a tripartite treaty with the Indo-British Government and Ranjit Singh in June, 1838, by which it was decided that Shah Shuja would be helped by the English and the Sikhs to recover the throne of Afghanistan from its ruler, Dost Mohammed. Thus began the First Afghan War (*q.v.*). Accordingly, Shah Shuja was triumphantly conducted by an Indo-British army through the Bolan pass to his capital in Kabul in August 1839; but the Afghans practically refused to accept him as their ruler. They rose against his English protectors and in April, 1842 he was assassinated by an Afghan patriot.

Shams-i-Siraj Afif—was the author of *Tarikh-i-Firoz-Shahi*, a contemporary history in Persian of the reign of Sultan Firoz

Shah Tughluq (*q.v.*). He was an officer under Firoz Shah and his work may be regarded as the official history of the Sultan's reign.

Shams-ud-din Atga Khan—was appointed by Emperor Akbar as his prime minister in 1561. His appointment was most distasteful to Akbar's foster-mother, Maham Anaga, and her son, Adham Khan. One day, soon after the appointment, Adham Khan walked into the office-room of Atga Khan in the palace and there stabbed him to death. The ruffian then made an attempt on the person of the Emperor himself, but was felled to the ground with a stunning blow by Akbar himself and then hurled to death from over the battlements.

Shams-ud-din Bahmani—the seventh Bahmani sultan, succeeded his brother, Ghiyas-ud-din in 1397, but was soon afterwards deposed, blinded and imprisoned.

Shams-ud-din Muzaffar Shah—an Abyssinian originally named Sidi Badr, rose to high offices under Nasir-ud-din Mahmud II, the last ruler of Bengal belonging to the house of Iliyas (*q.v.*). In 1490 Sidi Badr murdered his master and usurped the throne under the title of Shams-ud-din Muzaffar Shah. He proved to be a tyrant and widespread disorder prevailed throughout the kingdom. Unable to bear it, the nobles of Bengal under the leadership of his minister Ala-ud-din Hussain besieged him in his capital at Gaur for four months in 1493 in the course of which he died.

Shams-ud-din, Sultan of Kashmir—originally an adventurer named Shah Mirza or Mir, came from Surat, entered into the service of the Hindu raja of Kashmir and rose to be his minister. In about A.D. 1346 he deposed the Hindu raja and seized the throne of Kashmir. He ruled wisely till his death in about 1349. He founded the dynasty of the Muhammadan sultans of Kashmir who ruled in the valley until its conquest by Akbar in 1586.

Shastri, Lal Bahadur (1904-1966)—Prime Minister of India from May, 1964 to his death on 11 January, 1966, was born of poor parents in the Benares district, Uttar Pradesh, was a self-made man who raised himself by dint of his merits, ability and character from the humble position of a schoolmaster to the premiership of India in succession to Pandit Jawahar Lal Nehru. During his short term of office for only nineteen months he had no mean achievements in recognition of which India's highest honour, Bharat-Ratna, was conferred on him posthumously. He was a quiet and unostentatious but determined nationalist and though small in stature he was a great leader who did much to solve not only India's domestic problems of food and finance but also her almost war like relations with China and fought two actual wars with Pakistan over the latter's attempts at occupying the Rann of Kutch and Kashmir and Jammu. In the second war with Pakistan over Kashmir and Jammu he bravely and determinedly headed the united national effort of India and beat back Pakistan and simultaneously held China in a leash. The Kutch affair he agreed to submit to arbitration by an international tribunal and also agreed at the request of the UNO to a cease-fire on the Kashmir front when India was having the upper hand in the war. Later on, he went to Tashkent at the invitation of Russia to explore the possibilities of a peaceful settlement with Pakistan and, through the mediation of Russia, agreed with President Ayub Khan of Pakistan to an agreement known as the Tashkent Declaration (*q.v.*). The effort and strain brought about his end on 11 January, 1966, a few hours after he had put his signature to the document. Lal Bahadur Shastri was a martyr to the cause of peace between India and Pakistan.

Shariat-Ulla, Haji—a Muhammadan leader in the district of Faridpur, now in East Pakistan, started a movement for reforming Islam in East Bengal early in the nineteenth century. His movement came to be known as the Faraidhi (or Faraizi) movement. It developed into an agrarian movement, but it was generally peaceful. He is considered as one of the precursors of the revival movement amongst the Muhammadans in East Bengal.

Shaukat Ali, Maulana—was a prominent leader and politician amongst the Indian Muhammadans. Born in Rampur, near Benares, in 1873, he began his career as an employee in the Excise Department of the British Indian Government. After fifteen years' service he took to politics and was interned by the Government during the First World War. On his release he led, along with his brother Mohammed Ali, the *Khilafat* Movement in 1919-20. He also joined the Indian National Congress and its non-co-operation movement. But later on he left the Congress, identified himself with the Muslim League which he represented, along with others, at the Round Table Conference (*q.v.*). In 1934 he also became a Member of the Indian Legislative Assembly. But he and his brother, Mohammed Ali, were eclipsed with the rise of M.A. Jinnah (*q.v.*).

Shaukat Jang—was the son of the second daughter of Nawaq Ali Vardi Khan (*q.v.*) of Bengal and was thus a cousin of Ali Vardi's successor, Nawab Siraj-ud-daulah (*q.v.*). At the time of the death of Nawab Ali Vardi Khan in April, 1756, Shaukat Jang was the governor of Purnea. He disputed the right of Nawab Siraj-ud-daulah to the succession to the throne of Bengal and with the support of the disaffected nobles of Bengal he secured from the Mughul Emperor the *sanad* for the subadarship of Bengal. But before he could enforce his claim he was attacked by Siraj-ud-daulah, was defeated and killed late in 1756.

Shayesta Khan—was a maternal uncle of Emperor Aurangzeb (*q.v.*) who appointed him in 1660 as governor of the Deccan with the special mission of subduing Shivaji (*q.v.*). Shayesta Khan had at first some successes against Shivaji, but when in the rainy season he retired to Poona he was surprised by a night attack led by Shivaji in person and narrowly escaped death with the loss of three fingers and of his son. Shayesta Khan was then transferred to Bengal which province he administered for about thirty years with conspicuous success, suppressing the Portuguese pirates who infested the waterways of lower Bengal and conquering from the king of Arakan the Chittagong district in 1666. He died when over ninety years of age at Agra in 1694.

Sher Afghan—whose original name was Ali Quli Beg Istajhi, was a Persian adventurer who came to seek his fortune in the Mughul court. He married Mihr-un-nisa (*q.v.*) when she was seventeen years of age and received early in the reign of Jahangir (*q.v.*) the *jagir* of Burdwan and the title of Sher Afghan (tiger-thrower). In 1607 he fell under suspicion of complicity with the Afghan rebels in Bengal. Jahangir, therefore, ordered Qutb-ud-din Koka, who was then the governor of Bengal, to arrest Sher Afghan and to send him to the capital. But Sher Afghan resisted arrest and in the affray that followed Qutb-ud-din and Sher Afghan were both killed. Sher Afghan's widowed wife, Mihr-un-nisa, along with a daughter that had been born to her, were then sent to the court. Four years later she married Emperor Jahangir to whose youngest son, Shahriyar, was still later on married her daughter by Sher Afghan.

Sher Ali—was the Amir of Afghanistan, who succeeded his father Dost Muhammad (*q.v.*) in 1863, but was driven out of Kabul in 1866 and of Qandahar in 1867 and took refuge in Herat. He, however, regained Kabul and Qandahar in 1868. In the meantime Russia had extended her frontiers to the Khanates near the Caspian Sea and annexed Tashkent in 1865 and Samarkand in 1868. This advance of Russia towards Afghanistan made Sher Ali suspicious about her ultimate designs and in 1869 Sher Ali met at Ambala the Viceroy, Lord Mayo, to whom he made proposals for a definite treaty with the British Indian Government on certain terms aiming at strengthening his rule in Afghanistan so that he might be in a better position to resist further Russian expansion on the Afghan frontier. But Lord Mayo, acting under instructions from London, refused to enter into any such definite treaty. From about 1870 General Kauffmann, the Russian Governor-General in Turkistan since 1867, began a correspondence with Amir Sher Ali who in 1873, when Khiva was occupied by Russia, repeated his request to the Indian Government for a more definite treaty, but his request was again refused. But in 1876 the Government of India headed by Lord Lytton I (1876-80) suddenly changed its Afghan policy and offered to enter into a definitive treaty with Sher Ali, provided the Amir agreed to accept a British Resident at Herat. Knowing the Afghans as he did, Sher Ali felt sure that the acceptance of a British Resident within his dominions would be deeply resented by his Afghan subjects and his throne would be endangered, and consequently refused the British offer. But soon afterwards in revenge for British action in the Congress of Berlin, 1878, Russia sent a mission under General Stolietoff to Afghanistan which Sher Ali was obliged to accept. This supplied the Government of Lord Lytton I with an added justification for the British demand for the acceptance of a British mission by Sher Ali on whose refusal to do so the Indo-British Government declared war on Sher Ali in November, 1878. He could not resist the mighty force that immediately invaded his country and fled for safety to Russian Turkistan where he died in February, 1879. He was a victim of the ruthless ambitions and the selfish interests of his two powerful European neighbours viz., England and Russia.

Sher Ali Khan—an Afghan chief, was made by the British Indian Government the independent ruler of Western Afghanistan with his headquarters at Qandahar in 1879 and continued to rule there till 1891 when he was persuaded by the British Indian Government to abdicate and to retire to India.

Sher Khan Sur (1472-1545)—better known as Sher Shah, was the Emperor of India from A.D. 1539 to 1545 and established

the Sur dynasty which ruled over North India till 1556. Sher
Khan, whose original name was Farid Khan, was the son of
a petty Afghan *jagirdar* of Sasaram in Bihar, got a training in
administration in his father's estate, but the indifferent treatment that he received from his father turned him into a soldier
of fortune. In 1522 he entered into the service of Bahar Khan
Lohani who conferred upon him the title of Sher Khan, for
having killed a tiger single-handed. But he soon afterwards
entered the service of Babur who rewarded him with the
restoration of his father's *jagir* of Sasaram. Sher Khan on his
return joined the service of the Lohani king, Jalal Khan,
of Bihar, married the widow of Taj Khan, the lord of Chunar,
and got the important fort there. In 1531 when Chunar was
invaded by Emperor Humayun, Sher Khan cleverly saved himself
and retained the fortress. Two years later he defeated Mahmud
Shah, the king of Bengal, at the battle of Surajgarh and thus
became the undisputed ruler of Bihar. He then made two
attacks on Bengal and thus brought upon him an attack by
Humayun in 1537. Sher Khan inveigled him into Bengal, out-
generalled him and defeated him severely at the battle of
Chaunsa, near Buxar, in 1539. Humayun escaped by the skin
of his teeth, but Sher Khan now became the *de facto* ruler of the
whole of eastern India from Kanauj to Assam and assumed
the title of Sher Shah in order to signify his independent status.
Next year Sher Shah again defeated Humayun at the battle
of Bilgram (near Kanauj), marched on to Delhi which he
occupied and then occupied the Panjab. He subjugated Malwa
in 1542, took Raisin in 1543, followed up with the quick conquest of Sind and Multan, Marwar in 1544 and died as the
result of an explosion while engaged in besieging Kalinjar
which, however, fell. Thus within a short time Sher Shah
had ousted the Mughuls from Delhi and made himself the
Emperor of India. Sher Shah was no mere soldier; he was
also a great administrator who, within the short space of five
years of his rule, introduced many wise administrative reforms,
dividing the country into forty-seven units called *sarkars* (districts), each of which was subdivided into a number of
parganahs, establishing a revenue system based on the survey of
lands and collection of revenue direct from the cultivators who
were given *kubuliyats* in which their rights and liabilities were
precisely stated, reforming the currency based on a ratio of
64 copper coins for the silver tanka or *rupeya* i.e., the rupee,
improving trade and commerce by reforming the tariff and

removing vexatious customs duties, improving communication by the construction of trunk roads and by devising a system of horse-posts, reorganising the police system and improving the maintenance of peace and order by making each village responsible for the detection of local crimes, upholding justice impartially, showing tolerance to the Hindus of whom one at least (namely Brahmajit Gaur) rose to be one of his generals, and, last but not the least, reorganising and improving the army in which he introduced the system of direct recruitment and cash payments, and thus replaced the prevalent inefficient feudal levies by a regular army directly under the control of the sovereign. Many of his administrative reforms were later on adopted by the Mughul Emperor Akbar.

Sher Singh—was a reputed son of Maharaja Ranjit Singh of the Panjab, whom he succeeded in 1846, three years after the death of Ranjit, but he was murdered in 1843.

Sher Singh—son of Chatter Singh, was a Sikh leader who was at first trusted by the British who had defeated the Sikhs in their first war with them (*q.v.*). On the revolt of Mulraj (*q.v.*), the governor of Multan, in 1848 Sher Singh was sent with a large army against the rebels, but on reaching Multan he went over to the side of the rebellious Sikhs. His defection encouraged many Sikh leaders to rally round him and the revolt of Mulraj was turned into the Second Sikh War (*q.v.*). Sher Singh fought an indecisive battle with the English at Ramnagar on 16 November, 1848. He was also present at the battle of Chillianwalla which was fought in January, 1849, but failed to give the Sikh army a decisive lead and what was an indecisive battle was turned by Sher Singh's incapacity into a British victory. After the final defeat of the Sikhs in the battle of Gujarat on 21 February, 1849, he surrendered to the British and passed into oblivion.

Shiaism—is the faith of the section of the Muhammadans who consider that on the death of the Prophet his son-in-law, Ali, who had married the Prophet's only daughter, Fatima, should have been the Caliph. They, therefore, hold the first two Caliphs as usurpers and do not mention their names at the time of prayer. The Shias also hold that Ali's two sons were martyrs in the cause of true Islam and show honour to them by mourning their death annually in the month of Mohurrum. The section had its origin in Persia where Shiaism continues to be still very strong. Most of the Muhammadans in India are followers of Sunnism (*q.v.*) which was followed by the Sultans and Emperors of Delhi. The sultans of Bijapur and Golconda were Shias and this circumstance inflamed the passion of the Sunni Emperor Aurangzeb and led him to annex those states to his dominions. The Nawabs of Oudh as well as of Murshidabad were Shias, though the Muslim population in Oudh as well as in Bengal is largely Sunni.

Shihab-ud-din—*see* Muhammad Ghuri.

Shihab-ud-din—was a relation of Akbar's foster-mother, Maham Anaga. He was the governor of Delhi at the time of Akbar's accession. He was one of those who incited Akbar against the tutelage of Bairam Khan and caused his dismissal in 1560.

Shihab-ud-din Ghori—was the sultan of Malwa (1401-5). He was a descendant of the great Shihab-ud-din Muhammad Ghuri, the first Muhammadan sultan of Delhi. Taking advantage of the disorganisation that prevailed in the Delhi sultanate after the invasion by Timur in 1398 Shihab-ud-din, who was then the governor of Malwa, set himself up as an independent ruler of Malwa, with Dhar as its capital. The dynasty that sprang from him ruled up to 1432.

Shitab Rai—was a prominent man of Bihar who bore the title of Raja. On the grant of the *Dewani* to the East India Company Raja Shitab Rai was appointed as one of the two Deputy-Naibs and placed in charge of the collection of the revenue of Bihar. He was removed from the post in 1772 by Warren Hastings according to the orders of the Directors, arrested and put on trial on a charge of embezzlement, but he was honourably acquitted.

Shivaji (also spelt Sivaji)—was the founder of the independent Maratha kingdom. He was born in 1627 at Poona and was the son of Shahji (*q.v.*) and his first wife, Jijabai. Shahji was an officer in the Bijapur state and had practically discarded his wife soon after Shivaji's birth. Young Shivaji was brought up mainly by a local guardian named Dadaji Kondeo and her saintly *guru* Ramdas. They cared little for his literary education but his mother and Ramdas instilled into his mind that his duty was to free his country and people so that the gods, the Brahmans and the cows might be protected against the onslaughts of the Muhammadans. He kept company with the local hill people called the Mawalis and became very popular with them. Roaming about the countryside in their company he also acquired an intimate personal acquaintance with the passes and forts of the region and gathering round him a devoted band of Mawalis began his career at the age of nineteen by capturing the fort of Torna, about twenty miles from Poona. Conquests of other forts like Raigarh (1646), Chakan, Singhagarh and Purandhar, situated within the territories of the sultan of Bijapur, soon followed and by 1655 Shivaji had occupied Kalyan in Konkon and the fort of Javli, whose Raja, Chandra Rao, was treacherously murdered under his direction. These acquisitions provoked the sultan of Bijapur to send against Shivaji in 1659 a large army under a senior general named Afzal Khan. Both being unsure of success, opened negotiations and, at an interview that was arranged between the two, Afzal Khan attempted to strangle to death Shivaji, who having been prepared for such an eventuality, carried secretly with him a deadly weapon called tiger's claws with which he ripped up the bowels of the Muhammadan general who was killed on the spot. Soon afterwards Shivaji defeated the Bijapur army in an open pitched battle and thus practically stopped the hostility of Bijapur. He had now to face the much more powerful Mughul Emperor, Aurangzeb, who in 1660 sent against him a large army under his maternal uncle and general, Shayesta Khan, who first captured some of Shivaji's forts and then occupied Shivaji's headquarters, Poona, itself. Shivaji soon made a surprise night attack on Shayesta Khan who managed to escape with the loss of three fingers and of a son and got himself recalled. But Aurangzeb was persistent in his hostilities to Shivaji and sent against him new armies under new generals and the war continued. Though Shivaji was bold enough to plunder Surat in 1664 the Mughul general, Raja Jai Singh, took so many of his forts that in 1665 he made peace with the Mughuls by the treaty of Purandhar, surrendered 23 of his forts, keeping only 12 for himself and proceeded to the Mughul court at Agra under the promise of a safe conduct guaranteed by Raja Jai Singh. On his arrival at the imperial court in May, 1666, he was treated as a third grade *mansabdar* (*q.v.*) and was also placed under surveillance. Shivaji was, however, clever enough to escape, along with his young son, Sambhuji, who had accompanied him and his retinue from his place of confinement at Agra. Travelling in the guise of *sanyasins* and riding on swift horses he safely returned to his own country in December, 1666. Next year Aurangzeb made the best of a bad bargain by conferring upon Shivaji the title of Raja. Shivaji maintained peace with the Mughuls during the next two years which he devoted to the organisation of his own government. He resumed hostilities in 1670, exacted from the local Mughul officers

in some parts of Khandesh written promises to pay him the
Chauth, i.e., one-fourth of the estimated revenue, in return for
his protection and plundered Surat a second time. He thus
increased his power so much that in June, 1674, he had himself
crowned at Raigarh as the independent king of Maharashtra
and thus brought into existence a Hindu kingdom in the teeth
of the opposition of the Mughuls, the sultans of Bijapur, the
Portuguese of Goa and the Abyssinian pirates at Janjira.
Before his death, six years later, in 1680, he had extended his
dominions over the whole of the western Carnatic extending
from Belgaum to the bank of the Tungabhadra. He not only
raised himself from the position of a neglected son of a petty
jagirdar to the throne of an independent kingdom which was
his own creation, endowed it with an efficient administrative
and military organisation but had also carried his own people
with him. The spirit of independence which had inspired him,
he instilled so effectively in the minds of his countrymen that
they were able to maintain their independence against the whole
might of Aurangzeb who killed his son, made a prisoner of his
grandson and over-ran the whole country after Shivaji's death.
Phoenix-like, the Maratha kingdom rose from its ashes. Shivaji
was really a practical idealist; greater than Sher Shah, greater
than Ranjit Singh and even greater than Oliver Cromwell and
Napoleon, who were selfish egoists. (Sarkar, J. N., *Shivaji and
His Times;* Sen S. N., *Siva Chhatrapati*)

Shore, Sir John—was the Governor-General from 1793 to 1798.
He began his career as a lower officer in the Company's service
in Bengal and rose to be a member of the Calcutta Council
during the Governor-Generalship of Lord Cornwallis whom
he helped materially in reforming the administration. As the
Governor-General in succession to Lord Cornwallis he saw
to the enforcement and implementation of the reforms introduced by his predecessor. He adhered generally to the policy
of non-intervention in the affairs of the Indian states, remained
neutral in the war between the Nizam and the Marathas
culminating in the defeat of the former at the battle of Kardla
(*q.v.*) in 1795, but intervened in the affairs of Oudh upon
which he imposed a new treaty by which the Company got
Allahabad.

Shree Aravinda Ghose—*see* Ghose, Aravinda.

Shuja, Prince—was the second son of Emperor Shah Jahan. He
was a pleasure-loving prince, but was ambitious like his other
three brothers. In 1657 when Shah Jahan fell seriously ill

Shuja, who was then the governor of Bengal, was the first amongst his sons to claim his father's throne, proclaimed himself as the Emperor at Rajmahal, which was then the capital of Bengal and marched at the head of an army towards Delhi. But he was defeated by an Imperial army at the battle of Bahadurpur in February, 1658 and retired to Bengal. Later on after the defeat of Dara at the battles of Dharmat and Samurgarh Shuja felt emboldened and again took up arms. But he was defeated by Aurangzeb's general, Mir Jumla, fled to Arakan where he perished with all his family.

Shujaat Khan—a general in the service of Aurangzeb, was posted in the north-western frontier. In 1674 he and his forces were destroyed by the rebellious Afridis at the Karapa Pass. After this disaster the Emperor moved close to Peshawar and took measures which ensured peace on the frontier for a long period.

Shuja-ud-daulah (1754-75)—was the third independent Nawab of Oudh and was the son and successor of the second Nawab, Safdar Jang. Shuja-ud-daulah also enjoyed the dignity of being the *Wazir* of the Mughul Emperors, Alamgir II (*q.v.*) (1754-59) and Shah Alam II (*q.v.*) (1759-1806). But he practically did nothing to save or support the Emperor against Ahmad Shah Abdali who sacked Delhi in 1756, finally conquered the Panjab in 1759 and defeated the Mughul Emperor and his ally, the Marathas at the third battle of Panipat in 1761. He always looked after his own dynastic interests. In 1764 he entered into an alliance with Mir Qasim (*q.v.*), the fugitive Nawab of Bengal and Emperor Shah Alam II against the Company in Bengal but was defeated at the battle of Buxar. In 1765 he made peace with the English by surrendering the districts of Kora and Allahabad and by paying an indemnity of 50 lakhs of rupees. He also made a defensive alliance with the English whereby the Company engaged to provide him with troops for the defence of his frontiers and he consented to meet the cost of the army thus lent. In 1772 he made an agreement with the Rohillas to help them in case the Marathas invaded their state on condition of receiving a sum of 40 lakhs of rupees from the Rohillas if he succeeded in compelling the Marathas to withdraw. In 1773 the Marathas invaded Rohilkhand, but retired without fighting. Shuja-ud-daulah demanded the stipulated reward of Rs. 40,00,000 but the Rohillas evaded payment. Then in 1773 he made with the Company the Treaty of Benares by which he got back Kora and Allahabad for fifty lakhs of rupees in addition to a subsidy to be paid for the maintenance of a garrison of the Company's troops. At Benares Shuja-ud-daulah further got from Warren Hastings (*q.v.*), the Governor of Bengal, an assurance that, in return for a large subsidy, he would be helped with a British contingent for the purpose of forcing the Rohillas to pay him the stipulated sum of 40 lakhs of rupees which, in the view of Shuja-ud-daulah, they owed to the Nawab. Accordingly in 1774 Shuja-ud-daulah, aided by a brigade of British soldiers, invaded Rohilkhand, defeated and killed its ruler, Hafiz Rahamat Khan (*q.v.*) at the battle of Miranpur Katra and annexed Rohilkhand to his dominions. Next year Shuja-ud-daulah died.

Si—a viceroy of the Kushan king, Kadphises II (*q.v.*), led an expedition across the Pamirs into China, but was defeated.

Sibi, the—were a tribal people who lived in the Rechna Doab in the Jhang district. They were a rude people clad in skins and armed with clubs. Alexander, the king of Macedon, passed through the country of the Sibis who submitted to the Greek invader.

Sidi, the—were the chiefs of the Abyssinian pirates of Janjira on the western coast of India. They had to be chastised by Shivaji (*q.v.*).

Sikandar Shah—the second sultan (1489-1517) of the Lodi dynasty, was the son and successor of Buhlol Lodi (*q.v.*), the founder of the dynasty. He was a capable and pushing ruler. He suppressed the prevailing disorder, repressed the refractory provincial governors, chieftains and zamindars and thus restored the power and prestige of the Sultan. He checked the accounts of the leading Afghan jagirdars and thus increased the revenue. He extended his authority up to the frontiers of Bengal and made a treaty with Ala-ud-din Hussain Shah of Bengal by which each agreed not to encroach upon the territories of the other. He reduced to submission the chiefs of Dholpur and Chanderi and founded a new town in 1504 on the site of the modern city of Agra in order to control the neighbouring chiefs. He died in Agra in 1517, trying until his death in vain to suppress the disorder in his dominions.

Sikandar Shah—was the fifth and last ruler of Delhi belonging to the Sur dynasty founded by Sher Shah (*q.v.*) of whom he was a nephew. He was the governor of the Panjab in 1555 when he was declared Emperor by the Afghans but he was later in the year defeated by Humayun in a battle near Sirhind and retired to Siwalik Hills whence he was expelled by Akbar in 1557. He then fled to Bengal where he died some time in 1558-59.

Sikhs, the—are the followers of Guru Nanak (*q.v.*) (1469-1538). They generally belong to the Panjab. They were at first a peaceful sect which recognised no distinction of caste or creed amongst themselves, though most of the Sikhs were originally Hindus. They believe in the fundamental truth underlying all religions; they are non-sectarian in outlook and maintain harmony with secular life. After the death of Guru Nanak in 1538 the head of the Sikh community came to be called the *Guru*. There were nine such *Gurus*, namely, Angad (1538-52), Amardas (1552-74), Ramdas (1574-81), Arjan (1581-1606), Hargovind (1606-45), Har Rai (1645-61), Har Kishan (1661-64), Teg Bahadur (1664-75) and Govinda Singh (1675-1708). The fourth *Guru*, Ramdas, was so saintly a person that he was respected by Emperor Akbar who made a gift to him of a plot of land with a pool at Amritsar where was later on constructed the famous golden Sikh temple. It was the fifth *Guru*, Arjan, who compiled the scriptures of the Sikhs, called the *Adi Granth* or the First Sacred Book, by collecting select verses from the works of his four predecessors as well as those of some Hindu and Muhammadan saints. He also stabilised the finances of the Sikh Church by introducing the system of payment by every Sikh of 'a spiritual tribute' and by arranging for its collection by the *Guru's* agents called *masnads*. *Guru* Arjan was executed by the order of Emperor Jahangir on a charge of treason for having given shelter, out of pity, to the Emperor's rebellious and fugitive son, Prince Khusrav (*q.v.*). The next *Guru*, Har Govind, who was a son of *Guru* Arjan, gave a military turn to Sikhism by gathering round him a small army of Sikhs, rose against Shah Jahan (*q.v.*), defeated an imperial army on one occasion but was ultimately driven to take refuge in the Kashmir Hills where he eventually died. The next two *Gurus*, Har Rai and Har Kishan, were rather colourless, but they nursed with care the Sikh community which continued to develop on account of the fiscal policy of Arjan and the armed policy of his son. The ninth *Guru*, Teg Bahadur, incurred the displeasure of Emperor Aurangzeb who had him arrested and offered him a choice between death by execution and conversion to Islam. Teg Bahadur preferred death to conversion and was beheaded by Aurangzeb's order. This martyrdom had an important effect on his son and the next *Guru*, Govinda Singh (*q.v.*) as well as on the Sikh community.

Guru Govind (*q.v.*) deliberately followed the policy of transforming the peaceful Sikh sect into a militant body determined to resist Muhammadan aggression and atrocities and introduced such discipline amongst the Sikhs that they were turned into a military band to which he gave the name of *Khalsa* or Pure and gave them unity by requiring them all to wear five things *viz.*, long hair, short drawers, an iron bangle, a steel dagger and a comb. He fought with local Mughul officials many battles in the course of which he lost his two sons, but nothing daunted he carried on his work until his murder by an Afghan in 1708. His sayings were later on collected and formed a supplementary *Granth* or Scripture of the Sikhs. The community felt such respect for him that after his death the office of the *Guru* was abolished, though the immediate leadership passed to Banda (*q.v.*). He led the Sikhs in incessant opposition to the Mughuls from 1708 till his capture and cruel execution under the feet of elephants in 1716 by the order of Emperor Farruksiyar (*q.v.*) (1713-19). Hundreds of the ordinary Sikhs were subjected to cruel persecution by the Mughul government, but repression could not extinguish the military spirit of the Khalsa. In the absence of a *Guru*, leadership passed from an individual to a large body of men who organised their co-religionists as best as they could. Thus Kapur Singh of Fyzullapur started the *Dal Khalsa*, or the theocracy of the Sikhs. Other Sikh leaders availed themselves of the disorder and confusion that prevailed in the Panjab, following the invasion of Nadir Shah, increased the financial resources of the Sikhs, built a fort at Daliwal on the Ravi and carried plundering raids up to Lahore. The repeated invasions of Ahmad Shah Abdali, especially his invasion leading to the third battle of Panipat in 1761, helped the development of the Sikh power in the Panjab by entirely liquidating the Mughul rule in the province and putting into their hearts new hope and courage. They hung upon his rear, took to guerilla fighting and made his hold on the Panjab extremely precarious. Ultimately after his return to Afghanistan from India in 1767 the Sikhs by their valour and persistence brought under their control the entire plain and by 1773 their sway extended from Shaharanpur on the east to Attock on the west, and from Multan on the south to the hills on the north. Thus the Sikhs succeeded in carving out an independent state for themselves, but they lacked a unitary administration. They were divided into twelve *misls* or confederacies, namely, the

Ahluwalia, the Bhangi, the Dalewalia, the Fyzullapuria, the Kanheya, the Karora Singhia, the Nakai, the Nihang, the Nishanwala, the Phulkia, the Ramgarhia and the Sukerchakia. But with the collapse of the power of Ahmad Shah Abdali and of the Mughuls the Sikhs, freed from the fear of any external enemies, fell to fighting amongst themselves and might have been disintegrated into twelve bodies. That calamity was averted by the genius and ability of Ranjit Singh (*q.v.*) the leader of the Sukerchakia *misl*. Born in 1780, he got in 1799 from Zaman Shah, the king of Afghanistan, the governorship of Lahore which regularised his position in the estimate of the Muhammadans in the Panjab. There, in the course of the next six years, he made himself the master of all the trans-Sutlej *misls*. Though his efforts to bring the cis-Sutlej *misls* also under his control failed on account of the opposition of the leaders of those *misls* backed by the British power in India, Ranjit had developed before his death in 1839 the Sikhs "from a sect into a people" whom he endowed with an independent state extending from the Sutlej to Peshawar and from Kashmir to Multan protected by a strong army trained after the European fashion and equipped with powerful and large artillery. But he could not give the Sikhs a grown-up and capable son as successor who could carry on his work. The result was the succession of a number of weak puppet sovereigns and the predominance of unscrupulous politicians and ambitious generals whose intrigues and incompetence involved the Sikhs in the First and Second Sikh Wars (*q.v.*) within the short space of four years (1845-49), and brought about the destruction of the independent Sikh kingdom of the Panjab which had been built up through long years of sweat, tears and blood.

Sikh Wars, the—were fought in 1845-46 and 1848-49. The *First Sikh War*, which broke out six years after the death of Ranjit Singh (*q.v.*) in 1839, was caused as much by the annexation in 1843 of Sind by the English whose aggressive designs were once again demonstrated as by the unruliness of the Sikh army which forced Rani Jhindan, the mother and regent of the minor Sikh king, Dalip Singh, and her counsellors to authorize the invasion of British territory by crossing the Sutlej in December, 1845. It was a short sharp war lasting only three months during which four hard-fought battles took place at Mudki (18 December), Ferozeshah (21 and 22 December), Aliwal (28 January, 1846) and Sobraon (10 February, 1846) in all of which the Sikhs were defeated. The last battle opened the way to Lahore which was occupied by the victorious British headed by the Governor-General, Lord Hardinge (*q.v.*) who dictated the terms of peace. By the treaty of Lahore the Sikhs ceded to the British all lands on the British side of the Sutlej as well as the Jalandhar Doab lying between the Sutlej and the Bias and paid an indemnity of 50 lakhs of rupees in cash and ceded Jammu and Kashmir in lieu of another one crore of rupees which the Sikh Government was not in a position to pay in cash. Kashmir was, therefore, sold to Golab Singh, the Governor of Jammu, for a sum of one crore of rupees. The strength of the Sikh army was reduced to 20,000 infantry and 12,000 cavalry and a British Resident (Sir Henry Lawrence) was stationed at Lahore, where a British army was also to remain in occupation till the end of 1846. But before the year ended the treaty of Lahore had to be amended providing for the continuance of the army of occupation for eight years until Maharaja Dalip Singh should attain majority. The Resident, Sir Henry Lawrence, became the President of the Council of Regency which contained, amongst others, the Queen Mother, Rani Jhindan. But the terms of the treaty and the administration of the province under British guidance were soon found irksome by many Sikh leaders, especially by the Queen Mother who began intriguing against the British and was therefore deported. The demobilized Sikh soldiers continued to be a disturbing element in the state and discontent against the British increased. This was brought to a head when Mulraj, the governor of Multan, failing to render accounts, resigned. A Sikh successor was promptly appointed and was escorted to Multan by two British officers, but they were suddenly attacked and murdered in April, 1848. Taking this incident as an indication of popular resentment against the British, Mulraj took possession of Multan with its fort where he was soon afterwards besieged by a small locally collected British army. A small Sikh army sent under Sher Singh from Lahore went over to Mulraj. This incident turned a local rebellion into a general rising of the Sikhs who thus began the *Second Sikh War*. Like the First, the Second Sikh War was also a short, sharp contest lasting only a few months. The Sikhs fought a drawn battle with the British at Chillianwalla on 13 January, 1849; Multan surrendered nine days later and the main Sikh army was decisively defeated by the British on 21 February, 1849 at Gujarat. The whole of the Panjab lay prostrate at the feet of the British and Lord Dalhousie, who was then the Governor-

General, promptly ordered its annexation to the British Indian Empire, the minor Maharaja Dalip Singh was sanctioned an annual pension of £ 50,000 and sent to England for training, the *Khalsa* was broken up and the bearing of any arms except a small *Kripan* was forbidden. The British dominions in India were thus extended to the frontier of Afghanistan (Gough & Innes, *The Sikhs and the Sikh Wars*)

Simhavishnu Pallava—an early king of the Pallava dynasty of Kanchi, ruled in the last quarter of the sixth century A.D. and claimed to have defeated not only the Pandya, Chola and Chera kings but even the king of Ceylon. (*S.O.S.*)

Simla—is a hill-station and was the summer capital of the Government of India. It along with the neighbouring region came into British possession in 1815-16 after the Gurkha War (*q.v.*). Lord Amherst was the first Governor-General who spent a summer at Simla in 1827. It has ceased to be the summer capital of the Government of India since independence.

Simon Commission—was appointed in November, 1927, with Sir John (later on Viscount) Simon as the Chairman to enquire into and to report on the working of the constitution in India as established by the Government of India Act, 1919 (*q.v.*). All its members were Britishers and this 'all white' nature of its composition was deeply resented by the Indians. The Indian National Congress decided to boycott it and wherever the Commission went the people observed *hartals* which the Government resented and sometimes applied force to break on the plea of violence on the part of the observers of the hartal. Such incidents created profound resentment and led the Indian National Congress at its 1929 session at Lahore to declare independence to be the goal of Indian aspirations. The Report of the Simon Commission which was published in May, 1930 proved a further disappointment as it recommended the establishment of complete responsible government in the provinces only and the continuance of the prevailing system of administration at the centre under complete British authority and control until the whole of British and Indian India was combined in a federation which the Commission itself recognised as a very distant possibility. The Indian nationalists refused to accept the Commission's recommendations which, however, had some effect on the Government of India Act, 1935 and envisaged a federation of British and Princely India which became a reality after the inauguration of the Republic of India in 1947.

Simuka—was the founder of the Satavahana dynasty (*q.v.*). According to the Puranas he was a contemporary of the last king of the Sunga dynasty (*q.v.*), but his date is uncertain. Probably he flourished in the beginning of the second century B.C.. His kingdom lay in the district of Bellary in Madras Presidency and included some part of the Western Deccan. He was succeeded by his brother, Krishna.

Sind—is the name of the valley of the Indus below its junction with the Jhelum. It witnessed the birth and collapse of a prehistoric civilisation (*q.v.*) in about 3000 B.C. of which many relics have been recently discovered at Mohenjo-daro in the Larkana district. In the time of Alexander's invasion it was inhabited by various tribal peoples like the Mousikanos, the Sambas and the Brahmanas. They were all reduced to submission by the Greek conqueror whose navy sailed and the army marched down the Indus to the city of Patala at the apex of the Indus delta from where Alexander with his army started on its homeward march through Baluchistan while his fleet started on its voyage to Babylon. Sind was a part of the Maurya empire, and was also included within the empire of Chandragupta II who ruled in the fifth century A.D. Later on it passed under the rule of a Brahman dynasty of which the last king was Dahir. In A.D. 711 Sind was invaded by the Muhammadan Arabs led by Muhammad ibn Kasim who defeated and killed Dahir (*q.v.*), stormed the fort of Alor which was the capital and annexed Sind to the dominions of the Arabs who remained in possession of it until A.D. 1176 when it was conquered from the Arabs by Shihab-ud-din Muhammad Ghuri (*q.v.*) and thus became a part of the Delhi sultanate. Sind seceded from the Delhi sultanate towards the close of the reign of Muhammad Tughluq (*q.v.*) who died fighting for its reconquest and remained practically independent of Delhi in spite of two attempts at its reconquest by Sultan Firuz Shah Tughluq in 1361-62. Upper Sind, however, passed under the control of Babur (*q.v.*) on his conquest of Multan and it was at Umarkot on the fringe of Sind that Akbar was born in 1542. Lower Sind with its capital at Thattah was conquered by Akbar in 1591 and the whole of Sind thus again became a part of the Delhi empire. Late in the eighteenth century, with the decline of the Mughul power, Sind passed under the control of the Amirs of Sind (*q.v.*). But in the nineteenth century with the expansion of the British Indian empire the importance of Sind and of the Indus tempted the Indo-

British government to covet its possession and in 1832 a treaty
was made with the Amirs which opened up the Indus to navigation and trade by the British. Ten years later Sir Charles
Napier (*q.v.*), encouraged by the Governor-General, Lord
Ellenborough, provoked a war with the unoffending Amirs
who were defeated at the battles of Miani and Dabo and Sind
was annexed to the British Indian dominions. It remained a
part of the Bombay Presidency until April, 1936 when it was
created into a separate state. After the partition of India in
1947 Sind became a part of Pakistan and its capital, Karachi,
became the metropolis, which, however, has recently been
transferred to Rawalpindi.

Sind, the—is a river which rises in the Tonk district and flowing
through central India and Bundelkhand, falls into the Jumna.
It determined to a certain extent the British strategy in the
Pindari war.

Sindhu, the—is the Sanskritic Indian name of the river Indus.
Flowing through Kashmir and the Panjab where it receives the
Sohan, the Jhelum, the Chenub, the Ravi, the Bias and the Sutlej
and then through Sind it falls into the Arabian Sea. It has contributed a great deal to the economy of the states through which
it flows. According to one view it is the root from which the
word Hindu has been derived.

Sindhia, Daulat Rao—was the grand-nephew of Mahadaji Sindhia
whom he succeeded in 1794. He was a young man whose ambition was to control Peshwa Baji Rao II. He had a rival in
Jaswant Rao Holkar. His ambition was deeply resented by the
Peshwa who, however, sided with the Sindhia against the Holkar
in the battle of Poona on 25 October, 1802. The Sindhia was defeated and his defeat led Baji Rao II to flee to Bassein where
he concluded with the British the treaty of Bassein (*q.v.*) by
which he entered into a subsidiary alliance with the British
as the price of his restoration by the British and thus parted with
the independence not only of his own self but also of the whole
Maratha people. Naturally the Sindhia, along with the Bhonsla
and the Holkar, deeply resented this action of Peshwa Baji Rao II
and, the Sindhia, acting in conjunction with the Bhonsla, refused
to accept the treaty. This led to the Second Maratha War (*q.v.*)
(1803) in the course of which young Daulat Rao, pitted against
Arthur Wellesley (later on the Duke of Wellington) in the
Deccan and Lord Lake in north India, was defeated within
a short time at the battles of Delhi, Assaye, Laswari and Argaon
and obliged to make peace with the British by the treaty of

Surji-Arjungaon on 30 December, 1803 accepting the subsidiary alliance and surrendering much territory including Gwalior and his claim to interfere in Rajputana. Daulat Rao Sindhia was, later on, given Gwalior and freed from the restrictions on his right of interference in Rajputana which he continued to harry cruelly and much to his own harm. He also became a patron of the Pindaris, but he was so effectively isolated strategically at the beginning of the Pindari War (*q.v.*) which developed into the Third Maratha War (*q.v.*), that he was forestalled from taking any part in it and remained at the end of the war in possession of his considerable dominion which he held till his death as a subsidiary and protected Prince with his capital at Gwalior.

Sindhia, Mahadaji—was an illegitimate son and successor of Ranoji Sindhia (*q.v.*) who rose from a humble position to a high command under Peshwa Baji Rao I. Mahadaji was present at the Third Battle of Panipat (1761), received a wound which permanently lamed him, but escaped with his life. On his return to the Maratha territory he conducted himself and his affairs so well that he became the most prominent chief amongst the Maratha leaders and his one aim was to supersede Nana Faḍnavis (*q.v.*) as the guardian of the Peshwa at Poona. Though he failed in this object, he soon regained so much power and prestige in north India that in 1771 Mahadaji re-established Emperor Shah Alam II (*q.v.*) on the throne in Delhi and practically became the Emperor's protector. Mahadaji next acted as the mediator between the British and the Marathas who were then engaged in their first war (1775-82) and re-established peace between them by the treaty of Salbai (1782) (*q.v.*). This achievement raised him much in the estimate of the British. He also appreciated the superiority of the British military organisation and remodelled his army with the assistance of European officers like Count de Boigne turning it into a regular army equipped with powerful artillery. This army made him superior to many Indian princes, Rajput as well as Muhammadan. He defeated Ismail Beg of Rajputana at Patan in 1790, a combination of the Rajput princes at Mirtha in 1791, and the Holkar at Lakheri in 1792. Already he had secured from the titular Emperor Shah Alam II for the Peshwa the office of the *Vakil-i-Mutlak* or Vice-regent of the Empire, with which the Peshwa was solemnly invested at a ceremony held at Poona under the sponsorship of Mahadaji in 1792. What the Peshwa gained was merely symbolical, but the ceremony marked the highest point of success in the career of Mahadaji Sindhia who died in 1794. (Duff, Grant, *History of the Marathas*; Vol. III)

Sindhia, Ranoji (1726-50)—was the founder of the Sindhia family of Gwalior. Born in an ordinary Maratha family, he served so creditably under Peshwa Baji Rao I (*q.v.*) that after the annexation of Malwa to the Maratha State he was endowed with a part of Malwa. Gwalior became his headquarters.

Singhana—the most powerful king of the Jadava dynasty (*q.v.*) of Devagiri (*q.v.*), succeeded his father, Jaitugi, early in the thirteenth century and ruled till his death in 1246. He made extensive conquests and his kingdom included the whole of Central and Western Deccan. He was also a great patron of literature and art. His protégé Sarngadhara wrote a work on music called *Sangita Ratnakara* to which the king himself added a commentary. The study of astronomy was also patronised and a college was established for the study of *Siddhanta Siromani* written by Bhaskaracharya (*q.v.*).

Sinha, Satyendraprasanna, First Baron of Raipur (1863-1930)— was the first Indian to be appointed by the British Government as Governor of a province. Born in a middle-class family in the district of Birbhum in Bengal he joined the Bar and soon gathered a roaring practice. Late in life he took to politics, and presided over a session of the Indian National Congress held at Bombay in 1915. He was the first Indian to be appointed as a Member of the Viceroy's Executive Council in 1909 and was the Governor of the province of Bihar and Orissa from 1920 to 1924. He was the only Indian to be honoured with a peerage. He belonged to the Moderate party of Indian politicians and justified by his ability the right of the Indians to the highest offices in their country.

Sipihr Shikoh, Prince—was the youngest son of Prince Dara (*q.v.*) and a grandson of Emperor Shah Jahan. He was spared by Aurangzeb in consideration of his young age and was later on married to his third daughter.

Siraj-ud-daulah—was the Nawab of Bengal from April, 1756 to June, 1757. He was the favourite grandson of Nawab Alivardi Khan (*q.v.*) whom he succeeded. His claim to his grandfather's throne was contested by his cousin Shaukat Jang (*q.v.*) who was then the Governor of Purnea. Siraj was barely twenty years of age at his accession. His judgment was immature, his character not without blemish and he was surrounded by self-seeking, ambitious and intriguing courtiers. He was not the monster of cruelty and immorality that his English opponents have tried to prove nor was he a patriot who died for preserving the independence of Bengal, as some nationalist historians have attempted to establish. He acted in his own personal interest but failed on account of want of steadiness of purpose. He was no coward and was not afraid of fighting. He won a decisive victory over his cousin, Shaukat Jang, whom he defeated and killed in battle. What he lacked was steadiness of purpose. He had ample cause for complaint against the English in Calcutta who had strengthened their fort there without his permission and given refuge to a fugitive (Krishna Das, son of Raja Rajaballav) from his legal justice. The attack that he made on their settlement of Calcutta was well planned and well executed and Calcutta was seized very easily after only a four days' (16 June to 20 June, 1756) siege. The major portion of the English who were in Calcutta had already fled by ship down the river and the few who could not do so were made captives, kept in a cell called the Black Hole, which was within the fort and of the existence of which the Nawab was completely ignorant. Later on the survivors of the 'Black Hole tragedy' (*q.v.*) were permitted freedom of movement by the Nawab. But the success of Siraj stopped with the capture of Calcutta. He failed to appreciate the necessity of pursuing the fugitive English to Falta and destroying them there. Nor did he take any adequate steps for the defence of Calcutta and for the prevention of its recapture by the English. The result was that the English led by Clive and Watson recovered Calcutta in January 1757, practically without any opposition from the Nawab's side. Siraj then entered into negotiations with the English who in March, 1757, again transgressed his sovereignty by attacking and capturing the French possession of Chandernagore. Siraj allowed this act of high misdemeanour on the part of the English to pass with impunity. He even made with them the treaty of Alinagar (*q.v.*) but the English in utter disregard of that treaty entered into a treasonable conspiracy with the disaffected courtiers of the Nawab and, thus emboldened, sent on 13 June an army under Clive to "wait upon" the Nawab. Siraj naturally collected an army and advanced to stop the insolent progress of the English on whom no treaty seemed to be binding, but was defeated by the English, mainly on account of the treachery of his Muhammadan and Hindu generals, at the battle of Plassey on 23 June, 1757, fled to his capital at Murshidabad where nobody rose in his defence, became a fugitive, but was soon captured and beheaded. Siraj-ud-daulah fell; but, unlike Clive, Watson, Mir Jafar and Company who had conspired to bring about his downfall, he had deceived neither friend nor foe. (Maitra, A. K., *Siraj-ud-Daula*)

Sirhind—is a town in the Panjab, famous in the annals of the Sikhs.

Sisunaga—was, according to the Puranas, the founder of a dynasty of kings of Magadha, to which belonged Bimbisara (*q.v.*) a contemporary of Gautama Buddha and Vardhamana Mahavira. He has been assigned to the middle of the seventh century B.C. and his dynasty is said to have produced nine kings, namely, Kakavarna, Kshemadharman Kshemajit, Bimbisara or Srenika, Ajatasatru, Darsaka, Udashin or Udaya, Nandivardhan and Mahanandin, the last of whom was deposed and killed by Mahapadma Nanda, the founder of the Nanda dynasty in about 470 B.C. According to the Ceylonese sources, Sisunaga was the founder of a dynasty that followed that of Bimbisara who belonged to the Haryanka dynasty. (*see* also Saisunaga dynasty.) (*E.H.I. & P.H.A.I.*)

Sita—is the wife of Rama, the hero of the *Ramayana*. She is the traditional ideal of a wife in the estimate of the Hindus.

Sitabaldi, the battle of—was fought in November, 1817, between the Bhonsla Raja, Appa Sahib (*q.v.*) and the British during the Third Maratha War (*q.v.*). The Marathas under the Bhonsla were decisively defeated and Appa Sahib surrendered.

Siva—is a Hindu deity and is one of the Hindu Trinity. He is worshipped under various names and in different forms, his phallic emblem being the most popular form. It is difficult precisely to ascertain how old his cult is—specimens of his phallic emblem are believed to have been found amongst the relics of the prehistoric civilisation discovered at Mohenjo-daro (*q.v.*); his name Rudra is found in the *Rig-veda* and his image has been found on the coins of some of the Kushan kings (*q.v.*). Certainly his cult prevailed in the Gupta period (*q.v.*). Narayanapala, the fifth king of the Pala dynasty (*q.v.*) of Magadha, built one thousand temples to Siva whose worship was, however, more popular in Southern India than in Northern India and was carried to the snow-clad temples at Kedar-Badri as well as to Nepal by the great saint-philosopher, Sankaracharya (*q.v.*). Siva stands as the emblem of renunciation, so valued by Hindu saints and philosophers.

Skandagupta—was the last great emperor of the Gupta dynasty. He succeeded his father Kumaragupta in A.D. 455. As a Prince, he had repulsed an invasion by a tribe called the Pushyamitras, and soon after his accession he repelled an invasion by the Hunas. He ruled for thirteen years (A.D. 455-68) which were occupied in incessant war, for the Hunas made repeated raids which he repulsed at the cost of the economy of the state. Early in his reign he reformed the debased coinage of the closing years of Kumaragupta I by issuing coins of pure gold, silver and copper of standard weights, but the pressure of the Huna Wars obliged him in the latter part of his reign to debase the coinage again. He, however, found means to restore the great dam of the Sudarsana Lake, which had been first built by Chandragupta Maurya (*q.v.*), turned into an irrigation tank by his grandson Asoka (*q.v.*) and repaired by the Saka Great Satrap Rudradaman (*q.v.*). During his reign Parnadatta, his viceroy in Kathiawar, repaired and strengthened the dam in A.D. 456, and, two years later Parnadatta's son, Chakrapalita, built a temple to Vishnu on this dam. Skandagupta was the last of the great Gupta emperors.

Slave dynasty, the—was founded by Qutb-ud-din Aibak in A.D. 1206 in Delhi and lasted till A.D. 1290. It derived its name from the circumstance that its founder as well as some of his great successors, like Iltutmish and Balban, were all originally slaves who later on forged their ways to the throne of Delhi. Qutb-ud-din (1206-10) was originally a Turki slave of Shihab-ud-din Muhammad Ghuri (*q.v.*), had helped him materially in his victory at the second battle of Tarain in A.D. 1192, then occupied Delhi on behalf of his master, extended Muhammadan conquests to Gujarat on the west and to Bihar and Bengal on the east before his master's death in A.D. 1206 and had been manumitted and dignified by him with the title of the Sultan in A.D. 1203. Naturally he succeeded to his master's Indian dominions and became the founder of the Slave dynasty of the sultans of Delhi. He ruled till his death in 1210. His son and immediate successor, Aram Shah, ruled only for a year and was displaced in A.D. 1211 by his sister's husband Iltutmish (*q.v.*) who was an able administrator who ruled till his death in 1236. His immediate successor was his son, Rukn-ud-din (*q.v.*) who was a worthless debauchee and was replaced after only a few months of rule by his sister, Raziyyat-ud-din, better known as Sultana Raziya (*q.v.*) in 1237 who proved a competent ruler; but her sex was against her and she was deposed three years later in 1240. Her brother Bahram (*q.v.*), who succeeded her, ruled till his death by assassination in 1242. He was succeeded by Masud Shah, a grandson of Iltutmish, who became such a pleasure-loving tyrant that he was deposed in 1246 and was replaced by Nasir-ud-din, a son of Iltutmish. Sultan Nasir-ud-din was a man free from carnal vice, was temperate in his habits and fond of learning and had the fortune of having as his supporter a strong man in Balban who was one of the first forty slaves of Iltutmish and was also his father-in-law. He ruled for twenty years (1246-66). He was succeeded by his father-in-law Balban who was a ruthless king, freed the country from the inroads of the Mongols which had begun as early as the reign of Iltutmish, subdued all rebels, Muhammadan and Hindus, restored decorum in the court and peace and order in the state, suppressed the rebellion of Tughril Khan (*q.v.*) in Bengal and ruled till his death in 1286. A year earlier his favourite son, Prince Muhammad, had died in a battle with the Mongol raiders in the Panjab and his second son Bughra Khan, whom he had appointed as Governor of Bengal, refused to come to Delhi to occupy the throne of his dreaded father. In the circumstances Bughra Khan's son, Kaiquabad (*q.v.*) was installed as the sultan in 1286, but he turned into such a drunken reveller that the nobles rose against him and murdered him in 1290. Thus the Slave dynasty came to an inglorious end. The sultans of the Slave dynasty paid little attention to the welfare of their subjects and were generally more given to pleasure than to administration. Yet they have left behind them some remarkable architectural monuments of which the Qutb Minar (*q.v.*) still stands in all its grandeur, and some of them extended patronage to men of letters like Minhaj-ud-din Siraj, the author of the *Tabakat-i-Nasiri* (*q.v.*) and poets like Amir Khusru.

Slavery—as an institution existed in India in all ages. Though Megasthenes (*q.v.*) in the 4th century B.C. states that slavery was unknown to India, yet Kautilya's *Arthasastra* (*q.v.*) as well as Asoka's inscriptions refer to the existence of slaves in ancient India. Men were reduced to slavery for various causes like indebtedness and captivity in war, but slavery does not appear to have assumed in ancient India the magnitude and cruelty that marked it in Europe. In the Muhammadan period slavery increased in proportion, assumed an added cruelty by the practice of castration and continued to exist long after the establishment of British rule. It was in 1843 that an Act was passed for its suppression.

Sleeman, Sir William—was an officer in the service of the East

India Company in India. During the administration of Lord William Bentinck (*q.v.*) he took the leading part in suppressing the *Thags*. Later on he rose to be the British Resident in Oudh which post he held from 1848 to 1854. His reports on the prevailing misgovernment in Oudh led to its annexation in 1856.

Slim, Sir William—was an English general who during the Second World War was in command of the fourteenth army engaged in resisting the Japanese aggression in South-East Asia including India. The Seventh Division of his army stopped the Japanese advance at Kohima near Manipur in 1944 and thus prevented the entrance of the invading Japanese hosts into India.

Sobraon, the battle of—was fought on 10 February, 1846 between the Sikhs and the Indo-British army in the course of the First Sikh War. It ended in a decisive victory for the British, opened to them the way to Lahore which they promptly occupied and thus compelled the Sikhs to make peace by the treaty of Lahore.

Solankis, the—is a Rajput sect, also known as the Chalukyas (*q.v.*).

Solinger, the battle of—was fought in 1781 in the course of the Second Mysore War (1780-84) (*q.v.*) between Haidar Ali of Mysore and the English who won the battle.

Someswara I—the fifth king of the Chalukya dynasty of Kalyani, ruled from A.D. 1041 to 1072. He founded Kalyani which he made his capital. He had to fight with the Chola king, Rajendradeva (*q.v.*) who defeated him at the battle of Koppam (*q.v.*) and his successor Virarajendra who defeated him at the battle of Kudalasangamam. In spite of these defeats he left his kingdom intact.

Someswara II—the son and successor of Someswara I, the Chalukya king of Kalyani, ruled only for four years (A.D. 1072-76) and was deposed by his brother Vikramaditya VI (*q.v.*).

Someswara III—the eighth king of the Chalukya dynasty of Kalyani, was the son and successor of the seventh king Vikramaditya VI (*q.v.*) and ruled from A.D. 1126-38. His reign was tranquil. He is reputed to have been the author of various works on polity, administration of justice, medicine, astrology, arms, chemistry and rhetoric. But his versatility and erudition did not contribute to his military strength. It was during his time that the feudatories of the Chalukyas threw off their yoke and the decline of the Chalukya power commenced.

Somnath, the temple of—was a celebrated Hindu shrine built to Siva by the early Chalukya kings of Gujarat at Prabhasha on the coast of Kathiawar. It was an immensely rich temple being endowed with the revenue of ten thousand villages. The water of the Ganges was brought daily from northern India for the worship of its presiding deity. A thousand Brahman priests were engaged in the performance of its daily ritual and three hundred and fifty male and female musicians and dancers were attached to the temple which was daily visited by so many devoted Hindus that three hundred barbers found employment in shaving their heads. This rich temple was invaded by Sultan Mahmud (*q.v.*) of Ghazni in A.D. 1024 who sacked it after a fiercely contested battle in which fifty thousand Hindus are said to have been killed. Mahmud got possession of the fortified temple, broke into pieces the huge stone *lingam* which symbolised the presiding deity and returned with huge booty, after demolishing the temple and the fortifications. The temple was later on rebuilt.

Sopara—was an ancient port on the western coast of India through which much overseas trade was carried on.

Soter Megas—meaning the 'Great Saviour' was a title used in the coins supposed to have been issued by the Nameless king who probably reigned between the Kushan kings, Kadphises II and Kanishka (*q.v.*).

Souza, Manuel de—was the Portuguese captain of the port of Diu in 1539 when Sultan Bahadur Shah (*q.v.*) of Gujarat paid a visit there to confer with the Portuguese governor, Nuno da Cunha, on board a Portuguese ship in the port. There Bahadur Shah was treacherously attacked by the Portuguese sailors and in the tussle that followed Bahadur Shah was killed and de Souza lost his life.

Sravana Belgola—is situated in Mysore. According to Jain tradition, Chandragupta Maurya (*q.v.*) retired there after abdication and starved himself to death.

Sravasti—was the capital of the ancient kingdom of Koshala (*q.v.*). It was visited several times by Gautama Buddha and continued to be an important city till the ninth century A.D. It was situated on the Rapti and has been identified with the modern village of Sahet Mahet in Uttar Pradesh.

Srenika—was an alternate name of king Bimbisara (*q.v.*) of Magadha.

Srinagar—was the headquarters of the Raja of Garhwal who gave shelter to Prince Sulaiman (*q.v.*) the eldest son of Prince Dara, in 1658.

Srinagar—is the capital of the State of Kashmir.

Srirangam—is a city near Trichinopoly. It is renowned for its association with the great Vaishnava philosopher and teacher, Ramanuja (*q.v.*) who lived there, except for a short interval, until his death.

Sri Vijaya—was the name of a city and kingdom established by Indian colonists in the Malay Archipelago. The city has been identified with Palembang in Sumatra. (*see* Overseas, Indians.)

Srong-tsan-Gampo—was the most renowned king of Tibet who ruled from A.D. 629 to 650. He was thus partly a contemporary of King Harshavardhana (*q.v.*) after whose death in A.D. 646-47 he sent an expedition against the usurper, Arjuna, who had occupied Harsha's throne, defeated him, and occupied Tirhut. He embraced Buddhism and introduced the religion in Tibet. He founded the city of Lhasa and imported from India the alphabet now used in Tibet.

Stein, Sir Aurel—was a famous antiquarian, archaeologist and explorer. He carried on extensive excavations in Central Asia where he discovered the remains of many Buddhist stupas and monasteries, images of Buddhist and Brahmanical gods and manuscripts written in Indian languages and Indian scripts. He was also a great Sanskritist and translated into English the *Rajatarangini* by Kalhana (*q.v.*).

Stewart, General—was in command of a British army in Afghanistan during the Second Afghan War (1879-90). After the massacre of Cavagnari (*q.v.*), the British envoy in Kabul, on 24 July, 1879, General Stewart promptly reoccupied Qandahar which had been restored to the Amir by the treaty of Gondamak (*q.v.*) in 1879 and thus made feasible the subsequent retribution by the British army on the Afghans.

Sthanakavasi, **the**—is a Jain sect. It is a modern offshoot of the Svetambara Jains and rejects the use of images in worship.

Stolietoff, General—was the leader of the Russian embassy which reached Kabul in 1878 and had to be received publicly by Amir Sher Ali (*q.v.*). His reception by the Amir who, as an independent ruler, had every right to do so, was most unjustifiably made by the Viceroy, Lord Lytton I (*q.v.*), an excuse for declaring the Second Afghan War (*q.v.*) which lasted from 1878 to 1880.

Strabo—was a classical historian who has left an account of India at the time of Alexander's invasion, quoting many passages from the *Indica* of Megasthenes (*q.v.*).

Strachey, Sir John—was a distinguished member of the Indian

Civil Service who as well as his brother, Sir Richard, served with distinction during the Viceroyalties of Lords Lansdowne (q.v.), Mayo (q.v.) and Lytton I. Sir John regularised the financial relations between the Central and Provincial Governments in India. Sir Richard presided over a Famine Commission which drew up the Famine Code (q.v.).

Stuart, Charles—was a commercial expert on whose advice Lord Cornwallis (q.v.) depended a great deal in drawing up rules regulating the trade and commerce of the East India Company in India.

Stuart, General—was commended for his part in the battle of Porto Novo (q.v.) in 1781 in the course of the Second Mysore War. Later on he succeeded Sir Eyre Coote to the chief command of the British army, but failed to take advantage of the opportunity presented by Haidar Ali's death in 1782. Subsequently he fell out with Lord Macartney, the Governor of Madras, and this quarrel greatly hampered English operations.

Subhaschandra Bose—*see* Bose, Subhaschandra.

Subhagasena (spelt Sophagasenas by the classical historians) —was an Indian prince whose territories lay in the Kabul valley. He was attacked in about 208 B.C. by Antiochus the Great and was obliged to purchase peace by paying a large indemnity and surrendering many elephants.

Sudas—is a king mentioned in the Rig Veda, along with Bharata and Janamejaya.

Sudras, the—one of the four *varnas* in the caste system of the Hindus. (*see* caste system.)

Suez Canal, the—was opened in 1869 connecting the Mediterranean Sea with the Red Sea. This greatly reduced in length the direct sea-route between India and Europe. It not only quickened trade and commerce between the East and the West but also promoted the flow of European ideas into India. It was the work of a French engineer named de Lesseps.

Suffren de, Admiral—a French Admiral, arrived off the Indian coast in 1781, fought five naval battles with the English navy under Hughes, got control for some months over South Indian waters and captured Trincomale in Ceylon. But before his victories could effectively influence the fortunes of the Anglo-French War, peace was made between England and France by the treaty of Versailles in 1783.

Sufi-ism—is a branch of Muhammadanism. It is more philosophical and consequently more tolerant than Islam.

Sulaiman—an Arab merchant, visited the court of the Rashtrakuta king, Amoghavarsha (*q.v.*) (*c.* 815-77) whose power and wealth impressed him very much. He left an interesting account of what he saw in India in the first half of the ninth century.

Sulaiman Kararani—was the Afghan king of Bengal in the early part of the reign of Akbar (*q.v.*). He made formal submission to Akbar but retained practical independence. It was his son Daud (*q.v.*) who openly defied Akbar who defeated him in 1575 and again in 1576 when he was killed in battle.

Sulaiman Shikoh, Prince—was the son of Prince Dara Shikoh. On the outbreak of the War of Succession amongst the sons of Shah Jahan in 1657-58 Sulaiman was first sent against his uncle, Prince Shuja, whom he defeated at the battle of Bahadurpur near Benares in February, 1658 but was too far away to help his father either at Dharmat (*q.v.*) or at Samugarh (*q.v.*) and was forced to flee to the Garhwal hills, but he was soon betrayed to Aurangzeb who had him killed by slow poisoning in 1662.

Sullivan, Lawrence—was a director of the East India Company and an opponent of Robert Clive (*q.v.*).

Sultanate of Delhi, the—was set up by Qutb-ud-din Aibak (*q.v.*) in 1206 and was overthrown by Babur in 1526. During this period five dynasties ruled as sultans of Delhi. These were the Slave dynasty (1206-90), the Khalji dynasty (1290-1320), the Tughluq dynasty (1321-88), the Sayyid dynasty (1414-50) and the Lodi dynasty (1450-1526). (*See* under each separately.) Most of them were of Turki origin and most of the sultans were bloodthirsty tyrants. They had a sort of civil government, but they left no fruitful ideas or institutions behind them. Their government was an arbitrary despotism, practically unchecked except by the fear of rebellion and caring nothing for the Hindus who formed the majority of their subjects. They, however, developed in India a new language, namely Urdu, and a new style of architecture which combined the features of the buildings of Mecca and Damascus with those of India. As a consequence of the contact of Hinduism with Islam certain new religious sects like those founded by Nanak (*q.v.*), Kabir (*q.v.*) and Chaitanya (*q.v.*) arose which aimed, in spite of the ferocious fanaticism of the sultans of Delhi, at bridging the gulf between the Hindus and Muhammadans in India but they only had qualified success.

Sunga Dynasty, the—was founded in about 185 B.C. by Pushyamitra (also spelt Puspamitra) (*q.v.*) who was the Commander-in-Chief of the last Maurya king, Brihadratha (*q.v.*) whom he killed and whose throne he occupied. He ruled from 185 B.C. to 151 B.C. He kept practically intact the Magadhan empire in north India. But his authority was not unchallenged. Even if the view that the Kalinga king, Kharavela, was his contemporary and defeated him, is not considered tenable, there is hardly any doubt that his dominions were attacked by an Indo-Bactrian king, probably Menander (*q.v.*) whom, however, he repulsed. In any case he had such victories to his credit as justified him in celebrating the horse-sacrifice (*aswamedha*) twice in his reign and thus announcing the revival of Brahmanical Hinduism in India after its eclipse by Buddhism as the result of the religious propaganda carried on by the third Maurya emperor, Asoka (*q.v.*). The celebrated Sanskrit grammarian, Patanjali, is believed to have officiated as the priest at his horse-sacrifice. Pushyamitra was succeeded by nine kings, namely, Agnimitra, Jethamitra, Vasumitra, Bhadraka (identified with Kasiputra-Bhagabhadra mentioned in the Gaḍuḍa pillar inscription left by Heliodoros (*q.v.*) at Besnagar) three unnamed successors, then Bhagavata who ruled for 32 years and Debabhuti, the last king who was deposed and killed by his *amatya* or minister, Vasudeva, in about 73 B.C. The Sunga dynasty ruled for a hundred and twelve years. (*P.H.A.I.*, ch. vi)

Sunnis, the—are an Islamic sect comprising the majority of the Muhammadan population in India. Unlike the Shias (*q.v.*) they hold the first two Caliphs as duly elected leaders of Islam and join their names in their daily prayers along with that of the Prophet. They constitute the orthodox section of the Muhammadans and all the Delhi sultans as well as the Mughul emperors were Sunnis and often waged wars against the Shias who were considered as rather heretical.

Supreme Court of Judicature, the—was established in Calcutta by the Regulating Act (*q.v.*) in 1774 with a chief justice and three puisne judges who were all named in the Act which also fixed their salaries. It was thus to be entirely independent of the executive in India. The Court was vested with jurisdiction over all British subjects, not excluding the highest officials and all residents of Calcutta. No definite mention was made of the system of law that the Court was to administer and naturally enough Chief Justice Sir Elijah Impey (*q.v.*) and his three colleagues decided to administer justice according to the English law as it then existed. The judges of the Supreme Court were also very assertive of their rights, claimed and exercised jurisdiction over all persons and ignored the authority of the Company's courts. Their actions appeared to be vexatious and pretentious. When they sentenced Nandakumar (*q.v.*) to death on a charge of forgery the Indians were stunned, though the Governor-General, Warren Hastings and his friends were pleased. But the turn of the Governor-General to be bewildered came when in 1779-80 in the famous Cossijura case (*q.v.*) the Supreme Court threatened to charge the Governor-General and his Council with contempt of court. The threatened open war between the Council and the Court was cleverly averted by Warren Hastings who appointed Sir Elijah Impey, the Chief Justice of the Supreme Court, to be also the President of the *Sadar Diwani Adalat* on a high salary. This arrangement had the merit of improving the *Sadar Diwani Adalat* but it was soon upset, on account of its obvious defect of subordinating the highest judiciary to the executive. In 1797 the number of the judges was reduced to three and in 1781 its jurisdiction was clearly defined. In 1801 a Supreme Court was established in Madras and in 1823 another in Bombay. In 1833 the jurisdiction of the three Supreme Courts was precisely stated to be limited to (i) British-born subjects, (ii) persons residing within the boundaries of the three cities concerned and (iii) all persons who were directly and indirectly in the service of the Company. Finally, in 1861 by the Indian High Courts Act the Supreme Court of Judicature was amalgamated with the *Sadar Diwani Adalat* to form the High Court of Calcutta with original jurisdiction over the city of Calcutta and appellate jurisdiction all over Bengal, Bihar and Orissa. Similarly, the Supreme Courts in Madras and Bombay were turned into High Courts in those two Presidencies.

Supreme Court of India—was founded by the Constitution of India Act, 1949. It started functioning on 26 January, 1950. It is presided over by the Chief Justice of India (Sir Harilal Kania being the first incumbent) who is helped by a number of judges who hold office till the age of 65. It is a Court of Record and has both original and appellate jurisdiction. It is the highest court of appeal in India and no appeals lie on its decisions. It can issue directions or writs for the enforcement of any of the Fundamental Rights as laid down in the Constitution of India Act, 1949. (*q.v.*). (Shri Ram Sharma, *The Supreme Court in India*)

Sur dynasty, the—was founded by Sher Shah Sur in 1540. It ruled over the Delhi empire between the defeat of the second

Mughul Emperor, Humayun, in 1540 and the restoration of Humayun in 1555. During this short period of fifteen years the dynasty produced three sovereigns, namely, Sher Shah (*q.v.*) (1540-45), his son Islam (or Salim) Shah (1545-54) and his cousin Adil Shah (1554-56) whose general Himu (*q.v.*) or Hem Chandra was defeated and killed by Akbar in the second battle of Panipat in 1556 which marked the collapse of the Sur dynasty.

Sura dynasty, the—is traditionally associated with Bengal, more particularly with south-west Bengal. Tradition represents Adisura (*q.v.*) as the founder of the dynasty. He is said to have brought five Brahmanas from Kanauj and settled them in Radha (West Bengal) and Varendra (North Bengal). But there is no other independent epigraphic or numismatic evidence in proof of his existence, and, his date, which varies from the eighth to the eleventh centuries, is most uncertain. However, whatever may be the historical fact about Adisura, the Sura family continued to be powerful in Bengal as late as the eleventh century when king Vijayasena (*q.v.*) came to rule (*c.* A.D. (1095-1158). He has left on record that he married Vilasadevi, a princess of the Sura family to which perhaps had earlier belonged king Ranasura, who was ruling in southern Radha when it was invaded by Rajendra Chola (*q.v.*). The Sura dynasty fell after the rise of the Sena dynasty (*q.v.*). (*H.B.*, Vol. I.)

Suraj Mal—was the Jat ruler of Bharatpur (*q.v.*) on the eve of the third battle of Panipat (*q.v.*) in 1761. He was a very astute statesman and a wealthy prince. His help was sought by the Marathas as well as by Ahmad Shah Abdali (*q.v.*). At first he agreed to help the Marathas, but later on he withdrew from the fighting line on account of the arrogance of the Marathas and took no part in that battle which greatly influenced the history of India. He was, however, a very successful ruler in his own way. The adopted son and successor of the Jat chief, Badan Singh, Suraj Mal led the Jats from 1756 till his death in 1763, and created for them the kingdom of Bharatpur comprising the districts of Agra, Dholpur, Mainpuri, Hathras, Aligarh, Etawah, Meerut, Rohtak, Furruknagar, Rewari, Gurgaon and Mathura. The creation of such a large independent Hindu kingdom in close proximity to the Mughul capital, Delhi, bears testimony to his sagacity, intellect, vision and ability.

Surji-Arjungaon, the treaty of—was concluded in 1803 between the English and Daulat Rao Sindhia, bringing to a close the war between them. By this treaty the Sindhia accepted a British Resident at his court, recognised the treaty of Bassein (*q.v.*), definitely surrendered his claims on the Nizam and engaged to take into his service no foreigner except with the consent of the British. He further ceded to the British the Doab between the Ganges and the Jumna, which including Delhi and Agra thus became a conquered British province, and all his territories in the Deccan as well as in Gujarat. The Sindhia also had to agree to refrain from interfering in the politics of a great part of Rajputana. The treaty of Surji-Arjungaon thus marked the end of the existence of the Sindhia as an independent prince and the establishment of British sovereignty over the major part of northern India.

Surman, John—a young factor in the service of the East India Company in Calcutta, led an English embassy consisting of an Armenian, named Khwaja Sarhand, and an Englishman, named Edward Stephenson with Hugh Barker as the Secretary, to the Court of Emperor Farruksiyar (*q.v.*) in July, 1715 and obtained on 30 December, 1716, from the Emperor three separate *farmans* (imperial grants) addressed to the Mughul Governors of Bengal, Hyderabad and Ahmedabad confirming the right of the Company to duty-free trade on the payment of an annual tribute of Rupees Three Thousand only and to other trading facilities. This *farman* secured by Surman was so important in its provisions that this has been called the Magna Carta of the English trade in India. (Bhattacharya, S., *East India Company and Economy of Bengal*, pp. 27 ff.)

Sutras, **the**—are compendious treatises dealing with Vedic rituals as well as with customary law. They are written in a very compressed style and are not intelligible without the help of authoritative commentaries. The *Sutras* comprise the *Srauta* which describes the rituals of the greater sacrifices, the *Grihya* which explains the ceremonial of household worship and the *Dharma* which details social and legal usage.

Sutee—*see Sati.*

Svetambara Jains—form a sect of the Jains (*q.v.*) who, notwithstanding the injunction of Vardhamana Mahavira (*q.v.*) wear clothes and garments, all white.

Swain, Clara—was the first woman to practise Western medicine in India. She was of American birth and came to India in 1874. Six years later came the second female doctor, Fanny Butler, who was an Englishwoman. The first Indian woman doctor was Mrs. Kadambini Ganguli, a Bengali lady.

Swami Vivekananda—*see* Vivekananda Swami.

Syed Ahmed, Sir—*see* Sayyid Ahmed.

Sykes, Francis—was one of the four members who constituted the Select Committee to advise Robert Clive during the second term of his Governorship from 1765 to 1767. He, like his colleague Sumner (*q.v.*) was sent from England and came to Calcutta by the same boat as Clive and generally supported Clive.

T

Tabaqat-i-Akbari, **the**—is the official history of the time of Emperor Akbar. It was written in Persian by the court-historian, Nizam-ud-din Ahmad, and is most reliable for dates and topography.

Tabaqat-i-Nasiri, **the**—is the history of the early sultans of Delhi written by Minhaj-ud-din Siraj (*q.v.*) who enjoyed the patronage of Sultan Nasir-ud-din (*q.v.*) during whose reign he wrote the work.

Tagore, Abanindranath (1871-1951)—a renowned artist and littérateur, was the founder of the Indian Society of Oriental Arts. He re-established the old Indian system of art and painting in the esteem of the world. The more famous of his paintings were the 'Exiled Yaksha', 'The Death of Shah Jahan', 'Buddha and Sujata', 'Kach O Devyani', and 'Omar Kayyam'. He was the Vice-Principal of the Government School of Art in Calcutta from 1905 to 1916 and was for some time its Principal as well. He inspired a school of Indian artists of whom the most famous member was Nandalal Bose.

Tagore, Devendranath (1817-1905)—a renowned savant and religious leader, was a son of Dwarkanath Tagore of Calcutta who earned for his munificence the courtesy title of "Prince', and inherited from his father great social status as well as heavy debts. With an honesty which was uncommon in those days he cleared all his father's debts and by his erudition, bearing, character and contributions to culture he added to the social status of the Tagore family which continued for the next hundred years to be a centre of Indian culture and learning. He was a prominent member of the Brahma Samaj (*q.v.*) which he led with conspicuous success from 1843. He also founded in 1843 the famous journal *Tattvabodhini Patrika* through which he promoted serious thinking and earnest speaking amongst the children of the soil, emphasized the need of developing the mother-tongue, the need of studying science and theology, opposed prevailing superstitions and social evils and waged an unrelenting war against the proselytising activities of the Christian missionaries. Devendranath, like Ram Mohan Roy (*q.v.*), wanted the Indians to accept what was good in Western culture and to combine that with the best in Indian tradition, culture and religion. He thus never dissociated himself from the fold of Hinduism which he wanted not to destroy, but to reform. This lent a strain of conservatism to his religious ideas which eventually led to the breach with Kesab Chandra Sen (*q.v.*) who established the dissentient church of the New Dispensation (*Nava-Vidhan*) as well as with the radical Brahmas who still later established the *Sadharan Brahma Samaj*. But Devendranath, with saintly character and spiritual vision, continued to receive all through his life the respectful homage of his country-men who lovingly referred to him as the *Maharshi* (the Great Sage).

Next to religion, expansion of education was the principal object of Devendranath's activities. He was closely connected with various educational institutions in different parts of the province and it was in 1863 that he purchased the site of Santiniketan which he handed over to a body of Trustees in 1886 and where later on his illustrious son, Rabindranath, founded the *Visva-Bharati* (Centre of World Culture).

Primarily interested as Devendranath was in religion and education, the larger interests of the country also received his attention. He was the first Secretary of the British Indian Association (*q.v.*) which was founded in 1851, and which aimed at securing an increased and due share in the administration of the country for the children of the soil by constitutional agitation. He was one of the stalwarts amongst the few Indians who in the nineteenth century laid the foundation of modern India. (Chakrabarty, S., *Devendranath Thakurer Atmajivani*)

Tagore, Dwarkanath (1794-1846)—was the founder of the famous Tagore family of Jorasanko in Calcutta. He earned a lot of money in business which he transacted in friendly co-operation with the English merchants and started the Union Bank which was the first Bengali venture in the banking line. He supported the liberal movements of the day and was one of the earliest supporters of the Brahma Samaj founded by Raja

Ram Mohan Roy (*q.v.*) and led it till 1843 when he handed it over to his son Devendranath (*q.v.*). He visited Europe twice in 1842 and 1845 and was received in audience by Queen Victoria. He spent his large income with such extravagance that late in life he became involved in debts, though the recipients of his gifts conferred upon him the title of 'Prince'. He died in London in 1846.

Tagore, Rabindranath (7 May, 1861–7 August, 1941)—was the greatest Indian poet in modern times and one of the greatest poets ever born. He was a son of Devendranath Tagore (*q.v.*) and was born in Calcutta where he also breathed his last after gaining an international reputation and respect as the *Gurudeva* (the Preceptor). He began writing poetry even in boyhood and in 1882 his *Sandhya-Sangeeta* showed such proficiency that the celebrated Bengali novelist and littérateur, Bankimchandra Chatterjee (*q.v.*) who composed our national anthem, the *Vande Mataram*, honoured him by putting round his neck the garland that he himself was wearing. Rabindranath was a versatile genius who excelled not only as a poet but also as a dramatist, novelist, essayist and, in later life, even as an artist. He wrote innumerable poems, touching all the chords of human feelings, though his lyrics are the most famous. The publication of an English translation of his *Gitanjali* (Offerings of Songs) won him the Nobel Prize in 1912. The Calcutta University honoured itself by conferring the Doctorate degree (*honoris causa*) on him in 1912, and acted on his suggestions to correct Bengali spelling and to introduce Bengali as a subject for the examination for the highest degree of the University. The British Government conferred a knighthood on him in 1913. Honours came pouring on him from all parts of the world and Rabindranath put conquered India for the first time on the intellectual map of the world. He travelled widely over Europe, America and Asia and everywhere raised the prestige and honour of India. Pre-eminent as a poet, Rabindranath was no recluse. He was intensely patriotic and well in the forefront of the Swadeshi movement, though he disliked boycott. For, his patriotism was based not on selfish nationalism, but on catholic internationalism. He encouraged indigenous industries, rural reconstruction of which the Sree-niketan which he founded near Santiniketan was an example, as well as popular education, folk-songs and dances, indigenous arts and crafts and the co-operative movement. He generally kept himself aloof from the hectic political agitations of the day

but was never afraid of raising his stentorian voice in protest
whenever the alien Government in India took to unreasonably
harsh repressive measures. He gave voice to the pent-up feelings
of millions of Indians by resigning the knighthood that the
British Government had conferred on him as a protest against
the massacre perpetrated by the British at Jallianwala Bagh
(*q.v.*). His action was the severest condemnation of the British
system of administration in India. Rabindranath's great contribution to human culture was the foundation of the *Visva-
Bharati* at Santiniketan in 1901. Without any financial support
from the Government of the time Rabindranath maintained
this unique seat of world-culture out of the proceeds of the
sale of his books and other personal income for fifty long years.
It was ten years after his death that this beloved child of
Rabindranath was taken over by the Government of the
Republic of India which now maintains it as a university.
Poet and savant, Rabindranath was a seer, an Indian first
and an internationalist second, who was readily accepted as
friend, philosopher and guide by Mahatma Gandhi who, like
many others, endearingly and respectfully called him *Gurudeva*.
(Works of Rabindranath; Thompson, *Rabindranath*; Radha-
krishnan, S., *Philosophy of Rabindranath;* Dasgupta, S. N.,
Rabindra-Deepika)

Tagore, Satyendranath (1842-1923)—was the first Indian to
compete in the Indian Civil Service Examination. Born in
Calcutta, he was the second son of Devendranath Tagore (*q.v.*)
and the elder brother of Rabindranath. He entered the Indian
Civil Service in 1864 and was placed in the Bombay cadre.
Service conditions were then so adverse to Indians that
Satyendranath could only rise to be a District and Sessions
Judge before his retirement. He was also a poet and littérateur
who wrote several books in Bengali.

Tahmasp, Shah—the Emperor of Persia, with whom Emperor
Humayun (*q.v.*) sought shelter in 1544, granted asylum to the
fugitive Mughul Emperor and provided him with the military aid
that enabled Humayun to occupy Qandahar and Kabul in
1545 and eventually to recover his Indian dominions.

Taila (or Tailapa)—was the founder of the second Chalukya
dynasty which had Kalyani as its capital. He defeated the
last Rashtrakuta king, Kakka II (*q.v.*) in *c.* A.D. 972. The dynasty
founded by Taila ruled till A.D. 1190.

Taj, the—the most renowned monument of Mughul rule in India,
is a mausoleum built by Emperor Shah Jahan (*q.v.*) on the

tomb of his beloved queen, Mumtaz Mahal (*q.v.*) at Agra. It was begun in 1632, took about twenty-two years in building and was finished in 1653. It cost fifty lakhs of rupees in those days and is still rightly regarded as one of the wonders of the world for its beauty and magnificence. It was designed by an Indian architect named Ustad I'sá who might or might not have had some Italian or French collaborators. It still stands in all its glory on extensive grounds on the bank of the Jumna, near the city of Agra, and attracts thousands of visitors from all over the world. It has been called 'a dream in marble'. (Smith, V. A., *Hist. of the Fine Arts in India*)

Taj-ud-din Yildiz—*see* Yildiz.

Talikota, the battle of—was fought on the 23rd January, 1565, between Ramraja (*q.v.*) who led the army of Vijayanagar (*q.v.*) and the combined armies of the sultans of Ahmadnagar, Bijapur and Golconda. Ramaraja was defeated and killed and the Vijayanagar army was completely routed. It was a decisive battle which marked the complete collapse of the Hindu kingdom of Vijayanagar.

Talpur, the Amirs of—was one of the three branches of the Amirs of Sind (*q.v.*) who were defeated by the English in 1843, deposed and exiled.

Tamerlane—*see* Timur.

Tamilakam —the land comprising the three ancient kingdoms of the Pandya, Chola and Chela or Kerala, extended on the north to Pulicat and the Tirupathi hills, about 100 miles to the north-west of Madras, to Cape Comorin on the south and from the Coromandel coast on the east to the Western Ghats on the west. The language spoken by the majority is Tamil which has a rich and ancient literature. The people are of Dravidian origin, though later on they received a large element from the Aryan stock. The two are now inextricably intermingled and the Tamil language has also been much influenced and altered by Sanskrit grammar and diction. The most popular and famous works in Tamil literature are the *Kural*, the *Epic of the Anklet* and the *Manimekalai*. Of these again the *Kural* is "the most venerated and popular book south of the Godavari".

Tamralipti—an ancient town the site of which is now occupied by the modern town of Tamluk in Midnapur district in West Bengal, was situated very near the sea (modern Tamluk is deep in the interior on account of a shift in the river course) and was a busy port in the fifth century A.D. It was from Tamralipti that the famous Chinese pilgrim Fa-Hien (*q.v.*)

who visited India from A.D. 401 to 410, sailed homewards in a ship manned entirely by sailors from Bengal.

Tamraparni—is the name of a river in the Tinnevally district. It was also the name by which Ceylon is referred to by Asoka in his Rock Edicts II and XIII. (Bhattacharya, S., *Select Asokan Epigraphs*)

Tansen—a famous musician, adorned the court of Emperor Akbar. It has been observed that 'a singer like him has not been in India for the last thousand years'. He received his training at Gwalior during the reign of Man Singh (*q.v.*) and lies buried there. His arrival at the court of Akbar was such a remarkable event that Akbar had it portrayed in colours in 1562.

Tantia Jog—the minister of Jaswant Rao Holkar, greatly helped in the re-organisation and revival of the Holkar's state after the Third Maratha War (*q.v.*).

Tantia Topi—a famous general fighting on the side of the sepoys during the Sepoy Mutiny (*q.v.*), was a Maratha Brahman especially attached to Nana Shaheb (*q.v.*). He was the one capable general that the mutineers produced. His hostility to the English was implacable. He was present at the capture of Cawnpore by the sepoys and witnessed the massacre of the Europeans, men, women and children at Bibigarh. He showed great skill as a general, tactician and organiser. At the head of the Gwalior contingent of 20,000 soldiers he repulsed General Wyndham before Cawnpore. Defeated and driven out of Cawnpore by Sir Colin Campbell, Tantia joined the Rani of Jhansi and carried on a desperate fight in Central India, but he was again badly defeated by Sir Hugh Rose (*q.v.*) in the battle of the Betwa. Defeats, however, never overwhelmed Tantia. Within a few months Tantia, accompanied by the Rani, marched to Gwalior, won over the Sindhia's army, drove the Sindhia to take refuge with the English at Agra, proclaimed Nana Shaheb as the Peshwa and threatened to rouse the Marathas against the English. But he was again frustrated by Sir Hugh Rose who retook Gwalior, defeated him in the battles of Morar and Kotah in one of which the Rani fell fighting. Tantia again escaped, but would not surrender. Chased from place to place he evaded his relentless pursuers until at last he was treacherously betrayed in April 1859, to the English by Man Singh, a feudatory of the Sindhia. He was put on trial before a British court on charges of rebellion and murder; but he refused to recognise the court's right to try him, was sentenced to death and perished on British gallows.

Tara Bai—the wife of Rajaram (*q.v.*), the second son of Shivaji I, became on the death of her husband in 1700 the regent and guardian of their minor son, Shivaji III, in whose name she carried on the administration of the Maratha kingdom and the interminable war with the Mughul Emperor Aurangzeb. Under her inspiring leadership the Marathas again began to take the aggressive in raiding the imperial territories in Berar, Gujarat and Ahmadnagar and succeeded in getting much wealth and prestige. She was, however, put in a difficult situation when in 1707 Sahu or Shivaji II, the son and successor of her husband's elder brother Shambhuji, was released by the Mughuls and returned to Maharashtra to claim his patrimony. Sahu soon gathered round him a large body of supporters headed by Peshwa Balaji Vishwanath. Tara Bai proved no match for this combination and was obliged to recognise Sahu as the sovereign of the Maratha kingdom, though she succeeded in maintaining her son Shivaji III in some royal state in Satara. She had rendered great service to the Marathas by keeping up their unity and integrity during the critical years from 1700 to 1707. Her son Shivaji III was later on adopted as son and successor by Raja Sahu.

Tarain, the battles of—were fought between Prithviraj (*q.v.*), the Chauhan king of Delhi and Ajmer, and Shihab-ud-din Muhammad Ghuri in A.D. 1191 and 1192. In the first battle of Tarain Prithviraj defeated Shihab-ud-din, who was severely wounded, and put him to flight. But in the second battle which took place a year later in 1192, Shihab-ud-din defeated and killed Prithviraj. The victory of Shihab-ud-din in the second battle of Tarain was soon followed by the capture and occupation of Delhi by the Muhammadans and thus led to the establishment of their rule over northern India for several centuries.

Taranath—a Tibetan author and historian, flourished in the seventeenth century. His work affords an account of the history of India in the early period as preserved in Tibetan tradition. It is useful as corroborative evidence and also for filling in gaps left by indigenous sources.

Taraori, the battles of—*see* Tarain which is another name for Taraori.

Tardi Beg—a Mughul general, was entrusted by Bairam Khan (*q.v.*) with the defence of Delhi immediately after the death of Humayun (*q.v.*) in 1555. But he failed in his task and suffered Delhi to be captured and occupied by Hemu (*q.v.*) in

1556. For this failure he was executed by Bairam Khan's orders.

Tariff Board, the—was set up in 1923 for the purposes of safeguarding existing Indian industries and fostering new ones. It did good work by giving protection to the steel, textile, sugar and cement industries which have all prospered.

Tarmashirin—the Khan (ruler) of the Chagtai section of the Mongols, invaded India in 1328-29 and came up very near to Delhi. The sultan, Muhammad Tughluq, somehow persuaded him to cut short his raid and return.

Tashkent Declaration—was signed and issued jointly by Lal Bahadur Shastri, Prime Minister of India and Ayub Khan, President of Pakistan on 11 January, 1966 after a prolonged conference which was arranged at Tashkent by Mr. Kosygin, the Prime Minister of the Soviet Government of the U.S.S.R. The Declaration stated that India and Pakistan agreed not to have recourse to force and to settle their disputes through peaceful means, to withdraw all armed forces by 25 February, 1966 to the 5 August, 1965 line; to continue meetings both at the highest and at other levels on matters of direct concern to both countries; to base relations between the two countries on non-interference in the internal affairs of each other; to restore normal functions of diplomatic missions; to discourage any propaganda directed against each other; to consider measures towards the restoration of economic and trade relations, communication and cultural exchanges; to create conditions which will prevent exodus of people; to continue discussion of questions relating to the problem of refugees and eviction of illegal immigrants and to discuss the return of property and assets taken over by either side during the recent conflict. In implementation of this declaration the belligerent armies were duly withdrawn to positions occupied by them before the outbreak of the conflict; but it is as yet too early to judge the main effect of the Tashkent Declaration on the larger Indo-Pakistan relations, but the Declaration will be remembered on account of its pathetic association with the sudden death, within a few hours of its signing, of Lal Bahadur Shastri.

Tatas, the family of the—was founded by Jeejibhoy Jamshedji Tata (1783-1859). Jeejibhoy was born of a very poor family in the village of Naosari in Baroda state. He was a Parsee and by his industry, courage and business acumen made himself a great businessman who went to China in connection with his affairs. He accumulated two crores of rupees within 28 years of his business career. He was also very benevolent and gave away about fifteen lakhs of rupees in establishing and endowing charitable institutions in the city of Bombay. His son Jamshedji (1839-1904) took up the management of the business from 1858 and largely increased the activities as well as the wealth of the Tatas. He earned millions by exporting raw cotton from India to the U.S.A. during the American Civil War. He went to England, learnt the textile manufacturing industry at Manchester and foundedt he Empress Cotton Mill in 1877 and the Tata Swadeshi Mill in 1887. He also started the Lonavla Hydro-electric Scheme. His greatest achievement was the founding of the Tata Iron and Steel Company at Sankchi, now famous as Jamshedpur, which went into production in 1907 and is now one of the largest steel plants in the world. Like his father he also gave much for the public benefit, but his endowments were more purposeful. He endowed two scholarships to enable Indian students to learn technology in Europe and he left large endowments for the Bangalore Tata Scientific Research Institute which was established after his death. The Tatas have played a prominent part in the industrial regeneration of India by creating new industries and providing for research.

Tatar Khan—*see* Nasir-ud-din Muhammad Shah of Gujarat.

Taxila (Sanskrit **Takshashila**)—a very ancient city, was situated near the modern railway station of Sarai-Kala, twenty miles north-west of Rawalpindi in West Panjab. At the time of Alexander's invasion it was the capital of king Ambhi (*q.v.*) and had already earned a great reputation as a seat of medical science. Jivaka, the court physician of King Bimbisara (*q.v.*), is said to have taken a seven years' course of training in medicine at Taxila. Extensive archaeological explorations that have been carried out on the site have revealed monuments of pre-Maurya and Maurya times, of the Indo-Greek period and of the Kushan period. Taxila also occupies an important part in Hindu, Jain and Buddhist literatures. A Greek traveller named Apollonius who visited Taxila in about A.D. 43-44, has left an interesting account of the city. Taxila was the seat of a Viceroy during the reign of Asoka (*q.v.*) and continued to be an important political centre under the Indo-Bactrian and Kushan (*q.v.*) rulers. In the seventh century it became a part of the kingdom of Kashmir. It lost its pre-eminence and gradually became a deserted place after the conquest of the

Panjab by Sultan Mahmud (*q.v.*) early in the eleventh century. (Marshall, Sir John, *Guide to Taxila*)

Tea industry, the—was originated in India in the nineteenth century. In the eighteenth century the East India Company brought tea to India from China. Late in that century wild tea plants were found growing in Assam, but it was doubted whether these were genuine and their leaves were consumable. In 1834 Lord William Bentinck got tea-seeds and skilled labour from China and a Government garden was soon started, but it was sold to the Assam Tea Company when it was formed in 1839. The Company after some experiments succeeded in growing the tea plant in India with Indian labour and from 1850 the industry rapidly expanded. Tea which is now planted extensively not only in Assam, but also in Cachar, Darjeeling, Naini Tal districts as well as in the Kangra valley, has become one of the best gold-earning industries of India.

Tegh Bahadur (1664-75)—the ninth *Guru* of the Sikhs, was the son of the sixth *Guru*, Har Govind, and succeeded the eighth *Guru*, Har Kishan. He settled at Anandapur, near Kiratpur in the Panjab. He lived for a short time at Patna where his famous son and successor, Govinda Singh was born (1666). In 1668 he also went to Assam with Aurangzeb's army, but on his return to the Panjab he incurred the anger and hostility of Emperor Aurangzeb for having encouraged the Brahmans of Kashmir to resist certain repressive imperial measures. Tegh Bahadur was, therefore, arrested by imperial command and taken as a captive to Delhi where he was offered a choice between death and conversion. He preferred his faith to his life and was cruelly executed in 1675 by Aurangzeb's order. His mantle fell on his worthy son and successor who turned the peaceful Sikhs into a militant fraternity. Tegh Bahadur's martyrdom inspired the Sikhs with determination to avenge their wrongs on the Mughuls.

Teja Singh—was the Commander-in-Chief of the Sikh army on the eve of the outbreak of the First Sikh War (*q.v.*) (1845-46). He was more anxious to secure the goodwill of the hostile English than to win he war. He betrayed his trust and was largely responsible for the defeat of the Sikhs in the war.

Telegraph, the first line of—was laid in 1854 in India. It ran from Calcutta to Agra and covered a distance of 800 miles. It stood the British in good stead during the Mutiny. It was extended to Lahore and then to Peshawar by 1857. It has been since spread practically all over India and now connects India with the rest of the world as well.

Telugu—is one of the four principal languages spoken in the Deccan, the other three being Tamil, Malayalam and Kanarese. Telugu is spoken in the northern part of what was once the Madras Presidency. Telugu is the language of the majority of the people of the modern Andhra State, lying between Orissa and Madras. Telugu received the patronage of the kings of Vijayanagar, especially of king Krishnadeva Raya who himself was a great poet writing in Telugu as well as in Sanskrit. His court was adorned by eight great Telugu poets of whom Peddana was the greatest.

Terry, Edward—a chaplain, accompanied Sir Thomas Roe (*q.v.*) during his embassy to the court of Jahangir. He wrote an account of his visit to India and his book *Voyage to East India* is a very important source of information for men and events in contemporary India.

Thags, **the**—were bands of robbers and murderers. They generally moved about in small groups innocently garbed as travellers and killed their unsuspecting victims by tying a handkerchief with a ring round their necks when they were either asleep or not sufficiently careful and cautious and then robbed the victims of all their possessions. They abounded in Central India and it was only after years of careful preparation begun in 1830 that Col. Sleeman succeeded in uprooting them.

Thaneswar—an ancient city famous in Sanskrit literature, was situated to the north of modern Delhi and the ancient Indraprastha between Ambala and Karnal. It was the heart of the region called the *Bramhavarta*, the first sacred region in India occupied by the Indo-Aryans. Not very far from it lay the great field of Kurukshetra where was fought for eighteen days the great battle between the Kurus and the Pandavas which forms the main theme of the great epic, the *Mahabharata*. It was also called *Sthanvisvara* or *Sthanesvara* and was sacred to God Siva. Towards the close of the sixth century A.D. it became the capital of the Pushyabhuti dynasty and its reigning king Prabhakaravardhana made it the metropolis of a large kingdom comprising Malwa, north-western Panjab and part of Rajputana. It, however, lost its pre-eminence during the reign of Prabhakaravardhana's younger son, Harshavardhana (A.D. 606-647) who preferred Kanauj as the capital of his much larger dominions. Its status declined under the pressure of the Huna invasions of the later seventh and eighth centuries, but it continued to be a very sacred place to the Hindus. In A.D. 1014 it was raided and plundered by Sultan Mahmud and later on became a part of the Ghaznavid kingdom of the Panjab. It lay on the road to Delhi and in its vicinity were fought the two battles of Tarain (*q.v.*) and the three battles of Panipat (*q.v.*) which decided the fate of India four times. It became a part of the British Indian empire after the Third Maratha War (*q.v.*).

Thar desert, the—lying between Rajputana and the lower Indus valley, is entirely waterless and trackless and is negotiable only by caravans. It now forms the boundary between India and West Pakistan. It separates Sind from the Deccan as well as from north-west India and its existence was one of the factors that prevented the expansion of the Arab dominions beyond Sind which was conquered by the Arabs in A.D. 710. It also checked for some time the expansion of the British dominions into Sind which was very much coveted by the British on account of the access that it gave at once to Afghanistan and the Panjab. It passed under British control with the annexation of Sind (*q.v.*) to their Indian empire.

Thathah, the province of—comprised the lower Sind valley. In Akbar's time it was included within the province of Multan (*q.v.*) but was formed into a separate *suba* or province during the reign of Aurangzeb. The capital of the province was also called Thathah (or Tattah) and it was in the neighbourhood of this city that Sultan Muhammad Tughluq died in 1351.

Theosophical Society, the—was founded by Madame Blavatsky (*q.v.*) and Col H. S. Olcot in the United States in 1875. They came to India later on and established the headquarters of the Society in Adyar, a suburb of Madras. The Society became a great force in Indian life and politics after its great protagonist, Mrs. Annie Besant (*q.v.*) came and settled in India in 1893. Her exertions and eloquence soon led to the establishment of many branches of the Society all over India. The Society had little success as a religious cult in India, but it led to a revived faith in the minds of the Western-educated Hindus in the Hindu religion which it praised in Western terms. The revived faith in ancient Hinduism instilled into the minds of educated India a "new self-respect, a pride in the past, a wave of patriotic life and the beginning of the re-building of a nation", a culmination which was materially promoted by the way in which Mrs. Annie Besant, with whom the Theosophical Society in India came to be identified, threw herself into the Indian National movement as led by the Indian National Congress.

Thibaw—was the king of upper Burma from 1878 to 1886. His claim to have independent commercial and political relations with European countries other than Great Britian was the real cause that led the Viceroy, Lord Dufferin (*q.v.*), to declare a war against him in December, 1885 on the flimsy plea that he had refused commercial facilities to the British traders in Burma and misgoverned his subjects. Thibaw, however, failed to offer any practical resistance; his armies were easily routed; he surrendered unconditionally and was deposed and exiled to India where he lived till his death. His kingdom was annexed to the British Indian empire.

Tibet—has a long history of cultural relations with India. In the seventh century the Tibetan king, Srong-tsan-Gampo (*q.v.*) (*c.* A.D. 629-98) embraced Buddhism and sent to India a learned Tibetan, named Thonmi Sambhota, who collected some Buddhist texts and carried to Tibet the western Gupta script which was very similar to Devanagari and which became the basis of the Tibetan alphabet. It is probable that the celebrated sandalwood image of Buddha Avalokitesvara which is installed and worshipped even now in the Potala, the palace of the Dalai Lama, was originally brought to Tibet by Thonmi. King Srong-tsan-Gampo not only embraced Buddhism but also became a pupil of Thonmi, became literate and devoted himself to the preaching and propagation of Buddhism amongst the Tibetans, encouraging amongst them honesty, humanitarianism, pure and simple living, respect for learning and love of the motherland. Buddhism thus contributed much to the cultural and economic development of Tibet. The work of translating Sanskrit texts into Tibetan started by Srong-tsan-Gampo was carried on by his successors and led to the development of the Tibetan language into a polished and expressive literary medium. The establishment of Buddhism in Tibet led to the development of close intercourse between Tibet and India and visitors from Tibet to Indian centres of Buddhist learning, especially Nalanda and Vikramasila, as well as from India to Tibet became a regular feature of Tibeto-Indian relations. Thus the great Buddhist preachers, Santarakshita (*q.v.*) and Padmasambhava (*q.v.*), visited Tibet in the middle of the eighth century and Atisha (*q.v.*) in the middle of the eleventh century. This cultural contact led to the development and establishment in Tibet of Lamaism which attempts a synthesis of the Hinayana, Mahayana and Tantrayana forms of Buddhism and also effected a great change in the national character of the Tibetans who were gradually transformed from a warlike people into peaceful religious devotees amongst whom were born many spiritual teachers, competent scholars, able linguists and devout practisers of meditation. The combined efforts of Tibetan and Indian scholars at translating Indian Sanskrit texts into Tibetan were most fruitful and many Sanskrit works, whose originals are not to be found now in India, have been found in Tibet either in original Sanskrit or in Tibetan translation.

Political relations between Tibet and India were in the past very slender. Samudragupta (*q.v.*), the second Gupta Emperor, who prided himself on the submission of Nepal, makes no mention of Tibet in his Allahabad inscription in the fourth century. In the seventh century Harshavardhana (*q.v.*), who maintained friendly relations with China, sent an embassy there through Tibet with which evidently his relations were friendly. On his death his minister Arjuna who had usurped his throne, incurred the displeasure of the Tibetan king, Srong-tsan-Gampo, for having opposed the embassy of Wang-heun-tse (*q.v.*) and was defeated and deprived of Tirhut which, how-ever, threw off the Tibetan yoke in A.D. 1703. Thereafter Tibet ceased to have any *political* relations with India. The Muham-madan conquerors of India fought shy of the snow-clad heights of Tibet and none of them except Iktiar-ud-din Muhammad, son of Bakhtyar, who made a disastrously futile raid on Tibet in A.D. 1204, even attempted its conquest. But the commercial greed of the British knew no limits and as early as 1774-75 Warren Hastings (*q.v.*) sent George Bogle, a young officer of the Company, to visit the Tashi Lama who is the spiritual head of Tibet, but Bogle who left an interesting report of his journey could secure no advantage for the British, for Tibet since the early years of the eighteenth century had acknow-ledged the suzerainty of China whose authority over Tibet was represented by the presence at Lhasa, the capital of Tibet, of two Chinese Residents or Viceroys called *Ambans*. China and Tibet agreed upon keeping Tibet closed to the Britishers in India and succeeded in keeping out the British from Tibet till the close of the nineteenth century. In 1886 after the Third Burmese War (*q.v.*) the British Government made a conven-tion with China by which in return for an implied acceptance by the British of Chinese suzerainty over Tibet the Chinese

Government agreed to raise no objection to the British annexation of Burma. In 1887 the Tibetans invaded the British protected state of Sikkim but were easily driven back, and in 1890 the Tibet-Sikkim boundary was settled by a convention between China and Great Britain. In 1893 some commercial facilities to be given to the British in Tibet were also agreed upon, but were not actually made available. Thus in the beginning of the twentieth century Tibet still continued to be a forbidden country to the British and the first British subject who ventured to penetrate into Lhasa was a Bengali schoolmaster, named Saratchandra Das (*q.v.*), who made his way into Tibet and brought back valuable information about the political and religious condition in Tibet. Further, in the beginning of the twentieth century the Dalai Lama with the help of his tutor, Dorjieff, a Russian Buddhist, became eager to throw off the Chinese sovereignty, entered into some negotiations with the Government of Russia which filled the British Indian Government, then controlled by the prancing Viceroy, Lord Curzon (*q.v.*), with the fear that Tibet would soon be under Russian protection. The British Indian Government was determined to prevent this culmination and in 1903 sent an expedition, euphemistically called a mission, under Colonel Francis Younghusband, which entered into Tibetan territories without meeting with any opposition in July, 1903, easily defeated an ill-armed Tibetan army at Guru in March, 1904, and after defeating a larger Tibetan army in April, forced its entrance into Lhasa in August, 1904. There Younghusband dictated in September a treaty to Tibet by which the Tibetans agreed to open to the British three trade marts within Tibet, to pay an indemnity of 75 lakhs in as many annual instalments (subsequently reduced to 25 lakhs payable in three annual instalments), to allow the British to occupy the Chumbi valley lying between Sikkim and Bhutan until the indemnity was paid, to refrain from ceding any part of Tibetan territory to any foreign power and from granting any concessions for opening railroads in Tibet to any foreign power without granting similar facilities to the British Government. Thus Russian expansion into Tibet was forestalled, but British bungling soon led to turning the Chinese suzerainty over Tibet, which had so long been only nominal and theoretical, into a practical reality. China was allowed to pay off, on behalf of Tibet, the indemnity of 25 lakhs and the Chumbi valley had to be evacuated by the British. Further in 1906 England and China

concluded a convention by which England agreed neither
to annex any Tibetan territory nor to interfere in Tibet's
internal administration and in return China agreed not to allow
any foreign power to interfere with the internal administration
or territorial integrity of Tibet. Again in 1907 England and
Russia agreed to carry on political relations with Tibet through
China. Thus the suzerainty over Tibet was made a gift to
China which soon afterwards overran Tibet and sent the Dalai
Lama as a refugee to India. But the British Government protested
and the Tibetans, taking advantage of the disorders in China
due to internal revolution, overthrew Chinese suzerainty in
1918. The changes in Russia after the Revolution of 1917
and the confusion that arose about the same time in China,
relieved the British Indian Government of any menace of an
external enemy threatening British interests in Tibet and for
the next thirty years there was friendly understanding between the Governments of Tibet and India. But circumstances
altered in the late fifties of this century. China developed into
a great communist state; and, under the leadership of Mao
Tse-tung, determined to re-assert and exercise her right of
suzerainty over Tibet which she, accordingly, overran and
occupied in 1959 forcing the Dalai Lama to flee for his life
to India, while the recently established Government of the
Republic of India looked on supinely. Tibet was thus annexed
to the vast Chinese empire whose southern boundaries thus
became conterminous with the northern boundary of India,
making an eventual clash between the two almost inevitable.

Tilak, Bal Gangadhar (1857-1920)—was a famous Indian
nationalist leader and was also a very erudite scholar. Born
in a Maratha Brahman family of Ratnagiri, he was educated in
Deccan College, took a degree in law, sponsored the foundation
of the Fergusson College, and took to journalism as the editor of
two journals named 'Maratha' (English) and 'Kesari' (Maratha).
In 1897 he started the Shivaji festival and thus tried to revive
patriotic fervour amongst the Indians. His adverse criticism of
Government measures against the plague outbreak in Poona
led to his prosecution and conviction on a charge of sedition.
In 1907 he organised, along with Bepin Pal and Lala Lajpat
Rai, the extremist section amongst the Congressmen who held
that the usual Congress method of seeking redress of grievances
through resolutions was useless and that a more effective
method was required for compelling Great Britain to accede
to the Indian demands. Further, Tilak and his associates refused

to accept as the goal of the Indian National Congress the establishment in India of responsible Government of the type prevalent in the self-governing Dominions within the British empire. He demanded that India should have an autonomous government, absolutely free of the British control. Thus the differences between him and the moderate party of the Indian National Congress were fundamental and Tilak started in 1916 a Home Rule League. Tilak was not satisfied with the Government of India Act, 1919, but he died in August, 1920 and the Indian National Congress at its Nagpur session held in December, 1920, declared the attainment of Purna Swaraj or complete self-rule and not mere Dominion Status, by all justifiable and peaceful means, to be its goal. Tilak thus stood largely vindicated after his death. His implacable hostility to British domination led to long periods of imprisonment in British jails, but his spirit was never broken. He was calumniated by Sir Valentine Chirol in his *Indian Unrest* and went to England to sue him, but the English courts gave an adverse verdict. His two works, the *Geeta Rahasya* and the *Orion* are monuments to his erudition. (Parvate, T. V., *Bal Gangadhar Tilak*; Kelkar, N. C., *Landmarks in Lokamanya's Life;* Karmarkar, D. P., *Bal Gangadhar Tilak;* Ghose, Arabinda, *Speeches of B. G. Tilak:* Reisner and Goldberg, *Tilak and the Struggle for Indian Freedom*)

Timur (also called Timur-i-lang and Tamerlane) (1336-1405) —succeeded to his father's throne as the Amir of Samarqand in 1369 and soon afterwards started on a career of conquest. After overrunning Mesopotamia, Persia and Afghanistan he invaded India with a large army of cavalry in 1398 and advanced on Delhi after sacking many places and massacring thousands of persons on the way. He completely routed at the outskirts of Delhi the large army with which Sultan Mahmud Tughluq opposed his further advance, entered into Delhi on 18 December, 1398 and gave the city up to rapine and pillage by his soldiers for several days. He halted in Delhi for only fifteen days after which he started on his way back home, re-crossing the Indus in March, 1398, laden with the rich booty that he had taken in Delhi and all along his route. He left anarchy, famine and pestilence behind him and dealt a severe blow to the Delhi sultanate which hastened its decay.

Tipu Sultan—was the son and successor of Haidar Ali of Mysore. He ascended the throne of Mysore on his father's death in April, 1783, when Mysore was engaged in her second war with the English in India. Tipu, who was as brave and warlike

as his father, continued the war, defeated the army of Brigadier
Mathews whom he took captive and obliged the English to make
peace with him by the treaty of Mangalore in March, 1784
on the basis of mutual restitution of conquests. But the peace
proved temporary, for five years later the third war between
the English and Mysore broke out. Though the English were
aided by the Nizam and the Marathas, Tipu showed great
valour and astute generalship but was forced after three campaigns at the last two of which the Governor-General Lord
Cornwallis himself was in command, to make peace in 1792 by
the Treaty of Seringapatam by which he surrendered to the
victorious allies one-half of his dominions, paid an indemnity
of three crores of rupees and placed two of his sons as hostages
in the hands of the English. But Tipu Sultan continued to be
restive under this humiliating defeat. He began to look for
allies against the English, for another war with them he felt
was sure to break out sooner or later. He sent emissaries to
Arabia, Kabul, Constantinople, France, and to the French
colony of Mauritius seeking their help against the English,
but except at Mauritius he got no encouragement. On the
other hand, Lord Wellesley who came out as the Governor-
General in April, 1798, felt sure of Tipu's hostile intentions
and was determined to wage war against him. He, therefore,
called upon Tipu to accept a subsidiary alliance with the
English and on his refusal to do so Wellesley made a tripartite
treaty with the Nizam and the Marathas and declared war on
Tipu in March, 1799. Tipu fought with great gallantry, but
the odds against him were too heavy. Three allied armies
marched on Seringapatam from three different directions,
and besieged his capital which Tipu defended with great
courage. But he fell fighting before the walls of Seringapatam
which the English captured in May, 1799. Thus died Tipu
Sultan, a most remarkable personality in Indian history.
Hostility to him had so deeply darkened the vision of some contemporary English historians that they described him as
a religious fanatic and tyrannical ruler. But these charges
are all unfounded. He was a very diligent and capable ruler
and administrator who made Mysore a prosperous state in
spite of the wars that he had to fight. He was no fanatic and
generally treated his Hindu subjects with fair tolerance. He
was a diplomat with a large vision, and if his efforts to build
up an anti-British front in India failed it was not his fault.
Above all, he was the only Indian ruler who never allied him-

self with the English against any Indian ruler, Hindu or Muham-madan, though he had every reason for deeply resenting their conduct towards him. (Wilks, Mark, *H.S.S.I.* & Khan, M. H., *Hist. of Tipu Sultan*)

Tirumala—was the brother of Ramaraja (*q.v.*), the general of Vijayanagar, who lost the battle of Talikota in 1565. After the battle, Tirumala, along with the nominal ruler Sadasiva (*q.v.*) took refuge at Penugonda, but usurped the throne in about 1570. He ruled for only three years and founded the fourth or the Aravidu or Karnata dynasty of Vijayanagar. The last of his descendants was Ranga who lived in about the middle of the seventeenth century.

Tissa—was the king of Ceylon (*c.* 250 B.C. - 211 B.C.) on whose invitation Prince Mahendra (*q.v.*) went to Ceylon and pro-pagated Buddhism there. Tissa entered into an alliance with the Maurya Emperor Asoka (*q.v.*) and did all he could to foster the growth of Buddhism in Ceylon. He laid the foundation of the sacred city of Anuradhapur where a branch of the sacred Bo-tree from Bodh-Gaya was planted. This tree is shown even today.

Tissa, Thera—was a senior and learned Buddhist Indian monk who convoked and presided over the Buddhist Council (*q.v.*) held at Pataliputra in the reign of Asoka.

Tivara (or Tivala)—was a son of Emperor Asoka whom his second queen, Kaluvaki, bore. He is mentioned in the Queen's inscrip-tion of Asoka, but nothing else is known about him. (*S.A.E.*)

Todar Mal—was the Revenue Minister of Emperor Akbar (*q.v.*) and was honoured by him with the title of Raja. He was born of humble parents in Lahore in the Panjab and entered into Akbar's service in 1561. On the conquest of Gujarat by Akbar in 1573, Todar Mal was commissioned to make a revenue settlement there and it was first in Gujarat that Todar Mal made his first revenue settlement on improved principles of measurement of land according to a uniform standard of measurement, classification of land according to its fertility and settlement and collection of the Government share of one-third of the produce direct from the cultivator. This system was later on extended to the whole of the Mughul empire with necessary local alterations. Todar Mal was also a great general. He conquered Bengal in 1576 and was the *Subadar* or Governor of Bengal, Bihar and Orissa for a term from 1580. He was free from avarice and was one of the ablest officers of Akbar.

Tols—are indigenous Sanskrit schools, characteristic of the ancient

Hindu system of education. These were located in the houses of the *adhyapakas* (professors) who maintained the institutions at their own cost, finding accommodation and food, and in some cases even clothing, for the students who were admitted. The hours of teaching and reading were so arranged as to suit the convenience of the teacher and the taught. Close contact between the student and the teacher as well as the absence of any kind of monetary payment by the students were the main characteristics of the system. As the teacher had to maintain the student, naturally the former exercised some right in picking and choosing the students, who generally belonged to the caste of Brahmans, but teaching was available to meritorious students of other castes as well, if and when they could arrange for their food elsewhere. The *adhyapakas* whose precarious incomes depended on the generosity of local landlords and other men of piety, underwent much hardship in maintaining the *tols* which was considered as a bounden duty which every Brahman learned in the *Shastras* (sacred Sanskrit literature) owed to his religion. All branches of Sanskrit learning, especially grammar, literature, law (*smriti*), logic (*nyaya*) and philosophy (*Vedanta* or *Darsan*) were taught. Some *tols* are still in existence and to some Government now make monthly grants.

Tomaras, the—was a clan of the Rajputs (*q.v.*) who, according to some, were of foreign origin, like the Pratiharas and the Chouhans. This clan came to be the rulers of the modern Delhi region in the eleventh century. It was the Tomara chief Anangapal who founded the city of Delhi in the middle of the eleventh century. The celebrated iron pillar which records an eulogy of an unidentified king named Chandra, was removed by Anangapal to its present site in about A.D. 1052 as an adjunct to a group of temples which the later Muhammadan conquerors demolished, utilising their materials in building the mosque and the Qutb Minar.

Tonk, Nawab of—*see* Amir Khan.

Topra—was near Ambala in the Panjab. Here was situated a pillar containing a version of the Seven Pillar inscriptions of Asoka. The pillar attracted the notice of Sultan Firuz Shah Tughluq (*q.v.*) who had it transported to Delhi where it still stands and is known as Firuz Shah's *lat*. (Afif-i-Siraj, *Tarikh-i-Firoz Shahi*)

Toramana—a leader of the Huns, established himself in Malwa in about A.D. 500. He assumed the title of *Maharajadhiraja* (sovereign of *maharajas*) and his sway probably extended over the Central Provinces, Salt Range and Central India. Several of his silver coins have been found. He was succeeded in about A.D. 502 by his famous son, Mihirakula or Mihiragula (*q.v.*).

Torna—was a hill fort, about twenty miles to the south-west of Poona. Shivaji began his career at the age of nineteen by capturing the fort of Torna in 1646.

Tosali—was the seat of a *Mahamatra* at the time of Asoka (*q.v.*). It is mentioned in his first Separate Kalinga Edict which has been found at Dhauli in the Puri district of Orissa. (Bhattacharya, S., *Select Asokan Epigraphs*)

Tranquabar—was a port on the Coromandel coast where the Danes established a factory in 1620. It was a trading port and never had any political significance. It was sold to the British Government in 1845.

Trichinopoly—was a fortified city in the Carnatic where Muhammad Ali (*q.v.*), a claimant to the throne of the Carnatic, took refuge in 1751. It was besieged by the French and their protégé Chanda Shaheb but had to he relieved as a result of a diversion created by Robert Clive (*q.v.*) who seized Arcot. It was besieged again by the French in 1753, but was relieved by the English in 1754 and continued to be in the possession of the Nawab of the Carnatic until the annexation of his territories to the British Indian empire.

Trilochanapala—was installed as the king of Kanauj by the Chandella king, Ganda, in A.D. 1019 in place of the reigning king, Rajyapala, who was defeated and killed by Ganda. Later on in the same year Trilochanapala made an abortive attempt to prevent Sultan Mahmud from crossing the Jumna and perhaps perished in the effort. At any rate nothing more is known about him.

Trilochanapala—the penultimate Shahiya king of Ohind, tried ineffectually to resist Sultan Mahmud, was defeated in the battle of the Ramganga and was assassinated in A.D. 1021-22. His son and successor Bhima, who died in 1026, was the last Shahiya king.

Trimbakji—was a Maratha who enjoyed the favour and confidence of Peshwa Baji Rao II (*q.v.*) who appointed him as the governor at Ahmedabad. Trimbakji planned and brought about the murder of Gangadhar Shastri, Gaekwad's envoy, who had come to Poona under the promise of a safe conduct. The English deeply resented the murder and at the insistence of Elphinstone, the British Resident, Trimbakji was arrested and surrendered by the Peshwa to the English who kept him in detention at Salsette.

Tripartite Treaty, the—was concluded in 1838 during the administration of Lord Auckland amongst the British, Shah

Shuja, the fugitive Amir of Afghanistan and Maharaja Ranjit Singh of the Panjab. It provided that Shah Shuja was to be restored to the throne of Kabul with Sikh military and British financial help. In return Ranjit Singh was to be confirmed in all the territories that he had acquired and Sind was to be surrendered to the Afghan Government of Shah Shuja whom the British expected to control. This aggressive treaty eventually involved Lord Auckland's Government in the disastrous Afghan War of 1838-42 (*q.v.*).

Tughluq Shah—*see* Ghiyas-ud-din Tughluq.

Tughril Khan—a Turki noble, was appointed by Sultan Balban (*q.v.*) as the governor of Bengal, but in A.D. 1278 he assumed independence. He was suppressed and killed by Sultan Balban after a three years' campaign from 1279 to 1282.

Tukaram—a famous poet and saint of Maharashtra, was a senior contemporary of Shivaji I (*q.v.*) on whom his poems and teachings had a great deal of influence.

Tukaroi, the battle of—was fought in the Balasore district of Orissa in 1575 in which the Mughul army of Akbar, led by his general Munim Khan, defeated Daud Khan, the Afghan king of Bengal, who was, however, granted easy terms and lived to fight in 1576 another campaign in which he was defeated and killed.

Tukoji Rao Holkar I—was appointed Commander-in-Chief of the Holkar's army by Rani Ahalya Bai (*q.v.*) in 1767. On the Rani's death in 1795 he became the ruler of the Holkar state which he ruled till his death in 1797.

Tukoji Rao Holkar II—was the ruler of the Holkar state from 1843 to 1846. He was an efficient administrator who increased the wealth and prestige of the Holkar family.

Tukoji Rao Holkar III—the head of the Holkar state from 1903 to 1926, was forced to abdicate as he was held responsible for a murder outside the state.

Tulsi Bai—was a favourite mistress of Jaswant Rao Holkar (1798-1811). She was very clever and intelligent and became the Regent in the Holkar's state in 1808 when Jaswant Rao became insane. On the death of Jaswant Rao in 1811 she became the practical ruler of the state. She had the support of Holkar's minister, Balaram Seth, and of the Pindari chief, Amir Khan. Her administration was distasteful to the army which rose against her in 1817 and murdered her. The army was soon afterwards defeated by the British in the battle of Mahidpur (*q.v.*) in 1817.

Tulsidas—a famous saintly Hindi poet, lived from A.D. 1532 to

1623. He resided at Benares. He was the author of the famous work *Ramacharitamanasa* (The Pool of Rama's Life) which is a Hindi version of the Sanskrit epic the *Ramayana* and is read with loving respect by all Hindus, rich and poor alike, in upper India. He was not merely a poet of a high order as his work shows, but also a spiritual teacher of the people of Hindusthan who still hold his memory in high esteem.

Tuluva dynasty, the—was founded in Vijayanagar in about A.D. 1503 by Narasa Nayaka. The dynasty which ruled till 1565, comprised six kings, viz. Narasa Nayaka (1503-05), his son, Vira Narasimha (1505-09), his brother, Krishnadeva Raya (1509-29) (*q.v.*) who was the greatest king of the dynasty and under whom the kingdom reached its zenith, his brother Achyuta (1529-42), his son Venkata I (1542) and his cousin Sadasiva (1542-65). It was during the reign of the last king that Vijayanagar was defeated by the combined forces of the sultans of Bijapur, Golconda and Ahmadnagar in the battle of Talikota in 1565 and the city was pillaged and destroyed. Sadasiva fled as a refugee to Penugonda where he was killed in 1570 and the Tuluva dynasty of Vijayanagar was extinguished.

Tungabhadra, the—a river in the Deccan, rises in the Western Ghats and falls into the Krishna near Raichur where it forms a famous doab which was long a bone of contention between the Hindu kingdom of Vijayanagar and the Muhammadan Bahmani kingdom and the succession states.

Turushka-danda, **the**—was an additional tax which was levied by king Govindachandra of Kanauj (*c.* A.D. 1104-55) to meet the cost of resisting the Muhammadan invaders.

Tushaspa—was the governor of Gujarat and Kathiawar during the reign of Asoka (*q.v.*). He bore the title of Raja and reconstructed the embankments of the Sudarshana lake (*q.v.*) near Girnar so strongly that they endured for four hundred years and required no repair until the time of Satrap Rudradaman who rebuilt it in A.D. 150. Tushaspa has been taken to have been a Persian in the service of Emperor Asoka.

U

Udai Singh—the Rana of Mewar (1529-72), was the son and successor of Rana Sangram Singh (*q.v.*) who had fought against

Babur the battle of Khanua in 1527. Udai Singh, however, had none of his father's courage and patriotism, and had the misfortune of being pitted against the Mughul Emperor Akbar who invaded Mewar and besieged Chitor in 1567. Udai Singh took no personal part in the defence of Chitor which fell to Akbar after a four-month's siege. Udai Singh also made no effort to recover Chitor, but kept himself immersed in the pursuit of pleasures at his new capital which he founded at Udaipur and ruled ingloriously till his death in 1572 when he was succeeded by his illustrious son, Rana Pratap Singh (*q.v.*).

Udaipur, the treaty of—was concluded in 1818 between the Rana of Udaipur and the British Government represented by Sir Charles Metcalfe by which the Ranas of Mewar (Udaipur) passed under British protection.

Udaya (or Udasin)—a king of Magadha in about 443 B.C., was a grandson of Ajatasatru (*q.v.*) and son of Darsaka (*q.v.*). He built the city of Kusumapura on the Ganges, a few miles from Pataliputra on the Sone. Later on Kusumapura was merged in the larger city of Pataliputra (*.q.v.*).

Udgir, the battle of—was fought in February, 1760 between the Marathas led by Sadasiva Rao Bhao, the first cousin of the reigning Peshwa, Balaji Baji Rao (*q.v.*) and the Nizam of Hyderabad. The Nizam was decisively defeated and the ambition of the Marathas was greatly heightened.

Ujjaini (also called Avantika)—in Malwa, is one of the ancient cities of India. It is also one of the seven sacred cities of the Hindus in India. In the seventh century B.C. it was the capital of the kingdom of Avanti, known later on as Malwa. It passed under the rule of the Saka satraps (*q.v.*) in the early centuries of the Christian era, but was recovered in the fifth century by Chandragupta II, the third Gupta emperor, who made it his capital. The city figures prominently in the works of Kalidas who in his *Meghaduta* (*q.v.*) has left brilliant descriptions of the city, of the river Sipra on which it is situated and the many temples especially that of Siva (called Mahakala), which decorated the city.

Ulamas, the—are Muhammadan doctors of divinity who stood for orthodoxy as well as theocracy. They were opposed to strong Muhammadan rulers like Ala-ud-din Khalji (*q.v.*), Muhammad Tughluq (*q.v.*) and Akbar (*q.v.*). They had a great deal of influence on the illiterate and ignorant Muhammadan masses over whom they still continue to have much control.

Ulugh Khan—a general of Sultan Ghiyas-ud-din Balban (q.v.), defeated and overthrew Prataparudra, the Kakatiya king of Warangal in 1323.

Ulugh Khan Balban, Sultan—*see* Sultan Ghiyas-ud-din Balban.

Umarkot (also spelt Amarkot)—was a small Rajput principality near the border of Rajputana and Sind. The ruling chief, Rana Prasad, gave shelter to the fugitive Emperor Humayun (q.v.) in 1542 and it was at Umarkot that his son Akbar (q.v.) was born on 23 November, 1542.

Umdut-ul-Umara—was the Nawab of the Carnatic on whose death in 1801 Lord Wellesley (q.v.) took over the administration of the Carnatic on the ground that Umdut was in treasonable correspondence with Tipu Sultan (q.v.) of Mysore.

United Company, the—was the name given to the East India Company after its union in 1708 with the rival body called 'The English Company Trading to the East Indies' formed towards the close of the seventeenth century. The United Company, however, continued to be popularly known by the older name of the East India Company (q.v.).

United East India Company of the Netherlands—founded in 1602, was a Dutch venture with large financial resources and backing of the state of Holland. It established its headquarters at Batavia and concentrated its attention on the trade in spices with the Spice Islands. It effectively excluded the English from Java and the Moluccas. In India also it established factories at Pulicat, north of Madras, in 1609 and later on at Masulipatam and Surat. Their command of the spice trade, their wealth and the traditional industry and ability of the Dutch enabled them to secure a large share of the trade with India. In Bengal they had a settlement at Chinsurah and they resented the growth of the political influence of the English in Bengal after the battle of Plassey, but Robert Clive anticipated their hostility and attacked and defeated them at the battle of Biddera (q.v.) in November, 1759. Thereafter the Dutch abandoned all attempts to rival the English in the struggle for political power in India and continued only as a commercial people. On the outbreak of war between England and Revolutionary France war was also declared between England and Holland in 1791 and all the Dutch possessions in India passed under British control. Even Java was conquered in 1810, but was restored to the Dutch in 1816.

Universities Act, the—was passed in 1904 during the Viceroyalty of Lord Curzon (*q.v.*). It was based on the recommendations made by a Commission presided over by Mr. (afterwards Sir) Thomas Raleigh, the Law Member of the Viceroy's Executive Council. The Act tightened Government control over the Universities in India by limiting the numbers of senators and syndics and by creating a majority of nominated members in the Senate. The Act, therefore, provoked a great deal of popular agitation against itself. But it had one merit. It aimed at turning the Indian Universities which had so long been only examining bodies into teaching institutions as well, especially for Post-Graduate teaching. It provided for the appointment of University Professors and Lecturers and for the equipment of laboratories and museums. The Calcutta University under the guidance of Sir Asutosh Mookerjee, who became its Vice-Chancellor in 1906, availed itself of these provisions and opened, with generous public endowments, a teaching department which has done much for the advancement of learning not only in Bengal but also over the rest of India.

Universities, Indian—were first established in 1857 in Calcutta, Madras and Bombay on the model of the University of London. These were all at the beginning merely examining bodies. But in 1913 Sir Harcourt Butler, who was the first Education Member of the Viceroy's Executive Council, issued a Resolution recommending the establishment of teaching and residential Universities. Provincial patriotism combined with communal consciousness led in the second quarter of the twentieth century to the establishment of Universities at Patna, Lucknow, Aligarh, Benares, Agra, Delhi, Nagpur, Waltair, Dacca, Mysore, Hyderabad, Chidambram, Trivandrum, Gauhati and Poona. Some of these are residential and most of them are teaching Universities. At present there are more than sixty Universities in India including the *Visva-Bharati* founded by Rabindranath Tagore in 1921. The number is increasing every year. An autonomous body called the University Grants Commission has been constituted and is in charge of the distribution amongst the Indian Universities of whatever funds the Government of India may provide for higher University education in India.

Upagupta—a famous Buddhist monk, was the son of Gupta, a perfumer of Benares. He was the preceptor of Asoka whom he is believed to have converted to Buddhism. It is also believed that he accompanied his royal disciple on a tour of Buddhist holy places and pointed out to him the place of the nativity of

Gautama Buddha which is marked by the Rummindei Pillar Edict of Asoka. (Bhatacharya, S., *Select Asokan Epigraphs*, p. 59)

Upanishadas, the—are treatises dealing with the philosophical ideas and thoughts of the Vedic Indo-Aryans. These do not deal with rituals or sacrifices. These contain deep philosophical speculations regarding the ultimate truth and reality, a knowledge of which was considered sufficient to enable a person to attain *moksha* or emancipation. These revolve round the two conceptions of *Brahman* or the Absolute and the *Atman* or the individual self. The Upanishadas are generally in prose, but some are written in verse as well. These are sometimes parts of the *Aranyakas* and sometimes are separate treatises. At present more than a hundred treatises go by the name of *Upanishadas*, but only twelve on which commentaries were written by Sankaracharya (*q.v.*) are considered to be the original Upanishadic treatises. These twelve are—*Aitareya* and *Kausitaki* belonging to the *Rigveda* (*q.v.*), the *Chhandogya* and *Kena* appertaining to the *Sama Veda* (*q.v.*), the *Taittiria*, *Katha*, *Svetsvatara*, *Brihadaranyaka*, *Isha*, *Prasna*, *Manduka* and *Mandukya* which are parts of the *Yajur Veda* in its two branches. The Upanishadas are considered to be pre-Buddhistic in date, though some of them were certainly later compositions.

Upavedas, the—are subsidiary Vedas dealing with medicine (*Ayurveda*), archery (*Dhanurveda*), music (*Gandharvaveda*) and art and architecture (*Shilpa-shastra*). These were called *Upavedas* because every branch of learning was given a religious significance.

Upton, Colonel—was a military officer under the East India Company who made with the Marathas the treaty of Purandhar (*q.v.*) in 1776 which superseded the earlier treaty of Surat (*q.v.*). The treaty of Purandhar was never enforced.

Urdu language—was evolved as the result of a necessity for carrying on exchange of ideas between the conquering Muhammadans who spoke Turki and Persian and the conquered Indians who spoke Hindi. 'Urdu' is a Turki word meaning 'camp' and Urdu was originally a camp language containing words taken from Persian, Turki and Hindi. Its script is Arabic which is written from the right to the left and its grammar and structure are Hindi in the main. Urdu is spoken in northern India mainly by the Muhammadans and many Hindus also are adepts in it. It gradually developed a literature. Amir Khusru, the famous poet who enjoyed the patronage of Sultan

Ala-ud-din Khalji and who died in A.D. 1325, wrote in Urdu as well as in Persian. In modern times Sir Muhammad Iqbal was the greatest of the Urdu poets.

Usman Khan—a leader of the Afghans in Bengal, took advantage of the uncertainty created by the frequent change of governors in Bengal and roused the Afghan residents in Bengal to a rebellion against the Mughul Emperor Jahangir in 1612. But he was defeated by the Mughuls in March, 1612 and died from the effects of a severe wound received in his head during the battle.

Ustad Isa—was probably the architect who designed the Taj and supervised its construction.

Ustad Mansur—was a famous artist who enjoyed the patronage of Emperor Jahangir. Some of his paintings are still extant and justify the praise that contemporaries bestowed on him as a painter and artist.

Utpala dynasty, the—was founded in about A.D. 855 in Kashmir by Avantivarman (855-83). He was famous for the irrigation works that were carried out in Kashmir during his reign. His son and successor, Sankaravarman, (A.D. 883-902) at first extended the boundaries of his kingdom but was eventually killed by his own subjects whom he had harassed with extremely heavy taxation and by plundering temples. A period of turmoil followed as the result of which Kashmir suffered badly. Two later kings, namely, Partha and his son and successor, Unmattavanti, were bloodthirsty tyrants and the dynasty practically came to an end with the death of Unmattavanti in A.D. 939.

Uttara Kurus—were an Indo-Aryan tribe mentioned in the *Aitareya Brahmana*. They lived beyond the Himalayas.

Uttara Madras, the—were an Indo-Aryan tribe who, like the Uttara Kurus, lived beyond the Himalayas.

V

Vaisali—a famous city in the days of Gautama Buddha (*q.v.*), was the capital of the kingdom of the Lichchhavis (*q.v.*) which comprised the modern Muzaffarpur district in Bihar. Its ruins have been located at and near the village of Basarh near Hajipur on the north bank of the Ganges. In its heyday it was a noble city, ten or twelve miles in circuit, which had the honour of being visited by Gautama Buddha several times. It was conquered and occupied by king Ajatasatru (*q.v.*) of Magadha and passed under his rule. The city, however, continued to be important even in the fifth century A.D. when it figured as the seat of a governor under the Gupta emperor, Chandragupta II (*q.v.*).

Vaishnavism—was preached by four great teachers, namely Nimbarka, Ramanuja, Madhva and Vallabha. They differ in ritual but all agree in a form of modified monotheism and worship the Supreme Being under some such names as Rama, Krishna or Vasudeva. They all reject sacrifices and believe that salvation is attainable by devotion to the deity. They believe in the existence of God, the soul and matter. The soul is entangled in matter and, with the grace of God, struggles for close proximity to Him. The disciples of Nimbarka are numerous in North India, especially in Mathura and worship Krishna and Radha. Ramanuja (*q.v.*) is popular in South India where a form of Vaishnavism had already been preached by poet-saints called Arvars or Alvars who emphasized ecstatic devotion to God. Ramanuja called the Supreme Being Narayana and relied much on the *Bhagavad-Gita*. He held that God is omniscient, omnipresent, almighty and all-merciful and salvation meaning blissful existence near God can be obtained by those souls who constantly meditate on him. The Madhva school flourishes most in South Kanara. It claims that God is like a father to human beings who are like his sons and daughters. Their form of worship is very puritanical. The followers of Vallabha are numerous in Gujarat as well as in the Mathura region. They hold that since the individual and the deity are one, the body should be reverenced and indulged. Their system is, therefore, called the *Pushti-marga* or the path of well-being and comfort. Their doctrines led to much luxury, indulgence and indecency. The most powerful exponent of Vaishnavism in North India was Ramananda (*q.v.*) who flourished in the fourteenth century. He used the vernacular language, ignored caste rules, admitted all as equals—all worshippers of the true God. This God is Rama, rather than Narayana or Krishna. Ramananda took disciples from all classes and amongst his twelve chief disciples were the Muhammadan weaver Kabir (*q.v.*) and the leather-seller, Rai Das. Sri Chaitanya (*q.v.*) in Bengal and Orissa and Sankaradeva (*q.v.*) in Assam were also great exponents of Vaishnavism, though there was an essential difference between the two. Chaitanya idealised the love of Krishna and Radha and emphasized the importance of such ardent unsensual love as the means for attaining bliss, while Sankaradeva preferred to worship Krishna as the boy Gopala and had little to do with the love of Radha. Vaishnavism led to great development of vernacular literature as illustrated by the contributions of Jayadeva (*q.v.*) Vidyapati, Chandidas (*q.v.*) Mirabai, Tulsidas (*q.v.*) Kirtivasa, and Sankaradeva (*q.v.*) who was a poet and dramatist as well as a religious teacher. (Elliot, *Hinduism and Buddhism*, Vol. II)

Vaishyas, the—constituted the third group in the caste-hierarchy of the Hindus. It consisted of traders, merchants and agriculturists. (Dutt, N. K., *Castes in India*)

Vajheska—was probably the name of the father of the Kushan king, Kanishka (*q.v.*).

Vakataka dynasty, the—was founded in central India between Bundelkhand and the Penganga early in the fourth century A.D. by Pravarasena I, son of one Vindhyasakti. He was a powerful ruler who brought Berar under his control. On his death his kingdom was probably divided, the southern portion going to his son, Savasena, and the northern portion to his grandson, Rudrasena I, whose son and successor, Prithivisena I, was probably a contemporary of Samudragupta (*q.v.*) who, for reasons unknown, left Prithivisena I undisturbed in his possessions. Prithivisena's son and successor, Rudrasena II, married Pravatigupta, a daughter of the third Gupta Emperor, Chandragupta II, and very likely became a protected prince. The Gupta Princess had three sons namely, Divakarasena, Damodarasena and Pravarasena II who probably succeeded to the throne one after the other. The last king who ascended the throne in about A.D. 410 appears to have gradually shaken off the Gupta supremacy. Later on in the second half of the fifth century the Vakatakas temporarily became powerful in Malwa and their last king, Harisena, controlled central Deccan. But early in the seventh century the Vakataka dynasty disappeared. Some of the Ajanta caves were executed and dedicated during their supremacy. (*P.H.A.I.*, pp. 541 ff.)

Valabhi—was the name of a city and kingdom founded by the Maitrakas (*q.v.*) at the close of the fifth century A.D. The kingdom originally comprised eastern Kathiawar. The city is now represented by the village of Wala. The first king was Dronosimha who ruled early in the sixth century A.D. with the title of Maharaja. A branch of the dynasty established itself in Mo-la-po or Western Malwa and to this branch belonged King Siladitya-Dharmaditya who reigned in the first decade of the seventh century. The two branches became united during the rule of Siladitya's nephew Dhrubasena (also called Dhrubabhata) who married the daughter of King Harshavardhana and became a protected prince. After the death of Harsha the kingdom of Valabhi continued to be rich and powerful until it was overthrown by the Arabs in about A.D. 770. The city of Valabhi was rich and prosperous and was the residence of several renowned Buddhist teachers. It was also a great centre of learning and in the seventh century it rivalled Nalanda and attracted many students including the Chinese pilgrim, Hiuen Tsang.

Vallalasena—was the second king (*c.* A.D. 1158-79) of the Sena dynasty (*q.v.*) of Bengal. He succeeded his father Vijayasena. He probably defeated the Magadhan king Govindapala and also led an expedition into Mithila. At any rate his dominions comprised Vanga, Varendra, Radha, Bagdi and Mithila. He introduced various social reforms including *Kulinism* with a view to the revival of orthodox Hindu rites in Bengal. He was also a great scholar and author of repute and two of his works, the *Danasagara*, dealing with different kinds of gifts, and the *Adbhutasagara*, dealing with omens and portents, have come down to modern times. (*H.B.* I.)

Valmiki—was the sage (*rishi*) who is traditionally believed to have been the author of the great epic, the *Ramayana* (*q.v.*). He is also believed to have been the earliest of the poets (*adi-kavi*).

Vanavasi (also called Jayanti or Vaijayanti—a famous city on the upper Tungabhadra in the southern part of the Bombay state, came into prominence after the decline of the power of the Satavahanas in the middle of the third century of the Christian era and became very famous as the capital of the Kadambas (*q.v.*) who ruled in the region from the third to the sixth century. It was also known as Jayanti or Vaijayanti. It declined after the fall of the Kadambas.

Varahamihira—was a famous Hindu astronomer who flourished between A.D. 507 and 587. Traditionally he is associated with the court of the great king Vikramaditya of Ujjaini (*q.v.*). His works contain many Greek terms which show that he was deeply versed in Greek science.

Vardhamana Mahavira—*see* Mahavira.

Varthema, Ludovico di—was an Italian traveller who visited

Gujarat during the reign of Sultan Mahmud Bigarha (1459-1511). In his account he has related many fantastic stories about the personal habits of the Sultan.

Varuna—a Vedic deity, represented the Heaven or Sky. Striking invocations are addressed to him in the Rig and the Atharva Vedas.

Vasishka—was the elder son of the Kushan king, Kanishka (q.v.). He predeceased his father who was succeeded by his younger son, Huvishka (q.v.).

Vasishthaputra Pulumayi—was a Satavahana king who ascended the throne soon after A.D. 130. His capital was Baithan, i.e., Paithan or Pratisthana on the Godavari. He ruled till A.D. 154 over an extensive kingdom which included the Krishna-Godavari region as well as Maharashtra.

Vasishthaputra Sri Satakarni—was a Satavahana king whose exact position in the genealogical list has not yet been determined. He was perhaps the Satavahana king who married the daughter of the Great Satrap, Rudradaman (q.v.), was twice defeated in battle by his father-in-law, but was spared destruction on account of their close relationship.

Vasudeva—is the name of a deity whose worship was prevalent as early as the time of Panini, i.e., the fourth century B.C. It is only another name of the Great God Vishnu.

Vasudeva—was the founder of the Kanva dynasty of Pataliputra in succession to the Sungas (q.v.). He was a Brahman by caste and was the minister of the last Sunga king, Devabhuti or Devabhumi (q.v.) on whose assassination he occupied the throne in about 73 B.C. The dynasty which he founded comprised four kings, namely, Vasudeva who ruled for nine years, his son Bhumimitra, his son Narayana, and his son Susarman who was overthrown by Simuka (q.v.), the founder of the Satavahana dynasty in about 28 B.C.

Vasudeva I—the last of the great kings of the Kushan dynasty (q.v.) ruled probably from A.D. 155 to A.D. 177. His coins have been found in large numbers in Sind, the Panjab and Uttar Pradesh but none of his inscriptions has been found outside Mathura. This suggests the shrinkage of his dominions just as his name suggests a change in religion from Buddhism to the Brahmanical cult. He was probably a worshipper of Siva whose image has been found on many of his coins. The Kushan empire speedily declined after the death of Vasudeva I and nothing but the names are known of the later Kushan kings who are designated Vasudeva II and Vasudeva III.

Vasumitra—a renowned Buddhist philosopher and author, lived in the time of Kanishka (*q.v.*). He presided over the meeting of the Buddhist Church Council (*q.v.*) held in the reign of Kanishka in Kashmir. His main work was the *Mahavibhasa Sastra.*

Vatapi (or Badami)—the capital of the Chalukya dynasty of kings founded by Pulakeshin I in the sixth century A.D., was situated in the Bijapur district of the modern Bombay State.

Vayu Purana, **the**—is one of the oldest of the eighteen Puranas (*q.v.*). It probably got its present shape in the fourth century A.D., but its genealogical lists of the ancient Indian kings have been considered to be more reliable and complete than other such Puranic lists.

Vedangas, **the**—are supplementary sections of the Vedas. These are written in *sutra* style and deal with six subjects, namely, phonetics (*siksha*), religious practice (*kalpa*), grammar (*vyakarana*), metre (*chhandas*), etymology (*nirukta*) and astronomy or astrology (*jyotisha*).

Vedanta, **the**—is a collective designation for the philosophy of the *Upanishadas* (*q.v.*) which are integral parts of the Vedas. Literally the term means the end or goal of the Vedas. It is mainly based on the *Brahma-Sutra* by Badrayana and its greatest exponent was Sankara (*q.v.*) who summarised the main idea of his monistic Vedanta philosophy in half a sloka: *Brahma satyam jaganmithya jivo Brahmaiva kevalam* (Brahman is reality, the world is illusion and the soul is God). It further holds that religious rites like worship and meditation which make *Isvara* (God) their object, lead to heavenly bliss, but not to *moksha* or emancipation which is attainable only by one who knows that his true self is *Brahman.* Vedanta, however, was interpreted in a different way by other sages like Ramanuja (*q.v.*) who unlike Sankara, was a sectarian. He identified the Supreme Deity (*Brahman*) with Vishnu or Narayana who is in all elements and in all human souls and whose grace, attainable by and through *bhakti* or devotion and good works, releases the soul which does not merge with the lord but enjoys near him a personal existence of eternal bliss and peace. This system is known as *Visishtadvaita* or modified monism which is upheld by Vaishnavism (*q.v.*). The monism of Sankara and the modified monism of Ramanuja are the two principal systems of Vedanta philosophy, of which there are other interpretations like those of Nimbarka and Madva. (Hiriyana, *History of Indian Philosophy;* Swami Vivekananda, *The Vedanta,* Vols. I, III, VI and VIII of his works)

Vedas, the—are the most ancient sacred books of the Hindus, and probably the oldest of such works in the world. The Hindus believe that they are divine revelations made by the Supreme being to the various seers (*risis*) to whom the hymns are attributed, and are, therefore, eternal (*sanátana*). They are also called *sruti* (that which is heard) and were to be learnt by the disciple from the preceptor by hearing and repeating. The Vedas are four in number, namely, the Rig, the Sama, the Yajur and the Atharva, and are held to contain the basis of Hinduism. Modern Hinduism differs much from the Vedic religion, but it ever appeals to its authority. Each of the Vedas is divided into four parts, namely, *Samhita, Brahmana, Aranyaka* and *Upanishada.* The *Samhitas* are collections of hymns, divided into *Suktas* or hymns. The Rig-Veda Samhita, for example, consists of 1,028 *suktas* which are classified into 10 *mandalas* or books. The *Brahmanas* are prose texts containing observations on various sacrificial rites and ceremonies. The principal *Brahmanas* are the *Aitareya* and *Kausitaki* belonging to the Rig Veda, the *Tandya* and *Jaiminiya* attached to the Sama Veda, the *Taittiriya* and the *Satapatha* appertaining to the Yajur Veda and the *Gopatha* to the Atharva Veda. The *Aranyakas* or forest texts were more speculative than ritualistic and were meant for elderly persons who had retired from active domestic lives to completely secluded lives in forests. The *Aranyakas* are complements of the *Brahmanas,* each of which has an *Aranyaka* attached to it bearing the same name. Lastly, the *Upanishadas* (*q.v.*) are predominantly speculative and philosophical texts written generally in prose. They mark a reaction against a mere sacrificial religion and emphasizes what is believed to be the ultimate truth and reality, a knowledge of which was essential for securing the emancipation (*moksha*) of man. The Rig Veda is certainly the oldest of the four Vedas but its age has not been precisely fixed. It has been attributed by some to so ancient an age as the fourth millennium B.C., while some would not assign it an earlier date than five centuries before the Behistun inscription (*q.v.*) or the Avesta of the Zoroastrians. In any case, the Rig Veda represents the earliest of the literature of the ancient Hindus and affords the earliest account of the religious, social, economic life of the Indo-Aryans. (Tilak, B. G., *Orion;* Keith, A. B., *Religion and Philosophy of the Vedas*; Majumdar, R. C., *The Vedic Age; Cambridge History of Ancient India,* Vol. I; Dutt, R. C., *Rig Veda Samhita*)

Vellore, Mutiny of Indian troops at—was one of the earliest of the abortive mutinies in the Indian army. In 1806 the Indian troops at Vellore rose in mutiny in protest against certain new regulations which were considered to infringe on their religious practices. The Mutiny was forcibly suppressed within a short time, but its lesson was ignored with disastrous consequences later on.

Vengi, the kingdom of—situated between the Godavari and the Krishna, was conquered by Samudragupta (*q.v.*) in the fourth century B.C. when it was ruled probably by a Pallava prince. In about A.D. 611 it was conquered by the Chalukya king, Pulakeshin II, who established his brother, Kubja Vishnuvardhana, as his viceroy with his capital at Pishtapura, now Pithapuram, in the Godavari district. Four years later, Vengi was made an independent kingdom by Kubja Vishnuvardhana who founded there the line of the Eastern Chalukyas (*q.v.*) which lasted until A.D. 1070 when it was merged with the kingdom of the Cholas.

Venkata I—a king of the Tuluva dynasty of Vijayanagara, succeeded in 1542 his father Achyuta, but was murdered in the year of his accession.

Venkata—the third king of the Fourth or Aravidu dynasty of Vijayanagara (*q.v.*) which had been destroyed in 1565, removed the capital from Penugonda to Chandragiri. His rule began in 1585 and the date when it ended is uncertain. He was a generous patron of Telugu poets and Vaishnava authors.

Venkatadri—a brother of Ramaraja, who was practically the ruler of Vijayanagar (*q.v.*) during the reign of Sadasiva (1542-65), was a great general who perished in the battle of Talikota (*q.v.*) in 1565.

Ventura, General—an Italian soldier of fortune, was employed by Maharaja Ranjit Singh (*q.v.*) and helped him in organising the Sikh infantry. He was very generously treated by Ranjit Singh, was appointed by him as a provincial governor and was granted a whole village as a *jagir*. He, however, left the Panjab soon after the death of Ranjit Singh in 1839. (Sinha, N. K., *Ranjit Singh*)

Verelest, Henry—the Governor of Bengal (1767-69), was a person of only moderate ability, but knew how to make his way up the official ladder. He came out to Bengal as a writer in the Company's service and rose to be a member of the Select Committee of Four Advisers of Robert Clive (*q.v.*) during the latter's second term of Governorship (1765-67) and succeeded him on his retirement in 1767. As Governor he drew a remuneration of £ 27,093 per year in addition to his share in private trade. His administration was rapacious and was largely responsible for the terrible famine (*q.v.*) that visited Bengal in 1769-70 and carried off one-third of the population.

Vernacular Press Act, the—passed in 1878 by the Viceroy, Lord Lytton (*q.v.*) imposed restrictions on newspapers published in Indian languages not applicable to those published in English. This Act led to a great agitation amongst the Indians and was repealed by Lord Ripon (*q.v.*) in 1882.

Viceroy, the—was the official designation conferred on the Governor-General of India after the assumption of the administration of India by the Crown of England in 1858. Lord Canning, who was then the Governor-General, became the first Viceroy with effect from 1 November, 1858. The office was renamed Crown-Representative by the Government of India Act, 1935. Lord Linlithgow was the last Viceroy.

Victoria, Queen and Empress—(1819-1901)—ascended the throne of England in 1837 and bore the title of Queen of Great Britain and Ireland till 1877 when she was also proclaimed Empress of India. The administration of India was transferred from the East India Company to the Crown of England in 1858 and the Proclamation that was issued in the name of the Queen announcing the change, made her popular with the Indians, who believed that some of the liberal principles enunciated in the Queen's Proclamation (*q.v.*) owed their incorporation in the document to the personal liberal views of the Queen. She never visited India and in the matter of Indian administration she always acted as a constitutional sovereign giving approval to policies as advised by her responsible Ministers, yet she earned great popularity with the Indians and her death in 1901 was generally regretted all over India.

Victoria Memorial in Calcutta—was conceived and carried out by Lord Curzon (*q.v.*) who thought of founding a grand monument to British rule in India. It is a stately building in the midst of spacious grounds in the Calcutta Maidan, but it lacks the beauty as well as the grandeur of the Taj (*q.v.*) which Lord Curzon probably wanted to excel.

Vidarbha—was the ancient name of modern Berar (*q.v.*).

Vidisa—is an ancient town, now called Bhilsa.

Vidyasagar, Pandit Iswarchandra (1820-91)—was an eminent educationist and social reformer. Born in a poor Brahman family in the district of Midnapur in Bengal, he was educated in the Government Sanskrit College, Calcutta, where he became a Professor in 1851 and from which he retired in 1858 as its Principal. Originally a Sanskrit scholar, he later on learnt English of which he became a master. As early as 1847 he published his first Bengali prose work named *Betal-Pancha-vimsati* which was followed by other Bengali prose works which have earned for him the title of the father of Bengali prose literature. He was an orthodox Hindu who refused to attend Government functions where his garb of *dhoti*, *chaddar* and slippers was banned. His ideas of social life were liberal and advanced and his greatest achievement was the legalisation by the British Government of the remarriage of Hindu widows. He was a great personality, charitable, benevolent and unbending where self-respect was in question. He founded many schools and the Metropolitan College, now renamed after him the Vidya-sagar College, Calcutta, where Hindu students might get higher education on payment of such small tuition fees as were payable by Muslim students in Government Colleges as the result of the Mahsin endowments. A Brahman and a Sanskritist, he was an earnest advocate of Western education in Bengal and was opposed to the reservation of the Government Sanskrit College exclusively for the study of Sanskrit. He advocated the introduction of the study of Western philosophy and of the applied sciences in its curriculum so that his countrymen might not lag behind in materialistic knowledge. He was one of the towering personalities of Bengal who significantly contributed to its re-awakening in the nineteenth century.

Vigraharaja—was a name borne by four kings of the Chouhan dynasty of Ajmer. Of these four, Vigraharaja II ruled in the third quarter of the tenth century and Vigraharaja IV flourished in the middle of the twelfth century. He considerably extended his ancestral dominions. He was a patron of Sanskrit literature and was a dramatist himself who wrote the *Harakali-nataka*. He was the uncle and a predecessor of Prithviraja or Rai Pithora (*q.v.*).

Vijaya I (also called Vira-Vijaya)—was a king of the First dynasty of Vijayanagar (*q.v.*) who was associated for a short time with Devaraya II (*q.v.*) at the beginning of his reign which commenced in 1425, but was soon removed.

Vijaya II—was a king of Vijayanagar (*q.v.*) for only a year (1446-47).

Vijayanagar—was the name of a city as well as of a kingdom founded in the Deccan to the south of the Tungabhadra in about A.D. 1336 by two brothers, Harihara and Bukka, sons of Sangama. The foundation of the city was finished in 1343 and within the next ten years the kingdom extended from the Eastern to the Western Oceans across the Deccan. Harihara I ruled till his death in 1354-55 and the administration was run by his brother Bukka I for the next twenty-two years (1355-77). Neither of the two brothers assumed the royal title which was first adopted by Harihara II the son and, successor of Bukka I, who ruled from 1377 to 1404. The kings of Vijayanagar were called Rayas who ruled the country with great success and splendour up to 1565. During this period there were three dynasties of kings, namely, the First or Sangama dynasty comprising Harihara II (1377-1404), his son Bukka II (1404-06), Devaraya I (1406-22), Ramachandra (1422), Vira Vijaya (1422-25), Devaraya II (1425-47), Mallikarjuna (1447-65), Virupaksha (1465-85) and Praudhadevaraya (1485). The second or Saluva dynasty was founded by Saluva Narasimha who had been the minister of the later kings of the First dynasty which he overthrew. Narasimha ruled from 1486 to 1492 and was succeeded by his son Immadi Narasimha (1492-1503) who was the second and last king of the Saluva or Second dynasty which was overthrown by his minister Narasa Nayaka, who founded the Third or Tuluva dynasty which comprised six kings, namely, Narasa Nayaka (1503), his son Vira Narasimha (1503-09), Krishnadeva Raya (1509-29), Achyuta (1529-42), Venkata (1542), and Sadasiva (1542-65) whose reign closed with the disastrous battle of Talikota leading to the destruction of the city of Vijayanagar. Sadasiva fled to Penugonda where he was deposed in 1570 by Tirumalla who founded the Fourth dynasty which ruled from 1570-1642 with its capital, first at Penugonda, and, later on, at Chandragiri. But the history of the kingdom of Vijayanagar had practically ended with the destruction of the city. The most prominent characteristic of the history of Vijayanagar was its perennial struggle with its northern neighbours the Muhammadan Bahmani kingdom and its offshoots. The bone of contention between the two kingdoms was the Raichur Doab, besides the hostility due to the religious differences between the rulers of the two kingdoms. In this struggle the Bahmani sultans had generally the advantage. It was only during the reign of Krishnadeva Raya (*q.v.*) (1509-29) who was the greatest of the kings of Vijayanagar, that the Hindu kingdom had the advantage over its Muhammadan neighbours, regained Raichur, and defeated the sultans of Bidar and Bijapur. He extended his sovereignty over the whole of the old Presidency of Madras as well as over Mysore. But the advantages thus gained were not only lost, but the great city of Vijayanagar was destroyed by a combination of the Muhammadan sultans of Bijapur, Golconda, Ahmadnagar and Bidar who routed the Vijayanagar army in the battle of Talikota in 1565, forced the reigning king Sadasiva to save his life by flight to Penugonda in the interior of the kingdom and plundered and destroyed the city of Vijayanagar which was completely razed to the ground. All through its existence the city by its grandeur, wealth, fortifications and ample provisions extorted the admiration of foreign travellers like Nicolo Conti (1420), Abdur Razzak (1443), Paes (1522) and Nuniz (1535). Abdur Razzak went to the length of observing, "The city is such that the eye has not seen nor ear heard of any place resembling it upon the earth. It is so built that it has seven concentric fortified walls, one within the other." This city was not only densely populated but was also adequately provisioned. Yet its citizens did not offer, or even organise, any resistance to the Muhammadan invaders who proceeded leisurely to sack and destroy the city after their victory at Talikota. This circumstance certainly suggests that in spite of the prosperity of the kingdom the general mass of the population was never inspired by any devotion to, and love for, the ruling dynasty. The Vijayanagar kings were ardent patrons of Sanskrit learning. The great Vedic commentator Sayana (*q.v.*) and his equally learned brother, Madhava, served under the early kings of Vijayanagar. They were also great builders who evolved a distinct school of art, painting and architecture, excelling specially in building amply provided forts. (Sewell, R., *A Forgotten Empire;* Saletore, B.A., *Social and Pol. Life in Vijayanagar Empire*)

Vijnaneswara—a celebrated Hindu lawyer and jurist, lived in Kalyani, the capital of the Chalukyas, during the reign (A.D. 1076-1126) of Vikramanka (*q.v.*) (also called Vikramaditya Chalukya). His work, the *Mitakshara*, is considered the most authoritative exposition of the Hindu law of succession as prevailing over the whole of India outside Bengal and Assam where Raghunanda's (*q.v.*) *Dāyabhag* is followed.

Vikrama era—dates from 58 to 57 B.C. and is supposed to have been established by a king named Vikramaditya (*q.v.*). (*see ante* Eras, ancient Indian.)

Vikramaditya—meaning 'the Sun of Prowess' was a title assumed by various ancient Indian kings. Tradition associates it with a king of Ujjaini, in whose court lived nine learned scholars (*navaratna*) including Kalidas (*q.v.*), who was the repository of prowess and all virtues and who defeated the Sakas. The Vikrama era dating from 58-57 B.C. is also attributed to king Vikramaditya. But sober history does not know of any such powerful king with the said title ruling in western India in the second half of the first century of the pre-Christian era. It knows that the title was borne by several historical sovereigns, namely, Chandragupta II (A.D. 380-415), his grandson Skandagupta (A.D. 455-67), and several Chalukya kings, viz. Vikramaditya I (A.D. 655-80), Vikramaditya II (A.D. 733-46), Tribhuvanamalla (A.D. 1009-16), and Vikramaditya or Vikramanka (A.D. 1076-1125). Of these several kings Chandragupta II, the third Gupta emperor, who defeated the Saka satraps, who had his capital at Ujjaini and whose reign was marked by great intellectual achievements as well as by all-round peace and prosperity and in whose reign Kalidas probably flourished, has been considered to have had the best claims for being considered as the original king Vikramaditya who later on passed into legends. (Bhandarkar, R. G., *Hist. of the Deccan*)

Vikramanka (or Vikramaditya)—a Chalukya king of Kalyani (1076-1126), was a successful warrior and patron of literature. His court poet was Bilhana who wrote the biography of his royal patron in his work *Vikramanka-charita* and the great Hindu jurist, Vijnaneswara,t he author of the *Mitakshara*, the leading authority on Hindu law outside Bengal and Assam, enjoyed his patronage. He bore the title of Vikramaditya.

Vikramasila—the seat of a famous Buddhist monastery, was situated at Patharghata in the Bhagalpur district of Bihar. The monastery at Vikramasila was founded by the Pala king, Devapala (*q.v.*). It developed into a famous seat of learning and it was from here that the renowned Buddhist monk, Atisha (*q.v.*) went on invitation to Tibet in A.D. 1038.

Vinaya Pitaka, **the**—is the second of the three Pitakas (baskets) which constitute the Buddhist scriptures known as the *Tripitaka* (Three Baskets), the other two being the *Sutta* and *Abhidhamma* Pitakas. The *Vinaya Pitaka* deals primarily with the rules of monastic discipline. It is divided into three parts viz. *Suttabibhanga, Parivara* and *Khandaka.* The first again includes the *Patimakkha* which is a list of offences which a monk might commit and must confess and the last, *Khandaka,* is subdivided into two parts, namely, the *Mahavagga* and the *Chaluvagga.*

Vira Vallala—a Hoysala king (1173-1220) of Dvarasamudra (Mysore) was a grandson of the famous Hoysala king Vishnuvardhana (*q.v.*), extended his dominions to the north of Mysore, defeated the Yadavas of Devagiri and made the Hoysalas the dominant power in Southern India.

Vira-Narasimha—a king (1505-09) of Vijayanagar, killed Immadi Narasimha, the last king of the Saluva or Second dynasty of Vijayanagar and re-asserted the royal authority over the kingdom. He was succeeded by his half-brother, Krishnadeva Raya (*q.v.*), the greatest king of Vijayanagar.

Vira Saiva Sect.—*see* Lingayet sect.

Virupaksha I—a son of king Harihara II (*q.v.*) of Vijayanagar, seized the throne on the death of his father in A.D. 1404, but was promptly deposed and ousted by his brother, Bukka II (*q.v.*).

Virupaksha II—the penultimate king (1465-85) of the First dynasty of Vijayanagar, was given over to vices and was murdered by his eldest son who in his turn was murdered by his younger brother, Praudhadevaraya, the last king of the dynasty.

Visala-deva—the Chouhan king of Ajmer, led an Indian army collected at the request of king Anandapal (*q.v.*) of the Panjab against Sultan Mahmud in A.D. 1008, but was defeated.

Vishnu—an important deity of the Hindus, is worshipped as the Supreme God by the Vaishnavas. Along with Brahma and Maheswara (Siva) he forms the Trinity of the Hindus.

Vishnugupta—*see* Kautilya.

***Vishnu Purana,* the**—is one of the 18 Puranas of the Hindus and is considered to be one of the oldest. It best conforms to the five requirements of a Purana and treats with primary and secondary creations, genealogies of gods and patriarchs, reigns of various Manus and the history of ancient dynasties. It is specially consecrated to the glorification of God Vishnu.

Vishnuvardhana (also called Bittideva or Bittiga)—the Hoysala king of Dvarasamudra (A.D. 1110-41), waged many wars and extended his territories, but was partially subordinate to the Chalukyas. He occupied a very important place in the religious history of the time. He was originally a Jain, but he came under the influence of the renowned Vaishnava sage, Ramanuja and became converted to Vaishnavism. It was after his conversion that he dropped his former name of Bittideva or Bittiga and adopted the name of Vishnuvardhana. Thereafter he devoted himself to the glorification of his new faith by the construction of temples of unsurpassed magnificence some of which are still extant at Belur and Halebid and of which the best example is the temple of Hoysalesvara at Halebid which has eleven running friezes, each 700 feet or more in length, covered with elaborate sculptures depicting elephants, tigers, scrolls, horsemen and celestial beasts and birds, and which has been aptly described as 'one of the most marvellous exhibitions of human labour'.

Viswas Rao—was the eldest son and prospective heir of the Peshwa, Balaji Baji Rao (*q.v.*). At the age of 17 he was appointed Commander-in-Chief of the Maratha army that was sent to northern India to stop the progress of Ahmad Shah Abdali. The actual command was in the hands of his uncle, Sadasiva Rao Bhao. The expedition culminated in the Third Battle of Panipat on 13 January, 1761, where Viswas Rao was killed and the Marathas were defeated.

Vivekananda, Swami (1863-1902)—was a Hindu *sanyasi* who won international renown and organised the Ramakrishna Mission (*q.v.*). Born in a middle-class Bengali family in Calcutta, Swami Vivekananda whose original name was Narendranath Dutta, took the B.A. degree of the Calcutta University and was studying law when he became a disciple of Ramakrishna Paramahamsa (*q.v.*), renounced the world, became a *sanyasi*, travelled all over India from the Himalayas to Cape Comorin, was warmly received everywhere by princes as well as peasants and then in 1893 went to the United States to attend the famous Parliament of Religions at Chicago. He made his mark there by his very first speech and the many discourses that he delivered in different places in the U.S.A. brought him fame and friends. Several Americans, men and women, became his disciples and centres for the study of the teachings of Ramakrishna were established in the States. From America he went to England in 1896 where also he was warmly received by many and several Englishmen and women, including Miss Margaret Noble (Sister Nivedita) (*q.v.*), became his disciples. On his return to India in 1896, he received a hero's welcome and began to exercise a great deal of influence in moulding the religious and social ideals of his countrymen. To the catholicity and universalism of the religious teachings of Ramakrishna he added an emphasis on social service, on efforts to ameliorate the sufferings of men, to remove their ignorance and to help in their economic regeneration which was to be effected by improving character and developing the spirit of self-sacrifice. He organised the disciples of Ramakrishna first into a body known as the Ramakrishna Mission, founded a permanent home for it at Belur where he established the Belur Math and went on another tour all over India. He went to the U.S.A. again in 1899 and established at San Francisco a centre for the study of Vedanta and a branch of the Ramakrishna Mission. On his way back he toured several countries of Europe and felt and declared that Europe was on the verge of a war. On his return to India, he established a branch of the Ramakrishna Mission with a school and a hospital at Benares. Exertions, hardships of the life of a *sanyasi* and constant worry about the future of the organisations founded by him broke his health and he died in 1902 at the early age of thirty-nine. His speeches and writings which have been since collected and published by the Ramakrishna Mission, cover eight volumes, each running into about 600 pages of closely printed matter. Amongst his works the *Jnana-Yoga*, the *Raja-Yoga* and the *Bhakti-Yoga* are the most famous and were all originally written in English. The only book that he wrote in Bengali was *Prachya and Paschatya* (The East and the West) which reveals the depth of his vision and the ideals that he stood for. He was a tireless correspondent whose letters so far published run into several hundreds. He kept a diary which unfortunately has not yet been published. His greatness lies in the circumstance that in the nineteenth century when India was considered to be a very backward country which had everything to learn from Europe, he convinced Europe that India had a great culture and a great religion from which Europe and the world have much to learn. He thus instilled a new self-respect in his countrymen and thus prepared the way for their self-assertion. As Sree Chakrabarti Rajagopalachari observes, "Swami Vivekananda saved Hinduism and saved India. But for him we would have lost our religion and would not have gained our freedom. We, therefore, owe everything to Swami Vivekananda." (*Works of Swami Vivekananda*, 8 volumes; *Life of Swami Vivekananda* by His Eastern and Western Disciples; *Swami Vivekananda Centenary Memorial Volume*; ed. R. C. Majumdar)

Vizagapatam—is a port on the Coromandel coast of India. The English established a factory there early in the eighteenth century. Later on it became a part of the British Indian empire. It was bombed by the Japanese in 1942, but was not severely hit. It is now being developed into a modern port with shipbuilding facilities.

Vrijjis, the—were a tribal people, better known as the Lichchhavis, who gave their name to the locality now represented by Muzaffarpur district in Bihar. Their capital was at Vaisali (*q.v.*). They formed an aristocratic republic which was controlled by an assembly of the notables, each of whom had equal control over the administration. Their system of government was, however, so efficient that Gautama Buddha is said to have formed the organisation of the Buddhist Sangha on the model of the assembly of the Vrijjis. They were subdued by king Ajatasatru (*q.v.*) in the fifth century B.C., but continued to play an important part in Indian history till the beginning of the fourth century A.D. when a marriage with the Lichchhavi princess Kumara Devi enabled Chandragupta I (*q.v.*) who was then a petty ruler, to lay the foundation of the Imperial Gupta dynasty of Magadha.

Vyaghraraja—a king of a south-Indian kingdom named Mahakantara, is mentioned in the Allahabad Pillar inscription of Samudragupta (*q.v.*) as one of the several kings of south India who were vanquished by the Gupta Emperor, but was later on restored as a matter of grace.

Vyankaji (or Venkajee)—a younger step-brother of Shivaji I (*q.v.*) held the *jagir* in Bijapur state which had been granted by the sultan to their father, Shahji. His mother's name was Tuka Bai. He did not in any way help his elder brother, Shivaji, in founding the independent kingdom of Maharashtra.

Vyasa (better known as Vyasadeva)—was, according to Hindu tradition, a very learned sage to whom is attributed the great epic, the *Mahabharata*, the eighteen *Puranas* as well as the *Bhagavad Gita* and the *Vedanta Sutra*. His existence is vouched for by no other evidence than literary tradition which, however, is so strong and old that it cannot be brushed aside. It may, however, be true that his reputation as an author led many later writers to pass off their works under cover of his great name.

W

Wadgaon, the Convention of—was concluded in January, 1779, by Colonel Cockburn who was leading a British army against the Marathas during the First Maratha War. Cockburn suffered reverses in the Western Ghats at the hands of the

Marathas and escaped destruction by signing the Convention of Waḍgaon by which all territories acquired by the Bombay Government since 1773 were to be surrendered, the force that was to arrive from Bengal was to be recalled, and the Sindhia was to receive from the British a share of the revenues of Broach. The Convention of Waḍgaon was disowned by the Governor-General, Warren Hastings, who soon took measures to retrieve the position.

Wahabi movement, the—was a militant movement amongst the Indian Muhammadans directed against Western culture and Western rule. It began in the early nineteenth century and had its headquarters at Sitana, north of Peshawar. It established recruiting centres at Patna and in some places in Bengal and its influence spread far and wide through secret channels throughout India. Driven from Sitana in 1858 by a British punitive expedition the Wahabis established themselves at Malka and menaced the Panjab in 1863. A British army under Sir Neville Chamberlain captured and destroyed Malka in December, 1863 and the Wahahi movement was crushed.

Walajah, Nawab—*see* Muhammad Ali.

Wali-ullah Shah (1703-62)—was a famous Muhammadan theologian of Delhi. He translated the *Quran* into Persian and started a movement for reforming Islam from within. His disciple, Sayyid Ahmad of Bareilly, however, later on joined the militant Wahabi movement (*q.v.*).

Wandiwash, the battle of—was fought in January, 1760, between an English army led by Sir Eyre Coote (*q.v.*) and a French army led by Count de Lally (*q.v.*). The French were decisively defeated. Bussy (*q.v.*) was made a prisoner and Lally was driven to Pondicherry which also was forced to surrender in January, 1761. The battle of Wandiwash thus practically ended in British triumph the prolonged Anglo-French conflict in the Carnatic. The power of the French in India fell never to rise again.

Wang-hiuen-tse—a Chinese envoy, visited India three times in A.D. 643, 646-47, and 657. During his first mission Emperor Harshavardhana was alive, but the Emperor had died before Wang-hiuen-tse was in his capital on his second mission. On the death of Harsha his minister, Arjuna, who usurped Harsha's throne, attacked the Chinese mission, massacred the escort and robbed its property; but Wang-hiuen-tse succeeded in escaping to Tibet whose king Srong-tsan-Gampo (*q.v.*) placed at his disposal an army with whose aid Wang-hiuen-tse made a raid on Tirhut, defeated and captured the usurper, Arjuna, and returned in triumph to China. Wang-hiuen-tse came to India on his last visit of pilgrimage in A.D. 657, offered robes at Buddhist holy places like Vaisali and Bodh Gaya and returned through Afghanistan by the Pamir route.

War of the Austrian Succession—which was fought in Europe from 1740 to 1748, led to the outbreak of the First Anglo-French War in India (*q.v.*), generally known as the First Carnatic War.

Warangal—was the name of the city and of the kingdom of which it was the capital. It was ruled by kings of the Kakatiya dynasty (*q.v.*). It was over-run by Sultan Ala-ud-din Khalji in A.D. 1310 and was subsequently annexed to the Delhi sultanate.

Watson, Admiral—a naval officer under the East India Company, arrived in India in 1754 and remained in Madras waters till 1756 when he was sent at the head of a fleet of five men-of-war and five transports to help Robert Clive in re-capturing Calcutta (*q.v.*) which had been captured recently by Nawab Siraj-ud-daulah (*q.v.*). Watson had a very easy task, for he met with no opposition and easily recovered Calcutta in January, 1757, and occupied Hughli a few days later. Then in March, 1757 he sailed up the Ganges and bombarded from his ships the French forts at Chandernagore (*q.v.*) which was forced to surrender. He then entered, along with Clive, in the intrigues for deposing Nawab Siraj-ud-daulah, but he refused to put on the faked copy of the treaty meant for Omichand (*q.v.*) his signature which was forged by Robert Clive.

Wavell, Lord (formerly Sir Archibald) (1883-1950)—the Governor-General of India from 1943 to 1947 in succession to Lord Linlithgow (*q.v.*), was a great general and the C-in-C. of the Indian army from 1941 to 1943 and ousted the Japanese from their conquests in Burma and India. The first task that he performed was to tackle with military efficiency and promptitude the Bengal famine and the food position steadily improved. After the War it fell to him to arrange for the peaceful transfer of power of administration in India from British hands to those of Indians in accordance with the Government of India Act, 1935. The task was made difficult by Indian suspicions about the bona fides of British intentions as well as by the mutual distrust between the nationalist Congress which was a predominantly Hindu organisation and the exclusively communal Muslim League which was determined to resist Hindu predominance. He held several conferences between the Congress and Muslim League leaders, suppressed a short-lived naval mutiny in Bombay in February, 1946 which made him conscious of the narrow margin by which the British held power in India, received the Cabinet Mission (*q.v.*), and, on the failure of their plan, formed with the support of the Congress the Interim Government (*q.v.*) with Pandit Jawaharlal Nehru (*q.v.*) as the Vice-President. The League resented the step, and, proclaiming the 16th August, 1946 as a 'Direct Action Day', plunged India into bloody communal riots which Lord Wavell, with all his military fame and resources, failed either to forestall or to suppress promptly. Both communities suffered in localities where the one or the other was in the majority. In these circumstances, Lord Wavell was recalled in 1947 and was succeeded by Lord Mountbatten (*q.v.*). He died in 1950.

Wazid Ali Shah—the last Nawab of Oudh (1847-56) was deposed by Lord Dalhousie (*q.v.*) in 1856 on the ground of misgovernment and deported to Calcutta where he lived on a pension of twelve lakhs of rupees till his death.

Wazir Ali—an illegitimate son of Nawab Asaf-ud-daulah (1775-97) of Oudh, was recognised on his father's death in 1797 as the Nawab of Oudh, but was next year deposed and replaced by the British Government with his uncle Sa'adat Ali (1798-1814). Later on he became involved in the murder of the British Resident, Mr. Cherry, and attempted a rebellion which was suppressed.

Wazir Khan—the Mughul fouzdar of Sirhind, fought against Guru Govinda Singh (*q.v.*) and murdered his two sons. Soon after the death of Guru Govinda in 1708 Banda attacked Sirhind and defeated and killed Wazir Khan.

Waziris, the—are a frontier tribe living on the British side of the Indo-Afghan frontier as marked by the Durand line (*q.v.*). They gave their name to the territory occupied by them. They were a turbulent people and the Indo-British Government had to send several punitive expenditions against them in order to keep them under control.

Wedderburn, Sir William—was a distinguished member of the Indian Civil Service. After his retirement from the Indian Civil Service he took a leading part in encouraging the foundation of the Indian National Congress and attended its first session held in Bombay in December, 1885. Later on he also presided over two Congress sessions in 1899 and 1910 and continued to be a supporter of the Indian national cause till his death.

Wellesley, Arthur (later on Duke of Wellington) (1769-1852)—
was a younger brother of Lord Wellesley, Governor-General
in India (*q.v.*). He came to India as a military officer in 1797,
that it to say, a year earlier than his elder brother and continued to be in the Company's military service in India till
1805. He took a prominent part in the wars of the time,
especially in the Second Maratha War (*q.v.*) in the course of
which he won great renown by defeating the Marathas at
the battles of Assaye (*q.v.*) and Argaon (*q.v.*) in 1803. He also
evinced great diplomatic skill in negotiating the treaties of
Deogaon (*q.v.*) with the Bhonsla and of Surji-Arjangaon (*q.v.*)
with the Sindhia. After his return from India he won greater
fame as the British general who won the Peninsular War and
defeated Napoleon at the battle of Waterloo. In 1828 he became
for a short time the Prime Minister of England and continued
to be consulted on all military and Indian affairs till his death
in 1852.

Wellesley, Marquess Richard Colley—the Governor-General
in India from 1798 to 1805, was one of the greatest British
rulers of India. His administration was marked by great expansion of the British dominions in India which he effected by
war as well as by peaceful annexation. He deliberately gave
up the policy of Non-intervention (*q.v.*) and adopted the
aggressive policy of subsidiary alliance by which the Indian
Princes were required to come under British protection on
condition that they would maintain a contingent of British
troops within their states, accept a British Resident at their
headquarters, would have no relations with any foreign powers
except through the British and would not employ in their
services any foreigner without the previous consent of the
British Government in return for the Company's promise to
protect them against all foreign attacks as well as internal enemies. The Nizam accepted the subsidiary alliance and thus was
peacefully turned into a subordinate ally of the British. Tipu
Sultan (*q.v.*) of Mysore refused to accept it and Wellesley fought
against him the Fourth Mysore War (*q.v.*) in which Tipu was
defeated and killed and his dominions except Mysore and its
neighbourhood were annexed to the British empire. Over
Mysore also a Hindu Raja was set up as a subsidiary Prince.
Peshwa Baji Rao II accepted the subsidiary alliance by the treaty
of Bassein (*q.v.*), but as the Maratha chiefs would not accept it
Wellesley fought against them the Second Maratha War (*q.v.*)
which enabled him to annex to the British dominions the major

parts of the territories of the Bhonsla, the Sindhia and the Holkar, establishing British rule over Central India, Malwa, Gujarat, and Delhi. On the ground of misgovernment Wellesley also annexed the Carnatic, Tanjore and a large part of Oudh. His policy of continual aggression and annexations alienated the court of Directors and he was recalled in 1805. But at the end of his term of office Wellesley left the British undoubtedly the paramount power in India, Sind and the Panjab being the only two Indian states that remained outside the British empire.

Wemo—was a name of Kadphises II (*q.v.*).

Wheeler, Colonel—a military officer in the Company's service in Bengal, was appointed in 1776, on the death of Monson, to be a member of the Council of Warren Hastings (*q.v.*). Wheeler at first supported Francis, but later on he generally co-operated with Warren Hastings and gave him his support.

Wheeler, Major-General—an army officer in the Company's service, was in charge of the garrison at Cawnpore at the outbreak of the Sepoy Mutiny. He was 75 years old. When the sepoys attacked Cawnpore, he held out for three weeks in June, 1757, then surrendered on assurance of safe-conduct to Allahabad, but was attacked and killed by the sepoys with the other members of the British garrison when they were about to leave the place by boats.

White Huns, the—a branch of the Huns, invaded India in the eighth century. They are known as the Epthalites to anthropologists. (*E.E.C.A.*)

White Mutiny, the—is the designation given to a mutiny by the European troops in the Company's service in India against the Company during the second term of Robert Clive's office as Governor of Bengal. Clive, acting under instructions from the Directors of the Company in England, had reduced the *bhatta* or allowances of the white, i.e. the British soldiers in the Company's employ in India. This the British soldiers resented and they broke out in a mutiny which Clive suppressed with great vigour and promptness.

Wilkins, William—an Englishman in the service of the East India Company in Bengal during the administration of Warren Hastings (*q.v.*), was a good scholar in Sanskrit and Persian, received encouragement from the Governor-General in his oriental studies and translated the *Bhagavad-Gita* into English.

Willingdon, Lord (1865-1941)—the Viceroy and Governor-General of India from 1931 to 1935 in succession to Lord Irwin (*q.v.*), had been the Governor of Bombay from 1913 to 1919, and attended the League of Nations in 1924 as the representative of the Government of India. He had little sympathy with the nationalist movement in India and tried to play in Indian politics the role of a benevolent despot like Louis XIV of France whom he masqueraded in a Viceregal 'mask' held in Delhi during his regime. He definitely gave up the policy of conciliation which had been sedulously followed by his predecessor, Lord Irwin, put Mahatma Gandhi into prison in 1932 as soon as he returned from London after attending the second session of the Round Table Conference, declared the Congress illegal and resorted to severe repressive measures for suppressing the Civil Disobedience Movement which was started by the Congress. He attempted to impose upon India a constitutional settlement even though it might not meet with the approval of the Indian leaders. But the attempt failed and the Government of India Act which was passed by the British Parliament in 1935, could not be enforced by Lord Willingdon.

Wilson, Sir Archdale—a British general, rendered conspicuous service to the British in India. Soon after the outbreak of the Mutiny the quick death from cholera of two of his senior officers and the resignation of another through ill-health placed Wilson in command of the British army which had already occupied the Ridge which commanded the city of Delhi. But as the British army was very small and far from being able to prevent the sepoys from capturing Delhi it found itself practically besieged by them. Wilson resolutely held his position on the Ridge until Nicholson (*q.v.*) arrived with reinforcements with whose aid he recovered Delhi in September, 1858, after six days of desperate street fighting.

Wilson, Horace Hayman (1786-1860)—was a renowned English historian and orientalist versed in Sanskrit. From 1816 to 1832 he was employed in the Mint in Calcutta and was for 22 years (1811-33) the Secretary of the Royal Asiatic Society in Bengal. He was opposed to the policy of spending public funds exclusively for the expansion in India of Western learning which had the support of Lord Macaulay. His works were numerous including an *Anglo-Sanskrit Dictionary*, *Theatre of the Hindus* and translations into English of famous Sanskrit dramas, viz. *Meghaduta, Mrichchakatika, Malati-madhava, Uttara Ramacharita, Vikramorvarshi, Ratnavali* and *Mudra-Rakhshasa*. He was very much interested in the expansion of education amongst the Indians and was for many years a member of the Committee of Public Education, Calcutta.

Wilson, James—was the first Finance Member in the Viceroy's Executive Council. He joined in 1859 and died in harness only nine months later. He was an able financier who remodelled the system of financial administration in India, outlined important economies, imposed an income-tax for five years and introduced the practice of preparing annual budgets and statements of accounts.

Women, Emancipation of Indian—was largely promoted in the twentieth century. In spite of the tradition of the existence of learning and culture amongst Indian women in the past they were burdened with various social disabilities in the nineteenth and twentieth centuries—the prevalence of *sati*, female infanticide, child marriage, enforced widowhood amongst the Hindus, *purdah* or seclusion and polygamy. *Sati* and infanticide were stopped by legislation in the second quarter of the nineteenth century. At the instance of Pandit Iswarchandra Vidyasagar laws were passed raising the age of consent and legalizing the re-marriage of Hindu widows. The great obstacle in the way of female emancipation was the prevailing ignorance amongst them. This was gradually removed by the combined efforts of Christian missionaries, of reforming Hindu organisations like the Brahma Samaj and the Arya Samaj and of generous and liberal private Indian individuals. The Bethune School for girls was founded in 1849 and other educational institutions for women soon followed. Co-education has been introduced in educational institutions teaching humanities and sciences including medicine. Professor Karve established a Women's University at Poona. With the liberalisation of the political institutions in the country women came gradually to have a share in electing the nation's respresentatives to the legislature and at present every adult woman enjoys, like every adult man, the right of vote on the same conditions and terms. Rather, independent India has gone further in her advance in this direction than England and many other European countries. A distinguished Indian lady was her diplomatic representative in England and the U.S.S.R. and has also represented her in the United Nations Organisation. Another distinguished lady is now the Prime Minister of India and yet another the Governor of a premier state. Further, independent India has by legislation stopped polygamy amongst the Hindus and has also recognised the daughter's right to inheritance of her father's property. Indian women except the Muhammadans amongst them, are now as free as

Indian males and are making important contributions to the nation's progress.

Wood, Sir Charles—was the President of the Board of Control from 1854 to 1858. In this capacity he issued in 1854 the famous Despatch of 1854 which laid down the education policy of the Government of India, introduced the grant-in-aid system and sanctioned the establishment of Universities in Calcutta, Bombay and Madras. It also emphasized the importance of imparting education through the medium of Indian languages and solemnly declared that the education imparted in Government institutions should be "exclusively secular". Sir Charles Wood's Despatch led to the introduction and establishment throughout India of a graded system of educational institutions beginning with primary schools leading through higher schools and colleges to Universities. In pursuance of Sir Charles' Despatch the first Indian University was established in Calcutta in 1857 and two other Universities were soon afterwards established in Bombay and Madras.

World Wars the, and India—when the First World War broke out in 1914 Indians had absolutely no control over the administration of their own country. The British rulers of India voted a grant of 100 crores of rupees to England and sent large numbers of Indian soldiers and labourers to fight England's war in the various theatres of the War where they discharged their duties so well and contributed to such an extent to ultimate British victory that Britain acknowledged that "Without India, the war would have been immensely prolonged, if indeed without her help it could have been brought to a victorious conclusion." Further, repeated public declarations by British statesmen that the war was being fought for the protection of the smaller states and the declaration of President Wilson of the U.S.A., which was the ally of Britain, that the war was being fought for the purpose of allowing the smaller nations of the world the right of self-determination, naturally roused the political aspirations of the Indians. But after the ending of the First World War in the victory of the Allies it was soon clear that Great Britain was not prepared completely to implement her declared liberal intentions. All that Great Britain granted to India was the Government of India Act, 1919, which in spite of the announcement in the Preamble that the gradual establishment of self-governing institutions in India with a view to the ultimate establishment of responsible government was the aim of the British administration in India, only gave India the dyarchical system of provincial administration and a larger representation of the Indians in the Central as well as in the Provincial legislatures. Naturally, however, this very limited constitutional advance did not satisfy the hopes and aspirations of the Indians, and the nationalist movement continued unabated in India leading to the inauguration of the Non-co-operation Movement by the Congress in 1920 and the pursuit of a repressive policy by the British in India. In the economic sphere, however, the First World War had convinced Great Britain that in her own interests it was essential to develop some industries in India and obliged her to adopt gradually a policy of protection which benefited the steel, textile and sugar industries of India.

The Second World War which broke out in September, 1939 caught India divided in mind. Political consciousness had grown much greater than in 1914 and there was a section of Indian nationalists who wanted to take advantage of Great Britain's difficulties to promote the political interests of India. Some even thought of entering into an alliance with Germany and Japan, the two principal enemies of Great Britain, and ending British rule in India with the military assistance of the enemies of Great Britain. But the Indian National Congress under the idealistic leadership of Mahatma Gandhi would not accept such an opportunist policy. Under his guidance the Congress decided not to participate in the War efforts, but the British administrators made India contribute large sums of money to the war effort of Great Britain and also fully utilised the Indian army in fighting her wars in different parts of the world, especially in south-eastern Asia where the Japanese made dramatic and rapid advances, over-running not only the Malay Peninsula but also Burma and penetrating even into the North-Eastern Frontier State of Manipur and threatening Assam. When the British fled from Burma they left behind a large army of Indian soldiers as virtual prisoners of war in the hands of the victorious Japanese there. Netaji Subhaschandra Bose who had openly differed from Mahatma Gandhi on the Congress policy towards Britain's war, had stood for snatching from her embarrassments all possible advantages and escaped to Germany to avoid confinement in a British prison. He went from Germany to Japan and then to Burma where he organised the personnel of the Indian Army that the British had left there, into the Indian National Army, declared the establishment in Burma of an independent Indian state with himself as the Provisional head, began collaborating with the Japanese and set out at the head of the Indian National Army on a march which aimed at reaching Delhi and planting the Indian National Flag on the Red Fort there. But his army which was ill-equipped and ill-fed and lacked the essential support of an air-force, could come only as far as Kohima near Manipur from where it was beaten back by the numerically superior, better-fed, better-armed and better-served Indo-British army. Soon afterwards, Japan herself was ousted from the war as the result of the bombing of Hiroshima by the U.S.A. with atom bombs and Netaji's efforts to liberate India from the British rule by an open invasion from outside with foreign help ended in failure. Great Britain and her allies soon won the war, but the Indian National Congress under the leadership of Mahatma Gandhi was not conciliated. Great Britain tried to satisfy the political aspirations of India by declaring that 'Dominion Status' would be granted in fullness of time to India and at the same time promoted the communal aspirations of the Muhammadans in order to divide and weaken the Indians; but the Congress not only stuck to its already declared aim of independence but also started a campaign calling upon the Britishers to 'Quit India'. The movement gained great popularity; hostility to the Britishers pervaded all branches of the administration and spread even to the Navy. Great Britain, in spite of her victory in the war, was sorely hit by an excessive loss of man-power as well as of financial and other resources, made the best of an extremely adverse situation by deciding to withdraw from India and granted her independence in August, 1947.

Wynn, Charles W. W.—the President of the Board of Control, passed in 1827 the Jury Act by which he introduced religious distinctions into the judicial system in India by providing that while Christians, Europeans as well as Indians, would be entitled to sit as jurors in the trials of non-Christians as well as Christians, non-Christians like Hindus and Muhammadans would not be allowed to act as jurors in the trials of Christians. Raja Rammohan Roy submitted a petition against this provision which was eventually repealed.

X

Xavier, Father Jerome—a Jesuit Portuguese monk, came to India during the reign of Akbar (1556-1605). Father Xavier got into intimate contact with the Mughul Emperor by whom he was first received at Lahore in 1595. Father Xavier maintained contact with the Mughul court even during the reign of Jahangir (1605-27). He got from the Emperor permission for making converts, if he could, but he failed to secure any. He, however, secured from the Mughul Emperors certain advantages for the Portuguese in India. Father Jerome Xavier, as well as his colleague, Emmanuel Pinheiro, were excellent writers of letters which throw interesting light on the latter part of Akbar's reign and the earlier part of that of Jahangir. (Maclagan, Sir E., *The Jesuits and the Great Mughul*)

Xerxes—the Emperor of Persia (486 - 465 B.C.) and the son and successor of Emperor Darius I, held intact his father's Indian dominions including Gandhara, the Indus valley bounded on the east by the desert of Rajputana and probably Sind. According to Herodotus, the Greek historian, soldiers from Gandhara as well as from India were included in the expeditionary force that Xerxes led into Greece. The Gandharians were armed with bows of reeds and short spears while the Indians, clad in cotton garments, were armed with cane bows from which were shot arrows tipped with iron.

Y

Yadava dynasty, the—was founded in about A.D. 1191 by Bhillama with Devagiri (Daulatabad) as his capital. The most powerful king of the dynasty was Bhillama's grandson, Singhana, who ascended the throne in A.D. 1210. He conquered Gujarat and other neighbouring states and for a while the Yadava dynasty rivalled the Chalukyas. Its glory, however, was short-lived. In A.D. 1294 when Ramachandradeva (*q.v.*) was the reigning Yadava king, his kingdom was invaded by Sultan Ala-ud-din Khalji (*q.v.*) who sacked the capital, Devagiri, but spared the life of Ramachandradeva on the payment of a heavy indemnity which is said to have included six hundred *maunds* of pearls, two *maunds* of diamonds, rubies, emeralds and sapphires, much gold and many elephants. In 1309 the Yadava kingdom was again invaded by the Muhammadans led by Ala-ud-din's general, Malik Kafur (*q.v.*) and King Ramachandradeva who was still reigning, escaped annihilation by submission. He was the last independent king of the Yadava dynasty. After his death his son-in-law and successor, Harapaladeva, revolted against the sultan of Delhi in A.D. 1318, but was defeated, flayed alive and then beheaded. With his death the Yadava dynasty ended. The Yadava kings were patrons of Brahmanical Hinduism and of the Sanskrit language and literature. The renowned Sanskrit writer and Hindu jurist, Hemadri, flourished during the reign of Ramachandradeva.

Yadus, the—a tribal people, are mentioned in the *Rig-Veda*. According to later literary tradition the Yadus settled in western India near Prabhasa and Krishna, who is regarded as an *avatar* or incarnation of God, belonged to the Yadu tribe.

Yahiya-bin-Ahmad Sarhindi—was an early Muhammadan historian of the sultanate of Delhi.

Yajnavalkya—a famous *rishi* (sage), is associated by ancient tradition with the renowned philosopher-king and sage (*rajarshi*), Janaka of Mithila. Yajnavalkya occupies a high place amongst the ancient Hindu philosophers and sages and his name is very closely associated with the *Upanishadas*. He is said to have received the *Brahma-jnana* or knowledge of the *Brahman*.

Yajna Sri, Gautamiputra (A.D. 170-200)—was the most powerful of the later Satavahana (*q.v.*) kings. He recovered from the Western Satraps the Satavahana territories seized by them and issued a large series of silver, bronze and lead coins some of which bear the figure of a ship, suggesting that his rule extended to overseas dominions.

Yajurveda —is one of the four *Vedas*. The *Samhita* (*q.v.*) of the *Yajurveda* is a book of sacrificial prayer and contains not only some hymns taken from the *Rig-veda*, but also prose formulas to be recited by the priest who performed the manual work essential in connection with the due performance of a sacrifice. The *Yajurveda* has two different texts, namely, (a) the *Krishna Yajurveda* or *Black Yajurveda* and (b) the *Sukla Yajurveda* or *White Yajurveda*. To the former belong the *Taittiriya*, *Maitrayani* and *Kathaka* Brahmanas (*q.v.*) and to the latter belong the *Vajasaneyi* and the *Satapatha* Brahmanas. To the *Yajurveda* also belong the following *Upanishadas* (*q.v.*): *Taittiriya*, *Katha*, *Svetásvatara*, *Brihadáranyaka*, *Isa*, *Prasna*, *Mundaka* and *Mándukya*. The *Yajurveda* deals exhaustively with the rites and rituals pertaining to the performance of Vedic sacrifices.

Yakub Khan—the son and successor of Amir Sher Ali (*q.v.*), was recognised on his father's death in 1879 by the British as the Amir of Afghanistan. Yakub Khan concluded with the British the treaty of Gandamak (*q.v.*) in 1879 by which he practically agreed to be a protected protégé of the British on the throne of Kabul in return for a British promise of protection against foreign aggression and an annual subsidy of 6 lakhs of rupees. Such submission and subordination of their ruler to the British was most distasteful to the Afghans who, two months after the conclusion of the treaty, rose in rebellion against the Amir and his British patron, Cavagnari, the Resident at Kabul, and murdered him along with all the members of his escort. This led to a fresh outbreak of war between the Afghans and the British. Yakub Khan was easily driven out of Kabul and took shelter in the British camp. He was later on sent as a state-prisoner to Dehra Dun in India where he lived till his death in 1923. (*see* also the Second Afghan War.)

Yama—is the name of the Vedic god of the realm of the departed. He is believed to be a beneficent king, dispensing rewards and punishments according to justice. He is also, therefore, called *Dharma-raja*.

Yamunacharya—a famous preacher of Vaishnavism in South India, preceded Ramanuja (*q.v.*) who flourished in the twelfth century A.D.

Yandaboo, the treaty of—concluded in 1826, marked the close of the First Burmese War (*q.v.*). By this treaty the king of Burma purchased peace with the British by paying an indemnity of one crore of rupees, surrendering to the British the provinces of Arakan and Tenasserim, promising to abstain from all interference in Assam, Cachar and Jaintia which territories thus practically passed under British rule and by admitting a British Resident at Ava.

Yaqub—was the son and prospective successor of Yusuf Shah (*q.v.*), the sultan of Kashmir. He shared his father's defeat at the hands of the Mughuls in 1586 and lost his heritage.

Yaqub-ibn-Lais—the first independent Muhammadan ruler of Sind, received the sovereignty of the province as a gift from the Khalifah in A.D. 871.

Yaqut, Jalaluddin—an Abyssinian slave, acquired the favour of Sultana Raziya (*q.v.*), was promoted to the high post of the Master of Stables and was shown other favours by the Queen. This offended the pride of the nobles of the court and also roused their jealousy. The disaffected nobles led by Altuniya, the Governor of Bhatinda, rose against the Queen and in the battle that ensued Yaqut was defeated and slain and his patroness the Queen, was imprisoned.

Yasaskara—a king of Kashmir, was a Brahman by caste and

was raised to the throne by an assembly of Brahmans in the tenth century A.D. His rule lasted for only a short while.

Yaska—was an eminent ancient writer on *Nirukta* (etymology) which is considered as one of the six *Vedangas* (*q.v.*). His date is uncertain and he might have been practically a contemporary of the celebrated grammarian, Panini (*q.v.*).

Yasodhara—was one of the names of the lady who was married to Prince Siddhartha (Gautama Buddha) (*q.v.*) and bore him his only son. The other names by which she is known are Bhadda Kachchana, Subhadraká, Bimbá and Gopá.

Yasodharapura—was the capital of Kambuja-desha (Cambodia). The modern name of the city is Angkor Thom. It was founded by king Yasovarman (A.D. 889-908). The city was square in shape, each side being more than two miles in length. It was surrounded by a moat 330 feet broad and was enclosed by a high wall. It was decorated with many beautiful buildings and temples of which the Bayon, 150 feet high, was the most magnificent. Yasodharapura was one of the grandest cities in the world in that age.

Yasodharman—a king of Malwa, made himself famous in Indian history by defeating the Huna king, Mihiragula (*q.v.*) and breaking his power in about A.D. 528. He was probably helped by Narasimha Gupta Baladitya (*q.v.*). Nothing whatever is known about the ancestors as well as the successors of Yasodharman. The precise duration of his reign is also not known, but it is believed to have covered the first half of the sixth century A.D. He erected two columns of victory at Mandasor and, in the inscriptions recorded on them, Yasodharman is credited to have ruled over the whole of India from the Brahmaputra to the Western Ocean and from the Himalayas to Mount Mahendra which probably meant the Mahendragiri hill of the Western Ghats in the Travancore area. There is no independent evidence in support of these large claims made on behalf of King Yasodharman, who, in any case, must have been a great warrior and victorious king.

Yasomati—the queen of king Prabhakaravardhana (*q.v.*) of Thaneswar, was the mother of the renowned Emperor Harshavardhana (*q.v.*).

Yasovarman—was a king of Kambuja (Cambodia) who ruled from A.D. 889-908. He was a very powerful king who founded the great city of Yasodharapura (*q.v.*). He has left a large number of inscriptions in some of which the same text is written in the script ordinarily used in Kambuja and also in a script which is very similar to the Devanagari script as used in Northern India. The language used in both versions is Sanskrit.

Yasovarman—a Chandella king of Jejakabhukti (*q.v.*), modern Bundelkhand, ruled towards the close of the tenth century A.D., captured the fort of Kalanjar from the Pratiharas (*q.v.*) and compelled the Pratihara king, Devapala (*q.v.*), to surrender to him a much-prized sacred image of Vishnu which he installed in a temple which he built at Khajuraho (*q.v.*). He probably died in A.D. 950 and was succeeded by his son, Dhanga.

Yasovarman—a king of Kanauj, ruled in the first quarter of the eighth century. He sent an embassy to China in A.D. 731. Ten years later he was dethroned and slain by Lalitaditya Muktapida (*q.v.*), king of Kashmir. Yasovarman was the patron of the famous Sanskrit poet, Bhavabhuti (*q.v.*), the author of the *Malatimadhava* and also of Vakpati who wrote in Prakrit.

Yaudheyas, the—a tribal people, probably Kshatriyas, are mentioned in the Allahabad Pillar inscription of Samudragupta (*q.v.*) along with the Malavas, the Madrakas etc. as peoples who submitted to the control and sovereignty of the Gupta emperor. They probably lived at first in the valley of the Sutlej and later on expanded as far as the Mathura region. They had a republican form of government. (Law, B.C. *Some Ancient Mid-Indian Kshatriya Tribes*)

Yauvanasri—one of the queens of the Pala king, Vigrahapala III, (*q.v.*), was a princess belonging to the royal line of Chedi.

Yavanas, the—is a term that was used by Hindu writers originally to indicate foreigners of Greek extraction, but later on it was applied to Muhammadans as well. The word is etymologically derived from *Yauna* which is equivalent to Ionia and originally indicated the Ionians. (*S.O.S.*, pp. 321-27.)

Yen-Kao-Ching (or Yen-Kao-Chen)—the original of the Yuechi name of Kadphises II (*q.v.*).

Yildiz, Taj-ud-din—a rival of Sultan Iltutmish (*q.v.*), was originally a Turkish slave. At the time of the death of Qutb-ud-din, Yildiz held Ghazni and claimed that he had a better right to the throne of Delhi than anybody else. In 1214 Yildiz conquered the Panjab up to Thaneswar and tried to establish his authority over Iltutmish, but was defeated by the latter in a battle fought near Tarain in 1216. Yildiz was taken prisoner and sent to Badaun.

Yoga—one of the six systems of Hindu philosophy, is attributed to Patanjali. It is a system of practical philosophy and devotes itself mainly to the discussion of the cultivation of that frame of mind which leads to emancipation and prescribes for its achievements methods and exercises like discipline of the body, breath-control, sense-control and contemplation leading to *Samadhi*. Further, it recognises a supreme Being called *Isvara* who is pre-eminent, unequalled, unexcelled and omniscient. Yoga aims at the purification of the body, mind and soul, preparing them for the beatific vision. It holds that with a purified *citta* or mind and with faith in the soul it is possible for man to realise that there are other worlds beyond the universe which we see with our limited vision and animal senses. What is considered supernatural would then appear to be natural and it is feasible for a soul contemplating in solitude and silence to catch a steady vision of that supernatural or supramental state of bliss. It is the belief in such merits of *Yoga* that has attracted earnest minds amongst the Hindus from ancient to modern times to its practice. (Radhakrishnan, S., *Hist. of Ind. Philosophy*, Vol. II)

Yogavashishtha Ramayana, the—is a famous sacred Sanskrit text of the Hindus. It was translated by Prince Dara (*q.v.*) into Persian.

Yonas, the—are mentioned in Asokan edicts as a people amongst whom he claimed to have made many converts to Buddhism. They were a people of Hellenistic origin and some of them were certainly settled within his empire and were consequently his subjects, as is proved by the recently discovered bilingual Qandahar inscription of Asoka. (Bhattacharya, S., *Select Asokan Epigraphs*)

Younghusband, Sir Francis (1863-1942)—led a British Indian expedition to Tibet in 1903-04 by order of the Viceroy, Lord Curzon (*q.v.*). Younghusband reached Khamba Jeng, a place fifteen miles north of the Sikkim frontier and within Tibetan territories, in July, 1903. As the Tibetans refused to enter into negotiations with the British intruders until the latter would retire beyond their frontier so Younghusband proceeded, with the approval of the Government of India, further inside Tibet to Gyantse, after routing an ill-armed Tibetan army at Guru. But as Tibet still refused to negotiate Younghusband advanced further, defeated a second and larger Tibetan army in a battle fought at the Karo-la Pass amidst eternal snows and triumphantly entered the Tibetan capital, Lhasa, on 3 August, 1904. This success of Younghusband obliged the Tibetans to sue for terms and Younghusband imposed upon them the treaty of Lhasa (*q.v.*) on 7 September, 1904, triumphantly started on his return journey sixteen days later and completed it successfully. By the terms of the treaty of Lhasa as modified later on, Tibet was required to pay an indemnity of 25 lakhs of rupees in three years, to surrender the Chumbi valley for occupation by the British for 3 years and to permit a British agent to be posted at Gyantse. Younghusband was, on his return, warmly received and praised by the Viceroy, Lord Curzon. (Seaver, G. F., *Francis Younghusband*)

Yudhisthira—was the eldest of the five Pandava princes whose exploits and war with the Kurus form the main theme of the *Mahabharata*, one of the two great epics of India. He was the embodiment of truth and justice and was, therefore, called *Dharmaraja*.

Yueh-chis, the—were a nomadic people who originally occupied western China. Between 174 and 160 B.C. they were driven out of that region and migrated westwards to the region of the Gobi desert. Reaching the valley of the Jaxartes they expelled from there the Sakai who were in occupation. But ere long the Yueh-chis, in their turn, were vanquished by the Wu-sun and obliged to move to the valley of the Oxus as well as to Bactria. In course of time the Yueh-chis lost their nomadic habits and, becoming divided into five principalities, settled in Bactria. A century later, in about A.D. 40, the Kushan section or sept of the Yueh-chis under the able leadership of their chief named Kujula-Kara-Kadphises attained a predominant position over the other sections of the Yueh-chis, entered north-western India which they occupied and their chief became known in Indian history as Kadphises I, the founder of the Kushan dynasty of Indian kings. (*E.E.C.A.*)

Yule, George—was one of those rare non-official English merchant-princes who sympathised with the political aspirations of the Indians. He supported the Indian National Congress and presided over its fourth session held at Allahabad in 1888.

Yusuf Adil Khan (Shah)—the founder of the Adil Shahi dynasty of the sultans of Bijapur (*q.v.*), was said to have been a son of sultan Murad II of Turkey, who was brought up secretly in Persia and, for reasons of personal safety, had himself sold as a slave to Muhammad Gawan (*q.v.*), minister of the Bahmani sultan, Muhammad Shah III (*q.v.*). Yusuf made his way to high rank by his ability and was appointed by the Bahmani sultan as the Governor of Bijapur where, however, he set himself up as an independent ruler in A.D. 1489-90. He ruled till his death in 1510 and founded the Adil Shahi dynasty of Bijapur which ruled till 1686 when the last sultan, Sikandar, was defeated, captured and deposed by Emperor Aurangzeb. Yusuf Adil Shah was a capable administrator and a tolerant ruler who even appointed Hindus to high offices. He was a Shiah and married a Maratha lady to whom was given the name of Babuji Khanam and who became the mother of his son and successor, Ismail Shah. Yusuf Adil Shah was conscious of the importance of the port of Goa which was a favourite place for his occasional residence. In 1510 the Portuguese admiral, Albuquerque, took advantage of the negligence of the Sultan's local officers and seized the port, but Yusuf Adil Shah recovered the place six months later. He was a patron of men of letters and culture and died peacefully at the age seventy-four.

Yusuf Shah—the king of Bengal from A.D. 1474 to 1481, bore the royal title of Shams-ud-din Abul Muzaffar Yusuf Shah. He succeeded his father, Barbak Shah. He was a virtuous, learned and pious ruler who probably conquered Sylhet.

Yusuf Shah—the Muhammadan king of Kashmir, was attacked by Akbar, defeated and deposed by him in 1586 and Kashmir was annexed to the Mughul empire.

Yusufzais, the—were an Afghan tribe who were very restless. They rose in rebellion against Akbar and were forcibly reduced to submission. They rose again against the Mughul Emperor in 1667, killed Aurangzeb's Governor, Amir Khan, at Ali Masjid in 1672 and could be kept under subjection only by the personal presence of the Emperor at Peshawar. They continued to be a turbulent people even after their territories passed under British rule.

Z

Zafar Khan—the minister and general of Sultan Ala-ud-din Khalji, played a prominent part in the Sultan's various wars. He showed great skill and bravery in repelling the Mongol invasion which was led by Qutlugh Khwaja in 1299. His victory was purchased at the cost of his life.

Zafar Khan—was the founder of the Bahmani kingdom (*q.v.*) in the Deccan. His original name was Hasan who had rendered meritorious services to Sultan Muhammad Tughluq and was honoured with the name of Zafar Khan. In 1347 he was in charge of a large army at Daulatabad and this position he utilised to set himself up as an independent ruler in the south with Gulbarga or Kulbarga as his capital. On the assumption of independence and royalty he took the title of Abul-Muzaffar Ala-ud-din Bahman Shah. Firishta's statement that Hasan was originally a menial in the service of a Brahman astrologer named Gangu whose patronage helped him to rise in his career, lacks independent support. Hasan claimed descent from the famous Persian hero Bahman, son of Isfandiyar, and the dynasty that he founded came to be known as the Bahmani dynasty. He had to wage many wars with the neighbouring states, especially with the Hindu kingdom of Vijayanagar (*q.v.*) which also came to be founded in his time. He proved a victorious warrior and left at his death in 1358 a kingdom extending from the Wainganga river in the north to the Krishna in the south and from Daulatabad in the west to Bhongir in the east. He gave to his kingdom an efficient system of administration. He divided it into four *tarafs* or provinces, namely, Gulbarga, Daulatabad, Berar and Bidar. Each province was placed in charge of a governor, who maintained an army and appointed the necessary civil and military officers who were to work under him. He has been praised by historians as a just king who cherished his people. He was succeeded by his eldest son Muhammad Shah whom he had nominated as his heir on his death-bed.

Zafar Khan—a pretender to the throne of Bengal, was a son-in-law of Fakr-ud-din Mubarak Shah (*q.v.*) of Eastern Bengal. He fled to the court of Sultan Firuz Shah Tughluq (*q.v.*) and persuaded the Sultan to embark on an expedition against Bengal which, however, ended in failure.

Zafar Khan—the founder of the independent Muslim dynasty of the sultans of Gujarat, began his career as a general under the Tughluq sultan, Muhammad Shah, who appointed him in 1391 as the governor of Gujarat where he soon established peace and order. In 1396 taking advantage of the strife amongst the descendants of Firoz Tughluq, Zafar Khan set himself up as the independent ruler of Gujarat. He ruled peacefully for seven years at the end of which he was seized and imprisoned by his own son, Tatar Khan, who then proclaimed himself as the king. But Zafar Khan contrived with the aid of his brother the murder of his unnatural son, Tatar Khan, recovered his throne and assumed the name of Sultan Muzaffar. In spite of his advancing years Muzaffar (Zafar Khan) defeated the ruler of Malwa and installed his brother Nusrat as the king there. He died in 1411, leaving behind him a dynasty of independent sultans who ruled over Gujarat till 1572-73 when it was annexed by Akbar to the Mughul empire.

Zain-ul-Abidin—the eighth sultan of Kashmir, ruled from 1420 to 1460. His was a prosperous reign, based on the principle and practice of religious toleration. He repealed the *Jizya* (*q.v.*) on the Hindus and also allowed them to build temples. He abstained from eating flesh, prohibited the slaughter of kine and encouraged literature and the fine arts. He reduced the taxes and reformed the debased currency. He was proficient in Persian, Hindi and Tibetan and a munificent patron of learning, poetry, music and painting. He caused the *Mahabharata* (*q.v.*) and the *Rajatarangini* (Chronicles of Kashmir) (*q.v.*) to be translated from Sanskrit into Persian and also had some Persian works translated into Hindi. He lived a pure life and was devoted to his one wife. The last years of his life were embittered by the rivalries amongst his three sons for succession to the throne. On his death in 1470 his throne passed to his second son, Haji Khan.

Zakat, the—was a tax levied by the Muhammadan rulers in India on their Muhammadan subjects. It amounted to 2 per cent of one's income and its yield was earmarked for distribution as alms amongst the Muhammadans.

Zalim—means a tyrant. This sobriquet was applied to the Bahmani sultan, Humayun (1457-61) (*q.v.*).

Zalim Singh—the Rajput ruler of the state of Kotah in Rajputana, entered with the Company in 1817 into a treaty of defensive alliance, perpetual friendship, protection and subordinate co-operation and thus saved his state and family from Maratha aggression. His example was soon followed by the other Rajput princes of Rajputana.

Zaman Shah—the king of Afghanistan from 1793 to 1799, was a grandson of Ahmad Shah Abdali (*q.v.*) whose Indian exploits he wanted to emulate by invading India even in the year of his accession; but better sense prevailed and he decided to wait till his position was consolidated in Afghanistan itself. He, however, reduced Kashmir to submission in 1794 and also compelled the Amirs of Sind to pay him tribute. Then he started from Kabul on his way to India and had advanced up to Rohtas when he had to retrace his steps in order to suppress disorders that had in the meantime broken out within Afghanistan. The advance forces that he had sent into the Panjab were confronted with stiff opposition by the Sikhs and soon returned to Afghanistan without making any gains. Then in 1796-97 Zaman Shah again attempted an invasion of India advancing from Kabul to Peshawar and then marching through the Panjab to Lahore; but the Sikhs continued to oppose his march by making sudden attacks on his army and Zaman Shah took time in consolidating his hold on the Panjab. In the meantime troubles again broke out in Afghanistan forcing Zaman Shah to return to Kabul before he had proceeded beyond Lahore. Zaman Shah made his last attempt at the invasion of India in 1798 and easily advanced up to Lahore which he re-occupied, but again he had to leave his work unfinished and to retreat precipitately from the Panjab to Afghanistan which in the meantime had been invaded by the Persian emperor in collusion with Zaman's half-brother, Shah Mahmud, who eventually defeated and blinded Zaman Shah in 1799. He had, however, hovered over the Indian frontier for a sufficiently long period to paralyse the efforts of the kings in India to stop the advance of the British in the country. (Sinha, N. K., *Rise of the Sikh Power*)

Zeb-un-Nisa, Princess (1639-1709)—was a daughter of Emperor Aurangzeb. She was a very talented lady, well-read in Persian and Arabic, was an expert calligraphist who maintained a fine library of her own. She was also a fine poet and wrote a commentary on the Quran.

Zetland, Lord—was the Governor of Bengal from 1917 to 1922. He was more a man of letters than a capable administrator of a province like Bengal. His works were *Life of Lord Curzon* and the *Heart of Aryavarta* which he wrote when he was known by his earlier title of Lord Ronaldshay.

Zia-ud-din Barani—was a famous Muhammadan historian who enjoyed the patronage of Sultan Firoz Shah Tughluq (*q.v.*). His work *Tarikh-i-Firoz Shahi* contains practically a contemporary account of the reigns of his royal patron and his predecessor, Sultan Muhammad Tughluq (*q.v.*).

Zinda Pir, **the**—meaning a 'living saint', was the designation by which many Indian Muhammadans of the time of Aurangzeb referred to the Emperor.

Zoroastrians, the—*see* the Parsees in India.

Zulfikar Khan—a Mughul noble, rose to great power and prestige during the reign of Emperor Bahadur Shah (*q.v.*). He was the son of Asad Khan, the Prime Minister of Aurangzeb. After the death of Bahadur Shah, Zulfikar Khan intervened in the war of succession that broke out amongst the four sons of the late Emperor and helped Jahandar Shah to get the throne. Zulfikar wanted to play the king-maker, murdered Jahandar Shah in 1713, eleven months after his accession, and helped Farruksiyar to the Imperial throne, but was executed by the order of the Emperor in 1713.

IMPORTANT DATES

B.C.

c. 3102 — Commencement of the Kaliyuga Era; the Great War between the Kurus and the Pandavas.
c. 2700 — Date of Indus Valley seals found at Kish.
c. 817 — Traditional date of the birth of Parsvanatha.
c. 544 — Buddha's *Nirvana* according to Ceylonese account.
c. 527 — Traditional date of Mahavira's *Nirvana*.
c. 519 — Bahistun inscription of Darius I.
c. 486 — Buddha's *Nirvana* according to Cantonese record.
327-326 — Invasion of India by Alexander the Great.
325 — Departure of Alexander from India.
323 — Death of Alexander in Babylon.
c. 322 — Accession of Chandragupta Maurya.
c. 305 — Indian expedition of Seleucos Nikator.
c. 298 — Accession of Bindusara.
c. 273-232 — Reign of Asoka.
c. 187 — Overthrow of the Mauryas and the foundation of the Sunga dynasty.
c. 73 — Fall of the Sunga dynasty and rise of the Kanva dynasty.
c. 58 — Epoch of the Vikrama Era.
c. 50 — Kharavela—king in Kalinga.
c. 50 — Commencement of the Satavahana dynasty.
c. 20 — Fall of the Kanva dynasty.
c. 2 — Despatch of Buddhist missionaries from the Bactrian Court to the Chinese Emperor.

A.D.

c. 47 — Record of Gondophernes.
64 — Chinese Emperor Ming-ti sent agents to India for Buddhist texts.
c. 66 — Indian Buddhist monks, Kasyapa Matanga and Gobharana, arrived in China.
77 — Pliny's *Natural History*.
78 — Commencement of the Saka era. Consolidation of the Kushan dynasty in the Panjab.
c. 78-110 — Reign of Kadphises II.
c. 110-20 — Period of Nameless king.
c. 119-24 — Nahapana.

c. 120-62	— Reign of Kanishka.
c. 162-82	— Reign of Huvishka.
c. 182-220	— Reign of Vasudeva I.
226	— Establishment of Sassaninan dynasty in Persia.
320	— Commencement of the Gupta era. (26 Feby.)
c. 360	— Ceylonese embassy to Samudragupta.
405-11	— Fa-Hien travelled over India.
c. 415-55	— Reign of Kumaragupta I.
455-67	— Reign of Skandagupta.
476	— Birth of the astronomer Aryabhata.
c. 533	— Yasodharman defeated Mihiragula.
547	— Kosmas Indikopleustes.
c. 566	— Accession of the Chalukya king, Kirtivarman I.
606	— Accession of Harshavardhana.
609	— Coronation of Pulakeshin II.
619-20	— Sasanka in Eastern India.
622	— Commencement of the Hijra era.
629	— Hiuen Tsang begins his travels in India.
634	— Aihole inscription referring to Kalidas and Bharavi.
637	— Arab raid against Thana in Sind.
639	— Foundation of Lhasa by Srong-tsan-Gampo.
c. 642	— Death of Pulakeshin II.
c. 642-68	— Reign of the Pallava king, Narasinhavarman.
643	— Harsha meets Hiuen Tsang – Harsha's sixth quinquennial assembly at Prayag, departure of Hiuen Tsang.
645	— Hiuen Tsang returned to China.
c. 646-47	— Death of Harshavardhana.
c. 647-48	— Bhaskaravarman, king of Kamarupa, helped Wang-Hiuen Tse.
664	— Death of Hiuen Tsang in China.
674	— Vikramaditya I, Chalukya and Paramesvaravarman I, Pallava.
675-85	— I-tsing at Nalanda.
710-11	— Invasion of Sind by Muhammad bin Kasim.
712	— Arab conquest of Nirun and Alor – defeat and death of Dahir, King of Sind.
713	— Capture of Multan by the Muhammadans.
743-89	— Santarakshita and Padmasambhava in Tibet.
753	— Commencement of the Rashtrakuta dynasty.
783	—Vatsaraja started the Pratihara dynasty
815-77	— Reign of Amoghavarsha I.
829	— Harjara became the king of Kamarupa.

871-907	— Aditya I, Chola.
907	— Accession of the Chola king, Parantaka I.
c. 962	— Foundation of the kingdom of Ghazni.
973	— Commencement of the Chalukya dynasty of Kalyani.
977	— Accession of Sabuktigin.
985	— Accession of Rajaraja the Great, Chola.
986-87	— First invasion by Sabuktigin.
997	— Death of Sabuktigin.
998	— Accession of Sultan Mahmud.
1001	— Defeat and martyrdom of Jaipal.
1012-44	— Reign of Rajendra Chola I.
1018	— Seizure of Kanauj by Sultan Mahmud.
1026	— Sack of Somnath temple by Sultan Mahmud.
c. 1076-1148	— Anantavarman Choda Ganga, king of Orissa – construction of the temple of Jagannatha at Puri.
c. 1106-41	— Reign of Vishnuvardhana Hoysala – Ramanuja.
1175	— Shihab-ud-din Muhammad Ghuri invaded the Panjab which he occupied.
1178	— Defeat of Shihab-ud-din Muhammad Ghuri at the hands of Bhima, king of Gujarat.
c. 1185-1205	— Lakshmana Sena's rule in Bengal.
1191	— Defeat of Shihab-ud-din Muhammad Ghuri at the first battle of Tarain by Prithviraja.
1192	— Second battle of Tarain—defeat and execution of Prithviraja by Shihab-ud-din Muhammad Ghuri.
1192-93	— Capture of Delhi by Qutb-ud-din.
1194	— Defeat of Gahadvala king Jaychandra of Kanauj by the Muhammadans at the battle of Chandwar.
c. 1200	— Conquest of Bihar and Bengal by the Muhammadans under Ikhtiyaruddin (popularly called Bakhtiyar Khalji).
1206	— Death of Shihab-ud-din Muhammad Ghuri and the accession of Qutb-ud-din as the Sultan of Delhi. Commencement of the Sultanate.
1210	— Death of Qutb-ud-din.
1210-11	— Accession of Iltutmish.
1221	— Invasion by Chingiz Khan.
1228	— Conquest of Kamarupa by Sukhapa, the first Ahom king.
1231	— Foundation of the Qutb Minar.
1236	— Death of Iltutmish – accession and deposition of Firuz – accession of Raziya.
1240	— Deposition and murder of Raziya.

1246-66	— Reign of Sultan Nasir-ud-din.
1266-87	— Reign of Ghiyas-ud-din Balban.
1288	— Marco Polo at Kayal.
1290	— Fall of the Slave dynasty – accession of Jalal-ud-din Khalji.
1292	— Ala-ud-din Khalji captured Bhilsa – Mongol invasion.
1294	— Devagiri pillaged by Ala-ud-din Khalji.
1296-1316	— Reign of Ala-ud-din Khalji.
1297	— Conquest of Gujarat.
1301	— Ranthambhor captured by Ala-ud-din Khalji.
1302-03	— Ala-ud-din captured Chitor – Mongol invasion.
1305	— Ala-ud-din conquered Malwa, Ujjain, Mander, Chanderi and Dhar.
1306-07	— Kafur's expedition to Devagiri.
1308	— Expedition to Warangal by Ala-ud-din's army.
1310	— Kafur's expedition into South India.
1316	— Death of Ala-ud-din – death of Kafur.
1317-18	— Extinction of the Yadava dynasty.
1320	— Accession of Ghiyas-ud-din Tughluq.
1325	— Death of Ghiyas-ud-din – accession of Muhammad Tughluq.
c. 1327	— Transfer of capital from Delhi to Daulatabad.
c. 1329	— Issue of copper token currency in lieu of gold.
1334	— Rebellion of Madura.
1336	— Foundation of the kingdom of Vijayanagar.
c. 1337-38	— Expedition to Karajal.
1338-39	— Establishment of independent sultanate in Bengal.
1339	— Kashmir becomes independent under Shah Mir.
1342	— Ibn Batutah started on his mission to China.
1343	— Accession of Shams-ud-din Iliyas Shah in Bengal.
1347	— Foundation of the Bahmani kingdom.
1351	— Death of Muhammad Tughluq.
1351-88	— Reign of Firuz Shah Tughluq.
1393	— Establishment of the independent sultanate of Jaunpur.
1398	— Invasion of Timur.
1414	— Raja Ganesh in Bengal.
1420	— Nicolo Conti visited Vijayanagar.
1429	— Bahmani capital transferred from Kulbarga to Bidar.
c. 1430-69	— Reign of Rana Kumbha in Mewar.
1434-35	— Kapilendra, king of Orissa.
1443	— Abdur Razzak began his visit to India.

1451	— Fall of the Tughluq dynasty – accession of Bahlul Lodi.
1469	— Birth of Guru Nanak.
1472	— Birth of Sher Shah.
1481	— Murder of Muhammad Gawan.
1484	— Berar seceded from the Bahmani kingdom.
1489	— Accession of Sikandar Lodi – foundation of the independent sultanate of Bijapur.
1490	— Foundation of the independent sultanate of Ahmadnagar.
1493	— Husain Shah became the king of Bengal.
1494	— Babur ascended the throne of Farghana.
1497-98	— First voyage of Vasco da Gama.
1509	— Accession of Krishnadeva Raya – Albuquerque, Portuguese Governor in India.
c. 1509-27	— Reign of Rana Sanga in Mewar.
1510	— Capture of Goa by the Portuguese.
1512-18	— Foundation of the independent sultanate of Golkonda.
1526	— First battle of Panipat – accession of Babur to the throne of Delhi – commencement of Mughul rule in India.
1527	— Battle of Khanua and defeat of Rana Sanga.
1529	— Battle of the Gogra and Afghan defeat.
1530	— Death of Krishnadeva Raya – death of Babur – accession of Humayun.
1533	— Capture of Chitor by Bahadur Shah of Gujarat.
1534	— Humayun marched to Malwa.
1535	— Humayun defeated Bahadur Shah who fled.
1538	— Sher Khan defeated Mahmud Shah of Bengal – Humayun invaded Bengal – Death of Guru Nanak.
1539	— Sher Khan defeated Humayun at Chaunsa and assumed sovereignty.
1540	— Humayun was defeated at Kanauj and became a fugitive.
1542	— Birth of Akbar at Umarkot.
1544	— Humayun in Persia.
1545	— Death of Sher Shah – accession of Islam Shah.
1555	— Humayun recovered the throne of Delhi.
1556	— Death of Humayun – accession of Akbar – Second battle of Panipat.
1558	— End of the Sur dynasty.
1560	— Fall of Bairam Khan.
1561	— Akbar conquered Malwa.

1562	— Akbar married a Princess of Amber – end of petticoat government.
1564	— Akbar abolished the *jizya*, defeated Rani Durgavati and annexed her kingdom.
1565	— Battle of Talikota and destruction of the city of Vijayanagar.
1568	— Akbar captured Chitor.
1569	— Akbar captured Ranthambhor and Kalanjar – birth of his son, Salim.
1571	— Foundation of Fathpur Sikri.
1572	— Annexation of Gujarat by Akbar.
1573	— Surat surrendered to Akbar.
1575	— Battle of Tukaroi—defeat of Daud Khan by Akbar.
1576	— Akbar subjugated Bengal – death of Daud Khan – battle of Haldighat or Gogunda.
1577	— Invasion of Khandesh by Akbar.
1579	— Promulgation by Akbar of the "Infallibility Decree".
1580	— Rebellion in Bengal and Bihar.
1581	— Akbar's march against his brother Hakim and reconciliation with him.
1582	— Promulgation by Akbar of the "Din Illahi".
1586	— Annexation of Kashmir by Akbar.
1589	— Death of Todar Mal and Bhagwan Das.
1591	— Conquest of Sind by Akbar.
1592	— Annexation of Orissa to Akbar's empire.
1595	— Siege of Ahmadnagar by the Mughuls – acquisition of Qandahar by Akbar – annexation of Baluchistan to Mughul empire – death of Faizi.
1597	— Death of Rana Pratap.
1600	— Charter to the London East India Company – Ahmadnagar stormed by the Mughuls.
1601	— Capture of Asirgarh by Akbar.
1602	— Death of Abul Fazl – formation of the United East India Company of the Netherlands.
1605	— Death of Akbar – accession of Jahangir.
1606	— Rebellion of Prince Khusrav – investment of Qandahar by the Persians – execution of the fifth Sikh Guru, Arjan, by Jahangir's orders.
1607	— Qandahar relieved by the Mughuls – death of Sher Afghan – widowed Nur Jahan brought to the Mughul harem.
1608	— Recovery of Ahmadnagar by Malik Ambar.

1609	— Arrival of Hawkins at Agra – opening of a Dutch factory at Pulicat.
1611	— Jahangir married Nur Jahan – Hawkins left Agra – English factory at Masulipatam.
1612	— Prince Khurram married Mumtaz Mahal—English factory at Surat—annexation of Kuch Hajo to the Mughul empire.
1613	— Jahangir granted a *firman* to E.I. Co.
1615	— Submission of Mewar to Jahangir – arrival of Sir Thomas Roe in India.
1616	— Jahangir granted audience to Roe – Dutch factory at Surat.
1618	— Departure of Roe from the Imperial court.
1619	— Departure of Roe from India.
1620	— Mughuls captured Kangra – betrothal of Prince Shahryar to Nur Jahan's daughter – revolt of Malik Ambar.
1622	— Death of Prince Khusrav – Qandahar captured by Persia—Rebellion of Shah Jahan.
1624	— Shah Jahan's rebellion suppressed.
1625	— Dutch factory at Chinsura.
1626	— Death of Malik Ambar – rebellion of Mahabat Khan.
1627	— Death of Jahangir – birth of Shivaji (?).
1628	— Shah Jahan proclaimed Emperor.
1630	— Birth of Shivaji (?).
1631	— Death of Mumtaz Mahal.
1632	— Mughul invasion of Bijapur – Hughli sacked.
1633	— Extinction of the Nizam Shahi dynasty of Ahmadnagar.
1634	— Grant of *firman* permitting the English to trade in Bengal.
1636	— Mughuls made treaties granting respite to Bijapur and Golconda – appointment of Aurangzeb as Viceroy of the Deccan.
1638	— Recovery of Qandahar by the Mughuls.
1639	— Foundation by the English of Fort St. George at Madras
1646	— Shivaji captured Torna.
1649	— Qandahar captured again by Persia and lost by the Mughuls.
1651	— English factory at Hughli.
1653	— Dutch factory at Chinsura.
1656	— Annexation of Javli by Shivaji.

1657	— Illness of Shah Jahan – commencement of the war of succession.
1658	— Battles of Dharmat (April) and Shamugarh (May) – coronation of Aurangzeb.
1659	— Battles of Khajwah and Deorai – execution of Dara – captivity of Murad and of Shah Jahan – second coronation of Aurangzeb – death of Afzal Khan at the hands of Shivaji.
1660	— Prince Shuja driven from Bengal to Arakan – Mir Jumla governor of Bengal.
1661	— Cession of Bombay to the English – execution of Murad – Mughuls captured Cooch Behar and began invasion of Assam.
1662	— Mir Jumla over-ran Assam and forced the Ahoms to make peace.
1663	— Death of Mir Jumla – appointment of Shaista Khan as governor of Bengal.
1664	— Surat sacked by Shivaji – foundation of the French East India Company – assumption of royal title by Shivaji.
1666	— Death of Shah Jahan – Shivaji's visit to Agra and escape.
1668	— Aurangzeb issued new religious ordinances adversely affecting Hinduism – cession of Bombay to E.I. Co. – foundation of the first French factory at Surat.
1669	— Gokla, the Jat leader, rebelled.
1670	— Surat sacked a second time by Shivaji.
1671	— Chhatrasal Bundela rebelled.
1672	— Satnami rebellion – revolt of the Afridis.
1674	— Foundation of Pondicherry – assumption of the title of Chhatrapati by Shivaji.
1675	— Execution of the Sikh Guru, Teg Bahadur.
1677	— Shivaji's conquests in the Carnatic.
1678	— Death of Jaswant Singh – occupation of Marwar by Aurangzeb's orders.
1679	— Re-imposition of the *jizya* by Aurangzeb – Aurangzeb ordered invasion of Marwar.
1680	— Death of Shivaji – rebellion of Prince Akbar.
1681	— Assam re-asserted independence – Aurangzeb went on his Deccan visit.
1686	— Conquest and annexation of Bijapur by Aurangzeb.
1687	— Conquest and annexation of Golconda by Aurangzeb.
1689	— Execution of Shambhuji – accession of Rajaram and his retirement to Jinji.

1690	— Foundation of Calcutta by Job Charnock.
1691	— Jats defeated and subdued by the Mughuls – Aurangzeb at the height of his power.
1692	— Resumption of aggressive hostility by the Marathas.
1698	— Foundation of new English Company trading to the East Indies – acquisition by the East India Co. of zamindari of Sutanati, Kalikata and Govindapur.
1699	— First Maratha raid on Malwa.
1700	— Death of Rajaram – regency of Tara Bai.
1702	— Amalgamation of the English and the London East India Companies.
1703	— Berar raided by the Marathas.
1706	— Gujarat raided by the Marathas who sacked Baroda.
1707	— Death of Aurangzeb – battle of Jajau – accession of Bahadur Shah I.
1708	— Shahu, on his return from Delhi to Poona, became the king of the Marathas – death of Guru Govind Singh.
1712	— Death of Bahadur Shah I – accession of Jahandar Shah.
1713	— Accession of Farruksiyar – murder of Jahandar Shah.
1714	— Balaji Viswanath Peshwa – Hussain Ali viceroy of the Deccan – treaty between Hussain Ali and the Marathas.
1716	— Execution of Banda – Surman Embassy to the Imperial Court.
1717	— Emperor Farruksiyar's *firman* to East India Co.
1719	— Farruksiyar put to death – accession and deposition of puppet emperors – accession of Muhammad Shah.
1720	— Succession of Baji Rao I to the Peshwaship – fall of the Sayyid brothers.
1724	— Appointment of Sa'adat Khan as governor of Oudh – virtual independence of the Nizam in the Deccan – appointment of Qamar-ud-din as *wazir*.
1725	— Shuja-ud-din appointed governor of Bengal.
1735	— Recognition by the Emperor of Peshwa Baji Rao I as ruler of Malwa.
1739	— Nadir Shah took Delhi and sacked it – death of Suja-ud-din and appointment of his son, Sarfaraz, as Governor of Bengal – capture of Bassein and Salsette by the Marathas.
1740	— Alivardi Khan defeated and killed Sarfaraz Khan and became Nawab of Bengal – accession of Balaji

Baji Rao as Peshwa – invasion of Arcot by the Marathas and defeat and death of its Nawab, Dost Ali.

1742 — Marathas invaded Bengal – appointment of Dupleix as Governor of Pondicherry.

1744-48 — First Carnatic (Anglo-French) War.

1745 — Rohillas in occupation of Rohilkhand.

1746 — Capture of Madras by La Bourdonnais.

1747 — Invasion by Ahmad Shah Abdali.

1748 — Death of Nizam Chin Qlich Khan – death of Emperor Muhammad Shah – accession of Ahmad Shah.

1749 — Death of Shahu – restoration of Madras to the English.

1750-54 — Second Carnatic War.

1750 — Defeat and death of Nizam Nasir Jang – Muzaffar Jang became Nizam.

1751 — Capture and defence of Arcot by Robert Clive – death of Muzaffar Jang – accession of Salabat Jang as Nizam – conclusion of treaty by Nawab Alivardi Khan with the Marathas by surrendering Cuttack.

1754 — Recall of Dupleix – Godehu's appointment as governor and his treaty with the English – accession of Alamgir II.

1756 — Death of Alivardi Khan (21 April) – accession of Siraj-ud-daulah who captured Calcutta (20 June) – Seven Years' War (1756–63) – Third Carnatic War.

1757 — Recovery of Calcutta by the English (2 Jany.) – Delhi and Mathura sacked by Ahmad Shah Abdali (Jany.) – treaty of Alinagar between Siraj and the English – (9 Feby.) – capture of Chandernagore by the English (March) – battle of Plassey (23 June) – Mir Jafar installed as Nawab (28 June) – capture and execution of Siraj-ud-daulah (2 July).

1758 — Arrival of Lally in India – occupation of the Panjab by the Marathas – Masulipatam captured by Forde.

1759 — Battle of Bedara – Prince Ali Gauhar's futile invasion of Bihar – Emperor Alamgir II murdered by Ghazi-ud-din.

1760 — Battle of Wandiwash – battle of Udgir – installation of Mir Qasim as Nawab of Bengal – Vansittart appointed governor in Bengal.

1761 — Third battle of Panipat (14 January) – surrender of Pondicherry to the English – accession of Ali

Gauhar as Emperor Shah Alam II – appointment of Shuja-ud-daulah as *wazir* – death of Peshwa Balaji Baji Rao (23 June) – accession of Madhava Rao – Haidar Ali king of Mysore.

1763 — Treaty of Paris – Mir Qasim driven out of Bengal and Bihar.

1764 — Battle of Buxar.

1765 — Death of Mir Jafar – second Governorship of Clive in Bengal – treaty of Allahabad – grant of the Dewani of Bengal, Bihar and Orissa by Shah Alam II to the Company.

1766 — Acquisition by the Company of the Northern Circars.

1767 — Departure of Clive – Verelest, governor in Bengal – the First Mysore War (1767-69).

1770 — The Great Bengal Famine.

1772 — Warren Hastings appointed Governor in Bengal – death of Peshwa Madhava Rao – accession and murder of Peshwa Narayan Rao.

1773 — Enactment of the Regulating Act – Peshwaship of Raghunath Rao or Raghaba.

1774 — Accession of Narayan Rao as Peshwa – the Rohilla War – Warren Hastings installed as Governor-General – establishment of Supreme Court in Calcutta.

1775 — Trial and execution of Nanda Kumar – commencement of the First Maratha War which continued till 1782.

1776 — Treaty of Purandhar.

1779 — Convention of Wadgaon.

1780 — Gwalior captured by General Popham – Second Mysore War (1780-84).

1781 — Deposition of Chait Singh – Amendment of the Regulating Act.

1782 — Affair of the Begums of Oudh – the treaty of Salbai – death of Haidar Ali.

1783 — Fox's India Bill.

1784 — Treaty of Mangalore closed the Second Mysore War – Pitt's India Act.

1785 — Warren Hastings resigned Governor-Generalship.

1786 — Lord Cornwallis appointed Governor-General.

1790 — Commencement of the Third Mysore War (1790-92).

1792 — Treaty of Seringapatam ended the Third Mysore War – Ranjit Singh became the leader of a Sikh *Misl*.

1793	— Permanent Settlement of land-revenue in Bengal – renewal of of the Company's Charter – retirement of Lord Cornwallis – Sir John Shore Governor-General.
1794	— Death of Mahadaji Sindhia.
1795	— The battle of Kharda or Khardla – death of Ahalya Bai.
1796	— Death of Peshwa Madhava Rao Narayan – Baji Rao II Peshwa.
1797	— Zaman Shah in the Panjab – death of Nawab Asaf-ud-daulah of Oudh.
1798	— Lord Wellesley Governor-General – acceptance of subsidiary alliance by the Nizam.
1799	— Fourth Mysore War – death of Tipu – fall of Seringapatam – partition of Mysore – installation of the Hindu Raj family in Mysore – Ranjit Singh appointed Governor of Lahore by Zaman Shah – Malcolm led English mission to Persia – opening of the Baptist Mission at Serampore by William Carey.
1800	— Death of Nana Fadnavis.
1801	— Carnatic annexed to the British empire.
1802	— The battle of Poona – Treaty of Bassein.
1803	— The Second Maratha War (1803-05) – capture of Aligarh – battles of Delhi, Assaye, Laswari and Argaon – treaty of Deogaon and cession of Cuttack – treaty of Surji-Arjungaon.
1804	— War with the Holkar – defeat of Monson – battle of Deeg.
1805	— Failure of the English siege of Bharatpur – recall of Lord Wellesley – second term of Lord Cornwallis as Governor-General – death of Lord Cornwallis – Sir George Barlow Governor-General – treaty with the Holkar.
1806	— Outbreak and suppression of the Vellore Mutiny.
1807	— Lord Minto I appointed Governor-General (1807-13).
1808	— English Missions under Malcolm to Persia and under Elphinstone to Kabul.
1809	— Treaty of Amritsar between the English and Ranjit Singh.
1811	— Conquest of Java.
1812	— Pindari raid on Mirzapur – *Fifth Report*.
1813	— Company's Charter renewed – retirement of Lord Minto I – appointment of Lord Hastings as Governor-General (1813-23).

1814	— Outbreak of War with Nepal (1814-16).
1816	— Treaty of Sagauli closed war with Nepal.
1817-18	— The Pindari war and the Third Maratha War – battles of Kirkee and Sitabaldi – deposition of Appa Shaheb Bhonsla – battle of Mahidpur – treaty with the Holkar.
1818	— Battle of Ashti – defence of Koregaon – surrender of Peshwa Baji Rao II.
1819	— Capitulation of Asirgarh – abolition of the Peshwaship and retirement of Baji Rao II to Bithur as a British pensioner – protective alliances with the states of Rajputana – earthquakes – occupation of Singapore.
1820	— Starting of the *Samachar Darpan*, the first Bengali newspaper – appointment of Sir Thomas Munro as Governor of Madras (1820-27).
1823	— Departure of Lord Hastings – Mr. Adams acting Governor-General – deportation of the journalist, Mr. Buckingham – Lord Amherst Governor-General.
1824	— The First Burmese War (1824-26) – Barrackpore Mutiny.
1826	— Fall of Bharatpur – treaty of Yandabo – annexation of Assam, Arakan and Tennasserim.
1827	— The *Enterprise*, a man-of-war propelled by steam, lay off Madras.
1828	— Lord William Bentinck appointed Governor-General (1828-36).
1829	— Abolition of Suttee (*Sati-daha*).
1829-37	— Suppression of *Thuggee*.
1830	— Annexation of Cachar – Raja Rammohan Roy visited England.
1831	— Deposition of the Raja of Mysore and assumption of its administration by the English – journey of Burnes up the Indus – meeting at Rupar between Ranjit Singh and Lord William Bentinck.
1832	— Annexation of Jaintia.
1833	— Renewal of the Company's Charter – various reforms.
1834	— Annexation of Coorg – institution of Law Member in Supreme Council with Lord Macaulay as the first incumbent.
1835	— Foundation of Calcutta Medical College – Education Resolution – retirement of Lord William Bentinck – Sir Charles Metcalfe officiating Governor-General – abolition of Press restrictions.

1836	— Appointment of Lord Auckland as Governor-General (1836-42).
1837-38	— Famine in North India.
1838	— Tripartite treaty of the English with Shah Shuja and Ranjit Singh.
1839	— New treaty forced on the Amirs of Sind; death of Ranjit Singh – First Afghan War (1839-42) – Capture of Ghazni and occupation of Kabul.
1840	— Risings of Afghan tribes – deposition of Dost Muhammad.
1841	— Murders of Burnes and Macnaghten by the Afghans.
1842	— British disaster in Afghanistan – retirement to Jalalabad of Dr. Brydon alone – Lord Ellenborough became Governor-General (1842-44) – relief of Jalalabad – re-occupation of Kabul – restoration of Dost Muhammad – British evacuation of Afghanistan.
1843	— War with the Amirs of Sind – battles of Miani and Dabo – annexation of Sind – battle of Maharajpur – suppression of slavery.
1844	— Recall of Lord Ellenborough – Lord Hardinge became Governor-General (1844-48).
1845	— The First Sikh War (1845-46) – battles of Mudki and Ferozeshah.
1846	— Battles of Aliwal and Sobraon – treaties of Lahore.
1848	— Lord Dalhousie became Governor-General (1848-56) – revolt of Mulraj – the Second Sikh War (1848-49) – enunciation of the Doctrine of Lapse and annexation of Satara by the application of the Doctrine.
1849	— Battles of Chillianwalla and Gujarat – annexation of the Panjab – Bethune School for girls started in Calcutta – annexation of Jaitpur and Sambalpur.
1850	— Penal annexation of a part of Sikkim.
1852	— Second Burmese War – annexation of Pegu – death of ex-Peshwa Baji Rao II and stoppage of his pension.
1853	— Opening of first railway in India from Bombay to Thana – laying of telegraph line from Calcutta to Agra – annexation of Nagpur & Jhansi – cession of Berar by the Nizam – renewal of the Company's Charter; entrance into I.C.S. thrown open to competition.
1854	— Education Despatch of Sir Charles Wood.
1855	— The Santal insurrection.
1856	— Annexation of Oudh – the Indian Universities

Act – Religious Disabilities Act – Hindu Widow's Re-marriage Act – departure of Lord Dalhousie and appointment of Lord Canning as Governor-General – end of Crimean War – General Service Order – Persian War – war in China (1856-60) – introduction of the Enfield rifle and greased cartridges.

1857 — Local mutinies and incendiary fires at Barrackpore and Berhampore in Bengal (Jany. April) – outbreak of the Sepoy Mutiny at Meerut on 10 May, 1857 – occupation of Delhi by the sepoys and proclamation of Bahadur Shah as the Mughul Emperor of Delhi (May) – outbreaks at Lucknow and Bareilly (May) – occupation of the Ridge (June) by the British – massacres at Cawnpore (July) – recapture of Delhi, and murder of the Princes (Sept) – final relief of Lucknow and defeat of Windham at Cawnpore (Nov.) – recovery of Cawnpore (December); foundation of Calcutta, Bombay and Madras Universities.

1858 — Trial of Emperor Bahadur Shah (Jan-March) – recovery of Lucknow (March) – recovery of Jhansi (April) – recovery of Bareilly and Kalpi (May) – Rani of Jhansi and Tantia Topi spread the Mutiny to Gwalior and proclaimed Nana Shaheb as Peshwa (May) – defeat and death of Rani of Jhansi (June) – recapture of Gwalior and Jhansi – Proclamation of Peace by Lord Canning (July) – Act for the better government of India (August) – Queen's Proclamation (Nov.) – Lord Canning appointed Viceroy (Nov.).

1859 — Betrayal of Tantia Topi – withdrawal of Doctrine of Lapse – gradual restoration of order – indigo disputes in Bengal (1859-60).

1860 — Enactment of Indian Penal Code.

1861 — Indian Councils Act – establishment of High Courts – Civil Service Act – famine in N. W. India – enactment of the Code of Criminal Procedure.

1862 — Retirement of Lord Canning – Lord Elgin I appointed Viceroy (1862-63) – amalgamation of Supreme and Sadar Courts into High Courts.

1863 — Death of Dost Muhammad.

1864 — Sir John Lawrence appointed Viceroy (1864-68) – Bhutan War.

1865 — Orissa famine (1865-67) – opening of telegraphic communication with Europe.

1868	— Opening of railway from Ambala to Delhi – Sher Ali established as Amir of Afghanistan.
1869	— Lord Mayo became Viceroy (1869-72) – conference with Sher Ali at Umbala – visit of the Duke of Edinborough.
1872	— Murder of Lord Mayo – Lord Northbrook appointed Viceroy (1872-76).
1873	— Russians reduce Khiva – famine in Bihar (1873-74).
1874	— Disraeli Prime Minister in Britain; Bihar famine.
1875	— Deposition of Malhar Rao Gaekwar – visit of Edward, Prince of Wales.
1876	— Retirement of Lord Northbrook – Lord Lytton I became Viceroy (1876-80) – the Royal Titles Act – occupation of Quetta – outbreak of famine in the Deccan.
1877	— Delhi Durbar (1 Jany.) – Queen Victoria proclaimed Empress of India.
1878	— Vernacular Press Act – Second Afghan War (1878-80).
1879	— Abolition of Customs hedge.
1880	— Resignation of Lord Lytton I – Lord Ripon Viceroy (1880-84) – battle of Maiwand (July) – march of Roberts to Qandahar (August) – Abdur Rahman recognised as Amir of Afghanistan – reversal of Anglo-Afghan policy.
1881	— Rendition of Mysore – Factory Act – first general census.
1882	— Repeal of Vernacular Press Act; Hunter Commission.
1883	— Beginning of legislation establishing local self-government in India – the Ilbert Bill.
1884	— Resignation of Lord Ripon – Lord Dufferin Viceroy.
1885	— Panjdeh incident–Third Burmese War – First meeting of the Indian National Congress – Bengal Local Self-Government Act.
1886	— Annexation of Upper Burma – restoration of Gwalior fort – delimitation of the northern boundary of Afghanistan.
1887	— Queen Victoria's Jubilee.
1888	— Resignation of Lord Dufferin and Lord Lansdowne became Viceroy (1888-94).
1889	— Second visit of Edward, Prince of Wales.
1891	— Second Factory Act – Age of Consent Act – Manipur Rebellion.
1892	— Indian Councils Act.

1893	— Durand's Mission to Kabul; Vivekananda in U.S.A.
1894	— Lord Elgin II Viceroy (1894-99).
1895	— Chitral expedition.
1896	— Plague in Bombay 1896-1900 – famine (1896-97).
1897	— Tirah expedition – Famine Commission.
1899	— Lord Curzon Viceroy (1899-1905).
1900	— Famine – Land Alienation Act.
1901	— Death of Queen Victoria and accession of King Edward VII – North-West Frontier Province created.
1903	— Tibetan expedition (1903-04).
1904	— Indian Universities Act; Co-operative Society Act; Russo-Japanese War. (1904-5)
1905	— Partition of Bengal – Lord Minto II Viceroy (1905-10). Morley Secretary of State for India; Swadeshi and boycott.
1906	— Foundation of the Muslim League; Calcutta Congress – President Dadabhai Naoroji declared *Swaraj* as the goal of the Congress.
1907	— Anglo-Russian Convention; Congress split at Surat.
1908	— Newspapers Act.
1909	— Indian Councils Act (Morley-Minto Reforms) – terrorists' activities – first Indian (S. P. Sinha) appointed to the Viceroy's Executive Council.
1910	— Lord Hardinge Viceroy (1910-16).
1911	— King George V and his Queen visited India – Delhi Durbar – Partition of Bengal modified – transfer of capital from Calcutta to Delhi announced.
1912	— Removal of Imperial capital from Calcutta to Delhi – constitution of a separate province of Bihar and Orissa – Lord Carmichael Governor of Bengal – Lord Hardinge wounded by a bomb in Delhi.
1913	— Nobel Prize for Rabindranath Tagore.
1914	— The First World War – Declaration of War (4 Aug.) – landing of Indian troops in France (26 Sept.) – declaration of war by Great Britain against Turkey (5 Nov.).
1915	— Retreat of British force in Mesopotamia – General Townshend at the head of an Indo-British army entered Kut-el Amara – Defence of India Act.
1916	— Lord Chelmsford Viceroy (1916-21) – Turks captured Kut-el Amara and captured Townshend – Sadler Commission – the Lucknow Pact between the Con-

gress and the League – foundation of the Home Rule League – foundation of the Women's University at Poona.

1917 — Kut-el Amara retaken by the British – revolution in Russia leading to the fall of Tsardom – U.S.A. declared war on Germany – pronouncement by Mr. Montague, Secretary of State, in the House of Commons announcing that the policy of H. M. Government aimed at gradual development of self-governing institutions in India with a view to the progressive realisation of responsible government (27 Aug.) – Mr. Montague's visit to India.

1918 — Indians declared eligible for King's Commission – Indian National Liberal Federation – collapse of Russian power – British advance in Mesopotamia and commencement of German retreat in France – publication of Montague-Chelmsford *Report* and debate on the same in the Parliament – end of the First World War (1914-18).

1919 — Government of India Act, 1919 – Panjab disturbances – Royal Proclamation – abolition of the Khalif.

1920 — The Khalifat Movement – death of Bal Gangadhar Tilak; the Indian National Congress under the leadership of Mahatma Gandhi started the Non-cooperation Movement – Lord Sinha appointed Governor of Bihar and Orissa.

1921 — Continuance of Non-co-operation movement (1920-24) – Chamber of Princes – Moplah rebellion – visit of Edward, Prince of Wales – General Census – Lord Reading Viceroy (1921-26).

1922 — Resignation of Mr. Montague.

1923 — Foundation of Swarajist Party – certification of Salt Tax – decision to Indianise command of certain regiments of the Indian army.

1924 — Weakening of the Non-co-operation Movement.

1925 — Death of C. R. Das – formation of the Inter-University Board – Lord Lytton II officiated Viceroy.

1926 — Lord Irwin Viceroy (1926-31) – devaluation of the rupee.

1927 — Appointment of Simon Commission – National Congress at its Madras session adopted independence as the goal of Indian nationalist aspirations.

1928 — Amanullah, King of Afghanistan, deposed–All Parties

Conference – the Nehru Report – foundation of the
Independence League within the Congress, which,
however, agreed to accept Dominion Status, if
granted before the end of 1929 – Nadir Shah became
king of Afghanistan (1928-34).

1929 — Lord Irwin's announcement (31 Oct.) that the natural
issue of India's constitutional progress was the attainment of Dominion Status – the Lahore Session of the
Indian National Congress resolved that its goal was
the attainment of complete independence for India
(December).

1930 — Civil Disobedience Movement started on 6 April –
Report of Simon Commission – rebellion in Burma –
First Session of the Round Table Conference (Nov.-
Jany.).

1931 — Irwin-Gandhi Pact (5 March)– census of India –
Second Session of the Round Table Conference which
Gandhiji attended (Sept.-Dec.) – Lord Willingdon
Viceroy (1931-36).

1932 — Imprisonment of Gandhiji (Jany.) – Congress pros-
cribed–severe repression–Communal Award (Aug.) –
Gandhiji's fast – Poona Pact – foundation of the
Indian Military Academy at Dehra Dun.

1933 — White Paper on proposed reforms published – Joint
Select Committee.

1934 — Civil Disobedience Movement called off – Bihar
earthquake – Factories Act – Royal Indian Navy
created; murder of Afghan King Nadir Shah and
succession of Zahir Shah.

1935 — Government of India Act, 1935.

1936 — Death of King-Emperor George V – accession and
abdication of Edward VIII – accession of George VI –
Lord Linlithgow, Viceroy (1936).

1937 — Provincial autonomy inaugurated (1 April) – Interim Ministries – Viceregal statement (June) – formation of Congress Ministries in six provinces
(July) – Federal Court started – Lord Linlithgow,
Crown Representative and Governor-General
(1937-42).

1939 — Second World War (3 September) – Viceroy consulted Indian leaders – Congress demand an immediate definition of war aims – Viceroy's announcement (17 Oct.) of Dominion Status to be the goal of

constitutional development after the war – resignation of the Provincial Congress Ministries.

1940　— Muslim League declares for Pakistan – fall of France.

1941　—Japan declared war – Subhas Bose jumped home-internment and went overland to Germany.

1942　— British capitulation in Burma and evacuation leaving 90,000 Indian soldiers behind–Japan bombarded Vizag. (April) – Cripps Mission – 'Quit India' movement started–Civil disobedience–disturbances and repression – Bengal famine – imprisonment of Congress leaders.

1943　— The Bengal famine – Lord Wavell, Governor-General (1943-47).

1944　—Japanese invasion of Assam – I.N.A. – repulse of the Japanese and of the I.N.A. near Kohima in Manipur.

1945　—Japan surrendered – General Elections in India – Muslim League captured majority of Muslim seats in all provinces except N.W.F.P. while the Congress captured the majority of the general seats in all provinces and at the Centre.

1946　— Revolt of the R.I.N. (18 Feb.) – Cabinet Mission in India – Direct Action Day (16 Aug.) observed by the Muslim League with bloody communal riots in Calcutta – communal riots in Dacca (20 Aug.) – formation of the Interim Govt. (2 Sept.) – communal riots in Noakhali and Tipperah (14 Oct.) – communal riots in Bihar (25 Oct.) – Muslim League joined the Interim Govt. (26 Oct.) – first session of the Constituent Assembly (9 Dec.).

1947　— Lord Mountbatten Governor-General – communal riots in the Panjab – Mountbatten's announcement of the grant of independence on the basis of the partition of India into India and Pakistan (3 June) – Independence of India Act (15 Aug.) – creation of Pakistan – which attacked Kashmir–accession of Kashmir (Oct.) – Indian intervention.

1948　— Murder of Mahatma Gandhi (30 Jan.) – Rajagopalachari first Indian Governor-General (21 June) – India took Kashmir dispute to U.N.O. (July) – death of Jinnah (11 Sept.) – police action in Hyderabad and merger of the Nizam's dominions in Indian Republic.

1949　— Indian Constitution Act passed.

1950	— India declared a democratic Republic (26 Jan.) – Dr. Rajendra Prasad was elected President and Pandit Jawaharlal Nehru was appointed Prime Minister – establishment of diplomatic relations with China – India elected a member of the Security Council, U.N.O, for a term of 2 years – completion of the integration of Princely States.
1951	— Treaty of cession of Chandernagar – First Five Year Plan with a total outlay of Rs. 2,069 crores – General Census.
1952	— First General Election on the basis of universal adult suffrage.
1953	— Formation of Andhra State on linguistic basis – closure of Indian legation in Portugal.
1954	— Pancha Shila agreement signed – Chou En-lai's visit to India (June) – Jawaharlal Nehru's visit to China (Oct.).
1955	— Bandung Conference (April) – Nehru's visit to U.S.S.R. (June) – visit of Khrushchev and Bulganin to India (Nov.).
1956	— Second Five Year Plan with an outlay of Rs. 4,800 crores – States Re-organisation Act – India joined with Burma, Ceylon and Indonesia in demanding withdrawal of foreign troops from Egypt – signing of Indo-French treaty for the cession by France of Pondicherry, Karikal, Mahe and Yunnan.
1957	— Second General Election – Congress majority in all states except Kerala – adoption of the decimal system of coinage (1 April) – Communist-led Ministry in Kerala.
1958	— Dr. Graham's Report on Kashmir – formation of Oil India Ltd. and incorporation of Indian Refineries Ltd. – first atomic reactor in India goes into operation.
1959	— Dalai Lama and 14,000 Tibetan refugees, fleeing before the Chinese invaders, sought asylum in India – the Chinese kill 13 Indian army personnel at Longju and Ladakh which they occupied – dismissal of the Communist-led ministry of Kerala.
1960	— Nehru's visit to Pakistan – signing of the Indus Water Treaty – exchange of visits by the Presidents of India and U.S.S.R. – bifurcation of the state of Bombay into Maharashtra and Gujarat – abortive strike by 4 lakhs of Central Government employees.

1961 — General Census, including for the the first time Jammu & Kashmir, showing a population of 43.6 crores – Third Five Year Plan – Dowry Prohibition Act – liberation of Goa by the Indian army moving into the city at midnight on 17 December.

1962 — Third General Election – Congress majorities in every state and at the centre – Nagaland separated from Assam and formed into a separate State – Goa becomes Union territory – Metric system in linear, capacity and weight measures made compulsory – Noonmati (Assam) Refinery opened – China launched an aggressive attack on the Northern and North-Eastern borders of India ending in the Chinese imposition of a unilateral cease-fire.

1963 — Aeronautics India Ltd. established to manufacture aircraft – Colombo proposals accepted by India but rejected by China – Kamaraj Plan and re-organization of the Central Cabinet – Parliament approved use of English as an official language even after 1965.

1964 — Following communal riots in East Pakistan communal riots flared up in Calcutta, Jamshedpur and Rourkela – Home Minister, G. L. Nanda, launched anti-corruption drive – release of Sheikh Abdullah – Report of Mahalanobis Committee warning against concentration of economic power – Jawaharlal Nehru died on 27 May – Lal Bahadur Shastri appointed Prime Minister.

APPENDIX

LIST OF ABBREVIATIONS

A.H.D.	— Ancient History of the Deccan—G. Jouveau-Dubrueil.
A.M.A.I.	— Ancient and Medieval Architechure in India— E. B. Havell.
C.H.I.	— Cambridge History of India.
C.T.I.	— Cave Temples of India—Fergusson & Burgess.
D.H.I.	— Dynastic History of Northern India—H. C. Roy.
E.D.B.O.E.	— Economic Development of the British Overseas Empire—L.C.A. Knowles.
E.E.C.A.	— Early Empires of Central Asia—W. M. McGovern.
E.H.I.	— Early History of India—V. A. Smith.
E.I.	— Epigraphia Indica.
E.R.E.	— Encyclopaedia of Religion and Ethics.
F.M.R.I.	— Foundation of Muslim Rule in India – A. B. M. Habibulla.
H.B.	— History of Bengal (Dacca University), Vol. I, R. C. Majumdar & Vol. II, J. N. Sarkar.
H.I.E.A.	— History of Indian and Eastern Architecture—J. Fergusson.
H.O.	— History of Orissa—R. D. Banerjee.
H.I.I.A.	— History of Indian and Indonesian Art—Coomarswamy.
H.S.S.I.	— Historical Sketches of South India—M. Wilks.
I.C.D.	— Indian Constitutional Documents—A. C. Banerjee.
Ind. Ant.	— Indian Antiquary.
I.S.B.	— Independent Sultans of Bengal—N. K. Bhattasali.
J.B.O.R.S.	— Journal of Bihar & Orissa Research Society.
J.R.A.S.	— Journal of the Royal Asiatic Society.
P.A. & H.I.	— Prehistoric, Ancient and Hindu India—R. D. Banerjee.
P.H.A.I.	— Political History of Ancient India—H. C. Ray Chowdhury.
R.A.S.W.I.	— Report of Archaeological Survey, Western India—J. Burgess.
R.S.A.E.I.C	— The Rajput States and the East India Company— A. C. Banerjee.
S.A.E.	— Select Asokan Epigraphs—S. Bhattacharya.
S.O.S.	— Successors of the Satavahanas—D. C. Sircar.

ERRATA

Page	Line	*For*	*Read*
18	42	jaziya	jizya
56	8	Chand	Chanda
265	32	Auriel	Aurel
279	8	Pekin	Peking
329	34	Eastern Indonesia	Indonesia
341	29	Emperor's daughter	Emperor
350	26	Bamfylde	Bambfyld
378	3	Gladstone	Ripon
420	38	Hinaynana	Hinayana
601	6 *et al.*	Montgue	Montagu
676	35	Bengal	West Bengal
681	28	Pethwick	Pethick
827	5 *et al.*	Upanishadas	Upanishads